FOOD, HOPE & RESILIENCE

AUTHENTIC RECIPES AND REMARKABLE STORIES FROM HOLOCAUST SURVIVORS

JUNE HERSH

FOREWORD BY DANIEL BOULUD

AMERICAN PALATE

Published by American Palate
A Division of The History Press
Charleston, SC
www.historypress.com

Cover photos: blueberry pie and red stew, June Hersh; hummus, Pexels.com, user: eat-Kubba

Published by The History Press 2023
ISBN 9781467155397

This book is a revised edition of *Recipes Remembered, a Celebration of Survival*,
Published by Ruder Finn Press, 2011
ISBN 9781932646528

Manufactured in the United States

Library of Congress Control Number: 2023940702

Notice: The information in this book is true and complete to the best of our knowledge. It is offered without guarantee on the part of the author or The History Press. The author and The History Press disclaim all liability in connection with the use of this book.

This book is dedicated to those who are here and those who are not. I am forever humbled and honored to share your stories and recipes.

Inge Auerbacher, Arlette Levy Baker, Murray Berger and Fruma Gulkowich Berger, Nadzia Goldstein Bergson and Milton Bergson, Sonia and Zus Bielski, Edith Hamburger Blumenthal and Siggi Blumenthal, Luna and Haim Cohen, Michael and Florence Edelstein, Ruth and Julius Eggener, Mike and Frania Faywlowicz, Joan Ferencz, George and Ethel Feuerstein, Regina Schmidt Finer, Raymond Fishler, Mila Ginzburg Fishman, Stephen and Hela Fisk, Ida Frankfurter, Robert and Nella Frendel, Paula Gerson, Judith Koscianska Ginsburg and Marvin Mordechai "Motke" Ginsburg, Angie and Moritz "Moshe" Goldfeier, Natalie Gomberg, Elly Berkovits Gross, Henny Durmashkin Gurko and Simon Gurko, Reni Hanau, Celina Hecht, Peri Hirsch, Judita Hruza, the Jacobs family, Cecile and Simon Jeruchim, Lilly Schwarcz Kaplan, Ellen and Ernest Katz, Luna Kaufman, Celia Kener, Solomon and Koula Koen Kofinas, Ruth Kohn, Rae and Joseph Kushner, George Lang, Freda Lederer, Miriam Lesorgen, Stella Levi, Dina and Jacob Liverant, Greta Margolis, Lily Mazur Margules and Edward Margules, Miriam Margulies, Mary Fenyes Mayer, Marsha Meyer, Rachel Angelou Mosios, Katherine Wassermann Noir and Robert (Bela Schwartz) Noir, Kurt and Gisela Obernbreit, Ruth and Vittorio Orvieto, Sonya and Aaron Oshman, David and Mary May Prussin, Helen and Henry Ptashnik, Wolfgang "Wolfie" Rauner, Irma and Martin Reich, Melly Resnicow, Sara "Hannah" Rigler, Gita Karelitz Roback and Godel Roback, Sol and Sally Rosenkranz, Maks and Gita Rothman, the Rubach family, Ada Ehrlich Rubin and Leo Rubin, Evelyn Pike Rubin, Helena Pradelski Sabat and Benjamin Sabat, Olga Paverman Schaerf and Henry Schaerf, Doris Schechter, Ruth Schloss, Cantor Gershon Sirota, Ruth Baumwald Stromer and Moty Stromer, Fira Stukelman, Florence Tabrys, Ruth Goldman Tobias, the Turiel family, Berta Kiesler Vaisman, Jules Wallerstein, Hanna Kleiner Wechsler, Rachela Introligator Weisstuch and Victor Weisstuch, Dr. Ruth Westheimer, Chana Wiesenfeld, Matilda Winkler, Eva Young, Abraham and Millie Zuckerman

CONTENTS

FOREWORD

Food is a vital component of our lives. Our memories of food connect us to our family, heritage and each other. For that reason, when I was asked to contribute a recipe to the first edition of this book, I immediately said yes. To be part of a compendium that celebrated Holocaust survivors and their cherished recipes was an honor and a privilege. I am humbled to have the opportunity to become part of this newly revised edition. With the survivor community dwindling, books such as this one are even more vital today.

While reading the stories in the book, I found common roots and resonating themes. Being raised on a farm has always influenced my cooking. I came from a small town in Saint-Pierre-de-Chandieu, France, where I learned to respect food and cook at my grandmother's side. Most of the survivors within these pages were raised in small villages rather than big cities. In retelling their stories, they describe Friday night preparations for the Sabbath, much as I would prepare the chickens on our farm for our Friday night dinner. I learned to make goat cheese from my grandmother, as many of the survivors described learning how to make their family's cherished dishes. We share a respect for fresh and seasonal ingredients and the land and communities that grow them.

In the dedication to my book *Letters to a Young Chef*, I wrote how important it is to preserve the traditions of one's cuisine. *Food, Hope and Resilience* shows us how preserving one's cultural cuisine helps maintain the very existence of a people forced into diaspora. Despite hardship and upheaval, the contributors to this book managed to continue representing the food so important to their identity. That was their lifeline, their promise to those who did not survive and one of this book's greatest gifts. Every time I cook, I honor my family with flavors and techniques that celebrate our journey.

In *Food, Hope and Resilience*, you will be inspired by stories of perseverance and recipes that will bring a new dimension to your home cooking. The stories are more than just words, and the recipes are more than just ingredients. They speak to the need to embrace understanding and the danger of indifference. Their soulful flavors linger as you embrace their message and strive to create a world where we are truly responsible to and for one another.

—Daniel Boulud
Award-winning chef and restaurateur

ACKNOWLEDGEMENTS

This book has been a labor of love for so many; therefore, I have so many people to thank. I begin with "my" survivors. I looked forward to hearing their endearing and enduring accents every time we spoke. We *schepped nachas* (received joy) over births and graduations, weddings and *Bar Mitzvahs*. Together, we mourned many passings, including my mother's. She never lived to see this book in print but knew, in her heart, that it would be an eternal reminder of our strength as a people. This remarkable community of survivors showed me the true meaning of perseverance and perspective. I will always honor you and cannot thank you enough for your willingness to share your life-affirming stories and cherished recipes.

Thank you to my incredible family and friends whose support has been unwavering. You have encouraged me every step of the way and have championed this book since day one. A special thank-you to my husband, Ron, who took this book to heart and cleaned up my every mess, listened to my every revision and accompanied me on this journey from beginning to end. I could not have done this without you. Thank you to the original team at the Museum of Jewish Heritage, under the leadership of David Marwell, Director Emeritus, who initially greenlit the project. A special thank-you to Andy Smith, my literary angel, who brought this project to Ruder Finn Press, and to everyone there, especially the late David Finn and Susan Slack, who committed their talents and resources in preparing that book. To all the professional chefs, authors and restaurateurs who graciously and generously donated their recipes, thank you for letting me play in your kitchen. Your inclusion made the survivors blush with pride and joy that you were part of their process. The History Press championed this edition, under the incredible guardianship of Banks Smither. You demonstrated a bold commitment to remembering and honoring the legacy of Holocaust survivors, and your team has shown great respect to the subject matter. A special thank you to Abigail Fleming, my ardent copyeditor; Julie Foster, who faithfully designed the book; and Katie Parry, Maddison Potter and Caitlyn Post, who vigorously represent the book postproduction.

In the tradition of *l'dor v'dor*, from generation to generation, it is incumbent on the next generation to fulfill the obligation of preserving the legacy and lessons of the Holocaust. To that end, I leave this book and its mission in the hands of my family's next generation—Freya, Eloise, Jack, Daphne, Henry, Daisy and Aria—and trust that they will diligently pass on these stories and recipes, continue to be proud of their heritage and always bring tradition to the table.

Eat Well—Do Good
June Feiss Hersh

INTRODUCTION

While at its heart this is a book of recipes, in its soul it is a book of stories—life-affirming and uplifting stories about a community of remarkable people who have nourished and nurtured their families for decades. Plucked from their homes, our contributors were children of the Holocaust, thrown from comfort to chaos. Many survived death camps, displacement or years of hiding while others were sent to safety, arriving in unfamiliar places. We consider all these contributors survivors, as they survived the unimaginable and their lives were forever changed. Prior to the war, they had enjoyed memorable meals and family gatherings. They learned about secret ingredients and timeless traditions. They came from cities with regional specialties, indigenous spices, local flavors and distinctive techniques. Through it all, one important constant was the food they remembered. With this cookbook, we celebrate the survival of these miraculous people and their stories and RECIPES REMEMBERED.

THE STORIES

I embarked on this project not fully knowing what to expect. I am not the child of survivors and had little prior interaction with this community. What I did have was an association with the Museum of Jewish Heritage—A Living Memorial to the Holocaust. The Museum is dedicated to remembering the past while illuminating the future. This philosophy fell comfortably in place with the goals I had for this book. I wanted to retell the vital stories of Holocaust survivors and preserve their food memory to ensure the legacy of both. At the time of the first printing, this was a groundbreaking concept and the first book of its kind. You are holding a lovingly revised edition of *Recipes Remembered, a Celebration of Survival* with the same message and meaning as the original.

To bring these stories to life, I knew it was important to personally speak to every contributor, and over one hundred conversations later, I found myself not simply conducting interviews but making friends. The contributors became "my" survivors, my connection to the past and my reason to optimistically embrace the future. They reminded me with each and every conversation that although they lived through a tragic time, they were not tragic people. They turned their tragedy into triumph with every productive day they lived. Their stories share many commonalities, yet each is singularly their own. Many survived, having been saved by a benevolent neighbor, or a complete stranger who acted with courage now recognized as Righteous Among the Nations at Israel's Yad Vashem. There were those who sensed the impending upheaval and gained safe passage to unfamiliar places, many without their parents, whom they would never see again. Some escaped deep into the forest and fought as partisans, saving countless lives and subsisting in the woods building community and demonstrating resistance. Ghettos took the place of neighborhoods where families huddled together not knowing what the next day might bring. And too many were sent to death camps, where being instructed to stand on the left rather than the right was the difference between life and death. Was their survival luck, fate or divine intervention? Those in this book credit all three.

Upon liberation, having no family or home remaining, they found themselves once again living communally in displacement camps (hereafter known as DP camps), where they sought comfort and healing and the compatibility of other survivors. It was there that many met and married and where some brought new lives into the world. You'll see that most of the stories conclude with our noting how long the contributor was married and how many children, grandchildren and great-grandchildren they had at the time they were interviewed. This return to normalcy and the progeny they had was, as so many expressed, their best revenge, their reward for surviving. Since first writing this book, I sadly learned and noted after their story that a number of contributors have since passed. It is Jewish custom to say, "May his/her memory be for a blessing." Implicit in that phrase is the sentiment that the person's good works and their legacy should continue to flow and bless those who they leave behind. That is especially true for those this book honors.

I came to understand the psyche of each survivor and how their mind's eye saw the past and remembered their own personal truths. You need to understand that their stories reflect their perspective of their unique history. I consulted many sources for historical references, including the Museum of Jewish Heritage, the United States Holocaust Memorial Museum and the Jewish Virtual Library. However, I never questioned the accuracy of the story I was being told. The stories are in the survivors' voices, and they speak volumes, as do the photos that they graciously shared. Memories that cannot be conveyed in a word can be seen in a photo. We chronicled happier times with images of teenagers frolicking on a lakeside dock, children playing in their front yards, families gathering for life cycle events. They are moments captured, preserved and now shared in black and white so that these true expressions of better times may be a reminder for years to come.

Like the survivors' lives, which are a confluence of experiences, so was the language many used to tell their story. For those from central and eastern Europe, that would be Yiddish, a mash-up of German, Hebrew and other modern languages that defies definition but conveys so much nuance. You'll see lots of Yiddish words throughout the text. Like a sprinkling of salt, they add authentic flavor. We have placed Yiddish words and phrases in italics and provide a glossary in the back to help the uninitiated embrace this colorful idiomatic language. We used several reliable sources for the spelling of Yiddish words and places. So, don't make a *tzimmes* if our spelling differs from yours; there's more than one way to spell most of these words.

THE RECIPES

It might seem incongruous to include the word *food* in the title of a book about Holocaust survivors. Prior to writing this book, I would have agreed. I would think it insensitive, almost cruel, to discuss recipes in the context of such a horrific time when food was scarce and starvation prevalent. Yet after speaking to "my" survivors, I came to realize that memories of food led them to hope, and hope fed their resilience—hence the title. Thinking and talking about cherished food was not a reminder of what they did not have but created hope for what they might have again. Their food recollections provided foundation for them when they were in tenuous settings. It was a bond to those who longed for familiar tastes; it was a way to bring family back to life and bring life to those who felt lost.

As we moved from story to recipe, I saw smiles return and clenched hands ease. Food memory is transformative; it is a thread that weaves through all our lives. For Holocaust survivors, it brought them back to happier times. So many remarked that talking about the recipe, the preparation and the gathering around the table bridged their former to their current life. They drew on a recollection of their mother preparing *challah* for *Shabbos* or baking a potato *kugel* for what might be their last Passover *seder* together as a family. The constant in all the dishes they shared with me was they represent a memory of food that needs to be preserved.

I quickly discovered that Jewish food is hard to define. I began to question, what really makes a food Jewish? To a Sephardic Jew (one who can trace their roots to Spain after the inquisition), it is stuffed onions and chicken with okra that graced her holiday table. For a German survivor, it might be *arroz con pollo* and fried plantains that she learned to prepare as a refugee in the Dominican Republic, and for a Polish survivor, it is the coveted Shabbos dinner with chopped liver, matzo ball soup and roast chicken. The answer to my question was, more accurately, what isn't Jewish food? There were common features to survivors from particular regions in both their wartime experiences and their cooking style. That's why we arranged the book geographically, based on where the survivor was originally from.

Each chapter begins with brief historical context and some culinary insights. I invite you to delve more deeply into both. I know you will be welcomed by the traditional recipes that are associated with Jewish food, but I also know you will be inspired by the new interpretations and less familiar recipes that are presented in the book.

My first interview was with Regina Finer, the mother of Museum board member Evelyn Goldfeier. Evelyn explained to me that every question you ask a survivor is answered one or two hours later. You will hear about the cat's cough, an unforgettable trip to Israel or a visit to the dentist, and then your question will be answered. I was forewarned to be patient but dogged. If I let the interview get away from me, I might never get it back. I sat down with Regina, ready to listen and poised to ask numerous questions. I left my watch behind. She shared her moving story with me, and we both then gathered ourselves and moved on to her recipe.

ME: So Regina, tell me about a food that you remember enjoying as a child, something you still make today.

REGINA: Kluskies, potato dumplings.

ME: Do you have the recipe?

REGINA: I don't need a recipe to make them.

ME: Well, can you describe to me how you go about it, so I can share your "recipe" with others?

REGINA: Well, you take some potatoes.

ME: How many?

REGINA: How many? I never counted.

EVELYN: Mom, when you make dumplings, do you buy a bag of potatoes?

REGINA: Of course I buy a bag; the price is much better when you buy a bag.

EVELYN: And when you make your dumplings, do you use the entire bag?

REGINA: What, you think I would waste potatoes?

EVELYN: And can you carry the entire bag of potatoes?

REGINA: Who else is going to carry them for me?

EVELYN TO ME: Start with five pounds of potatoes.

Nearly every recipe unfolded this same way. I needed to be mindful that most were just children when their upheaval occurred. Recipes were another casualty, and faded memory became the source, as any true record of the recipe did not survive.

How do you write a cookbook based on loose formulas when most of these cooks prepare from instinct, taste and smell or by

shitteryne, a little of this and a little of that? How much is an eggshell of matzo meal or a glass of oil—back in the day it was a *Yahrzeit*, a memorial glass. Is a *bisel* a teaspoon or a pinch? And what about those recipes written in shorthand or scribbled as illegible notes stained with cooking oil and sauce? How do you assign servings when so many of the dishes can serve as an appetizer, light lunch or sweet dessert?

That's when I knew I needed to meticulously test and retest every recipe, so I could write each precisely, providing you with clear directions, accessible ingredients, consistent format and exact measurements.

The servings are Jewish portions (generous), and preparations are all kosher, out of respect for Jewish tradition. Prep time was tricky to determine as some of the dishes need to marinate for days and others assume you have three hands. (That's where my *Start to Finish* notation in the recipes comes in.) In some cases, I provide an alternate preparation and a notation I call *Feedback* where I share a variation, a reference to another's recipe or a food tidbit I learned along the way. Some recipes have been updated. No, bread crumbs were not a staple in most eastern European households, and food processors weren't machines but rather the people who did the laborious tasks of cutting and chopping.

However, even with all of this reconfiguring, the integrity of the recipe was maintained. All recipes were reviewed and approved by the contributor, and some even remarked that the small changes that were made created a version more reminiscent of what they remembered.

After a year of testing, my patient husband remarked, "For a year we have eaten like eighty-year-old Polish peasants," and he wasn't complaining a bit!

One thing I learned was the true definition of the two words I heard over and over: "The Best." Every contributor swore their gefilte fish or matzo ball soup was the best. How could that be? And then it hit me: the best had less to do with the ingredients and preparation and more to do with the association and tradition. The best soup I ever tasted was at my grandmother's table, surrounded by family, being shushed by my father and encouraged to misbehave by his. The soup might have been a little salty and the matzo balls sat like leaden spheres in my stomach, but I would have sworn that soup was perfection. Every recipe in this book represents someone's best, and there's a legion of loyal tasters who would swear to that. When you replicate a dish from this book, be faithful to the recipe, but be sure to include a piece of yourself in every preparation. Make it your own, make a food memory and tradition to make it the best your family ever tasted.

There are dishes that will appeal to your inner chef and others that are simple and straightforward. What they all have in common is the journey they have made, how they relate to the story that is being told and the survivor they honor. There were the recipes remembered that the survivor could not recreate, a technique that was watched but not learned, a flavor that was lost but not forgotten. That's when I developed my version (noted by JH in the recipe) and brought in our professional contributors. Their recipes were designed to complement, not replace, the survivors' recollections, and without exception, these talented chefs, cookbook authors and restaurateurs graciously stepped in.

Last and most importantly, you hold in your hands a piece of history, one that is fading due to time or indifference. It was my *bashert* to write this book and yours to read it thoughtfully, cook from it faithfully and share it generously. I spent hundreds of hours listening, learning, laughing and crying. I heard incredible stories of optimism, resolve, bravery and luck. I came home with recipes to test, savor, share and enjoy. The survivor community has so much to teach; I hope you will give voice to their photos, devour their words and savor their message as you welcome *Food, Hope and Resilience* into your home.

POLAND

It seems fitting to start the book with the stories and recipes from our Polish survivors. Not only do they represent the largest group of contributors, but their food represents many of the iconic Jewish classics as well. The German invasion of Poland on September 1, 1939, triggered World War II, although anti-Semitic sentiment and regulations had existed for many years before that. It was in Poland the Nazi regime established the most notorious death camps, including Belzec, Sobibor, Treblinka, Majdanek and Auschwitz-Birkenau, where alone more than one million souls perished. In all, 90 percent of the prewar Jewish Polish population were murdered, estimated at three million. Three million others who deviated from the Aryan standard perished as well.

After the devastating effects of the war, many of the survivors from Poland were sent to DP camps, as returning to a ravaged home was not an option. Those who could, immigrated to the United States, Canada or Israel (then called Palestine) and brought with them comforting preparations that have become a mainstay in our treasury of Jewish recipes. Meals would start with an appetizer known as *forshpeiz* and always end with something delectably delicious, like apple cake, made sweeter when prepared by a *Galicianer*, from southern Poland, or less so when baked by a *Litvak*, a Lithuanian Jew. While we have packed this chapter with surprises and culinary twists and turns, familiar dishes such as challah, chopped liver, gefilte fish, matzo ball soup, noodle kugel and brisket all appear in this section. You will find an array of foods, savory and sweet, familiar and unfamiliar, contributed by people from this region.

As we catch our collective breath, we read the stories and enjoy new interpretations and traditional recipes remembered from these resilient survivors.

There is an old eastern European folktale, the parable of stone soup, that captures the essence of Polish cooking. Like stone soup, Polish cuisine is a creative mix of available, affordable ingredients. A little of this and a bit of that, lovingly tossed together to make a nourishing, satisfying meal.

STONE SOUP

In a small shtetl in Poland, the people were struggling, and food was scarce. A soldier marched into the tiny village, hungry and tired, and asked for something to eat. The townspeople told him of their plight, and he reassured them that he could make a delicious soup from a stone. He dropped a stone into a pot of boiling water, and a crowd began to gather. They were skeptical, but the soldier assured them of a rich broth; so, they waited with great anticipation to taste the soup. He encouraged the villagers to contribute small offerings from their gardens and farms. Soon the villagers began tossing in bits of cabbage, carrots, mushrooms, onions and potatoes. Some threw in pieces of beef, turkey and chicken as the soldier encouraged them and told them how delicious the soup would taste. By the time the entire village had gathered to watch, the pot was filled with every vegetable grown in that small town and every cut of meat the butcher could find. Hand-rolled dumplings and homemade noodles filled the pot, and the aroma was splendid. The finished soup had an intense color and flavor, and the villagers and the soldier enjoyed a wonderful meal.

RECIPES

Regina Finer's *Kluskies*—Classic Potato Dumplings

Angie Goldfeier's Chicken Savoy Soup

Susie Fishbein*: Sesame Beef and Broccoli over Ramen Noodles

JH*: *Gribenes and Schmaltz*—Chicken Skin Cracklings and Rendered Fat

Eric and Bruce Bromberg*: Martha's Excellent Matzoh Ball Soup

Judith Ginsburg's Brisket

The Ginsburg Family Corned Beef

Rae Kushner's Potato Chip Kugel

Mark Bittman*: Simplest Whole Roast Chicken

Mark Strausman*: *Spaghetti al Rustico di Cipole*—Spaghetti with Onion and Tomato Sauce

Nadzia Bergson's Home Baked Challah

Faye Levy*: Apple Challah Bread Pudding

Ada Rubin's Chocolate Chip Cake

Frania Faywlowicz's Meat and Potato *Cholent*

Rhoda Fishler's Meringue Nut Cookie

Hela Fisk's Plum Cake

Joan Nathan*: Classic Gefilte Fish

Natalie Gomberg's *Mohn*—Poppy Seed Cookies

Henny Gurko's Roasted Chicken and Vegetables

Sara Moulton*: Esther's Chicken Fricassee

Celina Hecht's Fresh Yellow Pepper Soup

Gil Marks*: Bialys—Polish Onion Rolls

The Jacobs Family: Baba's Dough and Baba's Cheesecake

Michael Solomonov*: Beets with *Tehina* and Prepared *Tehina*

Celia Kener's *Holishkes*—Shortcut Unstuffed Cabbage

Miriam Lesorgen's *Kreplach*—Stuffed Noodle Dumpling

JH*: Orange Honey Ginger Soy Dipping Sauce

Dina Liverant's *Kutletela*—Small Chicken Burger

Lily Margules's *Tzimmes*—Chicken with Prunes

Mark Strausman*: *Involtini di Manzo*—Beef Braciole

Helen Ptashnik's Braised Red Cabbage and Apples

Arthur Schwartz*: *P'tcha*—Jellied Calf's Feet with Garlic

Gita Roback's Slow Simmered Sunday Sauce

Jeff Nathan*: Duck with Apple and White Raisin Sauce

Sally Rosenkranz's Honey Cake

Judy Bart Kancigor*: Louis Selmanowitz's Chopped Herring

Ina Garten*: Chopped Liver

Ruth Stromer's Honey and Lemon Stuffed Cabbage

Florence Tabrys's Sweet and Creamy Cheese Blintzes

David Waltuck*: Blintzes of Fresh and Smoked Salmon with Caviar Cream

Florence Tabrys's *Jablecznik*—Polish Apple Cake

Sabina Goldman's Bursting with Blueberries Tart

Ruth Tobias's Orange-Flavored Sponge Cake

Ruth Tobias's *Peperonata*—Bell Peppers

Hanna Wechsler's Strawberry-Filled *Naleshniki*—Blintzes

JH*: Strawberry Sauce

Michael Solomonov*: Tehina—Hummus

Jennifer Abadi*: *Chibiz*—Syrian Pita or Pocket Bread

JH*: Chilled Cherry Soup

Eva Young's Creamy Cheese Noodle Kugel

Millie Zuckerman's Sugar Cookies

*Indicates professional contributor

Regina Schmidt Finer

In her own words

Regina was the first person I interviewed for this book. She set the bar for everyone to come. Her humor and positive outlook immediately put me at ease. Regina left me smiling when she asked if I thought we might make it on to a national talk show to tell her story and demonstrate her cooking; she felt that would be a great outcome. I know she would be pleased that you are reading her moving story and preparing her cherished recipe.

I was a teenager when I was taken from my home, just outside of Warsaw, Poland. That was the last time I saw my parents. I was sent to the Warsaw ghetto along with my younger brother and sister and my aunt, who was two years older than me. For many months, we hid in a bunker in the ghetto and avoided being transported to a camp. Eventually, like all the others in the ghetto, we were discovered and sent to Majdanek. I went there with my sister and aunt; my brother was left behind, hidden in a kitchen cabinet. I fear he did not survive. In the camp, my sister and I were separated. I remember seeing her on that first day and she seemed angry that we were apart; I felt terrible. On the second day there, I looked but couldn't find her. I never saw her again. My aunt and I were moved to many camps, including Auschwitz. Although my aunt was older than me, I felt I was the stronger one and knew I had to protect her. The day of our last move, we were placed on different lines. I appealed to a guard to put us on the same line; I didn't care where it was going—I just wanted us to be together. Luckily, she was moved to my line, the one that survived.

We were marched on foot through the woods of Germany, heading to our next and final destination. We knew that this would be our last chance to escape. When it became dark, we escaped into the woods. We stole boys' clothing from a laundry line and found shelter at a farmer's home. He and his wife sheltered us for several months, until the Russian army liberated us. My aunt and I returned to Poland to find our home and family gone. My aunt wasn't well, and a very kind gentleman offered us a place to stay; he later became her husband. I traveled to a displacement camp, where I met and married my husband. We eventually came to America, where we raised our children. Through it all, there were so many memories of my childhood that helped me get through the difficult times.

So many of my memories revolved around traditions and food. I remember how our family and neighbors gathered in my mother's home for Shabbos. It was a competition to see who was the biggest *baleboste*—that was determined by who baked the best challah and made the best noodles for the kugel. Holidays were especially joyous; the house was freshly

Regina Schmidt Finer holding her son Arthur, surrounded by fellow passengers as they disembarked the SS *General Blatchford* at Ellis Island, having just arrived in America, in 1950.

painted, and the kitchen was cleaned spotless. The holidays meant get dressed, go to *shul*, come home and eat! My mother would call me to help her, "Rivkala, help me chop, help me bake the cookies, help me make the gefilte fish." In those days, the fish was stuffed into the head of a carp! I now make that same recipe for my family, but I leave the fish head out of it. I love to make potato dumplings, Polish cakes and kugel.

There is a feeling of community that binds us all. Everyone should treat everyone else with respect and respect his or her religion. And most of all, the message I pass on to my three children, three grandchildren and two great-grandchildren is: remember to be a *mensch.*

Author's Note: I sadly learned that Regina has passed away. She now has three great-grandchildren. May her memory be for a blessing.

Regina Finer's *Kluskies*—Classic Potato Dumplings

Think of this recipe as the little black dress of potato dishes. It goes with everything, and you can keep it basic or dress it up. Their firm but spongy consistency makes them perfect to soak up rich gravy or float happily in a bowl of soup. For a variation, Regina often sautéed some onions and spooned them over the dumplings. When preparing the dumplings, Regina suggested you have an old rag or *shmatte* handy to wring out the excess water from the grated potatoes. If you don't have a shmatte, no worries—a dishtowel or cheesecloth will do just fine.

Yield: About 30 dumplings
Start to Finish: Under 30 minutes

6 russet potatoes (about 2 pounds), peeled,
 then grated
3/4 cup all-purpose flour, sifted
1/4 cup matzo meal
1 egg, beaten

1/2 onion, grated (about 1/3 cup)
1 1/2 teaspoons kosher salt
6 turns grated black pepper

Bring a large pot of salted water to boil.

Grate the potatoes using a box grater or food processor fitted with the metal blade. If using a processor, do so in several batches and use the pulse feature to break up any chunks that do not finely grate. Place the grated potatoes in a towel and wring out the excess water.

Stir in the flour, matzo meal, beaten egg, onion, salt and pepper and mix thoroughly. Nothing works better than your hands, so get in there and knead the dough. You'll know it's ready when it is no longer sticky, adding a little extra matzo meal as needed. Roll the mixture in your hands and form small dumplings about the size of a walnut.

Drop the dumplings into the pot of salted boiling water. Do not over crowd the pot, as the dumplings will stick together; shake the pot while boiling to free those that cling to the bottom. Boil until they float to the top, about 5 minutes. Remove with a slotted spoon and allow them to drain. Serve while they are still nice and hot.

Angie Goldfeier and Moritz "Moshe" Goldfeier

As told by Angie and excerpted from Museum of Jewish Heritage material

Walking into Angie's home in Manhattan was like stepping into a beautiful china shop in eastern Europe. The only difference was this shop was run by a gracious Holocaust survivor with a terrific sense of humor and a flair for conversation and cooking. Her table displayed delicious desserts, and I nibbled marble sponge cake throughout our conversation.

Angie Goldfeier, in her own words
When the war began and affected Poland, I was only nine years old. Within three years, both of my parents were taken from our home. At first, I lived with strangers, and then I moved into the ghetto on the outskirts of town. Toward the end of 1942, my older sister Regina and I were moved from the ghetto and sent to the first of several camps we were in. I credit my sister, and a lot of luck, with my survival. When liberated from Bergen-Belsen, we returned to Poland to find our remaining family members. We found one sister and learned that our two brothers had survived and were living in Germany. For the next three years, I lived in Germany, with my sister at my side. When I came to the United States, I felt uncomfortable at first. While my husband attended to business in Germany, I moved to Florida to be with my sister; this helped me accept my new life. I am very grateful to this country, because sixty-five years ago, I would never dream I would be where I am today.

Angie Goldfeier and Moritz "Moshe" Goldfeier.

Moshe's story, based on material from the Museum of Jewish Heritage
Moshe was born in 1927 in Brzeziny, Poland, in a traditional home, where he was one of four children. His mother attended to the cooking and cleaning and made holidays memorable

and special. His grandfather was a rabbi, and he gave him a strong Jewish identity. In 1939, when Moritz was twelve, the family learned of the German invasion of Poland.

Fearing for their lives, his father and cousin fled to the Soviet Union, and Moshe's mother ultimately was held accountable for those actions. Friends and relatives stepped in to care for the children. Within months, a ghetto had been formed. Moshe's mother was able to find a teacher willing to give Moshe Jewish lessons. She then secretly gathered a *minyan* in a tailor shop and even obtained a Torah—all so he could celebrate becoming a Bar Mitzvah.

In May 1942, after Moshe lost his younger brother, the ghetto was liquidated, and the inhabitants were moved to another in Lodz. They worked and lived there until the summer of 1944, when this ghetto was closed as well. The two remaining brothers, their mother and sister were sent to Auschwitz. Moshe's mother and sister did not survive, but he and his brother, Berek, did, having been transferred to a labor camp, where they remained until they were liberated. After liberation, the two brothers headed to Germany in hopes of finding other family members. It was there Moshe met and married Angie. Moshe learned that his father survived and had immigrated to Israel. They reconnected and saw each other every year. Sixty-one years later, he and Angie are the proud parents of two children, five grandchildren and six great-grandchildren.

Author's Note: I sadly learned that both Angie and Moshe have passed away. May their memory be for a blessing.

Angie Goldfeier's Chicken Savoy Soup

Chicken soup was a staple in every Polish home. It would be prepared for Shabbos and stretched to last throughout the week. Every cook had her own variation. Angie's is really a departure from the usual, and the results are rich and satisfying. She combines three different meats to create the stock and lots of root vegetables and herbs. The crowning glory is the head of Savoy cabbage that flavors the broth and anchors the taste. Angie has a special way to prepare the flanken to prevent *schmutz,* an unpleasant foam, from, as she says, "ruining your soup." At the end, she adds one packet of chicken flavor seasoning to help bring all the flavors together.

Yield: About 12 servings
Start to Finish: Under 4 hours (for best results, refrigerate overnight)

1 pound beef flanken, boiled and rinsed
1 (3½- to 4-pound) chicken, quartered and rinsed
2 turkey wings, rinsed
1 head Savoy cabbage (about 1½ pounds), halved
4 carrots, rinsed and cut into chunks (about 2 cups)

2 turnips, washed and halved
2 parsnips, washed and cut into large chunks
4 celery ribs, rinsed, cut into large chunks (about 2 cups)
Kosher salt and pepper
½ cup chopped fresh dill leaves
1 packet G. Washington's Golden seasoning or 1–2 chicken bouillon cubes

Bring a medium pot of water to boil and add the beef flanken. Boil for 30 minutes, skimming off and discarding the foam that rises to the surface. While the beef cooks, put the chicken, turkey wings, cabbage, carrots, turnips, parsnips and celery in an extra-large soup pot. Fill the pot with enough cold water to cover all the meat and vegetables. Bring the water to boil, skimming and discarding any foam that rises to the surface.

Remove the flanken from the pot and rinse it quickly under cold running water. Pat the meat dry and add to the soup pot, adding more water if needed to cover the meat. Season with salt and pepper and simmer, covered, for 2 to 3 hours, until the soup taste has fully developed.

Strain the broth, discarding everything except the cabbage. Slice the cabbage and reserve; you will add it back to the soup when it is time to serve. If time allows, cool the soup in the refrigerator overnight so the fat will rise to the top and solidify, making it easy to remove and discard. Before serving, add the cabbage, dill and 1 seasoning packet or bouillon cube to the soup. Heat until the soup and cabbage are nice and hot.

Sonia Bielski and Zus Bielski

As told by their sons Zvi and Jay Bielski

If the name Bielski sounds familiar that could be because of the 2008 film *Defiance*, in which Daniel Craig and Liev Schreiber play the roles of two of the four Bielski brothers, who were responsible for saving over 1,200 Jews. These brave souls created a community and fought as partisans deep in the forest. They account for over 20,000 descendants who would not be here today had it not been for the heroic actions of the Bielski brothers. I spoke to proud family members Zvi and Jay, who shared their family story. Several other contributors to this book were part of the Bielski partisans and are quick to say they owe their lives to these courageous men.

Zvi Bielski

I remember when I was a soldier in the Israeli army, and I was with friends at the Yad Vashem Memorial. I was fooling around with my buddies, when one of them called out to me, "Bielski, we gotta go." A couple walked over to me and asked, "You Bielski? We know the Bielskis, are you related?" When I told them I was the son of Zus Bielski, they literally fell to their knees and cried uncontrollably. I can feel it in my bones even now. They began to tell me stories about how my family saved their family and how they would not be here today were it not for my father and his brothers. I felt very honored. At the time of the war, they were just a small group, my dad and uncles and a few other families, hiding in the forest that my father and uncles knew so well. They would send people into the ghetto to smuggle others out. They would bribe the guards, even get them drunk to enable those inside to escape under the fence. They were devoted to saving as many Jewish lives as possible.

One man came to my dad and said, "I have a cousin, maybe we should get her out too."

Zus Bielski.

My father brazenly asked, "Is she cute?" That woman was named Sonia. They sneaked her out; her parents had to force her to go. She hid during the day and traveled at night. When she arrived at the camp, she was so frightened; she was only seventeen at the time. When my mother joined the group, she was happy to find a woman whom she had known from home. The woman was Chaya, my uncle Asael's girlfriend. My mom jokingly asked Chaya if there was another commander, another brother, for her. It was then that she was introduced to my father, who was a strong, tall, good-looking guy (my parents were together for fifty-five years!). Days later, he arranged for my grandparents to escape the ghetto.

My father was always my hero; he was like a giant to me. I look back on my childhood and remember the impact of my father's story. I was a second or third grader, and I remember when the Beatles came to the United States. All my classmates felt the Beatles were their heroes. I tapped a classmate on the shoulder and said that if she really wanted to hear a story and meet a hero, she should meet my dad. That was my family history. Resistance in the purest sense is what they did. Resistance takes many forms, as even today we are still defying the Nazis by retelling these stories.

Jay Bielski
(a recollection of Sonia's cooking)
In 1970, we moved into our first American house; it was in Brooklyn, New York. Alex "Zus" and Sonia loved that house. It was the first house since before the war that we could all call our own. There it was a giant kitchen with a fan to blow out the heat; they were so proud. We were living the American dream. We lived ten minutes from Tuvia, Lilka and their three kids. Some weekends it was Sonia's turn to cook for Lilka's family. She had a giant pot in which she made *chaunt—*

that's beans, beef, potatoes, carrots, celery, onions, garlic and whatever was fresh in the season. In addition, the centerpiece would be the *kishke*. The kishke was made from a cow's intestines, which were thoroughly cleaned and stuffed with mincemeat, sometimes rice and vegetables and flour. People would drop by to socialize and recall the partisan days, have some chaunt, drink some vodka and tell the developing stories of their lives. They spoke of the new births, Bar Mitzvahs, weddings, deaths, birthdays and graduations of various kinds. What was left unsaid was that they were there in Zus and Sonia's house, with Tuvia's family, as well as Aaron, the youngest Bielski partisan. The whole thing was a miracle that they were alive.

Taeba Seltzer Bielski, who gave her infant daughter Lola to be raised by Polish peasants later retrieved by Zus with a gun, during the war, was there. Lola was now grown up and

Sonia Bielski.

married with kids. It was a group cook-off, just like in the woods of Belarus. They made veal ribs with pockets and tzimmes.

Those two main dishes were done for weekends, which inevitably featured Bielski partisans from all over the metropolitan area. They would come over and stay late to play cards, gin rummy mostly for the ladies. Some would smoke, and they gambled while the men played poker. Mostly they drank shots that they didn't have to duck from! We can't forget the butcher on 17th and M in Brooklyn. His name was Abie Kotler, and he was the chief butcher from the Bielski partisans. He would be the one to get the cow's intestines or the chicken feet (used for another great dish), which tasted like kosher shrimp, cooked over a slow fire with a tomato base with onions, garlic, carrots and celery. It was succulent! Everyone would just be sucking and sucking trying not to make too many unpleasant noises; these were cultured partisans, don't forget!

The women were educated back then, from good families, and fortunately they met up with some unruly Jewish menfolk who had the audacity to be defiant against ever-changing enemies: Nazis, Belarusians, Poles and the Cossacks, all out to destroy them. And so, in the end there are twenty to thirty thousand living Jews because of Tuvia, Zus, Asael and Aaron who all long to eat the foods of their Maccabees, the defiant Bielskis. I still cook for this Bielski clan, which includes three children, six grandchildren and one great-grandchild. They still can get a touch of partisan food on a regular basis. It's just difficult to get cow's intestines to stuff these days, so aluminum foil will have to do.

Sesame Beef and Broccoli over Ramen Noodles

Zvi laughed when I asked him what recipe his mother, Sonia, would like to contribute to the book. "If you were to ask her what she made for dinner on Sunday nights, she would have to say, 'reservations.' She loved to go to Chinatown for great Chinese food." In her honor, Susie Fishbein, best-selling author of the *Kosher by Design* series of books, provided a wonderful dish that Sonia just might have ordered on a typical Sunday night.

Excerpted from *Kosher by Design Entertains* (Artscroll/Shaar Press, 2005)
Yield: 6 servings

¼ cup reduced sodium soy sauce
3 tablespoons rice wine vinegar
2 tablespoons hoisin sauce
2 tablespoons dark brown sugar
1 tablespoon chopped fresh ginger or ¼ teaspoon ground ginger
2 teaspoons roasted or toasted sesame oil
2 teaspoons cornstarch
¼ teaspoon crushed red pepper flakes
2 pounds pepper steak sliced into long, thin strips

2 (3-ounce) packages beef or oriental [soy]-flavored ramen noodles (reserve 1 spice packet, discard the other)
4 scallions, sliced
1 teaspoon roasted or toasted sesame oil
1 tablespoon canola oil
3 cloves garlic, minced
12 ounces broccoli florets, cut into small pieces
Sesame seeds

In a Ziploc bag or non-reactive bowl, combine the soy sauce, vinegar, hoisin sauce, brown sugar, ginger, sesame oil, cornstarch and pepper flakes. Add the meat and marinate for 30 minutes in the refrigerator.

Place 4 cups water into a medium pot. Bring to a boil and add the 2 packages ramen noodles with one of the spice packets. Add the scallions and 1 teaspoon sesame oil. Remove from the heat; let stand, covered. Set aside.

In a large skillet or wok, heat the canola oil to medium heat. Remove the meat from the marinade, reserving marinade, and add the meat to the skillet. Cook for 3 minutes. Add in the minced garlic. Add the broccoli and sauté for 6–8 minutes. Add the marinade into the pan and stir until thickened. Toss to combine.

Serve over the ramen noodles. You can drain them or serve them in the broth. Sprinkle with sesame seeds.

Fruma Gulkowich Berger and Murray Berger

As told by their son Ralph Berger

The Museum of Jewish Heritage's amazing exhibit titled *Daring to Resist* has among its artifacts a simple fork and spoon. These innocuous utensils would seem commonplace were it not for the fact that they survived along with Ralph's mother, Fruma, as she lived in the woods of Poland as part of the "Bielski Brigade." Ralph shared with me some of his recollections of his parents and their life in America.

My father was from Wsielub, Russia, and my mom was from Korelicze, Poland. They met as fighters in the Bielski Brigade after they had escaped from the Novogrudok Ghetto. My father was an original member of the group, one of the fifteen men who elected Tuvia Bielski as commander of the brigade. My mom escaped after the ghetto *Aktion* on August 7, 1942, in which over four thousand innocent Jews were killed. My mother and her sister-in-law, Judy Gulkowich, escaped by hiding in a cesspool for six days without any food. My uncle, Ben Zion Gulkowich, rescued them. Soon thereafter, all three escaped into the woods and joined the Bielski partisans. My father would always say with a sly smile, "I found my wife in the woods." For nearly two and a half years, my parents were fighters in the Bielski Brigade, which they spoke openly about after the war. The spoon and fork displayed in the Museum exhibit were the only possessions my mother had left from her parents' home. She escaped from the ghetto with them, cooked with them while

in the brigade, carried them across Europe and displaced persons camps and then used them to prepare delicious meals for family and friends for the next fifty years.

My brother, Al, and I were born here in America and were raised in a traditional household. Every Friday night, it was chicken soup with matzo balls or noodles, chicken, potato kugel or noodle pudding, tzimmes and some kind of cake like *babka* or *zemmel*. My mom was a great cook, making everything from scratch. Her gefilte fish was really second to none. She and my dad would go from one fish store to another before the holidays to find the best fish. Growing up, the holidays were bittersweet. The food would be delicious, but our celebrations were different from those of the kids with American-born parents. We didn't have grandparents and lots of aunts and uncles and cousins surrounding the table and sharing in the holiday. For my family, you also could not have a celebration without great food.

I remember lots and lots of food on the table at the *Kiddush* in my parents' home following

Fruma and Murray Berger.

my Bar Mitzvah. Shortly after most of the company had left and the table was cleared, Tuvia Bielski, who lived across the street with his family, came in to tell us that he had just become a grandfather. Immediately. the food came back out. I can still picture Tuvia, my dad and my Uncle Ben doing shots and eating gefilte fish. One of my favorite dishes was *gribenes*, chicken cracklings. Even when I was in college and law school, I would bring gribenes back with me from my visits home and everyone would go crazy for it. I am spoiled by my mother's cooking, as even now I judge the traditional Jewish foods by what she would make, and they usually just don't compare. My parents were married for forty-eight years and had two children and two grandchildren.

Gribenes and Schmaltz—Chicken Skin Cracklings and Rendered Fat

Ralph is certainly not the only child of eastern Europeans who remembers the intense aroma or rich flavor of gribenes, a Jewish delicacy that has humble roots. Out of necessity, the Jewish homemaker would render her own chicken, duck or goose fat, and the by-product, crisp cracklings, would be shmeared on thick slices of challah bread, sprinkled with salt and devoured. For the most authentic chopped liver, delicious *pierogi* filling or to fry just about anything, try using the rendered chicken fat known as *schmaltz*. It will take your kitchen back in time and fill your senses with a sense of tradition.

Collect the fat from the excess skin of chicken, duck or goose. It might take time to do so; simply clip the fat and store it in the freezer in a tightly sealed bag until you have enough to render. Be careful not to clip any meat with the fat. When you have collected about 2 cups, you can render the fat and create gribenes from the combination of skin and onions. You might also ask your butcher to collect the trimmings for you.

Yield: About 2 cups schmaltz
Start to Finish: Under 1½ hours

2 cups chicken, goose or duck fat, cut into small pieces or strips

1 medium onion, sliced

Place the cut fat and about ½ cup of water (enough to cover the fat) in a heavy skillet or cast-iron pan and cook over low heat until the fat begins to liquefy and the water begins to evaporate. Stir the onions into the pan and continue cooking over very low heat until the skin and onions are very brown, but not burnt. Remove the bits of skin and onions with a slotted spoon and allow them to drain on a paper towel. Pour the fat into a jar that has a tight-fitting lid and refrigerate for up to 3 months or freeze for up to a year. Spread the cracklings on a slice of bread and sprinkle with kosher salt or use them to flavor a multitude of dishes.

JH

Eric and Bruce Bromberg

Professional contributors

No doubt Ralph would love to have a steaming bowl of his mom's chicken soup, just as he did every Friday night growing up. While Fruma is not here to provide that recipe, we have the real deal provided to us by Eric and Bruce Bromberg, chef/owners of the Blue Ribbon restaurants. Grandma Martha's chicken and matzoh ball soup is a mainstay on their brasserie menu.

Martha's Excellent Matzoh Ball Soup

Contributed by Eric and Bruce Bromberg, chef/owners of Blue Ribbon restaurant, New York City

Our Grandmother Martha's influence is everywhere in our restaurants but perhaps no more prevalent anywhere than in this dish, which defined her grace and profound understanding of all that is good in so many ways. Martha brought the matzoh balls and was often touted with delight at our family gatherings and holidays. It was said with resolve and relief as if it meant that everything was going to be just fine. It was a constant, something we could all always count on. It meant that even if the brisket was overcooked and the *blintzes* dry, the kugel too sweet and the chopped liver bland, the *haroset* overly alcoholic and the wine barely passable that everything would fall into irrelevance once you bit into those ethereal cloudlike matzoh balls and sipped her deceptively simple and transcending broth laden with dill, carrots and its luminescent golden puddles of schmaltz that danced and dipped on the turbulent surface.

There was a specific method to the recipe, a temperature for the eggs and other ingredients that were treated with love and reverence, a specific urn for transportation to a relative's house, a specific linen that shrouded that urn and even a wicker basket reserved for that occasion, and that occasion only, to transport the contents as if they were as precious as the sanctity of our beliefs or even baby Moses on his journey down the river Nile. Perhaps this is just a recipe, but for us and hopefully in its own way will be so much more for you as well. It is a way of life, a return to simpler things, simple things that if done just so can transform life and lead to so much more.

FOR THE BROTH

1 whole hen (3–4 pounds)

4 ribs celery with leaves, cleaned and chopped

3 carrots, cleaned and chopped

1 onion, chopped

2 leeks, cleaned and chopped

3 cloves garlic (whole)

4 sprigs flat parsley

3 sprigs dill

½ teaspoon black peppercorns

2 dried bay leaves

1 tablespoon kosher salt

GARNISH

Carrot rounds, blanched till soft

Chopped dill

Salt and pepper

FOR THE MATZOH BALLS

1 cup matzo meal

4 eggs

1 ounce rendered chicken fat (schmaltz)

½ ounce kosher salt

½ teaspoon double-acting baking powder

2 ounces seltzer

PROCEDURE BROTH

Rub chicken with kosher salt inside and out. Let stand 15 minutes. Rinse well under cold water. Pat dry with paper towel. Put chicken in a large pot of cold water covering chicken by 3 inches. Bring to boil. Impurities will rise to the top, then skim off and discard. Add everything. Bring back to boil, skim and then reduce to a simmer. Let simmer. After 45 minutes (or until chicken is cooked), remove chicken. Take meat off of bone (save meat for another meal), put bones back in pot. Cook for 1 hour more. Strain through a sieve and cheesecloth and let cool in refrigerator. When cool, fat will rise to the top and solidify, making it easy to remove.

PROCEDURE MATZOH BALLS

In large mixing bowl, add all ingredients except seltzer; mix well. Add seltzer water and let mixture sit covered and refrigerated for 1 hour. Fill a large-diameter pot ¾ full with water and bring to a simmer (190–200 degrees). With wet hands roll out 1-ounce balls. Lower balls into water. Cook until tender, approximately 45–60 minutes (test with toothpick or do the famous chef Eric cut in half). Balls should be light and fluffy in the center. Let matzoh balls cool.

FOR SOUP

Slice carrot into rounds. Chop 2 sprigs of dill. Bring broth to a boil with carrots and dill and matzo balls. Season to taste. Serve when matzoh balls are warm in center.

Judith Kosczianska Ginsburg and Marvin Mordechai "Motke" Ginsburg

As told by Judith and her daughter Fran

Judith described in great detail her experiences during the war. Judith was part of the Bielski partisans, and her husband, Motke, was an active resistance fighter throughout the war. Their story is inspiring, and her recipes, which were collected in a Ginsburg family cookbook, are delicious.

JUDITH

I was born in a town called Lida; it was in Poland but is now called Belarus. When I was sixteen, I was sent to the ghetto with my sister, her husband and their children. The rest of my family had perished. On May 8, 1942, our ghetto was liquidated, and we were marched to the train station; it was a three-kilometer walk. My sister told me to run (she could not because she had the children with her), saying, "One of us should survive." There was a young German soldier marching with us, and I don't know why, but he talked to me. He said, "I don't know where you are going, but it will be bad." I turned to the soldier and said, "I'm going to run, if you shoot me, shoot me." I don't know where I got the courage. A friend of mine was walking with her mother, and her mother told us both to run. We tore off our patches and did just that. We jumped over fence after fence and finally fell into a garden. We waited til we heard the trains leave, staying very quiet until it was pitch dark. We were wet, hungry and crying. This part of the city was unfamiliar to us, but we did know

German guards surrounded it. We encountered a stranger who told us to go with God. I know someone was watching over us that day; God was with us.

We knocked on a door, and while the woman of the house shooed us away, the husband invited us in. He gave us a jug of cold milk and said, "God sent you to my house." He promised that if we stayed the night, he would take us to the partisans. Fearing that this seemed too good to be true, we left during the night and wandered toward the area where we

Judith and Marvin Ginsburg in Foehrenwald DP camp with son Howard.

heard the partisans were hiding. The Russian partisans were looking for recruits, and we joined them. We had to carry guns and go out on actions during the day and defend the camp at night. My friend stayed with them, but after several months, I left that group and joined the Bielskis. The way they are shown in the movie *Defiance* is very accurate. Tuvia, the leader of our group, saved us all and took care of us. Every Jew meant so much to him. Survival there was like a movie. Some local farmers shared food with us; if they didn't, we took the food from them. When you have no choice, you go along with anything you need to do to survive. You learn to put on an act that you're not afraid. I fought with the partisans until we were liberated, after about one and a half years. Over 1,200 people survived because of Tuvia and his protection.

After the war, I returned to my hometown, where I got married to one of the Ginsburg brothers. Though considered heroes among the Russian partisans, they were not Communists and feared conscription. We fled Russia to Poland, Poland to Germany, arriving in Foehrenwald DP Camp. I gave birth to a son and daughter there. I believe our son was the first Jewish child born in that camp. We named him after my husband's younger brother, who was murdered after the liberation...another reason we ran. I wanted to bring young children into the world. There was survivor's guilt—why did I survive, why me? Every survivor feels this way. I knew we had to bring in new generations to build up; that's why my children and family are the most important things.

FRAN

My father, Motke, and his younger brother, Tzalke, were young, strong and heroic, risking their lives to save others in the ghetto. He and his brother joined *Iskra*, a Russian partisan group. They went back to help hundreds escape from the ghetto in Iwje (Iwye), their small hometown. They were valiant fighters who blew up many German transport trains and were responsible for significant acts of sabotage. After the Russians liberated the territory, my father was awarded the Order of Lenin. His family settled in Lida, as there was little left of his shtetl after the war. He shared a big house with his brother, sisters and father. One day, my father's sister saw my hungry mother returning to town and thought it would be nice to bring her home for dinner. The rest is history. My parents were married sixty-one years and have four children, ten grandchildren and fifteen great-grandchildren.

My father had family members in Troy, New York, who sponsored their trip to America. One

The Ginsburg family in Foehrenwald DP camp.

was a kosher butcher, one a turkey farmer. My father became a cattle dealer and dairy farmer, so meat and food were always plentiful in our house. I remember that food was extremely important and had special emphasis because of the times my parents didn't have it. We lived almost communally with my aunt, uncle and cousins; all the holiday cooking was done together. I have vivid childhood memories of my mother and aunt standing at opposite ends in the kitchen stuffing a huge kishke or cooking *taiglach* in a giant vat of honey We even *kashered* our own meat. Our freezer was always filled with amazing baked goods. Even now my mom bakes her own challah and famous *rugelach*. Our food memories were seasonal; in the summer, my father would come with a bushel of this or a sack of that, which could easily result in a night of making pickles. Even if we didn't have money, we always had food.

Author's Note: I sadly learned that Judith has passed away. Her progeny includes ten grandchildren and sixteen great-grandchildren. May her memory be for a blessing.

Judith Ginsburg's Brisket

Every family has a method for preparing brisket. There's the popular onion soup mix or splash of Coca-Cola. Judith's version has no gimmicks, just lots of fresh garlic and vegetables. There are two options when buying the brisket. First cut, commonly referred to as flat brisket, is a lean, carefully trimmed cut. It's a little less juicy and requires less cooking time. The alternative is the whole brisket, which includes the deckle, the top layer. It needs to cook longer to be tender, but the layer of fat lends lots of flavor to the dish. The choice is yours. The sauce is created afterward, and the brisket can be eaten right away or sleep in the sweet and sour gravy to be devoured the next day.

Yield: 8 servings
Start to Finish: Under 4½ hours

1 (5- to 6-pound) brisket
Kosher salt and pepper
2 tablespoons paprika
2 tablespoons garlic powder
1 pound carrots (about 5–6), peeled and cut into chunks
6 medium onions (about 2 pounds), cut into large chunks
8–10 cloves garlic, coarsely chopped

FOR THE SAUCE
1 (14.5-ounce) can condensed tomato soup
1 cup ketchup
2 tablespoons brown sugar
1 tablespoon white vinegar

Preheat the oven to 350 degrees.

Rub the brisket generously with salt, pepper, paprika and garlic powder. Place it in a covered roasting pan with the carrots, onions, garlic and ½ cup of water. Cover and roast until fork tender, about 4 hours, checking on the brisket every hour to see if additional water is needed to prevent the meat from scorching.

When the meat is done, remove it from the roasting pan and thinly slice it against the grain. To make the sauce, stir into the pan ½ cup water, the can of soup, ketchup, brown sugar and vinegar. Place the brisket slices back into the sauce. You can heat the sliced beef and sauce and serve at once or let the brisket soak up the big flavors overnight in the fridge. It will be worth the wait.

Feedback
Eastern European cooks have relied on ketchup as a recipe enhancer for many years. It is a great combination of sweet and sour. Concentrated tomatoes blend with vinegar and sugar and assorted spices, making it a terrific flavor balance in many of our recipes. If you want to bring sweet and sour in a tomato-based recipe, try adding ketchup.

The Ginsburg Family Corned Beef

Corned beef and brisket are the same cut of meat; the difference is that corned beef is brined (cured with large salt kernels), giving it its distinctive taste. The key to home-prepared corned beef is to baby the beef before cooking and be patient while it slowly simmers. It takes a little extra time and attention, but the end result is well worth it. Be warned, your house will smell like your local deli—not such a bad thing!

Yield: Depends on the weight of the beef, about ½ pound per person
Start to Finish: Step 1: 12 –24 hours to soak the beef and change the water,
Step 2: Based on weight, 50 minutes per pound.

1 prepackaged corned beef	3 sprigs fresh thyme
4 celery ribs, cut into bite-sized pieces (about 1½–2 cups)	5 bay leaves
	5 garlic cloves, coarsely chopped
1 medium onion, sliced	3 tablespoons kosher salt
3 sprigs fresh parsley	5 black peppercorns

STEP 1
Remove the meat from the package and rinse under cold water. Cover the beef in a cold-water bath, in the fridge, for at least 12 hours or up to 1 day. This will remove the intense saltiness and soften the meat. Change the water every 2–6 hours, more in the beginning, less as the day goes on. When ready to cook, remove the corned beef from the fridge, rinse and pat dry.

STEP 2
Place the beef in a large Dutch oven with all the remaining ingredients. Cover the meat with fresh cold water and bring to a boil. Lower the heat to a slow simmer and cook until a knife inserted in the center comes out easily, about 50 minutes per pound. The cooking is to tenderize the meat, as the corning process actually cures and "cooks" it. Allow the meat to cool in the liquid before carving into thin slices, against the grain.

If serving with vegetables or potatoes, simmer them in a separate pot, as the corned beef water tends to get fatty. If you reheat the corned beef, be sure to add water to the pot or dish; the beef dries out easily.

Feedback
The third version of this cut of meat is pastrami. It is seasoned with salt, garlic, pepper and spices. It is then smoked and steamed. It requires nothing more than a good piece of rye bread, tangy mustard and a crisp pickle. May we suggest you leave the pastrami to the experts? Go out and buy a good pastrami sandwich to enjoy while the house fills with the aroma of roasted brisket or simmering corned beef.

Rae Kushner and Joseph Kushner

Based on conversations with family members.

The Kushner family is rightfully proud of the bravery and resilience of their matriarch and patriarch. In speaking to their grandson Jared, I learned that he maintains the ancient daily ritual of laying Tefillin (leather boxes containing Torah scrolls, worn during morning prayers). He explained that when he learned that some prisoners in Auschwitz, amid the chaos and devastation, still practiced this daily covenant, he could not do any less. He is equally committed to remembering and honoring his grandparents Rae and Joseph Kushner, who survived the Holocaust.

Jared's grandmother Rae grew up in a middle-class home in Novogrudok, Poland. When the family was forced into the ghetto, they were part of a courageous group who dug a tunnel to freedom. Rae, her sister and their father worked tirelessly digging a tunnel that would lead them outside the ghetto. After many months, Jared's grandmother, aunt and great-grandfather successfully escaped the ghetto. Despite the fact that most of the young people were among the first to emerge, Jared proudly explained that Rae and her sister chose to remain in the rear with their father. Miraculously, they escaped into the woods, where they spent the balance of the war. At times, they hid to evade capture, while at other times they aligned themselves with the Bielskis. Jared's grandfather Joseph Kushner also survived the war by hiding in the woods, sometimes working with the partisans and other times on his own. Rae and Joseph met in the woods and were married in a group ceremony in Budapest. After the war, like so many others, they went to a DP camp in Italy.

Together they came to America, settling first in Brooklyn and then moving to New Jersey. Joseph rose from a standard carpenter to a homebuilder and eventually became a successful real estate developer.

Rae and Joseph Kushner.

When I asked Jared what he learned from his grandparents (he was only four when his grandfather died), Jared said, "I learned that life brings adversity, but you choose how you can respond to it." Jared's love for his grandmother was evident as he described her: "My grandmother always had a smile on her face. She saw horrible things in her life yet somehow remained an incredible optimist who espoused that she felt very blessed. She was always able to get us excited." He continued by saying, "I think it's important to be proud of being Jewish. My family's survival is a miracle, and it is the job of my generation to make sure we make the opportunity of life that we were given count." Together Rae and Joseph had four children, fifteen grandchildren and twenty-eight great-grandchildren!

Kaynahorah.

Rae Kushner's Potato Chip Kugel

This is not so much a recipe as a preparation, but that doesn't diminish the memory of noodles and eggs crisping up in a pan and being served every Shabbos. Jared remembers his grandmother sneaking him into the kitchen to snack on these noodles before dinner was served. They were never eaten sweet; as Rae's daughter Linda explains, "We were Litvaks, Lithuanian Jews," so leave the sugar and cinnamon in the cabinet. Be sure to fry the noodles until they are so crisp that they begin to resemble potato chips.

Yield: 8 servings
Start to Finish: Under 30 minutes

1 (12-ounce) bag no-yolk noodles
1 tablespoon vegetable oil

2 eggs, beaten
Salt and pepper

Boil the noodles according to package directions. If using leftover noodles, rinse them in warm water to bring them back to life. Heat the oil in a 12-inch skillet. Combine the cooked noodles and beaten egg, season with salt and pepper and pour into the heated pan. Cook, over medium heat, until the underside is golden brown. Flip (use a large spatula or use the two-dish method: slide the noodles onto a plate, cover that plate with a second plate and flip, revealing the cooked side on top. Slide back into the pan). Continue browning the second side until very crisp. To serve, cut into eighths. To reheat, wrap in foil, make a slit for the steam to escape and place in the oven on the warming temperature. Serve as a side dish or *nosh*.

Mark Bittman

Professional contributor

Friday night dinner was and still is a time for the Kushner family to come together. It features time-honored food, none more universal for Shabbos dinner than roast chicken. Mark Bittman, the man who knows how to cook everything, shares with us a classic preparation for this ever-present Friday night centerpiece.

Simplest Whole Roast Chicken

Excerpted from *How to Cook Everything* (Wiley 2008)
Yield: 4 servings
Start to Finish: About 1 hour

We justifiably associate roast chicken with elegance, but it can also be super weeknight food, cooked in just about an hour. This method works because the high heat provided by the heated skillet cooks the thighs faster than the breasts, which are exposed only to the heat of the oven. It gives you nice browning without drying out the breast meat, and it's easily varied. If at any point during the cooking the pan juices begin to smoke, just add a little water or wine (white or red, your choice) to the pan. This will reduce browning, however, so don't do it unless you must. I suggest serving the pan juices with the chicken (you can call it "sauce naturel" if you like).

1 whole chicken, 3–4 pounds, trimmed of excess fat	A few sprigs fresh tarragon, rosemary or thyme (optional)
3 tablespoons extra virgin olive oil	5 or 6 cloves garlic, peeled (optional)
Salt and freshly ground black pepper	Chopped fresh herbs for garnish

Heat the oven to 450 degrees. Five minutes after turning on the oven, put a cast-iron or other heavy ovenproof skillet on a rack set low in the oven. Rub the chicken with the olive oil, sprinkle it with salt and pepper and put the herb sprigs on it if you're using them.

When both oven and pan are hot, 10 or 15 minutes later, carefully put the chicken, breast side up, in the hot skillet; if you're using garlic, scatter it around the bird. Roast, undisturbed, for 40–50 minutes or until an instant-read thermometer inserted in the meaty part of the thigh registers 155–165 degrees.

Tip the pan to let the juices from the bird's cavity flow into the pan (if they are red, cook for another 5 minutes). Transfer the bird to a platter and let it rest; if you like, pour the pan juices into a clear measuring cup, then pour or spoon off some of the fat. Reheat the juices, if necessary, quarter the bird, garnish and serve with the pan juices.

Sonya Oshman and Aaron Oshman

In Sonya's words

Listening to Sonya retell her story in vivid detail was like an unimaginable history lesson. She survived so many remarkable events and was an active character in her story of resistance and refusal to give up. Her message to anyone who will listen is, "Hope lives when people remember. You must spread the message that hate is a failure and love a success."

I was born in Novogrudok, Poland, and was the second oldest in a family of five children. I had two wonderful parents who were successful business owners and very influential people. My father was a good friend of the governor, who lived across the street. I went to the best school and continued my studies at the *gymnasium* (secondary school) and dreamed of becoming a doctor. In 1937, when Poland was divided, we resided on the east side, which Russia controlled. Among other changes, we now had to learn to speak Russian. For several years, the Germans, much like Napoleon did in the 1800s, began invading our territory. It was in 1942 when we found ourselves ghettoized and under Nazi control. I was given the job of cleaning the streets of rubble caused by the constant bombing of our town. It soon became clear that our ghetto was being liquidated, and one by one, people were disappearing and not returning. I was part of a group of about 250 people who decided we had to do something to save ourselves. I was lucky to still have one brother, Saul, with me and began to make the acquaintance of Aaron Oshman, the man I would later marry.

We would work during the day at our regular jobs; then at night, tired and

Sonya Oshman.

exhausted, we would dig a tunnel to the outside. We had no real tools, so we used only forks and spoons. Fortunately, we had a carpenter in our group who would sneak lumber back into the ghetto in the sleeves of his coat and use it to shore up the tunnel as we dug. On the rainy evening of September 23, we decided to make our escape. The night would be long; the sky was dark, and an electrician in our group cut the wires that lit the area. One by one, we crawled like mice through the tunnel, praying that the wood beams would support the dirt above us and prevent the tunnel from caving in. When we crawled out the end of what I believe was an almost three-hundred-meter tunnel, we scrambled to safety. Most of our group survived. I escaped with my brother at my side; Aaron and his brother were safely in front of us. When we reached the end, we weren't sure which way to go. I knew that to the right was the ghetto and to the left was a large cornfield situated beside a road. I ran across that road and, for weeks, hid in the fields.

One day, I spotted a little house, much like the one in *Little House on the Prairie*. It was lit by a kerosene lamp, and I could see an elderly man who resembled Santa Claus, sewing. I knocked on his window, and he said in Polish, "Come in my child, don't worry, I will save your life." He had heard about our daring escape and quickly hid me in the potato cellar below the main floor of the house. Aaron was hidden as well, in another area. Every night, for weeks, the old man would bring me a little bread, some potatoes and water. He was a poor man but shared what he had with me. His house was near the forest where we had heard the Bielski partisans were hiding. The land around the forest had soft earth that was like quicksand. The Nazis avoided the area, fearing that they would fall into the dirt and never get out. The Bielskis

Aaron and Sonia Oshman (*seated*) with Matthew. Saul is standing behind them.

knew the land well, so they felt relatively safe in these familiar woods. The farmer took me to the partisans, where I remained until I was liberated. During those years, Aaron and I were able to sneak into his hometown, where a rabbi married us. He was my husband for over fifty-seven years.

After liberation, Aaron and I knew we wanted to go to Israel and that we needed to get to Italy for that trip. There were no trains or planes for us to travel on, so we walked the entire way. First, we crossed from Poland to Romania. When we were in Romania, I noticed a broken gold ladies' watch lying in the street. I wasn't sure I should pick it up, but luckily for us, I did. From Romania we walked to Switzerland, crossing the Alps that were in our path. As we crossed the border from Switzerland into Italy, Russian soldiers tried to hold us back. I took out the watch and said in the Russian I had learned years earlier that the soldier should give this watch to his wife. His eyes lit up, and he allowed us to cross into Italy. On foot, we had made it from Poland to Romania, Romania to Switzerland, Switzerland to Italy and then hopefully on to Israel. In Italy,

I gave birth to my first son and, because I was ill, gave up my dream of going to Israel. We remained in the DP camp for five years. After that time, Aaron; my now five-year-old son, Matthew; and I passed through Ellis Island and landed in America. We were housed on 34th Street, where the wonderful HIAS (Hebrew Immigrant Aid Society) set us up on the tenth floor of a place I used to call Hotel De *Vance*. Through it all, I am a very happy person. I thank God every day when I get up. From this sorrow that I went through, God compensated me with two wonderful children and four beautiful grandchildren.

Mark Strausman

Professional contributor

While in the DP camp in Italy, Sonya recalled, "I shared facilities with other refugees. I cooked a lot of spaghetti and tomato sauce, sprinkled with plenty of Parmesan cheese, what could be bad?" Italian cooking maestro Mark Strausman shares his recipe to honor all the nights that classic spaghetti and tomato sauce nourished Sonya's growing family.

Spaghetti al Rustico di Cipole

Spaghetti with Onion and Tomato Sauce

Excerpted from *Two Meatballs in the Italian Kitchen* (Artisan, a division of Workman Publishing Company Inc., 2007)

This is my favorite everyday pasta dish, and after twenty-five years of serving it to American customers, I can tell you that they like it too. There's nothing easier to make at home since you probably have all the ingredients in the house. It's a perfect example of the way Italian food can be very simple and very delicious at the same time. You'll notice that I sauté the onions in a little bit of butter, rather than olive oil. Over the years, I've found that if I cook the onions slowly in just a small amount of butter, the result is a very creamy sauce without any need to add cream.

Makes about 2 cups sauce
Serves 4–6

2 tablespoons (28 grams) butter
1 medium red onion, thinly sliced
2 cups (480 ml) canned Italian plum tomatoes,
  preferably San Marzano, with their juice,
  pureed in a food processor or food mill
2 tablespoons plus 1 teaspoon kosher salt

1 pound (454 grams) spaghetti or linguine
  (see tip)
¼ cup (1 ounce/28 grams) freshly grated
  Parmigiano-Reggiano cheese
1 tablespoon (15 ml) extra-virgin olive oil

Place the butter in a 10- to 12-inch skillet over medium heat. Add the onion and cook, stirring frequently, until soft, about 5 minutes. Add the tomatoes and 1 teaspoon of the salt. When the mixture starts to bubble, reduce the heat to very low and cook at a bare simmer for 5 minutes. Remove from the heat and set aside.

While the sauce is cooking, fill a 10-quart stockpot with 7 quarts (6.5 liters) of water and bring to a boil over high heat. Add the remaining 2 tablespoons kosher salt. Add the pasta, stir and cook until al dente.

Reserve ½ cup of the pasta cooking water and drain the pasta. Add the pasta to the skillet with the sauce. If the pasta looks dry, add the reserved cooking water 1 tablespoon at a time, tossing to combine between additions. While still tossing the pasta and sauce, slowly sprinkle on the cheese, and toss until all the cheese is incorporated. The dish should look creamy and moist. Serve immediately, drizzling each portion with a little bit of olive oil.

Tip: Look for #11 spaghetti—it's just the right thickness.

Nadzia Goldstein Bergson and Milton Bergson

As told by their children Jaffa Feldman and Simon Bergson

Both Jaffa and Simon recall that not until her later years did their mother, Nadzia, really talk about her experiences during the Holocaust. Had she, they might have learned more about Nadzia's role in the Sonderkommando Revolt that took place in Auschwitz in October 1944. This was the only organized uprising ever recorded at Auschwitz, involving the smuggling of gunpowder to help create the explosives used to destroy a crematorium at the camp. Nadzia was one of those brave women who worked in the clothing department at Auschwitz and aided in the endeavor. While we don't know the extent of her involvement, we do know these women, many from the same city in Poland, would sew "trapdoors" in the lining and hems of their clothing to transfer the gunpowder. Their plot not only resulted in the deaths of SS guards and a commander, but their courageous actions sent a clear message to the Nazi regime as well.

JAFFA

My mom was born and raised in Ciechanow, Poland, which was a relatively large town. She was the oldest of three children from a middle-class family. She had a younger brother and sister but was the only family member to survive the war. My mom was young, healthy and strong, and it certainly helped her survive three long years in Auschwitz. She talked little about the war, opening up more in her last years. She was very proud of her role in smuggling gunpowder through what she described as a women's underground. I know that was an outstanding memory for my mother. I had a lovely childhood; my parents were very social and hardworking. I never knew we were poor in the beginning. Our holidays were very traditional, very European.

Nadzia and Milton Bergson.

Even though we were not very observant, on Friday nights my mother would make the chicken soup and flanken and always enough food, so we didn't need to cook the entire weekend.

SIMON

My dad was also from Ciechanow and was nine years older than my mother. My dad was in three camps, Auschwitz being the third and last. When he arrived at Auschwitz, he was experienced with how to handle life in the camp; he had learned the ropes. So, when they asked for volunteers to work as glazers, my father volunteered. On weekdays he worked in the kitchen and was able to gather extra food, and on Sundays he would go to the women's camp, to fix their broken windows. Once there, he would also share what he had squirreled away. He would ask where the barracks were that housed the girls from Ciechanow. He wanted to speak with people from his hometown, spend time with them and share stories. He was able to find that barrack and took an instant liking to my mother.

When Auschwitz was being liquidated, they were marched from the camp. After the march, he and my mother took a train together to their hometown. They discovered that they were each the only surviving member of their family. Like so many, they married. They spent the next four years waiting to immigrate to America. My sister, Jaffa, was born in their hometown; I was born in a DP camp in Austria. My parents would both say that they had two birthdays, their biological birthday and then the date of their liberation. I learned so much, especially from my father. He spoke openly about the war, both positive and negative. My father had a philosophy about America, and it's one that I find to be so true: "The harder you work, the luckier you get!" My parents were married for over forty years when my dad died suddenly from a heart attack. They had three children, eight grandchildren and five great-grandchildren.

Nadzia and Milton (*standing on the right*) in their hometown, Ciechanow, 1945.

Nadzia Bergson's Home Baked Challah

There is nothing as satisfying as baking your own challah. It is a feast for all the senses: the tactile sensation of kneading the dough, the welcoming aroma in your home and the satisfying visual of braided bread with its golden, eggy crust. The recipe handwritten years ago by Nadzia is an authentic reminder that makes preparing this challah so meaningful. We've filled in some of the blanks, but Nadzia's recipe is the foundation. Her original notes were to make two loaves, which commemorates the double portion of manna that fell in the desert on Fridays when the Jewish people wandered for forty years after the exodus from Egypt. It is also traditional to cast off a small piece of challah into the oven as a nod to the ancient custom of providing a bit of challah as a tithe to the priests in the Temple in Jerusalem. For the home baker, two loaves can be hard to manage, so this recipe creates one large loaf. There are many braiding techniques, six strands being the most traditional, round for the New Year, and this version, which has three strands, a good place for the home baker to start.

Yield: 1 large loaf
Start to Finish: Under 4 hours

1½ teaspoons active dry yeast
1¼ cups warm water (yeast thermometer
  should read between 105 and 115 degrees)
½ cup sugar
2 tablespoons vegetable oil
1 egg

4 cups bread flour
1 teaspoon salt

EGG WASH GLAZE
1 egg, plus 1 tablespoon water, beaten

In the bowl of a standing mixer, combine the yeast, water and sugar and allow the yeast to bubble, about 10 minutes. Add the oil and egg; beat on low speed with the flat paddle until combined. Slowly begin adding the flour and salt and mix until all 4 cups have been incorporated. Turn the mixer to medium and mix for several minutes. Replace the beater with the dough hook and knead for 10 minutes longer, adding more flour if needed to create a smooth, firm, elastic, non-sticky dough. Turn the dough out onto a lightly floured surface and knead for a minute or two so you can judge if the dough is right. Pour a drop of oil into a bowl and then place the dough in the bowl, rolling it around so all sides are covered with oil; this will help prevent a crust from forming while the dough rises. Cover the bowl with plastic wrap and then drape with a towel. Let it rise in a warm place for at least 1 hour or until it has doubled in size. If baking the dough at a later time, you can refrigerate the dough overnight and proceed to the next step.

Turn the dough out onto a lightly floured surface and punch down several times, so that all the air is released from the dough. Return the dough to the greased bowl and cover in the same manner as before. Let the dough rise an additional hour.

Lightly flour a work surface and turn the dough out. Punch down the dough and separate into three equal parts. Roll the dough sections in your hands to form three ropes, each about 12 inches long. Squeeze out the air as you roll and gently pull on the ends, so the strand is thicker in the middle and narrower at the ends.

Place the three ropes on a lightly greased baking sheet. Pinch the ends together at one end and begin braiding the bread just like you would a ponytail, by moving the far-right piece over the middle piece, taking the far-left piece and bringing it over the middle piece. When done braiding, pinch the remaining ends together and then tuck them underneath to create a neat finish. Cover with plastic wrap and a towel and let the dough rise one more time, about 30 minutes. Preheat the oven to 350 degrees.

Prepare the egg wash, and using a pastry brush, coat the challah. Bake for 40 minutes or until the top is nicely golden brown. When you tap the bread, you should hear a hollow sound. Let the bread cool completely before slicing.

Feedback
1 cup of raisins can be mixed in for a sweet holiday version, and poppy or sesame seeds can be sprinkled on top right before baking.

Faye Levy

Professional contributor

Cookbook author and columnist for the *Jerusalem Post* Faye Levy has an excellent idea for what to do with that leftover challah, and it is way more interesting than French toast!

Apple Challah Bread Pudding

Excerpted from *1,000 Jewish Recipes* (Hungry Minds Inc., 2000)

Makes 6 servings

Bread pudding made with challah is a scrumptious dessert. This one is studded with apples and flavored with cinnamon and vanilla. It rises slightly and, like a soufflé, sinks when cool.

4 ounces (¼ of a 1-pound loaf) challah, day-old or stale
1¼ cups milk
1 pound sweet apples such as Golden Delicious

6 tablespoons sugar
2 large eggs, separated
1 teaspoon vanilla extract
1½ teaspoons ground cinnamon
2 tablespoons butter, cut into small pieces

Preheat oven to 375 degrees. Generously butter a 5-cup baking dish. Remove crust and cut challah into chunks. Put it in a large bowl. Bring the milk to a simmer in a small saucepan. Pour it over the bread and let it stand about 5 minutes to soften.

Peel, halve and core apples. Slice them very thin.

Mash challah with a fork. Add 4 tablespoons sugar, egg yolks, vanilla and 1 teaspoon cinnamon and mix well. Add apples and mix well.

Whip egg whites until they form soft peaks. Gradually beat in remaining 2 tablespoons sugar and beat until stiff and shiny. Gently fold whites, in 2 batches, into bread mixture. Transfer mixture to baking dish.

Sprinkle with remaining ½ teaspoon cinnamon and scatter butter pieces on top. Bake about 50 minutes or until a thin knife inserted in the pudding comes out dry.

The pudding is best served warm. Although it sinks when cool, it still tastes good.

Ada Ehrlich Rubin and Leo Rubin

As told by their granddaughter Jolie Feldman

Ada's story is intrinsically linked to Nadzia Bergson's story, not only because these two courageous women survived Auschwitz together, but because of what transpired decades later. Her granddaughter Jolie told me the beautiful story of a true bashert.

My grandmother Ada Ehrlich Rubin was born in Poland and was sent to Auschwitz during the war. There she met and befriended Nadzia Bergson. Luckily, they both survived the war and years later bumped into each other walking down the street in New York City. Both were now married and had families of their own. My grandmother married my grandfather Leo, also a survivor, who came to this country with nothing and worked what felt like a million jobs to make a life. He and my grandmother lived well in America, as did Nadzia and her husband. They became reacquainted, and the two families spent much time together, sharing the holidays and *simchas*. Because both had suffered such losses during the war, they regarded each other as family. My grandparents eventually moved to Florida, and although they stayed in touch with the Bergsons, they certainly were not as close as they were when they lived in New York.

Years later, although I was a native Californian, I made the decision to head east and study broadcast journalism at Syracuse's Newhouse School. My roommate was dating a really nice guy, and one day in 1995, he brought his good friend, Jason, over to meet me. We hit it off. Jason was a student at nearby Ithaca College. We certainly knew we had made a connection, but we didn't realize

Ada's original recipe notes.

how deep it ran. It was not until Jason told his parents about me that we learned that we were the grandchildren of those same two women who survived Auschwitz more than fifty years earlier. We were married in 2000, and happily, both grandmothers lived to see us as a couple. My grandmother Ada passed away knowing Jason and I were to be married. She could not have been happier, and it gave her and Nadzia the chance to reconnect once again.

While my grandparents didn't speak much of the war, in her later years my grandmother did write down some of her recollections. My grandparents were wonderful people who tried to give us everything they could, even when they couldn't. They were married over fifty years and had one child, two grandchildren and two great-grandchildren (my twin sons), who are named in memory of their great-grandmothers—these two amazing women.

Ada Rubin's Chocolate Chip Cake

This recipe was interpreted from handwritten notes that Ada wrote in her later years, making it even more special. The egg whites are whipped into a cloud-like state to create this airy cake studded with sweet, grated chocolate. Ada prepared the cake to be *pareve*, but we've offered a variation, using butter and milk. Either way, it's simply satisfying.

Yield: 10–12 servings
Start to Finish: Under 1½ hours

7 eggs, separated
1½ cups sugar
½ cup oil or ½ cup melted butter
2 tablespoons vanilla extract
¾ cup water or ¾ cup milk

2 cups all-purpose flour
3 teaspoons (1 tablespoon) baking powder
½ tablespoon cream of tartar
6 ounces semisweet or bittersweet chocolate, grated

Preheat the oven to 350 degrees and lightly grease a 9 x 3-inch springform pan.

Beat the egg yolks and sugar, in a large bowl, on medium speed, until light and creamy, about 3 minutes. Add the oil (or butter), vanilla and water (or milk) and combine. Sift the flour and baking powder together then add to the egg mixture, on low speed. Beat until the flour is incorporated, then increase to medium speed for several minutes.

In a separate bowl, beat the egg whites with the cream of tartar until they form stiff peaks. Gently fold the egg whites into the batter. Pour the batter into the prepared baking pan. Grate the chocolate in a nut or coffee grinder or on the largest hole of a box grater (hold the chocolate in place with a towel so the heat from your hands does not melt it). Sprinkle the chocolate with a light dusting of flour (this will prevent it from sinking into the batter) and then drop the chocolate, by handfuls, on top of the cake batter and blend the chocolate into the batter by dragging a knife in swirling motions through the cake.

Bake for 1¼ hours, or until the top of the cake is lightly browned and slightly crusty. A bamboo skewer inserted into the cake's center should come out clean.

Cool the cake before unmolding. You might need to run a knife around the edge to release it from the rim.

Frania Faywlowicz and Mike Faywlowicz

As told by their daughter Toby Schafer

There is a romantic element to the story of Toby Schafer's parents that makes you almost forget you are listening to a true wartime retelling and feel you are peering into a beautiful Hollywood love story.

Both my parents were from the same town of Piotrkó Trybunalski, Poland. My father was the youngest of ten children and two years older than my mother. My father worked as an apprentice tailor for my mother's father. When the Germans forced them into the ghetto, my father, who worked outside the ghetto as a tradesman, was able to sneak in food. He always had a soft spot for my mother, so he would sneak food to her as well. He worked in a glass factory near the train station, where he watched the train carrying his parents and siblings fatefully pull away. When my parents were liberated, they both went back to their hometown, where they found nothing was left and anti-Semitism was prevalent. They went to the DP camp in Foehrenwald, and there they planned to be married.

My father wanted to sew something special for his bride-to-be. He didn't have access to a fabric store, so he stole a U.S. military-issued blanket to make her a pair of pants. Two days before their wedding, my parents were bicycling around town, my mother sporting her new pants. The police arrested her for having stolen goods! In spite of that, two days later they were married in Foehrenwald—we believe it was the first wedding to take place in that camp. My mother proudly wore her U.S. Army

Frania (*center*) wearing the pants Mike (*on the right*) made for her, January 1947. Mike's oldest brother is pictured on the left.

blanket pants, and medical gauze served as her veil. Many brides married after her used her veil for their ceremony.

In 1950, my parents were sponsored by a relative and moved to Montreal, a community with a large number of survivors. They lived well, and I remember them speaking often about the Holocaust. My mother cooked very

European. Like most children, I wanted to eat out, and my dad would say, "If you want to eat out, go out on the porch." Nothing was as good as something that was made at home. When we moved to an apartment in Coney Island, I remember one dinner there as the best meal of my life. I don't know why it stands out; it was rye bread with schmaltz, dried salami and a little salt on the bread. I remember sitting in this new home and feeling very safe. I always wanted to make things better for my parents because of all they had gone through. In our home it was always family first. My parents had two children, four grandchildren and three great-grandchildren.

Author's Note: I sadly learned that Frania has passed away. May her memory be for a blessing.

Frania Faywlowicz's Meat and Potato *Cholent*

Cholent is considered a special dish by observant Jews who needed to prepare Saturday's midday meal before Friday at sundown. The combination of ingredients is as varied as the families who prepared them but traditionally included meat, potatoes, beans and barley. The common factor is the slow baking, up to 24 hours, at a very low temperature. The stew would be assembled at home, and then the pot would be brought to a local bakery Friday before Shabbos began, to bake overnight. Retrieving the pot from the bakery and eating the dish Saturday afternoon was almost a ritual itself.

Frania's version has two textures of potato, melding into beef flanken and creating a satisfying, comforting, full-bodied meal. If the aroma from your kitchen could be bottled, it would be called *haimish*. Frania recalled everyone coming over to enjoy this dish—not because its brownish color is divine, but the taste seems almost sanctified.

Yield: 4–6 servings
Start to Finish: 15 minutes prep, then slow roasted for up to 15 hours

2 russet potatoes, peeled and very thinly sliced, plus 1 russet potato, peeled and grated

2 teaspoons kosher salt
Fresh cracked black pepper, to taste
2 pounds beef flanken

Preheat the oven to 225 degrees and line the bottom of a heavy-lidded pot with waxed paper.

Slice 2 of the potatoes paper-thin. If you have a mandolin or professional vegetable slicer, now would be the time to use it. Cover the waxed paper with half the sliced potatoes. Sprinkle the potatoes with 1 teaspoon of salt and a few turns of cracked black pepper. Lay the flanken on top of the potatoes and surround the flanken with the grated potato. Season with the remaining salt and additional pepper.

Pour 2 cups of water into the pot and then spread the remaining sliced potatoes on top. Cover with a piece of waxed paper, which seals the ingredients and helps retain moisture while the dish bakes. Cover the pot and bake overnight. Do not stir the dish or disturb the ingredients while baking.

Take the cholent out of the oven, remove the waxed paper and dab a paper towel on top of the sauce to absorb any oil that has collected on the surface. Be sure when serving that you do not scoop up the waxed paper from the bottom of the pot.

Feedback
Did you know that the trendy short rib, which appears on nearly every menu today, is really good old-fashioned flanken, cut in a different direction? Short rib is cut parallel to the bone and looks meatier with one hefty chunk of meat, while flanken, which is crosscut, has several smaller bones.

Raymond Fishler

As told by his wife, Rhoda

Raymond spent much of the war in Plaszow, which was initially a forced-labor camp and ultimately a concentration camp in Cracow. Plaszow gained worldwide attention when it became the focus of the Steven Spielberg film *Schindler's List*. Raymond's wife, Rhoda, likened his emotions at seeing the film to "a cork being unleashed." She elaborated on his experiences.

Raymond was born near Cracow, Poland, one of six children. There were four boys and two girls; he and his father were the only family members to survive. When the war came to their hometown, the family became scattered. Raymond was just fourteen at the time. A non-Jewish family hid Raymond, until he ran away to the Cracow ghetto, where he volunteered to work at the airport. In 1943, he was taken from the airport to Plaszow, where he met up with a sister, one brother and his father. His brother and sister perished. While Raymond managed a sewing factory at Plaszow, he met many of the "Schindler Jews." He also had many encounters with Amon Göth, the sadistic commandant.

As the war was drawing to a close, the camp was liquidated, with many of the prisoners being transported to Auschwitz. Raymond and his father were among the fortunate because when their train pulled into Auschwitz, it was turned away. They were put on another transport and went from camp to camp, fortunately being turned away each time. Two days before the war ended, he and his father escaped and hid in a barn in the Bavarian woods. There were fifty other men in the barn. Amazingly, they turned out to be German Air Force deserters who were hiding from the authorities. He viewed the airmen with restrained emotion, as he felt "they were a different breed from the SS." He also realized they were frightened and feared capture as they began to ask Raymond more and more questions about the war. He said it was very bizarre. When the troops came through the woods, Raymond realized they looked different than the soldiers he was accustomed to seeing. That's when he knew the war had ended. He and his father

Raymond Fishler in DP camp in Altötting, Germany, 1947.

wanted to go back home, but they were told there was nothing to go back to. Raymond immigrated to the United States, while his father remained in Europe.

Being married to a survivor is a unique experience. I try to maintain the traditions that he grew up with. My cooking style is very much like what he had in his home, which was very traditional Jewish cooking. I enjoy cooking everything. My mother would make two specific cookies, one for Passover, one for Rosh Hashanah. They have become traditional in our home, which was always filled with the flavors of the holidays, much to the delight of our two children and four grandchildren.

Author's Note: I sadly learned that Ray has passed away. May his memory be for a blessing.

Rhoda Fishler's Meringue Nut Cookie

This delectably light and moist confection has a mere three ingredients and is a favorite at Rhoda's Passover table.

Yield: About 3 dozen cookies
Start to Finish: Under 30 minutes

2 cups (about ½ pound) finely chopped walnuts

¾ cup sugar
4 egg whites, beaten

Preheat the oven to 350 degrees and lightly grease a cookie sheet or line it with a piece of parchment paper or nonstick silicone mat.

Chop the walnuts in a food processor, nut grinder or by hand with a serrated knife in a rocking motion. Combine the sugar and the walnuts. In a separate bowl, beat the egg whites until stiff but not dry.

Gently stir the nuts into the beaten egg whites.

Drop by generous teaspoonfuls on the lined baking sheet, about 1 inch apart, as they spread while baking.

Bake for 20 minutes or until lightly brown. They should still be a bit sticky and soft in the center. Do not overcook, or they will become crunchy and hard to bite.

Variation: Stir in 1 tablespoon cocoa powder, with the walnuts and sugar, for a chocolaty version.

Feedback

Sometimes, when separating eggs, you are left with remaining yolks or whites. No worries, they won't go to waste. They can be kept in the fridge for up to 5 days, in an airtight storage container, or they can be frozen by placing them in a covered ice cube tray, for ease of use at a later date.

Hela Fisk and Stephen Fisk

As told by their daughter Pearl Fisk

The evolution of Hela Fisk's name is really so illustrative of the way so many survivors reinvented themselves throughout their lives. Her daughter Pearl explains.

My mother, one of six children, was born in Wolysk, Poland, a small town of about twenty thousand people. She was married prior to World War II in an arranged match, and at age twenty had a son Yankel (Jacob). After the German occupation of Poland, my mom and her family were forced into the Ludmir ghetto. On the day the Germans "liquidated" the ghetto, my mother was out of the ghetto searching for water for her son. She knew the area and its townspeople well and spoke Polish and Ukrainian. When she returned to the ghetto and saw what the Germans had done, she realized her son, spouse and extended family had perished. She hid on an existing rooftop, cried all night and asked, "Why?" The following morning, she escaped from the ghetto and a non-Jewish Polish woman hid her in a hole in her barn for six weeks as German soldiers and Ukrainian collaborators scoured the area for Jews. When it became too dangerous for my mother to continue hiding in the barn, she left and was turned in to the Germans by nearby townspeople who recognized her and confirmed she was a Jew. She was sent to slave labor at Budzyn and remained in slave labor until she was liberated at the end of the war.

In 1945, after liberation, my mother returned to her home village, searching for her family and remains of her family life. She soon learned she was the sole survivor. One brother survived in Russia but was killed at the end of the war. As a person without a home, without anything, my mother entered the first of several DP camps. My mother met my father in one of these camps, and they began dating. They each suffered similar losses. My father, who was from Slomniki/Cracow, Poland, was a survivor of Auschwitz. They both waited to go to America.

On Thanksgiving 1952, my parents finally left Germany and arrived in New York City on an American transport ship, the *General Eisenhower*. As they disembarked the ship, they said their goodbyes and promised to keep in touch. My mother was met by an HIAS representative and taken to the station for a train to Boston. A relative who had left Poland after World War I and resided in Ipswich, Massachusetts, met my mother at the train. My father remained in New York City. My mother was not happy in Ipswich, as no one understood what she had lived through and witnessed. Within two weeks, and with only twenty-five dollars in her pocket, she returned to New York and rented a room in a tenement in the Bronx. Soon after, my mother found a job in the garment district and called my father. They met for coffee the next day and married in 1953. My twin sister and I were born in January 1954—twenty-one years after the birth of my mother's first child. Our parents celebrated our birth yet mourned the children and extended family they lost in the Holocaust. Rose and I are named for our maternal grandmothers who perished. Our parents were only married fourteen years when our father

Hela, outside DP camp, Germany, 1946.

kept kosher and celebrated *Shabbos* and the Jewish holidays. Our mother worked full time yet always cooked all our meals. She was a wonderful baker, and our home always smelled of her baking and cooking. My sister and I recall the first time our mom saw a pineapple and the look on her face when she learned that *lokshen* could come out of a box!

The evolution of my mom's name: My mom's given name was Ruchel; it was changed to Helinka when she began using false papers in the ghetto. Helinka became Hela in either the concentration or DP camp. At the time my mother married my dad, she was known as Hela Aiken. I'm not sure if this was her maiden name or her first married name as she spoke very little of her first husband and son who perished in the ghetto in 1942. In 1952, my parents arrived in New York City. My parents married in 1953, and my mother became Hela Finkelstein. Years later (1959–60), when they became citizens, the judge could not pronounce Finkelstein so he asked my father if a new American name would be OK. Thus, Finkelstein became Fisk, and my mother became Hela Fisk.

died on February 13, 1967, after a long illness. Our mother died thirty-eight years later to the date. Together they had my sister and me and five grandchildren.

The foods in our home were traditional Jewish eastern European. We never ate out,

Hela Fisk's Plum Cake

Pearl remembers her mother baking this quintessential batter version of Polish plum cake for Shabbos and "always for company, delicious hot or cold!!!" Serve it hot for a luscious dessert or bake it the night before and enjoy the subtle sweet goodness of the plums with the acidic orange juice for a delicious breakfast. Make this from May to October when plums are at their peak.

Yield: 10 to 12 servings
Start to Finish: Under 1½ hours

FOR THE FILLING

2 pounds dark, sweet plums, pit removed, cut into thin slices
¼ cup sugar (increase the sugar to ½ cup if the plums are tart or add a touch of honey) mixed with 2 teaspoons cinnamon

FOR THE BATTER

4 eggs
1½ cups sugar
1 cup vegetable oil
½ cup orange juice
2 teaspoons vanilla extract
3 cups all-purpose flour
3 teaspoons baking powder
1 teaspoon salt

TOPPING

2 tablespoons sugar mixed with ¼ teaspoon ground cinnamon

Preheat the oven to 350 degrees and grease a 9 x 3-inch springform or tube pan.

To make the filling, toss the plums with the sugar and cinnamon.

Prepare the batter in a large bowl. Beat the eggs, sugar, oil, orange juice and vanilla, several minutes, on medium speed, until light and fluffy. In another bowl, sift together the flour, baking powder and salt. On low speed, slowly add it to the egg mixture. Increase the speed to medium and beat for several minutes, until all the ingredients are well combined and the batter is smooth.

Pour a third of the batter (about 1 to 1¼ cups) into the prepared pan and top with a third of the plums, repeat 2 more times, ending with a layer of plums on top. Sprinkle with the sugar and cinnamon topping. Bake for 1¼ hours or until a bamboo skewer inserted in the middle of the cake comes out clean. Let the cake cool completely before removing from pan. If the cake does not release easily, loosen it by running a knife around the edges.

Variation: To use a rectangular 13 x 9 x 2-inch baking dish, make only 2 layers and reduce baking time to 45–60 minutes.

The Rubach Family

As told by JoJo Rubach

JoJo credits the women in his life for teaching him to be strong and fearless.

My paternal grandmother, Genia, grew up in Wloclawek, Poland. She married my grandfather, Joseph, who in 1939 was taken into the army and never returned to his family. My grandmother, along with her two children, Leon (my father) and his brother, Marc, survived the war by hiding with relatives and strangers. During the last years of the war, a kind woman, Sophia Tomashevsky, saved my father, grandmother and uncle. In the ultimate coming full circle, my daughter, Tessa, and my wife, Elle, went to Cracow, Poland, and attended the ceremony when Sophia was inducted into the "Righteous Among the Nations."

My mother, Eva, who was from Budapest, Hungary, is also a survivor. My maternal grandmother was very resourceful and smart. She anticipated the problems coming to Hungary and urged my grandfather to change the family name from Israel to Iranyi. This definitely allowed them to stay under the radar and survive the war.

The importance of family and how a family sticks together is what got them through everything, and that's something I've learned

The Rubach family celebrating in Israel.

from them. While visiting Israel with my entire family, including my parents, we gathered at the kibbutz where my great-aunt settled after she immigrated to Israel. There were forty people there, and at the end of lunch, my uncle raised a glass and toasted, *"L'chaim Mishpocha* Rubacha." I couldn't help but feel this is the true meaning of generation to generation, as one generation of survivors toasted another. Enjoy! My parents were married forty-six years and had two children, five grandchildren and seven great-grandchildren, with a great-great-grandchild on the way.

For forty-five years, the Rubach family has had an annual tradition of preparing Genia's gefilte fish. It is a team effort with JoJo (a non–gefilte fish eater) at the helm. The important aspect of this laborious endeavor is the team effort and respect they are paying to their family's heritage. To celebrate this wonderful tradition, we invite you to enjoy Joan Nathan's gefilte fish recipe that follows her mother-in-law's story.

Author's Note: I sadly learned that Genia and her son Leon have passed away. May their memory be for a blessing.

Paula Gerson

As told by her daughter-in-law Joan Nathan

Anyone who knows Jewish cooking knows Joan Nathan. She is a best-selling cookbook author and award-winning television personality. What you might not know is that her mother-in-law, Paula (Peshka), survived the Holocaust. Joan shared her mother-in-law's story as well as her famous recipe for gefilte fish.

The Gerson Family.

Paula (Peshka) Gerson was my mother-in-law. She was from Zamosc, Poland, and was a wonderful seamstress before and during the war. When the war broke out, she went to Siberia with her husband and infant. Her expertise with her sewing machine (which she carried with her) saved her and her family. When the war was over, they went to Uzbekistan, where my husband, Allan, was born. From there they entered a DP camp in Germany. Using an assumed name, they came illegally to the United States.

I felt that it was bashert that we were connected. Paula had an amazing memory for life before the Holocaust, and I love to hear stories about that life. Every year before Passover, we would make gefilte fish together, with me taking notes and she, carefully, cooking, remembering every gesture from her childhood. At one point each year, she would put carrots in the eyes of the head of one of the fish and raisins in the nose. Then she would sigh. We all knew why she sighed. She was remembering her mother, who did exactly the same thing. Her mother died in the Belzec Death Camp. My husband was one of three children, and there are five grandchildren in the family.

Joan Nathan

Professional contributor

Excerpted from *Jewish Cooking in America* (Alfred A. Knopf, 1998)

Until I married into this "start-from-scratch" gefilte fish family, we graced our Passover table with the jarred variety. What a difference homemade makes! Now gefilte fish making has become a welcome twice-yearly ritual in our house—at Rosh Hashanah and Passover. At our Passover seder, we all wait with bated breath for my husband's opinion. "Peshka, your gefilte fish is better than ever!" gets a broad grin from his Jewish mother. The gefilte fish recipe we use today came with my husband's family from the DP camps.

Gefilte fish is one of those recipes where touch and taste are essential ingredients. A basic recipe goes this way: "You put in this and add that." If you don't want to taste the raw fish, add a bit more seasoning than you normally would. What makes this recipe Galicianer (southern Polish) is the addition of sugar. For some reason, the farther south in Poland, the more sugar would be added. A Lithuanian Jew would never sweeten with sugar but might add beets to the stock. I have added ground carrot and parsnip to the fish, something that is done in the Ukraine, because I like the slightly sweet taste and rougher texture. If you want a darker broth, do not peel the onions and leave them whole.

Classic Gefilte Fish

Yield: About 26 patties

7 to 7½ pounds whole carp, whitefish and pike, filleted and ground*
4 quarts cold water or to just cover
3 teaspoons salt or to taste
3 onions, peeled
4 medium carrots, peeled

2 tablespoons sugar or to taste
1 small parsnip, chopped (optional)
3 to 4 large eggs
Freshly ground pepper to taste
½ cup cold water (approximately)
⅓ cup matzo meal (approximately)

*Ask your fishmonger to grind the fish. Ask him to reserve the tails, fins, heads and bones. Be sure he gives you the bones and trimmings. The more whitefish you add, the softer your gefilte fish will be.

Place the reserved bones, skin and fish heads in a wide, very large saucepan with a cover. Add the water and 2 teaspoons of the salt and bring to a boil. Remove the foam that accumulates.

Slice 1 onion in rounds and add along with 3 of the carrots. Add the sugar and bring to a boil. Cover and simmer for about 20 minutes while the fish mixture is prepared.

Place the ground fish in a bowl. In a food processor, finely chop the remaining onions, the remaining carrot and the parsnip or mince them by hand. Add the chopped vegetables to the ground fish.

Add the eggs, one at a time, the remaining teaspoon of salt, pepper and the cold water, and mix thoroughly. Stir in enough matzo meal to make a light soft mixture that will hold its shape. Wet your hands with cold water and, scooping up about ¼ cup of fish, form the mixture into oval shapes, about 3 inches long. Take the last fish head and stuff the cavity with the ground fish mixture.

Remove from the saucepan the onions, skins, head and bones and return the stock to a simmer. Gently place the fish patties in the simmering fish stock. Cover loosely and simmer for 20 to 30 minutes. Taste the liquid while the fish is cooking and add seasoning to taste. Shake the pot periodically so the fish patties won't stick. When gefilte fish is cooked, remove from the water and allow to cool for at least 15 minutes.

Using a slotted spoon, carefully remove the gefilte fish and arrange on a platter. Strain some of the stock over the fish, saving the rest in a bowl.

Slice the cooked carrots into rounds cut on a diagonal about ¼-inch thick. Place a carrot round on top of each gefilte fish patty. Put the fish head in the center and decorate the eyes with carrots. Chill until ready to serve. Serve with a sprig of parsley.

Natalie Gomberg

Based on our conversation

Natalie is the sole survivor of her family, which included her parents and five siblings.

Natalie Gomberg.

Having been interned in several concentration and labor camps, Natalie was liberated by a Russian Jewish officer. Following her liberation, she went to Leipzig to look for family members who might have survived. Her search led her to the men's camp in Buchenwald, where she was told she might find more information.

Eventually, Natalie was among 350 Jewish children who were transferred from Germany to Switzerland for rehabilitation. Interestingly, it was a Jewish captain in the American army, named Herschel Schachter, who was responsible for that transfer.

Natalie was hoping that when she reached Switzerland, she would be able to continue her search for family members, as Geneva was a central and important location for listing survivors. She stayed in Switzerland for nearly three years, at which point, in 1947, she received a special visa to come to America, sent by her Canadian relatives. Once here, Natalie worked for thirty years as a social worker. For many years, she has been an active member of the Museum of Jewish Heritage Speakers Bureau, where she talks about her experiences during the Holocaust in an effort to inform and educate. Her son, three grandchildren and one great-grandchild, as well as her husband of sixty-one years, are certainly grateful that her strength and will prevailed.

Natalie Gomberg's *Mohn*—Poppy Seed Cookies

In her hometown of Opatow-Kielce, Poland, Natalie undoubtedly had lots of mohn cookies and cakes. Natalie's uncomplicated cookie features a hint of lemon, which plays nicely with the mildly sweet, crunchy poppy seeds. You can roll these out very thin and make crispy wafer-like cookies or press the dough in your hands for a bigger bite.

Yield: 2 dozen (thick) cookies or 4 dozen (wafer-like) cookies
Start to Finish: Under 30 minutes

½ cup vegetable oil
½ cup sugar
2 eggs
1 teaspoon fresh lemon juice

1 teaspoon salt
2 teaspoons baking powder
2½ cups all-purpose flour
¼ cup poppy seeds

In a medium bowl, beat the oil, sugar, eggs and lemon juice until all the ingredients are well blended. In a separate bowl, combine the salt, baking powder and flour. Slowly add the flour mixture to the oil mixture and blend completely. Stir in the poppy seeds. The dough will be very thick and sticky.

Chill the dough while you preheat the oven to 350 degrees and lightly grease a large baking pan.

When the oven is ready, roll the dough out on a generously floured board to ¼ inch thick and cut with a cookie cutter for a wafer-like cookie. For a thicker cookie, form small balls, about the size of a golf ball, 1½-inch diameter, and slightly flatten with your hands (a little oil on your hands will help). Place on the prepared pan. Both versions will bake for 10 to 15 minutes (depending on thickness) or until the edges are lightly browned.

Feedback
For a lemonier version, add additional lemon juice or the zested peel of 1 lemon.

Henny Durmashkin Gurko and Simon Gurko

*As told by their daughter Rita Lerner;
Recipe provided by their daughter Vivian Reisman*

Rita remembers her mother as a very positive person. She talks effusively about a house filled with love and music.

My mother was from Vilna, Poland, and came from a loving, musical family. She had a sister, Fanny, who played the piano and a brother, Wolf, who was the first Jewish conductor of the Vilna Philharmonic. My mother was the singer in the family. My grandfather was the head of the Vilna Choir, and he worked in the synagogue. When the Nazis came into Vilna, my grandfather was taken away and perished. The rest of the family went into the Vilna ghetto. Since the start of the war, my uncle no longer conducted the orchestra but helped out backstage. While in the ghetto, he was given a special pass that allowed him to go in and out of the ghetto so he could continue working. Amazingly, during that time, he took apart a piano and sneaked it piece by piece into the ghetto, where he faithfully rebuilt it. He formed a choir in the ghetto, and the Nazis would come and listen to them. (Tragically, he perished only one hour before liberation.)

When the ghetto was liquidated, my mother, her sister and my grandmother went by train to several camps and then eventually were sent to Dachau. There they were part of the

Henny Gurko.

concentration camp orchestra. After they were liberated, they continued to perform and called themselves the ex–concentration camp orchestra. Imagine the sight as a group of devastated survivors entertained other survivors who now resided in the DP camps. Shortly after liberation, Leonard Bernstein came to Germany to conduct the Munich Symphony Orchestra. In lieu of his fee, he asked for special permission to perform with my mother's group. My mother and aunt performed with him in three different DP camps. He was very kind and offered to help them in any way he could, should they come to the United States. My mom came to America on a boat, where she met my father, Simon, a Polish survivor who spent the war in Siberia. After the war, my father, heroically, was part of the Brihah, which in Hebrew means "flight" or "escape." This valiant group smuggled many Jews out of Europe and into Israel. My mother always sang in the house. She sang every year at the Vilna commemoration. Music was very much in our house growing up.

My mother was always in the kitchen cooking and singing. She really made the house fun. She was a wonderful cook, making many traditional Polish dishes. When she made cholent, just the smell in the room was delicious. We ate chicken every Friday night; her baked chicken was our favorite. My parents were married twenty-three years; they had three children and six grandchildren.

Henny Gurko's Roasted Chicken and Vegetables

What could be more comforting and satisfying than well-seasoned roasted chicken nestled on a bed of fresh vegetables? Vivian recalls that Henny used lots of onions as well as chunks of carrots, celery and sweet potatoes, which made the chicken intensely flavorful and succulent.

Yield: 4 servings
Start to Finish: Under 2 hours

2 large onions, thinly sliced
1 pound of carrots (5–6), peeled and cut into 2-inch pieces
4 celery ribs, cut into 2-inch pieces (about 2 cups)
4 sweet potatoes, peeled and cut into 2-inch pieces

Kosher salt and pepper
1 whole (3½- to 4-pound) chicken, cut into eighths
2 tablespoons sweet paprika
2 tablespoons garlic powder
1 tablespoon onion powder

Preheat the oven to 350 degrees.

Place the onions, carrots, celery and sweet potatoes on the bottom of a large roasting pan. Lightly season them with salt and pepper. Pour enough cold water into the pan to just barely cover the vegetables. Season the chicken on all sides with salt, pepper, paprika, garlic powder and onion powder. Place the chicken pieces in the pan on top of the vegetables.

Bake, skin side down, for 45 minutes. Turn the chicken pieces over and continue baking an additional 45 minutes or until the chicken is completely cooked through (an instant-read thermometer should register 165 degrees) and the potatoes are tender. Occasionally baste the chicken to keep it moist, adding more water if necessary to create a nice sauce and prevent the vegetables from scorching.

Sara Moulton

Professional contributor

In many eastern European homes, roasted chicken was a given for Friday night dinner. Henny's version was a nice departure bringing in new elements and flavors. Another popular variation on chicken was fricassee, which for the frugal homemaker was a terrific way to utilize the parts of the chicken that were collected every Shabbos and saved. Today we might consider these parts throwaway, but you'll discover this dish has tremendous flavor and history. Sara Moulton, formerly the executive chef of *Gourmet* magazine and a beloved television personality and cookbook author, shares her mother-in-law's recipe for this ultimate shtetl preparation.

Esther's Chicken Fricassee

Excerpted from *Sara Moulton Cooks at Home* (Broadway Books, 2002)

Esther Adler, my mother-in-law, gave birth to three sons in less than three years (yikes!) and a daughter three years later. All four kids had hearty appetites, and all four turned out to be fairly strapping individuals. I'll confess that I've often wondered how in the world she managed to feed them. This recipe is one answer.

Esther's wonderful chicken fricassee was a relatively rare treat. She served it only about once a month because that's how long it took to assemble the parts. Every Friday night she'd cook two chickens, roasting one and making soup out of the other, while putting aside the packet of giblets that accompanied each bird. After four weeks of this routine, she'd finally have enough giblets to make fricassee (as well as enough livers to make chopped liver). She'd put a big basket of fresh challah nearby, and they'd sop up the gravy. Truthfully, it is almost a meal in itself.

Serves 6

2 tablespoons vegetable oil
2 medium onions, finely chopped
4 chicken necks, trimmed and cut crosswise
  into 4 or 5 pieces
1 pound chicken gizzards, trimmed
6 chicken wings
Kosher salt and freshly ground black pepper
  to taste

1 pound ground beef
½ cup matzo meal
1 large egg
2½ teaspoons kosher salt
1 teaspoon sweet paprika
½ cup all-purpose flour
½ teaspoon freshly ground black pepper

Heat the oil in a large casserole over medium heat. Add the onions and cook, stirring often, until softened, about 5 minutes. Add the necks, gizzards and wings. Season with salt and pepper. Reduce the heat to low and cover. Cook, stirring often, until the chicken has lost all traces of pink, about 30 minutes.

Meanwhile, combine the ground beef, matzo meal, egg and 1½ teaspoons of the salt in a large bowl. Pour in ½ cup cold water, mix well and form into small meatballs about the size of a walnut. You should have about 3 dozen.

Bring 2 cups of water to boil and pour it into the chicken parts mixture. Increase the heat to medium-high and bring to a simmer. Add the paprika and season with salt and pepper.

Mix the flour with the remaining teaspoon of salt and ½ teaspoon pepper in a large bowl. Add the meatballs and roll until coated on all sides. Shake off the excess flour.

Drop the meatballs into the simmering liquid in the casserole. Reduce the heat to low, cover and cook until the chicken is falling off the bones and the broth is slightly thickened and concentrated, about 2 hours.

Celina Hecht

In her own words

Celina talked about food with such passion, yet as a child living a secret life in Poland, food was unimportant to her. As we spoke further, I realized that Celina is a passionate woman and whether we discussed her family, her life history or her cooking style, she exuded enthusiasm and zeal.

I was born in Warsaw, Poland, in 1933. I lived there with my parents and my twin sister and grandparents, the whole family, until the German invasion of Warsaw. My father escaped from Warsaw, and thereafter my mother, sister and I escaped to Bialystok, where my mother's parents lived. By then, the Russian army had occupied Bialystok. The Russians took away our father in a transport to Russia. We remained in Bialystok, where we attended the Russian elementary school. Then in September 1941, the Germans started the war against Russia, the Germans occupied Bialystok and the ghetto was formed.

We lived in the Bialystok ghetto for a year and a half. After her great efforts, my mother encountered a Polish peasant woman, at the marketplace, outside the ghetto walls, who was willing to listen to my mother's pleas to save her two children. Miraculously, it was this peasant woman, a widow, Mrs. Kaczynska, who agreed to take us into her farm. Previously, my mother obtained blank church forms of birth certificates, which were filled out as if my sister and I were Polish Catholics. Mrs. Kaczynska had her own two young sons. We were taken in as if we were Mrs. Kaczynska's

Celina Hecht, 1946.

nieces. At Mrs. Kaczynska's poor village home, everyone treated us in every respect as if we were part of the family. We attended church. In our minds, we transformed ourselves as genuine, fervent, believing Catholics. Our mother had dresses made for our communion. Mrs. Kaczynska, during her visits to Bialystok, kept in touch with our mother. This continued until 1943, when the ghetto of Bialystok was liquidated. After that time, there was no trace of my mother.

In the summer of 1944, the Red Army finally expelled the Germans. Then, Mrs. Kaczynska went to Bialystok to find Jewish survivors, specifically with the intention of finding our family. She did find an aunt, with whom we reunited shortly thereafter. Then through various organizations, our father was able to contact us from Russia.

Finally, in 1946, our father caught up with us in Germany. It was then that our father took over. Eventually, he was able to get papers for all of us to come to the U.S.A., where we settled in New York. I was married in 1962 to a survivor as well. We have two sons and five grandchildren, all of whom, without bragging, do like my cooking.

Celina Hecht's Fresh Yellow Pepper Soup

Celina's food memories are distinctly eastern European, but her cooking style is eclectic. As she explains, "A number of years ago, we were in Florence, Italy. We stayed in a lovely hotel near the Sephardic temple. We ventured into a restaurant that had no menu. The only fare was what the cook prepared for that particular evening. As a first course, there was a delicious yellow pepper soup. I could not resist asking how this delicious soup was prepared." The recipe below is Celina's interpretation of that memorable soup.

Yield: 6–8 servings
Start to Finish: Under 1 hour

3 tablespoons olive oil
2 medium onions, chopped (about 1½ cups)
1½ pounds yellow peppers, cored, seeded and
 rough chopped
1 celery rib, chopped (about ½ cup)
1 carrot, peeled and chopped (about ½ cup)

2 large or 3 medium potatoes, peeled and
 diced (about 3 cups)
5–6 cups of chicken broth
2 bay leaves
Kosher salt and pepper
Seasoned croutons, for garnish (optional)

Heat the olive oil in a large soup pot. Cook and stir the onions, over medium heat, until lightly browned, about 10 minutes. Stir in the peppers, celery, carrot, potatoes and enough broth to cover the vegetables (about 2 cups). Cover and cook on low heat for 25 to 30 minutes, until the vegetables are soft.

When finished cooking, puree the soup in batches. Return the pureed soup to the pot and add the remaining 3 to 4 cups of broth, depending on your desired consistency. Toss in the bay leaves and season to taste with salt and pepper. Cook for an additional 15 minutes until heated through. Remove the bay leaves and serve with seasoned croutons on top.

Gil Marks

Professional contributor

As you read in Celina's story, she spent much of her childhood in and around Bialystok. Gil Marks's recipe and detailed excerpt is a tribute to that region and assuredly will bring back food memories not only to Celina, but to all our Polish survivors. If you have never tried one, bialys are a cousin to the ubiquitous bagel and certainly deserve your attention.

Author's Note: I sadly learned that Gil Marks has passed away. May his memory be for a blessing.

Bialys—Polish Onion Rolls

Excerpted from *The Encyclopedia of Jewish Food* (Wiley, 2010)

Residents of the northeastern Polish town of Bialystok, which at its height before World War II boasted a Jewish community of more than fifty thousand, enjoyed an indigenous round onion-topped flat roll that they referred to as *kuchen*, but outsiders commonly called, after its home, a *Bialystoker kuchen* or simply bialy. Bialystoker kuchen is a variation of the widespread *Ashkenazi* onion flatbread *tzibele pletzl*, originating in the early nineteenth century corresponding to the emergence of technology and agricultural methods in Europe to produce inexpensive white flour. By the end of the century, nearly every street in the Jewish sections of Bialystok contained a small kuchen bakery. These breads were once part of every weekday meal, and sometimes constituting the entire meal, complementing both dairy (delicious with a *shmeer* of butter) and meat. During World War II, the once dynamic Jewish community of Bialystok was liquidated by the Nazis, with Jews as well as bialys actually disappearing from the city. Today, residents of Bialystok no longer have any recognition of the kuchen or the role it once played. However, towards the end of the twentieth century, an increasing number of bagel stores in America, many owned by non-Jews, began offering bialys as well. At the end of the 1990s, an entrepreneur opened a shop in Bialystok, ironically named "New York Bagels," which also offered bialys, reclaiming part of the city's heritage. Consequently, the bialy endures as an image of nostalgia and a symbol of the tenacity and determination of a displaced people and culture that survives.

Makes 12 small rolls

DOUGH

1 (1/4-ounce) package (2 1/4 teaspoons) active
  dry yeast or 1 (0.6-ounce) cake fresh yeast

1 1/4 cups water (105–115 degrees [40–46 C]
  for dry yeast; 80–85 degrees [26–30 C] for
  fresh yeast)

2 tablespoons sugar

2 teaspoons table salt or 4 teaspoons kosher
  salt

About 4 cups (20 ounces) high-gluten flour

TOPPING

1/3 cup minced onions

1 tablespoon vegetable oil

1 1/2 teaspoons poppy seeds

1/2 teaspoon kosher salt

TO MAKE THE DOUGH

Dissolve the yeast in 1/4 cup water. Stir in 1 teaspoon sugar and let stand until foamy, 5 to 10 minutes. Add the remaining water, remaining sugar, salt and 2 cups flour. Gradually add enough of the remaining flour to make a soft dough.

On a lightly oiled or floured surface, knead until smooth and elastic, about 10 minutes. Place in an oiled bowl, turning to coat. Cover and let rise until doubled in bulk, about 1 1/2 hours.

Punch down the dough and knead briefly. Return to the bowl, cover and let rise a second time until doubled in bulk, about 1 hour.

Punch down the dough and knead briefly. Divide into 12 equal pieces, roll into balls, cover and let stand for 10 minutes. On a lightly floured surface, roll each ball into a 3 1/2-inch round about 1/2-inch thick. Place on ungreased baking sheets dusted with rye flour or cornmeal, cover and let rise until puffy, about 30 minutes.

TO MAKE THE TOPPING

Combine the onions, oil, poppy seeds and salt.

Using your thumb or a glass with a 1- to 1 1/2-inch bottom, press down the center of the dough rounds, leaving a 1-inch rim. Sprinkle about 1 teaspoon onion mixture into each indentation. Cover and let rise until puffy, about 30 minutes.

Preheat the oven to 425 degrees.

Bake the bialys until lightly browned, switching the pans halfway through baking, about 12 minutes. If the onions are not browned, place under a broiler for about 1 minute. Transfer to wire racks and let cool slightly or completely. For softer rolls, place cooled bialys in a plastic bag.

The Jacobs Family

As told by Charles's daughter Lisa Jacobs

You cannot mistake the love and reverence Lisa has for her father, Charles, her aunt Rose and beloved grandmother, Baba. Although they are no longer here, their presence is felt in the value she places on family and traditions, certainly an influence that was imbued in her by these three special people in her life.

My dad, Charles, was the youngest of eight children born to a baker in Slomniki, Poland. He was the bravest and most humble person I've ever known. For all my life, my father's past was something "he put in a box on a shelf" except for one time. It was a Chanukah family gathering in 1997. My dad and his sister, Rose, and brother, Marvin, opened up, and each knew a bit of the story and the other could fill in the rest. That was the first and last time my father's life during the war was brought into focus. His family was not wealthy, and their lives centered on their bakery. Like in many towns, on Friday night, it bustled with people carrying their various pots of cholent to slow bake for the night. Before they were sent to the camps, my grandfather, who perished in Plaszow, defied the Nazis by selling white bread on the Black Market. The family was warned that the Nazis were coming and were advised to leave. They were so worried, but with all the children where would they go?

Aunt Rose remembers the Nazis coming to their house with big shotguns in the early morning. My dad hid in a neighbor's house under a bed. Someone told on him. The Ukrainian soldier who found him dragged him out and put a gun to his head. Uncle Marvin said that probably he was not killed because the Ukrainian did not have any bullets left.

The Jacobs family, with all eight children.

My dad said that the Ukrainian marched him through a field. They walked for miles, with a gun pointed at my father's back the entire time. My dad said that the field looked just "like that painting with the girl sitting in the field," referring to *Christina's World* by Andrew Wyeth. He was about nine at the time. Dad said that after they had walked for about two miles, the soldier told him to "Go back now. Run." He said that he ran back and that he was very scared. He walked very quietly back into his house, and there was a light on. He was amazed to find his mother, Baba, sitting in the kitchen and that everything was calm and "normal."

Eventually, my father was sent to Plaszow labor camp. One night, some men helped him escape through a hole in the wall of the Plaszow ghetto. The next morning, he returned. All the men were asking him, "What are you doing back here?" My father said he had no place to go, and he was more afraid of being caught by the Nazis than being in the camp. After he was held in several more camps, the Americans liberated my dad on April 29, 1945. He was on a train leaving Dachau heading nowhere and literally wrapped in newspapers. I have photos of him with American soldiers, sitting in their jeep and wearing an American army cap.

My aunt Rose was the second-oldest daughter. She had an influential boyfriend who worked on the Black Market and obtained false papers for her stating that she was Gentile. Rose recounted how her boyfriend had come to her house late one evening and told her she had to pick a non-Jewish last name, something she could remember. Aunt Rose said she was so frightened that she couldn't think of a last name that she could easily remember and then she saw a box of tea. That's how Rose Jakubowicz became Rose Wissotzky—it's the Lipton tea of Poland. Despite her new identity, she still became a prisoner in Auschwitz,

although she received better treatment because they thought she was not Jewish.

After she was liberated, she was walking with a group of non-Jewish girls whom she had befriended in the camp. A man from Slomniki recognized her as Rose Jakubowicz. Rose said that she was embarrassed in front of her friends because she did not want them to know the truth, that she was really Jewish, yet she was anxious to talk to the man and find out if he knew anything about her family. She told her friends to go ahead and that she would catch up with them later. She ran to speak to the man, who told her that my dad was alive and living in a DP camp in Frankfurt. Rose and my dad were the first two siblings to reunite after the war. Although my father was the youngest, he was very resourceful. He gave Rose a watch and told her to use it to get the rest of the family out of Poland and bring them to Germany. After some time passed, Rose returned with Baba and Uncle Marvin and the watch! They remained in the DP camp until they immigrated to New York in 1948.

In my father's family, there are barely any family heirlooms to pass down. Everything they had was either taken, lost or stolen. That is why this recipe is so precious and so dear to me. It's really a family treasure. I feel that my love for baking is a special gift from my dad's side of the family. Every time I bake, I am really honoring my wonderful father, my aunt Rose, my grandmother, as well as my grandfather, aunts and uncles who died in the war. I love to bake, and baking is a way of preserving their memory.

My dad had two children and two grandchildren.

Charles Jacobs and Aunt Rose in Frankfurt, circa 1947.

Baba's Dough

Warmly described by Lisa

This is the simple, traditional, perfect cookie dough that I associate with my wonderful Baba, and it was one of Aunt Rose's signature confections. Aunt Rose was an exceptional baker but not only that. She'd look as though she could be dining at the Ritz instead of baking in her kitchen. There she was in her jewelry, silk blouse, heels, and she never got a speck of anything anywhere. There were never any measuring cups in sight, and whenever I would ask her, *Baba how much*, she'd laugh and then she'd just say in Yiddish, *Nacht, shitteryne*, "Throw it in." Miraculously, Aunt Rose's hands were clean throughout the entire process. Dough never stuck to her fingers. Both Baba and Aunt Rose would make it with oil so no one would have to think about whether or not the cookies were pareve. I prefer to make them with butter (Pulgra brand), as they are even more scrumptious. This dough is a multitasker, as it makes the most delicious cookies, as well as crust for apple and blueberry pie.

Baba's Cheesecake

Baba's cookie dough is the foundation for this light ricotta cheesecake. Lisa has carried on the timeless "ritual" of making this dough completely by hand.

Yield: 10 to 12 servings
Start to Finish: Under 2½ hours

FOR THE CRUST

BABA'S ALL-PURPOSE COOKIE DOUGH
1½–2 cups all-purpose flour
1 egg
½ cup sugar
1 teaspoon vanilla
1 teaspoon baking powder
1 stick (½ cup) cold butter, cut into tiny pieces

FILLING
3 cups farmer's cheese
4 tablespoons (½ stick) butter
¾ cup sugar
4 eggs, beaten
1 tablespoon all-purpose flour
1 tablespoon sour cream

Preheat the oven to 250 degrees.

To prepare the dough by hand, create a well with the flour and slowly incorporate all the ingredients with a fork and your hands. If you prefer, you can use a food processor, fitted with the metal blade. When the dough is formed, press it into a 9-inch pie pan, and chill until ready to use.

Blend all the filling ingredients until they are well combined but retain some of the "lumpy" texture. Pour the filling into the unbaked crust. Bake for 25 minutes then raise the temperature to 350 degrees and bake for an additional hour, or until the pie is set but not dry. Serve warm or cold.

Variation: Divide the dough into 2 or 3 pieces and wrap in plastic wrap. Chill the dough for 15 minutes and then roll the dough out on a floured board to ¼ inch thick. Using a cookie cutter, or the rim of a glass, cut into any shape desired and dip the cookies in sugar. Bake at 350 degrees on a parchment-lined cookie sheet for 15 minutes or until very light golden brown.

Luna Kaufman

Based on my conversation with Luna

Luna is an activist, humanitarian, educator and author. Her memoir, titled *Luna's Life: A Journey of Forgiveness and Triumph*, tells the story of her struggles during the Holocaust and how she came to be a champion in the field of Holocaust studies. Luna and Sister Rose Thering, a remarkable Dominican nun, formed a friendship, and together they worked tirelessly to erase anti-Semitic references in Catholic textbooks. Luna stresses, "We have to learn to coexist. What we teach our children is that we should accept each other's opinions. Accept everyone for whatever they are." The State of New Jersey considers Luna a regional treasure and has honored her in many ways. The Center for Holocaust Studies at Brookdale Community College hosts an annual Writing & Art contest named for her, and Seton Hall University bestowed on her an honorary doctorate.

When I asked Luna, who was twelve at the time the war started in her home of Cracow, Poland, and spent most of the war in various concentration and labor camps, how she defines her life, she answered, "When people ask me what I do or what I did, I ask them when." As she said, "I've worked in everything under the sun." After the war, she returned to Poland and then immigrated to Israel, where she married her husband, Alex. It was his status as an American resident that helped her secure a visa in 1952. Luna holds a degree in musicology, but her talents run deep, having reinvented herself so many times. From a volunteer at the Lake Placid Olympics to the head of the New Jersey State Opera, Luna has done it all.

Possibly the most intriguing adventure in Luna's reinvented postwar life was on April 8, 1994, when she found herself among a group of one hundred survivors who were invited for the first concert of Holocaust music to be performed at the Vatican. Dressed in black,

Luna Kaufman and her mother, Krakow, 1946.

with her head covered, she awaited a meeting with Karol Wojtyla, Pope John Paul II. It just so happens that the Pope was a former classmate of Luna's when she attended the Jagiellonian University in Cracow. Luna remarked, "I had traveled a long way from the concentration camps to the Vatican. I thought, maybe the world will change after all." This trip strengthened Luna's determination to work with the Catholic Church to improve communication between Jews and Christians. It led to her relationship with Sister Thering and the good work they accomplished together. Luna has three children and six grandchildren.

Michael Solomonov

Professional contributor

In her moving memoir, Luna describes her arrival in Israel: "We had finally reached the port of Haifa. We had finally come home." She remained in Israel while waiting to immigrate to the United States. Luna closes her chapter by writing, "I wished that my two years in Israel could have lasted forever." To bring a bit of Israel to Luna's story, we have paired it with chef and restaurant owner Michael Solomonov's authentic Israeli beet recipe. And while we are sure Luna ate beets growing up in Poland, we are also sure they never tasted like these!

Beets with *Tehina*

Contributed by Chef Michael Solomonov, Zahav restaurant, Philadelphia

Serves 4

1 pound red beets, all roughly the same size
1 cup kosher salt, plus additional
4 ounces prepared *tehina* [sesame paste] (see recipe)
2 ounces fresh lemon juice

4 ounces extra virgin olive oil
4 tablespoons freshly chopped dill
1 tablespoon freshly chopped mint
Freshly ground black pepper
4 tablespoons lightly toasted chopped walnuts

Preheat oven to 350 degrees.

Scrub the beets under cool running water to remove all dirt and debris. Spread ½ cup of kosher salt on the bottom of a heavy-bottomed sauté pan. Place the beets on top of the salt and cover with the remaining ½ cup of kosher salt. Place sauté pan in the preheated oven and roast for approximately 90 minutes, or until the tip of a paring knife easily pierces the flesh of the beets. Remove the beets from the salt and allow to cool for 20 minutes. Remove skins from the beets while still warm by rubbing with paper towels. Cool beets completely.

Grate the beets using the coarse side of a box grater. Combine the grated beets, prepared tehina, lemon juice, olive oil and herbs in a large mixing bowl and combine thoroughly. Season to taste with black pepper and additional kosher salt, if necessary. Sprinkle the walnuts on top of the beets and serve at room temperature.

Prepared *Tehina*

2 garlic cloves, peeled, germ and root end removed

2 ounces fresh lemon juice

4 cups organic sesame paste (preferably unhulled)

3 cups warm water

1 teaspoon ground cumin

½ cup extra virgin olive oil

Kosher salt

Combine the garlic cloves and lemon juice in a blender and process until it forms a smooth paste. Let stand for 10 minutes. Add half of the tehina and water and blend until smooth. Add the rest of the ingredients and blend again until smooth. Season to taste with kosher salt. Refrigerate for at least 30 minutes.

Celia Kener

In her own words

I met Celia following a tour she conducted for inner-city students at the Museum of Jewish Heritage. Her energy and willingness to educate young people are consistent with the dedication, strength and resilience she has shown throughout her life.

I remember that day in June 1941, when I was six years old. I was an only child in a middle-class traditional home in Lvov, Poland, and I posed for a commemorative photo. I was dressed in a blue Shirley Temple–styled costume ready to perform in my dance recital, the one I had been looking forward to for so long. That was the day they forcefully took my father away to serve in the Russian army. Shortly after that, I was playing outside with some children who at one time were my friends. They alerted a guard that I was Jewish, and I was taken away in a truck filled with other Jewish children. I don't know how I got up the nerve, but I approached the guard and asked, "Why are you doing this to me?" I must have touched a chord, because the guard opened the door and tossed me out, essentially saving my life.

I returned home and, along with my mother, aunt, uncle and cousins, moved into the ghetto. My mother, a beautiful woman, was quickly recruited to work outside of the ghetto. Every several weeks, she would come in and check on me. As raids took place, I hid with my extended family, until one day there was no room for me to hide with them. My aunt told me to find a good spot so that the Germans would not find me. I found such a spot; however, the rest of my family was not as lucky. I remember hearing my aunt's voice calling to me in the streets as she was taken away, "Celia, survive and tell our story."

My mother sensed that I would no longer be safe in the ghetto, so one night she came and sneaked me out. She took me to a home in the forest where a devout Christian family had agreed to raise me as their own. They were very kind, and even though I could not

Celia's father carried this photo of his daughter in her recital costume with him throughout the war years.

go outside, be near windows or even leave my closeted space, I knew they were doing their best to protect me. I was an obedient child and lived with them for a year and a half. One day, a nearby family who was harboring a Jew was murdered as an example to everyone in the town. My new family panicked and decided to send me to an orphanage. Luckily, the mother could not bear to do this, so without her family's knowledge, she took me to their barn, promising to feed me every three days. When I climbed up the rafters to my new hiding spot, I was told there was another person there and not to be afraid. I had no idea that the person I would now share the barn with was my own mother. She had been hiding there for nearly nine months, having escaped her work camp. My mother was weak and infirm, so I took charge. I would climb down and take the feed intended for the animals.

My mother eventually gained her strength, and by the time we were liberated we were able to walk out of the barn together. When we returned to our home, we were met with letters from my father. He too survived the war in the Russian army, and eventually we were all reunited. Amazingly, there was one possession that my father had kept throughout his ordeal: the photo of me dressed in my dance recital costume. I feel my life started when I came to the United States. The war is a book I put on a high shelf and try never to take down. I do tell my story to schoolchildren who visit the Museum of Jewish Heritage. I would love to sit them all down and cook a traditional Polish meal for them. I think they would enjoy many of the foods I remember as a child. There are several I still make today for my husband of fifty-five years, and they take me back to a happy time in my home. My three children and seven grandchildren associate many foods with me. They love "Gigi's" (that's what they call me) inventive food. I hope you enjoy them as well and remember never to lose hope or faith. Sometimes, it's all we have.

Celia Kener's *Holishkes*—Shortcut Unstuffed Cabbage

The distinctive flavors of stuffed cabbage are a fine balance between sweet and sour. Traditionally, the sauce envelopes blanched cabbage leaves that are filled with a meat and rice mixture. The technique can be tricky and the process, time consuming. Celia's shortcut is to take these same pungent flavors and create a medley where the meatballs are nestled in shredded cabbage, allowing the sauce to gently bubble away and cook all the ingredients as one. Purists might balk, but you'll be the one with a few extra minutes to relax and enjoy the compliments.

Yield: 4 to 6 servings as a main course, 6 to 8 servings as a starter
Start to Finish: Under 2½ hours

FOR THE SAUCE
1 large green cabbage (about 2 to 2½
  pounds), cored and sliced
24 ounces ginger ale
2 tablespoons brown sugar
4 tablespoons honey

FOR THE MEATBALLS (ABOUT 30)
1½ pounds ground beef
1½ teaspoons kosher salt
3 tablespoons ketchup
¼ cup seasoned bread crumbs
1 egg
5 tablespoons uncooked long-grain rice

TO PREPARE THE SAUCE
In a large Dutch oven, combine the cabbage, ginger ale, brown sugar and honey (to help the honey ease off the spoon, coat the spoon in a dab of oil). Bring to a boil, cover and reduce the heat to low.

TO MAKE THE MEATBALLS
Mix together all the meatball ingredients. Form the mixture into small 1-inch-diameter meatballs, adding more bread crumbs if the meat does not hold together. Place the meatballs in the pot of cabbage and gently stir so they incorporate with the sauce. Cover and cook on low heat for 2 hours, until the cabbage is tender and the meatballs are firm but cooked through.

Feedback
For a stronger tomato flavor, add 1 (14-ounce) can of tomato sauce to the pot while the cabbage cooks. If you like it sour, add lemon juice, white vinegar or a little sour salt to achieve the perfect pucker.

Miriam Lesorgen

As told by her daughter Karen Banschick

Karen Banschick's mother, Miriam, came to America having survived the Holocaust with very little except her memories and ambition. She was a practical, pragmatic Polish-born woman who Karen remembers saying, "For what you spend to eat out one night, you could cook for a week." That prompted her to create meals that were versatile and relatively inexpensive. Through her cooking and her love, Miriam has undoubtedly left an everlasting legacy for her two children, six grandchildren and eight great-grandchildren.

Miriam Lesorgen's *Kreplach*—Stuffed Noodle Dumpling

Grandma Mancia, as Miriam was known, was famous for her *kreplach*. Her grandchildren swore that no deli in New York could duplicate their lightness and flavor. The key to good kreplach is to roll the dough thin enough so the dough is transparent, but thick enough to hold the filling when boiling. Karen's mom favored a beef filling, but we've included a chicken with scallion filling as a variation. If you prefer your kreplach as a trendy small bite, we've also included an easy dipping sauce to spice things up.

Yield: 24 kreplach
Start to Finish: Under 1½ hours

FOR THE KREPLACH DOUGH
1¾ cups all-purpose flour
½ teaspoon salt
2 eggs
3 tablespoons corn oil
1–2 tablespoons water

FOR THE BEEF FILLING
½ pound ground beef
1 tablespoon oil
1 small onion, grated
1 teaspoon kosher salt

FOR THE CHICKEN FILLING
½ pound ground chicken
1 tablespoon oil
3 tablespoons minced
 scallions
1 teaspoon garlic powder
1 tablespoon soy sauce

In a medium bowl or the bowl of a food processor, fitted with the metal blade, combine the dough ingredients, dry first then liquid, and process, adding a drop of additional water, if necessary, to create a smooth, elastic dough. Turn the dough onto a lightly floured surface and knead for a minute or two. Wrap the dough in a barely damp cloth and let it rest for 1 hour. While the dough sits, prepare the filling.

Heat the oil in a skillet, cook and stir in the ground beef or chicken, over medium heat, until nicely browned, about 10 minutes. Be sure to break up large pieces with the back of a fork or spoon. Remove the meat from the skillet with a slotted spoon and let the meat cool for a few minutes before adding the rest of the filling. Meanwhile, bring a large pot of salted water or broth to boil.

When the beef has cooled a bit, combine it with the grated onion and salt.

For the chicken, combine the scallions, garlic powder and soy sauce with the browned chicken.

On a floured board, roll the dough to ¼ inch thick; it will be very elastic. If you tug at it, it will just snap back; use the rolling pin to stretch. Using a cookie cutter or rim of a glass, cut the dough into 3-inch rounds. Have a small bowl of water standing by to dip your fingers. Place 1 teaspoon of filling in each round and seal by dipping your fingers in the water and dabbing the edges. Fold the circle into a half moon and pinch the edges closed. Drop a few filled kreplach at a time into the boiling liquid and cook about 20 minutes. Occasionally shake the pot to be sure no shy kreplachs cling to the bottom.

They are done when they happily float to the top and the dough is soft to the bite. If you cooked the kreplach in soup, do nothing more, just enjoy. If you cooked them in water, remove the kreplach with a slotted spoon and let them drain on a paper towel.

The kreplach can then be dropped into a bowl of soup or lightly fried. To fry the kreplach, heat 1 tablespoon of oil for every 8 kreplach and lightly brown, in a skillet, for several minutes. Drain on a paper towel and serve with the dipping sauce below.

Orange Honey Ginger Soy Dipping Sauce

The name of the recipe is also the list of the 4 basic ingredients.

2 tablespoons orange juice
2 teaspoons honey

½ teaspoon ground ginger
4 tablespoons soy sauce

Blend together and serve as a dipping sauce or light dressing.

JH

Dina Liverant and Jacob Liverant

As told by their daughter Dorothy Liverant Goldberg

In 1997, Dorothy Goldberg went with her family to Lublin, Poland, where her parents were before and during the Holocaust. Her father showed them Majdanek concentration camp, where he was imprisoned and from where he had escaped. He also showed them his former apartment and many places where he hid from the Nazis. He wrote his memoirs so that the family would always know what he endured. Dorothy shares some of that story with us.

Both my parents were from a city, not a small shtetl. My parents always felt proud that they had the opportunity for a good education and that my mother graduated from the gymnasium (secondary school). My mother survived the war by passing as a Christian woman. She got false papers and paid a Polish family to hide her. When her money ran out, she had to leave, and she hid wherever she could. She bleached her brown hair white using straight peroxide from the bottle to get all the color out. She was the only member of her family to survive. She never forgave herself for not being able to save her fifteen-year-old sister.

My father went to vocational school for bookkeeping before the war and then went into the Polish army. He learned the Christian prayers there, which later helped him survive. After the war started, he obtained documents to show he was Christian. The papers, which he acquired through the underground, were authentic, as they were from a deceased Gentile man. Even so, he was rounded up as a forced laborer and sent to Majdanek concentration camp, where he was imprisoned for fourteen months. In March 1944, he escaped from the Majdanek sub-camp on Lipowa Street, along with nine others, who

Dina and Jacob Liverant, with Dorothy.

dug a tunnel to freedom. He hid in the woods and joined the A.K. (Armia Krajowa), a Polish home army, for a short time. Throughout the entire war, he maintained his false identity as a Christian. Less than six months later, he was liberated and met my mother. They married in the fall of 1944. Many survivors needed to reconnect with people with whom they had something in common; my parents were no different. When I asked my father how he survived, he would tell me it was more luck than anything. He recalled a night where he said he had a bad feeling about his hiding place, so he didn't return the next night. It turned out that everyone who had hidden there was betrayed and captured. He attributed his survival not to intelligence or strength, but to fate.

I try to keep many of my family's traditions alive. It is important to me to preserve the holidays and the *alte heim*. My mom was a believer in continuing to cook traditional foods. I am always trying different ways to recreate what we ate as children. Her apple cake was delicious and is a very traditional Polish dessert. Our favorite was her *kutletela*, her version of a chicken burger, which my family still enjoys today. My parents were married for fifty-three years and had two children and three grandchildren in their lifetime. Since they have passed on, our family has grown to four grandchildren and two great-grandchildren (and two more on the way)!

Dina Liverant's *Kutletela*—Small Chicken Burger

Long before the ubiquitous turkey burger was on every menu, ground chicken cutlets were a regular meal in Polish households. A good way to stretch the protein was to grind the chicken and mix it with seasonings and sometimes vegetables. Some cooks poached the cutlets, while others like Dina would fry them as mini burgers. Top them as you wish or sandwich them in a bun and enjoy!

Yield: 4 servings
Start to Finish: Under 15 minutes

2–4 tablespoons canola oil for frying
1 pound ground white meat chicken
2 eggs, beaten
¼ cup seltzer
Scant ¼ teaspoon baking soda

¼ cup bread crumbs (or matzo meal at Passover)
1 teaspoon garlic powder
1 teaspoon kosher salt
Black pepper, to taste

Heat 2 tablespoons of oil in a large skillet over medium heat. Combine all the remaining ingredients, using a large wooden spoon or your hands. Wet your hands lightly and form 4 burgers. When the oil is hot, gently place the burgers in the pan. Fry until the bottom side is nicely brown and crisp, about 5 minutes. Flip the burgers and continue frying until the chicken is cooked through and both sides are brown and crisp, adding more oil to the pan if needed. Drain on paper towels before serving.

Feedback

If you prefer a firmer burger, omit the seltzer and baking soda (although Dina maintained the baking soda helped your digestion). You can add minced onion, garlic or scallions to the chicken mixture before frying, or change up the seasoning blend to your taste. To spice things up, Dorothy suggests a splash of Sriracha (a Thai-style hot sauce), sprinkled on the cutlets. The same chicken mixture can be poached for a lighter variation. Bring a large pot of chicken broth to boil. Form the chicken mixture into small ovals (like gefilte fish) or mini meatballs. Cook them for 20 to 30 minutes, until the chicken is completely cooked through.

Lily Mazur Margules and Edward Margules

In Lily's words

Lily Margules makes several things very clear, the most crucial being, "There are other things much more important than hate." Our conversation flowed, and her intellect showed through in everything she said and has written. Her parents were what Lily termed "assimilated intelligentsia," and they imparted to Lily the thirst for knowledge and culture. Her ease at writing has always been Lily's gift. "Ask me about two trains that are traveling at certain speeds in the same direction, which arrives first? I haven't a clue. But ask me to write, that's easy." Her book, *Memories, Memories*, is written in such a way as to help children understand her journey from Vilna to America, with, as she writes, "a few stops along the way."

My parents met when they were both students at the university during the Russian Revolution. My mother became a dentist, while my father studied to be a rabbi but changed his mind and studied to be a pharmacist instead. Although we lived in Vilna, Poland, in my early childhood we spoke only Russian, but later we spoke Polish as well. The first time I realized I was Jewish was as a student in an exclusive private school with other Jewish children. One day I sat down to eat my non-kosher lunch, which was made fun of. To pacify me, my mother bought a pair of silver candlestick holders and a bag of Shabbos candles and began lighting candles on Friday night. One of my biggest pleasures was to be invited to my friend's house when they celebrated Shabbos, with all the ceremony and traditional food. The best holiday in our house had to be Passover, as I was born on the first day of the seder, so my mother would shower me with presents.

I learned about anti-Semitism in 1935 when my father, who was a decent guy and employed at a big government pharmacy, was told he did not have enough education to be a pharmacist. This was a ruling directed only at Jewish pharmacists. He went back to school and passed his master's exam in Warsaw but was dismissed from his position one year later. The only way he could support his family was to buy his own pharmacy, and he could only do so by paying a Polish pharmacist under the table to buy the pharmacy in his name. I still remember his name, it was Wiscniewsty, and the pharmacy was in a small town called Soly. When the Germans came, my father sent first my sister and me, and later came himself, to Vilna to be with my mother's sister, Sonia Lipkowicz Perski. By this time, I was nearly a teenager and I had already suffered the loss of my mother. My father was taken from the pharmacy and deported to Estonia. I managed to see him one last time when he was in

Lily Mazur, age six, and her father, David, saying goodbye to his nephew Chacrel (Herschel), 1930.

Kaiserwald concentration camp. One day, a girl from our labor camp where I was working together with my sister, Rachel, told us that a man called David Mazur, who came with a transfer of prisoners from Estonia, was asking about his two little girls, Lily and Rachel. The only way I could go and see him was to pretend I had a toothache so they would send me to a dentist in Kaiserwald to have my tooth extracted. I boarded a truck to the camp, and I was looking for the barracks where the men were being held. I found my father, who was

so relieved to know that my sister, Rachel, and I were alive and together. I clearly recall his words, "No matter what happens, we will meet at the pharmacy in Soly. You are the oldest sister; take care of Rachel. Keep your head high and conduct yourself in accordance with our good family name." I don't remember everything, but certain things are engraved in my heart; I remember this. After we were liberated, we searched for our father but never saw him again.

It was on September 23, 1943, when Rachel, my aunt Sonia and I were awakened by screaming guards and ordered out of the ghetto. Rumblings in the crowd told us that the line to the right would live and to the left would not. Knowing my sister, Rachel, looked very young and small, my aunt removed her high heels and exchanged them with Rachel's shoes. Rachel now looked taller and older and, along with me, was spared, but my aunt Sonia was not. We were sent to the right, to live, and she was sent to the left, to die. Rachel and I moved through numerous work and concentration camps, and on March 11, 1945, the Russian army in a small village called Krummau in East Prussia liberated us. It was in Lodz, Poland, that we joined a group of Zionists who planned to go to Israel. We were now part of the Kibbutz, Ihud; we were young, idealistic and full of determination. We traveled from Poland to Prague, Prague to Munich and Munich to Italy. It was difficult for Jewish refugees to get the necessary documents, so we posed as Greek peasants who were seeking work in Italy's vineyards. On New Year's Eve 1946, our caravan of trucks stopped at the foot of the snow-filled majestic Alps. We had to climb to the other side to enter Italy. Much to our surprise, we were not the only refugees doing so. I had no idea that my future husband, Edward Margules, was also crossing the Alps on that same memorable night. He shared a bag of home-baked cookies with his fellow climbers; I ate them with zest, never suspecting that he and I would meet again and share a life together.

Upon reaching Italy, Rachel and I stayed in a DP camp in Grugliasco, near the city of Turin. We had heard that in Milan you were able to search for surviving family members, so we decided to go there to post notices. While in Milan, we would pass the hours by going to the movies. On one particular day, the movie was being shown in Russian. I helped translate the film for my sister, and this caught the attention of a young man sitting behind me. We were introduced a few days later, and on February 13, 1947, in an ancient synagogue in Turin, Italy, I married Edward Margules. The rabbi, who had all of three hairs in his beard, had survived Nazi occupation in a Jesuit monastery. This was the happiest day of my life.

Sometime later, we received a telegram from my father's brother, Isaac, who offered to sponsor our trip to join him in Buenos Aires. Although we never made our *aliyah*, Rachel, Eddie and I, while still in Italy, listened to the radio on May 14, 1948, when the dream for a Jewish homeland became a reality. I lived in Buenos Aires for nearly a decade and learned their traditions as well as maintaining my Polish heritage and that of my adopted home of Italy. It has been a long odyssey from Poland to America; I came here in 1956 with a family and a very strange accent. It was a little Russian, a little Polish, some Italian and some Argentinean. I was shy and quiet and often embarrassed by my unusual accent. I was liberated for a second time when Dr. Henry Kissinger became secretary of state, and I realized that it is what you say, how intelligently you present your ideas that matters, not your accent. It was then that I took a deep breath, opened my mouth and began to express my opinions. I haven't stopped since!

Together Edward and I have two children and one grandchild.

Author's Note: I sadly learned that both Lily and Edward have passed away. May their memory be for a blessing.

Lily Margules's *Tzimmes*—Chicken with Prunes

Lily very clearly remembers cooking with her aunt Fanny Mazur in Buenos Aires. "I didn't know how to boil a cup of tea. My aunt made a delicious tzimmes, a dish she ate in Vilna, with chicken parts, large slices of potatoes, sweet prunes, brown sugar and honey. It was cooked on the stove, a long time on a small flame, with my aunt adding water as necessary. The prunes would just melt in your mouth." Tzimmes, which in Yiddish means "a big fuss," is a good name for this dish inspired by Lily's memories, as everyone who enjoys it will make a big fuss over you.

Yield: 4 servings
Start to Finish: Under 2½ hours

4 tablespoons vegetable oil
1 (3½- to 4-pound) chicken, cut into 8 pieces
 (skin can be removed)
2 cups water
½ cup red wine (or broth)
2 tablespoons brown sugar

2 tablespoons honey
2 cups pitted prunes
Kosher salt and pepper
2 russet (or sweet) potatoes (about ¾ pound),
 peeled and cut into large chunks

Heat the oil in a large Dutch oven and brown the chicken parts on all sides, over medium heat, about 15 minutes. Pour off the fat and add 1 cup of the water, the wine (or broth), brown sugar, honey and prunes. Season the dish with salt and pepper and bring to a gentle boil. Reduce the heat to low, cover and cook for 1 hour and then add 1 more cup of water and the potatoes, being sure to tuck the potatoes into the sauce. Season to taste with salt and pepper. Continue cooking for 45 to 60 minutes or until the potatoes are fork tender. If the sauce is too concentrated, add some boiling water, heat through and serve.

Mark Strausman

Professional contributor

Lily fondly remembers her life in Argentina, where her Italian neighbors taught her to cook many Italian dishes. "I recall eating on Sundays a big Italian dinner, where we served meat slow cooked in tomato sauce. On Sundays it was really enjoyed as a big family lunch." The following recipe, contributed by Mark Strausman, honors those warm recollections.

Involtini di Manzo—Beef Braciole

Excerpted from *Two Meatballs in the Italian Kitchen*
(Artisan, a division of Workman Publishing, Inc., 2007)

My version of braciole isn't terribly dainty, but it is more moderately proportioned than the old-school dish. I like smaller bundles because then the taste of the flavorful filling doesn't get lost in pounds of meat. Use a cut of beef with a little bit of fat in it—I like top round—and pound the pieces thin to tenderize them and so they'll be easy to roll. Traditionally, the dish is served in two courses. First the sauce from the pan is served with some pasta....Then the meat itself is brought out, with a green vegetable on the side. But to make things simpler, I often cut up the braciole and serve them right on top of the sauced pasta, as one dish.

Serves 4

1 tablespoon (15ml) extra-virgin olive oil
1 medium yellow onion, chopped
2 garlic cloves, minced
1 (28-ounce, 794-gram) can Italian tomato
 puree, preferably San Marzano
1 cup (240ml) dry red wine
1 teaspoon oregano, preferably Sicilian
½ teaspoon kosher salt
Pinch of crushed red pepper flakes
A small Parmigiano-Reggiano cheese rind
 (optional) (see note below)

FOR THE FILLING
1 tablespoon (15ml) extra-virgin olive oil
1 medium red onion, minced
3 garlic cloves, minced
½ cup (120ml) dry white wine
2 teaspoons chopped fresh oregano
2 teaspoons finely grated lemon zest
½ cup (2 ounces/56 grams) freshly grated
 Parmigiano-Reggiano cheese (optional) (see
 note below)

FOR THE BRACIOLE

8 (3-ounce/85-gram) pieces of beef, top or bottom round, pounded to a thickness of 1/8 inch (0.3cm)

2 teaspoons kosher salt
1 teaspoon freshly ground black pepper
2 tablespoon (30ml) olive oil

TO MAKE THE SAUCE

Place a 10- to 12-inch skillet over medium-low heat, and when it is hot, add the olive oil. Add the onion and garlic and cook until wilted, about 5 minutes. Add the tomato puree, wine, oregano, salt, red pepper flakes and Parmigiano-Reggiano rind, if using, and bring to a boil. Remove from the heat and set aside.

Preheat the oven to 325 degrees.

TO MAKE THE FILLING

Place an 8-inch skillet over medium-low heat, and when it is hot, add the olive oil. Add the onion and garlic and cook until wilted, about 5 to 7 minutes. Add the white wine and simmer until it has evaporated, 5 minutes. Set aside to cool.

When the onion mixture has cooled, stir in the oregano, lemon zest and cheese, if using.

TO ASSEMBLE THE BRACIOLE

Lay the beef out on a cutting board or work surface and sprinkle both sides with the salt and pepper. Spread some of the onion (and cheese) mixture in the center of each piece of beef, leaving a 1-inch border uncovered. Starting from a short side, roll up the beef and close with a toothpick.

Place a 10- to 12-inch ovenproof skillet over medium-high heat, and when it is hot, add the olive oil. Add the beef and cook until deeply browned on all sides, about 8 minutes. Cover with the tomato sauce, transfer to the oven, and braise until the beef is tender, 1 to 1½ hours.

Serve immediately.

Editor's Note: The recipe calls for a traditional filling, which includes grated cheese. Obviously, if you are kosher, you will omit that ingredient from your preparation.

Helen Ptashnik and Henry Ptashnik

As told by their daughter Meira Fleisch

Meira describes the actions both her parents took during their ordeal; each in their own way exhibited heroism and resolve. While she recalls her parents saying, "They owe their lives to luck, their siblings and good people here and there," as their story shows, they were active participants in their fate.

Both my parents were from Stopnits (Stopnica), Poland, but because my father was ten years older than my mother, they didn't really know each other. You could say they were worlds apart. When my mom was a teenager of about fourteen and my father was in his early twenties, the war changed their lives. My parents were both sent to the same work camp, but both ended up in separate concentration camps. During their internment, my mother was with her two sisters and my father with his two brothers. They were both fortunate that they could be useful to the Germans, as this certainly kept them alive. My father was quite heroic and was responsible for saving many lives while interned. He and his brother, both carpenters, built a sliding door hideaway in the barracks. They essentially created a place for sick prisoners to hide. Doing so, they undoubtedly saved those people's lives. Decades later, I remember when my father was in the hospital and dying. A man in a wheelchair came to visit him, saying he owed his life to my father, who hid him during the war. I felt very proud, and my father was very honored.

After the war, my father went to a DP camp, while my mother was taken to a rehabilitation

Hella and Yeheskel (Helen and Henry), wedding photo, Israel, January 9, 1949.

camp in Italy. She was actually housed in one of Mussolini's former palaces. From there my mother went to Israel aboard a ship that the British initially turned away. In an active act of defiance, the passengers on board staged a hunger strike, and the British allowed her and eventually all the others to disembark. My father had also immigrated to Israel, and one day, while at what I believe was a government building, they bumped into each other. From that time on, my dad started visiting my mother's home. My mother thought he was courting her sister, as they were closer in age, but he was after my mother. My dad fought in the War for Independence, and they remained in Israel for over a decade; that's where I was born.

My mother always cooked fresh foods, never canned or packaged; there were no TV dinners in my house. I used to eat, in my early school days, an Israeli sandwich made from cream cheese and olives; they were the best. I remember loving her chicken soup and her *p'tcha*, with its highly seasoned flavor and lots of garlic. She was a refined cook; even in her noodle pudding, she always used fine noodles. Of her recipes, the one I remember now is a red cabbage dish that she served at holidays. My mother's strength was to make simple food well and focus on quality. What you put in is what you get out. My parents were married fifty-eight years and had two children and four grandchildren.

Helen Ptashnik's Braised Red Cabbage and Apples

This could very well be the ultimate sweet and sour recipe. Mild, sweet red onions and tangy cabbage meld together with tart, crisp apples, honey, lemon and brown sugar. The result is a mélange of flavors that roll off your tongue as authentic Polish cuisine. Just like a seesaw, you can tip the balance in whichever direction you please, adding more lemon for a sour flavor or brown sugar to make it sweeter.

Yield: 8 to 9 cups
Start to Finish: Under 2½ hours

2 tablespoons vegetable or canola oil
2 large red onions, thinly sliced
1 large red cabbage (about 2 to 2½ pounds), shredded
1 tablespoon kosher salt
4 apples (2 Granny Smith, 2 Cortland or McIntosh), peeled and sliced thin

¼ cup honey
¼ cup ketchup
2 tablespoons brown sugar
¼ cup tomato sauce
1 tomato, pureed or finely diced
Juice of 1 lemon

Heat the oil in a large sauté pan; cook and stir the onions, over medium heat, until just soft, about 10 minutes. While the onions cook, shred the cabbage. Add the shredded cabbage to the pan and sprinkle with the salt. Using a large pair of kitchen tongs, toss the cabbage and onions so the salt works its way into the dish. Continue cooking until the cabbage has cooked down and begun to release its liquid, about 10 minutes.

While the cabbage cooks, peel and slice the apples and prepare the remaining ingredients. Stir the apples into the pan. Add the honey, ketchup, brown sugar, tomato sauce, tomato and lemon juice. Cover the pan, reduce the heat to low and cook for 2 hours, stirring the cabbage every 30 minutes. Season to taste with salt and balance the sweet and sour to your liking. Serve hot as a side dish.

Arthur Schwartz

Professional contributor

Who but Arthur Schwartz would we turn to for an authentic, foolproof Yiddish recipe to honor Meira's food memory of her mother's flavorful p'tcha?

P'tcha—Jellied Calf's Feet with Garlic

Excerpted from *Jewish Home Cooking* (Ten Speed Press, 2008)

Most people remember p'tcha as jellied calf's feet with chopped raw garlic and, in some versions, slices of hard-cooked egg or chopped hard-cooked egg embedded in the firm gelatin (*yoich*) just to make it look a little better. In French, p'tcha would be called an aspic, which sounds elegant. But even with a name like p'tcha, the dish has a cult following. Hardly anyone makes it at home, and it is nearly impossible to find in a restaurant, so it has become legendary.

P'tcha possibly started out as a soup, not a jelly. Refrigeration is required to get the broth to jell. Maybe in the shtetls they chilled their p'tcha outside in the frigid air. In the following recipe, chopped fresh parsley is a contemporary touch to improve the looks of the jelly as well as its flavor. If, however, in your memory, p'tcha is not p'tcha if it doesn't resemble a brownish, suspiciously quivering brick, leave out the herb.

Serves 6 to 8

2 calf's feet or knuckles or both (about 3 pounds), sawed into 2-inch pieces by the butcher

10 cups water, plus additional water for soaking

2 medium onions, quartered

2 cloves garlic, coarsely chopped, plus more for the broth

1 teaspoon salt

¼ teaspoon white pepper

2 tablespoons distilled white vinegar

1 cup finely chopped fresh flat-leaf parsley, for garnish

3 egg yolks, for thickening the hot broth or 2 hard-cooked eggs, peeled and sliced or chopped, for garnish (optional)

Finely minced garlic, for garnish (optional)

1 lemon, cut into wedges, for garnish (optional)

Wash the meat thoroughly. Put the pieces into a large bowl, cover them with water, let soak for a few minutes, then drain. Scrape the skin with a sharp knife until it is smooth. (Sometimes, these days, the calf's feet are already cleaned.) In a 4-quart pot, bring the 10 cups of water to boil over a high heat.

Place the pieces in the boiling water along with the onions, the 2 cloves of coarsely chopped garlic, salt, pepper and vinegar. Continue to boil until the meat and gristle begin to separate from the bones, about 3 hours. You will probably have to add more water to keep the feet covered, but it is supposed to reduce. Strain the liquid, saving both liquids and solids.

Pull the meat from the bones and cut into small pieces. Taste the broth and adjust the salt, pepper and vinegar to taste. To serve hot, combine the meat and broth and return to boiling. Remove from the heat and add as much chopped raw garlic as you like. Do not simmer the broth after adding the garlic.

Serve hot in individual soup bowls with meat and garlic, garnished with fresh chopped parsley. Or beat the 3 egg yolks together in a mixing bowl, then mix in some hot broth. Pour this mixture into the broth; do not allow the broth to boil after adding the raw eggs or the eggs will curdle. Another way to serve the broth is with chopped hard-cooked egg, instead of the raw egg enrichment.

To serve cold, which is more typical, arrange the pieces of meat and gristle in a deep heatproof dish. Add the parsley and chopped garlic. Pour in the broth and refrigerate, covered. Before the gelatin firms completely, place slices of hard-cooked egg over the top. Or, alternately, chop the hard-cooked egg and add it to the broth before you refrigerate it and it starts to jell.

In either case, hot or cold, can be served with wedges of lemon.

Gita Karelitz Roback and Godel Roback

As told by their daughter, Rosy Granoff

Gita's intelligence and chutzpah were two characteristics that served her well. Even as a child, she was a nonconformist who envisioned a strong Jewish state. However, her legacy is here in America, as her daughter lovingly remembers her, as a brave, resourceful woman.

Gita and Godel Roback after liberation.

My mother was the youngest of three children, born to a well-to-do family in Baranów, Poland. My mom, who was just a kid before the war broke out, attended parochial school. She benefited from a very good education, and I am proud to say my mother spoke seven languages. She was also somewhat of a free spirit, very dissimilar to her siblings, shunning materialistic things and pursuing Zionist causes. As a young girl, she would sneak out of her house at night and attend meetings and rallies sponsored by Menachem Begin's right-wing organization. When the war broke out, she was working as a bookkeeper. Several members of her family were immediately deported to Siberia, and others followed after to find them; they were never heard from again.

When my mother was sent to the ghetto, she worked as an administrative assistant for a German officer. It is hard to imagine, but she witnessed her mother being rounded up and taken away. My mother wanted to go after her, but the officer convinced her to stay, explaining frankly that if she left, she would not survive. While in the ghetto, she and her first cousin plotted their escape, with hopes of joining the partisans. Through ingenious trickery, she arranged to sneak over the barbed wire and escape into the woods where they joined a small group of freedom fighters. They spent the next couple of years traveling by night and hiding by day. It was in this group that she met my father, Godel Roback.

After the war, my mother and father moved to Rome, Italy, where my two brothers were born. Their plan was to realize my mother's lifelong dream and go to Palestine (Israel). However, a family member from my father's side offered to sponsor their trip to America, and they accepted. My parents surrounded themselves with friends from the war; partisans became the relatives we never had the chance to meet. And while we had a traditional Shabbos dinner every Friday night, my mother's cooking traditions were more American and Italian than eastern European. A family tradition, which stemmed from the time she spent in Italy, was to have pasta every Sunday night. She and my dad were married over forty years, and together they had three children, six grandchildren and three great-grandchildren.

Gita Roback's Slow Simmered Sunday Sauce

Gita would begin her sauce with the tireless trio of onions, peppers and celery. Slow-cooked herbs, crushed tomatoes and tomato paste simmered the day away till a robust and aromatic sauce emerged. These same ingredients can easily create a quick sauce; you might sacrifice a little in flavor, but if time is crunching, it's still far better than store bought. Gita would bathe waiting pasta in the vibrant sauce and serve it alongside thick, juicy rib steaks, which were simply broiled. For a change of pace, burgers made from freshly ground beef and veal and seasoned with grated onion and garlic would be served bunless alongside the spaghetti.

Yield: 3 cups
Start to Finish: At least 4 hours or up to 6 hours; for quick sauce, under 1 hour

2 tablespoons olive oil
1 medium onion, finely chopped (about ¾ cup)
1 medium green pepper, cored, seeded and diced
2 celery ribs, finely chopped
2 pounds ripe plum tomatoes, peeled, seeded and chopped, or 1 (28-ounce) can whole tomatoes with their juice
1 heaping tablespoon tomato paste

1 (8-ounce) can tomato sauce
2 garlic cloves, minced
2 tablespoons freshly chopped oregano
2 tablespoons freshly chopped flat leaf parsley, plus additional for garnish
2 tablespoons freshly chopped basil, plus additional for garnish
2 bay leaves
Kosher salt and pepper

Heat the oil in a large saucepan; cook and stir the onions, peppers and celery over medium heat until lightly browned, about 10 minutes. Stir in the tomatoes, tomato paste, tomato sauce, garlic, oregano, parsley, basil and bay leaves. Season to taste with salt and pepper. Lower the heat to a simmer; cover and cook the sauce for at least 4 hours or up to 6. For quick sauce, cook for 30–60 minutes. In the last few minutes of cooking, add the additional parsley and basil. Before serving, remove the bay leaves and toss with your choice of pasta.

Feedback

In this slow simmered sauce, parsley and basil are added twice. First, they are cooked with the sauce to flavor it and meld with the aromatics. They are also added right at the end to appreciate their full flavor. Usually, the fresh spring taste of soft herbs such as parsley, dill and basil is best preserved if they are chopped right before using and added at the very end. With this recipe, you get the slow-cooked flavor from the herbs and their vibrant fresh boost at the end.

Sally Rosenkranz and Sol Rosenkranz

In Sol's words

Sol was a born teacher, spending much of his time educating children on the lessons of the Holocaust. Even at ninety-plus years, he recalled every name, every incident in such vivid detail that I listened with rapt attention. His is truly a story of perseverance and love.

I remember very clearly my childhood in Krosniewice, Poland. I was the youngest in the family, and I recall helping my mother, beginning on Thursday, to prepare for Shabbos. We lived well and had the money to buy chicken, duck, goose, eggs and butter from the peasants who sold their wares. In 1939, when I was twenty-one, Poland was fully affected by the Nazis. I came from a close-knit family, so much so that when the Nazis came for my older brother, who was married and a father, my middle brother took his place. My younger sister did the same for my older sister. They both did it out of love. When the town was ghettoized, our building, a corner stone house, became part of the ghetto. We considered ourselves lucky, taking in our aunts and uncles, filling our house with over twenty people. On March 1, 1942, we escaped the ghetto the night before it was liquidated. The story is one of great luck.

While in the ghetto, I was assigned to shine the boots of the German police who lived in a large building just outside the ghetto. I would go early in the morning and was warned not to wake them up, which was difficult because the floorboards squeaked. If you did wake them, as I did on my first day, you were beaten and told not to come back. One morning, in the first week of February 1942, I approached the gate and saw a family I did not recognize; it was a mother, father and two boys. I learned from the father, whose name was Harry Greenfield, that his family escaped from their nearby ghetto before it was liquidated. I brought the family home with me, and we listened to their warnings and escape plan. The following day, I released the bottom portion of the fence so they could sneak out.

I was asked back to the police station, as I was the last young fellow in the ghetto. Before the war, my family had been in the fur business, and we still had many of our goods. It was freezing cold, and I took a fur collar for the son of the German chief of police, Danksom Miller. In exchange, I asked him what was going to happen to the Jews. He told me not to be afraid until March 1, which was only two weeks away. On the last day in February, my friend Aaron Shulman, who took care of their horses, and I were given a very heavy assignment to fill up their stalls with heating supplies of coal and wood. While I was outside the ghetto, I used my time to convince five families in town to hide my family for the night. That evening, I sent my family out of the same opening in the fence, but I remained behind. In the morning, as I was collecting the boots to shine, I saw three trucks pull up in front of the police station. I camouflaged myself as a

Sally and Sol Rosenkranz.

worker, waited for the commotion to stop, and I was on their tail. I followed the police as they took up positions on the side of the ghetto. It was probably foolish of me, but I was brazen. I soon reconnected with my family, and we were on the road to escape.

We first went to Lodz, and we bribed a civil servant to direct us to a small cottage, where a woman hid my family in her attic. I decided not to go up to the attic but stayed downstairs in the hut about thirty to forty-five minutes. Later, a German border guard entered with a German shepherd. He sat opposite me and started a conversation since he noticed me wearing a watch. He spoke to me in German, asking to buy the watch. I

played dumb that I didn't understand German and responded in Polish and not about the watch. Instead, I spoke about the heavy snow and the severe weather. I must say, he was not a sophisticated border guard. He did not have the slightest clue who was up in the attic or that I was Jewish. Shortly after, we met up with the Greenfields in a city called Piotrkow/Trybunalski. In May, my brother and I were sent to work in separate factories. I worked in Kara, a glass factory beside the railroad. We worked all day but were allowed to return home at night. Beginning in August, the trains that ran there were taking Jewish people to Treblinka. Every day I would watch the trains, as people on the train would throw notes from the small windows. Kids would run and pick up the notes, and we would read them to see if we recognized any names. One evening in September, we went to the gates to leave for home after work, but they were shut and remained shut. We were now detained and cut off from our family. After about a week of being detained, I was opening the notes thrown from the train and sadly read the names of my family. I never saw them again.

I continued working from May 1942 to November 1944. The Germans feared the Russians were nearby, so they would scoop us up and move us. We did this over and over, until we arrived in Buchenwald. There I found my first cousin Phil. We volunteered to be transferred, one time near a gasoline factory, Rheinsdorf Leipzig, where we were almost killed by Allied bombs. We were not fed, and every day we each collected two cigarette rations in Buchenwald, which we later used to bribe a guard to transfer us to field work. We were again loaded on to trains, and by now we learned never to be the first and never to be the last. We stayed in the middle of a train that was nearly sixty cars long. We were lucky, because Allied planes dropped bombs that blew up the front of the train. We were in a large forest in Austria before approaching Strasbourg. We used that timing to run as fast and as far as we could, heading into the forest. Once again, we were scooped up and marched from town to town, through Strasbourg and into Czechoslovakia and ending up in Terezin. A few weeks later, the Russians liberated us. I survived because I always had an eye open, and I was very lucky.

My wife, Sally, came from a large family. She was second to the youngest and was thirteen when taken to the camps. Sally went through many camps in Poland and Germany. She ended up in Bergen-Belsen where the British liberated her. I also came to Bergen-Belsen after the war, and that's where we met. Sally learned she had family who had survived the war and were living in Stuttgart. She wanted to go there to find them. We had just gotten acquainted, but I took her to the train station. The train was packed.

Luckily, one window on the train was open, and I pushed Sally through the window onto the train on top of everyone's shoulders. This was the only way to go from place to place. She told her family all about me, and they invited me for *Pesach*. I went to Stuttgart, and I was given an interview by the family. A Jewish military chaplain married us on April 27. My future brother-in-law worked for an American military office, and he was given all the affidavits needed for all of us to come to America in July 1946.

Sally learned all the cooking and baking from her aunt Toby, also a survivor. She became an excellent cook and baker under Aunt Toby's guidance and then by figuring things out on her own. We had a truly wonderful life together, and I knew she was my bashert. After fifty years of marriage, Sally suffered a heart attack and, as fitting with our life story, died in my arms. We have three children and one grandchild.

Author's Note: I sadly learned that Sol has passed away. May his memory be for a blessing.

Jeff Nathan

Professional contributor

Sol remembers as a young boy preparation for Shabbos dinner beginning Thursday, and he recalls a home where chicken, goose and duck were enjoyed for Friday night dinner. Jeff Nathan adds, "There was a time in early Jewish American history when the duck for a Shabbos dinner was as commonplace as today's chicken. This recipe is classy, yet relatively easy to prepare with pantry ingredients."

Duck with Apple and White Raisin Sauce

Presented by Chef Jeff Nathan, host of Jewish Television Network's *New Jewish Cuisine*.
Yield: 4 servings

1 apple, quartered
1 orange, quartered
2 (5-pound) ducklings

Butcher cracked black pepper (also known as quarter cracked)

Preheat the oven to 450 degrees.

Place the quartered apple and orange in the cavity of each bird. Prick ducks with a fork all over. Season with pepper. Roast, breast side up on a foil rack in baking pan. Bake at 450 degrees for 1 hour.

Lower the temperature to 400 degrees for one half hour more.

Remove ducks from oven. Let them rest approximately 20 minutes. Carve or refrigerate overnight.

Apple with White Raisin Sauce

4 tablespoons sugar
1 piece star anise
1/4 cup apple cider vinegar
2 Granny Smith apples, peeled and cored, tossed with lemon juice

1/4 cup golden raisins
1/2 cup apple cider or juice
1/8 teaspoon ground cinnamon
Fruit liquor
Cornstarch

In a small saucepot, place the sugar, star anise and cider vinegar. Cook until caramel colored.

Carefully add the apples, raisins, cider and cinnamon. Slowly simmer until rich and flavorful. Thicken with a slurry of fruit liquor and cornstarch as needed.

Sally Rosenkranz's Honey Cake

Sally's daughter Rita writes, "My late mother, Sally Rosenkranz, who was from Radom, Poland, lost her mother in the Holocaust. Mom learned to cook and bake from her aunt, refining recipes over the years. I bake this crowd-pleasing honey cake for the holidays, and also freeze individual slices for drop-in guests."

Yield: Two 9-inch loaves, 12 to 16 slices each
Start to Finish: Under 1½ hours

½ cup brewed coffee, cooled
3½ cups sifted all-purpose flour
¼ teaspoon salt
2 teaspoons baking powder
1 teaspoon baking soda
1½ teaspoons ground cinnamon
¼ teaspoon ground nutmeg
⅛ teaspoon powdered cloves (optional)

1½ teaspoons powdered ginger (optional)
4 eggs
1 cup sugar
1 cup vegetable oil
2 cups dark honey
1½ cups coarsely chopped walnuts or
  almonds
1 cup raisins (optional)

Preheat the oven to 325 degrees and grease two 9-inch loaf pans or a 16 x 11 x 4-inch baking pan. Brew the coffee and set it aside to cool.

In a medium bowl, sift the flour, salt, baking powder, baking soda, cinnamon, nutmeg, cloves and ginger. In a separate large bowl, beat the eggs on medium speed, gradually adding the sugar and beating for several minutes, until the mixture turns a pale yellow. Beat in the oil, honey and cooled coffee. Gradually add the flour mixture to the egg mixture, beating on low speed to prevent the flour from flying out of the bowl. Turn the speed up to medium and beat for several minutes, until a smooth, thick batter is formed. Stir the chopped nuts into the batter. If adding raisins, stir them in at this time.

Fill the prepared pans halfway with batter. The cake rises considerably when baking. (Any extra batter can be used to make delicious muffins.) Bake for 1 to 1¼ hours until the top of the cake is a cinnamon brown, but not burnt, and a bamboo skewer inserted in the center comes out clean. This cake can deflate as it rests; while its sunken shape might look funny, it does nothing to the incredible taste.

Cool completely before slicing.

Maks Rothman and Gita Rothman

As told by their daughter Sylvia Rothman Nirenberg

Maks and Gita were a mixed marriage, he from Poland and she from Romania. We placed their story in the Polish section, as Sylvia's home traditions leaned more toward the Polish style.

Maks and Gita Rothman on their wedding day.

My parents began their new lives in Canada, but they started them in very different places. My father, Maks, was born and raised in Poland and, like so many others during the war, came home one day to find his house burned to the ground and his family gone. My dad was a resourceful teenager and spent the war years surviving on his own, hiding by day, scavenging for food at night. He drifted from border to border, always evading capture. Eventually, he immigrated to Israel and fought in the Israeli army. My father learned that most of his family had survived. He traveled to Canada to be reunited with his parents, two sisters and two brothers. Amazingly, another sister whom the family did not believe had survived resurfaced recently and was reunited with the rest of the family more than fifty years after she was presumed dead.

I know little about my mother's story during the war, as she was reluctant to talk about her experiences. I know that her family fled Romania to Siberia and that she eventually came to Canada, where she met my dad. When they moved to America, I remember my mother cooking the traditional Shabbos meal, and then we would eat the leftovers for days. My parents have two children, four grandchildren and one great-grandchild.

Judy Bart Kancigor

Professional contributor

Maks Rothman was famous for his pickled herring. Sylvia recalls, "When my father made it, I would run the other way. This was a dish he would make for breakfast gatherings at his synagogue." Not only did Polish Jews consume a lot of herring, but they were also herring traders and importers.

   Because the fish was pre-salted, and inexpensive, it became a staple in the diet of eastern European Jews. The great debate is wine sauce or cream sauce? You decide. To turn this recipe, contributed by Judy Bart Kancigor, into herring in cream sauce, simply cut the herring into bite-size pieces, stir in some sour cream and correct the taste with sugar.

Louis Selmanowitz's Chopped Herring

Excerpted from *Cooking Jewish: 532 Great Recipes from the Rabbinowitz Family* (Workman Publishing Company, Inc. 2007)
Serves 6

2 salted herrings, filleted
1 small white onion, chopped
1 large tart apple, peeled and finely chopped
2 tablespoons distilled white vinegar
1 large egg, hard-cooked and mashed

$\frac{1}{8}$ teaspoon freshly ground black pepper
Romaine lettuce, for serving
Grated hard-cooked egg and finely chopped
  onion, for garnish
Plain crackers, for serving

Soak the herrings in cold water to cover for 24 hours. Then rinse them well and grind them by hand.

Combine the ground herring, onion, apple, vinegar, egg and pepper in a bowl and mix thoroughly.

Spoon the mixture onto a platter lined with romaine lettuce leaves and garnish with grated egg and chopped onion.

To serve, schmear (spread) on plain crackers.

Helena Pradelski Sabat and Benjamin Sabat

As told by their daughter Anna Sabat

Many of Anna's childhood memories are built around food and family gatherings. With lots of humor and great respect for those traditions, she shares her memories with us.

My mother, whose maiden name was Helena Pradelski, was born on February 22, 1921, in Sosnowiec, Poland, the fourth of six children. Her brother, Henry, the eldest, was the only son. During the war, he was shuttled through various concentration camps, while my mother spent five years in one work camp, where she and other young women made machinery parts to be used in the war. Unlike my father, Benjamin Sabat, who was in Auschwitz, my mother had no number tattooed on her arm. When the war ended, my mother was deliriously happy to be finally reunited with her brother, Henry, but as they continued their search for the rest of their immediate family, they eventually learned that their parents and four sisters perished in the camps. As did many survivors, after the war, my mother quickly married and became pregnant (with me).

We came to America in the summer of 1949 and settled in Brooklyn, New York, where my sister Mary (!) was born in 1951. Of course, food took on a significant role in our household, almost becoming another member of the family. The centerpiece of many family stories focused on how I, at two years old, barely ate for the weeklong ship voyage to America. I remained quite thin throughout my girlhood and adolescence, despite my parents' never-ending quest to fatten me up. For Holocaust survivors, it was almost shameful to have a thin child. The following are some recollections, mostly brief sketches, related to food in the home where I grew up:

My mother shopped for food daily, buying just enough for that day's meals, as she had in Europe. Everything had to be fresh. Our freezer stored nothing but ice cubes. She was not much of a baker, but she visited Jeffrey's Bakery on Church Avenue daily for bread and cakes. At night, after dinner, my sister and I were served absurdly large pieces of cake, along with glasses of milk or sometimes malteds that my father picked up on his way home from work at the local candy store with a soda fountain. My favorites were Jeffrey's chocolate eggs, which were individual-sized

Anna Sabat with her parents, Helena and Benjamin, Regensburg, Germany.

oval-shaped yellow cakes covered with chocolate. The centers were filled with a buttercream that even now makes my mouth water as I think of them. While my sister and I ate those or strawberry shortcake or seven-layer cake, my parents usually had sponge cake and tea in glasses.

My father insisted on fresh rye bread with his meals. Sometimes on Saturday mornings I was sent out to fetch the bread, one-quarter to one-half loaf at a time, sliced without seeds, as my father liked it. I recall the bakery clerk selecting the bread, which had a sticker on the end (I guess to distinguish the seeded from non-seeded ryes), and then putting it through the slicer. Sometimes I nibbled on the end piece as I carried the wax bag home. However, the morning's bread would not do for dinner that same day. Once again, I or my sister or my mother (never my father) would go to the bakery to get another quarter loaf. Sometimes as I stood at the counter waiting my turn, I looked at the breads and rolls piled high on the shelves and thought of the stories my mother told of the days just before she and her sisters were sent away, when there was little food and they traded their beautifully embroidered nightgowns to townspeople, only to be given pieces of stale bread in return.

My mother made gefilte fish from scratch for all the holidays. She would cover her ironing board with a cloth and clamp on a metal hand grinder into which she fed the fresh fish that she then mixed with other ingredients, shaped into oval patties and cooked. My mother made the best potato latkes I've ever had. They were completely different from the dense ones I've been served throughout my adult life on many occasions and in various settings. My mother's were light, airy, golden and crisp, never greasy. We usually ate them with only a light sprinkling of sugar—no sour cream or applesauce. One of my biggest regrets is that I didn't get the recipe when she was alive. My mother regularly made chopped liver. I can still hear the rhythmic sound of her wielding a *hak messer* to mince chicken livers, hard-cooked eggs and onions in a round wooden bowl that was covered with tiny nicks from years of use.

Attempts at American fare resulted in hamburgers round and dense as baseballs. Chopped meat was mixed with eggs and garlic and served not on buns, but on white bread. She sometimes packed them for me to take to school for lunch. I was embarrassed about how un-American they looked, but my friends loved them and gladly traded their "American" peanut butter and jelly sandwiches for my "refugee" hamburgers.

When I'd balk at a family dinner as my mother filled my plate to the brim and cut those absurdly large pieces of cake, my uncle Henry would advise me to humor her. "You have to remember," he said, "the war made us all a little crazy about food." My parents were married thirty-one years, as we lost my mom at a relatively young age. She knew my son, Matthew, but not my daughter, Helena, who was born in 1979 and is named for the grandmother she never knew. She would have loved knowing that because of her survival she also has two great-grandchildren.

Ina Garten

Professional contributor

While we can't bring back the sound of the hak messer chopping liver, we can ignite Anna's memories with a new version. We are sure that Ina Garten's fabulous recipe will bring back great memories for Anna and will provide us all with a new way to make this timeless classic.

Chopped Liver

Excerpted from *Barefoot Contessa Parties!* by Ina Garten (Clarkson/Potter Publishers), Copyright 2001. All Rights Reserved

Around the Jewish holidays, all our (Barefoot Contessa) customers wait for us to make chopped liver. It's like your grandmother's, if you have a Jewish grandmother, but better. The Madeira adds a bit of sweetness without your knowing what it is. Be sure not to overprocess this spread; you want it chunky. I serve it with pieces of matzo.

Makes about 5 cups

2 pounds chicken livers
1 cup rendered chicken fat
2 cups medium-diced yellow onion (2 onions)
⅓ cup Madeira wine
4 extra-large eggs, hard-cooked, peeled and chunked

¼ cup minced fresh parsley
2 teaspoons fresh thyme leaves
2 teaspoons kosher salt
1 teaspoon freshly ground black pepper
pinch cayenne pepper

Drain the livers and sauté them in 2 batches in 2 tablespoons of the chicken fat over medium-high heat, turning once, for about 5 minutes, or until just barely pink inside. Don't overcook the livers or they will be dry. Transfer them to a large bowl.

In the same pan, sauté the onions in 3 tablespoons of the chicken fat over medium-high heat for about 10 minutes, or until browned. Add the Madeira and deglaze the pan, scraping the sides, for about 15 seconds. Pour into the bowl with the livers.

Add the eggs, parsley, thyme, salt, black pepper, cayenne and the remaining chicken fat to the bowl. Toss quickly to combine. Transfer half the mixture to the bowl of a food processor fitted with a steel blade. Pulse 6 to 8 times, until coarsely chopped. Repeat with the remaining mixture. Season to taste and chill. Serve on crackers or matzo.

Feedback

Ina Garten's chopped liver has a delicious gourmet twist and a perfect texture. The chicken fat added to the mixture makes it rich and smooth. If you are kosher, then you know you must broil the liver first.

Ruth Baumwald Stromer and Moty Stromer

As told by their daughters Nina Gaspar and Sue Talansky

Nina and Sue speak in tandem, as many sisters do; one begins a sentence and the other finishes. When they exuberantly spoke of their parents, you could hear the joy in their shared memories. They described their father as a character, their mother as a lady.

They also shared their dad's diary with me, published by Yad Vashem. *Memoirs of an Unfortunate Person* is Moty's accounting of his time in hiding. The first-person narrative is revealing and chilling and provides great insight into their father. What is written here comes from his diary and from the eloquent introduction written by Sue.

Our father, Moty, was born in 1910, in Kamionka-Strumilowa (Kaminke), in southeastern Poland. According to his diary, he enjoyed the period of time between August 1939 and June 1941, when this part of Galicia was under Soviet rule. Everything was forever destroyed on Sunday, June 22, 1941, when German tanks and troops entered Kaminke. Ten days later, his grandfather and great-uncle were murdered. Moty fled to the Lemberg ghetto, where he remained till it was liquidated in June 1943. By then he had lost much of his family. Soon after, Moty escaped from a transport train and fled into the woods. He tried to find shelter with people he knew before the war: Jozef and Rozalie Streker, an ethnic German couple who had a farm in an area called Jagonia. The Strekers, at great risk, hid him in their attic for ten months, until the approaching Soviet armies and the implicit threat they posed to ethnic Germans forced them to abandon their home and its terrified hidden tenant. Decades later, the Strekers

were honored at Yad Vashem as "Righteous Among the Nations."

It is in the last two months of hiding, from April 6 to June 2, 1944, that our father wrote his memoir. He asked for paper and pencil in order to write down his thoughts and memories. Writing in Yiddish, in painfully neat and tiny script, he recounted as best he could the fate of those he knew and loved. There is a sense of urgency in these lines, and the script becomes larger and larger, as if he

Ruth and Moty Stromer.

were shouting these directions on paper with his last ounce of mental and physical strength. He needed to do everything in his power to ensure this manuscript's survival, if not his own. He wrote:

With the help of God I am writing these words on the night before I have to leave my place, this attic, where I have been more than—or exactly—300 days and nights. The days in this place were no brighter than the nights; but what do I want? To be able to spend more time in this place—or find one like it. May God help me! Please convey this to my brother Meyer Stromer, or my sister in America Henia Edelstein, to let them know.

Today is Thursday, April 6, 1944 I had a difficult time trying to decide whether to write this or not, because I had always hoped I would live through the greatest disaster....Once everything is on paper, [will I find] the right person to hide the manuscript? God has helped me. The fact is that my personal tragedy is the tragedy of hundreds of thousands of Jews. But be it as it may, I hope that I survive long enough to see my remaining family. Then I will laugh at life, because on more than one occasion I have looked death in the eye.

Soon after the last page was written, the war came to an end and Moty returned to Kaminke. There he met our mother, Ruth Baumwald. She was a beautiful woman, twelve years our father's junior and, like his sister, Henia, a graduate of a Polish gymnasium (secondary school). Our mother was far more reticent

about her war experiences than our dad. We know that a Christian woman in Lemberg proper hid her. We know she spent much of the war terrified beyond description and we know she survived with her nuclear family intact—a miracle indeed. My parents-to-be fell in love and were married in 1947 by the chief rabbi of Cracow, who, years later, in New York, officiated at my wedding, as well as my sister's.

After a brief sojourn in Belgium, the family moved to the Upper West Side of New York City. Once transplanted to America, our mother learned English quickly, and her kitchen was the center of our household. She served up standard American fare, burgers and fries, spaghetti and meatballs, steak and mashed potatoes. Thursday night was always "dairy" with creamy potato soup, fried fish, lokshen and Schrafft's ice cream for dessert. Eastern European foods found their place on our Shabbos and holiday tables: gefilte fish, chicken soup, tzimmes and her wonderful chopped liver. Our mother's delicious stuffed cabbage took almost a full day to prepare. When I was first married and living on the north shore of Long Island, I taught classes till late on Friday afternoons in Manhattan. In the winter, I did not have a chance to prepare a Shabbos meal, so my mother would cook and pack up a five-course dinner and then meet me at the 103rd Street IRT subway stop and simply hand it to me when the train doors opened. All of a sudden, as we pulled out of the station, this subway car packed with harried New Yorkers, filled with the aroma of a shtetl Shabbos.

My father loved to cook chicken soup. He would put on a huge chef's apron and prepare gallons at a time. More than cooking, our dad loved food shopping. Every Sunday, he went to Zabar's to buy appetizing lox and all the trimmings for our lavish brunches. He especially enjoyed chatting with a *landsman* behind the counter. Moty later learned that this same man who sliced nova for him every Sunday was also a survivor. Moty hated the lines. Not to worry. He simply searched the floor for discarded numbers and then skipped to the head of the line. It's things like this that helped him survive; he was always resourceful and knew how to bend the rules. We had the typical upbringing of survivors' children. We rarely ate out, never had babysitters, avoided pets, paid in cash and stuck together. We were the center of our parents' universe, and as often as not, much of their attentiveness expressed itself in the foods they so lovingly prepared and served to us. Their true legacy is their seven grandchildren and seven great-grandchildren.

Ruth Stromer's Honey and Lemon Stuffed Cabbage

Pure genius! That's the only way to describe Ruth's technique for preparing the uncooperative cabbage leaves necessary for stuffed cabbage. Instead of battling with boiling water, Ruth would freeze the cabbage for about a week. The night before she was going to prepare the stuffed cabbage, she would thaw the frozen head (overnight in the fridge will do it). The next morning, as if to say, "Stuff me," the leaves would fall away, limp, pliable and ready to go. Granted you have to think ahead, but give this method a whirl when you have a premonition of craving stuffed cabbage.

Yield: 14 to 16 rolls
Start to Finish: Under 2½ hours (plus the time to freeze and thaw the cabbage)

1 medium head of cabbage, frozen for one
  week, and then thawed overnight in the fridge

FOR THE SAUCE
2 tablespoons olive oil
1 large onion, coarsely
  chopped
24 ounces canned tomato
  juice
2 beef bones (shin bones
  work well)
2 teaspoons kosher salt
½ teaspoon black pepper

FOR THE FILLING
1 cup cooked rice
1 pound ground beef
2 teaspoons kosher salt
½ teaspoon black pepper
1 teaspoon onion powder or
  minced dried onion
1 egg

TO FINISH THE SAUCE
½ cup honey
2 to 3 tablespoons lemon
  juice, or ½ teaspoon sour
  salt

After the cabbage has been thawed, separate the leaves. You will need to cut the hard end (tip of the core) so that the leaves release from the head and cut out the thick white rib on each leaf. You should have at least 14 to 16 leaves, large enough to stuff. Let the leaves drain and rest on a paper towel while you prepare the sauce and filling.

Heat the oil in a large Dutch oven, cook and stir the onions, over medium heat, until lightly browned, about 10 minutes. Pour in the tomato juice, add the bones and season with salt and pepper. Let the sauce simmer, uncovered, while you prepare the filling.

Cook the rice, according to package directions. Let the rice cool for a few minutes then combine it with the rest of the filling ingredients. Fill each leaf with about ¼ cup of filling; don't overfill (the amount depends on the size of the leaf). Roll the end toward the middle, tuck in the soft sides and roll into a tight package. Place the rolls in the sauce close together; this will help prevent them from unrolling while they simmer. Cook, covered, on a low heat, for about 1½ hours, and then push the cabbage rolls to the side so you can stir in ½ cup honey and fresh lemon juice or sour salt to the sauce. Gently stir and season to taste with salt and pepper. Cook, covered, for 30 minutes longer.

Feedback
There is no question that the texture of the cabbage leaves using this method is different than when boiled. This same recipe can be prepared using the more traditional method of boiling the cabbage to obtain the wilted leaves (see Freda Lederer's recipe on page 263 for that technique).

Florence Tabrys

In her own words

Florence imbued in her daughters the responsibility to continue the traditions rooted in her eastern European home. She didn't talk often about her experiences during the war, but she was more than willing to share her cherished recipes.

I was born in a small town called Szydlowiec, near Radom, in Poland. My family consisted of my parents and six other siblings. In September 1939, when I was fourteen years old, the Nazis occupied our town. For three years, we continued to live in our house along with the other people in the town. It was not a formal ghetto, but the Polish people and the Nazi SS surrounded us. We were forced to do various jobs and survived, as my father, a cobbler, bartered for food and supplies. In 1942, my younger sister and I were separated from the rest of our family, and we never saw them again. My sister and I were sent to a munitions factory, where we worked twelve-hour shifts and managed to stay alive. As the Russian army grew closer, the SS moved us from camp to camp, and while we were confined in Bergen-Belsen, the British army liberated us. Miraculously, I stayed with my sister the entire time.

After liberation, like many other displaced persons, I went to a DP camp. There I met and married my husband, Harry. Together we immigrated to the United States and raised two beautiful daughters, who gave

Florence and Harry Tabrys in the United States, circa 1949–early 1950s.

us four wonderful grandchildren. Despite the hardships I endured and the losses I sustained, I feel very lucky to have been able to rebuild my life. One of the things that kept me going during the war were memories of my family, and so many of those revolved around family gatherings and food. We would remind ourselves of the simplest things that we ate at home, especially during the holidays.

I would think about how I helped my mother prepare the necessary dishes such as gefilte fish, chicken with matzo ball soup, kreplach, stuffed cabbage and apple cake for Shabbos. I can still taste the sweet blintzes that my mother would make. Those memories came with me to America, and those are the recipes I still lovingly prepare today.

Author's Note: I sadly learned that both Florence and her husband have passed away. They would have been so happy to know that their family has grown to include four great-grandchildren. May their memory be for a blessing.

Florence Tabrys's Sweet and Creamy Cheese Blintzes

These cheese blintzes have always been a favorite with everyone in Florence's family. Serve them for a casual brunch or light lunch. The filling is a combination of soft cheeses that melt into the blintz for a sweet and creamy burst of flavor with every bite. They make a great late-night snack and ready-to-heat treat, as they freeze perfectly.

Yield: 10 blintzes
Start to Finish: Under 30 minutes

FOR THE BATTER
6 large eggs
1/2 cup warm water
1/2 cup whole milk
1 cup all-purpose flour

FOR THE FILLING
1 (4-ounce) package cream cheese, softened at room temperature
1 cup (7.5-ounce package) farmer's cheese
1 teaspoon melted butter
3/4 teaspoon ground cinnamon
1/2 cup sugar
1 egg, beaten
Butter for frying

TOPPINGS
Sweetened sour cream, cinnamon sugar, confectioners' sugar, orange zest (optional)

Prepare the batter by whisking together all the ingredients. The batter should be thinner than a pancake batter, and a golden yellow color. Refrigerate the batter while you prepare the filling. For the filling, combine all the filling ingredients and gently blend until smooth.

Heat a pat of butter in an 8-inch nonstick skillet. Ladle about 1/4 cup of batter into the center of the pan and quickly swirl the pan in a circular motion to evenly distribute the batter. Fry for 1 minute and then flip the blintz over. Cook for just a few seconds on the flip side and remove to a waiting paper towel. Cover with a second paper towel to prevent the blintzes from drying out. Wipe the pan clean of the residual butter, add a fresh pat and follow the same process until you have used all the batter.

When cool to the touch, begin filling the blintzes. A large tablespoonful plopped right in the middle of the blintz should do it. Fold the blintz, by bringing the two ends to the middle, and then fold the two sides into the middle, creating a little oblong package. Their irregular shape lets people know they are homemade, so don't fret if they don't look perfect. The blintzes are ready to fry. Heat several pats of butter in the same skillet you used to cook the pancake and fry them for several minutes or until golden brown. You can freeze the prepared blintzes and fry them at a later time.

Enjoy the blintzes as is, or top with any of the suggested toppings. A classic fruit sauce makes an elegant choice (see recipe on page 139). Don't be surprised if people begin calling your blintzes crepes—they mean it as a compliment.

David Waltuck

Professional contributor

So now that you have mastered sweet cheese blintzes, are you ready to tackle a gourmet interpretation of this classic dish? There is no one better to guide you than masterful chef David Waltuck. David discovered that his Jewish roots could be elevated to fine cuisine, as evident in the following recipe.

Blintzes of Fresh and Smoked Salmon with Caviar Cream

Excerpted from *Chanterelle* (Taunton Press, 2008)

Years ago, while dining at one of New York's finest restaurants—an upscale, American-owned establishment with French-leaning food—I was served a miniature bagel topped with a drizzle of truffle sauce. I was startled to see a Jewish American staple in that setting. I was instantly liberated. It had never occurred to me to bring foods from my own ethnic heritage into Chanterelle, but as I sat there eating this gussied-up bagel, I thought, "Why not?"

It wasn't long before little nods to knishes, blintzes and other Middle European favorites began to find their way onto my menu. This is one such dish, which combines the form of a blintz with another cornerstone of my culinary heritage, smoked salmon. To balance the flavor and make the dish suitable to the elegant surroundings of Chanterelle, I add fresh salmon and finish the blintzes with a simple caviar cream. Try to find a nice, smoky salmon, such as a Norwegian-style one.

Rather than make blintz dough, I use *feuille de brik*, the crepe-like wrappers found in North African cooking. They can be purchased from specialty suppliers and are usually sold frozen and are very much my first choice for this dish, as they are much thinner and more delicate than spring roll wrappers. That said, you may use spring roll wrappers as an alternative.

Makes 24 pieces, enough to serve 6

½ cup heavy cream, plus more for serving

3 tablespoons crème fraîche or sour cream

1 teaspoon sherry vinegar

1 cup diced (¼-inch) sushi-grade salmon with skin removed (from about an 8-ounce fillet)

¼ cup diced (½-inch) smoked salmon (about 4 ounces)

½ teaspoon freshly squeezed lemon juice, plus more to taste

Pinch of kosher salt

1 large egg

2 tablespoons cold water

6 (12-inch) feuille de brik sheets or large spring roll wrappers

Canola or other neutral oil, for frying

2 tablespoons American black caviar, such as paddlefish

To make the caviar cream, put the cream, crème fraîche and vinegar in a medium bowl and stir together. Cover with plastic wrap and set aside to thicken at room temperature for 10–30 minutes, then transfer to the refrigerator to chill for at least 1 hour and up to 2 hours. If it becomes too thick, stir in a teaspoon or two more cream to make it pourable.

Put the fresh and smoked salmon in a medium bowl. Add the lemon juice and salt, toss gently and set aside.

Prepare an egg wash by whisking together the egg and water together in a small bowl.

Arrange the feuille de brik sheets on a clean, dry surface, with one corner pointed at you. Using a pastry brush, brush each one with a thin coat of egg wash. Place 3 tablespoons of the salmon filling in the center of each wrapper. Then, if you think of each corner as a compass point, fold the south corner upward and hold it down with a thumb as your pointer fingers fold in the east and west corners, encasing the filling. Roll the feuille de brik carefully and tightly away from you, sealing the blintz with a bit more egg wash if necessary.

Line a plate with paper towels. Heat a wide heavy-bottomed sauté pan over medium heat for 3 to 4 minutes. Pour in the oil and heat until a scant drop of water sizzles when flicked into the pan, about 2 minutes. Carefully place the blintzes in the hot oil and fry until crispy (the filling will be slightly undercooked in the center), 2 to 3 minutes per side. Use tongs to remove them from the oil to drain on the paper towels.

Use a serrated knife to cut each blintz into quarters. Stir the caviar into the cream. Arrange the blintz pieces on a platter. Serve hot with the caviar cream alongside as a dip.

Florence Tabrys's *Jablecznik*—Polish Apple Cake

If Polish women are tired and cranky, I understand why! This cake is a lot of work, but the final result is worth it. A delectable compote of apples and raisins is baked between layers of crunchy dough to create the national treasure that is *jablecznik*, Polish for "apple pie." Florence's twist is an added layer of grape jelly that introduces another flavorful note to every bite.

Yield: 24 pieces
Start to Finish: Under 1½ hours

FOR THE DOUGH
4 eggs
4 tablespoons orange juice
1 teaspoon orange peel, zested
4 tablespoons vanilla extract
1⅓ cups sugar
2 rounded teaspoons baking powder
1 cup vegetable oil
5 cups all-purpose flour

FOR THE FILLING
2½ pounds (8–10) McIntosh apples, peeled, cored and grated
½ cup raisins, or more to taste
½ cup sugar mixed with 2 teaspoons ground cinnamon

TOPPING
¼ cup sugar mixed with 1 teaspoon ground cinnamon

FOR THE LAYERING
1 cup grape jelly, room temperature

Preheat the oven to 375 degrees and grease a 13 x 9 x 2-inch Pyrex baking dish.

To make the dough, in a large bowl, beat the eggs, orange juice, orange zest, vanilla, sugar and baking powder on medium speed until well blended and frothy. Pour in the oil and continue to mix on medium speed. Turn the speed to low, begin adding the flour. When you have added 5 cups, remove the dough from the bowl and begin kneading on a floured surface, by hand. It is the best way to determine if you need additional flour (up to ½ cup) to form a smooth, elastic dough. Let the dough rest, covered, while you prepare the filling.

For the filling, peel, core and grate the apples on a box grater or with a food processor shredding disc.

Spoon the apples into a bowl and stir in the raisins, sugar and cinnamon. Toss to completely coat the apples. On a floured board, roll out a little more than half the dough, to fit the bottom of the baking dish. Use the rolling pin to roll up the dough and carefully lay it in the bottom of the dish. Use your hands to evenly spread the dough, bringing it halfway up the sides of the dish and patching empty spots as needed with the excess dough you trim from the sides. Think of this as an edible arts and crafts project.

With an offset spatula, spread a thin layer of grape jelly on top of the dough. Sprinkle a light dusting of flour over the jelly and then spread the apple mixture, as you would pie filling. Roll out the remaining half of the dough and lay it on top of the apples. Smooth it out and cut off any excess.

Press down lightly on the sides to form a seal around the edges. Sprinkle with the sugar and cinnamon topping. Lightly score the cake into 24 pieces and bake for 1 hour, or until the top of the cake is golden brown. Allow the cake to cool completely, allowing the juices to settle, before cutting all the way through.

Be sure you get the largest slice and a back rub. You've earned it!

Ruth Goldman Tobias

In her own words

Ruth Tobias is all about family and community. The day I met her, she was cooking for an Orthodox Jewish tradition called Sheva Brochos—Seven Blessings, when the bride and groom celebrate their nuptials for one week. Ruth is a creative cook and, as a result of her internment in Italy during the war, has studied Italian cooking. I devoured her delicious mandelbrot, a biscotti-like cookie, a recipe that will remain Ruth's secret. However, she shared her story and several other wonderful recipes with me.

My parents both came from the same small city in Poland. My father, Avram, left prewar Poland and headed to Germany to study. Sabina, my mother, came from an Orthodox family and also went to Germany. There they met and married. The mood in Germany was changing, and my father knew they had to relocate. He traveled to Italy to secure passage on an illegal ship to Palestine (Israel). In a twist of fate, he met a man on the train who convinced him to go to Milan. My father took that man's advice, and together my parents left Germany to settle in Italy. On June 10, 1940, Hitler and Mussolini made a pact, and the following day the Allies bombed Milan. Shortly after the bombing, Sabina went into labor, and I was born on the holiday of Shavuot, the twelfth of June. A year later, my mother and I were sent to an internment camp in Potenza. My father was not home at the time and therefore continued to live in a "safe" house in Milan. Eventually, he was arrested and sent to Italy's largest concentration camp, Ferramonti. After some time, my father was able to transfer to Potenza, where we were reunited.

Growing up in an internment camp seemed normal to me. There, I played with friends, lived simply but comfortably and remember cooking with my mother. Although we were under the protection of the Italian people, we held on to our Jewish traditions. We baked matzo on a big open fire and observed Passover and the other Jewish holidays. Shortly after the

Germans took control of Italy in September 1943, our camp was dispersed, and we were sent to a small town called Tito, where several Jewish families were harbored. I remember the Italians being compassionate, and I am grateful to them for keeping us safe. We could have easily been transported to a death camp, but because of their protective nature, we were spared. The Canadians liberated us, and the two things I remember were tasting chocolate and gum for the first time.

I know my upbringing was far from conventional, yet through the disruption and movement, I learned many things. I am very family oriented because I felt so isolated growing up. I enjoy family gatherings and I cherish the traditions my parents imbued in me. Because of my love for Italy and the Italian people who saved me, I have spent time in Tuscany and Bologna learning to prepare the traditional Italian foods that I did not explore as a child. I prepare both the traditional Jewish specialties as well as my Italian dishes. But mostly, I learned how to look at life. My father always said, "Cope with the problems that life brings and be thankful for what you have." I remember my dad singing all the time and my mom maintaining an amazingly positive outlook.

No one goes through life without disappointment; it is how you handle it that makes you who you are. I have tried to pass that philosophy on to my three children and five grandchildren.

Sabina Goldman's Bursting with Blueberries Tart

There are two kinds of blueberries: those that are shy and drawn and not really worth eating, and those that are so ripe with blueberry flavor that they are ready to burst out of their skin—those are the blueberries you want for this simply divine tart. Ruth's mom, Sabina, added vinegar to the crust, which acts as a stabilizer and adds a subtle bite to balance the buttery flavor. The blueberries bubble and create their own sweet syrup.

Yield: About 8 servings
Start to Finish: Under 1½ hours

FOR THE CRUST
2 cups all-purpose flour
Pinch salt
3 tablespoons sugar
1 cup (2 sticks) cold butter or margarine
2 tablespoons white vinegar

FOR THE FILLING
4 cups fresh blueberries
½ cup sugar
⅛ teaspoon ground cinnamon
2 tablespoons all-purpose flour

GARNISH
2 cups fresh blueberries
Confectioners' sugar

Preheat the oven to 400 degrees.

In a medium bowl, or in the bowl of a food processor fitted with the metal blade, combine the flour, salt and sugar. Using a pastry blender or in the processor, cut in the chilled butter and pulse or blend to form a crumb-like consistency. Allow bits of butter to remain visible; they melt and create steam during the baking process for a very tender and flaky crust. Sprinkle with vinegar and blend until you have created a soft dough.

With lightly floured hands, press the dough into a 9 x 2-inch springform pan, or a 9 x 1-inch pie pan with a removable bottom. The crust should be about ¼ inch thick on the bottom; the sides should be a little thinner and come up about 1 inch (you might have some dough remaining). You can refrigerate the crust until ready to fill.

In a separate bowl, gently toss the filling ingredients. Spoon the filling into the pan and bake, on the lower rack, for 1 hour. When the tart cools, garnish with blueberries and a sprinkling of confectioners' sugar.

Ruth Tobias's Orange-Flavored Sponge Cake

Ruth's pure recipe will change your impression of sponge cake. Long considered the wallflower in the bakery that you are obligated to buy for the holiday, this version is moist, citrusy and sweet. For a nice variation, the cake can be made with lemon juice and zest instead of orange.

Yield: 10 to 12 servings
Start to Finish: Under 1½ hours

6 eggs, separated
1 cup sugar
1 orange peel, zested
Juice of half an orange

1 cup all-purpose flour
1 teaspoon baking powder
Pinch salt

Preheat the oven to 325 degrees.

Beat the yolks and sugar, in a large bowl, on medium speed, until light and fluffy. First zest (grate) the orange peel, and then squeeze it for the juice. Stir in the orange juice and grated peel. In a separate bowl, sift the flour and baking powder three times. Add the flour to the egg mixture, on low speed, and then beat for a minute or two on medium speed.

In a separate bowl, beat the egg whites with a pinch of salt until they are stiff but not dry. Gently fold the whites into the batter. Spoon the batter into an ungreased 9 x 3-inch tube springform pan and bake for 50 to 60 minutes. When done, the top will be golden brown and a bamboo skewer inserted in the center should come out clean. To cool, invert the cake on a wire rack and then remove from the pan. Sprinkle with a dusting of confectioners' sugar or garnish with candied orange peel.

Ruth Tobias's *Peperonata*—Bell Peppers

Certainly, this flavorful and colorful recipe was influenced by Ruth's adopted home, Italy. It makes a lively side dish or delivers a wakeup call for your taste buds as a savory starter. Try tossing the vibrant peppers with rigatoni or ziti for a sizzling hot dish or chilling the peppers and pasta for a fiery summer salad.

Yield: 4 servings
Start to Finish: Under 1 hour

4 tablespoons olive oil
1 medium red onion, sliced
1 garlic clove, crushed
2 medium red bell peppers (about 1 pound),
  cored, seeded and cut into chunks
2 medium yellow peppers (about 1 pound),
  cored, seeded and cut into chunks

½ cup tomato sauce or 2 ripe plum tomatoes,
  peeled, seeded and diced
Kosher salt
Freshly ground black pepper basil, for garnish

Heat the oil in a large skillet; cook and stir the onions, over medium heat, until lightly browned, about 10 minutes.

Add the crushed garlic and cook for 5 minutes longer. Stir in the peppers, tomato sauce, salt and pepper; reduce the heat to low, cover and cook for 15 minutes. Uncover the skillet and cook 30 minutes longer.

Garnish with fresh basil leaves.

Hanna Kleiner Wechsler

In her own words

Hanna was one of my last interviews and confirmed what I learned from my very first. Those willing to share their stories have an amazing spirit, an outlook on life that inspires and a perspective that we can all benefit from. Hanna began our conversation by saying, "If you overcome this, you can do anything. There are seven wonders in the world. I consider my survival the eighth." After speaking with her, and getting to know her well, I would have to agree!

I was born in my grandfather's house in Nowy Korczyn, a little town in Poland. I had a few nice years before the war, but my memory of those years is almost zilch. I was the first grandchild on either side, and within a few years of my birth, it was unquiet in Poland. At first, Polish people, for a very short time, hid us. We lived in their barn, underneath the floor. There were eleven people in a very small space. One night the lady of the house came down and told us that she felt her neighbors were suspicious and that she could not keep us anymore. We left at night in order not to give her away. We went to a place where the Jews were picked up in the morning to go to the Cracow ghetto. My whole family stayed there, with my parents going to work every morning. By some miracle, one of my uncles got a connection to the outside; with money, you really could still be a little bit innovative and help yourself. My mother, Rozalia, looked like a 100 percent Gentile woman with blonde hair, blue eyes, fair skin and very gutsy. There was a family meeting, and my mother volunteered to go to our connection on the outside and obtain papers, so we could sneak out of the ghetto. Now we retell these things in a quiet way, but at the time, this was all a

Hanna, Mordechai and Rozalie Kleiner, 1945.

matter of life and death. It was a hair-raising moment.

She boarded a tram where a German soldier said to her in German, "Please sit down young lady." She never stopped telling us where her heart was at that time; you can only imagine. She went to the address she had for the papers. At that time, there were rumors that in Romania and Hungary the situation was not so bad and even Polish Jews were fleeing to those countries. Our new name was Koslovska. She came back with the papers, and I remember all the time she was gone, praying, "Please let my mommy come back." When I saw her, you can imagine how happy I was; it was a happy, terrible feeling.

We got out, the whole group, sneaking out at night. One uncle, who was extremely shrewd, smart and capable, arranged for two men to act as guides who would help us cross into Czechoslovakia then to Romania and on into Hungary. Like when Moses took us out of Egypt, it worked. On the way, we lived on berries and water from the morning dew that collected on the leaves. The roads were extremely dangerous and hard to walk. I remember being carried on the shoulders of one of my family members. We went out and crossed most of the borders, except when we came to Romania. The guides suddenly left us in no-man's land. We realized we didn't know where to go; we didn't know what to do.

From out of nowhere, two shepherds showed up—they spoke Hungarian and Romanian, we spoke only Yiddish and Polish, but money was a common language. Guess what? They took us directly into a German police station. We were thrown into a prison, even though we claimed we were not Jewish.

Somehow, we got out, I don't remember how, and we lived for a short time in Hungary. We lived freely until they began collecting the Jews there. My mother and I were lucky. The guard at the prison where we were housed had a little more heart. I looked like his daughter; my mother looked like his wife. He never took advantage of my mother, which we feared he might. What did he do for us? Each time someone came in to transfer inmates, he would shuffle our papers underneath, so we were among the last to be shipped to Auschwitz. One day he disappeared; we suspected he had been sent to the Russian front as a punishment because he was too good to the Jews.

We were separated from my father; my mother and I were sent to a camp that had housed gypsies. It was liquidated in anticipation of the arrival of Hungarian Jews. We were also interned in Auschwitz, where we spent about six to seven months. Every night, my mother would sneak out of the barracks and go to a friend who had stolen food from the kitchen. I always say that my mother gave birth to me every day we lived in Auschwitz, because without her I would not have survived. I also know that I gave her a reason to survive. She was my God and my angel that protected me always. Mother kept telling me all the time not to be seen, not to be heard and to try and survive.

My father, Mordechai, was shipped to Dachau while the Russians freed my mother and me. We returned to Cracow after the war, hoping to be reunited with my father and the rest of the family. We registered with an organization that tried to reunite families. While my father was sitting at a train station in Germany, an acquaintance from his hometown

Hanna Kleiner, Chanukah, 1945.

noticed him, looking so despondent, and told him that my mother and I had survived. My father came to Poland to look for us. Meanwhile, we had notified the organization that we were living with a friend on Long Street, and a long street is what it was. Very much like Fifth Avenue, it went on forever. My father knew the name of the street but not the number. He was determined to find us but reluctant to give out our real name, as Poland was still so anti-Semitic. He asked everyone if they saw a blonde woman with heavy legs and a nine-year-old daughter. For four days and nights, my father walked up that street going door to door and floor to floor. On the fourth day, at 5:00 a.m. he rang our bell; we thought it was the milkman. When my mother's friend opened the door, my mother heard my father's voice and fainted.

We returned to Germany and then immigrated to Israel, where we had a very nice life. We always talked about Auschwitz; my mother never got over it. I married an American, and I reluctantly left Israel and moved here in 1968. But God was good to me, providing a wonderful husband, children and grandchildren. We moved to Paramus, New Jersey, which I have to admit, I thought was the sticks. I cooked very few things like my mother. I became a Hebrew teacher and a real estate agent, and I enjoyed them both tremendously. I have had much naches in my life.

Author's Note: I sadly learned that Hanna's husband, Harry, has passed away. May his memory be for a blessing.

Hanna Wechsler's Strawberry-Filled *Naleshniki*—Blintzes

Hanna Wechsler spoke lovingly of her mother's blintzes, a cross between a thin crepe and a traditional blintz. She recalled her mom filling them quite simply with strawberry preserves, chopped nuts and a touch of sugar. Hanna proudly says, "This recipe has continuity; it has endured for four generations." Pair it with Florence Tabrys's blintz recipe (see page 127) for a sweet variation and top with the strawberry sauce (recipe follows).

Yield: About 1 cup filling
Start to Finish: Under 15 minutes

1 cup strawberry preserves
¼ to ½ cup chopped almonds or walnuts, your choice
1 teaspoon sugar, more or less to taste

Combine all three ingredients in a bowl and use as filling.

Strawberry Sauce

While Hanna's mother served her blintzes with fresh fruit, a pureed strawberry sauce is a colorful topping and helps bring out the strawberry goodness packed inside the blintz.

Yield: 2 cups
Start to Finish: Under 30 minutes

1 (16-ounce) bag frozen strawberries
3 tablespoons sugar
¼ cup water

1 teaspoon cornstarch
Juice and grated peel of half a lemon

In a medium saucepan, cook the strawberries, sugar, water and cornstarch over medium-low heat until the berries are very soft, about 15 minutes. Puree the berries and stir in the lemon juice and grated peel. Serve hot or cold over blintzes, cake or ice cream. The sauce will hold for 1 to 2 weeks in the fridge. You can also follow the same preparation if using frozen blueberries or raspberries.

JH

Michael Solomonov

Professional contributor

There is nothing quite like fresh homemade Israeli hummus—just ask anyone, like Hanna, who has spent time in Israel. Before opening his popular Philadelphia restaurant, Chef Solomonov took his staff to Israel for inspiration. One day, they visited five hummus parlors. He spent months perfecting his signature dish, and he points out that "Americans have this misconception that hummus is strongly lemony and garlicky or worse that it comes in lots of flavors. Israelis don't do flavors." Here is his straightforward, smooth and creamy, perfectly flavored hummus that you can easily replicate at home, even if your home is in Paramus, New Jersey!

Tehina—Hummus

Contributed by Chef Michael Solomonov of Zahav restaurant, Philadelphia

Serves 6

1 pound dry chickpeas
1 tablespoon baking soda
1 whole head garlic with the skin on, plus one clove with the germ removed
2 ounces of fresh-squeezed lemon juice
12 ounces un-hulled sesame paste
Kosher salt

Ground cumin, to taste
¼ cup Italian parsley, chopped
Paprika (preferably sweet, smoked Spanish paprika)
4 ounces extra virgin olive oil (preferably from Lebanon or Israel)

Cover the chickpeas and baking soda with at least double their volume of water and soak, refrigerated, for 18 hours. Drain the chickpeas and rinse thoroughly in cold water. Place the chickpeas in a large pot with the whole head of garlic and cover with water. Bring the water to a boil and reduce the heat to low.

Simmer the chickpeas over low heat for approximately three hours, or until very tender. Drain the chickpeas, reserving one cup of the cooking liquid. Discard the garlic bulb.

In the bowl of a food processor, add the sesame paste and the cooked chickpeas. Puree the mixture with the olive oil and lemon juice, adding enough reserved cooking liquid to achieve a smooth, creamy consistency. Season to taste with kosher salt and ground cumin. Garnish with extra virgin olive oil, chopped parsley and paprika.

Feedback

Tehina (also called tahini or sesame paste) has a taste similar to peanut butter and a consistency to match. In Middle Eastern homes, tahini is used like peanut butter as a spread, a dip or to enhance other dishes. It is available in most supermarkets; look in the aisle with Asian/Middle Eastern foods or where the condiments are found. If your market does not stock it, you can find it in a Middle Eastern specialty market. While the chef feels this recipe serves 6, as a dip it can feed an army.

Jennifer Abadi

Professional contributor

What better way to enjoy homemade hummus than with homemade pita? Jennifer Abadi, an expert in Syrian and Middle Eastern cooking, guides us through the steps to making homemade pocket pita. I am not saying it is as easy as a trip to the store, but it certainly tastes more authentic.

Chibiz—Syrian Pita or Pocket Bread

Excerpted from A Fistful of Lentils: Syrian-Jewish Recipes from Grandma Fritzie's Kitchen, by Jennifer Abadi (© 2002, used by permission from The Harvard Common Press)

The pocket this bread forms when baking makes it perfect for sandwiches or scooping up all kinds of meats and dips. Fresh or toasted, you'll enjoy this low-calorie bread found everywhere in the Middle East.

3 teaspoons active dry yeast
2½ cups warm water
1 tablespoon honey or sugar

1 tablespoon vegetable oil
6 cups enriched white bread flour
2 teaspoons salt

In a small bowl, combine the yeast, ½ cup of the warm water and the honey. Let stand until slightly frothy, about 5 minutes. Add the oil and mix.

In a large bowl, combine the flour and salt. Make a well in the center of the flour and pour the yeast mixture into it, mixing it into the flour with a wooden spoon. Add the remaining 2 cups warm water, ½ cup at a time. Shape the dough into a sticky ball and knead on a clean, well-floured work surface until very smooth and elastic, a good 10 minutes (add more flour as needed, a little at a time, if your dough is too sticky to knead).

Place the dough in a greased glass or plastic bowl and cover with a towel. Let rest in a warm place for 1½ hours to rise and double in size.

Knead the dough on a floured surface for another 10 minutes (again, adding flour as needed) and roll it into a tube about 1 foot long and about 3½ to 4 inches in diameter. Using a sharp knife, mark 16 equal lines on the roll of dough, then break the dough into 16 pieces of equal size and roll each into a ball.

On the same floured surface, roll out each ball with a rolling pin or tall glass until the dough is ¼ inch thick and 6 inches in diameter, resembling a small pizza. Place each rolled-out piece of dough on a floured piece of foil cut to the same size as a baking sheet, 4 to 5 at a time, until all 16 have been made.

Cover the flattened dough pieces with a kitchen towel and let them rise in a warm spot for another 2 hours. (At this point, preheat the oven to 550 degrees for 2 hours. It is important to get the oven temperature as high as possible so that each pita bakes quickly and forms a pocket.)

Carefully lift up one sheet of foil with the risen dough pieces and place on a baking sheet. Bake on the middle rack in the oven for 4 to 5 minutes. *Do not open the oven more than a crack until you see the bread puff up*. Take the sheet out and remove the baked pita breads, placing them in a basket and covering them with a clean cloth to keep warm. Discard the used foil and transfer another sheet of unbaked pieces to the baking sheet. Continue to bake in this manner, one sheet at a time, until all the pitas are baked.

These really don't stay soft and fresh past a day, but if you have a lot leftover, store them in a Ziploc plastic bag for up to 2 days on the counter or 1 week in the freezer, toasting them in the oven when needed.

Rachela Introligator Weisstuch and Victor Weisstuch

As told by their son Mark Weisstuch

Mark, a Jewish scholar, retells his parents' story with great precision and love.

My parents were married in 1935 and living in Dabrowa, southwestern Poland, with their two daughters, Sarah and Hannah, when World War II began. Within a week of the Nazi invasion, their area was overrun. My father was taken to numerous forced labor camps. In one, which served as a construction site, he befriended a German worker. They developed a relationship, and my father asked him if he would be willing to find my mother, to give her a message and retrieve supplies from her. For several months, this German laborer was a go-between for my parents. My mother remained at home until mid-1943, when she, her two children, her sister and her daughter were taken to the Srodula ghetto. There they hid in a cellar for several months. On January

Victor and Rachela Weisstuch, Münchberg, 1946.

13, 1944, they were all put on the last transport out of the ghetto and were sent to Birkenau; it was the last time she saw her daughters. In winter of 1944–45, the Germans evacuated Birkenau, and my mother and aunt were force marched into the German heartland and eventually ended up in Bergen-Belsen.

They were liberated from that camp by the British army in April 1945.

Bergen-Belsen became a DP camp, and my mother and aunt stayed there to recuperate. My father, learning they had survived, journeyed to Bergen-Belsen to find them. He continued his journey and eventually found my mother. After she recovered, they stopped in one town and were walking in the street and chatting in Yiddish. They used the Yiddish word for spoon, *loffel*. Three guys who were following behind them inquired who they were and where they were from. They said, "I knew a guy in the camp who used the word spoon in the same dialect as you." They discovered that these strangers were talking about my father's brother, Karl. That's how they learned that my uncle was alive.

They settled in Münchberg, Germany, where I was born. It was a Yiddish household, like a little shtetl. My mother cooked Jewish, which is, of course, Polish. There is no such thing as Jewish food; matzo is the only real Jewish food, and the rest is all borrowed, adapted and adopted from other countries. My parents and I came to New York in 1949. One distinct memory I have is that whenever my parents got together with their friends, all of whom were survivors, they always ended up meandering into and focusing on their war experiences. I would remember often hearing it, like music playing in the background. My parents were married fifty-eight years, had one more child and two grandchildren.

Chilled Cherry Soup

Mark remembers a time his family visited Poland. They were in Galicia and stopped at a roadside restaurant for lunch. They served cold cherry soup. "I ate this soup and said, 'Oh my, this is what my mother used to make.' This extraordinary cold cherry soup is what my mother made as a dessert or entree. This is exactly the same thing." This recipe replicates that memory and captures the tart and sweet flavor of the black cherries in a cold soup balanced by sour cream and lemon.

Yield: 4 to 6 servings
Start to Finish: Under 30 minutes, then time to chill

2 packages frozen black cherries, thawed with
  their juice
1 cup bottled cherry juice (red wine can be
  substituted)
Juice of 1 lemon

1 cinnamon stick
¼ cup sugar
1 cup sour cream
¼ cup heavy cream

In a medium saucepan, simmer the cherries with their juice, 1 cup of water, bottled cherry juice, lemon juice (throw in the lemon), cinnamon stick and sugar. (If using red wine, simmer separately in a small saucepan to allow the alcohol to cook off, then add to the soup in place of the cherry juice.) Cover and cook over medium heat until the cherries are soft, about 15 minutes. If the soup is too tart, add additional sugar and continue to simmer. If too sweet, add more water or lemon juice.

When the cherries are soft, remove the lemon and cinnamon stick. Ladle ⅔ of the soup into a blender and process until smooth. Combine the pureed and un-pureed soup and chill in a large, sealed container for several hours or overnight until very cold. Remove from the fridge and stir in the sour cream. Ladle the soup into individual bowls. Gently swirl a spoonful of heavy cream into the bowl to create a white ribbon in the pink soup; the presentation is beautiful.

JH

Eva Young

In her own words

I met with Eva and her husband, Julius, in their New York apartment. I juggled my notebook while sipping delicious peppery cabbage soup. I peered into Eva's fridge and saw the wonderful array of foods she had prepared. Her New York City kitchen is stocked with all the best ingredients and a recipe file filled with traditional Polish and Hungarian dishes that all have the Eva touch. Her life has been filled with remarkable moments, all contributing to the independent and accomplished woman she became.

I was born to an affluent family in Wisla, Poland. I remember a childhood filled with holiday meals, stuffed Cornish hens and home-baked challah. I also remember the day my father hollowed out a tooth and hid a diamond inside it. He told me it was for me to use one day to save my life. In 1942, when I was fifteen, I was a prisoner working in a Polish labor camp, manufacturing weapons. I knew I could not survive much longer, so I used the diamond to bribe a guard. I shared the proceeds with another prisoner, and I feel that saved his life as well. Three years later, as we were marched through the woods of Germany, I escaped and found safety in a farmhouse, where I met other girls who were in hiding. I only had my uniform to wear, so one of the girls gave me a sheet, from which I made a skirt. That skirt survived with me and is now part of the Museum of Jewish Heritage's collection.

After the war, I went to Holland, arriving in May 1945. We were transported along with returning Dutch soldiers, and Queen Wilhelmina was there to greet them. Our picture was taken for public relations posters, as we were the first survivors to arrive in Holland. I also helped rescue and transfer children to Israel, where I eventually immigrated. Because I was multilingual and had weaponry experience during the war, I was recruited to work with the Israeli brigade in developing, among other things, the Molotov cocktail. Even my husband did not know the secretive and sensitive nature of my work. On a family trip to America, my husband became ill and died, leaving me with two children in a new and unfamiliar country. I chose to stay here and began taking classes and eventually received a degree in business. I accepted a job as a jewelry buyer for all of the Klein's department stores. I had a good business sense and developed a strategy to increase sales. I would collect small deposits on merchandise and hold the jewelry until it was paid in full. When my boss came to my counter to see what I was doing, I showed him how I put away jewelry and collected small weekly payments. I suppose you can say that I invented the layaway!

I was promoted and given tremendous responsibility, which weighed heavily on me.

I couldn't sleep at night. What was I going to do? So, I would head into the kitchen and come up with all sorts of ideas about cooking. I developed my own taste, which brought back memories from my mother. If I'm going to relax, I'm going into the kitchen, because cooking is a huge part of my life. I met my husband, Julius, when I was a jewelry buyer, and he was a jewelry manufacturer. During the war, as a Hungarian citizen, Julius served in the army and was captured, along with German soldiers, and become a Russian prisoner of war. After three years as a POW, Julius made his way to America.

I love to be inventive with my cooking. Whatever I cook is in one pot or one dish. Everyone is unique; cooking helps me share with people. I have been married to Julius for thirty-seven years and we have two children, six grandchildren and seven great-grandchildren.

Author's Note: I sadly learned that Julius has passed away. May his memory be for a blessing.

Eva Young's Creamy Cheese Noodle Kugel

"She makes the best noodle kugel," exclaims Eva's husband, Julius. Eva adds several secret ingredients, like sour cream and whipped egg whites, but the crowning glory is the buttery baked graham cracker topping. Warm or cold, it makes a sweet ending, a luscious starter or a terrific midday nosh.

Yield: Servings vary depending on how you cut the kugel, but Eva wants you to know, it feeds a big family
Start to Finish: Under 1½ hours

FOR THE NOODLES
1 (12-ounce) package uncooked broad
  noodles
6 tablespoons (¾ stick) butter
6 eggs, separated
1 (8-ounce) package cream cheese, softened
1 (16-ounce) container small-curd cottage
  cheese
1 pint (8 ounces) sour cream
1 teaspoon vanilla extract
½ cup sugar

FOR THE TOPPING
⅔ cups crushed graham crackers (about 8
  crackers)
½ cup sugar
1 stick (½ cup) butter, melted

Preheat the oven to 350 degrees and lightly grease a 13 x 9 x 2-inch baking dish.

Put a large pot of lightly salted water to boil and cook the noodles according to package directions; drain. Return the drained noodles to the pot and stir in the butter. In a separate bowl, beat the egg yolks, cream cheese, cottage cheese, sour cream, vanilla and sugar on medium speed until light and fluffy. Stir the egg mixture into the noodles.

In a separate bowl, beat the 6 egg whites until stiff but not dry. Gently fold the egg whites into the noodles. Pour the noodles into the prepared baking dish.

Prepare the topping by mixing together the 3 ingredients. Sprinkle the topping over the noodles and bake for 1 hour or until the top is lightly browned.

Millie Zuckerman and Abraham Zuckerman

Based on Abe's memoir

Drive through a number of New Jersey neighborhoods and you might notice an interesting trend with regard to the names of many of the streets. They all honor Oskar Schindler, who was responsible for saving the lives of 1,200 Jewish men, women and children. These street names would seem curious unless you knew the story behind the men who developed those communities. In his moving memoir, *A Voice in the Chorus: Memories of a Teenager Saved by Schindler*, Abraham Zuckerman recounts his good fortune of being a "Schindler Jew" and how he survived the Holocaust. The following is based on details described in his memoir and conversations with his son-in-law.

Millie and Abe Zuckerman in DP camp, Bindermichel, Austria.

Abe was born in Cracow, Poland, in 1924. He was fourteen years old when the war came to his beloved homeland. Abe recounts watching in horror as his parents and two sisters were taken by the Nazis. Abe managed to flee and stayed with a farmer in Wieliczka. He was chased by the Nazis on numerous occasions and was sent to several work camps. Eventually, he was sent to Plaszow work camp, where he was reunited with his childhood friend Murray Pantirer. Together they were selected to work in Oskar Schindler's enamelware factory. Abe describes Schindler as "a living saint." He recalls how Schindler greeted Abe when he saw him and how he was immaculately dressed and had a protective, fatherly feeling. "He was very handsome, like a statesman; with him I felt I might survive." In August 1944, Abe was moved from Plaszow to Mauthausen, where two American soldiers liberated him in May 1945. Following his liberation, Abe spent four years in a DP camp in Bindermichel, Austria. It was there that he met and married Millie, his life partner for more than sixty years.

Millie also had a protector—a Polish woman, Michalina Kedra. Before the war, Michalina had been a patron of the grocery store owned by Millie's dad. The Nazis liquidated the entire town of Humniska, where Millie was born and raised. For two years, Millie, her sister and their parents hid above a trapdoor in Michalina's barn, never seeing the light of day. It was in Bindermichel that Abe and Millie began a new life. After their liberation and immigration to the United States, the Zuckermans stayed in touch with Schindler and hosted him many times. Abe and Murray, who became business partners, were especially proud to drive him through their numerous residential developments and show him the more than twenty-five streets named in his honor.

There was never a festive meal that ended without her handmade sugar cookies. To this day, her three children, ten grandchildren and three great grandchildren enjoy them.

Millie Zuckerman's Sugar Cookies

While Millie's cookies are a nice blend of ingredients, her family feels "the most important ingredients included in Millie's cookies are her love, sweetness and kindness." A nice dusting of sugar gives the cookies a lovely crunch, but we are sure Millie wouldn't mind if you indulged in sprinkles, shredded coconut or ground nuts. For an extra kick, grate 2 tablespoons of orange peel into the dough. This is a very soft dough, which is why this cookie doesn't crumble, so work quickly and do not over roll it or it will become too hard to handle.

Yield: About 5 dozen 2-inch cookies
Start to Finish: Step 1: Under 30 minutes, then refrigerate at least 6 hours or up to 24,
Step 2: Under 30 minutes

½ pound (2 sticks) margarine, room
  temperature
2 egg yolks
¾ cup sugar
½ cup orange juice

1 teaspoon vanilla
3 cups all-purpose flour
1 tablespoon baking powder
Granulated or sanding sugar for topping

STEP 1
Beat the margarine, egg yolks and sugar in a large bowl on medium speed until smooth and creamy, about 3 minutes. Slowly pour in the orange juice and vanilla. The liquids will cause the mixture to separate, so continue beating and scraping down the sides until they are well incorporated. In a separate bowl, sift together the flour and baking powder. With the mixer on low speed, add the flour to the butter mixture and beat on medium speed, until all the ingredients are well combined. Divide the dough in half, flatten each into a disc and wrap tightly in waxed paper. Refrigerate 6 hours or overnight.

STEP 2
Preheat the oven to 375 degrees, lightly grease a large baking sheet and have sugar ready to sprinkle on top of the cut cookies.

Remove one piece of dough from the fridge and cut it in half (it's easier to roll). Place the remaining dough back in the fridge. Lightly flour a work surface and roll the dough to ¼ inch thick. Using a cookie cutter, or the rim of a glass, cut the dough into the desired size and shape.

Gather and re-roll the scraps. If the dough is too soft, place it back in the fridge. Place the cookies on the prepared baking sheet and sprinkle with sugar (or your choice of topping) and then gently pat down to help the topping adhere. Bake for 12 minutes, or until the cookies are a light golden color with lightly brown-tinged sides. Repeat with the remaining dough or freeze (wrapped tightly, thaw before baking) for later use.

Feedback

This same dough makes a terrific foundation for *hamantashen* (cookie resembling a three-cornered hat eaten at the festival of Purim). Following the same procedure as above, have preserves or your choice of filling ready to dollop in the center. Cut the dough into 3-inch rounds. Place a teaspoon of filling in the center, then pinch the dough to form the 3 points (the corners of Haman's hat). Bake as directed above. Yields about 3 dozen cookies.

GERMANY AND AUSTRIA

The start of the Nazi reign officially began in Germany in 1933 when Adolf Hitler was appointed Chancellor. Soon after, a series of anti-Jewish laws were established, as was Dachau, the first concentration camp. In 1938, Austria became part of the Nazi regime in an annexation known as the *Anschluss*. It was not long before anti-Semitism spread and the situation for Jewish citizens throughout the region was dire. Many German Jews realized they were no longer safe, and they fled Germany for America or other countries that were sympathetic to their plight. However, there were those who felt their German citizenship would protect them; in the end, we know they were very wrong. According to the Jewish Virtual Library, 69 percent of German and 35 percent of Austrian Jews were murdered in the Holocaust. A sign of the impending fate for German Jews came on the night of November 9–10 known as *Kristallnacht*, the night of broken glass. Thousands of Jewish businesses, synagogues and homes were destroyed, and tens of thousands of Jewish men were sent to concentration camps in Germany. By this time, it was too late for most to leave.

Many German and Austrian survivors clung to their social and culinary traditions, while others strove to distance themselves from anything associated with that horrific time. The food of Germany and Austria has always been influenced by its geographic location. The result is a flavorful blending of both western and eastern European cuisine. French influences are especially felt in southwestern Germany, where several of our survivors were born. Their recipes reflect a sophisticated style of cooking and ingredients that have a French flair. Rich chocolate, slow marinades and the restrained use of sweet, balanced by sour, are elements borrowed from their Polish and Czech neighbors and can be seen in many preparations from the contributors of this region. German and Austrian cooks brought many of their cooking traditions with them to America, but none have left as firm an imprint on the culinary landscape as their cakes and pastries. Buttery streusel, *mürbeteig* dough and twice-baked *mandelbrot* cookies were all popularized in this region and can still be found in most European bakeries today. Because Germany and Austria experienced a wave of emigration as unrest began to build, we have a number of contributors who found themselves as refugees, with one foot firmly planted on safe soil and another tenaciously grounded in the rich culture they left behind. The result was a curious melding of culinary customs that you will find interesting and unexpected. We invite you to explore the stories and prepare and enjoy the varied and creative recipes remembered by our stouthearted contributors from Germany and Austria.

RECIPES

Inge Auerbacher's *Weincreme*—Whipped Topping

Jonathan Waxman*: Sweet Onion Tart

Edith Blumenthal's Chocolate Macaroons

Edith Blumenthal's Streuselkuchen—Crumb Cake

Reni Hanau's *Waffeln*—Waffles

JH*: *Schlagzahne*—Whipped Cream

Reni Hanau's Winter Celeriac (Celery Root) Salad

Daniel Boulud* Tender Beef with Horseradish, Parsnips and Celery Root

JH*: *Gruenkern* Soup with Mini Turkey Meatballs

Ruth Eggener's Braised *Sauerbraten*—Marinated Roast

Ellen Katz's Apricot Squares

Ruth Kohn's *Arroz con Pollo*—Chicken and Rice

Ruth Kohn's Fried *Platanos*—Fried Plantains

Miriam Margulies's *Palatschinken*—Thin Pancakes

Marsha Meyer's Fruit-Filled *Knodels*—Dumplings

Gisela Obernbreit's Thin and Crispy *Wiener Schnitzel*—Breaded Veal Cutlets

Ruth Obernbreit's *Tres Leches*—Three Milk Cake

Ruth Orvieto's Risotto

Ruth Orvieto's *Gnocchi Alla Romana*—Semolina Gnocchi with Cheese

Judy Prussin's Spiked Mandel Bread

Wolfie Rauner's *Matzo Kloesse*—Dumplings

Henny Bachrach's Almond and Apple Cake

Melly Resnicow's Chocolate Roll

Evelyn Pike Rubin's Sweet Summer Peach Cake

Doris Schechter's Blackout Cake

Orange-Scented Sugar Syrup and Chocolate Pudding

Ruth Schloss's Spaetzle with Cooked Dried Fruit

Helen Wallerstein's Potato *Latkes*

Helen Wallerstein's *Gesundheit Kuchen*—Chocolate Cake

JH*: Chocolate Ganache

Dr. Ruth's Celebration Cake

*Indicates professional contributor

Inge Auerbacher

In her own words

Inge has been awarded numerous honors for her work as an author, lecturer and advocate for human rights. She is the recipient of the Ellis Island Medal of Honor; Woman of Distinction Award, given by the New York State Senate; the Louis E. Yavner Citizen Award; and an honorary Doctor of Humane Letters from Long Island University. She is the author of six books. In her first book, *I Am a Star*, Inge writes, "We must speak out against evil and injustice. Let us build bridges of understanding and love to join mankind in every land. My hope, my wish, and prayer is for every child to grow up in peace without hunger and prejudice."

I was the last Jewish child born in Kippenheim, a small village located in the southwestern portion of Germany. My father's family had lived there for over two hundred years, and our house still stands today. Although I was only three years old during *Kristallnacht*, I remember it very clearly. After being detained in Dachau for several weeks, my grandfather and father were released, and we chose to go to Jebenhausen, an even tinier village of only one thousand people, to live with my grandparents, who were the only remaining Jewish family in that town. My grandmother was a wonderful cook, and I remember eating many dishes that you would associate with Swabian (southern German) cooking. Albert Einstein's family once owned the bakery in the village where we brought our challahs and cakes to be baked in their ovens. Because my hometown, Kippenheim, was near Alsace, our food was influenced by French cuisine. My grandmother was deported to Riga in 1941, and we were moved to a designated Jewish house, where we stayed until August 1942, when my parents and I were deported to Terezin.

While we were imprisoned in Terezin, the International Red Cross requested permission to inspect a camp. The Nazis chose Terezin for that purpose. Certain parts of the camp were cleaned up. Some people were given new clothing and good food to eat. A few children received chocolates and sardine sandwiches just as the commission walked past them. I was not one of the lucky ones. The International Red Cross inspection team left the camp believing the immense deception that Terezin was a "model" place for Jews to live. The truth was, conditions in Terezin were very harsh and of the fifteen thousand children imprisoned there between 1941 and 1945, a very small number survived. I was one of them. I spent three birthdays there. One year I received a potato cake the size of my palm, prepared from a mashed boiled potato with just a hint of sugar in it. Another year my doll Marlene, which survived Terezin with me, was given a new outfit sewn from rags. On my tenth birthday, my gift was a poem my mother had written especially for me.

Miraculously, on May 8, 1945, the Soviet army liberated us. The first thing we did was

Inge, holding her favorite doll, with her family.

rip off the yellow star from our clothes. All of us felt joy, pain and relief. We first went to a DP camp, then back to Jebenhausen to look for surviving family members. When we arrived in Jebenhausen, we faced the awful truth. Grandma and twelve other family members had not survived. The new owners of Grandma's house prepared a room for us. Our return after so many years was greeted by a vase filled with field flowers, which stood on the table. We soon found more permanent living quarters in the neighboring town of Göppingen. The mayor invited us to visit him at city hall. As soon as we stepped into the mayor's office mama noticed the oriental carpet—it was ours. The mantel clock had a familiar chime; it too, had once been our property. Our new home became a familiar place for the American soldiers to stop by. They showered us with personal goods and candy. Some ran with their melting ice cream rations to our home so that I could have a special treat. To my knowledge, there were only two Jewish child survivors who

had been in concentration camps who were now in the state of Württemberg. I spent my eleventh birthday there; it was a sensation.

Life slowly returned to normal again, but it was still lonely. We took the first opportunity we could to immigrate to America, in May 1946. We arrived in New York Harbor at night. I stood in awe of the blinking lights of Manhattan, which seemed like a wonderland to me. Lady Liberty was especially bright as her lamp's light welcomed and guided us to a new life. The next morning, we disembarked just as the sun rose on a new day. In America, after I spent a few years fighting a serious sickness that I contracted in the camp, I was able to continue my education and not only graduated high school and college but also did postgraduate work in biochemistry. Since 1981, my mission has been to educate children about the Holocaust, which I have tried to do in all my books and in several documentaries that tell my story.

Inge Auerbacher's *Weincreme*—Whipped Topping

This custard-style preparation that Inge enjoyed every year as a Passover topping for nut torte (see Henny Bachrach's and Dr. Ruth Westheimer's recipes on pages 203 and 224) combines wine, sugar and a subtle lemon kick. Substitute apple juice or grape juice for the wine to create a child-friendly holiday treat.

Yield: 2 to 3 cups
Start to Finish: Under 30 minutes

1 cup dry white wine
3 tablespoons sugar
2 eggs, separated
Juice of 1 lemon
1/2 teaspoon grated lemon zest

1 teaspoon vanilla extract
2 tablespoons potato starch (1 tablespoon cornstarch can be used for non-Passover preparation)

In the top of a double boiler, over gently simmering water, combine the wine, sugar, egg yolks, lemon juice, zest, vanilla and 1 cup of water. Whisk until the mixture begins to thicken and develops a custard-like consistency, about 15 minutes.

Combine the potato starch with 1/2 cup of water and stir until you create smooth slurry. Slowly pour the slurry into the wine mixture, continuing to whisk so the custard thickens but does not clump. When the custard is thick like pudding, remove from the heat and cool.

When the mixture is cool and you are ready to serve, whip the egg whites, in a medium bowl, until stiff but not dry. Gently but thoroughly fold the egg whites into the mixture. Always stir up from the bottom to incorporate all the ingredients. Serve at once to prevent the whites from loosening and settling.

Feedback

To test when a custard or pudding preparation is thick enough, try a technique called "coating the back of a spoon." Take a large spoon, wooden works best, and dip the flat side into the mixture. Run your finger down the middle of the back of the spoon. If your finger leaves a trail, like the parting of the Red Sea, and the coating does not fill in the line, the custard is ready.

Jonathan Waxman

Professional contributor

While talking to Inge about her food memories, she described several dishes that have stayed with her over the years. One favorite is a sweet and salty onion tart that her grandmother would make and for which Inge no longer had a recipe. Jonathan Waxman, one of America's most beloved chefs, guides us in preparing his version of this established dish rooted in Alsace Lorraine, Inge's childhood backyard.

Sweet Onion Tart

Excerpted from A Great American Cook: Recipes from the Home Kitchen of One of Our Most Influential Chefs (Houghton Mifflin, September 2007)

The onion tarts I encountered in Europe were light, tasty and delicious. The versions I had eaten in America were leaden, coarse and often the pastry wasn't cooked through. The best of the versions in Europe were the ones made with puff pastry or semi-puff pastry. I decided to create a version as light as the European tarts. Not wanting to reinvent the wheel, I played around with an even lighter and fluffier tart that used fewer eggs and little cream. The trick was to extract as much liquid and flavor from the onions as possible without losing the texture components. This light but tasty tart tastes complex—with just six ingredients.

Yield: 6 servings

3 Maui onions, or other sweet onions, such as
  Vidalia or Walla Walla
2 tablespoons butter
½ cup balsamic vinegar
Salt and freshly ground black pepper

½ pound puff pastry
2 large eggs
½ cup heavy cream
Thyme blossoms, or 1 teaspoon fresh thyme
  leaves

Slice the onions crosswise as thinly as possible. Place a large skillet over very low heat. Add the butter, and when it melts, stir in the onions. Cook, stirring, for 30 minutes. Add the vinegar and cook until it's reduced, about 5 minutes. Let the mixture cool, and then season with salt and pepper.

Heat the oven to 400 degrees. Roll out the puff pastry as thinly as possible. Fit the pastry into an 8-inch tart pan. Dock the pastry by poking it all over with the tines of a fork. Bake the bare pastry for 25 minutes or until dark golden brown, especially the bottom crust. Don't be afraid that the tart will burn later when it is filled—the filling will prevent that from happening.

Whisk the eggs lightly in a bowl and add salt and pepper. When the pastry has browned properly, take it out of the oven and let it cool for 10 minutes. Spread the onion mixture evenly into the tart shell. Add the cream and the thyme blossoms or thyme leaves to the whisked eggs, blend well and then pour the mixture over the onions. Stir gently with a fork. Don't worry about mixing it perfectly. Bake the tart for 25 minutes or until just set. Remove and let the tart cool. Serve warm or at room temperature.

Edith Hamburger Blumenthal and Siggi Blumenthal

In her own words

Despite upheaval as a child and medical setbacks as an adult, Edith demonstrated a quiet inner strength and a gentle resolve. But the true measure of this woman was the love, respect and devotion shown to her by her youngest son, David, who joined in the interview, and her older son Michael, who participated via speakerphone. Humor permeated every aspect of our conversation, and together we marveled at Edith's organizational skills and keen memory.

My great-uncle Felix Levy was the second youngest of eight children born to my grandmother. Years before the war, a relative visiting from America suggested to my grandparents that they send Felix back with him to the United States. Felix was unmarried, and it seemed like a good idea. It wasn't until the 1930s that we realized what a good idea it really was. In 1938, on the night of Kristallnacht in our town of Hanau, Germany, many of the men were taken to a work camp. My father, Julius Hamburger, was one of those men taken. Oddly enough, among the things he took with him was a document that

Edith with her parents and brother Theodore.

said he had served in the First World War on the German side. It was just a coincidence that he had that with him. After three weeks, all the men with military papers indicating service in the German military were released from that camp, and my father returned home in January 1939.

It was very difficult to survive in Germany at a time when Jews were being persecuted for simply being Jews.

It was hard for my father to find work, and it was difficult for me, who was almost eleven, and my brother, Theodore, who was nine, to deal with the persecution and harassment in school. At that point, we were anxious to leave Germany. My family could have actually left Germany more than eighteen months earlier, but my father gave our papers to his pregnant sister, Ida, so she could travel safely to the United States and have her child. Uncle Felix arranged for our affidavits to be filed and sent for the entire family to join him in the United States. In March 1940, my parents, brother and I boarded the *Washington*, which I believe was the last ship to leave Italy for America. We finally arrived in New York in April 1940, after spending Passover on the ship. My late brother Theodore was the youngest boy on the ship and recited the Ma Nishtana (four questions) for everyone at the ship's seder. One of the treasured items that we brought on our voyage was a cookbook my mother had received from her mother. The book was called *Kochbuch für einfache und feine jüdischen Köche*, which roughly translates to mean "Cookbook, for Simple and Fine Jewish Cooks." We arrived in New York on the last day of Passover, April 12, 1940. My father, a religious man, insisted on walking to our next destination but was told at Ellis Island that walking to Manhattan was not possible. So, for the first and only time in his life, he rode in a car on a Jewish holiday.

My job was to learn and study. At first it was very hard since I spoke no English and was shy. I tried very hard to be a good student and I still have my very first report card where my teacher wrote when commenting on my first semester, "a courageous beginning." The following December, in seventh grade, I wrote an article for our school newspaper, titled "The Best Time I Ever Had." In it I wrote:

When I consider the best time I ever had I have to look back on my past life. I find that I had the best time right after the worst time. This was about six months ago when I arrived in this country. I realized then the difference between a free country and a land ruled by a dictator. In Germany, as a Jew, I was considered an outcast. My family was persecuted and my father was taken to a concentration camp. But in this country I have found friendship and understanding. I can associate with other girls of all creeds in the school I attend. I didn't understand the language but teachers as well as pupils realized my position and they helped me as much as they could. I will always consider the time when I came to the "Land of the free" as the best time of my life and will be grateful to this country, which gave me refuge. By being loyal and a law-abiding citizen, I can repay my new country for its kindness. Edith Hamburger, 7B1

I attended Washington Irving High School, where I was valedictorian, and then matriculated at Hunter College, where I majored in Spanish and was voted the girl most likely to succeed. I married Siegmund Blumenthal in May 1953.

My husband Siggi's life was challenging as well. When the Nazis came to power, his father, David Blumenthal, realized things could only get worse. He sold his farm, and the week after Siegmund's Bar Mitzvah, my husband; his brother, Alfred; and his parents, David and Johanna, left Germany for Catskill, New York. Siggi had very little schooling in New York, as he needed to work. Between 1934 and 1939, David, Johanna and their sons sacrificed and worked tirelessly and, during that five-year period, sponsored more than fifty family members and friends to come to America.

Shortly after Pearl Harbor, Siggi enlisted in the U.S. military and spent three years

Edith's mother, with a group of young women, pitting plums.

serving his country in active combat in the Pacific Theater. When he returned to the United States, he held a number of jobs in the food industry, and eventually he and his brother, Alfred, along with their father, David, opened a small supermarket in New York City on Columbus Avenue, between 86th and 87th Streets, where the two brothers worked side by side until 1981. Siggi then took a job at the local kosher market in Teaneck, New Jersey, where he befriended almost every child in Teaneck, until his death in 1990.

Siggi and I had two sons who married two wonderful women. I have nine grandchildren, two girls and seven boys. I am truly grateful to everyone who helped me arrive at this point in my life.

Author's Note: I sadly learned that Edith has passed away. May her memory be for a blessing.

Edith Blumenthal's Chocolate Macaroons

No need to wait until Passover to enjoy these light little flourless chocolaty treats.

Yield: 60 to 65 cookies
Start to Finish: Under 30 minutes

5 whole eggs
1 cup sugar
½ teaspoon ground cinnamon
1 tablespoon cocoa powder

½ pound ground semisweet chocolate
1 pound ground almonds (about 4 cups)
Sugar for dipping

Preheat the oven to 350 degrees and line a cookie sheet with parchment paper or a nonstick silicone mat. Beat the eggs with the sugar, ground cinnamon and cocoa powder in a large bowl, on medium speed, for several minutes, until the mixture is light and fluffy. Grind the chocolate with a coffee or nut grinder or with a box grater, holding the chocolate with a towel to prevent it from becoming too warm from your hands. Stir in the ground chocolate and almonds to form a stiff dough.

Pour about ½ cup sugar into a small bowl and have a second bowl of warm water nearby. Dip your hands into the water, shake off the excess and roll 1 teaspoon of dough in your hands to form a small ball about 1 inch in diameter, and then roll the ball in the sugar. Place on the prepared cookie sheet and bake for 10 minutes. Let the macaroons cool slightly before removing them to a plate.

Edith Blumenthal's Streuselkuchen—Crumb Cake

From the German *streusel*, meaning "strewn together," and *kuchen*, meaning "cake," we have the definitive German dessert. Edith's no-fuss version is delicious as is, but we thought a lovely addition would be to incorporate blueberries into the batter. While the cake is a wonderful way to end an evening, it is also an awesome way to start the day. Preparing the cake in a deeper dish creates a moister finish; however, the jellyroll pan is what a true German baker would use.

Yield: 12 servings
Start to Finish: Under 1½ hours

FOR THE BATTER
1 stick (½ cup) butter, room temperature
1 cup sugar
3 eggs
1 teaspoon vanilla extract
¾ cup whole milk
2½ cups all-purpose flour
2½ teaspoons baking powder
1 teaspoon salt
1 cup fresh or frozen blueberries (if frozen, thaw and drain) (optional)

FOR THE CRUMB TOPPING
½ cup granulated sugar
¼ cup brown sugar
2½ cups all-purpose flour
1 teaspoon salt
1 teaspoon ground cinnamon
2 sticks (1 cup) cold butter, cut into small pieces

Preheat the oven to 350 degrees and grease a 13 x 9 x 2-inch baking dish or 15½ x 10½-inch jellyroll pan. While the butter comes to room temperature, create the topping by combining the 2 sugars, flour, salt and cinnamon. Stir the ingredients until completely blended. Cut in the cold butter, using a pastry blender, a fork or your hands. Work the butter into the flour mixture until soft crumbles form. Resist the urge to break up all the large clumps; it's nice for the streusel to have different sizes and textures. Refrigerate the topping until ready to use.

Prepare the batter in a large bowl. Beat the butter and sugar on medium speed until light and creamy, about 3 minutes. Beat in the eggs, 1 at a time, mixing after each addition. In a small bowl, add the vanilla to the milk. In another bowl, combine the flour, baking powder and salt. While beating on low speed, begin adding the milk and flour to the butter mixture, alternating between the two, until all the ingredients are incorporated. The batter will be thick and gooey. Toss the blueberries, if adding, with a tablespoon of flour to help prevent them from sinking to the bottom of the batter.

Gently stir in the blueberries, and then evenly spread the batter into the prepared dish or pan.

Scatter the streusel topping over the entire cake and bake for 35 to 40 minutes, or until the top is lightly browned and a toothpick inserted in the center of the cake comes out clean. When cool, slice and serve just as is or sprinkled with confectioners' sugar.

Feedback

To make a terrific blueberry streusel muffin, follow the directions above. Spoon the batter ¾ of the way full, into a muffin pan that has been lined with 2½-inch muffin cups. Spoon 1 to 2 teaspoons of streusel on top of each and bake at 350 degrees for 20 minutes. You will have streusel topping leftover. You can cut the recipe in half or refrigerate any remaining topping in an airtight container for up to 2 weeks.

Reni Hanau

In her own words

Talking to Reni was like having a conversation with an old friend. She had a warmth, humor and vibrancy that pervaded the stories and memories she shared with Museum visitors in her role as a gallery educator. On a cold December day, she shared her remembrances with me.

I grew up in a small town in Germany where my father was a teacher of both religious and secular studies and director of rituals; he was the kosher butcher, known as a *shochet*—or, as I like to say, a one-man clergy. He worked for the German government, which, as you might know, has no political atheists. Despite his connection to the government, he was taken to Buchenwald, from which he was released after presenting his papers. Our family knew that now was the time to leave. We moved to Frankfurt, Germany, from our comfortable home, which was situated next door to the synagogue. In Frankfurt, my father applied for a visa to England, where they were proficient in deveining, among other meats, ox tails, which is very difficult. My father wanted to learn that skill. The visa was granted, and we made our way to London.

Our family was relieved to be leaving a hostile country for safe harbor in England. After all, England was an ally nation and we felt we would be safe there. However, upon arrival, our German passports were scrutinized, and the British government deemed us "enemy aliens." We were banished to the Isle of Man, where, although we were safe, we were not free. My mother and I lived apart from my father, as the men and women were separated.

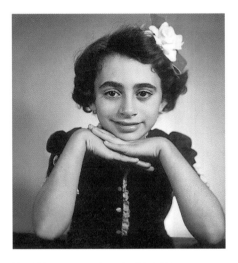

Reni Hanau, age ten, in America.

We were given chores to do, including cleaning the hotel where we resided. My mother, who had never done such housework, would pay a certain Christian "enemy alien" to do her work. She would say, "Don't spend my money on non-kosher lobster and shrimp!" We remained there until the end of the war when we departed for America.

When we arrived in the United States, a photographer on the dock wanted to snap my photo because I was declared the youngest prisoner of war. My mother would not allow the photo, and to this day I feel I was deprived this celebrity status. After my mother's passing, I found comfort in making the foods my mother used to make. If you make the same things your mother made, you feel a little less alone. That includes making Shabbos dinner the way I remember it.

There is a bakery in Washington Heights that makes a particular water challah that was so reminiscent of what I ate as a child. No wonder. It turns out that the baker is the son of the baker from my home village! The bread, which we called *berches*, is shaped like a rye bread, it has something like a braid on top and it is sprinkled with lots and lots of poppy seeds. Maybe people got a little high on that, who knows?

There are survivors who had the opportunity to save and bring to America, not only their traditions, but the actual utensils they used. It's like bringing a part of their old life into their new life. My husband, Walter, of fifty-five years, and our two sons and our seven beautiful grandchildren make my life richer.

Author's Note: I sadly learned that both Reni and Walter have passed away. May their memory be for a blessing.

Reni Hanau's *Waffeln*—Waffles

Reni left Germany as a child, but her memory of her mom's cooking traveled with her from Germany to England and on to America. Her snowy Sundays were warmed by these light waffles that scream with delight when covered in confectioners' sugar and fresh *schlagzahne*—whipped cream. In the time it takes to brew a good cup of coffee or squeeze fresh orange juice, you can have homemade waffles.

Yield: 4 to 6 servings
Start to Finish: 15 minutes

4 tablespoons butter, melted
½ cup sugar
1 cup whole milk
¼ cup sour cream

3 eggs, separated
1½ cups all-purpose flour
2 scant teaspoons baking powder

To create the batter, whisk together the butter, sugar, milk, sour cream and egg yolks in a large bowl. An old-fashioned eggbeater or wire whisk works great. In a separate bowl, combine the flour and baking powder. Stir the flour into the egg mixture until the flour is incorporated and the batter is smooth.

In a separate bowl, beat the whites until stiff but not dry, and gently but thoroughly fold them into the batter. The batter will be very light and airy. Let the batter rest while you heat the waffle iron. Ladle the batter onto the waffle iron, following the manufacturer's directions for how much batter the pan can hold; do not overfill. Cook until light brown, or the indicator on the waffle iron says they are done. Serve with a light dusting of confectioners' sugar or lightly sweetened whipped cream (recipe follows).

Feedback
If you do not have a waffle iron, you can turn these into delicious pancakes. Heat a large skillet or griddle with butter over medium heat. Drop a small ladleful of the batter and cook on the stove until lightly brown on both sides.

Schlagzahne—Whipped Cream

1 cup cold heavy cream
2 teaspoons vanilla extract

2 tablespoons confectioners' sugar (you can
  use regular sugar or even sugar substitute)

Make sure the cream, mixing bowl and utensil you are using are cold. Whip all the ingredients together, with a whisk, electric mixer or standing mixer fitted with the whisk attachment, until the cream forms firm but not hard peaks. Do not overwhip, or you'll end up with butter. You can add additional flavorings to taste such as almond extract or flavored liquor.

JH

Reni Hanau's Winter Celeriac (Celery Root) Salad

Reni enjoys this classic German provincial dish built around celeriac (aka celery root) that her mother would prepare. This alien-looking vegetable is not only homely but also suffers from an identity crisis. It has a taste similar to celery, with the texture more like a carrot. It stands up to pickling very well, stays in the fridge for days and makes a very healthful salad that Reni invites you to enjoy all winter long.

Yield: 6 to 8 servings (about 6 cups)
Start to Finish: Under 1 hour, then overnight

1 celery root (about 1½ pounds), peeled and
  cut into 1-inch chunks
3 carrots, peeled and cut into 1-inch chunks
½ cup diced kosher pickles
½ red onion or 2 to 3 shallots, finely diced

¼ cup olive or canola oil
½ cup white vinegar
Pinch of sugar
Kosher salt and pepper

Bring a medium-sized pot of salted water to boil and cook the celery root and carrots until tender, but not too soft, about 20 minutes. Drain and add them to a bowl along with the pickles, onion or shallot, oil, vinegar and sugar. Season to taste with salt and pepper. Cover tightly and refrigerate. The salad will marinate in the fridge; stir it occasionally so each ingredient has the chance to pick up all the flavors.

Daniel Boulud

Professional contributor

Now that we've gotten you to acknowledge the celery root, let's take it to another level, where the great Daniel Boulud introduces it to fresh horseradish in a deliciously rich beef dish.

Tender Beef with Horseradish, Parsnips and Celery Root

Excerpted from *Braise* (Ecco, 2006)

There's nothing that has quite the same extreme pungency as fresh horseradish. If you can't recall if you've ever eaten it, then you definitely have not. It's a forceful sensation you would remember, much more concentrated than the stuff in the jars. It's a classic accompaniment with braised fatty meat dishes, and for good reason. The sharpness is an excellent contrast to the richness of the meat.

You do need to take care when grating the horseradish, especially if your eyes are sensitive (though you will also feel it in your nose). If you use a food processor (and that's a good idea), whatever you do, don't lean over the machine when you take off the cover. Stand back!

Yield: 6 servings

1 (3-pound) beef bottom round
Coarse sea salt or kosher salt and freshly
  ground black pepper
1 tablespoon all-purpose flour
½ cup extra-virgin olive oil
1 large onion, peeled and cut into large dice
20 juniper berries (see note)
¼ cup red wine vinegar
1 tablespoon tomato paste
¾ cup vodka
¾ cup red wine

2 medium parsnips, peeled, trimmed and cut
  into large dice
1 large turnip, peeled, trimmed and cut into
  large dice
¼ celery root, peeled, trimmed and cut into
  large dice (about 1 cup)
3 bay leaves
2 tablespoons chopped fresh dill
5 ounces peeled, finely grated fresh
  horseradish (about ¾ cup; see note)
½ cup heavy cream (optional) (see Editor's
  note)

Center a rack in the oven and preheat the oven to 300 degrees.

Pat the beef dry and season with salt and pepper. Dust the beef with flour. In a medium cast-iron pot or Dutch oven over high heat, warm the olive oil. Add the beef and sear until golden brown on all sides, 12 to 15 minutes. Transfer the beef to a plate.

Lower the heat to medium. Add the onion, juniper berries and 1 teaspoon black pepper to the pot and cook, stirring 6 to 8 minutes, until the onions are translucent. Stir in the red wine vinegar and tomato paste and cook until almost all the liquid has evaporated. Pour in the vodka and red wine and bring to a boil. Add the parsnips, turnip, celery root, bay leaves, dill, ½ cup of the horseradish and 2 cups water. Return the beef to the pot and bring to a simmer.

Cover the pot and transfer it to the oven to braise for 2½ hours, turning the meat two or three times.

Editor's note: Mr. Boulud prepares a horseradish whipped cream to serve on the side. For those choosing to follow that preparation, we are including the final step. For those who are kosher, we suggest you serve the beef with the vegetables spooned on top of the meat and dollop a bit of the fresh horseradish on the side. You can also adjust the cut of meat.

Meanwhile, whip the heavy cream to medium peaks and stir in the remaining horseradish. Season to taste with salt and pepper. Serve the beef and vegetables with the horseradish whipped cream on the side.

Juniper berries: These small purple fruits of a high-altitude evergreen tree have a clean, resinous taste and are used to flavor meats, pâtés and marinades.

Horseradish: In the same family as cabbage and mustard, and a friend of both, the bitingly pungent horseradish root looks like a dirt-encrusted white carrot. It has to be peeled before cooking, and if it is tough, the root should be quartered lengthwise and the core cut away, jobs that will sting the eyes. The sharpness of raw horseradish, often mixed with vinegar or cream to be used as a relish, is lost when the root is cooked, as heat renders it a mild root vegetable with a pleasantly soft texture. Look for horseradish in well-stocked produce aisles, particularly around the spring Jewish holiday of Passover, during which it is used to represent the bitterness of affliction.

Gruenkern Soup with Mini Turkey Meatballs

Together, Reni and I developed this recipe, which features a uniquely German grain, rich chicken broth and mini turkey meatballs. *Gruenkern* has an interesting nutty flavor and is a nutritious substitute for rice, pasta or noodles in a soup, salad or as a side dish. It has similar properties to farro, spelt or wheat berries. While this forgotten grain is not easy to find, most German specialty stores or kosher suppliers can usually order it for you. It is a grain that both Reni and Edith Blumenthal remember fondly.

Yield: 6 servings
Start to Finish: Step 1: 6 to 8 hours or overnight, to soak the gruenkern, Step 2: Under 2 hours

FOR THE SOUP
1 cup gruenkern, soaked
3 tablespoons olive oil
1 large onion, finely chopped (about 1 cup)
2 carrots, peeled and finely chopped (about 1 cup)
2 celery ribs, finely chopped (about 1 cup)
2 quarts water or chicken broth (if using water, you will need to add a bouillon cube or chicken flavor seasoning packet)
Kosher salt and pepper
Soup bones (optional)

FOR THE MEATBALLS (MAKES ABOUT 30)
1/3 cup plain bread crumbs
2 teaspoons garlic, minced
3 tablespoons chopped fresh flat-leaf parsley
1 large egg
Kosher salt and pepper
1 pound ground turkey
Chopped fresh parsley for garnish (optional)

STEP 1
Soak the gruenkern for 6 to 8 hours or overnight, in cold water, enough to completely cover the kernels.

STEP 2
Heat the olive oil in a large soup pot; cook and stir the onion, carrots and celery over medium heat, until they have softened, about 15 minutes. Pour the broth (or water) into the pot; add the drained gruenkern. Season with salt and pepper. If you have any soup bones, feel free to add them to the pot for extra flavor. Cover and cook over low heat for 1 1/2 hours.

While the soup cooks, prepare the turkey meatballs. Preheat the oven to 350 degrees and lightly grease a baking sheet.

In a bowl, combine all the meatball ingredients, adding the turkey meat last. Form mini meatballs, about the size of a marble. Place them on the baking sheet and bake for 15 minutes. Turn them over and continue baking until they are lightly browned and cooked through, about 15 minutes longer.

Remove them from the oven and gently drop them into the soup. Add the bouillon cube or flavoring packet (if you used water). After 1½ hours, check to see that the gruenkern is done; it will retain a soft, slightly grainy bite. Serve piping hot with a sprinkle of chopped fresh parsley and a drizzle of olive oil.

JH

Ruth Eggener and Julius Eggener

As told by their daughter Evelyn Seroy

Evelyn's parents were among the fortunate group of German Jews who were able to obtain affidavits and immigrate to America before the full extent of Nazi oppression was felt. Evelyn became a tireless teacher on the subject of the Holocaust as part of the Museum of Jewish Heritage's Gallery Educator family.

My mother was the only child of Sol Stern and Henny Gerson. She was born in Fritzlar, Germany, in 1911 and attended a private girls' school taught by nuns. In 1933, her parents realized that there probably wouldn't be much of a future for her in Germany. Her paternal aunt signed the affidavit, and in February 1934, my mother set sail from Copenhagen for New York City. Upon arriving at her aunt's apartment, she was told that "tonight you'll sleep in the bathtub and tomorrow you'll get a job." My mother first worked as a governess, then as a housekeeper at the Essex House. She taught herself how to speak English by going to the movies.

My father, Julius, was born in Mayen, Germany. to Max and Caroline (Klein) Eggener. In 1938, my father came to America. How my parents met is a lovely story. From time to time, my mother would see my father on the subway. When she and a girlfriend went one evening to a dance, my mom told her chum, "That's the man I see on the train. I'm going to marry him." Her friend knew my father and introduced them. One month later, on the day that would have been her mother's birthday, my parents were married. The big

Ruth and Julius Eggener with their daughter, Evelyn, Fort Tryon Park, New York City.

splurge for them on their wedding night was to share a bottle of Coca-Cola.

My parents settled on Laurel Hill Terrace in Washington Heights. When they first married, my mother didn't know how to cook. She asked someone at the Essex House to give her seven recipes, one for each night of the week. After about a month, my father suggested that she should get seven more recipes, because he was tired of riding the subway up to Washington Heights, knowing what's for dinner. My mother prepared mostly German dishes. Everything she cooked and baked was always made from scratch with fresh ingredients. No shortcuts for her! My mother was still shopping and cooking and baking up until she died at the age of ninety-four. As her only child, I enjoy continuing her deeply rooted traditions.

I know that all children are proud of their parents. As a result of the training, which I received prior to becoming a gallery educator at the Museum of Jewish Heritage, I learned more of what my parents went through and am even prouder. I want to leave something so others will know my mother and father were here.

Ruth Eggener's Braised *Sauerbraten*—Marinated Roast

Sauerbraten translates to mean "sour roast," but that doesn't begin to convey the pungent and delicious result from marinating a simple cut of beef for several days in a mixture of wine, vinegar and spices.

Yield: 6 servings
Start to Finish: Step 1: Marinate 3 to 4 days, Step 2: Under 3 hours

MARINADE
½ cup apple cider vinegar
½ cup red wine
2 bay leaves
8 whole black peppercorns
¼ cup sugar
2 medium onions, sliced

1 (3- to 4-pound) chuck, rib, silver tip or
  French roast
Flour for dredging
2 tablespoons oil
Kosher salt and pepper

STEP 1
Bring all the marinade ingredients to boil in a medium saucepan. Reduce the heat, cover and simmer for at least 10 to 15 minutes. Allow the liquid to cool. Place the roast in a large resealable bag and pour the cooled marinade into the bag. Seal, then lay the bag in a shallow pan and refrigerate for 3 to 4 days. Turn the bag twice a day to evenly distribute the marinade.

STEP 2
Preheat the oven to 350 degrees and remove the roast from the marinade. Dry the meat with a paper towel and dredge in flour. Heat the oil in a Dutch oven or covered roasting pan and brown the meat on all sides. Strain the marinade, discarding the solids, and add half the marinade to the pot, reserving the rest of the marinade for later. Place the pot in the oven, cover and roast for 2½ hours or until the meat is tender, but not falling apart. Check the pot several times while roasting to add water as necessary to loosen the gravy. When the meat is nearly done, heat the remaining marinade in a small saucepan, bring to a boil and cook for 10 minutes, and then simmer uncovered, allowing it to reduce.

Reserve the marinade for the final step.

Remove the roast and slice thin. Add the sliced meat back into the pot. Pour the reserved marinade over the meat and season to taste with salt and pepper.

Feedback

Anytime you have a marinade that has come in direct contact with raw meat, you MUST boil it before reusing to reduce the risk of contamination from bacteria that can develop. The reduction also intensifies the flavor. Boil the marinade for 10 minutes, then lower the heat and let it simmer uncovered until it is reduced by half. The more it reduces, the more concentrated the flavor becomes. If you prefer, you can make a new batch of marinade and allow it to cook down and reduce by half before adding to the roast.

Ellen Katz and Ernest Katz

In their own words

Ellen and Ernest Katz smiled broadly as they listened to each other tell their respective stories. They both exuded a very positive attitude and built a beautiful life together. Ellen's outlook on life is, "You pick yourself up and dust yourself off." Ellen adds, "It is what we do. We always land on our feet."

ELLEN

I remember a very pleasant life as a little girl in Offenbach, Germany. I remember cooking with my mother when she baked. I would be licking the spoons like any child would. It wasn't until 1939 that we started to feel ostracized. I didn't look Jewish at all, because I was blonde with blue eyes, but when it came my turn to be waited on in a local store, I was told, "You can't have this." All of a sudden, I realized it was because I was Jewish. I was young, only twelve, so I was eligible to leave for America through an organized rescue effort known as the *Kindertransport*. My father arrived in America one month before me, while my mother stayed behind with my sister. My sister was over sixteen and too old to leave with me. She and my mother never made it out of Germany. I first went to Italy by train and met up with five or six other children and a woman who was in charge. We boarded a ship and came to America. I arrived in May 1940, and by the time I started school in September, I had no problem speaking English, as I had learned a little when I was in Germany. We

Ellen's travel document for the Kindertransport to America.

were determined not to speak German, we didn't want the culture, we wanted to forget. At first, we lived with my aunt and uncle, who had immigrated here a year earlier; then my father and I moved out and made it on our own.

ERNEST

Although I was born in Düsseldorf, I lived in the same town that Ellen did, as Offenbach was the center for handbag manufacturing, and that was my trade. I left Germany in 1938 and went to England, by way of Italy. When I arrived in England with my German papers, I was deemed an enemy alien, a prisoner of war, and sent to Australia. I was interned on a prisoner of war ship named the *Dunera*, which was actually hit by a torpedo in transit. We arrived in Sydney after two months and were put on a train for as far as it would go. I spent four years in a POW camp where we were treated fine and there was little anti-Semitism. The Australians eventually realized they had made a mistake and told us we could join the British army. I joined the Australian army instead and served for four years in the labor corps. My sister lived in America, so I came on a visit and decided to stay. (Ellen joins in the conversation: "Ernie had a girlfriend then, and it wasn't me! Eventually it was.") They were married over sixty years; they have two children and five grandchildren.

Author's Note: I sadly learned that Ernest has passed away. May his memory be for a blessing.

Ellen Katz's Apricot Squares

These sublime bites are Ellen's entrance fee when visiting her grandchildren. The dough is a classic mürbeteig: lightly sweet short crust pastry covered with flavorful apricot preserves, buttery streusel, crunchy walnuts and flaky coconut.

Yield: 40 mini squares
Start to Finish: Step 1: 15 minutes, then refrigerate at least 2 hours or up to 24 hours,
Step 2: Under 1 hour

FOR THE DOUGH
1 cup all-purpose flour
1 tablespoon sugar (more or less to taste)
Pinch salt
1 stick (½ cup) cold butter, cut into small
  pieces
1 egg yolk
1 tablespoon orange juice

FOR THE FILLING
1 cup apricot (or your favorite flavor) preserves

FOR THE CRUMBLE
1 stick (½ cup) butter, melted
⅔ cup all-purpose flour
1 cup sugar

FOR THE TOPPING
½ cup finely chopped walnuts (about 2 to 3
  ounces)
½ cup coconut flake

STEP 1
Mix the flour, sugar and salt in a food processor, fitted with the metal blade, or in a bowl using a pastry blender. Cut in the cold butter, egg yolk and orange juice. Pulse or blend the mixture. The dough will start out very crumbly but comes together as you pulse or blend it. Do not overprocess. The finished dough will be very soft but not sticky (add a drizzle more juice if the dough is dry). Press the dough into a 12 x 9-inch jellyroll pan. Spread the preserves over the dough, cover and refrigerate for 2 hours, or up to one day.

STEP 2
Preheat the oven to 350 degrees.

Create the crumble by melting the butter in a saucepan or in the microwave. Pour the melted butter into a small bowl and let it cool for a few minutes. Stir in the flour, then sugar, and mix with a fork to create crumbly, moist bits. Remove the dough pan from the fridge and sprinkle the crumbs all over the preserves. Sprinkle the nuts and coconut over the crumbs.

Bake for 35 minutes or until the crumble is lightly browned. When slightly cool, cut into bite-size squares. Allow the cookies to completely cool before removing from the pan. They store well in a closed container for several days.

Ruth Kohn

In her own words

Ruth Kohn proudly wears both an American flag pin and a Dominican Republic flag pin on her lapel, something you might not expect from a Jewish girl born in Germany. She happily shares her story and why her granddaughter says, "The sweet Dominican souls saved my grandma and grandpa."

I was six years old when Hitler came to power. Before then I remember a house where everyone was happy. We lived in Berlin from the time I was four until I was fourteen. My father had a cousin in America who wanted us to come, but my father, an Orthodox Jew and decorated German soldier, felt nothing would happen to us if we stayed. He once said, "If I ever leave Germany, it will be on the last train." That's exactly what happened. I had an uncle who was arrested on Kristallnacht. He paid the Nazis for his release. He traveled to Belgium, where he was arrested again. This time, he was sent to Portugal and was detained in a camp. He managed to escape by walking over the Pyrenees to Lisbon. Once in Lisbon, he met with the American Joint Distribution Committee, who told him of Sosua, a settlement in the Dominican Republic. Trujillo, the dictator there, was offering safe haven to Jews who would commit to agricultural work. My uncle accepted the offer and sent visas for us to join him. I was told we boarded the last train out of Germany. The age restrictions were changed the day after we left, and my parents would not have been able to leave if we had stayed one day longer.

We arrived in the Dominican Republic the day Pearl Harbor was bombed. "OK, now

Ruth Kohn, in Sosua, Dominican Republic.

what?" we thought. It was very bittersweet. We felt we were out of this world somewhere; the climate and the language in Sosua were so different. We went to a German school but had to learn Spanish, which was a very good thing. There were certain foods we could not get there, like white potatoes, so we adapted and ate sweet potatoes, fruits like plantains and papayas, all new foods to us.

The Dominicans were very kind; there was no anti-Semitism. It was a very strange feeling being able to walk down a street without harassment. When we first arrived, a young doctor from the hospital in town came and took our photos. The pictures were used for our Dominican documents. Years later, I worked as a nurse at that same hospital and dated that same doctor. I was later told that after he took my picture, he returned to the hospital and told everyone, "I am going to marry that girl someday." Six years later, he did. He waited for me! We were the first couple married at the Temple in Sosua.

My parents brought me up to be a happy person. I haven't forgotten anything, but I am happy. I really admire the Dominican people.

It was a horrible time, but they brought us through. We went from one dictator in Germany to another in the Dominican Republic, but the Dominican dictator saved our lives. Many Jews were saved by the Dominicans, seven hundred in Sosua alone. After the war I said, "What now?" It was like we were on hold, like you put clothes over the summer in mothballs. But my life now is really a happy ending. I was married forty-five years and have three children and two grandchildren.

Ruth Kohn's *Arroz con Pollo*—Chicken and Rice

This classic Latin American dish is a one-pot wonder. Juicy chicken, tender rice and a splash of green from the peas and olives make this a hearty and visually satisfying dinner.

Yield: 4 to 6 servings
Start to Finish: Under 2 hours

1 (3- to 4-pound) chicken, cut into 8 pieces
½ cup olive oil
Large onions, chopped (about 2 cups)
1 clove garlic, crushed
½ teaspoon crushed red pepper
1½ teaspoons kosher salt
½ teaspoon black pepper

2 cups, uncooked converted white rice
1 (28-ounce) can tomatoes, with their juice
1 (10½-ounce) can chicken broth
1 can green chili peppers, chopped (optional)
1 cup frozen peas
½ cup pimento-stuffed green olives, sliced
1 (4-ounce) can pimentos, drained and sliced

Preheat the oven to 325 degrees.

Wipe the chicken pieces with a damp paper towel. Heat the olive oil in a heavy 6-quart Dutch oven and brown the chicken, in batches, over medium heat, until golden brown on all sides. With a slotted spoon, remove the cooked chicken to a plate.

In the same pot, cook and stir the onions, garlic and red pepper over medium heat until golden, about 10 minutes. Stir in the salt, pepper and rice and cook for 10 minutes longer, stirring occasionally, until everything is lightly browned. Stir in the tomatoes and their liquid, chicken broth and chili peppers, if using. Place the chicken back into the pot (do not add the liquid that collected on the plate) and bring to a low boil. Place the covered pot in the oven and bake for 1 hour.

After one hour, add ½ cup of water, sprinkle in the peas, olives and pimento strips—do not stir. Cover and continue to bake for an additional 20 minutes. The chicken should be tender and moist and cooked through. Serve family style right from the Dutch oven.

Ruth Kohn's Fried *Platanos*—Fried Plantains

There is possibly no dish more iconic to Caribbean cuisine than fried plantains. Starchy foods normally eaten by eastern European Jews were not readily available on the island, so indigenous ingredients such as plantains and yucca were obvious substitutes. Don't confuse plantains with bananas: although from the same family, plantains are firmer, starchier and less sweet. Ruth enjoyed this preparation as a light dessert, with a preference for plantains that are dark yellow, black spots and all, but they can also be eaten as a side dish.

Yield: About 6 servings
Start to Finish: Under 15 minutes

Vegetable oil for frying
3 very ripe plantains, peeled and sliced
 lengthwise ¼ inch thick
Sugar for dusting

Heat several inches of oil in a large skillet until sizzling hot, about 350 to 375 degrees. Fry the plantains until golden, about 3 to 5 minutes per side. Drain on paper towels, then serve with a sprinkling of sugar on top. Omit the sugar if serving as a side dish.

Miriam Margulies

In her own words

Miriam spent most of the war years living in America as a new immigrant. Even as a child, she assumed many of the roles of a traditional homemaker while her mother worked to support them both. As a result, she is an accomplished and eclectic cook with German, Austrian, Hungarian and Czech specialties.

Miriam Margulies, 1950.

I was born in Vienna, Austria. My family enjoyed a very normal existence until I turned eight, when the Nazi regime took control. After two years living under Nazi rule, an uncle in America secured papers for my mother and me. We arrived in America in 1940 and took refuge in the German Jewish community of Washington Heights, New York.

Although I was only ten, I assumed many traditional roles, such as preparing meals. When you are a refugee coming to a strange country where you don't know the language or culture, you just do it!

After the war ended, we reunited with my father. I feel you should always be optimistic. It is wonderful living in this marvelous country that saved our lives, and we keep hoping for a good future. I have two children, seven grandchildren and one great-grandchild.

Miriam Margulies's *Palatschinken*—Thin Pancakes

This Hungarian-Viennese specialty is a very light and thin pancake, the Viennese version of a blintz on a diet. The filling is almost always preserves; Miriam favors apricot. Dust with confectioners' sugar for a light dessert or elegant breakfast. The pancakes freeze well, unfilled. To freeze, layer parchment or waxed paper in between each pancake and seal tightly.

Yield: 10 pancakes
Start to Finish: Under 30 minutes

1 cup sifted all-purpose flour
1 tablespoon sugar
1/8 teaspoon salt
1/2 teaspoon vanilla extract
2 eggs

1/2 cup water and 1/2 cup milk or 1 cup water
1 tablespoon butter, melted (you can substitute oil)
Confectioners' sugar, for sprinkling

Combine all of the ingredients in a blender and process until smooth. The batter should be thin, but not watery, so add more flour if needed to create a smooth, flowing batter.

Heat a touch of butter (or oil) in an 8-inch skillet over medium heat. When a drop of water dances in the pan, you are ready to add a small amount of batter, about 1/4 cup. Swirl the pan so the batter coats the entire bottom of the pan. When the pancake bubbles, turn it over and cook an additional 30 seconds.

Remove to a waiting plate and cover to prevent the pancakes from drying out. Continue this process until you have used all the batter.

Fill then roll the pancakes with any type of jam or preserves; apricot is most traditional. Sprinkle with confectioners' sugar just before serving.

Marsha Meyer

In her own words

I was born in a small town called Burghaun, Germany, that had about thirty Jewish families. In 1939, I was able to leave Germany and went to London, where I worked and lived with a Jewish family. I stayed only six months before coming to America. I enjoy cooking, and there are certain specialties I make that my two children and four grandchildren think are wonderful. My favorite recipe is for an unusual dumpling that you cannot buy in any store. It is a traditional German treat, called *knodels*. I serve it for dessert and stuff it with fresh or dried fruit. The late spring and early summer are the perfect time to prepare them when the plums and apricots are their ripest. It's quite a job to make, but my family is crazy about them. I like to set myself up at the kitchen table, turn on the TV and make these leisurely.

Marsha Meyer's Fruit-Filled *Knodels*—Dumplings

Yield: About 18 **knodels**
Start to Finish: Under 45 minutes

FOR THE DOUGH
½ pound red potatoes,
  peeled, boiled and mashed
½ pound (1 cup) ricotta
  cheese
2 cups all-purpose flour
2 egg yolks
Pinch of salt

FOR THE FILLING
18 dried pitted prunes or 36
  dried apricots or 18 fresh
  small plums or 18 fresh
  apricots
Sugar to sweeten the fruit

FOR THE TOPPING
½ stick (4 tablespoons)
  butter
½ cup unseasoned bread
  crumbs
3 tablespoons sugar
½ teaspoon ground cinnamon

To make the dough, bring a medium pot of water to boil and cook the potatoes until soft, about 15 minutes. Drain, then mash the potatoes by hand or use a ricer (creates a smoother texture). In a large bowl, combine the mashed potatoes with the ricotta cheese, flour, egg yolks and salt. Mix thoroughly and then knead on a lightly floured surface until a dough forms. If the dough is too sticky, you can add a little more flour.

Bring a fresh pot of salted water to boil.

Prepare the fruit by softening the dried apricots or prunes. Heat them for a few minutes with a little water in a small saucepan. Drain and dry them thoroughly. For the fresh fruit, simply wash the fruit. Marsha does not even remove the stone pit, but you can if you want to.

Separate the dough into manageable pieces for you to roll out on a floured board. Using a cookie cutter, cut the pieces large enough to wrap around the fruit that you will be using. For the fresh plums and apricots, the dough will need to be cut larger than for the dried fruits. For extra sweetness, dab a little sugar between the pieces of dried fruit before placing in the center of the dough.

Wrap the dough around the fruit, sealing all edges tightly. You should not be able to see the filling through the dough. If you can, you have stretched the dough too thin. Roll the filled dough in your hands to form the knodel. It is a very forgiving dough and easy to work with.

Drop the knodels in the boiling water and cook about 10 minutes. Gently move them around the pot so they don't stick to the bottom or to each other. Remove with a slotted spoon and allow them to drain on a paper towel.

While they drain, prepare the topping by melting the butter in a small skillet and lightly browning the bread crumbs with the sugar and cinnamon. After a few minutes, the topping should be light brown and you are ready to roll. Pour the topping into a small bowl and roll the knodel in the browned crumbs. If you like, you can sprinkle the knodels with vanilla sugar, confectioners' sugar or poppy seeds. Eat at once.

Feedback
Vanilla sugar is a favorite sweetener for many German cooks. Take one or two vanilla beans and split down the center. Place them in a tight container filled with confectioners' or granulated sugar. Let the flavor permeate the sugar for several days before using. Vanilla sugar is also sold in specialty food stores and online.

Gisela Obernbreit and Kurt Obernbreit

As told by Kurt's daughter, Ruth Obernbreit

Ruth is an accomplished writer with a colorful family history. Her father, an Austrian refugee, fled Nazi oppression for safe haven in the Dominican Republic. Ruth, Kurt's only child, wrote his story in a piece she titled "Paradise 1943." The following is an excerpt from that essay originally published in *The Westchester Review*. Ruth is especially proud of her two daughters who carry on their family traditions.

After the *Anschluss*, as Hitler marched into Austria in 1938, my father's family began to feverishly figure out how to leave Vienna. The small family included my grandfather, the fastidious Edmund; my grandmother, Gisela, a middle-class hausfrau; and my father, Kurt, an only child who at eighteen was a gymnasium (secondary school) graduate with an academic diploma. They were desperate. One afternoon, my grandmother was in the butcher store on the Wenggasse. She overheard a woman describe how her son was able to get out of the country. He had mailed the instructions written in invisible ink on the wrapping of a package. The directions were shared with my grandmother....In a certain village you bribed the local Nazi officer. You then found a certain spot at the end of the village and walked several hours in the woods where you were met by representatives of the "naturefriends" a group in Switzerland that housed refugees.... This is exactly what my eighteen-year-old father did.

He lived with the Swiss for two years while he looked for a place in the world that would take him. While my father and the other refugees were requesting visas, President Roosevelt was organizing an international

Kurt Obernbreit (*center*), Sosua, Dominican Republic.

conference in Evian, the one where the only head of state to offer refuge was a malevolent dictator (Trujillo) who said he would take 100,000 Jews. My father found out about this possibility and somehow in the first winter of the war, in 1940, he arrived in Portugal awaiting a ship to what was then called Santo Domingo. "It was like a kibbutz," my father would tell me of the living and working arrangements of Sosua. Every Jewish immigrant was given the equivalent of 80 acres, 10 cows, a mule and a horse. My father milked cows; he learned to love the smell of hay and manure. Whatever Trujillo's motivation, my father and his new friends were riding horses, planting tomatoes and were spared the ravages of the ghettos and concentration camps where others met their fate.

In 1943, my father was able to secure a visa for his father, Edmund, to come to Sosua. He was on the last shipload of settlers to arrive. Once there, he suffered a heart attack, and it was my father's obligation to write his mother and inform her of his death. At the time, his mother was working in England as a domestic. She was now able to secure a visa to Ecuador and persuaded my father to leave the Dominican Republic and meet her there. My father loved the Dominican people, knowing them to be warm and accepting of him and his people. They did not just save him physically, but more importantly, I think they saved his soul. (Kurt's progeny include Ruth, two granddaughters and two great-grandsons.)

Gisela Obernbreit's Thin and Crispy
Wiener Schnitzel—Breaded Veal Cutlets

Ruth relates memories of her grandmother Gisela's cooking: "My Viennese grandmother was a very fine cook. When I was a little girl, I would sleep over at her apartment on West 78th Street and she would make my favorite meal, *wiener schnitzel* and creamed spinach! Then we would watch *Lawrence Welk* together. The next day, in the afternoon, her lady friends would come over and visit. They knew each other from Vienna since they were children, even before World War I, yet they still referred to each other using last names only. She made all these things in a windowless kitchen, which clearly had been transformed from a closet, [with] a tiny stove, small fridge and little table on which she would pound, roll and mix by hand."

Yield: 4 servings
Start to Finish: Under 15 minutes

1 pound veal cutlets, pounded very thin
½ cup solid vegetable shortening (such as Crisco)
½ cup all-purpose flour, seasoned with kosher salt
2 eggs, beaten
¾ cup plain bread crumbs

GARNISH
Freshly chopped flat-leaf parsley and lemon wedges

Pound the veal until paper thin, using a meat mallet or the bottom of a heavy pan, to about ⅛ inch thick. The pounding not only thins the cutlets but also breaks down the sinewy tissue that makes the meat tough.

Heat the shortening in a skillet until it is very hot. You can use vegetable oil, but a solid vegetable shortening is preferred. The oil is ready when a few bread crumbs dropped in the pan sizzle and brown up quickly. True crispy schnitzel should soak up very little oil. Maintaining the proper temperature reduces the amount of oil absorbed.

Dip the veal first in the seasoned flour, then beaten eggs and then in the bread crumbs. Do not press the crumbs into the meat. Lightly shake off excess. Fry the veal, over medium heat, until crispy and golden brown, about 4 minutes on each side. Swirling the pan helps create those waves and ripples in the crust that schnitzel is known for. Serve immediately, sprinkled with freshly chopped parsley and a wedge of lemon. Boiled potatoes make a great accompaniment.

Ruth Obernbreit's *Tres Leches*—Three Milk Cake

Ruth recalls, "When my father was missing the Dominican Republic, he would have a yen for a really good cup of *café con leche* and a piece of this cake, which is totally out of this world. Don't be concerned that the cake seems soggy when first prepared. It absorbs the three varieties of milk as it sits overnight in the fridge."

Yield: 12 to 16 pieces
Start to Finish: Under 1 hour, then refrigerate for 6 to 8 hours or overnight

1½ cups all-purpose flour
1 teaspoon baking powder
1 stick (½ cup) butter, room temperature
1 cup sugar
5 eggs

½ teaspoon vanilla extract
1 cup whole milk
1 (14-ounce) can sweetened condensed milk
1 (12-ounce) can evaporated regular or skim
   milk

Preheat the oven to 325 degrees and grease and flour a 13 x 9 x 2-inch Pyrex baking dish.

Sift together the flour and baking powder. In a separate bowl, beat the butter and sugar on medium speed for several minutes until light and creamy. When the butter is a pale yellow, beat in the eggs, one at a time. Stir in the vanilla. With the mixer on low, begin adding the flour until all the ingredients are well combined. Pour the batter into the prepared baking dish and bake for 30 minutes, or until the top of the cake is a golden yellow color, firm to the touch, with brown tinged edges.

Let the cake cool for at least 10 minutes.

Combine the three milks and pour them over the cooled cake. Cover tightly with plastic wrap and refrigerate for 6 to 8 hours or overnight. Top with fresh whipped cream, smother with berries or a drizzle of melted chocolate—or all three!

Ruth Orvieto and Vittorio Orvieto

In Ruth's words

Ruth's story is very international. From a childhood in Germany, coming of age in Ecuador and a fifty-seven-year marriage to Vittorio, an Italian survivor, Ruth's life experiences have truly covered the globe.

I was born in Breslau, Germany, and had one older brother. On Kristallnacht, my sixteen-year-old brother was almost taken to a labor camp, so shortly after that my family shipped him off to Palestine (Israel). My father was sent to Buchenwald, and my mother went every day to the Gestapo to negotiate for his release. At that time, they would still let him go if she could secure a visa for him to another country. She secured visas for him alone to Shanghai, but he would not go without us. We scrambled and quickly got visas for the entire family to Ecuador instead. We arrived in Ecuador in 1939; I was twelve at the time.

Life was very different for us. In Germany, my father was a successful manufacturer; in Ecuador, he sold butter. Before leaving, we had packed our suitcases with items to use for bartering. When we arrived at the docks to leave Germany, the Gestapo confiscated our bags. We arrived in Guayaquil, Ecuador, literally with nothing but the clothes on our backs. When I was thirteen, I had to stop school and go to work to help support our family.

In Ecuador, I didn't consider myself to be German. I had only one dream and that was to get out of there and go to America. I had an affidavit, and I could have gone, but I met and married my husband, and we began raising a family. My husband, Vittorio, was born in Genoa, Italy, and left there at nineteen to escape the Holocaust. He often recalled the enormous kindness of the Italian people who helped him to board a ship to Ecuador. I always say that was the only good thing Hitler did for me.

After my second child was born, I knew I wanted to give my children a better life and a good education. We came to America in 1955, where we had our third child. I never felt German and preferred to cook the Italian food my husband enjoyed. We were married fifty-seven years and have three children, eight grandchildren and one great-grandchild.

Ruth Orvieto's Risotto

While Ruth's background is German, her husband, Vittorio, favored his familiar Italian dishes. Even when they lived in Ecuador, Ruth cooked in the Italian tradition. Risotto was one of her go-to dinners, studded with sweet onions, porcini mushrooms and lots of freshly grated Parmesan cheese. No doubt, you need to babysit risotto a little, while the crunchy outer kernels of the Arborio rice slowly absorb the white wine and hot broth. Be sure to use a dry white that is wineglass-worthy; never cook with wine that is not good enough to drink!

Yield: 4 servings as a main course, 6 servings as a starter
Start to Finish: Under 1 hour

1 (1-ounce) package dried porcini mushrooms
4–5 cups vegetable broth
3 tablespoons olive oil
1 small onion, chopped (about ½ cup)
3 tablespoons butter

2 cups uncooked Arborio rice
½ cup white wine
½ cup grated Parmesan cheese
Kosher salt and pepper
Chopped fresh flat-leaf parsley, for garnish

Soak the dried mushrooms in 1 cup of hot water for 30 minutes and then strain the mushrooms and their liquid, using a small piece of cheesecloth. You should have about ¾ cup of liquid reserved. In a medium saucepan, heat the vegetable broth and add the mushroom liquid. Cover and keep on a low simmer. Rinse and then chop the mushrooms, pat dry and reserve.

Heat the olive oil in a large skillet; cook and stir the onions over medium heat until they are just softening and translucent, about 5 minutes. Stir 1 tablespoon of butter in the pan and add the rice. Cook and stir the rice for several minutes (the rice will go from white to almost clear). Stir in the white wine and cook until the wine evaporates; this should only take a minute or two.

Using the back of the ladle, spread the rice out in the pan so it is in one thin layer. Begin stirring in your first ladle (about ½ cup) of heated broth. Keep the heat low; you don't want to rush this process. When the liquid is almost completely absorbed, stir in your next ladle. Continue adding the broth and stirring until you have used about half the liquid. Stir the reserved porcini mushrooms into the rice. Continue the ladling process until there are about 2 ladles of broth left in the pot. Stir the remaining 2 tablespoons of butter and grated cheese into the rice. Test the rice to see if it is al dente—you want it to be creamy but retain a little bite. Add the remaining broth or hot water until you achieve your desired consistency. Season to taste with salt and pepper. Serve immediately with a sprinkling of grated cheese, a drizzle of olive oil and a pinch of freshly chopped parsley.

Variations: Ruth suggests adding 1 cup of thawed frozen peas when you add the mushrooms.

For Risotto Milanese, Ruth would flavor the dish with saffron. Saffron is very expensive, but a little goes a long way. Omit the mushrooms and their liquid; they would overwhelm the subtle flavor of the saffron. Use 5 cups of broth and add ½ teaspoon of saffron to the broth as it heats. When you stir the broth into the rice, you will see the color begin to change to a mellow yellow. Threads of saffron will remain in the finished dish.

Ruth Orvieto's *Gnocchi Alla Romana*—Semolina Gnocchi with Cheese

Ruth's version of gnocchi, crusty, pillowy rounds of baked semolina layered with butter and Parmesan cheese, makes a beautiful presentation and a rich alternative to polenta or baked noodles.

Yield: 4 to 6 servings
Start to Finish: Under 1½ hours

2½ cups whole milk
¾ cup semolina flour
4 tablespoons butter divided (2 tablespoons cold, 2 tablespoons melted)

1 egg yolk, beaten
1 teaspoon kosher salt
¼ cup Parmesan cheese

In a medium saucepan, heat the milk till scalding (the point right before boiling, you'll see a skin begin to form on the top of the milk). Lower the heat to a simmer and begin adding the semolina, ¼ cup at a time. Stir with a whisk to avoid clumping. Once the semolina is completely incorporated, begin stirring with a wooden spoon; the mixture will look like mashed potatoes. On the lowest simmer possible, cook the semolina for 15 to 20 minutes; it will continue to thicken, and when you stir, it should pull away from the sides of the pot. It is done when it is very stiff and resembles wet dough.

Take off the heat and stir in 2 tablespoons of cold butter, the egg yolk, salt and half the cheese. The semolina will become very elastic and completely leave the sides of the pot. Clean and lightly dampen a large counter or a marble slab. Turn the semolina mixture onto the cool, clean, damp surface and, using a wet spatula or rolling pin, spread the semolina into a ½-inch layer. Let the mixture cool for at least 20 minutes. The dough should be cool to the touch before beginning the next step.

Preheat the oven to 425 degrees and lightly butter the bottom of an 11 x 7-inch rectangular baking dish.* In a separate small bowl, melt the remaining 2 tablespoons of butter and reserve.

Using a 1½-inch round cookie cutter, cut circles from the dough and begin layering them in the pan. Start with 24 rounds on the bottom (4 across, 6 down). Using a pastry brush, brush the rounds with the reserved melted butter and sprinkle a little of the remaining cheese on top. Cut 18 rounds for the next layer, and in a pyramid fashion, place those rounds on top of the first layer (3 across, 6 down). Brush with butter and sprinkle with cheese. Your next layer will be 12 pieces (2 across, 6 down), and the final layer will be 6 pieces, right down the center; brush with butter and sprinkle each layer with cheese. You will need to gather the scraps of dough and roll them out again in order to complete the layering. Pour any remaining butter on top and sprinkle with the rest of the cheese. Bake for 20 to 25 minutes or until the top lightly browns.

*You can also use an 8-inch round or 9-inch square pan, following the same layering patterns. You will need between 60 and 64 rounds.

Mary May Prussin and David Prussin

As told by their daughter Judy Prussin

Judy's parents, David and Mary May Prussin, both immigrated to the United States from Germany, as living there became ominously dangerous. Her father arrived in 1937, her mother in 1939. David and Mary's two children, two grandchildren and six great-grandchildren are happy they did.

Judy Prussin's Spiked Mandel Bread

Judy makes a traditional German cookie, mandelbrot, from the German meaning "almond bread." Judy's derives its almond flavor from a nice dose of amaretto, which she pairs with a variety of dried fruit and nuts. Judy's is a twice baked, stand-up-to-a-big-mug-of-coffee, crunchy, chocolaty delight. Think biscotti with an attitude.

Yield: 28 cookies
Start to Finish: Under 3 hours

1 stick (½ cup) butter, room temperature
¾ cup sugar
2 eggs
1 cup amaretto
2½ cups all-purpose flour, plus more if needed
⅓ cup unsweetened cocoa powder
1½ teaspoons baking powder

¼ teaspoon salt
1½ to 2 cups assorted nuts and dried fruit, almonds, hazelnuts, pistachios, macadamia nuts, dried cranberries and dried cherries (break up any large pieces)
1½ cups chopped white chocolate or 12 ounces white chocolate chips

Preheat the oven to 325 degrees and grease and flour a 20 x15-inch baking sheet.

Beat the butter and sugar in a large bowl, on medium speed, until light and creamy. Lower the speed and beat in the eggs and amaretto.

In a separate bowl, combine the flour, cocoa powder, baking powder and salt. On low speed, stir the flour into the butter mixture and then blend on medium speed until well combined. The dough will be thick, pasty and wet. If the dough is too wet to handle, add a little more flour. Thoroughly stir in the nuts, dried fruit and white chocolate. Divide the dough in half. On the prepared baking sheet, shape each half of dough into a log about 14 inches long x 1½ inches wide x 1½ inches high (lightly wet your hands or use the spatula to help shape the logs). Space the logs several inches apart, as they will grow while baking.

Bake for 30 to 45 minutes; the top of the cookie should be firm. Carefully transfer the logs from the baking sheet to a cooling tray and let them cool for 1 hour. You can turn the oven off and reheat it about 20 minutes before you need to bake the cookies for the second time. After an hour, using a serrated knife, slice the logs, on the diagonal, into pieces that are about 1 inch thick. Try not to use a rocking motion, which might break the cookies. Transfer the cut cookies back onto the baking sheet, standing them upright, about ¼ inch apart. Bake for an additional 30 to 45 minutes, depending on how crunchy you like them. Cool the cookies on a tray and store them in a sealed container.

Wolfgang "Wolfie" Rauner

In his own words

A little Henny Youngman, a bit master of ceremonies and completely charming, that's how I would describe Wolfgang "Wolfie" "Johnny" Rauner. He loves to cook, write and kibbitz.

I was born in Trier, the oldest city in Germany. My early childhood was spent in the southwestern portion of the country, close to Alsace Lorraine. Our cooking techniques borrowed heavily from the French. My mother learned the domestic arts in France, so her food not only tasted delicious but also was presented beautifully; a sandwich would look like a banquet. In 1935, my father anticipated the mounting turmoil in Germany and moved the family to nearby Luxembourg. It was easy for us to leave because we had very little in Germany so there was little to leave behind. For five years, we lived peacefully; however, my father struggled to support us. We attended public schools, which were staffed by nuns in the early grades. In May 1940, Hitler invaded Luxembourg, and we were now under German occupation. In 1941, we left Luxembourg for the United States.

I annually observe the anniversary of my arrival in this country, June 21, 1941, as a personal holiday, by proudly flying the Star-Spangled Banner. It was then that we settled safely in Washington Heights, New York, or, as we liked to call it, "the fourth Reich." Both of my older brothers were drafted into the armed forces, one in 1942 and the second in 1943. My first brother was part of the "Ritchie Boys" who worked intelligence during the war. The second brother was in the Airborne Infantry and served as a translator. He was wounded landing in a glider while crossing the Rhine.

I always worked, often in sales. At one time, while working for Buitoni, a large supplier of Italian prepared foods, I was instrumental in

Wolfie (*second from the left*) with his two older brothers, Ludwig and Edgar, and sister, Gertrude (Trudy).

bringing kosher supervision to the company. To this day, I love cooking Italian food; some of my most creative specialties are from that region.

Pesach in my home always included matzo balls. Not the usual preparation or serving style. In my mother's home growing up, they were boiled. In my father's, they were fried. It's funny because my parents grew up in towns very near each other, but they each had a different way to serve the matzo balls. In my home growing up, my mother, the diplomat, made both. Boiled were served with soup, the fried ones with the main dish. For over thirty years, this tradition has survived. These matzo balls are not like what we make today; they had their origin in the Alsatian kitchen. To this day, I'm still very much affected by the love my mother showed through her cooking. My wife and I have two children and five grandchildren.

Wolfie Rauner's *Matzo Kloesse*—Dumplings

Wolfie, with his usual witty style, describes in great detail the process for making this traditional Passover dish that he has eaten since he was a boy. When boiled, they are a replacement for matzo balls; when fried, they are a lot like falafel. "My grandfather on my father's side operated a small bakery in the town of Merzig and also owned the best-known matzo bakery in the entire region. Generations later, people asked me, on first meeting, if I was related to 'the Matzo Baker of Merzig.' Thus, in my parents' home, every Pesach my mother made two kinds of *Matzo Kloesse*. We called them '*Freudenburger*' and '*Merziger*.' Essentially, they were made of the same basic recipe, only Freudenburger were boiled and the Merziger were fried. When making these, I start by throwing everyone out of the kitchen. I end by cleaning up the mess, before my wife gets back in. Be sure they don't fall on the floor, because if they hit your foot, they could just break your toe! In my early married years and when my children were growing up, I remember standing the whole day before *Erev* Pesach, night before Passover, and making huge quantities of both varieties. Usually having guests at our seder and two growing boys, we managed to put away quite a few. Even in later years when we went for seder to my son's house I still had to bring them along."

Yield: 20 to 24 Matzo Kloesse
Start to Finish: Step 1: Under 30 minutes, then at least 2 hours or up to 24 hours in the fridge, Step 2: Under 30 minutes

2 tablespoons chicken fat or vegetable oil
2 large onions, chopped (about 2 cups)
4 sheets matzo, broken into small jigsaw puzzle–like pieces
3 eggs, beaten
1/4 cup chopped curly parsley

1/8 to 1/4 teaspoon ground ginger
2 teaspoons kosher salt
1/2 teaspoon pepper (white preferred)
Matzo meal
Oil for frying or broth or salted water for boiling

STEP 1

Heat the fat or oil in a large skillet; cook and stir the onions over medium heat until brown but not burnt, about 15 minutes. While the onions cook, soak the broken matzo in a bowl filled with cold water. After 10 minutes, squeeze all the water from the matzo and let them sit in between two pieces of paper towel to absorb any residual water. Stir the matzo into the cooked onions and cook over low heat until the mixture is dry, about 5 minutes.

Spoon the cooked matzo and onions into a bowl; let them cool down for 5 minutes, then stir in the eggs, parsley, ginger, salt and pepper. Using a wooden spoon, or your hands, combine the mixture thoroughly. The mixture might look wet, but it soaks up the eggs as it sits. Cover with a piece of plastic wrap and refrigerate for at least 2 hours or up to 1 day.

STEP 2
To Prepare "Freudenburger" —Boiled Matzo Kloesse

Take the mixture out of the fridge and bring a large pot of salted water or broth to boil.

Add ½ cup of matzo meal to the matzo ball mixture. This should help firm the mixture and prevent the matzo balls from falling apart when boiled. Roll the matzo mixture into 1-inch balls (a little oil or nonstick cooking spray on your hands will help). Drop the matzo balls into the boiling liquid, reduce the heat to medium and boil until the matzo balls fluff up and rise to the surface, about 15 minutes. Eat with the soup or serve with a helping of fried onions on top.

To Prepare "Merziger" —Fried Matzo Kloesse

Add ¼ cup of matzo meal to the matzo mixture. Sprinkle a little matzo meal on a flat plate. Roll the matzo mixture into 1-inch balls (a little oil or nonstick cooking spray on your hands will help), then roll the balls in the matzo meal crumbs for an extra crunch on the outside. Let them sit in the fridge while the oil heats.

Heat a skillet with ¼ inch of oil. When the oil is hot, carefully place the Matzo Kloesse in the pan and brown on all sides, over medium heat, for several minutes. They should be brown and crisp on the outside, soft inside. Drain on a paper towel and eat as a side dish.

Feedback
The matzo mixture, before it is boiled or fried, would make a terrific Passover stuffing.

Irma Reich and Martin Reich

As told by their daughter, Suzanne Schaps

Both of Suzanne's parents were Holocaust survivors; one endured internment, and the other was a refugee. Suzanne remembers a home where food took on such an important role. She recalls a Hebrew expression that her mom used that translated means, "Food is my life." That was the overwhelming feeling growing up in her home. Suzanne provides us with a glimpse into their experiences and shares one of her favorite family recipes.

Irma Hamburger Reich.

My mother, Irma, was one of two surviving children of Henny and Alfred Hamburger. She lived in a small town near Hamburg called Fürstenau, Germany. My mother was lucky enough to be a passenger on a Kindertransport, which in 1938 took children from Germany to England. She was eighteen years old at the time. Her brother had left Germany earlier and was living safely in Colombia, South America. To support herself, my mother first worked as a housekeeper in England. She had no language skills but was very bright and able to adapt. She was very unnerved by the bombings that took place in England. It was then that she made the decision to leave England to live with her brother in South America.

When she arrived, she was threatened with deportation but ultimately was able to stay.

My father Martin's experience was very different. I know he survived internment in France, in four different camps. When he came to America, he and my mother made a life together. I was raised very American, and my mother's cooking was not strictly "immigrant style." She was a phenomenal cook and always made delicious food and presented it with an elegant flair. As their only child, I try to keep the traditions alive and share them with my two daughters and four grandchildren so they will hopefully live on.

Henny Bachrach's Almond and Apple Cake

Suzanne was effusive when describing her grandmother's holiday cake. "I particularly remember the delicious nut cake my mother would make for us every year at Passover. It was a recipe handed down to her by her mother, my grandmother Henny Bachrach. It had small coffee beans as decoration and a wonderful mocha filling. Because my grandmother Henny didn't have measuring utensils, she would use the broken eggshells to measure the matzo meal. We left that in as a nod to my grandma's resourcefulness. Be sure to prepare the cake one day ahead; it makes it easier to frost and allows the ingredients to set. I hope you enjoy it as much as I did as a child."

Yield: 10 to 12 servings
Start to Finish: Under 1½ hours

FOR THE BATTER
8 eggs, separated
1 cup sugar
8 ounces ground almonds (about 1¾ to 2
  cups)
Zest of 1 lemon peel
Juice of half a lemon
(5 to 6) half eggshells matzo meal (a little less
  than 1 cup)
1 large unpeeled red apple, grated

MOCHA CREAM FROSTING OR FILLING
½ pint (1 cup) heavy cream
1½ teaspoons sugar
1 tablespoon brewed coffee
Cooled raspberry jam for filling (optional)
Mocha coffee beans for garnish (optional)

Preheat the oven to 350 degrees and grease a 9-inch springform pan.

To prepare the batter, beat the egg yolks and sugar in a large bowl on medium speed until pale yellow, about 4 minutes. Stir in the almonds, lemon zest, lemon juice, matzo meal and grated apple.

In a separate bowl, beat the egg whites to form stiff but not dry peaks. Gently fold the egg whites into the egg mixture. Pour the batter into the prepared pan and bake for 1 hour. Cool well before removing from pan.

While the cake cools, prepare the mocha cream by combining all the frosting ingredients and beating on high speed until the cream is thick but not hard. To assemble the cake, carefully slice the cake in half, through the middle, creating two layers. Spread either a layer of mocha frosting or a layer of raspberry jam (if using) in the middle. Place the second layer on top and frost the sides and top with the mocha frosting. Decorate with the mocha coffee beans (if using). The cake can be frozen in the springform pan and frosted at a later time.

Melly Resnicow

In her own words

Melly articulated her story of coming to America following Kristallnacht with passion and clarity. She explained the quota system, which was a calculated method for controlling Jewish immigration to the United States. Your status was linked to the country in which you were born. Those born in Germany received a more favorable number than those born in Poland. This system was responsible for dividing her family when they immigrated to the United States.

I was born in the Saxony region of Germany. The family settled in Munich and experienced Kristallnacht there. My father was arrested and taken to Dachau, but after two weeks he was released and ordered to leave the country within twenty-four hours, which we happily did! My mother was able to obtain visas to Switzerland for herself, my brother and me. My father had to wait for his quota number to come up. Because he was born in Poland, he was listed on the Polish quota, while we were part of the German quota. We arrived in America in December 1938; my father was able to join us in April 1939.

Melly Resnicow (*left*) with her mother.

I was comfortable being here, and after two years at PS16 in Williamsburg, I became editor of the school magazine. I had two teachers who worked with me to teach me English (I had some private lessons when I was in Munich but only learned a few words of what I call "British" English). In 1946, when I was twenty, I married my American-born husband; we were married for fifty-two years. Together we had four children, and I am the proud grandmother of six grandchildren.

I learned to cook in Germany when I was about seven or eight. We had a housekeeper who did the cleaning, but my mother always cooked. I started baking around that time, mostly "assisting" my mother when she was baking. Someone presented me with a cookbook for children, and then I really got going. I remember making lots of cookies, which my younger brother gladly consumed; he still has a "sweet tooth." I continue to cook and bake at home for holiday meals, and then I transport it to my children's homes; they refer to me as "the caterer" and are very appreciative!

Author's Note: I sadly learned that Melly has passed away. May her memory be for a blessing.

Melly Resnicow's Chocolate Roll

Melly is a home baker with professional skills and knowledge that could put Martha Stewart to shame. This light and elegant confection is a flourless chocolate cake filled with sweet whipped cream. It is certain to impress company and satisfy anyone seeking a delicious chocolate dessert. Don't let the steps intimidate you; as Melly says, "It's practically foolproof."

Yield: 10 to 12 servings
Start to Finish: Under 2 hours

FOR THE BATTER
6 ounces semisweet
  chocolate chips
3 tablespoons water
¾ cup granulated sugar
5 eggs, separated

FOR THE FILLING
1 cup heavy cream
2 tablespoons confectioners'
  sugar
1 teaspoon vanilla

FOR DUSTING THE CAKE
Dutch cocoa powder
Confectioners' sugar
  (optional)

Preheat the oven to 375 degrees.

Begin the batter by melting the chocolate and 3 tablespoons of water in a double boiler over simmering water, stirring occasionally to keep the chocolate smooth. Remove from the heat, transfer the chocolate to a large bowl and cool slightly. In a separate bowl, beat the sugar and egg yolks until light and fluffy. Stir the egg mixture into the cooled chocolate. In a medium bowl, beat the egg whites until stiff but not dry and gently fold them into the chocolate batter.

Grease a 15 x 11 x 2-inch jellyroll pan, then line with a piece of waxed paper with the ends of the paper hanging over the edges of the pan. This will help lift the cake off when it is done. Grease the waxed paper and spread the batter evenly in the pan. Bake for 15 minutes.

Dampen a dishtowel and wring out the excess water so it is barely wet. Remove the cake from the oven and cover with the towel until the cake is completely cooled, about 1 hour. Using a small knife, loosen the edges of the cake that might have attached to the sides of the pan and gently lift the cake off the pan (using the extended side pieces of waxed paper as handles). Sprinkle the cake with a dusting of cocoa powder (a small kitchen strainer works well). Cover the counter with 2 new overlapping pieces of waxed paper and then gently turn the cake over so that the bottom is now the top. Peel the waxed paper from the cake.

To make the filling, whip the cream, sugar and vanilla until firm. Spread evenly over the entire cake. To create a log that is 15 inches long x 3 inches wide, using the waxed paper as a guide, gently roll the cake away from you. After each turn, press down gently, sliding your hands over the roll. The "seam" should be on the bottom. Take a small knife and cut off the paper along the sides of the roll but leave the ends; this will facilitate lifting the roll onto a platter. Cut a thin piece of cake from each end on the diagonal (Melly says, "These are for the baker"); additionally, cut off the paper "handles." For presentation, you can leave the log whole or cut into slices. Confectioners' sugar can be sprinkled on top, and additional cocoa powder can be dusted on top to hide any small cracks.

Evelyn Pike Rubin

In her own words

Evelyn Pike Rubin is the author of *Ghetto Shanghai*, an amazing story of sanctuary and survival. The following is an edited excerpt from her book.

I was born in Breslau, Germany (now Wroczlaw, Poland), at the onset of the Nazi era to a religiously observant Jewish family. My parents owned and operated a wholesale paper and twine business that had been founded by my mother during World War I. My parents were vacillating between leaving Germany immediately or "waiting it out," as Jews had been doing during the two thousand years of the dispersion. In 1935, the Nuremberg Laws were promulgated. It was at that time that my parents were looking for countries we could immigrate to. They tried Brazil, Palestine (under British mandate), Cuba, England, America, all to no avail. When it seemed there was no way out of Nazi-ruled Germany, we heard about one little glimmer of hope. The conquering Japanese, victors of the Sino-Japanese War of 1937, had established the port of Shanghai, China, as an "open" city. There was a good possibility one could go there without a visa just for the price of a steamship ticket. My parents, however, decided to put the idea of going to Shanghai "on the backburner," still hoping to get an American affidavit from a great-aunt of mine living in Brooklyn, New York, in the near future.

When we finally received the affidavit, to our consternation, we were informed by the American Consulate that we were assigned to the Polish quota because, under the Versailles

Evelyn with her parents.

Treaty, after World War I, my father's place of birth was integrated into Poland. In 1938, that quota was filled, and we were assigned a high number. Kristallnacht—November 9–10, 1938—of course, was the beginning of the end for European Jewry. My father was among those arrested and sent to Buchenwald. During his incarceration, my mother purchased tickets for us to leave for Shanghai the following February. This was most fortuitous, for the Nazis had decided to release almost all those arrested during the Kristallnacht pogrom with the proviso that they would leave Germany within two months. My father was released in December. On February 9, 1939, we took the train to Naples, Italy, for the month-long voyage into the unknown—Shanghai, China.

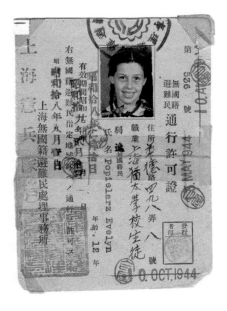
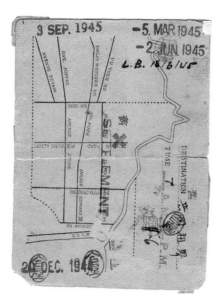

Evelyn's T'ung, Special Pass, Shanghai.

We arrived in Shanghai on March 14, 1939. My mother sold the personal possessions we had brought with us to purchase an apartment and to establish a typewriter business with my father doing the repairs with a hired Chinese mechanic and my mother taking care of the business end. My father's mother joined us in Shanghai in June 1940. The refugee population had reached approximately eighteen thousand by 1941. My father, whose war wound had acted up in Buchenwald and was left untreated, succumbed to these conditions at age forty-three, leaving my mother, my grandmother and me.

On February 18, 1943, the Japanese issued a proclamation to the refugee community, stating that we had three months to "relocate to a designated area." In effect we were going to live in a ghetto. The area was Hongkew. My mother sold her apartment to a Japanese family, and with three other families we moved into a four-room hovel: one bathroom, cold running water and no heat. A *t'ung*, "special pass," could be obtained from Mr. Goya, one of the Japanese ghetto administrators. Most, though not all, of the special pass applicants who could demonstrate they needed a pass to make a living outside the ghetto did receive such a pass. My mother also received one by applying as a typewriter mechanic, with customers in the French Concession. However, she used her pass for a different purpose. By visiting Chinese peddlers in parts of the city that Westerners did not often frequent, she purchased sundries (such as scarves, sunglasses, belts, etc.), which she brought back to the ghetto peddlers, who sold them on a consignment basis. That same year, my grandmother died at the age of seventy-four.

On July 17, 1945, American fighter planes bombed the ghetto. Some thirty refugees were killed, and hundreds more were wounded. Scores of Chinese inhabitants also were killed that day. Six weeks later, Major General Claire Chenault arrived in Shanghai from Chungking with the American Liberation Forces. Now the war was over for us also. Thus ended another chapter of Holocaust survival. When the world closed their doors to the beleaguered Jews of Europe, Emperor Hirohito had left one door open through which approximately eight thousand refugees, fleeing the Nazi terrorism, entered!

My mother and I arrived in the United States in March 1947 on an American troop transport, passing under the Golden Gate Bridge in San Francisco. I am the proud parent to six children and sixteen grandchildren.

Evelyn Pike Rubin's Sweet Summer Peach Cake

This easy-to-bake cake involves a rich batter layered with perfectly ripe fruit, capturing that just-picked summer fresh taste. Peaches are one of those fruits that jump out of the bushel and into your grocery cart when they are at their peak. They should be firm to the touch but smell sweet and ripe. In the fall, try making this with crisp apples. Follow the harvest and tailor this recipe to whichever fruit is in season.

Yield: 10 to 12 servings
Start to Finish: Under 2 hours

FOR THE BATTER
4 eggs
½ cup vegetable oil
1 cup apple juice
1 teaspoon vanilla extract
3 cups all-purpose flour
2 cups granulated sugar
1 teaspoon salt
3 teaspoons baking powder

FOR THE FILLING
1 pound peaches (about 3–4 medium), sliced
5 tablespoons sugar mixed with 3 teaspoons
  ground cinnamon

Preheat the oven to 375 degrees and grease and flour a 9-inch springform tube pan. (There are cooking sprays that have a touch of flour in them, perfect for this application.)

Prepare the batter by beating the eggs, vegetable oil, juice and vanilla in a large bowl on medium speed for several minutes. In a separate bowl, sift together the flour, sugar, salt and baking powder. A standard kitchen strainer makes a great sifter. On low speed, slowly add the flour mixture to the egg mixture and then beat on medium speed for several minutes, until smooth and thick. If you don't have an electric mixer, you can do it Evelyn's way, sifting together the sugar, flour, baking powder and salt then creating a well and using a wooden spoon, stirring in the juice, oil, vanilla and egg.

Start the filling by removing the pits from the peaches. A simple technique is to cut around the circumference of the peach and twist. The two halves should separate, and the stone pit will be easy to remove. Cut the peaches into ¼ -inch-thick slices. Sprinkle the cinnamon and sugar over the peaches and toss to coat. Don't let the peach mixture sit too long or it will become soggy.

Pour ⅓ of the batter (about 1 to 1¼ cups) into the bottom of the prepared pan. Top the batter with half the peaches, trying not to let them touch the sides of the pan. Spoon in the next third of batter and then the remaining peaches, finishing with the remaining batter. Bake for 1½ hours.

After 1 hour, check the cake to be sure the top is not browning too quickly. If it is, cover loosely with foil and continue baking. After 1½ hours, a bamboo skewer inserted into the center of the cake should come out clean; the cake should be golden brown and the texture firm to the touch. Allow the cake to cool completely before removing from the pan. Sliding a knife around the edges and underneath the cake will make transferring to a cake plate much easier.

Feedback

Cook any remaining peaches in a saucepan until they become very soft and the syrup thickens. Cool and enjoy as a topping for the cake. A dollop of whipped cream and a scoop of vanilla ice cream couldn't hurt. The cake has a texture similar to coffee cake, which makes it wonderful for breakfast the next day.

Doris Schechter

Doris is a unique contributor to the book, as she is both a survivor of the Holocaust and an accomplished baker, cookbook author and restaurateur. Her story is excerpted from her first book, *My Most Favorite Dessert Company Cookbook* (HarperCollins Publishers Inc., 2001), and from my interview with her. We devoured her freshly baked cookies as we spoke.

"I was born the year Hitler marched into Austria. My parents were living in Vienna at the time. I never learned how my father obtained the visa that allowed him to leave Vienna for Italy not long after the Anschluss. He sent for my mother and me a short time later. Italy became our adopted homeland....In 1944, my family was among the 986 refugees invited by President Roosevelt to spend the duration of the war in the United States. We crossed the Atlantic in a perilous journey on an army transport ship called the "Henry Gibbons."...In 1946, my family started a brand-new life in the Bronx....Our life was very family oriented with Friday night dinners that my grandmother Leah always prepared."

Doris married, had children and discovered her love for cooking after receiving a book on the cooking of Vienna. Her European background included baking with butter, but Doris was determined to prove that pareve baking could be delicious and elegant. It was from there that My Most Favorite Dessert Company was born. Her dream was for the company to have a Manhattan presence, as she called it "a little bit of Vienna uptown."

"The traditions of my faith and my heritage colored every aspect of my life and my family's lives....I have come full circle in my life. I am the sum total of my experiences. I came to this country as a Jewish refugee from Italy, having been born in Vienna. I became an American

Doris Schechter as a child with other refugee children in Upstate New York.

and have loved being an American. I started baking, with the aromas of Vienna filling my head....Tradition affects every aspect of my life and connects me to my background. I have five children and sixteen beautiful grandchildren."

Aside from being decadently delicious, Doris's Blackout Cake has a great history with the Museum of Jewish Heritage. When famed journalist and champion of Jewish refugees Dr. Ruth Gruber was being honored at the Museum, Doris prepared and donated five hundred chocolate chip loaves, based on this recipe, for the occasion. They were such a hit that annually Doris bakes these as a gift to the Museum. Doris calls it "an omen" that when she saw the photograph on the invitation for the event, she was stunned to see herself, as a six-year-old, in the group photo taken in Oswego, New York, where she lived with her family after coming to America.

Doris Schechter's Blackout Cake

Excerpted with permission from *My Most Favorite Dessert Company Cookbook* (HarperCollins Publishers Inc., 2001)

1 chocolate cake, cooled (recipe below)
About ¾ cup orange-scented sugar syrup
  (optional) (recipe follows)

Chocolate pudding (recipe follows)

Chocolate Cake

Makes 1 (10-inch) cake

1½ cups all-purpose flour
½ cup unsweetened cocoa powder
1 teaspoon baking soda
¾ teaspoon salt
¼ teaspoon baking powder

2 teaspoons pure vanilla extract
1 cup strong, freshly brewed coffee, cooled
8 tablespoons (1 stick) unsalted margarine
1½ cups sugar
4 extra-large eggs

Preheat the oven to 350 degrees. Grease the bottom and sides of a 10-inch cake pan. Cut out a round of parchment paper to fit the bottom and line the pan with it. Do not grease the paper.

Onto a sheet of waxed paper, sift together the flour, cocoa powder, baking soda, salt and baking powder. Stir the vanilla into the cooled coffee.

In the bowl of a standing electric mixer fitted with the paddle attachment, cream the margarine with the sugar on medium speed until lightened and fluffy. Scrape down the sides of the bowl with a rubber spatula. With the machine running, add the eggs, all at one time, and beat until incorporated.

Reduce the mixer speed to low and start adding the dry ingredients, alternating with the coffee mixture, beating until the batter is smooth and the ingredients have been fully incorporated.

Pour the batter into the prepared cake pan and smooth the top with the spatula. Bake for 45 minutes, or until a cake tester inserted in the center comes out clean. Remove the pan from the oven and let it stand 5 minutes. Unmold the cake, remove the paper liner and place the cake right side up on a wire rack to cool.

TO FREEZE

Wrap the cooled layer securely in plastic wrap, place it in a freezer bag and freeze for up to 1 month.

TO DEFROST

Unwrap it completely and let it stand at room temperature. Trim and frost as directed in the recipe.

Orange-Scented Sugar Syrup

Brushed on cake layers, it helps prevent them from drying out and can keep them tasting fresh for several days. A good syrup can also impart flavor to the cake layers.

Makes about 2½ cups

2 cups water
1 cup sugar

Peel of ½ medium orange

In a medium heavy-bottomed saucepan, bring the water, sugar and orange peel to a boil, stirring and washing down any sugar crystals on the sides of the pan with a pastry brush. Cook, stirring, until the sugar is dissolved. Then cook, without stirring, for about 5 minutes. Remove the pan from the heat and let the syrup cool. The syrup is ready to use.

Chocolate Pudding

Makes about 3½ cups

2 cups cold water, plus ½ cup
2 tablespoons unsalted margarine, cut into
 pieces
6 ounces bittersweet or semisweet chocolate,
 coarsely chopped

1 cup sugar
¾ cup unsweetened cocoa powder, sifted
⅓ cup cornstarch

In a medium saucepan, combine 2 cups cold water and the margarine over medium heat, stirring, until the margarine melts and the water comes to a boil. Add the chopped chocolate and the sugar and cook, stirring constantly, until the chocolate has melted and the mixture is smooth.

Add the cocoa to the chocolate mixture and stir to combine.

In a bowl, whisk together ½ cup water and the cornstarch until no lumps show.

Increase the heat under the chocolate mixture to medium-high and bring the mixture to a boil, whisking constantly. Add the cornstarch mixture and cook, whisking constantly and vigorously, until the pudding thickens and becomes shiny and smooth, 2 to 4 minutes. (Be sure to whisk the bottom and sides of the pan or the pudding will cook onto them.) Remove the pan from the heat.

Scrape the pudding into a large heatproof bowl and smooth the top. Press a piece of plastic wrap directly on the surface of the pudding to prevent a skin from forming and let the pudding cool. The pudding is ready to use as a filling or frosting or chill and serve at another time as a pudding.

TO ASSEMBLE THE CAKE
With a long-bladed serrated knife, horizontally slice off the crown of the cake to make a level layer. Be sure to reserve the trimmings (they become the crumbs).

With the knife, slice the cake into 3 thin, even layers. Reassemble the layers on top of each other and trim the edges of any hardened crust all the way around. Add all the trimmings to the reserved crown and hold at room temperature.

Place one of the layers on a cake stand or cake plate. Brush the top lightly with some of the orange sugar syrup, if desired. Measure about ¾ cup of the chocolate pudding and spread it evenly over the layer.

Brush one of the remaining cake layers with sugar syrup, if using, then invert it onto the cake on top of the pudding. Brush with sugar syrup.

Take another ¾ cup pudding and spread it evenly over the cake. Brush the remaining cake layer with sugar syrup and invert it onto the pudding. Brush with sugar syrup.

With a metal spatula, spread the remaining chocolate pudding evenly over the sides and top of the cake, using it as frosting.

Over a piece of parchment paper or small baking sheet, rub the reserved cake trimmings gently between the palms of your hands, crushing them to make fine cake crumbs. (You should have about 1½ cups crumbs.)

Dust the top and sides of the cake with the crumbs, covering it completely. Store leftover cake, covered with a cake bell or lightly with plastic wrap, in the refrigerator for 5 days, or perhaps as long as 1 week.

Feedback
For a non-pareve (contains dairy) version, room-temperature butter can be substituted for margarine in the cake and pudding recipes.

Ruth Schloss

In her own words

Ruth was one of 130 children who received kindness and protection from France's Baron Edouard de Rothschild. As a child, she went from Germany to France with a Kindertransport, ultimately arriving in America in 1947. She continues to press for recognition of Abbé (a French secular name for a priest) Glasberg, the man who saved her life, as a Righteous Among the Nations.

I was an only child born in Höheinöd, Pfalz, Germany, a small town near the French border of Germany. We had a beautiful big house, and I went to public school; everyone was my friend. In 1937, I was no longer allowed to go to school, and I had no friends. However, I was one of the lucky ones when in 1939, the Baroness de Rothschild brought me and 130 other children to live in her castle, Chateau De la Guette, near Paris, France. She was very kind and tried to help us as best she could. In the interim, my parents were deported to Camp de Gurs, in France, near the Spanish border. When I was thirteen or fourteen, the baroness arranged for me to see them. That was the last time I saw my parents; they were sent to Drancy, then Auschwitz. As a child, I did not appreciate the importance of that visit.

The baroness tried desperately to protect us during the war and to place us in safe houses. I was hidden in a foundling home where I cared for the babies there. When it became too dangerous to stay, I went into the woods with a friend named Danielle. For nearly three months, two lovely ladies from the French underground came and would care for us. One day, one of the women came and told us we

Ruth, age thirteen, with her parents.

were going to Switzerland where we would be safe. We crossed the border for a new life carrying with us the name and address of the person we were to meet. That person said, "I will take you to a farm and you can work there." Unfortunately, he took us instead to the police station in Geneva, and there the Swiss police gave us back to German authorities. They took us to prison, and after four days I was sent to Camp Rivesaltes. Three months after arriving at Rivesaltes, an abbé came into the camp to rescue us. He hid four of us under his coat. Outside the camp, there was a wagon filled with hay, and he hid us there. The German soldiers probed the wagon with pitchforks but could not find us. He took us to stay with a farmer in France. Once again,

I ended up in the woods and was eventually safely placed in St. Joseph's Convent.

The priest's name was Abbé Glasberg. I was a nosy little girl and wondered how could he be an abbé with that Jewish last name. We saw him after the war, and he told us that he was born in Russia to a very religious Jewish family. He had visions of the Virgin Mary, left Russia, went to France, converted and became an abbé. He checked up on us all the time, even when I was in the United States. When we asked him what we could do for him, he told us we must light candles every Friday night and that the boys must be Bar Mitzvahed. In addition, we must continue to be proud Jews and marry in the Jewish faith. I continue to press for Yad Vashem to recognize him as a "Righteous Among the Nations" for his selfless acts. At this time, Jewish converts cannot be recognized with that honor.

I came to America in August 1947. I spoke only French and German and worked as a domestic. I taught myself to read and write. When asked how I look at life, I would say don't ever, ever lose God, pray and think about the good things that were in your past as a child. I am married fifty-nine years, and together we have two children and three grandchildren.

Ruth Schloss's Spaetzle with Cooked Dried Fruit

Spaetzle noodles are traditionally eaten as a main course or a side dish to soak up a buttery sauce or rich gravy. Ruth's spaetzle becomes the comforting foundation for gently cooked dried fruit. Literally translated, spaetzle means "tiny sparrow," which describes the way these light noodle-like dumplings look as they flutter in the boiling water.

Yield: 4 servings
Start to Finish: Under 2 hours

FOR THE FRUIT
2 cups dried fruit: dates, figs, prunes, apricots
 or any combination you choose
1 tablespoon sugar (optional)

FOR THE SPAETZLE BATTER-DOUGH
1¼ cups all-purpose flour
Pinch of ground nutmeg (freshly grated is best)
Pinch of salt (optional)
1 egg, beaten with 8 ounces of water
2 tablespoons butter or oil, for frying
Cinnamon sugar for sprinkling (optional)

In a bowl, combine the dried fruit and add enough water to completely cover the fruit. Let the fruit sit for at least 45 minutes or up to 1 hour to soften and plump up. Cook the fruit over a low heat till soft. When the fruit is done cooking, let it remain in the pot while preparing the spaetzle.

In a small bowl, combine the flour, nutmeg and salt. Stir in the egg and water and mix until you have a wet elastic batter-dough.

Bring a large pot of salted water to boil. When the water boils, place the spaetzle dough on a cutting board and, using a knife, cut it into tiny pieces. Carefully push the pieces off the board into the pot of water.

You might need to dip the knife in the water to help slide the dough off the board. Do not overcrowd the pot or the spaetzle will stick together. Boil, uncovered, for 20 minutes. Drain the spaetzle in a colander.

To brown the spaetzle, heat the butter or oil in a skillet, cook and stir the spaetzle over medium-low heat until it is lightly browned and crisp on all sides, about 10 minutes. Spoon the spaetzle into a serving bowl and toss with the warm fruit. Ruth invites you to "enjoy with a good appetite."

Jules Wallerstein

As told by his wife, Helen

Jules was one of the 937 passengers who boarded the SS *St. Louis*, presumably for safe harbor in Cuba. The fate of this ship has been the subject of books and a Hollywood movie titled *Voyage of the Damned*. The story of the passengers and their circumstances are still debated today.

My husband, Jules, was born in Fürth, Germany. His father owned a jewelry store in town, which on Kristallnacht was ransacked and burned. His father was taken away for two days. Miraculously, he was returned. My husband's family had a very successful cousin who lived in America; he owned Bosco, the chocolate syrup company. It was this cousin, Leo Wallerstein, who provided visas for the family to escape Germany. When my husband was twelve years old, his family and a total of 937 people boarded the SS *St. Louis* headed for Cuba. Although they had all filed for and received proper documents, only 37 people were allowed entry when the boat arrived on Cuba's shores.

When the bulk of passengers were not allowed to disembark, the ship's Captain Schroeder sailed the boat within sight of Miami. Despite his hopes and the efforts of some members of the American government, the passengers were not allowed to enter the United States. The boat was ultimately turned away, and Captain Schroeder began desperately wiring other nations to see who would take these passengers. France, Holland, England and Belgium all agreed to take a portion of the people on board. My

Jules and Helen Wallerstein on their wedding day, May 31, 1953.

husband's family went to Belgium, and there he lived and even became a Bar Mitzvah. They lived peacefully with the Belgian people until the Germans invaded. Jules's father went to the bank to withdraw their money and unfortunately was stopped and arrested. He was sent to an internment camp in France. Once again, his family reached out to their cousin Leo, and in 1942, they joined his father in France and then came to America.

Three years later, now an American citizen, Jules was drafted into the army and sent overseas to serve as an interpreter and interrogator. He said it felt good this time "to be the one with the gun." To my husband, this was another adventure in his life.

In the year 2000, we received an invitation from "The Watchmen of the Nations." They invited us to Canada to be part of a ceremony where the Canadians apologized for not accepting any passengers from the SS *St. Louis*. This same group sent us to Florida in 2001, where over six hundred people gathered at the site where the ship had been anchored off the coast of Florida. We all said *Kaddish* (a prayer for the dead). It felt like the hands of the dead were reaching out. We then went with this group to Hamburg to see where the voyage began. We set out on a boat and reenacted the ship's departure. On the edge of the coast, there were Christian Germans waving Jewish flags to honor the survivors. It was unbelievably emotional and moving; we could never have imagined such a sight. Together we have two daughters and five grandchildren.

Author's Note: I sadly learned that Jules has passed away. May his memory be for a blessing.

Helen Wallerstein's Potato *Latkes*

With Helen's recipe you achieve latke nirvana: a potato pancake that is light and crispy. Helen grates her potatoes on the finer side, but you can shred them if you prefer more texture. Make sure you have plenty of sour cream, applesauce or simply sugar on hand to dunk, cozy up to or sprinkle on top.

Yield: 24 latkes
Start to Finish: Under 30 minutes

5 medium russet potatoes, peeled
1 medium onion, grated (use a large one if you
  like a strong onion flavor)
4 eggs, beaten

½ cup matzo meal
1–2 teaspoons salt
¼–½ teaspoon pepper
½ cup vegetable oil for frying

In a food processor using the metal blade, or using a box grater, finely grate the potatoes. Place them in a colander and squeeze out all the liquid. Grate the onion, using the food processor pulse feature to capture any small chunks. Stir the onions, eggs, matzo meal, salt and pepper into the potato mixture.

Heat ½ inch of oil in a nonstick skillet over medium heat until very hot (a drop of water should dance in the pan). To test the seasonings before frying the entire batch (you wouldn't want to taste the raw potato and egg mixture), drop one tablespoon of the mixture into the hot oil, fry for several minutes on each side and drain on a paper towel. Taste the latke and add more salt or pepper if needed. Now you are ready to make the rest. Drop a generous tablespoon of latke batter into the skillet and flatten the pancake with the back of a spatula. Turn the latkes over when the underside is nicely brown, about 3 to 5 minutes. Fry until golden on both sides. Drain on waiting paper towels.

Repeat this process, adding more oil to the pan and a touch more matzo meal to the mixture if needed to absorb the excess liquid that will collect in the bowl. Serve hot.

Feedback
Latkes play nicely with a variety of vegetables. Grate or shred 2 carrots or 1 large zucchini into the latke mixture for a unique taste.

Helen Wallerstein's *Gesundheit Kuchen*—Chocolate Cake

Helen calls this cake the "God Bless You Cake," but you can call it a light chocolate tea cake that is delicious and not too sweet. Drizzling the smooth chocolate ganache over the cake right before serving adds another layer of goodness.

Yield: About 8 slices
Start to Finish: Under 1½ hours

1 stick (½ cup) butter or margarine, room temperature
4 eggs, separated
¾ cup sugar
1 tablespoon zested lemon peel

½ cup whole milk
1 tablespoon cocoa powder, plus ½ teaspoon cocoa powder
1½ cups all-purpose flour
½ teaspoon baking powder

Preheat the oven to 350 degrees and lightly grease a 9-inch round cake pan.

Beat the butter, eggs and sugar several minutes, on medium speed, until light and fluffy. Add the lemon zest, milk and 1 tablespoon cocoa powder and continue mixing.

In a separate bowl, sift together the flour, baking powder and remaining ½ teaspoon cocoa powder. On low speed, add it to the egg mixture. Continue beating, on medium speed, for several minutes until all the ingredients are combined. Pour the batter into the prepared cake pan and bake for 50 minutes or until the cake is firm and a toothpick inserted in the center comes out clean. Dust with confectioners' sugar or chocolate ganache (recipe follows).

Chocolate Ganache

What sounds like such a complicated culinary confection is a simple two-ingredient wonder.

Yield: About 2 cups
Start to Finish: Under 15 minutes

8 ounces heavy cream

8 ounces semisweet chocolate or chocolate chips

Heat the heavy cream in a small saucepan, just until it is hot, but not scalding; you do not want a skin to develop. Place the chocolate in a medium-sized bowl. Take the pot off the stove and pour the warm cream over the chocolate, whisking to combine. Let the sauce sit and cool for a few minutes. The ganache will be thin enough to drizzle. If you prefer a thicker consistency, reheat and add more chocolate. Cooled thicker ganache can be used as a frosting or filling.

JH

Dr. Ruth Westheimer

In her own words

While you know that Dr. Ruth is an expert in her field, what you might not know is that she survived a traumatic childhood and fought in the Israeli Hagganah! She is known for her strength and moxie; after reading the story she shared with us, you will better understand why.

Cooking is important to every culture, but in cultures that always had a homeland, like the French or Italian or Chinese, cooking was only one aspect, as there was also the land, the great rivers, the mountains, the architecture. When you're French and surrounded by France, cooking is only a small part of who you are. But when you're a Jew and for thousands of years you didn't have a homeland, the food you ate became so much more integral to your identity. While I can guarantee that the "Celebration Cake" recipe described below will produce a delicious cake, I must also admit that the recipe isn't mine and no such dessert would ever be made by my hands. Let me explain to you why...

I was born in Frankfurt, Germany. In November 1938, when I was ten years old, the SS came to take away my father. Because of that, I met the qualifications to be sent with one hundred other children from Frankfurt to safety in Switzerland. In early January 1939, my mother and grandmother put me on a train, and the last time I would see them was as they were running alongside the train waving goodbye.

We were sent to a Swiss school for Orthodox children. We German Jewish children spent hours cleaning everything from top to

Dr. Ruth Westheimer.

bottom. During the first few years, we were given a rudimentary education, but when we were old enough to go to high school, only the boys were sent. We girls continued with our cleaning and so, as a result, when I left that school, it was with a Swiss diploma in housekeeping! Needless to say, it's not a diploma that I ever hung up on my wall.

As a result of my educational experience during that time period, I don't have any fondness for domestic duties. I had a husband and two children (and four grandchildren) and did what I had to do, but not with any joy, enthusiasm or much skill. My family was never hungry, but one can't say that they have fond memories of all those meals I made. And as soon as my fortunes changed (I was a college professor and then became Dr. Ruth), I gave up anything that even hinted that I was putting my Swiss diploma to use.

Dr. Ruth's Celebration Cake

Ruth explains the origin of this delicious cake. "I have a friend, Marga, who is a wonderful cook, especially when it comes to desserts. She is a cousin of my late husband, Fred, and for many years we were neighbors in Washington Heights. As often as Marga was willing to send over a care package of some of her delicious culinary skills, we gladly accepted. And later, when my grandchildren were born, Marga would always bake them birthday cakes; when they were older, she would bake with them. (While this recipe is from another cousin, Rose Westheimer, it's the one Marga has always used and I love.) Since Marga never had children, my grandchildren became her adopted grandchildren. If you follow this recipe, I'm sure that you're going to be rewarded with a lot of compliments from your friends and family. And rather than go through this whole story, go ahead and take credit for it. After all, you got it from me, and now that you know my background, you also know that the last thing I want credit for is as a baker!"

Yield: 10 to 12 servings
Start to Finish: Under 2 hours

THE BATTER	FROSTING 1	FROSTING 2	FOR GARNISH
12 large eggs, separated	16 ounces heavy cream	8 ounces heavy cream	Chocolate curls (optional)
1½ cups plus 2 tablespoons sugar	4 teaspoons sugar	2 tablespoons sugar	
2 tablespoons fresh-squeezed lemon juice		2 tablespoons cocoa powder, sifted	
3 cups (about 12 ounces) finely ground walnuts		1 teaspoon instant coffee granules	

Preheat the oven to 325 degrees.

Grease 3 (9-inch) round cake pans, line them with parchment paper and grease the paper and dust with flour. (Potato starch can be used for a Passover version.)

Beat the yolks in a large bowl on high speed with an electric mixer until thick. Add the sugar and lemon juice and continue beating until the mixture is a light yellow. Turn the beater off and stir in the nuts.

In a separate bowl, beat the egg whites, on high speed, until stiff peaks form. Fold the egg whites gently into yolk mixture.

Spoon ⅓ of the batter into each prepared pan (using a measuring cup will help ensure that you evenly distribute the batter). Bake for about 45 to 60 minutes, until golden brown. A tester inserted in center will come out slightly wet, as the cake will retain a moist pudding texture. Loosen the edges with a knife immediately after removing the pans from oven. Cool completely. Remove from pans and peel off parchment.

While the cakes cool, prepare the two frostings in separate bowls. Combine all the ingredients for each frosting and whip each at high speed until stiff peaks form. When the cakes are completely cooled, assemble the cake by placing the first cake layer on a plate. Top with a little less than half of Frosting #1. Place the second layer on top and spread Frosting #2. Top with the third layer and frost the top and sides with remaining Frosting #1. Using a vegetable peeler, shave small chocolate curls from a block of milk or dark chocolate.

Decorate the top of the cake with the curls. Chill before serving.

BELGIUM AND FRANCE

Belgium and France had different experiences during the war. In Belgium, there was considerable resistance, while France, claiming to be neutral, cooperated with the Nazi regime. Germany occupied Belgium in 1940, and between 1942 and 1944, most of the twenty-five thousand Jews deported from Belgium and eventually murdered in Auschwitz were actually Polish citizens or from other countries who fled to Belgium seeking protection. France was occupied at the same time as Belgium; however, it signed an armistice agreement with Germany. The new Vichy government was responsible for the deportation of tens of thousands of Jews residing in France, the majority not French citizens. They passed through transit camps such as Drancy and eventually were murdered in Auschwitz.

In addition to their beautiful accents and gracious manners, the contributors from these two countries display a flair for haute cuisine. Classic French and Belgian ingredients such as flavorful herbs, crisp white wine and stout are commonplace elements for our cooks from this region. We are fortunate to have several survivors representing these two countries. Their foods are indicative of the passion for cooking for which this region is known. We hope you will absorb the stories and welcome into your repertoire the recipes remembered by our spirited French and Belgian survivors.

RECIPES

Arlette Baker's *Poisson en Cocotte*—Fish Casserole

Arlette Baker's *Dinde Braiseé avec Choucroute*—Braised Turkey with Sauerkraut

Sonia Jeruchim's *Eingebrente*—Potato Soup

Cecile Jeruchim's Belgian Endives

Cecile Jeruchim's *Hachis Parmentier*—Cottage Pie

Arlette Levy Baker

In her own words

Arlette, an elegant and energetic woman, was very much affected by the Holocaust throughout her young life growing up in Paris. She maintains a strong French identity, as well as a commitment to teaching the lessons of the Holocaust. Her home and cooking reflect that passion.

Arlette Baker, photo from her French identity card.

I was very young when on December 30, 1942, the French police, who were working with the Nazis, came to our home. My father bought my life by bribing these men and insisted that our housekeeper be allowed to bring me to my grandparents' home. My father and my mother were taken to Drancy (a transit camp not far from Paris), and on February 13, 1943, I later learned they were sent to Auschwitz. I went to live with my grandparents in Paris. My grandmother had died, but my grandfather's second wife, a Catholic woman, raised me. I have always felt like a true Jew, even though my grandparents were very secular. Although I felt safe with my grandparents, they had my suitcase as well as theirs packed, just in case. As an adult, I came to America to marry my husband, William Baker; we raised two children who gave us three grandchildren.

Arlette Baker's *Poisson En Cocotte*—Fish Casserole

Arlette's fish with herbs is classically prepared in a *cocotte*, a small crock designed for cooking individual portions. You can use a Dutch oven or covered skillet and achieve the same result, a moist, flaky fish with a hint of herbs, lemon and wine. The potatoes gently cook in the sauce and provide a Provençal element to the dish.

Yield: 4 servings
Start to Finish: Under 45 minutes

1½ pounds (about 10–12) small Red Bliss
 potatoes, washed and quartered
4 tablespoons butter
4 thick-cut slices (about 6 ounces each) of
 fresh cod or halibut
1 medium onion, sliced
Juice of 1 lemon (about 2–3 tablespoons)

½ cup white wine or cognac
Pinch dried thyme
1 bay leaf
Kosher salt and pepper
1 tablespoon chopped fresh flat-leaf parsley,
 for garnish

Bring a medium size pot of salted water to boil and cook the potatoes until tender but not mushy, about 15 minutes. Drain and reserve.

Melt the butter over medium heat in a large skillet and lightly brown together the fish (on both sides) and onions for 5 to 10 minutes. Stir in the lemon juice, white wine or cognac, reserved potatoes, thyme and bay leaf. Season with salt and pepper. Cover and cook until the potatoes are very tender and lightly browned, about 10 minutes longer. Sprinkle with chopped parsley and remove bay leaves before serving.

Arlette Baker's *Dinde Braiseé avec Choucroute*—Turkey with Sauerkraut

Arlette clearly remembers her grandmother's Alsatian specialties simmering away in Le Creuset pots in their kitchen outside of Paris. In true Alsatian cooking, *choucroute* (French for sauerkraut) is a popular ingredient in slow simmering meat dishes. When braised, sauerkraut serves as the vegetable in the dish while cutting the grease and lending a sweet note.

Yield: 4 servings
Start to Finish: Under 1½ hours

7 tablespoons margarine or vegetable oil, divided

2–3 pounds turkey (wing, thigh, leg or breast)

2 medium onions, quartered

1 pound sauerkraut, washed and drained

½ cup cognac or brandy

1 carrot, peeled and diced (about ½ cup)

Kosher salt and pepper

Melt 5 tablespoons of the margarine or oil in a heavy pot or Dutch oven and brown the turkey and onions over medium heat for 20 minutes. (If cooking wings, separate at the joint for faster cooking and easier presentation.) In a separate skillet, lightly brown the sauerkraut in the remaining 2 tablespoons of margarine or oil. When the turkey and onions are brown, stir in the cognac, carrots and sautéed sauerkraut. Pour in 2 cups of water and season with salt and pepper. Cover and cook on the stove over medium-low heat for 1 hour, or until the turkey is fork tender and the sauerkraut is nicely brown.

ALTERNATE PREPARATION

Arlette is a devotee of the pressure cooker. Not only does she feel it cuts her cooking time dramatically, but she also loves the intense flavor it develops. For this dish, she uses a 6-quart pressure cooker. Arlette suggests browning the turkey and onions in the pressure cooker. She adds the cognac or brandy and then the balance of ingredients. Close the cooker securely and place pressure regulator on vent pipe and let it cook for 15 minutes with pressure regulator rocking slowly (stove switch at "low"). Let the pressure drop of its own accord. Arlette uses a 12-quart cooker to make a whole turkey in the same manner.

Cecile Jeruchim and Simon Jeruchim

In their own words

Cecile Rojer Jeruchim and Simon Jeruchim are a multitalented couple. Both are published authors, and both speak before children at schools and synagogues about their experiences during the war. But as their stories will show you, what they share most prominently is that they both survived the Holocaust as hidden children. Cecile benefitted from the kindness of the Belgian people and Simon from the French. Their stories are important reminders that even in the harshest times, there were good people who did good deeds.

CECILE

I was born in Brussels, Belgium, in 1931. I lived in Woluwe St. Pierre, a suburb of Brussels, with my Polish-Russian immigrant parents, Abraham and Sheva Rojer, and my two siblings, my older sister, Anny, and my younger brother, Charly. I had a wonderful childhood prior to the Nazi occupation, but the war changed everything. I will never forget a particular day in January 1943. I was sitting at the kitchen table eating my lunch, which had been prepared by my mother: steak, mashed potatoes and Belgian endives. I hated Belgian endives! Yet my mother, like most Belgian housewives, prepared and served them several times a week. I was about to finish my meal when my Gentile girlfriend came to my house asking if I wanted to accompany her to voice lessons, which I also used to take. Since Jews were restricted from going to school, I could only accompany my friend but was not allowed to participate. I asked my mother if I could go. She responded, "Not before you finish your endives, or I will save them for your dinner." I decided to leave with my friend, expecting the

Cecile (*center*) with brother Charly and sister Anny. Brussels, 1941.

endives to be waiting for me when I returned home. While I was away, the Nazis came to my house and arrested my parents. They were deported to Auschwitz, where they perished. That afternoon was the last time I ever saw my mother. My decision to go with my girlfriend separated me from my mother forever but also saved my life.

Today I often eat Belgian endives, as their subtle flavor gently brings me closer to my mother and reminds me of my lost childhood. Through the intervention of compassionate and courageous Gentiles, my sister, Anny, and I were hidden in a Catholic convent in Louvain, Belgium, where we were baptized and stayed until the war ended. My brother, Charly, who was hidden in the countryside, also survived. After spending the postwar years in homes for Jewish children, my sister, my brother and I immigrated to the United States in 1948 to live with relatives. I was always a talented dancer. My first job in the U.S. was as a ballroom dancing instructor. I also love writing. I am the author of *Hello do you know my name?*, an educational children's book, and of several short stories about my childhood. I have been married for the past fifty-three years to Simon Jeruchim, also a "hidden child" from France. We are the proud parents of two wonderful daughters, six beautiful grandchildren and five great-grandchildren, with two more on the way.

SIMON

I was born in Paris, France, in 1929. My parents were Polish-Jewish immigrants who settled in a Paris suburb where I lived happily with my two siblings, my older sister, Alice, and my younger brother, Michel. My father, Samuel, was a watchmaker and my mother, Sonia, a homemaker. I adored them, and to this day they still inspire me as role models. My mother was a free spirit, generous and optimistic, a lover of art and music. My father instilled in

me the love of books and his strong set of ethics. We lived comfortably in a middle-class neighborhood. My parents were not religious Jews, and I grew up with Gentile friends, not thinking that I was any different than they were. However, World War II shattered such a belief and also our lives when the Nazis invaded and occupied France in 1940.

Soon, anti-Semitic persecutions began with the wearing of the Jewish star and culminated in roundups and deportation. The defining moment of my life was July 16, 1942, when the French police, who collaborated with the Nazis, rounded up the Jews from Paris and its suburbs. By sheer luck, my mother had an appointment on that very day with her dentist, who confided that one of his patients, a police officer, told him of this impending major roundup. I remember vividly my mother relaying the news to my father, who dismissed it as just another rumor. But my mother persuaded my father for us to spend the night at our cleaning woman's home and thus we escaped arrest. For the following week, we hid in the back rooms of stores, and the people in our mostly non-Jewish neighborhood allowed us to stay a night at a time. Another miracle occurred with the intervention of a compassionate Gentile couple who, upon hearing of our plight, arranged for us children to go into hiding. We said goodbye to our parents, not realizing that it was the last time we would ever see them. My parents were arrested only a month later and were deported to Auschwitz, where they perished. My siblings and I were placed with farmers in Normandy. We pretended to be Christians by praying and going to church.

Simon, Alice and Michel in an orphanage near Paris, 1947–48.

Life was harsh and lonely. While in hiding, I met the village schoolteacher, who gave me a watercolor set and a sketchpad. I loved to draw. It was one of the most treasured gifts I ever received. I filled the pad with watercolors of people and places where I lived and luckily kept them for posterity. I was at the crossroads of the invasion when my village was liberated in August 1944 by American troops. Following the liberation, my siblings and I were placed in a series of Jewish children's homes by an uncle who had become our guardian. For the first time, I was taught about Jewish traditions. In one orphanage, I was asked to paint Hebrew letters on the dining room wall. That was the first time I felt some pride in being Jewish.

When I was fifteen, I became a Bar Mitzvah, in a simple ceremony.

My siblings and I immigrated to the United States in 1949 to live with relatives, hoping for a better life. However, my hopes were dashed when I was drafted in 1951 into the American army and sent to combat in Korea.

Luckily, I survived this conflict and found happiness when I met and married my wife, Cecile, and started a family of our own. I was also fortunate to fulfill my dreams of becoming a professional artist, as an award-winning package designer, graphic artist and book illustrator. My childhood watercolors are now in the permanent collection of the U.S. Holocaust Museum and my Korean drawings in the Korean War National Museum. Through my writings and talks, I keep alive the memory of my parents and all of the victims of the Holocaust. I wrote about my childhood in a book titled *Hidden in France—A Boy's Journey Under the Nazi Occupation* and a sequel, *Frenchy—A Young Jewish-French Immigrant Discovers Love and Art in America—and War in Korea.*

Sonia Jeruchim's *Eingebrente*—Potato Soup

Simon's sister, Alice, remembers fondly calling this family favorite *Farbrente* soup, but what we believe she meant was *eingebrente*, which in Yiddish loosely translates to mean "sautéed, almost burnt." The name derives from the classic lightly browned roux that is added in the last few minutes, amplifying the soup's simple flavors.

Yield: About 6 servings
Start to Finish: Under 30 minutes

4 russet potatoes, peeled and diced (about 4 cups)
Kosher salt and pepper
1 teaspoon onion powder

2 tablespoons cold butter
¾ cup all-purpose flour
Croutons and fresh-snipped chives, for garnish (optional)

In a medium soup pot, boil the diced potatoes with 6 cups of water. Season with salt, pepper and 1 teaspoon of onion powder. While the potatoes cook, combine the butter and flour in a small bowl and use a fork to blend and break up the mixture into tiny crumbs. Cook the flour and butter in a small skillet over low heat, stirring constantly, until the crumbs are a light brown, being careful not to burn them. Let them cool while the potatoes continue to cook.

When the potatoes are cooked fork tender, about 20 minutes, stir the slightly cooled browned crumbs into the potato soup. Cook for an additional 5 minutes. Season to taste with salt and pepper. If the soup is too thick, add some boiling water until you reach the desired consistency. Serve with croutons and fresh-snipped chives.

Cecile Jeruchim's Belgian Endives

Cecile credits this very Belgian vegetable for saving her life. As a child, she felt endives were bitter, but as an adult, she loves the flavor of lightly sautéed, curiously sweet endives.

Yield: 4 to 6 servings
Start to Finish: Under 30 minutes

3 large firm Belgian endives, split down the middle lengthwise
1 tablespoon butter

½ teaspoon sugar, or more to taste
2–3 tablespoons beer

To clean the endives, wipe them with a paper towel; do not rinse. Heat the butter in a medium skillet and sprinkle in the sugar, add the endives and cook, over medium heat, for several minutes, until brown on all sides. When the endives are nicely brown, stir in the beer. Cover and continue to cook over low heat for about 3 to 5 minutes, or until the endives are just beginning to soften, adding a touch more beer or sugar to taste.

Cecile Jeruchim's *Hachis Parmentier*—Cottage Pie

Every year, on June 13, Cecile prepares this dish that she remembers from her childhood. She invites her brother, Charly, over, and together they celebrate the day they arrived in America. This is the French version of cottage or shepherd's pie, with a fresh veggie mixed in for color and flavor. *Hachis* derives from the French "to chop," and Parmentier is the last name of the French man credited for having brought potatoes to France.

Yield: 4 servings
Start to Finish: Under 1 hour

1½ pounds Yukon Gold potatoes, peeled and quartered
2–3 tablespoons margarine (for mashing the potatoes)
1 pound fresh spinach leaves, carefully washed and stems trimmed

3 tablespoons vegetable oil
1 pound lean ground beef
1 medium onion, chopped (about ¾ cup)
2 cloves garlic, chopped
Kosher salt and pepper

Bring a medium pot of salted water to boil; cook the potatoes until fork tender, about 15 to 20 minutes. Drain, and then mash the potatoes, adding enough margarine to make them smooth and creamy. Using the same pot, steam the spinach leaves in about 3 inches of water, just until wilted, about 5 minutes. Remove from the water, and then drain and chop the spinach. Stir the spinach into the mashed potatoes.

Heat 1 tablespoon of oil in a skillet and cook the ground beef, over medium heat, until brown, about 10 minutes. Remove the meat with a slotted spoon and drain the fat from the pan. Stir the meat into the potato and spinach mixture. Add the remaining 2 tablespoons of oil to the skillet, cook and stir the onion and garlic, over medium heat, until lightly brown, about 10 minutes. Combine the onions and garlic with the meat and potato mixture. Season to taste with salt and pepper. The dish can be served just as is or spooned into a lightly greased casserole and baked at 325 degrees just until the top is crisp or browned under the broiler for an even crispier finish.

HUNGARY AND CZECHOSLOVAKIA

The war came late to Hungary, but the Final Solution, Hitler's plan to eradicate Jews from all of Europe, was swift and brutal. Between the start of their invasion in March 1944 until the end of the war, more than half a million Hungarian Jews were deported and murdered, mainly in Auschwitz-Birkenau. Czechoslovakia's trajectory was different from Hungary's, in that its land was annexed years before, as part of a concession to Germany by ally nations. In the end, their fates were similar, as more than a quarter of a million Czech Jews perished. You might notice that our Hungarian and Czech survivors were a bit camera shy, but that doesn't diminish their intense pride in their culture and culinary efforts.

These two countries share borders, which help define their shared cuisine. Their cooking highlights big flavors—handfuls of dill, potfuls of meat—and bellyfuls of rustic home cooking. Hungarian and Czech cuisine was very much influenced by the area's natural resources. Because this region is truly landlocked, fish preparations took a back seat to game, poultry and beef. There is a rich tradition of inventive vegetable preparations, hearty soups, rich goulash and everything paprikash! Hungary is forever linked to the small red pepper plant from which paprika is harvested. Many American cooks add paprika for the color it imbues rather than the flavor it imparts. Hungarians have known for centuries that paprika's spicy and potent properties help kick the taste up a notch. In a most interesting twist of fate, in 1937, Dr. Szent Gyorgyi, a Hungarian national, won the Nobel Prize for his work with paprika pepper pods. As the political climate began to change in Hungary, Dr. Gyorgyi facilitated the escape of his Jewish friends, worked with the underground resistance and even used his notoriety as a scientist to secretly negotiate with the Allies on behalf of his government. Our Hungarian and Czech survivors are a living reminder of staunch fortitude. It is with great respect that we present the moving stories and piquant recipes remembered by these intrepid survivors.

RECIPES

Joan Ferencz's Beef Goulash

Ethel Feuerstein's *Bab Leves*—Hungarian Bean Soup

Ida Frankfurter's Potato Kugel

JH*: *Granatos Kocka* (Grenadier March)—Potatoes and Pasta

Judita Hruza's Poached Carp in Aspic

Lilly Kaplan's Chicken Paprikash

Lilly Kaplan's Hungarian Butter Cookies

George Lang's *Húsvéti töltött csirke*—Stuffed Chicken for Passover

George Lang's Asparagus Pudding

George Lang's *Anyám cseresznyés lepénye*—My Mother's Cherry Cake

Freda Lederer's Passover Stuffed Cabbage

Gale Gand*: Cabbage Strudel

Greta Margolis's *Nockedly*—Hungarian Dumplings

Mary Mayer's Veal Paprikash

Mary Mayer's Raspberry Linzer Tarts

Katherine Noir's Mushroom Barley Soup

Matilda Winkler's "Mama's" Crunchy Beans

Gale Gand*: Myrna's Beef Short Ribs

*Indicates professional contributor

Joan Ferencz

In her own words

Joan greeted me with a broad smile that almost never left her face during our conversation. Her positive attitude came from what she called her philosophy of life. "I mourned for what I lost, but I knew I needed to make a life for myself, and I try very hard not to be bitter, nobody likes a bitter person."

I will never forget my childhood in Sziget, Hungary. I was the sixth child in a family of eight born to a father who was a small businessman and a mother who was a homemaker. What stands out for me were the holidays. Every holiday was observed, and every holiday was really very festive and social. Passover was my favorite because it was so exciting in my house. The Passover dishes were kept in the attic, and I remember running up the stairs to bring down the dishes, scrubbing and cleaning everything for the week ahead. At our seder, we would invite so many guests, and my father would sit at the head of the table, dressed in his white robe; I can just see it now. I was mesmerized by Elijah's cup, and when I was asked to open the door for Elijah, I remember being so scared that he might actually be standing there.

Our lives changed in 1944 when I was just a teenager, when Eichmann came to Hungary and hurried to finish the Final Solution. By spring, Hungary was occupied, and we were relocated to the ghetto. Within a month, we were ordered to pack our bags and report to the train station. I really didn't know what our fate would be. When you are a young girl, you listen, but the facts don't really penetrate. We made the trip to Auschwitz as a family, but once in the camp, only my two sisters and I remained together. I clearly remember a day when we were separated on two different lines, and I knew that one sister's line to the left would not survive. Slowly I crept toward my sister and stretched out my hand for her to take hold. I pulled her over to my line, to safety. She became a mother and a grandmother; that was my reward. The three of us were sent to several German towns, where we worked at oil refineries, repaired railroad tracks and ultimately on an assembly line inspecting bullets.

The Allies were continually dropping bombs, as our work camp looked very much like a military base. While sleeping in our barrack, a bomb dropped a mere half a yard away from me. Miraculously, it did not explode. The soft ground absorbed the bomb, and we were spared. I came out of the war without a scratch; others who worked beside me were not as lucky. The Russians liberated me after a six-week march that ended in Czechoslovakia. I returned to my hometown, where I went to a soup kitchen that some valiant Jewish men had stocked.

These returning prisoners of forced labor gathered linens and supplies from townspeople; all items had formerly been in Jewish households. I am proud to say I married one of those men. It didn't happen right away, and our story is pretty funny. I went to Prague to be with my sister and then from Prague to Paris to await the voyage to go to America. It was in Paris that once again, I bumped into my future husband, Michael. After we spent some time together, he proposed by saying the following, "If nobody marries you in America, I would like to." I left that January in 1947, and in August we reunited in America. He asked if I was married yet and I told him, "You are out of luck, you have to marry me." We were married fifty-two years and have two children and four grandchildren.

Author's Note: I sadly learned that Joan has passed away. May her memory be for a blessing.

Joan Ferencz's Beef Goulash

Joan's cooking style was not very Hungarian, as she embraced an American lifestyle, always cooking wholesome food, nothing from a can. However, one dish she remembers from her childhood was a very pure and authentic Hungarian goulash made simply with seasoned beef in slow simmered broth and thinly sliced potatoes that soften as they cook away in the robust sauce. When slow cooking, don't be tempted to use a higher-quality cut of meat; the cheaper cuts work better, as their extra fat helps the meat melt into assertive, flavorful bites.

Yield: 4 servings
Start to Finish: Under 2 hours

2 pounds beef chuck or shank, cut into 2-inch
  pieces
Kosher salt and pepper
2 tablespoons sweet Hungarian paprika
All-purpose flour, for dredging
3 tablespoons vegetable oil

2 large onions, sliced
2 cups beef broth
4 russet potatoes (about 1 1/2 pounds), peeled
  and cut into 1/2-inch-thick slices
1 teaspoon hot paprika (optional)

Pat the meat dry with a paper towel and season with salt, pepper and sweet paprika. Dredge the beef in the flour, shaking off the excess. Heat the oil in a medium-size Dutch oven or deep covered sauté pan and brown the beef (in batches if necessary) over medium heat for several minutes. When the meat begins to brown, add the sliced onions; continue to cook and stir, over medium heat, until the beef and onions are nicely brown, about 10 minutes longer. Stir in the broth, cover and cook over low heat for 1 hour. After 1 hour, add the sliced potatoes and season to taste with salt and pepper. For an extra kick, add hot paprika. Cover and continue to cook until the potatoes and beef are tender, about 30 minutes. If the sauce is too thick, add additional broth or water.

Ethel Feuerstein and George Feuerstein

In their own words

George Feuerstein and Ethel Duranter Feuerstein know all too well how life can change in an instant. They both know the power of love and the role fate and luck play in your life.

GEORGE

I remember March 19, 1944, as the Germans came into Hungary. Weeks later, I was arrested and put in a Hungarian work camp, a type of jail. After a few months, on October 6, 1944, all the Jews were collected and sent to Germany. I was a barber, and the Germans recruited me to shave and provide haircuts for the SS guards. I did that for six weeks. I was on many work details and always managed to get food to share with others. As the war was drawing to a close, we were moved from the camp and forced to walk twenty-five kilometers. It was on that march that the Americans liberated us. I was not in good shape and was sent to a hospital to recuperate. I looked out the window and saw a shining star. I knew it was my mother watching over me; I think that's why I survived. After recovering, I went to Israel, where I was met by kibbutzim and sent directly into the army as part of the elite guard. Although my siblings and I were separated during the war, we all survived. In 1962, I came to America to visit New York City. I met a woman, and we shared Friday night dinner. She showed me around her city, and on my next visit, just after knowing her thirty-six hours, I proposed.

ETHEL

I was from the town of Ungvár in Hungary. My sister was a seamstress of great talent and renown. Although I was not permitted to attend school, I learned to sew from her. Together we were sent to Auschwitz and left not knowing what had become of our mother. One day, my sister went to a bathroom in the camp and, as fate would have it, bumped into our mother. Because the barracks needed to account for each and every prisoner, you could not add someone to your barrack without sending someone in exchange. Luckily for us, our mother was able to switch with another prisoner, and we were reunited.

My mother told us that when she arrived, Josef Mengele was deciding who should live and who should die. He would point to one line for the sick and elderly and another for the young and healthy. He directed my mother to the line that would perish. She spoke up in German and told him that she was willing to work. He then pointed to the other line, and she was spared. In another twist of fate, my sister had, prior to the war, met a very handsome man while she was on vacation. They fell in love and communicated through the mail. The letters abruptly stopped, and my sister did not expect to ever see this man again.

Unbelievably, she found him in Auschwitz. While he still looked dashing, my sister was wearing ill-fitting clothing and certainly did not look her best. Although he did not recognize her, he recognized her voice. He was now engaged to a woman who had some clout in the camp, and at his request that woman watched over our family. Her protection, and the coincidence of meeting this man, helped us survive.

As the camp was liquidated, we were sent into the woods, where many were killed. Fate stepped in again, and we were saved by liberators who came through the woods on motorcycles. I spent time in a Swedish hospital, where I recuperated fully. While there, my abilities as a seamstress came into play. I met a woman from my hometown who I also knew from Auschwitz. I made a special dress for her that impressed the woman she worked for, who happened to be the Italian consul's wife. The diplomat's wife came to me in her chauffeur-driven limousine to ask me to design and sew clothing for her, explaining, "Why would I travel to Paris, when I could have custom-made clothing right in my own town?" This led to a string of jobs where I was designing and making clothing for some of Europe's most elegant and well-connected women. I was only twenty years old at the time.

Years later, now living in New York, I went on a blind date. George and I fell in love and were married soon after. Together we have three children and four grandchildren.

Ethel Feuerstein's *Bab Leves*—Hungarian Bean Soup

This melting pot Hungarian bean soup is inspired by Ethel's recollection of the flavorful soup she ate in Hungary and still prepares today. Hungarian soups are bountiful, incorporating a variety of vegetables, legumes and meat.

Yield: 8 to 10 servings
Start to Finish: Under 4 hours

2 cups dried beans: kidney, black-eyed, navy
 or mixed
5 tablespoons vegetable oil
2 large onions, diced (about 2 cups)
5 tablespoons all-purpose flour
4 carrots, peeled and diced (about 2 cups)
1 pound smoked turkey (if smoked turkey
 is not available, use smoked chicken or
 any meat of your choice. If the meat is not
 smoked, add a splash of liquid smoke to give
 the dish a smoky flavor)

4 teaspoons kosher salt
1 teaspoon black pepper
2 tablespoons sweet paprika
2 tablespoons finely chopped fresh flat-leaf
 parsley
2 teaspoons garlic powder

In a medium pot, boil the beans for several minutes, drain, then soak them in fresh cold water for 1 hour. Drain and reserve the soaked beans. While the beans soak, prepare the remaining ingredients.

Heat the oil in a large soup pot; cook and stir the onion, over medium-low heat, until soft and translucent, about 10 minutes. Stir in the flour, being sure to coat all the onions. Cook several minutes, allowing the onions to brown to a golden color before adding the beans, carrots, turkey, salt, pepper, paprika, parsley and garlic powder. Add 8 cups of water, or enough water to cover all the ingredients. Bring to a boil, then reduce the heat to low; cover and cook for 1½ to 2 hours or until the beans are tender, adding boiling water as needed if the soup becomes too thick. Cut the meat into bite-size pieces and blend into the soup or serve on the side.

Ida Frankfurter

In her own words

Ida has a war "souvenir" that few others would dare to keep. It became a focal point in her home as part of her Passover table.

I see my surviving as a double miracle, not just because I am alive, but also because I was on the line that was selected to die. We were marching, and two SS officers came to my line. One SS officer pointed to another woman, but the other said in German *andere*, which means "the other"—which was me. Because they miscounted when selecting the initial group, they needed two more people, and I was saved.

I was eighteen when I was transferred from Auschwitz to Peterswaldau in Ober Silesia, to work in a grenade factory. Right before I was liberated, the guard took two of us back to the factory and instructed us to throw the grenades into a swimming pool that the guards audaciously used at the camp. They foolishly thought this would prevent the liberators from discovering what they had been doing. I kept one grenade, the whole thing, but apparently the timer was not set and thankfully never went off. I kept it in my home in Hungary, carefully placing it in a china closet in my little apartment. When we left Hungary quickly, I didn't think about it and left it behind. An aunt of mine went into the apartment and thought it was valuable silver, so she took it for me. I still have it today. Every Pesach, I put it on the table as a reminder that we were slaves, like when we were slaves in Egypt. We are connected with that kind of idea.

I have been married for sixty-two years to my husband, George, also a survivor. I have two adopted children and seven grandchildren.

Ida Frankfurter's Potato Kugel

Like many cooks, Ida prepares familiar dishes with a little of this and a little of that. However, her potato kugel recipe was carefully written for her granddaughter, who wanted to duplicate her grandma's traditional dish. It can stand alone but makes a perfect foundation to soak up a hearty sauce.

Yield: 12 servings
Start to Finish: 1½ hours

5 pounds russet potatoes, peeled and grated
2 medium onions, grated (about 1½ cups)
5 egg whites or 3 whole eggs, beaten
1 cup vegetable oil
1½ to 2 cups all-purpose flour (matzo meal can be substituted at Passover)
2 teaspoons kosher salt
½ teaspoon black pepper

Preheat the oven to 350 degrees and lightly grease a 13 x 9 x 2-inch baking dish.

Grate the potatoes and onions, in batches, using the metal blade or fine shredding disc of the food processor; use the pulse feature to capture and process the small chunks. You can instead use a box grater. Spoon the mixture into a bowl. Add the eggs, oil and enough flour to absorb the liquid. The mixture should resemble thin rice pudding and a spoon should fall from side to side if placed in the mixture. Season with salt and pepper (see feedback).

Pour the batter into the prepared baking dish. Fill to 1 inch below the rim of the dish. (If you have any remaining potato mixture, refrigerate to make latkes at another time.) Bake uncovered for 1¼ hours, or until the kugel is a medium brown on top and set in the middle.

Feedback
Once a kugel is baked, it is impossible to adjust the salt and pepper. It is also hard to taste before cooking because of the raw ingredients. A simple solution is to fry a small amount of the mixture in hot oil, adjust the seasonings and then proceed with the remainder of the recipe.

Dr. Judita Hruza

In her own words

Judita grew up on the Hungarian border and, like many Hungarian Jews, lived a restricted but relatively safe life in Hungary, even as the war progressed. That was until 1944, when the Germans came and deported her parents. It was then that she was sent to a little town on the Hungarian-Austrian border where she worked digging trenches to buffer against Soviet army attacks. Her memories prior to the war were happy and typical. However, one memory, related to food, has an almost ironic meaning for her.

I was a laborer in a work camp in Austria when one day I was sent to clean a house on the grounds of the camp. I was very grateful for the assignment, as it was a break from the heavy work of digging trenches and I felt fortunate to be working indoors. While cleaning the house, I needed to get hot water, so I took my bucket and went to fill it, when I smelled something cooking in the kitchen. There was an old lady in there making something that smelled so wonderful. I recognized the aroma of sweet fried onions. The woman took pity on me, asking me if I was hungry. I, of course, said yes. She filled a little box for me with the food she was preparing. When I returned to the barrack, I hid it under my jacket because I was fearful that there was not enough to share with everyone. My mother's best friend was with me in the camp, and together we ate the dish in secrecy. Although it was now cold, I don't think I ever enjoyed any food as much as that.

I had never eaten a dish like this at home, as my mother was very health conscious, and we ate lots of vegetables. This dish, which was a combination of pasta, potatoes and fried onions, I later learned it is called Grenadier March. Although this is a dish I associate with a terrible part of my life, I continued to make it after the war because I have such a strong memory of enjoying it that day.

After the war, I went to a DP camp and then back to Hungary. I discovered my brother, who had obtained false papers, had also survived, but that most of my extended family, twelve members, had perished in Auschwitz. Eventually, I went to Sweden, where I earned my medical license and was a practicing pediatrician for twenty years. When I arrived in America, in 1970, I became a psychiatrist. I have two children and four beautiful grandchildren.

Granatos Kocka (Grenadier March)—Potatoes and Pasta

If it is true that armies march on their stomachs, then it is understandable how this dish evolved. This nutritious, carb-loving concoction was a favorite of Hungarian foot soldiers because it provided energy from potatoes, pasta and onions. It's really a deconstructed pierogi, with the potato and onion filling keeping company with the noodle, rather than being tucked inside it.

Yield: About 8 servings
Start to Finish: Under 45 minutes

1½ pounds potatoes (Red Bliss, Yukon Gold or russet), peeled and quartered
6 ounces uncooked pasta (can be broad noodles, bowtie, broken lasagna noodles, your choice)

½ cup chicken fat or vegetable oil
1 large onion, chopped (about 1 cup)
Kosher salt and pepper

Preheat the oven to 350 degrees. Bring a large pot of salted water to boil. Cook the potatoes until very tender, about 20 minutes. While the potatoes cook, bring another pot of water to boil and cook the noodles according to package directions, drain and reserve.

Heat the fat or oil in a large skillet; cook and stir the onions, over medium heat, until nicely browned, about 15 minutes. When the potatoes are ready, remove them from the pot with a slotted spoon and place them directly into the skillet with the cooked onions. Let them settle in and then lightly mash.

Season to taste with salt and pepper. Stir the pasta into the potato and onion mixture. Serve as is, or spoon into a lightly greased casserole and bake at 350 degrees for 20 minutes, until the top is lightly browned.

JH

Judita Hruza's Poached Carp in Aspic

Judita explains, "This dish has an extra special meaning for me. As a child I was a very poor eater; every meal was a cumbersome chore for me. I had a few favorites like this carp, which was on the top of my list. My grandmother used to make it for Passover dinner. One time she made it for me at a casual visit. Since we came between mealtimes, my grandma served my food to me on a tray and left me alone. I began to eat, and suddenly I felt very sad and started to cry. My grandma came running from the kitchen, alarmed: 'What's wrong? Don't you like it?' 'No,' I replied, 'It's not the same.' I was five, and I couldn't put into words what I was feeling. Looking back years later, I realized what had made me so sad. Sitting there alone, I was desperately missing the faces around the table, my extended family who had gathered here from all parts of the country for this one occasion, all in their fancy clothes, happy to see each other, me saying my *Ma Nishtana* (a reading from the Passover seder book *Haggadah*), the ceremonies, my little finger dipping in the wine, my grandfather telling the story that I never got tired of hearing again and again. The fish didn't taste the same eating it by myself in the big dining room. Luckily, we had several more Passover seders before the start of the war. Here is the dish I remember so vividly."

Yield: 6 to 8 servings
Start to Finish: 2 to 3 hours to salt the fish, then under 2 hours cooking time. The fish then chills for at least 4 and up to 24 hours.

1 whole carp* (about 5 pounds), cleaned, head and tail removed and reserved
Kosher salt
3 medium onions, sliced
2 parsley roots (parsnips), peeled and sliced ½ inch thick

3 carrots, peeled and sliced ½ inch thick
1 teaspoon paprika
1 package unflavored gelatin

Have your fishmonger clean and cut the fish for you. Liberally salt the fish and let it sit covered in the fridge for 2 to 3 hours. Place the vegetables in the bottom of a pot designed for poaching or use a shallow pot large enough to hold the fish submerged in water. Place the salted carp, head and tail on top of the vegetables, season with paprika and cover with cold water. Simmer on the stove, over low heat for 1 hour, or until the carp is moist and flaky and fully cooked.

Remove the carp and continue to let the vegetables, head and tail cook until the vegetables are very tender and the broth begins to thicken. Strain the broth, discarding the solids. Sprinkle a little of the gelatin into the broth and stir to dissolve. (Although the broth should gel on its own, the gelatin gives it a little extra help.) Put the carp in a dish deep enough to hold both the fish and the reserved liquid. Pour the liquid over the fish, cover and refrigerate several hours or overnight to allow the broth to set. Serve the fish with the jelly.

*Carp was a very popular fish in eastern Europe, and while still eaten today, especially at Passover, where it is a common component in gefilte fish, carp is not always readily available. It is also a very bony fish and difficult to filet. Pike or whitefish are easy substitutes for carp.

Lilly Schwarcz Kaplan

In her own words

Lilly Kaplan was always considered to be one of the most reputable and active realtors in New Rochelle, New York, my hometown. In addition to being a successful businesswoman, she was a wonderful homemaker, wife and mother to her two daughters. Her home always smelled of delicious home-cooked meals, which she loved to share with extended family and friends. In addition to her love of good food, Lilly instilled in her family a love of Israel, Jewish customs and values and the importance of *tikkun olam* (repairing the world) and *tzedakah* (charity).

I was born in Ungvár, the oldest child, having a younger sister and three younger brothers. Before the war, my family ran a wholesale bakery business. As a young teenager, I often worked alongside my parents. I was good in math and helped with the recordkeeping. On Fridays, people in town would bring us their pots filled with cholent so we could slow roast the cholent overnight in our commercial ovens. After Shabbos services, everyone would come to the bakery and collect their pots. I have to admit that on rare occasions, a few people were given someone else's pot, which got them upset. It struck me as funny that people would always know their own cholent from the dozens in the oven. I remember my mother inviting Yeshiva students who were coming through town to our Shabbos table.

Lilly Kaplan, Sweden, late 1940s–1950.

The war came to our area in 1944. Everyone in the family (except my father, who was forced to serve in a labor battalion) was deported to Auschwitz. On our arrival, I was separated from my family and chosen for work detail. My mother, grandmother and siblings were sent to the other group and perished. After I was liberated from Auschwitz, I was very ill with tuberculosis and typhus. I was fortunate to be sent to a hospital in Sweden. I received word in the hospital that my father had also survived, but I was hesitant about contacting him right away because I thought I was dying and wanted to spare him additional heartache. I did make a full recovery and made contact with my father. In Sweden, I received an education and got a job. I later reunited with my father in New York after trying for several years to get him out of a DP camp in Germany. I married my husband, Lew Kaplan, an American from the Bronx, shortly after I came to New York, and we were married for forty-seven years, until he passed away in 1998.

I didn't talk about the war very much when my children were growing up. I didn't want to burden them. I loved cooking and baking and felt it was one way that I was caring for my husband and girls. I always made everything myself. I relied on my instincts and educated guesswork to create meals for my family. My motto was, "If you can read, you can cook." After losing so many of my own family members in the war, I feel blessed that I have such a loving family especially my two wonderful daughters (and their husbands) and my four beautiful grandchildren.

Author's Note: I sadly learned that Lilly has passed away. Since that time she would have loved knowing that her family has grown to include five great-grandchildren. May her memory be for a blessing.

Lilly Kaplan's Chicken Paprikash

This authentic Hungarian specialty features plenty of paprika, which lends a rich red color and subtle spicy flavor to this popular chicken dish. While Lilly uses sweet paprika, for an extra jolt of flavor, add a teaspoon of hot or smoked paprika.

Yield: 4 servings
Start to Finish: Under 2 hours

3 tablespoons olive oil
2 medium onions, sliced
4 garlic cloves, chopped
4 pounds chicken parts, on the bone, skin
 removed
1 (14-ounce) can chopped tomatoes

1 cup chicken broth
¼ cup white wine
2 teaspoons sweet paprika
Kosher salt and pepper
1 green pepper, cored, seeded and sliced

Heat the olive oil in a large sauté pan; cook and stir the onions and garlic over medium heat until lightly browned, about 15 minutes. Remove with a slotted spoon and reserve. In the same pan (adding more oil if needed), brown the chicken pieces in batches and set aside on a plate. When all the chicken is browned, add the chicken (not the juice that has collected), onions and garlic back into the pan. Stir in the tomatoes, chicken broth, white wine, paprika, salt and pepper to taste. Top with the green pepper slices.

Simmer, covered, for 45 to 60 minutes, or until the chicken is tender and cooked through. Remove the chicken to a serving platter and bring the sauce to a slow boil. If the sauce is too thin, thicken it by creating a roux. In a skillet, heat 2 teaspoons of oil and then blend in 2 teaspoons of flour, stirring constantly to avoid burning the roux. You'll want it to be a light blonde color. Let the roux cool a bit, and then stir it into the sauce; cook for several minutes to let it do its thing. If the sauce is still not thick enough, repeat the above process. Pour the sauce over the chicken and serve with noodles or dumplings. See Greta Margolis's dumpling recipe (page 269).

Feedback
Paprika can be hot, sweet and several degrees in between. Look for pure Hungarian paprika; it's worth the difference. And be sure never to add paprika directly into a dry pan; it will burn quickly as it releases its natural sugar.

Lilly Kaplan's Hungarian Butter Cookies

Lilly maintains that it is easier to bake than to go to the bakery. Pretty funny when you consider her family was in the commercial bakery business. Her daughter adds, "We never had a bakery box in the house!" Lilly shares with us her simple, foolproof, light and crisp butter cookie recipe. The dough is delicate, so work quickly.

Yield: About 3 to 4 dozen cookies
Start to Finish: Under 30 minutes

1 stick (½ cup) butter, room temperature
¼ cup confectioners' sugar
½ teaspoon almond extract

1 cup all-purpose flour plus 2 tablespoons confectioners' sugar for dusting

Beat the butter, sugar and almond extract on medium speed until creamy. Lower the speed and slowly add the flour until a dough forms. Divide the dough into two pieces, flatten each into a disc and wrap in waxed paper. Chill the dough in the fridge while the oven heats.

Preheat the oven to 400 degrees and lightly grease a large baking sheet or line it with parchment paper or a nonstick silicone mat. When the oven is heated, remove the first piece of dough from the fridge.

Generously flour your work surface and the rolling pin and roll the dough to ¼ inch thick. Cut the dough with a cookie cutter, any size and shape you choose. Lilly would use the rim of a glass and overlap it to create half-moon shapes. Gently lift the cookies with a cookie spatula and place them on the prepared cookie sheet.

Bake for 10 minutes or until the cookies are a very light golden color. Do not overbake. The cookies will develop a burnt taste if they are too brown. When cool, sprinkle with confectioners' sugar.

Feedback

The grocery shelves are now lined with specialty extracts. The extracts are very concentrated and impart a real burst of flavor. In this recipe, you might try substituting lemon or orange extract for the almond; it adds a refreshing note.

George Lang

Based on our conversation and excerpts from his memoir

Stepping into the legendary restaurateur George Lang's office on New York's Upper West Side was like stepping into a perfect culinary library. I was surrounded by thousands of cookbooks, some dating to the nineteenth century. The cover of his memoir, *Nobody Knows the Truffles I've Seen*, terms him a restaurateur-raconteur extraordinaire. It didn't take long for me to realize that was not hyperbole. We talked about his transformation from Hungarian violin virtuoso to a beloved American restaurant consultant. Here is just a glimpse into his remarkable journey.

George remembers much about his childhood in Hungary, explaining,

George Lang as a child in Hungary.

> I was brought up in an unusual Jewish home. My father was a genius in 200 different ways, but he could barely read or write. He didn't believe in religion. My mother was very religious; her father was a Rabbi. Our kitchen was about as kosher as you could get. At Pesach (Passover), I particularly loved the after-dinner stories, but we practiced a particular Jewish, non-Jewish, Jewish. I felt ashamed of being a weak minority, but then I turned around. Every five seconds there was anti-Semitism in Hungary. I was an alien in my own hometown. Anti-Semitism was not institutionalized, though, like other Hungarian national sports; it enjoyed great popularity.

Life changed dramatically for George on February 6, 1944, the day he boarded the train to report to a forced labor camp. Prior to going, he and his father hid his prized violin and his mother's jewelry at a family friend's farm. Through a series of events, all orchestrated by George, he escaped the camp by obtaining false documents. He assumed the last name Hegedüs, which in Hungarian means "violinist." He made his way to Budapest, which was in upheaval. The ruthless Arrowcross Party had taken over the city, while the Russians were encroaching on the city's borders.

George made the daring decision to join the Arrowcross, not only to keep himself alive but also to facilitate lending a helping hand to other Jews caught in the turmoil.

> *During the next three weeks, we organized rescue missions in a number of safe-houses and yellow star ghetto buildings, and our little group succeeded in bringing out a couple of dozen people without a shot being fired.*

As the war ended, and the Russians took control of the city, George was charged with war crimes related to his brief service with the Arrowcross. After being incarcerated and standing trial, the judges of the People's Court weighed the evidence and concluded the following:

> *Based on all the facts, however, the activities of the accused were directed exclusively toward helping his despondent fellow humans living under abject conditions, bringing medicine, doctors and food to them, and these activities certainly did not help in the continuation of the power of the Arrowcross movement—which was the main point of the charges. Furthermore, his activities were actually instrumental in the cessation of Arrowcross power.*

It was now September 1945, and having been acquitted of all charges, George moved on with his life. He learned that both his parents were deported and perished in Auschwitz. He discovered few family members survived the war but was able to reunite with a cousin, Evi, and her new husband, Victor.

Both remained close to George over the next sixty years. George knew he needed to leave Hungary, so he connected with a group that smuggled people across the border into Austria. At the time, he didn't realize it would entail his hiding in a black coffin and traveling over the border in the back of a hearse. George remained in Austria, saving money and working with the HIAS for passage to America.

In July 1946, George left Vienna and boarded the SS *Marine Flasher*. He movingly describes the moment he entered New York Harbor:

> *Hundreds of my fellow refugees were crammed together into a single cheering crowd. With a few of them, I climbed to a small platform on the deck, and there she was, the Statue of Liberty, seemingly within touching distance. I had my trusty violin and my paper-mache valise (tied with a piece of string), and I was wearing a tie, since I felt I should be properly dressed for the occasion. I like to believe that everybody is entitled to one miracle in a lifetime. My allotment was the miracle of my survival between February 6, 1944, the first day of my life in the labor camp, and July 15, 1946, when I first saw Lady Liberty.*

Lang continued his musical aspirations, playing with such orchestras as the Dallas Symphony, but after hearing Jascha Heifetz play his beloved Mendelssohn, George realized he was never going to be the best violinist. Luckily for the food world, he directed his attention to the culinary arts. He started modestly, cleaning vegetables and then

George and his beloved violin.

What is important is to find out why the Jews took certain dishes from other countries. I can't think of a Jewish food that doesn't taste good. I've tasted every food on earth. I could live nicely without broiled steak, but not without fried chicken. I love dishes presented beautifully. I like the kind of dessert that if your mother is a very good baker, you would get the dessert you deserve.

As for Hungarian food, George maintains,

Even Hungarians don't agree on it. I discovered that cooking is influenced by the nature of your country. Every age of Hungarian cooking is defined not only by whom they conquered, but also by who conquered them. And I love paprika!

working at a banquet facility on the Lower East Side. George found his true talent, organizing and arranging the most lavish affairs. He had seamlessly made the leap from Hungarian Holocaust survivor to New York's premier restaurateur, bon vivant and master of fabulous fetes. He elevated dining to a new level and developed the concept of food as entertainment. He planned events for such dignitaries as Khrushchev and Queen Elizabeth. Possibly his crowning culinary glory was resurrecting Hungary's national treasure, Gundel, in Budapest. His pride and joy for nearly thirty-five years was New York's legendary Cafe des Artistes, which he bought in 1975. The Cafe, as he liked to call it, was run by his wife, Jenifer, whose cooking he touts as being "the best in the city." In turning his attention to food, George has some very strong beliefs.

At the Cafe, George would feature a Hungarian tasting menu and offer one dish daily that he called "poor people's good food." George confessed that sometimes that was his favorite dish of the day. "If I am inventive enough, I can come up with dishes, cooking methods, service, everything which has individual power and character that even though it doesn't have caviar and truffles, it becomes rich man's food."

When I asked what he has learned from his experiences during the Holocaust and what he wants his legacy to be, he answers quickly and assuredly:

I define myself in a number of ways, but I want to create things that are wonderful, beautiful and useful. I consider life fabulous and wonderful and it depends on what you do to it, not what people do to you. I have learned that no condition is so bad that you cannot survive it or on rare occasion, even change it.

George and Jenifer have two children.

With his gracious permission, I pored over George Lang's remarkable books to select the recipes to be included with his equally remarkable story. This was like letting a botanist loose in botanical gardens and telling him to pick the most fragrant flower. The history of Hungarian cuisine is poetically detailed in his eponymous *George Lang's Cuisine of Hungary* (Wings Books, 1994). It reads like a culinary journey and reveals how his love and respect for Hungarian cooking holds a deep-rooted meaning in his life. The journey begins, aptly, with soup and ends with a dessert that has special significance to George. As they say in Hungarian, *Elvéz!* Enjoy!

Author's Note: I sadly learned that George has passed away. May his memory be for a blessing.

George Lang's *Húsvéti töltött csirke*—Stuffed Chicken for Passover

Excerpted from George Lang's *Cuisine of Hungary* (Wings Books, 1994)

This matzo-stuffed chicken is Jewish family fare during Passover holidays. The stuffing is so different from the usual bread-based kind that regardless of religion or time of year, you should try it. If you are able, put some of the stuffing under the skin of the bird.

6 to 8 servings

1 fat fowl, 4 to 4½ pounds
3 whole pieces of matzo
½ small onion, chopped fine
¾ cup rendered chicken fat*
4 chicken livers, very carefully cleaned**
1 tablespoon chopped parsley
¼ pound mushrooms, chopped
Salt and pepper

2 eggs
2 tablespoons crushed matzo
1 medium-sized very ripe tomato, cut into
 pieces
1 medium-sized onion, sliced
1 green pepper, sliced
1 garlic clove, mashed

Soak the chicken in salted ice-cold water for 1 hour. Soak matzo in lukewarm water till soft, then squeeze until dry.

Cook chopped onion, covered, in 2 tablespoons of the chicken fat; do not brown. After 5 minutes add chicken livers, parsley and mushrooms. Cook, covered, for another 5 minutes. Let the mixture cool.

Add squeezed matzo and put the whole mixture through the grinder. Add salt and pepper to taste. Add eggs and crushed matzo and mix well. Let the stuffing rest for a couple of hours.

Mix in 6 tablespoons chicken fat.

Remove chicken from ice-cold water, wipe it well inside and outside and salt it. Fill with the stuffing. Sew up the opening.

Spread 2 tablespoons of chicken fat on the bottom of a baking pan. Put in tomato, sliced onion and green pepper. Add garlic, a sprinkle of salt and ¼ cup water. Spread remaining 2 tablespoons fat on top of the chicken, put the chicken in the pan, cover the pan and cook the chicken on top of the stove over low heat. Baste often.

Preheat the oven to 475 degrees F. When the chicken is done, take it out of the pan and keep it warm. Put vegetables through a sieve or blender to make sauce.

Put chicken back in the pan and place it in the preheated oven for about 10 minutes to make it brown and crisp.

Serve the sauce separately. Accompany with egg noodles, boiled and then sautéed in chicken fat for a few minutes, or rice.

*You can buy chicken fat at almost any market, or render your own (see recipe on page 33).
**For kosher preparation, broil the livers before adding them to the pan.

In his chapter on vegetables, Mr. Lang writes, "In Hungary, vegetables are not just *cooked*, they are *prepared*. The difference between an American vegetable dish and a Hungarian one is similar to the difference between plain boiled meat and a meat stew." You only need to visit his New York office to experience his love affair with asparagus. "I love single ideas, like asparagus," he explained as I gazed at the hundreds of asparagus-inspired objects that fill his office shelves. The following recipe is George's tribute to the simple stalk.

George Lang's Asparagus Pudding

Excerpted from George Lang's *Cuisine of Hungary* (Wings Books, 1994)

6 servings

1 pound fresh young asparagus	4 tablespoons butter
Salt	4 eggs separated
1 roll	4 tablespoons sour cream
½ cup milk	

Peel the asparagus and cut slantwise into 1-inch pieces. Place in a saucepan with 1 cup water and 1 teaspoon salt. Cook until done, but it should be almost crunchy and not soft. Drain.

Soak the roll in the milk, then squeeze. Thoroughly butter a pudding mold with 2 tablespoons of the butter.

Whip the rest of the butter till foamy. Add the roll, egg yolks, sour cream and 1 teaspoon salt. Whip till well mixed and fluffy.

Whip egg whites stiff and fold them in gently with a rubber spatula. Combine the mixture with the cooked asparagus; do it very carefully so as not to break the egg-white foam.

Pour the mixture into the buttered pudding mold. Do not fill mold more than ¾ full. Put on a tight-fitting top.

Fill a 4-quart pot half full of hot water. Set pudding mold into the pot and cook, with the cover on, for 1 hour.

Variation: To serve this as an appetizer, sauté 1 cup bread crumbs in ¼ pound butter until golden brown; pour crumbs on top of pudding or spoon a little over each slice. You may also combine the breadcrumb mixture with grated cheese.

George Lang's *Anyám cseresznyés lepénye*

My Mother's Cherry Cake

Excerpted from George Lang's *Cuisine of Hungary* (Wings Books, 1994)

Summer luncheons of my childhood often ended with this dessert. This cherry cake is all that a cake should be.

10 to 12 pieces

1 pound fresh cherries
³⁄₈ pound sweet butter
¾ cup granulated sugar
3 eggs, separated

1 cup flour
Pinch of salt
¼ cup bread crumbs
Vanilla sugar

Pit cherries, taking care not to split them. Set aside. Preheat oven to 375 degrees F.

Mix butter well with half of the granulated sugar. After a few minutes of vigorous whipping add egg yolks and continue whipping. Finally add flour and salt.

Beat egg whites with remaining granulated sugar till the mixture is stiff and forms peaks. With a rubber spatula, gently fold it into the butter mixture.

Butter a baking pan 10 x 6 inches and sprinkle it with bread crumbs. Put dough in pan, and top with cherries.

Bake in the preheated oven for 30 minutes. Before serving, sprinkle with vanilla sugar.

Freda Lederer

In her own words

My meeting with Freda was warm, friendly and full of positive energy. She credited her survival as "a combination of luck and perseverance." She was quick to point out, "You roll with the punches, instead of being bitter and complaining. Every day you have a new opportunity to make the best of this life and take the challenges that come your way."

Although I was born in Mukaevo (Mukacheve), Czechoslovakia, my new passport, which I renewed a few years ago, said I was born in the Ukraine, because the borders have changed. I was the only girl in a family of five children. We were a religious family, and my father was a small businessman. I was the only one who had gone through high school. At the time, it wasn't acceptable for a girl to be educated, but I was very adamant. I went to a public school and graduated in May 1944. After the school year was over, the graduates had to take oral and written tests to officially pass your graduation. At the time I had to take these exams, I was in the ghetto. I had a wonderful teacher who arranged for me to come and go out of the ghetto so I could take these tests. I was so naive; I didn't realize what was waiting for me. In June 1944, after I graduated, the entire ghetto was liquidated, and we were taken to Auschwitz. From the first minute on, I was separated from my family. I was only nineteen.

My first stroke of luck was that a German industrialist needed three hundred young people to work in his factory making radar parts. He pointed to me and asked if I spoke German; I answered him in German saying that I graduated from high school. He pushed me to the side where he was gathering people for work. After I was there for a few months, they needed people to work in a town near Hamburg. The Allies were bombing Hamburg day and night. The Germans marched us to the nearest camp, which was Bergen-Belsen. I think someone up in heaven was looking out for me because after three weeks, in April 1945, the British army liberated the camp. The British went out of their way; if not for them I would not be alive. I was very sick, and they requisitioned private German homes and made them into makeshift hospitals. A Swedish doctor came by and asked if I would like to go to Sweden to recuperate. I said yes and went to Sweden, where I stayed with a Jewish family for one year.

Through the Red Cross I found that three of my brothers survived as well and were in a DP camp in Germany. I left Sweden and we were reunited. At that time, President Truman mandated that ninety thousand refugees were permitted to enter the United States without a direct sponsor. I was sponsored by the Harrisburg community. That's where I settled; that's where I stayed. The rabbi there has said, "It was a good marriage." It takes time to become an American. At first, I saw myself as a refugee; you don't become an American instantaneously. I was married twenty-eight years and have three children, five grandchildren and two great-grandchildren.

Freda Lederer's Passover Stuffed Cabbage

Every year, Freda would host both seders at her house with her entire extended family. Her most famous dish was her stuffed cabbage. Freda says, "This is the original recipe" she ate as a child, but notes, "I had no idea how to make it then, and I really didn't care." Lucky for us, she does now. Freda's version is clean and simple with a definite sweet-and-sour tug-of-war. She prefers using a small head of cabbage, feeling the leaves are a better size to stuff and the head of cabbage is easier to handle.

Yield: 15 to 18 rolls
Start to Finish: Under 2 hours

1 small green cabbage (about 1½ pounds), boiled

FOR THE FILLING
3 tablespoons vegetable oil
1 pound ground beef
1 large onion, chopped (about 1 cup)
1 piece matzo, soaked until soft, then squeezed dry
2 eggs, beaten
½ cup water
¾ teaspoon kosher salt
¼ teaspoon black pepper

FOR THE SAUCE
1 (15-ounce) can tomato sauce
15 ounces water (fill the tomato sauce can)
2–3 tablespoons sugar
Juice of 2 lemons or a pinch of sour salt

Bring a large pot of salted water to boil. Prepare the cabbage by removing the center core. Cook the whole cabbage until the leaves begin to wilt, at least 15 minutes. Carefully remove the cabbage from the water (pierce the cabbage with a large serving fork to lift out of the water, support the cabbage underneath with a large, slotted spoon). Place the cabbage on a dish and let it cool so you can easily begin removing the outer leaves. Keep the water on a low boil in case you need to place the cabbage back in to help loosen the inner leaves. Begin peeling the cabbage; you will need 15 to 18 leaves. Cut a small V-shape in each leaf to remove the hard white rib. Let the leaves hang out on a paper towel to help absorb any remaining water.

Prepare the filling by heating 1 tablespoon of the oil in a skillet, cook and stir the beef, over medium heat, until nicely browned, about 10 minutes, breaking up any large pieces. Remove the meat with a slotted spoon. Discard the liquid from the pan and heat the remaining 2 tablespoons of oil, cook and stir the onions, over medium heat, until lightly browned, about 10 minutes. Combine the onions and meat and let them cool for a few minutes.

While the meat mixture cools, soak the matzo in cold water, until it is soft, but not mushy; it should resemble wet cardboard. Remove from the water and squeeze out as much liquid as possible. Add the matzo to the meat and onions and then stir in the eggs, water, salt and pepper.

In a Dutch oven or covered pot, combine the sauce ingredients. Bring to a boil, and then lower the heat to a slow simmer.

To stuff the cabbage, take a generous spoonful of meat filling and place it in the cabbage leaf. Use more for the larger leaves, less for the smaller. Roll the leaf to cover the meat, tuck in the sides and then continue rolling. You should have a nice, neat package. Place the stuffed cabbage rolls in the sauce, close together, layering if necessary. Cover and cook for 1 to 1½ hours, checking occasionally to see if water needs to be added to the sauce to prevent it from drying out. Serve family style with the sauce spooned over the cabbage rolls.

Variations: Stuffed cabbage was a favorite recipe, as there are several in the book. Lilly Kaplan shared with me an interesting twist to hers. Lilly lines the pot with sauerkraut—1 large can, rinsed and drained—before filling the pot with the cabbage rolls. Additionally, she chops the small inner leaves and adds those to the pot. When the pot is full, she dots the cabbage rolls with about 1 cup of dried Turkish apricots to add a layer of sweetness. If you don't have apricots, you could stir 1 cup of apricot preserves into the sauce instead.

Ruth Stromer also makes a wonderful stuffed cabbage and uses a different method to prepare the cabbage leaves (see page 124 for her recipe and technique).

Gale Gand

Professional contributor

While we have you thinking about cabbage and how it gathers a sweet mellow flavor when slow simmered, you might want to try premier pastry chef Gale Gand's family recipe, which takes cabbage from a main course to a sweet dessert.

Cabbage Strudel

Contributed by Gale Gand, executive pastry chef and owner of Tru restaurant, Chicago

This recipe came from my Hungarian great-grandmother Rose (Frankel) Simon, which she passed down to my grandma Elsie (Simon) Grossman. The story I was told was that my family was poor... so poor they couldn't afford apples for their apple strudel, so they used cabbage as a cheaper substitute, and with enough sugar and cinnamon, apparently it tastes practically like apples.

Makes 1 log or 8 servings

FILLING
¼ cup butter
½ green cabbage, shredded
¼ teaspoon salt
½ cup sugar
½ cup raisins
¼ cup walnut pieces, toasted

3 sheets phyllo pastry, thawed overnight in the refrigerator, if frozen kept moist
8 tablespoons (1 stick) butter, melted
½ cup sugar
1 cup walnuts, lightly toasted and finely chopped

FILLING
In a sauté pan, melt the butter. Heat it to medium-high heat and sauté the cabbage until tender. Add the salt and sugar and stir to dissolve. Add the raisins and cook a few minutes to reduce and thicken any juices. Stir in the walnuts and spread on a sheet pan to cool.

Preheat the oven to 375 degrees.

Line a sheet pan with parchment paper. Transfer 1 sheet of phyllo to the sheet pan. Using a pastry brush, brush the phyllo with butter. Sprinkle with ⅓ of the sugar and ⅓ of the chopped walnuts.

Repeat with the 2 remaining sheets of phyllo. Reserve the remaining melted butter and sugar. Turn the sheet pan so that the phyllo is horizontal to your body. Spoon the cooled cabbage filling 2 inches in from the left-hand edge of the phyllo, working from top to bottom, leaving 2 inches bare at the top and bottom. Turn the sheet pan ¼ turn and roll up the pastry to encase the filling, forming a log. Move the log to the center of the sheet pan and tuck the ends under to keep the filling from oozing out. Brush the surface with melted butter and sprinkle with sugar. Bake until golden brown, about 30 minutes. Let cool 10 to 15 minutes on the pan. Using a serrated knife, cut carefully into sections and serve warm.

Greta Margolis

In her own words

Greta had to assume many different personas to survive the war, first blending in as an Aryan peasant, then a partisan in the woods. Her sharp intellect certainly helped her understand the need to adapt.

I was born in 1937 in Czechoslovakia and was an only child. I remember my childhood very clearly. My father had a lot of friends in the government, and we did receive some protection for a while. My father was a government official, and we left only when his friends advised him it was no longer safe for us to stay. At that time, in 1943, many people had already been taken by trucks and trains and disappeared forever. We had papers with false names, and leaving everything behind, we traveled west to the capital of Slovakia. My parents felt that in a big city we could get lost. We stayed in a hotel for a while and then decided to move again to another town. We stayed there until the Germans invaded and then we ran for our lives.

Greta, age ten, at a ballet recital in 1947.

We wound up in a tiny farming village. Our being Jewish was always an issue, even though we had papers stating we were Aryan. However, we looked different, our demeanor was different and we did not blend in well. My father had money and paid a family so that we could live in their home. I didn't go to the school, which was in another village, but I helped my mother and the farmer's wife with the cooking, while my father did chores. I never felt like I was home. I didn't play with the neighbor's children, and I always understood the danger of being found. I stayed close to my parents.

Every so often, we would have to flee into the woods and join the partisans. We would stay in a bunker until it was safe to return. In 1945, the Russian troops came through the woods and liberated us. Trucks ran through the village, filled with Russian soldiers. It was on such a truck that I was returned to my home. The soldiers were friendly and nice; they knew we had been through a very traumatic period. I do remember that they took my father's watch. Some of the soldiers had their arms lined up and down with watches. We felt it was a small price to pay for our freedom. We returned home and found my grandparents, who lived in our same small town. Their house was intact, and they had survived, having been hidden by an uncle. I always knew we would come to America. My mother's entire family was here, but our papers had not come through in time to avoid the war. Right after we were liberated, my father began the process again. Three and a half years later, in 1948, we came to the Bronx, New York.

I was only eleven and spoke not a word of English. I started school right after Christmas, and by June, I was fluent. I skipped several grades and graduated from the sixth grade that summer. I enjoy the holidays and try to cook like my mom, who made many Hungarian dishes, even though we weren't Hungarian. My mother never taught me to cook, but I enjoy it and love incorporating all styles of cooking. I am married to my husband, Martin, almost fifty-two years. Together we have two sons and five wonderful grandchildren.

Greta Margolis's *Nockedly*—Hungarian Dumplings

Greta remembers her mother making these dumplings. "She would put the dough on a flat plate and with the side of a tablespoon, push little pieces into the pot of boiling water. These are excellent with any gravy or sauce."

Yield: 4 servings
Start to Finish: Under 30 minutes

1 cup all-purpose flour
2 eggs, beaten

Kosher salt and pepper
1 tablespoon water

Bring a large pot of salted water to boil.

Stir the flour into the beaten eggs, season with a pinch of salt and pepper and add 1 tablespoon of water to create the dough. Knead the dough for a couple of minutes; it should be smooth, elastic and not too sticky. If you need additional water or flour, feel free to add it to achieve the right consistency. When the water boils, place the dough on a plate, and using a tablespoon, cut the dough into 1-inch pieces, pushing the dough into the boiling water with the spoon. You might need to dip the spoon into the water to help slide the dumplings off the plate. Cover and cook until the water returns to a rapid boil. When the water boils, lower the temperature and gently boil, covered, for 15 minutes. Drain and rinse quickly in cold water.

Serve with gravy, sauce or lightly fried onions. These dumplings are an authentic addition to many Hungarian dishes. Try serving them with Lilly Kaplan's Chicken Paprikash (see page 252).

Mary Fenyes Mayer

In her own words

I met Mary at her home, and she greeted me at the door with an apology. She was sorry that she felt she had no story to tell. Three hours later, I left with a remarkable story, terrific Hungarian recipes and a care package of cookies for my husband.

I was born into a privileged family in Budapest, Hungary. My father was the president of an oil company, and my mother was a homemaker who had five servants to do much of the work. I sometimes compare my mother to the lead character in *A Streetcar Named Desire*. She was a good and loving mother who had an unusual view of the world. On September 1, 1939, after having spent the summer in Switzerland, one of my governesses came to take me home on a Red Cross train. My family felt there was little danger for us in Hungary, as my father was a decorated soldier and revered in our mostly non-Jewish community. Everything changed on May 23, 1944, when my father was first saluted, then arrested by the Gestapo. He was taken as a hostage, along with several Gentile executives, and held in a nearby hotel for ransom. Unbelievable amounts of money were paid for their freedom; however, they were taken away and never seen again.

At that time, my mother and I were given fifteen minutes to vacate our beautiful home, which had a wonderful rose garden. My mother remained in a "safe house" under the protection of Raoul Wallenberg. I was forced to work on a farm and then in a factory, where I worked very hard. A daily roll call stopped me from trying to escape, as we were told that if you were not accounted for, your family would be punished or shot. The first of several fortunate circumstances that changed my destiny occurred on a quiet July day. The factory I worked in was severely bombed on July 2, 1944. I was not in my usual bunker but in the Gentile section, which was off-limits during the week. I took the opportunity and the distraction the explosions created to escape. I remember calmly walking the twenty kilometers to my German governess's home and removing the yellow star from my clothing so people would not know I was Jewish. The next day, she arranged for me to have legal papers that had been secured by the daughter of my French governess. I assumed that young girl's identity. The risk these two loyal and loving women took by helping me was tantamount to being a Jew, since harboring or helping a Jew was punishable by death.

Circumstances continued to unravel as Hungary became more and more dangerous. I evaded arrest and capture several times, once because a stranger advised me not to return home. To this day, I believe that stranger was the angel Gabriel, sent to save me. I boarded a train to St. Endre, a village located north of Budapest on the Danube River. Upon arriving at the train station, I took a help wanted ad that was posted on a wall and decided to answer it. When I knocked on the door of the couple

Mary Mayer.

Once again, a stranger guided me to safety. This time, it was an important high-ranking Russian officer who was billeted with the couple I worked for. At first, I spoke to him in German but quickly realized that was offending him. I then spoke to him in French, explaining my circumstances. Miraculously, this Russian officer spoke French as well and, after hearing my story, provided me with a cadre of soldiers to escort me home to find my mother. He gave me a letter that would open every door; I called it a passport to safety. Unfortunately, when we got to the river, the Germans had blown up the bridges connecting the two sides of Budapest. I returned to St. Endre, crossed the frozen Danube and walked the twenty kilometers home! I finally made it and was reunited with my mother. I have gone from Hungary to America, where I built a life. I often question why I was spared, how I came to be so lucky. Maybe it was because my destiny was to give life to my wonderful son and daughter and enjoy my five grandchildren.

seeking help, they laughed that I certainly was not fit for the job. They were looking for a handyman, and I did not look the part. They did, however, provide me lodging for the night. When they awoke the next day, I had chopped the wood, built a fire and fetched buckets of water. The couple reconsidered, and I was safe once again.

Fortunately, I carried the fake documents that concealed my Jewish identity. It seemed ironic that I had grown up in a household where others did the cooking and cleaning for me and now I was doing the same for strangers.

Months passed, and on December 26, 1944, when I was working in the attic, I saw a very typical sight. A large black sedan driven by German soldiers sped through the town. That day something was different. A Russian tank almost collided with them coming from the opposite direction, killing the Germans. We had been liberated.

Mary Mayer's Veal Paprikash

Mary recalls eating everything paprikash when she was a child. Veal was a luxurious change from chicken or beef. In her home, goose fat was used to brown the meat, imparting a rich gamy flavor. Today's cooks tend to use olive oil, but chicken fat or goose fat will add an extra element to the sauce. Slow cook the dish for the most intense flavor and to ensure tender, juicy veal.

Yield: 4 to 6 servings
Start to finish: Under 2 hours

3–4 tablespoons vegetable oil
2–3 large onions rough chopped (about 2½–3 cups)
2 green peppers, cored, seeded and cut into chunks
2 pounds veal cut into 1- to 2-inch pieces

Flour for dredging, seasoned with kosher salt and pepper
1 (15-ounce) can tomato sauce
1 teaspoon sweet paprika
Kosher salt and pepper

Heat the oil in a large sauté pan or Dutch oven; cook and stir the onions and peppers over medium heat until lightly browned, about 10 to 15 minutes. Remove the vegetables from the pan with a slotted spoon and reserve.

Pat the veal dry, and then dredge the pieces in the seasoned flour. Add oil if needed to the sauté pan and brown the veal on all sides, about 3 minutes per side. If necessary, cook the veal in batches; do not overcrowd the pan or the pieces will steam, not brown. Have a plate standing by to hold the cooked meat.

When all the meat is browned, add it back to the pan with the cooked vegetables. Stir in the tomato sauce and paprika. Season to taste with salt and pepper. Cover and cook on the stove, over low heat for 1½ hours, or until the veal is fork tender and the sauce has taken on a burnt sienna color. The vegetables will have all but melted into the sauce.

Spoon the paprikash over a bed of noodles or potato dumplings. (See Regina Finer's recipe on page 23 or, for traditional Hungarian dumplings, see Greta Margolis's recipe on page 269.)

Mary Mayer's Raspberry Linzer Tarts

Linzer tarts come in all shapes and sizes, and Mary's are usually flavored with vanilla for a subtle sweet taste. For a nutty, marzipan flavor, add almond extract in place of vanilla. The cookies are delicate to handle but look so inviting with the preserves peeking out from the center. Only the shape of your cookie cutter and choice of filling limit your creativity.

Yield: 20–24 (1-inch) cookies, 16–18 (2-inch) cookies, 10–12 (3-inch) cookies
Start to Finish: Step 1: Under 30 minutes, then chill several hours or overnight,
Step 2: Under 30 minutes

FOR THE DOUGH

1 stick (½ cup) butter, room temperature
½ cup sugar
2 egg yolks
1 teaspoon vanilla extract or ½ teaspoon
  almond extract

1½ cups all-purpose flour
1 cup preserves, any flavor
Confectioners' sugar, for dusting

STEP 1

Prepare the dough by beating the butter and sugar on medium speed until light and creamy in a standing mixer, or you can use a food processor, fitted with the metal blade. Add the egg yolks, vanilla or almond extract and 1¼ cups flour. Mix the ingredients on low speed until they are completely incorporated. Remove from the processor and work the dough with your hands, on a lightly floured surface, slowly adding up to ¼ cup of the remaining flour to form a firm, nonsticky dough. Wrap the dough in plastic wrap and flatten into a thick disc. Refrigerate several hours or overnight.

STEP 2

When ready to bake, preheat the oven to 350 degrees and line a cookie sheet with parchment paper.

Remove the dough from the refrigerator and let it sit for about 10 minutes. Divide the dough into several pieces to make rolling easier. Generously sprinkle your work area with flour. Roll the dough to ¼ inch thick, and using a cookie cutter, cut into the desired size and shape. Create a small hole in the center of one half of the pieces by pressing a thimble or bottle cap into the dough; these pieces will be the tops of the finished cookie. Using a cookie spatula, place the cookies on the prepared cookie sheet.

Bake for 10–12 minutes or until they are a very light golden color. Gently lift the cookies off the baking sheet and allow them to cool before assembling. When the cookies are cool, turn the bottoms over (the ones without the hole) and dollop a teaspoonful of your favorite preserve. Cover with the top piece and press gently, allowing the filling to spill out of the hole, and then add an extra dollop of preserves right in the center. Sprinkle lightly with confectioners' sugar.

Katherine Wassermann Noir and Robert (Bela Schwartz) Noir

In her own words

Katherine Noir is a genuinely lovely woman who welcomed me into her home on a crisp, clear winter day. There was hot coffee waiting and three types of home-baked Hungarian pastries—all made even more remarkable by the fact that Katherine is legally blind. My memorable visit began with the retelling of her story.

We were three children in my home; my grandmother lived with us, and she was very strict around the kitchen, like a sergeant. My mother worked with my father, and they would close their beauty salon at lunchtime when we had our big meal. I was a lousy eater. The cuisine—we didn't call it that—was a mixture of Hungarian, Slovak and kosher Jewish. My father was a very bright man; he learned English by listening to the BBC on the radio. He taught us what was going on in the world. We learned Hebrew and Judaic studies from a private tutor that my parents hired. My parents felt I should learn a trade, so I went to beauty school and learned to be a hairdresser. After two years, I graduated with honors and even today have my original certificate!

In 1938, when I was thirteen, Czechoslovakia was dismembered. My father was sent to a slave labor camp where they were used on the front lines as buffers—expendable slave laborers, as most Jewish men were. One day, we were given two hours' notice to move into the ghetto. We were told we could take one change of clothing. My mother, who was very clever, advised us to layer, and we wore several pairs of socks and panties. We stayed in the ghetto only a short time, maybe six weeks, and worked as hairdressers. We were moved to Auschwitz, where my mother and brother perished. My sister, Suzi, and I worked in a munitions factory where, on an assembly line, I made the clocks for the grenades. We were eventually sent to Bergen-Belsen, and I became very ill. One day, I thought I was delirious, because I was certain I heard British voices. I wasn't dreaming. That was the day we were liberated. My sister, Suzi, and the British liberators saved me by taking me to the hospital. While recuperating in the hospital, we were invited by the king of Sweden to come to his country to receive medical attention and build a new life. We boarded an old ship and left for Sweden, where we stayed for two years. The Red Cross located an uncle of ours in New York, and he sponsored our trip to America. I found work as a hairdresser in the Bronx. I made fifteen dollars a week and twenty-five cents in tips. I was so happy.

My husband, who I was married to for fifty years, was also a hairdresser and a survivor. He was born in Hungary and lived in the same town as my cousin. Before the war, he actually had dinner at my home in Ungvár, Czechoslovakia. When the war started, he was sent to Auschwitz. While he was there, he overheard two SS guards discussing their wives. One was complaining that his wife needed a good haircut. My husband quickly spoke up. From then on, he became this woman's hairdresser. This connection earned him a spot in the kitchen, where he received extra bread that he shared with others in the barracks. It assuredly helped save his life.

When he came to America, he changed his name from Bela Schwartz to Robert Noir. He felt you needed a fancy name to own a hair salon in New York. He owned that salon, on 57th Street, for many years. I am not a big stomach person who loves to eat. In our home, I cooked Hungarian food for my husband and two children. I brought my traditions to this country.

Katherine Noir's Mushroom Barley Soup

Katherine's basic soup starter of onions, garlic, carrots and celery creates the perfect foundation for so many soups and inspired this mushroom barley. Katherine's husband used to joke, "Your soup is not edible." When Katherine would ask why, he would answer, "Because you didn't give me a spoon!" A spoon is all you'll need to enjoy this flavorful soup. For those who prefer to chew their mushroom barley soup, feel free to increase the amount of barley.

Yield: 8 servings
Start to Finish: Under 1½ hours

3 tablespoons olive oil
1 large onion, chopped (about 1 cup)
3–4 cloves garlic, chopped
2 celery ribs, chopped (about 1 cup)
1 large carrot, peeled and chopped (about ½ cup)
2 quarts beef broth or water

2 bay leaves
1 pound cremini mushrooms, cleaned and chopped
1 cup pearl barley
Kosher salt and pepper
¼ cup chopped fresh dill leaves

Heat the olive oil in a large soup pot; cook and stir the onions, garlic, celery and carrots over medium heat until they begin to soften, about 15 minutes. Add the water or broth, bay leaves, mushrooms and barley. Season with salt and pepper. Bring to a boil; then reduce the heat and cover and simmer for 50 minutes, adding boiling water if the soup becomes too thick. After 50 minutes, season to taste with salt and pepper. If you used water instead of broth, now would be the time to add 1 or 2 bouillon cubes to enhance the flavor. Stir in the chopped dill, and then continue cooking for 10 minutes.

Discard the bay leaf before serving.

Matilda Winkler

As told by her daughter, Susan Erem

Susan and I spoke while she was north of the border in neighboring Canada, visiting her mother, who had settled there after the war. Even as a child, her mom was incredibly responsible, acquiring her cooking talents at a very young age. With a lot of pride, Susan explains, "Whatever she did, she always did to the best of her ability."

Matilda and Miklos (Mendel) Winkler, 1948.

My mother was born in a small town in eastern Hungary on March 10, 1921. Her father died when she was very young, and her mom became a single working mother. My grandmother ran a tavern, and it became my ten-year-old mother's job to look after her brother, who was two years younger than she. That's how my mother learned to cook at such an early age; she took care of the household. Attached to the tavern was a general store, and she remembers making paper cones that she would fold and make into cups to fill with barley and grains. Cooking was always her thing. A lot of her self-worth was locked up in her cooking ability.

When the war broke out and the Nazis came to Hungary, her family first went into a ghetto and then were deported to Auschwitz. My mother remembers very well when she was separated from her mother at the train station. She naturally ran after her mother, but an SS guard pushed my mother aside, essentially saving her life. In Auschwitz, my mother was selected to work in the kitchen; she was about twenty-three at the time. Even the Germans were able to see that she was very capable. My mother would cook for her fellow prisoners, and she remembers that in order to wash the very large pots, she would have to climb inside them. After the war, women would often tell me how my mother had tried to grab extra food for them in Auschwitz.

After being liberated, she wanted to come to America. First, she returned to Hungary to see her brother, whom she learned had also survived. In 1948, she met and married my father, Miklos; I was born three years later. During the Hungarian Revolution in 1956, my parents decided to make their way to America. Once we made it to the DP camp in Austria, the International Red Cross processed us. They asked my father where he wanted to go. "America," he said. He was told that there was a three-month wait for America, but if Canada was ok, we could leave immediately. So, in February 1957, we arrived in Toronto. Our home was Hungarian with a Yiddish twist. There was always something good to eat; my mother was the best cook ever! I try to keep those traditions going for my two children and two grandchildren.

Matilda Winkler's "Mama's" Crunchy Beans

Susan's mom developed a unique way to prepare vegetarian cholent, which her granddaughter, Adina, lovingly dubbed crunchy beans. She would cook beans and barley each with onions, garlic and seasonings, then combine and roast them in a hot oven until they were crunchy and their distinctive nutty flavor was released. This prep is unlike conventional cholent, which slow bakes and becomes soft and mushy. You have to be a bean lover to love this dish, but if you are, this is the recipe for you.

Yield: About 6 to 8 servings (8 cups)
Start to Finish: 5 to 6 hours

1 pound dried kidney beans, combination of dried beans or a bag of cholent beans, rinsed, boiled and soaked
2 large onions, diced (about 3 cups) and divided
6 garlic cloves, crushed and divided

1 tablespoon paprika
½ cup olive oil, additional oil for baking
1 teaspoon kosher salt
½ teaspoon black pepper
1 cup dried pearl barley, rinsed

Matilda would use the overnight soak method for the beans, but the quick soak method works well for this dish. Boil the beans in a large pot of water for several minutes. Drain, then spoon into a bowl and cover with fresh cold water. Let the beans soak for about 1 hour. Drain and reserve.

In a large pot, combine the beans, 2 cups of diced onions, 4 garlic cloves, all the paprika and half the oil, salt and pepper. Cook the beans over medium-low heat for about 1½ hours or until the beans are very soft (they will not absorb all the liquid). Try not to over stir the mixture while it cooks; you don't want to break up the beans.

In a separate pot, combine the barley, the remaining 1 cup of diced onions, the remaining 2 cloves of garlic, ½ teaspoon salt, ¼ teaspoon of pepper and 2 cups of boiling water. Cover and cook on medium-low heat for about 30 minutes or until the barley and onions are very soft. If the water cooks out, add more hot water to the pot and continue cooking. Take the barley off the heat and wait for the beans to finish.

After the beans have been cooking for 1 hour, preheat the oven to 400 degrees and coat the bottom of a large roasting pan with the remaining ¼ cup of oil.

When the beans are ready, gently stir the barley into the beans, until they are completely combined. Spoon the entire mixture into the prepared roasting pan. Bake for 1 to 3 hours, stirring every 30 minutes and drizzling the top with olive oil after each stir. The dish is ready when the liquid is gone and the beans and barley have the desired crunch. For soft beans, figure 1 hour; crunchy beans 2 hours; and super crunchy 2½ to 3 hours. Serve as a side dish for meat or poultry.

Gale Gand

Professional contributor

Beans and barley make a fabulous side dish, as they can stand up to a rich stew that has a robust sauce and bold flavor. Gale Gand's family short ribs recipe is just the thing to hold its own alongside Matilda's crunchy beans. The following recipe suggests using potatoes, with a variation for parsnips. If serving with Matilda's crunchy beans, parsnips would be the way to go.

Myrna's Beef Short Ribs

Contributed by Gale Gand, executive pastry chef and owner of Tru restaurant, Chicago

This is my mother's recipe, which I remember her making as a child but never learned from her firsthand. My mother died when I was thirty-six and so later in my life, when I was having a craving for this dish, the only way to learn it was to slowly but anxiously hunt through her recipe card file and try to find it. You could always rely on my mother, and sure enough, there was the recipe, as if it were waiting for me to resurrect it. Complete with sidebars written in her distinct handwriting, with comments like "try this with parsnips next time." I felt like she was right there in the kitchen with me as I methodically worked my way through her instructions. It was like she was still with me...true eternal life!

Serves: 6 to 8

3 pounds beef short ribs, cut up
Salt
Fresh ground black pepper
Flour
2 tablespoons vegetable oil (we'd probably use canola oil now)
1 medium onion, sliced
½ cup celery leaves

2 sprigs of parsley
1½ cups beef stock or broth
2 cups canned tomato chunks
6 medium carrots, peeled and cut into chunks
8 small onions, peeled
4 medium potatoes or 2 parsnips, peeled and cut into chunks
1 teaspoon paprika

Remove any excess fat from the ribs. Sprinkle them with salt and pepper, then roll them in flour. In a Dutch oven, heat the vegetable oil and brown the short ribs on all sides. Add the sliced onions, celery leaves, parsley and beef stock. Cover and simmer on low heat for 2 hours or until the meat is very tender, adding more stock if needed. Add the canned tomato, carrots, onions, potatoes or parsnips and paprika. Season with a little salt and pepper and continue cooking, covered, another 30 minutes or until the vegetables are tender. Serve family style on a very large platter.

ROMANIA, RUSSIA AND THE UKRAINE

We would need a history professor or cartographer to fully understand the relationship geographically between Romania, Russia and the Ukraine. During the war, it was particularly complicated and would require a lengthy explanation of how these countries were affected by Nazi occupation and association. Suffice it to say that Romanian Jews found themselves deported to camps such as Transnistria and Auschwitz, where the death tolls exceeded a quarter of a million. The Ukraine is harder to assess, as its territory is so entwined with the Soviet Union. Ukraine was home to one of Europe's largest Jewish populations, and it is estimated that from starvation and systemized extermination more than one and a half million Ukrainian Jews perished. One of the more notorious mass murders was at Babi Yar, just outside of what was then Kiev (Kyiv). In just two days, more than thirty thousand Jews were killed. The Soviet Union was invaded by Romania and Germany in 1941, where in a series of *pogroms*, which in Russian literally means "to wreak havoc," thousands of Jews were murdered. It is estimated that of the four million Jews in the Soviet Union, by the end of the war, more than half died.

Despite this devastation, the traditions of this region are still strongly felt. So many hands have touched this area that their customs and foods absorbed flavors from every culture, all of which played a role in shaping the region. From Romania we got spicy, saucy, vibrant food that reflected a cosmopolitan bent. Czernowitz, where many of our contributors were from, was known as "Little Vienna" and was the home to intellectuals, poets and artists and can even lay claim to the melodic folk song "Hava Nagila." Their cooking was affected by proximity to Bulgaria, Turkey and Greece, imparting a Mediterranean note, which harmonized beautifully with their traditional fare. Ukrainian and Russian cooking packs bold soups with garlic and dill, laden with vegetables, and dishes featuring jewel-red beets were abundant. Filling, substantial and nourishing were the trademarks of foods from this region, while the influences from neighboring eastern European countries lent a Yiddish flavor to many preparations. Several of our contributors from this area found refuge in other parts of Europe or across the ocean. However, even in their new homeland, they flexed their Romanian and Slavic muscles and incorporated the cooking styles from home. Open your hearts to the incredible stories and your kitchens to the bold flavors of our recipes remembered from these hardy survivors.

RECIPES

Florence Edelstein's Robust Mushroom Soup

Mila Fishman's Cabbage Pie

Nella Frendel's Beef Bourguignon

Nella Frendel's Chocolate Mousse Cake

Olga Schaerf's Romanian *Karnatzlach*—Spicy Grilled Meat with Dipping Sauce

Olga Schaerf's *Salade De Bouef*—Beef Salami Salad

Elly Gross's Baby's Biscuits

Peri Hirsch's Rugelach

Peri Hirsch's Walnut Cookies

Hannah Rigler's Chocolate Thinsies

JH* *Schi*—Russian Cabbage Soup

Fira Stukelman's Summer *Borscht*—Beet Soup

Berta Vaisman's *Malai*—Corn Bread

Michelle Bernstein*: Duck Breasts with Jerez, Oranges and Spanish Almonds

Berta Vaisman's *Barenikes*—Pierogis

Chana Wiesenfeld's *Kasha Varnishkes*

Chana Wiesenfeld's Ukrainian Winter Borscht

*Indicates professional contributor

Florence Edelstein and Michael Edelstein

In their own words

I talked to Michael and Florence in the heart of their home, the kitchen, as it filled with the early aromas of the approaching Passover holiday. Michael quipped, "We are married fifty-three years, and in the end, I agree with whatever she says." They share a positive outlook, a close-knit family and a legacy of philanthropy.

MICHAEL

In 1999, fifty-four years after I was forced from my hometown of Skala in the Ukraine, I went back and retraced the steps of my escape from the ghetto. If you ask me what I had for dinner last night, I would have to ask the boss (he points to Florence), but I remembered everything about what happened fifty-four years earlier. My town had two thousand Jews before the war; I was one of only eighty that survived.

Nikola Gitman was one reason we survived, as he helped smuggle my father and me out of the Borshchiv ghetto. We hid in the back of his wagon, shielded by hay as he drove us out of the ghetto and toward town. From there we were able to remain hidden and eventually make our way to the woods.

I remember knocking on doors, hoping someone would help us. These were former neighbors, people who knew us, but they didn't help. In one case, a woman told us to come back the next day, when she would give us a loaf of bread. Instead, she called the police and tried to turn us in. In the summer, we hid in the woods, but when winter came, we knew that if we left deep footprints in the freshly fallen snow, it would be too easy to track and discover us. I recalled hearing a woman in the woods describe a bunker in town that her husband had dug. We went into the town and hid in that cellar. The bunker was so small that when my father turned in one direction, I would have to turn in the other.

Our second angel was Olenka Kowaleszen, who treated us with kindness and humanity. Once or twice a week, she would make soup for us or even polenta with onions. After liberation, this same woman helped me recuperate. I can still hear my father telling me, "Every day you gain, is one more day." Years later, we retold the story of these two courageous people, and they were fittingly honored as "Righteous Among the Nations" at Yad Vashem. Florence and I believe that when you do good, it comes back to you. When I reconnected with Olenka, I wanted to do something for her as a way of saying thank you. We helped her family establish a business, and I was happy to repay my gratitude by sending her grandchildren and great-granddaughters to college and medical school.

FLORENCE

I was born in Zamosc, Poland. My family were members of the Belzer sect of Hasidic Jews. When I was three years old, we left Poland for Russia. At the time, in 1939, Poland was divided between the Germans and the Russians. We chose the Russians and decided to run with the Russian army. My entire family survived because we made this choice. We lived in many parts of Russia and finally settled in Siberia. We were hungry and tired, but we did not fear for our lives. After the war, we went back to Poland and stayed in a DP camp in Germany. We wanted to go to Israel and applied for passage, but instead the HIAS was able to arrange our travel to the United States. We joined the Macabee Club, for new Americans; that's where I met Michael. Shortly after we met, he was drafted into the U.S. Army. Michael served two years in Korea, and when he returned, we were married. My life has been built on my firm belief that 90 percent of what you do is luck and the other 10 percent is guts. When you see a situation, grab it. In my wildest dreams, I could never imagine that we would accomplish for ourselves and for our three children and eleven grandchildren what we have. It's a dream come true.

Florence Edelstein's Robust Mushroom Soup

Florence told me how her grandmother, while they were barely surviving as refugees in Siberia, would scrounge up scraps of potatoes to nourish her family. Florence quickly learned that delicious soup can be built around any ingredient. The focus in this soup comes from the variety of mushrooms, concentrated porcini liquid and the array of fresh vegetables that Florence adds to the earthy mushroom base. Puree the soup for a creamy finish and indulge in a swirl of crème fraîche to lend a tangy, silky note.

Yield: 12 cups
Start to Finish: Under 2 hours

1 (1-ounce) package dried porcini mushrooms
6 tablespoons olive oil
2 medium-large onions, chopped (about 1½–2 cups)
1 large or 2 medium leeks, white part only, chopped and thoroughly rinsed (about 1 cup)
2 large carrots, peeled and diced (about 1 cup)
3 ribs celery, diced (about 1½ cups)
1 pound white mushrooms, coarsely chopped
½ pound shitake mushrooms, chopped (remove the stems and save them to flavor stock)
½ pound cremini mushrooms, chopped
2 medium russet potatoes, peeled and diced
Kosher salt and pepper
1 cup crème fraîche or light sweet cream
Freshly chopped dill leaves and crème fraîche, for garnish (optional)

Soak the dried mushrooms in 1 cup of hot water for 30 minutes.

Heat 3 tablespoons of the olive oil, in a large sauté pan, cook and stir the onions, leeks, carrots and celery over medium-low heat until they begin to soften, about 15 minutes. While the vegetables cook, chop the fresh mushrooms. When the vegetables are done, begin adding the mushrooms in batches. You don't want to overwhelm the pan, so allow each batch to cook down before adding the next. Once all the mushrooms are in the pan, let them cook with the onions over low heat for 15 minutes.

Spoon the cooked vegetables and the diced potatoes into a very large soup pot. By this time, the dried mushrooms should be done soaking. Using a small piece of cheesecloth (a strainer lined with a piece of lightly dampened paper towel or a coffee filter makes an adequate substitute), strain the dried mushrooms, reserving the liquid (you should have about ¾ cup). Add the reserved porcini liquid to the soup pot. Rinse and chop the porcini mushrooms and add them to the pot.

Lastly, add 6 cups of water or enough to cover all the vegetables. Season with salt and pepper, cover and cook, on low heat, until all the vegetables are soft, about 1 hour. If the soup becomes too thick, add boiling water to achieve the desired consistency.

Puree about ¾ of the soup. Pour the pureed soup back into the pot and stir in 1 cup crème fraîche or sweet cream. Season to taste with salt and pepper and heat through. Serve with a dollop of crème fraîche and a sprinkling of fresh chopped dill.

Feedback

Crème fraîche is a cross between heavy cream and sour cream. It has a slightly sour, nutty taste, which plays nicely against the sweet flavors of many stews and soups that contain slow-cooked root vegetables and onions. The beauty of crème fraîche is that its smooth texture won't curdle or separate when heated.

Mila Ginzburg Fishman

As told by her granddaughter Anna Moskovich

We're a family of women! My great-grandmother and her two daughters (my grandma and great-aunt) literally ran from the siege of Stalingrad as the German planes were shooting at people. They were from a small city near Moscow and fled to Siberia. After the war, when there was nothing left, my great-grandfather found a job and an apartment in Czernowitz, in the Ukraine. They shared this apartment with a non-Jewish family. Years later, when my father was twelve, he and his family actually wound up in the same apartment building, maybe even the very same apartment. It was then that my parents met; together they had two daughters who, between the two of them, had four more girls.

Mila Ginzburg Fishman.

The recipe I've provided, translated from Russian by my mother, is yummy. Just thinking of it, I can taste it! My memories are of my mother making it; her memories are of her mother and even grandmother making it. They had a small corner of a kitchen in the Ukraine where they made everything from scratch. She remembers her grandmother rolling the dough with her little hands, the smell of the dough rising.

Mila Fishman's Cabbage Pie

Yield: 15 to 20 pieces
Start to Finish: Step 1: Under 1½ hours, plus refrigeration overnight, Step 2: Under 1½ hours

FOR THE DOUGH
1 glass (8 ounces) whole milk
1 (¼-ounce) package or 2¼ teaspoons dry
  yeast
2 tablespoons sugar
½ teaspoon salt
1 tablespoon vegetable oil
4–5 cups all-purpose flour
1 egg, lightly beaten
1 stick (8 tablespoons) butter, cut into 8
  pieces

FOR THE FILLING
3 eggs
½ stick (4 tablespoons) butter or margarine
1 head green cabbage (about 2 pounds),
  cored and shredded
Kosher salt and pepper
Egg wash glaze: 1 egg plus 1 teaspoon of
  water, beaten

STEP 1

Begin the dough by warming the milk in a small saucepan, a little hotter than lukewarm (if you have a thermometer, it should read between 105 and 115 degrees). If microwaving, about 1 minute will do. Whisk in the yeast, sugar, salt and oil.

Pour 4 cups of flour into a large bowl, food processor with the metal blade or the bowl of a standing mixer, fitted with the paddle attachment. Slowly pour in the milk, beaten egg and 4 tablespoons of butter. Mix until the dough begins to form a ball. Remove from the mixer or bowl and work with your hands on a lightly floured surface for several minutes. If using a standing mixer, change from the paddle attachment to the dough hook and knead for several minutes. If the dough is sticky, add more flour, a little at a time. Cover the dough with a towel and let it rest for 1 hour. Leave the remaining butter out to soften.

While the dough rests, prepare the cabbage filling. Start by placing the eggs in a small saucepan and covering them with cold water. Bring to a rapid boil, reduce the heat to medium-low and cook for 10 minutes. Remove the eggs from the water and place them in ice-cold water until ready to peel. The ice water will help prevent that telltale green ring that sometimes develops on a hard-boiled egg yolk.

Heat the butter in a large skillet; cook and stir the shredded cabbage, over medium heat, for 10 minutes. Season to taste with salt and pepper. Spoon the cabbage into a bowl to cool. Peel the eggs, cut them into small pieces and add to the cooled cabbage. Cover the cabbage and refrigerate overnight.

Once the dough has risen, generously flour a work surface and roll the dough into a rectangle about ½ inch thick. Spread 2 tablespoons of the remaining butter or margarine on the dough. Fold the dough like an envelope, roll out again and spread the last 2 tablespoons of butter on top. Fold and roll twice more. Finally, fold the dough like an envelope, wrap in plastic wrap and refrigerate overnight.

STEP 2

Preheat the oven to 375 degrees and grease a 15½ x 10 ½-inch jellyroll pan.

Take the dough from the fridge and cut the dough in two pieces, making one piece slightly bigger than the other. Roll out the bigger one to about ¼ inch thick to fit the baking pan. Lay the dough in the prepared pan, bringing the dough up the sides. Spread the cabbage filling on top. Roll out the second piece of dough. Lay the second piece on top of the cabbage and pinch the edges to seal the pie. Brush the top with the egg glaze and then with a knife make 3 slits in the dough for the steam to escape. Bake for about 1 hour or until the top is golden brown. Serve the pie straight from the oven.

Nella Frendel and Robert Frendel

As told by their daughter, Paulette Mondschein

Paulette comes by her cosmopolitan elegance naturally. Both her parents were lovers of the arts and made sure they imbued their only child with a sense of security and an appreciation for culture.

My father and mother were both from Czernowitz, Romania, "Little Vienna." They were married in Romania when my mother was nineteen and my father was twenty-five. When the war broke out, they left their town and went to Bucharest, where they obtained fake documents. My father had light hair and baby-blue eyes; my mother had red hair and green eyes—they did not look Jewish. They stayed in people's homes and because they had money were able to evade arrest. They crossed the border from Hungary to Vienna. From Vienna they went to Paris with the help of the underground. They remained in Paris for seven years.

When they lived in Paris, my mother was a designer. Knowing how persuasive she could be, she probably talked her way into her job as Christian Dior's apprentice. When I was two years old, my parents, my grandfather and I immigrated to the United States. We traveled on a boat from Marseilles to New York. When we arrived here, a photographer for the *New York Herald Tribune* snapped my picture. I was wearing a French beret with my curly hair peeking out. The headline the next day read "New American." My parents loved this country, and they became very American. I never felt we had a Romanian identity; they spoke French, German or English. Every Friday night, we would have a traditional Shabbos meal. My mother was a phenomenal cook. She would also make delicious classically French dishes like chocolate mousse and beef bourguignon. As a child, I wanted to be an American; I didn't

Nella and Robert Frendel, with their daughter, Paulette, on the boat to America.

want parents who spoke different languages or cooked European foods. Looking back now, I know I should have felt differently.

What defined my parents was their ability to always make me feel safe and secure. They were wonderful parents, and we were a beautiful little family unit. My parents were extraordinarily elegant, exuding that old European charm and culture. I was always in Carnegie Hall or taking piano lessons (even though I wasn't very good). When they came here, the first thing they bought was a piano. I think that it was very important for Jewish people to expose themselves whenever they could to culture, books and learning because it was something no one could take away. They were married thirty years, I was the only child and they have two grandchildren and six great-grandchildren.

Nella Frendel's Beef Bourguignon

While Friday night dinners featured the traditional Jewish fare, Nella would wake up a weekday with a rendition of this classic and beautifully fragrant dish. Slow braised beef mingles with carrots, onions and potatoes in a rich wine sauce. Be sure to use a good deep red wine from the Burgundy region of France—it is the basis for the sauce and will infuse the beef and vegetables with an earthy flavor. If you can exhibit some self-control, let the finished dish sit overnight in the fridge; it intensifies the flavor and thickens the sauce.

Yield: 4 to 6 servings
Start to Finish: Under 5 hours

2 tablespoons olive oil
2½ pounds beef chuck, cut into 1-inch pieces
  and patted dry
2 cloves garlic, chopped
2 cups frozen pearl onions, thawed
2 large carrots, peeled and cut into 1-inch
  pieces (about 1 cup)
1 medium russet potato, peeled and cubed
  (about 1 cup)

1 generous tablespoon tomato paste
1 cup beef broth
3 cups red wine
1 teaspoon herbs de Provence
2 teaspoons kosher salt
Black pepper, to taste
2 bay leaves

Preheat the oven to 250 degrees.

Heat the oil in a large Dutch oven and brown the beef, over medium-high heat, for several minutes on all sides. You might need to brown the meat in batches. Do not overcrowd the pot, or the beef will steam, not brown. Remove the browned beef to a plate. In the same pot, cook and stir the garlic and pearl onions over medium heat for 2 to 3 minutes; add oil if needed. Stir in the beef, and its collected drippings, and the remaining ingredients. Place the covered pot in the oven and slow roast for at least 4 hours. Remove from the oven and check the sauce to see if it is thick enough. If not, create a slurry by mixing 1 tablespoon cornstarch with 2 tablespoons of water; stir into the sauce and cook 15 minutes longer. The dish can be refrigerated overnight and reheated the next day on the stove, over a low heat.

Feedback
Herbs de Provence is a unique blend of floral herbs containing dried basil, rosemary, tarragon, marjoram, thyme and parsley. Some preparations also contain lavender. If you do not have herbs de Provence, use a teaspoon of any of the abovementioned herbs, alone or in combination.

Nella Frendel's Chocolate Mousse Cake

Light, airy and just sweet enough describes this luscious French cake that Paulette's mother made for special occasions. The very proper ladyfingers serve as a foundation for this classic preparation. Ladyfingers hide in the market and can usually be found in the fresh fruit section alongside the berries. If ladyfingers are not available, or you want to simplify the preparation, prepare only the mousse and serve it from a large dessert bowl or in individual ramekins. The mousse is so decadently delicious that it can stand alone.

Yield: 10 to 12 servings
Start to Finish: Step 1: Under 1 hour, then chill 4 hours (if preparing the mousse only) or overnight (for the cake), Step 2: Under 15 minutes

FOR THE MOUSSE
2 (3-ounce) packages ladyfingers
12 ounces good semisweet chocolate or
  semisweet chocolate chips
2 whole eggs
4 eggs, separated
2 cups heavy cream

FOR THE TOPPING
1 cup heavy cream
2 teaspoons sugar
Chocolate shavings or mini chocolate chips
  (optional)

STEP 1

If preparing as a cake, arrange the ladyfingers vertically around the sides of an ungreased 9 x 3-inch springform pan with the rounded, finished sides against the pan; these will face out when you unmold the cake. Line the bottom with ladyfingers and set the pan aside. Save the remaining ladyfingers for another time. If making only the mousse, skip this step.

Prepare the mousse by melting the chocolate in a double boiler, over a simmering heat, stirring occasionally until completely melted and smooth. Once melted, pour the chocolate into a large bowl and allow it to cool completely. Beat the 2 whole eggs and stir into the chocolate. The texture of the chocolate will change immediately. Keep stirring vigorously until the chocolate is thick and has a deep, shiny, chocolaty color. Whisk in the 4 egg yolks, one at a time, stirring hard after each addition.

In a separate bowl, beat the 4 egg whites until stiff but not dry. Gently fold the egg whites into the chocolate mixture. Stir until the egg whites are completely blended, being sure to spoon the chocolate up from the bottom of the bowl in large but gentle circular motions. The mixture will be fluffy.

In a separate bowl, whip 2 cups of the heavy cream until very thick but not hard. Stir the whipped cream into the chocolate mixture. When completely incorporated, the color should resemble milk chocolate. Spoon into the prepared springform pan and chill overnight. If foregoing the cake presentation, spoon into one large dessert bowl or individual ramekins and chill for at least 4 hours.

STEP 2

Prepare the topping by whipping the heavy cream with the sugar. Beat until thick and shiny. Using a vegetable peeler, curl chocolate shavings. Spoon the whipped cream over the top of the cake and garnish with the chocolate shavings or chips. For the dessert bowl presentation, spoon a dollop of whipped cream over each serving and dot with the shaved chocolate or chips.

Olga Paverman Schaerf and Henry Schaerf

In Olga's words

Olga sits across the table from me, stark white hair perfectly coiffed, movie star eyes and a personality that screams, "I have some amazing stories to share." Fortunately for Olga and her America-raised husband, Henry, they escaped the brunt of Nazi oppression, having found refuge in France during the war. Olga told with remarkable clarity her story of how she came to France.

My husband, Henry, and I left Czernowitz, "Little Vienna," and went to Bucharest in the early 1930s because it was bigger, easier and there we did not stand out as Jews. Prior to the war, although my husband was born in Europe, he and his family had been living in the United States. His family remembered the life they had in Europe and longed for it, so they went back. Now he had to leave, again.

We stayed in Bucharest for many years until the Russians were getting close. At that time, you could pay to obtain a visa. We were able to secure one to South America, even though we knew that we did not want to settle there. It was a way for us to get out quickly. The visa was good for only a week or two. Fortunately, we were able to change our plans, and we made the decision to take a boat to France, as my brother lived in Paris and it seemed natural for us to move there. On the boat, I remember we had a very large suite, called the Royal Suite; it was the only room available. We took it and shared it with an unknown passenger. One day, my husband leaned across our balcony and saw that the man sharing our suite was a priest. That same day my, husband

Henry and Olga Schaerf, Italy 1950s.

went downstairs to the bar to buy an orange juice. He had only Romanian money, which the bartender would not take. The man sitting next to my husband at the bar said, "Put it on my tab." As it turned out, that man was the priest sharing our suite. We came to know him well. Monsignor Kirk was an emissary to the Pope and was planning to disembark when the boat made its first stop in Naples. One day, the priest asked my husband to watch his two suitcases. He would not tell us what was inside, but we suspected they were secret war-related documents he was carrying to the Vatican. We tried many times to locate him, to thank him for his kindness and tell him we were safe, but at the time were unsuccessful.

We arrived in Marseilles, and as was very typical, France was enduring a strike. We were unable to travel to Paris and reach my brother. My brother was very resourceful and had a plan. He rented an ambulance, knowing it would get through the snarled traffic, and made the trip from Paris to Marseilles. Together we remained in Marseilles for about one month before moving to Paris. Once there we lived well, as the people I came in contact with treated the refugees beautifully. I always felt that the French hated each other, but they liked us. Even when it came to rations, I felt we got more than our mandated share.

We came to America in 1949 but kept our Romanian traditions. Remarkably, years later, in an unbelievable coincidence, my son, Ray, who is a cardiothoracic surgeon, operated on a young priest. My son told his patient about our encounter with the monsignor. Not only did his patient know the priest, but he had also studied with him and knew that Monsignor Kirk had recently died. We thought it was very special that our son saved the life of this young man who was so personally connected to the man who helped us. If you ask me who I am, I would answer I am first a Jew, then an American. I try to look at things brightly and enjoy what I am doing. I am very happy with what I have. I have one son and four grandchildren.

Author's Note: I sadly learned that Olga has passed away. May her memory be for a blessing.

Olga Schaerf's Romanian *Karnatzlach*—Spicy Grilled Meat

Olga remembers devouring these garlicky little bites of beef for dinner or as a filling appetizer. Today in Romania they are called *mititei*, and they have become trendy street food. They are crowd pleasers at a summer barbecue hot off the grill and served on long bamboo skewers, or as finger food broiled in the oven and served like sliders or with the accompanying dipping sauce.

Yield: 12 pieces
Start to Finish: Step 1: 15 minutes, then refrigerate for at least 4 or up to 24 hours,
Step 2: Under 30 minutes

1 pound ground beef
4–5 cloves of garlic, grated
1 teaspoon kosher salt
1 teaspoon sweet paprika

½ teaspoon ground black pepper
1 generous splash Worcestershire sauce*
1 tablespoon ketchup
¼ cup finely chopped fresh flat-leaf parsley

STEP 1
In a medium bowl, combine the ground beef, garlic (grated over the meat so the garlic juice is incorporated), salt, paprika, pepper, Worcestershire sauce, ketchup and parsley. Combine with your hands to thoroughly blend. Cover and refrigerate at least 4 hours or up to 1 day.

STEP 2
Light the grill or preheat the broiler.

Wet your hands and form the meat into rounds the size of a golf ball, then elongate them into a thumb-like shape, about 3 inches long. Grill/broil, 5 inches from the heat source, for 4 to 5 minutes, turn over and continue to cook for 3 to 4 minutes longer. Serve as is or with the dipping sauce.

Dipping Sauce

Yield. About ¼ cup

4 tablespoons ketchup
2 tablespoons Dijon mustard

¼ teaspoon ground cumin
1 splash Worcestershire sauce*

Combine all the ingredients and serve on the side for dipping.

* Worcestershire sauce is a controversial ingredient in kosher cooking. Some approve of its use with meat; many others do not. Use your discretion when preparing this recipe and omit the Worcestershire sauce if it does not conform to your preferences.

Feedback
You can experiment with ground veal, lamb or turkey or a combination of meat. For the turkey, add a little extra Worcestershire and salt, as the turkey tends to be blander. You can spice these bites up even more by adding ½ teaspoon cumin to the meat or replacing the sweet paprika with hot. Some prefer a spongier texture, which can be achieved by adding ¼ cup seltzer and ¼ teaspoon of baking soda to the meat. This causes them to fluff up a bit when cooking.

Olga Schaerf's *Salade De Bouef* —Beef Salami Salad

Both Olga and her dear friend Nella Frendel (see page 289) regularly made this Provençal salad with a Jewish twist. It's a picnic in a bowl, with a French accent.

Yield: 6 to 8 servings (about 6 cups)
Start to Finish: Under 15 minutes

1 (8.5-ounce) can early peas, drained
1 (8.25-ounce) can diced or sliced carrots, drained
1 (12-ounce) whole beef salami, cut into bite-size pieces

1 pound mayo-based potato salad
5 teaspoons Dijon mustard
1 cup chopped sour pickles
Chopped fresh flat-leaf parsley and olive oil, for garnish

In a medium-size bowl, combine all the ingredients and gently stir to combine; you don't want to mash the peas when mixing. Chill in the fridge and serve as a side dish or lunch salad. Garnish with chopped parsley and a drizzle of olive oil.

Elly Berkovits Gross

In her own words

Elly is a woman on a mission. Through her talks at local schools and her five books, she feels she has "a commitment to remind the world that the tragedy that happened should never happen again." Thousands of children have heard and read her story, and as she explains, "They sometimes look at me like I'm from the moon, but if I can change the mind of one or two of them, then it's worth it." Apparently, Elly has done a wonderful job of doing just that, as one child wrote to her after reading her story, "You are an inspiration to all my friends....Your story makes me want to grow up and do everything I can to prevent anything like this from ever happening again."

I was born Elly Berkovits on February 14, 1929, in Simileu-Silvaniei, Romania. On March 16, 1939, my brother, Adalbert, was born. I loved the handsome little boy. That spring, Nazis invaded Czechoslovakia, and in 1942, my father, age thirty-six, was drafted into forced labor and forever disappeared from our lives. Beginning early in the winter of 1944, we Jews had to wear the yellow star. My mother tried to comfort me, saying, "Elly, you have to learn not to complain and take life as it comes." After Passover, we were ordered to leave our house. We were escorted to the ghetto, which was in a former brick factory at Ceheiu. In the ghetto, four females were ordered to peel potatoes, and by blind luck, at age fifteen, I was one of them. At night, I was allowed to take my mother and brother one or two potatoes. As long as I live, I'll never forget my little brother, who waited to see me, not for the potato, but because we loved each other. His handsome face got smaller day by day; my heart breaks when I think of him. In his short life few good days he had.

On Saturday, May 27, 1944, Erev Shavuot, we began our five-day journey to Auschwitz-Birkenau, where my mother and brother perished. I was put to work carrying water. In the end of August 1944, a group of us were transferred to Fallersleben, Germany, to work in a forced labor camp. Although I got a respiratory infection with fever, for some reason I was spared. The German officer in charge of our group ordered that I should not work in the factory but instead wash the living quarters' floor.

In early April 1945, we were shipped to Salzwedel, where I was reunited with my two cousins. On April 14, 1945, the Allies liberated us. Later we were moved to Hillersleben and, in a few months, returned home. In 1946, at the age of seventeen, I married Ernest Gross, a survivor of forced labor. We lived under the communist regime in Romania for twenty years and raised two children. In 1966, we moved to the United States. My husband and I worked long hours to support our family while our children focused on their education, and we

Elly Gross (*back row, third from the left*) school photo, 1936.

were able to reach the American dream. God bless America.

In 1998, I served as plaintiff on the case for reparations for all former slaves, Gentiles and Jews alike. That same year I took part in the "March of the Living" tour of Holocaust sites. While walking through Auschwitz-Birkenau, I found my mother and brother's picture in front of a boxcar taken when we had just arrived, on the morning of June 2, 1944. There I made a commitment that as long as I am able, I will remind everyone who will listen of our tragic past. In May 2005, I was invited to Germany and participated in one of their ceremonies. I also was invited to Fallersleben, where I had worked as a slave laborer at the age of fifteen. One part of the ceremony was especially emotional for me. From among all of the Holocaust victims, fifteen families were

selected for the permanent exhibition in the new Museum of Murdered European Jews in Berlin. My parents and brother were among the few selected for this high postmortem honor. It is a small, but nice, piece of closure of my struggle to leave a lasting memory for my family, which includes my husband of sixty-three years, one daughter, one son and five grandchildren.

Elly Gross's Baby's Biscuits

Reminiscent of the cookie we all gave our little ones, Elly's uncomplicated biscuits are great to make for children or with children. All they need is a quick dunk in a tall glass of milk or a soothing cup of tea.

Yield: About 3 dozen biscuits
Start to Finish: Step 1: 15 minutes then 6–8 hours or overnight, Step 2: Under 30 minutes

2 eggs
4 ounces (about 1 cup) confectioners' sugar
1 teaspoon vanilla extract

½ teaspoon baking powder
2 cups all-purpose flour

STEP 1

Whisk together the eggs and confectioners' sugar until the sugar is completely dissolved and no longer visible. Whisk in the vanilla and baking powder. Slowly begin adding the flour. You'll need to use a wooden spoon to stir the mixture as it thickens; the dough will be sticky. Scoop the dough onto a piece of waxed paper and tightly wrap the dough. Refrigerate for 6 to 8 hours or overnight.

STEP 2

Preheat the oven to 325 degrees and lightly grease a baking sheet.

Take the dough out of the fridge and divide it in half. Keep one half refrigerated while you work with the other. Very generously flour a work surface and roll the dough to ¼ inch thick. Cut with a 2-inch cookie cutter. Use a cookie spatula to place the rounds on the prepared baking sheet. Bake for 10 minutes; the cookies will remain a pale color with lightly browned edges. They harden as they sit, so do not overbake.

Peri Hirsch

In her own words

My husband joined me as I spoke with Peri. He was instantly smitten by her charm and demeanor. Equally delightful was her husband, Felix, who could have worked the Borscht Belt, and contributed one-liners and insights into the character and cooking talents of this wonderful, vibrant woman. While we savored her sweet rugelach and delicious walnut cookies, we listened to Peri retell her story and a remarkable ending that occurred more than fifty years later.

I was born in Transylvania, Romania, as one of nine children, and lived in an extended family with my parents and grandparents. I remember a very traditional home, where I loved watching my mother and grandmother prepare for Shabbos. My job on Friday was to shine all the shoes in the house, and if I was lucky, I would wash the dairy dishes as well. My father was in the meat business, so we ate well, and my mother, who was very good-natured, would share what we had with the neighbors who didn't have as much. My last Passover at home was in 1944, when the Germans officially came into our town. Within a few weeks, we were taken to the ghetto and then to Auschwitz-Birkenau.

At first, my entire family stayed together. I remember when they took us off the train in Birkenau and my mother was sent to a different line than me. I wanted so badly to go with her, but a Jewish man who was working the lines threw me to the other side, saving my life. I was lucky to still have my two sisters with me at that time. We were sent to a forced labor camp where we worked in factories located near the oil refineries and coal mines, which were targets for the Allied forces. I clearly remember September 11, 1944, the day a bomb exploded; it was like an atomic bomb. The SS cut the fence wires, and everyone scattered into the fields. One of my sisters was immediately killed by the blast, while my other sister was badly wounded. I had hidden under a bridge with a few other girls. A priest who saw us cowering under the bridge signaled us to run quickly into his house, and moments after we did, the bridge I was hiding under was destroyed.

I knew that a German doctor had taken my sister into a hospital, but I knew little else. I had actually visited her once but was not allowed to again. It was not until more than fifty years later that I would learn of the incredible compassion of this doctor, and the fate of my sister. As for me, I found some family members, and after being recaptured and marched through the woods, I eventually found safety in a farmer's home. I hid there with seven other girls until the Americans liberated us on April 14, 1945. Using cigarettes that we had collected, we bribed a German and hired a truck to take us to the DP camp. My hope was to go to Paris and then Israel. Instead, in 1946, I came to America aboard the SS *Marine Perch*.

Peri Hirsch.

More than half a century later, I returned to Germany, hoping to discover what happened to my sister. I connected with a wonderful woman, Dr. Marianne Kaiser, who was able to fill in the blanks for me. She told me that Dr. Rudolf Bertram was the German doctor who had established St. Joseph's Hospital near the factory where we were forced to work. He heroically rescued and treated eighteen Jewish girls in the basement of the hospital; my sister, Blanka, was one of those girls. I was told that when the Gestapo came to Dr. Bertram and demanded he release the girls, insisting they were strong enough to return to work, Dr. Bertram took a hard line. He told the SS that if he were forced to release even one girl, he would never treat another German soldier again. His defiance saved many of these girls; unfortunately, my sister was not among them. After a second bomb attack, she was sent to Bottrop, where she died of her injuries. In an act of unparalleled compassion, Dr. Bertram created a small plot where my sister and others were buried. On my trip to Germany, I was able to erect a proper headstone and honor my sister's memory. I have photos from a simple ceremony in Bottrop where a rabbi led us in saying Kaddish, the prayer for the dead, and unbelievably, where German citizens, out of respect for my sister, placed symbolic stones on her headstone. I wrote to Dr. Bertram to thank him for what he did for my sister; we corresponded until he died in 1975. His family became part of my family, and I will always be grateful to him for his kindness. For his heroism and humanity, Dr. Rudolf Bertram posthumously received the title of "Righteous Among the Nations" at Yad Vashem. Felix and I are married sixty years; we have three children and three grandchildren.

Author's Note: I sadly learned that Felix has passed away. May his memory be for a blessing.

Peri Hirsch's Rugelach

Peri's rugelach are jam-packed morsels, tender and flaky, with a subtle sweetness. Felix, Peri's husband, credits the family rolling pin for the perfection of these little bites of heaven. He says, "It has worked magic for generations." The beauty of this recipe is you can increase the sweet factor or nutty texture by adjusting the filling to your taste.

Yield: 32 pieces (recipe can easily be doubled to make 64 pieces)
Start to Finish: Step 1: Under 30 minutes, then chill at least 4 hours or overnight,
Step 2: Under 1 hour

FOR THE DOUGH
1 stick (½ cup) butter, room temperature
2 tablespoons sugar
1 (4-ounce) package cream cheese, softened at room temperature
1 tablespoon orange juice
1 egg
1 cup all-purpose flour
1 teaspoon baking powder

FOR THE FILLING
½ cup apricot preserves, room temperature
½ cup sugar plus 1–2 teaspoons ground cinnamon, more to taste
½ cup raisins
1 cup (4 ounces) chopped nuts, more to taste

FOR THE TOPPING
1 lightly beaten egg plus 1 tablespoon of water (egg wash)
Sanding sugar (optional)

STEP 1
Prepare the dough by beating the butter, sugar and cream cheese, just till soft and combined. Stir in the orange juice and egg. In a separate bowl, combine the flour and baking powder. Stir the flour mixture into the cream cheese mixture and combine, creating a soft, slightly sticky dough. Divide the dough into 2 pieces, flatten each into a disc and wrap in plastic wrap. Refrigerate at least 4 hours or overnight.

STEP 2
Take one package of dough out of the fridge and let it rest for 10 minutes. Keep the remaining dough chilled. Flour a work surface and roll the dough out into a 12-inch circle. With a spatula, spread half the preserves over the entire circle, and then sprinkle with half the sugar, raisins and nuts. Use the spatula to gently press the filling into the dough. Using a pizza wheel, cut the dough

into fourths, then cut each fourth into fourths. You should have 16 pieces. Some might be larger than others. No worries; it will give your cookies personality. Roll the wedges up starting at the widest end. When rolled, you should have a nice crescent shape.

Chill the rugelach while you preheat the oven to 350 degrees.

Remove the rugelach from the fridge and brush lightly with the egg wash. You can sprinkle with sanding sugar for a nice shine and sweet crunch or sprinkle additional cinnamon sugar on top. Bake for 25 minutes or until they are light brown. Repeat with the remaining dough.

Feedback
A good way to chop nuts is to use a serrated knife. Try rocking the knife back and forth over softer nuts like walnuts. Harder nuts, like almonds, might need the oomph that only a grinder or food processor can provide. Do not overprocess or you will have crumbs. 2 ounces shelled nuts equals ½ cup chopped nuts.

Peri Hirsch's Walnut Cookies

Sweet butter and crunchy walnuts combine with sugar and cinnamon for a crispy, light cookie.

Yield: About 4 dozen cookies
Start to Finish: Under 1 hour

½ pound (2 sticks) butter, room temperature
1 cup sugar
2 eggs
1 teaspoon vanilla extract
1½ teaspoons baking powder

2½ cups all-purpose flour
1 cup (about 4 ounces) finely ground walnuts
3 tablespoons sugar mixed with ½ teaspoon
  ground cinnamon
Whole walnuts

Beat the butter, sugar, eggs and vanilla for several minutes, on medium speed, until light and fluffy. In a separate bowl, combine the baking powder and flour. Stir the flour mixture into the butter mixture and mix thoroughly. Pour in the walnuts and mix by hand until evenly distributed. Divide the dough into 4 parts. On a lightly floured surface, using your hands (wet them to make it easier), roll each part into a log about 2 inches in diameter, wrap in plastic wrap and freeze.

When ready to bake, preheat the oven to 350 degrees.

Remove the dough from the freezer and cut it into ½-inch slices. Place on an ungreased baking sheet 2 inches apart. Sprinkle the cinnamon sugar over each cookie and bake for about 15 minutes or until light brown. When they come out of the oven, gently press a whole walnut in the center of each cookie.

Sara "Hannah" Rigler

Based on her memoir

Hannah was born Sara Matuson in Shavli, Lithuania, thirteen years before the Nazis invaded her town in 1941. Years later, she took the name Hannah to honor the memory of her sister, who perished along with the rest of her immediate family. Hannah is a doer. From the time she arrived in the United States in 1947, she involved herself in health services, community politics and Holocaust studies. Her life story is chronicled in her profound book, *10 British Prisoners-of-War Saved My Life*. Her story here is excerpted from that remarkable accounting of her childhood and experiences during the war. We have placed Hannah's story in the Russian section, as she was our sole contributor from Lithuania. Make no mistake, Hannah is proud of her Lithuanian roots and heritage.

We lived in a Jewish world. Our holidays were celebrated as a community, and each celebration was an event. My mother used to prepare for Passover weeks before the holiday. I went with Maryte, our live-in help, to the public baths to kosher the utensils for Passover. Today I think of the holidays as a time that brought us closeness and reverence to our family and bound us forever, a generation to generation with our people. The charmed life of my childhood came to a close in 1940; my family and I did not know the worst. The Russians invaded Lithuania and within a few weeks nationalized our factory. We were forced to share our home with a Russian pilot and his wife. They lived with us for a year when on June 22, 1941, the war started between Russia and Germany. Within a week, the Germans occupied Lithuania.

Through a series of events, her father was arrested and jailed, and she, her mother and sister were ghettoized. They remained in the ghetto for three years, and then they were moved by the Germans, first to Stutthof and then to several work camps. In December 1944, they were taken on a "death march," at which time Hannah made a life-changing decision.

My mother had hidden my father's diamond ring and I asked her to give it to me so that I could trade it for bread. I slipped out of line, eluding the guards and ran to the nearest barn. In the barn, I tried to trade the ring for bread, but a Polish man who was working there called the police, who chased me back to the line. I was a filthy, starving bundle of rags and yet I did not want to die and so I was running for my life. I ran and hid in another barn. After a few hours, a man entered the barn; he told me he was a British prisoner of war—Stan Wells. He told me the Germans had given up the search for me. He brought me something to eat, and then tried to figure out a way to save me. As he left, he said, "May God watch over you." Stan showed me there was still some decency in the world. Stan did return in the morning and told me the English POWs had decided to bring me back to their camp. On top of the barn was a hayloft and they had a plan to make a hole in the straw close to the chimney where I would lie, hidden all day. Late at night, Willy Fisher, one of the POWs, took me to his comrades. Neither Willy nor Stan came to see me again, but they did send me a kind and gentle substitute, Alan Edwards....In the morning I waited for Alan and my breakfast....In the afternoon I waited for Alan and supper. Alan stole a maroon coat, stockings, a pair of shoes and a sweater to go over my dress.

My dress had a large Mogen David on the back that no amount of washing could take out, so the sweater was designed to be my disguise. Alan went to look for my mother and sister in Praust but he could not get into the camp. One day, Alan decided to have me meet the other nine POWs. Each of the men gave me a small gift. After three weeks, Alan told me the Russians were close....He and the others were evacuated immediately. He offered to take me with them in place of Stan who had opted to stay behind. By shaving my head and disguising me as a boy, they hoped to save me. I stayed behind and was lucky to find a job working for a farmer named Heinrich Binder. He realized I was the Jewish girl that had escaped the Nazis several weeks earlier. He agreed not to turn me in, in return for my writing a note in Yiddish stating that he helped save my life. He felt this would help him as the liberating army was fast approaching. He saw me as a way of saving himself.

Mother, Father, Hannah, Sara and Liuba in Shavel, 1937.

Hannah's story did not end there; at one point she was arrested as a German spy, as she spoke both German and Russian so well. They believed her dress, with the Jewish star on the back, was part of her disguise. When she was finally vindicated, the interrogator suggested she write fiction, as he felt "nobody could go through what I experienced and live!" Months later, Hannah arrived in Bialystok, where she waited for news of her mother and sister. Hannah met a girl from her hometown of Shavli, who broke the news to her that her mother and sister had perished. She, however, remained in Bialystok, awaiting passage to Palestine or America.

Hannah came to America in 1947 and in 1952 married Bill, the love of her life. They have been married fifty-six years. For years, Hannah searched for the British men who had saved her life, writing letters to every Edwards in the London phone book. Through a series of lucky encounters, Hannah contacted Willy Fisher, one of the British POWs, whose diary verified Hannah's amazing but true story. And despite impossible odds, in 1972, after twenty-four years of searching, Hannah was eventually reunited with the men who saved her life. They met at the Portman Hotel in London.

My ten angels came with their wives to see a woman who was no longer a bag of bones but had a productive and satisfying life. They toasted their little sister who had found a special place in their hearts—and the stoic British cried. In 1989, they were honored at Yad Vashem...all of them designated as "Righteous Among the Nations." The message of my story is a simple one—never give up. The message of my book is to use the uniquely human trait of memory to connect the generations and to work unceasingly to leave this world a better place than when we entered it. This is a message I have tried to imbue in my two children and two grandchildren.

Hannah Rigler's Chocolate Thinsies

While living in Europe, after the war, Hannah received care packages from her aunt Mary in the States. One of her favorite treats were these wafer-like chocolate cookies, which taste like miniature ultra-thin brownies. They can be prepared in a snap with flour for anytime or with matzo cake meal for Passover.

Yield: About 60 cookies
Start to Finish: Under 30 minutes

3 tablespoons cocoa powder
½ cup sugar
¼ cup flour (or a little less matzo cake meal)
¼ cup vegetable oil
1 whole egg, or 2 egg whites
½ teaspoon vanilla extract
⅓ cup (about 1½ ounces) finely chopped nuts

TOPPINGS
Sprinkles, chocolate chips, chopped nuts
 (optional)

Preheat the oven to 400 degrees and line a 15½ x 10½ -inch baking sheet with parchment paper.

Stir together the cocoa, sugar and flour. Pour in the oil and stir. Stir in the egg and vanilla until all the ingredients are combined. Stir in the finely chopped nuts.

Spread the batter onto the prepared pan; the thinner you spread the batter, the crisper the cookies will be. Bake 10 minutes. Allow the cookie to cool slightly before cutting it into bite-size pieces (a pizza wheel works great). If any of the cookies are not crisp enough, pop them back into the oven for a minute or two. Remove them from the parchment paper when cool.

Cantor Gershon Sirota

Based on my family history

In 1943, one of the greatest voices in cantorial music was silenced forever. That voice belonged to Gershon Sirota, a close relative of my great-grandfather Rabbi Aaron Sirota. Hazzan Sirota, who was often referred to as the "Jewish Caruso," was a leading cantor in Europe at a time when cantorial music was as its height. He was born in the Odessa region of what is now the Ukraine but traveled extensively and unfortunately found himself in Poland during the war. He was one of the first cantors to ever record his music and sang throughout Europe and the United States in the early 1900s. In 1902, he honored the Zionist pioneer Theodor Herzl with his rich tenor voice. In New York City, a sold-out crowd at Carnegie Hall was treated to his haunting melodies.

Cantor Sirota fatefully returned to Europe and assumed the position as cantor at the prestigious Tlomackie Street Synagogue in Warsaw. He later relinquished that position, as his travels took him away from the Temple for prolonged periods of time. His final years were spent with his wife and children in the Warsaw ghetto, where they all perished.

As a child, I recall my parents playing on the phonograph the groundbreaking recordings my distant relative had made. At the time, I didn't appreciate the depth of his voice or the impact of his music. When my Hebrew schoolteachers, or choir directors, heard that I was related to the great Hazzan Sirota, they were awed, and I beamed proudly. However, I knew little of his life story and nothing of his tragic death.

Cantor Gershon Sirota.

My great-grandfather's Jewish roots ran deep. When he arrived here in the United States, his rabbinical obligations were paramount. He tended to small communities where rabbis were rare and sorely needed. In Moodus, Connecticut, he was not only the rabbi but also the shochet and a gentleman farmer. When I visited my great-grandfather, we never talked about his family that remained in Russia or those who did not survive the Holocaust. We did talk about Jewish traditions, one of which was blowing the *shofar* to call people to worship. He was a born teacher, and he taught me how to sound the shofar that he brought with him from Russia. Today, I replicate the ancient calls at my synagogue on Rosh Hashanah, to welcome in the new year. I feel it is a fitting way to honor my great-grandfather and the family I never had the chance to meet.

Schi—Russian Cabbage Soup

My grandma Rose Sirota Feiss kept many Russian traditions alive through her ethnic cooking. One of those dishes, *schi*, Russian cabbage soup, is a dish my grandmother taught me to make, and it has become a mainstay in my repertoire of family favorites. It is a dish they ate in Minsk, where she was born, and was popular throughout Russia. To honor Cantor Sirota, I have included my grandmother's version of Russian cabbage soup. Schi is a robust and rich soup with lots of cabbage and sauerkraut, mingling with beef short ribs and ultimately jumbo franks. It is a meal in itself; all you need is a chunk of crusty bread and a big spoon.

Yield: 10 servings
Start to Finish: Under 2 hours

1 large head green cabbage, cored and shredded
1 (28-ounce) can whole tomatoes, with ½ cup of its juice
3–4 pounds flanken/short ribs, cut into 2- to 3-inch pieces

1 (15-ounce) can sauerkraut, drained
2 quarts beef broth
8 jumbo hot dogs
Juice of 1–2 lemons
Kosher salt and pepper

Place the shredded cabbage in a very large soup pot. Add the tomatoes, crushing them over the pot with your hands, allowing the juices to stream in. Add ½ cup of the juice from the can. Tuck the ribs into the cabbage and top with the sauerkraut. Pour the broth into the pot and bring to a boil. Reduce the heat to low, cover and cook for 1½ to 2 hours. If the meat is not falling off the bone, cook an additional 30 minutes.

When the meat is cooked, remove it from the pot so you can trim the meat from the bones to make serving easier. Cut the meat into large chunks and reserve. Add the hot dogs and the juice from 1 lemon to the pot and cook for 15 minutes. Season to taste with salt and pepper.

If time allows, refrigerate the soup overnight so the fat rises to the top and solidifies. Remove this layer of fat, reheat and serve. Serve the soup with a piece of short rib in each bowl and extra lemon to squeeze for a sourer taste.

JH

Fira Stukelman

In her own words

Talking to Fira is like speaking to a college professor. She has a unique perspective, profound insights and a genuine respect for education. She remains strong-willed and fierce. Fira is a community leader and has worked with Congress and proudly calls Mayor Bloomberg a friend. In 1993, Fira founded the New York Holocaust Association, which is an active association of Holocaust survivors.

I was born on March 25, 1933, in Vinnytsya, Ukraine. In Russia, I never knew we were Jewish, because in Russia, everyone was Russian. It was not until the war broke out that we became more observant. A pogrom occurred in September 1941 and another in November, when German soldiers arrived on my street. My mother was taken away while I hid under the bed. I never saw my family again. I survived because a Christian woman came into the room and took me into her apartment. She put a scarf on my head and took me to live with my grandmother. During the day we stayed in the woods; at night we hid in broken and destroyed homes. One terrible night, my grandmother died in her sleep. I was eight years old and truly alone.

I spent the rest of the war in a camp and then the ghetto, until March 1944, when the Soviet army liberated us. I was sent to Chernovtsy, which was in Romania. I was sent to study in a trade school designed for young orphaned women. At sixteen, I graduated and worked in a sewing factory. I married and had a family while working two shifts and attending night school. I graduated from Moscow Textile Institute in 1961. At that time, I could feel an undercurrent of anti-Semitism. Life in

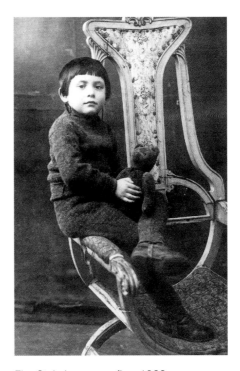

Fira Stukelman, age five, 1938.

Russia was not good, there was no freedom, and so, in 1979, we applied for documents to come to America. It took ten years for the gates to open. I always had the attitude that I would work and I would care about my family. I studied English and began a new life here in America. I would try and learn English everywhere I went. I paid attention at the store, at the bus stop, listening and learning always. In 1991, I went to Touro College, where I earned a degree in social work.

One thing that I miss about Russia is how the family all stays together. I try to keep our family, my two children and three grandchildren, together with the cooking traditions. I make mostly Jewish food, and I bake a lot. It wasn't until I married that I had parents (in-laws) who could teach me how to keep a Jewish home. I learned so much from my mother-in-law. She was really something. My husband and I were married for thirty-five years. The best of my life is here; every day I stand up and say God bless America.

Fira Stukelman's Summer *Borscht* (Beet Soup)

While hot *borscht* with vegetables and flanken warmed the cold nights, Fira's blazing red cold borscht turned vibrant fuchsia from a dollop of swirled sour cream cooled the hot summer days. Fira skips the middleman and boils the potatoes with the beets so they not only pick up the sweet flavor, but they become a colorful addition when served as well. For an authentic experience, have a chilled shot of *horilka* (Ukrainian vodka) standing by.

Yield: 8 to 10 servings
Start to Finish: Under 2 hours, then time to chill in the fridge

3–4 large beets (about 2 pounds), washed and scrubbed clean
2 medium red bliss potatoes, peeled and cut into eighths
3 carrots, peeled and grated on the large hole of a box grater
2 tablespoons sugar (more or less to taste)
1/2 teaspoon sour salt or 3 tablespoons lemon juice (more or less to taste)

2 teaspoons kosher salt
1/2 teaspoon black pepper

SUGGESTED GARNISH
Sour cream, fresh chopped dill leaves, hard-boiled eggs, chopped garlic, chopped sour pickles, grated carrot fried in a little butter

In a large pot, bring 8 cups of water to boil and cook the scrubbed beets over medium heat for 45 minutes. Remove the beets with a slotted spoon and allow them to cool for 30 minutes; do not discard the water. While they cool, cook the potatoes and grated carrots in the beet water. When the beets are cool enough to handle, trim the ends and peel the beets, using a paper towel to gently rub off the outer skin. Hold the end of the beet with the towel (or a tined gripper) and grate the beets on the largest hole of a box grater, directly into the soup pot. Cook, uncovered, over low heat for 1 hour. Stir in the sugar and sour salt or lemon juice and additional salt and pepper, adjusting to your taste. Transfer the soup to a large container and chill in the fridge until nice and cold.

Top the borscht with any or all of the suggested garnishes. If you prefer to serve the potatoes as a side dish, prepare the soup as directed above and boil the potatoes separately before serving.

Berta Kiesler Vaisman

As told by her daughter Juanita Siebenberg

Juanita comes by her cooking talent and warm South American ways naturally, as her mother, a Romanian refugee who found safe haven in Venezuela, brought all her traditions together in their home and in the kitchen.

Berta Kiesler in Romania.

My mother was born on March 12, 1919, in Czernowitz, Romania. She was married at the age of twenty and soon found herself living under Soviet occupation. In June 1941, her husband was taken prisoner by the Romanian army and was turned over to the Russian army, where he died serving on the front line. During this time, my mother was in the ghetto in Czernowitz. She was considered a valuable worker and therefore was not immediately deported to Transnistria, a part of the Ukraine that was conquered by the Germans and Romanians. On June 19, 1942, all that changed. She and her parents were sent by the Romanian government across the Dreister River to Transnistria.

They stayed on the Romanian side of the river for a short time before being transferred to a concentration camp. For more than a year, my mother worked on road construction. Learning that her parents had not survived the camp, she made the decision to return to Czernowitz, as repatriation was still legal. She returned to Czernowitz on March 22, 1944, crossing the border back into Romania. She eventually gained passage to South America, where one surviving brother lived. My father had gone to Venezuela years earlier, and my parents met and married in 1947. My sister, Melita, was born in 1949, and I followed two years later.

We came to America in 1980 and settled in New York. I was raised in Venezuela, and I am the first generation of my family to live in America. My mother was a terrific cook and loved to make Latin dishes. I try to carry on many of her traditions, both those from eastern Europe and Venezuela. My parents were married a short fifteen years when my father died. My parents had two children, five grandchildren and now five great-grandchildren.

Berta Vaisman's *Malai*—Corn Bread

While black bread or challah was the natural choice in Berta's native Romania, as an immigrant in Venezuela, Berta learned the regional specialties of her new home. Venezuelan cooking leans heavily on Caribbean influences, as evidenced in her creamy and subtle corn bread with its grainy texture and smooth filling.

Yield: 9 squares
Start to Finish: Under 1¼ hours

1 cup all-purpose flour
1 cup ground yellow cornmeal
2 cups whole milk
2 eggs
1 teaspoon baking powder

2 tablespoons vegetable oil
¼ teaspoon salt
½ cup (4 ounces) small-curd cottage cheese
  (optional)

Preheat the oven to 350 degrees and grease an 8 x 8-inch baking dish.

Combine all the ingredients, except the cottage cheese, and mix by hand with a wooden spoon. Pour half of the mixture into the prepared baking dish. Spread a layer of cottage cheese, and then top with the remaining batter. Bake for 1 hour or until the bread is firm and lightly brown.

Michelle Bernstein

Professional contributor

As a refugee in Venezuela, Berta adopted cooking techniques consistent with Spanish culinary influences in her South American home. The talented and warmly expressive Chef Michelle Bernstein infuses many of her dishes with ingredients that give a nod to Spain as well as her own South American heritage. As a Jewish American Argentinean chef, she uses these flavors to bring, as she says, "luxurious comfort food" to the table. The following recipe is a prime example of her culinary point of view.

Duck Breasts with Jerez, Oranges and Spanish Almonds

Contributed by Michelle Bernstein, chef/co-owner of Michy's, Miami

I wrote this recipe just for the book. It mixes old world with new, a hint of Jerez from Spain with the old French classic flavor of duck a l'orange. The duck is topped with Marcona almonds, my very favorite. The sauce is a delicious balance that just cuts through the fat of the duck. My mom always made whole roast duck for many of the holidays; I find the duck breasts in this presentation much easier on the home cook.

Serves 4

4 Peking or Maple Leaf duck breasts (2 whole breasts halved), scored in crosshatches
Salt and pepper
Juice and zest of 3 oranges
2 cups duck or chicken broth
2 shallots, minced
¼ teaspoon ground coriander seeds
Pinch ground cinnamon
1 star anise

2 tablespoons orange marmalade
2 ounces dry Jerez (Spanish sherry, I prefer amontillado for this recipe)
1 tablespoon sherry vinegar
2 tablespoons cornstarch mixed with 2 tablespoons water (slurry)
2 tablespoons finely chopped cilantro
1 tablespoon finely chopped Italian parsley
¼ cup Marcona almonds, chopped

Season the breasts with salt and pepper, set aside.

In a small saucepan, heat the orange juice. Reduce ¾ of the way down. Add the duck stock and reduce by about ¾.

Heat a sauté pan over medium-low heat; cook the duck breasts skin side down for 8–10 minutes or until golden brown. Remove the duck from the pan; set aside skin side up. Remove all but 1 tablespoon of duck fat from the pan. Add the shallots, spices, orange zest, marmalade, Jerez and vinegar and simmer for about 4 minutes. Add the orange-duck reduction. Place the duck breast into the pan. Heat the duck for 2 minutes (longer if you prefer the duck medium to medium-well done). Add the cornstarch slurry, whisking the sauce for 2 minutes. Remove the star anise. Add the cilantro and parsley. Season to taste with salt and pepper. Slice the duck, spoon the sauce over each and top with the almonds.

Berta Vaisman's *Barenikes*—Pierogis

Every culture has their version of a pierogi. The eastern European variety are usually filled with a flavorful potato and onion mixture that wants to burst out of its sealed pocket and dive right into a bowl of cold sour cream. You can finish them in the oven topped with fried onions or toss them into a hot skillet and brown them on the stove. Either way, make plenty—they disappear quickly.

Yield: About 30 pierogi
Start to Finish: Under 1½ hours

FOR THE FILLING
3 large Yukon Gold potatoes, peeled and
  quartered
½ cup (8 tablespoons) vegetable, canola or
  olive oil
3 medium onions, chopped (about 2¼ cups)
Kosher salt and pepper

FOR THE DOUGH
3 cups all-purpose flour
1 stick (½ cup) butter or margarine at room
  temperature
1 egg plus 1 egg yolk
1 teaspoon salt
½ cup reserved potato water

To prepare the filling, bring 3 quarts of salted water to boil and cook the potatoes until very tender, about 20 minutes. While the potatoes boil, heat 4 tablespoons of oil in a large skillet; cook and stir the onions over medium heat until lightly browned, about 15 minutes. Reserve the onions. Remove the cooked potatoes from the pot and reserve ½ cup of the potato liquid. Drain and reserve the potatoes.

Mash the potatoes and stir in half of the browned onions and 2 tablespoons oil. Season to taste with salt and pepper. Reserve the remaining onions and the remaining 2 tablespoons of oil for baking.

Preheat the oven to 325 degrees and bring a fresh large pot of salted water to boil.

FOR THE DOUGH
In a large mixing bowl, or the bowl of a food processor, fitted with the metal blade, combine the flour, butter, egg, egg yolk, salt and reserved potato water. When a ball forms, remove the dough from the bowl and knead with your hands for a couple of minutes. The dough should be smooth and elastic.

Divide the dough into two halves. Flour a work surface and roll the dough to a little less than ¼ inch thick (don't try to stretch, it will only tug back). Cut the dough into rounds using a 3-inch cookie cutter or the rim of a glass. Have a small bowl of water standing by to dip your fingers into. Place 1 teaspoon of filling in each round and seal by dipping your fingers in the water, running them along the rim of the dough, folding the circle into a half moon and pinching the edges closed.

Drop the pierogis one at a time into the boiling water and boil for about 5 minutes; do not overcrowd the pot. They will float to the surface when they are done. Drain on paper towels. Repeat with the remaining pierogis. When all the pierogis have been boiled, place them in a large Pyrex dish and cover them with the remaining onions and oil.

Bake for 30 minutes. If you prefer a crisper pierogi, do not bake them. Fry them in a large skillet, heated with the remaining olive oil. Drain on paper towels and serve with the remaining onions.

Chana Wiesenfeld

In her own words

Chana credits her willpower and drive for getting her through a very tough life. Her Romanian and Ukrainian roots show in her cooking style, which definitely reflects her rich heritage.

I was born in Buchovina, which has changed hands many times but is now considered the Ukraine. My father was a manager of sorts, supervising the forest workers, and my mother stayed at home. In 1941, when I was just a child, we went to the ghetto. My father had been taken away earlier and managed to escape through the woods and found us months later. We stayed there in the woods for three and a half years, at which point the partisans, and then the Russians, liberated us.

After being liberated, we returned to Czernowitz but found the Russians had plans for us, and we did not want to go along with their idea. We escaped from Romania, hoping to go to Palestine. I enlisted in a Zionist organization and boarded a train, which took thousands of children through Transylvania and then Bulgaria, Turkey and Greece. In 1946, I spent a year living in Cyprus before leaving for Palestine. We eventually traveled by boat to Palestine, where we lived in bunkers, because of the war. I was too young to enlist in the army, so I existed in limbo until I turned eighteen. I then served in the Israeli army, and in 1956 I was called up to serve again as a reservist. At that time, I met my husband and he had proposed. He returned to the States, and after eight months passed, he came back to Israel, and we were married. Together we came to the United States. I missed my family, I missed Israel, but I stayed here and made a life with my husband and two children.

We were married nearly twenty-five years when he passed away. I was lucky to meet and marry a second wonderful man, who I was married to for twenty-two years. I have five beautiful grandchildren and from them I shep naches. I would love to transmit to the younger generation there should be something leftover from their grandparents, when they start a conversation, there will be Jewishness so it wouldn't fade away. It is also good to bring up what happened. Let them know, let them teach, let them have an idea. They are starting to forget a little bit, I feel it in the air, and they shovel it away. Everyone will become better people by knowing what we went through.

Chana Wiesenfeld's *Kasha Varnishkes*

If we called this dish pasta with toasted grains and caramelized onions, it could easily appear on the menu of a trendy restaurant. But long before we realized whole grains were nourishing, filling, inexpensive and healthful, eastern European cooks discovered their goodness. Chana says her grandchildren "go bananas" for this dish, which works well as a side for stews, braised meat or a light lunch.

Yield: 6 to 8 servings
Start to Finish: Under 1 hour

1 (12-ounce) bag or box uncooked bow-tie
 pasta
3 tablespoons vegetable oil or butter
2 large onions, chopped (about 2 cups)
1 egg, beaten

1 cup kasha (buckwheat groats)
2 cups chicken or beef broth or water (broth
 will make the dish more flavorful)
Kosher salt and pepper

Bring a large pot of salted water to boil and cook the bow-tie noodles according to package directions, drain and reserve.

While the pasta cooks, heat the oil or butter, in a large skillet, cook and stir the onions, over medium heat, until they are very brown but not burnt, about 20 minutes. Using a slotted spoon, remove them from the pan and reserve. In a small bowl, mix the egg and kasha. Using the same pan you used for the onions, spread the kasha and egg mixture in a thin layer and cook, over medium heat, until the egg has cooked out and the kasha lightly browns, about 3 minutes. This step will help develop the kasha's nutty, toasted flavor.

In a small saucepan, bring 2 cups of broth or water to boil. Slowly pour the liquid into the skillet with the kasha and simmer, covered, for 15 minutes. Stir to completely break up any hardened bits of kasha. When the kasha is tender, combine the noodles and onions with the kasha. Generously season to taste with salt and pepper. If the mixture is too firm, add a touch more fat or liquid to loosen the mixture. Serve hot or cold.

Chana Wiesenfeld's Ukrainian Winter Borscht

Chana makes this wonderfully colorful and flavorful soup, chock-full of beets, vegetables and beef to warm even the coldest Russian night. While long considered peasant food by many, beets have been rediscovered for their amazing nutritional quality and sweet buttery taste. Beets have a high sugar content yet surprisingly low caloric count. They are rich in nutrients and vitamins and can be eaten cold in a salad or hot as in this authentic Ukrainian soup. Be sure to follow Chana's advice: "A good cook is the one that watches the pot."

Yield: 12 cups
Start to Finish: Under 2½ hours

1 pound beef flanken
4 large purple-red beets (about 2½ pounds), washed, peeled and halved
1 pound carrots (about 5–6), peeled and grated
1 small green cabbage (about 1 pound), shredded in long strips
1 whole onion, peeled

4 (8-ounce) cans tomato sauce
2 tablespoons chicken flavor powder (optional)
2 garlic cloves, chopped
¼–½ cup freshly chopped dill leaves
Kosher salt and pepper
Boiled new potatoes, for garnish (optional)

In a very large pot, bring 6 cups of water to boil and cook the flanken, skimming off and discarding any foam that rises to the surface. While the flanken cooks, prepare the vegetables for the soup. Take a spoon or small melon baller and scoop out the center of each cleaned and peeled beet half. Chana warns the centers are tough and sometimes bitter; discard them. Using a large box grater, grate the beets and carrots on the largest hole. Shred the cabbage into long strips and peel the onion but leave it whole. By this time, the flanken should be cooked.

Remove the flanken from the pot, rinse and pat dry. You can remove the meat from the bone and cut it into small chunks or leave it on the bone. Rinse out the pot and fill it with 8 cups of fresh water. Stir in the beets, carrots, cabbage, onion, tomato sauce and flanken. Cover and cook on medium heat for about 1½ hours, skimming off and discarding any foam that rises to the surface.

After 1½ hours, stir in the chicken-flavored powder (if needed to boost the flavor), garlic and dill and season to taste with salt and plenty of pepper. Cook an additional 5 to 10 minutes. Serve the soup hot with the traditional garnish of boiled potatoes.

Feedback

Chana makes another version called *knubble* (garlic) borscht. Eliminate the tomato sauce and add 4 tablespoons lemon juice (or a little sour salt) and 2 tablespoons of sugar in the last few minutes of cooking. This sweet-and-sour version also features lots of fresh dill tossed in at the end and plenty of garlic, 8 to 10 cloves, stirred into the soup before serving. Additionally, you can take thick slices of crusty black bread and coat them with the juice of freshly halved garlic cloves by rubbing the cut side of the garlic clove on the bread. This makes a delicious accompaniment.

GREECE

People tend to overlook the catastrophic loss in Greece during the Holocaust, as it seemed removed from the rest of Europe. Make no mistake, Greece suffered devasting losses. In one region known as Salonika, of the forty-three thousand Jews who resided there before the war, forty thousand were murdered. Greece experienced among the greatest loss by percentage. Unlike the other countries noted in the previous chapters, the Jews of Greece were Sephardic. That means their ancestors descended from those exiled during the Spanish Inquisition. Their culture and cooking style differ greatly from Ashkenazi Jews of central and eastern Europe. I began interviewing survivors from Greece just as I finished testing recipes from my Ashkenazi contributors. My kitchen was transformed; no gefilte fish poaching or crumb cake baking. Instead, it was filled with the aroma of fragrant oregano, sweetness from dark honey and a savory bite from salty feta cheese. Olive oil replaced chicken fat as the recipes from Sephardic survivors relate more to the Mediterranean style of eating than what we classically consider Yiddish cooking.

Despite tremendous losses during the war, or maybe because of them, the American Sephardic community remains strong and vibrant with a robust enjoyment of family, friends and food. With great respect for their Sephardic traditions and Greek roots, we present the fervent stories and flavorful recipes remembered by our gutsy Greek survivors.

RECIPES

Luna Cohen's *Fakee*—Greek Lentil Soup

Luna Cohen's *Tourlo*—Greek Ratatouille

Luna Cohen's *Loukoumades*—Greek Doughnuts

Koula Kofinas's *Fasülye*—Braised Marrow Bones with White Beans

Koula Kofinas's *Papoutsakia*—Stuffed Eggplant Skins

Solomon Kofinas's Roasted Baby Eggplant

Stella Levi's *Bamya*—Okra Stew with Chicken

Stella Levi's *Sevoyas Reynadas*—Stuffed Onions

Rachel Mosios's Roasted Lamb with Lemon Potatoes

Rachel Mosios's Spinach Pie

Mathilde Turiel's *Boyos*—Cheese and Potato Turnovers

Samuel Capsuto*: *Bimuelos de Patata*—Potato Pancakes and Raisin Syrup

Joe Dobias*: Horseradish Hanger Steak and Haroset

Jill Schulster*: The Drunken Pharaoh

*Indicates professional contributor

Luna Cohen and Haim Cohen

As told by their daughter Rachel Cohen

The Greek Sephardic community is a strong, proud group. Rachel is a product of that distinct culture and shared her family's story and treasured recipes with me.

My parents lived in Larissa, Greece, where my five siblings were born. My father was a broom-maker, my mother a homemaker. In 1942, when the Germans came into their town, they felt they would not be bothered. However, there came a time when Germans ordered the head of each household to report to the synagogue on a daily basis. My mother refused to let my father go. She felt it was very suspicious that only the Jews needed to report and that the other religious groups were not singled out. My parents felt it was obvious that they had to leave. Because of my father's occupation, he had many contacts with peasants who lived outside of the city; after all, he bought straw from them for his brooms. He felt the family would be able to blend in with the peasant community. Additionally, because my parents were simple people and not wealthy, they had little to leave behind by way of tangible items. They had not acquired an expensive home or other goods that they might regret leaving. They left with little, except their children and my teenage aunt and uncle.

Through the underground, my parents obtained documents saying they were a Christian family whose surname was Chiliakos. My parents fit the profile of this family, so it seemed like a safe solution. For years, my parents moved from town to town, where they were known as the Chiliakos family. In one town, my brother was a student in a Christian-

The Cohen family arriving at South Station, Boston, May 1956. *Left to right, front row*: Luna Maisis Cohen, Rachel, Rosa and Haim Cohen (shaking hands with HIAS representative); *second row*: Nissim, Solomon; *third row*: Isaac and Pinkhas.

run school. He attended church services, and he recalls when he was held up by the priest as an exemplary Christian student. Although I was not born during this period, my parents always talked openly about the war. I find there is a thread that runs through children of survivors. We worry about things other children might not even think about.

My childhood was very influenced by our Greek roots. I married an American man, but my cooking style is very Greek. I grew up eating what is now the trendy Mediterranean diet: for me, eating lentil soup, legumes, lots of salad and meat only once a week was a way of life. My parents were married sixty-one years and have six children and nine grandchildren.

Luna Cohen's *Fakee*—Greek Lentil Soup

This traditional lentil soup is a perfect example of bringing good, healthful ingredients together. What makes this soup Greek is the acidic "zing" that Rachel suggests you add right before serving.

Yield: 6 to 8 servings
Start to Finish: 1½ hours

2 tablespoons olive oil
1 medium onion, chopped (about ¾ cup)
2 cloves garlic, chopped
1 pound lentils, rinsed
2 celery ribs, diced (about 1 cup)
2 carrots, peeled and diced (about 1 cup)

2 bay leaves
Kosher salt and pepper
1 (6-ounce) can tomato paste
6–8 tablespoons balsamic vinegar, for serving

Heat the olive oil in a large soup pot; cook and stir the onions and garlic over medium heat until lightly browned, about 10 minutes. Add the lentils, celery, carrots, bay leaves and 6 cups of water. Season with salt and pepper. Cook, covered, on low heat for 50 minutes. Check the soup from time to time, adding boiling water as needed if the soup becomes too thick. After 50 minutes, stir in 1 can of tomato paste and cook for an additional 10 minutes. Don't overcook the soup; the lentils will become mushy and lose their nutty bite. Remove the bay leaves and drizzle 1 tablespoon of balsamic vinegar into each soup bowl right before serving.

Feedback

Lentils come in a variety of colors, but the brown and green lentils tend to hold their shape better. These legumes are rich in fiber and have been eaten since biblical times. It is written that Jacob used lentils to buy his birthright from his brother Esau, so they have deeply rooted significance.

Luna Cohen's *Tourlo*—Greek Ratatouille

Rachel makes this summer-fresh dish in the height of the season when the vegetables are abundant. *Soujouk*, authentic Mediterranean beef sausage, revs up the colorful and flavorful combination of peppers, zucchini and eggplant. The dried salted beef is spiced with garlic, pepper, cumin and a Turkish seven-spice mixture. Middle Eastern stores feature this variety, but it might be difficult to find a kosher version. If you cannot, substitute chicken, turkey or veal sausage and then add a pinch of cumin or red pepper flakes to enliven the dish.

Yield: 4 to 6 servings
Start to Finish: Under 2 hours

1 eggplant, cut into chunks, salted and drained
3–4 tablespoons olive oil
1 medium onion, chopped (about ¾ cup)
4 cloves garlic, chopped
2 zucchini, cut into bite-size chunks
2 tomatoes, cut into bite-size chunks
1 green pepper, cored, seeded and cut into
  chunks

1 red pepper, cored, seeded and cut into
  chunks
Kosher salt and pepper
½ teaspoon dried oregano
½ pound beef, turkey, chicken or veal sausage,
  chunked

Place the chunks of eggplant in a colander and sprinkle liberally with kosher salt. Place a plate on top of the eggplant to help weigh it down. Let the eggplant drain for 30 minutes. Rinse, dry and reserve. While the eggplant drains, prepare the remaining vegetables. Heat the olive oil in a large skillet, cook and stir the onion and garlic, over medium heat, until lightly browned, about 10 minutes. Stir in the zucchini, tomatoes, eggplant, green and red pepper. Cover and cook over low heat for 30 minutes.

While the vegetables cook, preheat the oven to 350 degrees.

Spoon the vegetables into a baking dish and season to taste with salt, pepper and oregano. Stir in the sausage and bake, uncovered, for 30 minutes.

Luna Cohen's *Loukoumades*—Greek Doughnuts

Few desserts have as rich a history as these small, sweet bites that are free-formed doughnuts. As early as the first Olympics, "honey tokens" were given to the victorious Olympians. Throughout Greece, *loukoumades* are sold at street fairs and pastry shops and served in Sephardic households as a celebratory treat anytime and especially at Chanukah. Rachel's recipe is pure and simple, with just the right ingredients to create these puffy delights. If you can find Greek honey, which is darker than most, it makes a wonderful finish to the dish.

Yield: 40 to 50 "doughnuts," about 10 to 12 servings
Start to Finish: Under 2 hours

FOR THE DOUGH
1 (¼-ounce) package or 2¼ teaspoons active
 dry yeast
1 teaspoon sugar
2 cups warm water
3–4 cups all-purpose flour
Oil for deep frying

TOPPINGS
Golden Greek honey, confectioners' sugar,
 ground nuts or ground cinnamon (optional)

To prepare the dough, you will need a large bowl, as the dough will rise to more than double its size. Dissolve the yeast and sugar in 1 cup of warm water (water temperature should be between 105 and 115 degrees). Allow the yeast to bubble for 5 to 10 minutes. (If it does not, either your water was not the correct temperature, or your yeast was not fresh. Discard and start again, as the dough will not rise or puff up properly.) Stir in 3 cups of flour and the remaining 1 cup of warm water. Mix until the dough is a very thick batter and sticky. It will resemble thick oatmeal, and when you tug on the dough, it will resist and pull back. You can add up to 1 more cup of flour to achieve this consistency. Cover the bowl with plastic wrap and let it double in size, about 1 to 1½ hours. The dough is ready when it has doubled and its craggy bumps resemble the surface of the moon.

In a saucepan or deep fryer, heat 3 to 4 inches of vegetable oil to 375 degrees. It is important to maintain that temperature to prevent the doughnuts from absorbing the oil. Have a bowl of warm water, 2 tablespoons and a plate with a paper towel ready. Dip the spoons in the warm water. Scoop out some dough onto one spoon and use the second spoon to push it into the hot oil. If the dough does not sizzle and immediately float and become golden brown, your oil is not hot enough. Begin dropping the dough into the oil, being careful not to let water from the spoons drip into the pot. Do not overcrowd the pot; it lowers the temperature, and the doughnuts will be greasy. The dough should quickly puff up and float to the top. They will become golden brown, and many will turn themselves over; nudge those that don't, so all sides become golden. When they are done, remove them with tongs, shake off the excess oil back into the pot and drain on the waiting paper towel.

Continue frying until all the doughnuts are cooked. Drizzle honey over the fried dough and have plenty of napkins standing by! You can also sprinkle them with confectioners' sugar and roll them in chopped nuts or cinnamon. They are best when eaten right away.

Koula Koen Kofinas and Solomon Kofinas

In their own words

I met Solomon and Koula at the Kehila Kedosha Janina Synagogue, a small New York landmarked temple that is nestled between Asian food stores and the trendy new establishments dotting New York's famed Lower East Side. This synagogue is the center of their lives, and the pride and respect they have for their Romaniote traditions permeated our conversation. Solomon is a human dictionary for Koula, and together they told me about their family history, lives in America and joy of cooking their Greek specialties.

KOULA

My family originally came from Ionannina, in the northwest part of Greece, but eventually settled in Larissa. I had one brother and two sisters. My father sold dry goods, traveling from bazaar to bazaar selling and trading his wares. In Greece, it was difficult for Jews to have regular jobs, so we created our own work and peddled to make a living. When I was about six, we began hearing how the Nazis were making life difficult for the Jews in Athens. My father moved us to a very small village, maybe only a few hundred people, where no one bothered anyone. We took non-Jewish Greek names and

Koula Kofinas and her wedding party.

spent the war years living there. Before that time, my parents had very lucky names: my dad was called *Siman Tov* and my mother *Mazel Tov* (meaning good sign and good luck); maybe the luck from their names brought us luck in surviving. I can still see my father and brother fishing out back and using the fish to barter for other food. When the war ended, we went back to Larissa and started from the beginning all over again. That's where I stayed until I came here in 1956.

SOLOMON

I was born in Athens, and when the war came to Greece, my brother and I ran away from our home and lived outside the city until the war ended. I lost the rest of my family in Auschwitz. After the war, we returned to our home and found out that German soldiers had lived there. We gained our house back by asking the Greek police to return it to us. I met Koula here in America, and we have been married for fifty-one years; we have two sons and two grandsons. I am proud to say that I married a Cohen, which is spelled Koen in Greek, because we do not have the letter *C* in our language. Our son now leads the service in the temple, and he is teaching our grandsons the same traditions.

Koula Kofinas's *Fasülye*—Braised Marrow Bones with White Beans

Koula recalls, "Friday nights we always had meat. Meat was reserved for celebrations like Passover and Rosh Hashanah, and of course, Shabbos. It's not the law, it's tradition. Some years we only had bones; this is why we made *fasülye* (beans), and we would make believe we were eating meat. We would eat the marrow from the bones; it was better than caviar." While this dish showcases the rich, buttery marrow, some prefer to have some meat on their bones. If that's the case, you can substitute short ribs.

Yield: 4 servings (about 2 bones per person)
Start to Finish: Under 3 hours

½ pound (about 1 cup) giant lima beans or any dried white bean
4 tablespoons olive oil
2 large onions, diced (about 2 cups)
2 carrots, peeled and finely chopped (about 1 cup)
2 celery ribs, finely chopped (about 1 cup)

4 cloves garlic, chopped
1 (28-ounce) can chopped tomatoes, with its juice
2 pounds (about 8 thick-cut) round marrowbones
2 teaspoons kosher salt
½ teaspoon black pepper

Bring a medium pot of water to boil and cook the beans for several minutes; drain and let the beans sit in a bowl of cold water for 1 hour. Drain and reserve. While the beans soak, prepare the remaining ingredients.

Heat the olive oil in a Dutch oven or covered pot; cook and stir the onions, carrots and celery over medium heat until just beginning to soften, about 10 minutes. Stir in the garlic and continue cooking for 5 minutes. Pour in the tomatoes with their juice; add the drained beans. Tuck the marrowbones in the sauce and add enough water to cover the bones by 3 inches (about 2 cups of water). Season with salt and pepper. Cover and cook, over low heat, for 2 hours or until the vegetables, beans and marrow are soft.

Check the pot occasionally to see if additional water needs to be added. If the center marrow begins to ooze from the bones, remove them from the pot and allow the beans to cook until tender. You don't want to lose the marrow in the sauce. In the end, if you find the sauce is too watery, Koula suggests you leave the lid off the pot for the last 15 minutes. Serve with plenty of crisp bread for dunking.

Koula Kofinas's *Papoutsakia*—Stuffed Eggplant Skins

Koula explains, "When we grew up, we made everything from scratch. It took me twenty years to buy anything from outside." Her ingredients represent the best of Greek cooking: fragrant parsley, flavorful oregano, good olive oil and fresh vegetables. Her stuffed eggplant brings in the salty addition of crumbled feta cheese, which melts into the meaty eggplant stuffing.

Yield: 4 servings
Start to Finish: Under 1½ hours

2 large eggplants, halved lengthwise (do not peel)
1 pound feta or farmer's cheese, crumbled (about 4 cups)
2 tablespoons finely chopped fresh flat-leaf parsley

½ cup seasoned bread crumbs
Kosher salt and pepper
1 egg
2–3 tablespoons olive oil

Preheat the oven to 375 degrees and coat the bottom of a baking dish with olive oil.

Bring a large pot of salted water to boil and cook the eggplants until they just start to soften. Do not let them fully cook or become too soft. Remove the eggplants from the pot and allow them to cool.

In a medium-size bowl, combine the feta, parsley, bread crumbs, salt (go light, the feta is salty) and pepper. When the eggplants are cool enough to handle, scoop out the meat, being careful not to scrape too deep or tear the skins; they need to be intact to stuff. As you are scooping out the meat, discard the large seeds; they are bitter. Chop the eggplant meat into small pieces and combine with the feta mixture. Crack the egg into the eggplant and feta and mix thoroughly. Fill each eggplant skin with ¼ of the eggplant and feta stuffing.

Place the eggplants, skin side down, in the prepared baking dish. Drizzle the tops with a little olive oil. Bake for 45 minutes or until golden brown. Serve with a drizzle of olive oil.

Feedback

When buying eggplants, Koula instructed me to buy the lightest in weight for its size, as that indicates an eggplant with fewer bitter seeds.

Solomon Kofinas's Roasted Baby Eggplant

Solomon credits his longevity to Koula's culinary talents: "I'm here after so many years because of her good cooking." But Koula is not the only chef in the house. Solomon enjoys preparing eggplant his way. He prefers the sweeter Japanese eggplant, which is much more like what they ate in Greece, small with few if any seeds. If you cannot locate Japanese eggplant, substitute small baby eggplant.

Yield: 4 servings
Start to Finish: Under 1 hour

1 pound Japanese eggplant or baby eggplant, quartered lengthwise
1 tablespoon finely chopped fresh flat-leaf parsley

Kosher salt and pepper
1 teaspoon dried oregano
Grated Parmesan cheese (optional)
3 tablespoons olive oil

Preheat the oven to 400 degrees. Toss the eggplant slices with the parsley, salt, pepper and oregano. Pour ½ cup water into a baking dish large enough to comfortably hold the eggplant. Place the eggplants in the dish. Bake for 45 minutes or until the eggplants are soft.

Periodically, check to see if water is needed to prevent the eggplant from scorching. Sprinkle with Parmesan cheese and a drizzle of olive oil before serving.

Feedback

While fresh herbs are almost always preferred, I actually recommend dried oregano in place of fresh. The flavor is a little less pungent and will not overwhelm the other ingredients. When adding dried oregano or any dried herb to a dish, gently rub it between your fingers to release its full flavor.

Stella Levi

In her own words

Stella is just one of those women. If you passed her on the street, you would marvel at her stature and elegance. If you spoke to her, you would be enthralled by her intellect and humor. Much of her time is devoted to New York's Centro Primo Levi, which "seeks to broaden the historical perspective of contemporary Jewish life and encourage understanding among different peoples." Her story is unfortunately typical for Greek Jews during the Holocaust, but her attitude is amazingly strong and positive.

I was born on the island of Rhodes, and as far as I know, so were many generations of my family before me. The Jewish community was considered Sephardic. I had a good childhood living in the "Juderia," the Jewish district of the walled city of the island. The other inhabitants within the walls were the Muslims of Turkish nationality. Rhodes and the other eleven smaller islands called Dodecanese were part of the Italian territory from 1912 till the end of the Second World War, when they were ceded to Greece.

Yes, I had a very pleasant childhood: summers at the beach nearby and mild winters that allowed the young people to go for long excursions outside the town to visit the recently excavated Greek classical monuments, an amphitheater and temple. To remember the weekly celebration of Shabbos brings still a pleasant feeling mixed with a strong sense of loss, the same that I have also for the many festivals that were always concluded with my mother and aunts and neighboring women singing beautiful songs in *Ladino* (an ancient Judeo-Spanish language) and Hebrew.

After the elementary Jewish school, I went to the Italian school run by Catholic nuns. It was an excellent school, but unfortunately the gates were to be closed to us (Jewish girls, and the same for the school for the boys) in September 1938 following the laws of "racial discrimination" against the Jews issued by the fascist government of Benito Mussolini. True, we at Rhodes did not experience the ferocious anti-Semitism and persecutions that plagued many Jewish communities in other European countries, but nonetheless we definitely bore material suffering and the emotional alienation and stigma of second-class citizens. The community saw a big emigration of young people, especially young men, going either to the then Belgian Congo and/or Rhodesia (today Zimbabwe). My brother left with them.

The war years were painful, what with shortages of food and the constant bombardments by the British and American air forces: the Juderia, being next to the commercial port, one of the main targets of the air raids, suffered much destruction and loss of lives. But the beginning of the end of the Jewish community of Rhodes and of the town of Rhodes as I knew it came in September 1943, when the Italian government surrendered. The country split in two: pro-Mussolini and the Germans against the rest who went with the king and General Badoglio. For reasons that I cannot still fathom, the government in Rhodes surrendered the island with some tens of thousands of Italian soldiers to the cunning Germans. The small Jewish community, unaware of the atrocities and mass killings already happening to their coreligionists in Poland and other countries under the Nazi regime, waited with dread nonetheless for the end of the war. But the end came in a manner so barbarous, so cruel and so inhuman that I still do not like to talk about or to think about it.

Suffice to say that we all ended up in Auschwitz-Birkenau, where most perished. A very small percentage of Jews from this region survived—among them were my sister and me.

In 1947, we arrived in New York to join some members of my family who had immigrated to the U.S.A. before the war. A few years later, I got married and had a son who lives in New Jersey and gave me the joy of having three good grandchildren.

Stella Levi's *Bamya*—Okra Stew with Chicken

One of Stella's favorite Greek specialties is *bamya*, Greek for "okra," which inspired this recipe. Chicken and okra stew is much like a New Orleans gumbo. Spicy cumin and aromatic coriander wake up the chicken and okra as they slow simmer with tomatoes, onions and garlic. Stella feels lamb or beef marries well with the sauce, so experiment with your favorite. A fresh squeeze of lemon adds a refreshing note at the end.

Yield: 4 servings
Start to Finish: Under 2 hours

1½ to 2 pounds chicken thighs
Kosher salt and pepper
¼ cup olive oil
1 pound fresh okra, rinsed and cut into 1-inch slices (remove the ends, they are tough)
2 medium onions, diced (about 1½ cups)

2 cloves garlic, chopped
2 cups chopped canned tomatoes, with their juice
1 teaspoon ground cumin
1 teaspoon ground coriander
Juice of 1 lemon (about 2–3 tablespoons)

Pat the chicken dry and then generously season the chicken with kosher salt and pepper. Heat the olive oil in a Dutch oven and brown the chicken in batches, on all sides, over medium heat. While they brown, prepare the okra, onions and garlic. When the chicken is browned, remove it to a waiting plate.

In the same pot, add a little olive oil if needed; cook and stir the onions over medium heat until lightly browned, about 10 minutes. Stir in the garlic and cook for an additional minute or two. Add the tomatoes, cumin, coriander, 2 cups of water and the juice of half the lemon. Add the chicken into the pot (not the liquid that has collected on the plate). Season with salt and pepper. Turn the heat to low, cover and cook for 45 minutes. After 30 minutes, preheat the oven to 350 degrees; the stew will finish cooking in the oven.

After 45 minutes, transfer the pot to the oven and bake, covered, for 30 minutes. Add water if the sauce is too thick: the okra is gummy and is a great natural thickener. If the sauce is thin, uncover the pot for the final 15 minutes. Squeeze the rest of the lemon juice over the finished dish just before serving.

Stella Levi's *Sevoyas Reynadas*—Stuffed Onions

While eastern Europeans prefer to stuff cabbage leaves, Greek cooks favor stuffing grape leaves and these delicious slow simmered sweet onions. We've added Stella's variation, which involves frying the stuffed onions. Either way you prepare this dish, it is a creative and bold way to serve this established favorite.

Yield: 25 rolls
Start to Finish: Under 2½ hours

5 large (about 5-inch diameter) onions, peeled, stem and root removed

FOR THE FILLING
1 pound ground beef or veal
3 tablespoons uncooked rice
1 tablespoon olive oil
1 tablespoon finely chopped fresh flat-leaf parsley
1 tablespoon tomato sauce, with pulp
1 tablespoon water
Kosher salt and pepper

FOR THE SAUCE
4 plum tomatoes, peeled and chopped into 1-inch pieces
3 tablespoons olive oil
Kosher salt and pepper
1 teaspoon oregano
Toothpicks to help close the rolls

Bring a very large pot (one that can hold all 5 onions submerged at one time) of salted water to boil. Gently place the onions in the water and boil for at least 20–25 minutes. While the onions boil, mix all the filling ingredients and reserve.

With a slotted spoon, carefully remove the onions from the pot but keep the water on a slow boil; you might need to drop the onions back in if the layers need additional coaxing. Let the onions cool, covered with a towel; this will help them steam, making them easier to peel. When the onions are cool enough to handle cut a slit in the onion vertically, from stem to root. (Imagine the onion is a globe of the earth; cut the onion from the North Pole to the South Pole, not around the equator!) Peel the onion, layer by layer; they should easily fall away and feel soft and pliable. You will need to continually trim the root and stem to help the layers fall off. Try to remove the thin film that you will find between the layers. Each onion should yield about 5 pieces, large enough to fill. Reserve the small inside portions to chop for the sauce.

Take an onion layer and fill it with a teaspoon of the meat filling. Roll the onion up: the onion will actually curl and form a tight roll on its own. Use a toothpick to close if needed.

To prepare the sauce, you will need to peel the tomatoes. Remove the small stem and then with a sharp paring knife, carefully remove the skin. If you are not confident with that method, bring a medium pot of water to boil. Prepare a bowl with ice water. Make a small X in the bottom of each tomato. Drop the tomatoes, one at a time, into the boiling water. After 30 seconds, remove with a slotted spoon. Plunge the tomato into the ice bath; the skin should begin to fall away. Chop the tomatoes into 1-inch chunks and reserve.

Roughly chop the small inner onion portions that you reserved. Heat the oil in a large sauté pan, cook and stir the chopped onions over medium heat until lightly browned, about 10 minutes. Stir in the chopped tomatoes and allow them to simmer with the onion. Pour 1 cup of water into the pan and then gently place the filled onions in the pot, nestling them in the sauce close together, layering them if necessary. Season to taste with salt, pepper and oregano. Cover and cook on medium-low heat for 45 minutes. After that time, add water if needed (you don't want the sauce too dry or diluted) and turn the onions over. Cover and continue to cook an additional 45 minutes. Serve by spooning the sauce over the onions, remembering to remove the toothpicks before eating.

Variation: Sometimes Stella fries the onion rolls before placing them in the sauce. Simply beat 2 eggs and dip the filled rolls into the beaten egg, then dredge lightly in flour. Fry in a large skillet coated with olive oil for several minutes on all sides, until lightly browned. Place the rolls in the sauce and continue as directed above.

Rachel Angelou Mosios

In her own words

Rachel spoke with a warm Greek accent and a personality to match. She is an Athenian Jew who, like many from her area, survived the war by living as a Christian in the Greek mountains. Both she and her husband came to America after the war, where they met in New York and built a home centered on Jewish traditions and wonderful Greek flavors.

I am very proud of where I came from, which is Athens, Greece. I was the oldest child, having no sisters and three brothers. The people in Athens were very close to the Jewish people. When things got bad, they gave us IDs with Christian names. The police tried to help other Greek Jewish people. We lived a very festive life. I remember very clearly a night where our family was at a great big party. Everyone was dancing and celebrating, yet they knew the war was approaching. From 1943 until 1944, we were okay. We had to hide occasionally from the Germans, but because my father was a very good businessman, we always had materials to trade with the farmers for food. My father had heard from his business partner, a man from Salonika, that it was unsafe to stay in Athens. My mother did not want to leave, but my father convinced her. On the last Passover that I spent in our hometown, I got very drunk! I was only nine, but I remember being so tipsy.

Soon after that holiday, we went into hiding. We went to a city called Pedely, a place that people would go to when they were ill. At first, we lived in a small cabin at the top of the mountains. One day, we found other members of our family and we went crazy with joy! We moved into a "villa" that we shared with them for the duration of the war. My father was always on the lookout, and fortunately for us, the Communists in the area hated the Germans more than they hated the Jews. When the Germans would approach, they would use a megaphone to warn us. I really believe they saved us many times.

After the war, we returned to our home, which was such a mess. The house was part of my mother's trousseau, and we were not going to leave it until we had to. When I was twenty, in 1954, my favorite aunt brought us to Astoria, Queens, which was a very Greek section of New York. I met my husband, Victor, who I am married to for fifty-one years. Together we have two children and six grandchildren. I was proud to learn that recently one of my granddaughters stood up at her school and told her classmates the importance of never forgetting the Holocaust. That is a lesson I am very happy to know she learned and is strong enough to pass on.

Rachel Mosios's Roasted Lamb with Lemon Potatoes

Sunday night meant leg of lamb for Rachel's family. She made the traditional roasted lamb and studded it with garlic, seasoned it with oregano and treated it to a splash of lemon, which adds an acidic note to the dish. The roasted potatoes linger in the oven after the lamb is cooked and pick up all the flavors of the zesty sauce.

Yield: 6 servings
Start to Finish: Under 2½ hours

1 (3-pound) leg of lamb
3–5 cloves garlic, peeled and halved
Kosher salt and pepper
1 teaspoon oregano

Juice of 1 lemon
8 red potatoes (about 2 pounds), peeled and cut into quarters or chunks

Preheat the oven to 350 degrees. With the tip of a sharp knife, pierce the lamb every 2 inches and insert the garlic. While the knife holds the slit open, sprinkle salt and cracked pepper into the roast. Season the entire lamb with additional salt, pepper, oregano and the juice of 1 lemon. Place the squeezed lemon in the bottom of the roasting pan and add ½ cup of water. Roast the lamb for 25 minutes per pound or until a meat thermometer inserted in the roast reads 150 to 155 degrees. Remove the lamb from the roasting pan and cover with foil; it will gain 5 to 10 degrees while it rests.

Raise the oven temperature to 400 degrees and add the potatoes and ½ cup water to the roasting pan. Cook for 45 to 60 minutes, checking the pan every 20 minutes to see if additional water is needed to prevent the potatoes from scorching. This also creates the sauce. When the potatoes are crisp on the outside and fork tender on the inside, they are done. Slice the lamb and place in the pan juices and reheat, if necessary, until warmed through. You can squeeze additional lemon juice into the pan if you prefer a tarter flavor.

Rachel Mosios's Spinach Pie

One of the reasons Rachel loves making this dish is because it boldly features dill, and as Rachel explains, "Greek Jewish people love dill!" While many spinach pies also pile on the parsley, Rachel feels it overwhelms the spinach and cheese and should be used in moderation. Resist the urge to cut this flaky pie into cute triangles; Rachel says they are not traditional. While her mother would make her own phyllo dough, we suggest store-bought frozen phyllo, which is readily available in most supermarkets. Phyllo is temperamental, so you might want to have an extra box on hand in case you need additional sheets.

Yield: 30 pieces
Start to Finish: 5 hours to thaw the phyllo, then under 1½ hours

1 box phyllo dough (large sheets), thawed

FOR THE FILLING

4 boxes chopped spinach, thawed and drained
1 tablespoon olive oil for frying
1 medium onion, chopped (about ¾ cup)
6 eggs, beaten
2 bunches scallions (about 12), white and light green portion only, chopped (about ⅔ cup)
1 pound feta cheese, crumbled (about 4 cups)
4 ounces (½ cup) small-curd cottage cheese or farmer's cheese

2 ounces (¼ cup) cream cheese, softened at room temperature
Kosher salt and pepper
1 large bunch of dill, leaves chopped (about 1 cup)
¼ cup finely chopped fresh flat-leaf parsley

FOR ASSEMBLY

1 cup olive oil
3 tablespoons freshly grated Parmesan cheese

Thaw the phyllo according to package directions, about 5 hours at room temperature or overnight in the fridge. At the same time, thaw and drain the spinach. Remove the liquid from the spinach by squeezing the spinach with your hands or placing it in an old dish towel and squeezing out the liquid.

Heat 1 tablespoon of olive oil in a large skillet over medium heat; cook and stir the onions until lightly browned, about 10 minutes. When the onions are translucent, add the spinach to the pan and continue cooking and stirring for several minutes. Place the spinach and onions into a large bowl; stir in the eggs, scallions, feta, cottage cheese, cream cheese, salt (go lightly, feta is a salty cheese) and pepper. Stir to combine all the ingredients, breaking up any large clumps of cheese. Add the chopped dill and parsley. Refrigerate until ready to bake.

Preheat the oven to 375 degrees and prepare a large 15 ½ x 10 ½-inch jellyroll pan by coating the bottom with olive oil. A pastry brush is very helpful for this and for the phyllo layering. Open the phyllo dough and cover the sheets with a piece of waxed paper, then a damp towel; this is to prevent the phyllo from drying out while you assemble the pie.

Place one sheet of dough on the bottom and brush with oil. Place the next two sheets in the pan so they meet in the middle and hang over the opposite sides. Brush with oil, lay two more sheets in the pan, draping those ends over the opposite side, and brush with oil. Continue layering the sheets in the center of the pan, brushing each sheet with oil. Do not be concerned if some of the sheets tear; there will be many layers and it will not matter in the end. Once you have used half the package (about 10 sheets), spread the spinach mixture in the pan, smoothing it out with an offset spatula, a piece of greased waxed paper or your lightly greased hands. Sprinkle the spinach with the grated Parmesan cheese. Fold the overhanging sheets over the mixture and begin layering the top sheets by brushing each with oil and layering them in the center of the pan. When you are done layering, tuck in any straggling edges and brush liberally with the olive oil. Score the pie (cut through the top layers, but not piercing the bottom) into 30 pieces and sprinkle a touch of water on top.

Bake for 1 hour. If the top browns too quickly, cover loosely with foil and continue baking. Serve warm or cold.

Feedback
Rachel's spinach filling is delicious and versatile and can be used in so many ways. It makes a terrific ingredient for stuffing or layering pasta or filling a prebaked pie shell to create a quick and easy quiche. If handling the phyllo seems daunting, a wonderful variation is to buy puff pastry shells. Bake them according to the package directions. When fully cooked, spoon the spinach filling into the shells and heat through. They make an elegant appetizer or a delectably light lunch. This recipe uses oil, but you can use melted butter if you prefer the flavor.

The Turiel Family

As told by Bernie Turiel

Bernie Turiel is a very articulate gentleman who credits Selahattin Ülkümen for having saved his family and dozens of other Jews from Rhodes. It is interesting to note that Ülkümen, a Muslim, was the reason the term "Righteous Christians/Gentiles" was changed. He was the first Muslim to be honored by Yad Vashem, and from that time on, those courageous men and women who risked their lives to save Jewish people were known as "Righteous Among the Nations."

I was born on the island of Rhodes in November 1934. At that time, Rhodes was an Italian possession. My immediate family consisted of my father, Daniel, mother, Mathilde Nahum, and younger brother, Elliot. My mother was born in Izmir, Turkey. When she married my father in 1933, she came to live in Rhodes. Because of her closeness with her family in Turkey, my mother made sure that she registered with the Turkish Consul in order to remain a citizen of Turkey. This turned out to be very fortunate for our family and the others who also registered.

In early September 1943, the Germans took possession of Rhodes. The adult male Jews were asked to report and register periodically with the German authorities. On the first day of Passover in 1944, after we had come home from synagogue, a severe air raid took place. While we were sitting having our lunch at home, a bomb dropped down the street from us and we saw the home that was hit go up in flames. My father became greatly alarmed as to what was happening in the city. He decided that it was time for us to move out of our home and move to a nearby village.

Our family had an old farm in a village outside the city, but it had no adequate living facilities. Abidin, a Turkish farmer who lived in the same village, was the caretaker of our farm and was a good friend of the family. Without announcement, we showed up at his doorstep after we left the city. He and his family welcomed us, and even though they had meager living facilities in their home, they emptied out one room, laid out mattresses on the floor, and we were welcomed to spend as much time as we needed with his family. We continued to live on the farm until July 1944. Living with this Turkish family was one of the happiest events of my life. Even though we did not live in comfort, we were welcomed into their home. I remember learning to ride horses on the farm, cultivate the fields, do the farming, pick fruits and nuts from the trees and join the sons of Abidin in work and play. We had become part of his family, and they had become part of ours.

In January 1943 a young Turkish diplomat, Selahattin Ülkümen, was appointed as the consul general to the island of Rhodes. On July 19, 1944, after the arrival of SS officers in Rhodes, a leader of the Jewish community was informed by a German officer that all Jewish males over the age of sixteen years had to report to a designated spot the following day. This time, when the adult male Jews were gathered, they were immediately placed in a detention center by a group of SS officers. Wives and children of all the men detained were ordered to report within forty-eight hours. Mr. Ülkümen was aware of what was going on in Europe, just as we all were aware of the existence of the concentration and extermination camps. He immediately went to confront the German commander on the island, General von Kleemann. Mr. Ülkümen demanded that all Turkish citizens and their families be protected since the Turkish Republic was a neutral country and not involved in the war. With his determination and energy, he got the German authorities to concede to the release of the Jews holding Turkish passports and their families. With his energetic and determined intervention on behalf of the Turkish Jews, he was also able to procure the release of my father and other heads of families from the detention center who were married to women who maintained their Turkish citizenship, even though there was no basis for this contention. He also made a valiant effort to seek the release of other Jews who had abandoned their Turkish citizenship.

Through his efforts, he was able to rescue forty-two persons who were either Turkish citizens or married to Turkish citizens. Within days, the Jewish community of Rhodes was placed on three small cargo boats and shipped to the Greek port of Piraeus near Athens, and from Athens they were transported to Auschwitz. In January 1945, we were given permission to leave Rhodes, and twenty-six of us embarked on a sailboat for a prolonged trip that started at dawn. We arrived at Marmaris, Turkey, at about 11:00 p.m. It was a treacherous and hard trip, but we were all happy to land on the shores of Turkey. After a short stay in Marmaris, we were able to travel to Izmir, Turkey, where we lived with my mother's family until we left for the United States in July 1946.

When we came to New York, and until she was in her nineties, my mother continued to make her delicious Sephardic dishes: *ojaldres* (baked phyllo triangles), *ooscas* (delicious sweetened rolls), *bimuelos* (potato pancakes), homemade haroset (a Passover relish of apples and walnuts) and so many more. I'm hungry now after just describing these dishes, but although I've made some of them, I think Mom had a secret ingredient because hers were always so much better.

In June 1990, Mr. Ülkümen was honored at Yad Vashem in Jerusalem, and his name was placed in the Avenue of the "Righteous Among the Nations" for his efforts in rescuing Jews from deportation from the island of Rhodes. My mother had the honor to be present at the ceremony. He will always be remembered in history as a kind, compassionate and righteous person. My parents had two sons—my brother and me—three grandchildren and six great-grandchildren.

Mathilde Turiel's *Boyos*—Cheese and Potato Turnovers

Mathilde's son Elliot and grandson Josh are the guardians of her potato and cheese stuffed *boyos* recipe. *Boyos*, from the Spanish for bun, are small "oil-dough" filled turnovers, which can be stuffed with a variety of savory fillings. Elliot recalls a close-knit community of Rhodes immigrants gathering on Saturday nights in New York to play endless poker and feast on Sephardic specialties such as these.

Yield: 20 to 24 pieces
Start to Finish: Step 1: 15 minutes, then refrigerate 6 to 8 hours or overnight,
Step 2: Under 45 minutes

FOR THE DOUGH
1 cup lukewarm water
1 tablespoon salt
2 tablespoons vegetable oil
2 tablespoons vinegar
3 cups all-purpose flour
Vegetable oil to soak the
 dough

FOR THE FILLING
½ russet potato, peeled and
 boiled
½ pound (or 7½-ounce
 package) farmer's cheese
2 eggs
¼ cup grated Parmesan
 cheese
¼ teaspoon baking powder
½ teaspoon salt

FOR ASSEMBLING
½ cup Parmesan cheese

STEP 1

In a medium bowl, prepare the dough by mixing the water, salt, oil and vinegar. Slowly sift in the flour and continue mixing until you have smooth, elastic dough. Cover the bowl with a damp cloth and let it sit for 30 minutes. After the dough has rested, form it into small 1½-inch-diameter balls (size of a golf ball). Place the dough balls in a shallow pan and cover generously with vegetable oil. Refrigerate, covered, for 6 to 8 hours or overnight.

Prepare the filling by bringing a pot of salted water to boil. Cook the potato until fork tender, about 20 minutes. Mash the potato and then stir in the farmer's cheese, eggs, grated cheese, baking powder and salt. Cover tightly with plastic wrap and refrigerate until ready to use.

STEP 2

Preheat the oven to 375 degrees, lightly grease a baking sheet and take the dough and filling out of the fridge.

Fill a bowl with ½ cup of grated Parmesan cheese. Place a ball of dough on a flat surface and begin stretching it, being sure not to tear it; the oily dough is not very elastic. Try to create a flat shape resembling a 4- or 5-inch square. Even though the dough is extremely oily, use a pastry brush to spread a little additional oil in the center of each piece (you can use the remaining oil from the pan that the dough rested in overnight). Sprinkle the center of the dough with a pinch of Parmesan cheese. Drop a generous teaspoon of filling in the center. Fold the opposite corners into the middle, making a neat package, being sure there are no openings in the dough. Sprinkle the top with additional Parmesan cheese and place, seam side down, on the prepared baking sheet. Continue this process until you have used all the dough. Bake for about 30 minutes or until the boyos are lightly browned.

Variations: There are many fillings that can be used for the boyos. Why not try our spinach filling (see page 340) or potato and onion filling (see page 318)?

Samuel Capsuto

Professional contributor

The Capsuto family and the Turiels have much in common. They both have their family roots imbedded in the Turkish culture and both enjoy bimuelos, a Sephardic take on the classic potato pancake. The following is a personal recipe from Samuel Capsuto's family that brings a regional element and surprisingly yummy flavor to the dish.

Author's Note: I sadly learned that Samuel passed away. May his memory be for a blessing.

Bimuelos de Patata—Potato Pancakes

Contributed by Samuel Capsuto, owner of Capsuto Freres, New York

Yield: 14 pancakes
Start to Finish: Under 45 minutes

3 russet potatoes, peeled, boiled and mashed
5 eggs, beaten
1 cup sharp grated cheese

½ teaspoon salt
Vegetable oil for frying

Bring a medium pot of water to boil and cook the potatoes until very soft, about 20 minutes. Drain then mash the potatoes. Add the eggs, cheese and salt. The mixture should be thick. In a large skillet, heat about 1 inch of vegetable oil. When the oil is about 375 degrees, drop the potato mixture, by generous tablespoons, into the oil. Cook until golden on each side, about 3 to 5 minutes per side. If you prefer to bake the pancakes, grease a baking sheet and bake at 375 degrees for 30 minutes.

Raisin Syrup

1 pound raisins
4 cups water

Lemon juice to taste

Bring all the ingredients to boil in a saucepan. Reduce the heat and cook until the liquid is reduced by ⅓. Strain the sauce and serve the syrup on the side or drizzled on the potato pancakes.

Joe Dobias and Jill Schulster

Professional contributors

Bernie Turiel fondly recalls his mom's homemade haroset (Passover relish), and while we don't have the recipe for her version, here is Chef Joe Dobias's. The following recipes are a playful spin on Jewish traditional dishes that were featured at a "progressive Passover seder" held at New York's Joe Doe Restaurant. The chef has paired it with a mouthwatering hanger steak and a pungent horseradish vinaigrette that awakens the taste buds. To wash it all down, blend an irreverent drink that Jill, Joe's wife and master mixologist, calls "The Drunken Pharaoh."

Horseradish Hanger Steak and Haroset

Contributed by Chef Joe Dobias

Yield: 6 servings
Start to Finish: Step 1: 15 minutes, then 8 to 10 hours or overnight to marinate,
Step 2: Under 30 minutes

MARINADE
½ cup ketchup
¼ cup Worcestershire sauce
½ small horseradish root, peeled and grated
⅛ cup maple syrup (natural good quality real syrup)
6 hanger steaks, 8 to 10 ounces each

HORSERADISH VINAIGRETTE
1 whole apple
½ piece horseradish root, grated fine
¼ cup cider vinegar
1 cup olive oil
1 tablespoon kosher salt
1 tablespoon black pepper

HAROSET
2 apples, sliced or diced (your preference)
3 tablespoons chopped almonds
3 tablespoons honey
1 tablespoon Manischewitz wine
½ tablespoon apple cider vinegar
Kosher salt and pepper

STEP 1
Clean the steak of all silver skin and fat. Mix all the marinade ingredients in a large bowl and then pour it over the steak. Refrigerate in the marinade for 8 to 10 hours or overnight.

In a blender, puree all the vinaigrette ingredients, season to taste with salt and pepper, cover and refrigerate until ready to serve.

For the haroset, in a small bowl, combine the ingredients and mix thoroughly. Season to taste with salt and pepper. Cover and refrigerate until ready to serve.

STEP 2
Remove the marinated steaks from the refrigerator and allow them to come to room temperature. Cook them as you choose: in the broiler, on a griddle or on the grill. Serve with the horseradish vinaigrette and haroset on the side.

The Drunken Pharaoh

If you see Elijah when you open the door, you've had too much!

FOR EACH DRINK
1 piece matzo
1 tablespoon confectioners' sugar
Simple syrup (a combination of 2 parts water
 and 1 part sugar boiled then cooled to make
 a sweet syrup) or light corn syrup

1½ ounces Old Pogue bourbon*
½ ounce fresh lemon juice
2 ounces Manischewitz wine
Club soda, to top off drink

Take a piece of matzo and crush it with the back of a spoon until it is coarse. Do not make it into powder. Mix in the confectioners' sugar.

Take a 10½- to 12-ounce glass. "Rim" (coat the rim of the glass with the simple syrup or corn syrup and then dip it right into the matzo to coat the entire rim). The syrup will help the crumbs adhere to the rim of the glass. Fill the glass halfway with ice.

In a shaker glass filled halfway with ice, add the bourbon, lemon juice and Manischewitz. Shake vigorously and then strain it into rimmed glass. Top the drink off with club soda. L'Chaim!

* If you would not drink bourbon at Passover, substitute another appropriate alcohol in its place.

GLOSSARY

This glossary of Yiddish words will not only help you navigate the book, but it will make you a Yiddish *maven* (expert) in a snap as well.

alte heim: old home
The aromas bring back memories of the alte heim.

baleboste: homemaker
If you make homemade noodles instead of opening a box, you're a real baleboste.

bashert: meant to be
It is bashert that all these wonderful recipes have been preserved.

bisel, a: a little
Add a bisel more sugar to make it a touch sweeter.

challah: yeasty egg bread traditionally made for the Sabbath meal
It's not easy to braid the challah with six strands.

forshpeiz: appetizer
Before there was tapas, Polish cooks always began a meal with forshpeiz.

haimish: homey
You always feel welcome in a haimish home.

hak messer: kitchen tool used to chop
The sound of the hak messer chopping onions can make you crazy.

kasher: to make kosher
The meat was kashered so it is fit and proper to eat.

kaynahorah: literally means to ward off the evil eye, the Jewish version of "knock on wood"
I think my honey cake is going to rise perfectly, kaynahorah.

kibbitz: to chat in a fun and congenial manner
It's always more fun to kibbitz when you have a little nosh to eat.

kiddush: Blessing over the wine, or a reception held after morning prayers
The grandfather at the reception said kiddush over the wine and then we all enjoyed a bountiful kiddush.

kishke: a blend of ground ingredients that were stuffed into a cow's intestinal lining; now synthetic casings are used. Idiomatically, it means someone's guts.
Please stop complaining, you're taking my kishkes out.

kugel: a pudding or casserole, often made with noodles or potato
I like my potato kugel savory and my noodle kugel sweet.

landsman: a fellow Jew who comes from your hometown
How comforting it was for a survivor to meet a landsman.

L'chaim: a Jewish toast, means to life
Let's make a toast to the remarkable survivors, L'chaim.

lockshen: Jewish egg noodle
A true baleboste makes her lokshen from scratch.

mensch: a person of integrity and honor
The Righteous Among Nations designation acknowledges the mensch who helped save their Jewish neighbors.

mishpocha: the entire family
When you make these recipes, be sure to invite the whole mispocha.

nosh: a light bite
Some of these recipes are big meals, others just a light nosh.

pareve: a neutral food that contains no dairy so it can be eaten with meat
If you add butter to the cake it won't be pareve.

schmutz: dirt
The foamy schmutz that rises to the top of soup needs to be removed.

shep naches: get pleasure
So many of the survivors shep naches from their children and grandchildren.

shitteryne: To cook without a recipe, throwing in a little of this and a little of that
It's much easier to cook with a recipe than by shitteryne.

shmatte: rag
Be sure to have a shmatte standing by when making latkes.

shochet: a ritual butcher to maintain kosher law
The local shochet was a very important man.

shtetl a small Jewish town in eastern Europe, a term used primarily before World War II
So many of our Polish survivors came from small shtetls.

shul: synagogue
The pious go to shul daily to pray.

simchas: a festive occasion
Simchas are so wonderful to celebrate.

tzimmes: a casserole, idiomatically used to imply that something is a big fuss
Don't make a tzimmes if the tzimmes doesn't come out well.

vance: bed bug, idiomatically used to mean someone who gets in trouble
If you continue to be a nuisance, I'll have to call you a little vance.

General terms used in the book that might not be familiar as they relate to Jewish holidays and traditions:

aliyah: when a Jewish person immigrates to Israel

Bar/Bat Mitzvah: when a Jewish boy/girl turns thirteen and accepts the responsibility of being a Jewish adult

Erev: the day before a Jewish holiday

gymnasium: a European term for secondary school

Haggadah: The book used to conduct the Passover seder

haroset: A compote made from nuts and wine eaten at Passover

Kaddish: A prayer for the dead

Ma Nishtana: a term for the four questions asked by the youngest person at a Passover seder

minyan: ten adult Jews (for the Orthodox must be men) required to conduct formal prayer

Palestine: a term for Israel prior to statehood in 1948

Pesach: an alternative Hebrew term for the Passover holiday

Rosh Hashana: The Jewish New Year

seder: Ritual dinner to celebrate the Passover holiday

Shabbos: a derivation of the Hebrew word *Shabbat*, indicating the Sabbath, celebrated by Jews from sundown Friday to sundown Saturday

Shavuot: a holiday to commemorate the Jews receiving the Torah and to celebrate the wheat harvest

Yahrzeit: anniversary of the death of a close relative, often marked with prayer and the lighting of a candle

ABOUT THE AUTHOR

June Feiss Hersh grew up in New Rochelle, New York. She graduated magna cum laude from the University of Pennsylvania with a degree in elementary education. She holds a master's degree in gifted and talented education and taught third and fourth grade before joining her family's lighting business. When her family sold the company in 2004, June's sister remarked, "We did well, now let's do good." That's when June embarked on her food writing career, penning cookbooks with a charitable flavor. She has authored five books with a focus on the Holocaust, Jewish food and food history, all of which have generated proceeds for charitable organizations. Proceeds from the sale of this book will benefit those committed to teaching the lessons of the Holocaust. June was a featured guest on QVC's *In the Kitchen with David*, has given hundreds of book talks in connection with her published works and writes extensively for food blogs and magazines. She is a member of the New York chapter of Les Dames D'Escoffier, a philanthropic organization of female leaders in the food, wine and beverage industry, and serves on the advisory board of the Catskills Borscht Belt Museum. When not cooking or writing, June enjoys traveling, playing with her dog Mallomar and, most of all, being called Nana by Henry, Daisy and Aria. She resides in Bedford, New York, with her husband of forty-seven years. To provide feedback, inquire about speaking engagements or just to chat, email: junehersh@gmail.com.

EAT WELL- DO GOOD
WWW.JUNEHERSH.COM

Other works by June Hersh

Recipes Remembered: A Celebration of Survival (Ruder Finn Press, May 2011)

The Kosher Carnivore (St. Martin's Press, September 2011)

Still Here: Inspiration from Survivors and Liberators of the Holocaust (2015)

Yoghurt: A Global History (Reaktion Books, 2021, available in English, Chinese, Japanese and Arabic)

Iconic New York Jewish Food: A History and Guide with Recipes (The History Press, February 2023)

junehersh@gmail.com   @JuneHersh   june.hersh.3

Fundamentals of
BIOFILM RESEARCH
Second Edition

Zbigniew Lewandowski
Haluk Beyenal

CRC Press
Taylor & Francis Group
Boca Raton London New York

CRC Press is an imprint of the
Taylor & Francis Group, an **informa** business

CRC Press
Taylor & Francis Group
6000 Broken Sound Parkway NW, Suite 300
Boca Raton, FL 33487-2742

First issued in paperback 2017

© 2014 by Taylor & Francis Group, LLC
CRC Press is an imprint of Taylor & Francis Group, an Informa business

No claim to original U.S. Government works

Version Date: 20131014

ISBN 13: 978-1-4665-5959-2 (hbk)
ISBN 13: 978-1-138-07437-8 (pbk)

Library of Congress Cataloging-in-Publication Data

Lewandowski, Zbigniew, author.
  Fundamentals of biofilm research / by Zbigniew Lewandowski, Haluk Beyenal. -- Second edition.
  p. ; cm.
  Includes bibliographical references and index.
  ISBN 978-1-4665-5959-2 (hardcover : alk. paper)
  I. Beyenal, H., author. II. Title.
  [DNLM: 1. Biofilms. QW 90]

  QR100.8.B55
  579'.17--dc23   2013026166

Visit the Taylor & Francis Web site at
http://www.taylorandfrancis.com

and the CRC Press Web site at
http://www.crcpress.com

Contents

Preface

The seven years that have passed since the publication of the first edition have brought significant advances in both biofilm research and biofilm engineering, some of which we have included in the text. As a result, many chapters have been updated and expanded with the addition of new sections reflecting changes in the status quo in biofilm research and engineering. We have also emphasized throughout the text that biofilm research and engineering have matured to the extent that biofilm-based technologies are now being designed and implemented. Two examples of such technologies are described in the first chapter: the use of biofilms in reactors for wastewater treatment and the use of biofilms in microbial fuel cells. The biofilm-based technologies used in wastewater treatment exemplify mature technologies: they are in use in large-scale reactors, even though the design of these reactors is still mostly empirical. Microbial fuel cells, exemplify emerging biofilm-based technologies that are still at the level of bench- and pilot-scale applications. The trend is obvious: In the future we will see more and more biofilm-based technologies, and biofilm research will need to include large-scale reactors and large-scale biofilm-based processes.

Not all the changes we intended to introduce in the second edition could be accommodated by expanding the existing chapters, though, and two chapters have been added: Chapter 2 (Imaging and Characterizing Biofilm Components) and Chapter 7 (Biofilms on Metals and Other Electrically Conductive Surfaces). Chapter 2 discusses techniques that are used to enhance the imaging of components of biofilm systems and includes not only the imaging of biofilm microorganisms using various types of optical and electron microscopy but also the imaging of the topography and chemistry of surfaces and of the hydrodynamics and mass transport in biofilms. Chapter 7 discusses new frontiers in biofilm research, energy conversion in biofilms, and the biofilm-based conversion of chemical energy to electrical energy. The effects of depositing biofilms on metals had been studied by biofilm researchers for a long time, mostly to quantify the mechanisms of microbially influenced corrosion (MIC). More recently, however, new branches of biofilm research have emerged, dedicated to the mechanisms of electron transfer between biofilms and metals, energy conversion in biofilms, and the generation of electricity in microbial fuel cells (MFC). The biofilms active in MIC and MFC are now seen to be electrochemically active biofilms (EABs). The processes driven by EABs have a common denominator, the mechanisms of electron transfer between microorganisms and solids. The studies initially concerned with electrically conductive surfaces converged with the existing research on microorganisms growing on minerals. These minerals are not necessarily electrically conductive, but they do serve as electron donors or acceptors in microbial metabolic reactions, giving rise to such terms as "mineral-respiring microorganisms." Not surprisingly, these processes are driven by microorganisms attached to the surfaces of minerals, or biofilms. The mechanisms of electron transfer between minerals and microorganisms are still under study, but the parallels to the mechanisms of electron transfer between micro-organisms and metals or other electrically conductive surfaces are obvious. The results of such studies apply to such diverse fields as corrosion protection, new types of power supplies and advanced techniques of bioremediation. When we were preparing the first edition of this text, it was the structure and complexity of microbial structures on surfaces (i.e., the biofilms) that stimulated the imagination and were imaginatively compared to cities built by microorganisms. Now, the applications of biofilm-based technologies stimulate the imagination. The edition of *Science Daily* (http://www.sciencedaily.com) published on December 15, 2009, extrapolated from a paper presented by a group of scientists from MIT in the Proceedings of the US National Academy of Sciences and summarized their findings in an article entitled "Rock-Breathing Bacteria Could Generate Electricity and Clean Up Oil Spills." We can only hope that by the time we prepare the next edition of this book, such applications will have become reality.

The main goals for this text remain the same as they were in the first edition. Specifically, the goals are to serve as

- A compendium of knowledge about biofilms and biofilm processes.
- A set of instructions for designing and conducting biofilm experiments.
- A set of instructions for making and using various tools useful in biofilm research.
- A set of computational procedures useful in interpreting results of biofilm research.
- A set of instructions for using the model of stratified biofilms for data interpretation, analysis, and biofilm activity prediction.

The book describes biofilm processes and biofilm-based technologies at a level adequate to help someone with a general knowledge of bioengineering but uninitiated in biofilm research to learn the tools and techniques used to study biofilm processes. Thus, interested researchers can start experimental explorations of biofilm processes armed with a basic knowledge of these processes and the tools useful for studying them. Once they start their own explorations, a more thorough literature search will be needed. We provide sources of relevant texts that we believe are interesting and constitute a good introduction to the subject.

As in the first edition, at the end of the book we attach a CD with software packages useful for facilitating procedures described in the text. Specifically, the CD contains the following:

- Computer programs for extracting numerical parameters from images of biofilms.
- Computer programs for computing the growth-limiting nutrient concentration profiles in stratified biofilms.
- Computer programs for calculating biokinetic parameters from growth-limiting nutrient concentration profiles measured using microelectrodes.
- Computer programs for controlling micropositioners and a data acquisition system for measuring chemical concentrations in biofilms using microelectrodes.

We refer to the use of MATLAB® throughout the book, both for calculations and to control instruments. The source codes of the MATLAB programs are given on the attached CD, and the use of the program is described in the corresponding chapters. Before using the CD, please copy its entire contents to your hard drive. If you use a different directory structure or folder names different from those used on the CD, you must revise the path definitions in the corresponding MATLAB programs; otherwise, you will receive error messages.

Many people contributed to the second edition of the book, most notably the generations of students and visitors who have worked over the years in the Biofilm Engineering Research group at Washington State University in Pullman and in the Center for Biofilm Engineering, Montana State University in Bozeman. Some of their names appear in the subtitles of figures, some appear in a list of references following a chapter, and some appear in the first edition of the book. Jerome Babauta provided expert comments on Chapters 4 and 7. His contribution to the subject of electrochemically active biofilms helped us to address future areas of research on EABs. We both acknowledge support from the Office of Naval Research, Department of Energy, National Science Foundation, and Department of Defense, which sponsored projects that allowed us to develop the methodology and results presented in this book. The expert comments and proofreading of the text by Lois Avci have improved it considerably. Finally, the generations of our students and visitors who have worked tirelessly over the years in the Biofilm Structure and Function Laboratory at the Center for Biofilm Engineering and in the Biofilm Engineering Research group at Washington State University are gratefully acknowledged.

MATLAB® and Simulink® are registered trademarks of The MathWorks, Inc. For product information, please contact:

The MathWorks, Inc.
3 Apple Hill Drive
Natick, MA, 01760-2098 USA
Tel: 508-647-7000
Fax: 508-647-7001
E-mail: info@mathworks.com
Web: www.mathworks.com

Authors

Zbigniew Lewandowski has been active in biofilm research for 30 years. He is a professor in the Department of Civil Engineering at Montana State University in Bozeman and conducts research at the Center for Biofilm Engineering there. Much of his research has been devoted to studying microscale biofilm processes and their relations to the performance of macroscale biofilm reactors, relations between microbial and physicochemical processes, mass transport in biofilm reactors, and energy conversion in biofilms. Most recently, he has been studying electrochemically active biofilms in such processes as microbially influenced corrosion and microbial fuel cells. He has published more than 100 papers and 12 book chapters on biofilms and biofilm processes. He coedited the book *Biofouling and Biocorrosion in Industrial Water Systems*. He chaired the Biofilm Specialist Group of the International Water Association (IWA), organized several international conferences, and presented short courses on biofilm processes in the US, Ireland, Poland, and China.

Haluk Beyenal is widely known for his biofilm engineering expertise in the areas of microscale biofilm characterization and electron transfer processes. The research in his laboratories has focused on a fundamental understanding of biofilm processes, and the characterization of biofilms and applications of biofilm processes to the environment, energy, and health. He and his collaborators have developed many research tools for understanding biofilm processes at the microscale, including microelectrodes for monitoring local chemistry inside biofilms and mathematical models for predicting biofilm activity, electron transfer rates, and biofilm structure. His research group pioneered the study of electron transfer processes in biofilms using microelectrodes. He and his collaborators developed an electrochemical nuclear magnetic resonance microimaging technique to study electron transfer processes in biofilms. The microscale techniques developed in his laboratory are crucial to the study of biofilms respiring on electrodes. His research group and his collaborators also developed technology to power remote sensors using energy harvested from microbial fuel cells. His research has been funded by the Office of Naval Research, the National Science Foundation, the Department of Energy, the Department of Defense, and the National Institutes of Health as well as by industry. He received an NSF-CAREER award in 2010. He has published more than 80 papers and eight book chapters on biofilms and biofilm processes. Currently, he is an associate professor at Washington State University, in the Gene and Linda Voiland School of Chemical Engineering and Bioengineering.

chapter one

Introduction to biofilms and to biofilm research

1.1   Introduction

Many natural and engineered systems are influenced by biofilms, microorganisms firmly attached to surfaces. From the human perspective, the effects of biofilms vary from desirable, through undesirable, to disastrous, depending on the locations where the biofilms are deposited and on their microbial community structures. Examples of desirable effects are the activities of biofilms accumulated in wetlands and in the trickling filters used in wastewater treatment plants. These biofilms remove organics from water. Examples of undesirable effects are the activities of biofilms accumulated in cooling towers and other heat exchangers. These biofilms increase heat transfer resistance. Finally, examples of disastrous effects are the activities of biofilms developing on tampons applied to absorb bleeding and the activities of biofilms developing on implantable prosthetic devices. The former biofilms can cause serious illnesses or the death of the infected patients, and surgery may be required to remove the latter. Irrespective of where the biofilms have accumulated and what their microbial compositions are, there is a common desire to control their activities either to promote their growth or to eradicate them. To facilitate biofilm control and to optimize biofilm processes, an entirely new branch of bioengineering has emerged: biofilm engineering. Most subjects covered by this book belong to the domain of biofilm engineering.

Biofilms affect such disparate processes as bioremediation of toxic compounds, oral hygiene, souring of oil formations, microbially influenced corrosion (MIC), wastewater treatment, and the use of implantable prosthetic devices, causing the development of biofilm research in the related disciplines of science and technology. The two types of biofilm-related research activities that have emerged from this complex picture are research devoted to understanding fundamental biofilm processes and research devoted to developing biofilm technology. Currently, the most active discipline in biofilm research devoted to understanding the fundamentals of biofilm processes is microbial ecology, in which biofilms are seen as highly organized structures of microorganisms having qualities comparable to those of tissues. Microorganisms in biofilms are not randomly distributed; instead, they aggregate in clusters resembling communities in which various microbial species have various tasks to accomplish, and they communicate with each other using chemical signals. This internal organization of bacterial biofilms, documented by confocal images and molecular probes, has stimulated imaginations and spawned new ideas, sometimes bordering on science fiction. *New Scientist*, the British science magazine, published an article in August 1996 emphatically comparing biofilms to cities built by microorganisms. This analogy reflects the popular image of biofilms as self-assembled microbial structures that are able to optimize their functions. Time has passed, and this paper is now a historical footnote, but the general idea it proposed not only survived but gained even more traction when cell–cell communication in biofilms was discovered. Since the publication of the paper in 1996, chemical substances have been identified that are used by biofilm micro-organisms to facilitate the exchange of information, a discovery that implies new possibilities in biofilm control. If these lines of communication could be intercepted, biofilms could be controlled in an entirely new way, and if such intervention is indeed possible, the implications go far beyond controlling biofilms. The research is ongoing, and it remains to be seen to what extent these expectations will be satisfied.

The effects of biofilms on various technological processes constitute the domain of biofilm engineering, which is mostly devoted to controlling biofilm processes. Among the various types of research projects oriented toward biofilm control, biomedical research attracts much attention. This area of biofilm research experiences the most spectacular development. According to the National Institutes of Health html document, "Guide: Research on Microbial Biofilms" released on December 20, 2002, biofilms are responsible for 80% of infections in the body. According to the Guide, these infections include "oral soft tissues, teeth and dental implants; middle ear; gastrointestinal tract; urogenital tract; airway/lung tissue; eye; urinary tract prostheses; peritoneal membrane and peritoneal dialysis catheters, indwelling catheters for hemodialysis and for chronic administration of chemotherapeutic agents (Hickman catheters); cardiac implants such as pacemakers, prosthetic heart valves, ventricular assist devices, and synthetic vascular grafts and stents; prostheses, internal fixation devices, percutaneous sutures; and tracheal and ventilator tubing." Graphic images of biofilms on nonhealing wounds and infected implantable prosthetic devices extracted during revision surgeries are convincing examples of the importance of biofilms and biofilm processes in biomedical research. However, biomedical research is not the only, and is perhaps not even the most active, area of research dedicated to developing biofilm technology. Much has been done to understand and to mitigate the effects of biofilms in nonbiomedical processes, such as the biodeterioration of stone, MIC, and the biofouling of filtration membranes. An example of an undesirable biofilm effect is shown in Figure 1.1, in which a biofilm is accumulating inside silicone tubing used to deliver nutrients to a biological reactor. As time progresses, the biofilm that has accumulated on the walls may close the conduit entirely.

Biofilms are also used to enhance desirable technological processes, such as the bioremediation of contaminated groundwaters and wastewater treatment. Establishing biofilm research as a discipline provides a common denominator to all these studies and generates interest in biofilms as a mode of microbial growth that may cause effects that are difficult to predict using the traditional model of microbial growth in suspension. A host of biofilm-based technologies have been implemented in biological wastewater treatment.

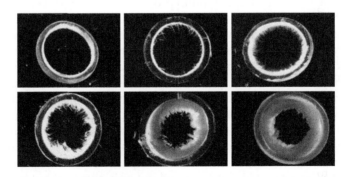

Figure 1.1 Biofilm formation in silicone tubing.

The study of biofilms entered the scene relatively late, but our current awareness of biofilms and knowledge of biofilm processes have changed our perception and our approach to many problems in everyday life. For example, microbial contaminations of surfaces, from those in households to those in hospitals, are now seen as biofilm problems. The rapidly developing interest in controlling biofilm processes, either stimulating or inhibiting them, has generated the field of research activities commonly called biofilm engineering; but there is no sharp division between the fundamental studies of biofilm processes and biofilm engineering, as there is no such division between any type of natural science and engineering, and we will not make such a distinction in this book. Quantifying biofilm processes at a fundamental level is the prerequisite to understanding biofilm control, whether for enhancement or inhibition. The physical, conceptual, and virtual tools described in this text can be used equally well in fundamental research on microbial community structure and activity and in research on controlling MIC.

The following text will introduce the basic vocabulary needed to discuss biofilm research. It is unfortunate that many terms used in biofilm research do not have precise meanings; for example, the term *biofilm activity* can be defined in more than one way. Without attempting to rectify this situation, the terms used here will be defined, and every attempt will be made to use them consistently throughout this text.

1.2   Terminology

1.2.1   Biofilms, biofouling, and biofouling deposits

There is no commonly accepted definition of the term *biofilm*. Although self-explanatory to biofilm researchers, it is regarded as controversial by many in other fields of research and for good reasons. One reason is that *film* semantically implies a continuous and relatively thin layer. Despite that implication, many biological structures regarded as biofilms are not continuous, and many others can hardly be called thin. The lack of a commonly accepted definition of a biofilm leaves it to the judgment of individual researchers whether, for example, microorganisms immobilized in polymers should be considered biofilms or not. In this text, a biofilm is considered to be an aggregate of microorganisms imbedded in a matrix composed of microbially produced extracellular polymeric substances (EPS) and attached to a surface. The aggregate does not have to form a continuous layer, and its thickness is not limited by any arbitrarily selected number, but it must be attached to a surface. This latter requirement specifically excludes suspended microbial flocks and microorganisms immobilized in polymer beads from the definition of a biofilm. It accepts immobilized microorganisms, though, as long as the substance in which they are immobilized is attached to a surface. Briefly, the definition says that biofilms are microorganisms attached to surfaces.

Definitions of biofilms are often challenged, and the definition given here will also be challenged. Challenging definitions of biofilms by asking apparently provocative questions, such as "How many microorganisms have to be on the surface to form a biofilm?" or "Should a deposit of dead microorganisms on a surface be considered a biofilm?" is more than just a frivolous and sometimes annoying activity. It has a deeper meaning and significance because it stimulates our understanding of biofilm processes. For example, the question "How many microorganisms are needed to form a biofilm?" can be answered if the notion is accepted that microorganisms growing in biofilms are significantly different from those growing in suspension. Biofilm researchers have demonstrated that microorganisms attached to surfaces consistently express different genes than the same species growing in suspension. If this notion is accepted, then the answer to the question is, "A single microbial cell attached to a surface can be called a *biofilm*, because it expresses the characteristic features of biofilm microorganisms." However, this is a rhetorical question, and our definition of a biofilm as "an aggregate of microorganisms imbedded in a matrix composed of microbially produced EPS and attached to a surface" does not specify the number of microorganisms that constitute a biofilm.

Some biofilm researchers argue that biofilms should be regarded as a mode of microbial growth, in the same manner as microbial growth in suspension is, rather than as physical structures formed by microorganisms attached to surfaces. Following their argument would produce definitions of biofilms that are different from the one accepted in this book. Defining biofilms as aggregates of microorganisms attached to surfaces, as is done here, is practical for those life scientists who study biofilm structure, biofilm activity, and microbial community structure in biofilms, and for those engineers who study rates of biofilm reactions and mass transfer in microbial aggregates. For others, alternative definitions of biofilms may be more suitable. Using alternative definitions of biofilms may be quite productive in some areas of biofilm research and may help in interpreting biofilm processes from a point of view other than that assumed in this book. Even though our definition of biofilm has been designed from the engineering point of view and to satisfy the needs of biofilm engineering, the definition suggested by the National Institutes of Health in the html document "Guide: Research on Microbial Biofilms," released on December 20, 2002, "A biofilm is an accumulation of microorganisms (bacteria, fungi, and/or protozoa, with associated bacteriophages and other viruses) embedded in a polysaccharide matrix and adherent to solid biologic or non-biologic surface," is quite close to our definition.

It is conceivable to avoid the controversial definition of a biofilm by not using the term *biofilm* at all: there are other terms that can be used instead. Another term often used when referring to attached microbial growth is *biofouling* (of surfaces). It is derived from the term *fouling of surfaces*, which refers to the process of contaminating surfaces with (usually) mineral deposits. In principle, the term *biofouling* refers to the same process as the term *fouling* does, but it emphasizes the fact that the deposits on the fouled surfaces are composed of mineral substances mixed with living microorganisms and macroorganisms and with EPS excreted by the microorganisms. The term *biofouling* is less controversial than the term *biofilm*, perhaps because *fouling* does not imply any geometrical form of the deposits, as *film* does. Even though the terms *biofouling* and *biofilm* are sometimes used interchangeably, they do not have the same meaning: biofouling is a process, whereas a biofilm is an object. The term *biofouling deposits* is considered an equivalent of the term biofilm, particularly in industrial settings, where it is used to emphasize the presence of scaling deposits or corrosion products imbedded in the EPS excreted by the microorganisms attached to surfaces. When larger organisms accumulate on surfaces, as is common in marine environments, for example, the term *macrofouling* is used, without referring to biofilms.

1.2.2   Biofilm systems, biofilm processes, and biofilm reactors

Besides the term *biofilm*, which refers only to a deposit on a surface, a broader term, *biofilm system,* is needed that includes other components affecting the rates of biofilm formation, biofilm structure, and activity. A *biofilm system* is defined as a group of compartments and their components determining biofilm structure and activity.

A biofilm system is composed of four *compartments* (Figure 1.2):

- The surface to which the microorganisms are attached
- The biofilm (the microorganisms and the EPS matrix)

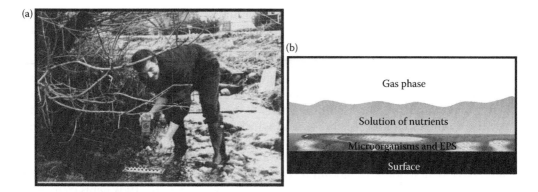

Figure 1.2 (a) Stainless steel coupons attached to a rack are immersed in a stream. The four compartments of this system are (1) all the surfaces on which the biofilms are deposited, including the stainless steel coupons, (2) the biofilms deposited on these surfaces, (3) the water, and (4) the air. (Reprinted from Braughton, K. R. et al., *Biofouling* 17: 241–251, 2001.) (b) Biofilm compartments: gas phase, solution of nutrients, biofilm and surface.

- The solution of nutrients
- The gas phase (if present)

It is convenient to identify components within biofilm compartments. The number of components in each compartment may vary, depending on the needs of a particular description. For example, in one study it may be convenient to identify two components of the biofilm: (1) the EPS (matrix) and (2) the microorganisms. In another study, it may be convenient to identify three components of the biofilm: (1) the EPS, (2) the microorganisms, and (3) the particulate matter trapped in the matrix. Similarly, it may be convenient to single out two components of the surface: (1) the bulk material and (2) the biomineralized deposits. Alternatively, if MIC is studied, it may be convenient to describe the surface by identifying three components: (1) the metal surface, (2) the corrosion products, and (3) the biomineralized deposits on the surface. The needs of the specific study dictate the number of components identified in each compartment of the biofilm system, as is exemplified in Figure 1.2.

The term *biofilm processes* refers to all physical, chemical, and biological processes in biofilm systems that affect, or are affected by, the rate of biofilm deposition or the microbial activity in biofilms. Examples of biofilm processes are attachment, detachment, and growth. In some texts, these three processes are considered *the* biofilm processes because other processes occurring in biofilm systems are related to this group of processes. This tendency to refer to only three biofilm processes originates from the mass balances in chemical and biological reactors in which the rate of change in the concentration of a selected component is quantified in the influent, in the effluent, and in the reactor, which is analogous to quantifying the rates of attachment, detachment, and growth in biofilms if we assume that the biofilm is the reactor. We do not think it is practical to restrict the number of biofilm processes to these three, because there are processes occurring in biofilms that may be difficult to associate with any of them, such as plasmid exchange and the buildup of resistance to antimicrobial agents.

Biofilm processes are quantified in *biofilm reactors*. Colloquially, biofilm reactors and biofilm systems have the same meaning. There is a subtle difference between these two terms, though: biofilm systems exist with or without our intervention, whereas biofilm reactors are created by our actions. Whenever a biofilm process is promoted or suppressed in a biofilm system, or even when a biofilm process in a biofilm system is quantified without its rate being affected, the biofilm system becomes a biofilm reactor. For example, wetlands exist in nature whether engineers designed them or not. Wetlands designed and constructed to remove contaminants are biofilm reactors because the biofilm processes were used to achieve the goal. However, even natural wetlands, once biofilm performance in them is monitored, become biofilm reactors. A special subgroup of engineered biofilm reactors is laboratory biofilm reactors (LBRs), which are constructed to emphasize selected biofilm processes or to facilitate selected types of measurements in biofilms. Chapter 3 is entirely dedicated to these biofilm reactors.

It is convenient to identify biofilm reactors with biofilm systems and to define biofilm reactors as a collection of four compartments and their respective components determining biofilm processes, e.g., a continuously stirred tank reactor (CSTR), a lake, a wetland, or a human body, without any implicit or explicit references to natural or engineered processes occurring in these systems. One benefit of this definition is that it is not restrictive: the reactor whose performance is affected by the presence of biofilms can be affected by the presence of another agent, biological or not. For example, a CSTR that is used to grow microorganisms in suspension can be, in addition to its main function of growing microorganisms in suspension, considered a biofilm reactor—if the researcher decides to quantify the effect of microbial growth on the walls. Several parameters are quantified in biofilm reactors, and their meanings must be defined.

1.2.3   Biofilm activity

Biofilm activity is defined here as the rate of nutrient utilization per unit of surface area covered with biofilm, which is consistent with the definition of biofilm activity in most biofilm engineering applications. In most studies, biofilm activity is evaluated based on the rate of utilization of the growth-limiting nutrient. However, in some instances, rates of change of substances other than the growth-limiting nutrient are selected to compute biofilm activity. The choice of the substance for evaluating biofilm activity is dictated by the process under study and sometimes by analytical convenience. If a biofilm reactor is operated to remove an undesirable substance from the solution, then the rate of removal of this substance is a natural choice for evaluating biofilm activity. Other choices include the substances serving as the main electron donor and the main electron acceptor in the respiration of selected groups of microorganisms residing in the biofilm. Biofilm activity can be computed from measurements at the macroscale or at the microscale, and we will call these overall and local biofilm activities, respectively.

1.2.4   Nutrient utilization rate and specific nutrient utilization rate

Nutrient utilization rate (NUR) and specific nutrient utilization rate (SNUR) are two parameters in common use for quantifying the rates of microbial reactions in suspension. For a chemostat operated at a steady state with volume V, volumetric flow rate Q, and cell density X (Equation 1.1), NUR is computed by multiplying the difference in nutrient concentration between the influent and the effluent of the reactor by the volumetric flow rate (Figure 1.3):

$$\text{NUR} = (C_{\text{Influent}} - C_{\text{Effluent}}) \times Q \qquad (1.1)$$

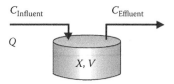

Figure 1.3 A chemostat operated at a steady state with volume V, volumetric flow rate Q, and cell density X.

The units of NUR are $\dfrac{g}{m^3} \times \dfrac{m^3}{s} = \dfrac{g}{s}$.

SNUR is NUR divided by the amount of biomass in the reactor ($X \times V$):

$$\text{SNUR} = \frac{(C_{\text{Influent}} - C_{\text{Effluent}}) \times Q}{X \times V} \tag{1.2}$$

The units of SNUR are $\dfrac{\dfrac{g\ nutrient}{s}}{\dfrac{g\ biomass}{m^3} \times m^3} = \dfrac{g\ nutrient}{g\ biomass \times s}$

NUR and SNUR have the same meanings in biofilm reactors as they have in reactors with suspended growth. Computing the amount of biomass accumulated in the biofilm needed to compute the SNUR is more challenging in a biofilm reactor than it is in a reactor with suspended microbial growth.

1.2.4.1   Biofilm activity from macroscale measurements: Overall biofilm activity

To evaluate biofilm activity from macroscale measurements (Equation 1.3), the concentration of the substance selected for evaluating biofilm activity is measured in the influent and in the effluent of a biofilm reactor, and the difference between these concentrations is multiplied by the volumetric flow rate and then divided by the surface area covered by the biofilm (Equation 1.3). The substance selected for the evaluation of biofilm activity must be actively utilized by the microorganisms, and it should not precipitate, evaporate, be deposited in the biofilm, or otherwise be removed from the reactor in any manner other than by microbial utilization (Figure 1.4).

$$\text{Biofilm activity} = \frac{(C_{\text{Influent}} - C_{\text{Effluent}}) \times Q}{A} = \frac{\text{NUR}}{A} \tag{1.3}$$

The unit of biofilm activity is $\dfrac{g}{s \times m^2}$.

One common error made when quantifying biofilm activity at the macroscale in LBRs is not taking into account biofilm growth in the tubing. To avoid this error, it is important to take the samples of the substance selected for the evaluation of biofilm activity from as close to the entrance and the exit of the reactor as possible. In particular, evaluating the concentration of the selected substance in the influent to the reactor based on its concentration in the container with the feed solution should be avoided, if possible. Estimating biofilm activity from macroscale measurements averages out the differences in biofilm

Figure 1.4 A continuous flow biofilm reactor. The reactor volume is V, the volumetric flow rate is Q, the surface area on which the biofilm grows is A, and the biofilm density is X_f.

activity that may exist in various parts of the reactor. Biofilms accumulate on all surfaces in the reactor, and these surfaces may be made of different materials or differently oriented in space. For example, if the reactor bottom is made of glass but the walls are made of polycarbonate, the biofilm on the bottom may have different activity than the biofilm on the walls. Also, the bottom of the reactor is oriented horizontally, whereas the walls are oriented vertically, which may affect the way the biofilms respond to shear stress. The differences in material and the differences in flow regime near these surfaces may cause the differences in activity of the biofilms accumulated on these surfaces. Biofilm activity estimated from macroscale measurements averages out all these differences and presents a biofilm of uniformly distributed activity. Macroscale measurements of biofilm activity can be quite adequate for estimating the overall reactor performance in wastewater treatment, for example; but in experiments designed to quantify the effects of hydrodynamics on biofilm accumulation or the effects of surface chemistry on biofilm accumulation and activity, biofilm activity should be estimated from microscale measurements, which deliver information about local biofilm activity, and the locations of the measurements should be chosen so they are relevant to the type of question addressed by the specific study.

1.2.4.2   Biofilm activity from microscale measurements: Local biofilm activity

Microbial activity at the microscale is identified with the flux, from the bulk solution to the biofilm surface, of the substance selected for evaluating biofilm activity. As in the measurements of biofilm activity at the macroscale, the selected substance typically used in these measurements is the growth-limiting nutrient. Measurements of biofilm activity at the microscale are determined by the availability of tools to a larger extent than measurements at the macroscale are. Because fluxes at the microscale are quantified locally, rather than averaged over the entire surface area as is done at the macroscale, the concentration profiles of the selected substance must be measured with adequate spatial resolution. For this purpose, microsensors sensitive to the selected substance are used. There is only a limited number of microsensors that are able to measure concentration, and the availability of these tools limits the choices of substances used to evaluate biofilm activity at the microscale.

The local microbial activity in the biofilm is computed as the flux of the nutrient across the biofilm surface at the location of the measurement, and the flux is evaluated by multiplying the slope of the concentration profile near the biofilm/bulk solution interface (within the diffusion boundary layer) by the diffusivity coefficient of the substance whose concentration was measured in water:

$$j_w = D_w \left(\frac{dC}{dz} \right)_w \qquad (1.4)$$

where D_w is the diffusivity in water of the substance selected for the evaluation of bio-film activity, C is the concentration of the substance, z is the distance, and $(dC/dz)_w$ is the slope of the concentration profile measured at the biofilm surface from the water side. The units of flux are the same as the units of biofilm activity determined from the macroscale measurements:

$$\frac{m^2}{s} \times \frac{g}{m^3} \times \frac{1}{m} = \frac{g}{m^2 \times s}$$

For each biofilm reactor, biofilm activity may be estimated at two scales of observation: the macroscale and the microscale. Biofilm activity at the macroscale is reported as a single number, whereas biofilm activity at the microscale is reported as a set of numbers because biofilm activity depends on the location of the measurement. The existing mathematical models of biofilm activity have difficulty reconciling the results of the measurements of biofilm activity at the macroscale with those at the microscale. It is expected that the two types of measurements should give the same overall biofilm activity. However, this expec-tation can be fulfilled only if the biofilm is uniformly distributed in the reactor and the microbial activity is uniformly distributed in the biofilm. Neither of these two conditions is satisfied in real biofilms, and the biofilm activity estimated from the microscale mea-surements, in general, is not equal to that estimated from the macroscale measurements. It is not clear how to compare these results or how to integrate the results of biofilm activity measurements at the microscale so that an overall biofilm activity equal to that measured at the macroscale can be achieved. The concept of stratified biofilms used to interpret the results of measurements has the potential of bridging the two scales of observation.

Even if it eventually becomes possible to arrive at the same biofilm activity from results from the two scales of measurements, the measurements at the microscale deliver information that cannot be extracted from the measurements at the macroscale. For some biofilm processes, it is important to quantify the extreme values of biofilm activity because the locations in the biofilm where these extreme values occur exhibit extreme properties. For example, in studying MIC, which causes highly localized damage to metal surfaces, it is important to quantify the extreme values of biofilm activity because the extreme, and highly localized, chemistry in biofilms determines the extent of microbial corrosion. The average biofilm activity estimated from measurements at the macroscale cannot deliver this information.

1.2.5   *Biofilm development and the concept of biofilm structure*

Biofilm formation begins with the adsorption of single cells from the solution. Microbial cells are transported with the stream of liquid above the surface. Cells from the solution hit the surface and interact with the conditioning film adhering to the surface. Some cells attach to the surface, produce EPS, and form a biofilm. Other cells attach and then detach and leave the surface. The initial colonization of surfaces is supported by three mecha-nisms of microbial transport: (1) diffusive transport, (2) convective transport, and (3) the active movement of motile bacteria. The highest rate of microbial transport is by convec-tion, which may exceed the other two rates by several orders of magnitude. After the microbial cells are in contact with the surface, they may adhere to it or not. The probability of lasting adsorption is termed *sticking efficiency,* which is a parameter that is computed as the ratio of the number of microorganisms attaching to a surface to the total number of microorganisms landing on the surface within the same time interval. Sticking efficiency depends on many factors, including the properties of the surface, the physiological state of the organisms, and the hydrodynamics near the surface.

Figure 1.5 shows the three characteristic stages of biofilm formation. The first stage, called *attachment*, is mostly affected by the surface properties and the rate of microbial transport to the surface. The second and third stages—*colonization* and *growth*—are both affected by such factors as the mass transport of nutrients to a larger extent than they are by the properties of the surface or the rate of microbial transport to the surface.

The adherence of bacteria to a surface is followed by the production of slimy adhesive substances, known as EPS. These are predominantly made of polysaccharides and proteins, and their role is elucidated later in this chapter. Although the association of EPS with attached bacteria has been well documented in the literature, there is little evidence to suggest that EPS participates in the initial stages of adhesion, except perhaps in the cases in which negatively charged bacteria attach to negatively polarized metal surfaces, in which the involvement of EPS has been hypothesized. However, EPS definitely assists the formation of mature biofilms by forming a slimy substance called the *biofilm matrix*. Figure 1.6a shows an image of bacteria attached to a surface imbedded in a slimy layer of EPS. The images were acquired using atomic force microscopy, and the biofilm was partially dried to enhance the visibility of the cells covered with EPS. Drying the samples

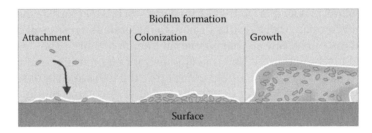

Figure 1.5 Stages of biofilm formation.

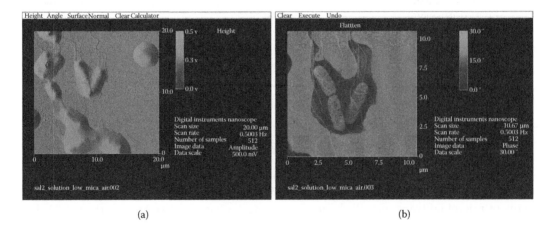

(a)   (b)

Figure 1.6 **(See color insert.)** Atomic force microscopy images of bacteria attached to a surface. The cells are imbedded in EPS that was (a) partially dried to expose the microorganisms and then (b) further dried. (Both images courtesy of Recep Avci of the Physics Department, Montana State University, Bozeman.)

somewhat longer produces an even more convincing image of the microorganisms imbedded in EPS, as seen in Figure 1.6b.

The first conceptual model of microbial biofilms assumed that the microorganisms are uniformly distributed in the matrix, as shown in Figure 1.7.

This model served the research community well for many years, and it is still useful in the mathematical modeling of some biofilm processes. However, as time passed and tools were developed for direct probing of the intrabiofilm environment with high spatial resolution, such as confocal microscopy and microelectrodes, it became obvious that some of the experimental results acquired using these tools were impossible to interpret using the conceptual model of biofilms in which microorganisms were uniformly distributed in a continuous matrix of EPS. One of the first signs that something might be wrong with the model came in 1993, when Drury injected micron-sized fluorescent latex particles into a biofilm reactor and studied their fate (Drury et al. 1993). The expectation was that these particles, after settling on the biofilm surface, would be pushed off by the growing and exfoliating bacteria. One of the popular notions in biofilm engineering at that time was that faster-growing microorganisms replace slower-growing microorganisms, analogous to the process occurring in continuous cultures of suspended microorganisms. The fluorescent beads were used to imitate bacteria having a growth rate equal to zero, and they were expected to be pushed away by growing biofilm microorganisms. After the experiment was terminated, the biofilm was sectioned and the beads were recovered. Surprisingly, many of them were found at the bottom of the biofilm, near the surface supporting biofilm growth. This contradicted one of the assumptions of the model: if the biofilm was a continuous gelatinous layer, as was stipulated by the model, then how did these beads get to the bottom of the biofilm? Clearly, the model of homogeneous biofilms could not explain this result. On the other hand, in a heterogeneous biofilm, this effect is actually expected: the beads penetrated and were trapped in interstitial voids, which frequently reach the bottom of the biofilm. Another controversial argument pointing toward the need to revise the conceptual model of biofilms came from the study of MIC. An argument often used when discussing MIC was that if biofilms formed continuous layers on metal surfaces, then they should decrease the corrosion rate, not increase it, by depleting the oxygen, the principal cathodic reactant in natural waters, near the surface. In light of that fact, the experimental observations indicating that biofilms increased the rate of corrosion were difficult to interpret. In the model of heterogeneous biofilms, oxygen freely penetrates to the surface through voids, causing the formation of differential aeration cells and accelerating corrosion; the parts of the surface covered by microcolonies are deprived of oxygen and become anodic, while the parts where oxygen reaches the surface become cathodic. A serious difficulty in interpreting experimental results arose when concentration profiles of

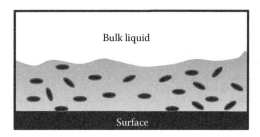

Figure 1.7 The model of biofilm structure created by early biofilm researchers assumed microorganisms randomly distributed in a continuous layer of EPS.

dissolved nutrients, e.g., oxygen, were measured to verify mathematical models of biofilm activity. The mathematical models referred to a single profile across the biofilm, and the profiles measured at different locations in the same biofilm were different to an extent that could not be ascribed to experimental errors only. As long as single profiles were analyzed, which was the case in most early publications, everything worked as expected. Mathematical models of biofilm activity, however, are intended to describe biofilm activity over a certain surface area, not just at a single location where measurements are taken. Attempts to find an average nutrient consumption rate over a certain area often generated surprising variability in that parameter. Because there was no independent technique for verifying microelectrode measurements, the suspicion was that the microelectrode measurements were not accurate. It is now well known that biofilm heterogeneity strongly influences the chemical profiles measured by microelectrodes and that measuring different nutrient concentration profiles at different locations in a biofilm is to be expected.

The difficulties with interpreting experimental results using the conceptual model of homogeneous biofilms continued to mount. In another set of experiments, profiles of flow velocity were measured near the biofilm surface using nuclear magnetic resonance imaging (NMRI). It was expected that biofilms covering walls of conduits would behave as if they just decreased the dimensions of the conduits. Flow velocity was expected to decrease on approaching the biofilm surface and to finally reach zero at the biofilm surface. Careful measurements of flow velocity distribution in biofilms demonstrated that the flow velocity reached zero at the conduit surface instead of at the biofilm surface as expected. Again, this effect is expected in heterogeneous biofilms, in which water can move in the interstitial voids.

All these effects that were impossible to interpret using the model of homogeneous biofilms—penetration of biofilms by small fluorescent beads, differential aeration cells, different concentration profiles at different locations, and flow of liquid through the biofilm—are expected and easily interpreted using the conceptual model of heterogeneous biofilms. For the purposes of this text we will be using the conceptual model of heterogeneous biofilms, i.e., biofilms in which microorganisms are assembled in clusters separated by interstitial voids (Figure 1.8). A heterogeneous biofilm is composed of (1) a densely compact sublayer, (2) round microcolonies, (3) interstitial voids, and (4) sometimes streamers,

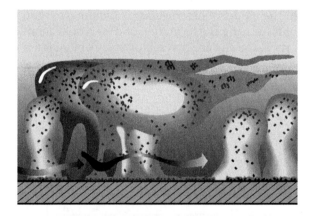

Figure 1.8 Heterogeneous biofilm. Microscopic observations indicate that biofilms are not flat and that the distribution of microorganisms is not uniform. Instead, multispecies biofilms form highly complex structures containing voids, channels, cavities, pores, and streamers, with cells arranged in microcolonies.

which are long strands of EPS extending from the microcolonies. The sublayer is not continuous and, in places, exposes the surface. Above the sublayer are dense, often round, microcolonies that are filled with EPS and densely packed with microorganisms. These may finish with elongated streamers extending downstream. Microcolonies are separated by interstitial voids forming a network of interconnected channels, giving biofilms their characteristic porous structure. Water can move freely within the network of these channels.

It is believed that microorganisms in biofilms are organized as communities. It is further hypothesized that these communities are assembled following a master plan, so that the cells of one species associate with those of another species for mutual physiological benefits. As time passes, the discrete microcolonies of microorganisms deposited on the surface grow in size, join, and form heterogeneous layers of microorganisms embedded in the polymer matrix covering the entire surface. Natural biofilms are even more heterogeneous than those grown in the laboratory because they contain adsorbed and entrapped materials including inorganic particles, such as clay or silt. The mixture of all these components forms the characteristic biofouling deposits, in which materials of nonbiological origin are imbedded in a matrix of EPS excreted by biofilm microorganisms. Images of mature biofilms are less clear than images of young biofilms because the visibility is obscured by the EPS excreted by the microorganisms and by the presence of other materials entrapped in the matrix of EPS. Figure 1.8 shows an idealized image of a heterogeneous biofilm. Such distinct structures are seen only in relatively young biofilms. As biofilms become older, the semicontinuous sublayer tends to become denser and thicker and to accumulate various particles from the system, while the upper layer, consisting of the characteristic round microcolonies and streamers, remains the same. New advances in understanding biofilm structure show that, as time passes, the bottom layers of biofilms become dense and compact and their porosity becomes much lower than the porosity of the upper layers. It is not known whether this decrease in porosity results from biofilm growth and expansion near the bottom or just from the accumulation of debris and pieces of biofilm sloughed off upstream.

Once a mature biofilm is established on a surface, it actively propagates and eventually covers the entire surface. The mechanisms of propagation in mature biofilms are more diverse than those of initial attachment; several of these mechanisms are depicted in Figure 1.9.

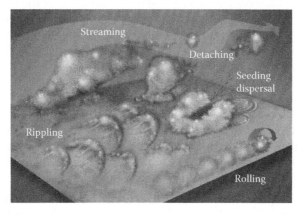

Figure 1.9 **(See color insert.)** Mechanisms of biofilm propagation. (Courtesy of P. Dirckx, MSU Center for Biofilm Engineering.)

Biofilm researchers see complex modes of biofilm propagation in everyday laboratory practice and have to take steps against some of them. Biofilms in tubing delivering nutrients to LBRs can spread in the direction opposing the direction of the flow and eventually invade the container with the nutrients. This fact clearly demonstrates that mature biofilms propagate in more complex ways—against the flow in this case—than just the simple attachment of the suspended microbial cells in the incoming stream of nutrients, which is characteristic of the initial stages of biofilm formation. Specially designed flow breakers are used to prevent the spread of biofilm in tubing used to deliver nutrients, and we discuss them in Chapter 9.

1.3   Characterizing selected parts of biofilm systems

In the previous sections we defined a biofilm system as a collection of four compartments: (1) the surface, (2) the biofilm, (3) the solution of nutrients, and (4) the gas phase. Much of biofilm research is about characterizing these compartments, their relations to biofilm processes, and relations among their components. A set of conceptual models has been developed to image and to interpret the physicochemical and biological processes occurring in these compartments. The following section describes these models and these processes. We characterize selected compartments and selected components of biofilm systems, those we usually characterize when describing biofilm processes from the engineering point of view.

1.3.1   Characterizing surfaces

Actually, there are two surfaces of interest in biofilm research: the surface to which the microorganisms are attached and the surface of the microorganisms—the microbial cell surface. However, only the surface on which a biofilm accumulates is identified here as a compartment of the biofilm system. Therefore, throughout this text, when we refer to the surface we mean the surface to which the microorganisms are attached, unless explicitly specified otherwise. The surface on which the microorganisms aggregate has acquired an unfortunate name in biofilm research—the substratum, which is easily confused with another important name often used in the same context—the substrate, which is the growth-limiting nutrient. To avoid confusion, it makes sense to use the term nutrient instead of substrate, whenever possible. We start the analysis of the effects of the surface on biofilm processes with a description of the effects of the surface on the initial events in biofilm formation, the microbial colonization of the surface. Despite an intensive research effort on the relations between the surface properties and the rate of microbial attachment to the surface, these relations are still not clear.

1.3.1.1   Surface properties and microbial colonization of surfaces

The process of biofilm formation consists of a sequence of steps and begins with the adsorption of macromolecules (proteins, polysaccharides, nucleic acids, and humic acids) and smaller molecules (fatty acids, lipids, and pollutants such as polyaromatic hydrocarbons and polychlorinated biphenyls) onto surfaces. These adsorbed molecules form conditioning films that may have multiple effects, such as altering the physicochemical characteristics of the surface, acting as a concentrated nutrient source for microorganisms, suppressing or enhancing the release of toxic metal ions from the surface, detoxifying the bulk solution through the adsorption of inhibitory substances, supplying the required nutrients and trace elements, and triggering biofilm sloughing. The properties of a conditioning film depend on the quality of the water in contact with the surface and may dramatically affect the surface properties. For example, in 1976, Loeb and Neihof demonstrated in electrophoretic studies that platinum particles suspended in seawater depleted of organic matter were electropositive before immersion and became electronegative upon immersion in natural water. Although there is no doubt that the conditioning film influences microbial colonization, this effect is difficult to evaluate because the conditioning film forms on surfaces immediately upon immersion and, consequently, there are no surfaces immersed in water that are without such a film to serve as a reference.

The possibility that the adhesion of microorganisms to inert surfaces is affected by electrostatic interactions has been explored with the hope that such interactions may help in establishing procedures for preventing biofilm formation on electrically conductive surfaces. Surfaces immersed in water acquire electrical charges owing to the preferential release of surface ions, the preferential adsorption of ions from the solution, or the surface equilibrating redox reactions in water. Also, most bacteria, algae, and detritus in natural waters carry a net electronegative surface charge. The effects of surface charge on microbial adhesion can be studied by applying known electrical potentials to metal surfaces, polarizing them. The expected consequence of applying a negative charge would be to repel the negatively charged microorganisms. However, this effect is mitigated by the presence of the adhesive substances produced by the microorganisms, EPS, which bridge the microbial cells with the surfaces. As a result of these interactions, negatively charged bacteria adhere to both negatively and positively charged surfaces.

Much attention has been devoted to studying hydrophobic effects on the attachment of microbes to each other and to surfaces. It is well known that certain materials can easily be covered with a film of water, while other materials resist wetting; the first are called hydrophilic and the latter hydrophobic. A well-known example of hydrophobicity is oil droplets on a water surface: the surface of oil resists wetting. Hydrophobic particles suspended in water prefer to interact with particles of their own kind, such as other hydrophobic particles, rather than with water. Because of this, hydrophobic particles immersed in water behave as if they were forming "voids" in a bulk solution. This behavior has consequences. Water is a highly structured polar solvent with individual particles connected by hydrogen bonds. Hydrophobic particles, by forming voids in the bulk solution, deform that structure, stretching and breaking the hydrogen bonds between water particles. This effect, the stretching and breaking of hydrogen bonds, promotes the coalescing of hydrophobic particles suspended in water through the following mechanism: when two hydrophobic particles suspended in water coalesce, the surface area of the combined particle is smaller than the sum of the surface areas of the coalescing particles. Consequently, the energy associated with the deformation of the water particles, which is proportional to the surface area of the particles, decreases as a result of coalescing, making the process of coalescing thermodynamically spontaneous. When two hydrophobic particles approach each other and coalesce, the free energy of the system decreases, favoring adhesion. Conversely, hydrophilic surfaces form structures with water particles that may be stronger than those due to hydrogen bonds between water particles. In summary, the more hydrophobic surfaces are, the more strongly they adhere to each other. This effect obviously attracted the attention of those searching for the reason microorganisms attach to surfaces and to each other and resulted in the hypothesis that hydrophobicity is the reason for microbial adhesion to surfaces.

Upon closer inspection, there are experimental difficulties in verifying the claim that microorganisms adhere to surfaces because of hydrophobic interactions. To quantify this effect, both the microorganisms and the surfaces to which they adhere would need to be hydrophobic. However, only small parts of microbial cells are hydrophobic: most of the surface of a microorganism is hydrophilic and for a good reason. If the surface of a microorganism were entirely hydrophobic, the microorganism would die from starvation because it could not absorb nutrients that were dissolved in water. However, many biofilm researchers hypothesize that the small hydrophobic areas present on the surfaces of microbial cells are responsible for the adherence of microorganisms to hydrophobic surfaces. To test this hypothesis, the hydrophobicity of many surfaces and the surfaces of many microorganisms have to be evaluated. Evaluating the hydrophobicity of surfaces is relatively simple, at least in theory, and relevant experimental protocols for evaluating the hydrophobicity of surfaces by measuring contact angles have been developed.

The hydrophobicity of a surface is evaluated by measuring the contact angle: a drop of water is deposited on the surface, and the angle between the surface and the drop is measured (Equation 1.5). If the contact angle is more than 90°, the water forms droplets and does not wet the surface (image on the left in Figure 1.10) and the surface is called hydrophobic. Water does not enter capillary pores in hydrophobic surfaces. If the contact angle approaches 0°, the water spreads over the surface without forming droplets. The contact angle can be evaluated precisely using sophisticated equipment provided by specialized vendors or, perhaps somewhat less precisely, using relatively simple, homemade equipment. The measurements are interpreted using thermodynamics by referring the contact angle to the interfacial free energies of the liquid, its vapor, and the surface (Figure 1.11). The results of testing the hypothesis that hydrophobic interactions are responsible for microbial attachment to surfaces have not been conclusive for several reasons. The current theory used to evaluate hydrophobicity from measurements of contact angle does not take into account factors besides hydrophobic interactions affecting the contact angle, such as surface roughness or the presence or absence of surface films. Interpreting the results of measurements remains controversial.

The contact angle θ is controlled by three interacting forces, the interfacial tension of each participating phase (gas [vapor, V], liquid L, and solid S). The relation among

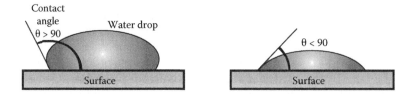

Figure 1.10 Measurement of the contact angle. A line tangent to the curve of the droplet is drawn at the point where the droplet intersects the solid surface. The angle formed by this tangent line and the solid surface on the side of the droplet is called the *contact angle*.

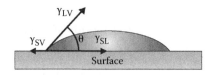

Figure 1.11 Forces acting on a drop of a liquid deposited on a surface.

these factors is quantified by Young's equation, and the contact angle is sometimes called Young's contact angle. Young's equation presents the horizontal components of the various surface forces as

$$\gamma_{SV} = \gamma_{SL} + \gamma_{LV} \times \cos(\theta) \tag{1.5}$$

From measurements of the contact angle, another parameter, the surface energy, can be computed. To visualize the meaning of the term, it is convenient to note that when a drop of water spreads over a surface, the cohesive forces that keep the drop of water together (surface tension) must be overcome by the adhesive forces between the liquid and the surface. If water wets the surface, then the energy needed to do the work of expanding the surface of the drop comes from its interaction with the surface. Consequently, if water droplets spread over a surface, the surface is referred to as a high-energy surface, and if water does not spread over the surface, the surface is referred to as a low-energy surface. Surface energy is measured in Newtons per meter (N/m) and is defined as the force along a line perpendicular to the surface or as the work done per unit area, which is proportional to the force $\gamma_{LV}\cos(\theta)$. Consequently, when θ approaches zero and $\cos(\theta)$ approaches one, for a perfectly wettable surface, the surface energy approaches a maximum. In Figure 1.11, γ_{SL} is the surface free energy of the solid surface covered with liquid, γ_{LV} is the surface free energy of the liquid–vapor interface, and γ_{SV} is the surface free energy of the solid surface in contact with vapor.

Despite the effort invested in quantifying the relation among hydrophobicity, surface energy, and the initial events of biofilm formation, the relation remains unclear. It appears that the techniques for measuring surface energy are too crude to provide an accurate estimate of hydrophobicity at a scale that is relevant to evaluating microbial attachment. Solid surfaces have heterogeneous chemistries and heterogeneous distributions of hydrophobicity and so do microbial surfaces. Surface chemistries show differences at the submicron scale, while the linear scale used to evaluate contact angle measurements is much larger than that. Measuring the contact angle calls for depositing drops of water on the surface. Drops of water are larger than typical microorganisms attached to surfaces. As a result, the measurements of contact angle average the properties of a large area of the surface, rendering the results less useful for evaluating the effects of hydrophobicity on microbial attachment, because microorganisms attach to a much smaller surface area. Not only are the individual microorganisms smaller than the droplets of water deposited on the surface, but also the parts of the microorganisms that are actually hydrophobic occupy only a small part of their surfaces. These differences between the scale of observation and the scale of the actual event may be one reason the relation between surface energy and biofilm formation is not as obvious as was initially assumed. As a result, the relation between microbial colonization and surface energy remains unclear: microorganisms, apparently unaware of the complexity of the situation, colonize both low- and high-energy surfaces.

Evaluating the hydrophobicity of microbial cells is controversial. There are no established rules or experimental protocols for measuring the hydrophobicity of microbial cells. For obvious reasons, measuring the contact angle on a microbial cell is not possible, so microbial cell hydrophobicity is evaluated by measuring the kinetics of microbial adhesion to surfaces of immiscible hydrophobic liquids added to water: droplets of a nonpolar (hydrophobic) solvent are suspended in water, and bacteria adhere to these droplets. The rate of change in microbial cell count in samples of water under some standardized conditions is a measure of microbial cell hydrophobicity. Measuring the hydrophobicity of microbial cells has been attempted by many researchers, but there is neither a uniform measure of microbial cell surface hydrophobicity nor any definitive scale of values for comparing hydrophobicities measured in different systems explored by individual researchers.

Microbially colonized surfaces can be studied from many branches of physical sciences, including chemistry and solid-state physics. Two characteristics of surfaces that are of particular interest to biofilm researchers are surface chemistry and surface topography. The extensive research done to relate surface properties to rates of biofilm accumulation has been only moderately successful, and the current thinking among biofilm researchers is that surface properties are important only for the initial attachment of microbial cells and, as the biofilm accumulates, the microbial cells that grow on top of the cells directly attached to the surface are not affected by the surface properties at all or are affected to a much smaller extent than the cells directly attached to the surface. This general statement may need to be modified in some instances. For example, at freely corroding metal surfaces, corrosion products imbedded in the biofilm matrix may provide additional surface area for microbial growth and may affect the rates and extents of biofilm growth and accumulation. The notion that microorganisms deposited within the biofilm matrix and away from the surface do not sense the properties of the surface is worth remembering when designing so-called anti-fouling surfaces, which, thus far at least, seem to delay microbial colonization rather than prevent it. Once microorganisms establish their presence on a surface, biofilm accumulation accelerates and the surface properties become less relevant, if they remain relevant at all.

1.3.2   *Characterizing hydrodynamics and mass transfer in biofilms*

In the preceding sections we defined the microbial activity in a biofilm as the rate of nutrient utilization per unit of surface area covered with the biofilm. In a biofilm system, the nutrient solution occupies the space above and within the biofilm compartment. However, if the surface is porous, the nutrient solution may also enter the pores of the surface. In some instances, as in the case of biofilms using electrodes as electron acceptors/donors, as in electrochemically active biofilms, the surface itself may be the substrate; we will cover this subject separately in Chapter 7, which is dedicated to biofilms on metals. The nutrient solution serves as the medium for delivering nutrients and other substances such as antimicrobial agents to the microorganisms imbedded in the biofilm matrix and removes the products of microbial metabolism from the space occupied by the biofilm. The rates of nutrient delivery and products removal affect the rates of biofilm processes. Many studies have quantified the rate of mass transport and the rate of microbial respiration in biofilms, as these two rates are equal in biofilms. With many simplifying assumptions, the process of mass transfer in biofilms can be quantified. However, some of the assumptions are not realistic: they are accepted because of computational convenience, not because they reflect truth about specific processes. For example, one of the most difficult factors to describe affecting mass transport in biofilms is hydrodynamics. The effect of hydrodynamics on biofilms is complicated for many reasons, among them feedback effects: the flow of nutrients affects the structure of the biofilm, and the structure of the biofilm affects the flow of nutrients. In the following section we will quantify some of the factors in this system, and we will make simplifying assumptions despite what was said above.

In flowing solutions of nutrients, there are two boundary layers above the biofilm surface: the concentration (mass transport) boundary layer and the hydrodynamic boundary layer. Above the respective boundary layers, nutrient concentration and flow velocity are uniformly distributed. Within the respective boundary layers, nutrient concentration and flow velocity are not constant but instead form gradients: the flow velocity and the nutrient concentration decrease toward the biofilm surface.

An axiom commonly accepted by biofilm researchers says that mass transport above biofilms is due to convection, while that within biofilms is due to diffusion. This axiom has been imbedded into many mathematical models of biofilm processes. However, several studies have documented that water actually does move in the space occupied by the biofilm, demonstrating that this axiom is not accurate. If water moves in the space occupied by the biofilm, then convective mass transport must be present in that zone. This is somewhat disconcerting, because at the same time many studies have shown profiles of various substances above and within the biofilms, demonstrating the existence of relatively thick mass boundary layers above the biofilm. We will return to this apparent controversy later, when we discuss the modified model of mass transport in biofilm systems. First, we will discuss the simplified model of hydrodynamics and mass transport in biofilms, shown in Figure 1.12. Even though we know that the model shown in Figure 1.12 is not accurate, it is simpler to discuss the meanings and the dimensions of the boundary layers in biofilm systems using a simplified model, and the conclusions we reach will not change the principles of why such layers exist or what they affect in biofilm systems.

In the simplified conceptual model of hydrodynamics and mass transport in biofilms (Figure 1.12), the flow velocity reaches zero at the surface of the biofilm surface (the nonslip condition). Because at the same time the flow velocity in the bulk solution is higher than zero, the flow velocity forms a profile near the biofilm, varying between the average flow velocity in the bulk solution and zero at the biofilm surface. Experimentally measured flow velocity profiles near biofilm surfaces look like the one shown in Figure 1.12. The overall flow velocity in the main stream is considered to be the average flow velocity. The flow velocity decreases near the surface of the biofilm and then reaches zero at the surface.

The layer of liquid in which the flow velocity decreases as a result of proximity to the surface is called the hydrodynamic boundary layer. It is marked by the letter ϕ in Figure 1.12. A direct consequence of the hydrodynamic boundary layer is the formation of the mass transport boundary layer, also called the diffusion boundary layer. Its existence is demonstrated by the gradient in nutrient concentration within the hydrodynamic boundary layer. As the flow velocity decreases near the biofilm surface, the mechanism of mass transport changes from being dominated by convection at locations away from the biofilm, where the flow velocity is high, to being dominated by diffusion at locations near the biofilm surface, where the flow velocity is low. Because the microorganisms in the biofilm can consume the nutrient at the rate that it is delivered by diffusion, the nutrient

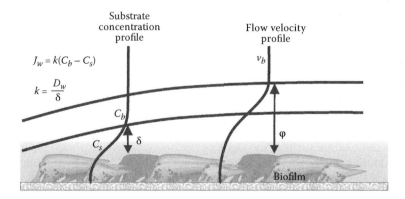

Figure 1.12 Substrate concentration profile and flow velocity distribution near and within an idealized biofilm.

concentration decreases near the surface, forming a concentration profile within the hydro-dynamic boundary layer. The layer of liquid above the biofilm surface where the nutrient concentration decreases as a result of biofilm activity and the diminishing rate of mass transport is called the mass transport boundary layer or the diffusion boundary layer. It is marked by the Greek letter δ in Figure 1.12.

There is a relationship between the thicknesses of the mass transport boundary and the hydrodynamic boundary layer. Both layers are affected by the transport of compo-nents toward the surface: the hydrodynamic boundary layer is affected by the transport of momentum, and the mass boundary layer is affected by the transport of nutrients. The rate of transport of a component is always described as the product of the gradient of the com-ponent being transported and a proportionality coefficient reflecting the physical nature of the transport of the component. The thickness of the hydrodynamic boundary layer is affected by the viscosity of water, and the thickness of the diffusion boundary layer is affected by the diffusivity of the nutrient; consequently, the proportionality constants in the relevant equations describing rates of momentum and nutrient transport are viscosity and diffusivity. The diffusivities of nutrients in water vary within narrow limits, about $2 \times 10^{-9}\,\mathrm{m^2/s}$. Meanwhile the kinematic viscosity of water at 20°C is about $1 \times 10^{-6}\,\mathrm{m^2/s}$, which is about 1000× higher than the diffusivity of small particles in water. As a result, the rate of momentum transfer vastly exceeds the rate of the transfer of nutrient particles toward the surface, and the hydrodynamic boundary layer is thicker than the mass trans-port boundary layer. The mass transport boundary layer is effectively buried within the hydrodynamic boundary layer, as shown in Figure 1.12. Some of the tools we use allow the experimental measurement of flow velocity gradients and nutrient concentration gradients and the determination of thicknesses of mass transport and hydrodynamic boundary lay-ers in biofilm reactors. To understand the entirety of the mass transport and hydrodynam-ics in biofilm systems, we need to include the intrabiofilm mass transport, and we will do so in Chapter 2. Just above the biofilm surface, the intensity of mass transport decreases, because flow velocity decreases near surfaces. As a result, the rate of nutrient consump-tion by the biofilm is determined by the rate of nutrient delivery by mass transport, and, in effect, the nutrient concentration decreases near the biofilm surface (Figure 1.12). The general shape of the nutrient concentration profile is affected simultaneously by the rate of mass transport and by the rate of microbial respiration. Figure 1.13 shows a profile of dissolved oxygen above and within a biofilm. In fact, the position of each point on the oxy-gen concentration profile shown in Figure 1.12 reflects a local equilibrium between these two processes, oxygen delivery and oxygen removal by microbial respiration. Above the biofilm surface, where the flow velocity is high, the concentration of microorganisms is negligible, microbial respiration is negligible, and mass transport is intensive because of convection. Near the biofilm surface, flow velocity decreases and so does the rate of mass transport. In that zone, there is no microbial nutrient removal, but the nutrient concentra-tion is affected by the microbial activity in the biofilm, located just below. To analyze the shape of the nutrient concentration profile inside the biofilm, microbial respiration and the nutrient removal that is associated with it must be taken into account. This new factor changes the curvature of the profile, from concave down, above the biofilm surface, to con-cave up, below the biofilm surface; the slope of the nutrient concentration profile increases faster than it would if the nutrient concentration were affected only by the mass transport limitations. Near the surface, the nutrient concentration is low and may reach zero even in relatively thick biofilms like the one shown in Figure 1.12. Because the parts of the oxygen concentration profile that are above and below the biofilm surface are affected by different factors, mathematically the overall profile shown in Figure 1.12 consists of two profiles,

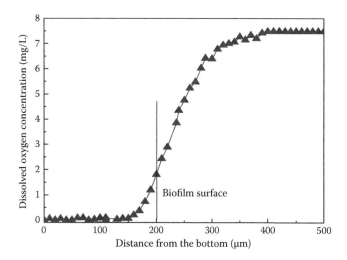

Figure 1.13 Oxygen concentration profile at one location on a biofilm. From the linear part of the middle section of the profile above the biofilm surface, between 300 and 200 μm, it can be estimated that oxygen decreases from 6.5 to 2.0 mg/L over a distance of 100 μm, giving the profile a slope of

$$450 \text{ mg/Lcm} = 0.45 \text{ mg/cm}^4 = \left(\frac{4.5 \text{ mg}}{100 \text{ L μm}} \frac{1 \text{ L}}{10^3 \text{ cm}^3} \frac{1 \text{ μm}}{10^{-4} \text{ cm}} \right).$$ The slope of the profile at the biofilm

surface is then multiplied by the molecular diffusivity of oxygen in water, 2×10^{-5} cm²/s, to yield the oxygen flux to the biofilm, 9×10^{-6} mg of oxygen/cm² × s, in accordance with Fick's first law.

that above the biofilm surface and that below the biofilm surface. The two parts are joined at the biofilm surface by the requirement of flux continuity across the biofilm surface.

Thus, when characterizing nutrient solutions in biofilm systems, we are mostly interested in two factors: (1) the distribution of the chemical components in the nutrient solution and (2) the distribution of the flow velocity in the nutrient solution. If the information about these two factors is sufficient, we can deduce the biofilm activity and mass transport in the biofilm system. Consequently, we will focus on evaluating these two factors in such a manner that the information can be used in mathematical models of biofilm activity and accumulation. To evaluate the distribution of the chemical components of a growth medium, we use a variety of microsensors, and to evaluate hydrodynamics, we use a variety of velocimetry techniques.

1.3.3 Characterizing the distribution of nutrients in biofilms

Two microsensors are particularly useful in determining biofilm activity: the oxygen electrode and the hydrogen sulfide electrode. In natural biofilms, oxygen is the most common electron acceptor if the solution is aerated, and sulfate is the most common electron acceptor in the absence of oxygen. The oxygen and hydrogen sulfide electrodes are used in the two respective situations. The following text refers to measurements done using oxygen microelectrodes but almost everything in it applies to hydrogen sulfide microelectrodes as well, once one adjusts for the fact that oxygen is consumed by microorganisms and hydrogen sulfide is produced by sulfate-reducing microorganisms: the hydrogen sulfide profile is inverted with respect to the oxygen concentration profile.

An oxygen concentration profile measured across a biofilm using an oxygen microelectrode is shown in Figure 1.13. Biofilm activity can be computed from these results by multiplying the slope of the concentration profile near the biofilm surface, from the solution side, by the diffusivity of oxygen in water. A system of coordinates with its origin at the biofilm surface is used in these calculations.

A concentration profile such as the one in Figure 1.13 is measured at a selected location in the biofilm, and the results are representative of that location only. It has been demonstrated that concentration profiles measured at different locations in the same biofilm are different. This creates a problem: which concentration profile is representative of the biofilm under study? This question cannot be properly addressed here; we will discuss it again in Chapter 6, where we use maps of oxygen concentrations at various levels in the biofilm to arrive at the representative oxygen concentration profile. Meanwhile, to evaluate the distribution of oxygen in a biofilm, the concentration profile can be measured at several locations. These locations do not have to be randomly selected: it is better if they are selected to form a pattern, which later helps in interpreting the results. Figure 1.14 shows the locations of a series of measurements; these locations were selected to be along a straight line transecting a microcolony. As a result, the profiles measured at the locations indicated in Figure 1.14 can be arranged and interpreted as a two-dimensional (2-D) distribution of oxygen across the selected transect, as shown in Figure 1.15.

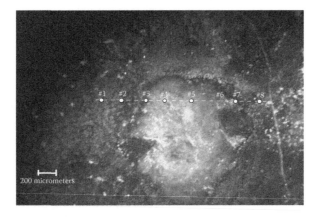

Figure 1.14 The strategy for taking microelectrode measurements if the data are to be presented in 2-D images. This approach is taken here to show the direction of the oxygen flux to the biofilm.

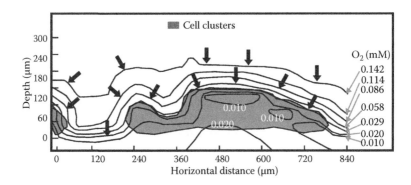

Figure 1.15 Oxygen concentration around a microcolony. The oxygen flux, which always follows the steepest gradient, is not always perpendicular to the surface. (Reprinted from deBeer, D. et al., *Biotechnology and Bioengineering* 43: 1131–1138, 1994.)

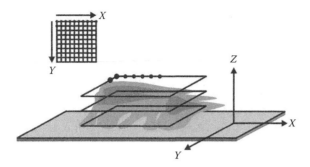

Figure 1.16 The strategy for taking microelectrode measurements if the data are to be presented in 3-D images. This approach is convenient when the data are to be compared with confocal microscopy images of the biofilm. First, the images, taken at the same distances from the bottom as the maps of the measured parameter, are quantified by computing appropriate parameters characterizing biofilm structure; then, the values of these parameters are plotted against the average concentration of each measured substance for each layer in the biofilm.

Continuous lines indicate isobars, and arrows indicate the directions of oxygen fluxes, which are always perpendicular to the active surface. Notice that the microcolony is anoxic in the middle, while oxygen is still detectable at the bottom, which demonstrates that the oxygen near the bottom was transported there via channels and voids, not just by diffusion through the microcolony. This conclusion demonstrates that the assumptions of one-dimensional biofilm models, that the direction of mass transport in biofilms is perpendicular to the surface and that it is entirely due to molecular diffusion, may not hold in heterogeneous biofilms. Two-dimensional images show a much more realistic picture of oxygen concentration in biofilms than individual profiles of oxygen concentration like the one shown in Figure 1.13. However, the true image of the oxygen distribution is 3-D. To provide the data for imaging the 3-D distribution of a component of a biofilm, measuring along a transect, as shown in Figure 1.15, is not adequate. A new approach needs to be implemented, and this approach is shown in Figure 1.16. To image the 3-D distribution of the oxygen concentration in a biofilm, we use measurements based on the concept of stratified biofilms. In this approach, a biofilm is subdivided into a finite number of discrete, uniform, and continuous layers. This procedure is explained in detail along with experimental measurements in Chapter 9.

1.3.4 Characterizing distribution of effective diffusivity and biofilm density

The most striking differences between the models of homogeneous and heterogeneous biofilms are related to the mechanisms of mass transport in the two systems: heterogeneous biofilms are porous, water moves within the space occupied by them, and their mass transport rates vary from one place to another. Particularly large differences in the mass transport rate are measured between the microcolonies and the voids because mass transport is controlled in the microcolonies by diffusion and in the voids by convection. These differences make using a single mass transport coefficient for the entire biofilm questionable. Whether using a single mass transport coefficient for the entire biofilm is justified or not depends on how much it varies from place to place. To evaluate the variation in mass transport rate among locations in biofilms, we introduce the concept of the local mass transport coefficient, the mass transport coefficient at a single point within the biofilm.

Evaluating the diffusivities of various substances in the matrix of EPS delivers information about mass transport within the EPS, but not necessarily about the mass transport within the biofilm. Because the biofilm is composed of microcolonies separated by interstitial voids, mass transport in the voids needs to be accounted for as well. In Chapter 2, we describe a technique we used to measure diffusivity in biofilms. It was based on injecting a tiny amount, measured in picoliters, of a fluorescent dye into a microcolony and measuring the rate of its dispersion using confocal microscopy. From such a set of data, diffusivity can be calculated. This technique was suitable for measuring diffusivity within individual microcolonies. For measurements of diffusivity in a biofilm composed of microcolonies and interstitial voids, the microinjection technique is not suitable because the plume of the injected substance disperses faster in the interstitial voids than it does in the microcolonies; in fact, in interstitial voids the tracer disperses faster than it is possible to monitor using microscopy. As a remedy, the concept of the local mass transport coefficient was introduced to quantify the distribution of the mass transfer coefficient and of the diffusivity in biofilms. The tools for evaluating the local mass transport coefficient are relatively simple and available in every microsensor laboratory: they are amperometric microelectrodes without membranes.

The idea of using amperometric microsensors without membranes goes against the usual principles of constructing such microsensors, as explained in Chapter 4. Amperometric microsensors are covered with membranes to mitigate the effects of mass transport known as the "stirring effect," because amperometric sensors without membranes are sensitive to mass transport in the vicinity of the sensor tips. This is an undesirable feature because the response of the sensor depends on two variables, the concentration of the solute and the rate of transport of the solute to the tip of the electrode. Applying a membrane with a diffusivity coefficient a few orders of magnitude lower than the diffusivity coefficient of the solute in water practically confines the entire mass transport resistance to the membrane and makes the sensor insensitive to the mass transport resistance in the vicinity of the sensor tip. Using amperometric sensors without membranes defeats this purpose and makes such sensors useless for determining the concentration of the solute. The principle of constructing sensors to determine the mass transfer rate includes keeping the concentration of the solute constant; then the sensor responds to the mass transport rate only. Such sensors are well known: rotating electrodes are built on this principle. Electrochemical sensors are also used to quantify mass transport rates to surfaces. To measure the distribution of the local mass transport coefficient in biofilms, we use mobile microsensors that can measure profiles of the mass transport coefficient across the biofilm or the mass transport coefficient at any selected location in the biofilm.

The choice of electrochemical reactant for the measurement of local mass transport coefficients in biofilm systems is narrowly restricted by the following criteria: (1) chemical stability; (2) high solubility; (3) low cost; (4) redox potential sufficiently different from that of hydrogen evolution (or oxygen evolution) to give long, well-defined limiting current plateaus within the water stability limits; and (5) low toxicity and negligible destructiveness to biofilm structure. One electrolyte system ($Fe(CN)_6^{3-}/Fe(CN)_6^{4-}$) meets most of the listed criteria and is selected for these measurements. Prior to measurement, the nutrient solution in the reactor is replaced with the electrolyte. After the electrolyte equilibrates with the biomass, the local mass transport coefficient is measured at selected locations on a grid. The local mass transport coefficients measured at the intersections of the grid lines are reported as maps of the distribution of the local mass transport coefficient at various distances from the bottom, as shown in Figure 1.17.

Studying the distribution of the local mass transport coefficient, particularly in comparison with the local biofilm activity, has proved to be very productive and explained

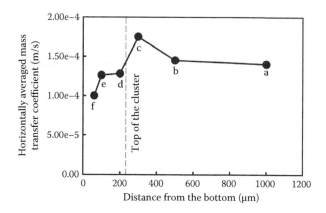

Figure 1.17 Distribution of local mass transport coefficient above and within a biofilm. Surprisingly, the local mass transport coefficient does not follow the shape of the oxygen concentration curve. We will explain this effect in Chapter 2. (Reproduced from Yang, S. N., and Lewandowski, Z., *Biotechnology and Bioengineering* 48: 737–744, 1995.)

some anomalies we had been measuring in biofilms (see Chapter 9 for details). However, biofilm modeling frequently uses effective diffusivity, and it is important to know how this parameter is distributed in biofilms. Biofilm reactions are heterogeneous, and in such reactions the rate of mass transport is balanced with the rate of reaction, such as the nutrient removal rate. Measuring local rate of reaction and local effective diffusivity at the same locations helps in understanding the relations between activity and mass transport at the microscale. We related local limiting current density to local effective diffusivity using layers of agar of different and known densities, and known effective diffusivities of ferricyanide. The effective diffusivity of ferricyanide in the agar layers was measured in a diffusion cell. A calibration graph was constructed to relate the limiting current density measured by the microelectrode and the effective diffusivity measured in the diffusion cell. This calibration graph was further used to calculate local effective diffusivity in biofilms from local limiting current density measurements, and prepare maps of local diffusivity distribution at various distances from the surface, as shown in Figure 1.18. Different biofilms were used to identify the effects of the growth conditions and the type of

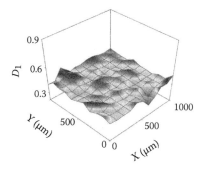

Figure 1.18 An example of local relative effective diffusivity (D_l) distribution at a selected distance from the bottom. (Reprinted from Beyenal, H. and Lewandowski, Z., *Water Research* 34: 528–538, 2000.)

microorganisms on the local effective diffusivity. Finally, we used an empirical equation reported in the literature to relate the local effective diffusivity to the local cell density.

The use of microelectrodes operated at the limiting current condition can be extended to quantifying other factors affecting rates of nutrient removal in biofilm reactors. If properly designed and calibrated, such electrodes can be used to measure profiles of diffusivity across biofilms. The variation of diffusivity in biofilms is a direct effect of the variation in local biomass density. Using simple equations relating effective diffusivity and biomass density (see Chapter 9 for details), profiles of effective diffusivity can be translated into profiles of biomass density across biofilms like those shown in Figure 1.19. These reveal a large difference in biofilm density between locations near the bottom and locations near the biofilm surface. The biomass density near the bottom approached 100 g/L.

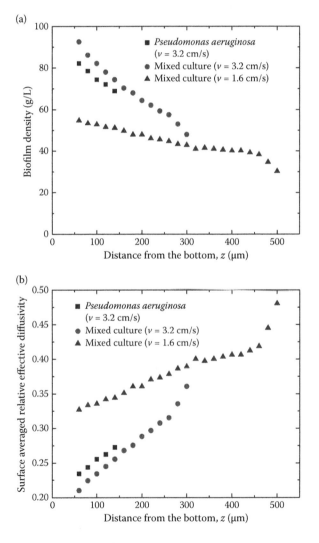

Figure 1.19 Variation of (a) biofilm density and (b) surface-averaged local effective diffusivity in the biofilms. (Reprinted from Beyenal, H. et al., *Water Science and Technology* 38: 171–178, 1998.)

1.3.5 Characterizing biofilm structure and its effects

Biofilm structure is defined as the distribution of biomass in the space occupied by a biofilm. Different biofilms have different structures (see Chapter 2), and the structure of the same biofilm varies over time. It has been hypothesized that the biofilm structure reflects certain functions of the biofilm and that a biofilm can optimize its structure to control the rate of nutrient delivery to the deeper layers of the biofilm. These and similar hypotheses based on visual analysis of various biofilms generated the need for quantifying biofilm structure. Large sections of this book are dedicated to quantifying biofilm structure.

1.3.5.1 Biofilm heterogeneities: Structural, chemical, physiological, and other

Biofilm heterogeneity is the extent of nonuniform distribution of any selected component in any of the compartments of the biofilm system, such as the distribution of the biomass, selected nutrients, selected products of microbial metabolism, or selected groups of microorganisms. Because there are many choices for the components selected to evaluate biofilm heterogeneity, the term biofilm heterogeneity is usually combined with an adjective referring to the selected component, such as structural heterogeneity, chemical heterogeneity, or physiological heterogeneity. The term biofilm heterogeneity was initially used exclusively for referring to the nonuniform distribution of the biomass in a biofilm. As time has passed, more types of heterogeneity have been described, and the term biofilm heterogeneity is not self-explanatory anymore. Colloquially, however, the original meaning of biofilm heterogeneity is often assumed: if no indication is given as to which component is referred to, the term heterogeneity refers to structural heterogeneity, defined as the nonuniform distribution of the biomass in the space occupied by the biofilm. Figure 1.20 gives an example of chemical heterogeneity in biofilms, a nonuniform distribution of oxygen.

Because the component used to evaluate heterogeneity is oxygen, this type of heterogeneity qualifies as chemical heterogeneity. There are important consequences of such heterogeneity. That there are different concentrations of oxygen at equal distances from the bottom indicates the existence of large horizontal gradients in the concentration of oxygen, which is the necessary precondition to horizontal mass transport in biofilms. The existence of horizontal mass transport in biofilms, in its turn, exposes the weakness of the assumption of many mathematical models of biofilm activity that the mass transport in biofilms is only from the bulk solution toward the bottom. To remedy this, it is important to relate biofilm heterogeneity numerically to the rates of mass transport. Quantifying biofilm heterogeneity is equivalent to quantifying the extent of nonuniform distribution. Several tools from a statistical toolbox are available for evaluating the extent of nonuniform distribution; the most popular is the standard deviation. For example, oxygen concentrations at locations equidistant from the surface are measured, and the differences among them are ascribed to chemical heterogeneity. The procedure for estimating the extent of heterogeneity of a selected component of a biofilm is identical with the procedure for evaluating the standard deviation of a set of experimental data, with one important difference: the deviations from the average are not due to errors in measurement but reflect a feature of the biofilm— heterogeneity. Using standard deviation as the measure of heterogeneity has a disadvantage: the standard deviation has the same units as the original measurement. Therefore, we prefer using the coefficient of variation instead, which is the standard deviation expressed as a percentage of the average (see Chapter 6). Still, every time biofilm heterogeneity is reported, even if it is expressed as a percentage of the average, the component chosen for the measurements should be reported as well. If the component is not reported, we assume that the measured heterogeneity refers to the distribution of the biomass.

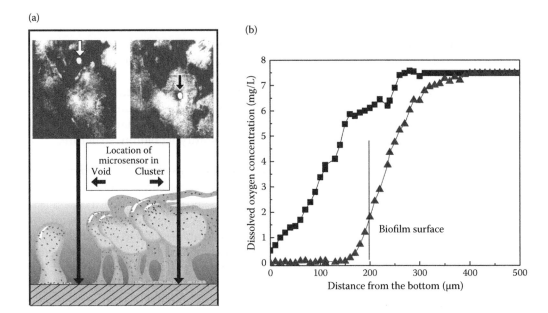

Figure 1.20 (a) Two profiles of dissolved oxygen concentration in a biofilm measured a few hundred micrometers apart in a biofilm. The results show that at the distance of 150 μm from the bottom, oxygen was depleted at one location and had a concentration comparable with that in the bulk solution at the other location. The image on the left shows that this is actually an expected effect in heterogeneous biofilms, which are composed of interstitial voids and microcolonies. (b) Dissolved oxygen concentration profiles measured at microcolonies are obviously different from dissolved oxygen concentration profiles measured at interstitial voids.

1.3.6   *Characterizing the flow of nutrients in biofilms*

The best technique for quantifying flow velocity distribution in the space occupied by a biofilm is NMRI, and we describe the use of this technique in Chapter 2. Using NMRI allowed us to demonstrate that water actually moved in the space occupied by a biofilm. The capability of averaging flow velocity over a slice of a reactor makes this technique attractive for describing the hydrodynamics in a biofilm reactor. However, this very feature, averaging the flow velocity, prevents the use of this technique to address the set of questions about the relations among flow velocity, biofilm structure, and biofilm activity. A measurement at a scale of resolution comparable with the scale of resolution of the microelectrodes measuring the profiles of nutrient concentration is needed. To some extent, this need has been satisfied by the development of microelectrodes that measure the local mass transport coefficient and the calibration of them to measure local flow velocity. Limiting current microelectrodes respond to the rate of mass transport to the tip of the electrode. For flowing liquids the major factor that determines the mass transport rate is the thickness of the mass transfer boundary layer, which, in turn, is affected by the local flow velocity. Because the response of the microelectrodes depends on local flow velocity, we relate the limiting current measured by an ammeter to the local flow velocity. The difficult part is to determine the local flow velocity in proximity to the tip of the electrode and use this set of data to calibrate the electrode. We use fluorescent beads and confocal scanning laser microscopy for particle tracking, as described in Chapter 2, to image the tip of the microelectrode and its immediate vicinity, and we measure the flow velocity by tracking the beads. From the images of the beads we compute the local flow velocity in the vicinity of the tip of the microelectrode, and we calibrate the limiting current microelectrode to measure flow velocity, as shown in Figure 1.21. The calibration of the electrode is described in Chapter 9.

Depending on the problem at hand, we may want to (1) image the flow velocity within a biofilm or in the individual channels of the biofilm or (2) image the flow velocity above the biofilm. These results carry different information. The flow velocity profile above the biofilm surface is used to evaluate the rates of convective mass transfer and shear stress above the biofilm, while the flow velocity within the biofilm is used to evaluate the rate of convective mass transport within the biofilm. One of the most important consequences of biofilm heterogeneity, from the engineering point of view, is that water actually flows through the space occupied by the biofilm. This affects the mass transport rate in that space by allowing for convective mass transport. However, convective mass transport affects only interstitial voids; mass transport in microcolonies is still dominated by diffusion. The complexity of mass transport within the space occupied by a biofilm is difficult to quantify or to model mathematically, and we are still waiting for an efficient mathematical model of microbial activity in heterogeneous biofilms.

We use all three techniques to measure flow velocity, as each of them has distinct advantages and disadvantages. NMRI and confocal laser velocimetry typically measure

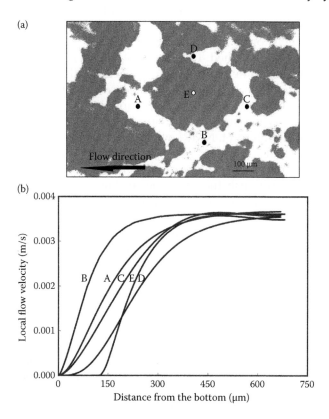

Figure 1.21 (a) A microscope image of a biofilm showing where the profiles were measured. White areas represent biofilm voids; dark areas represent cell clusters. (b) Local flow velocity profiles measured at the positions indicated in image A. (Reprinted from Xia, F. H. et al., *Water Research* 32: 3631–3636, 1998.)

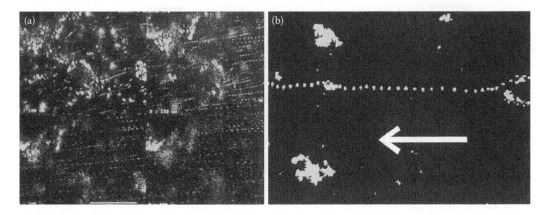

Figure 1.22 (a) Biofilm composed of cell clusters (white) and surrounding voids (black). The white dashes (one is shown by an arrow) in the voids are fluorescent particles used for velocity measurements; the bulk flow is from right to left. The scale bar is 100 μm. (b) To measure the flow velocity, one selected track is magnified.

only one component of the flow velocity vector. In the case of confocal laser velocimetry, this is an inherent problem, and the technique cannot be adjusted to measure the three components of the velocity vector. If a fluorescent bead starts flowing up or down in the biofilm, it leaves the depth of field, which is very shallow in confocal microscopy, and the measurement cannot be continued. Therefore, not one but many beads are injected into the space and at least some of them travel along trajectories that can be used to compute their flow velocity, as shown in Figure 1.22. In the case of NMRI this is not an inherent problem: NMRI can measure the flow velocity in any desired direction. However, components of the flow velocity measured in any other direction than along the main axis of the conduit are difficult to interpret. NMRI averages the results over a certain slice of the biofilm, so that they are not really local measurements, while confocal laser velocimetry can be used to evaluate flow velocity in a particular channel in the biofilm. Microelectrode measurements do not distinguish the direction of flow at all. The sensor responds to water movement without indicating in which direction it moved. The advantage of using a microelectrode is that we can measure profiles of flow velocity and correlate them with the profiles of substrate concentration measured by other electrodes.

1.3.7   *Characterizing structure and function of EPS*

Our knowledge of the structure and functions of EPS in biofilms is developing slowly, not because this component of the biofilm is underappreciated, but because of experimental difficulties. In contrast to the bewildering number of fluorescent stains available for micro-organisms in biofilms, there are no general stains for EPS. There are fluorescent stains for some types of polysaccharides but not for all those present in biofilms. It is possible to use fluorescent antibodies, but they are specific for the selected types of EPS for which they were developed. Some biofilm researchers use Alcian blue to stain EPS, but it targets anionic molecules only. The recent use of lectins, nonenzymatic proteins exhibiting a high affinity for polysaccharides (Neu et al. 2001), expands the availability of stains for EPS. The limited availability of stains inhibits the *in vivo* study of EPS in biofilms. In addition, the *in vitro* procedures for characterizing EPS are tedious and require disrupting the EPS matrix. The results of *in vitro* studies of EPS, although no doubt correct from the chemical point of view, may miss important effects resulting from complex interactions between the microorganisms and the polymeric matrix. For example, the hypotheses have been put forward that microorganisms in biofilms optimize the biofilm structure to increase the mass transport of nutrients to the deeper layers of the biofilm and that any mechanisms involved in changing biofilm structure would necessarily involve the composition of EPS. It is unlikely that such interactions could be deduced from *in vitro* studies using EPS extracted from biofilm organisms and disrupted for the purpose of their chemical analysis. The EPS in biofilms is one of the least understood components in the biofilm compartment, and some of its apparently vital components, such as extracellular DNA (eDNA) and lipids, have only recently gained the attention that they deserve.

The structure and function of EPS in biofilms are one of the frontiers of biofilm research. Although much progress has been made, our understanding of EPS is still being amended by new experimental data and new concepts derived from these experiments. It has been known for some time that the role of EPS in biofilms needs further study, but the scope of the functions of EPS that have been discovered is stunning, as shown in Table 1.1, and much still needs to be done before we fully understand the role of EPS in biofilms.

1.3.7.1   Chemical properties of EPS

EPS have many functions in biofilms and some of them are elucidated in Table 1.1, which is reprinted from an excellent review by H.-C. Flemming and J. Wingender that was entirely dedicated to the biofilm matrix. One of the most fundamental functions of EPS is to provide the matrix, the scaffolding supporting microbial structures. As research was done to characterize the matrix of extracellular polymers in biofilms and data accumulated, it became clear that EPS have many other functions besides serving as scaffolding, and the research toward elucidating these functions is still ongoing. Some of these functions are listed in Table 1.1, which demonstrates that EPS participate in the most vital sense in all activities in biofilms. The studies on the structure and function of EPS in biofilms described in this section provide a glimpse into one of the most exciting areas of biofilm research.

Initially, biofilm researchers believed that the main components of EPS were polysaccharides. It has been established that these polysaccharides are alginates, linear polysaccharides composed of two different sugar residues: 1,4-linked β-D-mannuronic acid (M) and its 5-epimer, 1,4-linked α-L-guluronic acid (G). Bacterial alginates, especially those produced by *Pseudomonas* sp., differ considerably from the well-known algal alginates (obtained from brown algae such as *Laminaria hyperborea* and *Macrocystis pyrifer*) that are used industrially as gelling agents. The polymer chains of algal alginates contain numerous blocks (>5 consecutive residues) of L-guluronic acid (G-blocks), which enable intermolecular cross-linking via the selective binding of Ca^{++} ions to form gels. In contrast, *Pseudomonas* alginates do not contain G blocks. Instead, their G residues (0%–40%) occur as single residues (MGM type), and their alginates may not form intermolecular junction zones with Ca^{++}. A commonly accepted hypothesis about polymer matrix formation in biofilms is that calcium ions bridge the alginates; this is called the "egg-box model" (Skjak-Braek et al. 1986) (Figure 1.23). It was inspired by a model that was suggested by Rees (1972) for algal alginates. Because microbial alginates do not have adequate numbers of G blocks, using this model to explain processes in bacterial biofilms is risky. Table 1.2 shows the composition of alginate that was recovered from *Pseudomonas aeruginosa* by precipitation with isopropanol and purified.

This model of calcium ions cross-linking strands of alginates was developed from an investigation of the calcium-ion-induced gel-solid transition of alginate from algae. In the absence of calcium ions, alginate from algae forms highly viscous aqueous solutions, which rapidly solidify upon the addition of calcium ions.

Table 1.1 Functions of EPS in Bacterial Biofilms

Function	Relevance to biofilms	EPS components involved
Adhesion	Allows the initial steps in the colonization of abiotic and biotic surfaces by planktonic cells and the long-term attachment of whole biofilms to surfaces	Polysaccharides, proteins, DNA, and amphiphilic molecules
Aggregation of bacterial cells	Enables bridging between cells, the temporary immobilization of bacterial populations, the development of high cell densities and cell–cell recognition	Polysaccharides, proteins, and DNA
Cohesion of biofilms	Forms a hydrated polymer network (the biofilm matrix) mediating the mechanical stability of biofilms (often in conjunction with multivalent cations) and, through the EPS structure (capsule, slime, or sheath), determining biofilm architecture, as well as allowing cell–cell communication	Neutral and charged polysaccharides, proteins (such as amyloids and lectins), and DNA
Retention of water	Maintains a highly hydrated microenvironment around biofilm organisms, leading to their tolerance of desiccation in water-deficient environments	Hydrophilic polysaccharides and, possibly, proteins
Protective barrier	Confers resistance to nonspecific and specific host defenses during infection and confers tolerance to various antimicrobial agents (e.g., disinfectants and antibiotics), as well as protecting cyanobacterial nitrogenase from the harmful effects of oxygen and protecting against some grazing protozoa	Polysaccharides and proteins
Sorption of organic compounds	Allows the accumulation of nutrients from the environment and the sorption of xenobiotics (thus contributing to environmental detoxification)	Charged or hydrophobic polysaccharides and proteins
Sorption of inorganic ions	Promotes polysaccharide gel formation, ion exchange, mineral formation, and the accumulation of toxic metal ions (thus contributing to environmental detoxification)	Charged polysaccharides and proteins, including inorganic substituents such as phosphate and sulfate
Enzymatic activity	Enables the digestion of exogenous macromolecules for nutrient acquisition and the degradation of structural EPS, allowing the release of cells from biofilms	Proteins
Nutrient source	Provides a source of compounds containing carbon, nitrogen, and phosphorus for utilization by the biofilm community	Potentially all EPS components

(continued)

Table 1.1 Functions of EPS in Bacterial Biofilms (Continued)

Function	Relevance to biofilms	EPS components involved
Exchange of genetic information	Facilitates horizontal gene transfer between biofilm cells	DNA
Electron donor or acceptor	Permits redox activity in the biofilm matrix	Proteins (e.g., those forming pili and nanowires) and, possibly, humic substances
Export of cell components	Releases cellular material as a result of metabolic turnover	Membrane vesicles containing nucleic acids, enzymes, lipopolysaccharides, and phospholipids
Sink for excess energy	Stores excess carbon under unbalanced carbon to nitrogen ratios	Polysaccharides
Binding of enzymes	Results in the accumulation, retention, and stabilization of enzymes through their interaction with polysaccharides	Polysaccharides and enzymes

Source: Reprinted from Flemming, H.-C. and Wingender, J., *Nature Reviews* 8: 623–633, 2010. With permission.

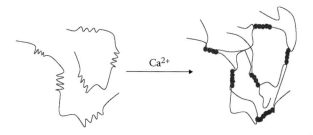

Figure 1.23 Egg-box model of calcium–alginate interaction (Reproduced from Gacesa, P., and Russel, N. J., *Pseudomonas Infection and Alginates: Biochemistry, Genetics, and Pathology.* London: Chapman & Hall, 1990.)

An extensive body of knowledge has accumulated on the chemistry of the extracellular (capsular or soluble) polysaccharides produced by industrially or medically important bacteria when they are cultured using conventional techniques. In contrast, little is known about the identity, concentration, or distribution of EPS in biofilms. A general problem is the lack of experimental methods that permit the identification and quantification

Table 1.2 Characteristics of Purified Alginate from *P. aeruginosa* Strain 8830

Property	Native	De-O-acetylated
Molecular weight (M_W) (g/moles)	1.8 (10^6)	1.5 (10^6)
Intrinsic viscosity (η mL/g)	29.0	–
O-acetyl content (moles per uronic acid residue)	0.69	–
Fraction of D-mannuronic acid (F_M)	n.d.[a]	0.95
Fraction of L-guluronic acid (F_G)	n.d.	0.05
Fraction of G units adjacent to a second G (F_{GG})	n.d.	0.00
Fraction of G units adjacent to a M (F_{GM+MG})	n.d.	0.05

Source: Reprinted from Abrahamson, M., Lewandowski, Z., Geesey, G., Skjak Braek, G., Strand, W., and Christensen, B. E., *Journal of Microbiological Methods* 26(1–2): 161–169, 1996.

[a] n.d., not determined.

(including spatial distribution) of specific EPS within biofilms, as opposed to the large number of methods that may be used for dissolved biopolymers. It is now recognized that the polysaccharides that are undisputed participants in the formation of the cohesive intercellular hydrated gel are just one of the components of EPS. Nongelling proteins and other macromolecules may have important functions in EPS even if they do not contribute to biofilm cohesiveness.

1.3.7.2   Chemical analysis of EPS

Before EPS can be chemically analyzed they must be separated from their biofilms. Currently, carbohydrate, protein, and DNA concentrations can be quantified using the phenol-sulfuric acid method, the BCA assay from Sigma, and PicoGreen dye from Invitrogen. However, these methods give the total amounts of the target compounds but no specific information about macromolecules. Recently, more advanced techniques have been applied to characterize EPS chemically (Cao et al. 2011) (Figure 1.24). The situation is complicated by the fact that there are two types of EPS in biofilms: the EPS constituting most of the biofilm matrix are loosely associated with the microbial cells (laEPS) (Figure 1.24a), and the rest are

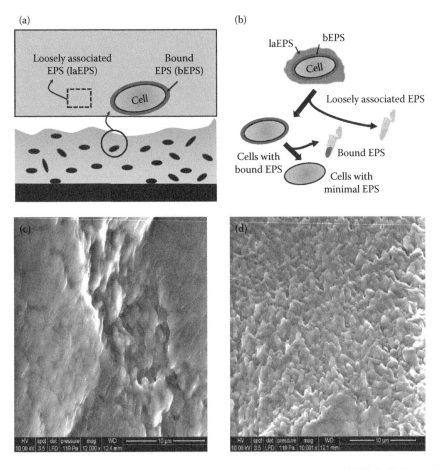

Figure 1.24 (a) Schematics of bound EPS (bEPS) and loosely associated EPS (laEPS) in biofilms. (b) Schematic illustration of cell preparation and EPS extraction for comparative analyses. Representative SEM images of *Shewanella* sp. HRCR-1 cells from HfMBR biofilms: (c) cells with bEPS and (d) cells with laEPS. (Reprinted from Cao, B. et al., *Environmental Science and Technology* 45: 5483–5490, 2011.)

tightly bound to the cell surface (bound EPS or bEPS) (Figure 1.24b). Loosely associated EPS can be separated by physical methods, but to separate bEPS, chemical methods need to be used; these methods are described in Chapter 9.

Once the bEPS and laEPS are separated from the microorganisms they can be characterized using a wide variety of techniques. We used quantitative chemical assays to determine the total protein and carbohydrate contents and compared the results with the results of Fourier transform infrared spectroscopy (FTIR) measurements (Figure 1.25). The ratios of carbohydrate to protein in the bound and loosely associated EPS samples were 0.77 and 3.64, respectively (Figure 1.25a). In environmental and laboratory-cultivated biofilms and planktonic cultures, the ratio of carbohydrate to protein in EPS is typically within the range of 0.2–4.2, and our results are within these limits. Because separating EPS from microorganisms is difficult, these results need to be scrutinized carefully: very low

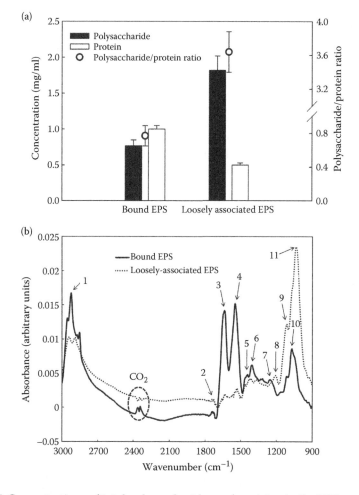

Figure 1.25 (a) Concentrations of total polysaccharides and proteins in the EPS samples. The polysaccharide/protein ratios for both bEPS and laEPS are also shown. The error bars represent standard deviation. (b) FTIR spectra of the bound and loosely associated EPS from a representative *Shewanella* sp. HRCR-1 biofilm. Band assignments: 1, 2 (membrane lipids and fatty acids); 3, 4, 5, 6 (proteins); 7, 8, 9, 10 (nucleic acids); 11 (polysaccharides). (Reprinted from Cao, B. et al., *Environmental Microbiology* 13: 1018–1031, 2011.)

carbohydrate-to-protein ratios in EPS samples may be indicative of contamination by lysed cell materials, while very high ratios may be a sign of inefficient EPS extraction. It is essential to be sure that there are minimal or no products of cell lysis in the extracted material.

The following section demonstrates the depth of the recent inquiries into the structure and function of proteins in EPS. The results exceed the scope of this text, but we decided to report them to indicate the direction of current studies and the kinds of results being found.

1.3.7.3   Proteomic analyses of EPS

One of the most powerful tools for the chemical characterization of EPS is mass spectroscopy. To identify the protein components associated with the EPS of *S. oneidensis* HRCR-1, we analyzed concentrated EPS samples using the liquid chromatography–mass spectrometry/mass spectrometry (LC-MS/MS) proteomic approach. One of the key processes is to find a database containing peptides and proteins. If genome sequences are available, they provide a database we can search for proteins. Because the genome of *Shewanella* sp. HRCR-1 had not been sequenced at the time of this work, peptides were identified by searching against *in silico* tryptic sequences derived from in-house *S. oneidensis* MR-1, MR-4, and MR-7 protein FASTA protein sequences (Turse et al. 2010). The results are summarized in Table 1.3. Of the proteins identified in the EPS fractions, seven were predicted to be extracellular and 51 were predicted to be bound to the outer membrane (OM) (Table 1.3). Most of the extracellular proteins (6 out of 7) were more abundant in the loosely associated EPS, while the majority of the OM proteins (28 out of 51) were more abundant in the bound EPS. Extracellular proteins are actively secreted by the cells and are not tightly associated with the cells or the bound EPS, enabling them to be readily separated through centrifugation. As a result, the extracellular proteins are mostly present in the loosely associated EPS.

Table 1.3 presents an enormous amount of data. The key question is what to do with these data. At this stage, a detailed literature search or genetic engineering could help us understand the data presented in Table 1.3. The secretion of a protein can be stopped by genetically engineering the organism, and the role of the protein can then be evaluated. For example, a protein with homology to biofilm-promoting protein BpfA (*S. oneidensis* MR-1 locus tag: SO4317) was identified in the loosely associated EPS (Table 1.3). BpfA is an unusually large protein (2768 amino acids, ~285 kDa) with glycine-rich domains for Ca^{2+} binding and also features ~100 amino acid tandem repeats characterizing Bap-family proteins, which are predominantly loosely associated with the bacterial OM (Theunissen et al. 2010).

1.3.7.4   Immunoblot analyses of the EPS proteins

Immunoblot analyses of EPS proteins are cheaper than proteomic analyses but give very limited information. Therefore, this technique is often used in conjunction with proteomics analysis. Figure 1.26 shows results from one-dimensional sodium dodecyl sulfate polyacrylamide gel electrophoresis (SDS-PAGE) and immunoblot analysis with cross-reactive antibodies toward OmcA, MtrC, MtrB, and MtrA. We expected to find outer membrane proteins OmcA, MtrC, MtrB, and MtrA in our samples, so we used antibodies against them. Figure 1.26a shows the separation of the EPS proteins, which were imaged using a general protein stain (GelCode). Multiple distinct protein bands associated with bound EPS could be observed. The sizes of the predominant proteins in bound EPS were estimated to be in the ranges of 60 to 90 and 30 to 40 kDa. The proteins in the loosely associated EPS were not well resolved, most likely because of interference from polysaccharides, considering the very high carbohydrate/protein ratio in this fraction relative to bound EPS

Table 1.3 Extracellular Proteins and OM Proteins Identified in Bound EPS (B) and Loosely Associated EPS (LA)

MR-1 locus tag	MR-4 locus tag	MR-7 locus tag	Protein description	B/LA ratio	Bias
SO0076	n.m.[a]	n.m.	Outer membrane MORN repeat variant protein	0.50	–
SO0144	MR4_0136	n.m.	Oligopeptidase B, PtrB	3	B
SO0300	MR4_3684	MR7_0261	Outer membrane lipoprotein, LppC	∞[b]	B
SO0322	**MR4_3651**	**MR7_0293**	**Conserved secreted protein of unknown function**	**4**	**B**
SO0403	n.m.	n.m.	Conserved outer membrane protein	0	LA
SO0404	n.m.	n.m.	Zinc-dependent metalloprotease domain lipoprotein	0.25	LA
SO0429	MR4_0433	MR7_3594	Oligopeptidase lipoprotein, M13 family	3.56	B
SO0518	MR4_0516	MR7_3515	Cobalt–zinc–cadmium cation efflux system outer membrane protein, CzcC family	13	B
SO0815	MR4_3302	MR7_0651	TonB-dependent vitamin B12 receptor, BtuB	2.20	B
SO0918	MR4_0760	MR7_3263	Acyl-homoserine lactone acylase, AaiD	1.26	–
SO1060	MR4_3039	MR7_0935	Conserved lipoprotein	∞	B
SO1215	n.m.	n.m.	Nucleoside-specific channel-forming outer membrane porin, OmpK	6	B
SO1295	MR4_2898	MR7_2980	Murein lipoprotein, Lpp	1.67	–
SO1429	n.m.	n.m.	Surface localized dimethyl sulfoxide reductase, molybdopterin-binding subunit, DmsA	0.80	–
SO1507	n.m.	n.m.	Putative outer membrane protein	4	B
SO1637	MR4_2633	MR7_2700	Beta barrel protein translocation component, BamA	∞	B
SO1659	MR4_2613	MR7_2680	Surface localized decaheme cytochrome *c* lipoprotein	6.20	B
SO1675	n.m.	n.m.	Conserved hypothetical lipoprotein	∞	B
SO1776	MR4_2512	MR7_2580	Outer membrane protein, MtrB	2.93	B
SO1778	MR4_2510	n.m.	Surface localized decaheme cytochrome *c* lipoprotein, MtrC	8.20	B
SO1779	MR4_2509	MR7_2577	Surface localized decaheme cytochrome *c* lipoprotein, OmcA	1	–
SO1854	**n.m.**	**n.m.**	**Secreted protein**	**0.28**	**LA**
SO1915	**n.m.**	**n.m.**	**Extracellular serine protease, subtilase family**	**0**	**LA**
SO2001	n.m.	n.m.	Bifunctional UDP-sugar hydrolase/5-prime-nucleotidase, UshA	0.08	LA

(continued)

Table 1.3 Extracellular Proteins and OM Proteins Identified in Bound EPS (B) and
Loosely Associated EPS (LA) (Continued)

MR-1 locus tag	MR-4 locus tag	MR-7 locus tag	Protein description	B/LA ratio	Bias
SO2427	MR4_1903	MR7_2075	TonB-dependent receptor	2.40	B
SO2715	MR4_2310	MR7_2380	Thiamine-regulated TonB-dependent receptor	3.50	B
SO2876	MR4_2350	MR7_2422	Conserved hypothetical lipoprotein	0.67	–
SO2907	MR4_1497	MR7_1564	TonB-dependent receptor	0.12	LA
SO2934	n.m.	n.m.	Extracellular lipase, Pla-1/cef family	1.40	–
SO3099	n.m.	n.m.	Outer membrane long-chain fatty acid transport protein, FadL-family	0.33	LA
SO3142	n.m.	n.m.	Peptidyl-dipeptidase, Dcp_1	∞	B
SO3193	n.m.	n.m.	Outer membrane polysaccharide export protein, OtnA	∞	B
SO3235	n.m.	n.m.	Flagellar filament capping protein, FliD	2.67	B
SO3237	n.m.	n.m.	Flagellin, FliC	4.68	B
SO3238	n.m.	n.m.	Flagellin, FliC	3.57	B
SO3247	MR4_1262	MR7_1332	Flagellar hook protein, FlgE	1	–
SO3309	n.m.	n.m.	Beta barrel protein translocation component, BamB	∞	B
SO3343	MR4_1202	MR7_1273	Conserved lipoprotein of unknown function	4.33	B
SO3357	n.m.	n.m.	Putative outer membrane protein	3	B
SO3525	n.m.	n.m.	Type IV pili-associated adhesin, PilY	1	–
SO3545	MR4_2966	MR7_3048	Outer membrane porin	1.05	–
SO3552	n.m.	n.m.	Lipoprotein with VWA and DUF3520 domains	1	–
SO3560	MR4_2981	MR7_3063	Subfamily M16B unassigned peptidases	∞	B
SO3564	MR4_1525	MR7_1592	Peptidyl-dipeptidase Dcp_2	0.43	LA
SO3565	MR4_1524	MR7_1591	Bifunctional 2-prime, 3-prime-cyclic-nucleotide 2-prime-phosphodiesterase/3'-nucleotidase, CpdB	0.67	–
SO3800	**n.m.**	**n.m.**	**Surface-associated serine protease**	**0**	**LA**
SO3811	MR4_3152	MR7_0815	Family 16 outer membrane lipoprotein of unknown function	1.50	–
SO3842	**MR4_3177**	**MR7_0789**	**Secreted low-complexity protein**	**0**	**LA**
SO3844	MR4_3179	MR7_0787	Oligopeptidase lipoprotein, M13 family	∞	B
SO3896	MR4_3228	MR7_0761	Outer membrane porin, Omp35	2.21	B
SO3904	MR4_3236	MR7_0753	Type I secretion outer membrane protein, TolC	∞	B

(continued)

Table 1.3 Extracellular Proteins and OM Proteins Identified in Bound EPS (B) and
Loosely Associated EPS (LA) (Continued)

MR-1 locus tag	MR-4 locus tag	MR-7 locus tag	Protein description	B/LA ratio	Bias
SO4080	MR4_3457	MR7_0493	Outer membrane lipoprotein, intimin-like	0.50	–
SO4317	**n.m.**	**n.m.**	**Biofilm-promoting protein, BpfA**	**0**	**LA**
SO4320	MR4_0381	MR7_3645	Type I secretion system, outer membrane component, AggA	1.13	–
SO4321	n.m.	n.m.	Pal-like T1SS-linked outer membrane lipoprotein	0.75	–
SO4561	**MR4_3756**	**MR7_3829**	**Putative extracellular protein of unknown function DUF2780**	**∞**	**B**
n.m.	MR4_2263	MR7_2335	TonB-dependent receptor	0.25	LA
n.m.	MR4_2681	n.m.	porin, Gram-negative type	1.50	–

Source: Reprinted from Cao, B. et al., *Environmental Microbiology*, 13: 1018–1031, 2011.

Note: Extracellular proteins are highlighted in bold. Unique peptide counts in three replicates for each EPS fraction were summed, and the B/LA ratio of peptide counts indicates relative abundance. Proteins with B/LA ratios higher than two or less than 0.50 were annotated as biased in abundance of B or LA, respectively.

[a] n.m.: no match in the protein database of the specific strain.

[b] ∞: not identified in LA.

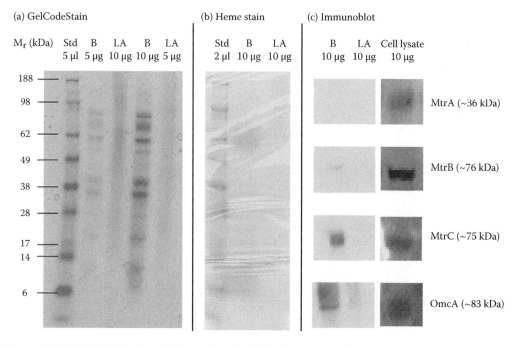

Figure 1.26 SDS-PAGE of the EPS proteins: (a) GelCode staining, (b) heme staining, and (c) immunoblot analyses. *Shewanella* sp. HRCR-1 whole-cell lysate is also shown in (c). Std: SeeBlue Plus 2 protein standard; B: bound EPS; LA: loosely associated EPS. (Reproduced from Cao, B. et al., *Environmental Microbiology* 13: 1018–1031, 2011.)

(3.64 vs. 0.77). SDS-PAGE with heme staining revealed the presence of proteins containing heme in both bound and loosely associated EPS (Figure 1.26b). The main heme proteins in the bound EPS were in the range of 60 to 90 kDa, while the loosely associated EPS heme proteins were greater than 70 kDa. The immunoblot analyses of the EPS proteins (Figure 1.26c) showed that (1) there was no MtrA homologue in either the bound or the loosely associated EPS; (2) homologues of MtrB, MtrC, and OmcA were detectable in the bound EPS; and (3) only the OmcA homologue was in the loosely associated EPS. The results from proteomics and immunoblot can be compared for consistency; in our case, the results of the immunoblot analyses were in agreement with those of the proteomics analysis.

1.3.7.5 *Viscoelastic properties of EPS*

Table 1.1 summarizes the most important functions of EPS from the life sciences point of view. From the engineering point of view, it is also important to quantify the effect of biofilm on the flow regime and vice versa. Designing conduits whose walls will become covered with biofilm requires that we understand the mutual relations between the biofilm matrix and the flow. Traditional approaches fail here because the viscoelastic properties of the biofilms are responsible for certain phenomena that are not fully understood. One effect of biofilms on the flow regime, specifically on the pressure drop in conduits, is to delay the onset of turbulence in conduits covered with biofilm; this is described in Chapter 2. Surfaces that damp turbulent eddies and delay the onset of turbulence in the flow near them are called compliant. Dolphin skin is one example of a compliant surface; biofilm appears to be another. Figure 1.27 shows a series of flow velocity profiles measured using NMRI in two rectangular conduits, one covered with biofilm and one without biofilm. Initially, when flow velocity was low, about 3 cm/s on average, the flow was stable in both reactors. Once the flow velocity increased to 8 cm/s, the flow in the reactor without biofilm lost stability, but that in the conduit with biofilm remained stable, which demonstrates that biofilms act as compliant surfaces and actively damp turbulent eddies initiated in conduits.

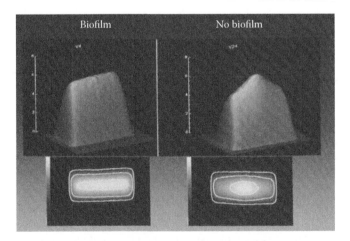

Figure 1.27 Flow velocity profiles in a rectangular closed conduit. Note that the flow velocity profile in the conduit without biofilm indicates the existence of a jet in the middle section of the reactor, while the flow in the reactor with accumulated biofilm is stable and its velocity profile is parabolic.

1.4 Characterizing microbial growth and biofilm formation

1.4.1 Microbial growth in suspension and in biofilms

Microorganisms use nutrients for growth, energy production, and product formation; this is summarized by the following expression:

$$\text{Nutrients} + \text{microorganisms} \rightarrow \text{more microorganisms} + \text{energy} + \text{products} \quad (1.6)$$

The microbial growth rate is defined as the temporal change in microbial cell concentration:

$$\text{growth rate} = \frac{dX}{dt} \quad (1.7)$$

Microbial growth is characterized by the *specific growth rate* (μ), which is defined as

$$\mu = \frac{1}{X}\frac{dX}{dt} \quad (1.8)$$

A plot of microorganism concentration versus time is called a *growth curve*; a typical curve for batch growth is shown in Figure 1.28. For practical reasons the concentration of the microorganisms is expressed as the logarithm of the cell concentration.

The growth curve shows five phases: (1) the lag phase occurs immediately after inoculation and is the time required for the adaptation of the microbial cells to the new environment; (2) the exponential growth phase, also known as the *logarithmic growth phase*, occurs when the number of microorganisms increases exponentially; (3) the deceleration phase follows the exponential phase—the growth decelerates because of the depletion of one or more essential nutrients or the accumulation of toxic microbial products; (4) the stationary phase starts at the end of the deceleration phase, when the net growth rate is equal to zero; and (5) the death phase (or decline phase) follows the stationary phase—during this phase the total microorganism concentration decreases.

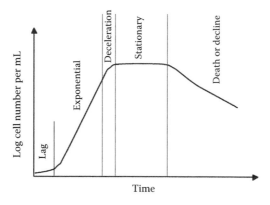

Figure 1.28 Typical growth curve.

1.4.2 Kinetics of microbial growth

Microbial growth kinetics is the relationship between the specific growth rate (μ) of a microorganism and the growth-limiting nutrient concentration (C). The most popular mathematical model that correlates these two parameters is the Monod equation (Monod 1949):

$$\mu = \mu_{max} \frac{C}{K_{sM} + C} \qquad (1.9)$$

Two constants are used to describe the growth rate in this equation: (1) μ_{max} is the maximum growth rate when the growth-limiting nutrient concentration is not limiting, and (2) K_{sM} is the Monod half-saturation constant. These constants are called biokinetic parameters, and they are quantified for various microorganisms (Figure 1.29).

Although the Monod equation is an empirical equation, its form reflects the assumptions about the underlying processes that were made to derive the Michaelis–Menten equation quantifying enzyme kinetics: on the surface of microorganisms, there exist a finite number of active sites that can be occupied by nutrient particles, so that once the binding sites are all occupied (saturated), the growth rate reaches a maximum. The assumption that reacting particles bind to a finite number of binding sites is used to model other processes as well. It always leads to similar mathematical equations represented by hyperbolas; these can be recognized in the equations quantifying the kinetics of adsorption (Langmuir equation) or the kinetics of ligand saturation (Scatchard equation).

Monod kinetics is not the only way to describe microbial growth in suspension. Modifying the assumptions leads to different forms of the kinetic expressions. Tessier (1942) hypothesized that the dependence of the specific growth rate on the growth-limiting nutrient concentration was proportional to the difference between μ and μ_{max}, which means that not all binding sites have the same affinity for the substrate:

$$\frac{d\mu}{dC} = \frac{1}{K_{sT}} (\mu_{max} - \mu) \qquad (1.10)$$

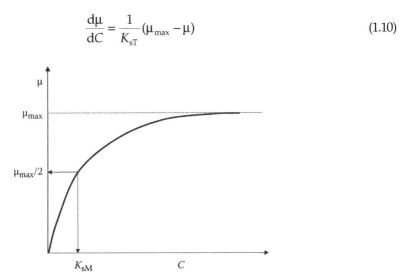

Figure 1.29 Effect of growth-limiting nutrient concentration on specific growth rate. K_s and μ_{max} can be calculated graphically.

Equation 1.10, when integrated, gives the well-known form of the Tessier equation (Tessier 1942):

$$\mu = \mu_{max}(1 - e^{-C/K_{sT}}) \qquad \text{(Tessier)} \tag{1.11}$$

There are other types of equations correlating specific growth rate with the growth-limiting nutrient concentrations (Mozer 1948; Contous 1959):

$$\mu = \mu_{max}(1 + K_{sMZ}\, C^{-\lambda}) \qquad \text{(Mozer)} \tag{1.12}$$

$$\mu = \mu_{max}\frac{C}{BX + C} \qquad \text{(Contois)} \tag{1.13}$$

In some instances, a high concentration of the growth-limiting nutrient(s) can inhibit the growth of microorganisms. In such instances, Haldane kinetics can be used:

$$\mu = \mu_{max}\frac{C}{K_s + C + C^2/K_I} \tag{1.14}$$

Haldane kinetics is a modified form of Monod kinetics, with the difference that as the growth-limiting nutrient concentration increases, at some concentration it starts to inhibit microbial growth and the growth rate decreases with the increasing concentration of the growth-limiting nutrient, as shown in Figure 1.30. This effect is called *substrate inhibition.*

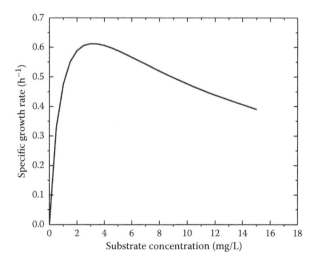

Figure 1.30 Effect of an inhibitive growth-limiting nutrient concentration on specific growth rate.

1.4.2.1　Multiple-nutrient-limited growth

Equations 1.10 through 1.14 describe single-nutrient-limited growth, and some have analogs in enzyme kinetics that can be derived using appropriate assumptions. A more modern approach recognizes that growth kinetics may depend on the concentration of more than one nutrient. For example, redox reactions may depend on the concentrations of the electron donor and the electron acceptor. In such instances it is logical to use the concentrations of both growth-limiting substances (electron donor [ed] and electron acceptor [ea]) in the kinetic equations, as is done in double-substrate Monod kinetics:

$$\mu = \mu_{max} \frac{C_{ed}}{K_{ed} + C_{ed}} \cdot \frac{C_{ea}}{K_{ed} + C_{ea}} \tag{1.15}$$

Multiple growth-limiting nutrients may have complicated effects on microbial growth kinetics. In general, three forms of multiple-nutrient growth kinetics can be considered.

(1) An interactive or multiplicative form,

$$\mu/\mu_{max} = [\mu(C_1)]\,[\mu(C_2)] \dots\dots [\mu(C_i)]; \tag{1.16}$$

(2) An additive form,

$$\mu/\mu_{max} = [\mu(C_1) + \mu(C_2) + \dots\dots + \mu(C_i)]/I; \text{ and} \tag{1.17}$$

(3) A noninteractive form

$$\mu/\mu_{max} = \min\,[\mu(C_1) \text{ or } \mu(C_2) \text{ or } \dots\dots \text{ or } \mu(C_i)] \tag{1.18}$$

1.4.2.2　Nutrient utilization rate

NUR in a batch reactor is defined as the change in the nutrient concentration over time:

$$-\frac{dC}{dt} = \frac{1}{Y_{x/s}} \frac{dX}{dt} \tag{1.19}$$

Equation 1.19 was originally introduced by Monod (1949); later Pirt (1975) and Powell (1974) added the maintenance term (Equation 1. 20) because Equation 1.19 could not represent their experimental data:

$$-\frac{dC}{dt} = \frac{1}{Y_{x/s}} \frac{dX}{dt} + mX \tag{1.20}$$

The rate of microbial growth in suspension is limited by the substrate concentration. The kinetics of microbial growth in suspension is limited by the substrate concentration and by the rate of substrate delivery, or mass transport. Assuming that the mass transport mechanism is diffusion, the growth kinetics are then described as diffusion with reaction. This is the simplest of the representations of microbial growth kinetics in biofilms, and the conceptual models that represent this mechanism are shown in Figure

1.31a and b. Figure 1.31a shows the nutrient concentration profile of a homogeneous biofilm, while Figure 1.31b shows the nutrient concentration profile of a stratified biofilm. A more detailed description of the nutrient concentration profiles of both models is in Chapter 6.

There are two profiles of substrate concentration in each conceptual model of the process shown in Figure 1.31: one is the substrate concentration profile external to the biofilm, and the other is the substrate concentration profile within the biofilm. The substrate concentration profile external to the biofilm surface is not explicitly modeled. Rather, the flux (J) of the substrate to the biofilm is related to the difference between the substrate concentration in the bulk solution (C_b) and that at the biofilm surface (C_s), the diffusivity of the substrate in water (D_w) and the thickness of the mass transfer boundary layer (δ) (Figure 1.12):

$$J_w = -\frac{D_w(C_b - C_s)}{\delta} \tag{1.21}$$

Since the thickness of the diffusion boundary layer is seldom known, it is often combined with the diffusivity of the substrate to give the mass transfer coefficient, which can be estimated experimentally:

$$k = \frac{D_w}{\delta} \tag{1.22}$$

to give

$$J_w = -k\,(C_b - C_s) \tag{1.23}$$

According to the conceptual model, the molecules of the substrate are transferred across the mass boundary layer by diffusion, enter the biofilm, and are used by the microorganisms attached to the surface. Within the biofilm the substrate is transported by diffusion and is removed by microbial reaction, hence diffusion with reaction. The rate of microbial consumption in biofilms is typically described using a Monod-type equation (Equation 1.4), while the

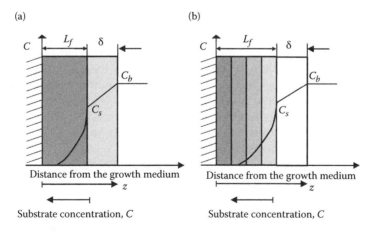

Figure 1.31 Conceptual models of nutrient concentration profiles in (a) homogeneous and (b) stratified biofilms.

rate of mass transport by diffusion is described using Fick's second law. At a steady state the rate of substrate delivery by diffusion equals the rate of microbial substrate utilization:

$$D_f \frac{d^2C}{dz^2} = \mu_{max} \frac{C}{K_{sM} + C} \frac{X_f}{Y_{x/s}} \tag{1.24}$$

Two boundary conditions are used to specify the substrate concentration at the bottom and at the surface of the biofilm:

$$\left(\frac{dC}{dz} \right)_{(z=0)} = 0$$

and

$$C_{(z=L_f)} = C_s \tag{1.25}$$

where D_f is the average effective diffusivity of the growth-limiting nutrient in the biofilm (m^2/s), z is the distance from the bottom (m), L_f is the thickness of the biofilm (m), X_f is the average biofilm density (kg/m^3), $Y_{x/s}$ is the yield coefficient (kg microorganisms/kg nutrient), μ_{max} is the maximum specific growth rate (s^{-1}), K_{sM} is the Monod half-rate constant (kg/m^3), C is the growth-limiting substrate concentration (kg/m^3), and C_s is the growth-limiting substrate concentration at the biofilm surface (kg/m^3).

The model in this equation describes the relatively simplistic case of diffusion with reaction. To reflect the true behavior of biofilm, more sophisticated models are needed, models that can accommodate what we know about biofilm mechanics, including the heterogeneous biofilm structure, complicated hydrodynamics, and gradients in effective diffusivity and density across the biofilm. Many attempts have been made to construct a comprehensive biofilm model, and the current state of affairs is that we have several models that address some of the issues discussed above, but none that addresses them all. Thus, the actual problem at hand determines which of the existing models is best to use. Biofilm structure is most often addressed using the cellular automata model, which was designed to produce structures resembling those reported by experimentalists. We present our own contributions to modeling biofilm processes in Chapter 8, where we introduce the model of stratified biofilms, which is consistent with the system of measurements we propose in this book. As expected, the more variables the models include, the more complicated and less user-friendly they become. The fundamental question of biofilm engineering—"How can we predict the performance of biofilm reactors based on our knowledge of microscale biofilm processes?"—is nowhere as obvious as it is in the mathematical modeling of biofilm processes. We offer an answer to this question in Chapter 8, where we introduce the model of stratified biofilms to interpret experimental data collected using the techniques described in this book.

1.5 Biofilm-based technologies

As our understanding of biofilm processes has improved, some of these processes have been found attractive enough to be implemented at larger than laboratory scales as biofilm-based technologies. In terms of environmental engineering, wastewater treatment offers several examples of biofilm-based technologies being successfully implemented, and we use it here to demonstrate the extent to which these technologies have been used in this particular application.

1.5.1 Biofilm-based technologies in wastewater treatment

Traditional wastewater treatment technologies, based on suspended cultures of microorganisms, such as the activated sludge process, must address the problem of separating the hydraulic retention time (HRT) from the solids retention time (SRT), and this separation is executed by using settling tanks to separate the biomass from the liquid. Part of the separated biomass is then recycled back to the reactor, and part is discharged for further treatment. Biofilm reactors offer an alternative way of separating HRT from SRT: immobilizing the biomass on surfaces. Separating HRT from SRT by immobilizing the biomass on surfaces has advantages over the traditional processes of separating the liquid from the biomass in settling tanks. One of the immediately apparent advantages is eliminating the necessity of building settling tanks, which take space and are notoriously difficult to operate, or pump stations to pump recycled sludge. Another, perhaps not as immediately apparent, advantage is the increased concentration of the biomass. The biomass concentration in activated sludge processes is typically less than 8 g/L of volatile suspended solids, while that in biofilms can exceed 80 g/L; this is at least a tenfold difference.

The designers of wastewater treatment processes have embraced biofilm-based technologies without hesitation. This is perhaps because biofilm-based technologies such as trickling filters and packed bed reactors were used in wastewater treatment long before they were called biofilm-based technologies. Packed bed reactors, which operate using biomass immobilized within the bed of the reactor, were initially filled with rocks and have recently been filled with various plastic media. Several types of biofilm reactors are in use in wastewater treatment, and Figure 1.32 presents a summary of their configurations.

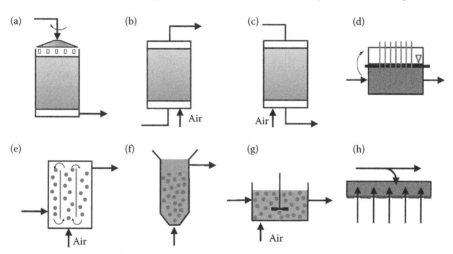

Figure 1.32 Configurations of engineered biofilm reactors used in wastewater treatment: (a) trickling filter, (b) submerged fixed bed biofilm reactor operated in an up flow mode or (c) a down flow mode, (d) rotating biological contactor, (e) suspended biofilm reactor including an airlift reactor, (f) fluidized bed reactor, (g) moving bed biofilm reactor, and (h) membrane-attached biofilm reactor. (Reprinted from Morgenroth, E., Modelling biofilm systems. In *Biological Wastewater Treatment—Principles, Modelling, and Design*. Henze, M., van Loosdrecht, M. C. M., Ekama, G., and Brdjanovic, D., Eds. London: IWA Publishing, 2008.)

Perhaps the most promising and popular biofilm technology in wastewater treatment is moving bed biofilm reactors (MBBR). The principles of the technology are similar to those of activated sludge except that the biomass in MBBR is immobilized on plastic biomass carriers instead of forming flocks as it does in the traditional activated sludge processes. Plastic biomass carriers made of high-density polyethylene are manufactured by several companies. Table 1.4 lists some of these companies and gives the dimensions of their biomass carriers. The manufacturers typically give proprietary names to their biomass carriers, but the overall design and principle of action are very similar. The biomass carriers have a specific gravity of about $0.95 \text{ g} \times \text{cm}^{-3}$, somewhat less than water, and are therefore slightly buoyant. Biomass accumulates on the carriers as biofilm, and the movement of the carriers in the reactor is propagated in aerated tanks by the air from the aeration systems or in anoxic/anaerobic tanks by mixers.

MBBRs have been successfully used in a variety of processes for carbon oxidation, nitrification, and denitrification. Wastewater treatment with MBBRs requires neither settling tanks nor sludge recycling, which simplifies the operation considerably. Before

Table 1.4 Companies Producing Biomass Carriers and the Dimensions of the Carriers

Manufacturer	Name	Bulk specific surface area, weight, gravity	Nominal carrier dimensions (depth, diameter)	Carrier photo
Veolia Inc.	AnoxKaldnes™ K1	500 m²/m³, 145 kg/m³, 0.96–0.98	7.2 mm, 9.1 mm	
	AnoxKaldnes™ K3	500 m²/m³, 95 kg/m³, 0.96–0.98	10 mm, 25 mm	
	AnoxKaldnes™ Biofilm Chip (M)	1200 m²/m³, 234 kg/m³, 0.96–1.02	2.2 mm, 45 mm	
	AnoxKaldnes™ Biofilm Chip (P)	900 m²/m³, 173 kg/m³, 0.96–1.02	3 mm, 45 mm	
Infilco Degremont Inc.	ActiveCell™ 450	450 m²/m³, 134 kg/m³, 0.96	15 mm, 22 mm	
	ActiveCell™ 515	515 m²/m³, 144 kg/m³, 0.96	15 mm, 22 mm	
Siemens Water Technologies Corp.	ABC4™	600 m²/m³, 150 kg/m³, 0.94–0.96	14 mm, 14 mm	
	ABC5™	660 m²/m³, 150 kg/m³, 0.94–0.96	12 mm, 12 mm	
Entex Technologies Inc.	BioPortz™	598 m²/m³	14 mm, 18 mm	

Source: Reprinted from Biofilm Reactors. *WEF Manual of Practice* No. 35. Prepared by the Biofilm Reactors Task Force of the Water Environment Federation, p. 215, 2010.

Figure 1.33 **(See color insert.)** Moving bed biofilm reactor (MBBR) at the Williams-Monaco Wastewater Treatment Plant, Colorado. (Reprinted from Biofilm Reactors, *WEF Manual of Practice No. 35*. Prepared by the Biofilm Reactors Task Force of the Water Environment Federation, p. 243, 2010.)

being discharged, treated wastewater passes through screens that separate out the floating biomass carriers and retain them in the reactor. MBBRs can handle higher loadings of contaminants than traditional activated sludge does, and many wastewater treatment plants that were using activated sludge are being retrofitted to use plastic biomass carriers. This gives welcome relief to many overloaded wastewater treatment plants. Reactors with plastic biomass carriers can be connected in series, thus facilitating all modern configurations used in combined organic carbon and nutrient removal processes. Figure 1.33 shows an example of a treatment plant implementing MBBR technology, the Williams Monaco Wastewater Treatment Plant, Colorado.

1.5.2   Biofilm-based technologies for energy conversion: Microbial fuel cells

We discuss the principles and show examples of microbial fuel cells (MFCs) in Chapter 7; here we focus on the use of MFCs as an example of biofilm-based technology. MFCs are energy converters in which microorganisms attach to the electrically conductive materials of the anode and the cathode and modify the redox potentials near their surfaces. Once the electrodes are connected, current flows between them. An external electronic circuitry is used to harvest some of the energy of the flowing electrons. Although MFCs are still a juvenile technology, at various stages of research and pilot-scale, rather than mature, full-scale commercial applications, the work promises the development of an attractive alternative power source that can be invaluable in carefully selected applications. MFCs therefore attract much attention within the community of biofilm researchers. An example of such a special application is the use of MFCs in the marine environment to replace sea batteries. MFCs that work as power sources in the marine environment are an example of a biofilm-based technology and present an opportunity to show the various stages of the technological development of new alternative power sources. They also show the difficulties researchers face in making the technology available for commercial use. Various submerged electronic devices, mostly sensors, are deployed in the sea at remote locations or at locations with denied access and are operated for long periods of time. One problem with powering such submerged electronic devices is the maintenance of the power sources. Sea batteries, often used for such purposes, rely on sacrificial anodes, which have a limited lifetime. Sea batteries need to be replaced every few months, which is a work- and time-consuming process. Considering their dimensions and weight, sea batteries probably do not qualify as portable devices. For example, the SWB 501 battery manufactured by Kongsberg Maritime AS is 1 m long and weighs 120 kg. The practical operational time of sea batteries is limited, and every time they need to be replaced, a team of divers has to be involved. Also, the replacement schedule is only loosely related to the frequency of actual use of the battery; once activated, sea batteries discharge whether they are used or not because sacrificial anodes dissolve spontaneously in seawater. The size and weight of sea batteries, combined with the often rigorous maintenance schedules of the devices they power, make using them particularly challenging at locations of difficult or denied access. Power supplies based on MFCs can be made smaller and lighter than sea batteries, and they are maintenance-free for their lifetimes. They do not discharge spontaneously, and once deployed they can be left unattended for years and retain their operational capabilities, unless physically destroyed.

As discussed above, the development of MFC technology is at various stages of research and using MFCs for field applications presents researchers with challenges that do not exist when MFCs are operated at the bench scale in the comfort of the laboratory environment. These challenges need to be addressed and successfully solved one by one until the technology is mature enough for commercial applications. The purpose of this section is to give an example of the development of a biofilm technology showing the challenges biofilm researchers face trying to scale up a process and use it outside their laboratories. For bench-scale MFCs in laboratories, oxidizable substances are delivered to the system as well-defined organics, making possible the use of thermodynamic tables and computations predicting and quantifying the electrochemical processes involved in generating electrical energy, as shown in Chapter 7. In field applications, however, researchers rely on the mixtures of mostly unknown reduced organics that are available in benthic deposits, which makes many thermodynamic computations difficult or impossible. MFCs work on the same electrochemical principles whether in the laboratory or in the field, but those used in the field are constructed differently than those typically used in the laboratory. Figure 1.34 shows the principle of a sediment microbial fuel cell (SMFC), also known as a benthic fuel cell.

The components of a sediment fuel cell are similar to those shown in Figure 7.43 except for the lack of a proton exchange membrane separating the anodic and cathodic compartments. In SMFCs the electrical neutrality of the environment surrounding the anodic and cathodic compartments is perturbed by the electrochemical reaction and restored by ions readily available in the solution, which spontaneously migrate in the electrical field surrounding the electrodes. Much of the effort in developing MFCs as alternative power sources for submerged electronic devices is oriented toward finding suitable oxidized and reduced substances in open waters and benthic sediments that can serve as reactants converting chemical energy to electrical energy. Not surprisingly, reduced substances are found in benthic deposits, and most of them are sulfides. However, it has been demonstrated that natural dissolved organic matter can also serve as the anodic reactant in MFCs.

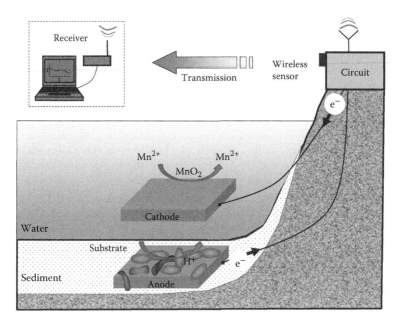

Figure 1.34 Sediment microbial fuel cell.

As for the cathodic reactant, most MFC researchers rely on reducing dissolved oxygen. The disadvantages of using oxygen as the cathodic reactant are well known and are related to the low solubility of oxygen in water and to the slow kinetics of oxygen reduction on metal electrodes. Therefore, we base our designs and our thermodynamic computations on biomineralized manganese oxides rather than depend on dissolved oxygen. The principles of using biomineralized manganese oxides as cathodic reactants, including thermodynamic computations, are explained and presented in Figure 7.44. In our results and the collected field data, the monitored cathodic potentials of the MFC electrodes are consistent with our thermodynamic computations, indicating that biomineralized manganese oxides develop on the cathodic members of our MFCs. The biggest advantage of using biomineralized manganese oxides is that they are solid reactants and therefore do not change activity when discharged (reducing dissolved oxygen relies on mass transport). The problem with biomineralized manganese oxides is that microorganisms cannot deposit the oxides and charge the electrodes fast enough when high power is in demand. Therefore, oxygen reduction often supplements the cathodic reaction and provides the cathodic current in the long-term operation of devices, particularly those using variable amounts of power. This exhibits itself as a mixed potential of the cathode. For sensors that can be powered intermittently, biomineralized manganese offers the advantage of a higher cathode potential but requires periods of the electronic circuitry waiting in sleeping mode until enough biomineralized manganese oxide has been deposited on the cathodes to switch the circuit to operational mode. Figure 1.34 shows the principle of the field-scale MFC based on using reduced substances in benthic deposits as the anodic reactants and biomineralized manganese oxides as the cathodic reactants. The electrochemical and microbial reactions active during the charging and discharging of the biomineralized deposits of manganese oxides are explained in Chapter 7. We tried SMFCs in two configurations. Initially, an MFC encased in a buoy with attached cathodes was anchored at a selected location. Later we changed the design, abandoned the buoy, and used cathodes immersed deeper into the water but suspended above the bottom by floats.

Figure 1.35 shows the principle of the MFC installed in a buoy (top) and the process of deploying the MFC in the ocean (bottom). The buoy was filled with electronics, including a data acquisition system and a radio transmitter sending the results of the measurements to a remote receiver located in the laboratory (this is the reason for the buoy in Figure 1.35 to have an antenna).

The configuration shown in Figure 1.35 was very attractive, but, unfortunately, it suffered from a fatal flaw: the excessive growth of seaweed on the cathodes, which were attached to the buoy. This prevented them from developing the desired cathodic potential. Figure 1.36 shows the buoy right after it was retrieved from the ocean after a few months of operation during which we tried, unsuccessfully, to revive its activity. The reason for the problem became obvious once the buoy was retrieved. As seen in Figure 1.36, the cathodes

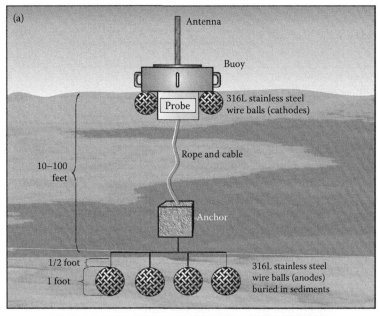

Figure 1.35 (a) The principle of the MFC installed in a buoy and (b) a team of divers deploying the buoy with the MFC in the ocean at Hatfield Marine Science Center, Newport, Oregon.

Figure 1.36 The buoy with an MFC retrieved from the ocean. The anodes (the balls of stainless steel wire at the left side of the buoy) were clean and developed their anodic potentials properly. However, the cathodes, attached to the buoy, were covered with seaweed and did not reach the desired cathodic potential.

(attached to the buoy) were entirely covered with seaweed, which effectively inhibited all available cathodic reactions, the deposition of biomineralized manganese oxides and oxygen reduction. We should note that the sediment microbial fuel cell worked perfectly for the first three months and failed after that, demonstrating the need for long-term testing of these devices.

As a result of this operational failure, we had to change the configuration of the MFC. In the following deployments we used cathodes suspended above the bottom, away from the water surface, where excessive seaweed caused the operational problems. The redesigned configuration is shown in Figure 1.37.

MFCs with cathodes suspended above the bottom, as in the configuration shown in Figure 1.37, were deployed and tested at two sites, both at the Pacific Ocean: the Hatfield Marine Science Center, Newport, Oregon and the Space and Naval Warfare Command Center, San Diego, California, where they worked successfully for an entire year. No problem with seaweed on the cathodes was reported at either deployment site. The only problem noticed was at the deployment site in San Diego, where, after a few months of MFC operation, shrimp became attracted to the anodes and dug holes in the sediment, which introduced oxygen into the benthic deposits, which affected the potential and decreased the efficiency of the buried anodes. This problem, however, can be easily fixed by installing plastic nets above the buried cathodes to serve as a physical barrier for the shrimp. A

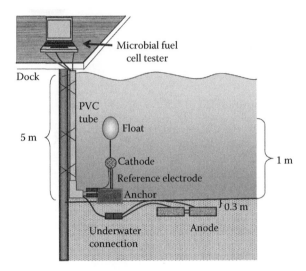

Figure 1.37 The redesigned configuration of the MFC, this time hard-wired to the data acquisition system and testing equipment. This configuration proved to be much more robust than the one shown in Figure 1.35.

potentially interesting research question emerges from this observation: Why were the shrimp attracted to the buried cathodes? Hypothetically, they followed the gradient in electrical potential, but this hypothesis would have to be tested in controlled experiments that exceed the scope of our work with MFCs.

Thus far, we have deployed several sediment microbial fuel cells designed like that shown in Figure 1.37 in Palouse River, near Washington State University, Pullman, and operated them for more than three years. We are continuing to operate them. Once the design was perfected and the requirements of long-term operation were satisfied, we were able to focus on practical and scientific problems related to the operation of the MFCs, such as increasing the power production, the mechanism of the anodic and cathodic reactions, and, above all, elucidating the mechanism of electron transfer from microbial cells to the solid electrodes.

A discussion on implementing biofilm technologies would not be complete without referring to the problems with scaling up biofilm processes. The main source of these problems is biofilm heterogeneity, which causes biofilm activity to vary from location to location. Biofilm models that describe biofilm processes on the scale of an entire reactor assume that the biofilm is uniformly distributed in the reactor. This assumption, which is fully justified in the case of well-mixed reactors, is inadequate in biofilm reactors, and we can use Figure 1.20 in this chapter to illustrate the magnitude of the problem. With the current sophistication in quantifying biofilm processes at the microscale, it is not surprising to observe that the local conditions quantified in biofilms deviate widely from the average conditions quantified for the entire reactor and from those predicted by biofilm models. The process of "calibrating" biofilm models typically adjusts the vital process parameters, such as the thickness of the mass transfer biofilm layer, as much as it takes to fit the model prediction to the experimental data. Such a procedure is obviously questionable. As for the deviations of the locally measured properties of the biofilms from the average, one hopes that they cancel each other and that overall, at the macroscale, the differences measured at the microscale do not matter much, but we do not really know for sure that this is the case. It actually gets worse: biofilms grown in two identically operated biofilm reactors have different structure. Figure 1.38 shows that biofilms in two laboratory reactors were similar

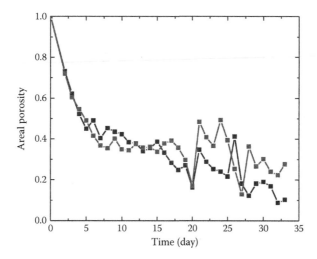

Figure 1.38 Areal porosity evaluated daily from 30 images taken at randomly selected locations in each of two biofilms (Lewandowski et al. 2004). The data show that the biofilms accumulated in these two reactors operated in parallel are similar only for a few days. After that, the biofilms gradually develop a different structure in each reactor. After the first sloughing event, on day 20, each biofilm shows a different growth pattern. (Reprinted from Lewandowski, Z. et al., *Water Science and Technology* 49: 359–364, 2004.)

only during the initial stages of operation. After just a few days, most likely after the first sloughing event, each reactor acquired different characteristics and a different pattern of biofilm accumulation. We used areal porosity, defined and explained in Chapter 6, to characterize biofilm structure in the reactors.

The oscillating pattern of biofilm accumulation demonstrates that biofilm structure never reaches a steady state in biofilm reactors and should be characterized as a sequence of sloughing and regrowth processes. However, all these observations originated from experimental studies using small-scale laboratory reactors. One may argue that the oscillating pattern of biofilm accumulation may not be relevant in larger-scale reactors, because the local deviations from the average may cancel each other when biofilms cover a large surface, but we do not know whether this is true. Besides, even if this argument is true, it also raises a question: How big must the biofilm reactor be to cancel the local oscillating patterns of biomass accumulation?

It is convenient and it simplifies mathematical description to assume that biofilm processes reach a steady state in biofilm reactors in the same manner as biological and chemical processes reach a steady state in reactors with suspended biomass. However, the indispensable condition for reaching a steady state in a well-mixed reactor with a growth of suspended microorganisms is that part of the biomass be removed from the reactor with the effluent. This is not the case in biofilm reactors: biomass in biofilm reactors is immobilized on surfaces of the reactors and is removed at unequal and unknown intervals in the form of biofilm sloughing. As above, one can argue that even if the biomass concentration never reaches a steady state at the microscale, the local deviations cancel each other and the substrate conversion rate reaches a steady state, and the counterargument to this statement is the same as the one we used above.

Scaling up biofilm processes is obviously a problem that needs to be addressed. However, there are also difficulties with interpreting results at the microscale. Above,

Figure 1.39 Image of a biofilm grown at a flow velocity of 0.81 m/s.

we criticized the procedure of calibrating biofilm models using the thickness of the mass boundary layer as the control parameter. The criticism is still valid, but we have difficulty in suggesting a better procedure. Figure 1.12 shows an idealized model of hydrodynamic and mass transfer boundary layers measured as distances from the biofilm surface to the locations where the respective factors, flow velocity and substrate concentration, are not affected by the presence of the surface or the biofilm. Obviously, to measure the thickness of any of these boundary layers, the position of the biofilm surface needs to be determined precisely. Here is the problem. The surfaces of biofilms grown at relatively low flow velocities, a few centimeters per second, have fairly well defined positions. However, the positions of the surfaces of biofilms grown at higher flow velocities are much less defined. Figure 1.39 shows the surface of a biofilm grown at a flow velocity 0.81 m/s. It is quite obvious that the position of the biofilm surface in Figure 1.39 would have to be chosen arbitrarily.

In practice, we locate the position of the biofilm surface at the inflection point of the dissolved oxygen concentration profile measured across the biofilm rather than using microscopy. This procedure provides a reproducible way of approaching the problem, but the problem is not solved. At some point we have to admit that the surfaces of some biofilms are ill defined and so are the thicknesses of the hydrodynamic and mass transfer boundary layers.

1.6   Strategy of biofilm research

Biofilm research develops around hypotheses based on conceptual models of biofilm processes. The conceptual models of biofilm processes are continually tested for consistency with the accumulated experimental results. If the accumulated results show that an entire model or a part of it is not consistent with the experimental evidence, these doubts are converted into relevant research hypotheses and further tested. If the tests corroborate the inconsistency between the conceptual model and the experimental evidence, the conceptual model is altered. An example of such a situation is the development of the conceptual model of biofilm structure shown in Figure 1.8. This model was introduced because several experimental results could not be explained within the framework of the then existing conceptual model of biofilm structure. Inconsistencies between experimental data and a conceptual model rarely require changing the entire conceptual model, however; more often, fragments of the conceptual model need revision. For example, the conceptual model of heterogeneous biofilms in Figure 1.8 shows a thin, discontinuous layer of

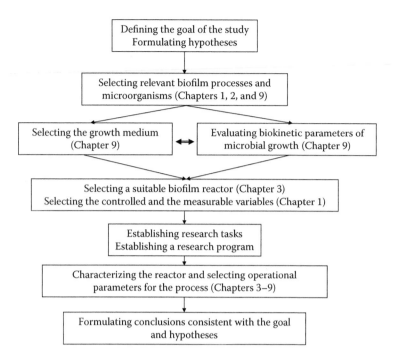

Figure 1.40 Sequence of steps in a typical biofilm study.

microorganisms at the bottom of the biofilm. This layer was introduced into the model to accommodate the concept of differential aeration cells in biofilms growing on electrically conductive surfaces, observed by the researchers who studied MIC. The process of developing conceptual models of biofilm processes and testing hypotheses derived from these models is perpetual and it refines the knowledge of biofilms and biofilm processes. This activity is consistent with Karl Popper's assertion that scientific theories cannot be proved, only disproved. It does not matter how many observations are consistent with the model; a single observation that is not consistent with the model invalidates it. If such observations accumulate, the model has to be changed.

Although it is impossible to give precise recipes for conducting biofilm research, biofilm studies usually have several identifiable steps, shown in Figure 1.40.

The sequence of steps in Figure 1.40 is not unique and may be modified depending on the nature of the project, but some components of the sequence, such as establishing the goal of the study, formulating the hypotheses, testing the hypotheses, and formulating the conclusions, can be identified in every research program. These common components will be addressed individually, starting with the most important component: the goal of the study.

1.6.1 The goal of the study

Clearly, every biofilm study must have a goal. It is best to put this goal in writing at the very beginning and keep it in mind at all times, because all other steps in the sequence need to be in agreement with the goal. If possible, the goal should be formulated in one sentence, which needs to be specific enough to communicate the purpose of the study yet general enough not to include practical details of the study. There is a delicate balance between going too far and not going far enough in specifying the goal. To give an example, the sentence "the goal of the study is to quantify the effect of hydrodynamics on the structure of a biofilm" is too general and needs to be restricted by defining what is meant by "hydrodynamics" and what is meant by "biofilm structure." It is better to formulate this goal as: "the goal of the study is to quantify the effect of flow velocity on the temporal development of porosity in biofilms of *Pseudomonas aeruginosa*." This goal will serve as an example in the following sections to show that all other steps in the sequence need to be consistent with the goal.

1.6.2   Hypotheses

If there is a reason for initiating a study, there is also an expectation with regard to the results of the study that can be formulated as one or more hypotheses. Following the example from the previous paragraph, the hypotheses for the project can be formulated as follows:

1. Biofilm porosity decreases with increased flow velocity
2. Biofilm porosity reaches a steady state
3. The time needed to reach a steady state is inversely proportional to the flow velocity in the reactor

1.6.3   The tasks

The goal of the study and the hypotheses define what is studied and what the expectations are. Typically, the study needs to be subdivided into manageable tasks that can be accomplished within the time designated for the study. Before formulating the tasks, many details of the research program need to be specified, such as the type of reactor to be used, the range of flow velocities to be studied, the type of analysis to be used to monitor the biofilm, and—this should be at least discussed at this stage—the type of analysis to be used to evaluate the results. The tasks may be something like the following:

1. Preparing the reactor and inoculating it with the selected microorganisms
2. Operating the reactor
3. Taking confocal images of the biofilm
4. Measuring flow velocity
5. Computing biofilm porosity from the images of the biofilm
6. Analyzing results
7. Preparing a report

The first five tasks will be repeated for the different flow velocities that are specified in the research program.

1.6.4   Selecting relevant experimental conditions

1.6.4.1   Selecting microorganisms and growth media

After the goal of the study and the hypotheses have been formulated, there are many choices to be made with respect to the experimental conditions of the study, such as selecting the reactor, the type of microorganisms, and the growth medium. These choices define the relevance of the study. To follow the example we started in the previous section, let us say that to study the effect of flow velocity on the temporal development of biofilm porosity, the researcher has selected the aerobic decomposition of glucose by *Pseudomonas aeruginosa* in a tubular reactor, which defines the microorganisms and the type of reactor. If possible, the microorganisms should be acquired from a certified source, such as the American Type Culture Collection (ATCC). This makes reporting the experimental procedure easier, and others can use the same source of microorganisms if they want to repeat the experiment and reproduce the data. Although the growth medium can also be acquired from the same source, ATCC, it often needs to be modified to satisfy the needs of a specific project. Typically, the media designed to grow microorganisms in planktonic form are much too concentrated to be relevant in environmental studies. Often, the carbon sources used to grow microorganisms are not particularly relevant in environmental studies. In the example discussed above, the researcher might decide to use glucose as the carbon source. However, if the goal of the study were changed to quantifying the effect of flow velocity on the temporal development of porosity in biofilms developing in constructed wetlands, using glucose as a carbon source would not add to the relevancy of the study.

The selection of a reactor is determined by the nature of the tests. This project will require taking images but not physical sampling of the biofilm. Therefore, a closed conduit reactor is a good choice. Because the biofilm structure will be evaluated at designed time intervals, it is probably better to use rectangular tubes so that they can be positioned on the stage of a confocal microscope. The dimensions of the reactor need to be checked to ensure that the desired flow velocity can be achieved, and the length of the reactor needs to exceed the entry length determined from the characteristics of the flow and the geometry of the reactor.

1.6.4.2   Selecting biofilm reactors

The type of reactor is selected to satisfy the needs of process control and analyses. The selected reactors need to be characterized. The extent of the characterization varies and depends on the nature of the study. In the project selected for the example, in which the flow velocity affects biofilm structure, it is certainly important to characterize the hydrodynamics and to make sure that the images of biofilm structure are collected where the flow is stable, at a distance from the entrance exceeding the entry length to the reactor.

1.6.4.3   Selecting operational parameters

1.6.4.3.1   Selecting control variables.   The control variables are those that the operator can set at a desired level. In each type of experiment there are variables that need to be controlled, either by keeping them constant or by changing them in a designed manner. In the project we are using as an example, the composition of the growth medium needs to be kept constant and the flow velocity needs to be changed from one run to another in a predesigned manner.

1.6.4.3.2   Selecting the measured variables.   The measured variables are those that are evaluated using appropriate procedures. Measured variables are quantified from two points of view: (1) experimentally and (2) using mathematical models. In the example discussed here, one of the measured variables is biofilm porosity. The researcher needs to decide what other parameters need to be measured, perhaps the concentrations of the growth-limiting nutrients in the effluent.

Table 1.5 An Example Research Program Timeline

Task number	Month 1	Month 2	Month 3
1. Preparing the reactor and inoculating it with the selected microorganisms	------------------		
2. Operating the reactor	------------------	------------------	---------
3. Taking confocal images of the biofilm	------------------	------------------	---------
4. Measuring the flow velocity	------------------	------------------	---------
5. Computing the biofilm porosity from the images of the biofilm		------------------	---------
6. Analyzing the results		------------------	-------------------
7. Preparing a report		------------------	-------------------

1.7   Research program

The research program elaborates on the tasks: it tells how the research will be carried out and specifies how many runs are needed and how many repetitions are to be scheduled. The research program should include a timeline describing the sequence in which the tasks are to be executed, the time needed for executing each task, and the possible overlaps in time in which the tasks are to be executed. Because the goal of the study in the example is to quantify the relation between flow velocity and the temporal development of biofilm porosity, the biofilm will have to be grown several times, at various average flow velocities. This can be done in parallel or in a consecutive fashion, depending on the number of required runs, and the number of available reactors, etc. One of the outcomes of a properly prepared research program is a timeline like that in Table 1.5. While evaluating the measured variables, the researcher needs to be sure that the results of these measurements are reproducible. Such issues as the number of repetitions, the use of legitimate analytical protocols, and the interpretation of data using recognizable statistical procedures need to be considered.

1.8   Interpreting results of biofilm studies

Interpretation of the results should be discussed before the study actually starts. On the basis of the list of analyses scheduled for the study, it is possible to visualize these data already existing and select a manner of presenting them that is consistent with the goal of the study and documents the data in such a manner that they can be interpreted. For example, plotting temporal variations in biofilm porosity for various flow velocities may be an acceptable approach. Before deciding how to present the data, it is important to review the hypotheses and verify that the type of presentation selected for the study will actually permit testing the hypotheses. In this example, just plotting biofilm porosity versus time for each flow velocity is not enough to test the hypotheses. Because the hypotheses refer to a steady state of porosity in the reactor, it is important to define a steady state of porosity. If the researcher decides, for example, that porosity has reached a steady state when it does not vary by more than 10% in five consecutive days of reactor operation, then it is possible to use each of the plots of porosity versus time to determine the time needed to reach the steady state. To test the hypothesis that biofilm porosity reaches a steady state, it would be helpful to limit the time of the test to a manageable length, say 60 days. If the biofilms reach a steady state within 60 days, then the hypothesis tests positive. If the porosities of biofilms grown at different flow velocities reach steady states at different times, then the time needed to reach a steady state can be plotted versus the flow velocity in the reactor, and from this set of data the third hypothesis can be tested.

Finally, the shortcomings of the study should be explicitly addressed. For example, in the study discussed above, the conclusion may emerge that the research program should have included the effect of shear stress on the development of biofilm porosity as well as the effect of flow velocity. Sometimes, the results can be recalculated to address the shortcomings; if not, the shortcomings should be specified as subjects of research needed in the future.

Nomenclature

Symbol	Meaning	Usual Units
B	Constant in Contois model	
C	Growth-limiting substrate concentration	kg/m^3
C_{ed}	Electron donor concentration	g/L, kg/m^3
C_{ea}	Electron acceptor concentration	g/L, kg/m^3
$C_{Effluent}$	Effluent nutrient concentration	g/L, kg/m^3
$C_{Influent}$	Influent nutrient concentration	g/L, kg/m^3
C_b	Bulk substrate concentration	g/L, kg/m^3
C_s	Growth-limiting substrate concentration at the biofilm surface	g/L, kg/m^3
D_f	Average effective diffusivity of the growth-limiting nutrient in the biofilm	m^2/s
D_w	Diffusivity in water of the substance selected for the evaluation of biofilm activity	
J_w	Flux	kg/m^2
k	Mass transfer coefficient	m/s
K_{sMZ}	Moser saturation constant	g/L, kg/m^3
K_s	Monod saturation constant	g/L, kg/m^3
K_{sT}	Tessier saturation constant	g/L, kg/m^3
K_I	Substrate inhibition constant	g/L, kg/m^3
K_{ed}	Monod constant for electron donor	g/L, kg/m^3
K_{ea}	Monod constant for electron acceptor	g/L, kg/m^3
L_f	Thickness of the biofilm	m, μm
m	Maintenance coefficient	h^{-1}
Q	Volumetric flow rate	L/h
t	Time	h
V	Volume	L, m^3
v_b	Bulk flow velocity	m
X	Planktonic cell density	g/L
X_f	Average biofilm density	kg/m^3
$Y_{x/s}$	Yield coefficient (kg microorganisms/kg nutrient)	
z	Distance from the bottom	m

Greek symbols

Symbol	Meaning	Usual Units
μ	Specific growth rate	s^{-1}
μ_{max}	Maximum specific growth rate	s^{-1}
γ_{SL}	Surface free energy of the solid surface covered with liquid	N/m
γ_{LV}	Surface free energy of the liquid–vapor interface	N/m
γ_{SV}	Surface free energy of the solid surface in contact with vapor	N/m
θ	Contact angle	degree
δ	Thickness of the mass transfer boundary layer	m
ϕ	Hydrodynamic boundary layer thickness	m

Abbreviations

Abbreviation	Meaning
bEPS	Bound EPS
CSTR	Continuously stirred tank reactor
EPS	Extracellular polymeric substances
HRT	Hydraulic retention time
laEPS	Loosely associated EPS
LBR	Laboratory biofilm reactor
MBBR	Moving bed biofilm reactor
MFC	Microbial fuel cell
MIC	Microbially influenced corrosion
NMRI	Nuclear magnetic resonance imaging
NUR	Nutrient utilization rate
OM	Outer membrane
SDS-PAGE	Sodium dodecyl sulfate polyacrylamide gel electrophoresis
SNUR	Specific nutrient utilization rate
SRT	Solids retention time

References

Cao, B., Shi, L. A., Brown, R. N., Xiong, Y. J., Fredrickson, J. K., Romine, M. F., Marshall, M. J., Lipton, M. S., and Beyenal, H. 2011. Extracellular polymeric substances from Shewanella sp HRCR-1 biofilms: Characterization by infrared spectroscopy and proteomics. *Environmental Microbiology* 13(4): 1018–1031.

Contous, D. E. 1959. Kinetics of bacterial growth: Relationship between population density and specific growth rate of continuous culture. *Microbiology* 21: 40.

Drury, W. J., Stewart, P. S., and Characklis, W. G. 1993. Transport of 1-mu-m latex-particles in *Pseudomonas-aeruginosa* biofilms. *Biotechnology and Bioengineering* 42(1): 111–117.

Lewandowski, Z., Beyenal, H., and Stookey, D. 2004. Reproducibility of biofilm processes and the meaning of steady state in biofilm reactors. *Water Science and Technology* 49: 359–364.

Monod, J. 1949. The growth of bacterial cultures. *Annual Review of Microbiology* 3: 371–394.

Mozer, A. 1948. *The Dynamics of Bacterial Populations Maintained in the Chemostat.* Publication 614. Washington, DC: The Carnegie Institution.

Neu, T. R., Swerhone, G. D. W., and Lawrence, J. R. 2001. Assessment of lectin-binding analysis for in situ detection of glycoconjugates in biofilm systems. *Microbiology* 147: 299–313.

Rees, D. A. 1972. Shapely polysaccharides. *Biochemical Journal* 126: 257–273.

Skjak-Braek, G., Grasdalen, H., and Laren, B. 1986. Monomer sequence and acetylation pattern in some bacterial alginates. *Carbohydrate Research* 154: 239–250.

Tessier, G. 1942. Croissance des populations bacterie'nnes et quantite'd'aliment disponible. *Reviews of Science,* Paris 3028, 209.

Theunissen, S., De Smet, L., Dansercoer, A., Motte, B., Coenye, T., Van Beeumen, J., Devereese, B., Savvides, S., and Vergauwen, B. 2010. The 285 kDa Bap/RTX hybrid cell surface protein (SO4317) of Shewanella oneidensis MR-1 is a key mediator of biofilm formation. *Research in Microbiology* 161: 144–152.

Turse, J., Marshall, M., Fredrickson, J., Lipton, M., and Callister, S. 2010. An empirical strategy for characterizing bacterial proteomes across species in the absence of genomic sequences. *PLOS One* 5(11): e13968.

Suggested readings

Reviews

Arciola, C. R., Alvi, F. I., An, Y. H., Campoccia, D., and Montanaro, L. 2005. Implant infection and infection resistant materials: A mini review. *International Journal of Artificial Organs* 28: 1119–1125.

Baker, J. S. and Dudley, L. Y. 1998. Biofouling in membrane systems—A review. *Desalination* 118: 81–89.

Branda, S. S., Vik, A., Friedman, L., and Kolter, R. 2005. Biofilms: The matrix revisited. *Trends in Microbiology* 13: 20–26.

Bridier, A., Briandet, R., Thomas, V., and Dubois-Brissonnet, F. 2011. Resistance of bacterial biofilms to disinfectants: A review. *Biofouling* 27(9): 1017–1032.

Carpentier, B. and Cerf, O. 2011. Review—Persistence of *Listeria monocytogenes* in food industry equipment and premises. *International Journal of Food Microbiology* 145(1): 1–8.

Casey, E., Glennon, B., and Hamer, G. 1999. Review of membrane aerated biofilm reactors. *Resources Conservation and Recycling* 27: 203–215.

Chandra, J., Zhou, G. Y., and Ghannoum, M. A. 2005. Fungal biofilms and antimycotics. *Current Drug Targets* 6: 887–894.

Chatterjee, S. N. and Chaudhuri, K. 2006. Lipopolysaccharides of vibrio cholerae: III. Biological functions. *Biochimica et Biophysica Acta-Molecular Basis of Disease* 1762: 1–16.

Chen, V., Li, H., and Fane, A. G. 2004. Non-invasive observation of synthetic membrane processes—A review of methods. *Journal of Membrane Science* 241: 23–44.

Cohen, M., Kofonow, J., Nayak, J. V., Palmer, J. N., Chiu, A. G., Leid, J. G., and Cohen, N. A. 2009. Biofilms in chronic rhinosinusitis: A review. *American Journal of Rhinology and Allergy* 23(3): 255–260.

Daigger, G. T. and Boltz, J. P. 2011. Trickling filter and trickling filter-suspended growth process design and operation: A state-of-the-art review. *Water Environment Research* 83(5): 388–404.

Devinny, J. S. and Ramesh, J. 2005. A phenomenological review of biofilter models. *Chemical Engineering Journal* 113: 187–196.

Dobretsov, S., Teplitski, M., and Paul, V. 2009. Mini-review: Quorum sensing in the marine environment and its relationship to biofouling. *Biofouling* 25(5): 413–427.

Eding, E. H., Kamstra, A., Verreth, J., Huisman, E. A., and Klapwijk, A. 2006. Design and operation of nitrifying trickling filters in recirculating aquaculture: A review. *Aquacultural Engineering* 34: 234–260.

Fux, C. A., Costerton, J. W., Stewart, P. S., and Stoodley, P. 2005. Survival strategies of infectious biofilms. *Trends in Microbiology* 13: 34–40.

Gaylarde, C. C. and Morton, L. H. G. 1999. Deteriogenic biofilms on buildings and their control: A review. *Biofouling* 14: 59–74.

George, R. P., Muraleedharan, P., Dayal, R. K., and Khatak, H. S. 2006. Techniques for biofilm moni-
    toring. *Corrosion Reviews* 24: 123–150.
Ghafari, S., Hasan, M., and Aroua, M. K. 2008. Bio-electrochemical removal of nitrate from water and
    wastewater—A review. *Bioresource Technology* 99(10): 3965–3974.
Hall-Stoodley, L., Costerton, J. W., and Stoodley, P. 2004. Bacterial biofilms: From the natural environ-
    ment to infectious diseases. *Nature Reviews Microbiology* 2: 95–108.
Harris, L. G. and Richards, R. G. 2006. Staphylococci and implant surfaces: A review. *Injury-
    International Journal of the Care of the Injured* 37: 3–14.
Hodkinson, B., Williams, J. B., and Butler, J. E. 1999. Development of biological aerated filters: A
    review. *Journal of the Chartered Institution of Water and Environmental Management* 13: 250–254.
Ivanovic, I. and Leiknes, T. O. The biofilm membrane bioreactor (BF-MBR)—A review. 2012.
    Desalination and Water Treatment 37(1–3): 288–295.
Jorge, P., Lourenco, A., and Pereira, M. O. 2012. New trends in peptide-based anti-biofilm strategies:
    A review of recent achievements and bioinformatic approaches. *Biofouling* 28(10): 1033–1061.
Kaplan, J. B. 2005. Methods for the treatment and opinion prevention of bacterial biofilms. *Expert
    Opinion on Therapeutic Patents* 15: 955–965.
Karunakaran, E., Mukherjee, J., Ramalingam, B., and Biggs, C. A. 2011. "Biofilmology": A multidis-
    ciplinary review of the study of microbial biofilms. *Applied Microbiology and Biotechnology* 90(6):
    1869–1881.
Kodjikian, L., Roques, C., Campanac, C., Doleans, A., Baillif, S., Pellon, G., Renaud, F. N. R., Hartmann,
    D., Freney, J., and Burillon, C. 2005. *Staphylococcus epidermidis* biofilms on intraocular lens sur-
    face: Review of the literature. *Journal Francais D Ophtalmologie* 28: 224–230.
Konaklieva, M. I., and Plotkin, B. J. 2006. Chemical communication—Do we have a quorum? *Mini-
    Reviews in Medicinal Chemistry* 6: 817–825.
Kumar, C. G. and Anand, S. K. 1998. Significance of microbial biofilms in food industry: A review.
    International Journal of Food Microbiology 42: 9–27.
Lasa, I. and Penades, J. R. 2006. Bap: A family of surface proteins involved in biofilm formation.
    Research in Microbiology 157: 99–107.
Levin, B. R. and Rozen, D. E. 2006. Opinion—Non-inherited antibiotic resistance. *Nature Reviews
    Microbiology* 4: 556–562.
Melchior, M. B., Vaarkamp, H., and Fink-Gremmels, J. 2006. Biofilms: A role in recurrent mastitis
    infections? *Veterinary Journal* 171: 398–407.
Momba, M. N. B., Kfir, R., Venter, S. N., and Cloete, T. E. 2000. An overview of biofilm formation in
    distribution systems and its impact on the deterioration of water quality. *Water SA* 26: 59–66.
Monds, R. D. and O'Toole, G. A. 2009. The developmental model of microbial biofilms: Ten years of
    a paradigm up for review. *Trends in Microbiology* 17(2): 73–87.
Mukherjee, P. K., Zhou, G. Y., Munyon, R., and Ghannoum, M. A. 2005. Candida biofilm: A well-
    designed protected environment. *Medical Mycology* 43: 191–208.
Patwardhan, A. W. 2003. Rotating biological contactors: A review. *Industrial and Engineering Chemistry
    Research* 42: 2035–2051.
Percival, S. L., Hill, K. E., Williams, D. W., Hooper, S. J., Thomas, D. W., and Costerton, J. W. 2012. A
    review of the scientific evidence for biofilms in wounds. *Wound Repair and Regeneration* 20(5):
    647–657.
Percival, S. L. and Walker, J. T. 1999. Potable water and biofilms: A review of the public health impli-
    cations. *Biofouling* 14: 99–115.
Pokhrel, D. and Viraraghavan, T. 2004. Treatment of pulp and paper mill wastewater—A review.
    Science of the Total Environment 333: 37–58.
Reij, M. W., Keurentjes, J. T. F., and Hartmans, S. 1998. Membrane bioreactors for waste gas treatment.
    Journal of Biotechnology 59: 155–167.
Sanz, M., Lau, L., Herrera, D., Morillo, J. M., and Silva, A. 2004. Methods of detection of *Actinobacillus
    actinomycetemcomitans*, *Porphyromonas gingivalis* and *Tannerella forsythensis* in periodontal micro-
    biology, with special emphasis on advanced molecular techniques: A review. *Journal of Clinical
    Periodontology* 31: 1034–1047.
Seth, A. K., Geringer, M. R., Hong, S. J., Leung, K. P., Mustoe, T. A., and Galiano, R. D. 2012. In vivo
    modeling of biofilm-infected wounds: A review. *Journal of Surgical Research* 178(1): 330–338.

Sharma, M. and Anand, S. K. 2002. Bacterial biofilm on food contact surfaces: A review. *Journal of Food Science and Technology-Mysore* 39: 573–593.

Sheikholeslami, R. 1999. Composite fouling—Inorganic and biological: A review. *Environmental Progress* 18: 113–122.

Simoes, M., Simoes, L. C., and Vieira, M. J. 2010. A review of current and emergent biofilm control strategies. *LWT-Food Science and Technology* 43(4): 573–583.

Sreenivasan, P. and Gaffar, A. 2002. Antiplaque biocides and bacterial resistance: A review. *Journal of Clinical Periodontology* 29: 965–974.

Steinberg, P. D., De Nys, R., and Kjelleberg, S. 2002. Chemical cues for surface colonization. *Journal of Chemical Ecology* 28: 1935–1951.

Stewart, P. S. 2012. Mini-review: Convection around biofilms. *Biofouling* 28(2): 187–198.

Stewart, P. S. and Costerton, J. W. 2001. Antibiotic resistance of bacteria in biofilms. *Lancet* 358: 135–138.

Subramani, K., Jung, R. E., Molenberg, A., and Hammerle, C. H. F. 2009. Biofilm on dental implants: A review of the literature. *International Journal of Oral and Maxillofacial Implants* 24(4): 616–626.

Szymanska, J. and Sitkowska, J. 2012. Bacterial hazards in a dental office: An update review. *African Journal of Microbiology Research* 6(8): 1642–1650.

Thevenot, D., Dernburg, A., and Vernozy-Rozand, C. 2006. An updated review of Listeria monocytogenes in the pork meat industry and its products. *Journal of Applied Microbiology* 101: 7–17.

Thrash, J. C. and Coates, J. D. 2008. Review: Direct and indirect electrical stimulation of microbial metabolism. *Environmental Science and Technology* 42(11): 3921–3931.

Tidswell, E. C. 2005. Bacterial adhesion: Considerations within a risk-based approach to cleaning validation. *PDA Journal of Pharmaceutical Science and Technology* 59: 10–32.

Walker, J. T. and Marsh, P. D. 2004. A review of biofilms and their role in microbial contamination of dental unit water systems (DUWS). *International Biodeterioration and Biodegradation* 54: 87–98.

Wang, W., Wang, J., Xu, H., and Li, X. 2006. Some multidisciplinary techniques used in MIC studies. *Materials and Corrosion* 57: 531–537.

chapter two

Imaging and characterizing biofilm components

In the first chapter we defined a biofilm system as a collection of four compartments: (1) the surface, (2) the biofilm, (3) the solution of nutrients, and (4) the gas phase. Much of biofilm research is about characterizing these compartments, relations among the compartments, and relations among their components. It often helps to image the components of interest before characterizing them, and this chapter discusses imaging techniques we find useful for that purpose. The term *imaging* is not limited here to optical imaging using various types of microscopy; instead, it is used broadly to refer to all activities aimed at enhancing the visibility of various components of biofilm systems. Surface topography may be imaged using optical microscopy, surface chemistry may be imaged using surface analytical techniques, and hydrodynamics in biofilms may be imaged using nuclear magnetic resonance imaging. Because specific imaging techniques can be used to study various compartments and components of biofilm systems, including optical microscopy used to image biofilms and surfaces, we will first describe the relevant imaging techniques and then give selected examples of their applications.

2.1   Microscopy

Microscopy is the most popular technique for imaging components of biofilm systems. It encompasses a variety of techniques in which an image of a sample is magnified to enhance its visibility. On the basis of the principles of image formation, the microscopy techniques popular in biofilm research can be divided into three categories: (1) optical microscopy, which uses the visible and the UV parts of the electromagnetic spectrum; (2) electron microscopy, which uses electron beams in transmitted and reflected modes; and (3) scanning probe microscopy, which uses a physical probe to scan a specimen, e.g., atomic force microscopy (AFM).

2.1.1   Optical microscopy

Optical microscopy (OM) refers to the techniques that use mainly the visible part of the electromagnetic radiation spectrum, in some applications near-UV or near-infrared (IR) light, to illuminate an object and magnify the image of it using optical lenses, as opposed to electron microscopy, which uses magnets as lenses. This is the type of microscopy that has been the most closely associated with the development of microbiology. By modern standards, the principles that govern classical optical microscopy are straightforward, and we will discuss them in the following paragraphs. The technique has been popular, but from its inception it has been known for having two limitations: (1) the resolving power of the optical microscope determines the minimum size of the objects that can be resolved, and (2) out-of-focus objects degrade the images of thicker specimens. These limitations have been addressed by recent advances, and the resulting improvements have reached levels that just a few decades ago were considered impossible because of the physical limitations of optical systems. Many of the recent advances in optical microscopy are results of advances in quantum optics combined with applications of the wonders of modern technology, such as the use of high-intensity monochromatic light sources—tunable lasers—to illuminate objects, digital imaging, modern computers and advanced software packages to handle image acquisition, image manipulation, and analysis. In fact, the recent advances in optical microscopy have been so overwhelming that only those who follow them closely can navigate the seemingly countless variations of the technique and the seemingly countless acronyms associated with them. Effective use of the complex tools offered by modern optical microscopy requires that the users understand the principles of the optoelectronic technology behind them, which can easily pose a problem. The goal of this section is to survey the popular techniques, explain their physical principles, discuss the terminology, and illuminate those applications that are useful in biofilm research.

Optical microscopy is used in biofilm research not only to characterize the compartments of biofilm systems but also as an aid in manufacturing tools, such as microelectrodes, and for monitoring their use in biofilms. It is used in combination with many other techniques that require monitoring or manipulation at a scale smaller than that normally visible by the unaided eye. The resolutions offered by optical microscopy are not as impressive as those of electron microscopy, but because of its relatively low magnification, optical microscopy offers a large field of view, which allows the imaging of larger parts of a sample, and does not require the extrapolation of information from very small fields of view that is necessitated by electron microscopy. Sample preparation in optical microscopy can be very simple or very complicated, depending on the application. More complex procedures of sample preparation are often required when fluorophores that can be identified in images are attached to various components of a sample. Images of biofilm components are further analyzed using various forms of morphometry to quantify factors characterizing the size and shape of the microorganisms, microcolonies, or EPS.

Depending on the nature of the sample and the illumination used, the objects under a microscope can be studied using reflected light or transmitted light. Reflected and transmitted light microscopy is likely to be the first in the sequence of techniques used to characterize surfaces and microbial deposits on surfaces. It is often used as a "let's see how it looks" type of technique, but in the hands of those who know what to look for when examining surfaces or microbial deposits, this is a powerful research tool.

2.1.1.1 *Resolution of optical microscopes*

Improving the resolution of optical microscopes has been the central problem occupying microscopists since the invention of the microscope and the leading motive in improving the performance of microscopes. In the initial stages of development, the quality of the lenses used to build a microscope was the limiting factor determining its resolving power. Later, as optical glass formulations improved and computers were used to design lenses, various optical aberrations were identified as limiting factors; many of these aberrations were eventually mitigated using lenses designed to correct them. The optical resolution of modern lenses approaches the theoretical limits specified by geometric optics. In an ideal optical system, devoid of all optical aberrations, the resolution of optical lenses is still limited by diffraction, which is a limitation imposed by natural laws: it can be manipulated to mitigate its extent, but it cannot be removed entirely.

The theoretical resolution of an optical microscope is defined as the smallest distance between two objects that can be separated in the field of view, and it is quantified as

$$d = \frac{\lambda}{2A_N} \qquad (2.1)$$

where d is the distance between the objects, λ is the wavelength of the light used to illuminate the objects, and A_N is the numerical aperture of the microscope, which characterizes the medium and the angle inside which the lens can accept light reflected from the illuminated object. Numerical aperture is defined as

$$A_N = n \times \sin(\theta) \qquad (2.2)$$

where n is the refractive index of the medium, equal to 1 in air, and θ is one-half of the largest angle at which the lens can accept light reflected from the object. The importance of determining the possible resolution of optical microscopy warrants a brief discussion of the limitations imposed on the factors in Equation 2.2. For example, this somewhat peculiar reference to the half-angle of acceptance, instead of to the entire angle of acceptance, has practical reasons. The total angle inside which a lens accepts light cannot exceed 180°, and half of that angle is 90°, which translates to $\sin(\theta) = 1$. If the entire angle of acceptance were used, then a lens with a light acceptance equal to 180° would have a numerical aperture described by a function of $\sin(\theta)$ that reaches a maximum at 90° and decreases to zero at 180°, as $\sin(180°) = 0$. Using the half-angle of acceptance bypasses this problem, so that the function reaches a maximum at 90°, where $\sin(\theta) = 1$. To reach the extreme angle of accepting the light reflected from an object, the lens would have to touch the object, making the distance between the lens and the object equal to zero. Lenses cannot focus so close, and therefore $\sin(\theta)$ is always smaller than 1. The refractive index of the medium refers to the substance between the lens and the object under the microscope. Typically, this is air, and the refractive index of air equals 1 by definition. In some techniques this medium is water or a specially formulated liquid that has a refractive index higher than 1, which increases the possible resolution of the microscope. To determine the highest theoretically possible resolution of optical microscopes using air as the medium, we can take the extreme values for all the parameters in Equation 2.1 and calculate the smallest distance d between two objects that can be resolved. As predicted by Equation 2.1, optical resolution can be improved by using short wavelengths to illuminate the object and by using an objective with the highest possible numerical aperture. To estimate the best possible resolution, we will use violet light, with $\lambda = 400$ nm; a half-angle of incidence of $\theta = 90°$, which gives $\sin(\theta) = 1$; and air as the medium, which has a refractive index equal to 1. Introducing all these factors into Equation 2.1 gives the smallest distance between two objects that can be resolved under this set of conditions, equal to $d = 200$ nm, or 0.2 μm, which is commonly considered to be the theoretical best resolution of the optical microscope. This distance is smaller than the size of many, but not all, bacteria.

The limit of optical resolution determined from Equation 2.1 is known as Abbe's limit, or the diffraction limit. Diffraction refers to the bending of light waves at the edges of opaque objects. Images in optical microscopy are formed by various proportions of diffracted and nondiffracted light reflected from an object. The smaller the object is, the higher the contribution of the diffracted light, which decreases the quality of the images. The diffraction of light is followed by the interference of the light waves: the waves of light bend at the edges of opaque objects (diffraction) and overlap each other, forming alternating bands of bright and dark zones (interference). This effect obviously degrades the quality of images, and the smaller the objects are and the closer they are to each other, the larger the contribution of the diffracted light is to the process of image formation and the more degraded the image quality is. If two small objects are placed in close proximity to each other and each of them diffracts the light waves that illuminate them, the light waves deflected at the edges of one object interfere with the light deflected at the edges of the other object, degrading the image quality. If these two objects are small enough and placed close enough to each other, they cannot be separated in the image. Hence the name, resolution limited by diffraction. The diffraction limit is quantified in terms of the wavelengths of the interfering light waves. This is often referred to as the Rayleigh criterion, which says that the resolution of a lens is considered diffraction-limited when the minimum of the light wave diffracted from one source point coincides with the maximum of the light wave diffracted from the other source point.

Equation 2.1 quantifies this effect in the most concise way: it says that under the most favorable conditions the images of two small objects under a microscope can be resolved if the distance between them is less than one half of the wavelength of the light that illuminates them, which is just another way of stating the Rayleigh criterion. Although the diffraction limit is imposed by natural laws, and therefore appears to be inviolable, it has been continually challenged by those attempting to improve the resolution of their optical tools. Improving the resolution beyond the limit imposed by geometric optics was finally accomplished with the help of quantum optics. Some of the improvements in resolution in optical microscopy are relevant to imaging biofilms, and it is worthwhile to look at them more closely. When the factors affecting the diffraction limit were first quantified, microscopists increased the resolution of optical microscopes by using immersion liquids with refractive indexes higher than one to increase the numerical aperture of the lens. The object under the microscope was covered with the immersion liquid and the lens was immersed in the liquid, which eliminated air from the space between the lens and the object. Because the immersion liquids had refractive indexes larger than 1, the numerical aperture in Equation 2.2 increased and *d*, the smallest distance between two objects that can be resolved, decreased. Immersion liquids are still in use, and those currently available have refractive indexes of about 1.5. Using immersion lenses improves the resolving power of the microscope, but it does not really defy the limitation by diffraction. It just manipulates one of the factors in Equation 2.2, the refractive index, to increase the resolving power of the microscope; the resolving power of the microscope is still determined by the diffraction. Conquering the diffraction limit required more sophisticated approaches and was finally accomplished with help from quantum mechanics and computer science. As a result of these advances, modern optical microscopy does not recognize the diffraction limitation defined by Equation 2.1 as the ultimate factor determining the resolving power of the optical microscope: resolutions exceeding those calculated from Equation 2.1 have been achieved in optical microscopy. The fact that better resolutions than those predicted by Abbe's limit have been accomplished by microscopists does not invalidate the law: researchers just found ways to work around the limitations imposed by the law. We will discuss some of these advances later in this text.

2.1.1.2 *Examples of optical microscopy applications*

Optical microscopes can be used in an upright or in an inverted configuration. The upright configuration has been, historically, the most common way of using these microscopes. In this configuration, the sample is placed on a stage below the objective lens. This configuration is ideal when the microscope is used to inspect a sample but poses severe limitations when the sample needs to be manipulated under the microscope, because the distance between the lens and the sample is too small for the introduction of any tools, such as microelectrodes. If the sample needs to be manipulated in any way, usually the inverted configuration is preferable. In this configuration the lens is positioned below the stage, leaving ample space for the sample to be accessed from above. Depending on the application, we use both configurations. In both configurations the sample can be illuminated by reflected light, in which case the light source is on the same side of the sample as the lens, or transmitted light, in which case the light source and the lens are on opposite sides of the sample. New microscopes allow the user to select the type of illumination, and in some cases both types of illumination are used at the same time. The selection of the illumination type depends on the nature of the sample to be imaged, as is explained below.

2.1.1.2.1   Example 1: Imaging microsensors during construction.   Constructing microsensors for use in biofilm research would be very difficult without the aid of optical microscopy. Many procedures for constructing microelectrodes are monitored using OM. The image in Figure 2.1 shows a setup we use for inserting a cathode into the shaft of a dissolved oxygen microsensor. The sensor is placed on the stage of an optical microscope, the cathode is inserted into the shaft using a micromanipulator, and the progress is monitored using a charged-coupled device camera while the image is displayed on the computer screen. The setup allows the operator full control over the process and improves the success rate for making microsensors. Many other procedures for making microsensors are also monitored under the microscope.

2.1.1.2.2   Example 2: Imaging biofilm distribution on a surface.   Figure 2.2 shows reflected light and transmitted light microscope images of biofilms in which microorganisms have established residence on a glass surface and excreted extracellular polymers.

Reflected light microscopes in inverted configurations are used mostly to monitor biofilm formation and to monitor the positions of microsensors. In this type of application, an inverted microscope is typically positioned below the bottom of a flat plate biofilm reactor and images are acquired through the transparent bottom of the reactor. Some reactors have multiple transparent walls, which gives us more freedom in positioning the light

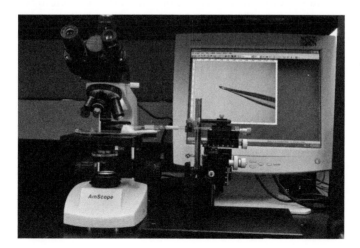

Figure 2.1 **(See color insert.)** The process of inserting a cathode into the shaft of a dissolved oxygen microsensor is monitored using an upright microscope and transmitted light. The microscope is connected to a camera for imaging.

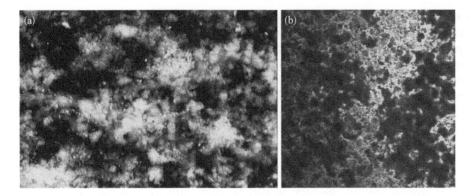

Figure 2.2 Biofilm images acquired using (a) reflected light microscopy and (b) transmitted light microscopy.

sources and the objective of the microscope: we can illuminate the sample from one side of the reactor and take the images from the opposite side to generate transmitted light microscopy images. Biofilm images acquired using reflected light appear different from those acquired using transmitted light. When transmitted light is used, the illuminated cell clusters appear dark on a light background (because of light reflection). When reflected light is used, the illuminated cell clusters appear light against a dark background (because of light absorption). Regardless of the type of illumination used, the images can be used to quantify a variety of structural parameters, such as textural entropy, homogeneity, energy, areal porosity, average horizontal/vertical run lengths, average/maximum diffusion distances, and fractal dimension, as described in Chapter 6.

2.1.1.2.3 Example 3: Identifying microorganisms from the morphology of microbial deposits. An example of how powerful simple direct microscopy can be is the use of reflected light microscopy to identify the type of microorganisms colonizing surfaces of stainless steels immersed in natural waters based on the morphology of the deposits. Note that the biofilm shown in Figure 2.2 is deposited on a glass surface and the cell clusters reflect more light than the surface. In Figure 2.3 the biofilm is deposited on a

Figure 2.3 Reflected light microscopy image of biofilm on a 316L SS coupon after 13 days of *in situ* exposure to fresh river water. (Reproduced from Dickinson, W. H. et al., *Corrosion Science* 38: 1407–1422, 1996.)

stainless steel surface and the surface reflects more light than the biofilm. Therefore, the background in Figure 2.2a is dark and the background in Figure 2.2b is bright. Using reflected light microscopy images of deposits on stainless steel surfaces in natural waters (Figure 2.3), microbial deposits were hypothetically ascribed to the activity of manganese-oxidizing bacteria Siderocapsaceae (Dickinson et al. 1996). This hypothesis was then tested and corroborated using other techniques of surface analysis, such as scanning electron microscopy (SEM) and energy dispersive spectroscopy (EDS), discussed later in this chapter.

2.1.2 Fluorescence microscopy

In its early stages of development, optical microscopy was exclusively based on illuminating the field of view using external light sources, and objects under the microscope were made visible by the differences in the intensity of the light that was reflected or absorbed by the objects and their backgrounds. The limitations imposed by Equation 2.1 assumed that the objects that needed to be resolved by the microscope were illuminated by the same light source and that the resolution was limited by the diffraction of the light illuminating both objects, as explained in the preceding section. The limitation was bypassed by using another type of illumination, fluorescence. In fluorescence microscopy the external light is used to stimulate secondary illumination, which is emitted by the object itself. More succinctly, in fluorescence microscopy the image of the object is formed by the light emitted by the object under the microscope.

Fluorescence is the property of a molecule to emit light of a longer wavelength when it is irradiated by light of a shorter wavelength. Typical excitation and emission spectra of a fluorescing molecule are shown in Figure 2.4. An example of a substance with such excitation and emission spectra is the common stain fluorescein.

The physical principles of fluorescence microscopy do not depend on the type of illumination. Whether the illumination is wide-field or scanning, electrons of the fluorescing molecules absorb photons from the illuminating light and increase their energy above that characteristic of their ground state. These excited molecules quickly lose their excess energy and return to their ground state. In the process most, but not all, of the energy gained by absorbing photons from the illuminating light is released by emitting photons with somewhat lower energy than those initially absorbed. The energy of the incoming

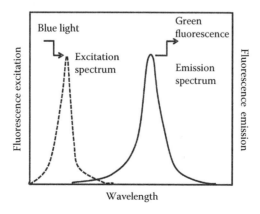

Figure 2.4 Excitation and emission spectra.

photons is related to the wavelength of the light used to illuminate the object by the Planck equation:

$$E = hc/\lambda \tag{2.3}$$

where h is Planck's constant, c is the speed of light, and λ is the wavelength. Because the emitted photons have a lower energy than the photons that stimulated the fluorophore, they generate light with a longer wavelength than that used to illuminate the fluorophore. The distance between the peaks of the adsorbed and emitted light spectra is called the Stokes shift and can be seen in Figure 2.4.

Depending on how the sample is illuminated, optical microscopy is often classed into two categories: (1) wide-field microscopy, in which the entire sample is illuminated, and (2) scanning microscopy, in which only part of the sample is illuminated at a time and the beam of illuminating light travels across the sample. Wide-field fluorescence microscopy is executed by using white light from mercury lamps and fluorescence microscopes equipped with filters to select the desired part of the spectrum from the white light. If the illuminating light is delivered through the objective, the name epifluorescence microscopy is often used. In scanning microscopy, the light is delivered by lasers. Most fluorescence microscopes use arch discharge sources of light, such as mercury or xenon lamps, but other sources can be used as well. Before hitting the specimen, the light is reflected by a dichroic mirror or a beam splitter, which reflects the UV part of the light toward the specimen and allows light with other frequencies than UV to pass through. The light reflected from the specimen passes again through the dichroic mirror, which reflects only the UV part of the reflected light toward the photodetector. Lasers are also used as sources of light, particularly argon-ion and argon-krypton lasers. The main benefit of using lasers is the delivery of a much higher intensity of light than arch discharge lamps can deliver. Some types of fluorescence microscopy, particularly multiphoton and confocal microscopy, rely on lasers and their ability to deliver high-intensity monochromatic light, but using lasers also limits the use of fluorescence microscopy to the wavelengths that can be delivered by the existing lasers. This disadvantage of using lasers is, however, slowly being mitigated by progress in laser technology and the development of tunable lasers that can deliver more than one wavelength of high-intensity monochromatic light. Some applications of optical microscopy, such as photobleaching and multiphoton and confocal microscopy, depend on a capability to illuminate objects with a narrow beam of monochromatic light: these applications would be difficult or impossible without lasers.

2.1.2.1 *Examples of applications*

In fluorescence microscopy, objects may exhibit natural fluorescence or, more often, microscopists may manipulate them into exhibiting fluorescence by attaching fluorescent stains. Most fluorescent stains have been developed with a particular application in mind, and they come with their specific excitation and emission wavelengths clearly specified. Their application is then linked to the ability of the user to generate the conditions under which they can be used, which are a source of light with suitable wavelengths for stimulating the fluorescent stains and the ability to record the fluorescent light emitted at its characteristic wavelengths. Among the many possible ways of staining biofilm components in fluorescence microscopy, four are very popular among biofilm researchers: (1) fluorescent *in situ* hybridization (FISH) probes, (2) fluorescent proteins used as reporter genes, (3) live versus dead stains, and (4) staining of the EPS. Incidentally, these techniques have revolutionized microbial ecology and had a pronounced impact on biofilm studies. Using fluorescent probes and suitable microscopes, the researcher can detect not only the presence of the selected microorganisms in the biofilm but also their location in the biofilm with respect to other microorganisms and their physiological activity. The application of FISH probes and the use of fluorescent proteins to identify microorganisms in biofilms make possible the study of population dynamics in biofilms. From a practical point of view, the main difference between these two techniques—FISH and fluorescent proteins—is that FISH staining is done on dead microorganisms while fluorescent proteins are expressed by living microorganisms. Both techniques are powerful, but the ability to monitor living microorganisms gives an advantage in studying mechanisms of biofilm processes that is difficult to overestimate. Live/dead staining is also very useful, particularly for monitoring the growth and accumulation of biofilms challenged with an antimicrobial agent.

2.1.2.1.1   Example 1: Fluorescent in situ *hybridization probes.*   DNA hybridization is a general technique popular in biomedical research. It is used, for example, to detect chromosomal abnormalities, such as Down syndrome. Hybridization probes are single-stranded fragments of DNA or RNA designed to attach to complementary nucleotide sequences in a sample. The probes have radioactive or fluorescent markers so that their locations in the sample can be determined using autoradiography or fluorescence microscopy. Hybridization protocols call for isolating and separating the DNA or RNA on a gel before the fluorescent probes are added to the sample. The *in situ* variety of the technique, which is extensively used in biofilm research, does not require isolating the DNA or RNA; instead, the probes are hybridized with the complementary nucleotide sequences inside microbial cells. *In situ* hybridization uses fluorescence-labeled complementary DNA or RNA probes, often derived from fragments of DNA that have been isolated from the target microorganisms, purified and amplified. In microbial ecology, ribosomal RNA in bacterial cells is targeted by fluorescence-labeled oligonucleotide probes. The large number of ribosomes in bacterial cells helps to achieve high signal intensity. Even though the protocols for using FISH have the same steps, the accessibility of the targeted site varies among strains of bacteria and the protocols need to be modified to account for these differences.

To accomplish *in situ* hybridization, the probe has to enter the microbial cell and hybridize with the nucleotides for which it was designed. Therefore, the cell membranes must be permeabilized using chemical agents, such as detergents, which make membranes porous by extracting lipids. The probe enters the cell and hybridizes with the nucleotides, and the residual probe that did not hybridize is washed out. Washing out the residual probe is an important step in the procedure. In the extreme case, in which none of the probe hybridized, the entire probe has to be washed out from the cell; otherwise, artifacts are created. Bacterial FISH probes are primers for the 16S RNA region, and in biofilms they are typically used to identify the microorganisms residing in the biofilm matrix.

Typical applications of FISH probes in biofilm studies require that the steps of known procedures be modified and adjusted to the existing conditions on a case-by-case basis. This usually calls for a tedious and time-consuming tweaking of the existing protocols. Biofilm is immobilized in a suitable epoxy resin and cut into thin slices using a microtome. The probes are applied to the slices and their distribution is imaged using fluorescence microscopy. FISH probes have become indispensable tools for studying biofilm processes at the microscale. Using these probes is most challenging at the step of optimizing the conditions under which they are applied, but from the point of view of microscopy, they do not present overwhelming difficulties and the results can be rewarding: not only can the microorganisms in the matrix be identified but, when confocal microscopy is used, the images show the locations of various physiological groups of microorganisms in the matrix of extracellular polymers. The main disadvantage of FISH, apart from time-consuming protocols, is that the microorganisms in the biofilm are killed in the process of preparing the samples for staining. The necessity of killing the microorganisms imposes limitations, but these limitations are often bypassed by the ingenuity of biofilm research-ers who design sophisticated experimental protocols mitigating the limitations of the tech-nique. FISH probes have opened new frontiers to biofilm researchers. Using these probes helped demonstrate the existence of clusters of physiological groups of microorganisms within biofilm microcolonies—microcolonies within microcolonies (Figure 2.5). FISH probes have become tools of choice for quantifying microbial community structures in biofilms and are used to study a variety of biofilm processes. For example, using time lapse sampling of biofilm combined with FISH it has been shown that as time passes and the chemistry in a biofilm changes, the motile microorganisms, those which can actively change their positions in the biofilm, move in search of a better environment (Figure 2.6).

Examples of applications are shown in Figures 2.5 and 2.6. Figure 2.5 shows the distri-bution of ammonia oxidizers and nitrite oxidizers in a microcolony of a nitrifying biofilm. As seen, these two groups of microorganisms are spatially separated in microcolonies, therefore constituting a secondary (physiological) heterogeneity in the biofilm.

Figure 2.6 shows a mixed-population biofilm in which the locations of *Leptothrix dis-cophora*, marked with a green probe, were established with respect to other groups of micro-organisms in this biofilm, marked with a red probe. It was demonstrated that *L. discophora*, a motile microorganism, had moved toward the top of the biofilm, where the microorgan-isms had access to oxygen. Once the various types of microorganisms in the microcolonies were separated by differently stained probes, not only their respective positions but also the ratios of their numbers at various locations in the biofilm could be compared.

2.1.2.1.2   Example 2: Fluorescent proteins.   Fluorescent proteins (FP) were initially extracted from *Aequorea victoria* jellyfish in the late 1960s and 1970s (Prendergast 1978). They quickly became recognized as valuable tools in microbial ecology. Since then, several other FPs have been discovered and isolated from various organisms, e.g., green fluores-cent protein (GFP) was cloned and expressed by Chalfie et al. (1994) and red fluorescent

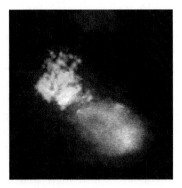

Figure 2.5 **(See color insert.)** A microcolony of a nitrifying biofilm. Molecular probes (fluorescent *in situ* hybridization probes) of different colors, red and green, attached themselves to different physiological groups of microorganisms occupying the microcolony: ammonia oxidizers and nitrite oxidizers. Note that the physiological groups of microorganisms are not mixed randomly but are, rather, spatially separated from each other, forming a secondary structure in the biofilm—physio-logical heterogeneity.

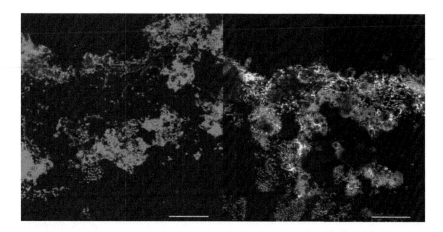

Figure 2.6 **(See color insert.)** FISH probes were used to find the locations of *Leptothrix discophora* (green probe) in a mixed-population biofilm. The red signal represents cells that were stained with propidium iodide, and green represents a fluorescent FISH probe. Yellow indicates a green and red overlay. The scale bar is 25 μm. (Reproduced from Campbell, S. et al., *Corrosion* 60: 670–680, 2004.)

protein by Matz et al. (1999). Many FPs have been optimized for use in fluorescence microscopy by genetic manipulations of the organisms that originally expressed them. When stimulated with light of the appropriate wavelength, an FP emits fluorescent light of a specific color, such as cyan, green, orange, yellow, or red, depending on the structure of the protein. Using fluorescent proteins has an advantage over using FISH probes to tag microorganisms, because FPs can be genetically encoded, tracked in living cells, and used as reporter genes.

Although the use of FPs to study the molecular biology of suspended microorganisms is widespread, their use in biofilm research is inhibited by some of their properties. When the genetic manipulation concerns a single species of microorganisms grown in suspension, the use of FPs is relatively straightforward. To make sure that the microbes in the culture carry the plasmid encoding the FP, an antibiotic resistance gene is inserted into the same plasmid. The microorganisms are grown in a growth medium containing the antibiotic to which they are resistant. The microbial cells that lose the plasmid cannot grow in this medium and, consequently, all microbial cells in the growing culture can express the fluorescent protein. This strategy works well for single-species microbial cultures. If a mixed population of microorganisms were used, and biofilms are inherently mixed population cultures, introducing an antibiotic into the growth medium would inhibit all microorganisms except those that carried the antibiotic resistance gene. It is conceivable to tag all the microorganisms with antibiotic resistance inserts, and only some of them with antibiotic resistance and FP, but such a protocol is not very practical. Another limitation on the use of fluorescent proteins in biofilms is imposed by the presence of oxygen. To enfold properly, fluorescent proteins need oxygen. In a culture of suspended microorganisms it is possible to keep oxygen at a constant level by aerating the growth medium. This does not work in biofilms, because aerating the bulk solution does not ensure that oxygen is available in deeper layers of the biofilm. For all these reasons, the use of fluorescent proteins in biofilm research is often limited to enhancing images of biofilm structure.

In special applications, it may be beneficial to use fluorescent proteins in single-species biofilms. Figure 2.7 shows a microcolony of a *Staphylococcus aureus* biofilm in which

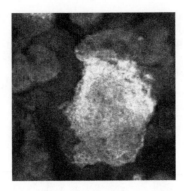

Figure 2.7 **(See color insert.)** A microcolony of *Staphylococcus aureus* expressing yellow fluorescent protein imaged using confocal scanning laser microscopy. (Reproduced from Beyenal, H. et al., *Microbiology Methods* 58: 367–374, 2004.)

the microorganisms express yellow fluorescent protein. The microorganisms expressing the fluorescent proteins have been genetically modified so that the fluorescent protein is expressed only when another protein is expressed, toxic shock syndrome toxin-1, which is responsible for toxic shock syndrome in humans. This protocol allows the study of the physiological responses of the microbes to various stimuli in terms of their expression of the protein of interest, toxic shock syndrome toxin-1. Having such genetically modified microorganisms allows the researcher to study factors that promote and inhibit the production of a dangerous bacterial toxin in biofilms of these microorganisms.

As indicated above, fluorescent proteins are used to enhance the visibility of bacterial cells in biofilms. Figure 2.8 shows an example of GFP-expressing *Pseudomonas aeruginosa* cells growing on a glass surface and imaged using epifluorescence microscopy. This image was taken using a 40× lens, while the image in Figure 2.7 was taken using a 10× lens. Because of the higher magnification, single cells are visible in Figure 2.8. Using a higher magnification, as in Figure 2.8, allows us to see individual cells but does not allow us to observe large cell colonies. Different magnifications are needed to address different research questions. One can quantify the structure of the biofilm (areal porosity or biovolume) from Figure 2.8. However, it would be difficult to calculate these numbers from the image in Figure 2.8.

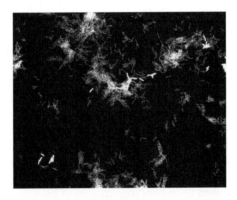

Figure 2.8 *Pseudomonas aeruginosa* cells expressing GFP (shown as gray) attached to a glass surface. We are able to see individual microbial cells on the surface.

2.1.2.1.3   Example 3: Live/dead stains and staining all microorganisms in a biofilm. Traditionally, the number of live microbial cells is quantified by culturing them in an appropriate growth medium. However, this technique cannot be used to assess the viability of bacterial cells *in situ* in a living, hydrated biofilm, and it gives no information about the number or location of the dead cells in a biofilm. In many biofilm studies in which bactericidal or bacteriostatic agents are used, it is important to monitor the effect of these agents on the microbial population in the biofilm with respect to the number of microbial cells affected and the location of the affected cells. In such studies, live/dead stains are used. The mechanism by which these stains act relies on the condition of the cell membrane. If the cell membrane has been compromised, as in a dead cell, the fluorescent stain penetrates the cell and stains either the entire volume of the cell or a specific component, depending on the type of stain used. Because, in principle, the stain penetrates the membranes of dead cells but not those of living cells, it results in a much stronger fluorescent signal from dead cells than from living cells, which can only absorb the fluorescent marker on their surfaces. The microbial cells that exclude the stain are considered viable. One stain, quite popular in biofilm research, that does not penetrate the membranes of living cells but does stain dead cells is a nucleic acid stain, propidium iodide. Because a live/dead stain is more effective on dead cells than it is on living cells, it is often used in tandem with a stain that can penetrate both living and dead cells, such as thiazole orange (Biosciences Catalog no. 349483 or 349480). Thiazole orange is a permeant dye: it enters all cells, live and dead. The combined use of both stains enhances the visibility of all the microorganisms in the biofilm and provides a fast and reliable method for distinguishing the live and dead bacterial cells. Although live/dead staining remains one of the most powerful staining techniques in biofilm research, the reproducibility of the results obtained using this technique is questionable. Among the many stains that are available for staining microorganisms in biofilms, the following three are quite popular (see also Table 2.1):

1. Acridine orange (3,6-dimethylaminoacridine) is a weak base. It is soluble in water and permeant to live and dead cells. It emits green fluorescence when bound to compact chromosomal DNA and red fluorescence when bound to the nonintact DNA of dead cells. Acridine orange is used as a general cellular fluorescent stain.
2. Propidium iodide is a popular red fluorescent nuclear and chromosomal counter stain. Because propidium iodide is not permeant to live cells, it is also used to

Table 2.1 Selected Dyes and Their Applications

Dye	Invitrogen catalog no.[a]	Excitation (nm)	Emission (nm)	Applications
SYTO 9	S-34854	485 (DNA) 486 (RNA)	498 (DNA) 501 (RNA)	Binds to DNA and RNA.
Acridine orange	A1301	500 (DNA) 460 (RNA)	526 (DNA) 650 (RNA)	Permeant to live and dead cells, binds DNA and RNA. Used for RNA/DNA discrimination.
Propidium iodide	P1304MP	485 490[b]	617 635[b]	Not permeant to live cells. Stains dead cells.

Note: Detailed information about the use of these stains and application notes can be obtained from https://www.invitrogen.com.
[a] The same products can be bought from other vendors.
[b] As a component of the live/dead BacLight Bacterial Viability Kit (catalog no. L7012).

detect dead cells in a population. This stain is one of the components of live/dead staining.

3. SYTO dyes are cell-permeant dyes. They are green fluorescent nucleic acid stains that show a large fluorescence enhancement upon binding nucleic acids. The SYTO dyes can be used to stain RNA and DNA in both live and dead eukaryotic cells, as well as in both Gram-positive and Gram-negative bacteria. The SYTO 9 kit from Invitrogen, for example, which stains both live and dead bacteria, comes with instructions on how to use it and is one of the most commonly used dyes in biofilm research. Figure 2.9 shows an example of using SYTO dyes to stain microbial cells in a *Campylobacter jejuni* biofilm. In the image the red-stained cells are dead and the green-stained cells are alive. The images of the red- and green-stained cells were taken separately and then combined so that both could be seen at the same time. The yellow color resulting from this superposition indicates a mixture of live and dead cells (Table 2.1).

2.1.2.1.4   Example 4: Staining biofilms to image the extracellular polymeric substances.   The extracellular polymeric substances consist of polysaccharides, proteins, nucleic acids, and lipids. In contrast to the large number of fluorescent stains available for microorganisms in biofilms, there are no general stains for EPS. There are fluorescent stains for some components of EPS, such as stains for selected polysaccharides, but not for all components of the biofilm matrix. This should not come as a surprise, considering that EPS are a mixture of many substances, and it is difficult to find a single stain that stains them all at the same time and does not stain anything else. Some biofilm researchers use Alcian blue to stain EPS, but it targets anionic molecules only. Lipid fractions have been stained using Nile red. The recent use of lectins, nonenzymatic proteins exhibiting a high affinity for poly-saccharides, expands the availability of stains for EPS. Components of the biofilm can be stained individually or using multiple stains. For example, Chen et al. (2007) used multiple stains to image total cells, dead cells, proteins, lipids, and alpha and beta polysaccharides in bioaggregates. Selected dyes used to stain EPS are listed in Table 2.2.

Figure 2.9 **(See color insert.)** Confocal images of *C. jejuni* in a five-day-old monoculture biofilm stained for cell viability. The biofilm contains a mixture of living (green) and dead (red) bacteria (magnification, 60×); yellow indicates a mixture of live and dead cells. (Modified from Ica, T. et al., *Applied Environmental Microbiology*, 78: 1033–1038, 2012.)

Table 2.2 Selected Dyes Used to Stain EPS

Dye	Invitrogen catalog no.	Excitation (nm)	Emission (nm)	Specificity
Tetramethylrhodamine Concanavalin A (lectin)	C860	555	580	Selectively binds to α-mannopyranosyl and α-glucopyranosyl sugars.
Lectin PNA from *Arachis hypogaea* (peanut), Alexa Fluor 488 conjugate (lectin)	L21409	552	656	Lectin PNA is specific for terminal β-galactose.
Nile red	N-1142	625	700	Used to localize and quantify lipids.
C_1-BODIPY 500/510 C_{12} (fluorescent fatty acid analog)	D-3823	500	510	Used for lipid trafficking studies.
FilmTracer SYPRO Ruby biofilm matrix stain	F10318	488	610	Stains biofilm matrix (labels most classes of proteins, including glycoproteins, phosphoproteins, lipoproteins, calcium-binding proteins, and fibrillar proteins).

2.1.3   Enhanced fluorescence microscopy

Imaging fluorescence opened new frontiers in microscopy and allowed the diffraction limit, as described by Equation 2.1, to be bypassed. In fluorescence microscopy, the object under the microscope is the source of light. The emitted light is stimulated by an external illuminating light, but the light that is used for imaging the objects under the microscope is emitted by the objects themselves. Because the imaged objects are the sources of light, the concept of optical resolution, as defined by Equation 2.3, needs to be adjusted in fluorescence microscopy by acknowledging that optical resolution depends not only on the distance between two points but also on the contrast difference between the images of the two points and that fluorescence microscopy can improve the latter. The Rayleigh criterion says that the resolution is diffraction-limited if the minimum of the light wave diffracted from one source point coincides with the maximum of the light wave diffracted from the other, which works well if both objects are evenly illuminated by an external light source but not necessarily that well if the objects themselves are the sources of light. As a consequence, several variations of fluorescence microscopy have been developed that seemingly defy the Rayleigh criterion. They depend on illuminating mostly one of two objects positioned closer to each other than half the wavelength of the illuminating light. Because the objects are illuminated differently, they can be distinguished in the image because of the contrast difference without violating the Rayleigh criterion. The following sections will discuss selected examples of applying the principles of fluorescence microscopy to reach resolutions better than that predicted by the Rayleigh criterion, which quantifies the diffraction-limited resolution of optical microscopes.

2.1.3.1   Stimulated emission depletion microscopy

Some of the procedures used to improve resolution in fluorescence microscopy rely on light quenching, in which additional pulses follow the excitation pulse and modify the energy delivered to the fluorophores. One example of such a procedure is stimulated emission depletion (STED) microscopy, which can lower the limit of resolution to about 70 nm, which is about two thirds less than the diffraction limit for optical microscopy— 200 nm— according to the computation shown at the beginning of this chapter. STED microscopy uses blue light to stimulate the fluorophore and orange light to quench the blue light. Light of a given color can be quenched using light of the complementary color, the one on the other side of the color wheel. According to color theory, if two complementary colors are mixed in equal proportions, they cancel each other, forming a shade of gray. The blue light is delivered in the form of a narrow beam to illuminate a small spot on the specimen. The orange light is delivered in the form of a doughnut around the small spot; it quenches the light around the spot illuminated by the blue light. In effect, the orange light shrinks the location that is illuminated by the blue light that can stimulate fluorescence, and the fluorescent light is emitted from a spot that is smaller than that illuminated by the blue light. The emitted fluorescent light is green. As a result, an illuminated object can be imaged even if it resides in close proximity to another object, because the other object is not illuminated. The resolving power of this technique is better than that predicted by the criterion quantifying diffraction-limited resolution. An image of the sample is formed by scanning the blue excitation spot over the sample and recording the emitted fluorescent light. The smaller the excitation spot is, the higher the resolution of the microscope. Because the STED beam is doughnut-shaped and centered over the excitation spot, it is possible to preferentially quench the outer edges of the excitation spot and stimulate fluorescence at the center only.

2.1.3.2 *Fluorescent resonance energy transfer microscopy*

In another variation of fluorescence microscopy that provides a resolution better than that limited by diffraction, one fluorophore transfers energy to another fluorophore. This type of interaction is called fluorescent resonance energy transfer (FRET), and it is possible only if the donor and the acceptor fluorophores are close to each other, separated by a distance of a few nanometers. In this type of interaction, the donor fluorophore is stimulated using light of an appropriate wavelength, as in traditional fluorescence microscopy. However, when the donor fluorophore dissipates the energy, some of the dissipating energy, instead of being emitted as photons, is transferred to another fluorophore, the acceptor, which in its turn emits photons. Because the light emissions produced by the two fluorophores have different wavelengths, the fluorophores can be resolved in an image. Specialized FRET microscopes are available, but the techniques depend more on the selection of the fluorophores than on specialized microscopy and can be executed using confocal microscopes. Multiphoton microscopy has also been successfully tried with FRET to make the method even more versatile.

2.1.3.3 *Two-photon microscopy*

As discussed above, fluorophores used to tag samples are stimulated using light with a high-energy short wavelength and, once stimulated, they emit lower-energy light with a longer wavelength. Two-photon microscopy reverses this process and seemingly achieves the impossible: the light emitted by the fluorophore has a shorter wavelength than the illuminating light, which at first glance can be interpreted as violating natural laws by gaining energy from nothing. This effect is equivalent to the negative Stokes shift in Figure 2.4, and the trick is accomplished with help from quantum mechanics. To stimulate electrons in a fluorophore, a precise amount of energy needs to be delivered, and the amount of energy that is released as photons is always lower than the amount of energy that stimulated the emission: this cannot be violated. In two-photon microscopy, the object is illuminated with photons delivered at short intervals using pulsating light. With this type of illumination, two photons can be absorbed by a fluorophore at a single location and, because the time between the deliveries of the photons is very short, on the order of femtoseconds, the total energy delivered to this location is the sum of the energies of these two photons. Before the energy of the fluorophore, increased by its absorption of the first photon from the illuminating light, is dissipated by the emission of a photon with a lower energy than the photon delivered by the illuminating light, the next photon is delivered by the illuminating light and increases the energy level of the fluorophore even further. Consequently, the energy of the two consecutive photons is accumulated by the fluorophore and the combined energies from two excitation photons dissipate at the same time. As part of this process, a single photon is emitted that has an energy higher than the energy of either of the two photons absorbed from the illuminating light. Because the emitted photon has an energy higher than that of an individual photon of the illuminating light, it projects itself as light of a shorter wavelength. For example, if the illuminating light is in the infrared range of the spectrum, the emitted photon will have the wavelength of green light. Two-photon microscopy does not violate any physical laws, even though it appears to do just that. There are advantages to using two-photon microscopy instead of one-photon microscopy. Because the fluorophore in the sample is excited at a single point, a two-photon microscope has an extremely high resolution and does not require the pinhole used in traditional confocal microscopy to reject out-of-focus fluorescent light. There are no out-of-focus objects: the object that is illuminated is the one that is in focus. Also, the light used in two-photon microscopy can penetrate deeper into the specimen than the light used in one-photon fluorescence microscopy. The ultraviolet radiation typically used in one-photon microscopy can cause many kinds of damage to living cells, while the infrared radiation typically used in two-photon microscopy can penetrate deep into a sample without damaging it, and the depth of penetration is important in biofilm research. The typical light source used in single-photon fluorescence microscopy is an ultraviolet laser, and the typical light source used in two-photon microscopy is an infrared laser, such as a titanium sapphire laser. The main disadvantage of two-photon microscopy is the cost of the instrument: the infrared pulsed laser and the necessity of using optics compatible with infrared light make the application of the technique expensive.

2.1.3.4 Confocal scanning laser microscopy

The first limitation of optical microscopy was related to lateral resolution: how close two objects can be to each other and still be resolved in an image. In the preceding sections, we tacitly assumed that these objects were positioned on the same plane with respect to the lens. Much changes when these objects are located on different planes with respect to the lens, and the extent to which such objects can be resolved in optical microscopy depends on the depth of field (DOF) of the lens. The DOF is the range of distance from the lens in which the objects appear to be sharply rendered. In principle, a lens can focus only on a single plane, but to the human eye there is a zone that has acceptable focus. This zone starts in front of and reaches behind the plane of true focus: it is identified as the DOF. A large DOF can render sharp images of objects positioned on different planes, even if these planes are separated by relatively large distances. DOF depends on many factors, including the numerical aperture of the objective and the distance between the object and the lens. When objects are very close to the lens and the lens has a high numerical aperture, which are the conditions common in high-resolution optical microscopy, DOF is very thin. If the objects are located on different planes, only one of them can be in focus.

Objects under a microscope that are thicker than the DOF pose difficulties in traditional optical microscopy, because parts of the image are inherently out of focus. This is a physical limitation characteristic of the optical system, and nothing can be done to change it; much, however, can be done to bypass it. Using traditional light microscopy, a series of images can be collected, one focal plane at a time. However, in each such image, only one focal plane is sharply in focus, while the remaining focal planes contribute images of the objects that are out of focus and degrade the overall image. Confocal microscopy uses a trick to mitigate this degrading effect due to out-of-focus images. The trick is based on an invention that preceded the invention of the optical microscope and was known to Aristotle: a camera obscura, or dark chamber. The device relies on an optical phenomenon that occurs when light passes through a small opening in a thin material—a pinhole. Part of the light does not scatter but instead passes undisturbed and forms an image of the object from which it was reflected. This manner of forming an image is different from how images are formed using lenses. A lens collects light reflected from objects positioned at various distances from the lens and then focuses the light. Because the objects are at different distances from the lens, they are on different focal planes and the light reflected from them passes through different parts of the lens: not all the light can be focused at the single point that defines the plane of focus. This explains why only one distance from the lens can be in sharp focus. When light passes through a very small opening, as in a camera obscura, many objects that are located on different focal planes are not imaged because the light reflected from them was not bent enough to find its way to the opening. As a result most out-of-focus objects do not show in the image. This effect, combined with the scanning of a sample using various focal lengths, is the basis of confocal microscopy, which performs optical sectioning of a sample using a lens with a very small DOF.

Confocal microscopy is not inherently fluorescence microscopy, but samples are often tagged with fluorescent markers to enhance the imaging of various biofilm components. Although the term *biofilm components* may encompass many substances in a biofilm, it usually refers to two, microorganisms and extracellular polymers, and the following sections will describe procedures used in staining these components. Staining has received much attention, and stains have been developed that can bind specifically to selected parts of specimens and enhance the visibility of various components of biological samples, including biofilm components. Images acquired by confocal microscopy can often be enhanced by staining biofilm components. There are general stains available, such as fluorescein isothiocyanide, which can be used to stain organic material in general and can also be used to image biofilm coverage. Confocal microscopy is often used together with FISH probes, as described above in the sections dedicated to fluorescence microscopy. There are many suppliers of fluorescent dyes useful in confocal microscopy, and their catalogs offer impressive numbers of choices, e.g., Molecular Probes, Inc. (Eugene, Oregon, http://www.invitrogen.com). Once the decision has been made about which biofilm component is to be stained, to select a suitable dye, the following factors need to be considered:

1. Excitation wavelength: The lasers available with a specific confocal laser scanning microscopy (CSLM) limit the dye selection. If a dye requires a 400-nm excitation wavelength and the CSLM does not support a 400-nm excitation wavelength, the dye cannot be used.
2. Optical filters available with the CSLM: Older CSLMs use removable optical filters to select specific wavelengths of the emitted light. Newer CSLMs use tunable filters.

3. Emission efficiency: To improve detection, the dye must fluoresce brightly and the intensity of its fluorescent light must be significantly higher than that of the autofluorescence of the biofilms.

4. Emission spectrum: The CSLM must have filters for emitted light that coincide with the emission spectra of the dyes; using dyes with narrow emission spectra is preferable. When multiple dyes are used, their emission spectra should not overlap.

5. Photobleaching: Some fluorophores are susceptible to photobleaching, e.g., fluorescein. Avoiding longer image collection times may alleviate this problem. Selecting a dye that is not susceptible to photobleaching addresses this problem directly.

6. Interference with metabolic processes: Most of the dyes disrupt metabolic processes within microbial cells. Many dyes are also sensitive to pH and ionic strength, and they may or may not be suitable for a particular application, depending on the pH and ionic strength of the solution.

7. Dye specificity: Highly specific dyes that stain the target but do not stain other components of the biofilm are preferable.

2.1.3.4.1 Examples of CLSM applications

2.1.3.4.1.1 Example 1: CLSM for imaging biofilm structure in 3-D. Confocal microscopy is currently a tool of choice in biofilm research, as it provides crisp images of fully hydrated biofilms. These images serve a variety of purposes, depending on the research question being addressed. In some of our own applications, we correlate the structure of biofilm with selected biofilm processes, such as intrabiofilm mass transport. The only way we can do this is by using confocal microscopy in conjunction with other tools we commonly use, such as microelectrodes, as we describe later in this chapter. CLSM is a unique type of microscopy in that it enables the optical sectioning of a biofilm into thin layers. The result is a set of images representing biofilm structure at various distances from the bottom, as shown in Figure 2.10.

A 3-D biofilm image like that shown in Figure 2.10b can be rotated and manipulated to reveal the pattern of biomass deposition, which in its turn is helpful for understanding the images of the distribution of biofilm activity. Rotated images of this reconstructed biofilm are shown in Figure 2.11. Such images can also be digitally cut using appropriate software to reveal the inner structure of the biofilm. Many modern confocal microscopes come with software for doing these manipulations.

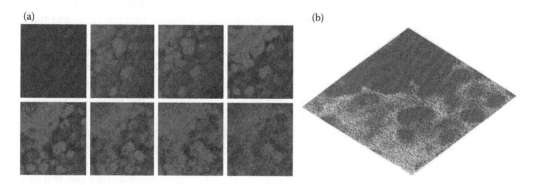

(a) (b)

Figure 2.10 **(See color insert.)** (a) A stack of biofilm images. The number of images in a stack is usually much higher: only selected images from the stack are shown to demonstrate the principle of the technique. (b) 3-D view of the biofilm reconstructed from the layers of images.

Figure 2.11 Rotated images of the reconstructed biofilm.

2.1.3.4.1.2   Example 2: CLSM in conjunction with microelectrode measurements.   As powerful a technique as CLSM is, it is even more powerful when combined with other tools and techniques used in biofilm research. The photograph in Figure 2.12 shows confocal microscopy combined with microsensor measurements. Simultaneous imaging of nutrient concentration and of the distribution of biomass in the vicinity of the tip of the microelectrode provides information that neither of these techniques alone, CLSM or microelectrode, could provide.

2.1.3.4.1.3   Example 3: CSLM velocimetry in biofilms.   It is well known that water moves through the channels and voids in the space occupied by a biofilm. To quantify the intensity of mass transport inside a biofilm, it is beneficial to measure the flow velocity in the inner space of the biofilm, and this can be done with the aid of confocal microscopy. A micrometer-sized fluorescent bead was injected into the space occupied by a biofilm and followed with confocal microscopy. Images were taken at a known time interval, and these images were superimposed to produce the composite image shown in Figure 2.13. Since the distances between positions occupied by the bead can be measured from the image, and the time elapsed between measurements is equal to the interval between the images being taken, the local flow velocities in the biofilm can be computed along the path of the bead.

2.1.3.4.1.4   Example 4: CLSM for characterizing mass transport in biofilms.   From the biofilm engineering point of view, EPS are materials that are responsible for much of the mass transfer resistance in biofilms. To reach the microorganisms, nutrients must diffuse in through the EPS matrix, and the products of microbial metabolism must diffuse out through the EPS matrix. Because mathematical models of biofilm activity are based on the equilibrium between the rates of microbial reactions and the rate of diffusion, diffusivity in EPS has been quantified by many authors. Measuring the diffusivities of specific substances in living, fully

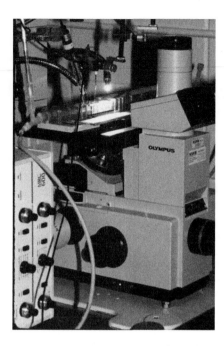

Figure 2.12 Inverted confocal microscope with a flat plate biofilm reactor. We insert microelectrodes from the top and image biofilm structure through the bottom.

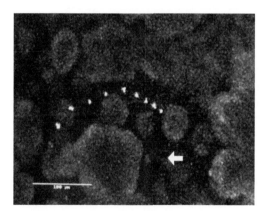

Figure 2.13 Neutral-density fluorescent latex spheres (density at 20°C, 1055 kg/m^3; excitation wavelength (Ex), 580 nm; emission wavelength (Em), 605 nm; diameter, 0.216 μm) from Molecular Probes, Eugene, Oregon were injected into a biofilm, and their movement was followed using confocal microscopy. The arrow indicates the direction of the water flow.

hydrated biofilms is challenging. Our group spent time developing tools for determining the diffusivities of small molecules in biofilm matrices by injecting picoliters of fluorescent dyes into biofilms and following the temporal distribution of the plumes using confocal microscopy (Figure 2.14). This is a tedious technique, but it is also one of the few techniques that can be used for truly *in situ* measurements of diffusivity in intact biofilms. The technique that we are now using, which is described later in this book, is based on electrochemical measurements. It requires drastic changes in the environment and is certainly much more intrusive

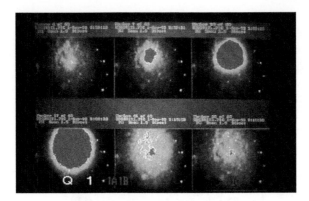

Figure 2.14 **(See color insert.)** Measuring diffusivity in a biofilm matrix using microinjections and confocal microscopy. (Reproduced from deBeer, D. et al., *Biotechnology and Bioengineering* 53: 151–158, 1997.)

than injecting picoliters of liquid into individual microcolonies. Its main advantage, besides convenience, is that we can measure diffusivity profiles at various locations in the biofilm, which is not possible using the microinjections technique. Figure 2.14 illustrates the principle of measuring diffusivity by microinjecting fluorescent dye and following the plume with confocal microscopy. The fluorescent dye is injected into a microcolony at time $t = 0$, which is imaged in the upper left-hand corner of the figure. As time passes, successive images are taken at a known time interval and the diameter of the plume is measured. The diffusivity of the injected substance is determined from the velocity at which the plume disperses.

2.1.4   Electron microscopy

Electron microscopy (EM) uses beams of electrons to illuminate a sample instead of the beams of light used in optical microscopy. There are two basic types of electron microscopes: the transmission electron microscope (TEM), in which the beam of primary electrons penetrates the sample, and the scanning electron microscope, in which the beam of primary electrons is reflected from the sample. In each of these two types of electron microscopes, the images are formed as a result of interaction between the beam of primary electrons and the sample, although the principles of image formation in TEM and SEM are somewhat different. Both microscopes require the use of a vacuum, although in a variety of SEM known as environmental scanning electron microscopy (ESEM) this requirement is somewhat relaxed, at least in the sample chamber.

2.1.4.1   Transmission electron microscopy
The electrons used to illuminate a sample in transition electron microscopy (TEM) are generated by an electron gun equipped with a heated tungsten or lanthanum hexaboride element. The electrons are directed toward the specimen through a condenser and a series of electromagnetic lenses. The beam of electrons is further accelerated toward the sample by applying a steep potential gradient in the column using high potentials, on the order of 100 kV. Once the primary electrons reach the sample, some penetrate the sample unscattered and some collide with the atoms of the sample and become scattered. Image formation in TEM depends on the ratio between the number of electrons that are scattered by the specimen and the number that are not. The dark areas of the image are formed by the scattered electrons; the light areas, by the unscattered electrons. In older instruments the image was formed on the surface of a cathode ray tube; in modern instruments the

image is projected on a computer screen. When primary electrons collide with the atoms of a sample, they can hit either the nucleus or another electron, and they scatter in both cases. The collision of a primary electron with the nucleus of an atom leads to so-called elastic scattering, and a collision with another electron leads to so-called inelastic scattering. This terminology originates from nuclear physics, where the term *elastic scattering* is used to describe a scattering event in which the kinetic energy of the scattered particle is mostly conserved; inelastic scattering means just the opposite. In elastic scattering the electrons lose little energy and are deflected at wide angles, which may approach 180°, leading to backscattering. Elastic scattering improves the contrast and the resolution of the image because the scattered electrons originate from a single point in the image, the nucleus. The higher the atomic number of the element (the bigger the nucleus), the more electrons are elastically scattered and the better the quality of the image is. When primary electrons collide with the electrons of a sample, they lose much more energy than they do in elastic scattering and are deflected at much smaller angles. Inelastic scattering is detrimental to the quality of an image in TEM: it causes a loss of contrast and resolution because the wave of scattered electrons is noncoherent and originates from various points in the image. Inelastic scattering may also lead to the emission of secondary electrons from the electron cloud if the energy of the primary electrons exceeds the ionization energies of the atoms with which they collide.

The image quality in TEM depends much on sample preparation. During image formation in TEM, primary electrons interact with the sample by (1) passing through the sample unscattered, (2) being elastically scattered by interacting with the nuclei, or (3) being inelastically scattered by interacting with the electrons. All three types of interactions are image-forming events in TEM. Elastic scattering contributes to the formation of the dark parts of the image, while the unscattered electrons contribute to the formation of the bright parts of the image. The inelastically scattered electrons contribute to the formation of grey areas in the image, which causes a loss of contrast and degrades the image quality. The quality of a TEM image depends on the thickness of the sample: using thin samples minimizes the effect of inelastic scattering and increases the number of unscattered electrons penetrating the sample. Typically, samples in TEM are slices of a specimen and their thickness is between 10 nm and 1 μm.

Even though TEM uses electrons to illuminate an object, instead of light, the resolution is still limited by diffraction, as described by Equation 2.1. The high resolutions of TEM result from the beam of primary electrons having a much shorter wavelength than the light illuminating samples in OM. The wavelength of the electrons is

$$\lambda = \frac{h}{mv} \tag{2.4}$$

where h is Planck's constant, m is electron mass, and v is electron velocity.

Also, we note that the kinetic energy of the electrons equals

$$\frac{1}{2}mv^2 = eV \tag{2.5}$$

where e is the electron charge and V is the potential through which the electrons are accelerated.

Combining Equations 2.4 and 2.5 gives

$$v = \sqrt{2eV/m} \tag{2.6}$$

and

$$\lambda = \frac{h}{\sqrt{2emV}} \tag{2.7}$$

Using values of $h = 6.62 \times 10^{-34}$ m² kg/s, $e = 1.60 \times 10^{-19}$ coulombs, $m = 9.109 \times 10^{-31}$ kg, and $V = 100$ kV gives a wavelength of $\lambda = 0.0038$ nm, about 0.004 nm, which is much shorter than the wavelength of the violet light we used in the example in Section 2.1.1.1. That was 400 nm, 5 orders of magnitude longer than the wavelength of the electron beam. The practical resolution in TEM does not reach the theoretical limits because of electromagnetic lens aberrations. Commercial microscopes, such as the JEOL 2010, reach a resolution of "only" 0.2 nm.

As discussed above, in the conventional applications of TEM, the image is formed by the scattered and unscattered electrons based on their energies. High-resolution transmitted electron microscopy (HRTEM) uses additional information, the phase of the wave of the scattered electrons and the interference pattern, to deliver a resolution of 0.2 nm.

2.1.4.1.1 Biofilm sample preparation and key factors for TEM. TEM is executed in a high vacuum, with pressure on the order of 10^{-5} mm Hg, for several reasons. The presence of gas in the column would cause the primary electrons to collide with the gas particles and degrade the image. Also, using a high voltage in TEM would cause ionization of the gas and arch discharges between the components of the instrument. However, using a high vacuum in TEM imposes limitations on the types of samples that can be imaged and can be a source of artifacts. In particular, biological specimens are typically highly hydrated and need to be dehydrated before they are placed in the vacuum chamber. Removing water may change the structure of the specimen and needs to be accounted for when one is making conclusions based on the shape of the specimen under the microscope. Attempts are made to minimize the consequences of removing water by "fixing" the samples, often by using cross-linking chemicals that help retain the original structure of the specimen after water has been removed. Biological specimens are made of elements with low atomic mass, which decreases the contribution of elastic scattering to image formation and degrades the quality of the images. This problem is sometimes addressed by staining samples to increase the contribution of elastic scattering. The stains use heavy elements, such as lead, tungsten, and uranium, and such substances as uranyl acetate and lead citrate are popular stains in TEM. They exhibit affinity for functional groups of proteins and are characterized by high levels of elastic scattering. As we noted above, the quality of the image is greatly improved when the sample is thin, which increases the contribution of the unscattered electrons to the image formation. To make a thin sample, the specimen is frozen or embedded in a solidified resin, after which thin slices of it can be cut using a microtome. These slices are often stained to further improve the quality of the image. Most biological samples are mounted on "grids," which are small discs with a fine mesh made of copper covered with graphite. One of the effects of irradiating a sample with a beam of primary electrons is that the temperature of the sample increases, which can be detrimental to a biological specimen. This effect is counteracted by using microscope stages cooled with liquid nitrogen or helium: cold stage. Despite all its limitations, TEM allows us to image the structure of a biological specimen in a unique way and has contributed to our understanding of the structure and function of various biological components.

2.1.4.1.2 *Examples of applications.* TEM and HRTEM with a resolution of 0.2 nm are used when analyses at a scale of resolution smaller than the dimensions of the microbial cells are required. These types of analyses are used when individual cells in the biofilm are responsible for the process under study and the analysis of individual cells can improve our knowledge of the biofilm process. For example, biofilms of sulfate-reducing bacteria reduce U(VI) to U(IV), and some of the uranium precipitates in the periplasmic spaces of the microbial cells. The mechanism of uranium removal is not entirely understood. The hypotheses have been put forward that some of the uranium precipitates outside the cells and that uranium reduction is caused by the proteins excreted by the microorganisms. Establishing the mechanism of uranium removal of these biofilms requires characterizing the biofilms and their components at a scale that can only be reached using transmission electron microscopy. Using the accepted terminology, the compartment of interest is the biofilm and the component under study is the microorganisms removing uranium. Figures 2.15 and 2.16 show examples of high-resolution microscopies being used

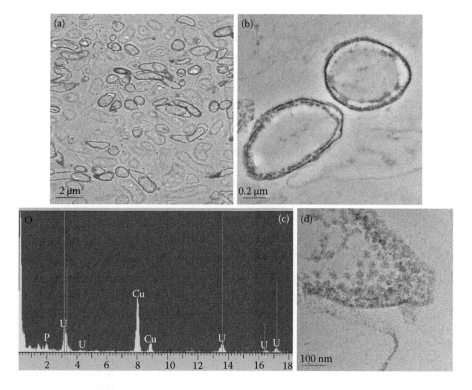

Figure 2.15 Images of biofilms in a reactor supplied with 30 mg/L uranium. (a) A low-magnification TEM image shows uranium-precipitating and nonprecipitating microbial cells. (b) At higher magnification, the microbial cells show a heavy precipitation of uranium on their membranes and in their periplasmic spaces. (c) Energy dispersive spectrometry analysis shows that the deposits contain uranium and phosphate (the peak of Cu is due to the sample grid). (d) The HRTEM image of the deposits shows poorly crystalline uranium in nodular agglomerates accumulated on microbial cell surfaces. (Reproduced from Marsili, E. et al., *Water Science and Technology* 52: 49–55, 2005.)

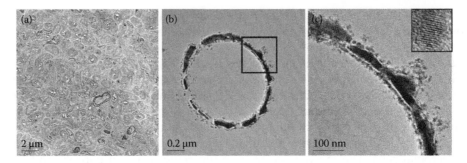

Figure 2.16 (a) TEM image of a cross section of biofilm showing cells with relatively low mineral precipitation. (b) Cells that precipitated uranium demonstrated the same site of reduction: the periplasm. (c) Cell with a pronounced lipid layer of plasma and outer membrane. High-resolution transmission electron microscopy revealed the well-defined nanocrystalline character of the precipitated uranium, with a crystal size of 2–5 nm (single crystal, inset in c).

to characterize biofilms of sulfate-reducing bacteria *Desulfovibrio desulfuricans* G20 reducing uranium U(VI) to U(IV) and precipitating it in the periplasmic spaces of individual microorganisms. To quantify this process, microbial cells have to be imaged with a spatial resolution better than the linear dimension of individual cells.

2.1.4.2 Scanning electron microscopy

In SEM, a sample is irradiated by a stream of electrons generated, as in TEM, by an electron gun. The incoming (primary) electrons in SEM interact with the sample similarly to those in TEM microscopes: they penetrate some distance into the surface, producing elastically and inelastically scattered electrons. However, in SEM the image-forming particles are all reflected from the surface: they do not penetrate the sample as they do in TEM. Also, in SEM the electron beam illuminating the sample is scanned across the sample and the image-forming particles either are reflected from the surface or actually originate from the surface. Scanning illumination is characteristic of SEM but not unique to it, as some modes of TEM operation use scanning beams of electrons as well.

SEM uses three image-forming particles: (1) secondary electrons, (2) backscattered electrons, and (3) x-ray photons. The inelastic scattering results in some electrons being ejected from the atoms at the surface, producing a wave of secondary electrons. The secondary electrons have low energies, below 50 eV, and are used to generate high-quality images reflecting surface topography. However, because the secondary electrons have low energies and form a noncoherent wave, they have to be attracted and accelerated toward the detector by a positively charged component placed in front of the detector. The secondary electron detector is positioned on the side of the sample, at an angle, and changing the angle affects the image. The elastically scattered electrons are backscattered, as they are in TEM. They have high energy, above 50 eV, and can provide information about the composition of the surface of the sample. The images formed by the backscattered electrons are not as sensitive to surface topography, but they are useful for showing other features: they are sensitive to the atomic number of the atoms residing on the surface of the sample, and therefore they display "atomic number contrast." As we discussed in Section 2.1.4.1, the bigger nuclei of heavier elements backscatter more electrons than the smaller nuclei of lighter elements. Finally, the high-energy primary electrons from the incident beam also scatter some inner shell electrons from the sample. When the missing electrons from the inner shells are replaced by electrons from the outer shells, which have higher energies than the electrons in the inner shells, the excess energy is released in the form of x-ray photons. Because the energy level of each shell is known for every element, the amount of energy released as x-ray photons carries information about the chemical composition of the surface. x-ray spectrometers collect the x-ray photons, measure the energy spectra and characterize the elements. This analysis is known as energy dispersive spectrometry (EDS). The energy spectra of the x-ray waves are imaged on plots on which the x-ray count is plotted on the vertical axis and the energy to which this count corresponds is plotted on the horizontal axis. The number of counts is proportional to the concentration of the element, and the energy level identifies the element. On the basis of the EDS information, SEM also generates maps imaging the spatial distribution of the elemental composition. Because of poor spatial resolution, x-rays are not used to generate images of the sample, but they are used to generate maps of the elemental composition of the sample.

2.1.4.2.1 Biofilm sample preparation and key factors for SEM. Conventional SEM operates in a high vacuum, and the samples must be dehydrated before use, usually in a series of solutions of increasing concentrations of ethanol. This can produce artifacts, particularly when highly hydrated biological samples are used. Also, the sample needs to be made electrically conductive because the electron beam charges the surface electrically in the vacuum, producing many kinds of artifacts, including interactions with the beam of primary electrons. The samples are thus coated with a thin layer of electrically conductive coating and ground to dissipate the electrical charge accumulating on the surface. Gold is often used for this purpose, but other conducting substances, even carbon, can be used. Coating the surface with a heavy element, such as gold, improves the resolution and contrast of the images but also produces artifacts. It may interfere with EDS analysis by absorbing x-rays, which gold does very efficiently. One of the perpetually repeated criticisms of SEM is that it images the coating, not the sample. The operator needs to be aware of the possible artifacts when interpreting the results of analyses. Almost all these problems are avoided in ESEM, in which the requirement of using a high vacuum is somewhat relaxed. We will discuss ESEM in the following sections.

2.1.4.2.2 Examples of applications

2.1.4.2.2.1 Example 1: Imaging biomineralized deposits on a metal surface. In biofilm research, SEM is particularly useful for examining mineral deposits on surfaces. It is less useful for analyzing microorganisms deposited on surfaces because it introduces artifacts resulting from the stringent methods used to prepare hydrated specimens. This technique uses a high vacuum, so for obvious reasons the samples must be dehydrated, usually in a series of ethanol solutions of progressively increasing concentration, before the analysis. Dehydrating does not change mineral deposits, but it does change the shapes of microorganisms and extracellular polymers. The SEM image in Figure 2.17, which was taken during the study described in the preceding sections, shows mineral deposits in the biofilm. These are the same deposits that were imaged using OM and shown in Figure 2.3.

SEM can be used to image microorganisms deposited on surfaces. However, as pointed out above, the drastic procedures used to dehydrate the samples cause artifacts that need to be taken into consideration when the images are interpreted. Other types of microscopy are more suitable for imaging microorganisms in biofilms than SEM is. However, in some types of biofilm research it is important to compare the location of the microorganisms on the surface with the topographical features of the surface, and for this application,

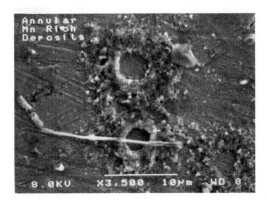

Figure 2.17 Scanning electron microscopy micrograph of annular deposits on a stainless steel coupon after exposure to fresh river water. The stainless steel substratum is visible within the central void. (Reproduced from Dickinson, W. H. et al., *Corrosion Science* 38: 1407–1422, 1996.)

SEM is a method of choice. SEM is also very useful for identifying features of interest on surfaces before other methods of surface analysis are used to further characterize them. Once the features of interest have been identified using SEM, there are many other surface analytical techniques that can be used to characterize the identified areas; some of these techniques are described in the following sections. Figure 2.18 shows the results of such a study, in which the surface features identified using SEM were further studied using AFM.

  2.1.4.2.2.2   Example 2: Imaging microorganisms in biofilms.   SEM offers a much better resolution than optical microscopy and is sometimes used to image microorganisms in biofilms. Such images show a distorted view of the inner space of biofilms by degrading the matrix of extracellular polymers. Extracellular polymers are highly hydrated, containing more than 90% water, and are therefore strongly affected by the dehydrating procedures used in preparing samples for SEM imaging. As a result, the initially slimy matrix of extracellular polymers is degraded and appears in SEM images as a network of randomly arranged strands, products of the polymeric matrix being dehydrated. This basically undesirable effect has one desirable consequence: it produces vivid images of

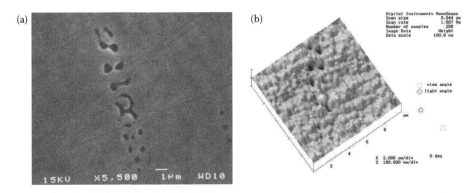

Figure 2.18 (a) An SEM image of surface damage caused by *Leptothrix discophora* SP-6 attached to a surface of 316L stainless steel. (b) An AFM image of the same area corroborated the conclusion that the surface had been damaged. (Reproduced from Geiser, M. et al., *International Biodeterioration and Biodegradation* 49: 235–243, 2002.)

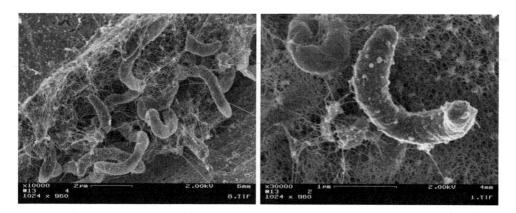

Figure 2.19 Scanning electron microscopy images of a biofilm and a single cell of *Desulfovibrio desulfuricans* G20 imbedded in extracellular polymers (EPS). The sample was dehydrated, and the slimy EPS shows as a mass of strands of dried extracellular polymers.

biofilm microorganisms devoid of the polymeric matrix, which when intact obstructs the view of the microorganisms. Figure 2.19 shows an image of microorganisms embedded in the matrix.

2.1.4.3   Environmental scanning electron microscopy

Both TEM and SEM require the use of a high vacuum to generate images. This requirement limits their applications to samples that are vacuum tolerant. Imaging biological samples, in which water content often exceeds 95%, requires extensive treatment of the samples, which is a source of many kinds of artifacts. Careful evaluation of the need for a high vacuum in SEM leads to the conclusion that it is required in the electron gun housing and in the column of the microscope, where the electrons generated by the electron gun are ushered into a cohesive beam and accelerated toward the sample in a high-voltage electrical field. The presence of any gas at these locations would lead to arch discharges among the components of the microscope because of gas ionization and deteriorate the quality of the image because of collisions between the primary electrons and molecules of the gas. However, once the electrons reach the sample the high-vacuum requirement can be somewhat relaxed. This has many advantages: it becomes possible to image hydrated samples and unnecessary to make samples electrically conductive. ESEM builds on these principles. To use a higher pressure in the sample chamber than in the column, ESEM has the sample chamber separated from the column by a series of (at least two) compartments, connected by small orifices. The gas pressure in the compartments gradually increases from the high vacuum in the column to a higher pressure, up to 50 mm Hg, in the sample chamber. This is much higher than the 6 mm Hg required to keep water in a liquid state at low temperatures and allows the imaging of hydrated samples, both conductive and nonconductive. The gas leaks slowly through the orifices between the compartments and is promptly removed to the desired pressure by vacuum pumps connected to each compartment. The entire system of gradually changing the pressure between the sample compartment and the column of the microscope is known as differential pumping. The small orifices limit the field of view of the microscope, because the beam of primary electrons needs to pass through the orifices, and the sample chamber needs to be constructed to limit the distance along which the electrons pass to limit the number of collisions with gas particles. Images are formed using the same principles as in SEM.

2.1.4.3.1   Examples of ESEM applications

2.1.4.3.1.1   Example 1: Imaging biofilm structure.   As we discussed in the section dedicated to SEM, dehydrating biofilms to prepare them for imaging at a high vacuum degrades the extracellular polymeric matrix and generates artifacts, as shown in Figure 2.19. Therefore, SEM has been most successfully used to image samples immune to dehydration, such as mineral deposits like those shown in Figure 2.17. The invention of ESEM opened new perspectives by allowing the imaging of fully hydrated biofilms and the testing of hypotheses based on the conceptual models of biofilm structure. One conceptual model of biofilm structure (see Figure 1.8) conjectured that biofilms were composed of microcolonies separated by interstitial voids. This model was generated based on a series of experimental results that could be reconciled only if biofilms were porous and allowed water to flow in the space occupied by the biofilm. At the time this model was conceived, there were few results corroborating what it postulated. The model was postulated to reconcile several experimental results that we could not explain using the then existing conceptual model of homogeneous biofilms, as explained in Chapter 1. The first results demonstrating that the model of heterogeneous biofilms largely depicted the structure of biofilms correctly came from confocal microscopy images, followed by ESEM images. Figure 2.20 shows examples of ESEM images and demonstrates what type of information can be obtained from such images. The image in Figure 2.20a shows a marine biofilm deposited on carbon steel with a microcolony and interstitial voids, just as predicted by the conceptual image in Figure 1.8. Figure 2.20b shows clusters of microorganisms in a pure culture biofilm of *Geobacter sulfurreducens*. In the clusters the cells are very densely packed. To demonstrate the type of artifacts produced by drying biofilms and imaging them in a high vacuum, Figure 2.20c shows an image of the biofilm presented in Figure 2.20b that was acquired using conventional SEM microscopy; there is little evidence in the SEM image that the microbes in the hydrated biofilm formed microcolonies separated by voids. Dehydration of the sample removes this information. Clearly, then, the type of microscopy used to acquire images of biofilms affects the information that is generated in the process of interpreting the images. ESEM is an excellent technique and highly recommended for use in biofilm research, rivaled perhaps only by CSLM.

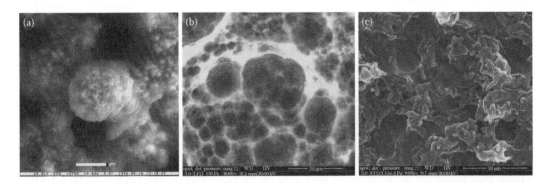

Figure 2.20 (a) ESEM image of a fully hydrated marine biofilm formed on carbon steel, following three weeks of exposure in Portsmouth Harbor, UK. Hydrated EPS, microcolonies, and pores characteristic of biofilm structure are clearly seen; photo courtesy of Iwona Beech, University of Portsmouth. (b) ESEM image of hydrated *Geobacter sulfurreducens* biofilm showing dense cells in cell clusters. (c) SEM image of the biofilm shown in (b). In this image, the microcolonies have been destroyed and the microorganisms dispersed. EPS is still visible.

2.1.5   Atomic force microscopy

In atomic force microscopy (AFM) a flexible cantilever is scanned over the surface of a specimen positioned on a piezoelectric scanner. The force between the cantilever and the surface, attributed to various forces resulting from overlapping electron clouds at the tip of the probe and at the surface, affects the position of the cantilever and is detected using optical detectors. Figure 2.21 shows the principle of AFM operation.

AFM can be operated in contact mode, noncontact mode or tapping mode. Contact mode is the simplest mode of operation: in it the cantilever is just scanned across the mapped surface. In the noncontact mode of operation, the cantilever oscillates as it is scanned across the surface. Tapping mode is essentially the same as noncontact mode, except that the amplitude of oscillations is bigger and the cantilever movement is affected by different forces. While noncontact mode can provide resolution on the atomic scale, tapping mode can provide resolution on the scale of individual molecules. The cantilever used in contact mode is elastic and deflects when reacting with surface forces, while the cantilevers used in noncontact and tapping modes are rigid. The detection system in the latter two modes is based on measuring the changes in the phase and amplitude of the oscillation of the cantilever, rather than the deflection of the cantilever, which is measured in contact mode. AFM was developed subsequent to scanning tunneling microscopy (STM). While STM can only be used to map conductive surfaces, AFM can be used to image any types of surfaces, including surfaces of biological specimens. For example, AFM can be used to image individual microorganisms deposited on various conductive and nonconductive surfaces, at least in the initial stages of biofilm formation, before the entire surface is covered with EPS. The initial stages of biofilm formation are well documented, mostly because acquiring images of microorganisms at this stage of biofilm formation is relatively easy. AFM gives images of microorganisms attached to surfaces with amazing clarity and resolution, superior to images of microorganisms acquired using SEM. The resolution of AFM is on the order of nanometers, which is orders of magnitude better than the resolution of optical microscopes.

2.1.5.1   Examples of AFM applications

2.1.5.1.1   Example 1: AFM used to map the topography of surfaces with attached microorganisms.   In biofilm research, AFM can be used to generate maps of surface topography. The AFM image in Figure 2.22 shows the initial stage of the colonization of 316 L stainless steel by manganese-oxidizing bacteria *Leptothrix discophora* SP6. The surface was carefully polished so that the shape of the microorganisms would be easily distinguishable from the morphological features of the surface.

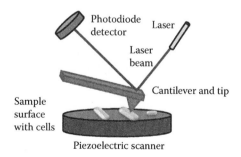

Figure 2.21 The main components of an atomic force microscope.

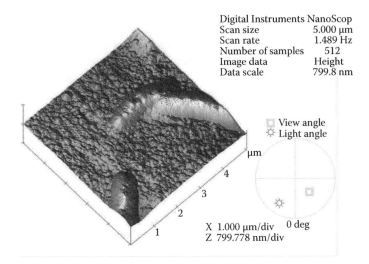

Figure 2.22 AFM image of manganese-oxidizing bacteria *Leptothrix discophora* SP6 attached to a surface of 316L stainless steel.

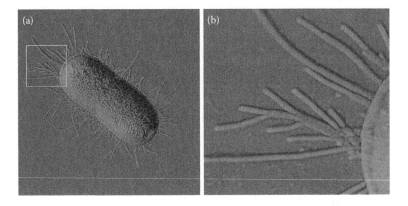

Figure 2.23 Phase images of *Salmonella typhimurium:* (a) 4.5 μm × 4.5 μm and (b) 1.0 μm × 1.0 μm. Both images were taken in air. (Images courtesy of Recep Avci of the Department of Physics, Montana State University, Bozeman. The technique of image acquisition is described in Suo, Z. et al., *Langmuir* 23(3): 1365–1374, 2007.)

2.1.5.1.2   Example 2: AFM used to image individual bacteria.   The recent progress in sample preparation and in encoding phase and amplitude in the noncontact mode of AFM operation has made it possible to acquire stunningly detailed images of individual bacteria. Figure 2.23 shows images of *Salmonella typhimurium* taken in air using noncontact mode with phase decoding.

2.1.5.1.3   Example 3: AFM used to image metal surfaces.   The ability of AFM to image surface topography is important in some types of biofilm research, such as studies on initial attachment and studies of microbially influenced corrosion. In our own microbially influenced corrosion studies we tried to associate the locations of microorganisms with the locations of corrosion cells and the locations of localized corrosion attack. For this we

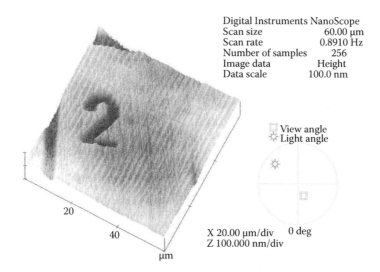

Digital Instruments NanoScope
Scan size   60.00 µm
Scan rate   0.8910 Hz
Number of samples   256
Image data   Height
Data scale   100.0 nm

▢ View angle
☼ Light angle

20

40

X 20.00 µm/div   0 deg
Z 100.000 nm/div

µm

Figure 2.24 Metal surface marked with a grid made by argon ion milling. (Reproduced from Geiser, M. et al., *International Biodeterioration and Biodegradation* 49: 235–243, 2002.)

needed to determine the positions of the microorganisms on the metal surfaces and correlate their distribution with the distribution of the surface chemistry. Figure 2.24 shows a mark, the numeral 2, made on a stainless steel surface to identify the location of a small square etched on the surface. Marking locations on metal surfaces was an essential part of our experiments evaluating the effect of microorganisms on electrochemistry near and at metal surfaces. As part of the study, the marked locations were analyzed before and after microbial colonization. Finding a location of a size comparable to the size of a single bacterium on a metal surface is not a trivial task. To make this task easier, the selected locations on the metal surface were subdivided into squares and each square was marked using ion beam milling prior to the analyses. The grids on the surface (see Figure 2.24) were milled using argon ion beams, and they subdivided the area of interest into squares. Each square on the surface was 180 × 180 µm, and each square had a numeral, also written using the ion beam milling technique. The following section in this chapter is dedicated to the use of time of flight secondary ion mass spectroscopy (ToF-SIMS) and shows images of such locations on 316L stainless steel surfaces prepared for elemental analysis (Figure 2.24). Before microbial colonization, surface chemistry was quantified on each square using ToF-SIMS. After the experiment, the biofilm was removed, the squares were located and identified, and the surface analysis was repeated. Comparing the results was useful in evaluating the effect of microbial colonization on surfaces. More about applications of this technique is in Section 7.7.1, which is dedicated to the mechanisms of microbially influenced corrosion.

2.1.6   Microscopy for surface analysis

Actually, there are two surfaces of interest in biofilm research: the surface to which the microorganisms are attached and the surface of the microorganisms—the microbial cell surface. However, only the surface on which a biofilm accumulates is identified here as a compartment of the biofilm system. Therefore, throughout this text, when we refer to the surface we mean the surface to which the microorganisms are attached, unless explicitly specified otherwise. The surface on which the microorganisms aggregate has acquired an unfortunate name in biofilm research—the substratum, which is easily confused with another important name often used in the same context—the substrate, which is the growth-limiting nutrient. To avoid confusion, it makes sense to use the term *nutrient* instead of *substrate*, whenever possible. We start our analysis of the effects of the surface on biofilm processes with a description of the effects of the surface on the initial events in biofilm formation, the microbial colonization of the surface. Despite an intensive research effort on the relations between surface properties and rates of microbial attachment to surfaces, these relations are still not clear.

Several instruments and analytical techniques are available for characterizing the chemistry and topography of surfaces. Each of them is designed to deliver some type of information about surface chemistry or topography and may be less suitable for delivering other types of information. We will briefly address the usefulness of the instruments and techniques we use. This description does not exhaust the available choices, and other instruments and other analytical techniques may be used to obtain the same results or to expand the analytical capabilities beyond those we have.

It is worth noting that the instruments of surface analysis help us to image the shape of the surface and the distribution of various elements and minerals on the surface; yet they provide little information about the mechanism or the rate of biofilm formation, as many other factors besides surface chemistry and topography affect biofilm formation. For example, characterizing the chemistries of surfaces before they are immersed in a solution of nutrients may give a false sense of confidence about the properties of the material that is being microbially colonized. In fact, the chemistry of a surface is rapidly modified upon immersion in a solution of nutrients by the formation of conditioning films, which are known to affect biofilm formation. The characteristics of conditioning films are not well known, and it is believed that they mostly affect the initial stages of microbial attachment, as discussed at the beginning of Section 1.3.1.1.

2.1.6.1   *Energy dispersive x-ray spectroscopy*

EDS is used to identify the elemental composition of materials imaged in a scanning electron microscope. To continue with the example introduced in Figures 2.17 and 2.18, the image in Figure 2.25 shows the elemental composition of those mineral deposits, acquired to verify the hypothesis that they were the result of the activity of the manganese-oxidizing bacteria. The SEM analysis of the mineral deposits was followed by the EDS mapping of the region shown in Figure 2.25. The analyses demonstrated the presence of Mn, Ca, O, and C in the annular deposits and corroborated the initial conclusion, that the contents of the deposits were consistent with those expected of manganese-oxidizing microorganisms, manganese and oxygen. The presence of carbon in the deposits was expected because the mineral deposits were mixed with the biomass of the microorganisms, and the presence of calcium was also expected because the deposits were formed in natural waters in which calcium was the main component of water hardness.

2.1.6.2   *X-ray photoelectron spectroscopy*

X-ray photoelectron spectroscopy (XPS), also known as electron spectroscopy for chemical analysis, is the most popular of the surface analytical techniques. It identifies the elemental composition and oxidation states of inorganic substances deposited on surfaces. The principle of the technique is to irradiate a surface with x-ray photons. When a photon encounters the atoms of a deposit or the base metal surface, it may pass unobstructed, it may collide with an electron and scatter with a partial loss of energy or it may collide with an electron and transfer all its energy to that electron, causing an electron emission. This

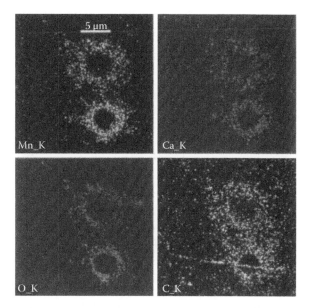

Figure 2.25 Energy dispersive x-ray spectroscopy maps of the annular mineral deposits shown in Figure 2.17, demonstrating the presence of oxygen, carbon, calcium, and carbon. (Reproduced from Dickinson, W. H. et al., *Corrosion Science* 38: 1407–1422, 1996.)

last possibility is the basis of XPS, and the basic equation that describes the photoemission of an electron is the Einstein equation for the binding energy of an electron (E_b):

$$E_b = h\nu - \text{KE} \tag{2.8}$$

where $h\nu$ is the energy of the x-ray photon and KE is the kinetic energy of the emitted electron. Thus, thc equation relates the energy of the irradiating photons to the binding energy of the emitted electrons. The binding energy is related to the electrostatic interactions between the positively charged nucleus and the negatively charged electron. If the kinetic energy of the emitted electron is measured, the binding energy can be calculated from Equation 2.8 and used to reveal information about the electronic structure of the chemical substance from which the electron was emitted. Thus, XPS spectra are plots of binding energies versus electron counts, as shown in Figure 2.26. Each peak in the spectrum is identified and, based on the electron binding energy, ascribed to a specific orbital of an atom of a specific element. Thus, the elemental composition of the sample is revealed, but not the formula for the particle to which the element belongs; that information can be revealed using time of flight secondary ion spectroscopy, which we discuss later in this chapter.

In practical terms, XPS uses low-resolution scans to deliver information about the chemistry of the first few atomic layers of a surface. Among other applications, it can be used to analyze the chemistry of deposits on metal surfaces. XPS uses monochromatized aluminum Al-Kα x-rays focused into a 20 to 200 µm beam to eject photoelectrons from the surface and the near-surface regions (0–50 Å). These photoelectrons are emitted from the core and valence levels of atoms and molecules. Because the core-level energy states, particularly those of shallow levels (e.g., Mn 3p), are perturbed by the local bonding and

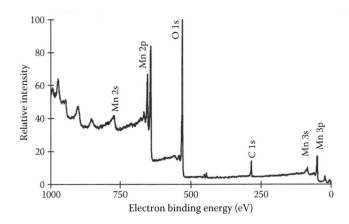

Figure 2.26 X-ray photoelectron spectroscopy spectrum of biofouling deposits of manganese-oxidizing bacteria.

charge states of species, small shifts in the binding energies (chemical shifts) provide a picture of the chemical environment of the elements and their abundance.

2.1.6.2.1 Examples of XPS applications

2.1.6.2.1.1 Example 1: Biomineralized deposits in a biofilm of manganese-oxidizing bacteria Leptothrix discophora *SP6.* The mineral deposits in a biofilm of manganese-oxidizing bacteria *Leptothrix discophora* SP6 are shown in Figure 2.27. These were identified as manganese oxides, consistent with the expectations based on a field experiment in which

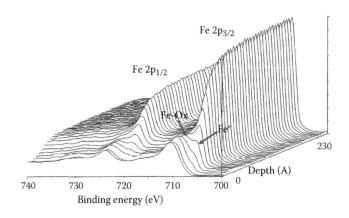

Figure 2.27 Using XPS to determine the thickness of a passive film on 316L stainless steel. As the sputtering progresses (removing the layers), the peak for iron oxides, Fe-O$_x$, is replaced by the peak for Fe°, which originates in the bulk metal. An 800-µm diameter equivalent area of the sample surface was analyzed while a 3 × 3 mm² area was sputtered using Ar⁺ ions for each cycle of depth profiling. In the sputtering process, Ar⁺ ions, accelerated to ~2 keV with a 0.25-µA current, were used to bombard the sample surface for selected time intervals (~0.5 min) until the Fe oxides were removed and the metallic Fe (bulk stainless steel) was reached. Judging from the scale, the iron oxides on this surface formed a layer about 50 A thick. (Reproduced from Yurt, N., *Leptothrix discophora* SP-6: Effects of biofilms on passive film chemistry of 316L stainless steel and modeling of growth. PhD dissertation, Montana State University, Bozeman, 2002.)

similar deposits were analyzed using EDS mapping, as shown in Figure 2.27. Following the conclusion of the field experiment, the same metal, stainless steel 316L, was colonized in a controlled laboratory experiment with manganese-oxidizing bacteria, and the biomineralized deposits were analyzed using XPS. The results, shown in Figure 2.26, identified the main components of the biomineralized deposits as manganese and oxygen, which was consistent with the expectation that the bulk of the deposits were composed of manganese oxides.

   2.1.6.2.1.2 Example 2: Thickness of the passive film on 316L stainless steel. Manganese-oxidizing bacteria have been implicated in the pitting corrosion of stainless steels, described in Chapter 7. Corrosion pits originate at sites on a metal surface where the integrity of the passive layer has been compromised, and part of the work related to the elucidation of the corrosion mechanism was to determine the thickness of the passive layer of 316L stainless steel before microbial colonization. We used XPS for that purpose. The chemistry and the distribution of the passive layer were quantified before and after exposure to a biofilm of manganese-oxidizing bacteria. Figure 2.27 shows a depth profile of the iron and iron oxides deposited on the surface. The surface of the stainless steel was sputtered using Ar^+ ions to remove layers of the passive film, and the chemistry of each layer was evaluated after each sputtering cycle.

2.1.6.3   ToF-SIMS

Secondary ion mass spectrometry (SIMS) uses mass spectrometry to identify the ionized particles emitted from surfaces bombarded by energetic primary ions in an ion beam. ToF-SIMS is considered the most versatile and sensitive surface analysis technique presently existing. It requires a high vacuum, on the order of 10^{-6} mm Hg, to prevent collisions between the primary beam of ions and gas particles. The instrument has the following essential components: a source of ions to form the ion beam, two mass analyzers, and an ion analyzer. The ions forming the ion beam can be generated in several ways. In the instrument we used, a field emission technique was used to generate Ga^+ ions: a tungsten needle covered with liquid gallium was placed in a high-voltage electrical field, and Ga^+ ions were extracted using a negatively charged electrode. The mass analyzers sort the captured ions based on their electrical charges and their magnetic properties. The electrical charge analyzer uses a static electrical field to sort the captured ions based on their electrical charge and kinetic energies. The magnetic analyzer uses a static magnetic field to further sort the captured ions based on their ratios of mass to electrical charge. Finally, the ion analyzer identifies the ions based on the information from the mass analyzers. In ToF-SIMS, the particles emitted from the surface are accelerated in an electrical field along a path of known length. The particles arrive at the flight analyzer at various times depending on their masses and charges, and the time of their flight is used to identify the particles. One of the prominent features of ToF-SIMS is its high spatial resolution: it easily reaches a resolution comparable with the sizes of individual microorganisms. ToF-SIMS is used to identify substances deposited on surfaces. In contrast to EDS, described above, which is used to identify the elemental composition of a surface, ToF-SIMS analyzes fragments of molecules detached from the surface and uses a library of fragments to identify the original substances deposited on the surface.

2.1.6.3.1   Examples of applications

   2.1.6.3.1.1 Example 1: Composition of microbial deposits in a biofilm sample from a creek.   In search of the mechanism by which manganese-oxidizing bacteria cause the corrosion of stainless steels and other passive metals and alloys, titanium corrosion coupons were immersed in a creek and allowed to be colonized by the native microorganisms for

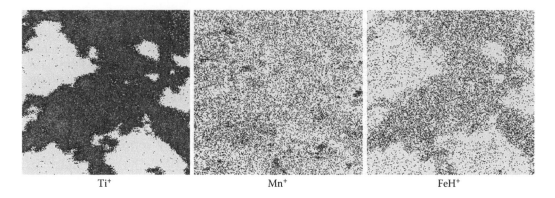

Ti⁺   Mn⁺   FeH⁺

Figure 2.28 ToF-SIMS images showing the distribution of secondary ions: Ti⁺, Mn⁺, and FeH⁺. The data were collected from a 180 × 180 μm² area on a Ti-6Al-4V coupon ennobled to +400 mVSCE in Roskie Creek near Bozeman, Montana. In the Ti⁺ map, the depleted signals in the white regions indicate that they are covered by residual biofilm, while the strong signals in the red regions indicate the absence of biofilm. In the regions not covered by biofilm, both Mn⁺ and FeH⁺ are enriched, which can be attributed to the presence of Mn-rich microbial deposits and Fe in the metal substratum. In the regions covered by biofilm, however, Mn⁺ is significantly enriched and FeH⁺ is also present, but Ti⁺ is depleted. This is an expected result if the Ti⁺ signal comes from the metal substratum only but the Mn⁺ and FeH⁺ signals come from both the deposits and the biofilm. Therefore, we conclude that there is biomineralized manganese as well as iron in the biofilm and microbial deposits.

several days. After the coupons were retrieved, the deposits on them were analyzed using ToF-SIMS. An example of the results is shown in Figure 2.28.

 2.1.6.3.1.2   Example 2: Analysis of biomineralized deposits in a biofilm of manganese-oxidizing bacteria on 316L stainless steel.   One of the challenges in studying microbially influenced corrosion is to relate the presence of specific groups of microorganisms, reactants, and products of metabolic reactions to the electrochemical reactions that control the corrosion process. In some instances this analysis can lead to revealing the mechanism of microbially influenced corrosion. It helps in this process to correlate the locations of the corrosion products, or the locations of corrosion damage, to the locations of the individual microorganisms colonizing the surface. ToF-SIMS is ideal for conducting such chemical analysis because it offers spatial resolution on a scale comparable to the size of individual microorganisms. However, the analysis of deposits or of changes in the chemical composition of the surface is conducted after the microorganisms have been mechanically removed from the surface, and it is not an easy task to find the locations where the microorganisms were located after they have been removed. To handle this task, we mark, using ion milling, a regular grid on the metal surface. The grid subdivides the selected location into squares, and we mark each of these squares with a numeral (as shown in Figure 2.24, where one such numeral was imaged using AFM). Having marked the squares on the metal surface, we colonize the surface with microorganisms and, after biofilm has been allowed to form for a suitable period, we determine, most often using optical microscopy, but sometimes SEM in cases where the deposits are too thick, the locations of microbial cells within individual squares, as shown in Figure 2.29. Then, after removing the microorganisms mechanically, we analyze the surface deposits within each square and correlate the composition of the surface with the locations where the microbial cells were detected.

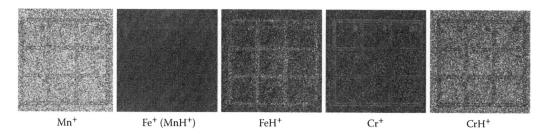

Mn$^+$	Fe$^+$ (MnH$^+$)	FeH$^+$	Cr$^+$	CrH$^+$

Figure 2.29 ToF-SIMS images of a surface of 316L stainless steel etched using argon ion beam milling to form a grid that can be found and analyzed after colonization with microorganisms. The squares are 180 μm × 180 μm. (Reproduced from Shi, X. et al., *Corrosion Science* 45: 2577–2595, 2003.)

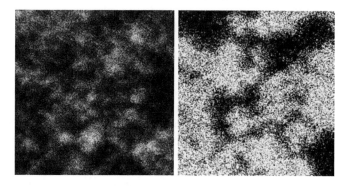

Figure 2.30 ToF-SIMS images of (left) Mn$^+$ and (right) Cr$^+$ at a depth of 420 Å. A Phi-Evan's Trift-I system was used for the ToF-SIMS experiments: this consists of a liquid metal (Ga$^+$) ion gun for obtaining high mass and high spatial resolutions for chemical imaging. In these experiments, 25-keV Ga$^+$ primary ions were used to generate secondary ions. These ions were separated and detected by a triple-pass 90° spherical sector electrostatic mass analyzer. (Reproduced from Yurt, N., *Leptothrix discophora* SP-6: Effects of biofilms on passive film chemistry of 316L stainless steel and modeling of growth. PhD dissertation, Montana State University, Bozeman, 2002.)

Figure 2.29 shows a set of such squares milled by argon ion sputtering on a surface of 316L stainless steel. ToF-SIMS was used to identify the deposits on the surface.

The spatial resolution of chemical analysis using ToF-SIMS can easily reach the size of individual microorganisms. Figure 2.30 shows a chemical analysis of the surface of one of the squares in Figure 2.29.

2.1.7 Nuclear magnetic resonance imaging

Flow velocity can be successfully measured in biofilms using CSLM velocimetry with fluorescent beads, as described earlier and shown in Figure 2.13, when the flow is steady and parallel to the bottom of the reactor. However, when the flow direction changes vertically, even slightly, the image of the bead disappears because the bead moves out of the thin layer in which objects are rendered in focus in CSLM. Other available techniques for measuring flow velocity distribution near surfaces are difficult to apply in biofilm systems. For example, laser Doppler velocimetry is only useful for measuring flow velocity distribution above the biofilm surface because the laser beam cannot penetrate the biofilm. Attempts to use hot-wire anemometry were entirely unsuccessful, because once the hot-wire probe touched the biofilm or was hit by a piece of biomass detached from the biofilm the measured signal was meaningless and the technique useless. In Chapter 4 we describe the use of a current-limiting electrode to measure flow velocity profiles, but its application is limited to measuring a profile of flow velocity at a single point in the reactor, and the measurement is quite tedious because it requires that the nutrient solution in the reactor be replaced with a solution of an electroactive reagent. The technique of choice for measuring flow velocity in biofilms is nuclear magnetic resonance imaging (NMRI).

NMRI is a popular imaging technique, particularly in medical facilities, where it is often called MRI because of the negative connotation of the word *nuclear* in medicine. The most popular version of the technique is based on imaging protons (^1H) in the liquid state. The nuclei of atoms that have odd numbers of protons or neutrons, such as 1H, 19F, 13C, 31P, and 15N, show magnetic properties and are sensitive to a magnetic field. If placed in a static directional magnetic field, the nuclei align themselves with the lines of the field and precess (wobble) about the lines of the magnetic field with which they have aligned. The frequency of the precession is predictable and given by the Larmor equation:

$$\omega_o = \gamma B_o \tag{2.9}$$

where ω_o is the frequency of precession in megahertz; γ is the gyromagnetic ratio, which for protons is 42.6 MHz/Tesla; and B_o is the strength of the static magnetic field in Tesla.

Precessing protons can absorb energy from external radio frequency (RF) pulses, but only if the pulses are delivered at the Larmor frequency as computed from Equation 2.9. The frequencies of the RF pulses may vary from 1 to 100 MHz. Once protons that were previously in equilibrium positions aligned with static magnetic field B_o absorb energy from a RF pulse, they are tilted away from their equilibrium positions. When the RF pulse is discontinued, they come back to their original positions at equilibrium, and while doing so they dispose of the excess energy they gained from the original RF pulse. This energy is emitted in the form of an RF signal, referred to as the free-induction decay (FID) signal. The strength of the FID signal is related to the density of protons in the volume of the sample. The process of returning to equilibrium is called relaxation, and it is characterized by two parameters: T_1, the longitudinal relaxation time, which reflects the time needed for the nuclei to return to equilibrium, and T_2, the transverse relaxation time, which is the time needed for the FID pulse to decay.

The principle of proton magnetic resonance imaging is using RF pulses to stimulate protons not in the entire volume of a specimen but only in a selected volume, such as a slice of the entire volume. This is accomplished by applying a gradient to static magnetic field B_o. The length of the sample is then exposed to the gradient in the magnetic field, and B_o in Equation 2.9 varies linearly from a maximum on one side of the sample to a minimum on the other side. The actual magnetic field intensity at a given location within the sample, B_o, depends on the position along the gradient, and so does the Larmor frequency, which becomes a function of the position. Because the sample is placed in the magnetic gradient, the applied frequency of the RF pulse stimulates only the protons in the volume (a slice in this case) that is exposed to the relevant intensity of B_o. To stimulate another slice of the sample, a pulse of another RF frequency needs to be used. The radio frequencies used to stimulate protons in separate slices vary linearly; thus it is possible to stimulate slices of the sample sequentially. Once the pulse is discontinued, the FID response is the signal that characterizes the concentration of protons in the individual slice rather than in the entire volume of the specimen. This approach can be further refined by applying gradients of the static magnetic field in more than one direction, which allows selecting not a slice but a small volume, a voxel, of the sample and stimulating protons within it.

If the protons are in a static position within the sample, the FDI signal comes from the same position as where the protons were stimulated by the RF. However, if the protons move, as they do in flowing water, the FDI signal comes from a different position than the one where the protons were stimulated by the original RF pulse. Encoding the distance between these positions and the time elapsed between the RF signal and the FDI response, the flow velocity of the selected voxels can be imaged, basically in any direction. It is instructive to image all three vectors of the flow velocity, but the information from such images is difficult to interpret. Therefore, velocity images provide maps of selected velocity components, typically measured along the main axis of the reactor. The NMRI we used was 2-D; i.e., a slice through the system was selected, and the parameters of interest were imaged in that slice. Images were calculated from the acquired data set through 2-D Fourier transformations of the signals. For the aqueous fluid used in these experiments, a significant time (on the order of 1 s) is required between successive repetitions, so the acquisition of an image using this technique requires that steady flow conditions be maintained for several minutes. NMRI delivers profiles of flow velocity for relatively low flow velocities, on the order of a few centimeters per second. Imaging the distribution of flow velocity using NMRI is an excellent technique, useful for fundamental biofilm research. It has delivered valuable information about biofilm systems performance in controlled conditions in laboratory biofilm reactors. However, the application of the technique to real-life biofilm reactors is severely limited. The most important factors limiting the use of NMRI in larger-scale, real-life reactors are (1) the reactor has to fit into the core of the available instrument, which restricts the size of the reactor, and (2) the reactor cannot have any metal components, which restricts the types of materials that can be used to construct the reactor.

2.1.7.1   Examples of applications

2.1.7.1.1   Example 1: Imaging flow around obstacles.   Measurements were made in a 10-cm-long polycarbonate bioreactor with a cross section 2 mm thick × 25 mm wide. A photograph of this reactor is shown in Figure 3.3 (Chapter 3). A row of four posts near the inlet and a second set of three posts were used to disturb the flow and provide a variety of local fluid mechanical conditions for possible biofilm accumulation. The imaging gradients were chosen to provide an image of the cross section, sensitivity to the axial velocity component, and approximately 0.1 mm of spatial separation between pixels.

Figure 2.31a shows the results of the measurements conducted without biofilm to characterize the reactor and see how the obstacles affected the distribution of the flow in the absence of biofilm. Figure 2.31b shows the flow velocity distribution in the horizontal projection of the reactor. The obstacles shown in Figure 2.31a have an obvious effect on the distribution of flow velocity. The results in Figure 2.31c show the same effect as that shown in Figure 2.31b using lines of the same flow velocity instead of color scale. Images of the flow distribution around obstacles can be superimposed on the pattern of biofilm development in this reactor once it is colonized with microorganisms. Finally, Figure 2.31d quantifies the distribution of flow velocity in the cross section of the reactor transecting the reactor across the row of four posts shown in Figure 2.31a.

2.1.7.1.2   Example 2: Distribution of flow velocity in a reactor with biofilm.   To measure profiles of flow velocity near and within biofilms, reactors similar to that shown in Figure 2.32 are used, but without the posts used as obstacles to the flow pattern.

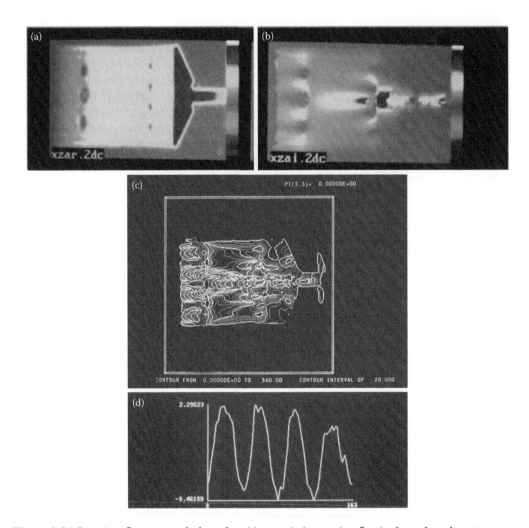

Figure 2.31 Imaging flow around obstacles: (a) a static image (no flow) of a polycarbonate reactor with a row of four posts near the inlet and a second set of three posts, (b) a color map showing a jet flow passing between the second and third posts in the polycarbonate reactor after the flow was initiated and the effects of the posts on the flow distribution, (c) a contour map of the flow shown in b, and (d) the flow velocity distribution around the three posts located in the middle section of the reactor.

Figure 2.32a shows an NMR image of the cross section of such a reactor, and the dark areas near the surface of the reactor are the biofilm. The average thickness of the biofilm in the reactor is 200 μm. The profile of flow velocity in this reactor, shown in Figure 2.32, demonstrates that the average flow velocity reached about 2.4 cm/s and that the flow velocity decreased to zero at the surface, as expected from the nonslip condition in hydrodynamics. What was unexpected in these results was that the flow velocity reached zero at the surface of the reactor, not at the surface of the biofilm. This result helped change the conceptual image of biofilm structure from the model of homogeneous biofilms to that of heterogeneous biofilms: the profile of flow velocity demonstrates water movement within the space occupied by the biofilm. Because the modernized model assumes that biofilms are

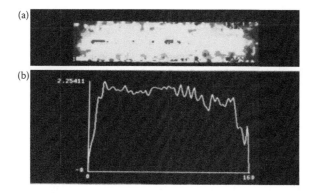

Figure 2.32 (a) A flow velocity field and (b) flow velocity profile measured by NMRI.

made of microcolonies separated by interstitial voids, it is no longer surprising to detect water movement in the space occupied by a biofilm.

The capability of averaging the flow velocity over a slice of the reactor makes NMRI attractive for describing the hydrodynamics in biofilm reactors. However, this very feature, averaging the flow velocity, prevents the use of this technique to address the set of questions about the relations between flow velocity and biofilm activity. A measurement at a scale of resolution comparable with the scale of resolution of the microelectrodes measuring the profiles of nutrient concentration is needed. To some extent, this need has been satisfied by the development of microelectrodes that measure the local mass transport coefficient and the calibration of them to measure local flow velocity.

2.1.7.1.3 Example 3: Distribution of effective diffusivities in biofilm. As biofilm research progresses, biofilm researchers find new applications for NMRI. Recently, a new use for NMRI in biofilm research was demonstrated by the research group led by Paul Majors at the Pacific Northwest National Laboratory: pulsed-field gradient nuclear magnetic resonance (PFG-NMR) for measuring water diffusion in live biofilms. The reactors used for this application are much smaller than those we use for imaging flow velocity. To measure rates of diffusion of water using NMR, the sample is subjected to a series of pulsed magnetic field gradients (PFG) that encode each hydrogen atom's displacement into its signal phase. This displacement information is preserved in the magnitude of the NMR signal, which represents the vector sum of all spins within the volume of measurement. The signal attenuation effects of molecular diffusion are described by the Bloch–Torrey differential equation for transverse magnetization in the presence of a magnetic field gradient (Torrey 1956). The general expression for NMR signal attenuation due to diffusion is given by

$$\ln (M/M_0) = -bD \tag{2.10}$$

where M is the observed NMR signal intensity, M_0 is the signal intensity in the absence of gradients, D is the diffusion coefficient, and b is the diffusion-weighting factor (Le Bihan 1990). The b factor is dependent on the timings (t) and amplitudes (G) of all the gradient pulses and the gyromagnetic ratio (γ) for the nucleus of detection, forming expressions of the general form:

$$b(\gamma, G, T) = \sum \gamma^2 G^2 t^3 \tag{2.11}$$

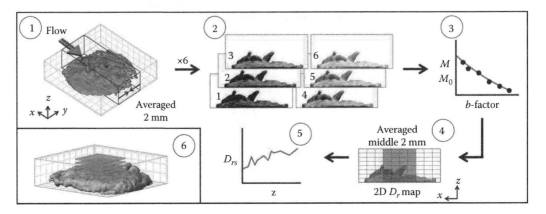

Figure 2.33 Steps for obtaining a diffusion coefficient profile: (1) The experimentally obtained NMR measurements provided averaging in the *y* direction. A 2-mm-thick slab aligned normal to that direction was selected and spatially resolved in the (phase-encoded) *x* and *z* directions. (2) A series of six diffusion-weighted 2-D images was collected, each having a unique *b* factor value. (3) A semi-logarithmic fit was performed to find the diffusion coefficient value for each pixel location. (4) The result is a 2-D (*x-z*) map of effective diffusion coefficients (in which the diffusion rate is modulated by spatial hindrance because of the presence of biomass). (5) To obtain the depth-resolved surface-averaged effective diffusion coefficient profiles, image pixels corresponding to the middle 2 mm of the sample were averaged along the *x*-axis. (6) A 3-D MRI image of the 10-day-old biofilm (yellow slices show the final shape and location of the apparent surface-averaging slices) was used to produce the diffusion coefficient profiles. (Reproduced from Renslow, R. et al., *Biotechnology and Bioengineering* 106: 928–938, 2010.)

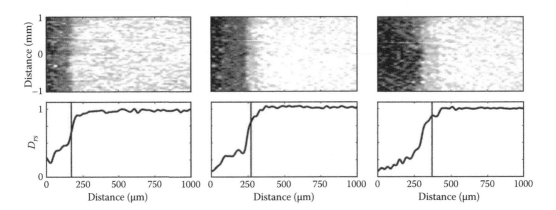

Figure 2.34 Diffusion mapping of a *G. sulfurreducens* biofilm over time. The top row shows 2-D De maps obtained using PFG-NMR, normalized against bulk diffusivity, of the middle 2 mm of the biofilm. The dark regions represent low De. The bottom row shows D_{rs} depth profiles derived by averaging the De of the middle 2 mm of the biofilm (shown in the maps). The top of the biofilm as determined using magnetic resonance imaging is indicated by the vertical lines. From left to right, the panels show the *G. sulfurreducens* biofilm at 24, 35, and 52 days old. (Reproduced from Renslow, R. S. et al., *Energy and Environmental Science*, 6: 595–607, 2013.)

where the sum includes cross product terms for interacting gradient pulses. Thus, by measuring the signal for a variety of b factors, it is possible to solve for D in Equation 2.10. Furthermore, because the NMR signal is spatially dependent in the presence of a gradient magnetic field, it is possible to obtain spatially resolved diffusion coefficient measurements (Figure 2.33).

NMR can be used to determine the diffusion coefficients of water because a substantial majority of the protons in the sample are bound in H_2O molecules (Figure 2.33). Owing to the self-ionization of water, a small fraction of the protons are found as hydronium ions. However, because the NMR signal is proportional to concentration, these hydrated protons ($\sim 10^{-7}$ molar) do not affect the measurement of the water (effective concentration of $\sim 10^2$ molar). Other protons that are present in the sample, such as those in various organic molecules, have a negligible effect because they also have very small concentrations and may be bound in the biofilm matrix or in the microbial cells, which further reduces NMR signal intensity. Therefore it is possible to measure the NMR signal of protons to determine the diffusion coefficients of water using Equation 2.10. The procedure is illustrated in Figure 2.34, which shows a 2-D relative effective diffusion coefficient (D_r) map of the NMR biofilm reactor obtained by PFG-NMR. Using this procedure, we can generate 2-D maps and stratified profiles of diffusivity, as well as profiles of metabolite concentrations. In this example, the diffusion mapping of a *G. sulfurreducens* biofilm over time is shown (Figure 2.34). Because NMR is noninvasive, we can monitor biofilm growth over time as well as generate diffusivity profiles in two dimensions (maps at the top) and surface-averaged profiles (below). Interestingly, these profiles are very similar to those we generated using microelectrodes (see Figure 1.19 for comparison). As expected, diffusivity in biofilms decreased toward the bottom.

References

Chalfie, M., Tu, Y., Euskirchen, G., Ward, W. W., and Prasher, D. C. 1994. Green fluorescent protein as a marker for gene-expression. *Science* 263(5148): 802–805.

Dickinson, W. H., Caccavo, F., and Lewandowski, Z. 1996. The ennoblement of stainless steel by manganic oxide biofouling. *Corrosion Science* 38(8): 1407–1422.

Le Bihan, D. 1990. Magnetic-resonance-imaging of perfusion. *Magnetic Resonance in Medicine* 14: 283–292.

Matz, M. V., Fradkov, A. F., Labas, Y. A., Savitsky, A. P., Zaraisky, A. G., Markelov, M. L., and Lukyanov, S. A. 1999. Fluorescent proteins from nonbioluminescent Anthozoa species. *Nature Biotechnology* 17(10): 969–973.

Prendergast, F. 1978. Chemical and physical-properties of aequorin and green fluorescent protein isolated from *Aequorea forskalea*. *Biochemistry* 17: 3448.

Torrey, H. C. 1956. Bloch equations with diffusion terms. *Physical Review* 104: 563–565.

Suggested readings

Biofilm imaging, microscopy, and characterization

Akiyama, H., Oono, T., Saito, M., and Iwatsuki, K. 2004. Assessment of cadexomer iodine against *Staphylococcus aureus* biofilm in vivo and in vitro using confocal laser scanning microscopy. *Journal of Dermatology* 31: 529–534.

Aldred, N., Ekblad, T., Andersson, O., Liedberg, B., and Clare, A. S. 2011. Real-time quantification of microscale bioadhesion events in situ using Imaging Surface Plasmon Resonance (iSPR). *ACS Applied Materials and Interfaces* 3: 2085–2091.

Alhede, M., Qvortrup, K., Liebrechts, R., Hoiby, N., Givskov, M., and Bjarnsholt, T. 2012. Combination of microscopic techniques reveals a comprehensive visual impression of biofilm structure and composition. *FEMS Immunology and Medical Microbiology* 65: 335–342.

Allan-Wojtas, P., Hildebrand, P. D., Braun, P. G., Smith-King, H. L., Carbyn, S., and Renderos, W. E. 2010. Low temperature and anhydrous electron microscopy techniques to observe the infection process of the bacterial pathogen *Xanthomonas fragariae* on strawberry leaves. *Journal of Microscopy* 239: 249–258.

Amano, A., Nakagawa, I., and Hamada, S. 1999. Studying initial phase of biofilm formation: Molecular interaction of host proteins and bacterial surface components. *Methods in Enzymology* 310: 501–513.

Angell, P. 1999. Understanding microbially influenced corrosion as biofilm-mediated changes in surface chemistry. *Current Opinion in Biotechnology* 10: 269–272.

Aoi, Y., Tsuneda, S., and Hirata, A. 2004. Transition of bacterial spatial organization in a biofilm monitored by FISH and subsequent image analysis. *Water Science and Technology* 49: 365–370.

Apilanez, I., Gutierrez, A., and Diaz, M. 1998. Effect of surface materials on initial biofilm development. *Bioresource Technology* 66: 225–230.

Arnold, J. W., and Bailey, G. W. 2000. Surface finishes on stainless steel reduce bacterial attachment and early biofilm formation: Scanning electron and atomic force microscopy study. *Poultry Science* 79: 1839–1845.

Bozorg, A., Gates, I. D., and Sen, A. 2012. Real time monitoring of biofilm development under flow conditions in porous media. *Biofouling* 28: 937–951.

Bremer, P. J., Geesey, G. G., and Drake, B. 1992. Atomic force microscopy examination of the topography of a hydrated bacterial biofilm on a copper surface. *Current Microbiology* 24: 223–230.

Bridier, A., Briandet, R., Thomas, V., and Dubois-Brissonnet, F. 2011. Resistance of bacterial biofilms to disinfectants: A review. *Biofouling* 27: 1017–1032.

Bryers, J. D. 2001. Two-photon excitation microscopy for analyses of biofilm processes. *Microbial Growth in Biofilms, Part B* 337: 259–269.

Caldwell, D. E., Korber, D. R., and Lawrence, J. R. 1993. Analysis of biofilm formation using 2D vs 3D digital imaging. 1993. *Journal of Applied Bacteriology* 74: S52–S66.

Camargo, G. M. P. A., Pizzolitto, A. C., and Pizzolitto, E. L. 2005. Biofilm formation on catheters used after cesarean section as observed by scanning electron microscopy. *International Journal of Gynecology and Obstetrics* 90: 148–149.

Cao, B., Majors, P. D., Ahmed, B., Renslow, R. S., Silvia, C. P., Shi, L., Kjelleberg, S., Fredrickson, J. K., and Beyenal, H., 2012. Biofilm shows spatially stratified metabolic responses to contaminant exposure. *Environmental Microbiology* 14: 2901–2910.

Cao, B., Shi, L. A., Brown, R. N., Xiong, Y. J., Fredrickson, J. K., Romine, M. F., Marshall, M. J., Lipton, M. S., and Beyenal, H. 2011. Extracellular polymeric substances from Shewanella sp HRCR-1 biofilms: Characterization by infrared spectroscopy and proteomics. *Environmental Microbiology* 13: 1018–1031.

Carpentier, B., and Cerf, O. 2011. Review—Persistence of *Listeria monocytogenes* in food industry equipment and premises. *International Journal of Food Microbiology* 145: 1–8.

Carr, J. H., Anderson, R. L., and Favero, M. S. 1996. Comparison of chemical dehydration and critical point drying for the stabilization and visualization of aging biofilm present on nterior surfaces of PVC distribution pipe. *Journal of Applied Bacteriology* 80: 225–232.

Chen, M. Y., Lee, D. J., Tay, J. H., and Show, K. Y. 2007. Staining of extracellular polymeric substances and cells in bioaggregates. *Applied Microbiology and Biotechnology* 75(2): 467–474.

Claret, C. 1998. A method based on artificial substrates to monitor hyporheic biofilm development. *International Review of Hydrobiology* 83: 135–143.

Cohen, M., Kofonow, J., Nayak, J. V., Palmer, J. N., Chiu, A. G., Leid, J. G., and Cohen, N. A. 2009. Biofilms in chronic rhinosinusitis: A review. *American Journal of Rhinology and Allergy* 23: 255–260.

Cross, S. E., Kreth, J., Zhu, L., Qi, F. X., Pelling, A. E., Shi, W. Y., and Gimzewski, J. K. 2006. Atomic force microscopy study of the structure–function relationships of the biofilm-forming bacterium *Streptococcus mutans*. *Nanotechnology* 17: S1–S7.

Daghighi, S., Sjollema, J., Jaspers, V., de Boer, L., Zaat, S. A. J., Dijkstra, R. J. B., van Dam, G. M., van der Mei, H. C., and Busscher, H. J. 2012. Persistence of a bioluminescent *Staphylococcus aureus* strain on and around degradable and non-degradable surgical meshes in a murine model. *Acta Biomaterialia* 8: 3991–3996.

Daigger, G. T., and Boltz, J. P. 2011. Trickling filter and tickling filter-suspended growth process design and operation: A state-of-the-art review. *Water Environment Research* 83: 388–404.

Daims, H., and Wagner, M. 2011. In situ techniques and digital image analysis methods for quantifying spatial localization patterns of nitrifiers and other microorganisms in biofilm and flocs. *Methods in Enzymology* 46: 185–215.

Darkin, M. G., Gilpin, C., Williams, J. B., and Sangha, C. M. 2001. Direct wet surface imaging of an anaerobic biofilm by environmental scanning electron microscopy: Application to landfill clay liner barriers. *Scanning* 23: 346–350.

Davit, Y., Iltis, G., Debenest, G., Veran-Tissoires, S., Wildenschild, D., Gerino, M., and Quintard, M. 2011. Imaging biofilm in porous media using x-ray computed microtomography. *Journal of Microscopy* 242: 15–25.

Dazzo, F. B. 2012. CMEIAS-aided microscopy of the spatial ecology of individual bacterial interactions involving cell-to-cell communication within biofilms. *Sensors* 12: 7047–7062.

DeVasConCellos, P., Bose, S., Beyenal, H., Bandyopadhyay, A., and Zirkle, L. G. 2012. Antimicrobial particulate silver coatings on stainless steel implants for fracture management. *Materials Science and Engineering C-Materials for Biological Applications* 32: 1112–1120.

Dorobantu, L. S., Goss, G. G., and Burrell, R. E. 2012. Atomic force microscopy: A nanoscopic view of microbial cell surfaces. *Micron* 43: 1312–1322.

Flemming, C. A., Palmer, R. J., Arrage, A. A., van der Mei, H. C., and White, D. C. 1999. Cell surface physico chemistry alters biofilm development of *Pseudomonas aeruginosa* lipopolysaccharide mutants. *Biofouling* 13: 213–231.

Franks, A. E., Nevin, K. P., Jia, H. F., Izallalen, M., Woodard, T. L., and Lovley, D. R. 2009. Novel strategy for three-dimensional real-time imaging of microbial fuel cell communities: Monitoring the inhibitory effects of proton accumulation within the anode biofilm. *Energy and Environmental Science* 2: 113–119.

Fulcher, T. P., Dart, J. K. G., McLaughlin-Borlace, L., Howes, R., Matheson, M., and Cree, I. 2001. Demonstration of biofilm in infections crystalline keratopathy using ruthenium red and electron microscopy. *Ophthalmology* 108: 1088–1092.

Ghafari, S., Hasan, M., and Aroua, M. K. 2008. Bio-electrochemical removal of nitrate from water and wastewater—A review. *Bioresource Technology* 99: 3965–3974.

Giaouris, E., Chorianopoulos, N., and Nychas, G. J. E. 2005. Effect of temperature, pH, and water activity on biofilm formation by *Salmonella enterica* Enteritidis PT4 on stainless steel surfaces as indicated by the bead vortexing method and conductance measurements. *Journal of Food Protection* 68: 2149–2154.

Gilbert, E. S., Khlebnikov, A., Meyer-Ilse, W., and Keasling, J. D. 1999. Use of soft x-ray microscopy for analysis of early-stage biofilm formation. *Water Science and Technology* 39: 269–272.

Gillis, A., Dupres, V., Mahillon, J., and Dufrene, Y. F. 2012. Atomic force microscopy: A powerful tool for studying bacterial swarming motility. *Micron* 43: 1304–1311.

Gjersing, E. L., Codd, S. L., Seymour, J. D., and Stewart, P. S. 2005. Magnetic resonance microscopy analysis of advective transport in a biofilm reactor. *Biotechnology and Bioengineering* 89: 822–834.

Gottenbos, B., van der Mei, H. C., and Busscher, H. J. 1999. Models for studying initial adhesion and surface growth in biofilm formation on surfaces. *Biofilms* 310: 523–534.

Hannig, C., Follo, M., Hellwig, E., and Al-Ahmad, A. 2010. Visualization of adherent micro-organisms using different techniques. *Journal of Medical Microbiology* 59: 1–7.

Harrison-Balestra, C., Cazzaniga, A., Rabassa, A., and Mertz, P. 2001. A wound-isolated pseudomonas aeruginosa grows a biofilm in vitro and is visualized by light microscopy. *Journal of Investigative Dermatology* 117: 436.

Heidrich, M., Kuhnel, M. P., Kellner, M., Lorbeer, R. A., Lange, T., Winkel, A., Stiesch, M., Meyer, H., and Heisterkamp, A. 2011. 3D imaging of biofilms on implants by detection of scattered light with a scanning laser optical tomograph. *Biomedical Optics Express* 2: 2982–2994.

Hidalgo, G., Burns, A., Herz, E., Hay, A. G., Houston, P. L., Wiesner, U., and Lion, L. W. 2009. Functional tomographic fluorescence imaging of pH microenvironments in microbial biofilms by use of silica nanoparticle sensors. *Applied and Environmental Microbiology* 75: 7426–7435.

Hoa, M., Tomovic, S., Nistico, L., Hall-Stoodley, L., Stoodley, P., Sachdeva, L., Berk, R., and Coticchia, J. M. 2009. Identification of adenoid biofilms with middle ear pathogens in otitis-prone children utilizing SEM and FISH. *International Journal of Pediatric Otorhinolaryngology* 73: 1242–1248.

Holman, H. Y. N., Miles, R., Hao, Z., Wozei, E., Anderson, L. M., and Yang, H. 2009. Real-time chemical imaging of bacterial activity in biofilms using open-channel microfluidics and synchrotron FTIR spectromicroscopy. *Analytical Chemistry* 81: 8564–8570.

Homan, N. M., Venne, B., and Van As, H. 2010. Flow characteristics and exchange in complex biological systems as observed by pulsed-field-gradient magnetic-resonance imaging. *Physical Review E* 82: 026310.

Hu, Y. F., Zhang, J. D., and Ulstrup, J. 2011. Investigation of *Streptococcus mutans* biofilm growth on modified Au(111)-surfaces using AFM and electrochemistry. *Journal of Electroanalytical Chemistry* 656: 41–49.

Hwang, B. K., Lee, W. N., Yeon, K. M., Park, P. K., Lee, C. H., Chang, I. S., Drews, A., and Kraume, M. 2008. Correlating TMP increases with microbial characteristics in the bio-cake on the membrane surface in a membrane bioreactor. *Environmental Science and Technology* 42: 3963–3968.

Iltis, G. C., Armstrong, R. T., Jansik, D. P., Wood, B. D., and Wildenschild, D. 2011. Imaging biofilm architecture within porous media using synchrotron-based x-ray computed microtomography. *Water Resources Research* 47: W20601.

Ivanovic, I., and Leiknes, T. O. 2012. The biofilm membrane bioreactor (BF-MBR)—A review. *Desalination and Water Treatment* 37: 288–295.

Ivleva, N. P., Wagner, M., Szkola, A., Horn, H., Niessner, R., and Haisch, C. 2010. Label-free in situ SERS imaging of biofilms. *Journal of Physical Chemistry B* 114: 10184–10194.

Jean, J. S., Tsao, C. W., and Chung, M. C. 2004. Comparative endoscopic and SEM analyses and imaging for biofilm, growth on porous quartz sand. *Biogeochemistry* 70: 427–445.

Johnson, M. A., and Ross, J. M. 2008. Staphylococcal presence alters thrombus formation under physiological shear conditions in whole blood studies. *Annals of Biomedical Engineering* 36: 349–355.

Jorge, P., Lourenco, A., and Pereira, M. O. 2012. New trends in peptide-based anti-biofilm strategies: A review of recent achievements and bioinformatic approaches. *Biofouling* 28: 1033–1061.

Kamjunke, N., Spohn, U., Futing, M., Wagner, G., Scharf, E. M., Sandrock, S., and Zippel, B. 2012. Use of confocal laser scanning microscopy for biofilm investigation on paints under field conditions. *International Biodeterioration and Biodegradation* 69: 17–22.

Karcz, J., Bernas, T., Nowak, A., Talik, E., and Woznica, A. 2012. Application of lyophilization to prepare the nitrifying bacterial biofilm for imaging with scanning electron microscopy. *Scanning* 34: 26–36.

Karunakaran, E., Mukherjee, J., Ramalingam, B., and Biggs, C. A. 2011. "Biofilmology": A multidisciplinary review of the study of microbial biofilms. *Applied Microbiology and Biotechnology* 90: 1869–1881.

Karygianni, L., Follo, M., Hellwig, E., Burghardt, D., Wolkewitz, M., Anderson, A., and Al-Ahmad, A. 2012. Microscope-based imaging platform for large-scale analysis of oral biofilms. *Applied and Environmental Microbiology* 78: 8703–8711.

Kielemoes, J., Bultinck, I., Storms, H., Boon, N., and Verstraete, W. 2002. Occurrence of manganese-oxidizing microorganisms and manganese deposition during biofilm formation on stainless steel in a brackish surface water. *FEMS Microbiology Ecology* 39: 41–55.

Kim, T. G., Yi, T., Lee, E. H., Ryu, H. W., and Cho, K. S. 2012. Characterization of a methane-oxidizing biofilm using microarray, and confocal microscopy with image and geostatic analyses. *Applied Microbiology and Biotechnology* 95: 1051–1059.

Kodjikian, L., Burillon, C., Lina, G., Roques, C., Pellon, G., Freney, J., and Renaud, F. N. R. 2003. Biofilm formation on Intraocular lenses by a clinical strain encoding the ica locus: A scanning electron microscopy study. *Investigative Ophthalmology and Visual Science* 44: 4382–4387.

Koley, D., Ramsey, M. M., Bard, A. J., and Whiteley, M. 2011. Discovery of a biofilm electrocline using real-time 3D metabolite analysis. *Proceedings of the National Academy of Sciences of the United States of America* 108: 19996–20001.

Larsen, P., Olesen, B. H., Nielsen, P. H., and Nielsen, J. L. 2008. Quantification of lipids and protein in thin biofilms by fluorescence staining. *Biofouling* 24: 241–250.

Lasa, I., and Penades, J. R. 2006. Bap: A family of surface proteins involved in biofilm formation. *Research in Microbiology* 157: 99–107.

Lenton, P., Rudney, J., Chen, R. Q., Fok, A., Aparicio, C., and Jones, R. S. 2012. Imaging in vivo secondary caries and ex vivo dental biofilms using cross-polarization optical coherence tomography. *Dental Materials* 28: 792–800.

Lenz, A. P., Williamson, K. S., Pitts, B., Stewart, P. S., and Franklin, M. J. 2008. Localized gene expression in *Pseudomonas aeruginosa* biofilms. *Applied and Environmental Microbiology* 74: 4463–4471.

Lerchner, J., Wolf, A., Buchholz, F., Mertens, F., Neu, T. R., Harms, H., and Maskow, T. 2008. Miniaturized calorimetry—A new method for real-time biofilm activity analysis. *Journal of Microbiological Methods* 74: 74–81.

Lim, J., Lee, K. M., Kim, S. H., Nam, S. W., Oh, Y. A., Yun, H. S., Jo, W., Oh, S., Kim, S. R., and Park, S. 2008. Nanoscale characterization of *Escherichia coli* biofilm formed under laminar flow using atomic force microscopy (AFM) and scanning electron microscopy (SEM). *Bulletin of the Korean Chemical Society* 29: 2114–2118.

Loehfelm, T. W., Luke, N. R., and Campagnari, A. A. 2008. Identification and characterization of an *Acinetobacter baumannii* biofilm-associated protein. *Journal of Bacteriology* 190: 1036–1044.

Lorenz, U., Schafer, T., Ohlsen, K., Tiurbe, G. C., Buhler, C., Germer, C. T., and Kellersmann, R. 2011. In vivo detection of *Staphylococcus aureus* in biofilm on vascular prostheses using non-invasive biophotonic imaging. *European Journal of Vascular and Endovascular Surgery* 41: 68–75.

Maddula, V. S. R. K., Pierson, E. A., and Pierson, L. S. 2008. Altering the ratio of phenazines in *Pseudomonas chlororaphis* (aureofaciens) strain 30-84: Effects on biofilm formation and pathogen inhibition. *Journal of Bacteriology* 190: 2759–2766.

Maeyama, R., Mizunoe, Y., Anderson, J. M., Tanaka, M., and Matsuda, T. 2004. Confocal imaging of biofilm formation process using fluoroprobed *Escherichia coli* and fluoro-stained exopolysaccharide. *Journal of Biomedical Materials Research Part A* 70A: 274–282.

Manz, B., Volke, F., Goll, D., and Horn, H. 2005. Investigation of biofilm structure, flow patterns and detachment with magnetic resonance imaging. *Water Science and Technology* 52: 1–6.

Manz, B., Volke, F., Goll, D., and Horn, H. 2003. Measuring local flow velocities and biofilm structure in biofilm systems with magnetic resonance imaging (MRI). *Biotechnology and Bioengineering* 84: 424–432.

McLean, J. S., Majors, P. D., Reardon, C. L., Bilskis, C. L., Reed, S. B., Romine, M. F., and Fredrickson, J. K. 2008. Investigations of structure and metabolism within *Shewanella oneidensis* MR-1 biofilms. *Journal of Microbiological Methods* 74: 47–56.

McLean, J. S., Wanger, G., Gorby, Y. A., Wainstein, M., McQuaid, J., Ishii, S. I., Bretschger, O., Beyenal, H., and Nealson, K. H. 2010. Quantification of electron transfer rates to a solid phase electron acceptor through the stages of biofilm formation from single cells to multicellular communities. *Environmental Science and Technology* 44: 2721–2727.

Milferstedt, K., Pons, M. N., and Morgenroth, E. 2008. Textural fingerprints: A comprehensive descriptor for biofilm structure development. *Biotechnology and Bioengineering* 100: 889–901.

Monds, R. D., and O'Toole, G. A. 2009. The developmental model of microbial biofilms: Ten years of a paradigm up for review. *Trends in Microbiology* 17: 73–87.

Muli, F. W., Struthers, J. K., and Tarpey, P. A. 1999. Electron microscopy studies on *Gardnerella vaginalis* grown in conventional and biofilm systems. *Journal of Medical Microbiology* 48: 211–213.

Navarro, G., Peach, K. C., Cheng, A., Bray, W. M., Yildiz, F. H., and Linington, R. G. 2012. An image-based 384-well high-throughput screening method for phenotypic discovery of biofilm inhibitors in *Pseudomonas aeruginosa*. *Planta Medica* 78: 1104–1105.

Neu, T. R., Manz, B., Volke, F., Dynes, J. J., Hitchcock, A. P., and Lawrence, J. R. 2010. Advanced imaging techniques for assessment of structure, composition and function in biofilm systems. *FEMS Microbiology Ecology* 72: 1–21.

Neu, T. R., Woelfl, S., and Lawrence, J. R. 2004. Three-dimensional differentiation of photo-autotrophic biofilm constituents by multi-channel laser scanning microscopy (single-photon and two-photon excitation). *Journal of Microbiological Methods* 56: 161–172.

Neut, D., Dijkstra, R. J. B., Thompson, J. I., van der Mei, H. C., and Busscher, H. J. 2012. A gentamicin-releasing coating for cementless hip prostheses—Longitudinal evaluation of efficacy using in vitro bio-optical imaging and its wide-spectrum antibacterial efficacy. *Journal of Biomedical Materials Research Part A* 100A: 3220–3226.

Nott, K. P., Heese, F. P., Hall, L. D., Macaskie, L. E., and Paterson-Beedle, M. 2005. Measurement of flow field in biofilm reactors by 3-D magnetic resonance imaging. *AIChE Journal* 51: 3072–3079.

Nott, K. P., Heese, F. P., Paterson-Beedle, M., Macaskie, L. E., and Hall, L. D. 2005. Visualization of the function of a biofilm reactor by magnetic resonance imaging. *Canadian Journal of Chemical Engineering* 83: 68–72.

Nott, K. P., Paterson-Beedle, M., Macaskie, L. E., and Hall, L. D. 2001. Visualisation of metal deposition in biofilm reactors by three-dimensional magnetic resonance imaging (MRI). *Biotechnology Letters* 23: 1749–1757.

Nunez, M. E., Martin, M. O., Chan, P. H., and Spain, E. M. 2005. Predation, death, and survival in a biofilm: Bdellovibrio investigated by atomic force microscopy. *Colloids and Surfaces B-Biointerfaces* 42: 263–271.

Packroff, G., Lawrence, J. R., and Neu, T. R. 2002. In situ confocal laser scanning microscopy of protozoans in cultures and complex biofilm communities. *Acta Protozoologica* 41: 245–253.

Palmer, R. J., Park, J., Pedraza, A. J., Suci, P., Geesey, G., Kolenbrander, P. E., and White, D. C. 1998. Flowcell for combined FTIR spectroscopy confocal microscopy applied to oral biofilm research. *Journal of Dental Research* 77: 287.

Palmer, R. J., and Sternberg, C. 1999. Modern microscopy in biofilm research: Confocal microscopy and other approaches. *Current Opinion in Biotechnology* 10: 263–268.

Pamp, S. J., Sternberg, C., and Tolker-Nielsen, T. 2009. Insight into the microbial multicellular lifestyle via flow-cell technology and confocal microscopy. *Cytometry Part A* 75A: 90–103.

Pasmore, M., Todd, P., Pfiefer, B., Rhodes, M., and Bowman, C. N. 2002. Effect of polymer surface properties on the reversibility of attachment of *Pseudomonas aeruginosa* in the early stages of biofilm development. *Biofouling* 18: 65–71.

Pasmore, M., Todd, P., Smith, S., Baker, D., Silverstein, J., Coons, D., and Bowman, C. N. 2001. Effects of ultrafiltration membrane surface properties on *Pseudomonas aeruginosa* biofilm initiation for the purpose of reducing biofouling. 2001. *Journal of Membrane Science* 194: 15–32.

Paterson-Beedle, M., Nott, K. P., Macaskie, L. E., and Hall, L. D. 2001. Study of biofilm within a packed-bed reactor by three-dimensional magnetic resonance imaging. *Microbial Growth in Biofilms, Part B* 337: 285–305.

Pecharki, D., Petersen, F. C., Assev, S., and Scheie, A. A. 2005. Involvement of antigen I/II surface proteins in *Streptococcus mutans* and *Streptococcus intermedius* biofilm formation. *Oral Microbiology and Immunology* 20: 366–371.

Peltola, M., Neu, T. R., Raulio, M., Kolari, M., and Salkinoja-Salonen, M. S. 2008. Architecture of *Deinococcus geothermalis* biofilms on glass and steel: A lectin study. *Environmental Microbiology* 10: 1752–1759.

Percival, S. L., Hill, K. E., Williams, D. W., Hooper, S. J., Thomas, D. W., and Costerton, J. W. 2012. A review of the scientific evidence for biofilms in wounds. *Wound Repair and Regeneration* 20: 647–657.

Phipps, D., Rodriguez, G., and Ridgway, H. 1999. Deconvolution fluorescence microscopy for observation and analysis of membrane biofilm architecture. *Biofilms* 310: 178–194.

Qian, Z., Stoodley, P., and Pitt, W. G. 1996. Effect of low-intensity ultrasound upon biofilm structure from confocal scanning laser microscopy observation. *Biomaterials* 17: 1975–1980.

Read, R. R., Eberwein, P., Dasgupta, M. K., Grant, S. K., Lam, K., Nickel, J. C., and Costerton, J. W. 1989. Peritonitis in peritoneal-dialysis—Bacterial-colonization by biofilm spread along the catheter surface. *Kidney International* 35: 614–621.

Renslow, R. S., Majors, P. D., McLean, J. S., Fredrickson, J. K., Ahmed, B., and Beyenal, H. 2010. In situ effective diffusion coefficient profiles in live biofilms using pulsed-field gradient nuclear magnetic resonance. *Biotechnology and Bioengineering* 106: 928–937.

Rodrigues, A. C., Wuertz, S., Brito, A. G., and Melo, L. F. 2003. Three-dimensional distribution of GFP-labeled *Pseudomonas putida* during biofilm formation on solid PAHs assessed by confocal laser scanning microscopy. *Water Science and Technology* 47: 139–142.

Sanford, B. A., de Feijter, A. W., Wade, M. H., and Thomas, V. L. 1996. A dual fluorescence technique for visualization of *Staphylococcus epidermidis* biofilm using scanning confocal laser microscopy. *Journal of Industrial Microbiology* 16: 48–56.

Sanford, B. A., Thomas, V. L., Mattingly, S. J., Ramsay, M. A., and Miller, M. M. 1995. Lectin-biotin assay for slime present in in-situ biofilm produced by *Staphylococcus epidermidis* using transmission electron-microscopy (TEM). *Journal of Industrial Microbiology* 15: 156–161.

Schaudinn, C., Carr, G., Gorur, A., Jaramillo, D., Costerton, J. W., and Webster, P. 2009. Imaging of endodontic biofilms by combined microscopy (FISH/cLSM–SEM). *Journal of Microscopy-Oxford* 235: 124–127.

Schmid, T., Burkhard, J., Yeo, B. S., Zhang, W. H., and Zenobi, R. 2008. Towards chemical analysis of nanostructures in biofilms I: Imaging of biological nanostructures. *Analytical and Bioanalytical Chemistry* 391: 1899–1905.

Semechko, A., Sudarsan, R., Bester, E., Dony, R., and Eberl, H. J. 2011. Influence of light attenuation on biofilm parameters evaluated from CLSM image data. *Journal of Medical and Biological Engineering* 31: 135–143.

Seth, A. K., Geringer, M. R., Hong, S. J., Leung, K. P., Mustoe, T. A., and Galiano, R. D. 2012. In vivo modeling of biofilm-infected wounds: A review. *Journal of Surgical Research* 178: 330–338.

Seymour, J. D., Codd, S. L., Gjersing, E. L., and Stewart, P. S. 2004. Magnetic resonance microscopy of biofilm structure and impact on transport in a capillary bioreactor. *Journal of Magnetic Resonance* 167: 322–327.

Sich, H., and Van Rijn, J. 1997. Scanning electron microscopy of biofilm formation in denitrifying, fluidised bed reactors. *Water Research* 31: 733–742.

Simoes, M., Simoes, L. C., and Vieira, M. J. 2010. A review of current and emergent biofilm control strategies. *LWT-Food Science and Technology* 43: 573–583.

Singhal, D., Boase, S., Field, J., Jardeleza, C., Foreman, A., and Wormald, P. J. 2012. Quantitative analysis of in vivo mucosal bacterial biofilms. *International Forum of Allergy and Rhinology* 2: 57–62.

Sjollema, J., Sharma, P. K., Dijkstra, R. J. B., van Dam, G. M., van der Mei, H. C., Engelsman, A. F., and Busscher, H. J. 2010. The potential for bio-optical imaging of biomaterial-associated infection in vivo. *Biomaterials* 31: 1984–1995.

Staal, M., Borisov, S. M., Rickelt, L. F., Klimant, I., and Kuhl, M. 2011a. Ultrabright planar optodes for luminescence life-time based microscopic imaging of O-2 dynamics in biofilms. *Journal of Microbiological Methods* 85: 67–74.

Staal, M., Prest, E. I., Vrouwenvelder, J. S., Rickelt, L. F., and Kuhl, M. 2011b. A simple optode based method for imaging O-2 distribution and dynamics in tap water biofilms. *Water Research* 45: 5027–5037.

Stewart, P. S. 2012. Mini-review: Convection around biofilms. *Biofouling* 28: 187–198.

Subramani, K., Jung, R. E., Molenberg, A., and Hammerle, C. H. F. 2009. Biofilm on dental implants: A review of the literature. *International Journal of Oral and Maxillofacial Implants* 24: 616–626.

Suci, P. A., Siedlecki, K. J., Palmer, R. J., White, D. C., and Geesey, G. G. 1997. Combined light microscopy and attenuated total reflection Fourier transform infrared spectroscopy for integration of biofilm structure, distribution, and chemistry at solid–liquid interfaces. *Applied and Environmental Microbiology* 63: 4600–4603.

Sun, C., Fiksdal, L., Hanssen-Bauer, A., Rye, M. B., and Leiknes, T. 2011. Characterization of membrane biofouling at different operating conditions (flux) in drinking water treatment using confocal laser scanning microscopy (CLSM) and image analysis. *Journal of Membrane Science* 382: 194–201.

Swope, K. L., and Flicklinger, M. C. 1996. The use of confocal scanning laser microscopy and other tools to characterize Escherichia coli in a high-cell-density synthetic biofilm. *Biotechnology and Bioengineering* 52: 340–356.

Szymanska, J., and Sitkowska, J. 2012. Bacterial hazards in a dental office: An update review. *African Journal of Microbiology Research* 6: 1642–1650.

Tendolkar, P. M., Baghdayan, A. S., Gilmore, M. S., and Shankar, N. 2004. Enterococcal surface protein, Esp, enhances biofilm formation by *Enterococcus faecalis*. 2004. *Infection and Immunity* 72: 6032–6039.

Thomas, J., Levos, K., Wratchford, R., Luong, N., and Crout, R. 2000. 3-D biofilm patterns in peri-odontal diseases defined by confocal microscopy. *Journal of Dental Research* 79: 483.

Thrash, J. C., and Coates, J. D. 2008. Review: Direct and indirect electrical stimulation of microbial metabolism. *Environmental Science and Technology* 42: 3921–3931.

Thurnheer, T., Gmur, R., and Guggenheim, B. 2002. Analysis of a six-species biofilm model using fluorescent oligonucleotide probes and confocal laser scanning microscopy. *Journal of Dental Research* 81: A393.

Van Houdt, R., and Michiels, C. W. 2005. Role of bacterial cell surface structures in *Escherichia coli* biofilm formation. *Research in Microbiology* 156: 626–633.

van Merode, A. E. J., van der Mei, H. C., Busscher, H. J., and Krom, B. P. 2006. Influence of culture heterogeneity in cell surface charge on adhesion and biofilm formation by *Enterococcus faecalis*. *Journal of Bacteriology* 188: 2421–2426.

Venkata, H. N. N., Nomura, N., and Shigeto, S. 2011. Leucine pools in *Escherichia coli* biofilm discov-ered by Raman imaging. *Journal of Raman Spectroscopy* 42: 1913–1915.

Von Ohle, C., Mack, A., Drews, U., and Brecx, M. 2003. Early stages of dental biofilm formation assessed by confocal microscopy. *Journal of Dental Research* 82: 510.

Waharte, F., Steenkeste, K., Briandet, R., and Fontaine-Aupart, M. P. 2010. Diffusion measurements inside biofilms by image-based fluorescence recovery after photobleaching (FRAP) analysis with a commercial confocal laser scanning microscope. *Applied and Environmental Microbiology* 76: 5860–5869.

Walker, J. T., Hanson, K., Caldwell, D., and Keevil, C. W. 1998. Scanning confocal laser microscopy study of biofilm induced corrosion on copper plumbing tubes. *Biofouling* 12: 333.

Wells, J., Gonzalez-Cabezas, C., and Miller, C. 1999. Scanning electron microscope monitoring of a dental unit waterline biofilm formation model. *Scanning* 21: 169.

Wirtanen, G., Alanko, T., and Mattila-Sandholm, T. 1996. Evaluation of epifluorescence image analy-sis of biofilm growth on stainless steel surfaces. *Colloids and Surfaces B-Biointerfaces* 5: 319–326.

Wirtanen, G., and Mattila-Sandholm, T. 1993. Epifluorescence image-analysis and cultivation of food-borne biofilm bacteria grown on stainless-steel surfaces. *Journal of Food Protection* 56: 678–683.

Yawata, Y., Toda, K., Setoyama, E., Fukuda, J., Suzuki, H., Uchiyama, H., and Nomura, N. 2010. Monitoring biofilm development in a microfluidic device using modified confocal reflection microscopy. *Journal of Bioscience and Bioengineering* 110: 377–380.

Zaura-Arite, E., van Marle, J., and ten Cate, J. M. 2001. Confocal microscopy study of undisturbed and chlorhexidine-treated dental biofilm. *Journal of Dental Research* 80: 1436–1440.

Zhang, W., Sileika, T. S., Chen, C., Liu, Y., Lee, J., and Packman, A. I. 2011. A novel planar flow cell for studies of biofilm heterogeneity and flow-biofilm interactions. *Biotechnology and Bioengineering* 108: 2571–2582.

Biofilm monitoring

Aoi, Y., Shiramasa, Y., Tsuneda, S., Hirata, A., Kitayama, A., and Nagamune, T. 2002. Real-time moni-toring of ammonia-oxidizing activity in a nitrifying biofilm by amoA mRNA analysis. *Water Science and Technology* 46: 439–442.

Benbouzidrollet, N. D., Conte, M., Guezennec, J., and Prieur, D. 1991. Monitoring of a *Vibrio natrie-gens* and *Desulfovibrio vulgaris* marine aerobic biofilm on a stainless-steel surface in a laboratory tubular flow system. *Journal of Applied Bacteriology* 71: 244–251.

Boe-Hansen, R., Martiny, A. C., Arvin, E., and Albrechtsen, H. J. 2003. Monitoring biofilm forma-tion and activity in drinking water distribution networks under oligotrophic conditions. *Water Science and Technology* 47: 91–97.

Bozorg, A., Gates, I. D., and Sen, A. 2012. Real time monitoring of biofilm development under flow conditions in porous media. *Biofouling* 28: 937–951.

Cloete, T. E., and Maluleke, M. R. 2005. The use of the rotoscope as an online, real-time, non-destructive biofilm monitor. *Water Science and Technology* 52: 211–216.

Giao, M. S., Montenegro, M. I., and Vieira, M. J. 2003. Monitoring biofilm formation by using cyclic voltammetry—Effect of the experimental conditions on biofilm removal and activity. *Water Science and Technology* 47: 51–56.

Gjaltema, A., and Griebe, T. 1995. Laboratory biofilm reactors and on-line monitoring: Report of the discussion session. *Water Science and Technology* 32: 257–261.

Helle, H., Vuoriranta, P., Valimaki, H., Lekkala, J., and Aaltonen, V. 2000. Monitoring of biofilm growth with thickness-shear mode quartz resonators in different flow and nutrition conditions. *Sensors and Actuators B-Chemical* 71: 47–54.

Jass, J., O'Neill, J. G., and Walker, J. T. 2001. Direct biofilm monitoring by a capacitance measurement probe in continuous culture chemostats. *Microbial Growth in Biofilms, Part B* 337: 63–70.

Kadurugamuwa, J. L., Sin, L., Albert, E., Yu, J., Francis, K., DeBoer, M., Rubin, M., Bellinger-Kawahara, C., Parr, T. R., and Contag, P. R. 2003. Direct continuous method for monitoring biofilm infection in a mouse model. *Infection and Immunity* 71: 882–890.

Kadurugamuwa, J. L., Sin, L. V., Yu, J., Francis, K. P., Kimura, R., Purchio, T., and Contag, P. R. 2003. Rapid direct method for monitoring antibiotics in a mouse model of bacterial biofilm infection. *Antimicrobial Agents and Chemotherapy* 47: 3130–3137.

Kadurugamuwa, J. L., Sin, L. V., Yu, J., Francis, K. P., Purchio, T. F., and Contag, P. R. 2004. Noninvasive optical imaging method to evaluate postantibiotic effects on biofilm infection in vivo. *Antimicrobial Agents and Chemotherapy* 48: 2283–2287.

Kjellerup, B. V., Veeh, R. H., Sumithraratne, P., Thomsen, T. R., Buckingham-Meyer, K., Frolund, B., and Sturman, P. 2005. Monitoring of microbial souring in chemically treated, produced-water biofilm systems using molecular techniques. *Journal of Industrial Microbiology and Biotechnology* 32: 163–170.

Leitz, M., Tamachkiarow, A., Franke, H., and Grattan, K. T. V. 2002. Monitoring of biofilm growth using ATR-leaky mode spectroscopy. *Journal of Physics D-Applied Physics* 35: 55–60.

Lewandowski, Z., and Beyenal, H. 2003. Biofilm monitoring: A perfect solution in search of a problem. *Water Science and Technology* 47: 9–18.

Lin, H., Ong, S. L., Ng, W. J., and Khan, E. 2004. Monitoring of bacterial morphology for controlling filamentous overgrowth in an ultracompact biofilm reactor. *Water Environment Research* 76: 413–424.

Milferstedt, K., Pons, M. N., and Morgenroth, E. 2006. Optical method for long-term and large-scale monitoring of spatial biofilm development. *Biotechnology and Bioengineering* 94: 773–782.

Mollica, A., and Cristiani, P. 2003. On-line biofilm monitoring by "BIOX" electrochemical probe. *Water Science and Technology* 47: 45–49.

Pereira, M. O., Morin, P., Vieira, M. J., and Melo, L. F. 2002. A versatile reactor for continuous monitoring of biofilm properties in laboratory and industrial conditions. *Letters in Applied Microbiology* 34: 22–26.

Pons, M. N., Milferstedt, K., and Morgenroth, E. 2009. Biofilm monitoring on rotating discs by image analysis. *Biotechnology and Bioengineering* 103: 105–116.

Tamachkiarow, A., and Flemming, H. C. 2003. On-line monitoring of biofilm formation in a brewery water pipeline system with a fibre optical device. *Water Science and Technology* 47: 19–24.

Wolf, G., Almeida, J. S., Crespo, J. G., and Reis, M. A. M. 2003. Monitoring of biofilm reactors using natural fluorescence fingerprints. *Water Science and Technology* 47: 161–167.

Yawata, Y., Toda, K., Setoyama, E., Fukuda, J., Suzuki, H., Uchiyama, H., and Nomura, N. 2010. Monitoring biofilm development in a microfluidic device using modified confocal reflection microscopy. *Journal of Bioscience and Bioengineering* 110: 377–380.

Yu, J., Wu, J., Francis, K. P., Purchio, T. F., and Kadurugamuwa, J. L. 2005. Monitoring in vivo fitness of rifampicin-resistant *Staphylococcus aureus* mutants in a mouse biofilm infection model. *Journal of Antimicrobial Chemotherapy* 55: 528–534.

Zinn, M. S., Kirkegaard, R. D., Palmer, R. J., and White, D. C. 1999. Laminar flow chamber for continuous monitoring of biofilm formation and succession. *Biofilms* 310: 224–232.

chapter three

Laboratory biofilm reactors and their applications

3.1   Introduction

In Chapter 1, biofilm reactors were defined as biofilm systems in which biofilm processes are controlled and/or measurements are performed to quantify these processes. Biofilm reactors can be natural or engineered: examples of natural biofilm reactors are lakes, rivers, and wetlands, and examples of engineered biofilm reactors are constructed wetlands, packed-bed reactors (PBRs), and trickling filters used in wastewater treatment plants. Many biofilm processes occurring in natural biofilm reactors can be imitated in the laboratory by constructing and operating suitable laboratory biofilm reactors (LBRs). Although many biofilm processes occurring in natural biofilm reactors can be imitated in LBRs, the complexity of the interactions among the various compartments of the natural biofilm reactors is usually compromised in LBRs, and this effect should be taken into consideration when the results of biofilm studies using LBRs are interpreted.

A variety of LBRs are typically used in research, and each of them has unique features that make it more suitable for some types of measurements and observations, but also less suitable for other types of measurements and observations. There are no universal LBRs that can satisfy all biofilm researchers and be suitable for all biofilm studies. LBRs that are used to quantify the effects of hydrodynamics on microbial activity in biofilms may not be suitable for quantifying biofilm structure using confocal microscopy and image analysis. LBRs are constructed to satisfy two requirements: (1) to facilitate the biofilm processes under study and (2) to facilitate the measurements characterizing the processes under study. By selecting an LBR for a particular study, the researcher makes several choices, consciously or not, such as which biofilm processes will be emphasized and which will be compromised, and which measurements will be possible and which will not. LBRs imitate various functions of natural biofilm reactors and offer the benefit of studying biofilm processes in isolation, but this benefit also imposes limitations on the relevance of the results, which are directly affected by the choices made by selecting the reactor and the experimental conditions. It is important to be aware of these limitations, even if the researcher later chooses to ignore some of them.

The terminology used here includes "relevance of the results." This is defined as the extent to which the results of a biofilm study in an LBR reflect the performance of natural and engineered biofilm reactors. The term *relevance of the results* reminds us that the results of a study in an LBR depend on the choices made with respect to the reactor and experimental conditions and that the results of biofilm studies in LBRs do not necessarily reflect the process in the natural or engineered reactors faithfully. By definition, the study of biofilm processes in LBRs, in isolation from their natural environment, limits the relevance of the results. Natural and engineered biofilm processes depend on complex interactions among the four compartments of the biofilm system: the surface, the biofilm, the solution of nutrients, and the gas phase. LBRs are not always able to reproduce these interactions faithfully. This inherent limitation imposed on the relevance of the results by studying biofilm processes in LBRs is magnified by the common desire of biofilm researchers to isolate the variables in biofilm processes and quantify the isolated effects of selected variables on selected processes, such as the effect of nutrient concentration on the rate of biofilm accumulation. Each attempt to isolate variables should be scrutinized for the effect it has on the relevance of the results, because attempts to isolate variables may compromise the interactions among the various compartments in biofilm reactors: rarely can one variable be manipulated in a biofilm reactor in isolation from other variables. Often, changing one variable causes a sequence of events—a domino effect—and the consequences of changing one variable may affect the biofilm process under study in a more complex manner than that expected and intended.

For example, changing the concentration of the growth-limiting nutrient in an attempt to change the microbial growth rate in a biofilm starts a chain of events that affects several variables besides the one intended (the growth rate). It changes the depth to which the growth-limiting nutrient penetrates into the biofilm, pH, oxygen concentration profile, and concentration profiles of all nutrients in the biofilm. In effect, changing the concentration of the growth-limiting nutrient changes the microbial growth rate, as intended, but also changes other biofilm processes in the reactor, and the results of the study may be more complex than those expected.

The intended and unintended consequences of interfering with biofilm processes are obviously an important aspect of biofilm control. The researcher interferes with biofilm processes by changing variables of these processes and evaluates the effects of these changes by quantifying other variables. To discuss the effects of the choices made when designing a biofilm study and the level of necessary interference in biofilm processes in such studies, the variables used to describe the performance of LBRs are divided into two groups: controlled variables and measured variables.

3.2   Variables in biofilm reactors

3.2.1   Types of variables

The variables are the factors affecting biofilm processes that are quantified in biofilm reactors. Examples of variables in biofilm processes are the concentration of the growth-limiting nutrient and the retention time. For practical reasons, it is convenient to distinguish two types of variables in biofilm reactors: (1) *controlled variables* and (2) *measured variables*. This terminology coincides with the terminology accepted in control theory, in which controllability and measurability are defined and evaluated. The terms controlled variables and measured variables are self-explanatory. The controlled variables are the factors affecting biofilm processes that the researcher decided to manipulate in the LBR, such as the retention time, nutrient concentration, and temperature. The measured variables are the factors that the researcher decided to measure in the LBR, such as the biofilm activity and biofilm thickness. The distinction between controlled and measured variables may be blurry on occasion. The decision whether a particular factor should be considered a controlled variable or a measured variable is made by the operator, and this decision is not irreversible. For example, the operator may use the concentration of the growth-limiting nutrient in the influent as a controlled variable, and then change his mind and decide to measure it.

These controversies arise when the selection of variables in general is discussed. In specific cases, it is usually easy to decide which variables are to be controlled and which are to be measured. Dividing the factors affecting biofilm processes into two groups—controlled and measured variables—makes it possible to define the goal of biofilm studies as finding functions relating the selected controlled variables to the selected measured variables. This goal of biofilm studies corresponds to the goal of biofilm engineering, which is to control biofilm processes. Going even further, and imitating the terminology used in mathematical analysis, the goal of biofilm studies in biofilm engineering may be thought of as mapping the set of controlled variables onto the set of measured variables. Unfortunately, because of the complexity of biofilm processes and the complexity of the interactions among the various compartments of biofilm systems, one-to-one mapping is the exception; the consequences of this fact will be discussed later in this text. The results of biofilm studies are shown as plots of controlled variables versus measured variables, such as a plot of flow velocity (controlled variable) versus biofilm density (measured variable) or a plot relating the biocide concentration (controlled variable) to the log reduction of the cell count (measured variable). Table 3.1 gives examples of controlled and measured variables.

Although selected measured variables in specific biofilm studies can be related to selected controlled variables, arriving at general relationships between the controlled and measured variables in biofilm processes is much more difficult. Because natural biofilm processes are simplified in LBRs, it is difficult to make general statements of the type that in all biofilm processes certain measured variables always respond to certain changes in the controlled variables in the same manner. Some of these difficulties in achieving general significance in the results of biofilm studies using LBRs are inherently related to the complexity of biofilm processes and there is little the researcher can do about them; however, some are related to the manner in which the researcher operates LBRs and interprets the results, and these can be restricted by keeping in mind the significance of the results while choosing reactors and experimental conditions. Biofilm processes are inherently complex, and operating an LBR is an attempt to simplify this complexity. Simplifying biofilm processes also changes them, and there is a limit beyond which simplifying a biofilm process actually produces a different biofilm process, which may have little to do with the original process the researcher was attempting to quantify. Biofilm processes are affected by a variety of factors arranged in a complex network of interactions among various compartments

Table 3.1 Examples of Controlled and Measured Variables

Controlled variables	Measured variables
Chemical components of the influent (i.e., glucose and oxygen concentrations, pH, etc.)	Chemical components of the effluent (i.e., glucose and oxygen concentrations, pH, etc.)
Available surface area for biofilm growth	Biofilm thickness
Shear stress on the clean surface	Biofilm density
Volumetric flow rate	Number of cells per unit surface area
Reactor volume	Biofilm structure
Retention time	Shear stress on the biofilm surface
Flow velocity	Flux of nutrients at a single location in the biofilm (local biofilm activity)
Recycle ratio	Pressure drop

and various groups of microorganisms, and the performance of a biofilm system depends on the complex interactions among the various occupants of the biofilm matrix and the various interactions among the compartments of the biofilm system.

In contrast, LBRs are constructed and operated to satisfy the reductionistic desire to isolate variables. This desire expresses itself in many ways, such as in growing biofilms composed of pure cultures of microorganisms, using growth media designed to satisfy the needs of selected groups of microorganisms only, exerting "selective pressure" on some groups of microorganisms and promoting the growth of other groups of microorganisms. Using mutated and otherwise genetically altered microorganisms is also a good example of an attempt to isolate variables. As a result, the results obtained by studying biofilms in LBRs do not have general significance; instead, they are related to the specific conditions under which the LBR was operated. LBRs are indispensable in biofilm research, but the conclusions from studies using LBRs are determined by the experimental conditions imposed on the process, and not necessarily by the inherent properties of the process.

Measured variables in LBRs are quantified from two points of view: (1) experimentally and (2) using mathematical models of biofilm processes. Ideally, the results of experiments and the solutions from mathematical models should be the same. This does not often happen, however, and when the results of an experiment disagree with the prediction of the model the question is always the same: Which one is correct, the experimental data or the prediction from the model? The popular notion among those who quantify biofilm processes experimentally is that only an experiment can reveal the truth about biofilm processes, that mathematical models are just accessory tools that may or may not reflect the behavior of the biofilm system correctly. This notion is reinforced by citing examples of mathematical models that produced solutions heavily biased by the questionable assumptions used to construct the model and to facilitate computations. In fact, there is no easy way to determine which result is correct, or whether any of them is correct for that matter: it all depends on what is considered to be correct, and it is questionable whether the term *correct* should be used on such occasions at all. The results of experiments can be affected by dubious experimental conditions to the same extent that the solutions of mathematical models are affected by dubious assumptions. By fixing the controlled variables of the biofilm process in the LBRs, the operator creates an artificial reality, a set of conditions that do not necessarily exist in nature, and the results of the measurements are consistent with the set of conditions chosen to create this artificial reality. The same goes for mathematical models: selecting assumptions creates an artificial reality, and the results of the computations are consistent with the set of conditions accepted to construct the model. In this sense, the term *correct* means that the results of the experiment are consistent with the experimental conditions and that the solutions of the mathematical model are consistent with the assumptions of the model. This does not mean, however, that either the experimental data or the predictions of the model reveal the truth about the natural biofilm processes under study. In an extreme example, the predictions of the model and the experimental results may agree well without either of them predicting the outcome of the natural biofilm process. Both results are correct, because they faithfully reflect the artificial reality created by the operator of the reactor who set the control variables and the modeler who accepted the assumptions, but neither the predictions of the model nor the results of the experiment reflect the effects of the variables of the natural biofilm process they both try to imitate. If the predictions of the model and the experimental results are consistent but do not reflect the performance of natural biofilm systems, then, using the definition of relevance, it is better to say that these results are consistent but not relevant, without referring to whether they are correct or not.

3.2.2   *Relating the measured variables to the controlled variables*

The goal of biofilm studies in biofilm engineering has been defined as an attempt to find functions relating the controlled variables to the measured variables. In the simplest of scenarios, the measured variable is considered to be a function of one variable, the controlled variable:

$$\text{measured variable} = F \text{ (controlled variable)} \tag{3.1}$$

as in the relation

$$\text{biofilm density} = F \text{ (shear stress)} \tag{3.2}$$

Such simple relations may be true only when many other variables are kept constant. Better approximations can be achieved by using functions of many controlled variables, as in the relation

$$\text{biofilm density} = F \text{ (shear stress, nutrient concentrations)} \tag{3.3}$$

This approach works well if the number of controlled variables is two, in which case the relation between the two independent variables (the controlled variables) and the dependent variables (the measured variables) can be conveniently imaged using 3-D plots. If the number of measured variables exceeds two, the function can be studied numerically, but the possibility of imaging the results by plotting them is reduced to special cases in which some of the controlled variables are kept constant. In the following example, five controlled variables are used.

$$\text{biofilm density} = F \text{ (shear stress, nutrient concentration, pH, time, temperature)} \tag{3.4}$$

If the experimental plan includes quantifying functions of many controlled variables, then the analysis of results can become quite complex. Texts devoted to experimental design should be consulted for details of designing such experiments (Montgomery 2006). Facing a system with multiple controlled variables affecting one measured variable, biofilm researchers often simplify the analysis by keeping the excess controlled variables constant, and studying a set of simplified relations between variables, like the one shown below:

biofilm density = F (shear stress)
biofilm density = G (nutrient concentration)
biofilm density = H (time), etc.

These simplified relations may be true only if the variables can be truly isolated, which means that there are no functional relations among the controlled variables; for example, the shear stress does not change with changing pH and remains constant over time. However, simplifying assumptions that some variables are constant may only be realistic in empty reactors, where the operator exercises a high level of control over the controlled variables. These assumptions may not be realistic in reactors with biofilms, where the operator does not have full control over the controlled variables: after the biofilm has accumulated, the controllability of some variables in biofilm processes decreases. For example, shear stress can be controlled in an empty reactor by fixing the flow rate and flow velocity, but controlling shear stress in a reactor with biofilm is another matter. Operators of LBRs have surprisingly little control over the variables affecting biofilm processes. As another example illustrating this point, the operator inoculates the LBR with a carefully selected mixture of microorganisms, but there is no guarantee that all these microorganisms will become members of the microbial community in the biofilm, which, using the terminology described previously, raises the question: Is microbial community structure in biofilms a controlled variable or a measured variable? Or a more general question: What is the level of control we have over the microbial community structure in biofilms? Similar questions can be asked with respect to many other controlled variables.

The desire to disassemble a system into simple objects and study them separately is not unique to biofilm researchers. Physicists do this and study the behavior of elementary particles, for example. However, their systems can be simplified to the level of elementary particles. The systems biofilm researchers deal with can only be simplified to the level of a single microorganism, which is still a pretty complex structure. The desire to control biofilm processes in LBRs leads the researchers to make the reactors and the biofilm processes as simple as possible by fixing various controlled variables, using pure cultures of microorganisms, well-defined solutions of nutrients, pH buffers, antibiotics to eliminate undesirable microorganisms, etc. This approach gives the operator a false sense of confidence that the results characterize the behavior of biofilms. Although this may be true with respect to the process in the LBR, it is quite possible that by fixing all these variables the operator has created a biofilm system that has no relevance to any real biofilm system. Fixing experimental conditions has consequences: the results of the experiments always reflect the conditions. If the experimental conditions are changed, the results may be different. Ironically, the more control that is exercised over the biofilm processes in LBRs, the less certain are the predictions of the outcome of a natural biofilm process based on the results of the studies.

Although the weaknesses of simulating natural biofilm processes in LBRs are easily exposed, there are no easy solutions to remediate these weaknesses. When biofilm processes are studied in LBRs, the researcher can quantify many factors affecting these processes, but may have doubts about the relevance of the results. On the other hand, making observations of natural biofilms establishes relevance beyond doubt, but the interactions among the various factors affecting biofilm processes are so complex that everything affects everything and the results of such studies may not be enlightening.

The relevance of the results of a biofilm study using an LBR has been defined as the extent to which these results reflect the performance of the natural and engineered biofilm reactors the study imitates. Apart from the desire to establish the relevance of the results, the researcher has the obligation to make the results of the study reproducible. Achieving reproducibility of results may be hindered by the same problem that affects the relevance of the study, which is the level to which the various controlled variables can really be controlled. As previously discussed in this chapter, the level to which the controlled variables are really controlled in LBRs varies, and this affects the reproducibility of the results in LBRs. The researcher cannot be sure whether the controlled variables are controlled to the same extent in different experiments. Establishing the flow rate and the flow velocity controls the shear stress in an empty reactor. After the biofilm accumulates, the shear stress changes and it is questionable to what extent the shear stress can be controlled by the operator and whether the level of control can be reproduced from one experiment to another. The operator cannot change this; all the operator can do is to ensure that the experimental conditions are reproducible. To put this more succinctly, the operator cannot make the results reproducible, but he or she can make the experimental conditions and the procedures used to evaluate the measured variables reproducible. One of the purposes of this book is to help in achieving reproducibility of experimental conditions and of procedures used to evaluate measured variables. Only when the experimental conditions and the procedures used to evaluate the measured variables are reproducible and certain can the reproducibility of the results be properly evaluated and addressed. In the following sections, steps will be described that help in establishing the reproducibility of experimental conditions. The problems related to using reproducible procedures to evaluate the measured variables are addressed in Chapter 9. The problems related to the reproducibility of results are discussed later in this chapter.

3.2.3   Hydrodynamics in LBRs

The term *hydrodynamics in LBRs* refers to such factors as the average flow velocity, the flow velocity distribution, and the average shear stress. Hydrodynamic parameters can easily be estimated for empty (without biofilm) reactors of well-defined geometries. In the presence of biofilms, however, these variables change in an unknown manner. Quantifying the effect of hydrodynamics on biofilm processes is not trivial; the hydrodynamics in such reactors is a subject of research. Hydrodynamics in LBRs refers to reactors without biofilm. After biofilm has accumulated, tools are available for quantifying hydrodynamics at the microscale at selected locations in the biofilm; however, it is not known how to integrate the results of these localized measurements over the entire reactor so that they are representative of the hydrodynamics in the reactor and not only at the selected locations.

3.2.3.1   Flow velocity

The most popular way of computing the flow velocity is to divide the volumetric flow rate by the surface area perpendicular to the flow, which gives the average flow velocity v_s:

$$v_s = \frac{\text{volumetric flow rate}}{\text{surface area perpendicular to flow}} \qquad (3.5)$$

Average flow velocity is an important parameter characterizing flow in the reactor, but its usefulness for characterizing biofilm processes is limited. The average flow velocity can be used to characterize the flow in the reactor by computing the Reynolds number.

3.2.3.2   Momentum

Momentum M is the product of mass and velocity, and in this context it is the product of the mass of the flowing water and its velocity.

$$M = mv_s \qquad (3.6)$$

Momentum and flow velocity are vectors: the momentum of the flowing water is considered in the direction of the flow. In isolated systems, momentum is conserved and changing the momentum requires force. This relation between momentum and force is seen in the following definition of the rate of change in momentum:

$$\frac{dM}{dt} = \frac{d(mv_s)}{dt} = m\frac{dv_s}{dt} = \text{mass} \times \text{acceleration} = \text{force} \qquad (3.7)$$

The terms in the above equation are useful in many branches of physics, but in hydrodynamics it is customary to use the volume of the water in computations, rather than the mass, and express the mass of the water as the product of the volume V and the density ρ:

$$m = \rho \times V \tag{3.8}$$

This makes the rate of change of momentum equal to

$$\frac{dM}{dt} = \frac{d(mv_s)}{dt} = \frac{d(\rho V v_s)}{dt} \tag{3.9}$$

It is also customary to express the volumetric flow rate, Q, as the product of the cross section of the conduit, A, and the flow velocity:

$$Q = A \times v_s = m^2 \times \frac{m}{s} = \frac{m^3}{s} \tag{3.10}$$

Using these relations, the mass flux, the rate at which a mass of water is transferred in a conduit, is defined as

$$\frac{m}{t} = \rho Q = \rho A v_s = \frac{kg}{m^3} m^2 \frac{m}{s} = \frac{kg}{s} \tag{3.11}$$

which shows that the mass transfer rate has the dimension of mass per time as expected. Similarly, the momentum change rate has the dimension of momentum per time and is defined as

$$\frac{mv_s}{t} = \rho A v_s^2 = \frac{kg}{m^3} m^2 \frac{m^2}{s^2} = kg \frac{m}{s^2} = mass \times acceleration = force \tag{3.12}$$

It results from Equation 3.12 that the momentum change rate has the dimension of force. This is an important conclusion, indicating that any change in momentum is equivalent to a force. For example, if two layers of water having different flow velocities slide against each other, then the layers have different momentums and the momentum difference is equivalent to a force one of these layers exerts on the other; this force is called the *shear force* or the *shear stress*.

3.2.3.3 *Reynolds number*

The Reynolds number characterizes the flow and serves as a numerical reference to the hydrodynamic conditions in the reactor. For the flows in two biofilm reactors to be similar, the reactors must have the same geometry and the same Reynolds number.

The Reynolds number is defined as

$$Re = \frac{\rho v_s}{\dfrac{\mu}{L}} \tag{3.13}$$

where v_s is the characteristic (average) flow velocity (m/s), L is the characteristic length (m), ρ is the fluid density (kg/m³), and μ is the (absolute) dynamic viscosity (kg/m s).

The unit of dynamic viscosity is (Pa s), which is equal to 1 N s/m², or 1 kg/(m s). The cgs unit for dynamic viscosity is the poise (P), and 1 poise = 100 centipoise = 1 g/(cm s) = 0.1 Pa s. Water at 20°C has a viscosity of almost exactly one centipoise: 1.0020 cP.

In the more formal derivation of the Reynolds number, the final form of the expression results from relating the inertial forces to the viscosity forces of the flowing water. The forces originating from the inertia of the flowing water depend on flow velocity:

$$\rho v_s^2 L^2 = \frac{\text{kg}}{\text{m}^3} \frac{\text{m}^2}{\text{s}^2} \text{m}^2 = \text{kg} \times \frac{\text{m}}{\text{s}^2} = \text{mass} \times \text{acceleration} = \text{force} \tag{3.14}$$

The forces originating from the viscosity are quantified as follows:

$$\mu v_s L = \frac{\text{kg}}{\text{ms}} \frac{\text{m}}{\text{s}} \text{m} = \text{kg} \times \frac{\text{m}}{\text{s}^2} = \text{mass} \times \text{acceleration} = \text{force} \tag{3.15}$$

The Reynolds number is the ratio of the inertia forces to the viscosity forces:

$$\frac{\rho v_s^2 L^2}{\mu v_s L} = \frac{\rho v_s}{\dfrac{\mu}{L}} = \text{Re} \tag{3.16}$$

Introducing the concept of kinematic viscosity υ simplifies the expression of the Reynolds number. Kinematic viscosity depends on the density of water:

$$\upsilon = \frac{\mu}{\rho} \tag{3.17}$$

where ρ is the density of water, 1000 kg/m³. Consequently, the unit of kinematic viscosity is

$$v = \frac{\dfrac{\text{kg}}{\text{m} \times \text{s}}}{\dfrac{\text{kg}}{\text{m}^3}} = \frac{\text{m}^2}{\text{s}} \tag{3.18}$$

In SI units, the kinematic viscosity is expressed as m²/s. In cgs units, the kinematic viscosity is expressed in stokes (abbreviated S or St: 1 stokes = 100 cS = 1 cm²/s = 0.0001 m²/s. The kinematic viscosity of water at 20°C is 1×10^{-6} m²/s. Table 3.2 gives values of υ and μ for various temperatures.

The kinematic viscosity of water is implicated in the formation of the hydrodynamic boundary layer. When boundary layers are formed—a mass boundary layer and a hydrodynamic boundary layer—the thickness of the hydrodynamic boundary layer is proportional to the kinematic viscosity of water and the thickness of the mass boundary layer is proportional to the diffusivity of the particles that are transported across the boundary

Table 3.2 Dynamic and Kinematic Viscosities of Water
at Various Temperatures

Temperature, T (°C)	Dynamic viscosity, μ 10^{-3} (N s/m^2)	Kinematic viscosity, υ 10^{-6} (m^2/s)
0	1.787	1.787
5	1.519	1.519
10	1.307	1.307
20	1.002	1.004
30	0.798	0.801
40	0.653	0.658
50	0.547	0.553
60	0.467	0.475
70	0.404	0.413
80	0.355	0.365
90	0.315	0.326
100	0.282	0.294

Source: http://www.engineeringtoolbox.com.

layer. The diffusivity has the same unit as the kinematic viscosity of water, m^2/s, and the numerical value of the kinematic viscosity of water can be directly compared to the numerical values of the diffusivities of various substances in water. Table 3.3 reports the diffusivities of various substances of potential interest in biofilm engineering.

The Reynolds number is expressed in terms of kinematic viscosity υ rather than the absolute (dynamic) viscosity, μ:

$$\mathrm{Re} = \frac{v_s L}{\upsilon} \tag{3.19}$$

In many situations, it is unclear what should be used as the characteristic length in Equation 3.19. Because the Reynolds number was introduced to describe the nature of flow in pipes, the diameter of the pipe is used as the characteristic length. In other geometries, the so-called *hydraulic radius* is used as the characteristic length. The hydraulic radius (R_h)

Table 3.3 Diffusivity of Molecules
in Aqueous Solution at 20°C

Substance	Molecular weight (g/mol)	Diffusivity (m^2/s)
Oxygen	32	21.0×10^{-10}
Glucose	180	6.7×10^{-10}
Sucrose	342	4.5×10^{-10}
Insulin	5,200	2.3×10^{-10}
Albumin	67,000	0.7×10^{-10}
Urease	480,000	0.3×10^{-10}

Source: Chaplin, M. and Bucke C., Effects of solute diffusion on the kinetics of immobilised enzymes. Section 3.5 of *Enzyme Technology*. http://www.lsbu.ac.uk/water/enztech/diffusion.html.

is computed as the ratio of the surface area perpendicular to the flow, A, divided by the wetted perimeter, W:

$$R_h = \frac{A}{W} \tag{3.20}$$

In circular pipes, it is customary to use the diameter of the pipe as the characteristic length, which in terms of hydraulic radius makes it equal to

$$\text{Re} = \frac{v_s}{\upsilon}\frac{4A}{W} \tag{3.21}$$

where $4A/W = d$, the diameter of the pipe.

In other types of conduits, such as rectangular conduits, the Reynolds number is computed using the following formula:

$$\text{Re} = \frac{v_s 4R_h}{\upsilon} \tag{3.22}$$

Equality of the Reynolds numbers in two reactors is one of the conditions of similarity between the flows in the two reactors. However, the flows in two reactors having identical Reynolds numbers does not necessarily mean that the hydrodynamic conditions for biofilm growth are the same in these reactors. The numerical values of Reynolds numbers result from a combination of flow velocity and reactor dimensions. Thus, it is possible to get the same Reynolds number for different flow velocities in reactors of different geometries. In Equation 3.21, kinematic viscosity υ is constant irrespective of the geometry of the reactor, and average flow velocity v_s and hydraulic radius R_h can be manipulated to give the same Reynolds number in an infinite number of combinations. Consequently, the biofilms in two reactors may grow under identical Reynolds numbers but different flow velocities and shear stresses, and so the structures of these biofilms may be different. Therefore, all the conditions of similarity—(1) geometric similarity (shape), (2) kinematic similarity (flow characteristics), and (3) dynamic similarity (forces acting on the biofilm)— must be met for the claim to be made that biofilms in two reactors are grown under identical conditions. The following sections give examples of other dimensionless groups that can be quantified in biofilm reactors.

3.2.4 *Dimensionless groups quantified in biofilm reactors*

The most frequently computed dimensionless group in biofilm reactors is the Reynolds number. However, to compare reactors and operational conditions, several other dimensionless groups can be quantified. For biofilm reactors the most important dimensionless groups are the Schmidt number, the Peclet number, and the Sherwood number.

The Schmidt number, Sc, is

$$\text{Sc} = \frac{\upsilon}{D_w} \tag{3.23}$$

where D_w is the diffusivity of the molecules in water. The Schmidt number characterizes the medium; in LBRs this is the solution of nutrients. It relates the kinematic viscosity of the solution to the diffusivity of the nutrients. In pure water, Sc = 1000. This relation was used before, in Chapter 1, during the discussion of hydrodynamics and mass transfer in biofilm systems; it was argued that the diffusion boundary layer is 1000 times thinner than the hydrodynamic boundary layer. This estimation was based on the fact that, for small molecules in pure water, diffusivity is about 1000× lower than viscosity, which equals the Schmidt number for pure water.

The Peclet number, Pe, is given by

$$Pe = Re \times Sc \tag{3.24}$$

The Peclet number represents the ratio of the rate of mass transport by convection to the rate of mass transport by diffusion. This number will be used later in this chapter to quantify the differences between the mass transport rate in microcolonies and that in interstitial voids in heterogeneous biofilms. If convection exceeds diffusion, which is almost always true in water solutions, then Pe > 1.

The Sherwood number, Sh, can be written as

$$Sh = \frac{L}{\delta} = \frac{k \times L}{D_w} \tag{3.25}$$

where k is the mass transfer coefficient.

The Sherwood number is the ratio of the characteristic length L selected to characterize the system to the thickness of the boundary layer, δ. When transformed, the Sherwood number is proportional to the mass transport coefficient. These relations are needed to discuss the concepts of overall and local mass transport coefficients in Chapter 4. When the overall mass transport coefficient is being computed, the term *diffusion boundary layer* refers to the diffusion boundary layer above the biofilm surface. When the local mass transfer coefficient is being discussed, the term *diffusion boundary layer* refers to the diffusion boundary layer surrounding the tip of the microelectrode that is used to measure the local mass transport coefficient.

Example 3.1

An open-channel flat plate reactor is 2.5 cm wide, 4.0 cm deep, and 34.5 cm long. If the volumetric flow rate is 1.5 cm³/s and the depth of water is 3 mm, calculate (1) the average flow velocity in this reactor and (2) the Reynolds number in this reactor.

Solution

The reactor is drawn in Figure 3.1.

Computing the average flow rate requires estimating the surface area perpendicular to the flow, and this is calculated from Equation 3.5.

$$A = 2.5 \times 10^{-2} \text{ m} \times 3 \times 10^{-3} \text{ m} = 7.5 \times 10^{-5} \text{ m}^2$$

$$v_s = \frac{1.5 \times 10^{-6} \text{ m}^3/\text{s}}{7.5 \times 10^{-5} \text{ m}^2} = 0.02 \text{ m/s}$$

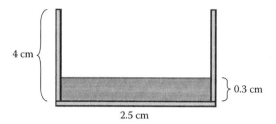

Figure 3.1 Cross section of an open-channel flat plate reactor.

$$W = 2.5 \times 10^{-2} \text{ m} + (3 + 3) \times 10^{-3} \text{ m}$$

$$R_h = \frac{2.5 \times 10^{-2} \text{ m} \times 3 \times 10^{-3} \text{ m}}{2.5 \times 10^{-2} \text{ m} + (3+3)10^{-3} \text{ m}} = 2.42 \times 10^{-3} \text{ m}$$

The Reynolds number is

$$\text{Re} = \frac{2 \times 10^{-2} \text{ m/s} \times 4 \times 2.42 \times 10^{-3} \text{ m}}{1 \times 10^{-6} \text{ m}^2/\text{s}} = 193$$

Although estimates vary somewhat, depending on the source, the flow in a conduit is characterized as *laminar* if the Reynolds number is below 2000 and as *turbulent* if it is above 4000 (Figure 3.2). For Reynolds numbers between these numbers, the flow is classified as *transient*. Consequently, the flow in this example is characterized as laminar, Re = 193. This example also illustrates one of the limitations of the open-channel flat plate reactors used in biofilm studies: it is difficult to set turbulent flow. The flow velocities in open-channel flat plate reactors are too slow to even approach a Reynolds number of 4000. For practical reasons, we assume here that the flow in the reactor is

- Laminar if Re < 2000
- Transient if 2000 < Re < 4000
- Turbulent if Re > 4000

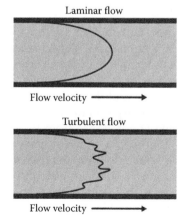

Figure 3.2 Patterns of flow velocity in laminar and turbulent flow regimes.

Example 3.2

The extent to which biofilm accumulation in a reactor affects the computation of the Reynolds number will be examined. Repeat the calculations from Example 3.1 assuming that the presence of the biofilm changes nothing but the dimensions of the conduit. Assume that there is a 200-μm-thick biofilm at the bottom of the reactor. The depth of water is still 3 mm because the biofilm is heterogeneous and the water shares the space with the biofilm.

Solution

The depth of the water layer includes the biofilm thickness. For that reason the depth of water over the biofilm will be 0.3 cm − 200 × 10^{-4} cm = 0.28 cm.

$$A = (2.5 \times 10^{-2} \text{ m}) \times (2.8 \times 10^{-3} \text{ m}) = 7.0 \times 10^{-5} \text{ m}^2$$

$$v_s = \frac{1.5 \times 10^{-6} \text{ m}^3/\text{s}}{7.0 \times 10^{-5} \text{ m}^2} = 0.0214 \text{ m/s}$$

$$W = 2.5 \times 10^{-2} \text{ m} + (2.8 + 2.8) \times 10^{-3} \text{ m} = 3.06 \times 10^{-2} \text{ m}$$

$$R_h = \frac{2.5 \times 10^{-2} \text{ m} \times 2.8 \times 10^{-3} \text{ m}}{2.5 \times 10^{-2} \text{ m} + (2.8 + 2.8)10^{-3} \text{ m}} = 2.287 \times 10^{-3} \text{ m}$$

The Reynolds number is

$$\text{Re} = \frac{2.14 \times 10^{-2} \text{m/s} \times 4 \times 2.287 \times 10^{-3} \text{m}}{1 \times 10^{-6} \text{m}^2/\text{s}} = 196$$

Comparing the results from Example 3.1 and Example 3.2, it is apparent that the presence of the biofilm increases Re inconsequentially. This computation does not reflect the real effect of the biofilm, which will be discussed later in this chapter.

3.2.5   *Hydrodynamic entry length*

In many biofilm studies, it is important to take microscale measurements at a location where the hydrodynamics are stable. In natural biofilm reactors, typical locations to avoid would be those near obstacles in the pathway of flow. Because obstacles to flow in an LBR can usually be avoided when the reactor is being designed, consideration should be given to other factors affecting flow stability, and the entry length to the reactor is one of these. For example, if the effect of flow velocity on biofilm structure is to be studied, then the biofilm images should be collected at a distance from the entry to the reactor exceeding the hydrodynamic entry length. Figure 3.3 shows a photograph of the reactor that was used during the nuclear magnetic resonance imaging (NMRI) measurements. Figure 2.31c shows how the entry to the reactor and obstacles near the entry to the reactor affect the pattern of flow. These data were generated using NMRI. The flow pattern near the entry to the reactor is complex, and the pattern of biofilm accumulation will reflect this complexity. In addition, this pattern of flow would be difficult to reproduce in another reactor in an attempt to reproduce the results of the biofilm study. It is much simpler to avoid the

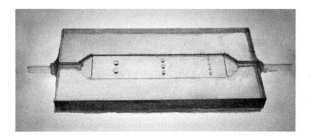

Figure 3.3 A photograph of the reactor that was used during the nuclear magnetic resonance imaging measurements.

problems with reproducing a flow pattern by making critical measurements at a distance from the entry that permits the flow to stabilize.

The hydrodynamic entry length is defined as the distance needed to develop a steady flow, after the water has passed through the entrance to the reactor. Computing the hydrodynamic entry length in an LBR is important in biofilm studies where the results of microscale measurements are sensitive to hydrodynamics. Only the part of the reactor in which the flow velocity profile is fully developed ensures reproducible hydrodynamic conditions for biofilm growth. Sampling the reactor at locations closer to the entrance than the hydrodynamic entry length is one of the reasons for which the results of biofilm studies may be difficult to reproduce. In pipes, the dimensionless hydrodynamic entry length number, E_l, is computed as

$$E_l = \frac{L_d}{4 \times R_h} \tag{3.26}$$

where E_l is the entry length number, L_d is the entry length (the distance from the entrance to the point where the flow profile is fully established), and R_h is the hydraulic radius of the pipe. The dimensional hydrodynamic entry length (the distance to the location where the flow is fully established) can be found by multiplying E_l by the hydraulic radius of the pipe. From empirical data, for laminar flow in pipes, $E_l = 0.06\text{Re}$, and for turbulent flow in pipes, the hydrodynamic entry length is $E_l = 4.4\text{Re}^{1/6}$.

The hydrodynamic entry length can be computed for an LBR that has the shape of a conduit. If the reactor is operated under laminar flow conditions, the hydrodynamic entry length is

$$L_d = 0.06\text{Re} \times 4 \times R_h \tag{3.27}$$

Example 3.3

In Example 3.1, it was calculated that the hydraulic radius of an open-channel flat plate reactor was equal to $R_h = 2.42 \times 10^{-3}$ m and that its Reynolds number was Re = 193. Using Equation 3.27, the hydrodynamic entry length to this reactor is

$$L_d = 0.06 \times 193 \times 4 \times 2.42 \times 10^{-3} = 0.112 \text{ m} = 11.2 \text{ cm}$$

If measurements of local biofilm properties are scheduled in this reactor, it is better to do them at a distance exceeding 11 cm from the entrance to the reactor. This way the flow characteristics can be reproduced from one study to another.

3.3   *LBRs as scale models*

LBRs are constructed to facilitate (1) the biofilm processes under study and (2) the measurements characterizing the processes under study. In principle, these conditions do not require that the LBRs be constructed as miniatures of large biofilm reactors, and they rarely are; the exact scaling of an LBR to imitate the dimensions of larger natural or engineered biofilm reactors is rarely an issue. Nevertheless, to increase the reproducibility of biofilm studies, it is desirable to construct and operate biofilm reactors as scale models not only in terms of linear dimensions but also in terms of fixing the controlled variables to ensure that the flow in the reactor and the forces acting on the biofilms are in constant relations to those existing in the reactor whose behavior is simulated. The importance of similarity of reactors is not limited to imitating large-scale reactors. Imitating LBRs from one study to another is equally important. If the biofilm processes in LBRs are to be reproducible from one study to another and from one reactor to another, the LBRs and the operational conditions need to satisfy as many conditions of similarity as possible. The most obvious condition to be satisfied is the geometric similarity: all linear dimensions in the model (LBR) should be in constant proportion to the respective dimensions of the object (large-scale reactor), so that

$$\text{ratio of the respective lengths} = \frac{x_{\text{model}}}{x_{\text{object}}} = \frac{y_{\text{model}}}{y_{\text{object}}} = \frac{z_{\text{model}}}{z_{\text{object}}} = L_r \tag{3.28}$$

where L_r is the ratio of the respective linear dimensions. Accepting a common ratio for all respective linear dimensions has further consequences. The surface areas and volumes in the model have constant ratios to the respective surface areas and volumes characterizing the object:

$$\text{ratio of the respective surface areas} = \frac{x_{\text{model}} \times y_{\text{model}}}{x_{\text{object}} \times y_{\text{object}}} = L_r^2 \tag{3.29}$$

and

$$\text{ratio of the respective volumes} = \frac{x_{\text{model}} \times y_{\text{model}} \times z_{\text{model}}}{x_{\text{object}} \times y_{\text{object}} \times z_{\text{object}}} = L_r^3 \tag{3.30}$$

The geometric similarity of the model to the reactor it imitates is important, but the conditions of similarity reach beyond simple geometric similarity. The necessary conditions include (1) geometric similarity (the dimensions of the model), (2) kinematic similarity (flow characteristics), and (3) dynamic similarity (forces acting on the biofilm). The conditions of similarity are characterized by dimensional analysis, which describes the properties of the system with as many dimensionless parameters as possible. Not all conditions of similarity can be characterized precisely enough in biofilm reactors to satisfy the requirements of dimensional analysis. Nevertheless, some dimensionless groups, such as the Reynolds number (characterizing the flow) and the shear stress (characterizing the forces acting on the biofilm), should be computed and reported for LBRs whenever possible. Reporting the dimensions of the LBR used is the easy part, and most published biofilm studies describe the dimensions of the reactors used in the study quite well. Flow characteristics and forces acting on the biofilm are more challenging to quantify, and many published studies give inadequate descriptions of these factors. The following sections describe how to characterize the flow and the forces acting on the biofilms in LBRs.

3.4   Factors affecting biofilm processes in LBRs

3.4.1   Stress and strain in the biofilm matrix

Forces due to flowing water acting on a biofilm can deform the elastic polymers that constitute the biofilm matrix. One of the important mechanical properties of biofilms is that the matrix made of extracellular polymers is elastic, which means that it can change its shape when subjected to external forces and return to its previous shape when these forces are removed. The forces applied cannot exceed the value for which catastrophic changes may occur, such as permanent disruption of the matrix—detachment. Forces acting on the polymeric matrix of a biofilm are characterized in the following sections as *stretching, compressing,* or *shearing.* In response to these forces, the polymeric matrix may change its shape and its volume. These changes can be quantified and the results used to characterize the mechanical properties of the polymeric matrix of a biofilm.

3.4.1.1   Compression and stretching

Stress is the force applied perpendicularly to an object per unit of the projected area. Stress can be compressive or tensile: it is compressive if it squeezes the object (compressive stress is called *pressure*), and it is tensile if it stretches the object. Strain is the relative change in the dimensions of the object subjected to stress. Stress and strain are, within limits, directly proportional (Hook's law). The elastic modulus, Y, also known as *Young's modulus,* is defined as the ratio of stress to strain, and it is a feature characterizing the mechanical properties of materials:

$$Y = \frac{\text{stress}}{\text{strain}} = \frac{\dfrac{F}{A}}{\dfrac{\Delta l}{L}} = \frac{\text{pressure (stress)}}{\text{relative change in length (strain)}} \tag{3.31}$$

Figure 3.4 illustrates the meaning of Equation 3.31.

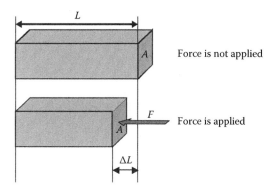

Figure 3.4 Stress and elastic modulus.

3.4.1.2   Shear deformation

Shear deformation is caused by forces acting parallel to the surface. The effect of shear on elastic materials is similar to the effect of stress, but in the case of shear the force is applied parallel to the surface. The deformation of the biofilm matrix can be quantified in terms of the material property called *shear modulus*. The shear modulus is defined in the identical manner as the elastic modulus, i.e., as the ratio of stress to strain.

Shear is the force acting on the biofilm along its surface. In response the biofilm changes its dimensions. Figure 3.5 illustrates the concepts of shear and shear deformation, also known as *shear strain*.

In Figure 3.5 a biofilm is attached to a surface and force *F* acts parallel to the surface. As a result of the shear force, the biofilm matrix is distorted by the top surface being shifted by ΔL in the direction of the applied force. Equation 3.32 defines the concept of shear modulus, and shear modulus can be measured in biofilm reactors.

$$\text{shear modulus} = \frac{\text{shear stress}}{\text{shear strain}} = \frac{\dfrac{F}{S}}{\dfrac{\Delta L}{H}} = G = \frac{\tau}{\tan \alpha} \tag{3.32}$$

where τ is shear stress and α is the shear angle. Shear strain can be also defined as the angle of distortion, $\Delta L/H = \tan \alpha$.

3.4.1.3   Elastic and viscoelastic deformations of biofilms

Elastic deformation of materials is reversible, and materials that obey Hook's law are called *elastic*. Elastic behavior, characterized by a linear relation between the stress and the strain, holds only up to a certain stress, beyond which it changes to plastic behavior, where small changes in stress cause large deformations. Finally, the changes in strain become catastrophic and the material breaks under stress. Figure 3.6 shows this type of behavior.

Attempts have been made to determine the elastic properties of biofilms (Stoodley et al. 1999). The authors determined the shear modulus in biofilms from the deformation of biofilm microcolonies caused by the flow of water. They estimated that the shear modulus of biofilm microcolonies was 27 N/m². The measurement was conducted in a tubular reactor, and Re = 3600 (Figure 3.7).

The shear strain ($\Delta L/H$) in Figure 3.5 equals the tangent of the shear angle, or the angle of distortion, α. If the angle of distortion is small, then sin α = tan α = α, which simplifies some computations, such as those in the example above. The authors computed that the

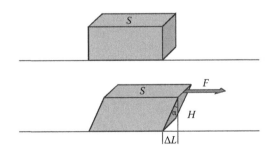

Figure 3.5 A biofilm microcolony is attached to a surface, and force *F* is applied parallel to the surface. As a result of the shear force, the biofilm matrix is stretched (distorted).

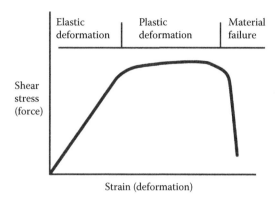

Figure 3.6 Elastic and plastic deformation of materials.

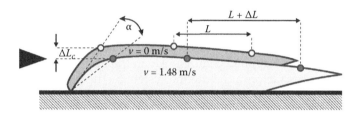

Figure 3.7 A cross section of a microcolony and a streamer showing how deformations in the shape of the microcolony were used to measure L and ΔL. The open circles represent fluorescent particles attached to the biofilm surface in a reactor with stagnant water. The closed circles show the locations of the fluorescent beads after the flow velocity increased to 1.48 m/s. The value of ΔL_c was found from the downstream displacement and the change in thickness of the microcolony. The value of ΔL was found by measuring the distance between two particles on the streamer at rest (L), and the extension (ΔL) was determined at various loading and unloading flow velocities. The large arrow indicates flow direction. (Modified from Stoodley, P. et al., *Biotechnology and Bioengineering*, 65, 83–92, 1999.)

Young's modulus of elasticity of the biofilm matrix was 64 N/m^2, or 64 Pa, which is a rather low number for this property of materials. Most materials have a Young's modulus on the order of gigapascals (GPa); 1 GPa = 10^9 pascal (Pa); 1 Pa = 1 N/m^2 = 1 J/m^3 = 1 kg m^{-1} s^{-2}. By comparison, rubber has a Young's modulus between 0.01 and 0.1 GPa, which is between 10^7 and 10^8 N/m^2, a few orders of magnitude higher than the values measured for the biofilm matrix.

An elastic material returns to its original form when the stress is removed. In viscoelastic materials, the relation between stress and strain depends on time, and removing the stress only partially reverses the strain. Viscoelastic materials have "memory," and this feature is advantageously used in biofilm studies by quantifying biofilm structure and judging the forces that caused the structural features of the biofilms. Biofilms grown at high flow velocities and high shear stresses, for example, have elongated streamers, and this feature remains even after the flow velocity and shear stress have decreased. This effect of changing shape permanently under stress, characteristic of viscoelastic materials, is known as *creeping*. Creeping relates to the situation in which the stress is constant and the strain increases, which translates to progressive deformation of the material over time. This effect has been used here to explain the formation of streamers in biofilms (see the model of heterogeneous biofilms, Chapter 1). Another effect characteristic of viscoelastic materials is mechanical damping: this is their behavior when exposed to stress that varies over time. Damping causes the decay of vibrations, and this effect is used in Section 3.4.1.3 to explain why the presence of biofilm delays the onset of turbulence in conduits covered with biofilm.

3.4.1.4   Shear stress

It is known that shear stress is responsible for at least one biofilm process, i.e., erosion. Erosion in a biofilm is the detachment of small pieces of biofilm matrix from the surface of the biofilm. As was demonstrated in the discussion of momentum, stress forces exist in flow velocity gradients when two sheets of water slide against each other and they have different flow velocities. These sheets (laminas) act on each other with a certain force due to water viscosity, which binds them together, and the applied force, which tries to separate them. By definition, in velocity gradients, adjacent particles of water have different flow velocities and, having equal densities, must have different momentums. Because the adjacent particles of water are bound by the viscosity forces, the difference in flow velocities causes strain on the continuous body of water. Figure 3.8 shows a conceptual image helpful in quantifying the shear force. The force acting in this model can be estimated by assuming that one of these sheets is stationary and the other one is mobile.

To sustain the motion of the upper sheet in Figure 3.8 at a velocity v with respect to the lower sheet, a force F must be applied continuously to the upper sheet. The magnitude of this force is related to other factors affecting the system by the following equation:

$$\frac{F}{S} = \frac{\mu \times v}{z} \tag{3.33}$$

where S is the surface area of each sheet, v is the relative velocity of one sheet with respect to the other, z is the distance between the sheets, and μ is the viscosity. The ratio (F/S) is called the *shear stress*, τ. It was used in Equation 3.32 to quantify the shear deformation. Shear stress is often computed at the location near the surface where dz and dv approach zero, which gives meaning to the derivative dv/dz:

$$\tau = \frac{F}{S} = \mu \frac{dv}{dz} \tag{3.34}$$

In the absence of a measurement of the flow velocity near the surface, the shear stress at the surface without the biofilm can be computed as a function of the friction factor, f (McCabe and Smith 1976):

$$\tau_w = \frac{f \rho v_z^2}{2} \tag{3.35}$$

where f is the friction factor (dimensionless), v_z is the average flow velocity (LT^{-1}), and ρ is the density of water (ML^{-3}). Figure 3.9 illustrates the concept.

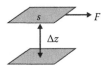

Figure 3.8 Concept of shear force. Force F acts on the upper sheet of liquid, separated by distance z from the lower sheet of water, considered to be stationary.

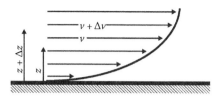

Figure 3.9 Flow velocity profile near a smooth surface.

3.4.1.5 Pressure drop

Liquid flowing in conduits experiences various forces, some of which promote the flow and some of which oppose it. An important group of forces opposing the flow results from the interactions between the liquid and the walls of the conduit. Even if the surface of the wall is perfectly smooth, the presence of the hydrodynamic boundary layer generates friction between particles in the liquid due to the gradient in flow velocity near the surface. The liquid particles do not move with the same flow velocity, and friction between particles moving at different velocities in the boundary layer causes an effect called *skin drag* or *wall drag*. Another group of forces that oppose water movement comes from the presence of stationary objects obstructing the flow. To bypass these objects, some particles of the liquid must change their paths, generating additional losses of energy due to friction. This effect is called *form drag*, and its magnitude depends on the geometry of the submersed objects. Specialized texts derive equations quantifying the form drag forces for simple geometric shapes such as spheres, cylinders, and discs.

If an object is immersed in flowing water, then the pressure of the flowing water on the object equals:

$$\text{dynamic pressure} = \frac{1}{2}\rho v_s^2 = \frac{\text{kg}}{\text{m}^3}\frac{\text{m}^2}{\text{s}^2} = \frac{\text{kg}}{\text{ms}^2} = \frac{\text{kg} \times \text{m}}{\text{m}^2\text{s}^2} = \text{kg}\frac{\text{m}}{\text{s}^2}\frac{1}{\text{m}^2}$$

$$= \frac{\text{mass} \times \text{acceleration}}{\text{area}} = \frac{\text{force}}{\text{area}}$$

This force is called *drag*, and it is defined as the force that pushes the object downward. It is equal to the dynamic pressure multiplied by the surface area projected in the direction of the incoming flow, *A*, and by an empirically determined drag coefficient, C_d.

$$\text{drag} = \frac{1}{2}\rho v_s^2 A C_d = \text{kg}\frac{\text{m}}{\text{s}^2}\frac{1}{\text{m}^2}\text{m}^2 = \text{kg}\frac{\text{m}}{\text{s}^2} = \text{mass} \times \text{acceleration} = \text{force}$$

Predicting pressure drop in conduits is an important part of designing pipelines, and several approaches are used in such computations. A popular way of predicting pressure drop in closed conduits is using diagrams which correlate the Reynolds number and the relative roughness of the wall to provide the engineer with the friction factor, *f*. The relative roughness is based on the relative height of the roughness elements, which is the ratio of the height of the roughness elements to the diameter of the conduit. Once the friction factor has been determined, the pressure drop, also known as the *head loss*, in circular conduits of diameter *d* is computed from the Darcy-Weisbach equation:

$$\Delta H_l = f\rho\frac{L_p}{d}\frac{v_s^2}{2g} = \frac{kg}{m^3}\frac{m}{m}\frac{\dfrac{m^2}{s^2}}{\dfrac{m}{s^2}} = \frac{kg}{m^2}$$

(3.36)

where ΔH_l is the head loss, L_p is the pipe length, v_s is the average fluid velocity, *g* is the gravitation constant, *d* is the pipe diameter, and *f* is the friction factor provided by the Moody diagram for clean new pipes.

Diagrams and equations used to predict pressure drop in conduits use the concept of roughness elements. The friction factor is a function of the Reynolds number, the height of the roughness elements, *e*, and the diameter of the pipe, *d*:

$$f = F\left(\text{Re}, \frac{e}{d}\right)$$

(3.37)

The effect of roughness elements on flow in conduits can be simulated by gluing grains of sand of various diameters to the walls of pipes. When the flow is laminar, the roughness elements are entirely buried in the hydrodynamic boundary layer and their effect on pressure drop can be predicted from theory. The ratio (e/d) is called the relative roughness. For laminar flow, the Reynolds number and the friction factor are related by

$$f = \frac{64}{\text{Re}}$$

(3.38)

When the flow velocity increases, the thickness of the boundary layer decreases and the roughness elements protrude through the boundary layer, further affecting the drag and the pressure drop. Empirical formulas are used to evaluate the friction factors for turbulent flow. One such formula was proposed by Colebrook (1938):

$$\frac{1}{\sqrt{f}} = -2\log\left(\frac{\dfrac{e}{d}}{3.7} + \frac{2.51}{\text{Re}\sqrt{f}}\right)$$

(3.39)

This equation is often shown as a plot of friction factor versus Reynolds number in the so-called Moody diagram (Figure 3.10). For high Reynolds numbers, the friction factor approaches a constant value.

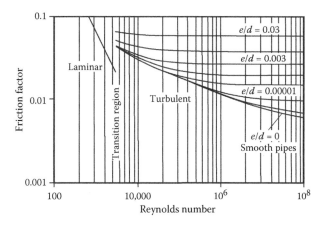

Figure 3.10 Moody diagram.

Example 3.4

Calculate the shear stress on the surface in the flat plate biofilm reactor described in Example 3.1.

Solution

In the reactor without biofilm, Re was determined to be equal to 193. The value of v_s was 0.02 m/s. The dimensionless fanning friction factor can be evaluated from Figure 3.10. For laminar flow, the friction factor is a simple function of the Reynolds number and is equal to

$$f = \frac{64}{\text{Re}} = \frac{64}{193} = 0.33$$

$$\tau_w = \frac{f\rho v_z^2}{2} = \frac{0.33 \times 1 (\text{kg/m}^3) \times 0.02^2 (\text{m/s})^2}{2} = 0.000066(\text{kg/ms}^2) = 0.000066 \text{ kg m/s}^2 \times 1/\text{m}^2 = \text{N/m}^2$$

Thus, the shear stress has the dimension of pressure, as it causes pressure loss in conduits.

The computation of shear stress above was done for the surface of the reactor without biofilm. It is assumed that this shear stress will also act on the biofilm after it is deposited on this surface. This assumption can only be justified if the surface of the biofilm is smooth and rigid, resembling the surface of the conduit. It is known that this is not true, and therefore the result of this computation is not certain for the reactor with biofilm. Parameters characterizing hydrodynamics in biofilm reactors, such as the Reynolds number and the shear stress, are based on assumptions that we know are not realistic.

Example 3.5

Calculate the friction factor for the following experimental system and operating conditions: v_s = 20 cm/s, the conduit is a circular tube with a 1-cm diameter, and T = 20°C.

Solution

The kinematic viscosity at 20°C is $1 \times 10^{-6}\,\text{m}^2/\text{s}$ (Table 3.2): $d = 1\,\text{cm} = 0.01\,\text{m}$ and $v_s = 20\,\text{cm/s} = 0.2\,\text{m/s}$.

$$\text{Re} = \frac{v_s d}{v} = \frac{0.2 \times 0.01}{1 \times 10^{-6}} = 2000$$

The flow is laminar, so we can use Equation 3.28:

$$f = \frac{64}{\text{Re}} = \frac{64}{2000} = 0.03$$

The same value can be read from Figure 3.10.

Unfortunately, the Moody diagram is of little help in predicting pressure drop in conduits covered with biofilms. Pressure drop in conduits covered with biofilms is caused by different factors than pressure drop in conduits without biofilms. These differences sometimes demonstrate themselves in the form of puzzling experimental results. Some biofilm reactors show higher pressure drops at low flow velocities than at high flow velocities. This effect is a consequence of the elastic and viscoelastic properties of biofilm. Microcolonies are made of bacterial cells imbedded in gelatinous extracellular polymers that can change shape under stress. At high flow velocities, the hydrodynamic boundary layer separates from the microcolonies, causing pressure drag downstream from the microcolony and pulling the material downstream. The microcolonies, being made of viscoelastic materials, slowly flow (creep) under the stress, forming elongated shapes called streamers (Figure 3.11). Such streamers are often seen when biofilms grow at high flow velocities. The streamers move rapidly and dissipate the kinetic energy of the flowing water, which is reflected in the pressure drop. The movement of the streamers is transmitted to the underlying microcolonies, which oscillate rhythmically (Figure 3.11).

The relation between flowing water and biofilms is determined by two facts: (1) biofilms are made of viscoelastic polymers that actively interact with the oscillations generated by the flow of water and (2) hydrodynamics can actively change biofilm structure. On the basis of the previous discussion, it is now expected that, at low flow velocities, biofilms can effectively smooth surfaces and stabilize the flow because the elastic polymeric

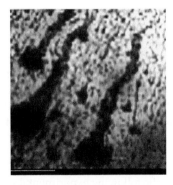

Figure 3.11 Surface of a biofilm with well-developed streamers. A sequence of images taken over time can give a planar view of the biofilm attached to the side wall of a reactor.

matrix can oscillate and effectively damp the vibrations coming from the flowing water. This effect delays the onset of turbulence in conduits covered with biofilm. However, as the flow velocity increases further, the elastic polymeric matrix must oscillate faster and faster and, eventually, the frequency of its oscillation cannot follow the frequency of the incoming eddies. At that point the biofilm oscillation is "out of phase" and the biofilm not only fails to damp the flow instabilities but actively introduces instability by randomly oscillating at a different frequency than the frequency of the incoming eddies. At that point the pressure drop in the conduit increases rapidly, exceeding by a few times the pressure drop predicted from computations assuming that the biofilm matrix is rigid. When the polymeric matrix is exposed to a high flow velocity for a longer time, the viscoelastic properties of the matrix cause the formation of streamers, such as those shown in Figure 3.11, and the situation becomes even more complicated because these streamers are another factor introducing flow instability. The existing mathematical models are entirely inadequate for dealing with this situation, and the pressure drops in such conduits cannot be accurately predicted.

3.4.1.6 Effect of biofilm on the flow in biofilm reactors

Computing the Reynolds numbers for empty reactors gives valuable insight into the nature of flow in these reactors. Once a biofilm develops, the nature of the flow changes, and there are no easy solutions to quantifying such flows. Nuclear resonance imaging of protons is a technique that has been successfully employed to answer critical questions, such as whether water flows through the biofilm, but it is too expensive to be used as a routine approach to quantifying flow in biofilm reactors and it is limited, thus far at least, to specialized research facilities. Examples 3.1 and 3.2, given earlier, show that biofilm accumulation on the walls does not change the Reynolds number significantly. However, this computation was carried out with the assumptions that the biofilm covers the surfaces uniformly and that the biofilm surface reacts with the flowing water in the same manner as the surface of the conduit does, and neither of these is true. The biofilm surface has different characteristics than the surface of the conduit, and it is not expected to inter-act with the flowing water in the same manner as the surface of the conduit. Examples 3.1 and 3.2 also show that it is not trivial to correct the hydrodynamic computations for the true effect of the biofilm on the Reynolds number. Before this can be done, the true mechanism of this effect must be determined. Besides, some of the parameters used to characterize the hydrodynamics in biofilm reactors are ill defined. For example, because biofilms are porous and water actually flows through the space occupied by a biofilm, the hydraulic radius and the wetted perimeter in such a reactor are not known. It is difficult to define these two parameters in biofilm reactors. Computing the Reynolds number and the hydraulic radius is meaningful only for reactors operated without biofilm. Once the biofilm starts to accumulate, it is not known how to compute the hydraulic radius and the meaning of the Reynolds number is dubious. Experimental evidence corroborates these doubts by showing that the predictions based on the equations used here are not accurate. In a study we conducted some years ago using flat plate biofilm reactors, one reactor was operated with biofilm, another was operated without biofilm, and the flow velocity profiles were acquired using proton NMR imaging. We expected that the presence of biofilm would increase the hydrodynamic entry length because the biofilm surface was uneven and thus should introduce turbulent eddies near the surface at relatively low flow veloci-ties. The flow velocity profiles, shown in Chapter 1 (Figure 1.27), were collected at the same distance from the entry to the reactor. The results are surprising: the entry length to the reactor with biofilm was shorter than the entry length to the reactor without biofilm. This is demonstrated by the existence of a jet in the middle section of the flow velocity profile of the reactor without biofilm: the flow in this reactor had not reached stability. On the basis of these results and other experimental data quantifying the nature of pressure drop in biofilm reactors, we concluded that biofilms act as so-called *compliant surfaces*. Because of the elastic nature of extracellular polymers, biofilms interact with flowing water is such a manner that they actually damp the oscillations of the flowing water and actively delay the onset of turbulence. This all shows that our knowledge of the interactions between flowing water and biofilms is inadequate and that our computational procedures do not reflect the effects of biofilms on hydrodynamics. Progress has been made since these results were published by including the effect of the elasticity of the extracellular polymers in the conceptual model of the interactions between biofilms and flow, but a theoretical treatment of the problem is still lacking.

3.4.2   *External mass transport in biofilms*

The hydrodynamics in a biofilm reactor affect not only the pressure drop but also the rate of transport of the nutrient from the bulk solution to the biofilm. In biofilm models the rate of reaction equals the rate of transport of the reactants to the surface of the biofilm. The conceptual model of mass transport toward the biofilm surface (Chapter 8) shows the diffusion layer near the surface of the biofilm and also assumes that this diffusion layer comprises all mass transport resistance to the biofilm. In this model, the rate of mass transport to the biofilm is computed as the flux of nutrients across the diffusion layer. Using the assumption that the nutrient concentration profile in this layer is linear, the flux of the nutrient can be computed from Fick's first law:

$$J = D_w \frac{C_b - C_s}{\delta} \tag{3.40}$$

To simplify computations, the diffusivity and the thickness of the mass transfer boundary layer are lumped together and their ratio is called the *mass transfer coefficient*:

$$k = \frac{D_w}{\delta} \tag{3.41}$$

From this, the flux of nutrients can be quantified as

$$J = k(C_b - C_s) \tag{3.42}$$

If the flow velocity increases, the thickness of the mass transfer boundary layer, δ, decreases, which, according to Equation 3.41, increases the mass transfer coefficient. The data needed to compute the local flux of a nutrient can be extracted from a profile of the nutrient concentration measured using suitable microelectrodes. The usual treatment of such data is to measure the gradient of the profile near the biofilm surface and multiply the gradient by the diffusivity of the nutrient in water. The result is the flux of the nutrient at that particular location:

$$J = D_w \frac{dC}{dz}\bigg|_{(z=z_s)} \tag{3.43}$$

Because the concentration profile also provides C_b and C_s, the mass transfer coefficient, k, can be estimated from Equation 3.42, and the thickness of the boundary layer can be estimated from Equation 3.41.

The results of these computations depend on the position of the biofilm surface on the concentration profile, but exact locating of the biofilm surface is not trivial. The problem of locating the biofilm surface on the nutrient concentration profile is serious enough to warrant separate study. The results in Figure 3.12 illustrate the nature of the problem. Conceptually, the biofilm surface is at the inflection point of the nutrient concentration profile. As can be seen in Figure 3.12, the position of the inflection point on such a profile is rather ill defined: it is not easy to decide where the inflection point is in Figure 3.12, and it is even harder for noisy signals, in which the data points are dispersed.

To find the biofilm surface on the nutrient concentration profile experimentally, we glued together an electrochemical microsensor for measuring oxygen and a fiber optic microsensor for measuring optical density so that their tips were at the same level. This combined sensor simultaneously measured the oxygen concentration profile and the optical density profile. It is difficult to locate the surface of the biofilm on the oxygen concentration profile because the flux of oxygen across the biofilm surface is continuous, so that there is not much difference between the oxygen concentration just above the biofilm surface and that just below the biofilm surface. The optical density profile, however, changes abruptly at the biofilm surface, as there is a large difference between the optical densities just above the biofilm surface and just below the biofilm surface. Superimposing these two profiles enabled exact locating of the biofilm surface on the oxygen concentration profile (Figure 3.13). The optical density profile in Figure 3.13 shows that the biofilm surface was at the end of the curved part of the oxygen concentration profile.

The result from locating the biofilm surface on the concentration profile using a combined microsensor came as a surprise. If we were to have chosen the inflection point in the oxygen concentration profile in Figure 3.13, we would have located it somewhere around 1.3 mm from the bottom, which would have been an entirely inaccurate estimate. This inaccurate estimate of the position of the surface would have led to an inaccurate estimate of oxygen flux from Equation 3.39 because the oxygen concentration at the distance of 1.3 mm from the bottom was about 4 mg/L, whereas the real concentration of oxygen

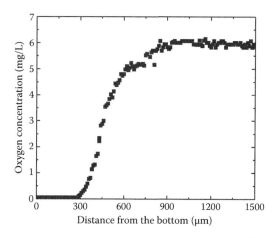

Figure 3.12 Oxygen concentration profile measured with a microelectrode. (Reprinted from Rasmussen, K., and Lewandowski, Z., *Biotechnology and Bioengineering*, 59, 302–309, 1998.)

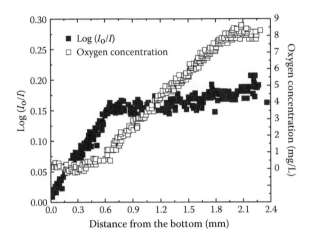

Figure 3.13 Profiles of oxygen concentration and optical density in a biofilm. A combined microsensor—an oxygen microelectrode and an optical density microprobe—permitted locating the biofilm surface 0.60 mm from the bottom. This distance, when marked on the oxygen concentration profile, indicated that the biofilm surface was at the beginning of the linear part of the oxygen profile within the mass transport boundary layer. I is the local light intensity, and I_o is the maximum light density. (Reprinted from Lewandowski, Z. et al., *Biotechnology and Bioengineering*, 38, 877–882, 1991.)

at the biofilm surface was only about 0.5 mg/L. It is quite tedious to construct combined microsensors, and we do not use them often. On the basis of the results in Figure 3.13, we have accepted as a rule that the biofilm surface is at the end of the curved part of the oxygen concentration profile of the biofilm. This rule has been corroborated by several other measurements, and we use it in all computations (Lewandowski et al. 1991). The following example of simple computations based on information extracted from oxygen concentration profiles demonstrates how this rule is used.

Example 3.6

A profile of oxygen concentration has been measured and is plotted in Figure 3.14. Estimate the oxygen flux, the mass transfer coefficient and the thickness of the mass boundary layer from these results.

Using the rule specified above (that the biofilm surface is at the end of the curved part of the nutrient profile), the surface of the biofilm is located approximately 0.025 cm from the bottom and it is estimated from the data in Figure 3.14 that the oxygen concentrations at the edges of the boundary layer are as follows:

Concentration of oxygen on biofilm surface, $C_s = 0.49$ mg/L = 0.49×10^{-3} mg/cm^3

Concentration of oxygen in the bulk solution, $C_b = 5$ mg/L = 5×10^{-3} mg/cm^3

For these computations, the data in Table 3.3 were used to evaluate the diffusivity of oxygen in water as $D_w = 2.1 \times 10^{-9}$ m^2/s = 2.1×10^{-5} cm^2/s.

A rough estimate of the nutrient concentration gradient at the biofilm surface is based on the assumption that the nutrient concentration in the boundary layer changes linearly:

$$\frac{dC}{dz} \approx \frac{(5-0.49)\times 10^{-3}}{0.1-0.025} = 0.06013 \frac{mg}{cm^4}$$

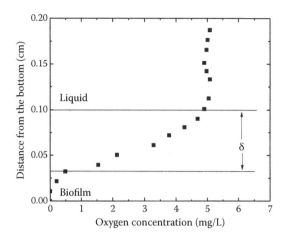

Figure 3.14 Oxygen concentration profile used in this example.

The flux of oxygen, from Equation 3.43, is

$$J = D_w \frac{dC}{dz} = 2 \times 10^{-5} \frac{cm^2}{s} \times 0.06013 \frac{mg}{cm^4} = 1.203 \times 10^{-6} \frac{mg}{cm^2 \times s}$$

The mass transfer coefficient, from Equation 3.42, is

$$k = \frac{J}{C_b - C_s} = \frac{1.203 \times 10^{-6} \dfrac{mg}{cm^2 \times s}}{(5 - 0.49) \times 10^{-3} \dfrac{mg}{cm^3}} = 2.665 \times 10^{-4} \frac{cm}{s}$$

The thickness of the boundary layer, from Equation 3.41, is

$$\delta = \frac{D_w}{k} = \frac{2 \times 10^{-5} \dfrac{cm^2}{s}}{2.665 \times 10^{-4} \dfrac{cm}{s}} = 0.075 \text{ cm}$$

Because the surface of the biofilm in Figure 3.14 has been located 0.0324 cm from the bottom and the thickness of the boundary layer has been estimated to be 0.0676 cm, the oxygen concentration should be constant at a distance from the bottom equal to 0.0324 + 0.0676 = 0.1 cm. A comparison of the data in Figure 3.14 with the computations shows that, indeed, the concentration of oxygen remains constant at distances from the bottom exceeding 0.1 cm. Therefore, the estimated thickness of the mass boundary layer is acceptable, which also demonstrates that the rule used to locate the surface of the biofilm on the nutrient concentration profile is acceptable.

3.5   *Operating modes of LBRs*

LBRs are used to study biofilm processes in controlled environments. As discussed at the beginning of this chapter, they are constructed to satisfy two requirements: (1) to facilitate the biofilm processes under study and (2) to facilitate the measurements characterizing the processes under study. LBRs can be categorized from various points of view, and they will be categorized here based on the distinct features of their design, such as flat plate reactors and rotating reactors. Categorizing LBRs from the point of view of their applications is more difficult, because identical reactors may be used in a variety of biofilm studies. The main goal of the procedures presented in this book is to quantify the relations between biofilm structure and biofilm activity, and the reactors suitable for studying these factors will be indicated here. From the definitions of biofilm structure and activity in Chapter 1, we can deduce that reactors for quantifying biofilm activity at the microscale should support microelectrode measurements and the imaging of biofilms. Several types of reactors are in use, and some are better suited to evaluating biofilm activity, whereas others are better suited to evaluating biofilm structure. In addition, it is beneficial if both types of reactors—those used to quantify biofilm activity and those used to quantify biofilm structure—permit the controlling or at least the quantifying of the hydrodynamics. There are no universal LBRs that satisfy all needs. Each reactor has limitations, and choices must be made when an LBR is selected for a particular study. The usefulness of various LBRs in particular studies will be discussed as well as the advantages and the limitations of the most popular LBRs. Also, each reactor can be operated in different modes. The selected mode of operation may, to some extent, mitigate the limitations of particular reactors. LBRs are typically operated in one of three configurations: (1) without recycle, (2) with recycle, and (3) with recycle and a mixing chamber.

The configuration of the reactor setup related to each of these modes of operation is shown in Figure 3.15 and addressed in the following sections.

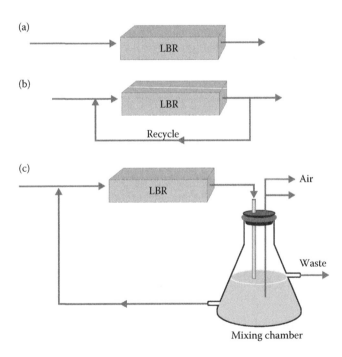

Figure 3.15 Operating modes of LBRs: (a) an LBR without recycle, (b) an LBR with recycle, and (c) an LBR with recycle and a mixing chamber.

3.5.1   LBRs without recycle: Once-through mode of operation

The operation of an LBR without recycle is known as a *once-through operation*. It is typically done at low flow velocities. When high flow velocities in the reactor are desired, the reactor is operated with recycle. The main advantage of using the once-through mode is the simplicity of the operation. The disadvantage of this mode of operation is the possibility of generating gradients of nutrient concentrations along the reactor. This possibility can be mitigated by using a short reactor, but then the hydrodynamic entry length may exceed the size of the reactor. Consequently, this mode of operation does not give much control over the conditions in the reactor. Such reactors are sometimes used just to grow biofilms that are later subjected to other studies.

If the limitations are acceptable, once-through is a convenient mode of operation. The once-through mode is often used in so-called "biomedical applications," in which potentially pathogenic microorganisms are grown and exposed to various concentrations of antimicrobial agents, after which the changes in biofilm activity are evaluated. The purpose of such studies is to grow biofilms and determine the efficacy of the selected antimicrobials. This is done by determining the activity before and after treatment, and how the biofilm was grown is of less interest in this type of study. In this case, accepting the limitations of the once-through operating mode is a fair trade for the convenience of the operation. The reactors used for this mode of operation are small, and many reactors can be operated in parallel. The single-pass mode of operation limits the possibility of microbial contamination because the number of connections and pumps is limited. We often operate the simplified open-channel flat plate reactors described in the following sections in this configuration.

3.5.2   LBRs with recycle

An LBR with recycle is the most usual mode of operating a biofilm reactor in our laboratory. When we grow biofilms in flat plate flow reactors, we recycle the solution to control the flow velocity. Also, in some studies, when we use growth media with high concentrations of nutrients, fast recycling increases the contact of the liquid with the air in the flat plate flow reactor and helps deliver oxygen to the liquid. The latter benefit of this mode of operation is restricted to the reactors that have an air space above the flowing liquid.

3.5.3   LBRs with recycle and a mixing chamber

When oxygen deficiency in the reactor is expected, and it cannot be overcome by increasing the recycle ratio to increase oxygen delivery through the surface of the liquid, we use in-line aerating chambers to transfer oxygen into the growth medium. This configuration is often used with tubular reactors, in which the contact of liquid with air is negligible. Such reactors need in-line aerators, particularly when a highly concentrated solution of nutrients is used. One difficulty in executing this mode of operation is preventing air bubbles from entering the reactor, where they can disturb the pattern of flow and make the hydrodynamics in the reactor nonreproducible.

3.6   LBRs and their typical applications

3.6.1   Flat plate reactors

This is probably the largest group of biofilm reactors. Although their geometrical configurations vary, they all operate on the same principle: biofilms are grown on the bottom and walls of a reactor operated under well-controlled conditions. The popularity of these reactors is determined by their convenience: they allow the monitoring of biofilm structure and activity at the same time.

3.6.1.1   Open-channel flat plate reactors

The main feature of an open-channel flat plate reactor is the channel, which is typically rectangular. When the reactor is operated, the channel is only partially filled with water. We use these reactors the most often because they are particularly suitable for quantifying relations between biofilm structure and activity. They permit (1) growing biofilms under well-defined hydrodynamic conditions, (2) using a variety of microscopic techniques to quantify biofilm structure, and (3) using microsensors to quantify chemical gradients in the biofilms. Flat plate reactors are all designed using the same principle, but we use many versions of open-channel flat plate reactors. Their designs vary depending on the type of biofilm process we want to emphasize or the type of measurement we want to use in a specific study. For example, if microscopic observations are important, the reactors are constructed with glass bottoms, whereas if only microsensor measurements are scheduled, the reactors are made with polycarbonate bottoms, which are less expensive and easier to make. In some studies, we place microscope slides at the bottom of the reactor, remove them at the end of the experiments, and use them to quantify biofilm structure using confocal scanning laser microscopy (CSLM) imaging or determine the number of cells per unit surface area. In some studies, the departure from the standard construction is quite dramatic, as in the case of flat plate reactors used to quantify processes in biofilms grown in the gas phase. Such reactors will be discussed at the end of this chapter.

In a biofilm laboratory, it is important to standardize as many procedures as possible, and constructing our open-channel flat plate reactors is an example of an attempt to standardize reactors.

Figure 3.16 gives an example of the construction. It shows a polycarbonate channel 2.5 cm wide, 4.0 cm deep, and 34.5 cm long (the same dimensions that we used in quantifying hydrodynamics in Examples 3.1 through 3.4). The reactor has a working volume of approximately 150 mL, including the volume of all tubings. The exact volume of the reactor is determined before every experiment because the volume of the reactor is used in many computations. The flow velocity in the reactor is controlled by recycling part of the flow, and the volume also affects the flow rate in the recycle line. All fittings have a 3/8-inch opening width with a 1/8-inch plastic pipe thread. All fittings are centered and placed close to the edge except the output line, which is positioned above the recycle line. The width of the channel is 2.5 cm so that microscope slides can be positioned at the bottom, if needed. Growing biofilm on microscope slides is useful in many studies in which biofilm samples must be removed from the reactor and each one treated differently, as in the case of testing antimicrobial efficacy or describing temporal biofilm accumulation.

Example 3.7

For the channel biofilm reactor we described in Example 3.1, the hydraulic radius was computed to be $R_h = 2.42 \times 10^{-3}$ m and the Reynolds number to be Re = 193. Using Equation 3.27, the hydrodynamic entry length to this reactor can now be calculated:

$$L_d = 0.06 \times 193 \times 4 \times 2.42 \times 10^{-3} = 0.112 \text{ m} = 11.2 \text{ cm}$$

Because the bottom plate of the reactor is 27.9 cm long (see Figure 3.16), only 27.9 − 11.2 = 16.7 cm of the reactor can be used for measurements that are sensitive to the

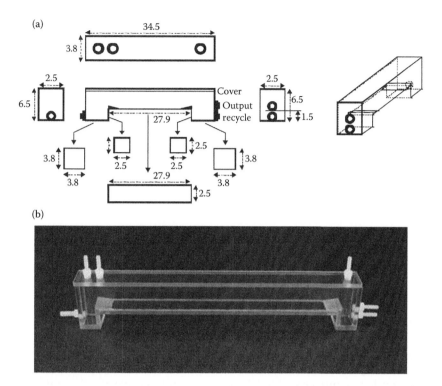

Figure 3.16 (a) An open-channel flat plate biofilm reactor. All dimensions are in centimeters, and the figure is sketched without scale. The water depth in this reactor is adjusted by the size of the triangular inserts (ramps) glued to the bottom of the reactor at the beginning and the end of the channel. Typically, the depth is set to 3 mm. (b) Photograph of the reactor.

nature of the flow. It is not advisable to use the part of the reactor in close proximity to the effluent, which limits the working range to about 15 cm. If biofilm measurements sensitive to hydrodynamics are to be conducted, we use two microscope slides with the dimensions 2.5 cm × 7.5 cm × 0.1 cm to grow biofilms in this reactor. These slides occupy a distance of 2 × 7.5 = 15 cm near the outlet of the reactor, and we assume that this location positions the slides beyond the hydrodynamic entry length to the reactor, in a zone of stable and well-developed flow. If more than three slides are needed, a longer reactor is used.

While operating open-channel flat plate reactors, we control the retention time and the flow velocity. The retention time is controlled by setting the nutrient delivery pumps, and the flow velocity is controlled by varying the recycle ratio. The following examples explain how to make appropriate computations to establish the retention time and the average flow velocity.

Example 3.8

The operator wants to operate the reactor described in Example 3.1 at an average flow velocity of 0.5 mm/s and a retention time of 2 h, and we need to define the settings on the nutrient delivery pump and the recycle pump. The depth of the liquid in the reactor is 3 mm.

According to Equation 3.5:

$$v_s = \frac{\text{volumetric flow rate}}{\text{surface area perpendicular to flow}} = \frac{q}{7.5 \times 10^{-5}\,\text{m}^2} = 0.5\,\frac{\text{mm}}{\text{s}}$$

Thus, the volumetric flow rate satisfying this requirement is

$$q = 0.5\frac{mm}{s} \times 10^{-1}\frac{cm}{mm} \times 7.5 \times 10^{-5} m^2 \times 10^4 \frac{cm^2}{m^2} = 0.0375\frac{cm^3}{s}$$

where A is the surface area perpendicular to the flow: 2.5×10^{-2} m $\times 3 \times 10^{-3}$ m $= 7.5 \times 10^{-5} m^2$.

Using this result, the flow rate of the nutrient solution can be adjusted to provide the desired retention time. However, the flow velocity adjusted for the flow of nutrients in the reactor is not the one at which we desire to operate the reactor.

If we applied the flow rate computed above, the retention time τ_r in the reactor would be

$$\tau_r = \frac{\text{volume of the reactor}}{\text{flow rate}} = \frac{V}{q_{total}} = \frac{7.5 \times 10^{-5} m^2 \times 10^4 \frac{cm^2}{m^2} \times 27.9\, cm}{0.0375\frac{cm^3}{s}} = 558\, s$$

This is roughly 9 hours, much longer than the 2 hours we need.

In conclusion, using reactors without recycle does not allow simultaneous control of the flow rate and the retention time. To control the retention time and the flow rate at the same time, a recycle line must be added. In a reactor with recycle, the flow rate in the nutrient line determines the retention time in the reactor and the combined flow rates in the nutrient line and the recycle line determine the flow velocity in the reactor. In the recycle line, part of the liquid from the effluent of the reactor circulates back to the beginning of the reactor at a flow rate which is consistent with the desired flow rate in the reactor. Because the liquid in the recycle line never leaves the system, the flow rate in the recycle line does not affect the retention time (Figure 3.17).

After recycle has been added, both the retention time and the flow velocity can be controlled. To control both, start by determining the desired flow rate to satisfy the designed retention time:

$$\tau_r = \frac{V}{q} = \frac{7.5 \times 10^{-5} m^2 \times 10^4 \frac{cm^2}{m^2} \times 27.9\, cm}{q} = 2\, h$$

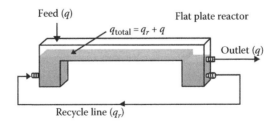

Feed (q)   Flat plate reactor

$q_{total} = q_r + q$

Outlet (q)

Recycle line (q_r)

Figure 3.17 Open-channel flat plate reactor with recycle.

From this, the required flow rate of nutrients may be computed:

$$q = \frac{7.5 \times 10^{-5}\,\text{m}^2 \times 10^4\,\frac{\text{cm}^2}{\text{m}^2} \times 27.9\,\text{cm}}{2\,\text{h}} = 10.46\,\frac{\text{cm}^3}{\text{h}}$$

The nutrient should be delivered at a rate of 10.46 cm^3/h. The total flow rate in the reactor, q_{total}, is composed of the fresh feed flow, $q = 10.46$ cm^3/h, and the unknown rate of flow of the recycled liquid, q_r:

$$q_{total} = q + q_r$$

The flow rate in the recycle line is found from the equation quantifying the flow velocity in the reactor:

$$v_s = \frac{\text{volumetric flow rate}}{\text{surface area perpendicular to flow}} = \frac{q + q_r}{7.5 \times 10^{-5}\,\text{m}^2}$$

$$= \frac{10.46\,\frac{\text{cm}^3}{\text{h}} \times 10^3\,\frac{\text{mm}^3}{\text{cm}^3} + q_r}{7.5 \times 10^{-5}\,\text{m}^2 \times 10^6\,\frac{\text{mm}^2}{\text{m}^2}} = \frac{10.46 \times 10^3\,\frac{\text{mm}^3}{\text{h}} + q_r}{75\,\text{mm}^2} = 0.5\,\frac{\text{mm}}{\text{s}}$$

$$q_r = 75\,\text{mm}^2 \times 0.5\,\frac{\text{mm}}{\text{s}} - 10.46 \times 10^3\,\frac{\text{mm}^3}{\text{h}} \times \frac{1\,\text{h}}{3600\,\text{s}} = 37.5\,\frac{\text{mm}^3}{\text{s}} - 2.9\,\frac{\text{mm}^3}{\text{s}}$$

$$= 34.59\,\frac{\text{mm}^3}{\text{s}} \times \frac{1\,\text{cm}^3}{1000\,\text{mm}^3} \times \frac{3600\,\text{s}}{1\,\text{h}} = 124.52\,\frac{\text{cm}^3}{\text{h}}$$

To satisfy the imposed conditions of the study—the flow velocity of 0.5 mm/s and the retention time of 2 h—the recirculation pump should be set to deliver 124.52 cm^3/h.

The recycle ratio (RR) in this reactor is

$$\text{RR} = \frac{q_r}{q} = \frac{124.52\,\frac{\text{cm}^3}{\text{h}}}{10.46\,\frac{\text{cm}^3}{\text{h}}} = 11.9$$

Example 3.9

Example 3.8 explains how to select the operational parameters of the reactor—the flow rate of the growth medium and the flow rate of the recycle. A reactor with a working volume of 100 mL will be used to demonstrate these procedures. If the growth medium is pumped through the reactor at a rate of 10 mL/h, then the retention time in the reactor is

$$\text{retention time} = \frac{\text{working volume}}{\text{volumetric flow rate}} = \frac{100\,\text{mL}}{10\,\text{mL/h}} = 10\,\text{h}$$

If the operator wants to set the recycle ratio to 320 (very high), what will the recycle flow rate q_r be?

$$\text{recycle ratio} = \frac{q_r}{q} = \frac{q_r}{10 \text{ mL/h}} = 320$$

$$q_r = 10 \text{ mL/h} \times 320 = 3200 \text{ mL/h}$$

3.6.1.1.1 Example of results from a biofilm study using open-channel flat plate reactors. Open-channel flat plate reactors are used in many biofilm studies. The first example presented here to demonstrate their use is related to the reproducibility of biofilm processes in LBRs. Our group has been attempting to grow structurally reproducible biofilms and create a model biofilm that has a reproducible structure. It would be desirable to have a model biofilm because various properties of the model biofilm could serve as a reference for the properties of biofilms grown in other studies. To ensure the reproducibility of biofilm processes, we methodically follow a procedure for growing our model biofilm in terms of microbial makeup, medium composition, temperature, surface preparation, etc. Despite all this effort, the reproducibility of our results for long-term growth is unimpressive. Discouraged by this series of failures, we asked the question: Are biofilm processes reproducible? To test whether model biofilms can be grown reproducibly, we operated two identical flat plate biofilm reactors under an identical and well-defined flow regime (Lewandowski et al. 2004). The biofilms were composed of *Pseudomonas aeruginosa* (ATCC 700829), *Pseudomonas fluorescens* (ATCC 700830), and *Klebsiella pneumoniae* (ATCC 700831). The fresh feed flow rate was 0.4 ± 0.1 mL/min. To maintain a reasonable flow velocity and shear stress, the recycle ratio was set to 300. The reactors were operated in parallel, they were inoculated with microorganisms from the same vessel, and the biofilms were grown using growth medium from the same container. As the parameter evaluated to test biofilm reproducibility, we selected the areal porosity of the biofilm measured at the level of the bottom. We hypothesized that structurally identical biofilms would grow as a result of identical biofilm processes. Therefore, with the biofilm processes identical in the two reactors, the areal porosities of the biofilms in the two reactors should be identical. The results were previously shown in Figure 1.38.

The conclusion of this study explains why we could not grow the model biofilm reproducibly. Each time we attempted it, the final structure of the biofilm was different. Biofilms grown in two identical and identically operated biofilm reactors have comparable structure only until the first sloughing event. After that, the biofilms have different patterns of accumulation. This conclusion is ominous not only because it shows that model biofilms may never materialize but also because of a more immediate consequence: it demonstrates our inability to select any particular time during the operation of these reactors when the results of the measurements will be representative of the biofilm structure. We consider the latter conclusion ominous because we cannot judiciously select any particular time to sample the reactor. All these conclusions lead us to the concept of a steady state in biofilm reactors. When we operate biofilm reactors, we assume that, after a few retention times, biofilm processes in the reactor reach a steady state and sampling the reactor at any time after the processes reach a steady state will give representative results. On the basis of the results in Figure 1.38, biofilm structure, and thus activity at the microscale, do not reach a steady state. We have reproduced this lack of reproducibility enough times to consider this effect a pattern characteristic of biofilm growth and accumulation.

An interesting speculation regarding the conclusion that biofilms accumulated under apparently identical conditions are different is the domino effect caused by changing a single variable in a biofilm process; we discussed this scenario in the introduction to this chapter in reference to the types of variables in LBRs. Hypothetically, this effect may amplify small differences between two reactors existing from the very beginning of their operation, perhaps concerning a single variable only. As we argued in the introduction, it is impossible to change only one variable in a biofilm reactor. We can also argue that it is impossible to run two identical reactors. Although all efforts are made to make the processes as similar as possible, it is unrealistic to expect that they are identical. Therefore, small differences between two apparently identical biofilm processes, perhaps concerning a single variable at the beginning, may affect many other variables, and as time passes these effects accumulate and cause what we have seen: two biofilm reactors operated identically showing different patterns of biofilm accumulation. Large differences in the final outcome of a process caused by minute differences in the boundary conditions are well-known features of nonlinear and chaotic processes. Biofilm accumulation exhibits similar behavior; minute differences in the operating conditions of two seemingly identical reactors lead to different patterns of biofilm accumulation.

Open-channel flat plate reactors are also used to measure concentration profiles of various nutrients using microelectrodes. This procedure is somewhat more complex than taking images of the biofilm and, in a sense, destructive. Microsensor measurements, although nondestructive, require removing the lid from the reactor, which exposes the contents of the reactor to air and contaminates the reactor. Therefore, microelectrode measurements are typically done at the end of the time the reactor is operated, as the last measurements before the operation is discontinued. Unless the biofilms are composed of undefined microbial populations, the reactor is open to the air during the operation, and contamination is not considered a problem. Microelectrode measurements are carried out in flowing water at a location where the flow is well established, beyond the reach of the hydrodynamic entry length to the reactor. The results we selected as an example of the measurements were obtained in channel flow reactors (see Figure 3.18) and show

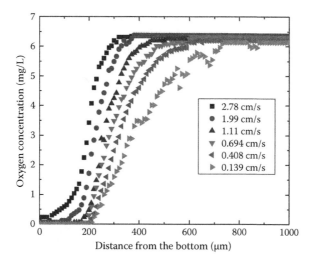

Figure 3.18 Oxygen concentration profiles measured in a flat plate channel reactor at various average flow velocities. As the flow velocity increases, the gradient of the profiles increases as well, and so does the flux of oxygen, which equals the gradient multiplied by the diffusivity of oxygen in water. (Reprinted from Rasmussen, K., and Lewandowski, Z., *Water Research*, 32, 3747–3755, 1998.)

that the gradients of the oxygen concentration profiles increase when the flow velocity increases. This is an expected effect of increasing the flow velocity because the gradient of these profiles determines the driving force of the mass transport: the higher the flow velocity, the higher the rate of mass transport. The rate of oxygen transfer across the biofilm surface can be quantified from the results in Figure 3.18 as an oxygen flux for each of the profiles. Such computations are reported by Rasmussen and Lewandowski (1998a, 1998b), and the reader may consult the original papers (Rasmussen and Lewandowski 1998a, 1998b). A change in the oxygen concentration profile can be caused by many factors, not only by a change in the flow velocity. It can change because the biofilm activity has changed, as when the biofilm is treated with antimicrobials. It is somewhat challenging to quantify the reasons that the shape of the concentration profiles changes because there are many causes that may have the same effect. For example, decreasing the flow velocity may have the same effect on the shape of the oxygen profile as treating the biofilm with an antimicrobial substance. In both cases, the slope of the profile at the biofilm surface will decrease. The researcher needs to make sure that the observed variations in the shape of the concentration profile are properly interpreted. This demonstrates how important it is to make sure that the hydrodynamics in the reactor are reproducible and the microsensor measurements are conducted at a distance from the entry to the reactor that exceeds the entry length of the reactor. If this condition is overlooked, the effects of unstable hydrodynamics can be confused with the effects of biofilm activity.

3.6.1.1.2 Example of results from a biofilm study using a modified open-channel flat plate reactor. Open-channel flat plate reactors can be modified to address various research questions, and their unique features make them amenable to many types of projects. Here we describe the use of an open-channel flat plate reactor in a study designed to quantify the rates of electron transfer between a biofilm and an electrode in a biofilm of *Geobacter sulfurreducens* and compare these rates with pH and redox profiles measured across the biofilm. The biofilm was grown at the bottom of an open-channel flat plate reactor operated with recycle. The reactor was equipped with three electrodes: a biofilm electrode (or working electrode), a counter electrode, and a reference electrode. Initially, the reactor was inoculated with *G. sulfurreducens*, and the biofilm was allowed to grow and accumulate on the biofilm electrode while it was polarized at +300 $mV_{Ag/AgCl}$. The growth medium was devoid of an electron acceptor so that the polarized electrode was the only electron acceptor available for the respiration of *G. sulfurreducens*. The experimental setup is shown in Figure 3.19.

The rate of electron transfer from the biofilm to the electrode was quantified as the current measured in the external circuit, and the results are shown in Figure 3.20a. To determine the relation between the rate of electron transfer and the potential of the electrode, we ran electrode polarization tests using a 1-mV/s scan rate. The polarization curve (Figure 3.20b) shows that a limiting current was reached at a polarization potential of + 0.2 $V_{Ag/AgCl}$; in practical terms, polarizing the electrode above 0.2 $V_{Ag/AgCl}$ would give the same current.

The versatility of the open-channel flat plate reactor made it possible to measure pH and redox profiles across a biofilm deposited on the surface of an electrode at the same time that electrochemical tests quantifying the rate of electron transfer between the biofilm and the electrode were performed. The pH and redox potential profiles were measured at two different phases of biofilm growth corresponding to two different currents, 1.05 and 1.85 mA. The results are shown in Figure 3.21. As time passed and the current increased from 1.05 to 1.85 mA, the pH profiles changed and the difference in pH between

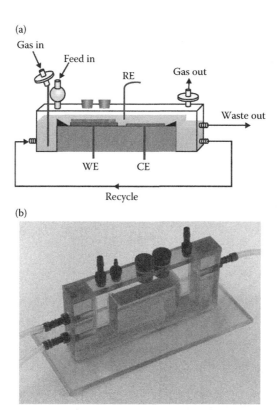

Figure 3.19 (a) A three-electrode bioreactor. The working, counter, and reference electrodes were housed in the same compartment. (b) A photograph of the reactor without electrodes. Note that (a) is not scaled.

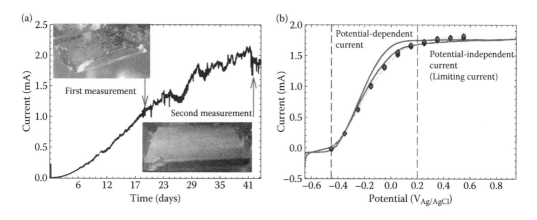

Figure 3.20 **(See color insert.)** (a) Current generation of the *G. sulfurreducens* biofilm over time. The red arrows show the times when the biofilm images were taken. (b) Steady state polarization curve superimposed on slow-scan CV (1 mV/s). At polarization potentials above 0.2 $V_{Ag/AgCl}$, a maximum current is achieved. (Reproduced from Babauta, T. J. et al., *Biotechnology and Bioengineering* 109: 2651–2662, 2012.)

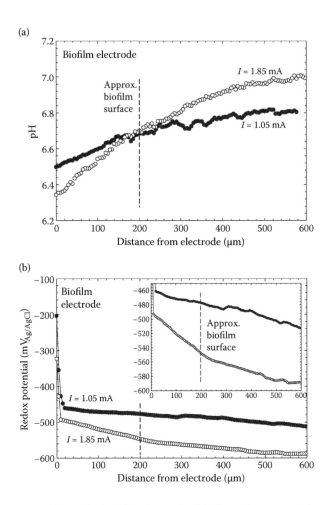

Figure 3.21 (a) The pH profiles at the biofilm electrode. (b) The redox potential profiles at the biofilm electrode. The inset shows the profiles over a smaller y-axis range for clarity. The biofilm electrode was polarized to 0.45 $V_{Ag/AgCl}$ during measurements. The solid circles represent profiles measured at a current of 1.05 mA. The open circles represent profiles measured at 1.85 mA. (Reproduced from Babauta, T. J. et al., *Biotechnology and Bioengineering*, 109, 2651–2662, 2012.)

the top and the bottom of the biofilm increased from 0.3 to 0.6 pH units, from pH 6.5 at 1.05 mA to pH 6.3 at 1.85 mA. Because the *G. sulfurreducens* biofilm was consuming acetate, the increasing rate of proton release must have corresponded to the increasing rate of the respiration reaction described by

$$CH_3COO^- + 3H_2O \rightarrow CO_2 + HCO_3^- + 8H^+ + 8e^- \tag{3.44}$$

The redox potential inside the biofilm increased from −500 to −460 $mV_{Ag/AgCl}$ and from −590 to −490 $mV_{Ag/AgCl}$ when measured at 1.05 and 1.85 mA, respectively. The inset in Figure 3.21b expands the data over a smaller y-axis range to show the redox potential change more clearly. The results in Figure 3.21b suggest that most of the current passing through the biofilm was not localized in the soluble aqueous phase and was unable to equilibrate with the redox microelectrode, consistent with the observation that replacing the growth medium did not affect the current. Otherwise, the redox potential profiles would have shown much larger changes for the given currents.

3.6.1.2 Flat plate vapor phase reactor

If needed, open-channel flat plate vapor phase reactors (VPRs) can be modified to accommodate measurements in the gas phase, such as in the reactor shown in Figure 3.22. Some applications include biofilms growing in contact with water vapor saturated with a contaminant that needs to be removed. In such processes, the biofilm reactor needs to be operated at a slightly increased gas pressure, and all measurements need to be done under this increased gas pressure. This requirement complicates the microsensor measurements because they must be done in a sealed and pressurized reactor. To make microelectrode measurements possible, we install, in the top plate of the reactor, ports covered with rubber sleeves which are gastight but permit microsensor measurements.

3.6.1.2.1 Example of results from a biofilm study using VPRs.
VPRs are used to study the decomposition of volatile organic compounds (VOCs) in biofilms (Villaverde et al. 1997). The overall layout of the VPR resembles that of the reactor shown in Figure 3.23, but the operating principles of the VPR are different from those described in the preceding sections. The substrate is delivered in the gas phase, not in the liquid phase. The reactor we use is 50 cm long, 5 cm wide, and 12 cm tall and is made of polycarbonate. A flat plate, 40 cm long and 5 cm wide, serves as the substratum for the biofilm growth. This is made of glass to facilitate biofilm monitoring through the bottom using an inverted microscope. Several glass coupons (12 × 12 × 0.1 mm) are positioned on the glass plate for biofilm sampling. These slides are usually retrieved after the experiment is completed, and the biofilm accumulated on the slides is characterized in a manner consistent with the reason for which the reactor was operated. The reactor lid is fastened to the reactor to form a gastight seal. Nine ports, each 2 cm in diameter, are distributed along the lid. These allow for sampling of the liquid and the biofilm on the

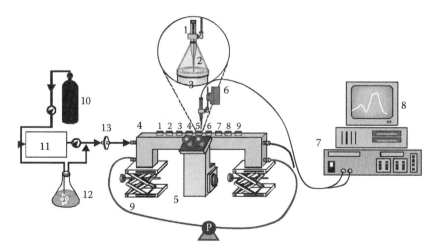

Figure 3.22 Flat plate vapor phase reactor arranged for the measurement of oxygen concentration profiles: (1) microelectrode, (2) latex glove finger, (3) sampling port, (4) flat plate VPR (with nine sampling ports), (5) inverted microscope, (6) micromanipulator, (7) picoammeter and voltage source, (8) PC, (9) lab jacks, (10) air tank, (11) humidifier, (12) source of volatile organic compounds, and (13) gas filter (0.2 μm).

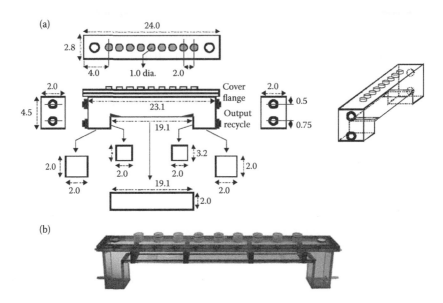

Figure 3.23 Flat plate vapor phase reactor: (a) Diagram (the dimensions in the diagram are in centimeters) and (b) photograph.

glass plate. The center of the first port is located downstream at 4 cm from the edge of the glass plate (9 cm from the gas inlet), the ninth is placed upstream at 4 cm from the other edge of the plate (9 cm from the gas exit), and the other seven ports are placed every 4 cm between the first and ninth ports. To prevent gas leaks, latex glove fingers are fastened onto the nine sampling ports using rubber O-rings. Ports on each end, each with a Teflon septum, permit gas and liquid sampling of the influent and effluent. The gases are delivered by two lines: one delivers compressed air bubbled through a humidifier, and the other passes through an Erlenmeyer flask containing the VOC under study, such as liquid toluene. The gas streams are combined and delivered through a 0.2-μm Teflon filter into the VPR and out to the atmosphere in a safety hood. Peristaltic pumps are used to provide sterile growth medium to the reactor at a constant flow rate. The growth medium is composed of mineral salts only; the sole external carbon or energy source during bacterial degradation is the selected VOC introduced in the vapor phase. The reactor is operated in countercurrent mode: the stream of gas is pumped in the opposite direction to the stream of liquid. The selected VOC diffuses into the liquid phase and serves as the carbon and energy source for the microorganisms.

We use this reactor to quantify toluene removal by *Pseudomonas putida* 54G biofilm grown on toluene vapor supplied as the sole external carbon and energy source. Oxygen profiles in the gas and liquid phases above the biofilm are used to evaluate the endogenous respiration rate of the biofilm (Figure 3.24).

3.6.1.3   *Simplified open-channel flat plate reactors*

Not all biofilm studies require the elaborate types of open-channel flat plate reactors shown in Figure 3.16. For example, we use simpler flat plate reactors to evaluate the antibacterial efficacy of selected antibacterial agents. There is no need to use elaborate flat plate reactors with controlled hydrodynamics in such studies, and simplified versions are used instead. Simplified versions of the open-channel flat plate reactors offer some, but not all, of the advantages offered by the more elaborate versions described above. The benefits offered by the simplified reactors are directly related to their small dimensions. Such reactors can

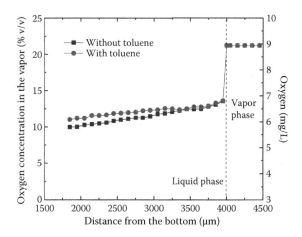

Figure 3.24 Oxygen concentration profiles in the vapor and liquid phases with 0.237 mg toluene/L in the liquid (circles) and in the absence of toluene (squares). (Reprinted from Villaverde, S. et al., *Biotechnology and Bioengineering*, 56, 361–371, 1997.)

easily be moved from location to location, positioned in temperature-controlled chambers, and attached to the stages of optical or confocal microscopes. In addition, if needed, several such reactors can be operated in parallel. The reactor system has a small footprint because the reactors are small, and the footprint can be further reduced by operating these reactors in a once-through mode. Many measurements that are typically conducted in the more elaborate reactors can be done in the simplified reactors as well. It is possible to use microsensors and to measure local biofilm activity in such reactors, and it is possible to take images of the biofilm and quantify biofilm structure. The main disadvantage of these reactors is that the experimental conditions may not be exactly reproducible because the hydrodynamics in such reactors are difficult to define. Therefore, the use of such reactors should be considered when the "before and after" effect is more important than exact reproduction of the conditions from one run to another. Figure 3.25 shows such a reactor. The retention time in this reactor is adjusted by setting the nutrient pump, and we operate such reactors in once-through mode, without recycle.

3.6.1.3.1   Example of results from a biofilm study using a simplified open-channel flat plate reactor.   One of the objectives of the study we have selected as an example of using simplified open-channel flat plate reactors was to measure fluorescence intensity and distribution in biofilms of *Staphylococcus aureus* genetically altered by inserting the TSST-1-yfpTM (yellow fluorescent protein) gene (Beyenal et al. 2004). Yellow fluorescent protein was expressed when the microorganisms produced the TSST-1 toxin. For the purpose of this measurement, we developed an optical microsensor which measures fluorescent light intensity distribution in biofilms. We also positioned the entire reactor on the stage of a CSLM and imaged the biofilm structure at the locations of the microsensor measurements.

The biofilm was grown in a growth medium made of 1% glucose, 10 μg/mL erythromycin R, 1/50 LB medium, and 0.200 mM dissolved oxygen. The reactor (Figure 3.25) was inoculated with a 24-hour-old culture of the organism, and the biofilm was grown statically for 24 hours. Flow of the growth medium at 30 mL/h was then initiated and continued for three days at 37°C in a reactor with a once-through mode of operation. The

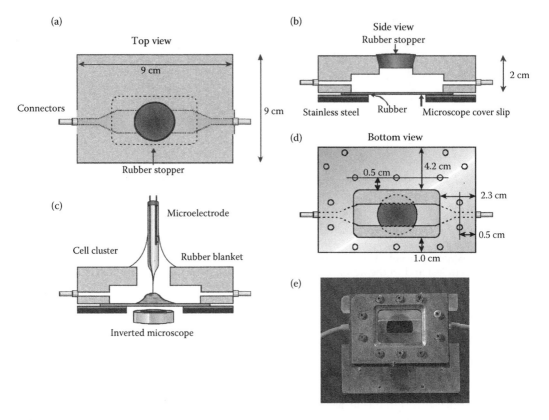

Figure 3.25 (a–d) A simplified flat plate reactor. (e) This photograph shows the bottom of the reactor. The biofilm is grown on the surface of the microscope slide and imaged using an inverted microscope. The rubber stopper is removed to open the top of the reactor. A microelectrode can be inserted through this hole to measure chemical profiles.

reactor was placed in a custom-designed, temperature-controlled chamber and mounted on an Olympus CK2 inverted microscope. The biofilm structure was monitored through a transparent window (cover slip) in the bottom of the reactor (Figure 3.25). This arrangement also allowed for monitoring the position of the tip of the microsensor when fluorescent light intensity profiles were measured (Figures 3.26 and 3.27).

3.6.1.3.2 Example of results from a biofilm study using a modified open-channel flat plate reactor. Open-channel flat plate reactors are often used in biofilm research to image biofilm structure while chemical profiling is done using microsensors, as described in Chapter 9. This is not, however, the limit of their applications. Open-channel flat plate reactors are probably the most versatile reactors used in biofilm research, and they can be adapted and modified to serve the needs of a variety of projects. The popularity of open-channel flat plate reactors stems from their unique features of providing direct access to the biofilm and allowing the control of the hydrodynamics: very few reactors offer such a combination of benefits. As an example of an application of such a reactor, we show here an open-channel flat plate reactor that was miniaturized and modified to fit the bore of an NMR instrument and used for imaging biofilms (Figure 3.28). We have selected this particular study to demonstrate the versatility of open-channel flat plate reactors; in this case the reactor was used to generate two-dimensional maps of effective diffusion coefficients

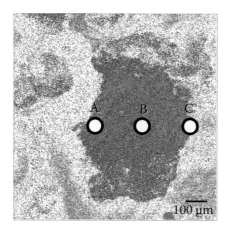

Figure 3.26 A microcolony of *Staphylococcus aureus* with the locations of the measurements marked. (Reprinted from Beyenal, H. et al., *Journal of Microbiological Methods*, 58, 367–374, 2004.)

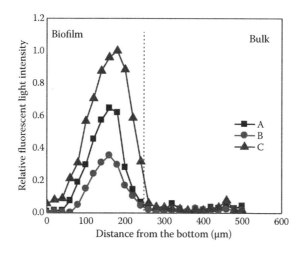

Figure 3.27 Depth profiles of the fluorescence intensity at the locations marked in Figure 3.26. (Reprinted from Beyenal, H. et al., *Journal of Microbiological Methods*, 58, 367–374, 2004.)

of water in *Shewanella oneidensis* MR-1 biofilms. The maps were generated based on *in situ* measurements of surface-averaged relative effective diffusion coefficient (D_{rs}) gradients using pulsed-field gradient nuclear magnetic resonance. The biofilm used in the measurements was grown in another reactor, a constant depth film fermenter (CDFF) (Peters and Wimpenny 1988), because that reactor generated multiple coupons of biofilms of the desired thickness and with very similar and reproducible structures. We describe the procedure for growing biofilms in CDFF reactors in Chapter 9. The coupons with the attached biofilm were removed from the CDFF reactor and fixed in the bottom of the flat plate reactor, as shown in Figure 3.1. Then the flat plate reactor was inserted into the bore of the 20-G NMR instrument. Immediately after this the nutrients needed for biofilm growth were pumped through the reactor using syringe pumps placed safely outside of the magnetic field lines of the NMR magnet. To prevent bubbles from forming and to generate a uniform field of flow, the solution of nutrients was made to enter the reactor from below.

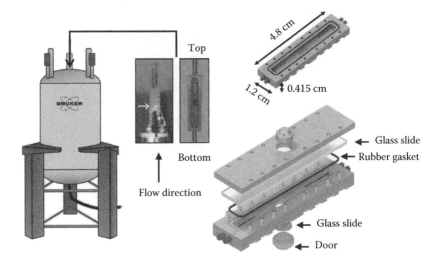

Figure 3.28 **(See color insert.)** NMR setup and NMR biofilm reactor. A glass disc (5 mm) completes the bottom flow channel wall, and the top wall is comprised of a glass coverslip sealed with a gasket. The photographs show that the NMR biofilm reactor is seated into a custom-built NMR probe. The white arrow shows the radio frequency coil. On the right, the NMR biofilm reactor is shown in detail.

Figure 3.29 shows MRI images of biofilms overlaid with their corresponding surface-averaged relative diffusivity (D_{rs}) profiles. These images were acquired for progressively older biofilms. For the 4-day-old biofilm the surface-averaged relative diffusivity decreased linearly across the entire thickness of the biofilm, which is similar to what we measured using microelectrodes (see Chapter 8). However, in biofilms older than 4 days the diffusivity profiles changed to those of characteristic two-layered biofilms, with a linear part of the diffusivity profile in the upper layer followed by a nonlinear part near the bottom of the biofilm. These nonlinear profiles of effective diffusivity in biofilms older than 4 days

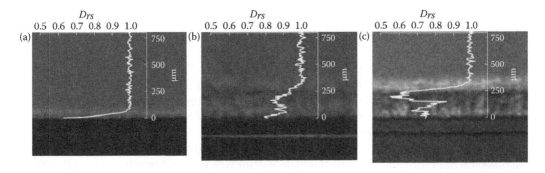

Figure 3.29 Surface-averaged relative effective diffusivity (D_{rs}) profiles overlaid with the corresponding water-selective 2-D MRI images of the flow chamber (and biofilms) for (a) the 4-day-old biofilm, (b) the 8-day-old biofilm, and (c) the 10-day-old biofilm. (Reproduced from Renslow, R. et al., *Biotechnology and Bioengineering* 106: 928–938, 2010.)

coincide with our conclusion, based on our attempts to grow reproducible biofilms, that after 4 days biofilm structure changes unpredictably (Figure 1.39).

3.6.2   *Rotating reactors*

Open-channel flat plate reactors, both elaborate and simplified, have a common weakness: they cannot be operated at high flow velocities or high shear stresses. It is practically impossible to operate these reactors at Reynolds numbers approaching those of turbulent flow. If an LBR needs to be operated at higher flow velocities than those conveniently reached in channel flow reactors, a possible choice is one of the rotating reactors. The principle of rotating biofilm reactors is to move the surface covered with biofilm with respect to the water rather than moving the water with respect to the surface, as is done in open-channel flat plate reactors. Rotating surfaces covered with biofilm offer more flexibility in controlling the hydrodynamics because the flow velocity does not depend on the flow rate through the reactor, and relatively high flow velocities near the surface can be achieved using low flow rates and long retention times in the reactor.

Rotating biofilm reactors have various physical configurations, but they all have one common feature: the flow velocity is controlled by controlling the relative velocity of the biofilm with respect to the bulk liquid. Some of them are closed and some are open. The closed reactors can be operated at higher flow velocities than the open reactors. Rotating reactors are a good choice in studies that require growing biofilms at a controlled shear stress. The nature of the operation prevents sampling of the biofilms during the operation. The reactors are equipped with polycarbonate slides on which the biofilm grows, and these slides can be removed from the reactor and the biofilms analyzed *ex situ*. The main disadvantage of using rotating reactors is that it is impossible to use microelectrodes to determine microscale biofilm activity while the reactors are operated.

3.6.2.1   *Rotating disc reactor*

A rotating disc reactor (RDR) imitates similar reactors used by chemical engineers and electrochemists to quantify the effects of mass transfer dynamics on the rates of heterogeneous reactions. In biofilm reactors, researchers do not have the luxury of using external circuits to monitor the progress of the reaction under study, but they use many concepts developed by the electrochemists to quantify various features in such reactors; for example, they measure the actual shear stress at various locations. Figure 3.30 shows the RDR we use in our laboratory.

The reactor vessel shown in Figure 3.30 is a square container made of transparent polycarbonate with a side length of 70 cm and a total height of 20 cm. A polycarbonate disc, 60 cm in diameter, rotates horizontally in the reactor. Six radial grooves are cut symmetrically into the lower side of the disc. Transparent polycarbonate slides, 3 cm long, are inserted into the grooves. Each groove contains nine slides. The disc rotates at a distance of 2 mm from the bottom of the vessel and is submerged 5 cm. An electrical motor is used to rotate the disc at a speed that can be controlled. An immersed thermostat is used to hold the water temperature constant.

We use this reactor to quantify the effects of flow velocity and shear stress on biofilm growth. It is essential to rotate the disc in a tight housing. If the gap between the rotating disc and the bottom of the reactor is smaller than the boundary layer thickness and the Reynolds number is smaller than 10^5, the variation of the tangential flow velocity across the gap becomes linear in the manner of Couette flow (Schlichting 1960). The following example illustrates the computational procedures we use to quantify the hydrodynamics in the reactor.

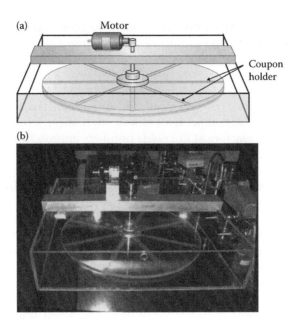

Figure 3.30 (a) Diagram of a rotating disc reactor and (b) photograph of the reactor.

Example 3.10

The reactor described above is operated with the disc suspended 2 mm above the bottom, and the rotating velocity of the disc is 1.05 rotations per second. The following computations describe the conditions in this reactor.

The Reynolds number for this reactor is calculated according to Schlichting (1960) to be

$$\mathrm{Re} = R^2 \frac{\omega}{\upsilon} \tag{3.45}$$

where R is the radius of the disc $[L]$, ω is the angular velocity $[1/T]$, and υ is the kinematic viscosity $[L^2/T]$. At 20°C, the kinematic viscosity evaluated from Table 3.2 is 1×10^{-6} m²/s. For the conditions reported above,

$$\mathrm{Re} = (0.3\ \mathrm{m})^2 \frac{1.05\ \mathrm{s}^{-1}}{1 \times 10^{-6}\,\mathrm{m^2\,s^{-1}}} = 9.45 \times 10^4 \tag{3.46}$$

The boundary layer thickness φ is calculated after von Kármán (1921):

$$\varphi = 2.58 \sqrt{\frac{\upsilon}{\omega}} \tag{3.47}$$

$$\varphi = 258 \sqrt{\frac{1 \times 10^{-6}\ \mathrm{m^2\,s^{-1}}}{1.05\ \mathrm{s}^{-1}}} = 2.51 \times 10^{-3}\ \mathrm{m} = 2.51\ \mathrm{mm}$$

In our example the boundary layer thickness is $\varphi = 2.51$ mm, which is more than the gap between the disc and the bottom, $s = 2$ mm. It is important to check that the thickness of the boundary layer is less than the gap between the bottom of the reactor and the rotating disc to ensure that the conditions for Couette flow are met.

The shear stress for Couette flow between rotating plates at a distance r from the axis is equal, at $r = R$, to

$$\tau = r\frac{\omega \times \mu}{s} = 0.3 \text{ m}\frac{1.05 \text{ s}^{-1} \times 10^{-3} \text{ N s m}^{-2}}{2 \times 10^{-3} \text{ m}} = 0.16 \text{ N m}^{-2} \tag{3.48}$$

where μ is absolute viscosity $[M/LT]$ and s is the gap between the rotating disc and the housing $[L]$; at 20°C, $\mu = 1 \times 10^{-3}$ N s m^{-2}, from Table 3.2, and $s = 2 \times 10^{-3}$ m. Note that the shear stress near the edge of the disc is orders of magnitude higher than that computed for the open-channel flat plate reactors in Example 3.4.

Linear flow velocity varies along the radius and at $r = R$ is equal to

$$v = \omega \times 2\pi r = 1.05 \text{ s}^{-1} \times 2 \times 3.14 \times 0.3 \text{ m} = 1.98 \text{ m s}^{-1}$$

Similar computations can be done for any length of the radius in this reactor, and thus the conditions for each location along the radius can be quantified uniquely.

A RDR is particularly suitable for studying the effects of hydrodynamics on biofilm accumulation because each location along the radius of the wheel has a different linear velocity and thus corresponds to a different flow velocity. Therefore, in a single experiment, a range of flow velocities can be covered. To get the same set of data using open-channel flat plate reactors, several reactors would have to be operated. After operating the reactor for the time appropriate for the study, the slides covered with the biofilm are removed from the disc and the biofilm is analyzed. Because there are six lines of slides, the study may include temporal changes in biofilm properties: the biofilm can be sampled at different times, allowing up to six analyses.

3.6.2.1.1   Example of results from a biofilm study using a RDR.   Figure 3.31 shows an example of results obtained from this reactor. The rotating velocity of the disc was selected so that the transition from laminar flow to turbulent flow occurred near the middle of the rotating disc. Biofilm thickness reached a maximum in the transition zone from laminar

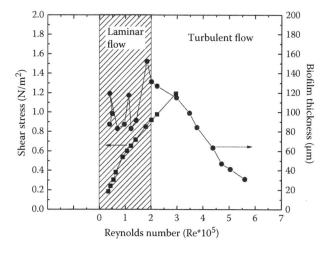

Figure 3.31 Biofilm thickness as a function of Reynolds number after three days of operation.

flow to turbulent flow. We interpreted this result as indicating that biofilm thickness was limited in the laminar flow zone by the mass transport of the growth-limiting nutrient and in the turbulent flow zone by the shear stress. Consequently, the conditions for biofilm accumulation were optimal in the transition zone from laminar to turbulent flow.

The RDR offers one more important convenience: measuring the mass transfer coefficient at various distances along the radius of the rotating disc. In Figure 3.30, below the rotating disc, positioned at about 11 o'clock, is a series of openings that are used to insert corrosion coupons made of 316L stainless steel (as shown in Figure 3.32). The coupons are imbedded in the holder shown in Figure 3.32 and screwed into the openings so that their surfaces are mounted flush with the bottom of the reactor.

To measure the distribution of the mass transfer coefficient along the radius, the reactor, without biofilm, is filled with ferricyanide, using the same solution as is used to measure the local mass transfer coefficient to microelectrodes. The procedure for measuring the mass transfer coefficient to each of the coupons along the radius is exactly the same as the procedure we use to measure mass transfer coefficients to microelectrodes, except that the surface area of each corrosion coupon used in the RDR is larger than the surface area of a typical microelectrode. As the electroactive reactant, we use a 25 mM solution of potassium ferricyanide, $K_3Fe(CN)_6$, in 0.2 M KCl. With proper experimental control, the ferricyanide is reduced to ferrocyanide, $Fe(CN)_6^{4-}$, at the surfaces of cathodically polarized electrodes:

$$Fe(CN)_6^{3-} + e^- \rightarrow Fe(CN)_6^{4-} \tag{3.49}$$

The flux of the ferricyanide, J, to the exposed surface of a coupon with sensing area A is related to the limiting current I by

$$J = \frac{I}{nAF} \tag{3.50}$$

Here, F is Faraday's constant and n is the number of electrons transferred in the balanced reaction. For practical reasons, the results of current measurements are reported as limiting current density (I/A), which describes the ratio of the limiting current to the

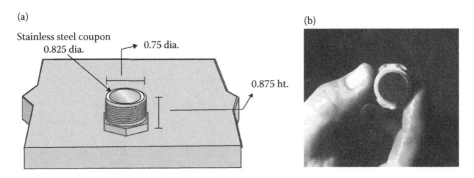

Figure 3.32 (a) Corrosion coupon in a plastic holder. Corrosion coupons mounted in a plastic holder are fixed at the bottom of the reactor. (b) Photograph of a coupon inserted into the bottom of the reactor.

reactive surface area of the microelectrode tip. The flux of ferricyanide to the electrode can also be expressed using Fick's first law:

$$J = \frac{D_w(C_b - C_s)}{\delta} = k(C_b - C_s) \tag{3.51}$$

When an individual coupon is polarized to a cathodic potential that causes the limiting current, the surface concentration of ferricyanide is $C_s = 0$ and the mass transfer coefficient can be computed from the measurements of the limiting current as

$$k = \frac{I}{nAFC_b} \tag{3.52}$$

If the mass transfer coefficient is known, then the Sherwood number can be calculated using Equation 3.25. A D_w value for ferricyanide in the electrolyte solution of 7×10^{-10} m²/s was used by Beyenal and Lewandowski (2001).

The mass transfer coefficient is measured separately for each coupon and for each selected rotating velocity of the disc. The results of the measurements characterize the distribution of the mass transfer coefficient in the empty reactor. Using this result to interpret the mass transfer coefficient in the reactor with biofilm requires a leap of faith and is probably not justified, but using these results to interpret the results of studies focusing on the initial attachment of microorganisms is justified.

3.6.2.2   Annular reactors

In annular reactors, one cylinder spins inside another cylinder. The inner cylinder rotates, and the outer cylinder is stationary. The torque needed to sustain the rotation is monitored and is related to biofilm buildup on the surfaces. In some reactors, polycarbonate slides are mounted in grooves cut in the stationary walls. When covered with biofilm, these slides can be removed for biofilm analyses. Figure 3.33 shows an annular reactor.

The principles of using annular reactors in biofilm studies are similar to the principles of using RDRs. In an annular reactor, a rotating cylinder rotates in a housing and the gap between the drum and the housing is kept small enough to produce Couette flow, in which the variation in tangential flow velocity across the gap is linear. Because in an annular reactor the entire surface of the rotating cylinder is at the same distance from the axis of rotation, the shear stress is the same everywhere. It does not vary with the distance from the axis of rotation as it does in a RDR. One benefit of having a single shear stress in the entire reactor is that it can be evaluated from the torque used to rotate the rotor. For a RDR we have to rely on the computation of shear stress done for the empty reactor; in an annular reactor we can actually determine the average shear stress as the biofilm accumulates. Simple torque meters, available from specialized vendors, are used to measure the torque needed to keep the rotating velocity of the inner cylinder constant. As the biofilm accumulates, the shear stress increases, and so does the torque. The measured torque is used to compute the shear stress in the following procedure (Roe et al. 1994). The shear stress in the reactor equals

$$\tau = \frac{T}{RA} \tag{3.53}$$

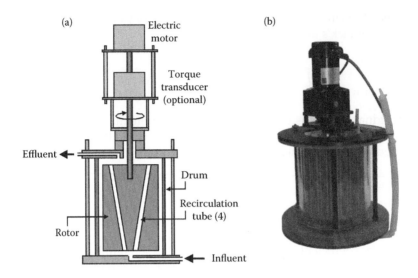

Figure 3.33 (a) Diagram of an annular reactor and (b) photograph of the annular reactor.

where T is the torque, R is the radius of the rotating cylinder, and A is the surface area of the rotating cylinder.

From the definition of torque:

$$T = FR \tag{3.54}$$

This, when substituted into Equation 3.53, gives the shear stress as a function of the measured variables:

$$\tau = \frac{T}{RA} = \frac{FR}{RA} = \frac{F}{A} \tag{3.55}$$

Torque meters are popular and inexpensive devices; many are computerized to simplify data acquisition, and they can be purchased from specialized vendors. Annular reactors are popular LBRs, particularly in industrial settings, where they are sometimes installed in bypass conduits to evaluate the rate of biofilm accumulation in the main conduits by approximating from the rate of torque increase.

If the conditions in the flat plate reactor described in Example 3.4, where the shear stress was 0.000066 N, were simulated using an annular reactor with an inner cylinder of diameter $d = 0.3$ m and height $H = 0.5$ m, the inner cylinder would have to be rotated using a torque that can be computed as follows:

The surface area of the inner cylinder, A, is

$$A = 2\pi RH = 2 \times 3.14 \times 0.5(0.3 \text{ m}) \times 0.5 \text{ m} = 0.471 \text{ m}^2$$

The torque is

$$T = \tau RA = 0.000066 \text{ kg m}^{-1} \text{s}^{-2} \times 0.5(0.3 \text{ m}) \times 0.471 \text{ m}^2 = 4.66 \times 10^{-7} \text{N m}$$

3.6.3 Tubular reactors

Tubular reactors are easy to operate, and the hydrodynamics in them are easy to evaluate. In contrast to the flat plate and rotating reactors discussed above, the flow velocities used in tubular reactors are limited only by practical considerations. We have used these reactors in biofilm studies where the flow velocity was a few meters per second. We use tubular reactors for two types of studies: (1) to study the effect of biofilms on the pressure drop in conduits covered with biofilms and (2) to study the effect of hydrodynamics on biofilm structure. In both cases, the reactors are just glass tubes attached to various external devices depending on the mode of operation. Because the reactors used to study biofilm structure have much smaller diameters than those used to study pressure drop in conduits, typically a few millimeters, they are referred to as "capillary reactors." Also, because capillary reactors are often positioned on the stages of microscopes to quantify biofilm structure, it is convenient to use square rather than circular tubes.

3.6.3.1 Example of results from a biofilm study using a tubular reactor to study the effect of biofilm formation on pressure drop

As discussed in the introductory section of this chapter, pressure drop in biofilm reactors is not caused by the biofilm acting as rigid roughness elements dissipating the energy of the flowing water; instead, it is caused by the elastic properties of the biofilm matrix and its interactions with the flowing water. The biofilm itself smoothes the walls, as shown in Figure 1.27; it is the interactions between the boundary layer and the biofilm matrix that are responsible for the pressure drop in conduits covered with biofilm. A typical setup for such measurements is shown in Figure 3.34. The reactor is just a glass tube connected to a high-output pump.

There is no adequate theoretical treatment that predicts the pressure drop in conduits covered with biofilm. The pressure drop in conduits covered with biofilm exceeds by 2 to 4 times the expected pressure drop computed using the Moody diagram. Therefore, many research projects are designed to target the relation between hydrodynamics and pressure drop in such conduits, and the suitable biofilm reactors, such as the one in Figure 3.34, are in frequent use. An example of an attempt to use the Moody diagram to evaluate the functional relation between accumulated streamer lengths (per unit volume of the tube) and the friction factor is shown in Figure 3.35.

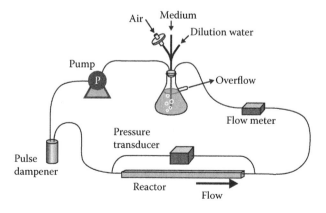

Figure 3.34 Tubular reactor system layout.

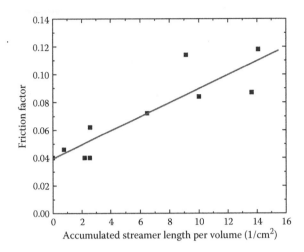

Figure 3.35 Plot of friction factor versus accumulated streamer length per unit volume of the tube. We cut a piece of the tube, measured the lengths of all the individual streamers and added them together to get the accumulated streamer length. The volume of the tube was calculated from the internal diameter and the length of the tube (Groenenboom 2000).

The results in Figure 3.35 demonstrate that increasing the length of the accumulated streamers has the same effect as increasing the surface roughness of the conduit, which corroborates our conclusions.

Studying the effects of biofilms on pressure drop in conduits is not the only application of tubular reactors. Because flow velocity in tubular reactors is restricted only by practical considerations, these reactors are used to study all kinds of relations between hydrodynamics and biofilm processes. The following example shows the use of these reactors in a study initiated to determine the distribution of flow velocity near the walls of conduits covered with biofilms. Such studies can be done using NMR imaging, but because NMR imaging is a highly specialized and expensive technique, we use other experimental techniques to acquire similar information. Because biofilms are porous and flow velocity reaches zero, not at the surface of the biofilm but at the surface of the conduit, it is interesting to see how the flow is distributed inside the biofilm. Figures 1.22 and 3.36 show results of such measurements. Liquid velocity measurements were done using a particle tracking technique described more fully in previous manuscripts (de Beer et al. 1994; Stoodley et al. 1994). Neutral-density fluorescent latex spheres (density at 20°C = 1055 kg/m^3, excitation 580 nm/emission 605 nm, diameter = 0.282 μm) were added to the reactor to achieve a final concentration of about 1×10^7 particles/mL. Particles traveling across the field of view during imaging with the CSLM appeared as dashed lines on the screen. After the lengths of these tracks (distance traveled) and the time taken to create them were measured, the velocity could be calculated. Velocity profiles in the reactor were obtained by capturing images at various focal depths after raising or lowering the motorized stage. Two flow velocity profiles are juxtaposed, one in the reactor without biofilm and one in the reactor with biofilm. As can be seen in the figure, the biofilm affects the flow velocity in the near-surface environment only. The water actually flows in the space occupied by the biofilm, and this effect influences the rate of mass transport in the biofilm.

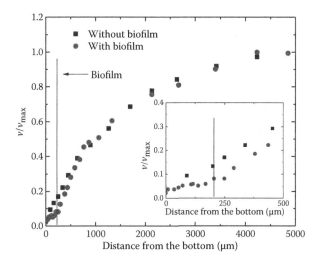

Figure 3.36 Flow velocity profiles in conduits with and without biofilm. (Reprinted from De Beer, D. et al., *Biotechnology and Bioengineering*, 44, 636–641, 1994.)

Figure 3.37 Photograph of a capillary reactor. The reactor is placed on the stage of a microscope, and the images of the biofilm are collected through the wall.

3.6.3.2   Tubular reactors for quantifying biofilm structure

Tubular reactors for quantifying biofilm structure are made of square-shaped glass tubes a few millimeters in diameter (Figure 3.37). They are positioned on the stages of light or confocal microscopes, and the images of the biofilms are collected through the glass wall. The need to collect images makes us use square tubes rather than round ones; it is easier to collect images through a flat wall than through a round one on the stage of a microscope.

3.6.4   Packed-bed reactors

Packed-bed reactors (PBRs) are suitable for quantifying neither biofilm structure nor biofilm activity. The retention time in the reactor is difficult to evaluate because the volume of empty spaces changes. The hydrodynamics are a mystery. There is no access to the biomass, no possibility of quantifying biofilm structure, and no way to make sure that the flow through the bed is uniform. Despite their obvious disadvantages, these reactors are quite popular in biofilm studies.

PBRs are popular because they imitate important processes in nature, such as flow through porous media (Figure 3.38). They are also successfully used in wastewater treatment plants and are easy to operate. For research purposes, PBRs should be avoided when

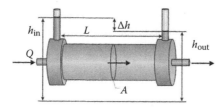

Figure 3.38 Schematic of the column of a packed-bed reactor.

possible. We do use these reactors to quantify biofilm processes in biofilms grown on various minerals. The PBRs are usually operated for a few months, after which they are disassembled and the mineral phase and the biofilm are evaluated. Results of studies in which biofilms of sulfate-reducing bacteria (SRB) were grown on calcite to evaluate the effect of carbonates on the process of reducing uranium (VI) to uranium (IV) with biogenic hydrogen sulfide are given in Chapter 1.

Flow through a porous medium is quantified using Darcy's law, which states as does Ohm's law, that the flow rate is directly proportional to the driving force and inversely proportional to the resistance. Darcy's law expresses this in the following form:

$$Q = KA\frac{\Delta h}{L} \tag{3.56}$$

where K is hydraulic conductivity $[L/T]$, A is the surface area of the flow, Δh is hydraulic head $[L]$ (potential), and L is length (resistance).

Permeability (K_p) for a PBR can be computed as $K_p = K\mu/\rho g$. Equation 3.56 for laminar flow in packed beds can be rearranged to include K_p, and the rearranged equation (Equation 3.57) shows that the flow rate is proportional to Δh and inversely proportional to viscosity μ and length L. This is the basis for Darcy's law for purely viscous flow in porous media:

$$v' = \frac{Q}{A} = \frac{K_p}{\mu\rho g}\frac{\Delta h}{L} \tag{3.57}$$

where v' is the superficial velocity based on the empty cross section in cm/s, Q is the flow rate in cm³/s, A is the empty cross section in cm², μ is the viscosity in cP, ΔP is the pressure drop in atm, ΔL is the length of the column in cm, and k is the permeability in (cm³ flow/s) (cP) (cm length)/(cm² area) (atm pressure drop). The units used for K_p are the darcy (1 cm² cP/s atm) and the millidarcy. If a porous medium has a permeability of 1 darcy, a fluid of 1 cP viscosity will flow at 1 cm³/s per 1 cm² cross section with a Δp of 1 atm/cm length. This equation is often used in measuring the permeabilities of underground oil reservoirs.

The dimensions of the reactors vary, depending on the needs of particular studies. In one of our studies using PBRs, SRBs were grown on calcite to evaluate the effect of carbonates on the process of reducing uranium (VI) to uranium (IV) with biogenic hydrogen sulfide. The reactors were clear polycarbonate tubes 2.54 cm in diameter and 40 cm long. Each column was filled with the crushed minerals and then sealed with epoxy resin. The flow was directed from the bottom upward, and to ensure that the flow was uniform we used flow distributors made of glass beads entrapped between two plastic sieves. These were placed in the inlets and outlets of the reactors. The mode of operation we used was with recycle and in-line aeration, as shown in Figure 3.39.

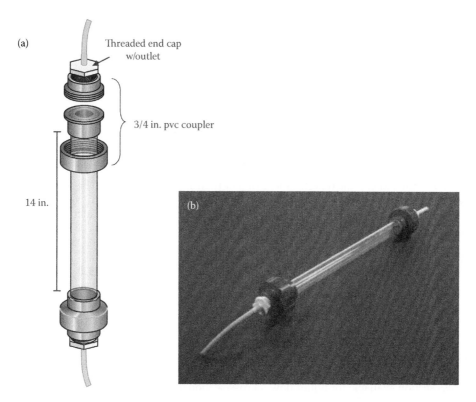

Figure 3.39 (a) Diagram of a packed-bed reactor and (b) photograph of the reactor.

Example 3.11

PBRs are often operated with recycle. The recycle ratio and the retention time are both set based on the measurement of the empty spaces (pore volume) in the packed bed. The relevant procedure for this measurement is given in Chapter 7. Consider a PBR described by the following set of parameters:

- Diameter of the column = 2.0 cm
- Length of the column = 40 cm
- Pore volume = 100 mL
- The flow rate of the nutrient solution is set to 10 mL/h

From this set of data, the reactor can be further characterized by computing the porosity of the packed bed. The porosity of the bed is defined as the ratio of the volume of the pores to the volume of the empty reactor.

Volume of the empty reactor = cross-sectional area × length = $\pi \times r^2 \times 40 = 3.14 \times (2/2) \times 40 = 125.6 \text{ cm}^3$

$$\text{porosity} = \frac{\text{void volume}}{\text{reactor volume}} = \frac{100 \text{ cm}^3}{125.6 \text{ cm}^3} = 0.8$$

This means that the pores constitute 80% of the packing material in the reactor. Assuming that the packing material and the pores are uniformly distributed throughout the reactor, this result can be interpreted as equivalent to the statement that 80% of the cross section of the reactor is available for liquid flow. This is an important conclusion because it allows computing of the average flow rate in the packed bed, after the flow rate in the recycle stream has been set.

The flow rate in the recycle stream can now be addressed. First, the retention time is computed, based on the flow of the nutrient solution:

$$\text{retention time} = \frac{\text{volume of liquid in the reactor (pore volume)}}{\text{flow rate of the nutrient solution}} = \frac{100\ \text{mL}}{10\ \text{mL/h}} = 10\ \text{h}$$

It is known that if the recycle ratio is higher than 40, then the PBR can be considered well mixed. If the operator wants to set the recycle ratio to 320 (very high), the flow rate in the recycle stream that will achieve the desired recycle ratio must be calculated:

$$\text{recycle ratio} = \frac{\text{recycle volumetric flow rate } (q_r)}{\text{nutrient solution flow rate}} = \frac{q_r}{10\ \text{mL/h}} = 320$$

$$q_r = 10\ \text{mL/h} \times 320 = 3200\ \text{mL/h}$$

On the basis of the conclusion that 80% of the surface area of the packed bed is available for flow, we compute the average flow velocity in the packed bed.

Cross section available for liquid flow = cross-sectional area × porosity = $\pi \times r^2 \times 0.8 = 3.14 \times (2/2) \times 0.8 = 2.5\ \text{cm}^2$

$$\text{average flow velocity} = \frac{\text{volumetric flow rate}}{\text{cross-sectional area available for flow}} = \frac{3210\ \text{cm}^3/\text{h}}{2.5\ \text{cm}^2} = 1286\ \text{cm/h}$$

Eventually, the reactor is operated using the following flow rates:

total flow rate = recycle flow rate + nutrient solution flow rate = 10 mL/h + 3200 mL/h = 3210 mL/h

3.6.5 Hollow fiber biofilm reactors

One of the limitations of flat plate reactors is that the ratio of the surface area available for biofilm growth to the total volume is low, which prevents the growing of large amounts of biomass in reactors of small volume. This limitation can be overcome by using a hollow fiber biofilm reactor (HFBR) with multiple hollow fibers. An additional benefit offered by the HFBR is the radial flow of nutrients, perpendicular to the biofilm (Figure 3.40), which improves biomass consolidation and facilitates nutrient delivery during biofilm growth. Also, the direction of the radial flow can be reversed to facilitate biofilm harvesting.

We used a HFBR to characterize the composition of extracellular polymeric substances (EPS) from *Shewanella* sp. HRCR-1 biofilms. Both bound and loosely associated EPS were extracted from *Shewanella* sp. HRCR-1 biofilms prepared using a HFBR. The detailed procedure used in EPS separation is given in Chapter 9, and the results of the EPS analysis are given in Chapter 2. The HFBR has limited use in fundamental biofilm research (it has its use in applied research dedicated to biofilm control on membranes), but this reactor is

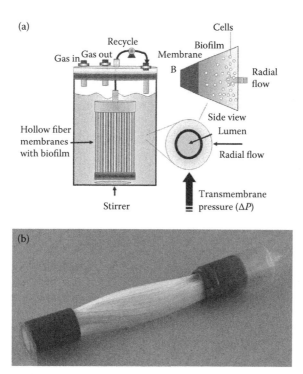

Figure 3.40 (a) A hollow fiber biofilm reactor. A 1-L flask is filled with individual hollow fibers. A transmembrane pressure is applied, and the liquid in the reactor is recycled through the biofilm. This eliminates the mass transfer limitation. (b) A photograph of a hollow fiber module.

uniquely useful for the simple task of growing large amounts of biofilm needed to conduct other tests.

3.7   Using LBRs in conjunction with other tools to explore biofilm processes at the microscale

This section discusses a selection of research projects related to biofilm structure and activity in which we used the conceptual, physical, and virtual tools introduced in this book. Like any other branch of life sciences or engineering, biofilm research develops in stages determined by the rate at which experimental and conceptual information is accumulated about the system under study: the biofilms. Each time a critical amount of information is accumulated, the conceptual models of biofilm processes are adjusted to accommodate the new information. Also, each time the conceptual models of biofilm processes are adjusted, new hypotheses are put forward based on the new models and the cycle continues: testing the new hypotheses leads to refining of the conceptual models and to adjusting them again. This is an important cycle, and to participate in it, the researchers need to know exactly the status of the knowledge about biofilm systems. The necessary knowledge can be acquired by reading review articles; better yet, it can be gained from participating in conferences and cultivating exchanges of information with other biofilm researchers. Review papers tend to emerge after major shifts in paradigms: they mark the end of one cycle and the beginning of another. Examples are given here of the refining of models of biofilm processes leading to the changing of conceptual models.

LBRs are essential research tools providing access to biofilm processes that would be difficult to study if we were using only natural biofilm reactors. As we stated at the beginning of this chapter, LBRs are constructed to satisfy two requirements: (1) to facilitate the biofilm processes under study and (2) to facilitate the measurements characterizing the processes under study. The use of individual reactors in specific measurements and to study specific effects, such as the effects of hydrodynamics on biofilm accumulations, has been discussed. Examples will now be given of using LBRs in conjunction with other tools described in this book to verify conceptual models of biofilm processes.

3.7.1 Quantifying mechanisms by which biofilm heterogeneity affects biofilm activity

The first project selected for discussion in this section belongs to the category of projects that are designed to demonstrate and quantify the mechanisms by which biofilm heterogeneity affects biofilm activity. To demonstrate these relations, we identified factors limiting hydrogen sulfide production in a two-species biofilm made of SRB (*Desulfovibrio desulfuricans*) and nonsulfate-reducing bacteria (*P. fluorescens*) (Beyenal and Lewandowski 2001). The tools and concepts we used in this work can easily be located in other chapters of this book.

The biofilm was grown in a flat plate flow reactor made of polycarbonate. The reactor was 3.5 cm deep, 2.5 cm wide, and 34 cm long, with a total working volume of 120 mL, operated at room temperature. The biofilm was grown at a flow velocity of 2 cm/s using Postage C growth medium under anaerobic conditions. Microscope slides (2.5×7.5 cm^2) were placed at the bottom of the reactor, and the biofilm that grew on these slides was later used for various analyses. After the biofilm accumulated, the slides with the biofilm were removed from the reactor and transferred to another reactor, which was positioned on the stage of an inverted microscope and operated using the same growth medium and other operational parameters as the reactor where the biofilms were grown. We used three types of microelectrodes in this study and measured H$_2$S concentration, pH, local mass transport coefficient, local effective diffusivity, and local flow velocity. The microelectrodes had tip diameters of less than 10 µm to prevent damaging the biofilm structure during measurements. The locations of the measurements were selected to emphasize the effect of biofilm structure on mass transport and microbial activity. Figure 3.41 shows an image of this biofilm, the distribution of cell clusters and interstitial voids, and the locations selected for sampling.

The image in Figure 3.41 shows typical features of heterogeneous biofilms: cell clusters and interstitial voids of various sizes. Using the tools described in this book, the mass transfer rate and the microbial activity in the vicinity of distinguishable features, such as the conditions in small voids versus those in large voids and the conditions in voids versus those in clusters, were quantified. The locations of the measurements are marked in Figure 3.41 using the numbers from 1 to 5, and these numbers are used to mark the plots in the corresponding figures where the results are presented. To study the effects of the flow velocity on mass transfer in cell clusters and in interstitial voids, we did all measurements at two flow rates: 2 and 0.8 cm/s.

Profiles of hydrogen sulfide measured in interstitial voids of various sizes are shown in Figure 3.42.

H$_2$S profiles measured at different locations are different, which is not surprising because this is one of the expected effects of biofilm heterogeneity. Also, the H$_2$S profiles look different from the profiles of oxygen in biofilms, shown in other chapters,

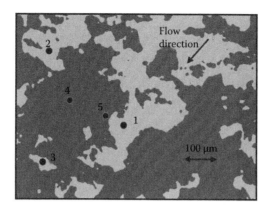

Figure 3.41 Image of a 5-week-old biofilm consisting of *Desulfovibrio desulfuricans* and *Pseudomonas fluorescens*. The light areas are voids and the dark areas are cell clusters. The numbers indicate the locations of the measurements: (1) big void, (2) medium-sized void, (3) small void, (4) cluster center, and (5) cluster edge. (Reprinted from Beyenal, H., and Lewandowski, Z., *AIChE Journal*, 47, 1689–1697, 2001.)

because hydrogen sulfide is produced in the biofilm and diffuses from the biofilm into the bulk solution, whereas oxygen diffuses from the bulk solution into the biofilm, where it is used. The concentration of hydrogen sulfide is highest near the bottom of the reactor and decreases toward the bulk solution, just the opposite of what is observed in oxygen concentration profiles. Inspection of the profiles of hydrogen sulfide measured in voids reveals that the highest concentration of hydrogen sulfide was observed at the bottom of the smallest void when the average flow velocity was high: 2 cm/s. The results can be interpreted by emphasizing the effects of flow velocity on mass transport: the flow velocity in the main channel is high, and the rate of sulfate ion delivery is high. If the flow velocity at the bottom of a small void is low, then the rate of hydrogen sulfide removal is low, which explains the results. These interpretations will remain hypothetical until the flow velocities at these two locations, at the top and at the bottom of this small void, are measured, and it is demonstrated that they do indeed relate to each other as expected. The slope of the concentration profile increases as the size of the void increases; this can be interpreted, again hypothetically, as the effect of intrabiofilm flow velocity being higher in the larger voids than it is in the smaller voids.

The profiles of hydrogen sulfide concentration in the microcolony at the locations specified in Figure 3.41 are shown in Figures 3.42 and 3.43.

Upon inspection of the profiles of hydrogen sulfide in the microcolony, it is evident that the highest concentration of hydrogen sulfide is at the bottom, near the middle of the large microcolony, at location 4. The concentration measured at the bottom at that location did not change in response to the change in flow velocity, which is consistent with expectations: water does not flow through microcolonies, so the water flow velocity in the main channel should not affect the concentration of hydrogen sulfide at the bottom of a microcolony. The profile of hydrogen sulfide measured near the center of the microcolony is steeper than that measured near the edge. This demonstrates that hydrogen sulfide is transported toward the biofilm surface at a higher rate near the center of the microcolony than near the edge. Because both profiles start from the same concentration near the bottom, clearly, hydrogen sulfide must also be transported somewhere else than toward the surface of the colony. The proximity of the void explains these differences between the two profiles: at the location near the interstitial void, hydrogen sulfide is transported toward

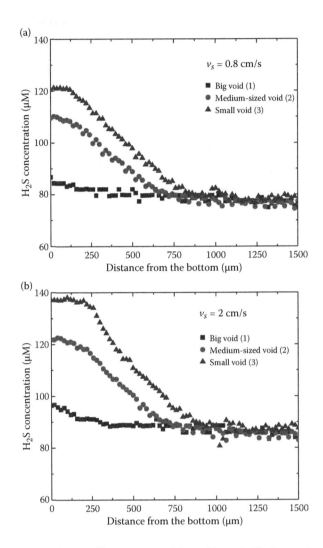

Figure 3.42 H$_2$S concentration profiles measured in voids at bulk flow velocities of (a) 0.8 and (b) 2 cm/s. (Reprinted from Beyenal, H., and Lewandowski, Z., *AIChE Journal*, 47, 1689–1697, 2001.)

the surface and toward the void. This demonstrates, again, that not only are nutrients in biofilms transported perpendicularly to the biofilm surface, but there is a lateral component to this mass transport as well.

Because the conclusion from inspecting the profiles of hydrogen sulfide in the voids depends heavily on the differences in intensity of mass transport among voids of different sizes, the profiles of local mass transport were measured at the same locations in the voids where the concentrations of hydrogen sulfide were measured. Figure 3.44 shows these profiles.

The measurements of the local mass transport coefficient are consistent with the hypothetical explanation of the shape of the hydrogen sulfide concentration profiles: mass transport is more intensive in large voids. This explains why the concentration of hydrogen sulfide reached its highest point at the bottom of the smallest void in Figure 3.41. To

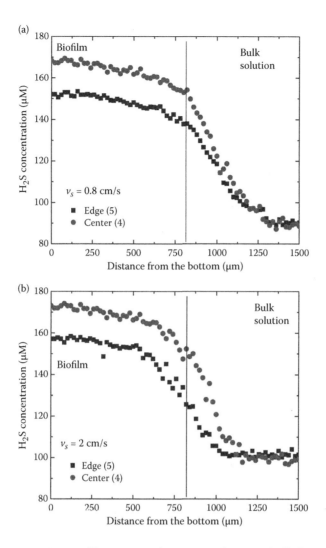

Figure 3.43 H$_2$S concentration profiles measured in microcolonies at bulk flow velocities of (a) 0.8 and (b) 2 cm/s. (Reprinted from Beyenal, H., and Lewandowski, Z., *AIChE Journal*, 47, 1689–1697, 2001.)

demonstrate the mechanism of this process, we measured the flow velocity distribution in the voids and show the results in Figure 3.45.

To interpret the results in Figure 3.42, we hypothesized that the differences in hydrogen sulfide concentration among these voids were a consequence of the differences in flow velocity among these voids. This hypothesis can now be tested using the results in Figure 3.45. The results show that the flow velocity reached an average value in the bulk solution, and the flow velocity profiles show that the flow velocity decreased rapidly in the interstitial voids. As hypothesized, the flow velocity in the largest of the voids was measurable all the way to the bottom of the reactor. In contrast, in the smallest of the voids, the flow velocity reached zero at some distance from the bottom. As a consequence, hydrogen sulfide generated in the biofilm was removed much more quickly from the large void than it was from the small void, which is consistent with the shape of the hydrogen sulfide

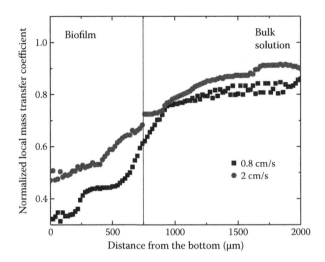

Figure 3.44 Normalized local mass transfer coefficient profiles measured at flow velocities of 0.8 and 2 cm/s. Increasing the bulk flow velocity increased the local mass transfer coefficient in the biofilm, showing that more substrate diffused into the biofilm. The continuous line shows the location of the biofilm surface. (Reprinted from Beyenal, H., and Lewandowski, Z., *AIChE Journal*, 47, 1689–1697, 2001.)

concentration profiles shown in Figure 3.42, indicating that the highest concentration of hydrogen sulfide was near the bottom of the smallest void. The biggest effect of the average flow velocity in the main channel on the profiles is that the slopes of the flow velocity profiles were steeper when the flow velocity in the main channel was 2 cm/s than when the flow velocity in the main channel was 0.8 cm/s.

Another interesting observation about this biofilm concerns the profile of local effective diffusivity measured across the microcolony, shown in Figure 3.46.

A smoothly evolving profile of effective diffusivity is not observed in Figure 3.46; instead, the profile appears to be composed of two parts. Hypothetically, this effect can be ascribed to the fact that the biofilm was composed of two types of microorganisms: sulfate-reducing microorganisms and non-SRBs. We suspect that the SRBs preferentially assumed locations near the bottom of the biofilm, where the redox potential may have been the lowest. This explanation remains hypothetical and subject to verification using FISH probes. Unfortunately, we did not expect this effect, and we did not plan on using FISH probes in this project, so the interpretation of this result remains hypothetical: it may warrant further study if the microbial community structure in such biofilms is of interest. If the hypothesis is true, then this result corresponds with the result shown in Chapter 2, in which microorganisms belonging to different physiological groups assumed different locations in the biofilm. The results in Chapter 2 also show that ammonia oxidizers and nitrate oxidizers in nitrifying biofilms may occupy different locations. Altogether, the hypothesis that the convoluted shape of the effective diffusivity profile may have something to do with the locations of different physiological groups of microorganisms in the biofilms is not without base.

Finally, we measured the pH profile in the biofilm. The reason for these measurements was the suspicion that the pH varied considerably across the biofilm, in which case the hydrogen sulfide microelectrodes would have to be recalibrated. Hydrogen sulfide is

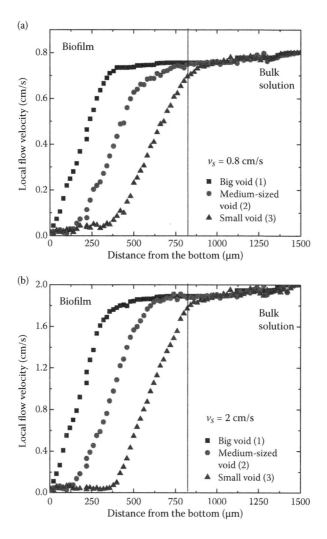

Figure 3.45 Local flow velocity profiles measured in voids at two average flow velocities: (a) 0.8 and (b) 2 cm/s. (Reprinted from Beyenal, H., and Lewandowski, Z., *AIChE Journal*, 47, 1689–1697, 2001.)

a diprotic acid, and there are three forms of sulfide present in water: H_2S, HS^-, and S^{2-}. If the pH varied, then the variation would affect the speciation of the sulfide species. The pH profile is shown in Figure 3.47, and we assumed, based on these results, that the pH variation measured across the biofilm, about 0.2 units, was negligible; it could not possibly change our general conclusions.

In summary, the biofilm had a heterogeneous structure consisting of cell clusters separated by voids. The H_2S concentration was lower in the voids than in the adjacent cell clusters, demonstrating that the voids acted as transport channels removing H_2S from the cell clusters. The extent of biofilm heterogeneity was directly correlated with the flux of H_2S from the cell clusters. At flow velocities below 2 cm/s, the flux of H_2S from the cell clusters depended on the flow velocity. We concluded that at these flow velocities the H_2S production rate was limited by the rate of delivery of sulfate ions to the biofilm. There was

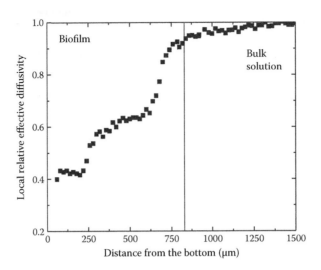

Figure 3.46 Variation of local relative effective diffusivity with respect to depth in the biofilm. The continuous line shows the location of the biofilm surface. (Reprinted from Beyenal, H., and Lewandowski, Z., *AIChE Journal*, 47, 1689–1697, 2001.)

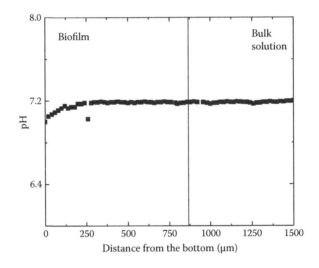

Figure 3.47 The pH as a function of distance from the bottom, measured at the center of the cluster (Figure 3.41). We measured similar pH profiles at other locations in the biofilm. The continuous line shows the location of the biofilm surface. (Reprinted from Beyenal, H., and Lewandowski, Z., *AIChE Journal*, 47, 1689–1697, 2001.)

no significant pH variation within the biofilm. Surprisingly, profiles of local relative effective diffusivity indicated that the biofilm was made up of two layers—a finding that could be related to the fact that the specimen was a two-species biofilm.

The study demonstrated that our basic understanding of the mechanism of mass transport and activity in heterogeneous biofilms is correct. All effects, with the exception of the convoluted profile of the effective diffusivity in microcolonies, are consistent with the expectations and with the hypotheses developed based on the conceptual model of heterogeneous biofilms discussed in Chapter 1. We have quantified these effects and increased the level of confidence that our understanding of biofilm processes in heterogeneous biofilms is basically correct. Such verification is reassuring but is not always the case, as will be demonstrated in Section 3.7.2.

The process of refining our knowledge of biofilm systems is iterative. Conceptual models of biofilm processes are hypothesized, and the hypotheses are tested. Most of the time, the predictions based on the conceptual models of biofilm processes are consistent with experimental results, but not always. If a hypothesis formulated based on the existing model tests negative, then the model is revisited and, if needed, revised. In the example given above, all the effects were consistent with the expectations. In the next example, we will see that this is not always the case and, sometimes, conceptual models need to be revised. The following example will illustrate a process in which inconsistencies were discovered between the measurements and the conceptual model.

3.7.2   Quantifying mechanisms of mass transport in biofilms

One of the known effects of biofilm heterogeneity is that water flows through the space occupied by the biofilm. This has a predictable effect on mass transport, which is expected to be due to convection in the bulk and in the voids of the biofilm. This prediction is, however, inconsistent with the measurements of oxygen profiles in biofilms, which persistently indicate the existence of a diffusion (mass) boundary layer above the biofilm surface (see Figure 3.48, in which the oxygen concentration decreases above the biofilm surface, or any other profile of oxygen in this book). It appears that there is a problem. On one hand, it is known that water flows inside the biofilm because it has been demonstrated experimentally. This is not a hypothesis—it is a fact. On the other hand, many profiles of oxygen concentration indicate a distinct diffusion boundary layer in the proximity of the biofilm

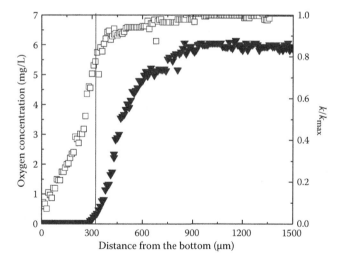

Figure 3.48 Superimposed oxygen concentration (▼) and local mass transport coefficient (□) profiles. The local concentration of oxygen is about 6 mg/L in the bulk and about 0.6 mg/L near the surface, which accounts for about a 90% decrease. This is a very steep concentration gradient, demonstrating a high mass transport resistance in that zone. The local mass transport coefficient is only about 10% smaller near the biofilm surface than it is in the bulk solution. (Reprinted from Rasmussen, K., and Lewandowski, Z., *Biotechnology and Bioengineering*, 59, 302–309, 1998.)

surface. If mass transport inside and outside of the biofilm is convective, this layer should not be there, or at least the concentration gradient near the biofilm surface should not be so steep. Experimental data show a higher mass transfer resistance near the biofilm surface than can be deduced from the existing conceptual models of biofilm processes. This apparent inconsistency between expectations and measurements, and between two types of measurements, warrants closer inspection, and this section is devoted to this problem. It also illustrates the iterative process of improving our knowledge of biofilm processes.

To address the inconsistency and inspect the nature of mass transport near the interface between water and biofilm, two profiles were measured at the same location: oxygen and the local mass transport coefficient. Because the local mass transport coefficient is a measure of the mass transport rate at the selected location, it is expected that the shape of the oxygen concentration profile will be related to the shape of the local mass transport coefficient profile when both are measured at the same location. It is further expected that at locations where the local mass transport coefficient is high, the local nutrient concentration will be high as well, higher than it is at a location where the local mass transport coefficient is low. Figure 3.48 shows profiles of oxygen concentration and the local mass transport coefficient measured at the same location in a biofilm (Rasmussen and Lewandowski 1998a).

It is clear from the data in Figure 3.48 that the variation in the mass transport coefficient does not correlate well with the variation in the oxygen concentration. Approaching the biofilm surface, the oxygen concentration decreases rapidly and reaches quite low levels at the biofilm surface, whereas the local mass transport coefficient remains quite high at that location. This observation is difficult to explain. Because there is no oxygen consumption in the bulk, the oxygen concentration profile should follow the shape of the mass transport coefficient profile much closer than it does in Figure 3.48. If the mass transport coefficient is high, then why is oxygen transported so slowly that it forms a steep concentration gradient? Strangely, although the two profiles in Figure 3.48 do not match, each of them is consistent with our knowledge of the behavior of the system. A low concentration of oxygen is expected at the biofilm surface; this result fits the concept of a mass transport boundary layer of high mass transport resistance above the biofilm surface. A high mass transport coefficient near the biofilm surface is also expected because water flows near and within biofilms and convection is the predominant mass transport mechanism in that zone. These two facts—high mass transport resistance and convection—cannot coexist. It is difficult to explain why the oxygen concentration decreases above the biofilm surface while the local mass transport coefficient remains almost constant.

To explain the nature of this discrepancy, the procedures we use to measure and compute the results that lead to the discrepancy need to be examined. Consider the flow velocity. All available flow velocity measurements in biofilms report only one component of the flow velocity vector: the one parallel to the bottom. On the basis of these results, we have developed the notion that mass transport near the biofilm surface and within the interstitial voids is controlled by convection.

The rate of convective mass transport from the bulk solution toward the biofilm equals the nutrient concentration times the flow velocity component normal to the reactive surface.

$$J = v \times C \tag{3.58}$$

where J is flux, v is the flow velocity normal to the reactive surface, and C is the concentration of the nutrient. The component of the flow velocity we measure is parallel to the surface and has nothing to do with the convective mass transport toward that surface.

Consequently, the estimate of the mass transport mechanism based on flow velocity holds only in the direction in which the flow velocity was measured. When the flow near a surface is laminar, as it is in the flat plate reactors where most of these results were measured, the laminas of liquid slide parallel to the surface and there is little or no convection across these layers; the mass transport parallel to the surface is convective, but the mass transport perpendicular to the surface is diffusive (Figure 3.49). Consequently, both conclusions are correct: the mass transfer near the biofilm surface is convective along the biofilm surface and diffusive parallel to the surface. This explains the results in Figure 3.48, in which the profile of oxygen concentration does not match the profile of mass transport. This is because the mass transport electrode does not distinguish directions: it does not matter for the measurement using this tool whether the mass flow is parallel to the surface or perpendicular to the surface. By definition, the local mass transfer electrode measures the rate of mass transfer to the electrode, not to the biofilm.

The effect of the diffusion layer on the mass transfer just above the biofilm surface needs to be addressed because it is in disagreement with the popular notion that mass transport within the biofilm is controlled by convection. The results given above demonstrate that, even though the mass transport of nutrients in the interstitial spaces in the biofilm is controlled by convection, the overall biofilm activity is still controlled by the rate of nutrient diffusion across the diffusion boundary layer above the biofilm. To better understand the mechanism of mass transport in biofilms, we will computationally verify the nature of the mass transport in the interstitial voids and in the microcolonies. The key factor controlling the mass transport mechanism is hydrodynamics, which determines the overall rate of nutrient delivery from the bulk solution into the biofilm and the distribution of nutrients within the biofilm. Flow velocity near a biofilm changes from a maximum in the bulk solution to zero near the surface, or bottom of the biofilm, forming a velocity profile similar to that formed by the nutrient concentration. Because of biofilm porosity, water moves in the space occupied by the biofilm, and the flow velocity reaches zero near the bottom (Lewandowski and Beyenal 2003). The rate of convection decreases near the

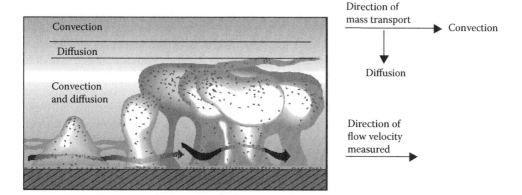

Figure 3.49 Alternating zones of convective and diffusive mass transport in heterogeneous biofilms. This hypothetical model of mass transport is consistent with the results in Figure 3.48. Mass transport in the space occupied by the biofilm is convective, but the amount of nutrient delivered to this space is limited by the diffusive mass transport just above the biofilm surface. (Reproduced from Lewandowski, Z., and Beyenal, H. Mass transfer in heterogeneous biofilms. In *Biofilms in Wastewater Treatment*, S. Wuertz, P. Bishop, and P. A. Wilderer, Eds., IWA Publishing, London, 2003, pp. 145–172.)

biofilm surface, because the flow velocity decreases there, and it is expected that molecular diffusion becomes the principal mechanism of mass transport in that zone.

Because we are suggesting changes to the existing conceptual model, it is important to support the new model, shown in Figure 3.49, with as many data as possible, including theoretical computations confirming that the mass transport dynamics within the space occupied by the biofilm are indeed consistent with the observations. To determine the mechanisms of mass transport near the biofilm surface and within the biofilm, a set of equations quantifying the rates of convection and diffusion will be used.

The time needed for a molecule to travel a distance L by diffusion is

$$t = \frac{L^2}{2D_w} \tag{3.59}$$

where D_w is diffusivity (cm²/s). The time needed for a molecule to travel a distance L by convection is

$$t = \frac{L}{v} \tag{3.60}$$

where v is flow velocity (cm/s). Equating the right sides of these equations and solving the resulting equation for the distance L, we arrive at the critical distance L_{crit}, which a molecule may travel during time t by either convection or diffusion; the mechanisms of transport are different but the distance is the same:

$$L_{crit} = \frac{2D_w}{v} \tag{3.61}$$

Thus, by measuring the distance traveled by a particle within the biofilm and knowing the diffusivity, the contributions from convection and diffusion in the overall mass transport may be distinguished. If the distance traveled by the molecule is longer than the critical distance, then the prevailing mass transport mechanism is convection. Alternatively, this calculation can be simplified by dividing Equation 3.59 by Equation 3.60 and concluding that when $Lv/2D > 1$, then convection exceeds diffusion.

In such analyses, it is important to select the characteristic distance the molecules have to travel in a way that is meaningful for the system under study. In our system, we believe that the thickness of the mass transport boundary layer is a good choice for the characteristic length; this can be calculated from Equation 3.59 for a given nutrient concentration profile. We assume that the molecular diffusivity of the dissolved nutrients (e.g., oxygen), D, is 2×10^{-5} cm² s⁻¹ (Beyenal et al. 1997) and that the characteristic distance L is the thickness of the boundary layer, e.g., 0.5 mm, which is equal to the thickness of the boundary layer in Figure 3.50. From Equation 3.60, it results that a molecule needs 62.5 s to diffuse 0.5 mm, which is equivalent to a linear velocity of 8 μm/s. Thus, 8 μm/s is the characteristic flow velocity in the system: it separates mass transport by diffusion from mass transport by convection. At locations where the flow velocity exceeds the characteristic flow velocity, mass transport is dominated by convection. Once the characteristic flow velocity has been estimated, the available experimental data reporting flow velocities near and within biofilms can be looked up and the locations in the biofilms where molecular diffusion

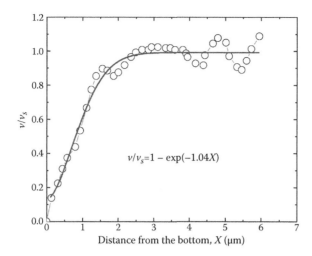

$v/v_s = 1 - \exp(-1.04X)$

Distance from the bottom, X (µm)

Figure 3.50 Flow velocity profile measured by nuclear magnetic resonance imaging. (Reprinted from Lewandowski, Z. et al., *Biotechnology Progress*, 9, 40–45, 1993.)

exceeds convection can be estimated. The results of flow velocity measurements, shown in Figure 3.50, will be used for another biofilm (Lewandowski et al. 1993).

The shape of the flow velocity profile near the biofilm is described by an empirical exponential equation:

$$\frac{v}{v_s} = 1 - \exp(-AX) \tag{3.62}$$

where X is the distance from the bottom, v is the local flow velocity, and v_s is the average bulk flow velocity in the conduit. The results in Figure 3.50 were collected at the average flow velocity in a conduit, $v_s = 4.6$ cm/s; parameter A was estimated to be 1.04×10^{-3} µm^{-1}. Note that A is expressed per micron, not per millimeter as in Figure 3.50. Solving Equation 3.62 for z indicates that the flow velocity exceeded 8 µm/s at distances exceeding 1.7 µm from the bottom, which is so close to the bottom that it is safe to assume that the mass transport in the biofilm voids is entirely due to convection. This conclusion satisfies those researchers who adopted the model of heterogeneous biofilms, because it reflects their expectations.

The flow velocity calculated in the previous paragraph is relevant to the interstitial spaces in the biofilm, but not to the inner spaces of the microcolonies. To test the mechanism of mass transport in the microcolonies, we use the same approach as above but assume that L, the characteristic length in the system, equals the size of a single microorganism in a microcolony, say 1 µm, and that D is the diffusivity in the matrix of extracellular polymers, say 2×10^{-5} cm^2 s^{-1}. The computational procedure used in the preceding paragraph shows that for convection to become the dominant mass transport mechanism, the flow velocity within the microcolony would have to exceed 40 µm s^{-1}, an unlikely event, as shown by Xia et al. (1998). Therefore, the dominant mechanism of mass transport within microcolonies is molecular diffusion, as expected.

In summary, we have demonstrated that molecular diffusion is the dominant mass transport mechanism in microcolonies and that convection is dominant within interstitial voids. These conclusions, although not unexpected, justify the popular notion that biofilm porosity increases mass transport rates within the pores but does not affect the mass transport within the microcolonies, at least not directly. An increase in mass transport outside of the microcolonies may affect the mass transport mechanisms within microcolonies indirectly by affecting the nutrient concentration surrounding the microcolonies in the pores deep in the biofilm. Nevertheless, the predominant mass transport mechanism within microcolonies remains diffusion.

The morphology of biofilms grown at low flow velocities often resembles the model with microcolonies separated by interstitial voids. There are enough experimental data to evaluate the nature of mass transport in such systems. For the purpose of discussing mass transport dynamics, the biofilm system is divided into two zones: the external zone, between the biofilm surface and the bulk solution; and the internal zone, between the bottom and the biofilm surface. The external zone can be further divided into two parts: (1) away from the biofilm surface, in the bulk solution and (2) in proximity to the biofilm surface. In the bulk solution, away from the biofilm surface, mass transport is controlled by convection if the water is flowing. Just above the biofilm surface, water flow is laminar. It is important to note that the water flow is parallel to the biofilm surface and the mass transport is normal to that surface. Therefore, nutrients are transported along the surface with the flowing water by convection and toward the surface by diffusion. This duality of the mass transport mechanism near the biofilm surface produces confusing experimental results because most tools used to study biofilms at the microscale do not discriminate between directions. Within the biofilm, the mass transport mechanism changes: the same component of flow velocity that was parallel to the bottom above the biofilm surface becomes perpendicular to some microcolonies below the biofilm surface. Therefore, the mass transport in biofilm channels is due to convection and, perhaps, dispersion, as the biofilm may act as a porous medium. Convection within biofilm pores makes mass transport quite efficient and may allow the nutrients to penetrate deep into the biofilm.

From all available information, mass transport within microcolonies is due to diffusion. In biofilms grown at low and moderate flow velocities, mass transport above the biofilm surface and below the biofilm surface is both convective and diffusive. Nutrients are transported along the biofilm surface by convection and toward the biofilm surface by diffusion. Below the biofilm surface, nutrients are transported in biofilm channels by convection and in microcolonies by diffusion. Consequently, microorganisms within microcolonies are supplied with nutrients from the bulk as the result of a chain of alternating convection and diffusion processes.

Mass transport in biofilms is affected by biofilm structure and by hydrodynamics. The fact that hydrodynamics also affects biofilm structure complicates the picture. To simplify matters, it is convenient to discuss biofilms grown at low flow velocities (a few centimeters per second) and biofilms grown at high flow velocities (a few meters per second) separately. Biofilms grown at low flow velocities and biofilms grown at high flow velocities have distinctly different morphologies. For biofilms grown at low flow velocities, the influence of biofilm structure on mass transport can be separated from the influence of hydrodynamics on biofilm structure because the effect of hydrodynamics on biofilm structure can be ignored. For biofilms grown at high flow velocities, this simplification is not warranted: at high flow velocities, hydrodynamics strongly affects biofilm structure. The available data on nutrient concentration gradients and flow velocity gradients are limited to biofilms grown at low flow velocities. Therefore, most information about the nature of mass transport in biofilms comes from measurements in biofilms grown at low flow velocities; very little is known about mass transport in biofilms grown at high flow velocities.

To summarize the dynamics of mass transport in biofilm systems, it is convenient to inspect how the mass transport resistance affects the nutrient supply to microcolonies. In slowly flowing water, the nutrient supply from the bulk to the biofilm is limited by diffusion across the mass transport boundary layer above the biofilm surface, a zone of high mass transport resistance. As a result, convection below the biofilm surface may help distribute nutrients within the biofilm, but the amount of nutrients available is determined by the zone of highest mass transport resistance above the biofilm surface. Convection in biofilm pores allows a deeper penetration of nutrients than previously suspected. Within microcolonies, mass transport is controlled by diffusion.

The procedure described above has been recalled to demonstrate the iterative process of improving our knowledge of biofilm processes. It also demonstrates how important it is to construct conceptual models of biofilm processes as we understand them. Not only do such models serve educational purposes, they are serious research tools. On the basis of these models, we formulate hypotheses. We also verify the results of biofilm studies against these conceptual models. If the results of a study are not consistent with the expectations based on the conceptual model, they warrant further inquiry. If the inconsistency is persistent, perhaps the model needs to be revisited.

3.8　*Functionality of LBRs*

There are no rigid rules guiding the selection of LBRs. Because there are no universal biofilm reactors, some desirable features must be compromised no matter which one is chosen. Table 3.4 specifies distinct features of popular LBRs and can be used as a guide to selecting LBRs for specific biofilm studies.

Knowledge of biofilm processes is accumulating based on observations and theoretical computations. Biofilm processes are studied in natural biofilm systems and in LBRs, where some variables are artificially set to the levels desired by the operator. The relevance of the observations of natural biofilm systems is unquestionable. However, the observations made in natural biofilm systems are affected by many factors outside of our control, and some of these factors may be unknown; it is difficult to study specific biofilm processes in natural reactors, where everything affects everything. LBRs have many disadvantages, but they allow the study of some biofilm processes in isolation. One may argue that such studies do not have the relevance of the studies of natural systems, and this is true: they do not have the same relevance. For better or worse, however, most of our current knowledge of biofilm processes was generated using LBRs and used to explain the behavior of natural biofilm systems, not the other way around.

The reactors discussed in this chapter do not exhaust the possible variety of LBRs constructed by biofilm researchers. Certainly, the selection of LBRs depends on the biofilm processes under study. Someone who studies microbially influenced corrosion may find that other types of reactors than those described here are more suitable for those studies. The reactors described here are suitable for studying the structure and activity of biofilms, but the problems addressed in the discussion of these reactors, such as the effect of hydrodynamics on biofilm processes, are common to all reactors and all applications. We also use other reactors in our laboratory, and we study other processes than those we have described here. We know that the selection of laboratory reactors has a certain number of common steps, and these steps do not depend on the application: they are universal. We have addressed as many of these steps as is practical in a text dedicated to biofilm structure and activity.

Table 3.4 Comparison of Functionality of LBRs

	Open-channel flat plate reactor	Simplified open-channel flat plate reactor	Rotating disc reactor	Annular reactor	Tubular reactor/ capillary reactor	Packed-bed reactor	Flat plate vapor phase reactor
Variable							
Average flow velocity in the reactor	Can be measured and controlled	Can be measured and controlled	No net flow	No net flow	Can be measured and controlled	Can be measured but is difficult to control because of biofilm growth	Can be measured and controlled
Local flow velocity	Can be measured	Can be measured	Cannot be measured	Cannot be measured	Can be measured	Cannot be measured	n/a
Shear stress	Can be measured and controlled	Cannot be measured or controlled	Can be measured and controlled	Can be measured and controlled	Can be measured and controlled	Cannot be measured	Can be measured and controlled
Average microbial activity	Can be measured	Can be measured	Can be measured	Can be measured	Can be measured	Can be measured	Can be measured
Local microbial activity using microelectrodes	Can be measured	Can be measured	Can be measured, but coupons with biofilm need to be removed from the reactor for the measurements	Can be measured, but coupons with biofilm need to be removed from the reactor for the measurements	Can be measured	Cannot be measured	Can be measured
Applications							
Biocide or antimicrobial efficiency testing	Can be used	Can be used	Can be used	Can be used	Can be used	Can be used	Can be used
Biofilm imaging and *in situ* structure quantification	Biofilm structure can be imaged	Biofilm structure can be imaged	—	—	Biofilm structure can be imaged and quantified	Biofilm structure cannot be imaged or quantified	Biofilm structure can be imaged and quantified

Nomenclature

Roman symbols

Symbol	Meaning	Usual units
A	Cross section of conduit	cm^2, m^2
C_b	Bulk substrate concentration	mol/cm^3
C_d	Drag coefficient	
C_s	Substrate concentration at the surface	mol/cm^3
d	Diameter of the pipe	cm, m
D_w	Diffusivity of the molecules in water	cm^2/s, m^2/s
e	Height of the roughness elements, m	
E_l	Hydrodynamic entry length number	
F	Force	Newton or C/mol
	Faraday's constant	
f	Friction factor	
G	Shear modulus	
H	Height of the object or cell cluster	m
ΔH_l	Head loss	
Δh	Hydraulic head	
I	Limiting current	A
J	Flux	$moles/m^2$
k	Mass transfer coefficient	cm/s, m/s
K	Hydraulic conductivity	m/s
K_p	Permeability	Darcy
L	Characteristic length	cm, m
	Length of a pipe	
	Length of a packed-bed reactor	
L_{crit}	Critical distance	m
L_d	Entry length	
L_r	Ratio of the respective linear dimensions	
m	Mass	kg
M	Momentum	kg m/s
n	Number of electrons transferred	
V	Volume	cm^3, L
v	Relative velocity of one sheet of liquid with respect to another	m/s
	Velocity of a molecule	
	Linear flow velocity	
v_s	Average flow velocity	cm/s, m/s
q	Reactor inlet or outlet flow rate	cm^3/s, L/s
v'	Superficial velocity in a packed-bed reactor based on the empty cross section	
q_{total}	Total flow rate	cm^3/s, L/s
q_r	Recycle flow rate	cm^3/s, L/s
Q	Volumetric flow rate	cm^3/s, L/s
R	Radius of the rotating cylinder or disk	m
R_h	Hydraulic radius	m, cm

S	Surface area at which force F is applied parallel to the surface	m^2
t	Time	s, h
T	Torque	N m
W	Wetted perimeter	cm, m
x	Distance	m
X	Distance from the bottom of the biofilm	m
Y	Elastic modulus	N/m^2
z_s	Biofilm surface	

Greek symbols

Symbol	Meaning	Usual units
ρ	Density	g/cm^3, kg/L
μ	Dynamic viscosity	$kg/m\ s$
υ	Kinematic viscosity	m^2/s
δ	Thickness of the boundary layer	m
τ	Shear stress	N/m^2
τ_r	Retention time	h
τ_w	Shear stress at the wall	N/m^2
α	Shear angle	
ω	Rotation rate	rotation/s
φ	Boundary layer thickness	m

Abbreviations

Abbreviation	Meaning
Pe	Peclet number
Re	Reynolds number
Sc	Schmidt number
Sh	Sherwood number

References

Beyenal, H., and Lewandowski, Z. 2001. Mass-transport dynamics, activity, and structure of sulfate-reducing biofilms. *AIChE Journal* 47: 1689–1697.

Beyenal, H., Seker, S., Tanyolac, A., and Salih, B. 1997. Diffusion coefficients of phenol and oxygen in a biofilm of *Pseudomonas putida*. *AIChE Journal* 43: 243–250.

Beyenal, H., Yakymyshyn, C., Hyungnak, J., Davis, C. C., and Lewandowski, Z. 2004. An optical microsensor to measure fluorescent light intensity in biofilms. *Journal of Microbiological Methods* 58: 367–374.

Colebrook, C. F. 1938. Turbulent flow in pipes. *Journal of the Institution of Civil Engineers* 11: 133–156.

De Beer, D., Stoodley, P., and Lewandowski, Z. 1994. Liquid flow in heterogeneous biofilms. *Biotechnology and Bioengineering* 44: 636–641.

Groenenboom, M. 2000. Increase of frictional resistance in closed conduit systems fouled with biofilms. Montana State University, Bozeman.

Lewandowski, Z., Altobelli, S. A., and Fukushima, E. 1993. NMR and microelectrode studies of hydrodynamics and kinetics in biofilms. *Biotechnology Progress* 9: 40–45.

Lewandowski, Z., and Beyenal, H. 2003. Mass transfer in heterogeneous biofilms. In *Biofilms in Wastewater Treatment*, Wuertz, S., Bishop, P., and Wilderer, P. A., eds. London: IWA Publishing, pp. 145–172.

Lewandowski, Z., Beyenal, H., and Stookey, D. 2004. Reproducibility of biofilm processes and the meaning of steady state in biofilm reactors. *Water Science and Technology* 49: 359–364.

Lewandowski, Z., Walser, G., and Characklis, W. G. 1991. Reaction-kinetics in biofilms. *Biotechnology and Bioengineering* 38: 877–882.

McCabe, W. L., and Smith, J. C. 1976. *Unit Operations of Chemical Engineering* (3rd ed.). McGraw-Hill.

Montgomery, D. C. 2006. *Design and Analysis of Experiments*. Hoboken, NJ: John Wiley.

Peters, A. C., and Wimpenny, J. W. T. 1988. A constant-depth laboratory model film fermentor. *Biotechnology and Bioengineering* 32: 263–270.

Rasmussen, K., and Lewandowski, Z. 1998a. The accuracy of oxygen flux measurements using microelectrodes. *Water Research* 32: 3747–3755.

Rasmussen, K., and Lewandowski, Z. 1998b. Microelectrode measurements of local mass transport rates in heterogeneous biofilms. *Biotechnology and Bioengineering* 59: 302–309.

Roe, F. L., Wentland, E., Zelver, N., Warwood, B., Waters, R., and Characklis, W. G. 1994. Online side-stream monitoring of biofouling. In *Biofouling and Biocorrosion in Industrial Water Systems*, Geesey, G. G., and Flemming, H.-C. eds. Ann Arbor, MI: Lewis Pub., pp. 137–150.

Schlichting, H. 1960. *Boundary Layer Theory*. New York: McGraw-Hill Book Co., pp. 66–67.

Stoodley, P., de Beer, D., and Lewandowski, Z. 1994. Liquid flow in biofilm systems. *Applied and Environmental Microbiology* 60: 2711–2716.

Stoodley, P., Lewandowski, Z., Boyle, J. D., and Lappin-Scott, H. M. 1999. Structural deformation of bacterial biofilms caused by short-term fluctuations in fluid shear: An in situ investigation of biofilm rheology. *Biotechnology and Bioengineering* 65: 83–92.

Villaverde, S., Mirpuri, R., Lewandowski, Z., and Jones, W. L. 1997. Study of toluene degradation kinetics in a flat plate vapor phase bioreactor using oxygen microsensors. *Water Science and Technology* 36: 77–84.

von Ka'rm'an, T. 1921. Uuber laminare und turbulent Reibung. *Z Angew Math Mech* 1: 233–252.

Xia, F. H., Beyenal, H., and Lewandowski, Z. 1998. An electrochemical technique to measure local flow velocity in biofilms. *Water Research* 32: 3631–3636.

Suggested readings

Boltz, J. P., Morgenroth, E., and Sen, D. 2010. Mathematical modelling of biofilms and biofilm reactors for engineering design. *Water Science and Technology* 62: 1821–1836.

Di Trapani, D., Mannina, G., Torregrossa, M., and Viviani, G. 2008. Hybrid moving bed biofilm reactors: A pilot plant experiment. *Water Science and Technology* 57: 1539–1545.

Gilmore, K. R., Little, J. C., Smets, B. F., and Love, N. G. 2009. Oxygen transfer model for a flow-through hollow-fiber membrane biofilm reactor. *Journal of Environmental Engineering-ASCE* 135: 806–814.

Goeres, D. M., Loetterle, L. R., Hamilton, M. A., Murga, R., Kirby, D. W., and Donlan, R. M. 2005. Statistical assessment of a laboratory method for growing biofilms. *Microbiology* 151: 757–762.

Griffin, P., and Findlay, G. E. 2000. Process and engineering improvements to rotating biological contactor design. *Water Science and Technology* 41: 137–144.

Ivanovic, I., and Leiknes, T. 2011. Membrane reactor design as a tool for better membrane performance in a biofilm MBR (BF-MBR). *Desalination and Water Treatment* 25: 259–267.

Kumar, A., Hille-Reichel, A., Horn, H., Dewulf, J., Lens, P., and Van Langenhove, H. 2012. Oxygen transport within the biofilm matrix of a membrane biofilm reactor treating gaseous toluene. *Journal of Chemical Technology and Biotechnology* 87: 751–757.

Logan, B. E. 2001. Analysis of overall perchlorate removal rates in packed-bed bioreactors. *Journal of Environmental Engineering-ASCE* 127: 469–471.

Martin, K. J., and Nerenberg, R. 2012. The membrane biofilm reactor (MBfR) for water and wastewater treatment: Principles, applications, and recent developments. *Bioresource Technology* 122: 83–94.

McQuarrie, J. P., and Boltz, J. P. 2011. Moving bed biofilm reactor technology: Process applications, design, and performance. *Water Environment Research* 83: 560–575.

Meyer, M. T., Roy, V., Bentley, W. E., and Ghodssi, R. 2011. Development and validation of a micro-fluidic reactor for biofilm monitoring via optical methods. *Journal of Micromechanics and Microengineering* 21.

Nicolella, C., van Loosdrecht, M. C. M., and Heijnen, J. J. 1999. Identification of mass transfer parameters in three-phase biofilm reactors. *Chemical Engineering Science* 54: 3143–3152.

Nott, K. P., Heese, F. P., Paterson-Beedle, M., Macaskie, L. E., and Hall, L. D. 2005. Visualization of the function of a biofilm reactor by magnetic resonance imaging. *Canadian Journal of Chemical Engineering* 83: 68–72.

Patwardhan, A. W. 2003. Rotating biological contactors: A review. *Industrial and Engineering Chemistry Research* 42: 2035–2051.

Pereira, M. O., Kuehn, M., Wuertz, S., Neu, T., and Melo, L. F. 2002. Effect of flow regime on the architecture of a *Pseudomonas fluorescens* biofilm. *Biotechnology and Bioengineering* 78: 164–171.

Qureshi, N., Annous, B. A., Ezeji, T. C., Karcher, P., and Maddox, I. S. 2005. Biofilm reactors for industrial bioconversion processes: Employing potential of enhanced reaction rates. *Microbial Cell Factories* 4.

Rittmann, B. E., Pettis, M., Reeves, H. W., and Stahl, D. A. 1999. How biofilm clusters affect substrate flux and ecological selection. *Water Science and Technology* 39: 99–105.

Rupp, C. J., Fux, C. A., and Stoodley, P. 2005. Viscoelasticity of *Staphylococcus aureus* biofilms in response to fluid shear allows resistance to detachment and facilitates rolling migration. *Applied and Environmental Microbiology* 71: 2175–2178.

Sarayu, K., and Sandhya, S. 2012. Rotating biological contactor reactor with biofilm promoting mats for treatment of benzene and xylene containing wastewater. *Applied Biochemistry and Biotechnology* 168: 1928–1937.

Seifi, M., and Fazaelipoor, M. H. 2012. Modeling simultaneous nitrification and denitrification (SND) in a fluidized bed biofilm reactor. *Applied Mathematical Modelling* 36: 5603–5613.

Stoodley, P., Dodds, I., De Beer, D., Scott, H. L., and Boyle, J. D. 2005. Flowing biofilms as a transport mechanism for biomass through porous media under laminar and turbulent conditions in a laboratory reactor system. *Biofouling* 21: 161–168.

Walters, E., Hille, A., He, M., Ochmann, C., and Horn, H. 2009. Simultaneous nitrification/denitrification in a biofilm airlift suspension (BAS) reactor with biodegradable carrier material. *Water Research* 43: 4461–4468.

chapter four

Sensors useful in biofilm research

4.1 Fundamental concepts in electrochemistry and principles of electrochemical sensors

Because large parts of this book are dedicated to electrochemical sensors and electrochemical techniques useful in studying biofilms, an introduction to electrochemistry is included to expose those aspects of the subject that may help in understanding how electrochemical sensors operate and why electrochemical techniques are used in studying biofilms. From our experience in teaching electrochemical sensors to graduate students, we know that it is not uncommon for students to have difficulties in applying the information in the classical texts on electrochemistry to designing electrochemical sensors and using electrochemical techniques. In part, these difficulties are caused by the fact that the terminology in electrochemistry is confusing and that mutually exclusive conventions are still in use. Whenever possible, the instances where the terminology is unclear or confusing are specifically pointed out. It is assumed that the reader is familiar with basic inorganic chemistry.

Electrochemistry quantifies the rates and mechanisms of electric charge transfer between two types of conductors: ionic conductors (those characteristic of chemistry, such as solutions of electrolytes) and electronic conductors (those characteristic of electronics, such as metal electrodes). Electric charge is quantified as a multiple of the electron charge (-1.6×10^{-19} coulombs) for negative electric charges and as a multiple of the proton charge ($+1.6 \times 10^{-19}$ coulombs) for positive electric charges. Electrically charged particles and molecules can move in each of these conductors: ions can move in ionic conductors, and electrons can move in electronic conductors. In addition, ions and electrons can penetrate interfaces between ionic and electronic conductors (metals). In this respect, the important difference between electronic and ionic conductors is that the metal ions that constitute the lattice of a metal electrode can move freely between the lattice of the metal and the aqueous solution, whereas the free electrons can move in the bulk of the metal only. In aqueous solutions, electrons are always associated with dissolved or precipitated substances. Interfaces between electronic and ionic conductors constitute the domain of electrochemistry. This is where electric charges are transferred between the two types of conductors. The rates and mechanisms of electric charge transfer across such interfaces are studied by electrochemists.

The general idea in developing a chemical sensor is to make it responsive only to the concentration of the substance that it is to measure while keeping all other factors affecting the sensor's response constant, negligible, or predictable and accounted for. Most chemical sensors discussed in this chapter belong to one of two categories: (1) potentiometric sensors, which reach chemical equilibrium with the analyte—the position of this equilibrium is evaluated from the electric potential difference between the sensor and a suitable reference electrode, and (2) amperometric sensors, which do not equilibrate with the analyte. Amperometric sensors react with the analyte. The rate of this reaction is equivalent to the electric current in the circuit between the sensor and another electrode, and it is a measure of the concentration of the analyte. One of the most serious obstacles to using electrochemistry in biofilm research, or in any other type of research for that matter, is the confusing conventions of polarity, resulting from the mixture of the various conventions used in thermodynamics and electronics. There are historical reasons for this state of affairs, and two examples will be presented here. The first example is that electric current was discovered before the discovery of electrons, and it was pragmatically decided that the carrier of current had a positive sign: Why should it have a negative sign? As a result, to this day, electrical engineers claim that the electric current flows from the positive terminal of a battery to the negative terminal, because that is how it was decided before electrons were discovered. This convention is, of course, opposed by chemists, who correctly claim just the opposite. Because the electrons are the true carriers of the electric current, the current flows from the negative terminal of a battery to the positive terminal. When chemistry amalgamates with electrical engineering to form electrochemistry, confusion arises. The second example is thermodynamics, which uses two opposing sign conventions to quantify the work done on a system. Before thermodynamics was established, those who worked on heat engines made the pragmatic decision that when energy is given up by the system (the engine), this is the desirable effect, and therefore the energy content associated with the change should carry a positive sign. After thermodynamics was established as a science, it was decided that just the opposite is true: when energy is given up by the system, the energy content of the system decreases, so the change in energy content associated with the change should carry a negative sign. All these opposing conventions are still in use, and they contribute to the confusion about polarity in electrochemistry. The only way to avoid the confusion is to start from the beginning and make conscious choices as to which conventions to use and explicitly realize the consequences of the choices. The following section will do just that.

4.1.1   Electric charges

4.1.1.1   Electric potential

Potential is the equivalent of energy. Absolute electric potential cannot be determined for a single point in space. It must be determined with respect to the potential of another point in space. The electric potential at location A with respect to location B is defined as the work needed to bring one unit of positive electric charge from location B to location A. Because the transfer of the charge originates at B, that location is assumed to be the reference location. The reference location may be at infinity, or it may be at a somewhat more accessible location, such as the ground (earth) or a suitable reference electrode. In the latter two cases, the electric potential of location A is defined as the work needed to bring a unit of positive electric charge from the respective reference location, the ground or the reference electrode, to location A. A location in space can have an electric potential even if there is no electric charge residing at that location. The electric potential of a location in space depends on the magnitude and distribution of all electric charges in that location. Even if no electrically charged particle resides at location A at all, if the space is occupied by other electric charges, that location will have an electric potential with respect to any arbitrarily selected reference location B. Quantifying electric potentials at selected locations in space with respect to a defined reference potential is conceptually easy, but the meaning of the computations is obscured by the conventions existing in various branches of physical sciences and engineering.

Although it is possible to work with a few different reference locations, it is practical to select only one and determine the electric potentials at all other locations in space with respect to that reference by moving an electric charge from the reference location to each location of interest and evaluating the work needed for this operation. The selection of the reference location depends on the field of study. Physicists use the location at infinity and define the electric potential at location A in space as the work needed to bring one unit of positive electric charge from infinity to that location. They assume that all locations at infinity have electric potentials equal to zero. Using a location at infinity as a reference point is an elegant solution, even if somewhat impractical. To be practical, it does not really matter which location is chosen as the reference location. What matters are the differences in electric potential among various locations in space: when these differences are computed, the electric potential of the reference location cancels out. For example, let us say the potential of an arbitrarily selected location C in space is used as the reference potential with respect to which the distribution of the potential in space is evaluated. Specifically, the difference in potential between two locations in space, A and B, is of interest. The difference in potential between A and B is computed as follows: At A, the potential equals the potential at A minus the potential of the reference location at C; at B, it equals the potential at B minus the potential at C. When the difference in potential between A and B is computed,

$$(\text{Potential at A} - \text{potential at C}) - (\text{potential at B} - \text{potential at C})$$
$$= (\text{potential at A} - \text{potential at B})$$

the reference potential at C cancels out. In conclusion, to compute the difference in potential between A and B, it does not matter where the reference point is located or what the magnitude of the potential at that reference location C is.

Electric charges distributed in a space affect each other and form an electric field. To characterize an electric field conceptually, a unit of electric charge, q_o, is transferred from one location to another, and the work needed to accomplish this transfer is measured. The test electric charge, q_o, should be inconsequentially small (one unit of the electric charge is used by convention) because its presence affects the other electric charges in the space. This effect should be negligible, so that the test electric charge will be significantly affected by the presence of all other electric charges in the space, but the other electric charges in the space will not be significantly affected by the presence of the test electric charge. Following the convention accepted in thermodynamics, to compute the energy used to transfer an electric charge from one location to another, the initial energy of the electric charge is subtracted from the final energy of the electric charge. If the charge is transferred from A to B, the work associated with this transfer (W_{AB}) is numerically equal to the electric potential energy at location B (EPE_B) minus the electric potential energy at location A (EPE_A).

$$
\begin{array}{ccc}
\text{A} & & \text{B} \\
q_o & \xrightarrow{\ W_{AB}\ } & q_o \\
EPE_A & & EPE_B
\end{array}
$$

The direction of the electric field at a location in space is determined by the direction of the spontaneous movement of a small positive electric charge released at that location.

Example 4.1

An electric charge q_o is transferred from A to B. Location A has electric potential energy EPE_A, location B has electric potential energy EPE_B, and the difference in electric potential energy between these locations is $EPE_B - EPE_A = EPE_{AB}$. The numerical values of EPE_A and of EPE_B are not known; only the difference between them, EPE_{AB}, is known: It is equal to the work needed to move the test electric charge from A to B. To make the result of the computation independent of the magnitude of the test electric charge, the energy change is computed per unit of the electric charge transferred:

$$\frac{W_{AB}}{q_o} = \frac{(EPE_B - EPE_A)}{q_o} = \frac{EPE_{AB}}{q_o} \tag{4.1}$$

The difference in electric potential energy of the unit positive electric charge between A and B is referred to as the *electric potential difference* between these two locations ($V_{AB} = V$):

$$\frac{EPE_{AB}}{q_o} = V_{AB} = V \tag{4.2}$$

Using SI units (joules for energy and coulombs for electric charge), a difference in electric potential energy in an electric field is expressed in volts:

$$\frac{1\,J}{1\,C} = 1\,V \tag{4.3}$$

The following computation illustrates the utility of these concepts.

Example 4.2

Transferring a test electric charge $(+)q_o = 1 \times 10^{-6}$ C from location A to B required 50×10^{-5} J of work. What is the potential difference between locations A and B?

This computation appears to be trivial, but it is not. Computing the numerical answer is straightforward, but a decision must be made as to what sign should be ascribed to the result, plus or minus. To proceed, one must decide whether the work used to transfer the electric charge from A to B had a positive or a negative sign. The problem of assigning signs to work and energy is well known in thermodynamics, where two opposing conventions are used. The so-called "scientific" convention assumes that the sign should be positive if the energy is delivered to the system. According to this convention, if energy is used to move an electric charge from A to B, the sign of the energy change associated with the move is positive. This convention is opposed by the so-called "engineering" convention, which takes a pragmatic approach to expending energy and to performing useful work: because it is desirable to have the system do the work, not the user, when the system does the work, the change is positive. According to this convention, if energy is used to move an electric charge from A to B, the sign of the energy change associated with the move is negative. The scientific convention will be used here: when work is done to move a (positive) test charge from location A to location B, location B has a higher electric potential than location A.

Having agreed on the sign convention, we can continue with the computation, which is now trivial:

$$EPE_B - EPE_A = (+)50 \times 10^{-5}\,J$$

The potential difference between the locations can now be computed:

$$\frac{(+)50 \times 10^{-5}\ \text{J}}{(+)1 \times 10^{-6}\ \text{C}} = (+)500\ \text{V}$$

and it has a positive sign.

As demonstrated, the choice of the reference location is not important for describing the distribution of electric potentials in space. What really matters are the differences in electric potentials between locations of interest. Therefore, various reference locations can be selected by the users, depending on the application. For example, physicists are quite satisfied with a reference location at infinity, but electrical engineers need a more practical reference location, something they can access empirically. Therefore, the electric potential at a location in an electronic circuit is defined as the work needed to transfer one unit of positive electric charge from the earth (ground) to that location; the electric potential of the earth is used as zero on this scale. When electrochemists refer to the electric potential of an electrochemical cell, they refer to the work needed to move one unit of positive charge from a standard hydrogen electrode (SHE) to the indicator electrode in that cell. However, when electrochemists refer to an electric potential in electronic circuitry, they use the convention used by the electrical engineers. It is important to be aware of these differences.

Using a positive electric charge to test the distribution of electric potential in electric fields complicates describing the electrical effects of charge transfer because the origin of electric charges is the excess or deficiency of negatively charged particles (electrons). Because a positive charge is used to test the electric potential distribution in electric fields, when electrons are moved in these fields, they move spontaneously from the location of lower electric potential to the location of higher electric potential, which is somewhat counterintuitive but is consistent with the manner in which electric field forces are quantified. For example, if a test electrode has a higher electric potential than the reference electrode, electrons will have the tendency to move from the reference electrode to the test electrode—from the lower electric potential to the higher electric potential. This can be visualized as the tendency of negatively charged particles (electrons) to move away from the locations with more negative electric potentials and move toward the locations with more positive electric potential.

4.1.1.2   Electrode potential and the Nernst equation

A redox reaction is composed of two half reactions: one substance donates electrons and the other substance accepts the electrons. The electrons have the tendency to move from the one substance to the other because the substance that donates the electrons has a lower affinity for the electrons than the substance that accepts them. As a result of electron transfer, the substance that donated the electrons is oxidized and the substance that accepted the electrons is reduced. The affinity of a substance for electrons can be evaluated and cataloged for the standard conditions as the potential of the half reaction in which this substance participates: the higher the potential of the half reaction, the higher the affinity of the substance participating in that half reaction for the electrons. As a result, substances can be compared by evaluating their affinity for electrons, and it can be predicted which substance will donate the electrons and which substance will accept the electrons—which substance will be oxidized and which will be reduced. Whether the actual transfer of the electrons occurs depends on kinetic limitations, and the kinetics of these reactions are determined experimentally. Technically, the difference between the potentials of the half reactions is called the *cell potential*, and it is proportional to the Gibbs free energy change resulting from transferring the electrons from one half reaction to another. In chemistry the tendency of reactions to occur is quantified by computing the Gibbs free energy change. In electrochemistry this same tendency is quantified by computing the cell potential. The two computations are equivalent: the cell potential is the Gibbs free energy change expressed in electrical terms, and the Faraday constant is used as the conversion factor.

The Faraday constant ($F = 96,485$ C/mol) is equal to the electric charge of one mole of electrons, and it appears in many electrochemical equations. To compute the Faraday constant the electrical charge of a single electron, which equals 1.602×10^{-19} coulombs, is multiplied by the number of electrons in one mole of electrons, which is equal to Avogadro's number, 6.0238×10^{23} particles per mole. The product of these two numbers is known as the Faraday constant, 96,485 coulombs per mole of electrons.

The common expressions in electrochemical calculations that use the Faraday constant are (1) the Faraday constant multiplied by the number of moles of electrons (n) transferred between locations, nF, which is equal to the electrical charge transferred between these locations, and (2) the electric charge transferred between locations multiplied by the potential difference between these locations expressed in volts, nFE, which is equal to the energy change. Actually, the latter expression should use ΔE instead of E, but it is customary to use E because potentials are always measured with respect to another potential, so E is always ΔE.

The electric charge transferred in a redox reaction, nF, and the energy change, nFE, are often used in electrochemical computations. From these relations, the Gibbs free energy change in an electrochemical reaction can be expressed as the equivalent of the potential difference:

$$-\Delta G = nFE \tag{4.4}$$

where ΔG is the Gibbs free energy change associated with the electron transfer. The accepted sign convention is consistent with the convention used in chemical thermodynamics: the energy of the reactants is subtracted from the energy of the products.

Because the Gibbs free energy change for a simple electrochemical reaction can be computed from thermodynamics and the free energy change in a redox reaction is equivalent to the potential difference, it is also possible to compute the equivalent potentials for these reactions. Such computations yield "half-cell potentials," which have exactly the same use as the computations of Gibbs free energy change in these reactions, but the half-cell potentials are expressed in a unit used in electrochemistry: volts. Computing cell potentials from Gibbs free energy changes does not add any additional information: the cell potential is just the Gibbs free energy change divided by the electric charge transferred in that reaction (nF). The sign convention is such that reactions are spontaneous when their cell potentials are positive:

$$E = \frac{-\Delta G}{nF} \tag{4.5}$$

This sign convention is consistent with the discussion above: electrons tend to move from locations with lower potentials to locations with higher potentials. If the thermodynamic convention is used, the sign of the potential of the final destination (the higher potential) minus the potential of the initial location (the lower potential) is positive, which indicates that the transfer of electrons between these locations is spontaneous. A negative change in Gibbs free energy is equivalent to a positive potential.

The cell potential E is just another way of expressing the Gibbs free energy change for that reaction, ΔG. For a redox reaction described by the following stoichiometry:

$$r(\text{reactant}) + ne^- \rightleftarrows p(\text{product})$$

the Gibbs free energy change is

$$\Delta G = \Delta G^\circ + RT \ln \left(\frac{\prod (\text{product activities})^p}{\prod (\text{reactant activities})^r} \right) \tag{4.6}$$

where (reactant) and (product) stand for activities of the reactants and products, typically substituted for by their molar concentrations, (reactant) = [reactants] and (product) = [products]; in practice, ion activities are substituted for by their concentrations, dissolved gasses are shown as their partial pressures, and solids have activities equal to one. Superscripts p and r stand for the stoichiometric coefficients associated with the reactant and the products, and the electron activity does not enter the equation because, by convention, the free energy of formation for electrons is equal to zero. Dividing both sides of Equation 4.6 by the charge transferred in the redox reaction, nF, and combining it with Equation 4.5, the relations quantifying the Gibbs free energy change yield

$$E = -\frac{\Delta G}{nF} = -\frac{\Delta G^\circ + RT \left[\ln \prod (\text{product activities})^p - \ln \prod (\text{reactant activities})^r \right]}{nF} \tag{4.7}$$

For standard conditions,

$$E^\circ = -\frac{\Delta G^\circ}{nF} \tag{4.8}$$

Equation 4.7 yields

$$E = E^\circ - \frac{RT}{nF} \ln \left[\frac{\prod (\text{product activities})^p}{\prod (\text{reactant activities})^r} \right] \tag{4.9}$$

If the reaction occurs at 25°C, this expression can be further simplified by substituting the constant values for the universal gas constant R, Faraday constant F, and absolute temperature T, equivalent to 25°C, and using decimal logarithms instead of natural logarithms:

$$R = 8.314 \text{ J/mol-K}$$
$$F = 96{,}485 \text{ C/mol}$$
$$T = 298 \text{ K } (25°C)$$

$$E = E^\circ - \frac{0.059}{n} \log \left[\frac{\prod (\text{product activities})^p}{\prod (\text{reactant activities})^r} \right] \quad (4.10)$$

To check this result, remember that changing from the natural to the decimal logarithm requires multiplying the result by 2.3: $\log(a) = 2.3 \ln(a)$. Equations 4.9 and 4.10 are two forms of the Nernst equation. The latter, written for 25°C, is used in most computations. To visualize the effects of the substrate and product concentrations on the cell potential, it is useful to modify the form of the Nernst equation by changing the negative sign to a positive sign and rearranging the logarithmic expression accordingly:

$$E = E^\circ + \frac{0.059}{n} \log \left[\frac{\prod (\text{reactant activities})^r}{\prod (\text{product activities})^p} \right] \quad (4.11)$$

Nernst equation is often presented in a more specific form by taking advantage of the convention that electrochemical reactions proceed forward if they are reduction reactions; thus we know that the reactants are the oxidized substances and the products are the reduced substances.

$$p \text{ ox} + ne^- \rightarrow r \text{ red}$$

Therefore, the Nernst equation can be written as

$$E = E^\circ - \frac{0.059}{n} \log \left[\frac{\prod (\text{red})^r}{\prod (\text{ox})^p} \right] \quad (4.12)$$

where (ox) and (red) are the activities of the oxidized and reduced substances, typically substituted for by the molar concentrations, ox = [ox] and red = [red].

The expression in the square brackets is the reaction quotient Q:

$$\left[\frac{\prod (\text{red})^r}{\prod (\text{ox})^p} \right] = Q \quad (4.13)$$

when $E = 0$, the reaction is at equilibrium, and the reaction quotient Q is equal to the equilibrium constant K:

$$0 = E^\circ - \frac{0.059}{n} \log K$$

This last equation demonstrates that computing standard potentials, $E°$, is just another way of quantifying the equilibrium constants for redox reactions:

$$K = 10^{\left(\frac{n}{0.059}E°\right)}$$

(4.14)

Earlier, it was concluded that cell potentials for redox reactions are equivalent to the Gibbs free energy changes for these reactions; it is now concluded that the *standard* potentials of half reactions are equivalent to their equilibrium constants. Reactions with numerically large equilibrium constants tend to proceed far to the right, and the same is true of reactions with numerically large potentials. This information is useful for interpreting the table of standard potentials (Table 4.1). The higher the reaction is on the scale of standard potentials, the stronger its tendency to proceed forward. Because, by convention, proceeding forward means reduction, the higher the reaction on the scale of potentials, the stronger its oxidizing power and the higher its affinity for electrons and its tendency to proceed forward. For example, the half reaction of reducing ozone to oxygen has a standard potential exceeding 2 V, which means that ozone is a strong oxidizer and the reaction will tend to go forward until the concentration of ozone is nearly exhausted.

To compute the potentials of reactions at nonstandard conditions, the Nernst equation is used. In practice, ion activities are substituted for by their concentrations, dissolved gases are shown as their partial pressures, and solids have activities equal to one. Standard potentials can be found in tables, such as Table 4.1.

It is convenient to visualize the potentials of various half reactions on a "potential ladder" in which individual half reactions represent rungs of the ladder. In this way, a certain energy is ascribed to each rung of the ladder and the direction in which electrons will flow in the electrochemical cell, if such a cell is assembled, can be predicted. This representation also helps in visualizing the computations that are needed to express the potentials of a given half reaction with respect to various reference electrodes. The reactants in the above half reactions have different affinities for electrons. To visualize how the reagents in two half reactions would interact in a solution, the cell potential must be computed using the actual concentrations of the reactants in both half reactions.

The half reaction of reducing protons to hydrogen has a special place in chemical thermodynamics. By convention, it is assumed that the Gibbs free energy of proton formation

Table 4.1 Standard Electrode Potentials of Selected Half Reactions in an Aqueous Solution at 25°C

Half reaction	Standard potential, $E°$ (volts)
$Li^+(aq) + e^- \rightleftarrows Li(s)$	−3.045
$K^+(aq) + e^- \rightleftarrows K(s)$	−2.92
$Ca^{2+}(aq) + 2e^- \rightleftarrows Ca(s)$	−2.76
$Na^+(aq) + e^- \rightleftarrows Na(s)$	−2.71
$Zn^{2+}(aq) + 2e^- \rightleftarrows Zn(s)$	−0.76
$2H^+ + 2e^- \rightleftarrows H_2$	0.00
$Cu^{2+}(aq) + 2e^- \rightleftarrows Cu(s)$	0.34
$O_3(g) + 2H^+(aq) + 2e^- \rightleftarrows O_2(g) + H_2O(l)$	2.07
$F_2(g) + 2e^- \rightleftarrows 2F^-(aq)$	2.87

and the free energy of electron formation are both equal to zero. This convention establishes the position of zero on the scale of potentials and provides a reference point for computing other potentials. Strictly speaking, only half reactions have potentials; entire reactions are characterized by free energy change. This is because each of the half reactions can be assembled as an electrochemical cell and its potential can be measured versus the potential of the SHE (Figure 4.1). Ascribing zero to the standard potential of the half reaction in which protons are reduced to hydrogen establishes the SHE. The standard potentials of other half reactions are compared to SHE. Standard potentials of half reactions do not have to be adjusted by subtracting their standard potentials from the standard potential of SHE, because the standard potential of SHE is always zero by convention. Consequently, any two electrochemical half reactions can be directly related to each other by comparing their standard potentials.

Computing a cell potential using the Nernst equation estimates the tendency of the reaction to occur expressed as the potential of an electrode immersed in a solution of the reactants specified in the half reaction. The results of these computations can be verified experimentally by assembling the half-cell(s) represented by the Nernst equation. Not all half reactions can be implemented in exactly the same way as shown in the table of standard potentials. Clearly, an oxygen electrode, for example, cannot be made. When it is not possible to make an electronic conductor (an electrode) of the reactant in a half equation, a substitute electrode made of a noble metal is immersed in the solution; platinum is the preferred metal for such electrodes. Using platinum electrodes where the reactants cannot be used as the electronic conductors in an electrochemical cell, each half reaction in the table of standard potentials can be represented by an electrochemical cell, and the results of the computations using the Nernst equation can be verified.

Because any half reaction in the table of standard potentials can be represented as an electrochemical cell, any half reaction in the table of standard potentials can be used as a reference electrode, at least in principle. However, not every half reaction makes a good reference electrode when represented as an electrochemical cell. Reference electrodes must fulfill many requirements, such as exhibiting stable and reproducible potentials, and only a few half reactions fulfill these requirements, such as those of SHE, the silver/silver-chloride electrode (SCE), and the calomel electrode. These half reactions have been successfully used as half-cells to compare their potentials with the potentials of other half-cells. For historical reasons, the potential of SHE is used as the universal reference potential, and the electrochemical potentials of other half-cells are reported with respect to the standard one molar SHE.

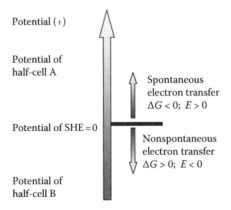

Figure 4.1 Relation between the Gibbs free energy change ΔG and the half-cell potentials.

The tables of standard potentials report the potentials of various half reactions with respect to the standard 1 M concentrations of the reactants and products. However, the popular reference electrodes used in the laboratory, such as the silver chloride and calomel electrodes, are, for practical reasons, filled with saturated solutions of chloride ions, not with the standard 1 M solutions. This is because it is quite difficult to keep the activity of 1 M solutions of any ion constant for a long time. With time, water evaporates and the concentrations of the solutes change. Therefore, it is convenient to use saturated solutions of chloride ions instead of normal solutions, because they do not change concentration when water evaporates. The advantage of using saturated solutions in reference electrodes is somewhat counterbalanced by the disadvantage of having to recalculate their potentials by adjusting the concentration of the electrolyte to the specific concentration in saturated solutions. Most tables of standard potentials, however, give the potentials of the standard and the saturated secondary reference electrodes (Ag/AgCl and SCE). Because the electrode potentials are measured with respect to the secondary reference electrodes and then recalculated to the potential of the hydrogen electrode, reasonable questions to ask are: (1) Why is the hydrogen electrode used at all? and (2) Why was the hydrogen electrode chosen as the universal standard electrode? The answers to these questions are buried in history. Reportedly, the strong personality of Nernst was as much behind the choice of the hydrogen electrode as the universal standard as the scientific merit supporting the choice.

4.1.1.3   Reference electrodes
If the potential of the indicator electrode in a half-cell is measured or computed with respect to a reference electrode other than SHE, the potential can easily be recalculated to the potential versus SHE because each secondary reference electrode has a known potential with respect to SHE. The computations are straightforward, and Figure 4.2 shows how to make them.

Potentials of half-cells with respect to reference electrodes other than SHE can be calculated as distances between the respective rungs on the potential ladder (Figure 4.2). For example, if an arbitrary half reaction A has a half-cell potential with respect to SHE equal to +0.362 V, then it has a half-cell potential of 0.362 V − 0.197 V = 0.165 V with respect to

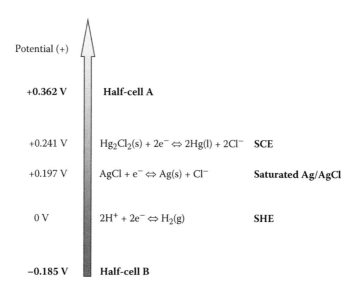

Figure 4.2 Potentials of various reference electrodes and their half-cell potentials.

the saturated Ag/AgCl electrode. Also, if the half-cell potential of an arbitrary half reaction B is −0.185 V with respect to SHE, then its half-cell potential with respect to SCE is −(0.241 V + 0.185 V) = −0.426 V. As for the signs of the computed potentials, if the half-cell potential of the arbitrary half reaction is above the potential of the selected reference electrode, the sign of the potential is positive and vice versa. Consequently, the computed half-cell potential for half reaction A is +0.165 V, while the half-cell potential for half reaction B is −0.426 V. If the half-cell potential of an arbitrary half reaction is between the potentials of SHE and, say, SCE, then it is positive with respect to SHE and negative with respect to SCE.

4.1.1.4   Electric current

Electric current is equivalent to the number of electric charges passing a cross section of a conductor, perpendicular to the flow of electric charges, in a unit of time. Because electrochemistry studies the interfaces between electronic conductors and ionic conductors, two types of currents are often referred to in electrochemistry: the electronic current (the flow of electrons) and the ionic current (the flow of ions). Because the current passing across an interface depends on the surface area perpendicular to the direction of current flow, the measured current is often related to the unit surface area of the electrode and called *current density*. Current densities are used to compare the performance of electrodes even if they have different geometries and surface areas. The fundamental law quantifying the flow of current is Ohm's law, which states that current is directly proportional to the potential and inversely proportional to the resistance. This statement holds in reference to both electronic currents and ionic currents.

4.1.1.5   Measuring potential and current

Although modern electronics offers digital instruments, the measurement of currents and potentials in electrochemical cells is best explained in terms of galvanometers. Galvanometers are devices constructed to measure small currents by quantifying the mechanical effects produced by current-carrying coils suspended in stationary magnetic fields. Figure 4.3 shows the principle of the measurement. A coil made of a wire carries current and generates

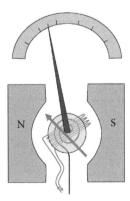

Figure 4.3 Principle of galvanometers. A needle is attached to an electromagnet, and it follows the movement of the electromagnet in the magnetic field of a stationary magnet. The electromagnet is made of a metal core around which a wire coil is wound. The ends of the wire are attached to the terminals of a battery or the electrodes of a galvanic cell. How far the needle is deflected depends on the current flowing through the coil. The needle is also connected to a spring, so that the magnetic forces deflecting the needle are equilibrated with the forces from the spring, and the needle reaches a stable position dependent on the current flowing through the coil.

a magnetic field. A metal core is inserted into this coil, so that the core consolidates the magnetic field lines and becomes an electromagnet. This electromagnet is mounted in a stationary magnet, and the magnetic fields of the two magnets, the coil and the stationary magnet, interfere with each other. The extent of this interference is proportional to the ratio of the magnetic fields of the two magnets. If the current flows through the coil, the electromagnet rotates in the stationary magnetic field in an attempt to align the two fields in the opposite direction: the negative pole of the electromagnet is attracted to the positive pole of the stationary magnet and vice versa. The interference between the magnetic fields rotates the electromagnet and the connected indicator needle by a force proportional to the current flowing through the coil and the field strength of the stationary magnet. All galvanometers use this relation to quantify the electric current in a coil.

Galvanometers are universal tools: they can be used to measure electric current, potential, and resistance. If a galvanometer is inserted into an electrical circuit in series, it measures the current passing through the location where the galvanometer is inserted. If the galvanometer is inserted in parallel, across a resistor, it becomes part of a potentiometer.

4.1.2   Electrochemical cells

An electrochemical half-cell is a physical representation of a redox half reaction, and it can be constructed by immersing appropriate electrodes in solutions of the electroactive substances (substances that can exchange electric charges with electrodes) specified in the half reaction which the half-cell represents. Two connected half-cells constitute an electrochemical cell. To complete the electrochemical cell, the half-cells are connected by an ionic conductor (salt bridge) and an electronic conductor (wire). Without these components the electrons will not flow between the cells, and the following section explains why, using an example of two metal electrodes immersed in solutions of their ions, forming two half-cells, as shown in Figure 4.4.

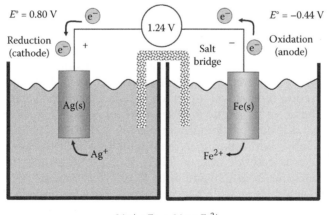

$$2Ag^+ + Fe \rightarrow 2Ag + Fe^{2+}$$

Figure 4.4 Electrochemical cell in which a silver electrode is immersed in a 0.5 M solution of Ag^+ ions in the half-cell on the left and an iron electrode is immersed in a 0.6 M solution of Fe^{2+} ions in the half-cell on the right. The potential of the cell is the difference in potential between the half-cell on the left and the half-cell on the right.

The potential of each half-cell can be computed from the Nernst equation with respect to the reference electrode of choice, and the entire cell voltage can be computed either as the difference between the half-cell potentials versus SHE or from the Nernst equation for the entire cell reaction. When the electrochemical cell is assembled and the electrodes in the two half-cells are connected by an electronic conductor, electric current flows from the half-cell with the substance of lower affinity for electrons to the half-cell with the substance of higher affinity for electrons. To restore its electrical neutrality, each electrode exchanges electric charges with its solution. As shown in Figure 4.4, Fe^{2+} ions are released into the solution in the half-cell on the right and Ag^+ ions are deposited on the silver electrode in the half-cell on the left. As a result, after a while the solution in the half-cell on the right loses some of its negative charge and becomes electrically positively charged and the solution in the half-cell on the left has an excess of negative charges and becomes electrically negatively charged. After several units of electrical charge have transferred across the metal/solution interface in each half-cell, the buildup of the potentials in the solutions prevents the further transfer of ions across the interface. The buildup of the positive charge in the half-cell on the right repulses the Fe^{2+} ions being released from the Fe electrode, and the buildup of negative potential in the half-cell on the left attracts the Ag^+ ions being deposited on the Ag electrode. Before further transfer of electrical charges can occur across the interface, the electrolyte solutions in the half-cells must be electrically neutralized. To prevent the buildup of electrical charges in the solution in each half-cell and to restore its electroneutrality, a salt bridge is used to connect the half-cells. A salt bridge can be made of agar saturated with potassium chloride, KCl. As the electrochemical reactions progress in the half-cells, and positive electric charges accumulate in the half-cell on the left and negative electric charges accumulate in the half-cell on the right, the salt bridge delivers the missing ions to each of the half-cells: it releases K^+ ions to the half-cell on the right and Cl^- ions to the half-cell on the left, thereby restoring the electrical neutrality of the electrolyte solutions in both cells. In a simplified version of the salt bridge, the half-cells are separated by a membrane or by a porous plug and the electroneutrality of the solutions on both sides of the membrane is restored by counterions transferring across the membrane or the porous plug. Without an arrangement restoring the electroneutrality of the solutions in the half-cells, an electrochemical cell would stop working after transferring just minute amounts of electrical charge.

When the electrodes in an electrochemical cell are connected and the electrodes have different potentials, the electrons flow from the location with the lower electric potential to the location with the higher electric potential. The electrode that is immersed in the half-cell in which the reactant in the solution is oxidized is called the *anode,* and the electrode that is immersed in the half-cell in which the reactant in the solution is reduced is called the *cathode.* The terms *anode* and *cathode* were reportedly first used by Faraday, and they remain in use to this day, particularly in corrosion studies. These terms are useful, but it is better to visualize which half reaction is reduction and which is oxidation rather than remember which is cathode and which is anode. Using these terms may cause confusion when switching from galvanic cells to electrolytic cells because the anodes and cathodes are reversed, as is explained in Chapter 7: the cathode in the galvanic cell becomes the anode in the electrolytic cell and vice versa. It is easy to determine which substance is oxidized and which is reduced from the Nernst equation, and the result of this computation holds as long as the electrodes are separated by an infinitely large resistance. The term used to describe this situation, the open circuit voltage, is discussed in detail later, in Section 4.1.2.

The cell in Figure 4.4 is composed of two half-cells:

$$2Ag^+ + 2e^- \rightleftarrows 2Ag; \quad [Ag^+] = 0.5 \text{ M}; \quad E^\circ = 0.8 \text{ V}$$

$$Fe^{2+} + 2e^- \rightleftarrows Fe; \quad [Fe^{2+}] = 0.6 \text{ M}; \quad E^\circ = -0.44 \text{ V}$$

The first half-reaction was multiplied by 2 to equalize the number of electrons transferred in the two half reactions. Multiplying half reactions by integers is done to adjust the numbers of electrons in the cathodic and anodic half reactions; the standard electrode potentials remain the same because they are calculated per one electron.

By convention, the cell potential is computed as

$$E_{cell} = E_{red} - E_{oxid} \quad \text{or} \quad E_{cell} = E_{cathode} - E_{anode}$$

To calculate the standard potential of the cell, the sign of the oxidation half reaction needs to be reversed to reflect the fact that it now proceeds in the opposite direction, and $E^\circ_{oxid} = -E^\circ_{red}$.

$$2Ag^+ + 2e^- \rightleftarrows 2Ag; \quad [Ag^+] = 0.5 \text{ M}; \quad E^\circ = 0.8 \text{ V}$$

$$Fe \rightleftarrows Fe^{2+} + 2e^-; \quad [Fe^{2+}] = 0.6 \text{ M}; \quad E^\circ = +0.44 \text{ V}$$

Now that the same number of electrons are transferred in the two half reactions, and the signs of the standard electrode potentials have been adjusted, we can add the reactions and their standard potentials, E°:

$$2Ag^+ + Fe \rightarrow 2Ag + Fe^{2+}; \quad E^\circ = 0.8 \text{ V} + 0.44 \text{ V} = 1.24 \text{ V}$$

This procedure is the practical approach to computing the standard potential of a cell. Because the signs for the standard potentials of individual reactions are subject to international conventions and are calculated for the reduction reactions, some textbooks advocate that we not emphasize reversing the sign of the oxidation reaction and that the correct notation for calculating the standard potential of the cell is to subtract the standard potential of the oxidation reaction:

$$E^\circ = 0.8 \text{ V} - (-0.44 \text{ V}) = 1.24 \text{ V}$$

The two procedures lead to the same numerical result, and the Nernst equation for the entire reaction is written as

$$E_{cell} = 1.24 + \frac{0.059}{2} \log \frac{[Fe^{2+}]}{[Ag^+]^2} \tag{4.15}$$

Substituting the concentrations of the iron and silver ions,

$$E_{cell} = 1.24 + \frac{0.059}{2} \log \frac{[0.6]}{[0.5]^2} = 1.26 \text{ V}$$

The potential of each electrode is determined by the concentration of the ions with which the electrode equilibrates, and the concentration of ions that matters is that near the surface of the electrode, not that in the bulk solution. If the current flows, Ag^+ ions are removed near the Ag electrode, and to sustain the current, they must be delivered from the bulk solution to the electrode by mass transport. In the other half-cell, Fe^{2+} ions are released into the solution from the Fe electrode and are removed by mass transport from there to the bulk solution. In both half-cells, mass transport is active when gradients in concentrations exist. As a result of the electrode reaction in each half-cell, the concentration of Ag^+ ions near the Ag electrode decreases and the concentration of Fe^{2+} ions in proximity to the Fe electrode increases. If the concentration of Fe^{2+} increases and the concentration of Ag^+ decreases, the ratio of these two concentrations in Equation 4.15 increases rapidly and so does the cell potential. Qualitatively, the increase and the cell potential depend on the current flowing between the half-cells and the rate of mass transport in each half-cell; the cell potential deviates from that computed using the Nernst equation.

The Nernst equation is valid only when the current is not flowing: it is an equation derived from thermodynamics. Once the current starts to flow, equations derived from kinetics, such as the Butler-Volmer equation, covered in Chapter 7, are used to quantify the *rate* of the electrode reaction. The potentials of individual electrodes cannot be predicted from these equations; they need to be measured.

4.1.2.1   Electrodes and the mechanisms of electric charge transfer

The term *electrode* is often loosely defined, which causes confusion. For example, various electrochemical sensors, such as oxygen and pH sensors, are called *electrodes*, and the half reactions in the table of potentials are sometimes called *electrodes*, as in the phrase "oxygen electrodes on metal surfaces." The term *electrode* will be used here, as consistently as is practical, only when referring to electronic conductors that exchange electric charges with ionic conductors. A visually identifiable example of an electrode is a piece of metal immersed in water. To make the terminology more flexible, adjectives will be used with the term electrode, referring to the designations of various electrodes, such as indicator electrodes, working electrodes, reference electrodes, and auxiliary electrodes.

Electrode potential is defined as the difference between the electrical potential of an electrode immersed in a solution and the electrical potential of a reference electrode. Electrode potential depends on the material of the electrode and the nature of the redox couples present in the solution of the electrolyte, specifically their ability to equilibrate using the metal electrode as a reactant. In this context, the electrode potential is a measure of the tendency of the redox couples in solution to undergo reduction using electrons from the metal electrode. Equilibrium potentials are measured under conditions that minimize current flow between the indicator electrode and the reference electrode; the equilibrium potential is also called the open circuit potential to underline that it is measured under a condition of suppressed flow of electric current.

A special place among electrode potentials is reserved for the potential of the redox electrode, which is technically defined as the potential of an inert electrode immersed in a solution. An inert electrode is made of a material that does not react with the species in the solution. Platinum is the material of choice for constructing redox electrodes. A redox electrode serves as a medium for electron transfer and ensures that the oxidants and reductants in the solution equilibrate with the electrode. The position of this equilibrium (the potential of the redox electrode) depends on the ratio of oxidizers and reducers in the solution.

To show how an electrode potential is established, we will consider three mechanisms of electric charge transfer across interfaces between electronic and ionic conductors, and two special cases of these mechanisms:

- Mechanism 1: Electric charge transfer between a metal electrode and a solution of its own ions
- Mechanism 1A, a special case of mechanism 1: Electric charge transfer between a metal electrode and a solution of ions that form sparingly soluble salts with the metallic ions
- Mechanism 2: Electric charge transfer between an inert electrode and a solution of reactive components of redox couples—redox potential
- Mechanism 2A, a special case of mechanism 2: Electric charge transfer between an electrode and a solution of reactive components of redox couples, one of which is a gas
- Mechanism 3: Electric charge transfer through membranes

Conceptually, all mechanisms of charge transfer across interfaces between electronic and ionic conductors can be considered charge transfers across membranes. In thermodynamics, a membrane can be anything that is permeable for one type of substance and not permeable for another. Consequently, the metal–solution interface is a membrane because it permits the transfer of its own ions and prevents the transfer of other ions. The electric potential that is established across such membrane is called the *electrochemical potential* because its value reflects the equilibrium between the chemical potentials of the species on the two sides of the membrane and their electrical charges contributing to the electric potential difference. This is further elaborated for mechanism 3.

4.1.2.1.1 Mechanism 1: Electric charge transfer between a metal electrode and a solution of its own ions.   Metals can exchange ions from their metallic lattices with ions of the same kind in a solution. As a result, metal electrodes can be in equilibrium with ions of their own kind in a solution. For example, an iron electrode can be in equilibrium with iron ions, Fe^{2+} (Figure 4.5). However, it cannot exchange Fe^{2+} ions with ions of another kind in the solution, such as Zn^{2+} ions, because Zn^{2+} ions do not fit into a metallic lattice composed of Fe^{2+} ions. Therefore, an iron electrode cannot be in equilibrium with zinc ions in a solution.

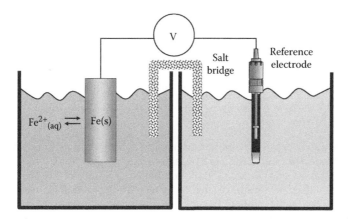

Figure 4.5 Iron electrode in a solution of its own ions.

The following reactions characterize an iron electrode immersed in a solution of its own ions and connected to a SHE:

$$Fe^{2+} + 2e^- \rightleftarrows Fe \quad \text{versus SHE:} \quad 2H^+ + 2e^- \rightleftarrows H_2$$

The standard electrode potential is evaluated from thermodynamic tables, and for this reaction it is $E° = -0.44$ V, as seen in the figure below:

Potential (+)

$E° = 0.0$ V $2H^+ + 2e \leftrightarrows H_2(g)$

$E° = -0.44$ V $Fe^{2+} + 2e^- \leftrightarrows HFe$

The Nernst equation predicts the cell potential for this reaction:

$$E_{cell} = E° - \frac{0.059}{n}\log\left[\frac{[Fe][H^+]^2}{[Fe^{2+}] \times p(H_2)}\right] \tag{4.16}$$

Because the iron electrode is assumed to be pure solid iron, its activity equals 1. By definition, proton activity [H$^+$] in SHE equals one. Hydrogen gas has a partial pressure $p(H_2)$ equal to 1 atm because the hydrogen gas in hydrogen electrodes is bubbled through the liquid and is subjected to atmospheric pressure, so its partial pressure must be equal to the atmospheric pressure (neglecting the hydrostatic pressure of the water).

$$E_{cell} = -0.44 - \frac{0.059}{n}\log\left[\frac{[Fe]}{[Fe^{2+}]}\right]$$

The ions in the metallic lattice of a metal electrode have different activities than the metallic ions in the solution. In an attempt to equilibrate the chemical potentials on the two sides of the interface, metal atoms can dispose of one or more electrons and become metal ions, soluble in aqueous solutions. This mechanism leads to the dissolution of the metal in water, and the process is called corrosion. The opposite may happen as well: a metal ion in the solution can accept an electron, become a metal atom, and be deposited on the metal surface. This process is called electrodeposition.

Mechanism 1 is exemplified by the following.

Example 4.3

Figure 4.6 shows a zinc electrode immersed in a 1 M solution of zinc ions connected to a reference electrode, the SHE. Zinc has a negative standard potential, which means that in the redox half reaction the oxidation of metallic zinc is preferred to the reduction of Zn^{2+} ions and that the Zn^{2+} ions have a tendency to leave the metallic lattice and become hydrated ions in the water solution. If some of these ions are transferred from the metal to the water, they leave behind an excess of electrons in the metal and the metal electrode acquires a negative potential.

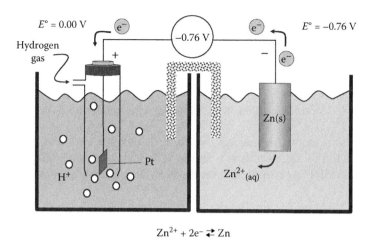

$$Zn^{2+} + 2e^- \rightleftarrows Zn$$

Figure 4.6 Zinc electrode in a solution of 1 M Zn^{2+} connected to SHE.

The potential of the zinc electrode is

$$E = E^\circ - \frac{0.059}{2} \log\left[\frac{[Zn]}{[Zn^{2+}]}\right] \tag{4.17}$$

where $[Zn^{2+}] = 1$ M (standard solution), $[Zn] = 1$ M (solid-state metal), and $E = E^\circ = -0.76$ V.

Figure 4.7 shows a silver electrode immersed in a solution of 1 M Ag^+. It has the opposite behavior. Silver is a noble metal, which means that it has a high affinity for electrons at a positive standard potential. As a result, the reduction of the Ag^+ ions is preferred to the oxidation of the metallic silver, so the positive ions from the metallic lattice do not easily transfer to the solution. When the activity of the silver ions in the solution is high enough, the positively charged silver ions in the solution have a tendency to penetrate the interface and become part of the metallic lattice, which shifts the potential of the silver electrode in the positive direction.

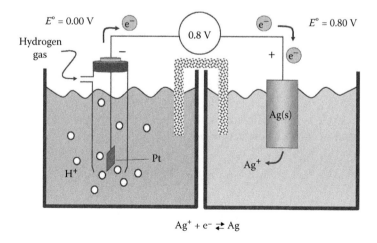

$$Ag^+ + e^- \rightleftarrows Ag$$

Figure 4.7 Silver electrode in a solution of 1 M Ag^+ connected to SHE.

The potential of the silver electrode is

$$E = E^\circ - \frac{0.059}{n} \log\left[\frac{[Ag]}{[Ag^+]}\right] \tag{4.18}$$

where $[Ag^+] = 1$ (standard solution), $[Ag] = 1$ (solid-state metal), and $E = E^\circ = +0.8$ V.

The potentials of metals immersed in solutions of their ions can be predicted from thermodynamics. If a metal electrode is immersed in a nonstandard solution of its ions, its potential against SHE is computed from the Nernst equation, as shown in Example 4.4.

4.1.2.1.2 Mechanism 1A: Electric charge transfer between a metal electrode and a solution of ions that form sparingly soluble salts with the metallic ions. All secondary reference electrodes are based on electric charge transfer between a metal electrode and a solution of ions that form sparingly soluble salts with the metallic ions. In principle, any half reaction can serve as a reference half reaction, but some half reactions are more suitable than others; the half reactions between metal electrodes and salts of sparingly soluble metal ions are considered suitable. Examples of reference electrodes built on this principle are the calomel and the silver chloride reference electrodes. In both of these, the electrode is made of silver and the ions establishing the potential of the electrode are chloride ions. However, as argued above, a silver electrode cannot be in equilibrium with chloride ions—it can only be in equilibrium with silver ions. To make it work, a clever mechanism is used that controls the potential of the silver wire. The chloride ions are in equilibrium with the sparingly soluble salts of mercury and silver: calomel (Hg_2Cl_2) in the calomel electrode and silver chloride (AgCl) in the silver/silver chloride electrode. These two sparingly soluble salts have two interfaces when deposited on silver wires: one with the solution of chloride ions and one with the surface of the silver wire. The chloride ions are in equilibrium with the deposited silver chloride, while the silver ions in the metallic lattice are in equilibrium with the silver ions in the solution. The concentration of the silver ions in the solution is determined by the solubility product of the sparingly soluble salts of silver. The following computations will illustrate this mechanism.

Silver/silver chloride (Ag/AgCl) is the most popular reference electrode for homemade electrochemical sensors because it is easy to make and its components are not toxic: the metal substratum in this electrode is silver, and the electrolyte is a solution of potassium chloride, KCl. The overall cell reaction is

$$AgCl \rightleftarrows Ag^+ + Cl^- \tag{4.19}$$

The silver electrode is in equilibrium with the silver ions in the solution. The following half reaction is used to compute electrode potential:

$$Ag^+ + e^- \rightleftarrows Ag \quad E^\circ = 0.8 \text{ V} \tag{4.20}$$

and the potential can be computed from the Nernst equation as

$$E = 0.8 + 0.059 \log[Ag^+] \tag{4.21}$$

To compute the potential of this half reaction, the concentration of the silver ions is needed. The concentration of the silver ions in the solution is controlled by the solubility of silver chloride. At equilibrium, the concentration of the silver ions in the solution can be computed from the solubility product and the concentration of chloride ions.

Silver chloride dissolves and dissociates:

$$AgCl = [Ag^+][Cl^-] \tag{4.22}$$

The solubility product, from thermodynamics, is $K_{sp} = 1.8 \times 10^{-10}$. Therefore,

$$[Ag^+][Cl^-] = 1.8 \times 10^{-10} \tag{4.23}$$

The chloride concentration is set near its saturation, 3.5 M; thus the concentration of the silver ions is

$$[Ag^+] = \frac{1.8 \times 10^{-10}}{3.5} = 5.14 \times 10^{-11} \tag{4.24}$$

With the concentration of the silver ions in the solution established, the electrode potential can be computed from the Nernst equation:

$$E = 0.8 + 0.059 \log(5.14 \times 10^{-11}) = 0.192 \text{ V} \tag{4.25}$$

Because the concentration of the chloride ions is constant and equal to their saturation concentration, the concentration of the silver ions is constant as well. As a result, the silver electrode exhibits a constant potential, and the entire assembly is used as a reference electrode to evaluate the potentials of other half-cells. Figure 4.8 shows a Ag/AgCl reference electrode.

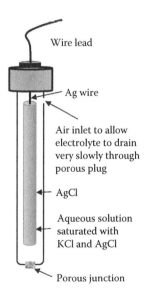

Wire lead

Ag wire

Air inlet to allow electrolyte to drain very slowly through porous plug

AgCl

Aqueous solution saturated with KCl and AgCl

Porous junction

Figure 4.8 Diagram of a silver/silver chloride electrode.

Calomel reference electrodes work on a similar principle, but the two electrochemical equilibriums are established between liquid mercury and calomel, and between a solution of chlorides and calomel. The overall electrode reaction is

$$Hg_2Cl_{2(s)} + 2e^- \rightleftarrows 2Hg_{(liq)} + 2Cl^- \tag{4.26}$$

Calomel electrodes are less popular for homemade chemical sensors because mercury salts are toxic and using them requires precautions that the user may not always be able to observe. Calomel electrodes are usually purchased from specialized vendors rather than constructed in the laboratory. Figure 4.9 shows a calomel reference electrode.

4.1.2.1.3 Mechanism 2: Electric charge transfer between an electrode and a solution of reactive components of redox couples—Redox potential. Redox potential E_h refers to the potential of an electrode made of a noble (nonreactive) metal immersed in an aqueous solution. Such an electrode acquires its potential as a result of exchanging electrons with the members of the redox couples in the solution, such as Fe^{+2}/Fe^{+3}. Redox potentials of solutions are measured as the potentials of platinized platinum electrodes versus suitable reference electrodes. The ideal redox electrode freely exchanges electrons with all redox couples in the solution. Platinum redox electrodes are not ideal, and it is known that some redox couples do not exchange electrons with platinum easily. This fact is referred to by the observation that "some redox couples do not equilibrate on platinum surfaces."

The potential of a redox electrode in an aqueous solution arises from the fact that members of redox couples in that solution attempt to equilibrate using electrons from the electrode or donating the excess of their electrons to the electrode. The redox potential of the solution, which is equal to the potential of the redox electrode, indicates the overall tendency of the electroactive species in the solution to extract electrons from and donate electrons to the redox electrode. Members of the redox couples in the solution attempt to equilibrate their chemical potentials by donating electrons to or acquiring electrons

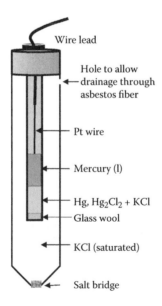

Figure 4.9 Diagram of a saturated calomel electrode.

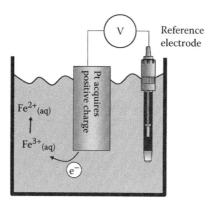

Figure 4.10 Mechanism 2: Electrons are transferred across the interface between the platinum and the solution in an attempt to equilibrate the members of the redox couple, whereas the iron ions are not (iron ions cannot equilibrate with the platinum electrode). This mechanism illustrates the formation of the redox potential E_h, when the chemical potential of the ferric ions exceeds the chemical potential of the ferrous ions and the redox couple attempts to reach equilibrium by extracting electrons from the electrode.

from members of other redox couples in the solution, and they may use the electrode as a member of a redox couple. For example, if the concentration of the reduced member of a redox couple, say Fe^{2+}, is in excess of that of the oxidized member of that redox couple, Fe^{3+}, the reduced member will donate some electrons to the metal electrode. As a result, the potential of the electrode will decrease. However, once the electrode potential decreases to a certain level, the transfer of electrons ceases because of electrostatic interactions: the negatively charged electrode will repel the reduced species and attract the oxidized, more positive, species. An electrochemical equilibrium is established when the repulsive forces are balanced by the forces causing the electron transfer. Such equilibriums have three participants: the two members of the redox couple and the electrode. Ideally, there is only one redox couple in the solution and the redox potential computed from the Nernst equation can be verified experimentally. In real situations, many redox couples exchange electrons with the electrode at the same time, making the electrode potential difficult to interpret.

Figure 4.10 shows an ideal situation, a platinum electrode in a solution of Fe^{2+} and Fe^{3+} ions. The redox potential of this solution can be predicted from the Nernst equation, and the potential of the platinum electrode should approximate this result.

Example 4.4

The redox potential of an acidified solution of ferrous (Fe^{2+}) and ferric (Fe^{3+}) ions will be computed (Figure 4.11). The solution needs to be acidified to prevent the precipitation of ferric salts. If this redox couple equilibrates on the surface of the platinum, which means that the members of the redox couple can exchange electrons with the electrode, the platinum electrode should exhibit a potential equal to the redox potential computed from the Nernst equation. As previously argued in this chapter, the potential of the platinum electrode in the solution of ferrous and ferric ions reflects the position of the electrochemical equilibrium between these two ions and the electrode in the solution. If the concentration of the ferric ions is in excess (with respect to the concentration at equilibrium), as is assumed in Figure 4.12, then in an attempt to reach equilibrium, electrons leave the platinum electrode and reduce some of the ferric ions to ferrous ions. When the platinum electrode donates electrons to reduce ferric ions, it loses negative electric charge and increases its potential. Not many electrons from the platinum wire can be transferred to the solution, however. The platinum electrode cannot deliver all the electrons needed to reach the equilibrium between the ferrous and ferric ions in the solution without being connected to an external source of electrons. As electrons are removed from the platinum wire, it acquires a higher potential, and as its potential increases, the wire starts attracting electrons and prevents them from leaving the metal. Eventually, the electrode reaches electrochemical equilibrium with the solution, by assuming an electrical potential that equilibrates the tendency of the redox couple to acquire electrons from the electrode and the electrostatic interactions that attract electrons.

$$E = 0.77 + 0.059 \log(1/0.1) = 0.77 + 0.059 \times 10 = 0.667 \text{ V}$$

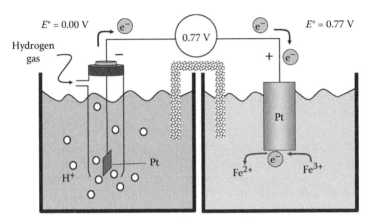

Figure 4.11 At standard conditions when $[Fe^{2+}] = [Fe^{3+}] = 1$ M, the potential of the redox electrode equals the standard potential for the half-cell, $Fe^{3+} + e = Fe^{2+}$, equal +0.77 V.

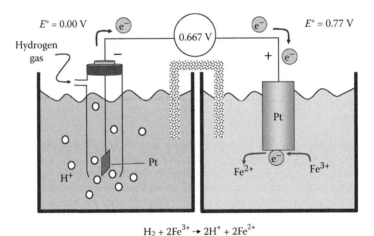

Figure 4.12 When the concentration of ferric ions exceeds the concentration of ferrous ions—$[Fe^{2+}] = 0.1$ M, $[Fe^{3+}] = 1$ M—the redox electrode transfers electrons to reduce some of the Fe^{3+} ions to Fe^{2+} ions. As a result, the electrode potential increases to +0.667; compare this to the 0.77 V measured in the solution of $[Fe^{2+}] = 1$ M, $[Fe^{3+}] = 1$ M in Figure 4.10.

Example 4.5

The redox potential of a solution of the Cr^{3+}/Cr^{2+} redox couple will be computed. If the solution is composed of equal concentrations of the ions, then the redox potential is directly equal to the standard electrode potential (Figure 4.13).

$$E = -0.41 - 0.059 \log(1/1) = -0.41 \text{ V}$$

When the solution in the half-cell on the right-hand side is replaced with a solution made of 1 M Cr^{3+} and 1×10^{-9} M Cr^{2+}, the electrode potential reverses, from negative to positive, because the concentration of the oxidized member of the redox couple, Cr^{3+}, exceeds the concentration which would equilibrate with Cr^{2+}. To reduce the excess of Cr^{3+} and reach chemical equilibrium, the redox couple attracts electrons from the platinum electrode, thereby increasing its potential (Figure 4.14).

$$E = -0.41 - 0.059 \log(1 \times 10^{-9}/1) = -0.41 + 9 \times 0.059 = 0.121 \text{ V}$$

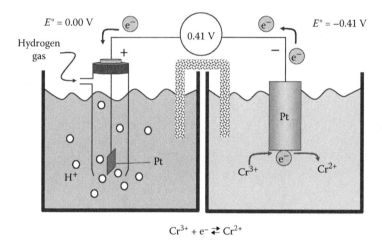

$$Cr^{3+} + e^- \rightleftarrows Cr^{2+}$$

Figure 4.13 Platinum electrode immersed in a solution of 1 M Cr^{3+} and 1 M Cr^{2+} and connected to the reference electrode, SHE.

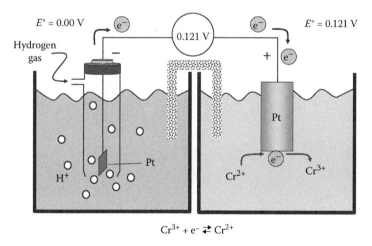

$$Cr^{3+} + e^- \rightleftarrows Cr^{2+}$$

Figure 4.14 Platinum electrode immersed in a solution of 1 M Cr^{3+} and 1×10^{-9} M Cr^{2+} and connected to the reference electrode, SHE.

4.1.2.1.4   Mechanism 2A: Electric charge transfer between an electrode and a solution of reactive components of redox couples, one of which is a gas.   A redox electrode may be in a solution of the constituents of a redox couple, one of which is a gas. One example of such an electrode is SHE, in which the constituents of the redox couple, H_2 and H^+, exchange electrons with the platinum and eventually equilibrate on the platinum surface (Figure 4.15). For this particular redox couple, platinum is an ideal material because gaseous hydrogen and protons equilibrate easily on platinum surfaces.

Other gases can also serve as members of redox couples, such as H_2S/HS^-, HCN/CN^-, and Cl_2/Cl^-. Figure 4.16 shows an example in which both half reactions include gaseous reactants.

In computing electrode potentials using the Nernst equation, the activity of the gas phase is approximated as the partial pressure of the gas. In standard gas electrodes the gas phase has a partial pressure of 1 atm.

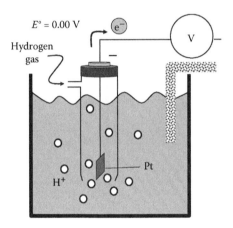

Figure 4.15 Standard hydrogen electrode, Pt in a solution of 1 M H^+.

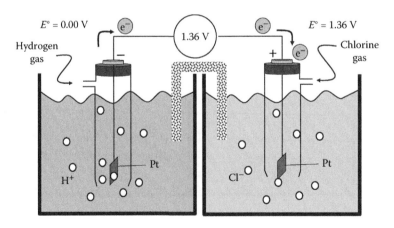

Figure 4.16 Standard chlorine electrode connected to SHE. The concentrations are 1 M Cl^- and 1 M H^+.

4.1.2.1.5 Mechanism 3: Electric charge transfer through membranes. Mechanism 3 refers to equilibrating electrochemical potentials in ionic solutions separated by membranes. Membranes, natural and engineered, selectively pass some substances while preventing other substances from passing. If a membrane separates two ionic solutions of different activities (concentrations), ions are transported across the membrane in the direction determined by the gradient in their concentrations. However, if the characteristics of the membrane are such that the counterions have restricted permeability, or, in an extreme case that is easier to visualize, only one type of ions can pass, the membrane separates the electrical charges and the solutions acquire different potentials. For example, if protons can cross a membrane but negatively charged counterions cannot cross it, then after a while the solution on each side of the membrane deviates from the electric neutrality ensured by the balance between the electric charges of the anions and cations. The solution on one side of the membrane acquires an excess of the positive charges and the solution on the other side an excess of the negative charges. With each proton passing across the membrane, the difference in potential between the two sides of the membrane increases. The increasing potential difference between the two sides of the membrane inhibits the transfer of protons across the membrane because the protons are repulsed from the solution on the positively charged side of the membrane and attracted to the solution on the negatively charged side of the membrane. Finally, the transport of protons across the membrane ceases because the buildup of the electric potential across the membrane counterbalances the difference between the chemical potentials of the two sides. This prevents the further transfer of electrically charged particles, a situation which is referred to as *electrochemical equilibrium,* and the difference in potential between the two sides of the membrane is called the *membrane potential.*

Membrane potentials can be evaluated from the Nernst equation. The membrane potential results from the fact that the membrane preferentially transfers one type of ions and does not transfer the counterions. Assume that the membrane preferentially transfers only Cu^{2+}: it does not transfer any other ions. Figure 4.17 illustrates the situation.

Because of the difference in copper ion activity (concentration) between the two sides of the membrane, copper ions are transported across the membrane from the left-hand side to the right-hand side, following the concentration gradient. Because no other ions are transferred across this membrane, the potential on the right-hand side of the membrane becomes more positive and that on the left-hand side becomes less positive. As time passes and the difference in potential increases, the transport of copper ions is inhibited by the electrostatic charges that have accumulated on the two sides of the membrane: negative on the left-hand side and positive on the right-hand side. The buildup of the electrical potential causes the copper ions passing across the membrane to be repulsed by the electrostatic charge that has accumulated on the right side and attracted by the electrostatic charge that

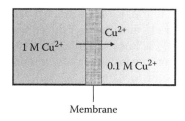

Figure 4.17 Transfer of electric charges across a membrane and buildup of a membrane potential.

has accumulated on the left side. After some time, the difference in chemical potential resulting from the difference between the concentrations of the ions on the two sides of the membrane is balanced by the difference in electric potential across the membrane, and the system reaches equilibrium. This effect can be quantified and used as a principle of constructing potentiometric sensors. The potential difference between the two sides of the membrane is proportional to the concentrations, so if the concentration of copper ions on one side of the membrane is known, the concentration of copper ions on the other side of the membrane can be estimated. This is the principle of chemical sensors based on measuring membrane potentials.

A sensor that measures the concentration of copper can be constructed based on these principles. Two electrochemical half-cells are separated by a membrane that allows the transport of copper ions and does not allow the transport of anions. To measure the potential on each side of the membrane, a copper wire is immersed in each of the half-cells. There are copper ions in the solution on each side of the membrane, but the concentration of copper ions on one side of the membrane is known. Following the principles discussed in the preceding sections, the copper wires acquire potentials with respect to SHE, and these potentials can be computed from the Nernst equation.

The electrochemical potential on each side of the membrane can be calculated from the Nernst equation, adjusted for the copper ion concentration on each side of the membrane.

$$Cu^{2+} + 2e \rightleftarrows Cu; \quad E^\circ = 0.52 \text{ V}$$

The electrode potential in the half-cell on the left-hand side of the membrane is

$$E_L = +0.52 + 0.059/2 \log[Cu^{2+}]_L$$

The electrode potential in the half-cell on the right-hand side of the membrane is

$$E_R = +0.52 + 0.059/2 \log[Cu^{2+}]_R$$

The difference in potential between the two sides of the membrane is

$$E_L - E_R = \{+0.52 + 0.059/2 \log[Cu^{2+}]_L\} - \{+0.52 + 0.059/2 \log[Cu^{2+}]_R\}$$
$$= 0.059/2 \{\log[Cu^{2+}]_L - \log[Cu^{2+}]_R\} \tag{4.27}$$

To construct a copper ion sensor based on measuring the membrane potential, the copper ion concentration must be kept constant on one side of the membrane. If this condition is ensured, the membrane potential is proportional to the copper ion concentration on the other side of the membrane. Let's assume that the concentration of copper ions on the right side of the membrane, $[Cu^{2+}]_R$, is known and equal to (C_{Cu}) and we want to determine the concentration of copper ions on the left side of the membrane, $[Cu^{2+}]_L$.

From Equation 4.27,

$$E = 0.059/2 \{\log[Cu^{2+}]_L - \log[Cu^{2+}]_R\} =$$

$$0.059/2 [\log[Cu^{2+}]_L - C_{Cu}] = 0.059/2 \log[Cu^{2+}]_L - (0.059/2)C_{Cu} \tag{4.28}$$

where $C_{Cu} = \log[Cu^{2+}]_R = $ constant because the copper ion concentration on the right-hand side of the membrane is known and constant. If the constant C_{Cu} is used, then Equation 4.28 can be converted to the form

$$E = B + (0.059/2) \log[Cu^{2+}]_L \tag{4.29}$$

where

$$B = -(0.059/2) C_{Cu} = const \tag{4.30}$$

The concentration of copper ions on the left-hand side of the membrane can be computed from Equation 4.29. This equation appears to have the same form as the Nernst equation. However, constant B is not equal to the standard potential of any redox half reaction. Instead, it depends on the concentration of the reacting substance on one side of the membrane, and it is usually evaluated experimentally, as the intercept of the calibration curve (copper concentration versus cell potential) with the y-axis.

A salt bridge is an indispensable component of an electrochemical cell. It allows the reestablishment of the electrical equilibrium affected by the charge transfer in each half-cell. However, it also behaves as a membrane and generates a membrane potential, which is an undesirable effect. An electrometer connected to the electrodes measures the sum of potential drops across all interfaces in the electrochemical cell, including the salt bridge. If the effect of the salt bridge is included, the overall potential measured by the electrometer is

$$E_{cell} = E_{ind} - E_{ref} + E_{l-j} \tag{4.31}$$

where E_{ind} is the potential of the indicator electrode, E_{ref} is the potential of the reference electrode, and E_{l-j} designates the liquid junction potential.

Because the potential drop across the salt bridge is difficult to evaluate, may vary over time, and depends on the measurement conditions, the readout of the potential difference is affected by the presence of the salt bridge to an unknown extent. To mitigate this effect, salt bridges should be designed so that the junction potential is small and reproducible, and much effort has been made by commercial manufacturers of electrochemical sensors to deal with this problem. One way to minimize the liquid junction potential is to use an electrolyte in the salt bridge composed of anions and cations having similar mobilities in electrical fields. Chloride ions and potassium ions have very similar mobilities, and potassium chloride is an often-used electrolyte in salt bridges. When chemical sensors are made in the laboratory, salt bridges are often replaced with porous ceramic plugs, which permit the transport of ions from the half-cells on both sides of the membrane to restore the electrical neutrality of the solutions.

4.1.3 Significance of the electrode potential

By measuring the potentials of electrodes with respect to a reference electrode, one can evaluate whether the electrons tend to move from the reference electrode to the indicator electrode or in the opposite direction. In simple cells in which all reagents and their concentrations are known, the direction of electron flow can be established using electrochemical computations. More often, however, this knowledge is inadequate, and direct measurements are made of the electrode potentials. Measuring electrode potentials in a meaningful way requires accepting certain conventions and then following them rigorously. This concerns the way in which the electrodes are connected to the electrometer.

Electrometers have two terminals, one marked red and one marked black. Depending on which terminal is connected to the reference electrode, the potential reading on the display will show with the sign negative or positive. The question is: Which of the terminals of the electrometer should be connected to the reference electrode? Most electrometers (but not all) are constructed in such a way that when the electrons transferred in the external circuit move toward the black terminal of the electrometer, the readout is positive.

To be consistent with the potential ladder, the reference and the indicator electrodes should be connected so that when the indicator electrode has a potential higher than the potential of the reference electrode, the number on the display is positive and vice versa. Figure 4.18 shows how to connect the electrodes when the potential of the indicator electrode is higher than the potential of the reference electrode, and Figure 4.19 shows how to connect the electrodes to the electrometer when the potential of the indicator electrode is lower than the potential of the reference electrode. Actually, a third case is also possible: the potentials of the indicator and reference electrodes may be equal, but this situation is trivial.

1. When the potential of the indicator electrode is higher than the potential of the reference electrode, the electrometer should display a positive potential. This can be accomplished by connecting the black terminal of the electrometer to the electrode that delivers the electrons to the external circuit. Because the electrons tend to move from the location of the lower potential (the reference electrode) toward the location of the higher potential (the indicator electrode), the reference electrode should be connected to the black terminal of the electrometer and the indicator electrode should be connected to the red terminal.

2. When the potential of the indicator electrode is lower than the potential of the reference electrode, the electrometer should display a negative potential. This can be accomplished by connecting the red terminal of the electrometer to the electrode that

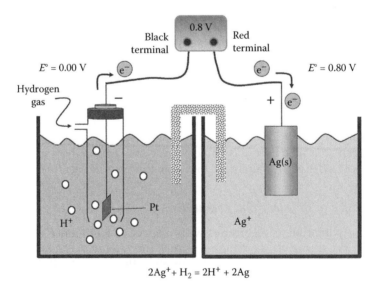

$$2Ag^+ + H_2 = 2H^+ + 2Ag$$

Figure 4.18 Silver electrode in a solution of 1 M Ag^+ connected to SHE. The potential of the indicator electrode is higher than the potential of the reference electrode. With the reference electrode connected to the black terminal of the electrometer, the electrons tend to move toward the black terminal, and the readout is positive.

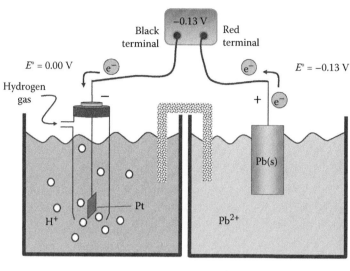

$$2H^+ + Pb \rightarrow H_2 + Pb^{2+}$$

Figure 4.19 Lead electrode in a solution of 1 M Pb^{2+} connected to SHE. The potential of the indicator electrode is lower than the potential of the reference electrode. With the reference electrode connected to the black terminal of the instrument and the indicator electrode connected to the red terminal, the electrons tend to move toward the red terminal and the readout is negative.

delivers the electrons to the external circuit. Because the electrons tend to move from the location of the lower potential (the indicator electrode) toward the location of the higher potential (the reference electrode), the reference electrode should be connected to the black terminal of the electrometer and the indicator electrode should be connected to the red terminal.

In both cases, following the accepted convention, the reference electrode is connected to the black terminal of the electrometer. With the reference electrode connected to the black terminal of the electrometer, the readout is positive when the potential of the indicator electrode is higher than the potential of the reference electrode and negative when the potential of the indicator electrode is lower than the potential of the reference electrode, which satisfies the convention accepted here. If the electrodes are properly connected to the electrometer, the sign of the potential on the display is meaningful, and it provides important information. It indicates (1) the direction in which the electrons tend to flow, (2) the direction in which the cell reaction is spontaneous, (3) the half reaction is oxidation and which is reduction, and (4) which reaction is anodic and which is cathodic.

In rare instances, instruments are wired in reverse and show a positive sign on the display when electrons tend to flow into the red terminal. If suspicion arises that this is the case, the instrument can be tested by arranging an electrochemical cell for which we know in which direction the electrons tend to flow. A practical approach is to connect a zinc electrode immersed in zinc chloride or zinc sulfate and connect it to a reference electrode through the electrometer. Because metallic zinc has a very low standard potential, the zinc electrode has a lower potential than the popular secondary reference electrodes.

After the meaning of the sign of the potential readout has been defined, the direction of the spontaneous reactions can be identified. For example, the half-cell in Figure 4.20 is a platinum electrode immersed in a solution of chromium (III) and chromium (II) connected

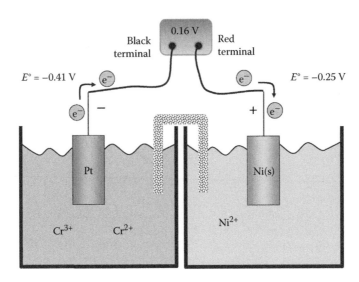

Figure 4.20 Platinum electrode immersed in a solution of 1 M Cr^{3+} and 1 M Cr^{2+} and connected to nickel electrode immersed in a solution of 1 M Ni^{2+}. In this example, electrons flow from the half-cell on the left to the half-cell on the right. This means that chromium Cr(II) is oxidized to chromium Cr(III) and the electrons are used to reduce nickel ions Ni(II) to elemental nickel Ni.

to a nickel electrode immersed in a solution of nickel ions. If the electrometer is connected as shown and the readout is positive, then the operator knows the electrons tend to flow toward the black terminal, which half reaction is oxidation (the one on the left), and which half reaction is reduction (the one on the right) even if the exact composition of each solution is not known.

4.1.3.1 *Galvanic and electrolytic cells*

When two electrodes made of dissimilar metals are immersed in solutions of electroactive reactants (chemicals that can exchange electric charges with the electrodes), each electrode acquires an electrical potential related to the electrochemical process (half reaction) occurring on it. The convention used to compute this potential from the half reactions assumes that the reduction reaction is the forward reaction and the oxidation reaction is the reverse reaction:

$$oxidized\ species + ne^- \rightarrow reduced\ species$$

From this assumption, the electrical potential (E) an electrode acquires is related to the free energy change in the half reaction occurring at that electrode:

$$E = -\frac{\Delta G}{nF} \tag{4.32}$$

where n is the number of electrons transferred in the half reaction, F is the Faraday constant, and ΔG is the Gibbs free energy change in the half reaction. In a galvanic cell, the electrode reaction occurring at the electrode characterized by the lower potential is called anodic (oxidation), while the electrode reaction occurring at the electrode characterized by the higher potential is called cathodic (reduction). This statement derives from the convention to which we referred above, that the reduction reaction is considered to proceed forward and the oxidation reaction to proceed in reverse. This convention is limited to redox reactions; for acid-base reactions, there is no convention that identifies which reaction proceeds forward and which proceeds in reverse. In these reactions the sign of the computed free energy change for the reaction indicates the direction in which the reaction proceeds.

To compute the cell voltage, the sign of the potential computed for the electrode at which oxidation occurs is reversed and the potentials of the two electrodes are added. In the accepted terminology, which we will follow here, a single electrode in an electrochemical cell is characterized by the *electrode potential* measured with respect to a reference electrode and the difference in potentials between the electrodes in the same electrochemical cell is called the *cell voltage*. Thus, we use the term electrode potential when referring to the difference in energy, expressed in volts, between the working and reference electrodes, and the term cell voltage when referring to the difference in energy, expressed in volts, between two metal electrodes in an electrochemical cell when neither of them is a reference electrode. An important starting point for describing an electrochemical cell is to measure the potential difference between its electrodes when the electrodes are not connected or are connected using a connector of infinitely high electrical resistance. The result of such a measurement is called an open circuit voltage (OCV). In many sources it is referred to as the open circuit potential, but the term OCV is consistent with the terminology we accepted above, as it refers to the *difference in potentials* and component potentials can vary for each of the electrodes in the cell. For example, the galvanic cell in Figure 4.21 has an OCV of 1.1 V, which is the difference between the equilibrium potentials of the two electrodes in the electrochemical cell. Electrode potential is always described against a specific reference electrode, and it is imperative to indicate which reference electrode has been used in the measurements. The primary reference electrode is the normal SHE.

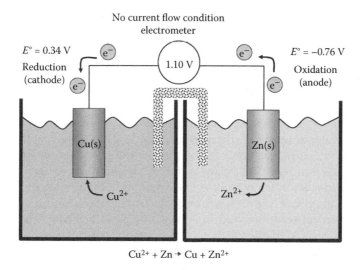

Figure 4.21 A galvanic cell in which the copper electrode in the half-cell on the left is immersed in a 1 M solution of Cu^{2+} ions and the zinc electrode in the half-cell on the right is immersed in a 1 M solution of Zn^{2+} ions. When no current is flowing, the cell voltage can be described as the OCV and the potential of each of the electrodes can be calculated from thermodynamics (Nernst equation).

If no indication is given of the reference electrode used, it is assumed that the reported electrode potential refers to SHE. For practical electrochemical measurements, researchers use either a saturated calomel electrode (SCE) or a saturated silver/silver chloride (Ag/ AgCl) electrode. These electrodes are known as secondary electrodes, and their potentials are related in thermodynamic tables to the potential of the primary reference electrode, SHE, so that an electrode potential measured with respect to one reference electrode can be easily recalculated and expressed with respect to another reference electrode. When the electrodes of an electrochemical cell are short-circuited using an electronic conductor of a reasonably low resistance, electric current flows from the electrode that has the lower electric potential to the electrode that has the higher electric potential. Such an arrangement is called a galvanic cell. Electrochemical reactions in galvanic cells are spontaneous, and the electrode that receives electrons from the electroactive reactants in the solution is called the anode while the electrode that donates the electrons to the electroactive reactants in the solution is called the cathode. As a result of the electrodes and the flow of the current being short-circuited, the potentials of the electrodes deviate from the equilibrium potentials they had at the OCV. The difference between the equilibrium potential of an electrode and the OCV is called its overpotential, and the overpotential of each electrode is described as

$$\eta = E_{OCV} - E_{equilibrim} \tag{4.33}$$

where η is the overpotential of the electrode and $E_{equilibrium}$ is the equilibrium potential. Each electrode of the cell has its own overpotential, so there are an anodic overpotential and a cathodic overpotential. Overpotentials result from various causes, but the two most recognized are the following: (1) An overpotential resulting from changes in the concentrations of the reactants near the electrodes is known as a *concentration overpotential*. When the current flows, the concentrations of the reactants change near the electrodes as a result of the electrode reaction combined with the mass transport limitations of the electroactive reactants and products. As the concentrations of the reactants near the electrodes are different from those in the bulk solution, the potential cannot be calculated from the Nernst equation, which is based on the concentrations of the electroactive species in the bulk solution. (2) The overpotential that results from the kinetic effects controlling the transfer of electrical charges between the electrodes and the electroactive reagents in solution, as in any other chemical reaction, is known as the *activation overpotential*. Thus, the voltage of the entire cell is composed of the equilibrium potentials and overpotentials of the anode and cathode, plus any ohmic resistances (IR) related to the flow of the current through the components of the cell, including the ionic current in the solution. It is possible in a galvanic cell to impose an external potential on any of the electrodes and change its overpotential. This process is called *polarization* of the electrode and, as with overpotentials, polarization can be anodic or cathodic. The polarization of electrodes plays an important role in the study of electrochemical reactions and in corrosion protection, which will be discussed later in this chapter and in Chapter 7.

The galvanic cell in Figure 4.21 is composed of two half-cells:

$$Cu^{2+} + 2e^- \rightleftarrows Cu; \quad E^o = 0.34 \text{ V}$$

$$Zn^{2+} + 2e^- \rightleftarrows Zn; \quad E^o = -0.76 \text{ V}$$

If both half-cells in Figure 4.21 are at the standard state, the zinc electrode donates electrons, becoming an anode, and the copper electrode accepts the electrons, becoming a cathode. The entire reaction in the galvanic cell is then

$$Cu^{2+} + Zn \rightarrow Cu + Zn^{2+} \quad E^o_{cell} = 0.34 - (-0.76) = 1.10 \text{ V}$$

The electrochemical cell voltage at the standard state is 1.10 V. In practical terms, this means that if we connect the black terminal of an electrometer to a Zn electrode and the red terminal to a Cu electrode, we measure +1.10 V, which is the OCV for this cell. When current flows between the electrodes in an electrochemical cell, each electrode acquires a potential different from that observed at OCV, when no current flows. Figure 4.21 explains the distribution of the electrode potentials in such a cell.

If the electrodes in the half-cells are connected with an electronic conductor of a reasonably low resistance, the current flows from the Zn electrode to the Cu electrode. To oppose this current, the negative terminal of an external DC power supply (a battery) can be connected to the Cu electrode and the positive terminal can be connected to the Zn electrode. The current flow in the galvanic cell is spontaneous. However, to change the direction of the current and make it flow in the opposite direction than in the galvanic cell, an excess potential over 1.10 V needs to be applied. Exactly how large the voltage should be depends on the true cell voltage (E'), which is composed of the equilibrium potentials of both electrodes, the overpotentials of both electrodes, and the ohmic resistance of the components of the entire electrochemical cell, such as the electrolyte, salt bridges, and membranes. It also depends on the rate at which the operator wants to drive the reaction. This requirement, the rate at which the operator wants to drive the reaction, is important in some applications, such as charging batteries or electroplating, which both benefit from slow rates of reaction. At the least, the applied potential needs to exceed the OCV, which encompasses the thermodynamic equilibrium potential, overpotentials, and ohmic resistance.

Rearranging Equation 4.33 gives the relation between OCV and the overpotential for a single electrode.

$$E_{OCV} = E_{equilibrim} + \eta \qquad (4.34)$$

Consequently, for the potential of the entire electrochemical cell, composed of two electrodes, two overpotentials need to be included, and because they have opposites signs, their absolute values need to be added:

$$E' = OCV + \sum \eta + IR_{cell} \qquad (4.35)$$

where I is the current passing between the two electrodes, and R_{cell} is the ohmic resistance of the components of the entire cell.

When a galvanic cell is connected to an external power source that can apply a voltage opposing that which is spontaneously generated in the cell, applying a voltage equal to that of the cell voltage, but of the opposite sign, stops the current (Figure 4.22). Applying an opposing potential exceeding the cell voltage actually reverses the current flow. Such an arrangement is called an electrolytic cell. Chemical reactions in electrolytic cells are nonspontaneous: they have to be enforced by the externally applied voltage. A typical example of such a situation is charging a car battery. The chemical that was oxidized in the galvanic cell is reduced in the electrolytic cell and vice versa (Figure 4.21). As a consequence,

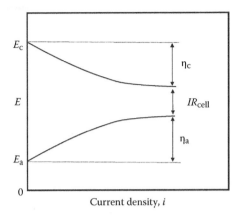

Figure 4.22 Anodic and cathodic overpotentials in a galvanic cell.

the electrode that was the anode in the galvanic cell becomes the cathode in the electrolytic cell and vice versa. The signs of the overpotentials are also reversed when cells are switched from galvanic to electrolytic (Figure 4.23).

Because the electrode that was the anode in the galvanic cell becomes the cathode in the electrolytic cell, and the electrode that was the cathode in the galvanic cell becomes the anode in the electrolytic cell, the terms anode and cathode do not describe the electrodes in electrochemical cells uniquely; they depend on the type of the cell, galvanic or electrolytic. In an electrolytic cell the reaction with the lowest polarized potential is the anodic reaction and the reaction with the highest polarized potential is the cathodic reaction, the opposite of the case in galvanic cells. To convert a galvanic cell into an electrolytic cell, an excess voltage over OCV must be applied, so that the current not only stops but flows in the opposite direction. The magnitude of this excess voltage depends on many factors related to the construction of the electrochemical cell and is therefore difficult to predict; it must be measured experimentally.

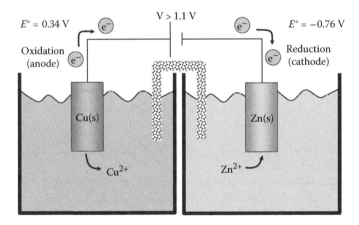

Figure 4.23 An electrolytic cell in which the copper electrode in the half-cell on the left is immersed in a 1 M solution of Cu^{2+} ions and the zinc electrode in the half-cell on the right is immersed in a 1 M solution of Zn^{2+} ions. To reverse the current that flows spontaneously in the galvanic cell, the applied potential must exceed the difference between the thermodynamic potentials of the half-cells plus the effects of the overpotentials.

4.1.3.2 Steady state diffusion near the electrode surface

Mass transport near electrodes is driven by three mechanisms: (1) diffusion, (2) migration, and (3) convection. Migration, which refers to the transport of charged particles in the electrical field, can be effectively eliminated by making measurements in high ionic strength electrolyte solutions of ions other than the constituents of the studied redox couples. Convection, which refers to the forced movement of particles in flowing solutions, can be effectively eliminated by making measurements in stagnant solutions. When migration and convection are suppressed, the mass transport of electroactive species to and from the electrode is dominated by diffusion.

In stagnant solutions of concentrated electrolytes, in which the main mechanism of the mass transport of ions and other electroactive reactants to and from the electrodes is diffusion, we assume that at ($t < 0$) the electrode exhibits the equilibrium potential. When a step potential of a magnitude that exceeds the electrode potential at equilibrium is applied to the electrode, as shown in Figure 4.24, current starts to flow and the concentration of the electroactive reactants in proximity to the electrode surface changes.

The rate of the electrode reaction is determined by the applied potential and by the concentration of the electroactive reactant in proximity to the electrode. As time passes, the electroactive reactant near the electrode is depleted by the reaction and replenished by the mass transport from the bulk solution. As a result, the concentration profiles evolve (Figure 4.24b) during the transient process, which lasts until the steady state is established. During the transient process, the concentration of the electroactive reactant in proximity to the electrode is described by Fick's second law of diffusion:

$$\frac{dC}{dt} = D\frac{d^2C}{dx^2} \tag{4.36}$$

where C is the concentration of the electroactive chemical reactant, t is time, x is the distance from the electrode surface, and D is the diffusion coefficient.

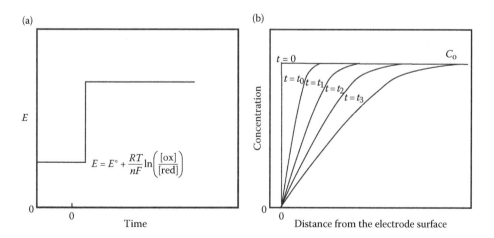

Figure 4.24 (a) An electrode is located in a stagnant solution and then a step potential is applied to the electrode, which raises the electrode potential above its potential at equilibrium. (b) The electroactive reactant concentration profiles change over time.

The initial conditions: $t = 0$ $C(x = 0) = C_o$.
The boundary conditions for this equation are

$$\lim_{x \to \infty} C(x,t) = C_o$$

$$C(x = 0, t > 0) = 0$$

The boundary conditions indicate that the bulk solution concentration is constant and the solution is not mixed. The solution to this equation, with the given initial and boundary conditions, is the Cottrell equation, which describes the transient response and the current in the circuit after a relatively large potential step is applied, assuming that the rate of the electrode reaction is limited by diffusion:

$$I = \frac{nFAD^{1/2}C_o}{\pi^{1/2}t^{1/2}} \tag{4.37}$$

where I is the current, n is the number of electrons exchanged during the electrode reaction, A is the surface area of the electrode, and F is the Faraday constant. Because the rate of the electrode reaction is determined by the diffusional mass transport rate, as the gradient concentration decreases, so does the reaction rate, as shown in Figure 4.25.

As time passes, the current, initially high, steadily decreases. Eventually, the process reaches a steady state characterized by a constant current known as the "limiting current." At the steady state the flux of the electroactive reactants is quantified by Fick's first law:

$$J = -D\left(\frac{dC}{dx}\right) \tag{4.38}$$

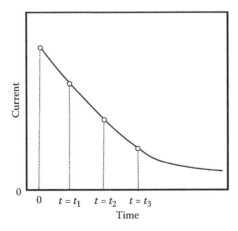

Figure 4.25 After a potential step is applied, the current initially increases to the maximum and then decreases following the Cottrell equation.

The flux of the electroactive reactants can be related to current density:

$$i = \frac{I}{A} = nFJ \tag{4.39}$$

and the current is

$$I = nFAJ \tag{4.40}$$

where F is the Faraday constant in coulombs mol^{-1}, D is the diffusion coefficient in cm^2/s, A is the surface area in cm^2, and dC/dx is in mol/cm^4.

The electroactive reactant react with the electrode at a rate depending on the applied polarizing potential and the concentration of the electroactive reactant (Figure 4.26). However, because the mass transport rate of the dissolved electroactive reactants toward the electrode is limited by diffusion, the rate of the reaction is ultimately limited by the rate of diffusion: the maximum rate of the electrode reaction equals the maximum rate of the delivery of the reactants. As this condition is approached, the concentration of the electro-active reactants near the electrode decreases and eventually reaches zero. When this happens, a further increase of the polarizing potential will not increase the current because at this stage the current is limited by the rate of mass transport and not by the applied potential. This state is referred to as the limiting current condition, and most amperometric sensors are operated at the limiting current, as we demonstrated earlier in this text.

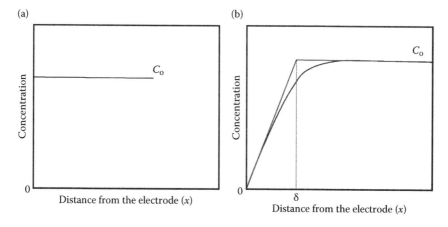

Figure 4.26 Possible concentration profiles of the electroactive reactants near the electrode surface in two extreme cases: (a) The case in which the electrode reaction is entirely controlled by the activation energy and the rate of mass transport of the electroactive reactants to the electrode surface is not the factor limiting the rate of reaction. (b) The case in which mass transfer controls the overall reaction rate. When the rate of the surface reaction reaches the rate of maximum mass transport under the given conditions, the electroactive reactants are distributed near the surface of the electrode as shown in (b), and the concentration of the reactant practically reaches zero at the surface of the electrode. Modern, and more accurate, approaches to electrode kinetics make this image more complicated (marked by the lower curve in (b)), but for the purpose of this exposition, we will use it in the form initially suggested by Nernst (marked by the upper curve in (b)). The value of δ is the thickness of the diffusion (mass) boundary layer, and x is the distance from the electrode.

Following Fick's first law and the simplified conceptual model shown in Figure 4.26b, the current can be described by

$$I = nFDA\left(\frac{C_o - C_s}{\delta}\right) \tag{4.41}$$

where C_o and C_s are the bulk and surface concentrations of the electroactive chemical reactants. If the current becomes limiting, $C_s = 0$ and the limiting current (I_{lim}) equals

$$I_{lim} = nFDA\left(\frac{C_o}{\delta}\right) \tag{4.42}$$

If we note that $D/\delta = k$, the mass transport coefficient, then the limiting current can be expressed more succinctly as

$$I_{lim} = nFDAkC_o \tag{4.43}$$

4.1.3.3 Membranes of amperometric sensors

The concept of a limiting current is critical to understanding the role of membranes in amperometric sensors. An amperometric sensor measures the current that results from the electrode reaction and, ideally, the electrode reaction includes only the analyte. To accomplish this, the working electrode of the sensor is polarized to a potential within the range of potentials that cause the limiting current for the electrode reaction with the analyte. Operating an amperometric sensor at the limiting current is convenient because the limiting current depends on the concentration of the electroactive species and does not depend, within limits, on the potential applied to the electrode. In this way, the response of the sensor is kept reasonably stable even if the polarizing potential fluctuates slightly. At the limiting current condition, the electrode response is constant at the applied potential only if the mass transfer rate is constant. Equation 4.42 shows that the limiting current depends on the thickness of the boundary layer, δ. The thickness of the boundary layer depends on the shear stress near the sensing tip of the sensor. This is referred to as the "stirring effect" in sensor terminology, because changing the rate at which the solution of the analyte is stirred during the measurement affects the response of the sensor. Sensors exhibiting serious stirring effect are unacceptable because they respond to two factors: the analyte concentration and the shear stress. To eliminate the stirring effect, the sensors are covered with membranes. The membranes are selected so that they that have a diffusivity for the analyte a few orders of magnitude lower than the diffusivity of that analyte in water. As a result, practically all the mass transport resistance of the solute to the electrode is confined to the thickness of the membrane. The rate of mass transport across the membrane establishes the magnitude of the limiting current, not the rate of mass transport to the membrane. In sensor terminology this is referred to as "confining the boundary layer to the membrane." Such membranes serve other purposes besides fixing the thickness of the boundary layer. They also protect sensors from the effects of aggressive environments and improve the selectivity of sensors. The limiting current in an amperometric sensor covered with a membrane is described by

$$I_{\text{lim}} = nFDC_{\text{bulk}}A \times \left(\frac{P_{\text{m}}}{d} \right) \tag{4.44}$$

where P_{m} is the permeability coefficient of the membrane and d is the thickness of the membrane.

4.1.3.4   *Functions of membranes on potentiometric and amperometric sensors*

Potentiometric and amperometric sensors are both covered with membranes. However, the membranes in these types of sensors play very different roles. In a potentiometric sensor the membrane is an indispensable part of the sensor: the sensor cannot function without the membrane, as the principle of the sensor is to measure the membrane potential. In an amperometric sensor the membrane is just a mechanical device that confines the thickness of the boundary layer and eliminates the stirring effect. Amperometric sensors can function without membranes if the rate of mass transport is constant, e.g., in stagnant solutions of the analyte.

The difference between the membranes on amperometric and potentiometric sensors can be emphasized in another way: as the effect of transducers. Transducers are devices that convert one type of energy to another type of energy, such as converting chemical energy to electrical energy. From this perspective, the membranes on potentiometric sensors are transducers: they convert chemical energy to electrical energy by generating membrane potentials. Membranes on amperometric sensors are not transducers: the energy does not change form because of the use of the membranes. In an amperometric sensor, chemical energy is converted to electrical energy on the surface of the working electrode.

4.1.4   *Amperometric sensors*

Figure 4.27a shows the principle of amperometric sensors. The electroactive analyte is transferred across a membrane and either oxidized or reduced on the surface of a polarized electrode. The current resulting from this process is proportional to the concentration of the analyte in the bulk solution. Figure 4.27b shows a first-generation amperometric sensor, in which the analyte is the reagent in the electrode reaction.

An example of the first generation of amperometric sensors is the oxygen sensor (Figure 4.28), also known as the *Clark sensor*, from the name of its inventor.

The first-generation amperometric sensors have limitations because not all substances of interest in analytical chemistry can be oxidized or reduced on metal electrodes. It was noticed that some substances that cannot be oxidized or reduced directly on metal electrodes can be oxidized or reduced by other dissolved substances, and these substances, if carefully selected, can be oxidized or reduced on metal electrodes. These substances are called *redox mediators*, and their use initiated the second generation of amperometric sensors. In a sense, these substances act as catalysts because they are regenerated in the electrode reactions and are not consumed. Redox mediators are sometimes called *electron shuttles*. Sensors operating on this principle are called *second-generation amperometric sensors* or *amperometric sensors with redox mediators*. Figure 4.29 shows the principle of such sensors.

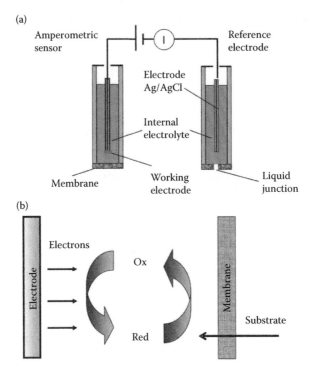

Figure 4.27 (a) Principle of amperometric sensors and (b) first-generation sensor. Electroactive analyte is transferred across a membrane and either oxidized or reduced on the electrode surface.

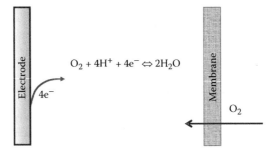

Figure 4.28 Principle of the oxygen sensor.

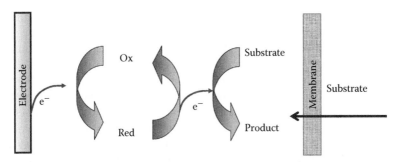

Figure 4.29 Second-generation amperometric sensor: a sensor with a redox mediator. Electroactive analyte is transferred across the membrane and either oxidized or reduced by the redox mediator.

An example of such a sensor is the hydrogen sulfide microelectrode described later in this chapter. It is difficult to oxidize hydrogen sulfide on metal electrodes. Therefore, hydrogen sulfide is instead oxidized by a redox mediator, ferricyanide, which as a result is reduced to ferrocyanide. In the next step, ferrocyanide is oxidized on the gold electrode to ferricyanide, and the cycle continues.

4.1.5   Potentiometric sensor

Potentiometric sensors, such as ion-selective electrodes, measure membrane potentials. The drop in potential caused by the development of the membrane potential becomes part of the resistance of the electrical circuit composed of all the components of the sensor. Figure 4.30 shows the components of such a circuit using a sensor with a membrane, generally a liquid ion exchanger (LIX). Equation 4.45 shows that the potential measured by the electrometer is composed of the potential drops across all interfaces in the system, including the LIX membrane:

$$E_{cell} = E_{int} - E_{ref} + E_{l-j} + E_{LIX} \tag{4.45}$$

The potential drops across the internal and external reference electrodes are known because the internal compartment of each electrode is filled with a solution of known composition. These potential drops do not change, because the internal solution in each reference electrode has a fixed composition. The potential drop at the liquid junction is constant if the bridge is properly designed. Consequently, the only variable potential drop in this circuit is the potential drop across the ion-selective membrane, and the magnitude of this potential drop depends on the difference in concentration of the analyte between the two sides of the membrane. The response of the electrode to various concentrations of the analyte in the external solution can be determined experimentally and plotted as a calibration curve.

4.1.6   Voltammetric sensors

Amperometric sensors describe a steady state, and potentiometric sensors describe an equilibrium. When using amperometric sensors, we keep the working electrode of the sensor at the predetermined polarization potential, wait until the limiting current reaches a constant value, and take the measurement. When using potentiometric sensors, we wait until the membrane potential reaches a constant value and take the measurement.

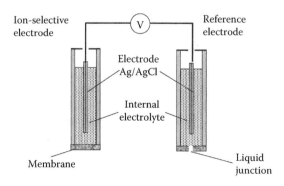

Figure 4.30 Principle of potentiometric sensors.

Voltammetric measurements are different: we control the potential and measure the current. The physical arrangement of a voltammetric sensor is composed of three electrodes—the working, counter and reference electrodes—and we use a potentiostat to apply a ramp of potential to the working electrode and measure the resulting current. There are several voltammetric techniques in use, and they rely on various types of potential ramps. In our work we have found that three are particularly useful in biofilm research: anodic stripping voltammetry, cyclic voltammetry, and square wave voltammetry. All three can be run using microelectrodes and are described in more detail in Chapter 7.

4.2   Microsensors

Microsensors, typically in the form of microelectrodes and microoptodes (fiber optic microsensors), are indispensable tools in biofilm research because they allow for the probing of local microenvironments and the quantification of local chemistries at the microscale with high spatial resolution, providing information that is difficult to get otherwise. In the metabolic activity of the microorganisms in a biofilm, some substances are consumed and some are generated. Both the consumption of substances dissolved in the bulk solution and the generation of products of microbial metabolism affect the distribution of these substances in the biofilm. The concentration profiles of these substances carry information about microbial activity and about mass transport. First, these profiles have to be experimentally measured, and then the microbial activity in the biofilm and the rate of mass transport need to be quantified. The measurement of concentration profiles is the subject of Chapter 9. The interpretation of results will be discussed in Chapters 8 and 9.

Microbiosensors are a separate category of microsensors used in biofilm research. They use biological material immobilized on a sensing tip to modify the chemical signal that reaches a transducer. Sensors built on this principle constitute the majority of macroscale biosensors, but their use to probe biofilms is severely inhibited by the technical difficulties caused by biosensor miniaturization. Reducing the tip size of the sensor to acceptable dimensions also reduces the space available for immobilizing biological materials, which decreases the sensitivity of the biosensor. Examples of successfully miniaturized biosensors are glucose, methane, nitrate, and nitrous oxide microsensors.

The majority of microsensors used in biofilm research are electrochemical sensors. Among them, the most useful are amperometric microsensors, which can be used to measure the concentrations of dissolved gases, ions, and organic and inorganic molecules. The chemistries involved in their operation are straightforward, and similarly constructed microsensors can be used to measure the concentrations of a variety of substances, depending on the potential to which the working electrode is polarized and the composition of the internal electrolyte. Care should be exercised when amperometric sensors are used to make sure that only one substance, the analyte, participates in the electrode reaction. It is important to note that amperometric sensors actually consume the reactant whose concentration they measure. Potentiometric microsensors, such as ion-selective microelectrodes, are popular for probing biofilms because they are easy to make, but they suffer from the disadvantages common to all ion-selective electrodes, such as poor selectivity, plus additional disadvantages related to two factors: (1) the fact that their tips have to be small and (2) the heterogeneous nature of biofilms. The small tip size makes them susceptible to electromagnetic noise, and the response time of some potentiometric microsensors is quite long. Potentiometric microelectrodes with small tip diameters are many times more susceptible to electromagnetic noise than large-scale, ion-selective electrodes because the small tip has a high electrical impedance. There are also objections to their use in biofilms of a more subtle nature. The signal measured by an ion-selective electrode is, in part, due to the activity of the measured ion and, in part, due to the activity of all other ions present in the solution, through the ionic strength of the solution affecting its activity. When macroscale ion-selective electrodes are used, it is a common practice to increase the ionic strength of the solution, using appropriate buffers, to make the electrode response less susceptible to changes in the ionic strengths of the ions originally present in the solution. This practice is obviously not possible when one is probing biofilms. Therefore, the response of an ion-selective microelectrode in a biofilm is affected, to an unknown extent, by the variation in ionic strength across the biofilm. The heterogeneous nature of biofilms defeats the basic principles of using ion-selective electrodes in analytical chemistry.

Following trends in the design and construction of macroscale biosensors, a few microbiosensors have been constructed with immobilized active biological materials, e.g., glucose, methane, nitrate, and nitrous oxide microsensors. It is encouraging to see that these are amperometric sensors and that they replace similar potentiometric sensors, such as the nitrate microsensor. However, microbiosensors are difficult to construct, and their performance is affected by factors difficult to isolate and to quantify, e.g., the effects of oxygen and pH on the activity of the biologically active materials immobilized on the sensor. Some of these problems can be traced to biofilm heterogeneity. When a macroscale biosensor is used to measure the concentration of an analyte in a homogeneous solution, some interfering effects can be mitigated by keeping their intensity constant, e.g., a constant and known oxygen concentration in the sample or a constant and known pH. This is obviously not possible when a heterogeneous biofilm is probed, and the variations in these parameters may affect the activity of the biological material immobilized on the sensor to an unknown extent. Microbiosensors have biological material immobilized on their sensing tips. The response of the sensor depends on the amount of material immobilized, and this conflicts with the necessity of keeping the tip diameter small, no more than about 50 μm. Not much biological material can be immobilized on such a small tip. Therefore, the microbiosensors described in the literature have tip diameters larger than 50 μm, which makes their use in thin biofilms questionable. These microbiosensors are quite popular for testing the chemistries in benthic deposits though.

A special group of microsensors comprises those used to quantify mass transport coefficient, diffusivity, and flow velocity. These microsensors are easy to construct and use, but their use requires a drastic invasion of the microbial environment, including killing the biofilm microorganisms, which makes their use limited. These sensors are not for routine use, but they help to characterize well-defined biofilms in laboratory biofilm reactors, and they are useful in fundamental studies of various biofilm processes.

Fiber optic microsensors (microoptodes) offer undeniable advantages over electrochemical sensors: they do not require external reference electrodes, and they are immune to electromagnetic noise. However, the available technology makes it difficult to manufacture fiber optic sensors with tip diameters small enough for probing biofilms. Microoptodes also have disadvantages. The optical signal generated at the tip of a fiber optic sensor often depends on a relatively complex, and sometimes poorly defined, chemistry between the reactant in the solution and the reactant immobilized on the tip of the sensor. In addition, the immobilized reactant may interact with the measured reactant or affect the microbial activity in the biofilm in an unknown way; this is particularly true if the immobilized reactant leaks because it has been poorly immobilized. When the tip diameter of the microoptode is less than 10 μm, the performance deteriorates rapidly because of light coupling problems. Therefore, the popular fiber optic microsensors have larger tip diameters, sometimes much larger than 20 μm.

There are many macroscale fiber optic sensors available, but not all of them can be miniaturized. Many of them use large-diameter fibers, often assembled in bundles, and these cannot be miniaturized to the size required for sensors to probe biofilms. Fiber optic sensors with small tips are difficult to construct and operate. Because the small tip diameter limits the amount of light that reaches the sample, and even more so the amount of light that comes back from the sample, lasers are typically used as powerful light sources to deliver the light to the sample and sensitive spectrophotometers are used to analyze the spectrum of the light that comes back. Consequently, using optical microsensors requires specialized equipment: lasers, optical benches, spectrophotometers that can accept fiber optic cables, lock-in amplifiers, and photomultipliers. All this makes using fiber optic microsensors more expensive than using electrochemical microsensors.

Interpreting microsensor measurements in biofilms is not trivial. The most popular application of microsensors in biofilm research is measuring the concentration profiles of various dissolved substances. In principle, using appropriate computational and experimental procedures, it is possible to quantify the kinetic parameters of microbial respiration, the dynamics of nutrient transport, and the depth of nutrient penetration from these profiles. However, the lack of adequate mathematical models of biofilm activity makes interpretation of the results difficult and conclusions uncertain. Much can be improved in the area of interpreting the results of biofilm studies, and the conceptual model of stratified biofilms described in Chapter 8 is an example of such improvements. The conceptual model of stratified biofilms, and the mathematical model based on this conceptual model, can accommodate microsensor measurements of biofilm activity and the quantification of biofilm structure using confocal microscopy and image analysis.

In probing biofilms, the design of the experimental system determines the quality of the acquired information to the same extent that the availability of specific microsensors does. To get full use of the information from microsensor measurements, experimental systems should be designed to allow unambiguous interpretation of the results. This may sound trivial, but, in practice, so much effort is devoted to constructing microsensors, to testing computer-assisted micromanipulation, and to coordinating sensor movement with data acquisition that this simple requirement can easily be overlooked. Microsensor response is affected by many factors, not only by the concentration of the measured substance, and the biofilm reactor in which the microsensor measurements are conducted must be designed in such a way that the interfering factors can be isolated. For example, when microsensors are used to determine local biofilm activity, it is important to control the hydrodynamics in the reactor. Hydrodynamics can affect the substrate concentration profiles to the same extent that microbial activity does. In a sense, the process of interpreting the results of microsensor measurements begins before a microelectrode measurement is taken, and it can be successfully completed only if the experimental system allows isolation of the interfering variables. For this reason alone, using microsensors to probe biofilms in natural systems, where interfering factors either are difficult to isolate or cannot be isolated, requires careful scrutiny so that the results of the microsensor measurements are properly interpreted.

The most useful microsensors in biofilm research have elongated shafts tapering down to a tip diameter of several micrometers. As a rule, the tip diameter should be small enough not to damage biofilm structure or produce other artifacts, e.g., excessive consumption of the measured reactant by amperometric microsensors. Because microsensors with submicron-sized tip diameters are notoriously fragile, the commonly used tip diameters are between 10 and 20 μm. Sensors with tip diameters of 50 μm or more should be evaluated for their possible effects on biofilm structure.

The term *microsensor* is often used to refer to small chemical sensors. However, the prefix "micro-" may refer to almost any linear dimension. Therefore, it is better to specify the required features that make a microsensor suitable for biofilm research rather than to try to justify any arbitrarily selected linear dimensions and refer to them as micro-. For example, a pH microelectrode with a tip diameter of 1 mm is too large for measuring pH profiles in biofilms, although it may be perfectly well suited to other microscale applications, such as measurements of pH in small volumes of water.

Figure 4.31b shows the shape of microsensors used to measure concentration profiles in biofilms. The most important part of such devices is the sensing tip, which is small, typically several micrometers in diameter. When microsensors are used to probe biofilms, it is tacitly assumed that their tips are small enough not to damage the biofilm structure. To justify this assumption, the microsensors used to probe biofilms have elongated shapes and are tapered to a sensing tip that is often less than 10 μm in diameter, although tip sizes vary and some sensors have tip diameters as large as 50 μm or even, on occasion, 100 μm. Sensors with tips larger than 100 μm are considered less useful in probing biofilms, unless they are used entirely outside of the space occupied by the biofilm; the possibility of damaging biofilm structure and thus producing artifacts increases with tip diameter.

Another reason for using sensors with small tip diameters is that the spatial resolution of the measurements is roughly equal to the tip diameter of the sensor. While the operator is measuring substrate concentrations across a biofilm, the locations of the measurements must be vertically separated by a distance equal to or exceeding the spatial resolution of the sensor, which is approximately the tip diameter of the sensor. Consequently, a microelectrode with a 10-μm tip diameter would allow for the collection of about fifty meaningful data points in a 500-μm-thick biofilm, whereas an electrode with a 100-μm tip diameter would allow for the collection of only about five. The quest for sensors with small tip diameters is limited by their mechanical properties: smaller tips are more prone to damage, and many microsensors have been destroyed by careless handling before they produced a single result. An acceptable compromise on tip size is microelectrodes with tip diameters between 10 and 20 μm: such tips are small enough not to damage biofilm structure (the

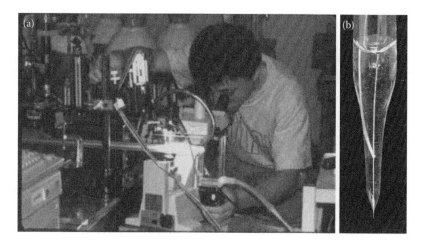

Figure 4.31 (a) One of our students using a popular microsensor: an oxygen microelectrode with a tip diameter of about 20 μm. (b) The shape of the microsensor, elongated and gradually tapered to a small tip, makes it ideally suited for use in biofilms.

measured profiles are reproducible), yet large enough to survive moderate abuse by the operator.

Among the many devices advertised as microsensors, two types are particularly useful with biofilms: electrochemical microsensors built as microelectrodes and optical microsensors built on fiber optic cables. Both types of microsensors can easily be manufactured with small, elongated tips. Useful electrochemical microsensors include potentiometric microelectrodes, which measure the potential across a membrane, and amperometric microelectrodes, which measure the current between the working and reference electrodes. Useful fiber optic microsensors, often called *microoptodes*, measure light absorption, light reflection, and fluorescence.

Potentiometric microsensors measure membrane potential, the potential difference between two reference electrodes immersed on either side of a membrane, as described earlier in this chapter. Amperometric microsensors measure current resulting from the transfer of electrons between members of redox couples and the sensing element of the microsensor. Typically, these microsensors are used in two-electrode configurations and the current is controlled by polarizing the indicator electrode (the sensor) to a known potential against a suitable reference (counter) electrode. The resultant current between the working electrode and the reference electrode is equivalent to the rate of the electrode reaction, and its magnitude depends on the reactant concentration and the mass transport rate in the vicinity of the electrode.

The available fiber optic sensors use photosensitive reagents that are (1) immobilized on their tips, (2) added to the solution, or (3) naturally present in biofilms. Examples of such sensors are those that measure the fluorescence of immobilized ruthenium salts sensitive to quenching by oxygen, those that measure light generated by fluorescently labeled antibodies, and those that measure the fluorescence intensity of fluorescent proteins expressed by biofilms, such as green fluorescent protein (GFP). The response of the fiber optic microsensors is interpreted using relevant equations quantifying light intensity:

1. If the analyte absorbs the light delivered to the sample, the sensor response is quantified using the Beer–Lambert law:

$$I_1 = I_{1o} \exp(-\alpha_1 L) \qquad (4.46)$$

2. If a fluorescent reagent is immobilized on the tip of the fiber sensor and the analyte quenches the fluorescence, the response of the sensor is quantified using the Stern–Volmer equation:

$$\frac{\tau_o}{\tau} = 1 + k_q \tau_o [C_q] \qquad (4.47)$$

The product ($k_q \tau_o$) is referred to as the Stern–Volmer quenching constant K_{SV}.

The fluorescence lifetime in the Stern–Volmer equation can be substituted for the fluorescence intensity:

$$\frac{I_{1o}}{I_1} = \frac{\tau_o}{\tau} \qquad (4.48)$$

Equation 4.48 describes the behavior of (micro)sensors based on fluorescence quenching. These can be operated in either of two modes: (1) measuring the fluorescence intensity or (2) measuring the fluorescence lifetime. Although measuring fluorescence intensity is simple, measuring fluorescence lifetime offers a distinctive advantage: the fluorescence lifetime does not depend on the amount of the fluorophore immobilized on the tip, so it is immune to changes in that amount that may occur during the measurement because of gradual leaking or photobleaching.

4.2.1 Potentiometric microelectrodes

The most popular potentiometric chemical sensors are ion-selective electrodes, and several of these can be miniaturized to make them useful in biofilm research. There is an inherent difficulty in using ion-selective microelectrodes in biofilms, however. By definition, these electrodes measure ion activities, which depend on ionic strength, which, in turn, is affected by all ions in the tested solution. For that reason, ion-selective electrodes are sensitive to the concentrations of all ions in the tested solution, not only the concentration of the one that is being measured. To counterbalance this effect, when ion-selective electrodes are used to measure the concentrations of ions in homogeneous solutions, special buffers are added to increase the ionic strength of the solution. This remedy cannot be used in biofilms, which are heterogeneous, and the spatial distribution of ionic strength in biofilms has an unknown effect on measurements using potentiometric microsensors.

4.2.1.1 Redox microelectrodes

As with macroscale redox electrodes, measurements with redox microelectrodes are easy to carry out but the results are difficult to interpret. There are some inherent difficulties related to the nature of biofilm systems and biofilm processes. Redox potential depends on pH, so if there is a significant gradient in pH across the biofilm, the effect of the pH variation should be taken into consideration. This means that another profile, of pH, should be taken at the same location and at the same time as the profile of redox potential. Fortunately, few biofilms show significant gradients in pH because most solutions have large enough buffering capacities and the mobility of protons is significant. These two effects prevent the formation of significant pH profiles across biofilms. Another well-known difficulty is that some redox couples do not equilibrate on platinum surfaces, and this effect must be taken into consideration for large and small redox electrodes. The effect is difficult to quantify, making the measurement difficult to interpret. Despite these difficulties, profiles of redox potential in biofilms can provide auxiliary information when combined with concentration profiles of the species that control the redox potential in natural waters, such as oxygen and sulfide. Measuring oxygen profiles, sulfide profiles, and redox profiles, and comparing the information they carry, gives the researcher confidence in the measurements.

Redox microelectrodes are easy to make: a platinum (Pt) wire (preferably platinized) is sealed in a glass capillary, and the flat tip of 10–15-μm Pt wire is exposed (Figure 4.32a). For our purposes, we also deposit platinum on the Pt wire tip, making what is called a platinized platinum bulb (Figure 4.32b). This additional step significantly increases the surface area of the redox microelectrode tip, which improves the response time. The electric potential at the redox microelectrode tip is measured against a suitable reference electrode (Bishop and Yu 1999; Zhang and Pang 1999).

The redox potential is used to quantify the overall composition of the surrounding solution in terms of its ratio of oxidized to reduced species. Redox potential correlates

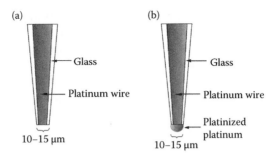

Figure 4.32 Redox potential microelectrode (a) with a flat platinum tip and (b) with a platinized platinum bulb tip.

with the dominant redox couples (e.g., oxygen–water) present in solution. When the dominant redox couple interacts with the electrode, the redox potential sensor can also freely exchange electrons with the electrode. The ratio of oxidized to reduced species is correlated with the Nernst equation for redox couples (Equations 4.49 and 4.50) and represents an electron pressure in the solution. The redox potential is affected by the ratio of oxidized to reduced species, the number of electrons transferred, the number of protons transferred, and the pH of the solution (Babauta et al. 2011).

$$OX + mH^+ + ne^- \leftrightarrow RED \tag{4.49}$$

$$E_h = E^\circ - \frac{59}{n} \log\left(\frac{RED}{OX}\right) - \frac{m}{n} 59 \, pH \tag{4.50}$$

In Equation 4.50, E_h is the redox potential (mV), E° is the standard reduction potential (mV; pH 0), n is the number of moles of electrons transferred per mole of the oxidized species, RED is the reduced species (M), OX is the oxidized species (M), m is the moles of protons transferred per mole of electrons transferred, and pH refers to the pH of the surrounding solution.

Typically, the redox microelectrode is operated using an external reference electrode, but it is possible to construct the redox microelectrode with an internal reference electrode, and Figure 4.33 shows the details of this construction.

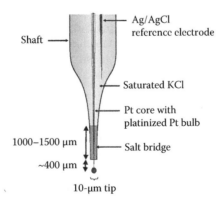

Figure 4.33 Redox microelectrode with internal reference electrode. (Reproduced from Babauta, T. J. et al., *Environmental Science and Technology*, 45, 6654–6660, 2011.)

4.2.1.2   Ion-selective microelectrodes

Two types of ion-selective microelectrodes with solid-state membranes have been used in biofilm studies: chloride microelectrodes based on Ag/AgCl membranes and sulfide electrodes based on AgS membranes. The chloride electrode behaves well but rarely is chloride concentration of any interest to the biofilm researcher; even if it is, one is unlikely to see chloride concentration profiles across a biofilm. The concentration of chloride can be measured in the bulk solution using the traditional methods of analytical chemistry, and the concentration of chloride ions in the biofilm is equal to that in the bulk solution. Measuring sulfide concentrations in biofilms, on the other hand, is very useful, mostly for quantifying the activity of sulfate-reducing bacteria in biofilms. However, the solid-state–membrane sulfide electrodes suffer from the disadvantages that are discussed below. They are easy to make but difficult to calibrate, and the results of measurements are difficult to interpret for the reasons specified in the next section.

4.2.1.3   Sulfide microelectrodes

Early sulfide ion-selective electrodes used solid-state silver sulfide membranes. The ion-selective sulfide microelectrodes are just miniature copies of their macroscale counterparts and have been used in microscale ecological research, in microbially influenced corrosion studies, and in combination with redox potential measurements in biofilms. They are easy to make: a silver wire, appropriately cleaned and sealed in a glass microcapillary, is immersed in a solution of ammonium sulfide or another sulfide, which causes spontaneous precipitation of the silver sulfide membrane, which is in equilibrium with the sulfide ions in the solution.

There is an inherent problem with using this construction, however. Lack of precise thermodynamic data prevents the calibration of sulfide electrodes based on AgS membranes with confidence. Because of the composition of the membrane, it is supposed to be equilibrated with the S^{2-} sulfides in solution. Sulfides in aqueous solutions equilibrate with bisulfide, HS^-, and the position of the equilibrium depends on pH:

$$S^{2-} = \frac{K_2[HS^-]}{[H^+]} \tag{4.51}$$

To calibrate the electrode, a series of solutions with known and constant concentrations of sulfide is needed. The concentrations of sulfide ions in these solutions are computed from Equation 4.51. This is trivial if the pH and K_2 are known. The pHs can easily be adjusted; the problem is the correct equilibrium constant K_2 for these computations. Many textbooks report a pK_2 for hydrogen sulfide around 14. However, a closer inspection of the reported equilibrium constants reveals that it is less certain than is usually assumed: the reported values vary from 13 to 21 (Giggenbach 1971; Myers 1986), a difference greater than 8 orders of magnitude. Because there is no indication of which value of the equilibrium constant should be used, the selection is arbitrary, so the results of calibration and the results of measurements are uncertain. Fortunately, there is another way of measuring sulfide concentration: using the amperometric sensors described later in this chapter. Using amperometric sensors, the researcher can avoid the controversial reported values of the second dissociation constant. The amperometric electrodes measure the concentration of hydrogen sulfide, and they can be calibrated using the first dissociation constant.

4.2.1.4 *pH microelectrodes*

Microelectrodes that measure pH are among the most popular and useful in biofilm research, and they have been constructed using various principles. The three most popular constructions of pH microelectrodes will be discussed here: (1) those made with LIX membranes, (2) those made with glass membranes, and (3) those made with metal oxides.

Microelectrodes with LIX membranes are easy to make and easy to use. The membranes are available from specialized vendors as ready-to-use cocktails composed of the ion exchanger, organic solvent, and stabilizers (see Chapter 5). The cocktail is applied to the tip of a micropipette by capillary action.

Glass pH microelectrodes are miniaturized versions of the macroscale pH electrodes (Figure 4.34). The ion-sensitive glasses used in these microelectrodes are provided by specialized vendors, e.g., Corning pH-sensitive glass no. 0150. Constructing glass microelectrodes is not particularly difficult, but they have a distinct disadvantage that limits their popularity for probing biofilms: the sensing tip is of considerable length. Figure 4.35b shows the construction: the sensor is made by fusing a micropipette made of pH-sensitive glass to another micropipette, made of lead glass, for example, which serves as the shaft of the microelectrode. The tip of the microelectrode is small, less than 20 µm, which qualifies the device as useful for probing biofilms. However, as seen in Figure 4.35b, the sensing tip protrudes from the shaft and its length can be 100 µm or more. Somewhere along this distance, pH is measured; however, it is not clear where. Therefore, glass pH microelectrodes are particularly useful for measuring pH gradients in thick layers, as in microbial mats or bottom sediments in rivers, whose thickness exceeds the *length* of the sensing tip by many times. For measurements in thin biofilms, however, their usefulness is questionable.

A separate category among pH electrodes is occupied by metal oxide pH electrodes (Figure 4.35c). An example is the iridium oxide pH microelectrode. The oxides of many noble metals are pH-sensitive and can be used to make pH microelectrodes. Such pH microelectrodes are not particularly difficult to prepare. The main difficulty is in oxidizing the noble metals, which requires using cyclic voltammetry because noble metals do not oxidize easily. Iridium oxide electrodes are prepared by potential cycling between

Figure 4.34 The pH microelectrode with a Corning 0150 glass membrane. The problem discussed above is quite obvious from this image; the electrode measures pH over a certain distance, roughly equal to the length of the protruding tip. For pH measurements with high spatial resolution this solution is unacceptable.

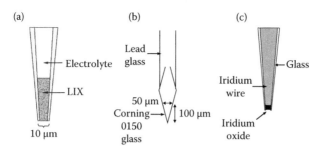

Figure 4.35 The pH microelectrodes: (a) a pH microelectrode with a liquid ion exchange membrane, (b) a pH microelectrode with a glass membrane (Jorgensen and Revsbech 1988), and (c) an iridium oxide microelectrode. (From Thomas, R. C., *Ion Selective Intracellular Microelectrodes: How To Make and Use Them*. Academic Press, London, 1978; Jorgensen, B. B., and Revsbech, N. P., *Methods in Enzymology*, 167, 639–659, 1988; Van Houdt, P. et al., *Biotechnology and Bioengineering*, 40, 601–608, 1992.)

−0.25 and +1.25 V SCE in sulfuric acid. Larger electrodes can be prepared by sputter deposition or thermal oxidation. However, sputtering and thermal oxidation produce predominantly anhydrous iridium oxide, whereas electrochemical oxidation of iridium produces predominantly hydrated oxides. The iridium oxide microelectrode is an excellent analytical tool, but its use is restricted in many environmental studies. Iridium oxide is unstable in the presence of H_2S, and probably of other reductants. This disadvantage practically disables the microelectrode when measurements are conducted in the presence of sulfate-reducing bacteria. However, many laboratory measurements are conducted in well-controlled conditions and in biofilms of pure culture microorganisms that are known not to reduce sulfate ions; in these conditions, the iridium oxide pH microelectrodes are exemplary.

The easiest pH microelectrodes to construct are those that are operated with an external reference electrode, but it is possible to construct them with an internal reference electrode, as shown in Figure 4.36.

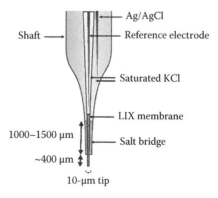

Figure 4.36 The pH microelectrode with internal reference electrode. (Reproduced from Babauta, T. J. et al., *Environmental Science and Technology*, 45, 6654–6660, 2011.)

4.2.1.5   Carbon dioxide microelectrodes

Carbon dioxide dissolves in water, and upon hydrolysis it forms a weak diprotic acid (carbonic acid) that then dissociates and affects the pH. Therefore, the concentration of carbon dioxide can be evaluated from changes in pH, if the experimental system is so designed that pH variation can be solely ascribed to carbon dioxide production or consumption. The principle of the measurement is based on buffer action. The internal electrolyte in the microelectrode shaft is (sodium) bicarbonate, which equilibrates with carbonic acid (carbon dioxide) (Figure 4.37).

During measurements, carbon dioxide dissolved in the external solution, $CO_2(g)$, diffuses through a gas-permeable membrane and reaches the internal solution, where part of it establishes the equilibrium:

$$CO_2(g) \rightleftarrows CO_2(aq) \tag{4.52}$$

The dissolved carbon dioxide, $CO_2(aq)$, undergoes hydration and forms carbonic acid, H_2CO_3:

$$CO_2(aq) + H_2O \rightleftarrows H_2CO_3 \tag{4.53}$$

The carbonic acid, H_2CO_3, dissociates in two steps. The first step produces bicarbonate ions:

$$H_2CO_3 \rightleftarrows H^+ + HCO_3^- \tag{4.54}$$

The internal solution is composed of carbonic acid and bicarbonate, and its pH can be calculated from the Henderson–Hasselbach equation:

$$pH = pK_a + \log \frac{\left[HCO_3^- \right]}{[H_2CO_3]} \tag{4.55}$$

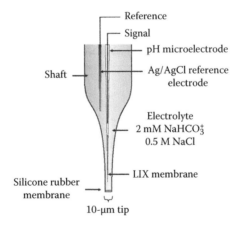

Figure 4.37 CO_2 microelectrode. (Modified from de Beer, D. et al., *Limnology and Oceanography*, 42, 1590–1600, 1997.)

From Equation 4.55, the concentration of carbonic acid, which for all practical purposes is equal to the concentration of carbon dioxide, can be estimated:

$$\log[H_2CO_3] = pK_a + \log\left[HCO_3^-\right] - pH \tag{4.56}$$

The internal electrolyte is prepared in such a way that the concentration of bicarbonate ions is exceedingly large, which makes the *change* in bicarbonate concentration, $\left[HCO_3^-\right]$, negligible, and therefore,

$$\log[H_2CO_3] \cong const - pH \tag{4.57}$$

In summary, the internal electrolyte is prepared with an excess of bicarbonate, so that the pH in the internal electrolyte is proportional to the activity of carbon dioxide in the external solution, which makes the electrode sensitive to carbon dioxide, even though it really measures pH. In our laboratory, CO_2 microelectrodes with tip diameters less than 20 μm are constructed routinely (Figure 4.37). In part, the construction is similar to that of the Clark-type dissolved oxygen microelectrode, in that the external micropipette is covered with a gas-permeable membrane, silicone rubber. The internal sensing device, however, is a pH microelectrode. The response time of CO_2 microelectrodes is long, between 2 and 5 min, which limits their usefulness in some applications.

The carbon dioxide microelectrode is calibrated in a series of solutions of different concentrations of carbonate buffer (pH-buffered solutions of $NaHCO_3$). Used in a biofilm, it measures the concentration of CO_2. The measurement is correct only if the pH does not vary across the biofilm, which is the case in most biofilms.

4.2.2 Amperometric microelectrodes

Amperometric sensors have proven to be reliable and very useful in biofilm research. In contrast to potentiometric sensors, they equilibrate relatively fast and, if properly designed and constructed, are easy to use. Whenever there is a choice of using an amperometric or a potentiometric microsensor in a biofilm study, using the amperometric sensor is advantageous. Later in this chapter, the amperometric sulfide microelectrode is described. This electrode has replaced the ion-selective sulfide microelectrode with a solid-state membrane described above. The amperometric microelectrode is so much better than the ion-selective microelectrode that we do not use the latter anymore.

4.2.2.1 Dissolved oxygen microelectrodes

Figure 4.38 shows the flagship of microsensors used to probe biofilms; the dissolved oxygen (DO) microelectrode. Because many microorganisms preferentially use oxygen as the terminal electron acceptor in respiration, oxygen electrodes are often used to quantify biofilm activity. In these cases, biofilm activity is identified with the oxygen consumption rate. Incidentally, oxygen microelectrodes are among the most reliable microsensors used in biofilm research.

In an oxygen microelectrode, oxygen diffuses through a silicone rubber membrane, arrives at a cathodically polarized working electrode, and is reduced to water (Figure 4.38). The device uses an Ag/AgCl half-cell as the counter electrode and a noble metal such as gold or platinum as the working electrode. The reduction of oxygen is achieved at potentials between –0.4 and –1.2 V. Applying –0.8 V typically satisfies the limiting current condition, and the measured current is proportional to the dissolved oxygen concentration in the vicinity of the sensor tip.

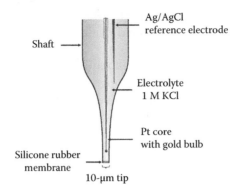

Shaft

Ag/AgCl
reference electrode

Electrolyte
1 M KCl

Pt core
with gold bulb

Silicone rubber
membrane

10-µm tip

Figure 4.38 Dissolved oxygen microelectrode. (Modified from Revsbech, N. P., *Limnology and Oceanography*, 34, 474–478, 1989.)

Oxygen is reduced on the platinum working electrode in the following half reaction:

$$2e^- + 1/2\,O_2 + H_2O \rightarrow 2\,OH^- \tag{4.58}$$

by the electrons derived from the anodic half reaction on the Ag/AgCl counter electrode:

$$2Ag + 2Cl^- \rightarrow 2AgCl + 2e^- \tag{4.59}$$

Oxygen microelectrodes are calibrated in water that is alternately aerated and de-aerated by purging with nitrogen and air. The measured current is typically between 10 and 150 pA for N_2-saturated water and between 100 and 700 pA for air-saturated water. Two-point calibration is sufficient because the calibration curve is linear. The response time of a good oxygen microelectrode is 1–5 s (95% of the maximum current), and stirring the solution should not increase the current by more than 5%.

4.2.2.2 Sulfide microelectrodes

The development of reliable sulfide microelectrodes was an important task in environmental research because sulfate is an important terminal electron acceptor in anaerobic microbial respiration. Initially, the microelectrodes for measuring sulfide ion concentration were built as potentiometric devices with a silver sulfide membrane. Later, this construction was eclipsed by the amperometric sulfide microelectrode. Amperometric sulfide electrodes measure the dissolved hydrogen sulfide concentration rather than the sulfide ion concentration, and therefore avoid the controversies about the correct pK_2 for hydrogen sulfide. A sulfide microsensor is shown in Figure 4.39. During measurements, the gas (hydrogen sulfide) penetrates the gas-permeable membrane (silicone rubber) and dissolves in the internal electrolyte. The internal electrolyte includes a redox mediator, ferricyanide $[Fe(CN)_6]^{-3}$, which is reduced by the hydrogen sulfide to ferrocyanide, $[Fe(CN)_6]^{-4}$, and then reoxidized on a platinum electrode. The sequence of the reactions involved in this process follows:

1. Hydrogen sulfide gas penetrates the membrane and dissolves in the internal electrolyte:

$$H_2S_{(g)} \rightleftarrows H_2S_{(aq)} \tag{4.60}$$

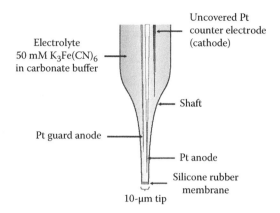

Figure 4.39 Sulfide microelectrode. (Modified from Jeroschewski, P. et al., *Electroanalysis*, 6, 769–772, 1994.)

2. Aqueous hydrogen sulfide dissociates to bisulfide, HS^-, and protons:

$$H_2S_{(aq)} \rightleftarrows HS^- + H^+ \tag{4.61}$$

3. Bisulfide is chemically oxidized by ferricyanide to elemental sulfur, while ferricyanide is reduced to ferrocyanide:

$$HS^- + 2[Fe(CN)_6]^{-3} \rightarrow 2[Fe(CN)_6]^{-4} + S_o + 2H^+ \tag{4.62}$$

4. Ferrocyanide produced in step 3 is reoxidized electrochemically to ferricyanide at the platinum electrode:

$$[Fe(CN)_6]^{-4} \rightarrow [Fe(CN)_6]^{-3} + e^- \tag{4.63}$$

The internal platinum anode, placed 10 μm behind the silicone membrane, and the guard anode, placed behind the internal anode, are polarized to (+)100 mV against the uncovered platinum counter electrode. The purpose of the guard anode is to oxidize the excess ferrocyanide that was not oxidized at the working electrode and prevent its accumulation in the electrode shaft. The response time of a good sulfide microelectrode is less than 3 s and the results are linear over a large range of H_2S concentrations, from 0 to 2000 μM H_2S. Sulfide microelectrodes are calibrated in solutions of H_2S, and the current generated by oxidizing ferrocyanide to ferricyanide is proportional to the H_2S concentration near the tip of the microelectrode.

The microelectrode is calibrated in a series of solutions of different concentrations of H_2S. Used in a biofilm, it measures the concentration of H_2S. The measurement is correct only if the pH does not vary across the biofilm, which is the case in all but a few biofilms.

4.2.2.3 Microelectrodes for measuring the concentrations of oxidants

Much biofilm research is devoted to removing undesired biofilms. One way of accomplishing this is to kill the biofilm microorganisms using strong oxidants, such as chlorine or hydrogen peroxide. Therefore, there is strong interest among biofilm researchers in developing microelectrodes that can take profiles of the oxidants used as antimicrobial agents. The principles of making and using these devices will be discussed in Chapter 5, using hydrogen peroxide microelectrodes as an example.

4.2.2.4   Hydrogen peroxide microelectrodes

An electrode that measures an oxidant concentration in a biofilm is an amperometric device that either reduces the oxidant by delivering electrons from an external circuit or further oxidizes the oxidant by accepting electrons from the oxidant and transferring them to an external circuit. This latter principle is exemplified by the hydrogen peroxide microelectrode, which oxidizes hydrogen peroxide to oxygen at the tip of a platinum wire (Figure 4.40).

The microsensor consists of a platinum wire sealed in glass and covered with a cellulose acetate membrane. The electrical circuit is completed by an external secondary reference electrode, such as a saturated calomel electrode (SCE), used as the counter electrode, and a picoammeter to measure the current. To facilitate the electrode reaction, the oxidation of hydrogen peroxide, the platinum working electrode is polarized anodically at +0.8 V against the SCE:

$$H_2O_2 \rightarrow O_2(g) + 2H^+ + 2e^- \tag{4.64}$$

The electrons are used in the cathodic half reaction at the counter electrode (SCE):

$$Hg_2Cl_2(s) + 2e^- \rightarrow 2Hg(l) + 2Cl^- \tag{4.65}$$

A hydrogen peroxide microelectrode can also be constructed with an internal reference (counter) electrode, as shown in Figure 4.41.

The microelectrodes are calibrated by plotting the measured current versus the concentrations of H_2O_2 in standard solutions. Calibration curves are electrode-specific because the measured current depends not only on the concentration of hydrogen peroxide but also on the active surface area of the electrode, which is unknown and not trivial to measure.

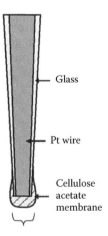

Figure 4.40 Hydrogen peroxide microelectrode.

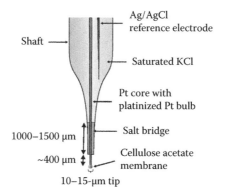

Figure 4.41 Hydrogen peroxide microelectrode with internal reference electrode.

4.2.2.5   Hydrogen microelectrode

The hydrogen microelectrode is an amperometric microelectrode, similar to the DO microelectrode in construction, except that the gold bulb is replaced with a platinized Pt tip (platinum bulb) because hydrogen has the highest exchange current density on platinized platinum. A positive 0.6-V polarization potential against the Ag/AgCl electrode is usually applied to satisfy the limiting current condition, and the measured current is proportional to the hydrogen concentration in the vicinity of the sensor tip. During the measurement, dissolved hydrogen from the environment diffuses through the silicone membrane, reaches the platinum bulb tip of the anodically polarized electrode, and is oxidized to protons:

$$H_2 \rightarrow 2H^+ + 2e^- \tag{4.66}$$

On the cathode side, silver chloride is converted to silver by receiving electrons:

$$2AgCl + 2e^- \rightarrow 2Ag + 2Cl^- \tag{4.67}$$

The hydrogen microelectrode is calibrated in the gas phase of 10% hydrogen in nitrogen and pure nitrogen (zero hydrogen). Figure 4.42 shows a diagram of the hydrogen microelectrode.

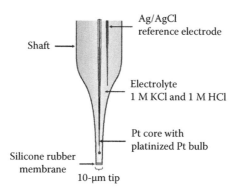

Figure 4.42 Hydrogen microelectrode.

4.2.3   Voltammetric microelectrodes

4.2.3.1   Flavin microelectrode

In Chapter 7 we describe the use of electroactive biofilms (EABs). The mechanism of electron transfer between biofilm microorganisms and metal electrodes is a matter of intensive research, and one of the hypotheses in these studies is that the microorganisms generate redox mediators, which they then use to facilitate electron transfer to metal electrodes. One group of such substances is flavins, which include flavin mononucleotide, riboflavin, and flavin adenine dinucleotide. It is therefore interesting to measure the concentration of flavins in biofilms directly, and for that purpose we constructed a flavin electrode (Nguyan et al. 2012) made of a glass-covered carbon wire microelectrode, a Ag/AgCl reference electrode, and a Pt counter electrode, all encased in a Pasteur pipette, as shown in Figure 4.43. To facilitate the exchange of ions and the restoration of electrical neutrality, the microelectrode is also equipped with an agar salt bridge layer. The electrolyte in the shaft of the microelectrode is saturated KCl.

4.2.4   Microbiosensors

Microbiosensors use biological material immobilized on a sensing tip to modify the chemical signal that reaches a transducer. Sensors built on this principle constitute the majority of macroscale biosensors, but their use to probe biofilms is severely inhibited by the technical difficulties caused by biosensor miniaturization. The main problem is that reducing the size of the sensor tip to acceptable dimensions also reduces the space available for immobilizing biological materials, which decreases the sensitivity of the biosensor. Examples of successfully miniaturized biosensors are glucose, methane, nitrate, and nitrous oxide microsensors. Because only glucose microsensors can be constructed with a tip diameter less than 20 μm, we discuss these below.

4.2.4.1   Glucose microsensors

Although glucose is not a particularly relevant reagent in environmental studies, many biofilm researchers use glucose as an electron donor to grow biofilms in laboratories. Because glucose sensors are among the most intensively studied biosensors for biomedical applications, there are several constructions available that can be used as models for

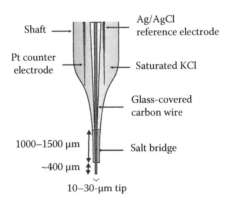

Figure 4.43 Flavin microelectrode.

constructing glucose microsensors to probe biofilms. The one that has been successfully miniaturized is an amperometric microsensor that measures hydrogen peroxide, H_2O_2, generated by the oxidation of glucose catalyzed by glucose oxidase enzyme immobilized on the tip of a microelectrode:

$$\text{Glucose} + O_2 \rightarrow H_2O_2 + \text{D-gluconolactone} \tag{4.68}$$

$$H_2O + \text{D-gluconolactone} \rightarrow \text{D-gluconic acid} \tag{4.69}$$

A glucose microsensor is shown in Figure 4.44. The construction is simple: platinum wire is sealed in a glass capillary, and the tip of the wire is exposed and platinized to obtain a porous matrix for immobilizing glucose oxidase enzyme. To immobilize the enzyme, the tip is dipped in the enzyme solution and then covered with a thin layer of glutaraldehyde. To measure glucose concentration, the platinum wire is polarized to +0.8 V against a SCE, in a similar manner to the sensors used to measure hydrogen peroxide. The measured current is linearly correlated with the glucose concentration near the tip of the microsensor.

The response of the glucose microsensor depends on the oxygen concentration and the pH in the external solution, because enzyme activity is affected by these factors. For this reason, the microelectrode must be calibrated in solutions of known and constant oxygen concentration and pH. To evaluate the glucose concentration in a biofilm, it is necessary to measure oxygen, pH, and glucose at the same location, which is a complex operation limiting, for practical reasons, the use of glucose microsensors. The sensor calibrates linearly between 0 and 3 mM when the oxygen concentration is kept near saturation and pH = 6.8. The response time is several seconds.

4.2.5   Microelectrodes for quantifying mass transport rates in biofilms

Amperometric microelectrodes are covered with membranes that confine the mass transport resistance of the measured substance. Such microelectrodes are not sensitive to the mass transport rate of the measured substance in the bulk solution or any

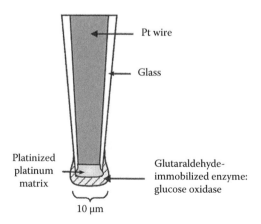

Figure 4.44 Glucose microsensor. (Modified from Cronenberg, C. C. H., and van den Heuvel, J. C., *Biosensors and Bioelectronics*, 6, 255–262, 1991.)

conditions determining this rate (e.g., the flow rate). The membrane shields the device from variations in the external mass transport rate. In many biofilm studies, however, these variations in the local mass transport rate are important, which prompted us to develop microelectrodes that quantify the local mass transport rate. These microelectrodes are constructed by removing the membranes from amperometric microelectrodes and making them sensitive to the mass transport rate. The principle of the amperometric sensors was to keep the mass transport resistance constant, so that the response of the sensor depended on the concentration of the measured solute only. The principle of the microelectrodes for quantifying mass transport rates is to keep the concentration of the solute constant so that the response of the sensor depends on the mass transport rate only. To quantify mass transport dynamics in biofilms, we use amperometric sensors without membranes, which makes them sensitive to the mass transport rates in the solution. Such devices have been used in studies on the effects of hydrodynamics on mass transport rates in various systems. Two differences distinguish our sensors from those described in the literature: (1) our sensors have tip diameters less than 10 µm and (2) they are mobile.

To use limiting current microelectrodes to quantify mass transport rates in biofilms, two conditions must be satisfied: (1) the only sink for the electroactive substance must be the microelectrode tip, and (2) there can be only one electroactive substance available for the electrode to process at a time. After a suitable electroactive substance has been selected and introduced into a biofilm, a microelectrode, polarized to an extent that satisfies the limiting current condition, reduces (or oxidizes, depending on the procedure) this substance. The electroactive substance is then removed (converted to another substance) at the tip of the microelectrode, thereby decreasing the concentration of this substance in the vicinity of the microelectrode tip. After a few seconds, equilibrium is established between the rate at which the electroactive substance is locally removed by the electrode reaction and the rate at which it is supplied by the mass transport. The limiting current reflects the position of this equilibrium. If, for any reason, the rate of mass transport of the electroactive substance to the tip of the microelectrode varies, the limiting current varies as well, and this is the principle of the local mass transport microelectrode. We use mobile microelectrodes and expose their tips at various locations in biofilms. The electroactive reactant we use is a 25 mM solution of potassium ferricyanide, $K_3Fe(CN)_6$, in 0.2 M KCl. With proper experimental control, the ferricyanide is reduced to ferrocyanide, $Fe(CN)_6^{4-}$, at the surfaces of cathodically polarized microelectrodes:

$$Fe(CN)_6^{3-} + e^- \rightarrow Fe(CN)_6^{4-} \tag{4.70}$$

Increasing the polarization potential applied to the microelectrode increases the rate of the electrode reaction (i.e., the rate of reduction of ferricyanide to ferrocyanide) until the rate reaches its limit for the existing set of conditions. At the limiting current, the concentration of ferricyanide at the electrode surface is zero and the concentration gradient cannot increase any further. Figure 4.45 shows the results from a microelectrode immersed in a solution of ferricyanide, polarized with respect to a reference electrode, and measuring the limiting current.

For such conditions, the concentration of ferricyanide at the electrode surface is zero ($C_s = 0$), whereas in the bulk solution it remains C_o. The concentration gradient is said to be confined entirely within the mass transfer boundary layer, δ. The flux of ferricyanide,

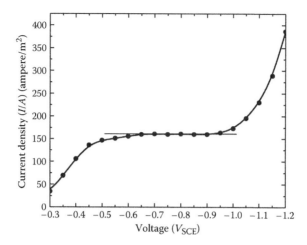

Figure 4.45 Limiting current. The electrode is polarized stepwise, from −0.3 to −1.2 V, and the current is measured. The range of potentials corresponding to the plateau (between −0.5 and −0.9 V) designates the potential range in which the limiting current is measured. If the working electrode is polarized to a potential somewhere in the middle of this range, small deviations in the applied potential do not affect the measured current. The line in the figure shows the limiting current.

J, to the exposed surface of a microelectrode with sensing area A is related to the limiting current, I_{lim}, by

$$J = \frac{I_{lim}}{nAF} \tag{4.71}$$

For practical reasons, the results of current measurements are reported as the limiting current density (I_{lim}/A), which describes the ratio of the limiting current to the reactive surface area of the microelectrode tip. The flux of ferricyanide to the electrode can also be expressed using Fick's first law:

$$J = \frac{D(C_o - C_s)}{\delta} = k(C_o - C_s) \tag{4.72}$$

Here, D is the diffusivity of ferricyanide, C_o is the concentration of ferricyanide in the bulk solution, C_s is the concentration of ferricyanide at the surface of the microelectrode, k is the mass transport coefficient, and δ designates the thickness of the diffusion boundary layer, which is controlled by the local shear stress and flow. In stagnant water, δ is controlled only by the diffusivity of ferricyanide. A properly arranged experimental system using a mobile microelectrode allows for measuring the rate of transport of ferricyanide to the microelectrode tip, and this transport rate is equivalent to the nutrient transport rate at that location in the biofilm.

If the electrode is polarized to such an extent that the current becomes limiting, C_s in Equation 4.72 equals zero and

$$J = \frac{D(C_o - C_s)}{\delta} = kC_o \tag{4.73}$$

If the right-hand sides of Equations 4.71 and 4.73 are equated, the local mass transfer coefficient can be computed from the limiting current measured at the selected location:

$$k = \frac{I_{lim}}{nAFC_o} \tag{4.74}$$

Using mass transport microelectrodes requires extensive modifications to the experimental procedure to make sure that the variables are properly isolated and that the system responds to one variable only, the one selected by the operator. Because the application of limiting current sensors requires the introduction of ferricyanide, which inactivates metabolic reactions in biofilms, measurements of mass transport dynamics must be conducted separately from the measurement of the primary substrate utilization rate. Because measurements of mass transport rates are destructive in terms of biofilm activity, the local substrate utilization rates, which are needed to quantify biofilm activity, are measured first, and then the nutrient solution is replaced by the electrolyte and the factors affecting mass transport dynamics are quantified.

Depending on the experimental arrangement used, mass transport microelectrodes can measure (1) the local mass transport coefficient, (2) the local effective diffusivity, or (3) the local flow velocity. To measure local effective diffusivities, mass transfer electrodes are calibrated in agar solutions of known diffusivities. To measure local flow velocity, mass transfer electrodes are calibrated in water flowing at a known flow velocity. Examples of such applications are described in Chapter 9.

4.2.6   Fiber optic microsensors

At the current state of technology, fiber optic microsensors are used in biofilm research to quantify the concentrations of chromophores added to a biofilm or present in the biofilm microorganisms rather than immobilized on the tip of a fiber. An example of such an application is the sensor we developed to measure the intensity of fluorescent light emanating from microorganisms tagged with a reporter gene and expressing yellow fluorescent protein, YFP. In this section, two fiber optic sensors that were constructed and used in our laboratory will be discussed: (1) an optical sensor to measure backscattered light intensity and (2) an optical sensor to measure fluorescent light intensity in biofilms. The construction of the sensor tip is the same in these two cases. What is different is the electronics used to run the sensor and collect the data.

The intensity of backscattered light is a function of local properties of the biofilm matrix such as the density of the microbial cells and the concentration of mineral deposits. In our applications, the main driving force behind using such a sensor was the hope that we could replace the measurements of diffusivity with measurements of backscattered light intensity. Measuring diffusivity in biofilms is a time-consuming procedure, and because of the nature of the setup (see Chapter 9) it can only be used in laboratory conditions. Backscattered light intensity and effective diffusivity are both functions of biofilm density, so we intended to calibrate the fiber optic sensor that measures backscattered light intensity in the units of effective diffusivity. The principle of measuring backscattered light intensity is shown in Figure 4.46.

The sensor proved to be more responsive than we expected: it responded not only to variation in biofilm density but also to variation in the concentration of particulate matter in the biofilm, an effect that is predictable from the principles of backscattered light

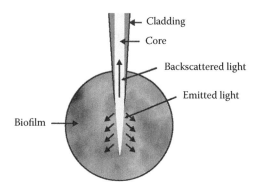

Figure 4.46 Fiber optic sensor for measuring backscattered light intensity in a biofilm.

measurements. Backscattered light can be caused by Fresnel reflection at the fiber tip, fluorescence in the biofilm, or backscattering from microstructures in the biofilm. Fresnel reflection is described as the reflection of a portion of the incident light from a discrete interface between two media having different refractive indices (e.g., the tip of a fiber optic cable and a biofilm). Scattering due to microstructures in the biofilm is another cause of the observed backscattered light. Scattering of light by particles or refractive index inhomogeneities of a size on the order of the wavelength of interest is called Mie scattering. Dimensionless parameter q is used to characterize an optical scattering process:

$$q = 2\pi n' r_o / \lambda_o \tag{4.75}$$

where n' is the refractive index of the medium in which the scatterers are immersed, r_o is the average scatterer radius, and λ_o is the wavelength of light in free space (Born and Wolf 1980). When the particle size is small compared to the wavelength of the light, $q \ll 1$, the resulting Rayleigh scattering has a scattering dependence which, for a fixed particle size, r_o, varies as λ_o^{-4} (Born and Wolf 1980). As the particle size becomes comparable to the wavelength, $q \geq 1$, the resulting Mie scattering develops a complicated dependence on λ_o. For very large particles, $q \gg 1$, geometric optics are used to describe the scattering process. All of these scattering processes depend linearly on the volume density of the light-scattering particles in the medium. Although measuring backscattered light has not replaced the measurement of effective diffusivity, the sensor has the potential for evaluating the concentration and/or the size distribution of particulate matter imbedded in biofilm matrix.

Figure 4.47 shows a schematic diagram of our fiber optic system. As the source of light, we use a laser diode, which is the preferred light source because of its high light coupling efficiency. A coupler is used to couple the light to the sensor and to couple the backscattered light to the measurement system. The reference and backscattered light intensities are measured using photodiodes.

The second application of fiber optic sensors that we have explored is measuring fluorescent light intensity in biofilms. The fiber optic part of the sensor is identical to that described in the previous section, but the optical system differs slightly from that shown in Figure 4.46. The most important difference is perhaps the necessity of selecting the light source according to the application, which is not always possible because the choice is limited. Laser diodes are available at certain frequencies and not available at other frequencies. For example, to measure green fluorescent light intensity in biofilms, a light source at 488 nm is used because GFP is excited at 488 nm. Fluorescent light is measured

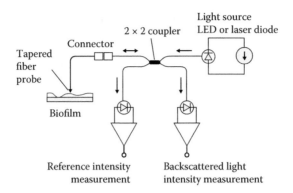

Figure 4.47 Schematic diagram of fiber optic system.

at 515 nm because GFP emits light at 515 nm. However, when we designed our optical system, 488-nm laser diodes were not available and we had to use a 405-nm laser diode instead. Figure 4.48 shows the setup we used.

Fiber optic sensors offer important advantages over electrochemical sensors: freedom from electromagnetic interference, internal optical reference, compactness, and geometric versatility. Some optical fibers can withstand high temperatures, aggressive chemicals, and other harsh environments. However, technical difficulties in making fiber optic sensors with small tips, which are required to make them useful in biofilm research, inhibit both the construction of fiber optic microsensors and their application to probing biofilms. The main problem is that when the size of the tip of the fiber optic sensor is decreased, the performance of the sensor deteriorates rapidly because of light coupling problems. Therefore, typical fiber optic microsensors have tip diameters much larger than 20 μm, and such sensors may damage biofilm structure. Attempting to immobilize various substances on the tips of such sensors makes them even bigger, so that their use in biofilm studies is questionable. We constructed and successfully used backscattering and fluorescent light intensity microsensors in biofilms and managed to keep their tip diameters reasonably small because we did not need to immobilize any reagents on their tips. It is unfortunate that the impressive advances in developing macroscale fiber optic sensors have not been paralleled by advances in developing fiber optic microsensors useful for studying biofilms.

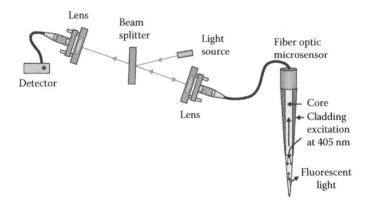

Figure 4.48 Fiber optic sensor for measuring fluorescent light intensity in biofilms.

Nomenclature

Subscripts

a   Anodic
b   Cathodic

Roman symbols

Symbol	Meaning	Usual units
A	Surface area	m^2, cm^2
B	Constant	V
C	Concentration of electroactive chemical reactant	Mol/m^3
C_o	Concentration in the bulk solution	Mol/m^3
C_s	Concentration on the electrode surface	Mol/m^3
d	Thickness of the membrane	m
D	Diffusion coefficient	m^2/s
E	Potential of an electrode against a reference	V
E^o	Standard potential of an electrode	V
	Standard emf of a half-reaction	V
	Standard redox potential	
E'	Potential of the entire electrochemical cell	V
E_{1-j}	Potential across the liquid junction membrane	V
E_{cell}	Potential across the electrochemical cell	V
E_{red}	Reduction potential	V
E_{oxid}	Oxidation potential	V
$E_{cathode}$	Cathode potential	V
E_{anode}	Anode potential	V
$E^o_{cathode}$	Standard cathode potential	V
E^o_{anode}	Standard anode potential	V
E_{int}	Potential across the interface of the internal reference electrode	V
E_h	Redox potential	V
E_L	Electrode potential in the half-cell on the left-hand side of the membrane	V
E_R	Electrode potential in the half-cell on the right-hand side of the membrane	V
E_{ind}	Potential of the indicator electrode	V
E_{ref}	Potential of the reference electrode	V
E_{1-j}	Liquid junction potential	V
E_{LIX}	Potential across the liquid ion exchange membrane	V
$E_{equilibrium}$	Actual potential of the electrode	V
E_{OCV}	Open circuit cell voltage	V
E_{ref}	Potential across the interface of the external reference electrode	V
EPE_A	Electric potential energy at location A	V
EPE_B	Electric potential energy at location B	V
F	Faraday constant: charge of one mole of electrons	$C\ mol^{-1}$
G	Gibbs free energy	kJ, kJ/mol
ΔG	Gibbs free energy change in a chemical process	kJ, kJ/mol
ΔG^o	Standard Gibbs free energy change in a chemical process	kJ, kJ/mol

i	Current density	$A/m^2, A/cm^2$
I	Current	A
I_l	Light emission intensity in the absence of the quencher	
I_{lim}	Limiting current	A
I_{lo}	Light emission intensity in the presence of the quencher	
J	Flux of electroactive chemical to the electrode surface	$Moles/m^2 h$
k	Mass transport coefficient	m/s
K	Equilibrium constant	
k_q	The quencher rate coefficient	L/mol s
K_{SV}	Stern–Volmer quenching constant	L/mol
L	Path length	cm
m	Number of protons generated in the reaction	
n	Stoichiometric number of electrons involved in oxidation/reduction reactions	
n'	Refractive index	
P_m	Permeability coefficient of the membrane	cm^{-1} or m/s
R	Ideal gas constant	J/mol K
R_{cell}	Ohmic resistance of the components of the entire cell	Ω
Q	Reaction quotient	
q_o	Electric charge	C
r_o	Average scatterer radius	M
x	Distance from the electrode surface	m
T	Absolute temperature	K
t	Time	S
V	Electric potential	V
V_{AB}	Electric potential difference between A and B	V
W_{AB}	Energy used to transfer an electric charge from location A to location B	J

Greek symbols

Symbol	Meaning	Usual units
τ	Fluorescence lifetime in the presence of the quencher	s
τ_o	Fluorescence lifetime in the absence of the quencher	s
λ_o	Wavelength of light in free space	nm
α_l	Absorption coefficient	cm^{-1}
η	Overpotential	V
δ	Thickness of the diffusion (mass) boundary layer	cm, m

References

Babauta, T. J., Nguyen, H. D., and Beyenal, H. 2011. Redox and pH microenvironments within *Shewanella oneidensis* MR-1 biofilms reveal electron transfer mechanisms. *Environmental Science and Technology* 45: 6654–6660.

Bishop, P. L., and Yu, T. 1999. A microelectrode study of redox potential change in biofilms. *Water Science and Technology* 39(7): 179–185.

Born, M., and Wolf, E. 1980. *Principles of Optics*, 6th ed. New York: Pergamon Press.

Cronenberg, C. C. H., and van den Heuvel, J. C. 1991. Determination of glucose diffusion coefficients in biofilms with microelectrodes. *Biosensors and Bioelectronics* 6: 255–262.

De Beer, D., Glud, A., Epping, E., and Kuhl, M. 1997. A fast-responding CO_2 microelectrode for profiling sediments, microbial mats and biofilms. *Limnology and Oceanography* 42: 1590–1600.

Giggenbach, W. 1971. Optical spectra of highly alkaline sulfide solutions and second dissociation constant of hydrogen sulfide. *Inorganic Chemistry* 10: 1333.

Jorgensen, B. B., and Revsbech, N. P. 1988. Microsensors. *Methods in Enzymology* 167: 639–659.

Myers, R. J. 1986. The new low value for the second dissociation constant for H_2S. *Journal of Chemical Education* 63: 687.

Nguyan, H. D., Renslow, R., Babauta, J., Ahmed, B., and Beyenal, H. 2012. A voltammetric flavin microelectrode for use in biofilms. *Sensors and Actuators B: Chemical* 161: 929–937.

Van Houdt, P., Lewandowski, Z., and Little, B. 1992. Iridium oxide pH microelectrode. *Biotechnology and Bioengineering* 40: 601–608.

Zhang, T. C., and Pang, H. 1999. Applications of microelectrode techniques to measure pH and oxidation-reduction potential in rhizosphere soil. *Environmental Science and Technology* 33(8): 1293–1299.

Suggested readings

Amman, D. 1986. *Ion-Selective Microelectrodes: Principles, Design, and Application.* Berlin: Springer-Verlag.

Bard, E. J., and Faulkner, L. R. 2000. *Electrochemical Methods: Fundamentals and Applications.* New York: John Wiley.

Harris, D. C. 1991. *Quantitative Chemical Analysis.* New York: W.H. Freeman.

Istanbullu, O., Babauta, J., Nguyen, H. D., and Beyenal, H. 2012. Electrochemical biofilm control: Mechanism of action. *Biofouling* 28: 769–778.

Jeroschewski, P., Haase, K., Trommer, A., and Grundler, P. 1994. Galvanic sensor for determination of hydrogen sulfide. *Electroanalysis* 6: 769–772.

Revsbech, N. P. 1989. An oxygen microsensor with a guard cathode. *Limnology and Oceanography* 34: 474–478.

Sawyer, D., Sobkowiak, A., and Roberts, J. L. Jr. 1995. *Electrochemistry for Chemists.* New York: John Wiley.

Thomas, R. C. 1978. *Ion Selective Intracellular Microelectrodes, How to Make and Use Them.* London: Academic Press.

Turner, A. P. F., Karube, I., and Wilson, G. S. (Eds.). 1987. *Biosensors, Fundamentals and Application.* New York: Oxford University Press.

Wang, J. 2006. *Analytical Electrochemistry.* New York: John Wiley.

Yu, T. R., and Ji, G. L. 1993. *Electrochemical Methods in Soil and Water Research.* Oxford: Pergamon Press.

chapter five

Microsensors: Construction, instrumentation, and calibration

5.1   Introduction

Two types of microsensors are popular in biofilm research: microelectrodes and microoptodes. Both deliver information about the physical and chemical characteristics of biofilms that is difficult to obtain otherwise. The necessity of penetrating biofilms without changing their structure determines the shape of the microsensors—elongated narrow tools, tapered to a small tip at the sensing end. Some types of microsensors useful in biofilm research are available commercially, but the mainstream of biofilm research still relies on individual researchers who manufacture their own microsensors. The procedures used in constructing microelectrodes and microoptodes will be discussed here, as well as the instruments used to operate and to calibrate them. These procedures have been tested in our laboratory, and they deliver serviceable microsensors.

Manufacturing microsensors requires a commitment of time and resources. If just a few measurements in a biofilm are needed, it is better to either buy the microsensors or collaborate with someone who makes them rather than try to construct them in the laboratory. Constructing microsensors remains a craft that is learned by trial and error. Procedures for making new microsensors or improving existing ones are often disseminated as informal communication among researchers rather than as precise protocols listing the materials and procedures used in their manufacture. Before starting your own microsensor laboratory, it is important to actually visit a laboratory manufacturing microsensors and get a sense of what is required to start this activity. Our own involvement in manufacturing microsensors started in the 1980s with our visits to the laboratory of Niels Peter Revsbech at the University of Aarchus in Denmark and has continued with our collaboration with that group of researchers. Over the years, we have developed our own procedures and modified some of the existing procedures, and we now offer a series of workshops to help others who want to start constructing microsensors on their own. Much of the material in this chapter has been extracted from the notes and handouts we use during these workshops. These procedures for developing microsensors have been tested and refined by a number of biofilm researchers. They work well in our laboratory, and we have examples of other laboratories that have started to construct microsensors based on these notes.

We show here a set of tools and procedures that we use in our laboratory; some of these tools and procedures can, and probably should, be modified to fit the needs of your laboratory and to reflect the personal preferences, manual skills, and financial resources available. The set of tools we are using is not invariable: new tools and procedures are being developed all the time in our laboratory and in other laboratories. We constantly monitor, by personal communication and by reading published papers, the procedures used in other laboratories developing microsensors similar to those we construct. From these contacts, we know that even when the tools that biofilm researchers use to make microsensors have the same names, the actual design of the tools can vary considerably from one laboratory to another. These differences, to some extent, reflect the personal preferences of the researchers who manufacture the microsensors and, to some extent, reflect the availability of funds designated for the operation of the microsensor laboratory. Researchers who want to develop their own microsensor laboratories often ask about the initial investment. There is no precise answer to this question, of course. One aspect of the answer is, however, worth exposing. Without attempting to deny the importance of adequate funding, we always assure the participants of our workshops that the ingenuity of the researchers manufacturing the microsensors is at least as important as the funds available for purchasing specialized equipment. Microsensors can be manufactured in an elaborate and expensive way or in a less glamorous, but much more affordable, way. The materials used and the steps in the procedures for manufacturing parts of microsensors vary from one laboratory to another, depending on the preferences of the researchers and the available equipment. However, the availability of funds is not necessarily the primary factor that limits the initial development. Dedication to the task, commitment of the time, knowledge and ingenuity of the researchers, and available resources—in that order—will decide whether a newly established laboratory will succeed in manufacturing microsensors. It is also important that the researchers involved have a good grasp of the electrochemical principles involved in designing and using microsensors. These principles have been delineated in Chapter 4.

Typically, laboratories manufacturing microsensors designate a dedicated space for this activity. Not much is needed initially, but with time and developing expertise, the space required will expand. It is better to start making microsensors using primitive, homemade devices and practice various steps of constructing microsensors before buying specialized equipment. This way, the researcher developing the microsensors evaluates which procedures could be made more efficient or accurate by using specialized equipment and establishes priorities for purchasing equipment based on the problems he or she has to solve in particular steps of constructing microsensors rather than spending time mastering exotic pieces of equipment before the real needs have been assessed. It seems to be the rule rather than the exception that researchers who have succeeded in manufacturing microsensors and established their own microsensor laboratories were frugal and preferred to exercise total control over each piece of equipment they were using. They gained this level of control by designing their equipment and assembling it from parts, often salvaged from other instruments. In particular, in the initial stages of organizing a microsensor laboratory, the users should remember that the goal of establishing a microsensor laboratory is to make meaningful measurements using microsensors, not just to test new procedures and improve existing procedures. Falling into this trap is a real and present danger in all microsensor laboratories, such as those just starting and those already well established. It is wise to remember that even after spending weeks in the laboratory developing a new procedure and glamorous-looking microsensors, we have the microsensors, but we still do not have any results.

It is difficult to make the process of manufacturing microsensors a string of routine procedures, and the success of each procedure depends on the experience and manual skills of the operators. In the following section, we show several items of equipment that are useful for constructing microsensors. These pieces of equipment work for us, but they can be substituted for by similar devices or bypassed altogether if the researcher invents his or her own path to developing the final product using different procedures than those we use. In most cases we provide all the information about the manufacturer and where the equipment can be purchased. In some cases this was not possible because the manufacturer went out of business or could not be located.

5.2   Constructing microelectrodes

5.2.1   Materials

5.2.1.1   Platinum wire

Platinum (Pt) is a soft metal that is easy to work with. It is commonly used by electrochemists to manufacture various electrodes, and we use Pt wires to construct the working electrodes in several microelectrodes. Platinum is reasonably nonreactive in water solutions, and it is well known that protons in water easily equilibrate with hydrogen on platinum surfaces and that the exchange current density for hydrogen evolution is higher on platinum than it is on surfaces of other metals. Because of this, platinum is the electrode material of choice in the standard hydrogen electrodes (SHEs). To increase their reactive surface area, platinum wires are often covered with finely dispersed platinum particles (called *platinum black* or *platinized platinum*). We use 99.99% pure platinum wires, with diameters of either 50 or 100 µm, from the California Fine Wire Company (Figure 5.1). We start with wires of different diameters, depending on the desired tip diameter of the sensor: when we need to etch the tip of the wire to a diameter of approximately 1–2 µm, we start with the thinner wire, the 50-µm-diameter wire, but when we need to etch the tip of the wire to a diameter of approximately 5–10 µm, we start with the thicker wire, the 100-µm-diameter wire. To taper the tip of the wire to the desired diameter, the wire is etched electrochemically in potassium cyanide, KCN. Etching produces the best results when the Pt wires are used "as drawn" (not annealed). The as-drawn, unannealed platinum wires are made of long, fibrous grains, while the annealed wires are made of compact crystal grains of various sizes (Figure 5.1). These compact crystal grains do not change their sizes during etching; instead, they detach from the surface, leaving behind cavities, which produces rough, unevenly etched wires.

Figure 5.1 A roll of Pt wire. It is best to buy large quantities of Pt wire, a few hundred feet at a time, because the price per foot of the long wire is dramatically lower than the price per foot of short pieces of exactly the same wire.

5.2.1.2   Silver wire

Silver (Ag) is a soft metal that is easy to work with. We use silver wires of various diameters to construct Ag/AgCl internal and external reference electrodes (Figure 5.2). Depending on the application, we use either 100-μm-diameter wire from the California Fine Wire Company or 0.25-mm-diameter wire from Aldrich; both are 99.9% pure silver. As with platinum wire, the price per foot of the wire is much lower when you are buying a few hundred feet than when you are buying short pieces.

5.2.1.3   Iridium wire

We use iridium (Ir) wires to construct a certain type of pH microelectrodes that is based on the properties of iridium oxides. We do not describe this construction here, but you may find it described in our published papers (Van Houdt et al. 1992; Beyenal et al. 2004). Iridium is the most corrosion-resistant metal known: It is resistant to the common mineral acids at all temperatures and to cold and boiling aqua regia. Iridium wires are drawn at 600°C–700°C, which is below the recrystallization temperature. Wires that are drawn in such a way have a fibrous structure. In contrast to Pt or Ag wires, Ir wires are difficult to work with. Etching iridium wires is quite difficult in comparison to etching platinum or silver wires. We etch iridium wires using anodic polarization (at 10 V DC versus a graphite electrode) for 10 min in 0.5 M H_2SO_4. Iridium wire is much more expensive than silver and platinum wires are. We use a 75-μm-diameter iridium wire.

5.2.1.4   Wires for making heating elements

Much of the glasswork must be done under a stereomicroscope, and the glass must be softened and shaped appropriately. Glass components are mounted in the field of view of the microscope using various tools described later and heated using electrical heating elements made of wires of various diameters. The shape and diameter of these wires vary, depending on the procedure in which they are used; they may also vary depending on the stage of the procedure in which they are used. Two factors determine the diameter of the wire needed at a specific stage of a procedure: (1) the rate of heat delivery and (2) the dimensions of the heated zone. The best materials for the heating elements are wires made of metals with high melting points, and we use a variety of these. In the initial stages of manufacturing microelectrodes, when the glass micropipettes have thick walls and a substantial input of heat is needed to soften the glass, we use thicker, 0.02–0.026 inch, wires made of nickel-chrome alloy (Nichrome) (Figure 5.3a). In the later stages of

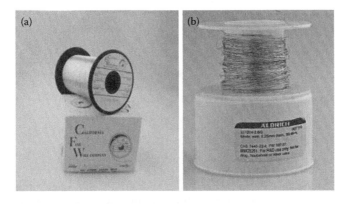

Figure 5.2 Two rolls of Ag wire: (a) 100 μm in diameter and (b) 0.25 mm in diameter.

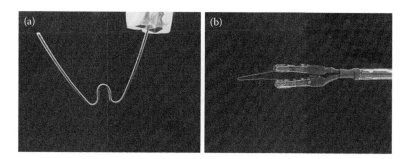

Figure 5.3 (a) An appropriately shaped Nichrome wire is used in the initial stages of construction. (b) A 100-μm Pt wire is used as a heating element when precise heat delivery is needed.

construction, when the micropipette walls are thinner and the heat must be delivered precisely to a restricted zone of the glass, we use heating elements made of 100-μm-thick platinum wires, which are the same wires we use to make the microelectrodes (Figure 5.3b). Heating elements are attached to various tools that help in positioning the heating elements in proximity to the zone that needs to be heated. Typically, in the initial stages of the procedures, when we work with components made of thicker glass, the heating elements are attached to stationary objects and the glass pipettes are attached to micromanipulators. Later, when the glass walls are thin, the heat delivery needs to be more precise, so the heating elements are attached to tools mounted on micromanipulators. The current delivered to the heating element is controlled using an adjustable power supplier, as will be described in this chapter.

5.2.1.5   Graphite rods

Graphite is a chemically resistant and electrically conducting material that has many applications in electrochemical studies (Figure 5.4). It can be purchased from specialized vendors in various shapes and sizes. It is desirable to use high-density, nonporous graphite, such as glassy graphite. We use graphite rods of various diameters to make counter electrodes for the electrolytic cells used to etch the tips of platinum and iridium wires.

Figure 5.4 A graphite rod installed in an electrolytic cell we use to etch the tips of Pt wires. The rod is connected to a DC source using an alligator clip.

5.2.1.6 Glasses

The variety of glass available on the market is impressive, and the task of finding the right type of glass can be confusing. Fortunately, there is no need for using exotic glasses to fabricate microelectrodes, and we try to keep our selection of glasses as simple as possible, limiting it to two or three types of glass. Limiting the number of glasses used has an important practical aspect. Each glass behaves differently when worked with, and testing too many types of glass for their usefulness in various procedures may easily become a project in itself. Glasses used to construct microelectrodes should satisfy simple requirements. For all procedures it is important to select glasses that soften at temperatures that are easily achieved using propane torches and electric heating elements. Using quartz glass is not a good idea, unless there is a valid reason for doing so. When glasses need to be fused, it is important to use glasses with similar coefficients of thermal expansion. Fused glasses having different thermal expansion coefficients will break near the fusing location. When an electrical wire is to be sealed in glass, it is better to use a glass with a high electrical resistance. A few parts of microelectrodes require glass with low electrical conductivity, but other parts can be made of inexpensive glass.

Some microsensors consist of several components combined in a common outer case. The material used for the outer case is not very demanding; we use the disposable glass Pasteur pipettes for the purpose (Figure 5.5a). They are made of a borosilicate glass, are inexpensive, soften at reasonable temperatures (about 785°C), and are reasonably strong. To make the internal components of the microelectrodes, we use glasses with low electrical conductivity, such as Corning 8161 (Potash Rubium Lead) Patch Clamp Glass, 1.5-mm outer diameter (Figure 5.5b). This glass has good electrical properties and is suitable for low-noise recordings. It has a softening point of about 600°C.

We prepare our microelectrodes using Corning 8161, which is designed for low-noise recordings. However, it is quite acceptable to use the less expensive ordinary lead glass instead of the more expensive Corning 8161 (http://www.macbicnj.com/). Ordinary lead glass behaves very similarly to that made by Corning. The background current of the sensors made using the Corning 8161 glass is lower than the background current of the sensors made of ordinary lead glass, but both glasses can be used. When buying lead glass, it is advisable to find a general supplier of glass and buy a reasonably large supply of 1.5- or 2-mm tubes. We buy bulk lead glass from general suppliers rather than precut small pieces of glass from specialized vendors; it is much less expensive this way.

We have spent some time experimenting with another type of glass with good electrical properties, Schott 8533, known as *green glass* (Schott Glaswerke, F.R.G.) (Revsbech

Figure 5.5 (a) Pasteur pipettes (Fisher #13-678-20C). (b) Corning 8161 (Potash Rubium Lead) patch clamp glass, 1.5-mm outer diameter.

1989). This glass has very good electrical properties, and microelectrodes sealed in it have negligibly small residual currents. However, it is quite expensive compared to the other glasses we use, and the procedure for its use is difficult. Because of its high cost, it is used for the tips of the electrodes only, so it must be fused to another capillary, made of less expensive glass, such as lead glass. Fusing two glasses increases the number of steps in the procedure and increases the probability that something will go wrong. After the glasses are fused, the remaining steps of the procedure are the same as those described here for capillaries made of a single piece of Corning 8161 glass. When using the green glass, make sure that the fusion of the two glasses is done properly, with no leaks. If the fusing is faulty, the microelectrode will not work.

5.2.1.7   Liquid ion exchangers

Liquid ion exchangers (LIXs) are often used as membranes in ion-selective electrodes. LIXs have three components: (1) the ion-selective compound or carrier (most often a neutral ligand), (2) a membrane solvent or plasticizer in which the carrier is dissolved, and (3) a membrane additive (a lipophilic salt). The carrier is dissolved in the solvent, which must be nonpolar (to reject hydrophilic ions and allow the solubilization of lipophilic compounds) and of moderate viscosity (to allow a microelectrode to fill easily). Additives produce significant improvements in selectivity and decrease membrane electrical resistance and response time. There are many neutral carriers or ligands available to bind a variety of ions that are biologically important: Na^+, K^+, H^+, Ca^{2+}, Mg^{2+}, and Cl^-. We use Fluka® chemicals to prepare the membranes of pH microelectrodes, and we use two types of membranes: (1) ready-to-use membranes, when available, and (2) membranes that we prepare in our laboratory.

5.2.1.7.1   Ready-to-use membranes.   We use a cocktail, Fluka 95297, as the LIX for pH microelectrodes (Figure 5.6). The cocktail is made of the following components: The carrier is 4-nonadecylpyridine (6%), the solvent is 2-nitrophenyloctylether (NPOE), and the additive that reduces the resistance of the membrane is potassium tetrakis (4-chlorophenyl) borate (1%). If needed, the membranes can be solidified with high-molecular-weight PVC (Fluka #81392) added to a final concentration of 10%–30% PVC. Before use, the PVC

Figure 5.6 Photo of liquid ion exchange (LIX) containers: (left) An ionophore container; (middle) an empty container that we use for homemade cocktails; (right) a ready-to-use cocktail. The ionophore containers have conically shaped inner walls because the volume of the solution is low (100 µL) and the conical shape of the walls increases the depth of the container and facilitates handling the liquid.

is dissolved in tetrahydrofuran (THF, Fluka #87369). Do not use laboratory-grade THF, because it contains stabilizing agents that destroy the membrane carrier. The PVC solution and the carrier can be mixed and stored for several months in a well-sealed container at room temperature, kept in the dark. As an additional solidifying agent, 5% nitrocellulose can be added. Solidified membranes are preferred when there is a high shear in the measurement system. High shear dislocates the liquid membranes and causes noisy measurements. It is important to keep all chemicals clean: dust particles have a deleterious effect.

5.2.1.7.2 Membranes that we prepare in our laboratory.   We prepare membranes for pH microelectrodes by mixing the following cocktail (all reagents from Fluka, names followed by the catalog number):

   1.0 wt.% Hydrogen ionophore I (95292)
   65.50 wt.% Bis(I-buthylpentyl) decane-1, 10-diyl diglutarate (30585)
   0.50 wt.% Potassium tetrakis (4-chlorophenyl) borate (60591)
   33.00 wt.% High-molecular-weight poly(vinyl chloride) (81392)

This cocktail is dissolved in 2–3 times its volume of tetrahydrofuran. To improve the mechanical properties of the membranes, an additional solidifying agent, 5% nitrocellulose, can be added if the measurements are conducted at high flow rates (above 10 cm/s linear liquid flow velocity). When making membranes for microelectrodes other than pH microelectrodes, only the ionophore has to be replaced. For example, to make microelectrodes sensitive to ammonium, we use an ammonium ionophore (09877) instead of the hydrogen ionophore listed above.

5.2.1.8   List of materials we use to construct microelectrodes

Table 5.1 summarizes the materials we use to construct microelectrodes. Some of the ion-selective microelectrodes based on LIX membranes constructed in our laboratory are listed in Table 5.2. You may refer to http://www.sigmaaldrich.com/ for more information about various ionophores available from that vendor for making ion-selective microelectrodes. Also, Fluka Chemie AG publishes a catalog, "Selectophore®, Ionophores for Ion Selective Electrodes and Optodes," which contains detailed information about numerous products useful for constructing ion-sensitive electrodes.

5.2.2   Tools and instruments for constructing microelectrodes

5.2.2.1   Micropipette pullers

Microelectrodes are often used by researchers in electrophysiology, and there is a large market developed to satisfy their demands. One of the many devices available for constructing microelectrodes is the microelectrode puller, which, in principle at least, simplifies making micropipettes. Micropipette pullers available on the market can be very complicated and quite expensive. Some pullers are vertical, and some are horizontal. The micropipettes that can be mounted and pulled are relatively small, often limited to 1 mm in diameter and a few centimeters in length, which restricts the usefulness of these devices for constructing microelectrodes for biofilm studies. The diameters of the outer cases or shafts of these microelectrodes often exceed 1 mm.

Some micropipette pullers are entirely controlled by microprocessors and allow the user to design the pulling of micropipettes in several stages and to control the temperature and the tensile strength applied to the ends of the micropipette at each stage. In principle,

Table 5.1 Materials We Use to Construct Microelectrodes

Components	Sources
Platinum wire	100 or 50 µm in diameter, 99.99% pure, as drawn http://www.calfinewire.com
Silver wire	100 µm in diameter, 99.99% pure http://www.calfinewire.com For thicker wires: http://www.sigma-aldrich. com/, catalog no. 327034
Iridium wire	100 µm in diameter, http://www.engelhard.com
Heating elements	Nichrome coiled heating elements http://www.aeroconsystems.com/electronics/ nichrome.htm
Graphite rods	www.sigma-aldrich.com/, catalog no. 496537
Glass	Pasteur pipettes from Fisher (http://www. fisherscientific.com/) catalog no. 13-678-20C Corning 8161 (Potash Rubium Lead) http://www. corning.com/ Schott 8533 http://www.us.schott.com/english/ index.html http://www.macbicnj.com/ We buy large quantities of glass tubings with various diameters from them. You can obtain information about standard wall tubing from Corning and Kimble.
Borosilicate, aluminosilicate, and pH-sensitive glass, fused and theta-style capillaries, Teflon-coated silver wire	http://www.warnerinstrument.com/
Glass, including thick-septum theta tubing, membrane solutions	World Precision Instruments, Inc. http://www.wpiinc.com/
Liquid membrane solutions and components for practically all ions, silanizing agents	Fluka Chemie AG, CH-9470 Buchs, Switzerland In the US, Fluka products are distributed by Sigma Aldrich at http://www.sigmaaldrich.com

Note: We do not promote any of the products specified in the table. We use these products, and we are satisfied with their performance, but there are other vendors and other products that may be used as substitutes with equally good results. Use the table as a point of departure to establish your own network of suppliers.

Table 5.2 Ion-Selective Microelectrodes Constructed in Our Laboratory

Measured ion	Liquid membrane	Filling solution (mmol/L)	Comments
H^+	Fluka 95292 (see custom membrane preparation for details)	NaCl–100 KH_2PO_4–250 Na_2HPO_4–250	For pH 4.5–11
H^+	Fluka 95297 (ready-to-use liquid membrane)	NaCl–100 KH_2PO_4–250 Na_2HPO_4–250	For pH 1.3–9.8
NH_4^+	Fluka 09879	NH_4Cl–10	

these devices allow the user to pull micropipettes reproducibly. We have tried some of these pullers and found them unnecessarily complicated and not particularly useful for constructing the types of microelectrodes we use. In our opinion, micropipette pullers have limited application in constructing microelectrodes for biofilm research. We still use components of one vertical puller, Stoelting Co., catalog no. 51217, which has a very sturdy construction and allows the pulling of glass pipettes up to a few millimeters in diameter. Most of the time, however, we use only the rack and the heating components of the puller and attach our own micromanipulators and illuminators to the rack. We do not use the magnetic puller of the device at all because we can control the shape of the tip by adjusting the amount of heat and using the force of gravity with much greater precision than can be achieved using magnetic pull. This puller is rigidly constructed, and it is a central piece on the workbench where we construct microelectrodes (Figure 5.7).

To pull glass micropipettes using gravity, we use heating elements made of wires of various diameters to deliver heat; after the glass softens, it slowly slides down, pulled by gravity. We monitor the area where the heat is delivered using a stereomicroscope and control the amount of heat delivered during the process, depending on how the glass behaves.

5.2.2.2 *Antivibration tables*
Antivibration tables are available from specialized vendors. The tops of these tables float suspended on the air cushions of a pneumatic system. We use a table (LW Series Light Load Vibration Isolation Workstation, LW-3060-0321) from Newport. We found the antivibration function of the table neither necessary nor desirable; if anything, we found it annoying. We use the table because it is very heavy and very sturdy, and because it has a metal top to which we can attach various tools using magnetic holders. By sheer weight this table provides stability to the components mounted on its top. However, if available resources are limited, a heavy metal plate placed on a sturdy lab table is probably equally useful.

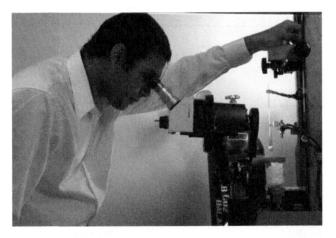

Figure 5.7 A large vertical microelectrode puller is useful, although it is not indispensable. We use a puller made by Stoelting Co., catalog no. 51217, http://www.stoeltingco.com/, Stoelting Co., 620 Wheat Lane, Wood Dale, Illinois 60191, USA. The puller allows one to change the level of the heating element. To adjust the position of the micropipette, we use a micromanipulator attached to the puller. Once the micropipette separates, it is cached in the small beaker at the bottom.

5.2.2.3   Stereomicroscopes and microscope holders

In many steps in the process of constructing microelectrodes, the components are too bulky to be placed under light microscopes and are monitored using stereomicroscopes. Besides that, the initial phases of construction use a large amount of heat, which would damage an optical microscope. We use Leica Stereo Zoom 7 microscopes (Figure 5.8) with zoom optics (from 10× to 70× magnification). All our microscopes have attachments for cameras; the image in the field of view of the operator is also shown on the screen of a TV monitor. If the available resources permit, it is best to have a few such microscopes and have some of them dedicated to certain tasks to avoid the necessity of constantly transferring microscopes from one location to another and changing their adjustments. We have three stereomicroscopes: One is attached to the micropipette puller, one is attached to the microgrinder, and one is not designated for any specific procedure. The microscope attached to the micropipette puller is mounted on a very sturdy holder (Figure 5.8b) and is positioned so that the heating element is visible in its field of view. It is equipped with a circular illuminator to improve the visibility of the component positioned in the field of view. When heat is applied to the heat element, and the glass starts to flow, the operator monitors the glass flow through the stereomicroscope and, based on the progress, decides whether to increase the heat, decrease the heat, or discontinue heating. The stereomicroscope attached to the grinding wheel is used to monitor the progress of grinding the tips of microelectrodes. To improve the visibility of the tip being ground, this microscope is attached to an adjustable holder. This holder is less sturdy than the one we use with the stereomicroscope used to monitor micropipette pulling, but it offers movements in many directions, which is essential in monitoring this procedure. The operator monitors the process of grinding and, depending on the progress, decides whether to lower the micropipette further or discontinue the grinding.

5.2.2.4   Light microscopes

We use upright and inverted microscopes. The upright microscopes are almost exclusively used during the construction of the microsensors, and the inverted microscopes are used during the measurements.

5.2.2.4.1   Upright microscopes.   Several steps in constructing microelectrodes, such as electroplating the tips of the electrodes and mounting the sensors in a common case,

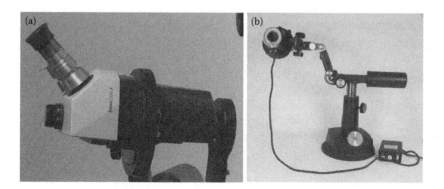

Figure 5.8 (a) Stereomicroscopes are useful during microelectrode pulling and when the tips of micropipettes are being ground. We use optics with a wide-angle zoom, from 10× to 70× (7:1 zoom). (b) The stereomicroscope holder.

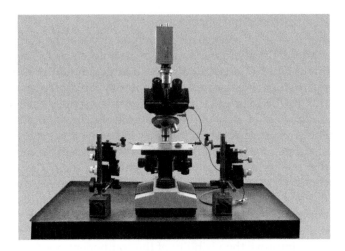

Figure 5.9 Microelectrodes under an upright light microscope. The microscope is placed on a metal base so that we can attach magnetic holders supporting micromanipulators.

require using light microscopes. The stages of these microscopes are not always used: some components we work with are mounted in micromanipulators, and their positions are adjusted so they are focused on the field of view. Because some components of the microelectrodes are opaque and some are transparent, it helps to illuminate these components using a mixture of light from above and light from below. One of our microscopes, a Nikon Optiphot-POL (Figure 5.9), has two illuminators, one above and one below, allowing us to mix transmitted and reflected light. With the microscopes for which this feature is not available, we use the transmitted light from the illuminator built into the microscope and reflected light from external fiber optic illuminators. We use upright microscopes (Figure 5.9) during microelectrode construction to inspect the tips of the microsensors and to diagnose the reasons for sensor malfunction. Sometimes the tip of a sensor is cracked, which is impossible to detect with an unaided eye. A quick inspection of the microsensor tip can often answer the question of why the sensor is not responding the way it should.

5.2.2.4.2 Inverted microscopes. For many measurements it is desirable to monitor the structure of the biofilm and the position of a microsensor in the biofilm at the same time. The upright microscopes do not have enough space between the lens and the object for a microsensor to be inserted. We have to insert the microsensor from the top and monitor the biofilm from the bottom. Inverted microscopes are useful tools in such instances. We position flat plate biofilm reactors on the stages of these microscopes and monitor the biofilm structure and the position of the microsensor tip through the bottom. Because biofilm reactors typically are attached to the microscopes and remain there for weeks, the inverted microscopes need to be rather sturdy. We use Olympus CK2 (Figure 5.10) or IMT-2.

5.2.2.5 Grinding wheels

When micropipettes have been drawn to the proper tip diameters, the tips of the micropipettes need to be trimmed and polished. Grinders useful for this purpose are available on the market. Their grinding wheels are covered with diamond particles and are suspended on air bearings to prevent vibrations. During the grinding process, the micropipette,

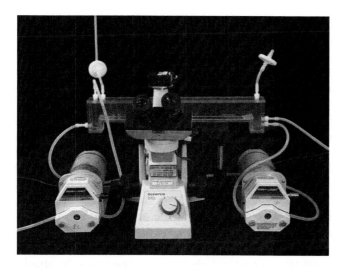

Figure 5.10 An inverted microscope. We place the biofilm reactor on top of the microscope and image the biofilm and the location of the microelectrode tip from the bottom.

attached to a micropositioner, is slowly lowered until its tip touches the rotating wheel. The surface of the grinder is illuminated using a fiber optic illuminator, and the progress of grinding the tip is monitored using a stereomicroscope. We use a diamond grinding wheel (Narishige, Model EG-4) (Figure 5.11) and we monitor the image of the tip being ground using a Leica Stereo Zoom 7.

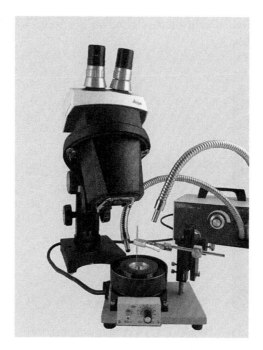

Figure 5.11 The grinder we use to polish the tips of glass micropipettes. The tip of the micropipette is illuminated using a fiber optic illuminator, and the grinding process is monitored using a stereomicroscope.

5.2.2.6   Micromanipulators

Many types of micromanipulators can be purchased from specialized vendors, and some are very precise and expensive. There are three types of procedures in microsensor laboratories that require micromanipulators: (1) positioning and holding in place various parts of microelectrodes during their construction, (2) positioning microelectrodes in biofilms during measurements, and (3) positioning biofilm reactors. Depending on the needs, we use one-dimensional (1-D) positioners (linear positioners), two-dimensional (2-D) positioners (positioning tables), and three-dimensional (3-D) positioners (micromanipulators). The most useful for constructing microelectrodes are the 3-D micromanipulators, which are truly indispensable pieces of equipment in microsensor laboratories. They do not have to be extremely precise, but they do have to be rigid and sturdy enough to hold the microsensor in place and to control its movement during various steps of construction. The entire setup used to construct microelectrodes must be heavy and rigid; otherwise, parts of the microelectrodes will vibrate in the field of view of the microscope, making it difficult to monitor the progress of the construction. The 3-D micromanipulators we use (from World Precision Instruments) are not particularly heavy, so they must be attached to heavy, rigid stands. Magnetic holders are often used to hold micromanipulators, and they are very convenient and handy; we have several magnetic holders from Narishige®. They are not very heavy, but they are rigid and firmly attached to the metal top of the table, which needs to be heavy and rigid. Using magnetic holders requires that you either have a heavy metal table or cover a part of the construction bench with a heavy metal plate that can hold magnetic holders. We place the light microscopes on such plates, so that we can attach magnetic holders with micromanipulators holding the parts of the microelectrodes with which we are working (Figure 5.12). Magnetic holders can easily be attached and detached from the table.

The use of 1-D positioners will be discussed in Section 5.4.3, where microelectrode measurements are described.

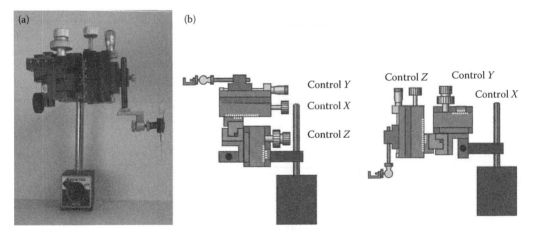

Figure 5.12 A micromanipulator (World Precision Instruments) with a microelectrode attached using a microelectrode holder: (a) mounted on a metal base using a magnetic stand (GJ-1 Magnetic Stand, Narishige) and (b) attached to magnetic stands to facilitate precise movement using control Z in the horizontal or lateral direction.

5.2.2.7   Microelectrode holders

Micromanipulators are not equipped with microelectrode holders; these holders need to be purchased separately. We use very convenient holders made by World Precision Instruments. These holders have a ball head that can be adjusted at various positions, providing additional degrees of freedom when manipulating microelectrodes (Figure 5.13).

5.2.2.8   Illuminators

Various types of illuminators can be purchased from specialized vendors, and these are truly indispensable pieces of equipment in the microsensor laboratory. Most procedures for manufacturing microelectrodes require good illumination, often combined with magnifying devices, such as stereomicroscopes and loupes. In some procedures it is challenging to illuminate the work space because of all the equipment needed for constructing microelecrodes: we use stereomicroscopes, micromanipulators, micropipette holders, and heating elements with holders, all at the same time. It is difficult to illuminate such a work space using stationary light sources because, with so many pieces of equipment crammed into a small space, the components of the setup cast shadows on each other, and it is impossible to find a good position for the illuminator. In such cases, fiber optic illuminators are indispensable. The flexible optical cables can be woven among other tools and illuminate the workplace even when we use many tools at the same time. We use fiber optic illuminators from Cuda Products and circular illuminators, attached to stereomicroscopes, from MicroLite (Figure 5.14). Stationary lamps are useful, too, particularly when the procedures require illuminating larger areas of the work bench. Specialized illuminators that can be attached to certain tools are also available, and some are useful. For example, the circular illuminators that can be attached to the front parts of stereomicroscopes and illuminate the object in the field of view are very useful (Figure 5.14).

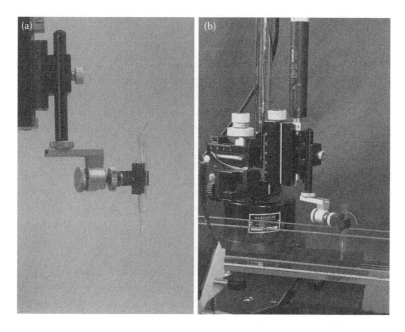

Figure 5.13 A microelectrode holder (a) holding a pH microelectrode and (b) in the reactor.

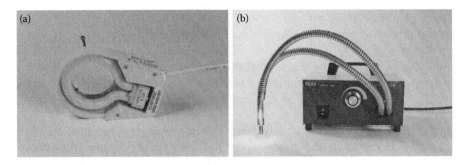

Figure 5.14 (a) A fluorescent circular illuminator that can be attached to a stereomicroscope and (b) a light source with a fiber optic illuminator (Cuda Products).

It is important that all illuminators allow for the continuous control of light intensity. Often the right mixture of lights of different intensities from multiple sources produces the most desirable effect. Light microscopes come equipped with illuminators. However, except for specialized microscopes such as those used by metallurgists, the illuminators are designed to illuminate transparent objects. This type of illumination is not necessarily the best for manufacturing microelectrodes because some components of microelectrodes, such as wires, are opaque and others, made of glass, are transparent. Fiber optic illuminators can be combined with light microscopes and used as external sources of light to illuminate objects positioned on the stages of light microscopes. The light from a fiber optic illuminator is directed onto the object under the microscope from above, and the appropriate mixture of transmitted and reflected light can be set to maximize the visibility of the object under the microscope. We also have a Nikon Optiphot-POL microscope, which is equipped with two illuminators, one for transparent specimens and one for opaque specimens. The two illuminators can be used simultaneously to achieve the right mixture of illumination.

5.2.2.9 Power supplies

Power supplies, both AC and DC, have many uses in laboratories manufacturing microsensors. We use them to control the electric current delivered to (1) the heating elements, (2) the electronic circuits used for etching wires, and (3) the electrodes during electroplating of the tips of the microelectrodes. Power supplies can be purchased from specialized vendors, but they may also be available from local hardware stores. Not all of the commercially available power supplies are directly applicable in the procedures for making microelectrodes, though. To obtain the right combination of current and potential to achieve the desired effects, for some procedures, additional electronic components are added. For example, for etching the tips of wires, we use the AC source shown in Figure 5.15 and the wiring diagram shown in Figure 5.16. The power supply used to power heating elements is shown in Figure 5.17.

5.2.2.10 Storing microelectrodes and parts of microelectrodes

During various stages of development, parts of microelectrodes need to be stored safely until they are used in the next stage (Figure 5.18a). In principle, all parts need to be stored in a dust-free environment, which essentially means in closed containers. For practical reasons, however, we often keep parts of microelectrodes in racks, shown in Figure 5.18b, and hold only the finished products in closed containers, such as those shown in Figure 5.18c

Figure 5.15 A custom-made AC source for etching tips of wires.

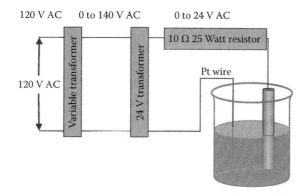

Figure 5.16 A custom-made variable AC source, which we use to etch the tips of Pt wires: a variable transformer made by Powerstat (voltage: 120 V AC, output voltage: 0 to 140 V AC, power: 1.4 KW), a transformer (120 V primary and 24 V, 2A), and a resistor (10 Ω, 25 W) used to limit the current in case of short-circuiting, i.e., the Pt wire touching the graphite electrode directly. It protects the 24-V transformer from burning in case of accidental short-circuiting.

Figure 5.17 HY1803D variable single-output DC power supply, digital (0-18VDC @ 0-3 A, Omnitronelectronics).

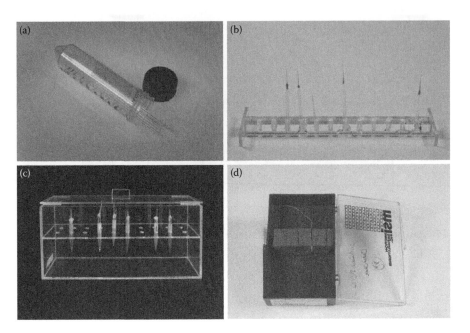

Figure 5.18 Various racks and containers for storing microelectrodes. (a) A tube used to store custom-cut glass in a dust-free environment. (b) A holder for cathodes. (c) A closed case holder for long-term storage. Note that dissolved oxygen microelectrodes are placed in 1000-μm disposable pipettes. (d) A closed container for storing glass-covered wires or microsensors. A hydrogen peroxide microelectrode is stored in the picture.

and d. However, if the construction of the microelectrodes lasts longer than one day, we keep the parts of the microelectrodes overnight in closed containers.

Table 5.3 specifies the tools we use and, when possible, gives the information about the manufacturer.

5.2.2.11   Auxiliary tools
In Figure 5.19, small tools used in constructing microelectrodes are shown.

5.2.2.12   Vacuum pumps
We use a small laboratory-type vacuum pump to remove air bubbles from the outer cases of electrodes (Figure 5.20).

5.2.2.13   Propane torches
We use small propane torches from hardware stores to heat glass capillaries in the initial stages of making micropipettes (Figure 5.21).

5.2.2.14   Instruments used to operate the microelectrodes
The instruments used in microelectrode measurements must be able to monitor low-level electric signals reliably. The main problem with these measurements is that they are prone to being affected by electromagnetic noise. This is not a surprise because low-level signals are often affected by electromagnetic noise and high-quality instruments are needed to ensure that the measurements are reliable. Possible sources of electromagnetic noise in laboratories include computer monitors, fluorescent light fixtures, and magnetic stirrers.

Table 5.3 Tools and Sources We Use to Construct Microelectrodes

Tools	Source
Fiber optic illuminators, light sources, and fluorescent circular illuminator	http://www.microlite.com/ http://www.cuda.com/ http://www.meyerinst.com/html/fiboptic.htm
Power supply Variac (Variable transformer)	Omnitronelectronics, HY1803D variable single-output DC power supply, digital (0-18VDC/@0-3 AMP), http://omnitronelectronics.net/ http://www.variable-transformer.com/ http://www.instserv.com/stacovt.htm
Micropipette puller	Stoelting Co., Catalog no. 51217, http://www.stoeltingco.com/
Antivibration tables	LW Series light load vibration isolation workstations, LW-3060-0321, http://www.newport.com/
Stereomicroscope	Leica Stereo Zoom 7 or Leica GZ7, http://www.leica-microsystems.com/
Upright or inverted microscopes	Nikon Optiphot-POL (upright), http://www.nikon.com/ Olympus CH-2 (upright), CK2 (inverted), IMT-2 (inverted), http://www.olympusmicro.com/
Grinding wheels	EG-4 micropipette grinder (the one which we have in the lab) EG-44 micropipette grinder (This is the new model, similar to ours, needs camera, etc.), http://www.narishige.co.jp/niusa/index.htm EG-400 micropipette grinder (integrated with microscope), http://www.narishige.co.jp/products/group1/eg-400.htm
Micromanipulators, magnetic stands, and microelectrode holders	World Precision Instruments: Micromanipulator model M3301R and microelectrode holder model #500475, http://www.wpiinc.com/ Narhishige magnetic stand model GJ-1, http://www.narishige.co.jp/

It is possible to design filters to mitigate some persistent sources of electromagnetic noise, such as the fluorescent lights in a laboratory, but these filters tend to affect the measured signal. If electromagnetic noise is a serious problem, it is best to shield the microelectrode, or the entire setup used in the measurements, by placing it in a Faraday cage. Sometimes just placing the entire measuring setup in a fume hood makes a difference.

Three types of operations requiring electrochemical equipment are common in measuring with microelectrodes: (1) measuring the current between electrodes, (2) measuring the potential of an electrode, and (3) polarizing an electrode. We use an HP 4140B pA meter/DC voltage source to measure current. This instrument also serves as a DC voltage source to polarize amperometric sensors. To measure electric potential, we use a Keithley Model 6517A electrometer/high-resistance meter. Both instruments are shown in Figure 5.22.

(a) A small stand we use to hold microelectrodes and other parts.

(b) A Petri dish used to silanize tips of microelectrodes.

(c) A 30-ml scintillation vial used to store electrolytes.

(d) Five-minute epoxy for gluing microelectrode parts.

(e) A trimmer (nail cutter) for cutting thin wires.

(f) A small beaker used to cushion the fall of shafts or outer cases. The edges are covered with modeling clay, and the beaker is filled with pieces of cut-up rubber gloves.

(g) A holder made of glass tubing that is connected to an alligator clip using silicone rubber tubing. The alligator clip tips are covered with silicone rubber tubing to prevent damage to glass microelectrodes.

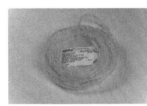

(h) Silicone rubber tubing (Masterflex #6412-16). A larger or smaller size can be used. Any heat-resistant silicone rubber tubing can be used for flexible connections.

(i) Some 100-μL disposable pipette tips used to construct a filling apparatus for micro-electrodes. We use a glass container to keep the filling apparatus in a dust-free environment.

(j) Electrical wire used to connect microelectrodes to external electrometers.

(k) Some 600-grit sandpaper cut into small pieces (~2 cm × 2 cm).

(l) A saturated calomel reference electrode.

Figure 5.19 Small items needed to construct microelectrodes.

(m) A hazardous chemical waste bottle.

(n) An etching station located in a well-ventilated, secured hood.

(o) A pen with diamond tip used to cut glass.

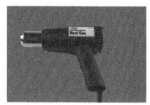

(p) An air gun used to pump hot air when needed.

(q) A small sonicator needed to clean glass and wires.

(r) Triangular files handy for cutting glass.

Figure 5.19 (Continued) Small items needed to construct microelectrodes.

Figure 5.20 Vacuum pump we use in our laboratory.

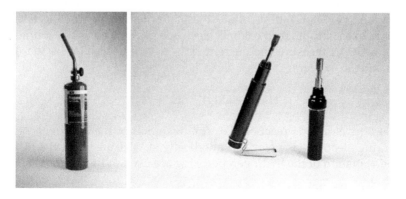

Figure 5.21 Propane torches we use in our laboratory.

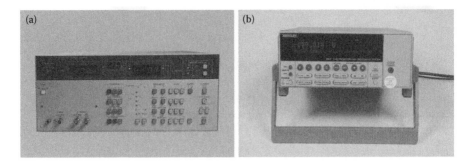

Figure 5.22 Good-quality electrometers are needed to make reliable microelectrode measurements. (a) An HP 4140B pA meter/DC voltage source used as a potential source and to measure current. (b) A Keithley Model 6517A electrometer/high-resistance meter (high-input impedance) used to measure the potential of potentiometric microelectrodes such as the ion-selective microelectrodes.

5.2.3   Constructing selected microelectrodes

The following sections explain how to construct microelectrodes. The useful procedures are exemplified by the sequences of steps for constructing three types of microelectrodes: (1) hydrogen peroxide microelectrodes (HPM), (2) dissolved oxygen microelectrodes (DOM), and (3) pH microelectrodes.

5.2.3.1   Constructing hydrogen peroxide microelectrodes

Hydrogen peroxide is a relatively mild oxidant occasionally used to eradicate biofilms from microbially contaminated surfaces. For various reasons it is important to know how the oxidant reacts with the biofilms. Microorganisms have developed various defense mechanisms to protect themselves against antimicrobial agents. Most of these mechanisms are still being investigated, but the defense mechanism used against hydrogen peroxide is known: some microorganisms use an enzyme, catalase, to decompose hydrogen peroxide to oxygen and water. Hydrogen peroxide electrodes are useful tools in studies of the defensive mechanisms of biofilms against toxic agents and of the effectiveness of hydrogen peroxide as an antimicrobial agent used to eradicate biofilms. We have used this electrode on many occasions, and it is a reliable microsensor. Figure 5.23 shows how it is constructed.

The HPM is an amperometric sensor. It is made of a platinum wire inserted into a glass capillary and covered with a cellulose acetate membrane. The electrical circuit is completed by an external standard calomel electrode (SCE) used as the counter electrode, and a picoammeter to measure the current. The electrode reaction is the oxidation of hydrogen peroxide to oxygen:

$$H_2O_2 \rightarrow O_2(g) + 2H^+ + 2e^- \tag{5.1}$$

To facilitate the electrode reaction (i.e., the oxidation of the hydrogen peroxide), the platinum working electrode is polarized anodically at +0.8 V against the SCE. The electrons from the oxidation of the hydrogen peroxide are used in the cathodic reaction at the counter electrode:

$$Hg_2Cl_2(s) + 2e^- \rightarrow 2Hg(l) + 2Cl^- \tag{5.2}$$

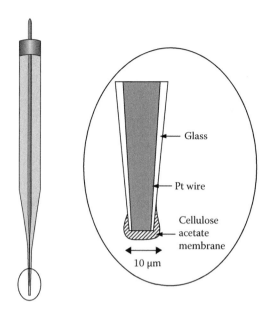

Figure 5.23 Hydrogen peroxide microelectrode.

The construction of a HPM consists of the following steps:

1. Making a shaft using Corning 8533 glass
2. Etching the Pt wire to a tip diameter of a few micrometers
3. Sealing the Pt wire in the shaft
4. Grinding the tip of the shaft
5. Applying a cellulose acetate membrane
6. Making the electrical connections
7. Calibrating the microelectrode

5.2.3.1.1   HPM step 1: Making a shaft using Corning 8161 glass.   Wash a glass tube (Corning 8161 glass) with acetone, then with deionized (DI) water, and then with acetone again. Allow the acetone to evaporate fully. Cut the glass tube into sections that are approximately 10 cm long. This can be accomplished by scoring the glass with a file and breaking it. The ends of the pipette should be fire-polished. Set up and ignite the propane torch. Keep one end of the tube in the flame of the propane torch until the edge of the glass is smooth. Put the glass aside for a while. *Do not touch the fire-polished end of the glass: it is hot.* When the glass cools off, repeat the procedure with the other end of the glass tube.

The shafts of the microelectrodes must be tapered to a tip diameter of several hundred micrometers. This tapering is done in a few steps. Start by pulling the glass by hand. Hold the middle of the sectioned glass tube over the flame, rotating the glass slowly (Figure 5.24a). As the glass is heated, it becomes soft. When it is sufficiently soft, pull apart the two ends (Figure 5.24b). Try to pull them apart straight so that the capillary linking the ends does not bend. Use the edge of the file to score the glass, and break the capillary in the middle (Figure 5.24c). Set these two pieces aside in a dust-free place. The next step is to etch the Pt wire (Figure 5.25).

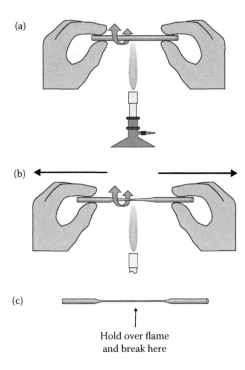

Figure 5.24 (a) Borosilicate glass (or Corning 8161) is placed above the burner until it softens. (b) The glass is pulled in the direction of the arrows. (c) The drawn capillary is broken in the middle, making two identical parts that can be used in the following steps.

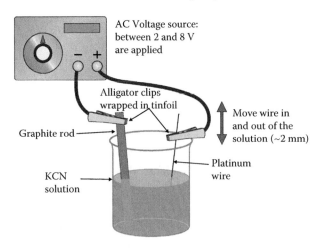

Figure 5.25 Components of the etching station.

    5.2.3.1.2   HPM step 2: Etching the pt wire to a tip diameter of a few micrometers.   Pt wires are etched electrochemically in concentrated potassium cyanide, KCN. *This is a highly toxic material, and it is important to work under a working fume hood* (Figure 5.26).

    Make sure that you know and understand the safety procedures relevant to working with potassium cyanide. One important requirement is that no acids be allowed in or near the fume hood in which the etching stand is located.

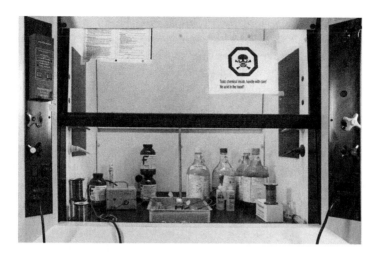

Figure 5.26 The etching station assembled under the fume hood.

We prepare the KCN solution in scintillation vials by dissolving 8 g cyanide KCN in 30 mL of DI water. Allow the chemical to dissolve completely. Freshly prepared KCN solutions etch wires faster than old and exhausted solutions. The principle of the etching process is that during the anodic cycle of the AC current the platinum dissolves into platinum ions in the solution. The platinum ions are complexed with the KCN, and they cannot precipitate during the cathodic cycle of the AC current. An important implication of this process is that the concentration of KCN becomes exhausted over time. You will notice that the initially colorless solution gains a yellowish brown tint over time. When the time needed to etch wires increases dramatically, it is time to change the potassium cyanide solution. Remember to dispose of the old solution safely.

To prepare for etching, attach the vial with the cyanide solution to a sturdy stand and assemble it in the fume hood near an AC voltage source. Insert the counter electrode, a graphite rod (Aldrich, 49654-5, 3 mm in diameter), into the cyanide solution. For etching, use either 50- or 100-μm-thick Pt wire. It does not matter which you use, but it may be easier for beginners to use the thicker wire; either way, the steps are the same. First, cut the wire into sections of 2–4 cm. The exact length of the wire depends on the length of the electrode you need to construct. Wash the wire with DI water. Attach the end of the wire to one of the terminals of the AC voltage source using an alligator clip with the tips wrapped in tinfoil (Figure 5.25). Hold the alligator clip, with the wire attached, and submerge about 1 cm of the wire into the cyanide solution. Hold the alligator clip with one hand and turn the voltage on with the other hand. Keep increasing the voltage until you see gas bubbles rising from the Pt wire. Approximately 2–8 V are used during the etching. Using smaller voltages extends the time of etching, but the tips of the Pt wires are smoother than those etched using higher potentials. Slowly move the wire up and down in the cyanide solution. Opinions vary on whether the wire should be removed partially or entirely from the solution with each vertical stroke. Try both procedures and choose the one you like better. After a few strokes, remove the wire from the solution and inspect it to see whether the tip diameter is in the range of 5–10 μm. If not, proceed with the etching as described above until the desired tip diameter results. With some experience you should be able to determine whether the tip diameter is within the specified range without using any measuring devices. Once the wire has the desired diameter, turn the potential off, detach the wire, and rinse it first with DI water and then with diluted H_2SO_4 (0.1–0.5 M). (*Remember not to keep the acid anywhere near the solution of cyanide.*) By rinsing the Pt wire with the dilute sulfuric acid solution we remove the residual cyanide from the Pt surface. Complete the procedure by washing the wire with DI water. Figure 5.25 shows the components of the etching station, and Figure 5.26 shows the entire etching station assembled under the fume hood.

5.2.3.1.3 HPM step 3: Sealing the Pt wire in the shaft. In this step, the Pt wire must be sealed in a glass capillary so that only its etched tip is exposed. Insert the Pt wire into the thick part of the glass shaft, etched end first. Be careful to insert the wire without bending the fragile, etched tip. If the tip is bent, the wire is useless and a new one must be etched. Place the glass capillary under a microscope with the wire inside and inspect the position of the wire that you have just inserted (Figure 5.27). Check whether the tip of the Pt wire is straight, and push the wire deeper into the shaft until its tip enters the capillary at the end of the shaft. Use a thin wire that can be inserted into the shaft to push the wire deeper into the capillary. Mark the location of the tip of the wire in the capillary using a Sharpie®. This mark will help you position the shaft near the heating element in preparation for sealing the wire. Attach a small ball of modeling clay to the fat end of the shaft. In the next step, the glass shaft will be pulled using heat from the heating element and gravity, and adding some weight to the shaft increases the level of control over this process. Some find adding weight helpful, and some do not; whether or not to use clay to increase the weight of the shaft is your decision. Try pulling glass with and without clay, and choose the procedure you like better. Suspend the shaft from the microelectrode puller using an alligator clip as shown in Figures 5.28 and 5.29.

Position the glass pipette near the heating element and in the field of view of the stereomicroscope, so that the tip of the wire is visible in the top part of the field of view of the stereomicroscope. Using the micromanipulator, move the shaft up, so that the tip of the wire is about 1.5 cm above the heating element. Turn the DC current source on and allow the heating element to warm up until it is glowing red hot. Monitor the glass flow using a stereomicroscope. The glass flow is clearly visible in the field of view of the microscope. It helps to have a zoom optic available in the stereomicroscope so that the size of the field of view can be controlled without the necessity of exchanging the optical components. When the glass softens, the shaft starts to drop slowly. Use the micromanipulator to slowly lower the shaft as the glass is dropping. This action coincides with the direction of the glass flow

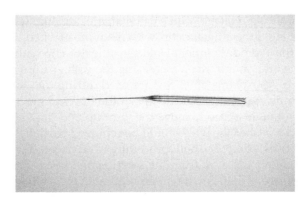

Figure 5.27 An etched Pt wire is inserted into a capillary. The location of the tip is marked with a Sharpie colored pen.

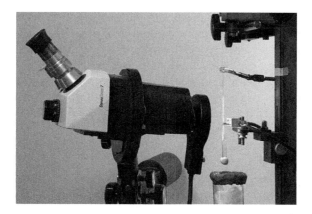

Figure 5.28 A photograph taken during the sealing process.

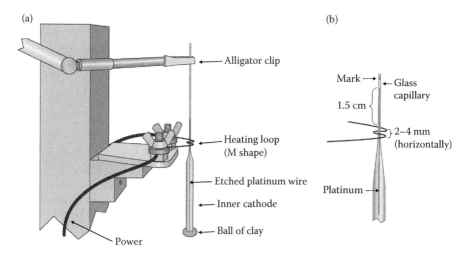

Figure 5.29 (a) Setup of pulling process. (b) Close-up view of the heating element.

and is designed to even the heat distribution so that the tip is uniformly covered with glass. Eventually, the glass will disconnect and the shaft will drop into the small beaker filled with pieces of rubber to prevent damage to the glass shaft. Inspect the shaft under a light microscope. The glass should seal the Pt wire within the capillary tightly, without air bubbles, dirt or debris trapped between the melted glass and the Pt wire. Air bubbles result from overheating the glass. If you see air bubbles, try decreasing the temperature of the heating element. Unevenly distributed glass over the Pt wire indicates that the heat was applied nonuniformly to the glass or that the shaft was swinging erratically during heating.

5.2.3.1.4 HPM step 4: Grinding the tip of the shaft.   Assuming that the Pt wire was successfully sealed in the shaft, the glass will be either sealing the tip of the wire or protruding past the tip, like a pigtail. In either case, the excess glass must be removed by grinding to leave a flat surface with an exposed tip of the Pt wire. The grinding wheel used in our laboratory was designed for grinding tips of microelectrodes (Figure 5.11). The micropipette is attached to a micromanipulator. The shaft is placed vertically, perpendicular to the grinding wheel, with the tip in close proximity to the surface of the wheel. The grinding wheel is turned on, and the shaft is slowly lowered onto the wheel until the tip touches the wheel. The shaft is slowly lowered using the micromanipulator, and the grinding continues until the glass and the Pt wire are flush with each other and the tip is flat and has an external diameter of about 10 μm (Figure 5.30). The setup for this procedure is shown in Figure 5.31. The micropipette is removed from the micromanipulator, and the tip is rinsed with DI water and acetone in a sonicator bath to remove any debris attached to the tip during the grinding.

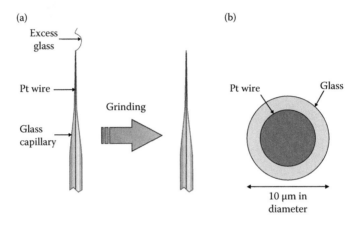

Figure 5.30 (a) The excess glass, the pigtail, must be removed by grinding. Sometimes the excess glass just seals the tip, without forming a pigtail. This must also be removed to expose the platinum wire. (b) The tip of the electrode after grinding.

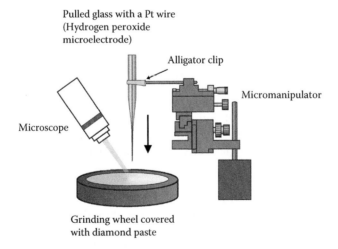

Figure 5.31 The grinding setup for hydrogen peroxide electrodes. We use a stereomicroscope to image the location of the microsensor tip.

5.2.3.1.5   HPM step 5: Applying a cellulose acetate membrane.   As explained in Chapter 4, Section 4.1.4, amperometric devices are covered with membranes to fix the thickness of the mass transfer boundary layer. A cellulose acetate (Sigma 180955) solution (5% (w/w), in acetone) is used as the membrane in hydrogen peroxide sensors. Before the membrane is applied, the electrode is cleaned in the sonicator bath, first in DI water and then in acetone. To apply the membrane, the tip is briefly dipped into the cellulose acetate solution prepared as described above (Figure 5.32). The electrode is set aside to allow the membrane to cure for at least 4 h. If possible, leave it for 24 h. The construction is complete, and the final step is to make the electrical connection between the Pt wire sealed in the shaft and the external electrical circuit.

The cellulose acetate membrane is attached to the tip by adhesive forces only. In some applications, such as when the tip is exposed to flowing water, the adhesive forces are too weak to keep the membrane in place and the attachment needs to be reinforced. In this case, we recess the Pt wire a few micrometers inside the capillary by etching the Pt wire using the procedure described earlier in this chapter. This causes part of the membrane to be within the recess, which reinforces the attachment of the membrane.

5.2.3.1.6   HPM step 6: Making the electrical connections.   To connect the electrode to the external circuitry, the Pt wire inside the shaft of the electrode needs to be soldered to a copper wire, which is then attached to the external circuitry. Put a small piece of the solder wire into the capillary and push it all the way down, until it reaches the narrow part where the end of the Pt wire is. Insert the copper wire until it touches the piece of solder wire. Heat the shaft at the location where the Pt wire, the copper wire, and the solder wire are located with a heat gun. As soon as the solder starts to melt, push the copper wire into the molten solder. Discontinue heating and allow the solder to harden (Figure 5.33). The sensor can now be attached to the external circuitry and is ready to be calibrated.

5.2.3.1.7   HPM step 7: Calibrating the microelectrode.   To calibrate the HPM, we apply +0.8 V between the anode (Pt wire) and a SCE and measure the current (Figure 5.34). We use the HP 4140B pA meter/DC voltage source to polarize the electrode and to measure the current. The current is proportional to the hydrogen peroxide concentration in the solution, and the concentration of hydrogen peroxide can be found using the calibration curve (Figure 5.35).

Figure 5.32 The hydrogen peroxide microelectrode is dipped in 5% (w/w) cellulose acetate solution in acetone for 2–3 s to form a membrane at the tip.

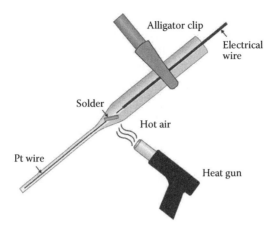

Figure 5.33 Soldering the Pt wire to the copper wire.

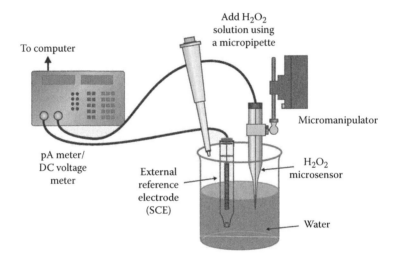

Figure 5.34 Electrical connection of the hydrogen peroxide microsensor and calibration setup. Note that the solution is gently mixed using a magnetic stirrer.

For calibration, we use a 8.8 M stock solution. We place the microelectrode in a beaker filled with 100 mL of water and place the beaker on a magnetic stirrer operated at a low agitation rate. We add 10 μL of stock solution each time to increase the H_2O_2 concentration to 0.88 mM in the beaker (Figure 5.34). If needed, the standard solution can be verified by titrating with 0.1 N $KMnO_4$.

The microelectrodes are immersed in the standard solutions, and the current is measured and plotted against the known concentration of hydrogen peroxide present in each sample, as shown in Figure 5.35.

5.2.3.2 Constructing dissolved oxygen microelectrodes

Oxygen microelectrodes are the most popular microsensors in biofilm research. Many microorganisms use oxygen as the terminal electron acceptor, and aerobic reactions in biofilms are intensively studied. Dissolved oxygen microelectrodes (DOMs) are amperometric devices: oxygen dissolved in water diffuses through a silicone rubber membrane,

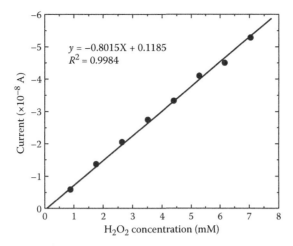

Figure 5.35 Calibration curve for the H_2O_2 microelectrode.

arrives at a cathodically polarized working electrode, and is reduced to water (Figure 5.36). The device uses an Ag/AgCl half-cell as the counter electrode and a noble metal such as gold or platinum as the working electrode. Applying –0.8 V typically satisfies the limiting current condition, and the measured current is proportional to the dissolved oxygen concentration in the vicinity of the sensor tip. The electrode reaction is the reduction of oxygen:

$$2e^- + 1/2\, O_2 + H_2O \rightarrow 2\, OH^- \tag{5.3}$$

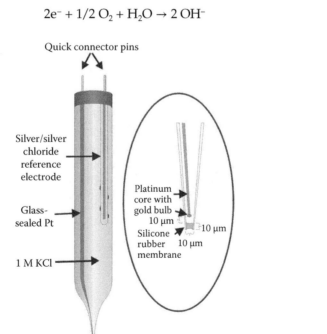

Figure 5.36 Dissolved oxygen microelectrode. The insert shows the position of the cathode, the reference electrode, and the silicone rubber membrane.

The anodic reaction is the anodic dissolution of silver at the Ag/AgCl counter electrode:

$$2Ag + 2Cl^- \rightarrow 2AgCl + 2e^- \tag{5.4}$$

Figure 5.36 shows the components of the oxygen microelectrode.

The construction of a dissolved oxygen microelectrode consists of the following steps:

1. Making an outer case
2. Opening the tip of the outer case
3. Applying a silicone rubber membrane
4. Etching the Pt wire to a tip diameter of a few micrometers
5. Making a shaft using Corning 8161 glass or Schott 8533 glass
6. Sealing the Pt wire in the shaft
7. Recessing the tip of the shaft
8. Electroplating the tip of the Pt wire with gold
9. Making the electrical connections
10. Preparing the Ag/AgCl reference electrode
11. Assembling all of the components
12. Filling the outer case with the electrolyte
13. Calibrating the microelectrode

5.2.3.2.1 DOM step 1: Making the outer case.   Start with a disposable glass Pasteur pipette (Fisher no. 13-678-20C). Score the pipette with a triangular file approximately halfway down, in the thick portion of the pipette (Figure 5.37a). Break the pipette at the score mark (Figure 5.37b). This step determines the length of the microelectrode, which can be shorter or longer according to the use of the individual electrode. Be sure that the broken glass parts do not fall inside the Pasteur pipette.

The cut end of the pipette should be fire-polished. This is accomplished by inserting the pipette into the flame of a propane fuel cylinder equipped with a nozzle until the edge of the glass is smooth. This reduces the possibility of cutting one's fingers against the sharp edges. The smooth edges will later also make it easier to introduce other components into the capillary. *Do not touch the glass: it is hot.*

The outer case is now ready to be thinned down to the 10-μm tip diameter typical of such microelectrodes. Put the thin end of the outer case through the heating element shaped in the form of a loop and attach the end to the micromanipulator using the alligator clip. The micromanipulator is positioned above the heating element and attached to the micropipette puller, as shown in Figure 5.38.

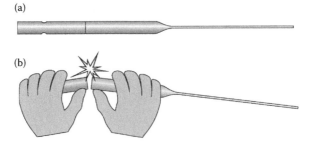

Figure 5.37 (a) Picture of Pasteur pipette showing the approximate position of the score mark made with a triangular file. (b) Breaking the pipette at the score mark.

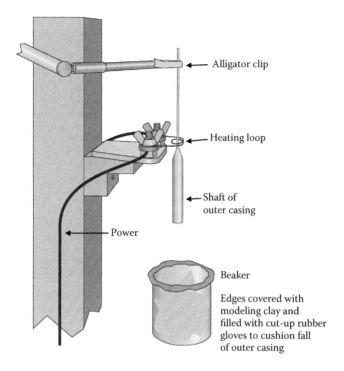

Alligator clip

Heating loop

Shaft of
outer casing

Power

Beaker

Edges covered with
modeling clay and
filled with cut-up rubber
gloves to cushion fall
of outer casing

Figure 5.38 Position of the outer case in the puller. Make sure that the pipette is dangling straight and that it does not touch the heating element.

Lower the pipette to the desired position to start the necking down of the pipette. The location of the correct position is somewhat arbitrary, but it should be close to the tapered region so that the first tapered part—the one generated by pulling the pipette by hand—becomes a part of the second tapered region. Ideally, the two tapered zones should have a smooth transition. The glass will slide down somewhat, but not too far, just enough to make the tip diameter smaller than what you had after drawing the pipettes by hand. The tip diameter will still be large; it will be reduced by the next stage of pulling.

As construction progresses, the precision of the procedures increases. The first pull, by hand, is the least precise. The second, shown in Figure 5.39, targets a specific part of the glass, the tapered zone, which resulted from pulling the glass by hand. The third stage of pulling is the most precise, and the most difficult to master. The final tapering of the micropipette, shown in Figure 5.39, is done using a heating element made of a 100-μm Pt wire, which can heat a very small surface of the glass at a precisely selected location.

Position the tapered part of the micropipette in the field of view of the stereomicroscope. Reposition the pipette so that the heated spot is now next to the heating element. However, this time, use the thinner heating element, made of 100-μm Pt wire, as shown. Increase the current through the heating element until it is glowing red. Then move the Pt wire near the glass. When the glass begins to melt and the pipette begins to drop, quickly turn off the current to the heating element. Controlling the heat source is the key to this procedure. Mastering this part is tricky, and the best results will come through trial and error. Sometimes you may need to turn the heat on and off during melting to control the heat. If too much heat is applied, the glass pipette will melt completely through and fall down. A heating element device is used for necking down the outer case. Repeat the above

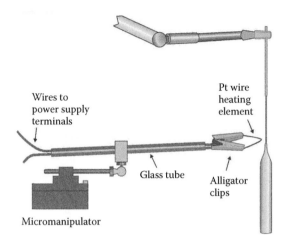

Figure 5.39 Third stage of pulling the micropipette. The outer case remains suspended from an alligator clip, but the heating element is now also attached to a micromanipulator.

procedure, by stopping the current flow through the heating element when the pipette begins to drop. Reposition the pipette so that the heating element is near the thin part and repeat the previous steps of the procedure. Two applications of this procedure should sufficiently taper the outer case. However, results may vary, so keep repeating this step until the glass diameter is less than a few micrometers. The casing can be allowed to drop after the taper is sufficiently thin (Figure 5.40).

5.2.3.2.2 DOM step 2: Opening the tip of the outer case. After the glass pipette has been successfully tapered, its tip is usually sealed. There may be a thin tail of glass extending from the tip. The tip must be opened, by breaking off the tail and exposing the inner part of the outer case. This can be accomplished by breaking off the tip under a microscope using a glass rod with a ball at the end. A technique for making a rod with a glass ball is shown in Figure 5.41.

Now, mount the outer case on the microscope stage using modeling clay. On the side of the microscope toward which the tapered edge of the casing points, set up a micromanipulator. Insert a glass rod with a ball on the end into the micromanipulator (Figure 5.42a).

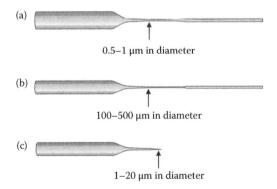

Figure 5.40 (a) Pipette after first pulling (by hand). (b) Pipette after second pulling (by puller). (c) Pipette after third pulling (using precise heating).

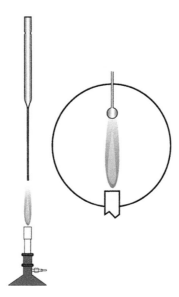

Figure 5.41 Technique for making a glass rod with a glass ball. A Pasteur pipette is heated over a burner until it melts. The melted glass develops a ball. The ball should be cooled for at least 1 min.

Bring the outer case into focus using the 10× objective (total of 100× magnification) on the microscope. Then move the stage far enough so that the fragile tip of the outer case is out of the way. Using the micromanipulator, move the glass ball under the microscope and bring it into focus (the end of the ball should be visible in the microscope's field of view, but not take up more than half of the field of view). Then bring the outer case back into the field of view. The two objects should both be in focus (Figure 5.42b). It helps to move the micromanipulator until the glass ball comes into focus while the tip of the outer case remains in focus. Having both objects in focus ensures that they are at the same level under the microscope.

Back the outer case up a little and jam it into the glass ball. Make sure this is done lightly, so the casing does not break lower down the outer case, past the 10-μm width. Keep jamming the casing into the ball until the end of the casing is 10 μm in diameter. Back the outer case up, so that it is out of the field of view of the microscope. Replace the glass rod in the micromanipulator with the device fashioned with a heating element at the end of it (Figure 5.3).

Bring the heating element into focus under the microscope and then move it to the edge of the field of view. Reposition the broken tip of the outer case so that it is back in focus in the other half of the field of view, just as in the previous procedure (see Figure 5.42c). Keep the heating element on until it is glowing red hot. Slowly move the broken tip toward the heating element, until it starts to melt and smooth out. Be careful not to let the tip of the outer case close completely. If this happens, the outer case is ruined! If the glass pipette is properly finished, the next step is to apply the silicone rubber membrane.

5.2.3.2.3   DOM step 3: Applying a silicone rubber membrane.   Put the glass rod with a ball back into the micromanipulator, this time with a tiny drop of silicone rubber on the end of the ball. Bring the ball on the glass rod into focus as before, then move it back to the edge of the field of view. Bring the tip of the microelectrode outer case into focus. Slowly advance the outer case toward the silicone rubber on the end of the glass rod. Insert the tip of the outer case into the surface of the silicone rubber (Figure 5.43a). Allow the silicone

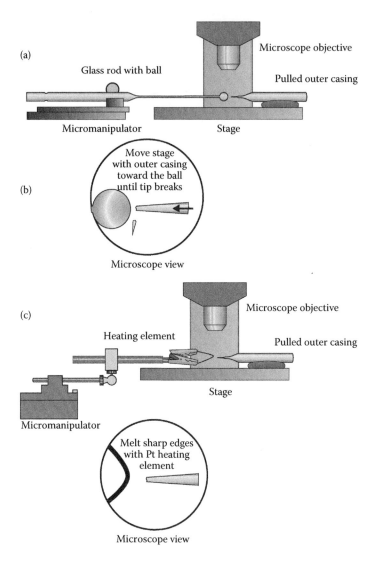

Figure 5.42 (a) Setup for breaking the outer case capillary. (b) View through the microscope. (c) Smoothing the broken glass tip by heating under the microscope.

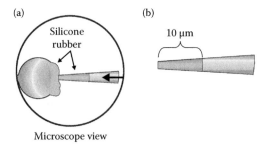

Figure 5.43 (a) Microscopic view of the procedure for applying a silicone rubber membrane. (b) Final view of membrane-filled capillary.

rubber to advance up the tip of the outer case, by capillary action, until the silicone rubber is 10 μm thick at the tip (Figure 5.43b). Remove the outer case, set aside, and dry for 24 h. The outer case is now completed. Construction of the inner cathode can continue while the membrane is drying. If the cathode is made before the outer case, the construction can continue until it is time to fill the electrode with electrolyte.

5.2.3.2.4 DOM step 4: Etching the Pt wire to a tip diameter of a few micrometers. This step is identical to HPM step 2 (Section 5.2.3.1.2).

5.2.3.2.5 DOM step 5: Making a shaft using Corning 8161 glass or Schott 8533 glass. For shafts made of Corning 8161 glass (white glass), this step is identical to HPM step 1

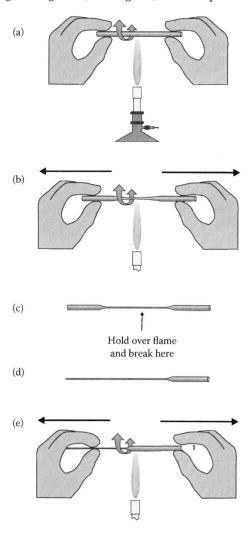

(a)

(b)

(c)

Hold over flame
and break here

(d)

(e)

Figure 5.44 Preparing the green glass microcapillary for the front part of the shaft. (a) Green glass is placed above the burner until it softens. (b) The glass is pulled in the direction of the arrows. (c) The drawn capillary is broken in the middle, making two identical parts that can be used in the following steps. (d) The pulled glass is cut to a manageable length. (e) Another pulling is performed very close to the neck of the pulled glass. The result is shown in Figure 5.45a.

(Section 5.2.3.1.1). However, for precise measurements where a low background current is needed, we use Schott 8533 glass, 3.3 mm outside diameter (Revsbech 1989). Schott 8533 has a characteristic green color, and we call it green glass. Because green glass is expensive, we do not make the entire shaft of the green glass: we only use the green glass to construct the front part of the shaft, and we fuse it with the shaft made of Corning 8161 glass. This procedure is illustrated in Figure 5.44.

The result of the pulling should be a piece of glass shaped as shown in Figure 5.45a, a thicker part with a microcapillary on each end. The thicker part in the middle is marked using a diamond pen and broken as cleanly as possible in the middle. The result is two identically shaped parts, each like the one shown in Figure 5.45b. Each of these two parts is a useful tip for a shaft under construction. Select one of the parts and insert the etched Pt wire into the green glass (Figure 5.45c). Now attach the green glass to the front part of the shaft. Prepare the back of the shaft made of white glass (Corning 8161). Cut the shaft (as in HPM step 1, Section 5.2.3.1.1) from the neck (Figure 5.45d), insert the narrow opening of the capillary made of white glass into the wide opening of the capillary made of green glass, and fuse the glasses over a propane flame, as shown in Figure 5.45e.

To test the quality of the seal between the green glass and the white glass, seal the tip by applying heat (the glass will shrink), then fill the inside of the shaft with alcohol and apply a vacuum (Figure 5.46). If the seal is faulty, air bubbles will appear where the two glasses were fused. If there is a leak the microelectrode will not work. After evaporating the alcohol you may try to seal it again and retest for possible leaks.

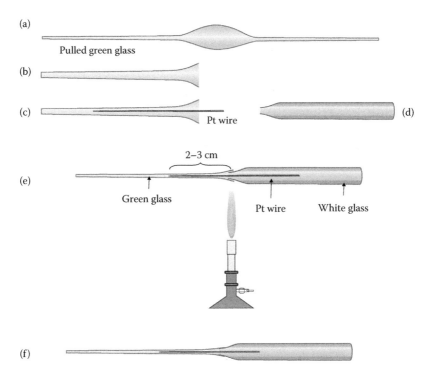

Figure 5.45 Fusing the glasses. (a) Thin capillary made of green glass. (b) The thin capillary is cut in the middle, and (c) a Pt wire is inserted into the capillary. (d) Prepared shaft made of white glass. (e) The green glass and the white glass are fused. (f) Final assembly of the shaft made of green glass (front part) and white glass (back).

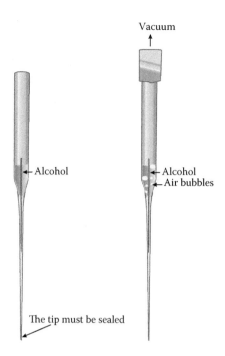

Figure 5.46 The quality of the connection between the green glass and the white glass must be tested as described above. Using alcohol and a vacuum helps in detecting faulty fusion: if the fusion is faulty, the air is sucked in from the outside and air bubbles are visible inside the shaft.

5.2.3.2.6   DOM step 6: Sealing the Pt wire in the shaft.   This step is identical to HPM step 3 (Section 5.2.3.1.3), except that this time green glass is used at the tip of the shaft. Working with the green glass is easier because its melting temperature is low.

5.2.3.2.7   DOM step 7: Recessing the tip of the shaft.   In preparation for the next step in the construction, which is electroplating the tip of the Pt wire with gold, the glass at the tip of the shaft is recessed to expose the tip of the Pt wire.

Put the heating wire assembly used for making the shaft (shown in Figure 5.47) into the micromanipulator. Bring the tip into focus and move it to one side of the field of view. Mount the pulled inner cathode onto the microscope stage using clay. Bring the tip into focus as described previously (Figure 5.47a). Keep the heating element on until it is glowing red hot. Slowly advance the electrode toward the heating element. Be careful not to touch the two together. Allow the glass covering the tip of the electrode to melt back, exposing 5–20 µm of the Pt wire (Figure 5.47b).

5.2.3.2.8   DOM step 8: Electroplating the tip of the Pt wire with gold.   The reason for electroplating the tip of the Pt wire with gold is to make the electrode resistant to contamination with hydrogen sulfide. Hydrogen sulfide is present in anaerobic biofilms, below the zone where oxygen is present. As a gas, it penetrates the silicone rubber membrane and contaminates the platinum tip. Gold is much more resistant to the presence of hydrogen sulfide than platinum is. If you are sure that the biofilm you are about to study does not generate hydrogen sulfide, this step may be omitted.

For this step, leave the electrode mounted on the stage of the microscope, but replace the heating element in the micromanipulator with the electroplating device (Figure 5.48).

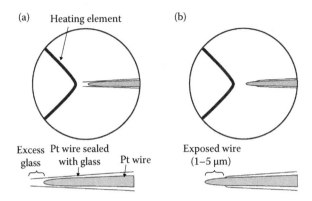

Figure 5.47 (a) Microscopic view of the heating element and the cathode. Below it is a close-up of the cathode tip prior to the glass being melted back. (b) View through the microscope of the melted and recessed glass at the tip. Although the figure is shown with a 5-μm piece of exposed Pt wire, this length may vary between 5 and 20 μm. Below it is a close-up of the exposed tip, after the glass has been melted back.

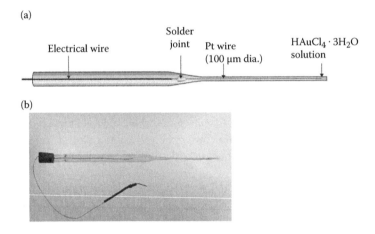

Figure 5.48 (a) Schematic diagram of the electroplating device. (b) Photograph of the electroplating device. The device is a Pasteur pipette with a platinum wire extending to a point just short of the tip. It is soldered to an insulated electrical wire.

Prior to placing the electroplating device under the microscope, touch the tip to DI water and then to the gold chemical. Two types of gold compounds can be used to electroplate platinum tips with gold: $HAuCl_4$ and $KAu(CN)_2$. We prefer to use $HAuCl_4 \cdot 3H_2O$ (Sigma, #G-4022) because it has better solubility and produces a more porous gold tip with a larger surface area, which results in a very stable signal. Place a small volume of the saturated $HAuCl_4 \cdot 3H_2O$ solution (it does not need to be exactly at the saturation concentration, i.e., any concentration close to saturation should be good enough) in the end part of the electroplating device. This is done by inserting the tip into the solution and using capillary forces. Place the device under the microscope using the micromanipulator and bring it into focus. Connect the other wire coming off of the power supply to the piece of Pt wire hanging out of the back of the electrode (Figure 5.49). A large resistor (about 1 MΩ) should be inserted into the circuit to prevent the deposition of an excessive amount of gold. Apply 0.5–1 V to the cell. The $HAuCl_4 \cdot 3H_2O$ solution is the electrolyte.

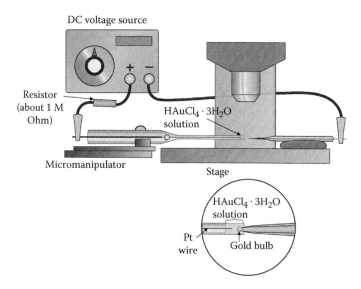

Figure 5.49 Electroplating setup. The inset shows a microscopic view of a gold ball being electroplated onto the end of a cathode tip.

When all parts are positioned under the microscope and sharply in focus, and the electrical connections are ready, slowly insert the tip of the cathode, using the micromanipulator, into the liquid solution that is in the tip of the electroplating device. Plate until the ball at the end of the Pt wire is 5–15 µm in diameter (Figure 5.49, inset). Rinse the tip with DI water. Store this in a safe place. The cathode is ready.

5.2.3.2.9   DOM step 9: Making the electrical connections.   This step is identical to HPM step 6 (Section 5.1.3.1.6).

5.2.3.2.10   DOM step 10: Preparing the Ag/AgCl reference electrode.   The "reference" electrodes used with dissolved oxygen electrodes are not really reference electrodes but counter electrodes. The counter electrode reaction delivers the electrons to reduce oxygen to water at the tip of the cathodic part of the sensor. However, because the counter electrodes used in oxygen sensors are typically the electrodes that are used as the reference electrodes in potentiometry, the name *reference electrode* is commonly used for the counter electrodes used in amperometric sensors. In principle, dissolved oxygen electrodes can be operated with external or internal reference electrodes; we use internal reference electrodes and place them inside the outer cases of the microelectrodes. The position of the reference electrode—inside the electrode outer case or outside it—is not only a matter of cosmetics or the elegance of the design: it affects the performance of the electrode. Specifically, inserting the reference electrode into the outer case decreases the level of electromagnetic noise experienced during measurements. All our dissolved oxygen electrodes are constructed with internal reference electrodes. The following paragraph describes the procedure we use to prepare an internal reference electrode.

Cut a piece of silver wire (0.25 or 0.5 mm in diameter, Aldrich #32703-4) 3–7 cm or the desired length. It should be long enough to reach about three quarters of the way down the electrode outer case and stick out the back of the electrode enough to be connected to an alligator clip later. Clean the surface of the silver wire with 600-grit sandpaper, dip the wire in 3 M HNO_3, and rinse with DI water. Connect the silver wire to the anode of the

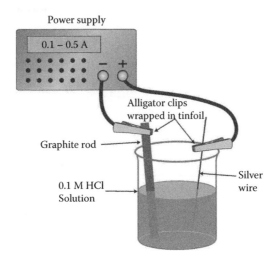

Figure 5.50 Diagram of the setup for preparing the Ag/AgCl wire.

power supply, and close the circuit by connecting a graphite rod (Aldrich #49654-5) to the cathode of the power supply. Place both the silver wire and the carbon rod into a 0.1 M HCl solution (Figure 5.50). Turn the electrometer on, set the voltage between 0.1 and 0.5 V DC, and leave the electrodes, the silver wire, and the carbon rod in the HCl for about 90 min. Applying a low voltage (0.1 V DC) and leaving it on overnight produces a smoother, more even AgCl layer on the silver wire; if there is no hurry to complete the electrode, we recommend applying a lower voltage and waiting overnight. Select the voltage to be used by slowly increasing it until small gas bubbles are observed on the silver wire. After chlorinization, the electrode should be aged for 1–2 days in dilute HCl (0.1 M). This aging is not a critical step but it stabilizes the electrode potential. To obtain electrodes with a stable potential, high-purity silver with a smooth surface and high-purity HCl should be used.

5.2.3.2.11 DOM step 11: Assembling all of the components. Before starting the final assembly, make sure that you have 6 to 10 of each component (cathodes and outer cases). Before a cathode is inserted into an outer case, you need to make sure that the cathode will fit into it. For that reason, the diameters of the cathodes and the diameters of the outer cases need to be measured at two locations (see Figure 5.51). Using the results of these

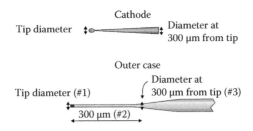

Figure 5.51 Measuring the diameters of the cathode and the outer case: First, measure the tip diameters of the cathode and the outer case; then, measure their diameters about 300 μm from the tip. The distance of 300 μm is our preference; however, depending on the shape of the outer case you may need to adjust this length. Refer to Table 5.4 below for an example of a set of data resulting from such measurements.

Table 5.4 Match Table for the Dimensions of the Outer
Cases and Cathodes

No.	Outer cases	No.	Cathodes
1	10-300-55	1	9-300-20
2	15-300-50	2	10-300-35
3	20-300-55	3	3-300-7
4	50-300-100	4	12-300-37
5	14-20-50	5	18-300-40
6	10-400-45	6	20-300-60
7	10-500-400		
8	20-400-48		
9	7-300-40		
10	20-300-60		

Note: Refer to Figure 5.51 for the meanings of the first, second,
and third numbers.

measurements, prepare a match table (see the example in Table 5.4), to determine which
cathode should be inserted into which outer case.

From the set of measurements shown in the match table, we selected the following
pairs of outer cases and wires to make sure that the cathodes would fit in the outer cases.

Outer case–Cathode

4–6
10–4
2–2
3–1
1–3

Some of the cathodes and outer cases are left unused in this selection process because
they do not match each other. Keep the unused components for later use, when constructing another batch of microelectrodes. Be careful to store the unused components in a dust-
free environment and not to keep them there for too long.

Mount an outer case on the microscope stage, keeping the tip in focus. Attach the cathode that matches the outer case to a micromanipulator and carefully insert the cathode
into the outer case, using the micromanipulator and the microscope stage to keep the tip of
the cathode in the field of view at all times (Figure 5.52a). Keep inserting the cathode until
the tip is ~10 μm from the silicone rubber membrane.

Back the cathode off just a few micrometers. Mix some 1-min epoxy, and place it on the
part of the cathode shaft that protrudes from the outer case. Move the cathode back into
the position where its tip is 10 μm from the silicone rubber (Figure 5.52b). The epoxy should
contact the outer case and the shaft. Allow the epoxy to set and dry. Once it is dry, proceed with mounting the reference electrode. Insert the reference about halfway down the
length of the outer case. Apply a tiny drop of epoxy to attach it to the outer case and hold it
in place. Allow the epoxy to set and dry. Remove the assembly from the microscope stage.

5.2.3.2.12 DOM step 12: Filling the outer case with the electrolyte. We use a solution
of 0.3 M K_2CO_3 (41.46 g/L), 0.2 M $KHCO_3$ (20.02 g/L) adjusted to pH 10.3, and 1 M KCl

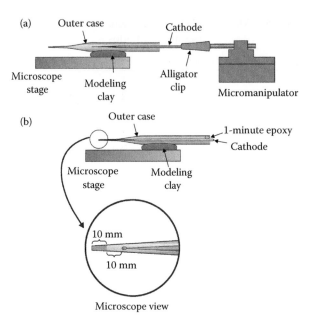

Figure 5.52 Steps for placing a cathode in an outer case. (a) The cathode is inserted into the outer case. (b) The cathode is glued to the outer case. Note the location of the glue.

(74.55 g/L) as the internal electrolyte for oxygen microelectrodes. A reasonable compromise between a relatively high pH and tolerable decomposition rates of microsensor components is obtained at a pH of 10.3. Before adding the electrolyte to the microelectrode, be sure that the solution does not contain air bubbles. If there are air bubbles visible, use a sonicator to remove them. Also, be certain that the electrolyte solution is clean and fresh. We use a stock solution of the electrolyte (approximately 1 L), and when we need electrolyte, we filter 30 mL of the stock solution through a 0.2-μm syringe filter. Leftover solution is discarded, and a new batch is filtered weekly.

It is difficult to fill the tip of the outer case, which is only a few micrometers in diameter. We use a simple tool made of a disposable plastic syringe to help in this procedure. The tip of the syringe is heated and pulled until it makes a very fine tip (Figure 5.53). This

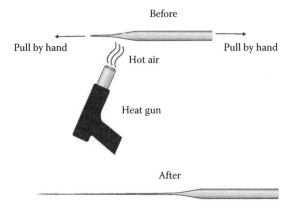

Figure 5.53 A disposable 200-μL pipette tip is pulled by applying heat using a heat gun. Later, this pulled tip is attached to a 1-mL syringe. The pulled part is cut to be 5–10 cm long.

tip can be inserted deep into the outer case and deliver the electrolyte close to the membrane in the narrow part of the outer case (Figure 5.54). Use the syringe to fill the tube with the electrolyte and deliver it as close to the tip of the outer case as possible. There will be some air remaining between the electrolyte and the membrane. We will remove this air using a vacuum.

Insert the outer case into a rubber stopper. The safe way to do this is to slit the stopper on the side and insert the outer case through the slit. Insert the assembly into a test tube, place the test tube in a vacuum flask, and apply the vacuum (Figures 5.55 and 5.56). Leave the assembly in for 1–2 min. Do not keep the electrode in the vacuum for an extended period of time, because the liquid evaporates. Check the tip of the outer case under the

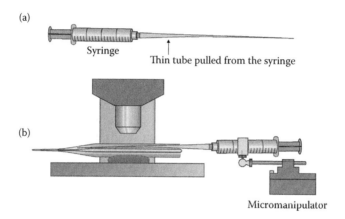

Figure 5.54 (a) Syringe with a thin tube for filling the electrode with electrolyte. (b) Filling of pulled micropipette with electrolyte solution.

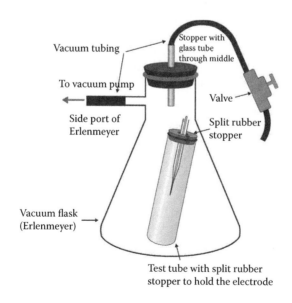

Figure 5.55 A test tube with a rubber stopper split down the side is used to hold the electrode. A vacuum is applied to rid the tip of any air bubbles trapped between the silicone rubber membrane and the electrolyte solution.

Figure 5.56 Photograph of a setup for removing air bubbles. The test tube with a rubber stopper holds the dissolved oxygen microelectrode. We use two test tubes: the first (outer) one is used to place everything inside the vacuum flask, and the second (inner) one holds the microelectrode. This way, we avoid damaging the microelectrode.

microscope to make sure there are no air bubbles left near the silicone rubber membrane. Apply the vacuum again if an air bubble remains. Then, fill the rest of the outer case with the electrolyte, and seal the back of the outer case shut with epoxy or silicone rubber. This completes the construction. Figure 5.36 shows a finished electrode.

5.2.3.2.13 DOM step 13: Calibrating the microelectrodes. During the measurements, the electrode is polarized cathodically by applying –0.8 V between the working electrode (gold) and the reference electrode (Ag/AgCl wire). The current between the working electrode and the reference electrode is directly proportional to the concentration of oxygen in the solution. The setup is shown in Figure 5.57. We use a HP 4140B pA meter/DC voltage source to polarize the electrode and to measure the current.

The oxygen microelectrodes are calibrated in water equilibrated with N_2 and in air. The measured current is typically in the range of 10–150 pA for N_2 and 100–700 pA for air-saturated water. The dissolved oxygen concentrations are 0 and 7.8 mg/L in water (at 25°C and 1 atm pressure) saturated with pure N_2 and in air, respectively. Two-point calibration, in N_2 and in air, is sufficient because the calibration curve is linear. The electrode is moved from air to N_2-saturated water (or vice versa) to check the response time of the electrode

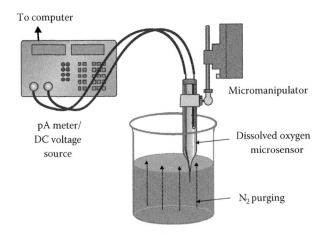

Figure 5.57 The dissolved oxygen microelectrode is calibrated in N_2 and air-purged water.

(time to reach 95% of the saturation value). This is typically 1–3 s. The current measured should be independent of whether the solution is stirred. A difference of 5% between the currents measured with and without stirring is considered acceptable. An example of this calibration procedure is shown in Figure 5.58.

The data in Figure 5.58 show that the average background current and the average current measured when the water is saturated with oxygen are 9.8 and 559 pA, respectively. The saturation concentration of oxygen in Bozeman, Montana (1700 m above sea level) at 25°C is 6.7 mg/L. The two-point calibration equation is thus

$$\text{Dissolved oxygen concentration} = 0.0122 \times \text{Current (pA)} - 0.1196 \qquad (5.5)$$

5.2.3.3 Constructing pH microelectrodes with liquid ion exchanger membranes

Measuring pH in biofilms is one of the more popular applications of pH microelectrodes. Many biofilm reactions affect the pH. However, the results of measurement are often disappointing because the buffering capacities of most natural waters and most growth media used in laboratories to grow biofilms are high enough to hide any possible changes in pH. Nevertheless, pH microelectrodes (PHMs) remain one of the more popular devices, and the following will describe a procedure for making a PHM with a membrane made of a liquid ion exchanger. A PHM is a potentiometric device. The principle of the measurement is measuring the potential across the LIX membrane, as explained in Chapter 3.

A PHM with a liquid ion exchanger is shown in Figure 5.59.

In the past, we used lead glass to make pH microelectrodes, but now we use two types of glass almost exclusively: Pasteur pipettes (Fisher, #13-678-20C) and borosilicate glass (Corning 7056).

In our experience, tubing rarely needs cleaning. However, we always wash the glass tubes with acetone and rinse with distilled water. There are mixed opinions about the

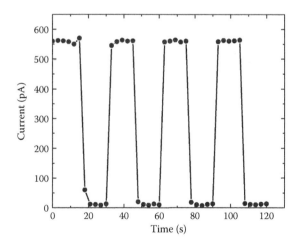

Figure 5.58 Current measured during the calibration procedure. The average currents measured at zero oxygen concentration (N_2 purged) and at oxygen saturation (air purged) are used for calibration. Note that the background current measured in the absence of oxygen depends on the electrical properties of the glass used to make the shafts: the better the glass, the lower this residual current. Background currents of about 100 pA are typical of electrodes with tip diameters of about 15 μm and shafts made of Corning 8161 glass. However, when we use green glass (Schott 8533), the current at zero oxygen concentration is below 10 pA.

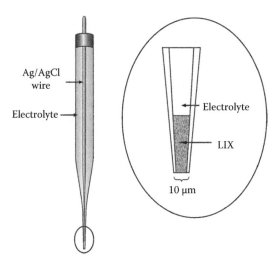

Figure 5.59 Diagram of a pH microelectrode with a LIX membrane.

usefulness of this cleaning and about the procedures used for it. The reason for these discrepancies in opinion is in one of the following steps in constructing the microelectrode, the silanization of the tip. The silanization does not always work, and the suspicion is that some cleaning procedures change the properties of the glass surface and cause the failure in silanization. There is no clear evidence that the cleaning procedures have anything to do with this effect, but the recommendations vary from avoiding cleaning to very effective washing procedures. If silanization fails persistently, we soak the glass tubes overnight in butanol, rinse in distilled water and ethanol, and finally dry at 200°C. It also helps to prepare the micropipettes just before the silanization. Pulling micropipettes is not a particularly time-consuming procedure, and it is best to pull the micropipettes on the same day they will be used. For all practical purposes, we consider pH microelectrodes disposable.

The following steps are used in constructing this type of microelectrode:

1. Making an outer case using borosilicate glass
2. Opening the tip of the outer case
3. Silanizing the tip of the outer case
4. Applying the LIX membrane
5. Filling the outer case with the electrolyte
6. Preparing the inner Ag/AgCl reference electrode
7. Calibrating the microelectrode

5.2.3.3.1 PHM step 1: Making an outer case using borosilicate glass. Except for the glass used, Corning 7056, this procedure starts with pulling the glass tubing as explained for DOM step 1 (Section 5.2.3.2.1). See also Figure 5.40.

5.2.3.3.2 PHM step 2: Opening the tip of the outer case. This procedure is identical to that described for DOM step 2 (Section 5.2.3.2.2).

The tip of a pH microelectrode should have a diameter between 2 and 10 μm. The tip region should be 200–500 μm long. The tapered part should be 1000–3000 μm long, as shown in Figure 5.60.

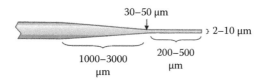

Figure 5.60 Final dimensions of pH microelectrode.

5.2.3.3.3 PHM step 3: Silanizing the tip of the outer case. The organic liquid membrane must adhere to the glass wall of the electrode; otherwise, the aqueous electrolyte solution will find a pathway along the luminal glass surface, thus short-circuiting the membrane and destroying the membrane potential. This requirement creates some problems because LIX membranes are hydrophobic liquids and do not adhere well to hydrophilic glass surfaces. This problem is handled by making the glass surface hydrophobic through silanization. Reactive silanes replace hydroxyl groups on the glass surface and bind to it with covalent bonds, resulting in a monomolecular hydrophobic coating (Ammann 1986). Vapor treatment with *N,N*-dimethyltrimethylsilylamine (TMSDMA; Fluka #417-16) is a very effective and widely used silanization method. Another method is to use Fluka #85120 silanization solution. The major disadvantages of using TMSDMA are that this compound has a high vapor pressure, evaporates easily, and is extremely toxic. Therefore, TMSDMA should always be kept and handled in a fume hood. *Check the safety data sheets before working with this substance.* To silanize the tip of a pipette, the tip is briefly dipped into the silanization solution as shown in Figure 5.61. Remove the tip promptly, and place the entire outer case in a Petri dish (all under the fume hood).

The micropipettes with the silane in their tips are mounted horizontally in a petri dish (Figure 5.62) and put into an oven, where they are baked at 200°C for 15 min. The micropipettes are now silanized and are ready for the membrane to be applied. They may be stored in the oven at 110°C, but we usually keep them in a closed Petri dish on a laboratory bench for a day. Storing silanized pipettes for longer periods should be avoided. Some laboratories store silanized pipettes in a hot oven or in desiccators to keep them dry. Despite all efforts, you may find resilanization necessary if the pipettes have been stored for several days. The silanization temperatures used in different laboratories range from 110°C to 200°C, but we have found that, within these limits, higher temperatures give

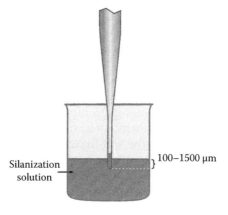

Figure 5.61 The electrode tip is dipped into silanization solution. After dipping, immediately put the electrode into a Petri dish (Figure 5.62).

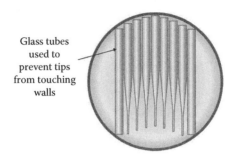

Glass tubes used to prevent tips from touching walls

Figure 5.62 The pulled pipettes are mounted in a glass petri dish with a lid to protect them from dust. They can also be cooked in the same manner.

better results. It has been reported that silanization may fail if the oven is contaminated with other organic substances that have evaporated and stuck to the inside surfaces of the oven. Cleaning the inside surfaces of the oven with a solvent and/or prolonged baking at a temperature much higher than that needed for silanization may help in such instances.

5.2.3.3.4 PHM step 4: Applying the LIX membrane. Unless we need to use other types of pH microelectrodes, such as glass membrane microelectrodes, we use ready-to-use liquid membrane solutions, "cocktails" that are commercially available for H$^+$ from Fluka Chemie AG (see Table 5.2).

We use the back-filling method, in which we first fill the tip with LIX and then fill the outer case from the back with the electrolyte. The membrane is applied by dipping the silanized tip of the micropipette into the membrane solution. The membrane is held in place by capillary forces and by adhesion of the hydrophobic solution to the hydrophobic surface of the glass. Dip the tip of the capillary into the liquid membrane solution (in the same manner as during silanization).

5.2.3.3.5 PHM step 5: Filling the outer case with the electrolyte. The electrolyte filling solution must contain the ion to be measured in addition to chloride, which is required for stable operation of the Ag/AgCl electrode. Some examples of filling solutions are given in Table 5.2. To fill the outer case with the electrolyte, it is necessary to use a very thin pulled syringe, which is described in Figure 5.53. The challenging part is to deliver the electrolyte to the thin end of the micropipette without trapping an air bubble. Problems may occur if the tip tapers at a steep angle, i.e., if its diameter changes rapidly. With this type of pipette tip, the release of pressure after filling may be followed by air being taken up into the tip. This does not happen if the tip has a gradual taper. The entire operation is done under a microscope, as illustrated in Figure 5.63.

Sometimes air bubbles appear in the filling solution within the shank of the microelectrode. Some procedures recommend using glass pipettes with internal filaments, which are easier to fill with the electrolyte. Unfortunately, filamented glass tubing does not help in this case because, after silanization, the self-filling properties with aqueous solutions are lost. If the air bubble is small and it is attached to the inner glass wall, a gentle tap can usually break it down. If that does not work, try pushing a thin fiber (some suggest a cat's whisker or a hair) through the bubble to disrupt it.

Small bubbles often consist of air that was originally dissolved in the filling solution. The reduction in pressure during suction or a slight increase in temperature during handling will favor bubble formation because the solution becomes oversaturated with air. If

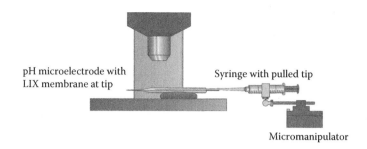

Figure 5.63 Back-filling of pulled micropipette with electrolyte solution. A disposable 200-µL pipette tip or a 1-mL syringe tube is pulled in a process similar to that applied to glass to make a syringe with a pulled fine tip.

bubbles occur frequently, it is a good idea to degas all electrolyte filling solutions occasionally. This can be done either by shaking the solution under low pressure or at a slightly elevated temperature (about 40°C) or by sonicating the electrolyte solution.

When the tip of the pH microelectrode is examined under a microscope, the membrane column should appear as a 50–400 µm long continuous region ending in a concave surface against the electrolyte filling solution. This also indicates proper silanization of the glass. A convex membrane–water interface, a LIX phase broken into multiple sections, and withdrawal of the LIX phase into the shank are typical signs of inadequate silanization (see Figure 5.64).

5.2.3.3.6 PHM step 6: Preparing the inner Ag/AgCl reference electrode. This step is identical to DOM step 10 (Section 5.2.3.2.10).

5.2.3.3.7 PHM step 7: Calibrating the microelectrode. We calibrate pH microelectrodes using standard pH buffers. The microelectrode and an external reference, a SCE, are immersed in a solution of known pH and the potential difference between the internal and external reference electrodes is monitored (Figure 5.65). The positive terminal of the voltmeter is connected to the pH microelectrode, and the negative terminal is connected to a SCE. A sample calibration curve is shown in Figure 5.66.

5.2.3.4 Constructing redox potential microsensors

The redox potential is used to express the overall oxidizing/reducing tendency of a solution in volts. The reference point for assessing this tendency is the potential of the hydrogen evolution reaction, which has a redox potential set to zero by definition. Solutions with a redox potential above the potential of the hydrogen evolution reaction have a tendency to accept electrons and are therefore oxidizing, and solutions with redox potentials below the

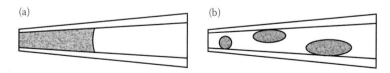

Figure 5.64 (a) In a properly silanized micropipette, the liquid membrane solution forms a uniform column with a concave interface against the aqueous filling solution. (b) In a poorly silanized micropipette, the organic membrane solution is easily replaced by water at the hydrophilic glass surface. This results in convex interfaces and, often, breaking of the membrane column.

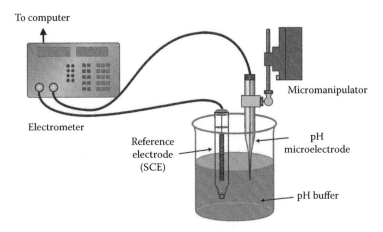

Figure 5.65 Setup and connections used to calibrate pH microelectrode. Note that the negative terminal is connected to the reference electrode.

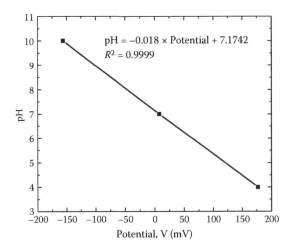

Figure 5.66 A sample calibration curve. The value of 1/slope is equal to ΔPotential/ΔpH = −55.5 mV/pH. The theoretical value is 59.

potential of the hydrogen evolution reaction have a tendency to donate electrons and are therefore reducing. The redox potential of a water solution is identified with the potential of a platinized platinum electrode reported with respect to a normal hydrogen electrode. Platinized platinum is used because it gives the highest exchange current density for the hydrogen evolution reaction, as shown in Figure 7.10. In natural waters, the redox potential often reflects the concentrations of the members of the dominant redox couple (e.g., oxygen in aerobic solutions or hydrogen sulfide in anaerobic solutions). If the members of the dominant redox couple exchange electrons with the redox electrode, the redox potential can be used to identify the composition of the solution. The redox potential depends on the ratio of the oxidized to the reduced members of all redox couples in the solution that can exchange electrons with a platinum electrode. For solutions composed of single redox couples, redox potential can be computed from the Nernst equation (Equation 5.6), which is identical to Equation 7.37, and are repeated here to expose the fact that the measured redox potential depends not only on the concentrations of the reduced and oxidized members of the redox couples but also on the pH.

$$OX + mH^+ + ne^- \leftrightarrow RED \tag{5.6}$$

$$E_h = E^o - \frac{0.059}{n} \log\left(\frac{RED}{OX}\right) - \frac{m}{n} 0.059 \text{ pH} \tag{5.7}$$

where E_h represents redox potential (mV), E^o is the standard reduction potential (mV; pH 0), n is the moles of electrons transferred per mole of oxidized species, RED is the reduced species (M), OX is the oxidized species (M), m is the moles of protons transferred per mole of electrons transferred, and pH refers to the pH of the surrounding solution.

Redox electrodes are potentiometric devices that measure the potential of the platinized platinum electrode with respect to a suitable reference electrode. Redox electrodes used in natural waters and in soils are usually connected to external reference electrodes. To measure redox potential profiles in biofilms, however, it is more convenient to use internal reference electrodes. Because the combined device uses two miniaturized electrodes (i.e., the working electrode (platinum) and the internal reference electrode), it is appropriate to call it a redox microsensor (RM) rather than a redox microelectrode, noting that the redox microelectrode is part of the redox microsensor. The redox microsensor we use is shown in Figure 5.67. The sensing tip of the microsensor, the platinized platinum wire, is sealed in an outer case made of Corning 8161 glass. Silver wire anodized in HCl to form a layer of AgCl is immersed in the internal solution, saturated KCl, and used as the reference electrode. The electrical connection between the tip of the redox microelectrode, which is exposed to the external solution, and the internal reference electrode is provided through the agar-based salt bridge placed at the tip of the outer shaft, as shown in Figure 5.67.

The construction of a RM consists of the following steps:

1. Making a shaft using Corning 8161 glass
2. Etching the Pt wire to a tip diameter of a few micrometers
3. Sealing the Pt wire in the shaft
4. Grinding the tip of the shaft
5. Electroplating the tip of the Pt wire with Pt
6. Making the electrical connections
7. Calibrating the microelectrode

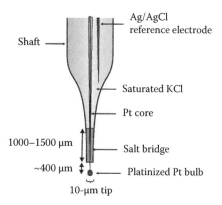

Figure 5.67 Redox microsensor.

5.2.3.4.1   RM step 1: Making a shaft using Corning 8161 glass.   This step is identical to HPM step 1 (Section 5.2.3.1.1).

5.2.3.4.2   RM step 2: Etching the Pt wire to a tip diameter of a few micrometers.   This step is identical to HPM step 2 (Section 5.2.3.1.2).

5.2.3.4.3   RM step 3: Sealing the Pt wire in the shaft.   This process is identical to HPM step 3 (Section 5.2.3.1.3).

5.2.3.4.4   RM step 4: Grinding the tip of the shaft.   This process is identical to HPM step 4 (Section 5.2.3.1.4).

5.2.3.4.5   RM step 5: Electroplating the tip of the Pt wire with Pt.   For this step, 30 mL of a solution of 0.02 M H_2PtCl_6 (8.20 g/L, Sigma Aldrich #262587–10 mL) in 1 M HCl (Sigma Aldrich #H1758) is prepared. This amount of solution suffices to platinize 300–500 redox microelectrodes. A diagram of the setup used to electroplate platinum is shown in Figure 5.68. To prevent evaporation of the platinum chloride solution and to keep it clean, the solution is kept in a vial and the cap of the vial is closed immediately after each deposition process is finished. During the electroplating, Pt ions are electrochemically deposited on the etched Pt wire tip using a three-electrode system: a working electrode (the sealed Pt wire in the shaft), a saturated calomel reference electrode, and a 100-μm-diameter Pt wire (counter electrode). All the electrodes are immersed in the solution of platinum chloride, H_2PtCl_6. To secure the setup mechanically, the working electrode is attached to a micromanipulator and the counter electrode is taped to the reference electrode. All the electrodes are connected to the Gamry Reference 600 Potentiostat/Galvanostat/ZRA. To electroplate platinum, we use the chronoamperometry option of the Gamry instrument and adjust the application parameters to the values given in Table 5.5. Although we use a Gamry© potentiostat, any other brand will work, as will simple homemade electrochemical setups.

After Pt ions have been electrochemically deposited and formed a ball of Pt on the tip of a platinum wire, the Pt wire, sealed in its glass shaft, is carefully dismounted from the micromanipulator, rinsed with distilled water to remove any traces of the platinum chloride, and then kept in a dust-free container. Figure 5.69 shows the consecutive stages of work on the tip of a Pt wire. Figure 5.70 shows a SEM image of a wire tip with an electroplated Pt ball.

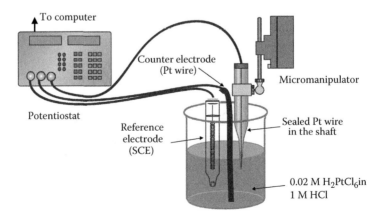

Figure 5.68 Diagram of the setup for electroplating the tip of a sealed Pt wire.

Table 5.5   Typically Used Values in the Gamry Framework of
Chronoamperometry for Depositing Pt Ions onto the Tip of an Etched Pt Wire

Application parameter	Value	Application parameter	Value
Step 1 voltage (V)	−0.29	I/E range	Fixed
Step 1 time (s)	690	Max current (mA)	0.1
Step 2 voltage (V)	−0.29	Limit I (mA/cm²)	800
Step 2 time (s)	5	IR compensation	None
Sample period (s)	5	PF Correction (ohm)	None
Cycle no.	1	Equilibrium time (s)	0

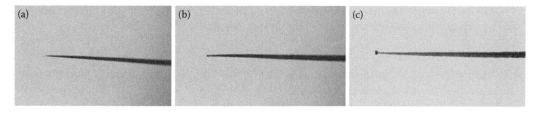

Figure 5.69 Stages of preparing the tip of a platinum wire: (a) The platinum wire protrudes from the outer case. (b) The platinum wire has been ground off. (c) A ball of Pt has been electrodeposited onto the tip of the Pt wire.

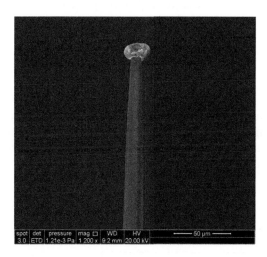

Figure 5.70 SEM image of the tip of a redox microelectrode with a ball of platinum electrodeposited onto the tip of the platinum wire.

5.2.3.4.6   RM step 6: Making the electrical connections.   This step is identical to HPM step 6 (Section 5.2.3.1.6).

5.2.3.4.7   RM step 7: Calibrating the microelectrode.   In principle, redox electrodes do not require calibration. However, it is important to test whether a constructed sensor responds in a predictable manner when immersed in a solution of a known redox potential. We use Zobell solution (YSI Inc., YSI 3682) for this purpose. Zobell solution is made of 0.0033 M $Fe(CN)_6^{-4}$, 0.0033 $Fe(CN)_6^{-3}$, and potassium salts, and it has a theoretical redox potential of +237.5 $mV_{Ag/AgCl}$. We use this solution to test our electrodes by measuring their potentials with respect to the Ag/AgCl reference electrode using a Keithley model 6517 electrometer/high-resistance meter. The potentials measured for various electrodes vary between +235 and +240 $mV_{Ag/AgCl}$ at 20°C. These numbers deviate by ±2.5 mV from the standard value of 237.5 $mV_{Ag/AgCl}$ provided in the calibration manual for Zobell solution.

Notes:

1. If the redox potential of your RM in Zobell solution deviates by more than ±2.5 mV from the theoretical value, discard the RM. If the measured deviations are consistent, check Note 2 first.
2. Zobell solution is photosensitive, so it is important to keep the solution in the dark between measurements. Once exposed to light its redox potential and color change.
3. Pay attention to the temperature. The redox potential varies with temperature.

5.2.3.5 Constructing flavin microelectrodes

To determine the role of flavins in extracellular electron transfer in biofilms, it is important to measure flavin concentration profiles directly using microelectrodes. Flavins exist in three forms: flavin adenine dinucleotide, flavin mononucleotide, and riboflavin (RF), as shown in Figure 5.71.

The flavin moiety can undergo a two-step redox reduction (Miyuki et al. 2002). When fully oxidized, or in the flavoquinone form, it can undergo a single-electron reduction to the flavosemiquinone form and then a second single-electron reduction to the flavohydroquinone form. This is shown for RF as an example; the reaction form is identical for all of the flavins:

$$RF + H^+ + e^- \rightleftarrows RFH \tag{5.8}$$

$$RFH + H^+ + e^- \rightleftarrows RFH_2 \tag{5.9}$$

It has been found that flavosemiquinones generally exist in low concentrations in solution (around 2%, although they were previously believed to be present in much higher concentrations), as they are rapidly converted through the fast reaction of two flavosemiquinones to one flavoquinone and one flavohydroquinone:

$$RFH + RFH \rightleftarrows RF + RFH_2 \tag{5.10}$$

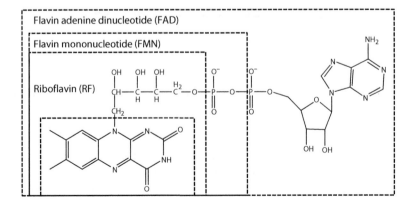

Figure 5.71 Chemical structure of flavins.

The full reduction of flavoquinones to flavohydroquinones is very rapid and can be considered a single two-electron reduction step, as shown in Figure 5.72:

$$RF + 2H^+ + 2e^- \rightleftarrows RFH_2 \tag{5.11}$$

To measure the concentration of flavins in biofilm we run a potentiodynamic measurement, square-wave voltammetry (SWV), using a flavin microsensor (FM), shown in Figure 5.73. The microsensor is composed of three miniaturized electrodes: a graphite working electrode, a platinum counter electrode, and a Ag/AgCl reference electrode. The graphite microelectrode is sealed in borosilicate glass, and only its tip is exposed to the external solution, as shown in Figure 5.73. The counter and reference electrodes are immersed in the internal KCl solution. The electrical connection between the external and internal solutions is provided by the agar-based salt bridge located at the tip of the outer case, which contains the internal solution and the counter and reference electrodes. All the electrodes are connected to the potentiostat, which runs potentiodynamic, three-electrode electrochemical measurements at the tip of the graphite microelectrode. The procedure for making a FM is described in this section. Several steps in the procedure are identical to steps described previously. However, the tip of this microsensor is more difficult to construct, which necessitates the adjustment of several steps of the previously described procedures. The modifications are usually minor and do not require modification of the standard equipment described in other sections.

The construction of a FM consists of the following steps:

1. Making an outer case
2. Opening the tip of the outer case
3. Making a shaft using Corning 8161 glass
4. Sealing the carbon fiber in the shaft

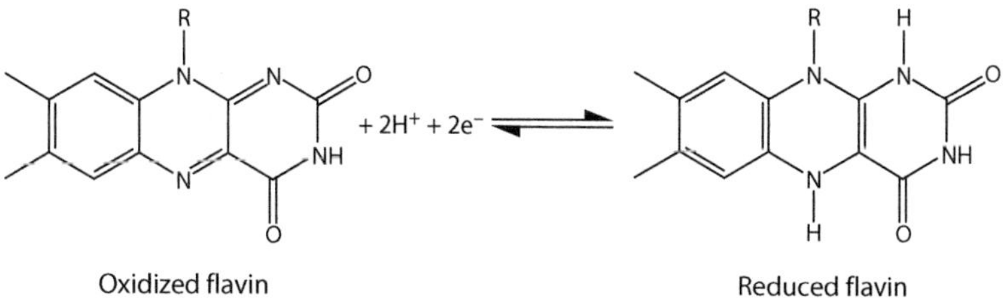

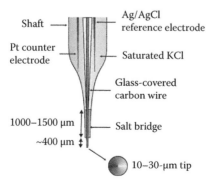

Oxidized flavin $\qquad$ Reduced flavin

Figure 5.72 Oxidized and reduced forms of flavins.

Figure 5.73 Flavin microelectrode.

5. Grinding the tip of the shaft
6. Making the electrical connections
7. Preparing the Ag/AgCl reference electrode
8. Assembling the components
9. Applying a salt bridge solution to the tip of the outer case
10. Filling the outer case with the electrolyte, and putting the reference and counter electrodes in place
11. Preconditioning the microelectrode
12. Calibrating the microelectrode

5.2.3.5.1 FM step 1: Making an outer case. This step is identical to DOM step 1 (Section 5.2.3.2.1).

5.2.3.5.2 FM step 2: Opening the tip of the outer case. Although for this type of microsensor the final tip diameter of the outer case is larger than those we described previously, mechanically this step in the procedure is identical to DOM step 2 (Section 5.2.3.2.2). The outer case is jammed into a glass ball until the glass tip breaks and the opening in the tip of the casing is about 100 μm (Figure 5.73). This allows glass-sealed carbon fiber wire to be inserted into the opening in the outer case. Figure 5.74 shows the stages of breaking open the tip of the outer case.

5.2.3.5.3 FM step 3: Making a shaft using Corning 8161 glass. This step is identical to HPM step 1 (Section 5.2.3.1.1).

5.2.3.5.4 FM step 4: Sealing the carbon fiber in the shaft. This process is identical to HPM step 3 (Section 5.2.3.1.3), except that in this case a carbon fiber is used instead of a platinum wire. The carbon fiber is 30 μm in diameter and electrochemically activated (World Precision Instruments, #C3005). A piece of carbon fiber approximately 5 cm long is inserted into one of the glass capillaries and pushed deeper into the shaft by a thin wire, leaving approximately 1 cm of the carbon fiber exposed at the end to be electrically connected to a copper wire. Because of the high temperatures used during the glass pulling, the carbon fiber tip ends up partially burned and with a tip diameter smaller than the 30-μm starting diameter. This process is similar to that for sealing Pt wire, except that the material we use is carbon, not platinum. Note that the mechanical strengths of Pt and

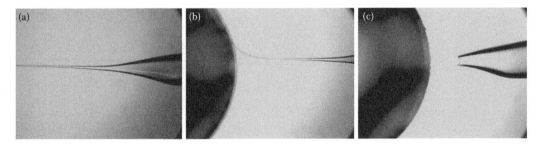

Figure 5.74 Light microscopy images of the tip of an outer case. (a) After pulling, the tip diameter is less than 10 μm. (b) The glass tip is broken by pushing the outer case against the glass bulb. (c) The tip of the outer case is opened to 100 μm. This procedure is identical to that shown in Figure 5.42, except that the final tip diameter of the outer case is larger, about 100 μm.

carbon fiber are different. Carbon fiber breaks easily, so working with carbon fiber is more difficult than working with platinum wire.

5.2.3.5.5 FM step 5: Grinding the tip of the shaft. This step is identical to HPM step 4 (Section 5.2.3.1.4). During the grinding process, part of the carbon fiber is also ground away to refresh the burned tip and expose the electrochemically active layers. The final flat tip diameter is between 10 and 30 μm. It is important to note that the larger the diameter is, the lower the detection limit of the FM will be.

5.2.3.5.6 FM step 6: Making the electrical connections. This step is identical to HPM step 6 (Section 5.2.3.1.6).

5.2.3.5.7 FM step 7: Preparing the Ag/AgCl reference electrode. This step is identical to DOM step 10 (Section 5.2.3.2.10).

5.2.3.5.8 FM step 8: Assembling the components. The sealed and ground carbon fiber shaft (working electrode) and the outer case are assembled under 40× microscope magnification using micromanipulators (Figure 5.75). The sealed carbon fiber is carefully attached to a micromanipulator, and the outer case is mounted on the microscope stage. Following this, the sealed carbon fiber is inserted into the outer case with its tip positioned approximately 400 μm outside the tip of the outer case. It is then glued to the outer case using 1-min epoxy near the fire-polished end of the outer case. The epoxy is allowed to set and dry completely, leading to the formation of a strong bond between the two glass walls. Note that after this process there is a gap between the tip with its sealed carbon fiber and the outer case. This will be filled with agar later.

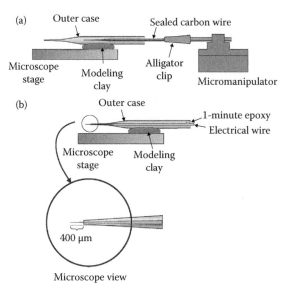

Figure 5.75 Setup for assembling the components. (a) The sealed carbon fiber inserted into the outer case. (b) The outer case and sealed carbon fiber are glued. The circled area shows a microscope view of the tip.

5.2.3.5.9   FM step 9: Applying a salt bridge solution to the tip of the outer case. A salt bridge is needed to separate the external solution from the internal solution and the reference and counter electrodes. We make a salt bridge using 1.812 g Agar R2A, 100 mL distilled water, and 1 mL 0.1 M Na_2SO_4 (14.40 g/L) mixed in a flask.

The R2A agar powder is dissolved in 100 mL of distilled water with 1 mL of 0.1 M Na_2SO_4 in an Erlenmeyer flask. The flask is placed on a Cloth Hemisphere-Mantle Bottom (Fisher Scientific #11-472-66) hot plate and the solution is boiled. Catching the boiling moment is important; otherwise, the solution runs over and becomes useless, not to mention the mess it makes. The flask is removed from the hot plate, and the solution is left to cool down to 40°C–50°C. During the cooling time the air bubbles disappear from the solution. While it is still warm, the salt bridge solution is applied to the tip of the outer case up to a depth of 1–1.5 mm, using a plastic capillary tube custom-made from a disposable pipette tip (Figure 5.76). The procedure for preparing the plastic capillary tube is described in DOM step 12 (Section 5.2.3.2.12). The agar salt bridge becomes solid after 10 min. Note that if the agar is applied directly after boiling, air bubbles will form and the salt bridge will be inadequate. If the temperature of the agar is too low during the application, the agar will solidify too quickly, making it difficult or impossible to apply. The arrangement during the agar and electrolyte filling processes and the salt bridge solution/air interface inside the outer case are shown in Figure 5.77.

5.2.3.5.10   FM step 10: Filling the outer case with the electrolyte and putting the reference and counter electrodes in place. In this step, the outer case is filled with the electrolyte filling solution made of saturated KCl saturated with AgCl (Fisher Scientific). Finally, the Ag/AgCl reference electrode and a counter electrode consisting of two twisted 100-μm

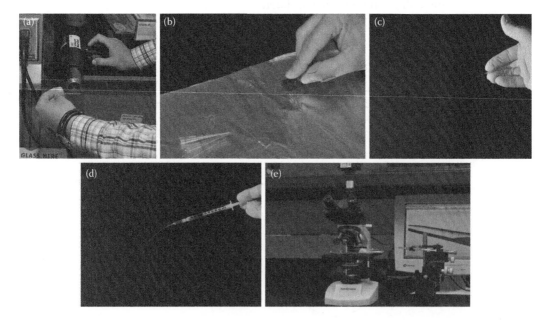

Figure 5.76 Components and steps for creating a thin tube to apply the salt bridge solution and fill the outer case with the electrolyte: (a) A 200-μL micropipette tip is pulled using a heat gun. (b) The tip of the pulled pipette is cut off. (c) Final view of pulled tip. (d) The pulled tip is attached to a syringe. (e) The syringe is mounted on a micromanipulator and used to inject electrolyte into the outer case tip.

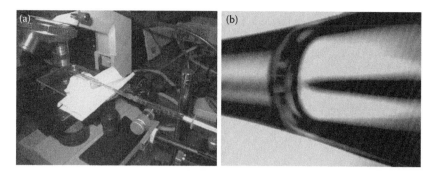

Figure 5.77 (a) The arrangement during the agar and electrolyte filling processes and (b) the salt bridge solution/air interface inside the outer case.

platinum wires (California Fine Wire Company #21884, 99.9999% pure) are inserted and glued using 1-min epoxy.

5.2.3.5.11   FM step 11: Preconditioning the microelectrode.   In order to enhance the signal, the microelectrode is preconditioned using chronoamperometry and cyclic voltammetry (CV). First, the clean microelectrode is polarized at a potential of +1800 mV$_{Ag/AgCl}$ for 300 s in a 10 mM phosphate buffer (0.5075 g/L NaH$_2$PO$_4$ and 0.8195 g/L Na$_2$HPO$_4$). Then, CV is performed at 100 mV/s from −800 mV$_{Ag/AgCl}$ to +1000 mV$_{Ag/AgCl}$ in the same solution for 30 cycles. The purpose of the preconditioning step is to create hydroxyl functional groups on the carbon surface as shown:

$$-C = O + H^+ + e^- \rightleftarrows -C - OH \tag{5.12}$$

Hydroxyl functional groups increase the number of active sites for flavin oxidation/reduction at the electrode surface and enhance the electron transfer capacity. Additionally, the electrode surface becomes more porous after this treatment and the effective electrode surface area increases. The flavin microelectrode needs to be reconditioned after each use by repeating the procedure. We obtain reproducible calibration curves after each use. A similar procedure was used by Brendel and Luther (1995).

Table 5.6 Parameter Values Used for Flavin Microelectrode Square-Wave Voltammetry

Square-wave voltammetry parameters for flavin microelectrode	Optimized values
Starting potential	+700 mV$_{Ag/AgCl}$
Final potential	−700 mV$_{Ag/AgCl}$
Equilibrium time	5 s
Potential step height	5 mV
Pulse potential	40 mV
Scan frequency	20 Hz

Note: Equilibrium time, potential step height, pulse potential, and scan frequency were chosen to optimize flavin detection. (Reproduced from Nguyen, H. et al., *Sensors and Actuators B: Chemical*, 161, 929–937, 2012.)

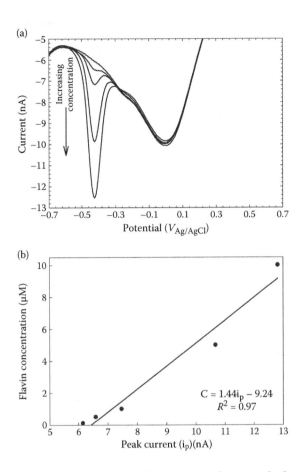

Figure 5.78 (a) Square-wave voltammetry (SWV) responses for several riboflavin concentrations, starting at 0.1 μM and increasing by half-decades to 10 μM and (b) the calibration curve of the flavin microelectrode, based on the SWV peak currents at −424 mV$_{Ag/AgCl}$. (Reproduced from Nguyen, H. D., Renslow, R., Babauta, J., Ahmed, B., and Beyenal, H. A voltammetric flavin microelectrode for use in biofilms. *Sensors and Actuators B: Chemical*, 161, 929–937, 2012.)

5.2.3.5.12 FM step 12: Calibrating the microelectrode. Square-wave parameters, including equilibrium time, pulse potential, and scan frequency, are optimized in a 5 μM riboflavin solution to hone the microelectrode sensitivity specifically for flavins. The operational parameters we use are given in Table 5.6. The flavin microelectrode is calibrated in riboflavin solutions with concentrations ranging from 10^{-7} to 10^{-5} M. Riboflavin powder (Sigma-Aldrich, #R4500) is diluted in the biofilm growth medium and used for both the optimization and the calibration. An example calibration curve is shown in Figure 5.78.

5.3   Constructing fiber optic microsensors

In this section, we describe two fiber optic sensors that we construct and use in our laboratory: (1) an optical sensor for measuring backscattered light intensity and (2) an optical sensor for measuring fluorescent light intensity in biofilms. These two sensors are constructed in a similar manner. The difference between them is in the operating procedures and the electronic setups used to measure the backscattered or the fluorescent light coming back from the tip. Also, we use a single-mode fiber to construct the sensors to measure

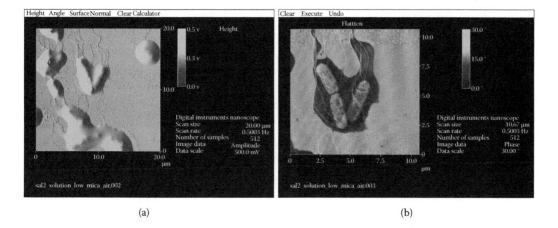

(a)   (b)

Figure 1.6 Atomic force microscopy images of bacteria attached to a surface. The cells are imbedded in EPS that was (a) partially dried to expose the microorganisms and then (b) further dried. (Both images courtesy of Recep Avci of the Physics Department, Montana State University, Bozeman.)

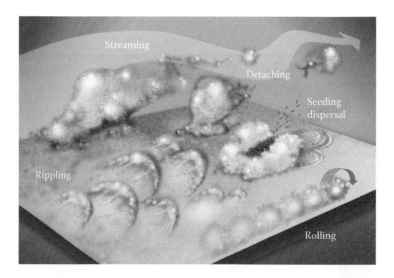

Figure 1.9 Mechanisms of biofilm propagation. (Courtesy of P. Dirckx, MSU Center for Biofilm Engineering.)

Figure 1.33 Moving bed biofilm reactor (MBBR) at the Williams-Monaco Wastewater Treatment Plant, Colorado. (Reprinted from Biofilm Reactors, *WEF Manual of Practice* No. 35. Prepared by the Biofilm Reactors Task Force of the Water Environment Federation, p. 243, 2010.)

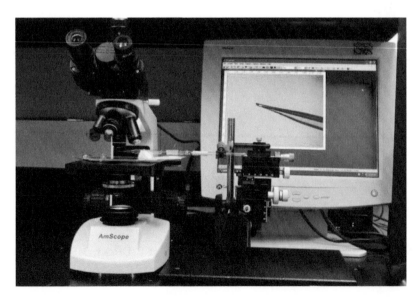

Figure 2.1 The process of inserting a cathode into the shaft of a dissolved oxygen microsensor is monitored using an upright microscope and transmitted light. The microscope is connected to a camera for imaging.

Figure 2.5 A microcolony of a nitrifying biofilm. Molecular probes (fluorescent *in situ* hybridization probes) of different colors, red and green, attached themselves to different physiological groups of microorganisms occupying the microcolony: ammonia oxidizers and nitrite oxidizers. Note that the physiological groups of microorganisms are not mixed randomly but are, rather, spatially separated from each other, forming a secondary structure in the biofilm—physiological heterogeneity.

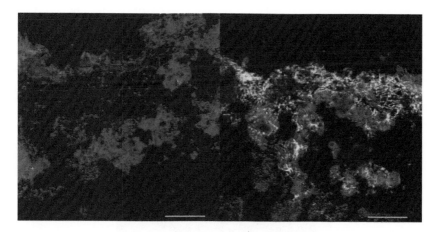

Figure 2.6 FISH probes were used to find the locations of *Leptothrix discophora* (green probe) in a mixed-population biofilm. The red signal represents cells that were stained with propidium iodide, and green represents a fluorescent FISH probe. Yellow indicates a green and red overlay. The scale bar is 25 μm. (Reproduced from Campbell, S. et al., *Corrosion* 60: 670–680, 2004.)

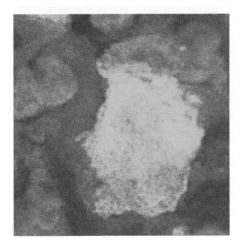

Figure 2.7 A microcolony of *Staphylococcus aureus* expressing yellow fluorescent protein imaged using confocal scanning laser microscopy. (Reproduced from Beyenal, H. et al., *Microbiology Methods* 58: 367–374, 2004.)

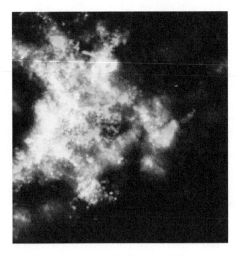

Figure 2.9 Confocal images of *C. jejuni* in a five-day-old monoculture biofilm stained for cell viability. The biofilm contains a mixture of living (green) and dead (red) bacteria (magnification, 60×); yellow indicates a mixture of live and dead cells. (Modified from Ica, T. et al., *Applied Environmental Microbiology*, 78: 1033–1038, 2012.)

(a)

(b)

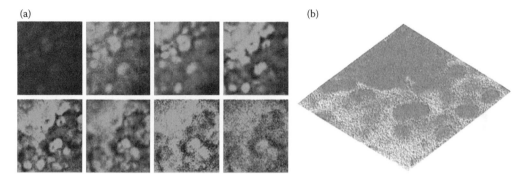

Figure 2.10 (a) A stack of biofilm images. The number of images in a stack is usually much higher: only selected images from the stack are shown to demonstrate the principle of the technique. (b) 3-D view of the biofilm reconstructed from the layers of images.

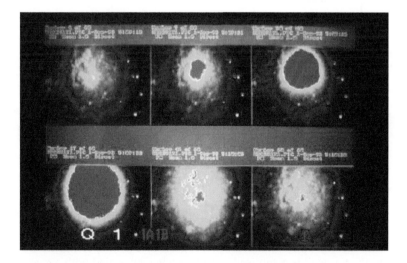

Figure 2.14 Measuring diffusivity in a biofilm matrix using microinjections and confocal microscopy. (Reproduced from deBeer, D. et al., *Biotechnology and Bioengineering* 53: 151–158, 1997.)

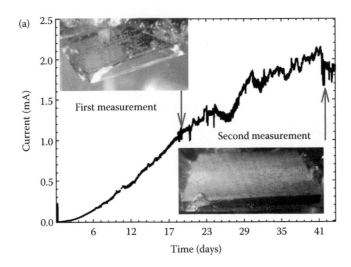

Figure 3.20 (a) Current generation of the *G. sulfurreducens* biofilm over time. The red arrows show the times when the biofilm images were taken. (Reproduced from Babauta, T. J. et al., *Biotechnology and Bioengineering* 109: 2651–2662, 2012.)

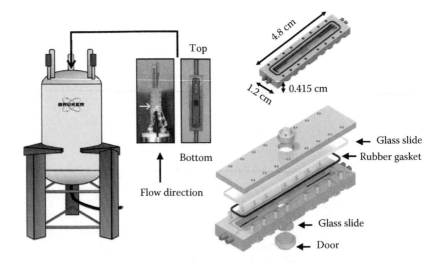

Figure 3.28 NMR setup and NMR biofilm reactor. A glass disc (5 mm) completes the bottom flow channel wall, and the top wall is comprised of a glass coverslip sealed with a gasket. The photographs show that the NMR biofilm reactor is seated into a custom-built NMR probe. The white arrow shows the radio frequency coil. On the right, the NMR biofilm reactor is shown in detail.

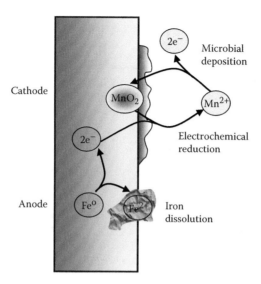

Figure 7.40 Redox cycling on metal surfaces: hypothetical mechanism of microbial involvement in the corrosion of stainless steels and other passive metals.

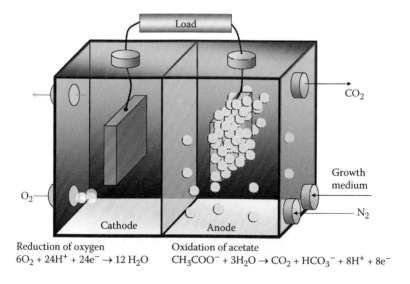

Reduction of oxygen
$$6O_2 + 24H^+ + 24e^- \rightarrow 12\ H_2O$$

Oxidation of acetate
$$CH_3COO^- + 3H_2O \rightarrow CO_2 + HCO_3^- + 8H^+ + 8e^-$$

Figure 7.43 MFC based on oxidizing acetate and reducing oxygen.

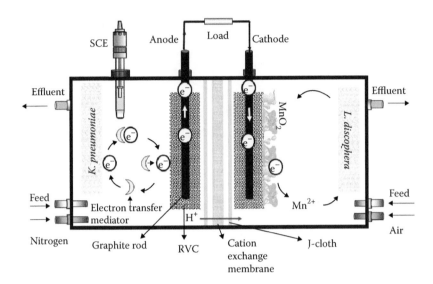

Figure 7.45 Schematic of designed MFC. Glucose was oxidized in the anodic compartment, and the electrons were transferred via an electronic conductor to the cathodic compartment, where they reduced microbially deposited manganese oxides. In the anodic compartment we used a redox mediator, HNQ, to facilitate the electron transfer from the glucose to the graphite electrode. In the cathodic compartment, manganese oxides were deposited on the graphite electrode and reduced directly, without any redox mediator, by the electrons derived from the anodic reaction. (Reprinted from A. Rhoads et al., *Environmental Science and Technology*, 39, 4666–4671, 2005.)

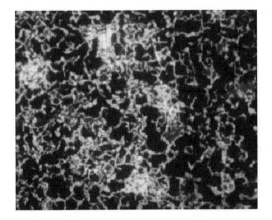

Figure 9.31 Live/dead image of *P. aeruginosa* PAO1. The red cells are dead, and the green cells are alive.

backscattered light intensity and a multimode fiber to measure the intensity of fluorescent light in biofilms. As will be demonstrated, single-mode fibers can be used to make smaller sensor tips. We had to use a multimode fiber to measure fluorescent light intensity because it was impossible to couple enough light to excite the biofilm using a single-mode fiber optic cable.

5.3.1   Tools and procedures for constructing fiber optic microsensors

Many tools we use to construct microelectrodes are also useful for constructing fiber optic microsensors. Those uniquely used to construct fiber optic microsensors are described here. We buy most of them from FIS (http://www.fiberinstrumentsales.com/) and Newport (http://www.newport.com/) (Figure 5.79).

5.3.1.1   Construction of the optical microsensor tip

We use the same procedure to make the tip of a fiber optic microsensor to measure backscattered light intensity as we do to make one to measure fluorescent light intensity in biofilms. However, depending on the microsensor, we use either a single- or a multimode cable. Figure 5.80 shows a drawing and a photograph of a fiber optic microsensor tip.

A fiber optic cable consists of three components (Figure 5.81): the core (the thin glass center of the fiber where the light travels), the cladding (the outer optical material surrounding the core that reflects the light back into the core), and the buffer coating (the

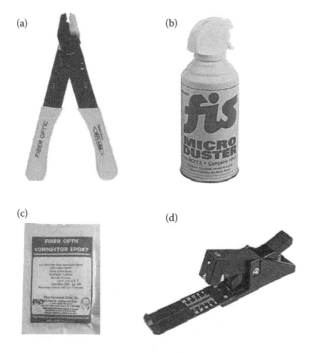

Figure 5.79 Tools, supplies, and instruments used to construct fiber optic microsensors. (a) A precision wire stripper. (b) Canned air. (c) FIS quick-cure epoxy, which exhibits a long pot, excellent glass-to-ceramic bonding, and a color change from amber to red upon curing. (d) A FIS field cleaver. This is suitable for use with quick-term connectors and optimal for mechanical splicing. It provides a guide for variable cleave lengths from 5 to 20 mm. Sometimes we use a diamond pen rather than a cleaver.

(a)   (b)

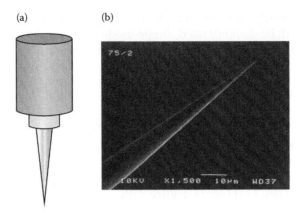

Figure 5.80 (a) Schematic drawing and (b) Scanning electron microscopy micrograph of a fiber optic microsensor tip.

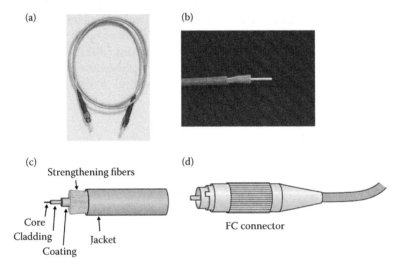

Figure 5.81 (a) Single-mode patch cord. The core diameter of the fiber optic depends on the wavelength. (b) Before the tip is constructed, the cable jacket should be stripped, the fiber should be strengthened, and the fiber optic cable should be coated. (c) A stripped cable and components. (d) Ferrule connector. One side of the cable must have an ferrule connector (FC) (a slotted screw-on connector). To make the tip, remove one of the connectors.

plastic coating that protects the fiber from mechanical damage and from moisture). Single-mode cables are single strands of glass fiber with a diameter of less than 10 μm and one mode of transmission. The section below explains how to calculate the number of modes transmitted in fiber optic cables. In single-mode fibers, light travels parallel to the axis, creating little pulse dispersion. Such cables require light sources with a narrow spectral width. A single-mode fiber is shown in Figure 5.82.

We use different single-mode fiber optic cables, depending on the wavelength to be used. The relevant properties are clearly described when you attempt to buy a single-mode fiber optic cable. We prefer to use single-mode cables because of their small core diameter, which actually makes for a very small sensing area at the tip.

Figure 5.82 A single-mode fiber optic cable.

The number of modes in a fiber optic cable is determined by computing the V parameter (Wilson and Hawkes 1998):

$$V = \frac{2\pi a}{\lambda_o}\left(n_1^2 - n_2^2\right)^{0.5} \qquad (5.13)$$

where a is the radius of the core, λ_o is the wavelength of the light, and n_1 and n_2 are the refractive indexes of the core and the cladding, respectively. A fiber can support only one mode when $V < 2.405$, but when $V \gg 1$ the number of modes that can be supported, N_m, is given by

$$N_m = \frac{V^2}{2} \qquad (5.14)$$

Example 5.1: Number of modes in a fiber

Consider a fiber where $n_1 = 1.48$, $n_2 = 1.46$, $\lambda_o = 630$ nm, and the core radius is 65 µm. Calculate V and the number of modes.

$$V = \frac{2\pi \times 65 \times 10^{-6}}{0.630 \times 10^{-6}}(1.48^2 - 1.46^2)^{0.5} = 157.1$$

Because $V \gg 1$, the number of modes is $N_m = (157.1)^2/2 = 12{,}342$.

5.3.1.2 Constructing fiber optic holders

Because the fiber optic tip is very thin and flexible, we use a holder to hold it in position when we use it in biofilms. The holder is made of a glass tube approximately 1–3 mm in diameter. First, we strip the cable jacket and the strengthening fibers and expose approximately 4–6 cm of the coated part of the fiber. Then, we strip the coating using a cable stripper (Figure 5.79) as shown in Figure 5.81b. It is important to use an optic cable stripper that is designed to be used for the specific cable; e.g., use a 250-µm stripper for a 250-µm fiber optic cable. After the cladding is exposed, we use a ferrule (FIS, catalog #conn 628) to reinforce the fragile optic tip and then glue the ferrule to a glass tube. These processes are demonstrated in Figure 5.83.

The tip is etched in hydrofluoric acid (HF). The insulation near the fiber tip is mechanically stripped, the tip is cleaned with isopropyl alcohol and cleaved (Figure 5.84), and the core to be etched is exposed. The core is carefully cut so that only the desired length of the core is exposed. We use a diamond pen or a cleaver for this purpose. A flat tip improves the chances of successful etching resulting in a tip looking like the one shown in Figure 5.80.

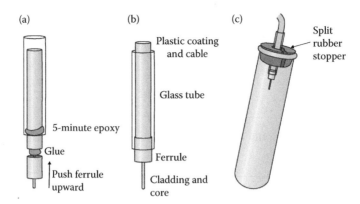

Figure 5.83 Construction of a fiber optic tip. (a) First place quick-cure epoxy onto the cladding, push the ferrule close to the cable, and let it dry for 30 min. Then add 5-min epoxy to the inside of the glass tube to glue the plastic coating to the cable. (b) Final diagram of assembled fiber optic tip. (c) An assembled tip is kept inside a glass tube, as shown.

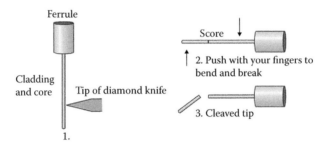

Figure 5.84 Cleaving of a fiber optic tip.

5.3.1.3   Cleaving and etching the tip

After cleaving, the tip is cleaned with isopropyl alcohol. The quality of the cleaving is tested by measuring the backscattered signal in air and in water (Beyenal et al. 2000). The tip is etched in HF under a fume hood. *It is important to take all necessary precautions during this procedure, as hydrofluoric acid can cause severe burns.* For etching, we use 37.5% HF placed in a plastic cup (Figure 5.85). Approximately 1 mm of the tip of the fiber optic cable is immersed in the HF solution. We move the tip in and out of the solution every 2 min to inspect the process of etching. The tip should be ready in no more than 15 min. The quality of the etching is determined by checking the tip under light microscopy. Usable tips have a smooth tapered length of 500–1000 μm. Tapering should be limited to the core, which allows the light to remain well guided until it reaches the actual sensing region, where the taper begins to cut into the core (Figure 5.80).

5.3.1.4   Fiber optic microsensor for measuring backscattered light intensity in biofilms

The setup for measuring backscattered light intensity in biofilms is shown in Figure 5.86. Although in our laboratory we use custom-designed instruments, we describe here the commercially available instruments that can be used for these measurements.

We use laser diodes as light sources. The light from a laser diode is injected into a coupler and from there into a fiber optic microsensor. Fifty percent of the laser light goes to a

Figure 5.85 Etching of a fiber optic tip. Use a well-ventilated hood for the hydrofluoric acid etching in this process.

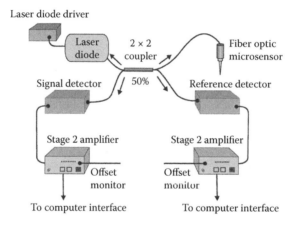

Figure 5.86 Schematic diagram of a fiber optic system.

reference detector, which gives a reference measurement for light intensity that is expected to be the same as the light intensity at the microsensor tip. The backscattered light from the microsensor is split in the coupler, and we detect 50% of the backscattered light in the signal detector. The signals are detected as current, which is translated to voltage (by transimpedance, a current-to-voltage instrument described later in this chapter) and collected as data through a computer interface.

5.3.1.5 Fiber optic cables

Table 5.7 describes selected single-mode fiber optic cables we use. Note that each light source requires the use of a different cable depending on the wavelength.

We use different cables, depending on the wavelength used in the measurement; single-mode fiber optic cables are clearly marked when you attempt to buy a single-mode fiber optic cable. Each light source of a different wavelength requires the use of a different

Table 5.7 Selected Single-Mode Fiber Specifications

Model	Operating wavelength (nm)	Numerical aperture (NA)	Mode field diameter, nominal (μm)	Cladding diameter (μm)	Coating diameter (μm)	Cut-off wavelength (nm)
F-SA/F-SA-C	488/514	0.10–0.14	3.4	125 ± 1	245 ± 12	400 ± 50
F-SV/F-SV-C	633	0.10–0.14	4.3	125 ± 1	245 ± 12	550 ± 50
F-SE/F-SE-C	780	0.10–0.14	5.4	125 ± 1	245 ± 12	680 ± 70
F-SF/F-SF-C	820	0.10–0.14	5.7	125 ± 1	245 ± 12	730 ± 70
F-SC/F-SC-C	980/1550	0.17–0.19	4.5/7.5	125 ± 1	245 ± 12	920 ± 50
F-SY/F-SY-C	980/1064/1550	0.13–0.15	5.8/6.2/10.4	125 ± 1	245 ± 12	920 ± 50

Source: http://www.newport.com/.

cable, and the fiber optic sensors that measure backscattered light intensity also use different cables, depending on the wavelength of the light used. For the measurements at 670 nm, we use a 4.3-μm core fiber with NA = 0.11 (Newport #F-SV/F-SV-C). For the measurements at 1320 nm, we use a 9-μm core fiber with NA = 0.11 (Corning SMF-28). If the backscattered light intensities of other wavelengths are measured, appropriate cables are selected from Table 5.7 or from specifications obtained from other vendors.

5.3.1.6 Fiber couplers

Fiber couplers are devices that distribute light to several outputs. We use the couplers specified in Table 5.8 to split light beams. For example, the 50:50 single-mode coupler in Figure 5.87 distributes 50% of the laser light to the microsensor and 50% to the reference. The backscattered light from the fiber optic microsensor is again split 50:50, and we detect this light in the signal channel.

Table 5.8 Selected Coupler Specifications

Model	Type	Operating wavelength (nm)
F-CPL-S12635	1 × 2 Single wavelength	633
F-CPL-S12135	1 × 2 Single wavelength	1310
F-CPL-S22635	2 × 2 Single wavelength	633
F-CPL-S22135	2 × 2 Single wavelength	1310

Source: http://www.newport.com/.

Note: "1 × 2" refers to one input and two outputs or vice versa.

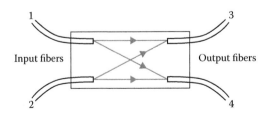

Figure 5.87 Schematic representation of a 2 × 2 fiber coupler. The light from either fiber 1 or fiber 2 is distributed to fibers 3 and 4.

5.3.1.7 Laser diodes

A laser diode converts an electrical signal into a corresponding light signal that can be injected into a fiber (Figure 5.88). Laser diodes are important components and the most costly components of the system. They are semiconductors that convert electrical current into light. The conversion process is fairly efficient in that it generates little heat compared to incandescent lights. Five inherent properties make laser diodes attractive for our purpose: (1) they are small; (2) they exhibit high radiance (i.e., they emit lots of light across a small area); (3) the emitting area is small, comparable to the dimensions of optical fibers, which is a desirable feature for coupling light to fiber optic cables; (4) they have a long life and high reliability; and (5) they can be modulated (turned off and on) at high frequencies. Despite these obvious advantages of laser diodes, some biofilm researchers use light-emitting diodes (LEDs) to construct fiber optic sensors because LEDs are less expensive than laser diodes. Recently, however, the components of optical systems, including laser diodes, are becoming more affordable: a laser diode that costs a few thousand dollars a few years ago costs a few hundred dollars now. From the point of view of selecting light sources for coupling light to single-mode fiber optic cables, laser diodes have a large advantage over LEDs because they have much smaller beam sizes than LEDs do and can deliver more light into single-mode fibers. Much of the light delivered by an LED does not enter the single-mode fiber because the diameter of the beam is much larger than the diameter of the fiber. We use a connectorized fiber-pigtailed FC and Fabry–Perot laser diodes as light sources. Table 5.9 compares characteristics of laser diodes and LEDs.

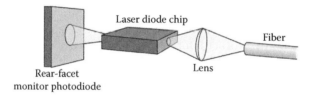

Figure 5.88 Coupling light from a laser diode to a fiber optic cable.

Table 5.9 Comparison of Some of the Characteristics of Lasers and LEDs

Characteristic	LEDs	Lasers
Output power	Linearly proportional to drive current	Proportional to current above the threshold
Current	Drive current: 50–100 mA Peak	Threshold current: 5–40 Ma
Coupled power	Moderate	High
Speed	Slower	Faster
Output pattern	Higher	Lower
Bandwidth	Moderate	High
Wavelengths available	0.66–1.65 µm	0.78–1.65 µm
Spectral width	Wider (40–190 nm)	Narrower (0.00001–10 nm)
Fiber type	Multimode only	Single-mode, multimode
Ease of use	Easier	Harder
Lifetime	Longer	Long
Cost	Low ($5–$300)	High ($100–$10,000)

Source: http://www.fiber-optics.info/articles/laser-diode.htm.

Laser diodes are typically constructed of GaAlAs (gallium aluminum arsenide) for short-wavelength devices. Long-wavelength devices generally use InGaAsP (indium gallium arsenide phosphide). We use Fabry–Perot lasers because they are the least expensive.

The light coupling does not have to be done manually: the devices on the market are composed of a laser diode coupled to a short piece of fiber optic cable (called a *pigtail*). These are available from various vendors. Newport's fiber-pigtailed laser diodes, for example, consist of Fabry–Perot devices with fiber pigtails precisely attached for optimum coupling efficiency. For our purpose, all fiber pigtails must be terminated with FC-style fiber optics. We generally operate laser diodes below threshold (typically $I = 0.7$ Ith) to improve signal stability, reduce noise intensity, and minimize coherence effects.

5.3.1.8   Laser diode drivers

Laser diodes need to be powered using appropriate power sources; these are called *laser drivers*. Laser drivers deliver the required current and potential to the laser diode. We use custom-built laser drivers. However, they are available from a variety of sources (http://www.thorlabs.com, http://www.newport.com/, etc.).

5.3.1.9   Photodiodes

Laser diodes are devices that convert electrical current into light; photodiodes work in the opposite direction. Photodiodes are semiconductor devices that convert light to electrical current. We use the PIN photodiodes shown in Figure 5.89.

To construct sensors that measure backscattered light intensity in biofilms, we use Si or InGaAs PIN photodiodes from Hamamatsu (http://sales.hamamatsu.com/). However, Hamamatsu sells bare photodiodes, and they need to be connected to an FC connector using procedures that may be difficult for laboratories without expertise in making these types of connections. An alternative to the Hamamatsu photodiodes is fiber-coupled InGaAs photodiodes (direct FC-coupled), which are available from various sources, such as http://www.roithner-laser.com, http://www.thorlabs.com/(FGA0), and http://www.edmundoptics.com/(NT55-757).

5.3.1.10   Detecting signals/amplifiers

The current generated by photodiodes must be amplified and measured. We use a UDT Tramp amplifier (http://www.udtinstruments.com) for this purpose (Figure 5.90). It is a transimpedance (current-to-voltage) instrument, providing a low-input impedance to

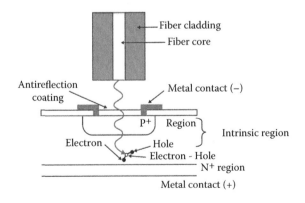

Figure 5.89 A PIN photodiode (P⁺ region, intrinsic region, and N⁺ region).

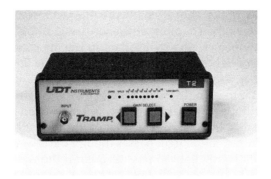

Figure 5.90 A UDT Tramp amplifier (http://www.udtinstruments.com), which is a transimpedance (current-to-voltage) instrument.

measure accurately the short-circuit current of phototransducers such as silicon and germanium photodetectors, vacuum photodiodes, photomultiplier tubes, and PIN photodiodes. The model we use provides multiple gain selections and utilizes a common BNC connector for the input and output connections. The output voltage from the amplifier is recorded in a computer and can then be used for calculation of signal-to-reference ratio.

5.3.1.11   Computer interface
A UDT Tramp amplifier receives current and converts it to voltage, and this voltage is read using an analog-to-digital/digital-to-analog card connected to a computer. The data acquisition system and the microsensor movement are combined in custom-made software written in MATLAB®. This is the same software we use to collect data from microelectrode measurements; it is described in the section on microelectrodes.

5.3.1.12   Fiber optic microsensors for measuring
fluorescent light intensity in biofilms
The setup for measuring fluorescent light intensity in biofilms is shown in Figure 5.91. We use it to measure yellow fluorescent light intensity in biofilms. Yellow fluorescent light is emitted by yellow fluorescent protein (YFP) expressed by genetically modified bacteria. Yellow fluorescent protein is excited by signals with a wavelength of 405 nm and emits light on wavelengths between 480 and 540 nm. To measure fluorescent light intensity, we use a different setup than that which we use to measure backscattered light intensity, because (1) the wavelength of the emitted light is different from that of the light used to stimulate fluorescence, (2) fiber couplers have a low coupling efficiency at 405 nm, and (3) there is dispersion and loss of 405-nm light in the fiber. It is well known that when a

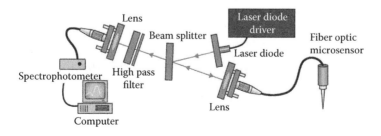

Figure 5.91 Fiber optic sensor for measuring fluorescent light intensity in biofilms.

light beam is coupled into a fiber with a small core diameter, some of the light does not enter the fiber, which lowers the coupling efficiency. In addition to the coupling ineffi- ciency, the light reflects, disperses, and is absorbed in the fiber, causing further losses of light; the size of the beam of light needs to match the size of the fiber optic cable.

We use a laser diode as the light source. The light from the laser diode is split by a beam splitter and focused into a single-mode fiber using a lens. The light at 405 nm causes light emission in the biofilm, and the emitted light is transferred back through the fiber optic cable toward the beam splitter. However, because the emitted light has a wavelength higher than 450 nm, all of the emitted light passes though the beam splitter. We add a high pass filter that does not allow any light to pass through if the wavelength is higher than 550 nm. Again, we use a specific lens to couple emitted light into a multimode fiber, and the multimode fiber is connected to a detector that is a spectrophotometer.

5.3.1.13   Constructing the tips

We use multimode fiber optic cable (140 µm/62.5 µm, Corning) for microsensors and to couple light into the spectrophotometer. All the procedures used in constructing the tip are the same as those described in Section 5.3.1.1.

5.3.1.14   Components of the measurement system

5.3.1.14.1   Laser diode.   We use a violet laser diode at 405 nm (5 mW CW power, single transverse mode, Nichia Chemical Industries, Ltd.) as a light source.

5.3.1.14.2   Beam splitter.   In contrast to the setup for measuring backscattered light intensity, in the setup for measuring fluorescent light intensity we use a beam splitter. A beam splitter is an optical device that is used to divide an optical signal beam into two (or more) directions. The laser beam is reflected by a beam splitter, LWP-30-RS400-TP450-PW-1012-UV from CVI Laser, Inc. (http://www.cvilaser.com), and focused onto the front end of the fiber by a lens. Our beam splitter is a long-wave pass dichromic, custom-built by CVI Laser, Inc. It reflects laser light at 400 nm (RS 400), is one inch in diameter and 0.25 inches thick (PW-1012), and transmits and polarizes any light above 450 nm. The incidence angle is 30°.

5.3.1.14.3   Lens.   A lens is used to focus the light into the core of a fiber optic cable. We use a single molded glass aspheric lens (C230TM-A 350–600 nm 0.55NA moderate size aspheric lens, Thorlab, Inc., Newton, NJ) to collimate the light from the laser diode without introducing aberrations.

5.3.1.14.4   High-pass filter.   The fluorescent light from the biofilm is collected at the fiber tip and passes through the beam splitter and a long-pass filter with a cutoff wave- length at 450 nm (Colored Glass Filter, Rolyn Optics, Inc., Covina, CA). It is collimated by a lens that is the same as the one described above.

5.4   Controlling microelectrode movements and data acquisition

5.4.1   Measuring instruments

The instruments required to perform the measurements are described in the sections on electrochemical and fiber optic microsensors (Chapter 4). The instruments used for micro- electrode measurements must be able to monitor low-level electrical signals reliably. The main problem with these measurements is that they are easily affected by electromagnetic noise. This is not a surprise, because low-level signals are often affected by electromagnetic noise. High-quality instruments are needed to ensure that the measurements are reliable. Possible sources of electromagnetic noise in laboratories include computer monitors, fluorescent light fixtures, and magnetic stirrers. It is possible to design filters to mitigate some persistent sources of electromagnetic noise, such as the fluorescent lights in the laboratory, but these filters tend to affect the measured signal. If electromagnetic noise is a serious problem, it is best to shield the microelectrode, or the entire setup used in the measurements, by placing it in a Faraday cage. Sometimes just placing the entire measuring setup in a fume hood makes a difference.

5.4.2   Data acquisition and microsensor movement control

The microelectrode movement system consists of a linear actuator and a controller. The tip of the linear actuator is moved using a stepper motor. The stepper motor controller provides voltage and current to rotate the stepper motor, which, in turn, moves the tip of the linear actuator. We use a custom-made MATLAB program to communicate with the stepper motor controller, to rotate the stepper motor by the desired number of turns, and to move the linear actuator in the desired direction. Figure 5.92 shows how the data acquisition system is coordinated with the sensor movements.

The data acquisition system reads a signal from an ammeter or an electrometer in the form of potential and stores the datum in the computer. After the datum is accepted and stored, the actuator moves the sensor to the next position. Both the data acquisition and the sensor movement are controlled using MATLAB programs, which are on the attached CD. The following section describes components of this system.

5.4.2.1   Data acquisition

The microelectrode produces a response in the form of electrical current or voltage. The data acquisition system accepts only voltage. Consequently, a signal in the form of a voltage is directed to the data acquisition system, while a signal in the form of a current is first converted to an equivalent voltage before it is directed to the data acquisition system. This conversion is done by the instruments we use (Figure 5.22): the picoammeter produces a voltage output between 0 and 2 V that corresponds to the current on the display. Before reaching the data acquisition system, the voltage signal is converted to a digital code so

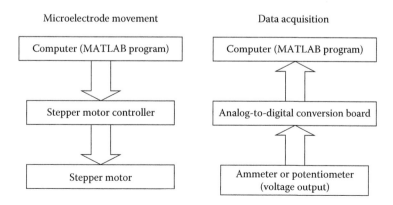

Figure 5.92 Operational diagrams of the data acquisition system and sensor movement control.

that it can be stored in the computer and then plotted on the display. For this purpose, we use an analog-to-digital conversion (ADC) system. The ADC system reads the voltage and converts it to an equivalent digital code and sends this to the computer. To simplify the description, the following acronyms are used:

AD: analog-to-digital
DAC: digital-to-analog
ADC: analog-to-digital conversion
ADCS: analog-to-digital conversion system
DACS: digital-to-analog conversion system
USB: universal serial bus

5.4.2.1.1   Selection of DAC system.   The parts of the ADC system (ADCS) are selected according to the following criteria:

1. Voltage range: An ADCS can accept a voltage input within a particular range only, for example 0 to 10 V (unipolar) or –10 to 10 V (bipolar). Some ADCS allow the user to select the voltage range using a software interface. The voltage input range of the ADCS should be equal to or greater than the range between the minimum and the maximum voltage outputs from the picoammeter. This is important: if a voltage is higher than what the ADCS can accept, it may damage the ADCS.
2. Resolution: The resolution represents how accurately the ADCS system can convert the analog voltage to a digital code. Consider an ADC with a voltage input range of –10 to 10 V and a resolution of 16 bits. The smallest voltage signal value that the ADC can convert is calculated as

$$\frac{abs(10) + abs(-10)}{2^{16}} = 305 \ \mu V$$

For a high resolution, this value should be as small as possible so that the ADCS can respond to even small changes in the voltage input.
3. Sampling rate: the sampling rate is defined as the number of AD conversions the system can perform in a second. A higher sampling rate means a shorter time to perform a single conversion. Because microelectrode measurements may be performed frequently, it is desirable to have a high sampling rate, so that the delay caused by the ADCS is negligible.

Because the current output of the microelectrode is on the order of a picoampere, it may be affected by electromagnetic noise. To eliminate the noise from the signal, the voltage must be sampled multiple times in a small time interval and then averaged. The higher the number of samples, the lower the noise component.

Example 5.2

Consider an ADCS system with 50,000 samples per second. Say that we want to take 100 samples and average them: the time needed for the ADCS can be calculated as

$$\frac{1 \ s}{50,000 \ samples} 100 \ samples = 0.002 \ s = 2 \ ms$$

5.4.2.1.2   ADC converter board.   We selected the USB-1608FS ADC module (Figure 5.93) from Measurement Computing®. The following criteria were considered when making the selection:

1. Low cost
2. Good resolution (16-bit)
3. High sampling rate (50,000 samples/s)
4. USB interface
5. Native support by MATLAB
6. Software-selectable voltage input ranges (±10, ±5, ±2, and ±1 V)
7. Eight ADC channels (even though we are using only one ADC channel, having more channels means that we can use it for capturing other signals or for future expansion)

5.4.2.1.3   Connecting the ADC board, computer, and ammeter or potentiometer.   The connections for the ADC board, computer, and ammeter or potentiometer are shown in Figure 5.94.

Figure 5.93 USB-1608FS ADC module from Measurement Computing (http://www.measurement computing.com).

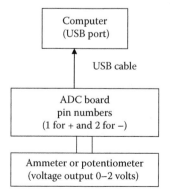

Figure 5.94 The connection of the ADC board, computer, and ammeter or potentiometer. Our MATLAB program requires the use of specific pin numbers to read the data.

5.4.2.1.4 MATLAB program for reading and recording potential. We use a simple MATLAB program (`Readthedata.m`) that initializes communication with the ADC from Measurement Computing, then triggers the DAC and collects the requested number of samples, averages them, and displays the result. The operator specifies the number of input data. The system reads that many data from the ADC board and then averages them and reports the result. For example, for the system to read 500 data and output the average of these readings, the operator needs to write the following comment in the command window:

> Readthedata(500)

The program outputs:

> Average of 500 reading is 0.25 V

5.4.3 Microelectrode movement control

5.4.3.1 Linear actuator

The first step in designing a microelectrode movement system is to find a suitable linear actuator and then a stepper motor controller. We use a linear actuator M-230.10S from Physik Instrumente (PI), GmbH & Co. KG, controlled by a stepper motor (http://www.physikin strumente.com/en/products/prdetail.php?VID = ZqS8AShcQcZEXNnF&sortnr = 703400). This linear actuator has a travel distance of 25 mm (Figure 5.95). It is equipped with a bidirectional two-phase stepper motor that drives a nonrotating tip via a flexible coupling. It comes with a permanently attached 0.5-m cable with a 15-pin sub-D connector. A minimum incremental motion of 0.05 μm is possible with this linear actuator, as is a maximum velocity of 2 mm/s.

The linear actuator needs to be connected to a 3-D micromanipulator. Because the tip of the stepper motor is nonrotating, it can easily be connected to a regular micropositioner, as shown in Figure 5.96.

5.4.3.2 Stepper motor controller

We selected the SSMicro stepper motor controller (Figure 5.97) from Simple Step®. The following criteria were considered when making this selection:

1. The controller should be able to drive a bidirectional two-phase stepper motor.
2. The stepper motor power driver in the controller should be able to meet the voltage and current requirements of the stepper motor coil.

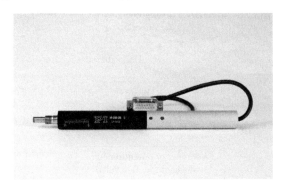

Figure 5.95 M-230.25S linear actuator, which can move the microelectrode with a minimum step size of 0.05 μm and a maximum velocity of 2 mm/s.

Figure 5.96 Photograph of M-230.25S stepper motor connected to a micromanipulator. The manipulator is the same as the one shown in Figure 5.12; we removed the fine adjustment control knob of the micromanipulator and installed the stepper motor head.

Figure 5.97 SSMicro stepper motor controller (http://www.simplestep.com/products/ssxymicro.html).

3. The controller should have the ability to read the origin and limit the sensor output from the linear actuator.
4. The controller should have a standard serial interface so that control commands can be sent using generic programs such as MATLAB.

The SSMicro controller manufactured by Simple Step met the requirements for controlling the selected linear actuator. This controller accepts commands in the form of ASCII codes using the serial port interface. Any program that is able to send an ASCII command to the serial port should be able to communicate with the controller.

5.4.3.2.1 Interfacing the linear actuator and the controller with the computer. The connections between the motor coil and the controller are shown in Table 5.10. The motor comes with a D15 cable on which the pins are clearly marked. We use appropriate pin numbers to connect the motor to the controller.

5.4.3.2.2 Controller-to-computer connection. We use the serial port of the computer for this connection. The serial port cable (DB-9) has nine pins, each numbered. One side of the cable is connected to the serial port, and the other side of the cable is connected manually to the pins on the controller (Table 5.11).

5.4.3.3 Limit sensing

The stepper motor moves within the limits for which it was designed and constructed. Any movement out of the limits will damage the stepper motor. To prevent this from happening, the stepper motor has a position controller that sends a signal if it is out of the limits. The controller receives this signal through the connection given in Table 5.10.

5.4.3.4 MATLAB program for controlling the stepper motor

We provide a simple MATLAB program (`movethemicroelectrode.m`) that moves the microelectrode in the requested step size. The program accepts the step size as an input parameter and moves the microelectrode the given distance. For example, to move the microelectrode 1000 µm, you need to write the following comment in the command window:

Movethemicroelectrode(1000)
The program outputs
Microelectrode moved 1000 microns

Table 5.10 Motor Coil, Controller, and Power Supply Connections

Motor: sub-D15(m)	Controller: J5 connector
Pin 1	Pin 1
Pin 9	Pin 2
Pin 2	Pin 3
Pin 10	Pin 4
Power supply to the controller	
Power supply	Controller Power (J1)
+24 V	Pin 1
– (Ground)	Pin 2
Home/limit sensor connections	
Motor: sub-D15(m)	Controller: J4 Connector
Pin 14	Pin 3 (Limit)
Pin 8	Pin 6 (Home)
Power supply to limit/home sensor electronics in the actuator	
Motor: sub-D15(m)	Controller: J3 Connector
Pin 6	Pin 5 (+5 V out)
Pin 7	Pin 6 (Ground)

Table 5.11 Controller-to-Computer Connection

Computer interface connection via DB-9 cable to serial port (pin numbers are given for cable)	Controller: J2 connector
Pin 5	Pin 1 (Ground)
Pin 2	Pin 2 (RxD)
Pin 3	Pin 3 (TxD)
24-V Adapter	J1 Connector
+	Pin 1
−	Pin 2

After the microelectrode has been moved to the desired position, the data acquisition system reads the signal from the electrode. The sensor movement and the data acquisition must be coordinated, as described in the next section.

5.4.3.5 Simultaneous movement of microsensor and data acquisition

In this chapter we provide the reader with a means of controlling microelectrode movement and reading data. The MATLAB programs on the CD provide these controls. However, this is a simplified system oriented toward beginners. The interface allows a user to move a sensor and collect data step by step. In our laboratory, we have gone one step further and use custom-developed software called Microprofiler® using Labview®. With this software, sensor movement and data acquisition are entirely automatic. This helps with sensitive measurements for which the presence of the operator may introduce undesirable electromagnetic noise. The programs described in this chapter and provided on the CD are sufficient to move the sensor, take measurements, and record the data at a basic level.

References

Beyenal, H., Davis, C. C., and Lewandowski, Z. 2004. An improved Severinghaus-type carbon dioxide microelectrode for use in biofilms. *Sensors and Actuators B, Chemical* 97: 202–210.

Brendel, P. J., and Luther, G. W. 1995. Development of a gold amalgam voltammetric microelectrode for the determination of dissolved Fe, Mn, O2, and S(-II) in porewaters of marine and freshwater sediments. *Environmental Science and Technology* 29: 751–761.

Miyuki, Y., Rosatto, S. S., and Kubota, L. T. 2002. Electrochemical comparative study of riboflavin, FMN and FAD immobilized on the silica gel modified with zirconium oxide. *Journal of the Brazilian Chemical Society* 13(5).

Revsbech, N. P. 1989. Microsensors: Spatial gradients in biofilms. In *Structure and Function of Biofilms*, W. G. Characklis and P. A. Wilderer (Eds.). New York: John Wiley pp. 124–144.

Van Houdt, P., Lewandowski, Z., and Little, B. 1992. Iridium oxide pH microelectrode. *Biotechnology and Bioengineering* 40: 601–608.

Wilson, J., and Hawkes, J. 1998. *Optoelectronics: An Introduction*, 3rd ed. Upper Saddle River, NJ: Prentice Hall.

Suggested readings

Reviews

Ammann, D. 1986. *Ion-Selective Microelectrodes.* Berlin: Springer-Verlag.

Beyenal, H., Lewandowski, Z., Yakymyshyn, C., Lemley, B., and Wehri, J. 2000. Fiber optic microsensors to measure back scattered light intensity in biofilms. *Applied Optics* 39: 3408–3412.

Jorgensen, B. B., and Revsbech, N. P. 1988. Microsensors. *Methods in Enzymology* 167: 639–659.
Kuhl, M. 2005. Optical microsensors for analysis of microbial communities. *Methods in Enzymology* 397: 166–169.
Lee, J.-H., Seo, Y., Lee, W. H., Bishop, P., and Papautsky, I. 2010a. Needle-type multi-analyte MEMS sensor arrays for in situ measurements in biofilms. *Emerging Environmental Technologies* II: 115–145.
Lewandowski, Z., and Beyenal, H. 2001. Limiting-current-type microelectrodes for quantifying mass transport dynamics in biofilms. *Methods in Enzymology* 331: 337–359.
Lewandowski, Z., and Beyenal, H. 2003. Use of microsensors to study biofilms. In *Biofilms in Medicine, Industry and Environmental Biotechnology—Characteristics, Analysis and Control.* Lens, P., O'Flaherty, V., Moran, A., Stoodley, P. and Mahony, T. (Eds.). London: IWA Publishing, pp. 375–412.
Revsbech, N. P. 2005. Analysis of microbial communities with electrochemical microsensors and microscale biosensors. *Methods in Enzymology* 397: 147–166.
Revsbech, N. P., and Jørgensen, B. B. 1986. Microelectrodes: Their use in microbial ecology. In *Advances in Microbial Ecology*, K. C. Marshall (Ed.). New York: Plenum, pp. 293–352.
Revsbech, N. P., Jorgensen, B. B., and Blackburn, T. H. 1983. Microelectrode studies of the photosynthesis and O_2, H_2S, and pH profiles of a microbial mat. *Limnology and Oceanography* 28: 1062–1074.

Amperometric microelectrodes

Bai, X., Dexter, S. C., and Luther, G. W. 2006. Application of EIS with Au-Hg microelectrode in determining electron transfer mechanisms. *Electrochimica Acta* 51: 1524–1533.
Beyenal, H., and Lewandowski, Z. 2001. Mass-transport dynamics, activity, and structure of sulfate-reducing biofilms. *AIChE Journal* 47(7): 1689–1697.
Boessmann, M., Neu, T. R., Horn, H., and Hempel, D. C. 2004. Growth, structure and oxygen penetration in particle supported autotrophic biofilms. *Water Science and Technology* 49: 371–377.
De Beer, D., Srinivasan, R., and Stewart, P. S. 1994. Direct measurement of chlorine penetration into biofilms during disinfection. *Applied and Environmental Microbiology* 60: 4339–4344.
De la Rosa, C., and Yu, T. 2006. Development of an automation system to evaluate the three-dimensional oxygen distribution in wastewater biofilms using microsensors. *Sensors and Actuators B-Chemical* 113: 47–54.
Jeroschewski, P., Haase, K., Trommer, A., and Grundler, P. 1994. Galvanic sensor for determination of hydrogen sulfide. *Electroanalysis* 6: 769–772.
Jeroschewski, P., Steuckart, C., and Kühl, M. 1996. An amperometric microsensor for the determination of H_2S in aquatic environments. *Analytical Chemistry* 68: 4351–4357.
Kato, D., Kunitake, M., Nishizawa, M., Matsue, T., and Mizutani, F. 2005. Amperometric nitric oxide microsensor using two-dimensional cross-linked Langmuir–Blodgett films of polysiloxane copolymer. *Sensors and Actuators B-Chemical* 108: 384–388.
Lee, J.-H., Seo, Y., Lim, T.-S., Bishop, P. L., and Papautsky, I. 2007. MEMS needle-type sensor array for in situ measurements of dissolved oxygen and redox potential. *Environmental Science and Technology* 41: 7857–7863.
Nguyen, H. D., Renslow, R., Babauta, J., Ahmed, B., and Beyenal, H. 2012. A voltammetric flavin microelectrode for use in biofilms. *Sensors and Actuators B-Chemical* 161: 929–937.
Peteu, S. F., Emerson, D., and Worden, R. M. 1996. A Clark-type oxidase enzyme-based amperometric microbiosensor for sensing glucose, galactose, or choline. *Biosensors and Bioelectronics* 11: 1059–1071.
Quintana, J. C., Idrissi, L., Palleschi, G., Albertano, P., Amine, A., El Rhazi, M., and Moscone, D. 2004. Investigation of amperometric detection of phosphate: Application in seawater and cyanobacterial biofilm samples. *Talanta* 63: 567–574.
Rasmussen, K., and Lewandowski, Z. 1998. The accuracy of oxygen flux measurements using microelectrodes. *Water Research* 32(12): 3747–3755.
Revsbech, N. P. 1989. An oxygen microsensor with a guard cathode. *Limnology and Oceanography* 34: 474–478.

Stewart, P. S., Rayner, J., Roe, F., and Rees, W. M. 2001. Biofilm penetration and disinfection efficiency of alkaline hypochlorite and chlorosulfamates. *Journal of Applied Microbiology* 91: 525–532.

Xia, F., Beyenal, H., and Lewandowski, Z. 1998. An electrochemical technique to measure local flow velocity in biofilms. *Water Research* 32: 3637–3645.

Yang, S., and Lewandowski, Z. 1995. Measurement of local mass transfer coefficient in biofilms. *Biotechnology and Bioengineering* 48: 737–744.

Yu, T., de la Rosa, C., and Lu, R. 2004. Microsensor measurement of oxygen concentration in biofilms: From one dimension to three dimensions. *Water Science and Technology* 49: 353–358.

Potentiometric microelectrodes

Bates, R. G. 1954. *Electronic pH Determinations, Theory and Practice.* London: John Wiley.

Baumgarten, C. M. 1981. An improved liquid ion exchanger for chloride ion-selective microelectrodes. *American Journal of Physiology* 241: C258–C263.

Bishop, P., and Yu, T. 1999. A microelectrode study of redox potential changes in biofilms. *Water Science and Technology* 7: 179–186.

Bissett, A., Reimer, A., de Beer, D., Shiraishi, F., and Arp, G. 2008. Metabolic microenvironmental control by photosynthetic biofilms under changing macroenvironmental temperature and pH conditions. *Applied and Environmental Microbiology* 74: 6306–6312.

De Beer, D., Glud, A., Epping, E., and Kuhl, M. 1997. A fast-responding CO_2 microelectrode for profiling sediments, microbial mats and biofilms. *Limnology and Oceanography* 42: 1590–1600.

De Beer, D., Schramm, A., Santegoeds, C. M., and Kuhl, M. 1997. A nitrite microsensor for profiling environmental biofilms. *Applied and Environmental Microbiology* 63: 973–977.

Fresser, F., Moser, H., and Mair, N. 1991. Intra- and extracellular use and evaluation of ammonium-selective microelectrodes. *Journal of Experimental Biology* 157: 227–241.

Gillam, D. E., Bishop, P. L., and Love, N. G. 2005. A study of glutathione-gated potassium efflux in biofilms using potassium microelectrodes. 5. *Environmental Engineering Science* 22: 489–495.

Hidalgo, G., Burns, A., Herz, E., Hay, A. G., Houston, P. L., Wiesner, U., and Lion, L. W. 2009. Functional tomographic fluorescence imaging of pH microenvironments in microbial biofilms by use of silica nanoparticle sensors. *Applied and Environmental Microbiology* 75: 7426–7435.

Hinke, J. 1969. Glass microelectrodes for the study of binding and compartmentalization of intracellular ions. In *Glass Microelectrodes*, Lavalle, M., Schanne, O. F., Hebert N. C. (Eds.). London: Science, pp. 349–375.

Lee, W. H., Pressman, J. G., Wahman, D. G., and Bishop, P. L. 2010. Characterization and application of a chlorine microelectrode for measuring monochloramine within a biofilm. *Sensors and Actuators B-Chemical* 145: 734–742.

Luther, G. W., Brendel, P. J., Lewis, B. L., Sundby, B., Lefrancois, L., Silverberg, N., and Nuzzio, D. B. 1998. Simultaneous measurement of O-2, Mn, Fe, I-, and S(-II) in marine pore waters with a solid-state voltammetric microelectrode. *Limnology and Oceanography* 43: 325–333.

Okabe, S., Ito, T., Satoh, H., and Watanabe, Y. 2003. Effect of nitrite and nitrate on biogenic sulfide production in sewer biofilms determined by the use of microelectrodes. *Water Science and Technology* 47: 281–288.

Pucacco, L. R., Corona, S. K., Jacobson, H. R., and Carter, N. W. 1986. pH microelectrode: Modified Thomas recessed tip configuration. *Analytical Chemistry* 153: 251–261.

Suzuki, H., Arakawa, H., Sasaki, S., and Karube, I. 1999. Micromachined Severinghaus-type carbon dioxide electrode. *Analytical Chemistry* 71: 1737–1743.

Thomas, R. C. 1978. *Ion-Sensitive Intracellular Microelectrodes, How to Make and Use Them.* New York: Academic Press.

Thomas, R. C., and Cohen, C. J. 1981. A liquid ion-exchanger alternative to KCl for filling intracellular reference microelectrodes. *Pflügers Archiv* 390: 96–98.

Xu, K., Dexter, S. C., and Luther, G. W. 1998. Voltammetric microelectrodes for biocorrosion studies. *Corrosion* 54: 814–823.

Zhang, T. C., and Pang, H. 1999. Applications of microelectrode techniques to measure pH and oxidation–reduction potential in Rhizosphere soil. *Environmental Science and Technology* 33: 1293–1299.

Zhao, P., and Cai, W. J. 1997. An improved potentiometric pCO_2 microelectrode. *Analytical Chemistry* 69: 5052–5058.

Microbiosensensors

Andersen, K., Kjaer, T., and Revsbech, N. P. 2001. An oxygen insensitive microsensor for nitrous oxide. *Sensors and Actuators B-Chemical* 81: 42–48.

Cronenberg, C. C. H., and van den Heuvel, J. C. 1991. Determination of glucose diffusion coefficients in biofilms with micro-electrodes. *Biosensors and Bioelectronics* 6: 255–262.

Damgaard, L. R., and Nielsen, L. P. 1997. A microscale biosensor for methane containing methanotrophic bacteria and an internal oxygen reservoir. *Analytical Chemistry* 69: 2262–2267.

Damgaard, L. R., Nielsen, L. P., and Revsbech, N. P. 2001. Methane microprofiles in a sewage biofilm determined with a microscale microsensor. *Water Research* 35: 1379–1386.

Damgaard, L. R., Nielsen, L. P., Revsbech, N. P., and Reichardt, W. 1998. Use of an oxygen-insensitive microscale biosensor for methane to measure methane concentration profiles in a rice paddy. *Applied and Environmental Microbiology* 64: 864–870.

Kim, J. K., and Lee, Y. H. 1988. Fast response glucose microprobe. *Biotechnology and Bioengineering* 31: 755–758.

Larsen, L. H., Revsbech, N. P., and Binnerup, S. J. 1996. A microsensor for nitrate based on immobilized denitrifying bacteria. *Applied and Environmental Microbiology* 62: 1248–1251.

McLamore, E. S., Shi, J., Jaroch, D., Claussen, J. C., Uchida, A., Jiang, Y., Zhang, W. et al. 2011. A self referencing platinum nanoparticle decorated enzyme-based microbiosensor for real time measurement of physiological glucose transport. *Biosensors and Bioelectronics* 26: 2237–2245.

Revsbech, N. P., Nielsen, L. P., Christensen, P. B., and Sørensen, J. 1988. Combined oxygen and nitrous oxide microsensor for denitrification studies. *Applied and Environmental Microbiology* 54: 2245–2249.

Fiber optic microsensors

Beyenal, H., Davis, C. C., and Lewandowski, Z. 2004. An optical microsensor to measure fluorescent light intensity in biofilms. *Journal of Microbiological Methods* 58: 367–374.

Broschat, S. L., Loge, F. J., Peppin, J. D., and White, D. 2005. Optical reflectance assay for the detection of biofilm formation. *Journal of Biomedical Optics* 10.

Buhlmann, P., Prestsch, E., and Bakker, E. 1998. Carrier-based ion-selective electrodes and bulk optodes. 2. Ionophores for potentiometric and optical sensors. *Chemical Reviews* 98: 1593–1687.

Ganesh, A. B., and Radhakrishnan, T. K. 2007. Fiber-optic sensors for the estimation of pH within natural biofilms on metals. *Sensors and Actuators B-Chemical* 123: 1107–1112.

Ganesh, A. B., and Radhakrishnan, T. K. 2008. Fiber-optic sensors for the estimation of oxygen gradients within biofilms on metals. *Optics and Lasers in Engineering* 46: 321–327.

Grunwald, B., and Holst, G. 2004. Fibre optic refractive index microsensor based on white-light SPR excitation. *Sensors and Actuators A-Physical* 113: 174–180.

Holst, G., Glud, R. N., Kuhl, M., and Klimant, I. 1997. A microoptode array for fine-scale measurement of oxygen distribution. *Sensors and Actuators B-Chemical* 38: 122–129.

Jorgensen, B. B., and Desmarais, D. J. 1986. A simple fiberoptic microprobe for high-resolution light measurements—Application in marine sediment. *Limnology and Oceanography* 31: 1376–1383.

Klimant, I., Holst, G., and Kuhl, M. 1997. A simple fiberoptic sensor to detect the penetration of microsensors into sediments and other biogeochemical systems. *Limnology and Oceanography* 42: 1638–1643.

Klimant, I., Kuhl, M., Glud, R. N., and Holst, G. 1997. Optical measurement of oxygen and temperature in microscale: Strategies and biological applications. *Sensors and Actuators B* 38–39: 29–37.

Klimant, I., Meyer, V., and Kuhl, M. 1995. Fiber-optic oxygen microsensor: A new tool in aquatic biology. *Limnology and Oceanography* 40: 1159–1165.

Kuhl, M., Lassen, C., and Revsbech, N. P. 1997. A simple light meter for measurements of PAR (400 to 700 nm) with fiber-optic microprobes: Application for P vs E-0(PAR) measurements in a microbial mat. *Aquatic Microbial Ecology* 13: 197–207.

Lerchner, J., Wolf, A., Buchholz, F., Mertens, F., Neu, T. R., Harms, H., and Maskow, T. 2008. Miniaturized calorimetry—A new method for real-time biofilm activity analysis. *Journal of Microbiological Methods* 74: 74–81.

Liebsch, G., Klimant, I., Frank, B., Holst, G., and Wolfbeis, O. S. 2000. Luminescence lifetime imaging of oxygen, pH, and carbon dioxide distribution using optical sensors. *Applied Spectroscopy* 54: 548–559.

Neurauter, G., Klimant, I., and Wolfbeis, O. S. 2000. Fiber-optic microsensor for high resolution pCO(2) sensing in marine environment. *Fresenius Journal of Analytical Chemistry* 366: 481–487.

Preininger, C., Klimant, I., and Wolfbeis, S. O. 1994. Optical fiber sensors for biological oxygen demand. *Analytical Chemistry* 66: 1841–1856.

General procedures for constructing microelectrodes

Brown, K. T., and Flaming, D. G. 1975. Instrumentation and technique for beveling fine micropipette electrodes. *Brain Research* 86: 172–180.

Kaila, K., and Voipio, J. 1985. A simple method for dry beveling of micropipettes used in the construction of ion-selective microelectrodes. *Journal of Physiology* 369.

chapter six

Quantifying biofilm structure

6.1   The need to quantify biofilm structure

The need to quantify biofilm structure became apparent when biofilm researchers discovered that it affects the rate of nutrient transport to the deeper layers of biofilms and, ultimately, influences microbial activity and the rate of biofilm accumulation. Detailed studies have since documented that biofilm structure determines the mass transport mechanism in the space occupied by a biofilm and mass transport rates near and within biofilms. The structural features of different biofilms are visually different, and it is possible that these differences are the effects of environmental factors that are known to control the rates of biofilm accumulation and activity, such as the hydrodynamics and chemical composition of the solution and the chemical and physical properties of the surface supporting biofilm growth. It is also possible that the structure of a biofilm reflects the fundamental processes that occur in a biofilm: attachment, detachment, and growth. If these hypotheses are verified and these relationships between biofilm structure and biofilm processes are true, then quantifying biofilm structure will provide access to the study of biofilm processes. To verify these hypotheses, biofilm structure needs to be quantified, and the parameters describing biofilm structure numerically need to be correlated with the rates of the biofilm processes they possibly reflect.

Thus far, most of the effects that biofilm structure has on biofilm processes are hypothetical, and they will remain hypothetical until tools are developed to quantify biofilm structure and to correlate the structure with the intensity of the processes the structure allegedly influences or reflects. Quantifying the relationships between biofilm structure and biofilm processes will open new avenues in biofilm research, as biofilm structure not only affects biofilm processes but is also a testimony to the history of a biofilm and can be used to determine the past events that occurred during its formation. For example, it is known that biofilms grown at high shear stress develop elongated microcolonies. It is also known that dense biofilms develop either as a result of high shear stress or as a result of starvation. Therefore, if a biofilm researcher samples an unknown biofilm having high density, the shape of the microcolonies may tell whether the density increased as a result of starvation or as a result of exposure to a high shear stress.

For the purposes of this chapter, it is important to define two terms: *biofilm structure* and *biofilm heterogeneity*. Biofilm researchers initially used *biofilm structure* when referring to the physical structure of biofilms (morphology), and the term was considered self-explanatory. However, as time progressed, many authors started to use this term as a synonym for biofilm heterogeneity, implicitly referring to various kinds of heterogeneity in biofilms: physiological, chemical, and genetic. Because the term biofilm structure is no longer self-explanatory, it must be defined every time it is used. In this writing, the initial meaning of *biofilm structure*—the distribution of biomass in the space occupied by the biofilm—is used. *Biofilm heterogeneity* is used when referring to the nonuniform distribution of any feature within the space occupied by a biofilm, e.g., the nonuniform distribution of the biomass, chemistry, or physiological group of microorganisms. These are referred to as structural heterogeneity, chemical heterogeneity, and physiological heterogeneity, respectively.

Biofilm structure—the spatial distribution of biomass within the space occupied by a biofilm—needs to be quantified from a set of refined measurements sensitive to the presence of the biomass. This can be done, for example, from a set of local effective diffusivity profiles measured as described in Chapter 9. Effective diffusivity is quantitatively related to biomass density, and profiles of effective diffusivity can be converted to profiles of biomass density. However, profiles of effective diffusivity are measured at selected locations in the biofilm, and many such measurements would have to be made to determine the distribution of the biomass in the space occupied by the biofilm. Therefore, determining the distribution of a biomass from effective diffusivity profiles, although possible, is clearly not very practical. The most practical approach to the problem is to quantify the distribution of the biomass from biofilm images, particularly from confocal microscopy images. Images taken with confocal laser microscopes are particularly useful because they provide information about biofilm distribution using the same field of view but various distances from the bottom. Using appropriate software, sequences of two-dimensional (2-D) confocal microscopy images acquired using the same field of view and several distances from the bottom are used to reconstruct biomass distribution in three-dimensional (3-D) space. This process aids imaging of the distribution but does not necessarily quantify it. Biomass distribution needs to be expressed numerically to be correlated with biofilm activity.

Images of biomass distribution in the space occupied by a biofilm are used to compute several parameters characterizing biofilm structure. These parameters by themselves do not necessarily reflect any fundamental biofilm processes. They are values of mathematical functions characterizing the distribution of the pixels in the biofilm images. Some of these functions are conceptually simple, such as the ratio of the number of pixels representing biomass to the number of pixels representing voids, and some are complex, such as the probability that the gray-scale intensity of two neighboring pixels is higher than a certain value. Many such functions have been devised and are routinely computed in image analyses of all sorts. Some of these functions are more and some are less suitable for quantifying biofilm images. For example, if the value of a function can be computed only if the edges within the image are well defined, that function may not be very useful for biofilm image analysis because the edges in biofilm images are notoriously ill defined. From a rich library of functions quantifying the distribution of pixels in images, several that appear promising have been selected. The values that these functions deliver are called "parameters describing biofilm structure." The remainder of this chapter is dedicated to explaining how these parameters are computed, what their meanings are, and how representative they are of the underlying biofilm processes. Scrutinizing the parameters for relevance is important because, in most cases, it is not clear which of these parameters are better and which are worse descriptors of the underlying biofilm processes. Whether the selected parameters are good descriptors of biofilm structure and reflect the underlying biofilm processes must be verified by testing them in various analyses of biofilm processes. Ultimately, the truly useful parameters should be useful for mathematical models of biofilm activity and accumulation.

In the following sections of this chapter, hands-on examples are given to explain the meanings of the parameters and the computational procedures. Relevant MATLAB® programs that perform these calculations automatically are also provided. These programs are used to compute structural parameters from the sample biofilm images saved on the CD and from simple images presented in matrices in this chapter.

The attached CD lists the individual functions that are used to perform specified tasks. Most of the file names are self-explanatory and indicate what the program does. For example, the file named `Arealporosity.m` can be used to compute areal porosity (AP) from binary images. The programs discussed in this chapter have been written as M files. M files are either script files or functions. Script files are simply files containing a sequence of MATLAB commands. Using script files eliminates the need to write individual function calls or use variable assignments. Functions make use of their own local variables, accept input arguments and, in some cases, produce output arguments. For example, the function named `Arealporosity.m` accepts a binary image matrix and returns the AP value. The attached M files are combined in a package for biofilm image analysis software called ISA. To run the functions described in this tutorial, first copy and save the relevant files from the CD to a computer and set the working directory in the C drive to C:\Fundamentals of Biofilm Research\6 QUANTIFYING BIOFILM STRUCTURE.

It is expected that the users have a basic knowledge of MATLAB and are able to install MATLAB and Image Analysis Toolbox on their computers. MathWorks offers a free trial of MATLAB and Image Processing Toolbox. Detailed information about downloading and installing the programs is on the provider's Web page (http://www.mathworks.com/).

6.2   Types of images

Biofilm images are acquired using either light microscopy or confocal scanning laser microscopy (CSLM). Once acquired, the images should be saved as TIFF files. Saving images as JPEG files should be avoided because information in this type of file is easily distorted because of compressing and decompressing during opening and closing of the file. If the images were acquired as red–green–blue (RGB) images, they must be converted to gray-scale images that can then be converted to binary images if needed. Figure 6.1a shows an RGB image of a biofilm which is converted to a gray-scale image, Figure 6.1b, and to a binary image, Figure 6.1c.

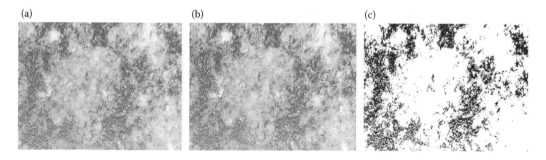

(a)   (b)   (c)

Figure 6.1 A biofilm image in different formats. The image size is 640 × 480 pixels, and the bright and dark areas show biomass (cell clusters) and voids, respectively. (a) RGB image, 16.7 million colors, 901 KB in size. The RGB image is saved on the CD, and the file name is "2D-test-biofilm-RGB.tif." (b) Gray-scale image, 256 levels of gray, 302 KB in size. The file name on the CD is "2D-test-biofilm-GrayScale.tif." (c) Binary (bilevel, or thresholded) image in black and white (two colors), 37.7 KB in size. The file name on the CD is "2D-test-biofilm-Binary.tif." (Reprinted from Beyenal, H. et al., *Biofouling*, 20, 1, 2004. With permission.)

From the gray-scale images (Figure 6.1b), textural parameters are computed. From the thresholded images (Figure 6.1c), areal parameters are computed. Thresholded images are also used to compute structural parameters in 3-D space from stacks of biofilm images.

6.2.1   Gray-scale images

There are 256 shades of grey, resulting from using eight bits of information at two levels, zero and one ($2^8 = 256$). If the biofilm images were RGB images, each of the three colors—red, green, and blue—would have 256 levels, and each pixel would have to be described as one of $256^3 = 16,777,216$ levels. This would create computational difficulties related to handling large files. To speed up the computations, the RGB images are converted to gray-scale images. Each pixel in the gray-scale image (Figure 6.1b) corresponds to an integer from 0 to 255, reflecting the intensity of the light. Thus, such images can be represented by matrices in which each pixel of the image has a value from 0 to 255, representing the level of the gray scale (Figure 6.2).

6.2.2   Binary images

Each pixel of the biofilm image is represented as one of 256 levels on the gray scale. To compute some of the parameters characterizing biofilm structure, it is important to ascribe each pixel in the image either to the biomass or to the interstitial void. For that purpose, the gray-scale image in Figure 6.2 is converted to a black and white image (Figure 6.3) by segmenting using a thresholding algorithm. Thresholding is based on selecting a gray level below which all levels are equated to zero and above which all levels are equated to one. The segmenting level may belong to either category, depending on the algorithm.

6.2.3   Stacks of CSLM images

Confocal scanning laser microscopy produces images of a field of view at different distances from the bottom of the biofilm. As a result, CLSM images are composed of many layers (Figure 6.4). Each image in Figure 6.4a is a gray-scale image, and the stack of images can be used to reconstruct the biofilm in 3-D space (Figure 6.4b and c).

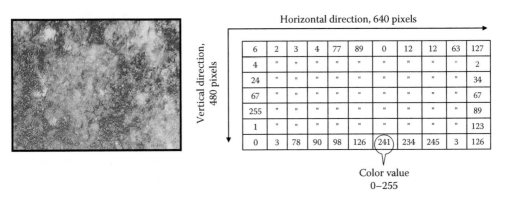

Figure 6.2 A gray-scale biofilm image (left). Each pixel has an intensity value represented by an integer from 0 to 255. This image is 640 × 480 pixels, and the bright and dark areas show biomass (cell clusters) and voids, respectively. (Reprinted from Beyenal, H. et al., *Biofouling*, 20, 1, 2004. With permission.)

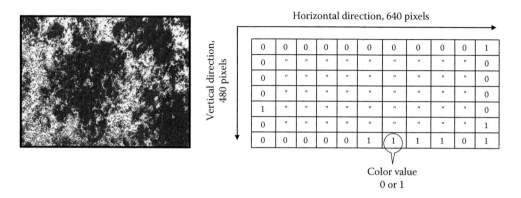

Figure 6.3 Binary image of a biofilm. When a gray-scale biofilm image (see Figure 6.2) is converted to a binary level image, the intensity of the gray level is represented by a one or a zero for each pixel. In the figure, black and white areas show biomass (cell clusters) and voids, respectively. In some cases, it is preferable to image the cell clusters as black because it is more visible. This is not a critical issue for the calculations as long as it is known which color belongs to cell clusters and which belongs to voids. (Reprinted from Beyenal, H. et al., *Biofouling*, 20, 1, 2004. With permission.)

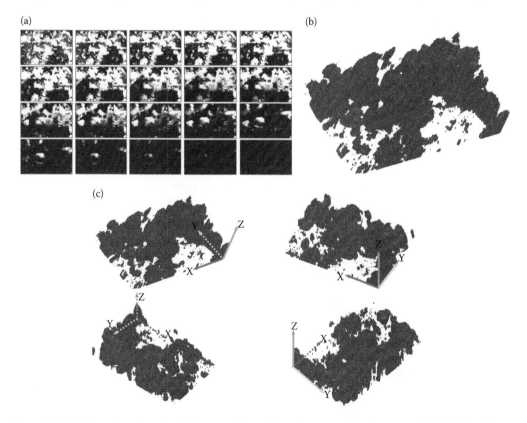

Figure 6.4 (a) A series of confocal images taken from the top to the bottom of the biofilm (upper left corner to lower right corner). (b) A 3-D reconstruction of the biofilm from the stack of confocal images shown in (a). (c) The 3-D image rotated and inspected from various angles. The 3-D reconstruction can also be cut digitally in any direction to inspect the inner space of the biofilm. (Reprinted from Lewandowski, Z. and Beyenal, H., *Water Science and Technology*, 47(5), 9–18, 2003.)

CSLM images can be saved as single layers of images, or they can be saved as an image stack. Saving the images separately is more convenient, because in this form they are ready for image analysis. Images saved in a single file (as an image stack) must be transferred to individual files before image analysis. This can be done manually using commercial software (most CSLM software packages have this option), or it can be done automatically using the MATLAB code shown below.

6.2.4 Converting CSLM image stacks to single images

On the CD is an image stack (saved as CSLMstack.tif) that is 24.1 MB and contains three different channels of 96 single-layer CSLM images in RGB planes. Only the first 32 images should be analyzed, because these images show the biomass distribution. For this application, these 32 images will be saved for further analysis in a directory called CSLMstackimages. To do this, the following steps should be taken:

1. Run MATLAB.
2. Change the current directory to "C:\Fundamentals of Biofilm Research\6 QUANTIFYING BIOFILM STRUCTURE" by typing "cd('C:/Fundamentals of Biofilm Research/6 QUANTIFYING BIOFILM STRUCTURE')."
3. To get image info, type

   ```
   x = imfinfo('CSLMstack.tif')
   ```

   The following should appear:

   ```
   x = 96x1 struct array with fields:
   Filename
   FileModDate
   ......... .
   ```

4. To find out how many image layers are in the stack, type

   ```
   size(x)
   ans = 96 1
   ```

5. Our stack of images is composed of 96 layers, so size(x) returns 96. Because there are three channels in this image stack, 96/3 = 32 is the total number of images in each channel.
6. Open "CSLMStackReader.m" and run it.
7. After MATLAB finishes running the codes, go to "C:\Fundamentals of Biofilm Research\6 QUANTIFYING BIOFILM STRUCTURE\CSLMstackimages". Thirty-two images, numbered sequentially 1.tif, 2.tif...32.tif, should appear.
8. These images are ready to analyze.

6.2.5 Converting digital images to data matrices

6.2.5.1 Images in MATLAB

The basic data structure in MATLAB is the array, an ordered set of real or complex elements. MATLAB stores single-layer images as 2-D arrays (i.e., 2-D matrices) in which each element of the matrix corresponds to a single pixel in the displayed image (see Figures 6.2 and 6.3). For example, an image composed of 480 rows and 640 columns of different colored dots is stored in MATLAB as a 480 × 640 matrix. For image analysis, all RGB or other formatted images must be first converted to gray-scale images because they contain unwanted information.

6.2.5.2   Converting RGB images to gray-scale images

The biofilm image on the CD named "2D-test-biofilm-RGB.tif" is an RGB true-color image, and it will be converted to a gray-scale image. There is a script file (converttograyscale.m) on the CD that can be used for this purpose. This conversion can be done using the command window in MATLAB by typing the following commands in the script file:

1. Read the image:

```
I = imread('2D-test-biofilm-RGB.tif');
```

2. Display the image:

```
imtool(I);
```

3. Convert to gray scale:

```
GLI = rgb2gray(I);
```

4. Write image with a new name:

```
imwrite(GLI,'graylevel-I.tif');
```

5. Display the image:

```
imtool(GLI);
```

The same calculations can be performed by running "converttograyscale.m".

A stack of CSLM images should first be converted to single 2-D images as described above and then converted individually to gray-scale images.

6.2.5.3   Converting gray-scale images to data matrices

The biofilm image on the CD named "graylevel-I.tif" is a gray-scale image. To convert it to a data matrix,

1. Read the image and assign it to 2-D matrix "I":

```
I = imread('graylevel-I.tif');
```

2. Learn the matrix size:

```
size(I)
ans = 480 640
```

This demonstrates that the size of matrix I is 480 × 640 pixels. It is a 2-D matrix.

6.3 Computing parameters from biofilm images

6.3.1 Textural parameters computed from single images

Texture, described as a repeating pattern of local variations in image intensity, provides information about the spatial distribution of gray-scale intensity levels in a neighborhood. In computer science literature, texture is often used to partition images into regions of interest and classify those regions.

Textural parameters quantify biofilm structure by comparing the size, position, and/or orientation of the visual components. Each textural parameter measures the gray-level variation in the cell clusters and in the interstitial spaces based on the likelihood that pixels of similar or dissimilar types will be neighbors. In these analyses, the following textural parameters described by Haralick et al. (1973) are computed: (1) textural entropy (*TE*), (2) energy (*E*), and (3) homogeneity (*H*).

The calculations described here are based on descriptions given by Haralick et al. (1973), and the textural parameters are computed from a gray-level co-occurrence matrix (GLCM). This matrix contains information about the positions of pixels having similar gray-level values, and it is computed from the spatial dependence matrices in the horizontal and vertical directions. Horizontal and vertical spatial dependence matrices show intensity variations for their respective directions.

The terms *energy* and *entropy*, when used in reference to images, are somewhat confusing, particularly to life scientists, who immediately associate them with the laws of thermodynamics and Clausius's entropy. The terms energy and entropy are used in other sciences, and their meanings are analogous to those in thermodynamics, but they are not identical. In image analysis, the term *energy*, introduced by Haralick et al. (1973), is a measure of directionally repeating patterns of pixels. The term entropy is also used in other sciences. Entropy in communication, defined by Shannon in 1948, measures uncertainty of information, and increasing entropy is associated with a loss of information. Energy and entropy in sciences other than thermodynamics are dimensionless. The following section defines energy and entropy as used in reference to images.

6.3.1.1 Calculating a normalized spatial dependence matrix

The following example shows an image as a 4×4 matrix with four gray levels (0–3).

0	0	1	1
1	2	0	1
2	3	1	0
2	2	2	3

The horizontal spatial dependence matrix (P_H) of this image is computed as

$$P_H = \{p_H(a,b)\} = \begin{bmatrix} p_H(0,0) & p_H(0,1) & p_H(0,2) & p_H(0,3) \\ p_H(1,0) & p_H(1,1) & p_H(1,2) & p_H(1,3) \\ p_H(2,0) & p_H(2,1) & p_H(2,2) & p_H(2,3) \\ p_H(3,0) & p_H(3,1) & p_H(3,2) & p_H(3,3) \end{bmatrix} = \begin{pmatrix} 2 & 3 & 1 & 0 \\ 3 & 2 & 1 & 1 \\ 1 & 1 & 4 & 2 \\ 0 & 1 & 2 & 0 \end{pmatrix}$$

where $p_H(a,b)$ is the number of changes in the gray scale between a and b in adjacent horizontal locations in the image, moving in either direction. For example, $p_H(0, 1)$ is the number of changes in the gray scale between 0 and 1 in the horizontal direction. There are two such changes moving from left to right and one moving from right to left, for a total of three. Because direction is not considered, the matrix is symmetrical around the diagonal.

Similarly, the vertical spatial dependence matrix (P_V) is

$$P_V = \{p_V(a,b)\} = \begin{bmatrix} p_V(0,0) & p_V(0,1) & p_V(0,2) & p_V(0,3) \\ p_V(1,0) & p_V(1,1) & p_V(1,2) & p_V(1,3) \\ p_V(2,0) & p_V(2,1) & p_V(2,2) & p_V(2,3) \\ p_V(3,0) & p_V(3,1) & p_V(3,2) & p_V(3,3) \end{bmatrix} = \begin{pmatrix} 0 & 4 & 1 & 1 \\ 4 & 2 & 2 & 0 \\ 1 & 2 & 2 & 2 \\ 1 & 0 & 2 & 0 \end{pmatrix}$$

where $p_V(a,b)$ is the number of changes in the gray scale between a and b in adjacent vertical locations in the image, moving in either direction. The spatial dependence matrix (P_{HV}) is the sum of the horizontal and vertical spatial dependence matrices

$$P_{HV} = P_H + P_V = \{p_{HV}(a,b)\} = \begin{pmatrix} 2 & 7 & 2 & 1 \\ 7 & 4 & 3 & 1 \\ 2 & 3 & 6 & 4 \\ 1 & 1 & 4 & 0 \end{pmatrix}$$

where $p_{HV}(a,b)$ is the total number of intensity variations from a to b and from b to a in the horizontal and vertical directions. Normalization is accomplished by summing the elements of the spatial dependence matrix and dividing each element by the sum.

$$\text{sum} = \sum_a \sum_b P_{HV}(a,b) = 48$$

$$P_N(a,b) = \frac{P_{HV}}{\text{sum}} = \begin{pmatrix} 0.0417 & 0.1458 & 0.0417 & 0.0208 \\ 0.1458 & 0.0833 & 0.0625 & 0.0208 \\ 0.0417 & 0.0625 & 0.1250 & 0.0833 \\ 0.0208 & 0.0208 & 0.0833 & 0 \end{pmatrix}$$

The textural parameters that can be defined from GLCM $(P_N(a,b))$ are

$$\text{Textural entropy, } TE = -\sum_{a,b}\sum_{P_N(a,b)\neq 0} P_N(a,b)\ln(P_N(a,b)) \qquad (6.1)$$

$$\text{Energy, } E = \sum_a \sum_b \{P_N(a,b)^2\} \qquad (6.2)$$

$$\text{Homogeneity, } H = \sum_a \sum_b \frac{1}{1+(a-b)^2} P_N(a,b) \tag{6.3}$$

In this example, the computed parameters are

Textural entropy = $-[0.0417 \times \ln(0.0417) + 0.01448 \times \ln(0.01458) + \dots 0.0833 \times \ln(0.0833)] = 2.51$

Note that to calculate textural entropy we use only nonzero values.

$$\text{Energy} = (0.0417)^2 + (0.01448)^2 + \dots + (0.0833)^2 + (0)^2 = 0.094$$

$$\text{Homogeneity} = \frac{1}{1+(1-1)^2}0.0417 + \frac{1}{1+(1-2)^2}0.1458 + \dots + \frac{1}{1+(4-4)^2}0 = 0.571$$

6.3.1.2 Calculating textural entropy, energy, and homogeneity

In this example, there is a 4 × 4 image matrix with four different gray levels (0,1,2,3). The "GLCM2DMATLAB.m" function on the CD will be used to calculate its textural parameters.

1. Read image to analyze:

$$X = \begin{array}{cccc} [0 & 0 & 1 & 1 \\ 1 & 2 & 0 & 1 \\ 2 & 3 & 1 & 0 \\ 2 & 2 & 2 & 3] \end{array}$$

Note that matrices in MATLAB are denoted by square brackets.

2. Run the function "GLCM2DMATLAB.m":

```
[TE,E,H] = GLCM2DMATLAB(X,4)
```

Note that the number 4 after X shows the number of gray levels in the image. The output of the program is

```
TE = 2.5091
E = 0.0938
H = 0.5708
```

6.3.1.3 Calculating textural parameters from a biofilm using MATLAB

In this example, textural parameters are computed for the image shown in Figure 6.1b.

1. Read the biofilm image:

```
X = imread('2D-test-biofilm-GrayScale.tif');
```

2. Run the function from the command window:

```
[TE,E,H] = GLCM2DMATLAB(X,256)
```

Note that the number after 4 has changed to 256 because the biofilm image has 256 gray levels.

3. The following results are computed:

```
TE = 9.3647
E  = 2.0174e-004
H  = 0.0954
```

6.3.1.4   Meanings of textural parameters

The meanings of the textural parameters and the procedures used to compute them are explained using the images in Figure 6.5.

6.3.1.4.1   Textural entropy.   Textural entropy (*TE*) is a measure of the randomness in the gray scale of an image. The higher the *TE*, the more heterogeneous the image. Figure 6.5a shows an image with no structure, composed of only white pixels (i.e., a void). The *TE* computed for this image is zero, showing there is no tonal variation in the pixels or heterogeneity in the image. Figures 6.5b,c, and d contain increasing numbers of pixel clusters and the *TE* increases accordingly.

6.3.1.4.2   Energy.   Energy (*E*) is a measure of directionally repeating patterns of pixels, and it is sensitive to the orientation of the pixel clusters and the similarity of their shapes. Smaller energy values mean frequent and repeated patterns of pixel clusters, and a higher energy means a more homogeneous image structure with fewer repeated patterns. In Figure 6.5a, the energy equals one, showing that there are no repeating patterns in that image. As the number of repeating clusters increases, the energy value decreases (Table 6.1).

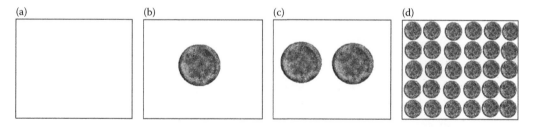

Figure 6.5 Custom-generated images introducing textural parameters of images: (a) a white area, (b) a single circular cell cluster, (c) two cell clusters, and (d) many cell clusters. The textural parameters computed from these images are shown in Table 6.1. (Reprinted from Beyenal, H. et al., *Biofouling*, 20, 1, 2004. With permission.)

Table 6.1 Textural Parameters Computed for the Images Shown in Figure 6.5

Image	TE	E	H
Figure 6.5a	0	1	1
Figure 6.5b	0.60	0.78	0.94
Figure 6.5c	1.02	0.59	0.88
Figure 6.5d	1.97	0.19	0.66

Source: Reprinted from Beyenal, H. et al., *Biofouling*, 20, 1, 2004.

6.3.1.4.3   Homogeneity.   Homogeneity (*H*) is a measure of spatially repeating patterns of pixels. It measures the similarity of the clusters: A higher homogeneity indicates a more homogeneous image structure. Homogeneity is normalized with respect to the distances between changes in texture, so it is independent of the locations of the pixel clusters in the image. In Figure 6.5a, the homogeneity equals one, showing there are no repeating spatial patterns in the image; the amount of homogeneity decreases with an increasing number of clusters (Table 6.1).

6.3.1.4.4   Homogeneity versus energy.   The definitions of homogeneity and energy are similar, and the meanings of these parameters require further explanation. This may be done by comparing the images in Figure 6.5. Figure 6.5c contains one more cluster than Figure 6.5b, and the additional cluster is shifted horizontally. Consequently, there is a pattern of repeating pixel clusters in the horizontal direction. However, the shapes of the two clusters are identical. Therefore, comparing the computed parameters, it is not surprising that the energy decreases more than the homogeneity does ($\Delta E = 0.19$ and $\Delta H = 0.06$). Indeed, ΔE is more than three times higher than ΔH, showing that there is significant directional variation between the image in Figure 6.5b and that in Figure 6.5c. Similarly, when Figures 6.5b and d are computed, $\Delta E = 0.59$ and $\Delta H = 0.28$. This shows that the decrease in homogeneity is caused by the repeating pattern of pixel clusters, while the accompanying decrease in energy is caused by directional variations in the pattern of pixel clusters in these images.

6.3.1.5   Examples of textural parameters computed from biofilm images

Two biofilm images are compared in Figure 6.6; Figure 6.6a shows large clusters, and Figure 6.6b shows small clusters. The textural parameters computed from these images are given in Table 6.2.

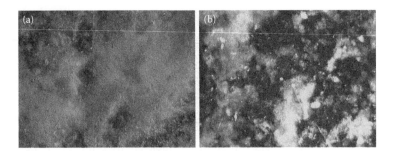

Figure 6.6 Two biofilm images compared qualitatively, above, and numerically, in Table 6.2. (Reprinted from Beyenal, H. et al., *Biofouling*, 20, 1, 2004. With permission.)

Table 6.2 Textural Parameters Computed from the
Images in Figure 6.6

Image	TE	E	H
Figure 6.6a	5.070068	0.01731	0.548574
Figure 6.6b	7.059066	0.003081	0.135297

Source: Reprinted from Beyenal, H. et al., *Biofouling*, 20, 1, 2004.

The biofilm in Figure 6.6a shows large clusters with small intensity variations, and it is expected that it will have a lower *TE* than the biofilm in Figure 6.6b. Because more repeating microstructures are seen in Figure 6.6b than in Figure 6.6a, it is expected that *E* and *H* will decrease. The decrease in *H* is more pronounced than the decrease in *E*, showing that directionally repeating patterns (or cell clusters) are more dominant in Figure 6.6b.

6.3.2   *Areal parameters computed from single images*

Areal parameters describe the morphology of biofilms; they are concerned with the size and shape/orientation of the constituent parts. Each parameter measures a unique characteristic feature of either the biomass or the interstitial space in the biofilm. Because of this, the first action that is performed in image analysis is to separate cell clusters from interstitial voids. This is done by image segmentation (explained in Section 6.3.2.1) separating an image into distinct components. The parameters are initially computed using pixels rather than distances. However, because the pixels have known dimensions, the computed parameters can easily be converted to linear scales.

A common method of segmenting an image is thresholding, in which all pixels with gray levels below a particular value (the threshold) are changed to zero and all above the threshold are changed to one. The resulting black and white image has two visible components (Figure 6.3).

6.3.2.1   *Thresholding biofilm images*

As discussed in Section 6.2.2, thresholding is a segmentation method that compresses the color scale, typically to two colors. For biofilm images, thresholding reduces the 256 gray levels to 2 gray levels to separate the image into biomass and interstitial space. The operator subjectively selects 1 of the 256 gray levels as the threshold. Computer software then segments the image(s) into two parts, with all gray levels less than or equal to the threshold becoming black and all higher gray levels becoming white.

To extract statistically meaningful morphological parameters from a series of images, the thresholding must be reproducible. The choice of threshold is subjective, so the choice of gray-scale intensity selected to segment the images depends on the operator's understanding of the image content and the desired relationship between the two segments in the final image. The operator uses his or her best judgment and sets the gray level in such a way that the binary image appears to capture the essence of the biofilm structure. Because the parameters computed from thresholded images depend on the selected gray level, their values are subjective. Variability among operators in choosing the threshold adversely affects the measurements obtained from the binary image.

Figure 6.7 shows the impact that the threshold has on the calculation of biofilm areal porosity. Different operator preferences for the threshold doubled the estimate of biofilm areal porosity in some cases.

Because there is no absolute measure of correctness for the threshold, it was assumed that an acceptable automatic thresholding method should give a value approaching the average value determined by a panel of human experts (Yang et al. 2001; Xavier et al. 2001). It was assumed that an automatic procedure that had sufficient precision could yield more reproducible results than human operators. To evaluate the efficiency of selected automatic image thresholding procedures, the following needed to be tested: the variability among thresholds set manually by different operators, the variability among thresholds set automatically using known thresholding algorithms, and the agreement between the thresholds set manually and those set automatically.

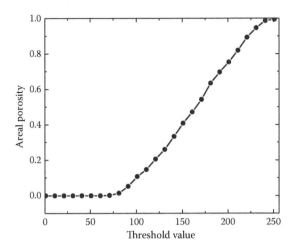

Figure 6.7 The gray-scale biofilm image shown as Figure 6.2 was used to test the variation of areal porosity (AP) with threshold value. The AP was 0.1 and 0.4 for gray-scale thresholds of 100 and 150, respectively. (Reprinted from Beyenal, H. et al., *Biofouling*, 20, 1, 2004. With permission.)

Most thresholding algorithms described in the literature were based on measuring boundaries and edges, and they were tested on objects having well-defined boundaries such as microbes or fluorescent particles (see review paper by Wilkinson [1998]). Using these boundary- and edge-detecting algorithms for biofilm images has been attempted. However, the cell clusters in biofilms do not have clearly marked boundaries, so the applicability of these algorithms is questionable. Our focus was on testing techniques that use entropy and histogram properties, and the following five methods of automatic thresholding available in the computer science literature were chosen: (1) local entropy (Pal and Pal 1989), (2) joint entropy (Pal and Pal 1989), (3) relative entropy (Chang et al. 1994), (4) Renyi's entropy (Sahoo et al. 1997), and (5) iterative selection (Ridler and Calvard 1978). The images of biofilms were generated by reflected light microscopy, transmission light microscopy, and CSLM. To generate a reference set, 10 researchers from the Center for Biofilm Engineering at Montana State University, Bozeman manually thresholded the same images. The results of the different automatic thresholding procedures were compared with each other and with the results of manual thresholding. Only the iterative selection method was found satisfactory in that it consistently set the threshold level near that set manually (Yang et al. 2001). For this reason, only the iterative selection method is described in this chapter, rather than all the applicable methods. In addition, for comparison purposes, Otsu's method was selected to calculate the thresholds of biofilm images because Otsu's method is a given MATLAB function.

6.3.2.2 *The iterative selection method for thresholding biofilm images*

The iterative selection method assumes that there is a mean value that is the optimal threshold value for both background and foreground pixels. As can be seen in Figure 6.8, $t_{opt} = (t_{back} + t_{fore})/2$ must be computed iteratively using the following algorithm: t_{opt} is the optional threshold value, t_{back} is the average of background pixels, and t_{fore} is the average of foreground pixels.

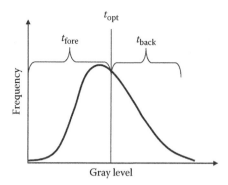

Figure 6.8 Schematic representation of optimum thresholding (t_{opt}) on a histogram. (Reprinted from Beyenal, H. et al., *Biofouling*, 20, 1, 2004. With permission.)

Iterative selection algorithm:

1. Select t_{opt}, called t_{optS} (start from 1 and increase accordingly).
2. Compute $t_{opt} = (t_{back} + t_{fore})/2$.
3. If $t_{opt} = t_{optS}$ it is the correct threshold value; stop iteration.
4. If $t_{opt} \neq t_{optS}$ go to step 1.

The value of t_{optS} starts from 1 and increases until the condition in step 3 is satisfied.

6.3.2.3   Calculating threshold value

The following example shows an image as a 4 × 4 matrix with four gray levels (0–3), from which the threshold value is computed below.

0	0	1	1
1	2	0	1
2	3	1	0
2	2	2	3

A 4 × 4 matrix with four gray levels (0 – 3).

Gray level	Bin
1	4
2	5
3	5
4	2

Gray level versus bin number. To calculate the bin number for gray level 1, just count the number of "1"s in the image matrix at the left. These values are used to compute the threshold value.

To compute the threshold value, first plot a histogram of the matrix. Note that the index starts at 1, corresponding to gray level 0.

Figure 6.9 shows each gray-level value and the bin number that is the total number of occurrences of that gray level. This image has four gray levels; a background and a foreground threshold value will be computed for each gray level, and a table will be prepared.

For $t_{optS} = 1$, the foreground and background averages are computed as follows:

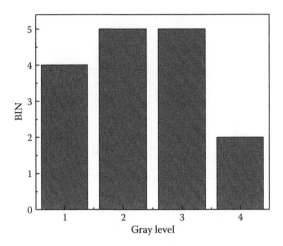

Figure 6.9 Histogram for the matrix in this section.

First, all pixels equal to or lower than 1 will be foreground, and any pixel having a value higher than 1 will be called background. Now the averages can be computed.

$$\text{Average foreground} = t_{\text{fore}} = \frac{\sum_{i=1}^{t_{\text{optS}}} \text{Gray level} \times \text{Bin}}{\sum_{i=1}^{t_{\text{optS}}} \text{Bin}}$$

$$\text{Average foreground} = t_{\text{fore}} = \frac{1 \times 4}{4} = 1$$

$$\text{Average background} = t_{\text{back}} = \frac{\sum_{i=t_{\text{optS}}+1}^{N} \text{Gray level} \times \text{Bin}}{\sum_{i=t_{\text{optS}}+1}^{N} \text{Bin}}$$

$$\text{Average background} = t_{\text{back}} = \frac{2 \times 5 + 3 \times 5 + 4 \times 2}{5 + 5 + 2} = \frac{33}{12} = 2.75$$

Compute $t_{\text{opt}} = (t_{\text{fore}} + t_{\text{back}})/2$

$$t_{\text{opt}} = (2.75 + 1)/2 = 1.875$$

For $t_{optS} = 2$ the foreground and background averages are computed as follows:

$$\text{Average foreground} = t_{\text{fore}} = \frac{1 \times 4 + 2 \times 5}{4 + 5} = \frac{14}{9} = 1.5556$$

$$\text{Average background} = t_{\text{back}} = \frac{3 \times 5 + 4 \times 2}{5 + 2} = \frac{23}{7} = 3.2857$$

$$t_{\text{opt}} = (3.2857 + 1.5556)/2 = 2.42$$

For $t_{optS} = 3$ the foreground and background averages are computed as follows:

$$\text{Average foreground} = t_{\text{fore}} = \frac{1 \times 4 + 2 \times 5 + 3 \times 5}{4 + 5 + 5} = \frac{29}{14} = 2.0714$$

$$\text{Average background} = t_{\text{back}} = \frac{4 \times 2}{2} = \frac{8}{2} = 4$$

$$t_{\text{opt}} = (2.0714 + 4)/2 = 3.0357$$

Calculations for $t_{optS} = 4$ are not performed because it does not allow any background. Table 6.3 summarizes the above calculations.

According to the iterative selection algorithm, the correct threshold value must give $t_{\text{opt}} = t_{optS}$. Mathematically, this may not always be possible because t_{optS} is an integer and t_{opt} is a real number. To avoid these difficulties, the smallest differences between t_{opt} and t_{optS} [Abs($t_{\text{opt}} - t_{optS}$)] are selected. If there are multiple minimum values (less than 1) of Abs($t_{\text{opt}} - t_{optS}$), the first t_{opt} is selected that provides a [Abs($t_{\text{opt}} - t_{optS}$)] value less than 1. Note that in this algorithm t_{optS} starts at 1 and increases in increments of 1. This sets the criterion for the selection of t_{opt}. For the above matrix, the threshold value is 1.875. This means any gray level equal to or smaller than 2 (closest integer to 1.875) represents the foreground, and any gray level higher than 2 represents the background. For biofilm images the background is selected to represent the voids in the biofilm image. However, for the threshold calculations the selection of the background or the foreground to represent voids does not make any difference.

In the examples that immediately follow this section the results of thresholding are compared using the iterative selection algorithm and Otsu's method on (1) a small matrix computed from a hypothetical biofilm image and (2) a large matrix computed from an actual biofilm image. For the large matrix the two methods found an almost identical threshold value. However, for the small matrix they gave different results. Otsu's method

Table 6.3 Computed Average and Foreground Values for Different Selected Threshold Values and Corresponding Optimum Threshold Values

t_{optS}	Foreground	Background	t_{opt}	Abs($t_{opt} - t_{optS}$)
1	1	2.75	1.875	0.875
2	1.5556	3.2857	2.42	0.42
3	2.0714	4	3.0357	0.0357

is used as an alternative method of thresholding images when the result obtained using the iterative selection method is not satisfactory, which happens occasionally.

6.3.2.4   *Thresholding using MATLAB for a given matrix*

Open the "threshold Matrix.m" file and run it.

```
threshold_from_otsu = 0.4980
threshold_from_iterative_selection = 0.4688
```

Note that 0.4688 is equal to 1.875/4, which was calculated manually as the threshold value in the above example. However, when an image is thresholded, the computer rounds this real number to the nearest integer.

6.3.2.5   *Thresholding a biofilm image using MATLAB*

To threshold the biofilm image, follow these instructions:

1. Read biofilm image to analyze:

```
X = imread('2D-test-biofilm-GrayScale.tif');
```

2. Run the function

```
threshold(X,256)
```

3. The output of the program is

```
threshold_from_otsu = 0.6706
threshold_from_iterative_selection = 0.6746
```

Note that the computed threshold values are normalized by dividing by the maximum gray level in the image, which is 256. This normalization procedure was used because MATLAB only accepts threshold values between 0 and 1.

6.3.2.6   *Thresholding a biofilm image and saving it as a*
thresholded image using MATLAB

For areal parameters to be computed, the gray-scale images need to be converted to binary images. An example of this procedure is given in the "Read_threshold_and_save.m" script file. The procedure in the script file is described below.

1. Read image:

```
X = imread('2D-test-biofilm-GrayScale.tif');
```

2. Assign a threshold value. This was computed previously to be

```
t = 0.6746;
```

3. Show original image and assign a title:

```
subplot(2,2,1), imshow(X);
title('GL Image');
```

4. Convert the gray-scale image to a binary image using the assigned threshold value:

```
bwOriginal = im2bw(X,t);
```

5. Show thresholded image and assign a title:

```
subplot(2,2,2);
imshow(bwOriginal);
title('Thresholded Image');
```

6. Write image to the disk for further use:

```
imwrite(bwOriginal,'BW-thresholded_image.tif');
```

Instead of typing all the codes, the "Read_threshold_and_save.m" script file can be opened and run. The thresholded image (BW-thresholded_image.tif) will be used to compute the areal parameters in the following examples.

6.3.2.7   *Calculating areal parameters*

The following sections give the definitions of several area parameters and relevant procedures for their computations. In particular, areal porosity, average run length, average diffusion distance, perimeter, and fractal dimension are defined and calculated.

6.3.2.8   *Areal porosity*

The AP is defined as the ratio of void area to total area:

$$\text{Areal porosity} = \text{AP} = \frac{\text{Number of void pixels}}{\text{Total number of pixels}} \tag{6.4}$$

6.3.2.8.1   Calculating AP.   In the following binary image, the number of void (zero) pixels is 27, and the total number of pixels is 36, so AP is 27/36 = 0.75. AP can be expressed as a percent by multiplying the ratio by 100. The AP of this image is thus 75%.

0	0	0	0	0	0
0	1	1	0	0	0
0	1	1	1	0	0
0	1	1	1	1	0
0	0	0	0	0	0
0	0	0	0	0	0

6.3.2.8.2   Calculating areal porosity from a sample data set using MATLAB.   The MATLAB program used to compute areal porosity is "Areal_porosity.m". To use this function, the user needs to read the binary matrix above and then pass it to the Areal_porosity.m function to compute the AP of the matrix. This can be performed as follows:

1. Read the matrix:

$$X = \begin{bmatrix} 0 & 0 & 0 & 0 & 0 & 0 \\ 0 & 1 & 1 & 0 & 0 & 0 \\ 0 & 1 & 1 & 1 & 0 & 0 \\ 0 & 1 & 1 & 1 & 1 & 0 \\ 0 & 0 & 0 & 0 & 0 & 0 \\ 0 & 0 & 0 & 0 & 0 & 0 \end{bmatrix}$$

2. Run "Arealporosity.m" to compute the AP:

```
Arealporosity(X)
```

3. The program output is

```
ArealPorosity = 0.7500
```

The Arealporosity function also shows the thresholded image.

6.3.2.8.3 Calculating areal porosity from a biofilm image using MATLAB. The MATLAB program for computing AP, "Areal_porosity.m", is given on the attached CD. To use this function, the user needs to read a binary image and then pass it to the Areal_porosity.m function to compute the AP of the selected biofilm image. This can be performed as follows:

1. Read the biofilm image:

```
X = imread('BW-thresholded_image.tif');
```

2. Run "Arealporosity.m" to compute the AP:

```
Arealporosity(X)
```

3. The program output is

```
ArealPorosity = 0.3181
```

Note that the original biofilm image is a reflected light microscopy image; therefore, in the thresholded image shown by MATLAB, voids are black.

6.3.2.9 Average run length

The average run length is the average number of biomass pixels representing cell clusters found consecutively in the image. Both the horizontal and the vertical average run lengths are used to provide additional information about directionality. These values provide a measure of the expected dimensions of a cell cluster and are therefore a measure of the average cluster size.

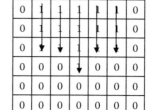

Number of horizontal runs = 4   Number of vertical runs = 5

6.3.2.9.1   Calculating average run lengths.   Average horizontal and vertical run lengths are computed by dividing the total number of pixels by the total number of runs in the horizontal or vertical direction. The binary biofilm image shown above has an average horizontal run length (AHRL) of $(5 + 5 + 5 + 1)/4 = 16/4 = 4$ pixels and an average vertical run length (AVRL) of $(3 + 3 + 4 + 3 + 3)/5 = 16/5 = 3.2$ pixels. The total numbers of runs in the horizontal and vertical directions are 4 and 5, respectively. The total number of biomass pixels is 16.

6.3.2.9.2   Calculating average run lengths from a sample data set using MATLAB.   The program "`Runlengths.m`" computes average run lengths. To compute the average run lengths of the below matrix,

1. Read the matrix:

$$X = \begin{bmatrix} 0 & 0 & 0 & 0 & 0 & 0 & 0 \\ 0 & 1 & 1 & 1 & 1 & 1 & 0 \\ 0 & 1 & 1 & 1 & 1 & 1 & 0 \\ 0 & 1 & 1 & 1 & 1 & 1 & 0 \\ 0 & 0 & 0 & 1 & 0 & 0 & 0 \\ 0 & 0 & 0 & 0 & 0 & 0 & 0 \\ 0 & 0 & 0 & 0 & 0 & 0 & 0 \end{bmatrix}$$

2. Run the MATLAB function:

```
Runlengths(X);
```

3. The output of the program is

```
AVRL  = 3.2000
AHRL  = 4
```

6.3.2.9.3   Calculating average run lengths from a biofilm image using MATLAB.   The program "`Runlengths`" computes the run lengths for a binary biofilm image. To compute the run lengths for the "`BW-thresholded_image.tif`" image,

1. Read the image:

```
BW = imread('BW-thresholded_image.tif');
```

2. Run the MATLAB function:

```
Runlengths(BW);
```

3. The output of the program is

```
AVRL = 10.4088
AHRL = 10.5888
```

6.3.2.10   Average and maximum diffusion distances

A diffusion distance in an image is defined as the minimum distance from a cluster pixel to the nearest void pixel. Two diffusion distances are considered: average and maximum. The average diffusion distance (ADD) is the average of the minimum distance from each cluster pixel to the nearest void pixel over all cluster pixels in the image. A larger diffusion distance indicates a larger distance for substrate to diffuse into the cell cluster. The maximum diffusion distance (MDD) is defined as the distance from the most "remote" pixel in the cell cluster to the nearest void cluster.

The definition of ADD refers to computing the shortest distance, but it does not specify how to compute it. To compute ADD, the Euclidean distance mapping algorithm is used (Breu et al. 1995). The Euclidian distance is calculated as $\sqrt{x^2 + y^2}$. For the cluster cells that do not border void cells, the distance from the cluster pixel to the nearest void pixel in the horizontal and vertical directions is computed.

6.3.2.10.1   Calculating average and maximum diffusion distances.   The diffusion distance is the minimum distance from a biomass cell to interstitial space: it is intended to measure the distance to nutrients. An example of a diffusion distance calculation using Euclidean distance is shown below.

0	0	0	0	0	0
0	0	1	1	0	0
0	1	1	1	1	0
0	0	1	1	0	0
0	0	0	0	0	0

0	0	0	0	0	0
0	0	1	1	0	0
0	1	1.41	1.41	1	0
0	0	1	1	0	0
0	0	0	0	0	0

Original image   Euclidian distance map

ADD is the average of the diffusion distances computed for all the cells in a cluster. A slightly different measure is the MDD, which is the largest of the diffusion distances computed for all the cells in the cluster. For example, in the Euclidian distance map, the ADD is the average of all the distances = $(1 + 1 + 1 + 1.41 + 1.41 + 1 + 1 + 1)/8 = 8.82/8 = 1.1$ pixels and the MDD is 1.41 pixels.

6.3.2.10.2   Calculating diffusion distances from a sample data set using MATLAB.   The program "Diffusiondistances.m" computes diffusion distances for a 2-D matrix.

1. Read the matrix:

$$X = \begin{bmatrix} 0 & 0 & 0 & 0 & 0 & 0 \\ 0 & 0 & 1 & 1 & 0 & 0 \\ 0 & 1 & 1 & 1 & 1 & 0 \\ 0 & 0 & 1 & 1 & 0 & 0 \\ 0 & 0 & 0 & 0 & 0 & 0 \end{bmatrix}$$

2. Run the MATLAB function:

```
Diffusiondistances(X);
```

3. The output of the program is

```
ADD = 1.1036
MDD = 1.4142
```

6.3.2.10.3   Calculating diffusion distances from a biofilm image using MATLAB.   The program "`Diffusiondistances`" computes the diffusion distances for a binary biofilm image. To compute the diffusion distances for the "`BW-thresholded_image.tif`" image,

1. Read the image:

```
BW = imread('BW-thresholded_image.tif');
```

2. Run the MATLAB function:

```
Diffusiondistances (BW);
```

3. The output of the program is

```
ADD = 4.6366
MDD = 32.9848
```

6.3.2.11   Perimeter

The perimeter (P) is defined as the total number of pixels at the cell boundary, so only pixels in contact with interstitial space are counted.

0	0	0	0	0	0
0	0	1	1	0	0
0	1	1	1	1	0
0	0	1	1	0	0
0	0	0	0	0	0

The perimeter of the above image is $1 + 1 + 1 + 1 + 1 + 1 = 6$. The shaded pixels are boundary pixels, and the total number of these pixels is the perimeter.

6.3.2.11.1   Calculating the perimeter from a sample data set using MATLAB.   The program "Perimeter" computes the perimeter for a binary biofilm image. To compute the perimeter for the matrix shown above,

1. Read the matrix:

$$X = \begin{bmatrix} 0 & 0 & 0 & 0 & 0 & 0 \\ 0 & 0 & 1 & 1 & 0 & 0 \\ 0 & 1 & 1 & 1 & 1 & 0 \\ 0 & 0 & 1 & 1 & 0 & 0 \\ 0 & 0 & 0 & 0 & 0 & 0 \end{bmatrix}$$

2. Run the MATLAB function:

```
perimeter(X);
```

3. The output of the program is

```
Perimeter = 6
```

6.3.2.11.2   Calculating the perimeter from a biofilm image using MATLAB.   The program "Perimeter" computes the perimeter for a binary biofilm image. To compute the perimeter for the "BW-thresholded_image.tif" image,

1. Read the image:

```
BW = imread('BW-thresholded_image.tif');
```

2. Run the MATLAB function:

```
perimeter(BW);
```

3. The output of the program is

```
Perimeter = 53596
```

6.3.2.12   Fractal dimension

In 2-D space, the fractal dimension measures the degree of irregularity in the perimeter of an object; it varies between 1 and 2. The higher the fractal dimension, the more irregular the perimeter of the object (Kaandorp 1994). For the purpose of our analysis, the higher the degree of variability in the biofilm cluster boundary, the higher the fractal dimension.

The Minkowski sausage method is used to compute the fractal dimension (Russ 2002), primarily because it relates to image processing techniques. The Minkowski method measures the fractal dimension by determining the rate of change in the perimeter of an object as the thickness of the perimeter line is increased. As the iterations proceed, the long and highly irregular perimeters become shorter because the irregularities are smoothed when thicker perimeter lines are used. From an image processing viewpoint, dilation (moving a circle around the boundaries as shown in Figure 6.10a) is used to accomplish the

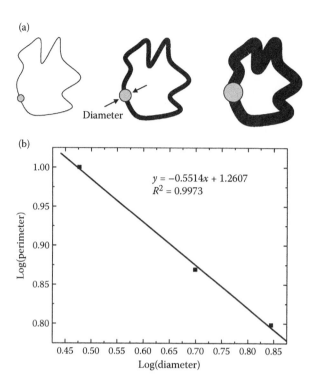

Figure 6.10 Minkowski sausage method of computing fractal dimension. (a) A circle of a particular diameter sweeps the perimeter of the object, producing a new perimeter. (b) Log(diameter) versus log(perimeter). (Reprinted from Beyenal, H. et al., *Biofouling*, 20, 1, 2004. With permission.)

smoothing of the perimeter line. Each circle of a particular radius sweeps the perimeter of the object, producing a new perimeter.

The gray-level value of the pixels at the boundary is set to zero and that of all other pixels is set to one (shown below). The Euclidean distance is then computed to obtain the distance to the boundary for each pixel. The dilation area is computed by varying the circle radius and counting the number of pixels at a distance smaller than the radius value. Then, the perimeter is computed as

$$\text{Perimeter} = \frac{\text{Dilated area}}{\text{Diameter}} \tag{6.5}$$

Plotting the logarithm of the dilation circle diameter against the logarithm of the measured perimeter produces a straight line. The fractal dimension is defined as

$$\text{Fractal dimension} = \text{FD} = 1 - \text{slope} \tag{6.6}$$

6.3.2.12.1   Calculating fractal dimension.   Calculating the fractal dimension is demonstrated for the binary image below.

0	0	0	0	0	0	0	0
0	0	0	0	0	1	1	1
0	0	0	0	0	1	1	1
0	0	0	0	1	1	1	1
0	0	0	0	0	1	1	1
0	0	0	0	0	0	1	1
0	0	0	0	0	0	0	0

1. Replace the boundary pixels with zeros and mark the remaining pixels with ones (see below).

1	1	1	1	1	1	1	1
1	1	1	1	1	0	0	0
1	1	1	1	1	0	1	1
1	1	1	1	0	0	1	1
1	1	1	1	1	0	0	1
1	1	1	1	1	1	0	0
1	1	1	1	1	1	1	1

2. Compute the Euclidian distances for the image generated in step 1 (see below).

5	4.12	3.16	2.24	1.41	1	1	1
4.47	3.61	2.83	2	1	0	0	0
4.12	3.16	2.24	1.41	1	0	1	1
4	3	2	1	0	0	1	1.41
4.12	3.16	2.24	1.41	1	0	0	1
4.47	3.61	2.83	2.24	1.41	1	0	0
5	4.24	3.61	2.83	2.24	1.41	1	1

To make this calculation easier, the border pixels have been replaced with zeros. It is also assumed that if there is a cell cluster pixel at the border of the image, that the next pixel is not a void.

3. Compute the perimeter for each dilation: Count the total number of pixels that have a distance less than the radius of the dilation circle.

5	4.12	3.16	2.24	1.41	1	1	1
4.47	3.61	2.83	2	1	0	0	0
4.12	3.16	2.24	1.41	1	0	1	1
4	3	2	1	0	0	1	1.41
4.12	3.16	2.24	1.41	1	0	0	1
4.47	3.61	2.83	2.24	1.41	1	0	0
5	4.24	3.61	2.83	2.24	1.41	1	1

For a radius value of 1.5 pixels, the dilated area is 30 pixels (see above). To compute the dilated area, all pixels that have a distance of less than 1.5 (the radius of the dilation circle) are counted. The perimeter value is 30/3 = 10.

4. Plot the logarithm of the diameter versus the logarithm of the perimeter and compute the slope of the linear function as shown in Figure 6.10. Fitting the data to a line gives a slope value of −0.55, so the fractal dimension is 1 − (−0.55) = 1.55.

As is the case for a few other parameters characterizing biofilm structure, the relation between fractal dimensions computed from biofilm images and underlying biofilm processes remains debatable and needs to be quantified. From the definition of the fractal dimension, it is known that the higher the fractal dimension, the rougher the surface of the microcolonies and the larger the surface area exposed to the solution of nutrients. Hypothetically, the fractal dimension should be related to the specific substrate utilization rate (nutrient utilization rate per unit volume of the biomass) and, perhaps, to biofilm activity.

6.3.2.13   Notes about MATLAB calculations

MATLAB marks perimeter pixels slightly differently from how they are marked in the example above. This difference is important when fractal dimension is calculated for the small-sized images used in these examples. However, this difference is negligible when the fractal dimension of a biofilm image is calculated because the image size is generally higher than 480 × 640. How this calculation is done using MATLAB is described below.

Assign X to the matrix generated using the image from the previous example:

$$X = \begin{bmatrix} 0 & 0 & 0 & 0 & 0 & 0 & 0 & 0 \\ 0 & 0 & 0 & 0 & 0 & 1 & 1 & 1 \\ 0 & 0 & 0 & 0 & 0 & 1 & 1 & 1 \\ 0 & 0 & 0 & 0 & 1 & 1 & 1 & 1 \\ 0 & 0 & 0 & 0 & 0 & 1 & 1 & 1 \\ 0 & 0 & 0 & 0 & 0 & 0 & 1 & 1 \\ 0 & 0 & 0 & 0 & 0 & 0 & 0 & 0 \end{bmatrix}$$

Mark the border pixels using a four-connected neighborhood. In this process, only the pixels that have at least one void in their immediate neighborhoods, in the horizontal or in the vertical direction, are marked as pixels belonging to the perimeter.

```
Perimeter_mark = bwperim(X,4)
```

The output is

```
Perimeter_mark =
   0 0 0 0 0 0 0 0
   0 0 0 0 0 1 1 1
   0 0 0 0 0 1 0 1
   0 0 0 0 1 0 0 1
   0 0 0 0 0 1 0 1
   0 0 0 0 0 0 1 1
   0 0 0 0 0 0 0 0
```

As shown, MATLAB marks edge pixels differently than has been done previously in this chapter. MATLAB considers any hypothetical pixel outside of the image to be a void pixel. For that reason, in this algorithm, all the edge pixels are removed to eliminate errors introduced at the edges. This procedure does not introduce significant error into parameter estimation when biofilm images are analyzed. Also, note that MATLAB marks boundaries with a 1 rather than a 0 as is done here.

6.3.2.13.1 Calculating fractal dimension from a biofilm image using MATLAB. The program "FractalDimension.m" computes fractal dimension for a binary biofilm image. To compute the diffusion distances for the "BW-thresholded_image.tif" image,

1. Read the image:

   ```
   BW = imread('BW-thresholded_image.tif');
   ```

2. Run the MATLAB function:

   ```
   FractalDimension(BW);
   ```

3. The output of the program is

   ```
   FractalDimension = 1.6996
   ```

The program also shows two figures: the biofilm image with a marked perimeter and a plot showing the correlation between log(diameter) and log(perimeter). Using this program to compute the fractal dimension of the matrix above may produce different results because an algorithm is used here to trim the pixels at the edges, eliminating the edge effects. This effect is not noticeable for large matrices, but it is very significant for small image matrices like the example shown above.

6.3.3 The meanings of the areal parameters of single images

To expose the meanings of the areal parameters, a set of hypothetical images (Figure 6.11) is generated and the areal parameters for each of them are computed. Figure 6.11a shows a single cell cluster; Figure 6.11b, two cell clusters; Figure 6.11c, three cell clusters; and Figure 6.11d, four cell clusters. The areal parameters computed from these images are shown in Table 6.4.

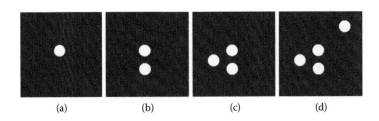

(a)   (b)   (c)   (d)

Figure 6.11 (a) A single cell cluster, (b) two cell clusters, (c) three cell clusters, and (d) four cell clusters. (Reprinted from Beyenal, H. et al., *Biofouling*, 20, 1, 2004. With permission.)

Table 6.4 Areal Parameters Computed for Each Image in Figure 6.11

Image	AP	ADD (pixels)	MDD (pixels)	AHRL (pixels)	AVRL (pixels)	P (pixels)
Figure 6.11a	0.983	9.65	27.46	44.02	44.80	160
Figure 6.11b	0.966	9.65	27.46	44.02	44.80	320
Figure 6.11c	0.949	9.65	27.46	44.02	44.80	480
Figure 6.11d	0.932	9.65	27.46	44.02	44.80	640

Source: Reprinted from Beyenal, H. et al., *Biofouling*, 20, 1, 2004.

As seen in Table 6.4, the ADD, MDD, AHRL, and AVRL are the same for each image. This is expected because identical cell clusters should have identical ADD, MDD, AHRL, and AVRL values, and the number of cell clusters in the image is irrelevant. The perimeter value increased linearly with the increasing number of cell clusters, as expected. Similarly, AP decreased with the increasing number of cell clusters.

6.3.3.1   Areal parameters computed from biofilm images

Two biofilm images are compared in Figure 6.12; Figure 6.12a shows a few small, elongated clusters, and Figure 6.12b shows a single, less elongated cell cluster. The areal parameters computed for these images are given in Table 6.5.

Because the image in Figure 6.12a has a few small, elongated clusters, it has a lower ADD than the cluster in Figure 6.12b. The perimeters are similar for these two images. Because the biofilm shown in Figure 6.12a has a lower ADD, a more efficient internal transfer of substrate is expected in that biofilm than in the biofilm in Figure 6.12b. Such analyses can be helpful in interpreting the results of chemical analyses of bulk solutions and in explaining differences in substrate consumption rates.

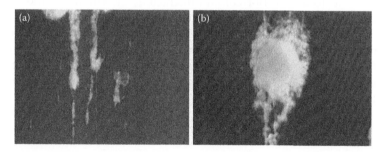

Figure 6.12 (a) Image of a biofilm with small, elongated clusters. (b) Image of a biofilm without such clusters. This biofilm has a higher ADD than that in (a) and thus may be less efficient at transferring substrate internally. These biofilms are compared numerically in Table 6.5. (Reprinted from Beyenal, H. et al., *Biofouling*, 20, 1, 2004. With permission.)

Table 6.5 Areal Parameters Computed for the Images in Figure 6.12

Image	ADD (pixels)	MDD (pixels)	AHRL (pixels)	AVRL (pixels)	FD	P (pixels)	AP
Figure 6.12a	7.623214	36.35932	25.35278	49.46883	1.097069	1722	0.940579
Figure 6.12b	30.37936	102.4597	79.17414	152.7074	1.115244	1698	0.804642

Source: Reprinted from Beyenal, H. et al., *Biofouling*, 20, 1, 2004.
Note: Before the analysis, the images were filtered using a 5 × 5 size median filter to remove noise.

6.4   Quantifying biomass distribution in 3-D from stacks of biofilm images

Quantifying biofilm structure from an individual biofilm image can only provide information about the biofilm structure at the distance from the bottom at which the image was taken, and this is not enough. For example, light microscopy images show only the bottom or the surface of a biofilm; they do not reveal information about the distribution of biomass in the entire biofilm, which, by definition, is the structure of the biofilm. To evaluate biofilm structure, the distribution of biomass in the biofilm, the biomass distribution, must be analyzed in 3-D. This analysis can be performed with stacks of biofilm images acquired using CSLM. The principle of this analysis is expressing the information about the pixel distribution in each image in the stack in a 2-D matrix, as discussed above, and then converting the stack of 2-D matrices into one 3-D matrix characterizing the entire stack of images. The parameters computed from 3-D matrices have the same names as those computed from 2-D matrices; however, the analysis of 3-D matrices is somewhat more complex.

The dimensions of a pixel in a single layer are controlled by the magnification of the microscope. For example, the pixel dimensions may be $dx = dy = 1$ μm. Note that for any microscopy technique, $dx = dy$ will always be the case. However, for 3-D images, the vertical dimension of the pixels is determined by the vertical distance between the images in the stack. To make the vertical dimension of the pixels equal 1 μm, the spaces between images in the stack are filled with interpolated images, and as many images are computed as are required for the distance between individual images to be equal to 1 μm. This is done by interpolating from the values of neighboring pixels in the vertical direction. Using pixels of equal dimensions in all three directions simplifies the analysis because the volume of the voxels, pixels in 3-D, does not have to be addressed. If the voxels have vertical dimensions different from their horizontal dimensions, the volume of the voxel must be computed for each stack of images. In this system, this process is vastly simplified because the volume of a given structure in a biofilm can be computed just by adding up the number of voxels representing the biomass in all matrices in the stack. If the size of the pixels in an image is other than 1 μm × 1 μm, the distance between the layers must be adjusted accordingly. Basically, the final dimensions of a voxel and the distance between layers will be $dx = dy = dz = k$.

6.4.1   Layers of CSLM images

Figure 6.13a shows the coordinate system used in this book. CSLM images are acquired in layers parallel to the biofilm surface. Each layer corresponds to an image in the X and Y directions, and the layers are arranged in the Z direction. A diagram of a single layer is shown in Figure 6.13b, where each pixel is represented as an (x,y,z) triplet, and dx and dy are defined as the size of a pixel in the X and Y directions. For all CSLM images $dx = dy$, and for this example it is assumed that $dx = dy = 1$ μm (Figure 6.13b).

The additional layer shown in Figure 6.13c introduces dz', the distance between layers in the image set. Because of computer memory limitations, users typically acquire CSLM images with dz' greater than dx or dy. Having $dx = dy \neq dz'$ biases the calculation of some parameters from stacks of biofilm images. To avoid this problem, additional layers are computed by interpolation so that the pixel size is the same in all three directions, $dx = dy = dz$ (Figure 6.13d).

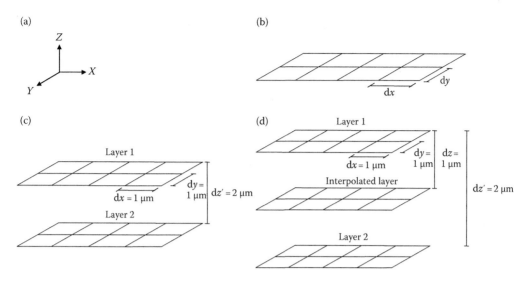

Figure 6.13 (a) Coordinate system used in this chapter, (b) single layer of image, (c) image with two layers with a distance between layers of dz′ = 2 μm, and (d) layer 1, layer 2, and the interpolated layer; dx = dy = dz = 1 μm. (Reprinted from Beyenal, H. et al., *Journal of Microbiological Methods*, 59, 395, 2004.)

6.4.1.1   Generating 3-D matrices from stacks of 2-D matrices

Relatively small images are used in the hands-on examples of computing parameters from stacks of biofilm images. In these examples, each image is represented by a 2-D matrix. The matrices are arranged in a stack, one above another. The user is required to convert the stacks of 2-D matrices into a 3-D matrix. This is done by first arranging a set of 2-D images into a stack of 2-D matrices and then converting the stack of 2-D matrices to a 3-D matrix. This process can be done automatically using the attached MATLAB programs. In this example, a 3-D matrix will be generated from layers of images represented by 2-D matrices. For this purpose, the MATLAB program "MatrixConstruct3D.m", which does not accept an input but outputs a 3-D matrix, is used.

1. Run MatrixConstruct3D.m and assign the output to D3:

   ```
   D3 = MatrixConstruct3D()
   ```

2. The output of the program is

   ```
   D3(:,:,1) =
      10 8 9 5
      11 7 8 7
   D3(:,:,2) =
      1 0 2 7
      3 0 3 1
   ```

3. After running the program, learn the size of the created 3-D matrix:

   ```
   size(D3)
   2 4 2
   ```

This matrix will be used in our first example of image interpolation, given below.

6.4.1.2 Example of generating 3-D matrices from stacks of 2-D matrices

A stack of single-layer images is converted to a 3-D data matrix by reading all the individual images and converting them to 2-D matrices and then converting the stack of 2-D matrices to a 3-D matrix. The program named "`ReadImagesGenerate3DMatrix.m`" on the CD is designed to perform this task. The program reads a given number of images in a given directory. In this example, four single images in the directory "`C:\Fundamentals of Biofilm Research\6 QUANTIFYING BIOFILM STRUCTURE\ThreeDmatrixImages`" will be read, and a 3-D matrix will be generated from the four layers of CSLM images by following the procedure below:

1. Define the location of the images as the directory:

   ```
   directory = 'C:\Fundamentals of Biofilm Research\6 QUANTIFYING
   BIOFILM STRUCTURE\ThreeDmatrixImages'
   ```

2. Run the MATLAB function:

   ```
   ThreeDMatrix = ReadImagesGenerate3DMatrix(directory,4);
   ```

3. After running the program, learn the size of the created 3-D matrix:

   ```
   size(ThreeDMatrix)
   ans = 512 512 4
   ```

MATLAB function `ReadImagesGenerate3DMatrix` produces a 3-D matrix that will be used to compute structural parameters from stacks of biofilm images.

6.4.1.3 Interpolation into stacks of biofilm images

A simple method of interpolation is the linear method, which looks at the same (x,y) coordinates in successive layers to compute the average pixel values and form the interpolated layer. For example, in Figure 6.14, the values of the pixels at location (1,1) in layer 1 and layer 2 are 10 and 1, respectively. The value of the pixel at (1,1) in the interpolated image is 6 because $(10 + 1)/2 = 5.5$, and 5.5 is rounded to the nearest integer, 6, because pixel values

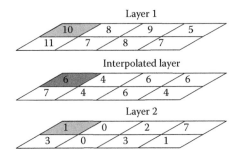

Figure 6.14 Linear method of interpolation. The CSLM images for layer 1 and layer 2 were acquired. The interpolated layer was generated to make dx = dy = dz and produce more accurate results. (Reprinted from Beyenal, H. et al., *Journal of Microbiological Methods*, 59, 395, 2004.)

must be integers. The pixel values for the other (x,y) coordinates in the interpolated layer are computed in the same manner.

If the user can acquire confocal images with $dx = dy = dz$, interpolation is not necessary. We need to interpolate layers of images because our computing resources are insufficient to handle very large sets of CSLM images. Interpolation works only for gray-scale images because binary images lack the critical information for interpolation.

6.4.1.4 *Interpolation of a sample data set using MATLAB*

The program "interpolation.m" interpolates data sets or biofilm images.

Create a 3-D matrix for the data shown in Figure 6.14 (exclude the interpolated layer, which we will calculate). This can be done as described above or by using "Figure14.m".

1. Assign dxy and dz' distances:

```
dxy = 1;
dzz = 2;
```

2. Assign the 3-D matrix shown in Figure 6.14:

```
F14 = Figure14()
```

3. Run interpolation.m:

```
IT = interpolation(F14,dxy,dzz)
```

The output of the program is

```
k = 2
IT(:,:,1) =
    10 8 9 5
    11 7 8 7
       IT(:,:,2) =
    6 4 6 6
    7 4 6 4
       IT(:,:,3) =
    1 0 2 7
    3 0 3 1
```

Note that IT(:,:,2) corresponds to the interpolated layer in Figure 6.14.

6.4.1.5 *Interpolation of biofilm images using MATLAB*

To make the software generate additional images, follow these steps:

1. Define the location of the images as the directory:

```
directory = 'C:\Fundamentals of Biofilm Research\6 QUANTIFYING
BIOFILM STRUCTURE\ThreeDmatrixImages'
```

2. Run ReadImagesGenerate3DMatrix.m and assign the output to the ThreeDMatrix matrix:

```
ThreeDMatrix = ReadImagesGenerate3DMatrix(directory,4);
```

3. Assign d*xy* and d*z'* distances

```
dxy = 1;
dzz = 2;
```

4. Run interpolation.m

```
BI = interpolation(ThreeDMatrix,dxy,dzz);
```

5. The program will generate three additional layers of biofilm images, and the size is

```
size(BI)
ans = 512 512 7
```

6.5   Computing 3-D parameters from stacks of biofilm images

From stacks of biofilm images, two classes of parameters can be computed: textural and volumetric. Textural parameters show the microscale heterogeneity of biofilms, and volumetric parameters describe the morphology of the biomass in a biofilm.

6.5.1   Textural parameters

Textural parameters quantify the gray-scale intensity variations in biofilm images as shown in Figure 6.2, where the gray-scale values vary from 0 to 255. Three textural parameters are computed: textural entropy, energy, and homogeneity. Textural parameters quantify biofilm structure by comparing the intensity, position, and/or orientation of the pixels. Each textural parameter measures the character of the cell clusters and interstitial spaces based on the likelihood that pixels of similar or dissimilar types will be neighbors. In our analyses, textural parameters are computed from stacks of biofilm images according to Haralick et al. (1973), using the GLCM computed for the *X*, *Y*, and *Z* direction dependence matrices. The GLCM represents the distribution of changes in gray-level value between neighboring pixels in the *X*, *Y*, and *Z* directions. The gray-scale image layers are eight-bit; thus the color values vary from 0 to 255.

6.5.1.1   Calculating a gray-level co-occurrence matrix

For simplicity, the example data set shown in Figure 6.15 only varies in gray-level value from 0 to 3.

The GLCM is computed from the spatial dependence matrices. Note that the size of the spatial dependence matrix is equal to the maximum gray level in the image: for a 256-gray-level biofilm image the size of the spatial dependence matrix is 256 × 256. The *X*-spatial dependence matrix (P_X) is defined and computed as

$$P_X = \{P_X(a,b)\} = \begin{bmatrix} P_X(0,0) \ P_X(0,1) \ P_X(0,2) \ P_X(0,3) \\ P_X(1,0) \ P_X(1,1) \ P_X(1,2) \ P_X(1,3) \\ P_X(2,0) \ P_X(2,1) \ P_X(2,2) \ P_X(2,3) \\ P_X(3,0) \ P_X(3,1) \ P_X(3,2) \ P_X(3,3) \end{bmatrix} = \begin{bmatrix} 2\,3\,4\,1 \\ 3\,2\,1\,2 \\ 4\,1\,2\,2 \\ 1\,2\,2\,4 \end{bmatrix}$$

where $P_X(a,b)$ is the number of times the gray-level changes from *a* to *b* between neighboring pixels in the *X* direction (moving in both directions on the *X* scale) integrated for all layers.

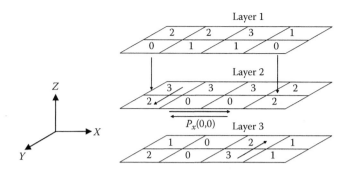

Figure 6.15 Stack of biofilm images with gray level values varying from 0 to 3, for a total of four different gray levels. (Reprinted from Beyenal, H. et al., *Journal of Microbiological Methods*, 59, 395, 2004.)

For example, $P_X(0,0)$ is 2 because in all layers there are two cases where pixels that are neighbors in the X direction (positive and negative) are both zero (see arrows in Figure 6.15). Similarly, $P_X(0,1)$ is 3 because there are three locations where pixels with values of 0 and 1 are neighbors, one in the left-to-right direction and two in the right-to-left direction.

The Y and Z dependence matrices are computed in the same manner: For example, $P_Y(3,2)$ is 2 because in all layers there are two instances where the pixel value changes from 3 to 2 between neighbors along the Y axis (see arrows in Y direction in Figure 6.15). Similarly, $P_Z(0,2)$ is 2 because, in all layers, there are two instances where the pixel value changes from 0 to 2 between neighbors in the Z direction (see arrows in Z direction in Figure 6.15).

$$P_Y = \{P_Y(a,b)\} = \begin{bmatrix} P_Y(0,0) & P_Y(0,1) & P_Y(0,2) & P_Y(0,3) \\ P_Y(1,0) & P_Y(1,1) & P_Y(1,2) & P_Y(1,3) \\ P_Y(2,0) & P_Y(2,1) & P_Y(2,2) & P_Y(2,3) \\ P_Y(3,0) & P_Y(3,1) & P_Y(3,2) & P_Y(3,3) \end{bmatrix} = \begin{bmatrix} 2 & 1 & 1 & 2 \\ 1 & 2 & 2 & 1 \\ 1 & 2 & 2 & 2 \\ 2 & 1 & 3 & 2 \end{bmatrix}$$

$$P_Z = \{P_Z(a,b)\} = \begin{bmatrix} P_Z(0,0) & P_Z(0,1) & P_Z(0,2) & P_Z(0,3) \\ P_Z(1,0) & P_Z(1,1) & P_Z(1,2) & P_Z(1,3) \\ P_Z(2,0) & P_Z(2,1) & P_Z(2,2) & P_Z(2,3) \\ P_Z(3,0) & P_Z(3,1) & P_Z(3,2) & P_Z(3,3) \end{bmatrix} = \begin{bmatrix} 2 & 2 & 2 & 2 \\ 2 & 0 & 3 & 1 \\ 2 & 3 & 2 & 2 \\ 2 & 1 & 3 & 2 \end{bmatrix}$$

The spatial dependence matrix is computed by summing the three dependence matrices:

$$P_{XYZ} = P_X + P_Y + P_Z$$

P_X

2	3	4	1
3	2	1	2
4	1	2	2
1	2	2	4

+

P_Y

2	1	1	2
1	2	2	1
1	2	2	2
2	1	2	0

+

P_Z

2	2	2	2
2	0	3	1
2	3	2	3
2	1	3	2

=

P_{XYZ}

6	6	7	5
6	4	6	4
7	6	6	7
5	4	7	6

The GLCM is computed by normalizing P_{XYZ} by dividing by the sum of all the counts

$$[\text{GLCM}] = \frac{[P_{XYZ}]}{\sum P_{XYZ}} \tag{6.7}$$

The sum of the elements in P_{XYZ} is $6 + 6 + 7 + 5 + 6 + 4 + 6 + 4 + 7 + 6 + 6 + 7 + 4 + 5 + 7 + 6 = 92$, so the GLCM is

$$\text{GLCM} = \frac{[P_{XYZ}]}{92} =$$

0.0652	0.0652	0.0761	0.0543
0.0652	0.0435	0.0652	0.0435
0.0761	0.0652	0.0652	0.0761
0.0543	0.0435	0.0761	0.0652

This procedure converts the elements in the GLCM into probabilities, so $P(a,b)$ is the probability of finding a and b as the gray-level values of neighboring pixels. Note that although variations in gray level in 3-D have been used, this GLCM is identical to the GLCM calculated above for a single biofilm image (refer to Section 6.3.1). This occurs because the GLCM can only show the possible color intensity variations.

6.5.1.2   Calculating GLCM from a sample data set using MATLAB

The program "glcm3D.m" can be used to compute the GLCM of an image. In this example, GLCM is calculated for the matrix shown in Figure 6.15.

1. Create a 3-D matrix for the data shown in Figure 6.15. This can be done as described above or by using "Figure15.m":

```
F15 = Figure15()
```

2. Run the MATLAB function:

```
GL3D = glcm3D(F15,4)
```

3. The output of the program is

```
ans =
    0.0652 0.0652 0.0761 0.0543
    0.0652 0.0435 0.0652 0.0435
    0.0761 0.0652 0.0652 0.0761
    0.0543 0.0435 0.0761 0.0652
```

Note that the number 4 is the number of gray levels in this image. For a biofilm image, it is 256.

6.5.1.3   Calculating textural parameters

From the GLCM the textural parameters can be computed according to Haralick et al. (1973). Note that the equations used to calculate TE, energy, and homogeneity from a stack of CSLM images are identical to those used to compute GSLM from single images (see Equations 6.1, 6.2, and 6.3.) Textural parameters are discussed in Section 6.3.1, and they have the same meanings for single biofilm images and 3-D biofilm images. However, for clarity, the meanings of textural parameters computed from stacks of biofilm images are discussed in Section 6.5.1.6.

In this example, the computed parameters are

$$TE = -[(0.0652 \times (Ln(0.0652)) + 0.0652 \times (Ln(0.0652)) + 0.0761 \times (Ln(0.0761))$$

$$+ 0.0543 \times (Ln(0.0543)) + 0.0652 \times (Ln(0.0652))........]$$

$$TE = 2.756$$

$$E = (0.0652^2 + 0.0652^2 + 0.0761^2 + 0.0543^2 + 0.0652^2 + ...$$

$$E = 0.065$$

$$H = \frac{1}{1+(0-0)^2} \times 0.0652 + \frac{1}{1+(0-1)^2} \times 0.0652 + \frac{1}{1+(0-2)^2} \times 0.0761$$

$$+ \frac{1}{1+(0-3)^2} \times 0.0543 + \frac{1}{1+(1-0)^2} \times 0.0652 + ...$$

$$H = 0.504$$

6.5.1.4   Calculating textural parameters from a sample data set using MATLAB

The program "textural3D.m" can be used to compute textural parameters from a sample data set. In this example, the GLCM computed in Section 6.5.1.2 will be used to compute textural parameters.

1. Be sure to compute GL3D (previous example).
2. Run the MATLAB function:

```
[TE,Energy,Homogeneity] = textural3D(GL3D)
```

3. The output of the program is

```
TE = 2.7558
Energy = 0.0645
Homogeneity = 0.5043
```

6.5.1.5   Calculating textural parameters from a biofilm image using MATLAB

The program "textural3D.m" can be used to compute textural parameters from a biofilm image. In this example, the GLCM of a biofilm will be computed and used to compute textural parameters.

1. Define the location of the images as the directory:

```
directory = 'C:\Fundamentals of Biofilm Research\6 QUANTIFYING
BIOFILM STRUCTURE\ThreeDmatrixImages'
```

2. Run the MATLAB function to generate a 3-D matrix from the single images:

```
ThreeDMatrix = ReadImagesGenerate3DMatrix(directory,4);
```

3. Compute the gray-level co-occurrence matrix. Note that 256 refers to the number of gray levels in our image:

```
GL3D = glcm3D(ThreeDMatrix,256);
```

4. Run the MATLAB function:

```
[TE,Energy,Homogeneity] = textural3D(GL3D)
```

5. The output of the program is

```
TE = 6.7454
Energy = 0.0148
Homogeneity = 0.2738
```

6.5.1.6 The meanings of the textural parameters computed from stacks of biofilm images

The meanings of the textural parameters are elusive. The following explanations have been found to be helpful in demonstrating the meanings of the textural parameters computed from biofilm images. Figure 6.16 shows simplified situations in which a space is filled with familiar geometric objects—spheres—that are arranged in several ways. Each sphere imitates a cell cluster in a biofilm, and for each arrangement of the clusters, textural parameters are computed and interpreted.

6.5.1.6.1 Textural entropy.
Figure 6.16a shows an image with no structure, composed of only white pixels, or voids. The TE computed for this image is zero, showing there

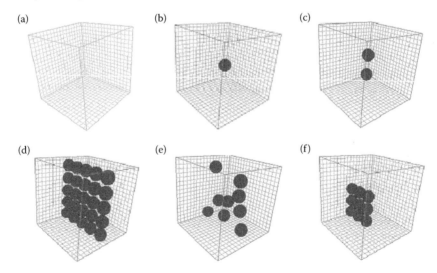

Figure 6.16 Simple images used to discuss the meanings of the textural parameters: (a) empty image (all voids), (b) a single cell cluster made up of a sphere, (c) two cell clusters, (d) many cell clusters repeating regularly, (e) nine irregularly repeating cell clusters, and (f) nine cell clusters placed regularly. The images were generated using MATLAB. The textural parameters for these images are given in Table 6.6. (Reprinted from Beyenal, H. et al., *Journal of Microbiological Methods*, 59, 395, 2004.)

is no gray-scale variation in the pixels or heterogeneity in the image. Figures 6.16b through d contain an increasing number of clusters, and the TE increases accordingly. Figures 6.16e and f contain the same number of cell clusters (identical), but they are oriented differently. They do not show significant gray-level variation, so the *TE* values are similar. An increased number of cell clusters increases textural entropy (compare Figures 6.16d and f) because of increased gray-level variability and structural heterogeneity in the images.

6.5.1.6.2   Energy.   In Figure 6.16a, the energy is one, indicating that there is no regularity in that image, but as the number of repeating clusters increases, the energy value decreases (Table 6.6).

6.5.1.6.3   Homogeneity.   In Figure 6.16a, the homogeneity equals one, indicating a homogeneous image; the homogeneity decreases with an increasing number of clusters (Table 6.6).

6.5.1.6.4   Homogeneity versus energy.   Figure 6.16d contains 23 more clusters than Figure 6.16c. Consequently, there is a pattern of repeating pixel clusters in the Z direction. However, the shapes of the clusters are identical. Therefore, comparing the computed parameters, it is not surprising that the energy increases more than the homogeneity does ($\Delta E = 0.129$ and $\Delta H = 0.028$). Indeed, ΔE is almost 4.5× higher than ΔH, showing that there is significant directional variation between the structures in Figure 6.16d and those in Figure 6.16e. When Figure 6.16e and f are compared, ΔE and ΔH are very low, showing that having identical cell clusters and gray-level variations maintains the values for energy and homogeneity. This shows that the decreases in homogeneity and energy are also caused by the number of cell clusters.

6.5.2   Volumetric parameters

Volumetric parameters are computed using the voxels representing biomass in an image. Each parameter quantifies a unique feature of the 3-D biofilm image. The volumetric parameters described here are average run lengths (in X, Y, and Z directions), aspect ratio, ADD, MDD, and fractal dimension. These parameters are computed from binary images in which only two gray levels are allowed. The resulting black and white image has two visible components, as shown in Figure 6.3. Thresholding procedures are described earlier in this chapter.

Table 6.6 Textural Parameters Computed for the Images in Figure 6.16

Image	TE	E	H
Figure 6.16a	0	1	1
Figure 6.16b	0.022837	0.99416	0.998767
Figure 6.16c	0.041726	0.988306	0.997531
Figure 6.16d	0.336192	0.859457	0.969088
Figure 6.16e	0.148825	0.947748	0.988684
Figure 6.16f	0.148364	0.947984	0.988631

Source: Reprinted from Beyenal, H. et al., *Journal of Microbiological Methods,* 59, 395, 2004.

6.5.2.1   Thresholding layers of biofilm images and generating a binary 3-D matrix using MATLAB

In this example, a 3-D matrix will first be generated using the program "Binary3Dmatrix.m". The function accepts the location of the images (directory) and the number of images (noi) to be added to the 3-D matrix. Note that all the images must be numbered, such as "1.tif".

1. Define the location of the images as the directory:

```
directory = 'C:\Fundamentals of Biofilm Research\6 QUANTIFYING
BIOFILM STRUCTURE\ThreeDmatrixImages'
```

2. Assign the number of images:

```
noi = 4
```

3. Run the MATLAB function to generate a 3-D matrix from the single images:

```
B3D = Binary3Dmatrix(directory,noi);
```

The B3D matrix is composed of binary data generated by thresholding 2-D matrices representing gray-level images. It will be used in further examples of calculating volumetric parameters from biofilm images.

6.5.2.2   Average run lengths

A run length measures the number of consecutive biomass pixels representing cell clusters in a given direction, and the average run length measures the average number of consecutive biomass pixels in the measurement direction. If a biofilm has a large average X-run length (AXRL) and a small average Y-run length (AYRL), then the biofilm appears stretched in the X direction, and this may indicate the presence of streamers. It is important to consider the direction of a run length (X, Y, or Z) before making conclusions, because each run length is valid only for one direction (Figure 6.17).

6.5.2.2.1   Calculating run lengths.   The calculation of an X-run length sweeps the image in the X direction, counting consecutive biomass pixels. Figure 6.18a shows the X-direction runs marked with arrows.

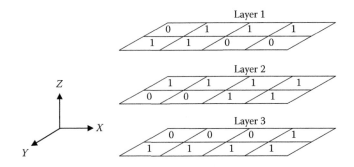

Figure 6.17 Binary images in 3-D space used to compute average run length. (Reprinted from Beyenal, H. et al., *Journal of Microbiological Methods*, 59, 395, 2004.)

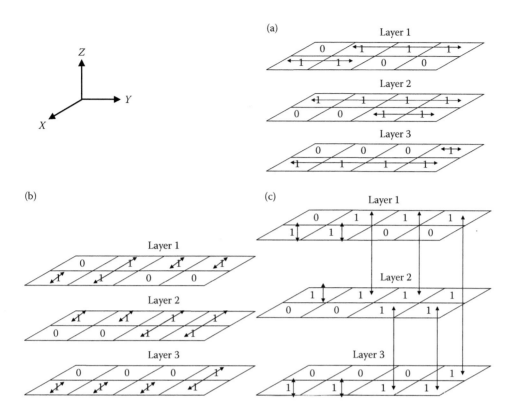

Figure 6.18 (a) Biofilm image in 3-D space with *X*-direction runs marked. (b) Biofilm image in 3-D space with *Y*-direction runs marked. (c) Biofilm image in 3-D space with *Z*-direction runs marked. (Reprinted from Beyenal, H. et al., *Journal of Microbiological Methods*, 59, 395, 2004.)

Starting at the top in Figure 6.18a, the runs in the *X* direction are (3 + 2) + (4 + 2) + (1 + 4) = 16. The number of runs (total number of arrows) is 6. Therefore, the AXRL is 16/6 = 2.67. The AYRL and average *Z*-run length (AZRL) are computed in the same manner:

```
AYRL = [(1 + 2 + 1 + 1) + (1 + 1 + 2 + 2) + (1 + 1 + 1 + 2)]/12 =
1.3333
AZRL = (1 + 1 + 1 + 1 + 1 + 2 + 2 + 2 + 2 + 3)/10 = 1.6000
```

6.5.2.2.2   Calculating run lengths from a sample data set using MATLAB.   The program "runLengths3D.m" can be used to compute the run lengths of an image. In this example, run lengths are computed from the matrix in Figure 6.17 (Figure 6.18 shows the principles of the calculations).

1. Create a 3-D matrix for the data shown in Figure 6.17. This can be done as described above or by using "Figure17.m":

```
F17 = Figure17()
```

2. Run the MATLAB function:

```
[AXRL,AYRL,AZRL] = runLengths3D(F17)
```

3. The output of the program is

```
AXRL = 2.6667
AYRL = 1.3333
AZRL = 1.6000
```

6.5.2.2.3   Calculating run lengths from a biofilm image using MATLAB.   In this example, run lengths are computed from a stack of biofilm images.

1. Define the location of the images as the directory:

```
directory = 'C:\Fundamentals of Biofilm Research\6 QUANTIFYING
BIOFILM STRUCTURE\ThreeDmatrixImages'
```

2. Assign the number of images:

```
noi = 4
```

3. Run the MATLAB function to generate a 3-D matrix from the single images:

```
B3D = Binary3Dmatrix(directory,noi);
```

4. Run the MATLAB function:

```
[AHRL,AVRL,AZRL] = runLengths3D(B3D)
```

5. The output of the program is

```
AHRL = 1.4072
AVRL = 1.3269
AZRL = 1.2285
```

6.5.2.3   Aspect ratio and its calculation

The aspect ratio is defined as the ratio of AXRL to AYRL. It indicates the symmetry of cluster growth in the X and Y directions.

$$\text{Aspect ratio} = \frac{\text{AXRL}}{\text{AYRL}} \tag{6.8}$$

If the aspect ratio remains constant during biofilm growth, the biofilm microcolonies grow symmetrically in the X and Y directions. If shear stress or any other action tends to deform the microcolonies in one direction, that effect is reflected in a changing aspect ratio.

The aspect ratio for the image shown in Figure 6.18 is

$$\text{Aspect ratio} = \frac{2.67}{1.33} = 2$$

Aspect ratios can be calculated in a similar manner for the other directions: AXRL/AZRL and AYRL/AZRL.

6.5.2.4 Average and maximum diffusion distances

A diffusion distance in 3-D space is defined as the linear distance from a cluster pixel to the nearest void pixel in the image. ADD is the average distance from each cluster pixel to the nearest void pixel over all pixels representing biomass in the image. From a process viewpoint, a larger diffusion distance indicates a larger distance over which substrate must diffuse in the cell cluster. MDD is computed as the distance from the most "remote" pixel in a cell cluster to a void pixel.

The definition of diffusion distance refers only to the shortest distance, and it is independent of the direction. To compute MDD, the Euclidean distance-mapping algorithm for 3-D space (Friedman et al. 1997) is used and the minimum distance from each cluster pixel to a void pixel is computed.

6.5.2.5 Calculating diffusion distances

A six-layer image with pixels representing biomass marked as ones (before Euclidean distance mapping) is shown in Figure 6.19, and Euclidean distance mapping is applied to produce the distance map:

Layer 1

0	0	0	0	0	0	0	0
0	0	0	0	0	0	0	0
0	0	0	0	0	0	0	0
0	0	0	0	0	0	0	0
0	0	0	0	0	0	0	0
0	0	0	0	0	0	0	0
0	0	0	0	0	0	0	0
0	0	0	0	0	0	0	0

Layer 2

0	0	0	0	0	0	0	0
0	0	0	0	0	0	0	0
0	0	0	1	1	0	0	0
0	0	1	1	1	1	0	0
0	0	1	1	1	1	0	0
0	0	0	1	1	0	0	0
0	0	0	0	0	0	0	0
0	0	0	0	0	0	0	0

Layer 3

0	0	0	0	0	0	0	0
0	0	0	0	0	0	0	0
0	0	1	1	1	1	0	0
0	0	1	1.7	1.7	1	0	0
0	0	1	1.7	1.7	1	0	0
0	0	1	1	1	1	0	0
0	0	0	0	0	0	0	0
0	0	0	0	0	0	0	0

Layer 4

0	0	0	0	0	0	0	0
0	0	0	0	0	0	0	0
0	0	1	1	1	1	0	0
0	0	1	2	2	1	0	0
0	0	1	2	2	1	0	0
0	0	1	1	1	1	0	0
0	0	0	0	0	0	0	0
0	0	0	0	0	0	0	0

Layer 5

0	0	0	0	0	0	0	0
0	0	0	0	0	0	0	0
0	0	1	1	1	1	0	0
0	0	1	1	1	1	0	0
0	0	1	1	1	1	0	0
0	0	1	1	1	1	0	0
0	0	0	0	0	0	0	0
0	0	0	0	0	0	0	0

Layer 6

0	0	0	0	0	0	0	0
0	0	0	0	0	0	0	0
0	0	0	0	0	0	0	0
0	0	0	0	0	0	0	0
0	0	0	0	0	0	0	0
0	0	0	0	0	0	0	0
0	0	0	0	0	0	0	0
0	0	0	0	0	0	0	0

In layer 3, the internal points for which the nearest void pixel is located on layer 2 are marked as 1.7. For the upper left pixel marked with 1.7 in layer 3 at (4,4,3), the nearest void is at (3,3,2). The calculation is as follows:

$$\text{Diffusion distance} = \sqrt{\Delta X^2 + \Delta Y^2 + \Delta Z^2} \qquad (6.9)$$

At that location, the diffusion distance is $\sqrt{(-1)^2 + (-1)^2 + (-1)^2} = 1.7$. The other internal points on layers 3 and 4 have been computed in the same manner. The 2s on layer 4 represent a distance of 2 pixels to the nearest void.

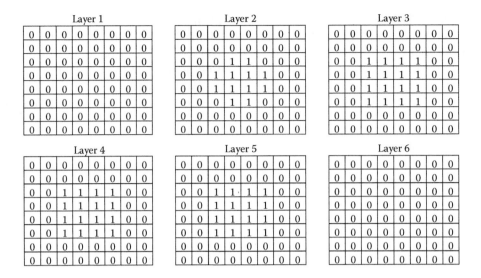

Figure 6.19 Biofilm image in 3-D space used to compute diffusion distances. (Reprinted from Beyenal, H. et al., *Journal of Microbiological Methods*, 59, 395, 2004.)

ADD is the average of all the diffusion distances, and MDD is the longest of all the diffusion distances in the image. For this example, there are 60 biomass pixels, so adding their diffusion distances and dividing by 60 produces 66.8/60 = 1.1133. MDD is 2.

6.5.2.5.1 Calculating diffusion distances from a sample data set using MATLAB. The program "DiffusionDistance3D.m" can be used to compute average and maximum diffusion distances from a stack of images. In this example, ADD and MDD are computed for the matrix shown in Figure 6.19.

1. Create a 3-D matrix for the data shown in Figure 6.19. This can be done as described above or by using "Figure19.m":

   ```
   F19 = Figure19()
   ```

2. Run the MATLAB function:

   ```
   [ADD,MDD] = DiffusionDistance3D(F19)
   ```

3. The output of the program is

   ```
   ADD = 1.1155
   MDD = 2
   ```

6.5.2.5.2 Calculating diffusion distances from stacks of biofilm images using MATLAB. In this example, ADD and MDD are computed from a stack of biofilm images. First, a B3D matrix must be made.

1. Define the location of the images as the directory:

   ```
   directory = 'C:\Fundamentals of Biofilm Research\6 QUANTIFYING
   BIOFILM STRUCTURE\ThreeDmatrixImages'
   ```

2. Assign the number of images:

```
noi = 4
```

3. Run the MATLAB function to generate a 3-D matrix from the single images:

```
B3D = Binary3Dmatrix(directory,noi);
```

4. Run the MATLAB function:

```
[ADD,MDD] = DiffusionDistance3D(B3D)
```

5. The output of the program is

```
ADD = 1.0673
MDD = 8.4853
```

6.5.2.6   Fractal dimension

Fractal dimension is a measure of the roughness of the boundaries of cell clusters; a higher fractal dimension indicates a more irregular cell cluster surface. In 3-D space, the fractal dimension varies from 1 to 3. Fractal dimensions in 3-D space are computed from stacks of biofilm images, and they are computed in a similar manner to fractal dimensions from images in 2-D space, except that instead of an area being swept out with increasing dilation of a circle, a volume is swept out with increasing dilation of a sphere. Instead of a logarithmic relationship between the perimeter and the diameter of the dilation circle, there is a logarithmic relationship between the volume of the layer surrounding the clusters and the radius of the dilation sphere.

The Minkowski sausage method has been modified to compute the fractal dimension from a stack of biofilm images because it relates naturally to image processing techniques (Russ 2002). The modified Minkowski method measures the fractal dimension by determining the rate of change in the boundary of an object as the volume of the boundary line is increased. As the iteration proceeds, the irregularities of the boundaries are smoothed by the progressively thicker boundaries marked by the spheres of increasing diameters.

From an image-processing viewpoint, dilation is used to accomplish the smoothing of the boundary line as a sphere sweeps out the boundary. The value of the boundary pixels is changed to zero and that of all other pixels is set to one (see example shown below), and then the Euclidean distances in 3-D space are computed to obtain the distance to the boundary for each pixel. The dilation volume is computed by varying the sphere radius and counting the number of pixels at a distance smaller than the radius value.

Plotting the natural logarithm of the dilation sphere radius against the natural logarithm of the measured volume produces a straight line, and the fractal dimension is defined as

$$\text{Fractal dimension} = FD = 2 - \text{slope} \qquad (6.10)$$

6.5.2.6.1   Calculating fractal dimension.   In this example, the image data shown in Figure 6.20 are used.

Layer 1

0	0	0	0	0	0	0	0
0	0	0	0	0	0	0	0
0	0	0	0	0	0	0	0
0	0	0	0	0	0	0	0
0	0	0	0	0	0	0	0
0	0	0	0	0	0	0	0
0	0	0	0	0	0	0	0
0	0	0	0	0	0	0	0

Layer 2

0	0	0	0	0	0	0	0
0	0	0	0	0	0	0	0
0	0	1	1	1	1	0	0
0	0	1	1	1	1	0	0
0	0	1	1	1	1	0	0
0	0	1	1	1	1	0	0
0	0	0	0	0	0	0	0
0	0	0	0	0	0	0	0

Layer 3

0	0	0	0	0	0	0	0
0	0	0	0	0	0	0	0
0	0	1	1	1	1	0	0
0	0	1	1	1	1	0	0
0	0	1	1	1	1	0	0
0	0	1	1	1	1	0	0
0	0	0	0	0	0	0	0
0	0	0	0	0	0	0	0

Layer 4

0	0	0	0	0	0	0	0
0	0	0	0	0	0	0	0
0	0	1	1	1	1	0	0
0	0	1	1	1	1	0	0
0	0	1	1	1	1	0	0
0	0	1	1	1	1	0	0
0	0	0	0	0	0	0	0
0	0	0	0	0	0	0	0

Layer 5

0	0	0	0	0	0	0	0
0	0	0	0	0	0	0	0
0	0	1	1	1	1	0	0
0	0	1	1	1	1	0	0
0	0	1	1	1	1	0	0
0	0	1	1	1	1	0	0
0	0	0	0	0	0	0	0
0	0	0	0	0	0	0	0

Layer 6

0	0	0	0	0	0	0	0
0	0	0	0	0	0	0	0
0	0	0	0	0	0	0	0
0	0	0	0	0	0	0	0
0	0	0	0	0	0	0	0
0	0	0	0	0	0	0	0
0	0	0	0	0	0	0	0
0	0	0	0	0	0	0	0

Figure 6.20 Biofilm image data in 3-D space used to compute fractal dimension. (Reprinted from Beyenal, H. et al., *Journal of Microbiological Methods*, 59, 395, 2004.)

Layer 1

0	0	0	0	0	0	0	0
0	0	0	0	0	0	0	0
0	0	0	0	0	0	0	0
0	0	0	0	0	0	0	0
0	0	0	0	0	0	0	0
0	0	0	0	0	0	0	0
0	0	0	0	0	0	0	0
0	0	0	0	0	0	0	0

Layer 2

0	0	0	0	0	0	0	0
0	0	0	0	0	0	0	0
0	0	1	1	1	1	0	0
0	0	1	1	1	1	0	0
0	0	1	1	1	1	0	0
0	0	1	1	1	1	0	0
0	0	0	0	0	0	0	0
0	0	0	0	0	0	0	0

Layer 3

0	0	0	0	0	0	0	0
0	0	0	0	0	0	0	0
0	0	1	1	1	1	0	0
0	0	1	1	1	1	0	0
0	0	1	1	1	1	0	0
0	0	1	1	1	1	0	0
0	0	0	0	0	0	0	0
0	0	0	0	0	0	0	0

Layer 4

0	0	0	0	0	0	0	0
0	0	0	0	0	0	0	0
0	0	1	1	1	1	0	0
0	0	1	1	1	1	0	0
0	0	1	1	1	1	0	0
0	0	1	1	1	1	0	0
0	0	0	0	0	0	0	0
0	0	0	0	0	0	0	0

Layer 5

0	0	0	0	0	0	0	0
0	0	0	0	0	0	0	0
0	0	1	1	1	1	0	0
0	0	1	1	1	1	0	0
0	0	1	1	1	1	0	0
0	0	1	1	1	1	0	0
0	0	0	0	0	0	0	0
0	0	0	0	0	0	0	0

Layer 6

0	0	0	0	0	0	0	0
0	0	0	0	0	0	0	0
0	0	0	0	0	0	0	0
0	0	0	0	0	0	0	0
0	0	0	0	0	0	0	0
0	0	0	0	0	0	0	0
0	0	0	0	0	0	0	0
0	0	0	0	0	0	0	0

Fractal dimension is computed using the following steps:

1. Mark only the border pixels as ones and mark the remaining pixels as zeros (see below): i.e., mark boundaries with ones.

Layer 1

0	0	0	0	0	0	0	0
0	0	0	0	0	0	0	0
0	0	0	0	0	0	0	0
0	0	0	0	0	0	0	0
0	0	0	0	0	0	0	0
0	0	0	0	0	0	0	0
0	0	0	0	0	0	0	0
0	0	0	0	0	0	0	0

Layer 2

0	0	0	0	0	0	0	0
0	0	0	0	0	0	0	0
0	0	1	1	1	1	0	0
0	0	1	1	1	1	0	0
0	0	1	1	1	1	0	0
0	0	1	1	1	1	0	0
0	0	0	0	0	0	0	0
0	0	0	0	0	0	0	0

Layer 3

0	0	0	0	0	0	0	0
0	0	0	0	0	0	0	0
0	0	1	1	1	1	0	0
0	0	1	0	0	1	0	0
0	0	1	0	0	1	0	0
0	0	1	1	1	1	0	0
0	0	0	0	0	0	0	0
0	0	0	0	0	0	0	0

Layer 4

0	0	0	0	0	0	0	0
0	0	0	0	0	0	0	0
0	0	1	1	1	1	0	0
0	0	1	0	0	1	0	0
0	0	1	0	0	1	0	0
0	0	1	1	1	1	0	0
0	0	0	0	0	0	0	0
0	0	0	0	0	0	0	0

Layer 5

0	0	0	0	0	0	0	0
0	0	0	0	0	0	0	0
0	0	1	1	1	1	0	0
0	0	1	1	1	1	0	0
0	0	1	1	1	1	0	0
0	0	1	1	1	1	0	0
0	0	0	0	0	0	0	0
0	0	0	0	0	0	0	0

Layer 6

0	0	0	0	0	0	0	0
0	0	0	0	0	0	0	0
0	0	0	0	0	0	0	0
0	0	0	0	0	0	0	0
0	0	0	0	0	0	0	0
0	0	0	0	0	0	0	0
0	0	0	0	0	0	0	0
0	0	0	0	0	0	0	0

2. Invert the pixels: change the ones to zeros and the zeros to ones (see below).

Layer 1

1	1	1	1	1	1	1	1
1	1	1	1	1	1	1	1
1	1	1	1	1	1	1	1
1	1	1	1	1	1	1	1
1	1	1	1	1	1	1	1
1	1	1	1	1	1	1	1
1	1	1	1	1	1	1	1
1	1	1	1	1	1	1	1

Layer 2

1	1	1	1	1	1	1	1
1	1	1	1	1	1	1	1
1	1	0	0	0	0	1	1
1	1	0	0	0	0	1	1
1	1	0	0	0	0	1	1
1	1	0	0	0	0	1	1
1	1	1	1	1	1	1	1
1	1	1	1	1	1	1	1

Layer 3

1	1	1	1	1	1	1	1
1	1	1	1	1	1	1	1
1	1	0	0	0	0	1	1
1	1	0	1	1	0	1	1
1	1	0	1	1	0	1	1
1	1	0	0	0	0	1	1
1	1	1	1	1	1	1	1
1	1	1	1	1	1	1	1

Layer 4

1	1	1	1	1	1	1	1
1	1	1	1	1	1	1	1
1	1	0	0	0	0	1	1
1	1	0	1	1	0	1	1
1	1	0	1	1	0	1	1
1	1	0	0	0	0	1	1
1	1	1	1	1	1	1	1
1	1	1	1	1	1	1	1

Layer 5

1	1	1	1	1	1	1	1
1	1	1	1	1	1	1	1
1	1	0	0	0	0	1	1
1	1	0	0	0	0	1	1
1	1	0	0	0	0	1	1
1	1	0	0	0	0	1	1
1	1	1	1	1	1	1	1
1	1	1	1	1	1	1	1

Layer 6

1	1	1	1	1	1	1	1
1	1	1	1	1	1	1	1
1	1	1	1	1	1	1	1
1	1	1	1	1	1	1	1
1	1	1	1	1	1	1	1
1	1	1	1	1	1	1	1
1	1	1	1	1	1	1	1
1	1	1	1	1	1	1	1

Steps 1 and 2 mark the boundaries of the cell clusters with zeros. Note that the boundary is defined for every direction.

3. Use Euclidian distance mapping in 3-D space (see the example in Section 6.5.2.5 of computing the diffusion distance) to compute the distance to a void (zero) pixel for each biomass pixel (Friedman et al. 1997).

Layer 1

3	2.4	2.2	2.2	2.2	2.2	2.4	3
2.4	1.7	1.4	1.4	1.4	1.4	1.7	2.4
2.2	1.4	1	1	1	1	1.4	2.2
2.2	1.4	1	1	1	1	1.4	2.2
2.2	1.4	1	1	1	1	1.4	2.2
2.2	1.4	1	1	1	1	1.4	2.2
2.4	1.7	1.4	1.4	1.4	1.4	1.7	2.4
3	2.4	2.2	2.2	2.2	2.2	2.4	3

Layer 2

2.8	2.2	2	2	2	2	2.2	2.8
2.2	1.4	1	1	1	1	1.4	2.2
2	1	0	0	0	0	1	2
2	1	0	0	0	0	1	2
2	1	0	0	0	0	1	2
2	1	0	0	0	0	1	2
2.2	1.4	1	1	1	1	1.4	2.2
2.8	2.2	2	2	2	2	2.2	2.8

Layer 3

2.8	2.2	2	2	2	2	2.2	2.8
2.2	1.4	1	1	1	1	1.4	2.2
2	1	0	0	0	0	1	2
2	1	0	1	1	0	1	2
2	1	0	1	1	0	1	2
2	1	0	0	0	0	1	2
2.2	1.4	1	1	1	1	1.4	2.2
2.8	2.2	2	2	2	2	2.2	2.8

Layer 4

2.8	2.2	2	2	2	2	2.2	2.8
2.2	1.4	1	1	1	1	1.4	2.2
2	1	0	0	0	0	1	2
2	1	0	1	1	0	1	2
2	1	0	1	1	0	1	2
2	1	0	0	0	0	1	2
2.2	1.4	1	1	1	1	1.4	2.2
2.8	2.2	2	2	2	2	2.2	2.8

Layer 5

2.8	2.2	2	2	2	2	2.2	2.8
2.2	1.4	1	1	1	1	1.4	2.2
2	1	0	0	0	0	1	2
2	1	0	0	0	0	1	2
2	1	0	0	0	0	1	2
2	1	0	0	0	0	1	2
2.2	1.4	1	1	1	1	1.4	2.2
2.8	2.2	2	2	2	2	2.2	2.8

Layer 6

3	2.4	2.2	2.2	2.2	2.2	2.4	3
2.4	1.7	1.4	1.4	1.4	1.4	1.7	2.4
2.2	1.4	1	1	1	1	1.4	2.2
2.2	1.4	1	1	1	1	1.4	2.2
2.2	1.4	1	1	1	1	1.4	2.2
2.2	1.4	1	1	1	1	1.4	2.2
2.4	1.7	1.4	1.4	1.4	1.4	1.7	2.4
3	2.4	2.2	2.2	2.2	2.2	2.4	3

The above matrix shows Euclidian distance mapping.

For each dilation, count the number of pixels with distances less than or equal to the sphere radius. This example starts from 1 and increases by 0.5 because the image matrix is very small compared to biofilm image matrices. For example, if the radius value is 1.5, count the number of pixels less than or equal to 1.5. Sum one layer at a time, 32 + 36 + 36 + 36 + 36 + 32 = 208. Then compute the volume/radius ratio, which is 208/1.5 = 138.66. This process is repeated for increasing radius values. Plotting the natural logarithm of the sphere radius versus the natural logarithm of the volume/radius ratio produces a straight line, as shown in Figure 6.21. Note that plotting log(volume/diameter) versus log(diameter) gives the same slope as plotting log(volume/radius) versus log(radius).

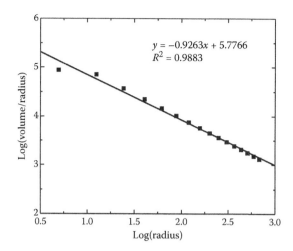

Figure 6.21 Log(volume/radius) versus log(radius). Some researchers use natural logarithms, and some use decimal logarithms. Actually, it does not matter which are used because the slope of the double log plot does not depend on the base of the logarithm used, as long as the logarithms on both axes use the same base. (Reprinted from Beyenal, H. et al., *Journal of Microbiological Methods*, 59, 395, 2004.)

In this example, the slope of the line is −0.93. Thus, the fractal dimension is 2 − (−0.93) = 2.93. In 3-D space, FD is 1 for a line and 2 for a sphere. For an extremely rough boundary structure, the fractal dimension approaches a limit of 3.

6.5.2.6.2   Calculating fractal dimension from a sample data set using MATLAB.   The program "FractalDimension3D.m" can be used to compute the fractal dimension of the 3-D matrix shown in Figure 6.20.

1. Create a 3-D matrix for the data shown in Figure 6.20. This can be done as described above or by using "Figure20.m":

```
F20 = Figure20()
```

2. Run the MATLAB function:

```
[FD] = FractalDimension3D(F20)
```

3. The output of the program is

```
FD = 2.9263
```

6.5.2.6.3   Calculating fractal dimension from a stack of biofilm images using MATLAB.   In this example, fractal dimension is calculated from a stack of biofilm images.

1. Define the location of the images as the directory:

```
directory = 'C:\Fundamentals of Biofilm Research\6 QUANTIFYING
BIOFILM STRUCTURE\ThreeDmatrixImages'
```

2. Assign the number of images:

```
noi = 4
```

3. Run the MATLAB function to generate a 3-D matrix from the single images:

```
B3D = Binary3Dmatrix(directory,noi);
```

4. Run the MATLAB function:

```
[FD] = FractalDimension3D(B3D)
```

5. The output of the program is

```
FD = 2.9186
```

6.5.2.7 Porosity

Porosity (P) is defined as the ratio of void volume to total volume. To simplify computations, images are interpolated so that the distance between consecutive images in a stack of images is equal to the dimension of one pixel ($dx = dy = dz$). This simplifies the computations because to compute the total volume of voids or the total biofilm volume, for example, you multiply the volume of each pixel, which is $dx^3 = dy^3 = dz^3$, by the total number of pixels. The following formula can be used to compute biofilm porosity:

$$\text{Porosity} = \frac{\text{Total void volume}}{\text{Total biofilm volume}} = \frac{\text{Total number of void pixels}}{\text{Total number of pixels}} \tag{6.11}$$

6.5.2.7.1 Calculating porosity. To compute porosity, the number of void pixels is summed over all layers. In Figure 6.22, there are 4, 3, and 5 void pixels in layers 1, 2, and 3, respectively. The total void pixel count is $4 + 5 + 3 = 12$, and the total pixel count is $8 + 8 + 8 = 24$. The porosity = total void pixel count/total number of pixels = 12/24 = 0.5.

6.5.2.7.2 Calculating porosity from a sample data set using MATLAB. The program "Porosity3D.m" can be used to compute the porosity of an image. In this example, porosity is calculated for the matrix shown in Figure 6.22.

1. Create a 3-D matrix for the data shown in Figure 6.22. This can be done as described above or by using "Figure22.m":

```
F22 = Figure22()
```

2. Run the MATLAB function:

```
P = Porosity3D(F22)
```

Layer 1			
0	1	1	0
1	1	0	0

Layer 2			
1	1	1	0
0	0	1	1

Layer 3			
0	0	0	0
0	1	1	1

Figure 6.22 Three-dimensional matrix used to compute porosity.

3. The output of the program is

```
P = 0.5000
```

6.5.2.7.3   Calculating porosity from a stack of biofilm images using MATLAB.   In this example, porosity is calculated from a stack of biofilm images.

1. Define the location of the images as the directory:

```
directory = 'C:\Fundamentals of Biofilm Research\6 QUANTIFYING
BIOFILM STRUCTURE\ThreeDmatrixImages'
```

2. Assign the number of images:

```
noi = 4
```

3. Run the MATLAB function to generate a 3-D matrix from the single images:

```
B3D = Binary3Dmatrix(directory,noi);
```

4. Run the MATLAB function:

```
P = Porosity3D(B3D)
```

5. The output of the program is

```
P = 0.8836
```

6.5.2.8   Biovolume

The biovolume of a biofilm is the total volume of its biomass. It is computed by summing the number of biomass pixels in the stack of matrices representing images of the biofilm and multiplying the result by the distance between layers (dz) and the dimensions of each pixel (dx, dy) in the image.

$$\text{The total number of biomass pixels} = \sum_{x=1}^{N_x}\sum_{y=1}^{N_y}\sum_{z=1}^{N_z} B(x,y,z) \qquad (6.12)$$

In the equation, $B(x,y,z)$ is the value of the pixel at (x,y,z) in the thresholded image set, which only has pixel values of zero and one. The number of biomass pixels is converted to the volume by multiplying the distance between layers (dz) and the dimensions of the pixels (dx, dy), $k^3 = dx^3 = dy^3 = dz^3$, by the number of pixels representing biomass.

$$\text{Biovolume} = k^3 \times (\text{The total number of biomass pixels in all layers}) \qquad (6.13)$$

6.5.2.8.1   Calculating biovolume.   The sample 3-D matrix used to compute biovolume is shown in Figure 6.23.

The total number of cell pixels is $4 + 4 + 4 + 4 = 16$. If the distance between layers and the size of a pixel is $k = dx = dy = dz = 1.25$ µm, then the biovolume is $16 \times k^3 = 16 \times 1.25$ µm $\times$ 1.25 µm $\times 1.25$ µm $= 31.25$ µm^3.

Layer 1				Layer 2				Layer 3				Layer 4			
0	0	0	0	0	0	0	0	0	0	0	0	0	0	0	0
0	1	1	0	0	1	1	0	0	1	1	0	0	1	1	0
0	1	1	0	0	1	1	0	0	1	1	0	0	1	1	0
0	0	0	0	0	0	0	0	0	0	0	0	0	0	0	0

Figure 6.23 Three-dimensional matrix used to compute biovolume.

6.5.2.8.2   Calculating biovolume from a sample data set using MATLAB.   The program "biovolume.m" can be used to compute biovolume from Figure 6.23.

1. Create a 3-D matrix for the data shown in Figure 6.23:

```
F23 = Figure23()
```

2. Run the MATLAB function:

```
Biovolume = biovolume(F23)
```

3. The output of the program is

```
Biovolume = 16
```

Note that the program output is 16 pixels. The user needs to convert this to a volume; e.g., if $k = dx = dy = dz = 1.25$ μm, the biovolume $= 16 \times (1.25 \text{ μm})^3 = 31.25$ μm^3.

6.5.2.8.3   Calculating biovolume from a stack of biofilm images using MATLAB.   In this example, biovolume is calculated from a stack of biofilm images.

1. Define the location of the images as the directory:

```
directory = 'C:\Fundamentals of Biofilm Research\6 QUANTIFYING
BIOFILM STRUCTURE\ThreeDmatrixImages'
```

2. Assign the number of images:

```
noi = 4
```

3. Run the MATLAB function to generate a 3-D matrix from the single images:

```
B3D = Binary3Dmatrix(directory,noi);
```

4. Run the MATLAB function:

```
Biovolume = biovolume(B3D)
```

5. The output of the program is

```
Biovolume = 122020
```

6.5.2.9   *Average and maximum biomass thicknesses and biomass roughness*

The average biofilm thickness is the volume of the biofilm divided by the total surface area of the substratum, whereas the biomass thickness is the volume of the biofilm divided by the area of the substratum that is covered by the biomass. The average biomass thickness is computed from the same results as the biofilm thickness. However, the locations where the biofilm thickness is equal to zero are rejected from the computation. In a sense, biomass thickness is the average thickness of the biofilm on the combined surface area of the substratum that is covered by the biofilm, specifically excluding the combined surface area of the substratum that is not covered by the biofilm. Figures 6.24 and 6.25, and the calculated average biofilm and biomass thicknesses (Table 6.7) can be used to understand these parameters better.

Average biomass thickness ($AT_{biomass}$) is computed as follows:

$$AT_{biomass} = \frac{k}{N_{biomass}} \sum_{1}^{N_{biomass}} T_{biomass}(x,y) \tag{6.14}$$

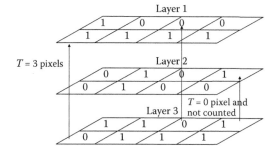

Figure 6.24 Stack of binary images of a biofilm used to compute the average and the maximum biomass thicknesses, the average and the maximum biofilm thicknesses, the biomass roughness, and the biofilm roughness. If there is no biomass at a location ($T_{biomass}(x,y) = 0$), the biomass thickness at that location is not included in the average biomass thickness calculations. However, $T_{biomass}(x,y) = 0$ is used in biofilm thickness calculations. Note that layer 1 refers to the top of the biofilm.

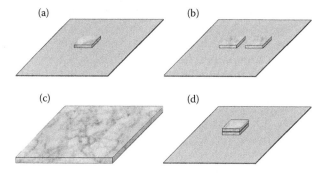

Figure 6.25 Hypothetical biofilms consisting of cell clusters of various sizes. These images are discussed in Section 6.5.2.11 biomass thickness versus biofilm thickness.

Table 6.7 Average Biomass Thicknesses and Average Biofilm Thicknesses of the Biofilm Images in Figure 6.25

Image	Average biomass thickness (μm)	Average biofilm thickness (μm)
Figure 6.25a	100	4
Figure 6.25b	100	8
Figure 6.25c	4	4
Figure 6.25d	200	8

The constant k is equal to the distance between layers, or to the dimension of the pixels ($dx = dy = dz$); $N_{biomass}$ is the total number of biomass thickness measurements; and $T_{biomass}(x,y)$ is the individual biomass thickness (in pixels) for each (x,y) location at the substratum. If biomass is not present at a specified location, this location does not contribute to the calculation of biomass thickness.

The maximum biomass thickness is the average of an arbitrarily selected fraction of the local biomass thicknesses. The maximum biomass thickness might be misleading if it were based on the distance between the bottom and a single point on the biofilm surface. Basing computations on the position of one point might subject the results to artifacts. For this reason, the maximum biomass thickness will be defined as the average of the highest 5% of biomass thicknesses computed for the surface area of the substratum.

The biomass roughness is a modified version of the surface roughness described by Murga et al. (1995); it quantifies the variation in biomass thickness. The biomass roughness is computed from the average biomass thickness as shown below:

$$\text{Biomass roughness} = \frac{1}{N_{biomass}} \sum_{1}^{N_{biomass}} \frac{\left| T_{biomass}(x,y) - AT_{biomass} \right|}{AT_{biomass}} \tag{6.15}$$

6.5.2.9.1 Calculating average and maximum biomass thicknesses and biomass roughness. The average and the maximum biomass thicknesses, the average and the maximum biofilm thicknesses, the biomass roughness and the biofilm roughness are all calculated from stacks of binary images, as shown in Figure 6.24.

When computing biomass thickness, it is important to disregard pores in the biofilm near the bottom of the biofilm. For $(x,y) = (1,1)$ the values are 1, 0, and 1 for layers 1, 2, and 3, respectively. The biomass thickness at that location is 3 pixels because the most remote pixel is located 3 pixels away from the bottom. This process is repeated for each location in the field of view, $T(x,y)$. The sum of thicknesses at all locations (expressed in pixels) is $(3 + 3 + 3 + 2 + 1 + 3 + 2) = 17$. Note that the 0 thickness is not included, so the total number of measurements is 7.

The thickness of a single layer is $k = 1$ μm. Therefore,

$$\text{Average biomass thickness} = (k/N_{biomass}) \times (3 + 3 + 3 + 2 + 1 + 3 + 2) = (k/7) \times 17$$

$$= (1 \ \mu m/7) \times 17 = 2.4286 \ \mu m$$

Five percent of the total number of measurements is $(17 \times 0.05) = 0.15$. The nearest nonzero integer to 0.15 is 1, so only the highest thickness value is used. Note that 0.15 is rounded to 1 because the maximum thickness must be based on at least one measurement. Thus the maximum thickness is $3 \times 1 = 3$ µm.

If the highest 50% of thicknesses is selected to represent the maximum thickness for this example, the thicknesses must be sorted into descending order (see the table below). Because there are seven measurements, 50% of them is $(7 \times 0.5) = 3.5$. This is rounded to the nearest integer: 4. Therefore, the first four thicknesses will be used to calculate the maximum biofilm thickness. The sum of the first four thicknesses is $(3 + 3 + 3 + 3) = 12$, and the average is $12/4 = 3$.

Rank	Thickness (µm)
1	3
2	3
3	3
4	3
5	2
6	2
7	1

Note that for biofilm images there are generally thousands of measurement points. For example, for 1000 thickness measurement points, the average of the 50 highest biofilm thicknesses (highest 5%) is computed for the maximum biofilm thickness as described above.

6.5.2.9.2 Calculating biomass roughness. For the biofilm in Figure 6.24, the biomass roughness is

Biomass roughness

$$= \frac{1}{N_{biomass}} \left(\frac{|3 - 2.4286|}{2.4286} + \frac{|3 - 2.4286|}{2.4286} + \frac{|3 - 2.4286|}{2.4286} + \frac{|2 - 2.4286|}{2.4286} + \frac{|1 - 2.4286|}{2.4286} + \frac{|3 - 2.4286|}{2.4286} + \frac{|2 - 2.4286|}{2.4286} \right)$$

$$\text{Biomass roughness} = \frac{1}{7}(0.23528 + 0.23528 + 0.23528 + 0.17648 + 0.58824 + 0.23528 + 0.17648)$$

$$\text{Biomass roughness} = \frac{1}{7}(1.8823) = 0.2689$$

6.5.2.9.3 Calculating average and maximum biomass thicknesses and biomass roughness from a sample data set using MATLAB. The program "BiomassthicknessesandRoughness.m" can be used to compute the average thickness, the maximum thickness, and the roughness of an image. In this example, these parameters are computed for the matrix shown in Figure 6.24.

1. Create a 3-D matrix for the data shown in Figure 6.24. This can be done as described above or by using "Figure24.m":

```
F24 = Figure24()
```

2. Before running the MATLAB function assign the following variables:

```
PMaxT = 0.05;
TORB = 1;
```

3. PMaxT refers to a percentage of local thicknesses, and TORB refers to the position of the first layer. In Figure 6.24, the first layer refers to the top of the biofilm, so its value is equal to 1. Therefore, the direction in which the biofilm thickness must be computed is known. This parameter is required because CSLM users sometimes acquire the first image at the bottom of the biofilm.

4. Run the MATLAB function:

```
[ATbiomass,MaxbiomassT,Biomassroughness] = BiomassthicknessesandRoug
hness(F24,PMaxT,TORB)
```

5. The output of the program is

```
ATbiomass = 2.4286
MaxbiomassT = 3
Biomassroughness = 0.2689
```

6.5.2.9.4 Calculating average and maximum biomass thicknesses and biomass roughness from a stack of biofilm images using MATLAB. In this example, average thickness, maximum thickness, and roughness are calculated from a stack of biofilm images.

1. Define the location of the images as the directory:

```
directory = 'C:\Fundamentals of Biofilm Research\6 QUANTIFYING
BIOFILM STRUCTURE\ThreeDmatrixImages'
```

2. Assign the number of images:

```
noi = 4
```

3. Run the MATLAB function to generate a 3-D matrix from the single images:

```
B3D = Binary3Dmatrix(directory,noi);
```

4. Before running the MATLAB function assign the following variables (same as above):

```
PMaxT = 0.05;
TORB = 1;
```

5. Run the MATLAB function:

```
[ATbiomass,MaxbiomassT,Biomassroughness] = BiomassthicknessesandRoug
hness(B3D,PMaxT,TORB)
```

6. The output of the program is

```
ATbiomass = 2.7921
MaxbiomassT = 4
Biomassroughness = 0.3403
```

6.5.2.10 Average and maximum biofilm thicknesses and biofilm roughness

Average biofilm thickness is the average thickness of a biofilm. The thickness for any (x,y) location is the distance from the bottom layer to the outermost cell, ignoring any pores inside the biofilm. Average biofilm thickness $(AT_{biofilm})$ is computed as follows:

$$AT_{biofilm} = \frac{k}{N} \sum_{1}^{N} T_{biofilm}(x, y) \tag{6.16}$$

The constant k is equal to the distance between the layers, or the linear dimension of the pixels, $dx = dy = dz$; N is the number of biofilm thickness measurements, including voids; and $T_{biofilm}(x,y)$ is the individual thickness (in pixels) for location (x,y) on the substratum. Note that even if no biomass is present at a specified location, that location does contribute to the biofilm thickness calculation; it is excluded from the biomass thickness calculations.

The maximum biofilm thickness is defined as the average of a percentage of the local biofilm thicknesses. It is believed that defining a single point as the maximum biofilm thickness may be misleading because a single point may be a noise at that location. For that reason, the maximum biofilm thickness is defined as the average of the highest 5% of biofilm thicknesses. The selection of 5% is arbitrary; any other number can be used.

The biofilm roughness describes how much the biomass thickness varies in the Z direction. Biofilm roughness is a modified version of the surface roughness described by Murga et al. (1995). The biofilm roughness is computed using the average biofilm thickness as shown below:

$$\text{Biofilm roughness} = \frac{1}{N} \sum_{1}^{N} \frac{\left| T_{biofilm}(x, y) - AT_{biofilm} \right|}{AT_{biofilm}} \tag{6.17}$$

6.5.2.10.1 Calculating average biofilm thicknesses. The data in Figure 6.24 are used in this example. When making thickness calculations, it is important to include zero thicknesses inside the biofilm. For $(x,y) = (1,1)$, the values are 1, 0, and 1 for layers 1, 2, and 3, respectively. Therefore, the thickness is 3 pixels because the most remote pixel is located 3 pixels away from the bottom. This process is repeated for each $T(x,y)$. The sum of all the thicknesses (in pixels) is $(3 + 3 + 3 + 2 + 1 + 0 + 3 + 2) = 17$. The total number of measurements (N) is 8, which can also be considered the total field of view in pixels. The thickness of a single layer is $k = 1$ μm. Therefore,

$$\text{Average biofilm thickness} = (k/N) \times (3 + 3 + 3 + 2 + 1 + 0 + 3 + 2) = (k/8) \times 17$$

$$= (1 \text{ μm}/8) \times 17 = 2.125 \text{ μm}$$

6.5.2.10.2 Calculating biofilm roughness. For the biofilm shown in Figure 6.24, the biofilm roughness is

$$\text{Biofilm roughness} = \frac{1}{N} \left(\begin{array}{l} \dfrac{|3 - 2.125|}{2.125} + \dfrac{|3 - 2.125|}{2.125} + \dfrac{|3 - 2.125|}{2.125} + \dfrac{|2 - 2.125|}{2.125} + \dfrac{|1 - 2.125|}{2.125} \\[2ex] \dfrac{|0 - 2.125|}{2.125} + \dfrac{|3 - 2.125|}{2.125} + \dfrac{|2 - 2.125|}{2.125} \end{array} \right)$$

Biofilm roughness

$$= \frac{1}{8}(0.41176 + 0.41176 + 0.41176 + 0.05882 + 0.52941 + 1 + 0.41176 + 0.005882)$$

$$\text{Biofilm roughness} = \frac{1}{8}(3.2941) = 0.4118$$

Note that if five-digit precision is used in the above calculations, the sum is calculated to be 3.241152 instead of 3.2941. Use at least eight digits to get 3.2941.

6.5.2.10.3   Calculating average and maximum biofilm thicknesses and biofilm roughness from a sample data set using MATLAB.   The program "BiofilmThicknessesandRoughness.m" can be used to compute average thickness, maximum thickness, and roughness from Figure 6.24.

1. Create a 3-D matrix for the data shown in Figure 6.24. This can be done as described above or by using "Figure24.m":

```
F24 = Figure24()
```

2. Before running the MATLAB function assign the following variables:

```
PMaxT = 0.05;
TORB = 1;
```

3. PmaxT refers to a percentage of maximum local thicknesses, and TORB refers to the position of the first layer. In Figure 6.24, the first layer refers to the top of the biofilm. Therefore, the direction in which the biofilm thickness must be computed is known. This parameter is required because CSLM users sometimes acquire the first image at the bottom of the biofilm.
4. Run the MATLAB function:

```
[ATbiofilm,MaxT,Biofilmroughness] = BiofilmThicknessesandRoughness
(F24,PMaxT,TORB)
```

The output of the program is

```
ATbiofilm = 2.1250
MaxT = 3
Biofilmroughness = 0.4118
```

6.5.2.10.4 Calculating average and maximum biofilm thicknesses and biofilm roughness from a stack of biofilm images using MATLAB. In this example, average thickness, maximum thickness, and roughness will be calculated from a stack of biofilm images.

1. Define the location of the images as the directory:

```
directory = 'C:\Fundamentals of Biofilm Research\6 QUANTIFYING
BIOFILM STRUCTURE\ThreeDmatrixImages'
```

2. Assign the number of images:

```
noi = 4
```

3. Run the MATLAB function to generate a 3-D matrix from the single images:

```
B3D = Binary3Dmatrix(directory,noi);
```

4. Before running the MATLAB function assign the following variables (same as above):

```
PMaxT = 0.05;
TORB = 1;
```

5. Run the MATLAB function:

```
[ATbiofilm,MaxT,Biofilmroughness] = BiofilmThicknessesandRoughness(B
3D,PMaxT,TORB)
```

The output of the program is

```
ATbiofilm = 0.9290
MaxT = 4
Biofilmroughness = 1.3346
```

6.5.2.11 Biomass thickness versus biofilm thickness

The difference between biomass thickness and biofilm thickness is best explained using hypothetical biofilms such as those in Figure 6.25. Figure 6.25a shows a hypothetical biofilm consisting of one cell cluster in the shape of a cube which is $100 \times 100 \times 100\ \mu m^3$ in size. Figure 6.25b shows a hypothetical biofilm consisting of two such cubes, each $100 \times 100 \times 100\ \mu m^3$. Figure 6.25c shows a hypothetical biofilm consisting of one cell cluster in the shape of a cube which is $500 \times 500 \times 4\ \mu m^3$ in size, covering the entire surface area of the bottom. Figure 6.25d shows a hypothetical biofilm consisting of one cell cluster in the shape of a cube which is $100 \times 100 \times 200\ \mu m^3$ in size. The field of view remains $500 \times 500 = 250,000\ \mu m^2$ in all cases.

The average biomass thickness and average biofilm thickness values of the hypothetical biofilms in Figure 6.25 are computed in Table 6.7.

This example shows that reporting the average biofilm thickness is not particularly informative. The average biomass thickness is more informative, and it reflects the physical dimensions of the biomass deposited on the surface in a more precise way. For example, the cell clusters in Figure 6.25a and b are identical. They have identical average biomass thicknesses but different average biofilm thicknesses. This example also demonstrates that using the average biofilm thickness as the only parameter for comparing biofilm structure is misleading.

6.5.2.12 *Surface area of the biomass in the biofilm*

The surface area of the biomass in the biofilm is defined as the area of the interface between the biomass and the liquid. Because the overall substrate utilization rate depends on the surface area, biofilms with higher biomass surface areas may show higher activity.

6.5.2.12.1 Calculating the biomass surface area. The first step in finding the biomass surface area of a biofilm is marking the biomass borders with ones. In Figure 6.26, below, an image in 3-D space is shown before the borders are marked and after. The biomass surface area is computed as

$$\text{Surface area} = k^2 \times \sum \text{Surface pixels} \tag{6.18}$$

In the stack of binary images in Figure 6.26, the pixels residing on the interface between the biofilm and the liquid are marked as ones. Layer 1 is located at the top of the biofilm, and layer 3 is located at the bottom of the biofilm. The pixels residing in the inner space of a microcolony are not counted. However, all biomass pixels in the top layer (layer 1) are considered surface pixels because they all reside at the interface.

Layer 1

0	0	0	0	0	0	0	0
0	0	0	0	0	0	0	0
0	0	1	1	1	1	0	0
0	0	1	1	1	1	0	0
0	0	1	1	1	1	0	0
0	0	1	1	1	1	0	0
0	0	0	0	0	0	0	0
0	0	0	0	0	0	0	0

Layer 2

0	0	0	0	0	0	0	0
0	0	0	0	0	0	0	0
0	0	1	1	1	1	0	0
0	0	1	0	0	1	0	0
0	0	1	0	0	1	0	0
0	0	1	1	1	1	0	0
0	0	0	0	0	0	0	0
0	0	0	0	0	0	0	0

Layer 3

0	0	0	0	0	0	0	0
0	0	0	0	0	0	0	0
0	0	1	1	1	1	0	0
0	0	1	0	0	1	0	0
0	0	1	0	0	1	0	0
0	0	1	1	1	1	0	0
0	0	0	0	0	0	0	0
0	0	0	0	0	0	0	0

The surface area is found by summing the number of surface pixels and multiplying by k^2. The total number of surface pixels, summing a layer at a time, is $16 + 12 + 12 = 40$. The pixel sizes are $dx = dy = dz = 2\ \mu m$, so $k^2 = (2\ \mu m)^2 = 4\ \mu m^2$. Therefore,

Layer 1

0	0	0	0	0	0	0	0
0	0	0	0	0	0	0	0
0	0	1	1	1	1	0	0
0	0	1	1	1	1	0	0
0	0	1	1	1	1	0	0
0	0	1	1	1	1	0	0
0	0	0	0	0	0	0	0
0	0	0	0	0	0	0	0

Layer 2

0	0	0	0	0	0	0	0
0	0	0	0	0	0	0	0
0	0	1	1	1	1	0	0
0	0	1	1	1	1	0	0
0	0	1	1	1	1	0	0
0	0	1	1	1	1	0	0
0	0	0	0	0	0	0	0
0	0	0	0	0	0	0	0

Layer 3

0	0	0	0	0	0	0	0
0	0	0	0	0	0	0	0
0	0	1	1	1	1	0	0
0	0	1	1	1	1	0	0
0	0	1	1	1	1	0	0
0	0	1	1	1	1	0	0
0	0	0	0	0	0	0	0
0	0	0	0	0	0	0	0

Figure 6.26 Binary images used to compute biomass surface area.

Surface area $= k^2 \sum$ Surface pixels $= k^2(16 + 12 + 12+) = k^2 \times 40 = (2\ \mu m)^2 \times 40 - 160\ \mu m^2$

6.5.2.12.2   Calculating biomass surface area from a sample data set using MATLAB. The program "SurfaceArea.m" can be used to compute the biomass surface area in an image. In this example, we compute the surface area for the matrix shown in Figure 6.26.

1. Create a 3-D matrix for the data shown in Figure 6.26. This can be done as described above or by using "Figure26.m":

```
F26 = Figure26()
```

2. Run the MATLAB function:

```
[SA] = SurfaceArea(F26)
```

3. The output of the program is

```
SA = 40
```

6.5.2.12.3   Calculating biomass surface area from a stack of biofilm images using MATLAB.

1. Define the location of the images as the directory:

```
directory = 'C:\Fundamentals of Biofilm Research\6 QUANTIFYING
BIOFILM STRUCTURE\ThreeDmatrixImages'
```

2. Assign the number of images:

```
noi = 4
```

3. Run the MATLAB function to generate a 3-D matrix from the single images:

```
B3D = Binary3Dmatrix(directory,noi);
```

4. Run the MATLAB function:

```
[SA] = SurfaceArea(B3D)
```

5. The output of the program is

```
SA = 119866
```

6.5.2.13   Ratio of biovolume to biomass surface area

The ratio of biovolume to biomass surface area is used to compare various biofilms, and it is computed as

$$V2SA = \frac{BV}{SA} \tag{6.19}$$

For example, for a biofilm with a biomass surface area of SA = 160 µm^2 and a biovolume of BV = 16 × 3 × 2 µm^3 = 384 µm^3, the ratio of biovolume to biomass surface is V2SA = 384/160 = 2.4 µm.

A low ratio of biovolume to biomass surface area indicates a high biomass surface area per unit volume and may be associated with high biofilm activity.

6.5.2.14 Meanings of the volumetric parameters

To illustrate the meanings of the volumetric parameters, we have generated a set of hypothetical biofilm images with spherical cell clusters, seen in Figure 6.27.

As seen in Table 6.8, the ADD, MDD, AXRL, AYRL, and AZRL are the same for all the images. This is expected because identical cell clusters should have identical parameters. Although all the spheres are identical, slight variations in fractal dimension values are caused by the proximity of the spheres resulting in newly developed borders.

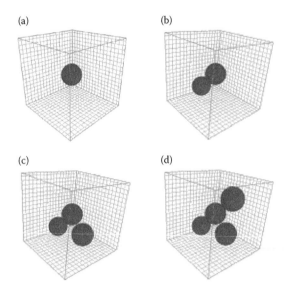

Figure 6.27 (a) A single cell cluster, (b) two cell clusters, (c) three cell clusters, and (d) four cell clusters. (Reprinted from Beyenal, H. et al., *Journal of Microbiological Methods*, 59, 395, 2004. With permission.)

Table 6.8 Areal Parameters Computed for the Images in Figure 6.27

Image	ADD (µm)	MDD (µm)	AXRL (µm)	AYRL (µm)	AZRL (µm)	FD
Figure 6.27a	4.03	15	20.08	20.08	20.08	2.11
Figure 6.27b	4.03	15	20.08	20.08	20.08	2.03
Figure 6.27c	4.03	15	20.08	20.08	20.08	1.99
Figure 6.27d	4.03	15	20.08	20.08	20.08	1.98

Source: Reprinted from Beyenal, H. et al., *Journal of Microbiological Methods*, 59, 395, 2004a. With permission.

6.5.2.15 Textural and volumetric parameters computed from biofilm images

Two biofilm images are compared in Figure 6.28. The biofilm was composed of sulfate-reducing bacteria *Desulfovibrio desulfuricans* G20 that were used to reduce dissolved uranium. To acquire the images and analyze the biofilms, a Leica TCS-NT confocal scanning laser microscope with 488-nm excitation and a 510-nm emission filter was used. The voxel width, height, and depth were all equal to 1.5 μm, which in this notation is $k = dx = dy = dz$. The textural and volumetric parameters described in this section and additional parameters were computed with ISA-2 following the descriptions given here and are given in Table 6.9.

The biofilm in Figure 6.28a has more cell clusters than that in Figure 6.28b. However, the clusters in the biofilm in Figure 6.28a have similar sizes, whereas the sizes of the cell clusters in Figure 6.28b vary widely. Intuitively, it is expected that Figure 6.28a should have a larger *TE* than Figure 6.28b because of the higher gray-level variations in Figure 6.28b. Homogeneity is higher for Figure 6.28a, as it has fewer spatially repeating gray-level variations than Figure 6.28b. However, both images have very low energy, showing directionally repeating variations.

(a) (b)

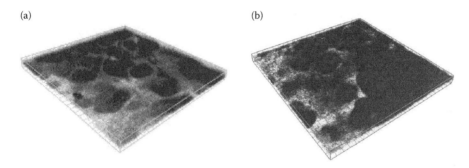

Figure 6.28 Textural and volumetric parameters computed from these two biofilm images are compared in Table 6.9. (Reprinted from Beyenal, H. et al., *Journal of Microbiological Methods*, 59, 395, 2004. With permission.)

Table 6.9 Textural and Volumetric Parameters Computed from the Images in Figure 6.28

| Image | Textural parameters | | | | | Volumetric parameters | | | | |
	TE	E	H	ADD (μm)	MDD (μm)	FD	AXRL (μm)	AYRL (μm)	AZRL (μm)	AR
Figure 6.28a	7.31	0.0015	0.2941	2.36	14.65	2.91	12.31	11.51	4.36	1.07
Figure 6.28b	8.78	0.00051	0.2224	2.59	22.65	2.84	11.82	11.09	4.28	1.07

Additional volumetric parameters[a]

Image	Biovolume (μm³)	Biomass volume to biomass surface area ratio (μm)	Porosity	Biomass surface area (μm²)	Average biofilm thickness (μm)	Maximum biofilm thickness (μm)	Biofilm roughness
Figure 6.28a	12×10^6	1.93	0.57	6.3×10^6	46.20	52.73	0.162
Figure 6.28b	86×10^6	2.05	0.68	4.2×10^6	39.93	46.88	0.165

Source: Reprinted from Beyenal, H. et al., *Journal of Microbiological Methods*, 59, 395, 2004.

[a] Additional parameters were computed with ISA-2 following the descriptions we give in this chapter.

From visual inspection, it is expected that the biofilm in Figure 6.28b will have bigger cell clusters than that in Figure 6.28a, i.e., higher ADD and MDD. As expected, ADD is slightly higher and MDD is 1.8× higher for Figure 6.28b (because it has a large cluster). The aspect ratio is close to 1 for both images, showing the circularity of the cell clusters. The results in Table 6.9 correspond to expectations, showing that the parameters reflect visual observations.

The results in Table 6.9 can be used to compare the biofilm images in Figure 6.28. Making such comparisons, it is assumed that identical biofilms should have identical structures. A comparison of the parameters characterizing biofilm structure shows that biofilms can have some parameters similar, such as the biofilm roughness in Table 6.9, and other parameters significantly different. This complicates the analysis because it can only be stated that two biofilms have certain parameters similar; rarely, if ever, can it be said that two biofilms have all the same structural parameters. This raises the question of when two biofilms should be considered identical. Perhaps an even more general question should be asked: Are there identical biofilms? Can identical biofilms be produced? If not, then how do we ensure the reproducibility of biofilm studies if every study starts with a different biofilm? These questions reveal the nature of the problem that is experienced when one is trying, for example, to generate reproducible biofilms to test the effects of antimicrobial agents on biofilm activity. From what is currently known, it is practically impossible to grow identical biofilms, particularly mature biofilms.

6.6   Interfering effects

Parameters computed from images of biofilms are affected by the procedures used to acquire the images and by the procedures used to compute the parameters. Some of these effects are undesirable and difficult to control. In this section, several of these factors are presented and their effects demonstrated.

6.6.1   Effects of image orientation and image inverting

In the process of inverting, binary images are converted to their negatives, in which the dark areas become light and vice versa. Textural parameters reflect the distribution of gray-scale intensity, and it is important to determine whether they are affected by the image orientation or the microscopy technique used. Figure 6.29a is rotated in Figure 6.29b and inverted in Figure 6.29c.

All the textural parameters computed for the images in Figure 6.29a through c are identical ($TE = 5.6547$, $E = 0.0052$, and $H = 0.3656$), showing that the parameters are invariant with regard to orientation and chromatic inversion. This is important because simple image manipulations are common in the process of analyzing biofilm images. For example, textural parameters do not give useful information about the effect of the flow rate on the cell clusters. Cell clusters become elongated in high-flow-rate environments, but the textural parameters can only detect repeating patterns of gray scale, which are not affected appreciably by the elongation. Such effects should be quantified using areal parameters (Table 6.10).

Image rotation changes only the values of AHRL and AVRL. Inverting an image affects all the parameters because it replaces voids with cell clusters and vice versa.

6.6.2   Effects of image filtering

Digital image filtering is the modification of individual pixels based on the properties of surrounding pixels. It is a common procedure in image manipulation and in image analysis,

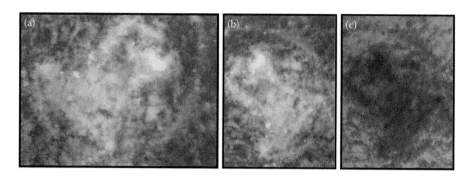

Figure 6.29 Three images of the same biofilm: (a) Original image, (b) image rotated to the left, and (c) image inverted. For all three images, the textural parameters are the same ($TE = 5.6547$, $E = 0.0052$, $H = 0.3656$), showing that the textural parameters do not depend on the position of the biofilm or the microscopy technique used (reflected or transmitted light). (Reprinted from Beyenal, H. et al., *Biofouling*, 20, 1, 2004.)

Table 6.10 Areal Parameters Computed for the Images in Figure 6.29

Image	AP	FD	ADD (pixels)	MDD (pixels)	AHRL (pixels)	AVRL (pixels)	P (pixels)
Figure 6.29a Original	0.473	1.231	20.386	85.586	53.293	50.170	8683
Figure 6.29b Rotated left	0.473	1.231	20.386	85.586	50.170	53.293	8683
Figure 6.29c Reversed	0.527	1.236	16.739	123.794	41.662	41.155	10286

Source: Reprinted from Beyenal, H. et al., *Biofouling*, 20, 1, 2004.

and it is reasonable to be concerned about possible impacts on computed textural and areal parameters. The biofilm image in Figure 6.30 was used to quantify the effects of image filtering on the textural and areal parameters. Median filtering, a nonlinear operation often used in image processing, was used to reduce "salt and pepper" noise. Median filtering is more effective than convolution when the goal is to reduce noise and preserve edges simultaneously (Lim 1990; MATLAB Version 6.5, Release 13, medfilt2 help file). MATLAB's built-in median filter (medfilt2(A,[m n]) was used to perform median filtering on matrix A (the image) in two dimensions. Each output pixel contains the median value in the $m \times n$ neighborhood around the corresponding pixel in the input image. A symmetric filter with $m = n$ was used, and its size is reported as the filter size in Figures 6.31 and 6.32.

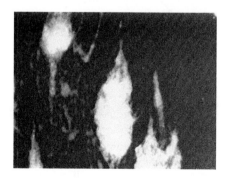

Figure 6.30 Biofilm image used to test the effects of filtering. (Reprinted from Beyenal, H. et al., *Biofouling*, 20, 1, 2004.)

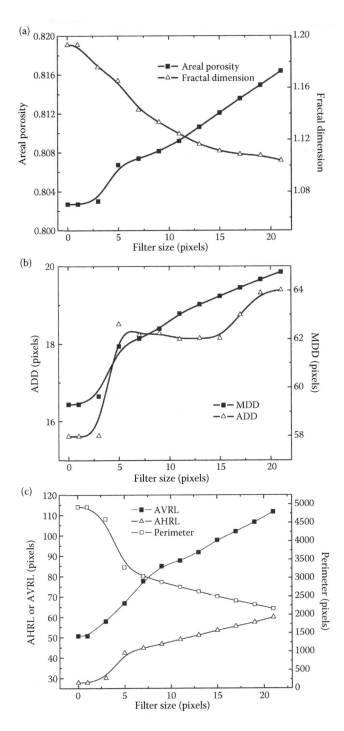

Figure 6.31 Effects of filter size on (a) the areal porosity and fractal dimension, (b) ADD and MDD, and (c) average horizontal and vertical run lengths and perimeter computed for the image shown in Figure 6.30. The binary images were filtered using a median filter with filter size [*x,x*]. The images were filtered *after* being thresholded. (Reprinted from Beyenal, H. et al., *Biofouling*, 20, 1, 2004. With permission.)

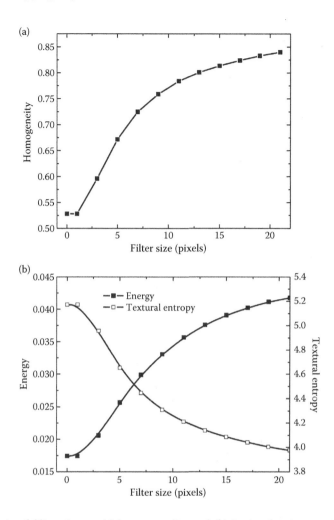

Figure 6.32 Effects of filter size on (a) homogeneity and (b) textural entropy and energy. The filter size is given by the value of x; the applied filter size is [x,x]. (Reprinted from Beyenal, H. et al., *Biofouling*, 20, 1, 2004. With permission.)

6.6.3   Effects of image filtering on areal parameters

This section evaluates the effects of filtering on the areal parameters computed from the biofilm image in Figure 6.30. The results are shown in Figure 6.31. All the areal parameters were affected, although to different extents.

6.6.4   Effects of image filtering on the textural parameters

A median filter [x,x] was applied to the biofilm image in Figure 6.30, and the effects of the filtering on the textural parameters are shown in Figure 6.32. The filter clearly affected the computed textural parameters. Energy increases logarithmically when the applied filter size is greater than one pixel in diameter. It follows from the one-pixel neighborhoods used to compute the GLCM that any filter with a size greater than one will have some effect on textural parameters. This should be taken into consideration when selecting the extent of filtration, particularly because there are no algorithms for selecting the correct filter size for gray-scale images and the effects of filtering vary from one image to another. It is important to report the type and the size of a filter that was used to manipulate an image before the textural parameters were computed.

6.6.5 Effects of image focus

Another important question that is frequently asked by the researchers who analyze biofilm images is whether image focusing affects computed parameters. To quantify this effect, the lens was focused on the bottom of the biofilm in Figure 6.33a to get the best focus. To decrease the image quality progressively, it was then focused 100 and 200 μm below the best focus and 100 and 200 μm above the best focus. The computed parameters are in Table 6.11. The areal parameters vary predictably, and they show maxima or minima at the best focus. However, *TE* and homogeneity vary randomly without showing a trend. Visually, there is little difference among these images. However, as seen in Table 6.11, the computed parameters are different, showing that image quality is important and that it affects the computed parameters. If two operators collect the same images but each focuses differently, they will compute different parameters.

6.6.6 Effects of magnification

To quantify the effects of magnification on computed parameters, one biofilm image was taken at 100× magnification (Figure 6.34a) and another was taken at the same location but using 40× (Figure 6.34b). Of course, when the magnification changed, the coverage area changed as well, so that the image in Figure 6.34b covers more area than that in Figure 6.34a. To evaluate the effects statistically, 20 images were taken at randomly selected locations of the same biofilm using 100× and 40× magnifications, and the areal and textural parameters were computed. The results for the images in Figure 6.34 are shown in Table 6.12, and the results for the other 20 images of the same biofilm, along with the statistical analysis, are in Table 6.13.

These results show that image magnification affects some of the parameters, but not others. To quantify the effects of image magnification, the ratio (R) of the value a parameter has at 100× to the value it has at 40× is used. In cases where the image magnification is not critical, $R = 1$. The following table shows the results obtained from an analysis of 20 images of the same biofilm acquired using 40× and 100× magnifications.

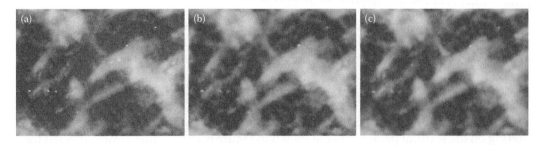

Figure 6.33 The same biofilm image but focused differently: (a) Focused at the bottom, (b) focused 100 μm below the bottom, and (c) focused 100 μm above the bottom. Visually, the images look similar, but the areal parameters differ. (Reprinted from Beyenal, H. et al., *Biofouling*, 20, 1, 2004. With permission.)

Table 6.11 Structural Parameters Computed from Images Collected at the Same Location but Focused Differently

Position (µm)	AP	FD	ADD (pixels)	MDD (pixels)	HRL (pixels)	VRL (pixels)	P (pixels)	E	TE	H
-200	0.578265	1.21822	20.94607	81.32035	55.64308	39.89537	7357	0.001835	6.806218	0.392095
-100	0.56242	1.20777	19.14667	80.61017	52.791	38.40468	8141	0.001576	7.034068	0.355179
0	0.641921	1.21487	17.8444	76.48529	45.33151	30.14895	7971	0.001957	6.784296	0.364352
100	0.580937	1.17529	19.02531	82.73452	57.20146	40.79987	7222	0.001641	7.00746	0.360304
200	0.59367	1.20722	21.39081	81	59.1484	41.58336	6806	0.001854	6.823609	0.391096

Source: Reprinted from Beyenal, H. et al., *Biofouling,* 20, 1, 2004b. With permission.

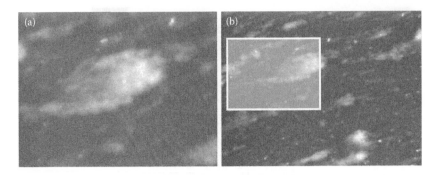

Figure 6.34 (a) A biofilm image taken using 100× magnification and (b) an image of the same location taken using 40×. Note that image b covers more area than image a. The cell cluster in image a is marked in image b. (Reprinted from Beyenal, H. et al., *Biofouling*, 20, 1, 2004. With permission.)

For AP and *TE*, *R* is close to one, showing that these parameters are not greatly affected by the magnification. *R* is slightly lower for FD, MDD, AHRL, AVRL, *P*, *E*, and *H*, showing that these parameters are slightly affected by magnification. Average diffusion distance is the parameter that is affected the most: $R = 3.24$. Because in some cases *R* is close to one but not exactly equal to one, the *t*-test was used to compute the statistical significance of these data and compute *p* values using the null hypothesis that the parameters are identical at the 5% level of significance.

The results in Table 6.13 show that energy and *TE* do not depend on image magnification. Areal parameters other than AP do depend on the magnification. Using 100× magnification, more detail can be seen in the image, such as small cell clusters, which are not seen with 40×. The most important conclusion to be drawn from the results in Table 6.13 is that when comparing images of different biofilms it is critical to use the same magnification.

6.6.7   Effect of illumination intensity on areal porosity

As expected, the intensity of the light used to illuminate a biofilm affects the computed AP. This effect is especially significant when biofilms are highly illuminated. Increased light intensity makes more areas visible in the biofilm; however, it also increases light reflected by the biofilm, causing bleaching. The effect of light intensity decreases with decreasing AP because there is enough biomass to reflect the light (see Figure 6.35).

Similar observations are valid with respect to CSLM images. The intensity of the laser light and the photomultiplier setting affect calculated parameters in a similar way to that described for light microscopy images.

6.7   Testing available software packages quantifying biofilm structure

There are several software packages available for quantifying biofilm structure from biofilm images. Before using any of these software packages, including the one described here, test whether the software computes the parameters correctly. To test the software, it is best to generate custom images of simple geometrical figures, from which structural parameters can be computed using a hand-held calculator. Below, we describe how to generate custom images of spheres and cubes. We then, analyze these images using ISA-2

Table 6.12 Structural Parameters Computed from the Images in Figure 6.34

	AP	FD	ADD (µm)	MDD (µm)	AHRL (µm)	AVRL (µm)	P (µm)	E	TE	H
40×	0.85021	1.2788	6.053965	40.388	15.109	7.760388	16477.5	0.02239	4.50579	0.3277972
100×	0.79535	1.4273	6.70264	34.9285	9.85085	4.70217	5905	0.01781	4.65018	0.3452019
Ratio = R (100×/40×)	0.93	1.12	1.107149	0.8648	0.65198	0.605919	0.358367	0.795	1.03	1.05

Source: Reprinted from Beyenal, H. et al., *Biofouling*, 20, 1, 2004. With permission.

Table 6.13 Structural Parameters Computed from 20 Images of the Same Biofilm Acquired Using 40× and 100× Magnifications

	AP	FD	ADD (µm)	MDD (µm)	AHRL (µm)	AVRL (µm)	P (µm)	E	TE	H
40×—average	0.8071	1.319	26.4	78.2125	29.83875	14.65415	12565	0.01732	4.83272	0.343235
SD	0.0578	0.043	5.94125	26.9625	11.22263	5.781558	4157.5	0.00468	0.22892	0.013783
100×—average	0.7589	1.421	3.2605	43.955	14.9795	6.51836	5354	0.01849	4.72513	0.369305
SD	0.101	0.078	2.988	13.665	4.9531	2.188209	2616.5	0.00537	0.19683	0.032455
p value	0.0718	<0.0001	<0.0001	<0.0001	<0.0001	<0.0001	<0.0001	0.4671	0.1193	0.0021
Comment	This difference is not statistically significant	This difference is statistically significant	This difference is statistically significant	This difference is statistically significant	This difference is statistically significant	This difference is statistically significant	This difference is statistically significant	This difference is not statistically significant	This difference is not statistically significant	This difference is not statistically significant
Ratio = R (100×/40×)	1.07	0.93	3.24	0.71	0.80	0.90	0.94	0.94	1.03	0.93

Source: Reprinted from Beyenal, H. et al., *Biofouling*, 20, 1, 2004.

Note: The level of significance is 0.05.

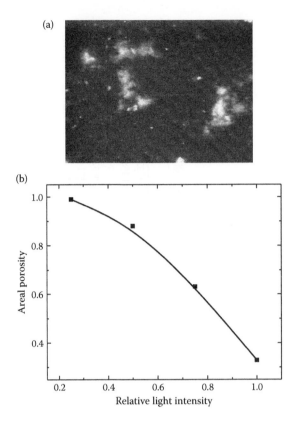

Figure 6.35 Effect of relative light intensity on computed AP values. The image in (a) was acquired using reflected light microscopy. (b) The relative light intensity, computed as the ratio of applied power to maximum power, is plotted against the computed AP values. (Reprinted from Beyenal, H. et al., *Biofouling,* 20, 1, 2004.)

software, which was developed by this research group. Note that ISA-2 is a combination of all the programs given in this book.

6.7.1 Generating images of cubes using MATLAB

The program "Generatecube.m" can be used to generate a custom image of a cube in a Cartesian coordinate system. In this example, 10 layers of images are generated. The function Generatecube(ms,cs,Xl,Yl,hi) accepts four parameters. Matrix size is represented by *ms*, *cs* is the size at the bottom of the cube ($X = Y$), and *hi* is the height of the cube. To generate a cube located at $X = Y = 1$ in a 5 × 5 matrix with a height of 2 pixels inside a 10 × 10 × 10 3-D matrix,

1. Assign the variables:

```
ms = 10
cs = 2
Xl = 4
Yl = 4
hi = 2
```

2. Run the MATLAB function:

```
DS = Generatecube(ms,cs,Xl,Yl,hi)
```

The program generated 10 layers of images and wrote them to the given directory (stated in the first few lines of `GenerateSphere.m`) as "`cd('C:\Fundamentals of Biofilm Research\6 QUANTIFYING BIOFILM STRUCTURE\cube')`". If needed, change this directory and write the images to a different location. DS is a 3-D matrix which includes data from stacks of biofilm images. These images were analyzed using ISA-2, and the following results were computed.

BV	8
SA	8
AR	1
MaxTbiofilm	2
V2SA	1
FD	1.778756
TE	0.077323
Biofilm roughness	1.92
P	0.992
AXRL	2
E	0.976484
ATbiomass	2
ADD	1
AYRL	2
H	0.992593
MaxTbiomass	2
MDD	1
AZRL	2
ATbiofilm	0.08
Biomass roughness	0

The theoretical values are computed as follows:

Biovolume (BV) = $2 \times 2 \times 2 = 8$
Surface area (SA) = $2 + 2 + 2 + 2 = 8$ (note that bottom pixels are not considered in the surface)
Porosity (P) = (total volume – biovolume)/total volume = $(10^3 - 8)/10^3 = 0.992$
Average diffusion distance = 1 (hand-computed; see examples)
Maximum diffusion distance = 1 (hand-computed; see examples)
Average X or Y or Z run length (AXRL = AYRL = AZRL) = 2, because the cube height is 2
Average biofilm thickness (ATbiofilm) = $(2 + 2 + 2 + 2)/(10 \times 10) = 0.008$
Maximum biofilm thickness (MaxTbiofilm) = 2 (cube size)
Biofilm roughness = 1.92 (hand-computed; see examples)
Average biomass thickness (ATbiomass) = $(2 + 2 + 2 + 2)/4 = 2$
Maximum biomass thickness (MaxTbiomass) = 2, because the cube height is 2
Biomass roughness = 0 (hand-computed; see examples)

The theoretical values computed using a hand-held calculator and those computed by the software match each other.

6.7.2   *Generating an image of a sphere using MATLAB*

The program "GenerateSphere.m" can be used to generate a custom sphere in a Cartesian coordinate system. In this example, 101 layers of images which have already been used in earlier examples are generated. The function "GenerateSphere(rad,Xloc,Yloc,Zloc,Matsize)" accepts four parameters. The radius of the sphere is rad, and Xloc, Yloc and Zloc are the location of the center with respect to the *X*, *Y*, and *Z* coordinates. Matsize is the size of the matrix in which the sphere will be located. Make sure that the boundaries of the sphere are not set out of the sphere. To generate a sphere with a 20-pixel radius, located at $X = Y = Z = 50$ and with a matrix size of $101 \times 101 \times 101$,

1. Assign the variables:

```
Rad = 20
Xloc = 50
Yloc = 50
Zloc = 50
Matsize = 101
```

2. Run the MATLAB function:

```
DS = GenerateSphere(Rad, Xloc, Yloc, Zloc, Matsize);
```

   The program generated 101 layers of images and wrote them to the given directory (stated in the first few lines of GenerateSphere.m) as "cd ('C:\Fundamentals of Biofilm Research\6 QUANTIFYING BIOFILM STRUCTURE\Sphere')". If needed, change this directory and write the images to different locations. DS is a matrix which includes data from stacks of images. These images were analyzed using ISA-2, and the following results were obtained:

BV	33371 μm^3
SA	7010 μm^2
AR	1
MaxTbiofilm	71 μm
V2SA	4.760485
FD	1.97179
TE	0.158629
Biofilm roughness	1.7559 μm
P	0.96761
AXRL	26.804 μm
E	0.934278
ATbiomass	64.902 μm
ADD	5.252543 μm
AYRL	26.804 μm
H	0.997559
MaxTbiomass	71 μm
MDD	20 μm
AZRL	26.804 μm
ATbiofilm	7.921 μm
Biomass roughness	0.0597 μm

It is assumed that $k = dx = dy = dz = 1$ μm.
The radius of our sphere was 20 pixels, so the theoretical values are

$$\text{Volume of the sphere} = \frac{4}{3} \times \pi \times r^3 = \frac{4}{3} \times \pi \, 20^3 = 33510 \, \mu m^3$$

$$\text{Surface area of the sphere} = 4 \times \pi \times r^2 = 4 \times \pi \, 20^2 = 5026 \, \mu m^2$$

$$\text{Ratio of volume to surface area} = \frac{33510}{5026} = 6.6673$$

Although the theoretical values are close to the computed values, there are some differences. The reason for these differences is that it is impossible to generate a smooth sphere surface using voxels shaped as cubes. This type of difference between computed and theoretical values was not seen when cubes were generated because cubes can be accurately generated using cubic voxels. Even for the images of the sphere, some parameters computed theoretically are the same as those computed by the software; for example, MDD equals the radius of the sphere (20). All of the run lengths (AXRL, AYRL, and AZRL) are equal, and the aspect ratio is 1, as expected.

6.7.3   Computing volumetric parameters for known shapes using ISA-2

In addition to the above computations, images of spheres with different radii were generated, and the volumetric parameters of these images were computed to test the relationships among these parameters and to reveal their physical meanings. Selected results are shown in Figure 6.36. As expected, MDD corresponds to the sphere radius. For a sphere, AXRL, AYRL, and AZRL are equal because the numbers of runs in the X, Y, and Z directions are equal. In other words, the aspect ratio is equal to 1.

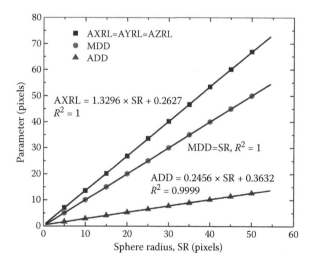

Figure 6.36 Variation of ADD, MDD, AXRL, AYRL, and AZRL for spheres with different radii. (Reprinted from Beyenal, H. et al., *Biofouling*, 20, 1, 2004.)

Before it was accepted for routine use in the laboratory, ISA-2 was first tested using images of custom-generated known shapes. Then, the software was tested using images of fluorescent beads 15 μm in diameter (distance between layers = $dx = dy = k = 1.46$ μm), acquired using CSLM. For these images, ISA-2 computed an MDD equal to 16.7 μm. Even though MDD should have been equal to the diameter of the beads, 15 μm, 16.7 μm was considered to be an acceptable result because it was close enough to the expected result and because it was unclear whether all the beads used were exactly 15 μm in diameter.

The tests demonstrate that ISA-2 can compute volumetric parameter values with reasonable accuracy. Similar tests should be conducted whenever new software is used to compute parameters characterizing biofilm structure from biofilm images, or whenever a new parameter is added to the list of parameters computed by the existing software.

6.8 Directions of future research on quantifying biofilm structure

To determine the best parameters for describing biofilm structure, those that could be used as descriptors of the underlying biofilm processes, the measured parameters are correlated with the rates of various biofilm processes, such as the rates of attachment, detachment, and growth. On the basis of these measurements, it is already known that biofilm porosity is a good descriptor of biofilm structure because it is correlated with the rate of biofilm accumulation. It is also known that some of the areal parameters computed from biofilm images seem to be linearly related. Therefore, at least some of the related parameters should be rejected as redundant. The areal parameters of known shapes such as circles are evaluated in the search for the relationships among these parameters. Figure 6.37 shows an example of such an analysis, a correlation of ADD with MDD and average horizontal and vertical run lengths (AHRL and AVRL) for circular cell clusters.

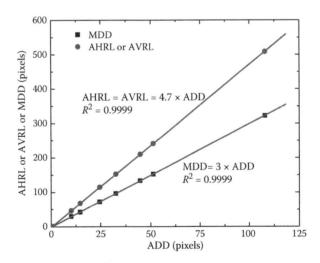

Figure 6.37 Variation of AHRL, AVRL, and MDD with ADD for a circle. To obtain a different ADD, the diameter of the circle is increased. (Reprinted from Beyenal, H. et al., *Biofouling*, 20, 1, 2004.)

Some simple relationships between biofilm descriptors are revealed in such analyses. For circles, AHRL/AVRL = 1 because the numbers of runs in the horizontal and vertical directions are the same. For a circle,

$$MDD = 3 \times ADD \tag{6.20}$$

Such simple analyses often help in understanding the results computed from real experiments. For example, in some biofilms, linear correlations between AHRL and AVRL were noticed, indicating symmetrical cluster growth. To further refine this relation, another useful parameter, the aspect ratio, has been defined as shown in Equation 6.8.

$$\text{Aspect ratio} = \frac{AHRL}{AVRL}$$

If the aspect ratio remains constant during biofilm growth, the biofilm microcolonies are growing symmetrically in the horizontal and vertical directions. If, however, shear stress, or any other action, tends to deform the microcolonies in one direction, then this tendency is reflected by a changing aspect ratio.

Several research groups quantify biofilm structure in an attempt to correlate biofilm structure with the rates of various biofilm processes. Because of these concentrated research efforts, a large number of parameters characterizing biofilm structure from biofilm images have been proposed and quantified. However, it is not yet known which parameters characterizing biofilm structure are better and which are worse descriptors of the underlying biofilm processes. Moreover, it is not known how many parameters are needed to describe biofilm structure uniquely. Hypothetically, if parameters computed from the image of a biofilm could be used, through independent methods, to reconstruct the biofilm image, that would demonstrate that enough parameters had been measured to describe the biofilm uniquely. This can be done using computer-based image reconstruction. For image reconstruction to be useful, the reconstructed and the original image must be comparable. Obviously, the original and reconstructed images are expected to have identical structural parameters. However, they should also look similar, which can be assessed using various methods. On the basis of our previous experience, this is best done using human judgment. The steps used in the process of reconstructing an image are shown in Figure 6.38. Following these steps we have reconstructed images having structural parameters identical to those of biofilm images described in this book.

We described the process of reconstructing biofilm images in the work of Renslow et al. (2011). Here, we report only the main steps to illustrate the process and to discuss the implications. The purpose of image reconstruction is to computer-generate an abstract image that has the same values for areal parameters as the target image of the real biofilm. We used one to seven areal parameters calculated from the biofilm images that we tried to reconstruct. The values of the computed areal parameters were used as targets for the reconstruction, and at the end of the iterative process designed to improve the matching level between the abstract computer-generated image and the biofilm image, the computer-generated image was expected to have its values for the areal parameters selected for reconstruction closely resemble the values of those parameters computed for the original biofilm image. The computer-generated images were constructed one pixel at a time using the algorithm in Figure 6.39.

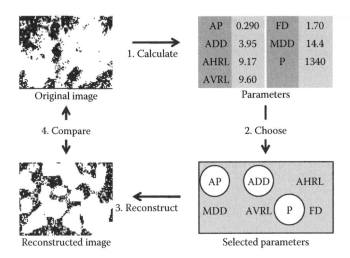

AP	0.290	FD	1.70
ADD	3.95	MDD	14.4
AHRL	9.17	P	1340
AVRL	9.60		

Figure 6.38 Steps in the process of constructing an image having structural parameters identical to those computed from a biofilm image. (1) Calculating parameters characterizing biofilm structure from the biofilm image. (2) Choosing the combination of calculated parameters to be used in the image reconstruction. The number of selected parameters can range from one to several. (3) Using the selected parameters to construct an image that has the selected structural parameters identical to those computed from the biofilm image. (4) Comparing the reconstructed image with the original image of the biofilm from which the parameters characterizing structure were computed. (Reprinted from Renslow, R. et al., *Biotechnology and Bioengineering*, 108, 1383–1394, 2011.)

The algorithm in Figure 6.39 was integrated into a MATLAB program and run on an 8-core, 64-bit Microsoft Windows Vista computer with 16 GB of RAM. First, a target biofilm image was uploaded to the computer and the algorithms described in this chapter were used to quantify the selected areal parameters characterizing the biofilm image. The areal parameters for image reconstruction can be selected arbitrarily as long as the selection includes AP. The reconstruction process progressed as the sequence of steps depicted in Figure 6.39. First, the program randomly generated an image that had the same AP and dimensions as the original image. Because AP is the only areal parameter not sensitive to the location of the pixels, it was used as a bootstrapping parameter. To generate an image with matching AP, biomass pixels were added, one at a time, to randomly chosen locations on an initially void-covered image until the AP of the computer-generated image matched that of the original biofilm image (step 1 in Figure 6.39). Once the computer-generated image had the same AP as the target biofilm image, the values of the areal parameters selected for the reconstruction were calculated for that image (step 2 in Figure 6.39). Obviously, the values of these parameters did not initially match the values computed from the original biofilm image, so the next steps in the procedure were designed to bring these values as close to each other as possible by minimizing the objective function described in Equation 6.25. The sum of squared differences (SSD) between the values of the structural parameters of the computer-generated image and those computed from the original biofilm image as computed (step 3 in Figure 6.39). To bring the values of the selected areal parameters closer together, an iteration process was implemented in which two disparate pixels (one void pixel and one biomass pixel) of the reconstructed image were chosen at random and their locations were swapped (step 4 in Figure 6.39). Swapping the pixels changed the areal parameters of the computer-generated image, so the new set

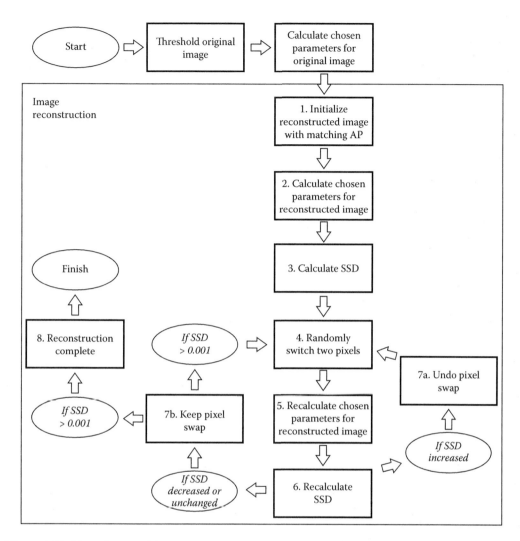

Figure 6.39 Algorithm used for reconstructing biofilm images. Biofilm structure quantification steps are shown outside the large box, and image reconstruction steps are shown inside the large box, starting at step 1. (Reprinted from Renslow, R. et al., *Biotechnology and Bioengineering*, 108, 1383–1394, 2011.)

of values of the chosen structural parameters had to be calculated (step 5 in Figure 6.39). To estimate whether swapping the pixels improved the level of matching, the new SSD was calculated (step 6 in Figure 6.39). If the SSD increased as a result of the pixel swap, the pixel swap was considered unsuccessful and the pixels were returned to their previous positions (step 7a in Figure 6.39). If, however, after the pixels were swapped the SSD remained the same or decreased, the pixel swap was considered successful and the pixels remained at their new locations (step 7b in Figure 6.39). Steps 4–7 were repeated until SSD was below 0.001, at which time the image reconstruction was considered complete and the resulting computer-generated image was accepted as the reconstructed image of the biofilm.

The main premise of the reconstruction algorithm in Figure 6.39 is that all areal parameters other than AP are sensitive to the locations of the pixels. Therefore, forcing the parameters to match was achieved by randomly switching the locations of pixels until the following objective function was minimized:

$$SSD = \sum_{i=1}^{N} \left(\frac{y_{reconstructed,i} - y_{original,i}}{y_{original,i}} \right)^2 \tag{6.21}$$

where N is the total number of parameters used for reconstruction, i is the arbitrary index value (from 1 to N) of a structural parameter (AP, ADD, etc.), $y_{reconstructed,i}$ is the structural parameter i value calculated from the computer-generated image and $y_{original,i}$ is the structural parameter i value calculated from the original image. The difference between $y_{reconstructed,i}$ and $y_{original,i}$ was normalized against $y_{original,i}$, so each selected parameter was weighted equally in the reconstruction. To avoid introducing a bias from the order in which parameters were considered, all parameters were matched concurrently. During image reconstruction, the locations of pixels were continually swapped in the reconstructed image to minimize SSD, while AP remained constant. At the end of the reconstruction, the new image and the original image had nearly identical values for the selected parameters, with the target SSD < 0.001.

Figure 6.40 shows the selected biofilm images and the computer-reconstructed images. The reconstructed images have the same structural parameters as the original images but

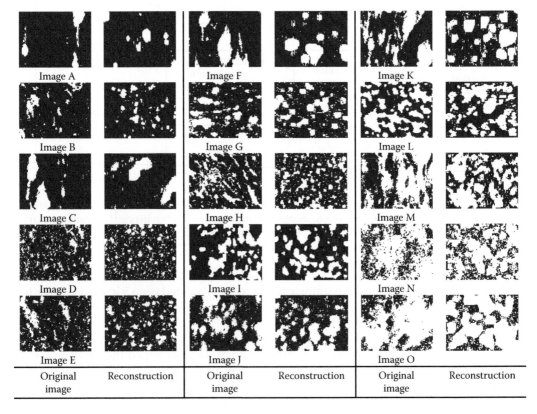

Figure 6.40 Fifteen sets of biofilm images and corresponding reconstructed images exhibiting the same AP, ADD, MDD, AHRL, AVRL, FD, and *P*. (Reprinted from Renslow, R. et al., *Biotechnology and Bioengineering*, 108, 1383–1394, 2011.)

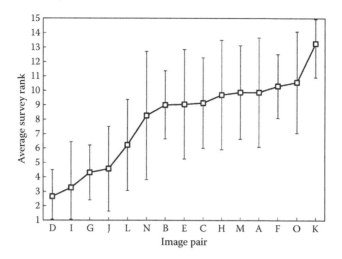

Figure 6.41 Results of the survey asking 22 volunteers to arrange the 15 pairs of biofilm images and corresponding reconstructed images in a sequence based on similarity, 1 being "most similar" and 15 being "least similar." The data points are the average ranks received for the individual pairs from all participants, and the bars show the standard deviation for each pair of images. (Reprinted from Renslow, R. et al., *Biotechnology and Bioengineering*, 108, 1383–1394, 2011.)

do not necessarily look similar to the original biofilm images. Figure 6.41 shows the results of a survey in which volunteers were asked to rank the similarity of the pairs of images shown in Figure 6.40. The pairs of images selected as most similar are for images D, G, I, J, and L. There was a high level of agreement among the participants that these five pairs of images were similar, and the corresponding standard deviations were relatively low (average of 2.6). The next nine pairs had higher standard deviations (average of 3.4) and similar ranks. For these nine pairs, the participants of the survey judged that the level of success in reconstructing the original biofilm image was similar. The least successful pair, for image K, was nearly three ranks away from the next worst pair, clearly identifying this pair of images as being the "least similar." Closer analysis of the results and the images demonstrates that humans tend to selectively focus on the predominant features of images, such as similarities and differences among large cell clusters and tend to ignore the smaller features, such as similarities and differences among small cell clusters. Thus, we believe that despite the unique features of human judgment—or perhaps because of them—in this case machine judgment is less biased and therefore more appropriate for evaluating the level of success in image reconstruction. Therefore, future researchers should focus on developing machine-dependent, rather than human-dependent, methods for comparing original and reconstructed images. An objective quantitative method for testing the level of success in image reconstruction is needed to ensure further progress in this effort.

Nomenclature

a	Integer number
ADD	Average diffusion distance
AHRL	Average horizontal run length

AP	Areal porosity
AR	Aspect ratio
AT_{biofilm}	Average biofilm thickness
AT_{biomass}	Average biomass thickness
AVRL	Average vertical run length
AXRL	Average X-run length
AYRL	Average Y-run length
AZRL	Average Z-run length
b	Integer number
BV	Biovolume
$\mathrm{d}x$	Size of a pixel in the X direction
$\mathrm{d}y$	Size of a pixel in the Y direction
$\mathrm{d}z$	Distance between interpolated image layers
$\mathrm{d}z'$	Distance between CSLM images before interpolation
E	Energy
FD	Fractal dimension
H	Homogeneity
k	Thickness of a single-layer CSLM image ($= \mathrm{d}x = \mathrm{d}y = \mathrm{d}z$)
Maxbiomass$T$	Maximum biomass thickness
Max$T$	Average biofilm thickness for the given percentage (PMax$T$) of biofilm locations with maximum values for biofilm thickness
MDD	Maximum diffusion distance
N	Number of biofilm thickness measurements
N_{biomass}	Total number of biomass thickness measurements
N_X	Total number of pixels in the X direction
N_Y	Total number of pixels in the Y direction
N_Z	Total number of pixels in the Z direction
P	Perimeter
P_{H}	Horizontal spatial dependence matrix
$p_{\text{H}}(a,b)$	Number of changes in the gray scale between a and b in adjacent horizontal locations in the image, moving in either direction
P_{HV}	Sum of the horizontal and vertical spatial dependence matrices
$p_{\text{HV}}(a,b)$	Total number of intensity variations from a to b and from b to a in the horizontal and vertical directions
PMax$T$	Percentage of locations with maximum local thicknesses
$P_{\text{N}}(a,b)$	Normalized spatial dependence matrix, or gray-level co-occurrence matrix (GLCM)
P_{V}	Vertical spatial dependence matrix
$p_{\text{V}}(a, b)$	Number of changes in the gray scale between a and b at adjacent vertical locations in the image, in all directions on the scale
P_X	X-spatial dependence matrix
$P_X(a,b)$	Number of times the gray level changes from a to b between neighboring pixels in the X direction, in both directions on the X scale integrated over the entire image
P_{XYZ}	Spatial dependence matrix in 3-D
P_Y	Y-spatial dependence matrix
$P_Y(a,b)$	Number of times the gray level changes from a to b between neighboring pixels in the Y direction, in both directions on the Y scale, integrated over the entire image

P_Z	The Z-spatial dependence matrix
$P_Z(a,b)$	The number of times the gray level changes from a to b between neighboring pixels in the Z direction, in both directions on the Z scale, integrated over the entire image
SR	Sphere radius
t_{back}	Average of background pixels
$T_{biofilm}(x,y)$	Individual thickness for each (x,y) location on the substratum
$T_{biomass}(x,y)$	Individual biomass thickness for each (x,y) location on the substratum
TE	Textural entropy
t_{fore}	Average of foreground pixels
t_{opt}	Optimum thresholding
t_{optS}	Optimum thresholding used during iteration
TORB	Integer used to identify whether the first image is numbered as 1
V2SA	Ratio of biovolume to surface area

References

Beyenal, H., Lewandowski, Z., and Harkin, G. 2004a. Quantifying biofilm structure: Facts and fiction. *Biofouling* 20(1): 1–23.

Beyenal, H., Donovan, C., Lewandowski, Z., and Harkin, G. 2004b. Three-dimensional biofilm structure quantification. *Journal of Microbiological Methods* 59(3): 395–413.

Breu, H., Gil, J., Kirkpatrick, D., and Werman, M. 1995. Linear time Euclidean distance transform algorithms. *IEEE Transactions on Pattern Analysis and Machine Intelligence* 17(5): 529–533.

Chang, C. I., Chen, K., Wang, J., and Althouse, M. L. G. 1994. A relative entropy-based approach to image thresholding. *Pattern Recognition* 27: 1275–1289.

Friedman, J. H., Bentley, J. L., and Raphael, R. A. 1997. An algorithm for finding best matches in logarithmic expected time. *ACM Transactions on Mathematics Software* 3(3): 209–226.

Haralick, R. M., Shanmuga, K., and Dinstein, I. 1973. Textural features for image classification. *IEEE Transactions on Systems Man and Cybernetics* SMC3(6): 610–621.

Kaandorp, J. 1994. *Fractal Modeling Growth and Form in Biology*. Berlin: Springer Verlag.

Lewandowski, Z., and Beyenal, H. 2003. Biofilm Monitoring: A perfect solution in search of a problem. *Water Science and Technology* 47(5): 9–18.

Lim, J. S. 1990. *Two-Dimensional Signal and Image Processing*. Englewood Cliffs, NJ: Prentice Hall, pp. 469–476.

Murga, R., Stewart, P. S., and Daly, D. 1995. Quantitative analysis of biofilm thickness variability. *Biotechnology and Bioengineering* 45: 503–510.

Pal, N. R., and Pal, S. K. 1989. Entropy thresholding. *Signal Process* 16: 97–108.

Renslow, R., Lewandowski, Z., and Beyenal, H. 2011. Biofilm image reconstruction for assessing structural parameters. *Biotechnology and Bioengineering* 108: 1383–1394.

Ridler, T. W., and Calvard S. 1978. Picture thresholding using an iterative selection method. *IEEE Transactions on Systems, Man, and Cybernetics* SMC-8: 630–632.

Russ, J. 2002. *The Image Processing Handbook*. Boca Raton, FL: CRC Press.

Wilkinson, M. H. F. 1998. Automated and manual segmentation techniques in image analysis of microbes. In *Imaging, Morphometry, Fluorometry and Motility Techniques and Applications*, Wilkinson, M. H. F., and Schut, F. (Eds.). John Wiley and Sons.

Xavier, J. B., Schnell, A., Wuertz, S., Palmer, R., White, D. C., and Almeida, J. S. 2001. Objective threshold selection procedure (OTS) for segmentation of scanning laser confocal microscope images. *Journal of Microbiological Methods* 47(2): 169–180.

Yang, X. M., Beyenal, H., Harkin, G., and Lewandowski, Z. 2001. Evaluation of biofilm image thresholding methods. *Water Research* 35(5): 1149–1158.

Suggested readings

Testing reproducibility of biofilm structure

GrayMerod, R., Hendrickx, L., Mueller, L. N., Xavier, J. B., and Wuertz, S. 2005. Effect of nucleic acid stain Syto9 on nascent biofilm architecture of *Acinetobacter* sp BD413. *Water Science and Technology* 52(7): 195–202.

Heydorn, A., Ersboll, B. K., Hentzer, M., Parsek, M. R., Givskov, M., and Molin, S. 2000. Experimental reproducibility in flow-chamber biofilms. *Microbiology* 146: 2409–2415.

Jackson, G., Beyenal, H., Rees, W. M., and Lewandowski, Z. 2001. Growing reproducible biofilms with respect to structure and viable cell counts. *Journal of Microbiological Methods* 47(1): 1–10.

Lewandowski, Z., Beyenal, H., and Stookey, D. 2004. Reproducibility of biofilm processes and the meaning of steady state in biofilm reactors. *Water Science and Technology* 49(11–12): 359–364.

Teles, F. R., Haffajee, A. D., and Socransky, S. S. 2008. The reproducibility of curet sampling of subgingival biofilms. *Journal of Periodontology* 79: 705–713.

Wroblewska, M. M., Sawicka-Grzelak, A., Marchel, H., Luczak, M., and Sivan, A. 2008. Biofilm production by clinical strains of *Acinetobacter baumannii* isolated from patients hospitalized in two tertiary care hospitals. *FEMS Immunology and Medical Microbiology* 53: 140–144.

Quantifying biofilm structure

Daims, H., Lucker, S., and Wagner, M. 2006. Daime, a novel image analysis program for microbial ecology and biofilm research. *Environmental Microbiology* 8(2): 200–213.

Daims, H., and Wagner, M. 2011. In situ techniques and digital image analysis methods for quantifying spatial localization patterns of nitrifiers and other microorganisms in biofilm and flocs. *Methods in Enzymology* 496: 185–215.

De Paz, L. E. C. 2009. Image analysis software based on color segmentation for characterization of viability and physiological activity of biofilms. *Applied and Environmental Microbiology* 75: 1734–1739.

Heydorn, A., Nielsen, A. T., Hentzer, M., Sternberg, C., Givskov, M., Ersboll, B. K., and Molin, S. 2000. Quantification of biofilm structures by the novel computer program COMSTAT. *Microbiology-UK* 146: 2395–2407.

Kuehn, M., Hausner, M., Bungartz, H. J., Wagner, M., Wilderer, P. A., and Wuertz, S. 1998. Automated confocal laser scanning microscopy and semiautomated image processing for analysis of biofilms. *Applied and Environmental Microbiology* 64(11): 4115–4127.

Lewandowski, Z. 2000. Notes on biofilm porosity. *Water Research* 34(9): 2620–2624.

Merod, R. T., Warren, J. E., McCaslin, H., and Wuertz, S. 2007. Toward automated analysis of biofilm architecture: Bias caused by extraneous confocal laser scanning microscopy images. *Applied and Environmental Microbiology* 73: 4922–4930.

Mueller, L. N., de Brouwer, J. F. C., Almeida, J. S., Stal, L. J., and Xavier, J. B. 2006. Analysis of a marine phototrophic biofilm by confocal laser scanning microscopy using the new image quantification software PHLIP. *BMC Ecology* 6: 1.

Posch, T., Franzoi, J., Prader, M., and Salcher, M. M. 2009. New image analysis tool to study biomass and morphotypes of three major bacterioplankton groups in an alpine lake. *Aquatic Microbial Ecology* 54: 113–126.

Xavier, J. B., White, D. C., and Almeida, J. S. 2003. Automated biofilm morphology quantification from confocal laser scanning microscopy imaging. *Water Science and Technology* 47(5): 31–37.

Yang, X. M., Beyenal, H., Harkin, G., and Lewandowski, Z. 2000. Quantifying biofilm structure using image analysis. *Journal of Microbiological Methods* 39(2): 109–119.

Selected computer science literature describing algorithms used in biofilm image analysis

Sahoo, P. K., and Arora, G. 2004. A thresholding method based on two-dimensional Renyi's entropy. *Pattern Recognition* 37(6): 1149–1161.

Sezgin, M., and Sankur, B. 2004. Survey over image thresholding techniques and quantitative performance evaluation. *Journal of Electronic Imaging* 13(1): 146–168.

Factors affecting biofilm structure

Allan, V. J. M., Callow, M. E., Macaskie, L. E., and Paterson-Beedle, M. 2002. Effect of nutrient limitation on biofilm formation and phosphatase activity of a *Citrobacter* sp. *Microbiology* 148: 277–288.

Battin, T. J., Kaplan, L. A., Newbold, J. D., Cheng, X. H., and Hansen, C. 2003. Effects of current velocity on the nascent architecture of stream microbial biofilms. *Applied and Environmental Microbiology* 69(9): 5443–5452.

Christensen, B. B., Haagensen, J. A. J., Heydorn, A., and Molin, S. 2002. Metabolic commensalism and competition in a two-species microbial consortium. *Applied and Environmental Microbiology* 68(5): 2495–2502.

Davey, M. E., Caiazza, N. C., and O'Toole, G. A. 2003. Rhamnolipid surfactant production affects biofilm architecture in *Pseudomonas aeruginosa* PAO1. *Journal of Bacteriology* 185(3): 1027–1036.

Downing, L. S., and Nerenberg, R. 2008. Effect of oxygen gradients on the activity and microbial community structure of a nitrifying, membrane-aerated biofilm. *Biotechnology and Bioengineering* 101: 1193–1204.

Ferreira, J. A. G., Carr, J. H., Starling, C. E. F., de Resende, M. A., and Donlan, R. M. 2009. Biofilm formation and effect of Caspofungin on biofilm structure of Candida species bloodstream isolates. *Antimicrobial Agents and Chemotherapy* 53: 4377–4384.

Hentzer, M., Teitzel, G. M., Balzer, G. J., Heydorn, A., Molin, S., Givskov, M., and Parsek, M. R. 2001. Alginate overproduction affects *Pseudomonas aeruginosa* biofilm structure and function. *Journal of Bacteriology* 183(18): 5395–5401.

Heydorn, A., Ersboll, B., Kato, J., Hentzer, M., Parsek, M. R., Tolker-Nielsen, T., Givskov, M., and Molin, S. 2002. Statistical analysis of *Pseudomonas aeruginosa* biofilm development: Impact of mutations in genes involved in twitching motility, cell-to-cell signaling, and stationary-phase sigma factor expression. *Applied and Environmental Microbiology* 68(4): 2008–2017.

Klausen, M., Heydorn, A., Ragas, P., Lambertsen, L., Aaes-Jorgensen, A., Molin, S., and Tolker-Nielsen, T. 2003. Biofilm formation by *Pseudomonas aeruginosa* wild type, flagella and type IV pili mutants. *Molecular Microbiology* 48(6): 1511–1524.

Lewandowski, Z., and Beyenal, H. 2005. Biofilms: Their structure, activity, and effect on membrane filtration. *Water Science and Technology* 51(6–7): 181–192.

Liu, H., Yang, F., Shi, S., and Liu, X. 2010. Effect of substrate COD/N ratio on performance and microbial community structure of a membrane aerated biofilm reactor. *Journal of Environmental Sciences-China* 22: 540–546.

Liu, J., Ling, J.-Q., Zhang, K., Huo, L.-J., and Ning, Y. 2012. Effect of sodium fluoride, ampicillin, and chlorhexidine on *Streptococcus mutans* biofilm detachment. *Antimicrobial Agents and Chemotherapy* 56: 4532–4535.

Mah, T. F., Pitts, B., Pellock, B., Walker, G. C., Stewart, P. S., and O'Toole, G. A. 2003. A genetic basis for *Pseudomonas aeruginosa* biofilm antibiotic resistance. *Nature* 426(6964): 306–310.

Nostro, A., Cellini, L., Di Giulio, M., D'Arrigo, M., Marino, A., Blanco, A. R., Favaloro, A., Cutroneo, G., and Bisignano, G. 2012. Effect of alkaline pH on staphylococcal biofilm formation. *APMIS* 120: 733–742.

Paul, E., Ochoa, J. C., Pechaud, Y., Liu, Y., and Line, A. 2012. Effect of shear stress and growth conditions on detachment and physical properties of biofilms. *Water Research* 46: 5499–5508.

Purevdorj, B., Costerton, J. W., and Stoodley, P. 2002. Influence of hydrodynamics and cell signaling on the structure and behavior of *Pseudomonas aeruginosa* biofilms. *Applied and Environmental Microbiology* 68(9): 4457–4464.

Semechko, A., Sudarsan, R., Bester, E., Dony, R., and Eberl, H. J. 2011. Influence of light attenuation on biofilm parameters evaluated from CLSM image data. *Journal of Medical and Biological Engineering* 31: 135–143.

Stapper, A. P., Narasimhan, G., Ohman, D. E., Barakat, J., Hentzer, M., Molin, S., Kharazmi, A., Hoiby, N., and Mathee, K. 2004. Alginate production affects *Pseudomonas aeruginosa* biofilm development and architecture, but is not essential for biofilm formation. *Journal of Medical Microbiology* 53(7): 679–690.

Venugopalan, V. P., Kuehn, A., Hausner, M., Springael, D., Wilderer, P. A., and Wuertz, S. 2005. Architecture of a nascent *Sphingomonas* sp biofilm under varied hydrodynamic conditions. *Applied and Environmental Microbiology* 71(5): 2677–2686.

Wood, S. R., Kirkham, J., Shore, R. C., Brookes, S. J., and Robinson, C. 2002. Changes in the structure and density of oral plaque biofilms with increasing plaque age. *Fems Microbiology Ecology* 39(3): 239–244.

Yildiz, F. H., Liu, X. S., Heydorn, A., and Schoolnik, G. K. 2004. Molecular analysis of rugosity in a *Vibrio cholerae* O1 El Tor phase variant. *Molecular Microbiology* 53(2): 497–515.

Biofilm structure and biofilm modeling

Boel, M., Moehle, R. B., Haesner, M., Neu, T. R., Horn, H., and Krul, R. 2009. 3D finite element model of biofilm detachment using real biofilm structures from CLSM data. *Biotechnology and Bioengineering* 103: 177–186.

Chang, I., Gilbert, E. S., Eliashberg, N., and Keasling, J. D. 2003. A three-dimensional, stochastic simulation of biofilm growth and transport-related factors that affect structure. *Microbiology* 149: 2859–2871.

Hermanowicz, S. W. 2001. A simple 2D biofilm model yields a variety of morphological features. *Mathematical Biosciences* 169(1): 1–14.

Kwok, W. K., Picioreanu, C., Ong, S. L., van Loosdrecht, M. C. M., Ng, W. J., and Heijnen, J. J. 1998. Influence of biomass production and detachment forces on biofilm structures in a biofilm airlift suspension reactor. *Biotechnology and Bioengineering* 58(4): 400–407.

Miller, J. K., Badawy, H. T., Clemons, C., Kreider, K. L., Wilber, P., Milsted, A., and Young, G. 2012. Development of the *Pseudomonas aeruginosa* mushroom morphology and cavity formation by iron-starvation: A mathematical modeling study. *Journal of Theoretical Biology* 308: 68–78.

Picioreanu, C., van Loosdrecht, M. C. M., and Heijnen, J. J. 2000. Effect of diffusive and convective substrate transport on biofilm structure formation: A two-dimensional modeling study. *Biotechnology and Bioengineering* 69(5): 504–515.

Pizarro, G. E., Teixeira, J., Sepulveda, M., and Noguera, D. R. 2005. Bitwise implementation of a two-dimensional cellular automata biofilm model. *Journal of Computing in Civil Engineering* 19(3): 258–268.

Volcke, E. I. P., Picioreanu, C., De Baets, B., and van Loosdrecht, M. C. M. 2012. The granule size distribution in an anammox-based granular sludge reactor affects the conversion—Implications for modeling. *Biotechnology and Bioengineering* 109: 1629–1636.

Xavier, J. B., Picioreanu, C., and van Loosdrecht, M. C. M. 2004. Assessment of three-dimensional biofilm models through direct comparison with confocal microscopy imaging. *Water Science and Technology* 49(11–12): 177–185.

Xavier, J. B., Picioreanu, C., and van Loosdrecht, M. C. M. 2005. A framework for multidimensional modelling of activity and structure of multispecies biofilms. *Environmental Microbiology* 7(8): 1085–1103.

Xavier, J. D., Picioreanu, C., and van Loosdrecht, M. C. M. 2005. A general description of detachment for multidimensional modelling of biofilms. *Biotechnology and Bioengineering* 91(6): 651–669.

Zacarias, G. D., Ferreira, C. P., and Velasco-Hernandez, J. 2005. Porosity and tortuosity relations as revealed by a mathematical model of biofilm structure. *Journal of Theoretical Biology* 233(2): 245–251.

Thresholding biofilm images

Chu, C. P., Lee, D. J., and Tay, J. H. 2004. Bilevel thresholding of floc images. *Journal of Colloid and Interface Science* 273(2): 483–489.

Jubany, I., Lafuente, J., Carrera, J., and Baeza, J. A. 2009. Automated thresholding method (ATM) for biomass fraction determination using FISH and confocal microscopy. *Journal of Chemical Technology and Biotechnology* 84: 1140–1145.

Rojas, D., Rueda, L., Ngom, A., Hurrutia, H., and Carcamo, G. 2011. Image segmentation of biofilm structures using optimal multi-level thresholding. *International Journal of Data Mining and Bioinformatics* 5: 266–286.

Rojas, D., Rueda, L., Urrutia, H., and Ngom, A. 2009. Efficient optimal multi-level thresholding for biofilm image segmentation. In *Proceedings of Pattern Recognition in Bioinformatics*, Kadirkamanathan, V., et al. (Eds.). Sheffield, UK: Springer, pp. 307–318.

Yerly, J., Hu, Y., Jones, S. M., and Martinuzzi, R. J. 2007. A two-step procedure for automatic and accurate segmentation of volumetric CLSM biofilm images. *Journal of Microbiological Methods* 70: 424–433.

chapter seven

Biofilms on metals and other electrically conductive surfaces

7.1 Introduction

This chapter introduces a fruitful and dynamic field of biofilm research that developed as a result of the study of microbial respiration in biofilms deposited on electrically conductive surfaces, particularly on metals. Microbial respiration is based on electron transfer from electron donors to electron acceptors in a series of reactions facilitated by a cascade of energetic reactants; these are well-known reactions described in the literature. The donors and acceptors of electrons in these reactions are typically dissolved reactants, but some microorganisms can use chemical constituents of solid materials as electron donors or acceptors in respiration, such as redox-sensitive minerals and metals (Nealson and Finkel 2011). When microorganisms use minerals for these purposes, the term "mineral-respiring microorganisms" is used. When microorganisms use electrodes for respiration, the term "electrode-respiring microorganisms" is used. The exact mechanisms of electron transfer between microorganisms and solid reactants, or metal electrodes, remain a matter of intensive debate in the literature. Free electrons do not exist in aqueous solutions, and in redox reactions electrons are transferred across distances comparable to the length of molecular bonds, at least in classical physics. Therefore, microorganisms, being much larger than the distances along which electrons are transferred, cannot approach surfaces closely enough to accept electrons from or donate electrons to the constituents of solid reactants directly. Consequently, if microorganisms exchange electrons with solid chemicals, there must be a mechanism that overcomes the problem of transferring electrons over distances exceeding those of molecular bonds. Two points of view, not necessarily conflicting with each other, are usually presented in this debate: (1) the recently proposed point of view, that electrons are transferred between microorganisms and solids by electrical conduction either through specifically designed proteins in the outer membranes of the microbes or through extracellular elongated appendages called nanowires, and (2) the more traditional point of view, that the electrons are transferred by redox mediators, small molecules that can, for example, approach the active center of an enzyme to accept or to donate an electron. These small molecules are also known as electron shuttles because they continuously move between electron donors and electron acceptors. Electron transfer by redox mediators does not necessarily require physical movement of these molecules: a chain of redox mediators can transfer electrons between microbial cells and solid surfaces. This mechanism is known as "superexchange" and is exemplified by the electron transfer along a chain of cytochromes produced in a *Geobacter sulfurreducens* biofilms. When microorganisms respire on minerals, a third mechanism may be implicated: solubilization of the minerals by microbially produced chelators. The production by *Shewanella oneidensis* MR1 biofilms of flavins that can diffuse out and oxidize solid manganese oxides, MnO_2, exemplifies this mechanism. It is difficult to select one of these mechanisms as the one that dominates the electron transfer processes between microbes and solids based on the published papers. Actually, the image that emerges from the published data indicates that the predominant electron transfer mechanism between microbes and solids depends on the type of the microorganisms, the environmental conditions, and the experimental system used to study the process. For the experimentalists, the message here is that to generate reproducible results that can also be compared with the data published by others, it is imperative that all components of the experimental system used to study the electron transfer mechanisms between microorganisms in a biofilm and solids be carefully selected and precisely controlled during the experiment. Ideally, the research protocols used in these studies would be identical, but, unfortunately, biofilm researchers often disagree on protocols for growing biofilms and making measurements.

A biofilm that can interact electrochemically with an electrode and regulate its microbial metabolism using the electrode either as a source or as a sink for electrons transported in the metabolic chain of reactions is known as an electrochemically active biofilm (EAB). Structurally, EABs look and act just as all other biofilms described in this book do; the name EABs refers to their most prominent function, the ability to exchange electrons with metal electrodes or with redox-sensitive minerals. EABs are also known under several other names, such as electricigens, electrochemically active microbes, exoelectrogenic bacteria, and anode-respiring or anodophilic species. Because the hallmark of these biofilms is their ability to exchange electrons with solid surfaces, such as electrodes in electrochemical cells, we believe that the term electrochemically active biofilms refers directly to the function of these biofilms, and we use it in this book. As we pointed out above, when EABs grow on electrodes, electrons from metabolic reactions can be exchanged with the electrode by (1) direct electron transfer from the microorganisms through membrane proteins or nanowires and (2) electron transfer mediated by soluble exogenous, or electron transfer, mediators (Figure 7.1).

Metabolically active microorganisms are efficient energy converters, and the energy transfer and conversion of the metabolic processes occur via sequences of redox and acid-base reactions that have been studied for centuries. These reactions, which occur mostly within microorganisms, are active in microorganisms residing in biofilms just as they are in suspended cultures of microorganisms. Regardless of the growth mode, suspended or attached growth, the pathways of electron transfer lead from the dissolved electron donors to the dissolved electron acceptors. On a larger scale of observation, the microorganisms active in these processes are mediators of electron transfer between substances dissolved in the solution of nutrients and the microorganisms benefit from these processes by sequestering part of the transferred energy. In EABs, the electrons are transferred between

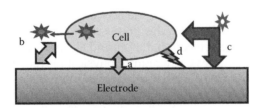

Figure 7.1 Accepted electron transfer mechanisms from a microbial cell to an electrode: (a) direct electron transfer through membrane proteins, (b) electron transfer through indigenous electron shuttles, (c) electron transfer through exogenous electron shuttles, and (d) electron transfer through nanowires. Note that electrons can be transferred in both directions (from the microbial cell to the electrode and vice versa). For simplicity, instead of a biofilm we show a single cell in this figure.

the chemical constituents of the solids covered by the biofilms and the reactants dissolved in the solution. Again, on the larger scale of observation, the biofilms in these processes are mediators of electron transfer between the substances dissolved in the solution of nutrients and the solids on which the biofilms are deposited, and the biofilm microorganisms benefit from these processes by sequestering part of the transferred energy. However, the processes of electron transfer between the microorganisms in EABs and the chemical constituents of solid surfaces introduce a novel component into the mechanisms of electron transfer, the solids; they therefore exhibit new properties and have new consequences that do not exist in suspended cultures of microorganisms. Two such processes have consequences of technological relevance that is serious enough to attract the attention of biofilm researchers and subsequent research funding: microbially influenced corrosion (MIC) and microbial fuel cells (MFCs). Both of these involve biofilms deposited on electrically conductive surfaces, mostly metals. In many ways these two processes operate on the same principles; however, while MIC occurs spontaneously, MFCs are actually engineered to harvest some of the energy transferred in the associated microbial and electrochemical processes. Mechanisms of MIC are also included in a much broader field of exploration, the biodeterioration of materials, where they are linked to other forms of microbial corrosion, such as the well-known corrosion of stone affecting ancient artifacts. We will focus here only on biofilm effects on metals and other electrically conductive surfaces. We will examine the consequences of these effects on the integrity of materials in the case of MIC and the possibility of harvesting energy and using it for practical purposes in MFCs. In addition, we will describe how to use electrochemical techniques to study these processes and to model biofilm and electrochemical reactions occurring on metal electrodes.

From the human point of view, on the one hand, MIC, just like galvanic corrosion, wastes the energy spent on the metals and alloys during the mining and the metallurgical treatment of the metal ores. MFCs, on the other hand, are considered useful devices that can capture chemical energy and convert it to a more useful form, electricity. The two processes are based on similar electrochemical principles: MIC and MFC both rely on a flow of electrons from an electrochemical half-cell characterized by a higher activity of electrons to an electrochemical half-cell characterized by a lower activity of electrons. From the electrochemical point of view, the main difference in the physical arrangements of these two processes is that the electrochemical half-cells in MIC are located on the same piece of metal, and therefore the metal can be characterized by a single electrical potential—the corrosion potential—while the electrochemical half-cells in MFC are located on two pieces of metal with different electrical potentials. The origin of the electrical potential is also different in these processes. MFCs use electrodes made of noble metals or inert materials such as graphite that do not corrode easily, so their electrical potential is set by the redox couples in the solution near the surface of the electrode. In MIC, one of the reactants is the electrode itself and the electrical potential of the metal is affected by the concentration of the corroding metal ions in the solution. The electrochemical half-cells in MFCs are connected through electronic circuits, and some of the energy transferred between these half-cells is harvested using suitable electronic devices. In both processes, MIC and MFC, the metabolic reactions of the microorganisms increase the difference in electron activity between the respective electrochemical half-cells involved in the process, which otherwise would exhibit little or no difference in electron activity. In both processes the electroneutrality of the solution is retained because the electrochemical reactions are associated with the external transfer of counter ions in the solution surrounding the electrodes.

As we pointed out above, MIC, on the one hand, is a detrimental process because it leads to the aimless dispersion of the energy accumulated in the metal. MFCs, on the other hand, are useful devices and when properly engineered can be used as power sources for electronic devices, particularly those requiring limited power. As the two processes work on the same principles, to control them, we try to inhibit in MIC the same reactions we try to enhance in MFCs. Although it has proven difficult to succeed fully in controlling either MIC or MFCs, the attempts to control these processes have had a very useful side effect: They have created a fruitful field of study for biofilm researchers, because closer inspection of the processes involved in energy flow and conversion revealed how surprisingly little we knew about the mechanisms of electron transfer between microorganisms in biofilms and the solid materials on which the biofilms are deposited. The studies of MIC and MFC have posed interesting questions and generated fundamental knowledge about the interactions of biofilms with solid surfaces more than they have produced the practical applications for which they were initiated. In the process, a common denominator of the two processes has been established through the introduction of the concept of electrochemically active biofilms, which we will explore in greater detail later in this chapter.

Studying the mechanisms of energy flow and conversion between chemical constituents of solid materials covered with biofilms and dissolved reactants in bulk solution, across the biofilms, has become a fruitful field of biofilm research, and we will introduce the main conceptual and physical tools needed to conduct such studies. Actually, many of these physical and conceptual tools have existed for a long time. The corrosion of metals has been studied for centuries, and electrochemical tools and suitable theories for studying the corrosion of metals and electron transport between conductive surfaces and dissolved reactants in solution are readily available and constitute the domain of electrochemistry. The same is true for studying the flow and conversion of energy in microorganisms, which constitute the domain of microbial energetics. The main challenge when studying energy flow and conversion in biofilms is therefore not a lack of conceptual and physical tools, but the steep learning curve facing biofilm researchers involved in these studies. It is the challenge of using these tools and reporting the results in meaningful ways that help in explaining the mechanism of energy transformations in such systems. The reasons for difficulties stem from the same base as they do in other multi- and cross-disciplinary research fields. The flow and conversion of energy between metals and dissolved reactants via biofilms are typically studied either by life scientists, who may have limited training in electrochemistry and in using electrochemical concepts, methods, and instruments properly to produce meaningful results, or by electrochemists, who may have limited training in the methods used in life sciences and microbial energetics to appreciate the complexity and the requirements of the living system that controls the results of the processes they study.

This chapter introduces a selection of conceptual and physical tools that are needed to study energy flow and conversion between biofilms and electrically conductive surfaces. The basic premise of the chapter is that the subjects of these studies are chemical reactions, related either to microbial metabolism or to the electrochemistry of metals, and, consequently, the concepts that apply to these studies originate from the thermodynamics and kinetics of chemical, electrochemical, and biochemical reactions. As in the other chapters in this book, we illustrate these principles using results of our own studies of MIC and MFCs that have been published over the years in various journals and presented at various conferences dedicated to life sciences and to physical sciences. A selection of protocols useful in such studies is also offered, in part here and in part in Chapter 9, which is dedicated to protocols intended to serve mostly as examples to guide the researchers in making their own modifications consistent with the goals of their particular studies. For practical purposes, and to make the exposition of these complex topics more manageable, we start with an introduction of basic concepts useful in these types of studies.

7.2   Basic electrochemical concepts relevant to understanding the effects of biofilms on metals

7.2.1   The rate of electrode reactions: The Butler–Volmer equation

The fundamental equation in potentiometry is the Nernst equation, which quantifies the electrode potential at equilibrium, and the fundamental equation in amperometry and voltammetry is the Butler–Volmer equation, which quantifies the rates of the electrode reactions. We will go through the basic steps in the derivation of the Butler–Volmer equation, as we went through the basic steps in the derivation of the Nernst equation in Chapter 3.

When current flows and electrical charges are transferred between an electrode and the dissolved reactants in a solution, the electrode acts as a chemical reactant and the rules of chemical kinetics apply as they do in reactions involving dissolved reactants. However, the existence of an electrical field in proximity to the surface of the electrode introduces additional factors that need to be taken into consideration in quantifying the kinetics of the reaction. The potential difference between the electrode and the solution generates an electric field. The electroactive reactants, the reactants in the redox reactions, are subjected to this electric field and behave differently than they behave in the absence of such a field. Some electrically charged particles will find it easier to approach the surface of the electrode because they are electrostatically attracted to the surface, and other electroactive reactants in the solution will find it difficult to approach the surface of the electrode because they are repulsed by the electrical field. To exchange electrical charges with the electrode, the electroactive reactants in the solution must approach the electrode. A detailed description of this situation is beautifully described in a book by Bockris and Reddy, *Modern Electrochemistry*; see the list of suggested readings at the end of the chapter.

In reversible electrode reaction process $M^{n+} + e^- \rightleftarrows M^{(n-1)+}$ at equilibrium, there is no net current flow, and the fluxes of the electrical charges across the interface are equal in the two directions. When this electrode is connected to another electrode in the same solution, the current measured in the external circuit is the result of the net difference between the flux of electric charges across the interface in one direction and that in the other direction. Whether the electrode is at equilibrium or not, two reactions, oxidation and reduction, are always occurring at the electrode surface. The following formalism is accepted when discussing electrode kinetics:

Forward reaction: ox + e$^-$ → red
Reverse reaction: red → ox + e$^-$

In the electrode reaction we are considering ox = M^{n+} and red = $M^{(n-1)+}$.

Following the convention accepted in electrochemistry and the assumptions we use for this conceptual model, the forward reaction is the reduction of cations by electrons from the metal electrode. We call this reaction cathodic and assign the subscript "c" to all relevant symbols. The reverse reaction, in which the less positive ions donate electrons to the electrode, is oxidation; we call this reaction anodic and assign the subscript "a" to all relevant symbols.

The derivation of the Butler–Volmer equation starts with an idealized concept of energy distribution near the surface of an electrode (Figure 7.2).

Assuming that the metal electrode has a higher potential than the solution, to accept an electron from the electrode, the cations must be near the electrode. Before an electron

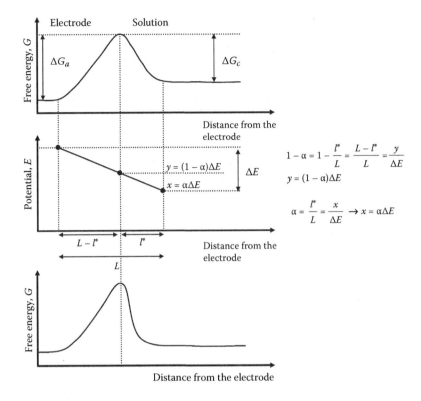

$$1 - \alpha = 1 - \frac{l^*}{L} = \frac{L - l^*}{L} = \frac{y}{\Delta E}$$

$$y = (1 - \alpha)\Delta E$$

$$\alpha = \frac{l^*}{L} = \frac{x}{\Delta E} \rightarrow x = \alpha\Delta E$$

Figure 7.2 Energy distribution near the surface of an electrode for reversible process $M^{n+} + e \Leftrightarrow M^{(n-1)+}$. To accept an electron from the electrode, the oxidized ions (M^{n+}) approaching the electrode from the bulk solution must surmount the free energy barrier, the activation energy for the cathodic reaction, ΔG_c, and part of the electric potential barrier, $\alpha\Delta E$. When the reduced ions ($M^{(n-1)+}$) transfer an electron to the electrode, they must surmount the free energy barrier, the activation energy for the anodic reaction, ΔG_a, and part of the potential barrier, $((1 - \alpha)\Delta E)$.

can be transferred from the electrode to the oxidized ion, the oxidized ion must surmount the activation energy barrier ΔG_c and part of the electric potential barrier $\alpha\Delta E$, where

$$\alpha = \frac{\text{distance between the location at the beginning of the double layer}}{\text{thickness of the double layer, } L}$$

$$\alpha = \frac{l^*}{L}$$

The electric potential barrier ΔE, which repulses the positively charged ions from the positively charged electrode, results from the fact that the metal electrode has a higher potential than the solution. The activation energy barrier, ΔG_c, has the same meaning as it does in the kinetics of homogeneous reactions.

Figure 7.2 shows that that there is a difference in the manner in which the two energy barriers are distributed: the potential energy barrier reaches its maximum at the surface of the electrode, while the activation energy barrier reaches its maximum away from the surface. When the energy barriers are superimposed, the resulting combined energy barrier that the cations must surmount has a maximum away from the surface, at the same distance from the surface as the maximum of the activation energy barrier, ΔG_a. As a consequence, once the cations have surmounted the activation energy barrier, ΔG_a, the combined energy barrier decreases. This effect must be taken into consideration when the minimum energy for the ion to approach the electrode successfully is quantified. To quantify it, the distance between the solution and the electrode is divided into two parts, separated at the location of the peak in the activation energy barrier. The electrical contribution to the overall energy barrier is

$$\Delta G_e = \alpha F \Delta E \tag{7.1}$$

The sum of energies contributing to the energy barrier for the cathodic reaction is

$$\Delta G_{Tc} = \Delta G_c + \alpha F \Delta E \tag{7.2}$$

The remaining part of the potential barrier amounts to $(1 - \alpha)F\Delta E$; it does not affect the cathodic reaction, but it does affect the anodic reaction in which the reduced electroactive reactants, less positively charged ions, donate electrons to the electrode and move away from the electrode. These ions must surmount activation energy ΔG_a plus the remaining part of the potential barrier, $(1 - \alpha)F\Delta E$. The sum of the energies contributing to the barrier for the anodic reaction is

$$\Delta G_{Ta} = \Delta G_a - (1 - \alpha)F \Delta E \tag{7.3}$$

Once we have quantified the energy barriers, we can use the Arrhenius equation, $k = A' \times \exp\left(\dfrac{-\Delta G_{activation}}{RT} \right)$, to evaluate the reaction rate constants, assuming that the reaction is first-order.

For the cathodic reaction this is

$$r_c = A' \times \exp\left(\frac{-\Delta G_{Tc}}{RT} \right) \times A \times [ox] = A' \times \exp\left(\frac{-(\Delta G_c + \alpha F \Delta E)}{RT} \right) \times A \times [ox] =$$

$$= A' \times \exp\left(\frac{-\Delta G_c}{RT} \right) \times \exp\left(\frac{-\alpha F \Delta E}{RT} \right) \times A \times [ox] \tag{7.4}$$

$$= k_c \times \exp\left(\frac{-\alpha F \Delta E}{RT} \right) \times A \times [ox]$$

where A' is the Arrhenius frequency factor, k_c is the reaction rate constant for the cathodic reaction, and A is the surface area of the electrode.

The cathodic current density is then

$$i_c = \frac{r_c \times F}{A} = k_c \times F \times \exp\left(\frac{-\alpha F \Delta E}{RT} \right) \times [ox] \tag{7.5}$$

Similarly, the rate of the anodic reaction is

$$r_a = A' \times \exp\left(\frac{-\Delta G_{Ta}}{RT}\right) \times A \times [\text{red}] = A' \times \exp\left(\frac{-\left[(\Delta G_a - (1-\alpha)F\Delta E)\right]}{RT}\right) \times A \times [\text{red}]$$

$$= A' \times \exp\left(\frac{-\Delta G_a}{RT}\right) \times \exp\left(\frac{(1-\alpha)F\Delta E}{RT}\right) \times A \times [\text{red}] \tag{7.6}$$

$$= k_a \times \exp\left(\frac{(1-\alpha)F\Delta E}{RT}\right) \times A \times [\text{red}]$$

where k_a is the reaction rate constant for the anodic reaction.

The anodic current density is then

$$i_a = \frac{r_a \times F}{A} = k_a \times F \times \exp\left(\frac{(1-\alpha)F\Delta E}{RT}\right) \times [\text{red}] \tag{7.7}$$

The potential difference between the electrode and the solution, ΔE, is the nonequilibrium potential, and it is composed of the equilibrium potential and the overpotential:

$$\Delta E = \Delta E_{eq} + \eta \tag{7.8}$$

where ΔE_{eq} is the potential of the electrode in thermodynamic equilibrium with the electroactive substances in the solution and η, the overpotential, is the part of the potential applied to the electrode that accounts for the deviation from the equilibrium. An overpotential can be applied to an electrode by a researcher using a potentiostat. As we discussed in Section 4.1.3.1 on electrolytic cells, the overpotential equals the difference between the actual potential of the electrode and the potential of the electrode at equilibrium. Electrodes whose potentials are higher or lower than at equilibrium are called polarized. Electrodes are polarized using external power sources:

$$\eta = \Delta E - \Delta E_{eq} \tag{7.9}$$

The part of the overpotential that results from changes in the concentrations of the reactants near the electrodes is known as the *concentration overpotential*, η_c. Besides concentration overpotentials, there are also kinetic effects inhibiting the transfer of electrical charges between electrodes and electroactive reagents in solution, and these effects cause the *activation overpotential*, η_a. The activation overpotential is applied to overcome the kinetic limitations of an electrical charge transfer across an interface of electrodes and solutions. Further, the current flowing in the electrolytic cell is described by Ohm's law, which says that the current in a circuit is proportional to the applied potential and inversely proportional to the resistance. Assuming that the resistance of the electronic conductors (electrodes and wires) is negligible, the resistance of the ionic conductor (electrolyte) must still be accounted for and overcome by applying a potential of somewhat greater magnitude. The additional potential that needs to be applied is called the *iR* drop, because its magnitude is evaluated as the product of the current flowing and the resistance of the electrolyte. In summary, the total overpotential in an electrolytic cell is equal to

$$\eta_{\text{total}} = iR + \eta_c + \eta_a \tag{7.10}$$

where i is current and R is resistance.

In terms of the overpotential, the cathodic and anodic current densities are expressed as

$$i_c = \frac{r_c \times F}{A} = k_c \times F \times \exp\left(\frac{-\alpha F(\Delta E_{eq} + \eta)}{RT}\right) \times [\text{ox}] \tag{7.11}$$

$$i_a = \frac{r_a \times F}{A} = k_a \times F \times \exp\left(\frac{(1-\alpha)F(\Delta E_{eq} + \eta)}{RT}\right) \times [\text{red}] \tag{7.12}$$

The net current density crossing the interface between the electrode and the solution is the difference between the current densities in the two directions, anodic and cathodic. It does not really matter which one is subtracted from which, anodic from cathodic or vice versa, as long as we follow the sign convention. The term *polarization* means that the potential of the electrode has been shifted from the potential at equilibrium. When we shift the potential of an electrode to a potential lower than that at equilibrium, we call this shift cathodic polarization. When we shift the potential of an electrode to a potential higher than that at equilibrium, we call it anodic polarization.

From the definition of overpotential, $\Delta E = \Delta E_{eq} + \eta$, we assign

$$\text{Cathodic polarization: } \eta = \Delta E - \Delta E_{eq} < 0$$

$$\text{Anodic polarization: } \eta = \Delta E - \Delta E_{eq} > 0 \tag{7.13}$$

It is important to follow the sign convention above. Results of voltammetric measurements are typically plotted on voltammetric axes. These axes are constructed in such a way that cathodic current is positive and anodic current is negative, which is consistent with subtracting the anodic current from the cathodic current: note that this convention is in agreement with Example 7.2, in which we use anodic and cathodic polarization and compute the net current. The following illustrates the computations when the electrode potentials vary over a certain interval, as is common in voltammetric methods.

$$i = k_c \times F \times \exp\left(\frac{-\alpha F(\Delta E_{eq} + \eta)}{RT}\right) \times [\text{ox}] - k_a \times F \times \exp\left(\frac{(1-\alpha)F(\Delta E_{eq} + \eta)}{RT}\right) \times [\text{red}]$$

$$= k_c \times F \times \exp\left(\frac{-\alpha F\Delta E_{eq}}{RT}\right) \times \exp\left(\frac{-\alpha F\eta}{RT}\right) \times [\text{ox}] \tag{7.14}$$

$$- k_a \times F \times \exp\left(\frac{(1-\alpha)F\Delta E_{eq}}{RT}\right) \times \exp\left(\frac{(1-\alpha)F\eta}{RT}\right) \times [\text{red}]$$

If the electrode is at equilibrium, $\eta = 0$, then the rate of the anodic reaction is equal to the rate of the cathodic reaction and the anodic current density equals the cathodic current density. This special case of current density at equilibrium, called the exchange current density, i_o, reflects the rate of the reversible electrode reaction at equilibrium. It cannot be measured in the external circuit: at equilibrium the current in the external circuit is equal to zero. The exchange current density depends on the type of reaction and on the material of the electrode. For the reduction of protons it varies widely, depending on the material of the electrode, as can be seen in Figure 7.3, which shows the exchange current density for the reaction $2H^+ + 2e \rightleftarrows H_2$ on various electrodes. For this particular reaction, the exchange current density is the smallest on mercury electrodes, where it is approximately 10 orders of magnitude smaller than on platinized platinum electrodes, which explains why platinized platinum electrodes are used in redox measurements and to construct SHE. Differences in exchange current density affect polarization curves: for the same applied overpotential, the current may vary by orders of magnitude depending on the electrode material.

The exchange current exists only at the interface between the electrode and the solution.

$$i_o = k_c \times F \times \exp\left(\frac{-\alpha F \Delta E_{eq}}{RT}\right) \times [ox] = k_a \times F \times \exp\left(\frac{(1-\alpha)F\Delta E_{eq}}{RT}\right) \times [red] \qquad (7.15)$$

which simplifies Equation 7.14 to the following form:

$$i = i_c - i_a = i_o \left[\exp\left(\frac{-\alpha(F\eta)}{RT}\right) - \exp\left(\frac{(1-\alpha)F\eta}{RT}\right)\right] \qquad (7.16)$$

In Equation 7.16 the cathodic current is positive and the anodic current is negative, which is consistent with the convention accepted in voltammetry.

When the electrode is cathodically polarized, $\eta < 0$, the cathodic current dominates, and the anodic current is negligible at higher cathodic overpotentials:

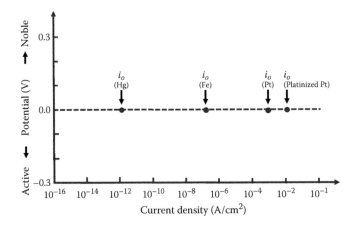

Figure 7.3 Hydrogen-proton exchange current densities. (Modified from M. Fontana and N. D. Green, *Corrosion Engineering*. McGraw-Hill, NY, 1967, p. 308.)

$$i = i_c - i_a = i_o\left[\exp\left(\frac{-\alpha F(-\eta)}{RT}\right) - \exp\left(\frac{(1-\alpha)F(-\eta)}{RT}\right)\right]$$

$$= i_o\left\{\left[\exp\left(\frac{\alpha F\eta}{RT}\right) - \exp\left(-\frac{(1-\alpha)F\eta}{RT}\right)\right]\right\} \approx i_o\exp\left(\frac{\alpha F\eta}{RT}\right) \tag{7.17}$$

Note that when the cathodic current dominates, then the overall current has a positive sign, which is consistent with the manner in which the voltammetric axes are arranged. When the electrode is anodically polarized, $\eta > 0$, the anodic current dominates, and the cathodic current is negligible at higher anodic overpotentials:

$$i = i_c - i_a = i_o\left[\exp\left(\frac{-\alpha F(+\eta)}{RT}\right) - \exp\left(\frac{(1-\alpha)F(+\eta)}{RT}\right)\right]$$

$$= i_o\left\{\left[\exp\left[-\left(\frac{\alpha F\eta}{RT}\right)\right] - \exp\left(\frac{(1-\alpha)F\eta}{RT}\right)\right]\right\} \approx -\left[i_o\exp\left(\frac{(1-\alpha)F\eta}{RT}\right)\right] \tag{7.18}$$

When the anodic current dominates, the overall current has a negative sign, which is consistent with the manner in which the voltammetric axes are arranged. To assign specific parts of the energy barrier to specific reactions, we assign: $\alpha = \alpha_c$ and $(1-\alpha) = \alpha_a$, which leads to the following expression:

$$i = i_o\left[\exp\left(\frac{-\alpha_c F\eta}{RT}\right) - \exp\left(\frac{\alpha_a F\eta}{RT}\right)\right] \tag{7.19}$$

where $\alpha_c + \alpha_a = 1$.

Equation 7.19 is known as the Butler–Volmer equation. For most computations it is enough to assume that $\alpha_c = \alpha_a = 0.5$, which translates to a symmetrical distribution of the electrical potential on the two sides of the activation energy barrier.

The use of the Butler–Volmer equation is restricted by the assumptions imposed when the equation was derived. It describes the kinetics of simple electrochemical reactions involving one electron exchange: a single anodic reaction and a single cathodic reaction occurring on the electrode. This idealized image of electrode reactions may be imitated in simple electrochemical cells. In more complex, and more real cells, more than one reaction may occur on the electrode at the same time. In such cases the overall current density has contributions from all reactions occurring on the electrode. For m separate half reactions:

$$i = \sum_{j=1}^{m} i_j \tag{7.20}$$

where j is the number of a reaction and i_j is the net current that this reaction contributes to overall net current i. Also, the equation was derived assuming a single electron transfer in the electrode reaction. If more than one electron is transferred in the electrode reaction, the Butler–Volmer equation does not really apply because each of the consecutively transferred electrons may be transferred at a different overpotential. However, if more than one electron is transferred in one step, at a single overpotential, then the Butler–Volmer equation can be modified to a more general form to account for the possibility that more than one electron is transferred:

$$i = i_o\left[\exp\left(\frac{-\alpha_c nF\eta)}{RT}\right) - \exp\left(\frac{\alpha_a nF\eta}{RT}\right)\right] \tag{7.21}$$

where $\alpha_c + \alpha_a \neq 1$.

It is worth stressing that the Butler–Volmer equation is a mathematical model quantifying electrode kinetics and as such it has its limitations. For example, the Butler–Volmer equation predicts that when the overpotential increases to infinity, so does the current. This prediction contradicts the empirical findings, which show that the current follows the Butler–Volmer equation only in a limited range of overpotentials and that outside of this range it reaches its limiting value, which is not affected by a further increase in potential, at least until the increase in potential is high enough to activate another electrode reaction. This effect is caused by the fact that the electrode current is limited not only by the overpotential, as the Butler–Volmer equation says, but also by the rate at which the electroactive reactants arrive at the electrode.

Example 7.1

Compute the anodic, cathodic, and net current densities in the following system:

$\alpha_a = \alpha_c = 0.5$
$i_o = 1\ \text{mA/cm}^2$
Surface area of the electrode, $A = 1\ \text{cm}^2$
Using (1) cathodic polarization $\eta = -0.1$ V and (2) anodic polarization $\eta = +0.1$ V
To simplify computations, note that $F/RT = 38.95$ coulombs $\times\ \text{J}^{-1}$
For the cathodic polarization, $\eta = -0.1$ V

$i_\text{net} = \exp[(-0.5) \times (38.95) \times (-0.1)] - \exp[(0.5) \times (38.95) \times (-0.1)] = 7.01 - 0.14 = 6.86\ \text{mA/cm}^2$

For the anodic polarization, $\eta = +0.1$ V

$i_\text{net} = \exp[(-0.5) \times (38.95) \times (0.1)] - \exp[(0.5) \times (38.95) \times (0.1)] = 0.14 - 7.01 = -6.86\ \text{mA/cm}^2$

When discussing the consequences of the Butler–Volmer equation, the first thing that is pointed out in textbooks is the fact that the net current does not depend on the applied potential E but on the overpotential. The exchange current density, i_o, controls the sensitivity of the electrode kinetics to the rates of change in the applied potentials: the higher the exchange current density, the faster the electrode responses and the steeper the slope, $di/d\eta$. Consequently, electrode processes with high exchange current densities are highly sensitive to a changing electrode overpotential, and vice versa: electrode processes with low exchange current densities respond slowly to a changing electrode overpotential.

The Butler–Volmer equation in the form shown in Equation 7.19 refers to the current density. To compute the current I, the current density i must be multiplied by the surface area of the electrode, A.

$$\frac{I}{A} = i = i_o\left[\exp\left(\frac{-\alpha_c nF\eta}{RT}\right) - \exp\left(\frac{\alpha_a nF\eta}{RT}\right)\right] \tag{7.22}$$

Example 7.2

For initial conditions $i_o = 1$ mA/cm², $n = 1$, and $\alpha = 0.5$, sketch the current density as a function of applied overpotential between the limits of −0.2 V and +0.2 V (Figure 7.4).

In terms of overpotential, the current away from the electrode (cathodic) is

$$i_c = \frac{r_c \times F}{A} = k_c \times F \times \exp\left(\frac{-\alpha F(\Delta E_{eq} + \eta)}{RT}\right) \times [\text{ox}] \tag{7.23}$$

and the current toward the electrode (anodic) is

$$i_a = \frac{r_a \times F}{A} = k_a \times F \times \exp\left(\frac{(1-\alpha)F(\Delta E_{eq} + \eta)}{RT}\right) \times [\text{red}] \tag{7.24}$$

The net cathodic current density is $i = i_c - i_a$.

As we have demonstrated, when we polarize the electrode cathodically by applying a potential in the negative direction, $\eta < 0$, the overall current density computed from the Butler–Volmer equation effectively becomes

$$i_c \approx i_o \exp\left[-\frac{\alpha n F(-\eta)}{RT}\right] = i_o \exp\left[\frac{\alpha n F \eta}{RT}\right] \tag{7.25}$$

The accepted set of conventions indicates that the cathodic current has a positive sign. Similarly, when we polarize the electrode anodically, $\eta > 0$, the overall current density computed from the Butler–Volmer equation effectively becomes

$$i_a \approx -i_o \exp\left[\frac{(1-\alpha)n F \eta}{RT}\right] \tag{7.26}$$

and the set of accepted conventions indicates that the anodic current has a negative sign.

To evaluate the exchange current density far from the equilibrium potential or at large overpotentials, it is convenient to take logarithms of the expressions in Equations

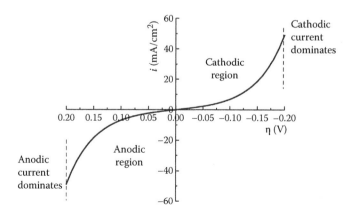

Figure 7.4 Relationship between overpotential η and current density i between −0.2 and +0.2 V.

7.25 and 7.26. This can be done for the anodic and cathodic current densities. For the cathodic polarization, taking logarithms of both sides of Equation 7.25 gives

$$\ln(i_c) = \ln(i_o) + \frac{\alpha nF}{RT}\eta$$

Similarly for the anodic polarization

$$\ln(i_a) = \ln(i_o) - \frac{(1-\alpha)nF}{RT}\eta \tag{7.27}$$

which shows that when the electrode is polarized, the logarithm of the current density is a linear function of the overpotential. This last relation corresponds to the so-called Tafel equation, and it is used to determine the exchange current density experimentally. From the Tafel equation it is possible to calculate the overpotential for a reaction.

$$\eta = \frac{RT}{\alpha nF}[\ln(i_c) - \ln(i_o)] = \frac{2.3 \times RT}{\alpha nF}\log(i_c) - \frac{2.3 \times RT}{\alpha nF}\log(i_o)$$

or

$$\eta = \frac{RT}{(1-\alpha)nF}[\ln(i_a) - \ln(i_o)] = \frac{2.3 \times RT}{(1-\alpha)nF}\log(i_c) - \frac{2.3 \times RT}{(1-\alpha)nF}\log(i_o) \tag{7.28}$$

The same equation can be derived for the anodic overpotential, and the result is the same as that in Equation 7.28, except for the change in the signs in the parentheses. Because the expression $\frac{2.3 \times RT}{\alpha nF}$ is composed of constants, it is also constant, and the general relation between the overpotential and the cathodic and anodic current densities can be written as

$$\eta = a \pm b\log(i)$$

where

$$a = \frac{2.3 \times RT}{\alpha nF}\log(i_o) \quad b = \frac{2.3 \times RT}{\alpha nF} \tag{7.29}$$

Here a and b are constants characteristic of the electrode system, and b is called the Tafel slope.

The relation in Equation 7.29 is plotted as the so-called Tafel plot, from which exchange current density can be evaluated as the current when the overpotential equals zero. The relation in Equation 7.29 has been derived assuming that for each type of polarization, cathodic or anodic, the magnitude of polarization is high enough that the net current is practically equal to the current resulting from applying the overpotential and that the opposing current is negligible. This is the "high

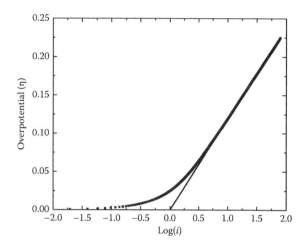

Figure 7.5 Estimating exchange current density. For overpotentials exceeding an absolute value of 0.1 V, the relation $\log(i) = f(\eta)$ can be approximated by a straight line. For overpotentials lower than 0.1 V, the relation between $\log(i)$ and the overpotential is more complex. From Equation 7.29 the intercept of the tangent line with the line $\eta = 0$ occurs at $\log(i) = \log(i_o) = 0$ and i_o is equal to 1 mA, coinciding with the data in Example 7.1.

field approximation," and it is true when the magnitude of the overpotential, in any direction, exceeds 100 mV. The effect of this assumption will be evident in the following example.

Example 7.3 Estimating the exchange current density, i_o, from the experimental data

We will use the same set of hypothetical data as we used in Figure 7.5, but we will apply much smaller overpotentials. The exchange current density will be estimated from the position of the intersection between the tangent to the plot of the experimental data and the $\log(i)$ axis. Figure 7.5 gives a rough estimate of the exchange current density. The estimate is rough because the $\eta - \log(i)$ curve is not really linear: after reaching a short linear segment, the current becomes limiting, a phenomenon that will be explained later.

7.2.2   Butler–Volmer equation when the electrode is not polarized

The Butler–Volmer equation describes the kinetics of electrode reactions. For these reactions to proceed preferentially in one or the other direction, the electrode must be polarized. An interesting exercise is to examine how the Butler–Volmer equation handles the situation in which the electrode is not polarized and is at equilibrium and the rates of the anodic and cathodic reactions are equal.

$$k_c \times [ox] = k_a \times [red] \tag{7.30}$$

We can rearrange this equation to the following form:

$$[ox] \times \exp\left[-\frac{\alpha nF(E-E^\circ)}{RT}\right] = [red] \times \exp\left[\frac{(1-\alpha)nF(E-E^\circ)}{RT}\right] \tag{7.31}$$

$$\frac{[\text{ox}]}{[\text{red}]} = \frac{\exp\left[\dfrac{(1-\alpha)nF(E-E^\circ)}{RT}\right]}{\exp\left[-\dfrac{\alpha nF(E-E^\circ)}{RT}\right]} = \exp\left\{\left[\frac{(1-\alpha)nF(E-E^\circ)}{RT}\right] - \left[-\frac{\alpha nF(E-E^\circ)}{RT}\right]\right\} \quad (7.32)$$

$$\ln\left(\frac{[\text{ox}]}{[\text{red}]}\right) = \left[\frac{(1-\alpha)nF(E-E^\circ)}{RT}\right] - \left[-\frac{\alpha nF(E-E^\circ)}{RT}\right] \quad (7.33)$$

$$\ln\left(\frac{[\text{ox}]}{[\text{red}]}\right) = \frac{nF}{RT}(E-E^\circ)[(1-\alpha)+\alpha] \quad (7.34)$$

$$\ln\left(\frac{[\text{ox}]}{[\text{red}]}\right) = \frac{nF}{RT}(E-E^\circ) \quad (7.35)$$

$$\frac{RT}{nF}\ln\left(\frac{[\text{ox}]}{[\text{red}]}\right) = E-E^\circ \quad (7.36)$$

$$E = E^\circ + \frac{RT}{nF}\ln\left(\frac{[\text{ox}]}{[\text{red}]}\right) \quad (7.37)$$

This is the Nernst equation as described in Chapter 4. Thus, when the electrode is not polarized, the Butler–Volmer equation reduces to the Nernst equation, as expected. This exercise may be of little practical value, but it demonstrates that the system of equations we use is inherently consistent.

7.2.3 *Mixed potential*

In previous diagrams, metal electrodes were shown in equilibrium with their own ions. This means that the forward and reverse reactions use the same reactants but proceed in the opposite directions. For example, if an iron electrode is immersed in a solution of ferrous ions, the forward reaction is $Fe^{2+} + 2e^- \rightarrow Fe$ and the reverse reaction is $Fe \rightarrow Fe^{2+} + 2e^-$. If the iron electrode is immersed in a solution of acid, however, there is another reversible reaction that is in equilibrium with the iron electrode: the forward reaction is the reduction of protons, $2H^+ + 2e^- \rightarrow H_2$, and the reverse reaction is the oxidation of hydrogen, $H_2 \rightarrow 2H^+ + 2e^-$.

Each of these reactions, iron oxidation and proton reduction, can be studied in isolation, and each has its own equilibrium potential depending on the composition of the solution. However, they can also occur simultaneously on the same piece of metal, and the metal cannot have two different potentials consistent with two equilibrium potentials measured in isolated studies. The metal will acquire a potential that is somewhere between these equilibrium potentials, and this is called a "mixed potential." In this scenario the forward and reverse reactions are not the same reaction going in opposite directions; they are different reactions. The intercept of the anodic part of the reaction with the lower thermodynamic equilibrium (iron oxidation in this example) with the cathodic part of the reaction with the higher cathodic equilibrium (proton reduction in this example) represents the corrosion current (i_{corr}) and the corrosion potential (E_{corr}). This is consistent with the conditions that apply to the corrosion of metals: (1) a metal can have only one electrical potential and (2) the anodic current must be equal to the cathodic current. The intercept of the lines in Figure 7.6 satisfies both requirements.

Figure 7.6 is an idealized image used to elucidate the meanings of the corrosion potential and corrosion current. Such representations use many simplifying assumptions, such as normal concentrations of protons and ferric ions and a lack of kinetic limitations for any of the reactions. Based on such simplifying images, diagrams exposing the main features of the corrosion process, such as the Evans diagrams shown in Figures 7.6 and 7.7, are constructed. Real corrosion processes are more complex than that shown in Figure 7.6. When we superimpose the concepts of mass transport resistance, electrode polarization, overpotential and limiting current on this idealized image, we arrive at a more realistic graphical representation of corrosion processes, such as that for the corrosion of iron shown in Figure 7.7.

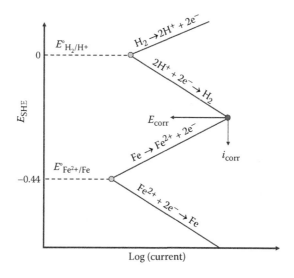

Figure 7.6 Idealized potentiodynamic polarization curves for an iron electrode immersed in a 1 M solution of ferric iron ions at pH = 0 demonstrate the meaning of mixed potential E_{corr} and corrosion current i_{corr}. Corrosion potential E_{corr} can be measured with respect to a suitable reference electrode (see also Figure 7.7, which shows such a measurement run for a real sample). Corrosion current i_{corr} cannot be measured directly, unless the anode and the cathode are separated, but it can be estimated using other electrochemical techniques based on disturbing the potential of the electrode, such as linear polarization resistance, described in Section 7.3.2.3.

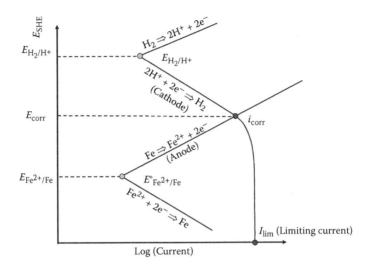

Figure 7.7 Diagram of anodic and cathodic polarization curves representing the corrosion of iron. The anodic reaction is the dissolution of iron, and the cathodic reaction is the reduction of protons. The delivery of the cathodic reactant, protons, is diffusion-limited, and at significantly low potentials the cathodic current reaches its maximum, characterized by the limiting current, as described in Chapter 4. For specific corrosion processes, such diagrams are often simplified to show only the anodic and cathodic reactions.

7.3   Abiotic corrosion of active metals: Iron

The term corrosion can be defined in various ways, and there are many forms of corrosion and many materials that can corrode—both metallic and nonmetallic. Among the well-known processes of nonmetallic corrosion are the corrosion of stone and its effect on ancient artifacts. Here, we restrict the meaning of corrosion and define it as the anodic dissolution of metals. Among the many anodic reactions that may occur at the surface of a metal, the one in which the metal itself is the chemical reactant subjected to oxidation is singled out and termed corrosion. Noble metals, such as platinum and gold, do not easily undergo an oxidation reaction and serve only to facilitate charge transfer between external redox reactants. In contrast, active metals such as iron are oxidized. This process contributes to the net anodic reaction rate and is typically the dominant anodic process for freely corroding metals. On corroding metals, anodic reactions are coupled with cathodic reactions (reduction). In aerated water solutions, the dominant cathodic reaction is the reduction of dissolved oxygen, while in anaerobic solutions, the reduction of protons is the dominant cathodic reaction; this is typically represented as the reduction of water for neutral and basic solutions. Active metals are characterized by high electron activity combined with low ionization energy. They readily donate electrons to other reactions, forming metal ions as a result; iron is an example of an active metal. Equations 7.38 through 7.43 show the relevant half reactions, followed by the corresponding net reactions, for the corrosion of iron in aqueous solutions.

Anaerobic

$$Fe \rightarrow Fe^{2+} + 2e^- \quad anodic \tag{7.38}$$

$$2H_2O + 2e^- \rightarrow H_2 + 2OH^- \quad cathodic \tag{7.39}$$

$$2H_2O + Fe \rightarrow Fe(OH)_2 + H_2 \quad net \tag{7.40}$$

Aerobic

In aerobic solutions, the basic anodic reaction is of course the same as the one described by Equation 7.38, the dissolution of iron, but the products of the reaction, ferric ions, are hydrolyzed and further oxidized by the available oxygen in the reactions summarized below:

$$4OH^- + 4Fe(OH)_2 \rightarrow 4Fe(OH)_3 + 4e^- \quad anodic \tag{7.41}$$

$$O_2 + 2H_2O + 4e^- \rightarrow 4OH^- \quad cathodic \tag{7.42}$$

$$4Fe(OH)_2 + O_2 + 2H_2O \rightarrow 4Fe(OH)_3 \quad net \tag{7.43}$$

7.3.1 Thermodynamics of iron corrosion

Using the terminology accepted in electrochemical studies, a metal immersed in water is called an electrode. The potential of an electrode in an aqueous solution depends on the rates of the anodic (oxidation) and cathodic (reduction) reactions occurring at the metal surface. When these rates are at equilibrium, thermodynamics can be used to quantify the electrode potential. When these rates are not at equilibrium, thermodynamics cannot be used to find the electrode potential: it needs to be found empirically. Corrosion reactions are not at equilibrium, and the potentials of corroding metals cannot be predicted from thermodynamics.

To illustrate the thermodynamic principles of galvanic corrosion, we will select a set of conditions and compute the potentials of the reactions participating in the corrosion of iron. For the anodic reaction,

$$Fe^{2+} + 2e^- \rightarrow Fe \quad E^o = -0.44 \ V_{SHE} \tag{7.44}$$

the Nernst equation quantifies the half-cell potential for iron oxidation as

$$E = E^o - \frac{0.059}{n} \log \left[\frac{1}{[Fe^{2+}]} \right] \tag{7.45}$$

Iron is a solid metal and its activity equals one. Consequently, the potential of the anodic half reaction depends on the concentration of ferrous ions in the solution and is computed as

$$E = -0.44 + (0.059/2) \log [Fe^{2+}] \tag{7.46}$$

Selecting the concentration of ferrous iron, $[Fe^{2+}] = 10^{-6}$ M, the potential equals $E = -0.62 \ V_{SHE}$.

The cathodic reaction, the reduction of oxygen, is

$$O_2 + 2H_2O + 4e^- \rightarrow 4OH^- \quad E^o = +0.401 \ V_{SHE} \tag{7.47}$$

The Nernst equation quantifies the half-cell potential for oxygen reduction:

$$E = E° - \frac{0.059}{n} \log \left[\frac{[OH^-]^4}{pO_2} \right] \tag{7.48}$$

The potential of this half reaction depends on the partial pressure of oxygen and on the pH. Noting that $\log [OH^-]^4 = 4 (-pOH) = -4(14\text{-pH})$, Equation 7.48 can be expressed as

$$E = 0.401 + 0.059/4 \, [\log (pO_2) + 4(14\text{-pH})] \tag{7.49}$$

Assuming that $p(O_2) = 0.2$ atm and pH = 7, the potential of the cathodic reaction is $E = 0.804 \, V_{SHE}$.

If only one of these reactions were occurring on the metal surface, the metal would assume the potential specified for that reaction. For example, if only the cathodic reaction were taking place, the metal would have the potential $+0.804 \, V_{SHE}$, and if only the anodic reaction were taking place, the metal would have the potential $-0.62 \, V_{SHE}$. This can be demonstrated in electrochemical studies in which the anode and the cathode can be separated, placed in different half-cells, and studied in isolation. However, in corrosion, both reactions occur on the same piece of metal and at the same time, and the potential of the metal can have only one value. As a result, the potential of the corroding metal is somewhere between the potential of the anodic half reaction, $-0.62 \, V_{SHE}$, and the potential of the cathodic half reaction, $+0.804 \, V_{SHE}$. The exact potential of the corroding metal depends on the kinetics (reaction rates) of the anodic and cathodic reactions; it can be measured empirically and interpreted from the theory of mixed potentials. Here, for the purpose of this simplified argument, it is enough to assume that the potential of the corroding iron is between the potentials of the anodic and cathodic half reactions, say, in the middle: $E = (-0.62 + 0.804)/2 =) = 0.092 \, V_{SHE}$. Setting the potential of the metal between the potentials of the anodic and cathodic half reactions has consequences: it sets the position of the equilibrium for each of the participating reactions. If the potential were equal to that computed for either of the half reactions, anodic or cathodic, that half reaction would be at equilibrium. If the potential of the corroding iron is exactly halfway between the potentials computed for the two half reactions, then neither of the half reactions (Equations 7.38 through 7.43) is at equilibrium and each of them proceeds in the direction that approaches the equilibrium. To quantify the consequences of this departure from the equilibrium, we can inspect the Nernst equation describing the potentials of anodic and cathodic half reactions when the potentials are shifted from their respective equilibrium potentials. If the potential of the corroding iron is $0.092 \, V_{SHE}$, it is higher than the equilibrium potential for the anodic reaction and lower than the equilibrium potential for the cathodic reaction. As a consequence, each reaction will proceed spontaneously toward the equilibrium determined by the potential of the metal, with the concentrations of the reactants and products adjusted to satisfy the equilibrium for the given potential.

The potential of the anodic reaction, $Fe^{2+} + 2e^- \rightarrow Fe$, must be adjusted to $+0.092$ V.

$$+0.092 = -0.44 + (0.059/2)\log [Fe^{2+}] \tag{7.50}$$

If separated from the cathodic reaction, this reaction has a potential of $E = -0.62 \, V_{SHE}$. When connected to the cathodic reaction, this reaction has a new equilibrium potential, of $E = +0.092 \, V_{SHE}$. To reach the new equilibrium potential, the concentration of ferric ions must increase. Consequently, the reaction proceeds to the left, to increase the concentration of ferric ions in the solution. Iron dissolves in this reaction.

The cathodic reaction, $O_2 + 2H_2O + 4e^- \rightarrow 4OH^-$, must adjust its potential to +0.0092 V as well:

$$+0.092 = 0.401 + 0.059/4 \left[\log(pO_2) + 4(14\text{-pH})\right] \tag{7.51}$$

If separated from the anodic reaction, this reaction has a potential of $E = +0.804$ V_{SHE}. When connected to the anodic reaction, it has a new equilibrium potential, $E = +0.092$ V_{SHE}. To reach this new equilibrium potential, the reaction proceeds to the right, to decrease the partial pressure of oxygen. Oxygen is consumed in this reaction.

As a result of the metal potential being located between the equilibrium potentials for the anodic and cathodic half reactions, the anodic reaction spontaneously proceeds toward dissolution of the iron and the cathodic reaction spontaneously proceeds toward reduction of the oxygen. Both reactions proceed until one of the reactants is exhausted or until the concentrations of their respective reactants adjust to reach the new equilibrium at 0.092 V_{SHE}. The thermodynamics of the corrosion processes explain why the processes occur but of course cannot predict the anodic or cathodic reaction rates. Kinetic computations are needed to refine our observations about thermodynamic considerations. Looking at the corrosion process from either the kinetic or the thermodynamic point of view gives only limited access to the nature of the corrosion process: The two approaches need to be combined to enhance our understanding of it.

7.3.2 *Quantifying corrosion potential and corrosion current*

7.3.2.1 *Potentiodynamic polarization techniques for studying anodic and cathodic reactions*

When the anodic and cathodic sites on a metal surface are electrically isolated, the equilibrium of each one with the electroactive reactants in the solution can be calculated from thermodynamics. However, the kinetics of the anodic and cathodic reactions must be quantified empirically. For that purpose an electrochemical arrangement is often set up in the laboratory in which the anodic and cathodic reactions are studied separately using polarization methods. However, in corrosion, the anodic and cathodic reactions are not at equilibrium because the electric current flows between them. They remain related to each other by two requirements:

1. The two reactions progress on the same piece of metal, so the metal can be characterized by one electrical potential.
2. The electrons extracted in the anodic reactions are used in the cathodic reactions; therefore the anodic current and the cathodic current must be equal.

These two requirements combined are used to quantify the thermodynamics and kinetics of the corrosion process and characterize the main parameters determining the corrosion process—the corrosion potential and the corrosion current. To study the anodic and cathodic reactions separately, polarization techniques can be used. Figure 7.8 shows the experimental setup used in such tests. The electrochemical cell is filled with the electrolyte and three electrodes are used: the working electrode, the counter or auxiliary electrode, and the reference electrode. The tested electrode is called the working electrode. All the electrodes are connected to a potentiostat, which is programmed to run the entire test. The electric potential, anodic or cathodic, is applied between the working electrode and the counter electrode. The applied potential is gradually increased, starting from the equilibrium potential, and is recorded against the measured potential of the working electrode.

During the anodic polarization, an increasing positive potential is applied to the electrode, and during the cathodic polarization a negative potential is applied. The anodic and cathodic potentials are applied in separate measurements. The experimental setup is shown in Figure 7.8. The results are plotted as log current density versus potential, as shown in Figure 7.9.

7.3.2.2   Visualizing factors affecting the kinetics of corrosion processes: Evans diagrams

The combined effect of the anodic and cathodic processes on the corrosion potential and on the corrosion current can be visualized using Evans diagrams, like the one shown below, which reflects the numerical example we have used to demonstrate that in corrosion

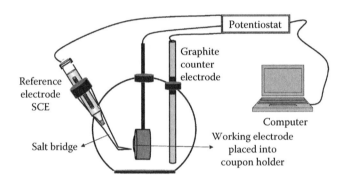

Figure 7.8 Experimental setup used in potentiodynamic polarization.

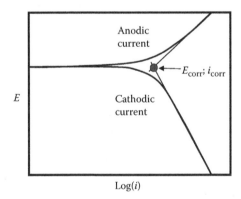

Figure 7.9 The intersect of the extrapolated anodic and cathodic potentiodynamic polarization curves demonstrates the meaning of corrosion potential E_{corr} and corrosion current i_{corr}. Corrosion potential E_{corr} can be measured with respect to a suitable reference electrode. Corrosion current i_{corr} cannot be measured directly, unless the anode and the cathode are separated, but it can be estimated using other electrochemical techniques based on disturbing the potential of the electrode. The slopes of the anodic and cathodic polarization curves are Tafel slopes b_a and b_c, respectively.

processes both the anodic reaction and the cathodic reaction are spontaneous. Each of these reactions can be studied separately by immersing the metal in a solution and changing the potential of the metal while measuring the current with respect to a suitable auxiliary electrode, which produces polarization curves (potential versus current density). The measured anodic and cathodic polarization curves can then be plotted in the same diagram, ignoring the fact that these two currents have different signs, to illustrate how each of the reactions affects the corrosion potential and corrosion current. The equilibrium potentials that we used above would produce the diagram shown in Figure 7.10.

Evans diagrams help us visualize important features of the corrosion process. The slopes of the lines in the diagrams represent the sensitivity of the respective reactions, anodic and cathodic, to changes in the potential. The purpose of the diagrams is more to help us grasp the relation between the anodic and cathodic reactions than any computational purpose. The main deficiency of these diagrams is that they use a linear scale on the horizontal axis, representing the current, so that the diagram oversimplifies the relation between the overpotential and the current and presents it as linear, while it actually is logarithmic, as shown in the Tafel relations. Nevertheless, these diagrams are very useful for visualizing the meaning and the relations among the various parameters and their effect on the overall corrosion process. The sensitivity, which reflects the changes in the relevant reaction rate (the current) in response to changes in potential, is presented in the Evans diagrams as $\Delta i/\Delta V$. The slopes in the diagram need to be interpreted carefully, because the current is represented on the horizontal axis and the slopes of the curves in the diagram, say $\Delta V/\Delta i$, are actually the reciprocals of the reaction sensitivities to the changes in the potential. The point where the lines intercept designates corrosion potential E_{corr} and corrosion current i_{corr}. In the simple example we considered above, we assumed that the metal would reach a corrosion potential exactly halfway between the equilibrium potentials of the anodic and cathodic reactions. Usually, however, one of the reactions, anodic or cathodic, is more sensitive to changes in potential than the other reaction. The anodic and cathodic potentials at equilibrium can be evaluated from thermodynamics. The corrosion potential and corrosion current, which are found at the intersections of the lines representing the relevant reactions, have to be measured: they cannot be found from thermodynamics. Figure 7.11 shows more realistic examples, in which the anodic and cathodic reactions show different sensitivities to the applied changes in potential.

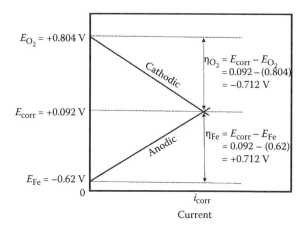

Figure 7.10 Evans diagram based on the equilibrium potentials used in Equations 7.46 and 7.49.

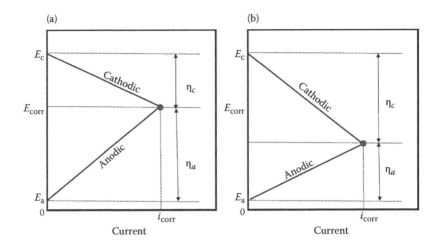

Figure 7.11 Evans diagrams for corrosion processes that are under (a) anodic control and (b) cathodic control.

The results in Figure 7.11 show slopes representing sensitivities of the anodic and cathodic reactions to changes in potential that are not the same. The reaction that is less sensitive to changes in potential controls the process. The process on the left is controlled by the anodic reaction, while the process on the right is controlled by the cathodic reaction: the slowest reaction controls the rate of corrosion. This leads us to the topic of quantifying the effects presented in these diagrams by deriving appropriate kinetic equations.

If the rate of the cathodic reaction changes, the corresponding rate of the anodic reaction changes. In the corrosion reaction, the electrons liberated from the anodic reaction are used in the cathodic reaction. If we deliver electrons to the corroding piece of metal externally, then they replace those derived from the anodic reaction and the corrosion rate decreases. This is the principle of the cathodic protection of metals, which requires connecting the corroding metal to another metal that is polarized to a lower potential. Figure 7.12 indicates how cathodic overpotentials affect corrosion currents and potentials.

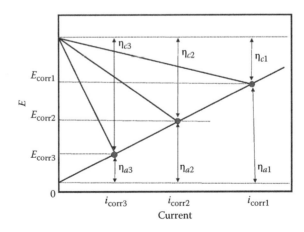

Figure 7.12 Evans diagram for overpotentials applied to a cathodic reaction. The higher the overpotential, the more resistance there is to the reaction proceeding.

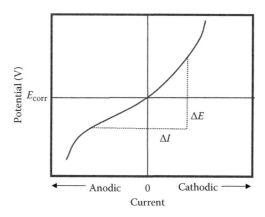

Figure 7.13 Determining the linear polarization resistance.

As will be demonstrated in following sections, some of the mechanisms of MIC cause increases in the rate of the cathodic reaction, causing the opposite effect, an increase in the corrosion current.

7.3.2.3 Corrosion rate: Linear polarization resistance

Linear polarization resistance is measured to assess the corrosion rate, or i_{corr}, of a sample of corroding metal on which the anodic and cathodic reactions cannot be separated and studied in isolation. The technique requires the potential to be scanned over a small range, 20 to 25 mV, around the open circuit voltage (OCV), as shown in Figure 7.13.

Because the range of applied potentials is small, the current varies linearly with the applied potential. This is analogous to the location near the origin of the axes in Figure 3.2. In this case the slope, $\Delta E/\Delta i = R_p$, constitutes the polarization resistance. Corrosion current i_{corr} can be calculated from the Stern–Geary equation:

$$R_p = \frac{b_a b_c}{2.3 i_{corr}(b_a + b_c)} \tag{7.52}$$

where b_a and b_b are Tafel slopes. These must be determined from separate measurements, as described by Equation 7.29.

7.4 Abiotic corrosion of passive metals

7.4.1 Passive metals and alloys

One possibility in the corrosion of metals is the formation of insoluble oxides on the surface of the metal. Such oxides form a barrier that, at only a few nanometers of thickness, slows down the anodic dissolution, or corrosion, of the metal. An example of such a passive film is the iron oxide that forms on the surface of corroding iron. This is not a very good passive film, because this particular oxide is porous and does not adhere to the surface very well. A similar reaction for chromium leads to the formation of an oxide layer of much better quality that is stable at the low pH and low reducing potentials where iron oxides are unstable. Because the quality of such protective layers depends on the presence and quality of metal oxides, it is important to identify the stability of these oxides as a function of pH and redox potential E_h. The stability of various ions and solid-state reactants in water solutions is indicated in E_h–pH diagrams, also known as Pourbaix diagrams, which show lines representing the equilibriums between neighboring reactants. Detailed explanations of how to construct such diagrams are available in many sources, and we will limit the discussion of them here to the necessary minimum showing the utility of these diagrams in selecting metals for applications in water solutions of known compositions. There is only a narrow band where water itself is stable, and this band is limited by the upper and lower water stability limits.

The upper stability limit for water is determined by the reaction

$$1/2O_2(g) + 2e^- + 2H^+ \leftrightarrow H_2O, \text{ with } E^\circ = 1.23 \text{ V}$$

characterized by the Nernst equation:

$$E = E^\circ - \frac{0.0592}{2} \log \frac{1}{p_{O_2}^{1/2} a_{H^+}^2}$$

$$E = 1.23 + 0.0296 \; \log p_{O_2}^{1/2} a_{H^+}^2$$

where p_{O_2} is the partial pressure of oxygen gas above the water surface and a_H is the proton activity. Since the line representing this equation in Figure 7.14 indicates the water stability limit, water is on one side of the dividing line and water oxidized to pure $O_2(g)$ is on the other side. Therefore, the partial pressure of oxygen in this equation is assumed to be equal to one. This simplifies the equation to

$$E = 1.23 - 0.0592 \times \text{pH}$$

The lower water stability limit is determined by the reaction $H^+ + e^- \leftrightarrows 1/2H_2(g)$ with $E^\circ = 0$ V characterized by the Nernst equation:

$$E = E^\circ - \frac{0.0592}{1} \log \frac{p_{H_2}^{1/2}}{a_{H^+}} \tag{7.53}$$

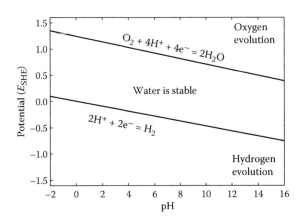

Figure 7.14 Water stability diagram.

where p_{H_2} is the partial pressure of hydrogen gas above the water surface and a_H is the proton activity. Since the line representing this equation in Figure 7.14 indicates the water stability limit, water is on one side of the dividing line and water reduced to pure $H_2(g)$ is on the other side. Therefore, the partial pressure of hydrogen in this equation is assumed to be equal to one, which simplifies the equation to

$$E = -0.0592 \times pH \qquad (7.54)$$

Other lines in E_h–pH diagrams are drawn using similar principles, and they indicate the equilibrium concentrations of the reactants. For example, if we are interested in the line indicating the position of the equilibrium between solid iron and ferrous iron, the appropriate reaction is

$$Fe^{2+} + 2e^- \rightarrow Fe \text{ with } E^\circ = -0.440 \text{ V}$$

and the Nernst equation is

$$E = -0440 - \frac{0.0592}{2} \log \frac{1}{a_{Fe^{2+}}}$$

For a selected activity of Fe^{2+}, usually 10^{-6} M if there is no more precise information, this line can be identified, as in Figure 7.15a, as a horizontal line separating the solid iron from the ferrous iron. It is worth noting that areas between lines represent a predominance of particular reactants, which does not mean that other reactants do not exist within these limits; they are just not predominant. Figure 7.15b shows the distribution of the iron and chromium oxides. It is apparent that the chromium oxides are stable at much lower redox potentials and much lower pH values, which makes chromium a desirable alloying component. It is able to produce stable chromium oxide and protect steel from corrosion

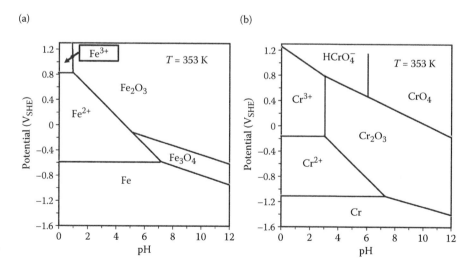

(a)   (b)

Figure 7.15 Comparison of the stability of iron and chromium oxides. Lines a and b represent the upper and lower water stability limits, respectively. (Modified from J. Huang et al., *Corrosion Science*, 51, 2976–2982, 2009.)

over a much broader range of pH and E_h values. It is particularly important that chromium oxides are stable at the relatively low redox potentials where oxides of iron can be reduced and removed from the metal surface, leaving it unprotected.

7.4.2 *Potentiodynamic polarization of passive metals and alloys*

Passive layers with much better properties are obtained when chromium is added as the alloying agent to iron. Polarization curves explain the mechanism of corrosion protection by passive films. Passive metals and alloys show a different mechanism of corrosion than active metals do. The best known passive alloys are stainless steels, and much research has been done on MIC of these materials. The corrosion reactions for stainless steels are the same as those for iron. However, stainless steels are alloys and some of their components, when oxidized, form dense layers of oxides and passive layers, which prevent further corrosion. Passivated alloys can resist corrosion in the presence of strong oxidants that would cause corrosion on unalloyed metal. This protection works to a certain extent only, however. When a cathodic reactant polarizing the metal has a high enough oxidation potential, localized corrosion, called pitting, occurs as a result of localized damage to the passive layer. The mechanism of this process is shown in Figure 7.16.

As shown in Figure 7.17, when a passivating alloy is subjected to anodic polarization, i.e., to an increasing electrode potential, the corrosion current initially increases. This increase continues until the polarization potential reaches a critical value, called the passivation potential. At this potential, the alloying constituents of the metal are oxidized and form dense layers on the metal surface, which slows down the corrosion of the metal, as is demonstrated by the decreasing corrosion current. As the polarization potential increases further, the metal first reaches a passive zone, in which it is immune to the increase in the polarization potential until the polarization potential reaches a critical value, called the pitting potential. When the polarization reaches and exceeds the pitting potential, the corrosion current gradually increases, as a result of localized damage to the passive layers. The damaged areas are small compared to the surface of the metal: the damage to the surface has the form of small pits, and this type of corrosion is called pitting corrosion. Because the damaged areas become anodic sites, their small combined surface area makes

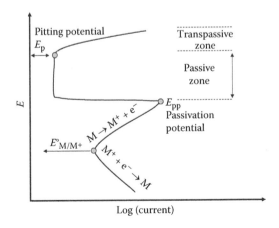

Figure 7.16 Potentiodynamic polarization curve of a passive metal; thermodynamic principles of passivation and pitting corrosion.

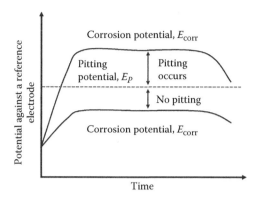

Figure 7.17 When the corrosion potential, E_{corr}, reaches the pitting potential, E_p (dashed line), of the metal in the given solution, pits are initiated. (Redrawn from J. Sedriks: *Corrosion of Stainless Steels*, 2nd ed. P. 106. 1996. Copyright Wiley-VCH Verlag GmbH & Co. KGaA. Reproduced with permission.)

the localized corrosion process particularly dangerous for the integrity of the metal. The anodic current densities can reach high values, and localized damage of the material can progress much faster than it does in cases of general corrosion, in which the anodic current densities are much smaller.

Passive metals and alloys, such as stainless steels, can be used within the passive zone, where the oxidation potentials of the available oxidants do not exceed the pitting potential. Microbial interference that accelerates the corrosion of such surfaces is then necessarily related to two possible mechanisms: microbially generated oxidants (cathodic reactants) can have higher oxidation potentials than the pitting potential, and microbially stimulated localized damage to the passive layers can decrease the pitting potential.

The first mechanism is related to the deposition of biomineralized manganese oxides, which can raise the potential of the passive metal above the pitting potential. The second mechanism is related to microorganisms in biofilms damaging the passive metal surface. We will discuss these mechanisms in more detail later in this chapter.

Figure 7.17 shows the relation among the corrosion potential, pitting potential, and probability of pits initiation, redrawn from Sedriks (1996). The potential (E_{corr}) of a metal such as stainless steel is measured against time. If the potential of the stainless steel is higher than the pitting potential (E_p), the stainless steel develops pits that initiate corrosion. If the potential of the stainless steel is less than the pitting potential, pits cannot develop. The pitting potential can be determined using standard electrochemical techniques, which are described elsewhere (Cramer and Covino 1987).

Pitting corrosion occurs on passive metals such as aluminum, stainless steel, and titanium. These metals form a layer of oxides on their surfaces that protects them from general corrosion in natural settings. There are three phases through which a pit evolves. First, chloride ions or other aggressive ions attack the passive layer and promote local defects (pit initiation). Second, the active metal begins to dissolve, but this may stop if the critical conditions are not adequate (metastable pitting). Third, when the critical conditions are met the pit grows and the process of metal dissolution becomes autocatalytic, meaning the metal dissolution rate increases. Eventually, the local dissolution of the metal may reach the point where the structure fails.

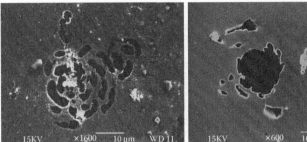

Figure 7.18 Scanning electron microscope images of pits initiated by anodic polarization of 316 SS in 0.1 M NaCl. (left) Groups of holes in the thin metal sheath covering the mouth of the pit (right). Small holes surrounding a large one also indicate a partial thin metal sheath. (Reprinted from M. Geiser et al., *International Biodeterioration and Biodegradation*, 49, 235–243, 2002.)

To show the structure of corrosion pits on stainless steel we anodically polarized 316L stainless steel in 0.1 M NaCl to cause pitting (Figure 7.18). The pits were bowl shaped with a thin metal sheath covering their mouths. They were on average 60.7 μm long and 50.2 μm wide.

7.5 Quantifying electron transfer processes in electrochemically active biofilms

In the introduction we pointed out that the most prominent function of electrochemically active biofilms (EABs) is to exchange electrons with metals and redox-sensitive minerals. Possible mechanisms of electron transfer between EABs and electrodes are depicted in Figure 7.2. However, the published data do not identify any of these mechanisms as universal or even predominant in most systems. Instead, the conclusion based on the existing literature is that the predominant mechanism of electron transfer in EABs depends on the type of the microorganisms, the environmental conditions and the experimental system used to study the process. To generate reproducible results, it is therefore imperative that all components of the experimental system used to study the electron transfer mechanisms between microbial cells in EABs and solids be carefully selected and precisely controlled during the experiment. On the basis of our experience, the following factors need to be carefully considered when experiments involving EABs are being designed: (1) selecting the material of the electrode on which the biofilms are grown, (2) selecting the type of the reactor, (3) identifying the current-limiting electrode in the experimental setup, and (4) selecting the procedure for conditioning the biofilms. We address these factors below.

7.5.1 Selecting the material of the electrode on which the biofilms are grown

It is not surprising to find that the electrode material is one of the most critical factors affecting the mechanism of electron transfer, because the redox couples in the solution equilibrate with the electrode material and the kinetics of the electrochemical reactions depend on the material of the electrode. Ultimately, the concentrations of the electroactive reagents and the equilibrium potentials of the redox couples in the solution determine the electrode potential, whether it is covered with biofilm or not. For the results of individual studies to be compared, it is critical for all of them to have been conducted using the same electrode material and, if possible, the same experimental setup. Most of the studies in the literature report using electrodes made of porous materials, such as graphite, carbon paper, carbon granules, carbon brushes, or carbon felts. These materials are relatively inexpensive, and they work well as electrodes in MFCs used to generate electricity, but they are much less useful in fundamental studies of electron transfer mechanisms in EABs because they all exhibit a high background current. Background currents can mask the electrochemical signals resulting from the processes involved in electrons being exchanged among electrodes, microbes, and dissolved electroactive reagents. On the basis of our experience, we recommend using electrodes made of other types of materials than those specified above. In particular, electrodes made of glassy carbon are suitable for such studies, as the background current from glassy carbon electrodes is practically negligible. The downside of this choice of material is that glassy carbon electrodes are quite expensive. They do offer superb quality and smooth, nonporous surfaces, which makes it possible to determine the surface areas of the electrodes from their geometric features. When biofilms grow on the surfaces of porous materials, some of the microbial cells grow in the pores, which creates a variety of artifacts. Figure 7.19, which shows *Geobacter* cells growing on a porous graphite electrode, demonstrates this effect. Some cells grow within the pores, which makes it difficult to determine the surface area of the electrode with which the microbial cells interact. In addition, the variation of the diffusion rates of the redox species between the flat parts of the electrode and the pores affects the results of the electrochemical experiments in an unpredictable manner.

One disadvantage of glassy carbon electrodes is that they are opaque. Therefore, if in a particular study biofilm structure needs to be monitored together with electrochemical measurements, using electrodes made of glassy carbon may not be advisable. In such instances, glass slides covered with gold or indium tin oxide (ITO) can be used. The reagents for preparing such electrodes are available from Sigma, Fisher, and other large suppliers of chemicals. The use of these electrodes has side effects, though. For example, gold may interact with the proteins secreted by EABs and modify their properties. ITO has optical properties similar to those of glass, which may be desirable for some applications, but it also exhibits high and variable electrical resistivity. Also, ITO-covered electrodes are not very durable. Platinum electrodes may exhibit unanticipated effects due to their catalytic activity.

All these considerations are important when one is selecting suitable materials for making working electrodes. The requirements that need to be imposed on materials for making counter electrodes are much less demanding, as a counter electrode serves only

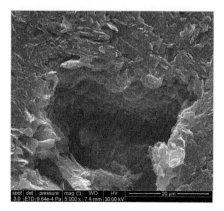

Figure 7.19 *Geobacter* biofilms growing in a pore of a porous graphite electrode.

as the electron source/sink for the electrons derived from the biofilm. Graphite electrodes with sufficiently large surface areas are quite suitable for use as counter electrodes.

7.5.2 Selecting the type of the reactor

Laboratory reactors used to study EABs are constructed to satisfy the needs of specific experiments and are subject to all the rules we discussed for LBRs in Chapter 3. The electrochemical configurations of these reactors are shown in Figure 7.20. From the functional point of view, they are all microbial fuel cells, MFCs, equipped with a variety of electrochemical instrumentation to satisfy the needs of specific measurements. In the simplest configuration, the reactor is just a MFC (Figure 7.20a), which is a useful configuration for generating electricity but not very useful for studying mechanisms of electron transfer. The electrodes are connected by a resistor, and typical measurements in such a reactor include the current and the potential drop across the resistor. The data are used to compute the electric power generated by the MFC:

$$V = IR \tag{7.55}$$

$$P = VI = I^2R \tag{7.56}$$

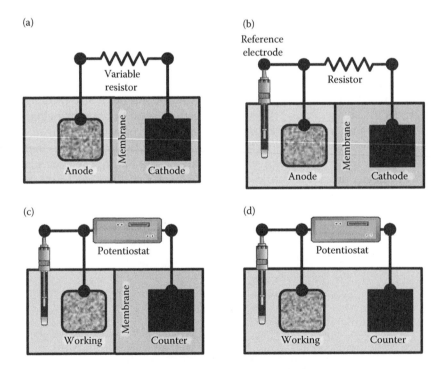

Figure 7.20 EABs can be studied using four configurations: (a) MFC, (b) MFC with a reference electrode, (c) MFC mode with a reference electrode and a potentiostat to control the potential of the working electrode, and (d) an electrochemical cell with a reference electrode and a potentiostat to control the potential of the working electrode but no ion exchange membrane. (Reprinted from T. J. Babauta et al., *Biofouling*, 28, 789–812, 2012. With permission.)

where V is the potential difference between the anode and the cathode, R is the resistance of the resistor, and I is the current passing through the resistor.

The configuration shown in Figure 7.20a demonstrates that a MFC can produce electricity but that to characterize its electrochemical performance additional equipment needs to be added. When current passes across the resistor, the potentials of both electrodes change. To study electron transfer mechanisms, it is important to characterize the electrode reactions, and the first step in this direction is to determine the electrode potential. This measurement can be accomplished by adding a reference electrode, as in the configuration shown in Figure 7.20b. This configuration is still a MFC, but it can be operated as a three-electrode electrochemical cell. In this arrangement the current passing across the resistor is limited by the rate of the electrode reaction on one of the two electrodes. The electrode that limits the current is appropriately called the current-limiting electrode, and it is important to identify which of the two electrodes limits the current. This can be done in a variety of ways, of which the simplest is using a variable resistor. Changing the resistance changes the potential of each of the electrodes, and the potential of each of the electrodes can be measured against the reference electrode. The electrode that exhibits the largest change in electrode potential in response to a change in resistance is the current-limiting electrode. It is important for many reasons to identify which of the electrodes limits the current. For example, if the goal of the work is to improve the performance of a MFC, one possible way to improve its performance is to modify the current-limiting electrode.

Changing the resistance in the configuration shown in Figure 7.20a changed the potential of the current-limiting electrode, and this effect was used to identify which of the two electrodes was limiting the current. Once the current-limiting electrode has been identified, an electrochemical system can be characterized further by quantifying its response to changes in the potential of the current-limiting electrode. In the configuration shown in Figure 7.20c, a potentiostat is used to control the potential of the current-limiting electrode. Following the common terminology, the electrode whose potential is being controlled is called the working electrode and the other electrode is called the counter electrode. In typical measurements in such systems, the current across the resistor is measured and plotted as a function of the potential applied to the working electrode. This is analogous to measuring polarization curves characterizing electrode reactions, with the additional complication that the electrons are exchanged between the electrode and the biofilm.

The reactor configurations in Figure 7.20a through c are microbial fuel cells, and the electrochemical half-cells are separated by ion exchange membranes. In the configuration shown in Figure 7.20d the ion exchange membrane has been removed. The ion exchange membrane is a substitute for the salt bridge in an electrochemical cell. It helps to restore the electrical neutrality of the solution in each of the half-cells. Removing the membrane connects the two half-cells, and this configuration resembles the three-electrode electrochemical setup shown in Figure 7.20d. This configuration is used for special purposes, such as generating hydrogen on the counter electrode to be used as the electron donor by a biofilm growing on the working electrode.

Example 7.4: Identifying the current-limiting electrode

As was explained above, the current-limiting electrode in an electrochemical cell can be identified in a variety of ways. We described the procedure for identifying the current-limiting electrode by connecting the electrodes through a variable resistance and examining the potentials of the electrodes in response to changes in the electrical resistance. In

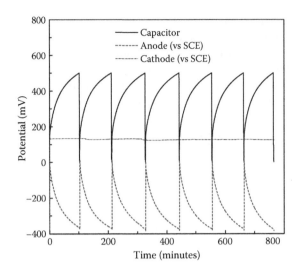

Figure 7.21 A MFC was used to charge a capacitor. When the potential of the capacitor reached 500 mV, the capacitor was discharged through a resistor. (Reprinted from A. Dewan et al., *Journal of Power Sources*, 195, 90–96, 2010.)

this example we use another method: we charge a capacitor using a MFC and examine the electrode potential in response to the charging and discharging of the capacitor. First, the capacitor is charged using the energy delivered by the MFC. When the capacitor reaches a preset potential (500 mV in this example), it is discharged and then charged again. During the charging and discharging cycles, the anode and cathode potentials vary and are measured with respect to a reference electrode. The results are shown in Figure 7.21. On the basis of these data, determine which electrode limits the current in this setup.

As seen in Figure 7.21, during the charging and discharging cycles, the cathode potential of the MFC remained constant but the anode potential varied significantly by nearly 400 mV; thus the anode was the current-limiting electrode.

7.5.3   *Selecting the procedure for conditioning the biofilms*

Growing biofilms on electrodes is similar to growing biofilms on other surfaces, except that biofilms growing on electrically polarized surfaces benefit from acclimatization. Acclimatization gives microorganisms time to adjust to the conditions of growth on an electrified interface. Biofilms can be grown on the electrodes of electrochemical cells in any of these possible configurations:

1. Closed circuit acclimatization: the biofilm electrode and the supporting electrode are short-circuited or connected across a resistor.
2. Open circuit acclimatization: the biofilm electrode is left disconnected.
3. Controlled cell potential acclimatization: a constant potential is applied between the biofilm electrode and the supporting electrode.
4. Controlled electrode potential acclimatization: a constant polarization potential is applied between the biofilm electrode and the reference electrode.

The closed and open circuit configurations are the simplest methods of acclimatizing biofilms. Acclimatization using the closed circuit configuration allows the biofilm electrode to reach a steady state cell potential. This configuration enhances steady state electron transfer. The resistor used to connect the electrodes needs to be carefully selected, as it controls the amount of current allowed to pass and the potential of the biofilm electrode. Open circuit acclimatization allows the biofilm electrode potential to develop freely until it reaches a steady potential with respect to a suitable reference electrode.

Figure 7.22 shows an example of electrode potential evolution during open circuit acclimatization. The electrodes were deployed in a river. The anode was buried in the sediments, and the cathode was suspended in the bulk solution. Initially, both electrodes exhibited potentials around 100 mV$_{SHE}$. After 10 days of exposure the individual electrodes reached steady potentials and the electrochemical cell reached a steady OCV. This method is virtually identical to growing biofilms on inert surfaces but provides additional information about the dynamics of the electrode potentials and the dynamics of the OCV evolution. The potentials of the individual electrodes characterize the relevant electrode reaction occurring on each electrode and provide information useful in controlling the performance of the system. For example, from the data in Figure 7.22, it is known that connecting the cathode to any electrode with a potential lower than 506 mV$_{SHE}$ will generate current. This current will of course depend on the actual OCV and on the electrical resistance, as predicted by Ohm's law.

Using a configuration of acclimatization with either a controlled cell potential or a controlled electrode potential requires the use of a potentiostat. Although both methods are described in the literature, we believe that only acclimatization with electrode potential control is justified. The cell voltage tells nothing about the potentials of the individual electrodes. If the cell voltage is set to, say, 0.5 V, this can be accomplished through an infinite number of combinations of the potentials of the two electrodes. If the electrode potential is set to 0.5 V against a specified reference electrode, this gives precise and reproducible information about the electrode, information that others can use to reproduce the results.

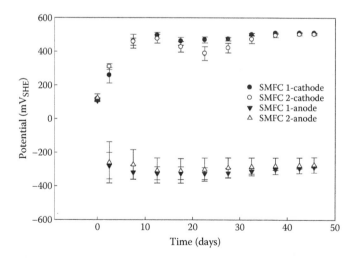

Figure 7.22 Potentials of cathodes and anodes in sediment microbial fuel cells (SMFC). The electrodes in each SMFC were run in duplicate. The cathodes reached an average potential of +506 mV$_{SHE}$, and the anodes reached an average potential of –280 mV$_{SHE}$. Thus, the OCV of the cell was 0.786 V. Each error bar shows a single standard deviation computed from several measurements of the individual potential. (Reprinted from R. Renslow et al., *Physical Chemistry Chemical Physics*, 13, 21573–21584, 2011.)

Controlled potential acclimatization is often used to select strains of microorganisms that can operate on electrically polarized surfaces or to study microbial community dynamics as a function of applied potential.

In conclusion, to grow biofilms on electrically polarized electrodes, the procedures for growing biofilms on inert surfaces can be used. The only difference between growing biofilms on inert surfaces and growing them as EABs on electrically polarized electrodes is that in the case of EABs we are usually interested in quantifying the rate of electron transfer between the biofilm and the electrode. Because current, resistance, and potential are connected by Ohm's law, to generate reproducible results, the potential of the electrode must be controlled while the current is being measured. The resistance is assumed to be constant and it can be measured, if needed. There is extensive literature discussing the polarization potential used to grow biofilms but, not surprisingly, there is no consensus among researchers as to the exact magnitude of that potential. It is practical, when growing EABs, to try various conditions and determine the optimum conditions for the specific biofilms under study. Once biofilms have been grown under well-controlled, reproducible conditions, electrochemical techniques can be used to quantify the rate of the electron transfer between the biofilm and the electrode.

7.6 Electrochemical techniques for studying electrochemically active biofilms

There is an impressive number of electrochemical techniques available for studying electrode processes in the absence of microorganisms, and there are many textbooks describing these techniques. Using these techniques when the electrodes are covered with biofilms is unconventional, and the applied methods need to be scrutinized for relevancy: not all electrochemical techniques used to study electrode processes give meaningful results when biofilms have been deposited on the electrode surface. Here, we discuss the techniques we use to study electrode processes in the presence of electrochemically active biofilms.

7.6.1 Long-term electrode polarization of electrochemically active biofilms

Studying biofilms on electrically polarized surfaces is relatively new in biofilm research, and many fundamental questions cannot yet be answered with certainty. One such question is the dynamics of the microbial community deposited on an electrically polarized surface. The working hypothesis is that the microbial community will change to select the microorganisms better adapted to operating on such surfaces. Better adapted microorganisms may or may not increase the efficiency of the electron transfer between the electrodes and the biofilm: the selection may favor survival skills for the extreme conditions on the surface of polarized electrodes but not the ability of the microorganisms to transfer electrons with increased efficiency. Studies addressing these types of questions necessarily depend on the long-term polarization of electrodes colonized by biofilms. In this configuration, biofilm reactors are inoculated with selected microorganisms while the electrode is polarized to a selected potential and the corresponding current is measured over time. Such studies can be conducted in a batch reactor or in a flow-through reactor. Figure 7.23 shows results from such a study. The electrode in this project was used as the electron acceptor, and the reactor was flow-through and continuously fed with the nutrient solution. The electrode potential was set using a potentiostat and the current was monitored.

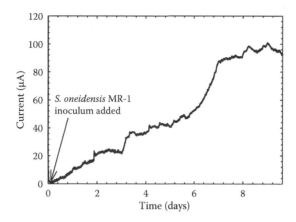

Figure 7.23 Current generation by a *Shewanella oneidensis* MR-1 biofilm growing on a graphite electrode under anaerobic conditions in the reactor configuration shown in Figure 7.20c. The current increased steadily over a period of nine days and reached a sustainable value. The polarization potential was $0~\mathrm{mV_{Ag/AgCl}}$. (Reprinted from T. J. Babauta et al., *Biofouling*, 28, 789–812, 2012. With permission.)

The data show that the microbial community responded with increasing current generation and that the current eventually reached a steady state.

7.6.2   Voltammetric techniques

The most popular sensors in biofilm research are amperometric and potentiometric devices, and some of them have been described above. We use them to either measure the current flowing between the working electrode and the counter electrode (amperometric sensors) or the electrode potential against a suitable reference electrode (potentiometric sensors). In this sense, the dissolved oxygen sensor does not measure dissolved oxygen and the pH sensor does not measure pH. They each measure an electrical property of the system, and it is up to the researcher to make sure that the electrical property measured by the sensor is proportional to the component of interest, dissolved oxygen or proton concentration in these cases. In some instances, however, neither potentiometric nor amperometric sensors are adequate. For example, if the researcher is interested in measuring the concentrations of several substances at the same time, or just does not know how many substances of interest are in the solution, amperometric and potentiometric sensors are of little help. Voltammetric techniques can help in such situations, as a voltammetric signal is specific to the substance that is measured and the technique can be used to detect many electroactive substances in a single experiment. The principle of voltammetry is to scan the potential of the working electrode between the potentials at which the electroactive substances in the solution are expected to discharge (exchange electrons with the electrode); the presence of each substance shows as a peak on the voltammogram. Many materials can be used to construct voltammetric electrodes. Four of them are favored for their performance: carbon, gold, mercury (film or drop), and bismuth (film). Diagrams of three electrodes made of these materials are shown in Figure 7.24.

Voltammetric techniques are very sensitive and are often used to detect and measure traces of substances present in nanomolar concentrations. The sensors used in these techniques can be miniaturized. For example, a gold microelectrode with a diameter of 25 μm,

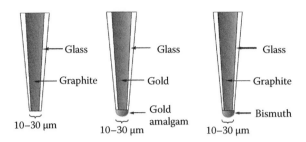

Figure 7.24 Typical materials used to construct voltammetric electrodes.

used to detect traces of copper Cu^{2+} with a detection limit of 0.3 nM, was described by Jianmei Zhuang et al. (2011). In Chapter 5 we described the construction of our own flavin microelectrode, which we use in studying EABs. Voltammetry is a potentiodynamic electroanalytical technique which depends on applying various forms of potential ramps to working electrodes and measuring the current as the various redox species discharge at their characteristic potentials. We will give examples of the use of voltammetric techniques when we describe our measurements of copper and lead in water. We used graphite as the substratum, electrodeposited a thin layer of mercury, and applied the analytical procedure known as anodic stripping voltammetry (ASV). The procedures for preparing electrodes for ASV can be found in various textbooks on analytical electrochemistry, such as the book by Wanf (1994).

7.6.3   Anodic stripping voltammetry

ASV is one of the simplest voltammetric techniques, and it is intuitive enough to be used as an example of voltammetric techniques in general. To detect lead and copper in water we use a graphite electrode on which a thin layer of mercury has been electrodeposited by cathodically polarizing the electrode in a solution of mercuric ions (Hg^{2+}), according to the reaction:

$$Hg^{2+} + 2e^- \rightarrow Hg \tag{7.57}$$

Figure 7.25 illustrates the procedure and the setup used for the cathodic polarization of the electrode.

Once the electrode is prepared, the analysis begins with the preconcentration of heavy metals dissolved in the layer of mercury on the graphite substratum. These form, respectively, lead and copper amalgams according to the reaction:

$$Me^{2+} + ne^- + Hg \rightarrow M(Hg) \tag{7.58}$$

To preconcentrate the metals from the water solution, the thin mercury layer is cathodically polarized at the deposition potential, which is usually about 0.5 V lower than the standard electrode potential for the metal to be determined. The duration of this step depends on the concentration of the metal in the water and needs to be optimized experimentally. The time needed to preconcentrate the metals is usually on the order of a few minutes. Once enough of the metal or metals from the solution have dissolved in the mercury layer and formed their respective amalgams, the setup is ready for stripping analysis.

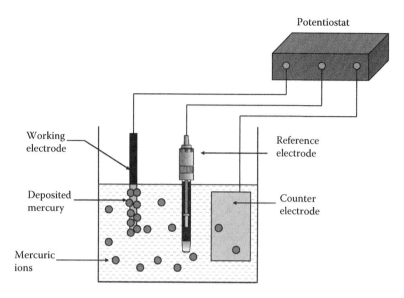

Figure 7.25 A graphite working electrode is cathodically polarized in a solution of mercuric ions so that a thin layer of mercury is deposited on the surface of the carbon.

This step starts from the cathodic (negative) potential used in the preconcentration phase and involves applying a ramp of potential toward the anodic (positive) potentials. As the potential is gradually increased, when it reaches the decomposition potential of a metal dissolved in the layer of mercury, the reaction proceeds in reverse:

$$M(Hg) \rightarrow Me^{2+} + 2e^- + Hg \tag{7.59}$$

The electrons released in the reverse reaction cause a current in the anodically polarized electrode. This is marked as a peak on the voltammogram, as shown in Figure 7.26. The height of the peak, or in more precise analyses the surface area under the peak, is proportional to the concentration of the metal. The actual concentration of the metal can be found from the calibration curve, which is prepared by running ASV in a series of solutions with known concentrations of the metal.

7.6.4   Cyclic voltammetry

Cyclic voltammetry (CV) is a potentiodynamic measurement in which the potential of the working electrode is linearly increased from the initial potential to the final potential. The initial and final potentials are set by the user. When the final potential is reached, the direction of potential change is reversed and the potential proceeds toward the initial potential. The current passing through the working electrode during the potential sweeps is plotted versus the potential to produce a voltammogram. CV can be used to identify the potential(s) at which active redox couples in the biofilm are oxidized or reduced. The potential scan rate must be determined by the user, and most of the time its selection is critical for the studied process. CV can be used to determine whether EABs have the capability for electron transfer, whether freely diffusing species or surface-adsorbed species contribute to electron transfer, and whether biofilms engage in catalytic activity toward specific substrates. We used this technique to characterize electrode processes on glassy

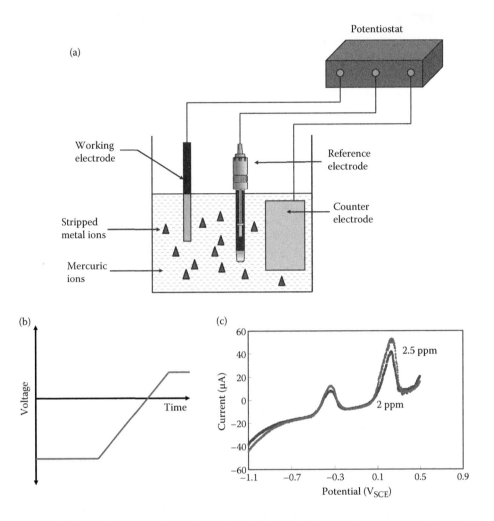

Figure 7.26 (a) Once the metals have been dissolved in the layer of mercury and formed their respective amalgams, (b) the anodic ramp of potential is applied to reverse the metal deposition reaction and produce a voltammogram, such as the one shown in (c).

carbon electrodes covered with *Shewanella* or *Geobacter* species. Figure 7.27a shows CV scans for a *Shewanella oneidensis* MR-1 biofilm grown on glassy carbon. Figure 7.27b shows CV for a *G. sulfurreducens* biofilm grown on glassy carbon. CV peaks measured with electrodes covered with biofilms are typically broad and difficult to interpret. In some cases they are actually composed of many individual overlapping peaks responding to specific redox couples. One method we use to gain information about how biofilms affect electrode processes from CV spectra is taking CV scans right after placing the biofilm electrode in fresh growth medium and another scan after physically removing the biofilm. Figure 7.27 shows examples of such scans. The differences between the CVs of electrodes with and without biofilm show the electrochemical reactions caused by electrochemically active species on the electrode surface. Figure 7.27 shows that *Shewanella* secretes electroactive compounds that are detected by the CV scan, while *Geobacter* appears to transfer electrons directly to the electrode.

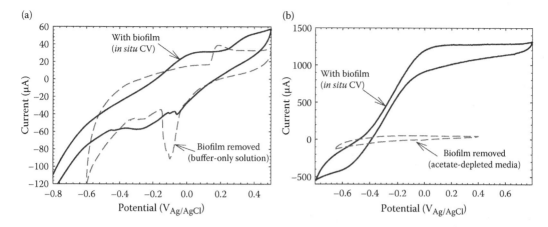

Figure 7.27 (a) *In situ* CV of *S. oneidensis* MR-1 (black line). The biofilm was physically removed from the biofilm electrode and a second CV was performed (dashed line). A glassy carbon electrode (10 mm × 10 mm) was used. The scan rate was 10 mV/s. (b) *In situ* CV of *G. sulfurreducens* (black line). The biofilm was physically removed from the biofilm electrode and a second CV was performed (red dashed line). A glassy carbon electrode (25 mm × 25 mm) was used. The scan rate was 10 mV/s for the first CV and 1 mV/s for the second CV. (Reprinted from T. J. Babauta et al., *Biofouling*, 28, 789–812, 2012. With permission.)

If needed, more information can be obtained by using mutants of the microorganisms under study. CV can provide useful information about the mechanisms of electron transfer between electrodes and EABs. However, CV studies do not reflect the ability of biofilms to produce long-term, sustainable current, which should be tested using long-term electrode polarization experiments, such as the one illustrated in Figure 7.8.

7.6.5 Square-wave voltammetry

As we mentioned above, there are a variety of amperometric techniques and many of them use more elaborate shapes for potential ramps than the linear ones used in ASV or in CV. Square-wave voltammetry (SWV) uses a potential ramp consisting of large-amplitude variations of potential that form characteristic rectangle-like steps. The amplitude of the potential variation in each step is selected such that both the oxidizing and the reducing current can be measured at each potential of the linear ramp. Because of this design, SWV can be used to assess the reversibility of the redox reactions involved. The square wave is superimposed on the linear ramp. The example in Figure 7.28 is a section of the potential sweep used when the flavin electrode was used in a biofilm.

The current is sampled at the ends of each pulse, and the difference between the measured values is plotted as the voltammogram. The main advantage of SWV is that it can detect low concentrations of electrochemically active reactants not easily detectable by CV. However, this technique is somewhat less popular than CV because of its complexity. Figure 7.29 shows the response of the flavin microelectrode described in Chapter 4 to various concentrations of flavin. The concentration of flavin can be measured by preparing a calibration curve using SWV in solutions of various concentrations of flavin, as shown in Figure 7.30.

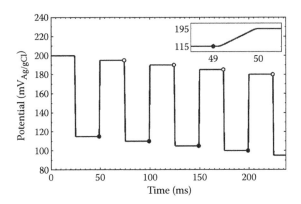

Figure 7.28 Section of a square-wave potential sweep, with parameter values matching those found to give optimum experimental results for the flavin microelectrode. The final SWV signal comprises the difference between the current measured at the end of the peak potential (open circles) and that measured at the end of the trough potential (closed circles). The inset figure shows an example of how the changes between the low and high potentials are smoothed using a spline function consisting of two quarter-sine waves connected by a straight line. This is done to avoid a jump discontinuity, which would prevent the model from converging. (Reprinted from H. D. Nguyen et al., *Sensors and Actuators B: Chemical*, 161, 929–937, 2012.)

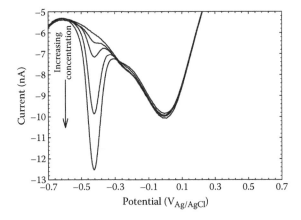

Figure 7.29 SWV responses to riboflavin concentrations, starting at 0.1 μM and increasing by half-decades to 10 μM. Figure 7.30 shows the calibration curve of the flavin microelectrode, based on the SWV peak currents at −424 $mV_{Ag/AgCl}$. (Reprinted from H. D. Nguyen et al., *Sensors and Actuators B: Chemical*, 161, 929–937, 2012.)

7.6.6   Use of coupled research techniques to explain the processes in electrically active biofilms

The overall complexity of the voltammograms of EABs requires the use of multiple research techniques to make progress in understanding the electron transfer mechanisms comprising them. Individual techniques, no matter how sophisticated, can only provide pieces of information, so additional techniques may be needed to corroborate the results. For example, electrochemical techniques alone, such as those presented above, cannot explain the

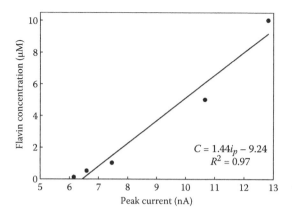

Figure 7.30 Calibration curve for the flavin microelectrode. (Reprinted from H. D. Nguyen et al., *Sensors and Actuators B: Chemical*, 161, 929–937, 2012.)

mechanisms of electron transfer processes in EABs. These techniques must be supported by physical and chemical evidence so that the reasons for the observed electrochemical responses can be determined. For example, the current peak at -450 mV$_{Ag/AgCl}$ in SVW in Figure 7.29 is generally accepted as being due to flavin. However, this hypothesis must be tested by running a CV in the clean electrochemical system with flavin. Alternatively, this hypothesis can be tested by adding flavin to the system: the flavin peak should increase after the addition of flavin. In addition, molecular techniques such as generating mutants with different gene/protein expression levels provide a physiological link to electrochemical investigations. For example, a flavin deletion mutant can give more information about the role of flavin in biofilms. The electrochemical techniques presented here describe the nature of the electron transfer event in the presence of biofilms (reversibility, mass transfer limitations, properties of redox couples, and reaction steps). However, they do not give any information on how biofilms participate in the electron transfer or what aspects of biofilm processes promote electron transfer. For example, the presence of redox couples in biofilms does not necessarily imply that they participate in electron transfer. A good example is flavin secreted by a *S. oneidensis* MR-1 biofilm. Hypothetically, the addition of flavin should increase the current, but the current is not sustainable, which raises questions about the role of flavin as an electron transfer mediator.

The chemistry inside a biofilm and the physical structure of the biofilm can be coupled to the results obtained using electrochemical techniques to understand electron transfer processes. The chemistry inside a biofilm can be determined using microelectrodes, and the physical structure of the biofilm can be imaged using microscopy techniques presented in this book. Microelectrode measurements allow us (1) to measure the kinetics of redox mediators inside biofilms directly, (2) to resolve local concentrations of chemical species inside biofilms, and (3) to determine the physical locations of electrochemically active species *in situ*.

7.6.7   Using microelectrodes in electrochemically active biofilms on electrically polarized electrodes

Microelectrodes can be used in conjunction with electrochemical techniques in two modes. In the first mode, depth profiles can be taken during constant polarization, which is similar to what we have described in this book. The second mode of measurement requires placing a microelectrode tip at a predetermined distance from the bottom and monitoring the response while changing the potential of the electrode. Figure 7.31 shows pH and redox profiles measured in a *G. sulfurreducens* biofilm at different growth stages. The first profile was taken while the biofilm was generating 1.05 mA of current, and the second profile was taken while the biofilm was generating 1.85 mA of current. As shown in Figure 7.31a, the pH difference between the bulk and the bottom of the biofilm increased with the increased current. Similar measurements are presented for redox potential. The redox potential increased toward the bottom of the biofilm (Figure 7.31b).

The second mode is shown in Figure 7.32. A hydrogen peroxide microelectrode (Figure 7.32a) was placed ~100 μm above a glassy carbon electrode. The glassy carbon electrode potential was changed linearly from a positive potential to a negative potential to investigate oxygen reduction. One by-product of oxygen reduction is hydrogen peroxide,

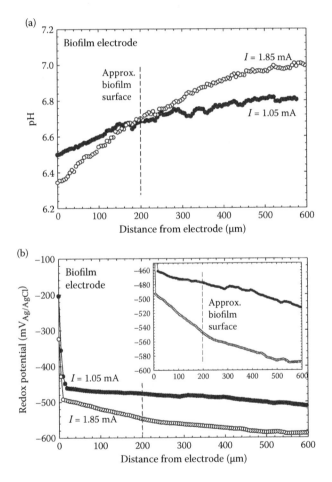

Figure 7.31 The pH and redox profiles measured in a *G. sulfurreducens* biofilm at different growth stages. (a) The pH profiles at the biofilm electrode. (b) The redox potential profiles at the biofilm electrode. The inset shows the profiles over a smaller *y* axis range for clarity. The biofilm electrode was polarized to 0.45 $V_{Ag/AgCl}$ during measurements. The solid circles represent profiles measured at 1.05 mA. The open circles represent profiles measured at a current density of 1.85 mA. (Reprinted from T. J. Babauta et al., *Biotechnology and Bioengineering*, 109, 2651–2662, 2012.)

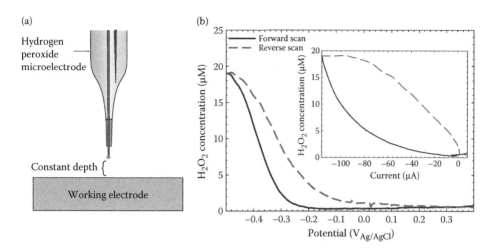

Figure 7.32 (a) Diagram of a hydrogen peroxide microelectrode. The bracket shows the distance between the electrode surface and the microelectrode tip. (b) Hydrogen peroxide concentration measured ~100 μm above a glassy carbon electrode during a CV scan. The inset shows current versus hydrogen peroxide concentration.

and a hydrogen peroxide microelectrode was used to detect hydrogen peroxide generation during the CV scan. Keeping the microelectrode position at a constant depth allows us to monitor hydrogen peroxide concentration variation with potential and corresponding current. Figure 7.32a shows that hydrogen peroxide was produced at potentials below $-200\ mV_{Ag/AgCl}$. The inset in Figure 7.32b shows how the hydrogen peroxide concentration correlated with the measured current. The forward and reverse currents are well separated, demonstrating the effect of diffusion processes.

Figure 7.33 shows combined measurements of variation in the oxygen and flavin concentrations in a *S. oneidensis* MR-1 biofilm. The dissolved oxygen concentration started slightly under the oxygen saturation concentration at ~8 mg/L and dropped to 0 mg/L

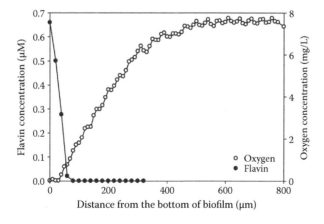

Figure 7.33 Flavin and oxygen concentration profiles in a *S. oneidensis* MR-1 biofilm. The thickness of the biofilm was approximately 300 μm. (Reprinted from H. D. Nguyen et al., *Sensors and Actuators B: Chemical*, 161, 929–937, 2012.)

near the bottom of the biofilm. The flavin concentration was below detection in all locations except for a spike near the bottom of the biofilm, where oxygen was depleted. These results demonstrate that flavins are produced in the anaerobic zone to act as intermediate electron acceptors in the deeper parts of the biofilm. The reduced flavins can then be transported to the aerobic zones, where they transfer the electrons to oxygen, which acts as the terminal electron acceptor.

7.6.8   Microscopy

Light microscopy is the first choice of researchers for techniques for imaging biofilms on electrodes. The main challenge is that high-quality electrodes are usually made of opaque materials that do not allow light penetration. Therefore, the reactors should be modified so that biofilm growth can be imaged *in situ*. An example of these reactors is shown in Section 3.5.1. The use of microscopy is critical to correlating biofilm structure with biofilm function related to electron transfer. Figure 7.34 shows an example of this. Figure 7.34

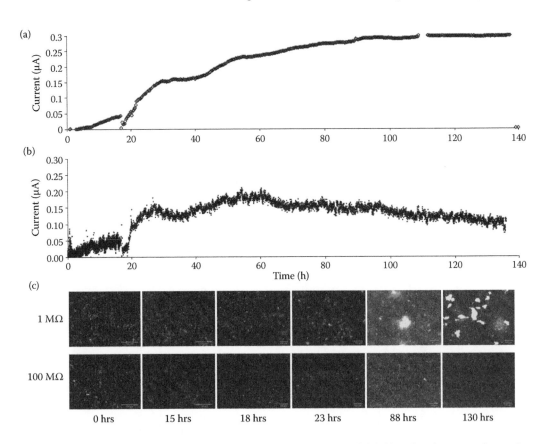

Figure 7.34 Simultaneous monitoring of current generation and biofilm development from single attached cells using epifluorescent imaging. Temporal variation in current in the imaging-compatible MFC for two different biofilms growing on anodes with external resistances of (a) 1 MΩ and (b) 100 MΩ. (c) Concurrent image data taken over the course of the experiment for both biofilms growing on anodes. Differences in biofilm development were clearly visible by 88 hours. The scale bars are equal to 10 μm for 0 and 15 hours and to 100 μm for 18–130 hours. (Reprinted from S. J. McLean et al., *Environmental Science and Technology*, 44, 2721–2727, 2010.)

shows current generation and biofilm development, from single attached cells to micro-colonies, using epifluorescent imaging and concurrent image data taken over the course of an experiment on biofilms on anodes. Differences in biofilm development were clearly visible by 88 hours. This difference was caused by the current accepted by the electrodes, which eventually affected the biofilm growth rates.

7.6.9   Modeling electrochemically active biofilms

The main goal of modeling biofilm processes is generally to predict the nutrient consumption rate, as discussed in this book. However, when electrochemically active biofilms are modeled, the main goal is to predict electron transfer rates to the electrode surface. Predicting the current generation from a biofilm through both mediated and conductive electron transfer mechanisms is a way to confirm the experimental results. The models developed were able to fit experimental data from *Geobacter* biofilms successfully. These models considered both mediated electron transfer, modeled using Butler–Volmer kinetics (Equation 7.60), and conductive electron transfer, modeled using the Nernst–Monod equation (Equation 7.61). The common form of the Butler–Volmer equation is given by

$$i = nFk^0 \left(X_{red} e^{(1-\alpha)f\left(E-E_X^{0'}\right)} - X_{ox} e^{-\alpha f\left(E-E_X^{0'}\right)} \right)$$

(7.60)

where n is the number of electrons transferred; i is the current density (A/m²); k^0 is the standard heterogeneous rate constant (m/s); X_{red} is the concentration of the reduced form of the redox couple at the biofilm electrode surface (mM); X_{ox} is the concentration of the oxidized form of the redox couple at the biofilm electrode surface (mM); α is the charge transfer coefficient (unitless); f is the grouped term of Faraday's constant, F (s A/mol) divided by the temperature, T (K), and the universal gas constant, R (J/K mol), thus nF/RT (1/V); E is the biofilm electrode potential (V); and $E_X^{0'}$ is the standard reduction potential of the redox couple (V). The Butler–Volmer equation is useful for modeling mediated electron transfer mechanisms because it couples the concentration of the electron mediator in both its oxidized and its reduced form at the biofilm electrode surface and the biofilm electrode potential to the production of current. This equation is often coupled to the diffusion of electron transfer mediators through biofilm to provide a method of calculating both current and depth profiles of mediator concentrations.

The Nernst–Monod equation is generally used to model conductive electron transfer:

$$\frac{i}{I_{lim}} = \left(\frac{1}{1+e^{-f(E-E_{KA})}} \right) \left(\frac{C}{K_S+C} \right)$$

(7.61)

where I_{lim} is the limiting current density (A/m²), E_{KA} is the potential at which the current is half the limiting current (V), C is the concentration of the electron-donating substrate (mM), and K_S is the Monod half saturation constant for that substrate (mM). The Nernst–Monod equation is a special form of a multiplicative Monod equation, where the electron acceptor is assumed to be a solid electron acceptor, accessible via instantaneous conduction, as opposed to a soluble electron-accepting molecule.

In addition to the complete mathematical modeling of a biofilm growing on an anode, empirical equations are used to predict current-voltage dependence in biofilms growing on electrodes. The Butler–Volmer–Monod model was fitted to experimental data to simulate biofilm electrode polarization curves and cellular kinetics as a function of potential and substrate concentration (Hamelers et al. 2011):

$$\frac{i}{I_{\lim}} = \frac{1 - e^{-f(E - E_{S/P})}}{K_1 e^{-(1-\alpha)f(E - E_{S/P})} + K_2 e^{-f(E - E_{S/P})} + \dfrac{K_M}{S} + 1}$$

(7.62)

where K_1 and K_2 are lumped parameters (unitless), $E_{S/P}$ is the thermodynamic electrode potential, and K_M is the substrate affinity constant (mM). It is important to note that the substrate affinity constant is not identical to the Monod half saturation constant in the Nernst–Monod equation. The model demonstrated that the apparent Monod constant was a function of anode potential and that, therefore, it is only at sufficiently high overpotentials (large $E - E_{S/P}$ values) that K_m is equivalent to K_S. Both K_1 and K_2 are complex terms that appear to be functions only of electrode potential and the microorganism used. K_1 can be understood as the ratio of the rate of biochemical substrate utilization to the rate of electrochemical exchange current density, while K_2 can be understood as the ratio of the rate of product formation to the rate of substrate formation inside the microorganism.

7.7 Examples of technologically relevant electrochemically active biofilms

7.7.1 Microbially influenced corrosion of metals

The terms "microbially influenced corrosion" (MIC) and just "microbial corrosion" have been added to the terminology used by corrosion scientists and engineers relatively recently. Once these terms established their presence, however, a tendency developed among corrosion professionals to blame microorganisms for all unexplained material failures: If you do not know what caused a material failure, it was probably MIC. As microbes may or may not have been involved in specific cases of material failure, it is reasonable to ask: "How do we know that the corrosion process was actually influenced by microorganisms?" The mere presence of microorganisms on the corroding metal does not demonstrate their involvement in the corrosion processes, as materials are rarely used in sterile environments. To address the question of whether a material failure was mediated by the presence of microorganisms, many research groups have attempted to identify fingerprints of MIC, i.e., specific characteristics distinguishing microbially stimulated corrosion from ordinary galvanic corrosion. Despite significant research efforts, universal characteristics of MIC have not yet been identified, and there are reasons to believe that the fingerprints of MIC have not been found because a universal mechanism of MIC does not exist. Instead, in the process of searching for a universal mechanism, several specific mechanisms by which microorganisms affect rates of corrosion have been identified, and the diversity of these mechanisms is such that it is difficult to expect that a single unified concept can bring them all together. It has been demonstrated by numerous researchers that the accelerated corrosion of metals in the presence of microorganisms stems from microbial modifications to the chemical and electrochemical reactions occurring near metal surfaces. Such modifications depend, of course, on the properties of the metal, the microbial community structure in the biofilm deposited on the metal surface, the water chemistry, and possibly a number of other factors that are relevant in specific cases of material failure.

To examine the possible microbial effects on the corrosion of metals, we will use the terminology introduced earlier in this book. As described in detail in Chapter 1, biofilm is composed of four compartments: (1) the surface to which the microorganisms are attached, (2) the biofilm (the microorganisms and the matrix), (3) the solution of nutrients, and (4) the gas phase. Each compartment consists of several components, and the number of components investigated may vary depending on the type of study. For example, in some MIC studies it is convenient to distinguish four components of the surface: (1) the bulk metal, (2) the passive layers, (3) the biomineralized deposits on the surface, and (4) the corrosion products. Microorganisms can modify each of these components in a way that enhances corrosion of the metal surface. Components of the other compartments of the biofilm can be modified in ways that affect the corrosion reactions as well. Modifications in the solution compartment may include the chemical composition of the water solution, the hydrodynamics and the mass transfer rates near the metal surface; modifications in the biofilm compartment may include the microbial community structure and the composition of the extracellular polymers (EPS). Each of these modifications may be complex in itself, each may affect the corrosion reactions in many ways, and the modifications may have synergistic effects.

When biofilms accumulate on metal surfaces, reactants and products of microbial metabolic reactions occurring in the space occupied by the biofilm affect the chemistry of the solution and the surface chemistry, and both types of modification may interfere with the electrochemical processes naturally occurring at the interface between the metal and its environment. The reactants and products of electrochemical reactions occurring at a metal surface interact in a complex way. Some of these interactions accelerate corrosion, and some may inhibit corrosion. The interactions that accelerate corrosion, and are characteristic enough, are called mechanisms of MIC. To approach the task of quantifying these mechanisms in an organized manner, we will start by describing the reactions characterized as galvanic corrosion and then assess the effects of various metabolic reactions on these reactions. Corrosion science has developed a succinct system of quantifying various forms of corrosion, and we will use this system to quantify the effects of microbial metabolic reactions on corrosion by referring to the principles of the chemistry and electrochemistry of metals immersed in water solutions. Traditionally, the mechanisms of corrosion are quantified using thermodynamics and kinetics, and we will follow this tradition here. The corrosion reaction described by Equations 7.38 through 7.43 can be modified by the metabolic reactions in biofilms in many ways, and we will discuss four possible modifications here:

1. Biofilms consuming oxygen, the cathodic reactant.
2. Biofilm matrix increasing mass transport resistance near a metal surface.
3. Metabolic reactions in biofilms generating corrosive chemicals, such as acids.
4. Metabolic reactions in biofilms generating products that serve as cathodic reactants.

These four possible interactions do not exhaust the possible effects of microorganisms on corrosion reactions. The reason we have selected these four interactions is that they have been extensively studied, so that we know more about them than we know about other interactions. Other mechanisms are continually being proposed and studied.

7.7.1.1   Mechanisms by which metabolic reactions in biofilms can affect the processes of corrosion

7.7.1.1.1   Mechanism 1: Biofilms create oxygen heterogeneities.   At first glance, the interaction between metabolic activity in biofilms and corrosion reactions appears to be trivial: microorganisms use the cathodic reactant, oxygen, which makes it unavailable for the corrosion reactions and, as a result, the corrosion rate should decrease. Because numerous researchers have demonstrated that biofilms accelerate corrosion, this simplistic approach is obviously not valid and more complex interactions need to be taken into account. Because biofilms are not uniform and microbial activity is not uniformly distributed in biofilms, oxygen consumption rates and oxygen concentrations vary from one location to another in biofilms, which leads to more interesting interactions than the simple removal of oxygen. Areas covered with biofilm exhibit lowered oxygen concentrations and become anodic, while those with less biofilm exhibit higher oxygen concentrations and become cathodic. As a result of the nonuniform coverage of a surface by a biofilm, anodic and cathodic areas are created and fixed at different locations on the metal surface, forming what is known to corrosion scientists as differential aeration cells. Different concentrations of oxygen at different locations on a metal surface can be caused by the active consumption of oxygen by microorganisms in biofilms nonuniformly distributed on the metal surface, but they can also be caused by a passive mechanism in which access to oxygen is physically obstructed in some areas. Placing an O-ring on a metal surface is an example of such a mechanism, but other, more subtle, scenarios are possible as well. One such scenario is based on partially covering a metal surface with a material that has a nonuniformly distributed diffusivity for oxygen. Access to oxygen is more difficult at some locations on the metal surface that at other locations on the same surface, and differential aeration cells are formed.

These speculations lead to the question of whether depositing microbial extracellular polymeric substances (EPS) on a metal surface would cause the formation of differential aeration cells and to a more general question: what is the role of EPS in microbially influenced corrosion? It is well known that polysaccharides, the main constituent of EPS, can be cross-linked with metal ions. In principle, then, if EPS covers a corroding site, the metal ions can cross-link with the polysaccharides and affect the position of the equilibrium between the corroding metal and its ions, thus accelerating corrosion. This mechanism is analogous to the formation of differential aeration cells, and in corrosion science both mechanisms are called differential *concentration* cells. Thus, the differential aeration cell described in the preceding paragraph is a specific case of a differential concentration cell. Metal concentration cells do not seem to affect MIC to a large extent, but doubt remains about the passive effect of EPS, which changes the access to oxygen of the various locations on the metal surface.

To address the question posed at the end of the previous paragraph, we will first demonstrate the thermodynamic principles of corrosion by differential aeration cells and determine the variables that need to be measured to resolve whether this mechanism is active in biofilms. If the anodic reaction is the oxidation of iron, $Fe \rightarrow Fe^{2+} + 2e^-$, and the cathodic reaction is the reduction of oxygen, $O_2 + 2H_2O + 4e^- \rightarrow 4OH^-$, then the overall reaction describing the process is

$$2Fe + O_2 + 2H_2O \rightarrow 2Fe^{2+} + 4OH^- \tag{7.63}$$

The Nernst equation quantifying the potential for this reaction is

$$E = E^\circ - \frac{0.059}{4} \log \frac{[Fe^{2+}]^2[OH^-]^4}{p(O_2)} \tag{7.64}$$

If the oxygen concentrations at two adjacent locations on an iron surface are different, given the same concentration of ferrous iron and the same pH, the cell voltages at these locations are different as well. Specifically, the location where the oxygen concentration is higher will have a higher potential (more cathodic), while the location where the oxygen concentration is lower will have a lower potential (more anodic). The difference in potential will give rise to current flow from the anodic location to the cathodic location and to the establishment of a corrosion cell. This is the mechanism of differential aeration cells, and the prerequisite to this mechanism is that the concentration of oxygen vary among locations. Indeed, many measurements using oxygen microsensors have demonstrated that oxygen concentrations in biofilms can vary from one location to another and that the mechanism by which differential aeration cells are formed, in which a thin layer of biofilm on the surface of the substratum is discontinuous, is consistent with the current model of biofilm structure, shown in Figures 1.8 and 2.2.

One of the most dangerous forms of localized corrosion of mild steel is tuberculation, which is the development or formation of small mounds of corrosion products; tubercle formation originates from a differential oxygen concentration cell (Figure 7.35).

7.7.1.1.2   *Mechanism 2: Biofilm matrix increases the mass transport resistance near the metal surface, thus changing the kinetics of the corrosion processes.*   Once the mechanism of differential aeration cell formation in biofilms had been demonstrated and explained, the immediately following question could be asked: Is microbial activity in biofilms a necessary prerequisite to the formation of differential aeration cells, or, perhaps, does the presence of extracellular polymers on the surface suffice? The idea that the presence of EPS on the surface might suffice is related to the known mechanisms of corrosion initiation based on different resistances to mass transport for oxygen at different locations on metal surfaces, similar to the initial stages of crevice formation. The possibility that the active removal of oxygen by biofilm microorganisms was not necessary to the initiation of a differential aeration cell was discussed by MIC researchers, but it was usually dismissed on the grounds that extracellular polymers are composed of 98% water and their layers on metal surfaces are only a few hundred microns thick, so that the increase in diffusion resistance

(a)   (b)

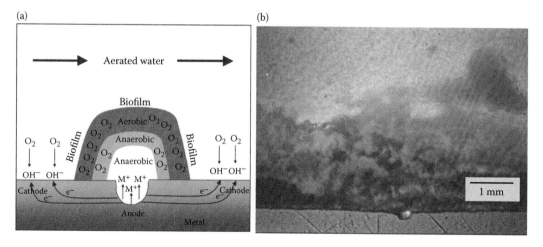

Figure 7.35 (a) Biofilm heterogeneity results in differential aeration cells. This schematic shows pit initiation due to oxygen depletion under a biofilm, following the sketch in the work of Borenstein (1994). (b) An anodic site and pit under a biofilm, and corrosion products deposited on mild steel.

resulting from the deposition of extracellular polymer could not possibly be significant. Nevertheless, the hypothesis was formulated that the deposition of extracellular polymer on a metal surface would form differential aeration cells, and an appropriate experiment was designed and executed (Roe et al. 1996). As a model of extracellular polymer, calcium alginate was used. Alginate is an extracellular biopolymer excreted by biofilm microorganisms. If alginate initiated differential aeration cells, then the oxygen concentrations at the locations covered with alginate should be higher than those at the locations not covered with alginate. Also, the pH should be higher at the locations covered with alginate than at the locations not covered with alginate. These expectations are consistent with the anodic and cathodic reactions: the anodic reaction decreases pH because ferrous ions hydrolyze and precipitate as hydroxides, and the cathodic reaction increases pH, as shown in Equation 7.54, because it consumes protons. Two drops of sodium alginate were deposited on the surface of a corrosion coupon made of mild steel and exposed to a calcium solution that cross-linked the sodium alginate and formed a calcium alginate gel on the surface. The variations in oxygen concentration and pH above these spots were measured using scanning microelectrodes. In addition, a scanning vibrating electrode was used to determine the distribution of the electrical field above the surface, and it was expected that this electrode would detect the positions of the anodic and cathodic sites. The results, shown in Figure 7.36, demonstrated that the mere deposition of a thin layer of alginate on mild steel is enough to fix anodic sites and initiate corrosion. All the characteristics of differential aeration cells were present in the system: the pH was lower near the sites that were covered with alginate than near the sites that were not covered; the oxygen concentration was lower near the sites that were not covered, and, as demonstrated by the image

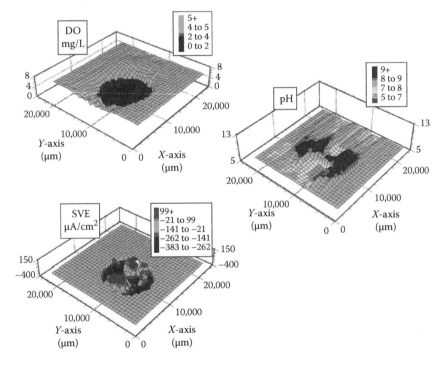

Figure 7.36 Two spots of calcium alginate deposited on a surface of mild steel fix anodic sites. (Reprinted from F. L. Roe et al., *Corrosion*, 52, 744–752, 1996.)

of the electric field distribution provided by the scanning vibrating electrode, there were anodic and cathodic sites fixed on the surface of the metal. This result, somewhat unexpected at that time, had further implications: it demonstrated that merely killing biofilm microorganisms using biocide(s) or antimicrobial(s) does not necessarily stop MIC. Once a biopolymer has been deposited on the surface, the active consumption of oxygen in the respiration reaction enhances the formation of differential aeration cells, but even without it differential aeration cells can form. This conclusion coincides with the general notion that removing the biofilm is more important than killing the biofilm microorganisms.

Once a differential aeration cell has been established, corrosion proceeds according to the mechanism described by Equation 7.63, which is also illustrated in Figure 7.35.

7.7.1.1.3 *Mechanism 3: Metabolic reactions in biofilms generate corrosive chemicals. Sulfate-reducing bacteria corrode mild steels.*
MIC due to the formation of differential aeration cells can be called a nonspecific mechanism, because it does not depend on the physiology of the microorganisms that deposited the extracellular polymers. There are, however, other mechanisms that are closely related to the type of microorganisms active in the biofilm and to their metabolic reactions. An example of such a mechanism is corrosion mediated by sulfate-reducing bacteria (SRB).

The corrosion of mild steel caused by SRB is probably the best known case of MIC because it provides a direct, easily understood link between microbial reactions and electrochemistry. Despite progress in research and in our understanding of the process, little can be done to prevent or to stop this type of corrosion once initiated, and SRB corrosion is still considered the main type of MIC.

SRB produce hydrogen sulfide by reducing sulfate ions. According to the mechanism that was proposed by Von Wohlzogen Kuhr in 1934, SRB oxidize cathodically generated hydrogen to reduce sulfate ions to H_2S, thereby removing the product of the cathodic reaction and stimulating the progress of the reaction. Over the years it became obvious that the mechanism must be more complex than that initially suggested, and it is now certain that the possible pathways for cathodic reactions are more complex and can, for example, include sulfides and bisulfides as cathodic reactants.

Hydrogen sulfide itself can be a cathodic reactant:

$$2H_2S + 2e^- \rightarrow H_2 + 2HS^- \tag{7.65}$$

Ferrous iron generated at anodic corrosion sites precipitates with the metabolic product of microbial metabolism, hydrogen sulfide, forming iron sulfides, FeS_x.

$$Fe^{2+} + HS^- \rightarrow FeS + H^+ \tag{7.66}$$

This reaction may provide protons for the cathodic reaction.

The precipitated iron sulfides form a galvanic couple with the base metal. For corrosion to occur, the iron sulfides must have electrical contact with the bare steel surface. Once contact is established, the mild steel behaves as an anode and electrons are conducted from the metal through the iron sulfide to the interface between the sulfide deposits and water, where they are used in a cathodic reaction. What exactly the cathodic reactants are is still debatable.

Surprisingly, the worst cases of SRB corrosion occur in the presence of oxygen. Because the SRBs are anaerobic microorganisms, this fact was difficult to explain. The effect is based on mechanism 3: Iron sulfides (resulting from the reaction between iron ions and sulfide and bisulfide ions) are oxidized by oxygen to elemental sulfur, a chemical known to be a strong corrosion agent (Lee et al. 1995). Biofilm heterogeneity plays an important role in this process, because the central parts of microcolonies are anaerobic while the outside edges remain aerobic. This arrangement makes this mechanism possible, because the oxidation of iron sulfides produces highly corrosive elemental sulfur, as in the following reaction:

$$2H_2O + 4FeS + 3O_2 \rightarrow 4S^o + 4FeO(OH) \tag{7.67}$$

Hydrogen sulfide can also react with the oxidized iron to form ferrous sulfide and elemental sulfur, thereby aggravating the situation by producing even more elemental sulfur and closing the loop through production of the reactant in the first reaction, FeS.

$$3H_2S + 2FeO(OH) \rightarrow 2FeS + S^o + 4H_2O \tag{7.68}$$

The product of these reactions—elemental sulfur—accelerates the corrosion rate. Schmitt (1991) has shown that the corrosion rate caused by elemental sulfur can reach several hundred milli-inches per year (mpy), and we know that elemental sulfur is indeed deposited in the biofilm during SRB corrosion (Nielsen et al. 1993). It is also well known that the sulfur disproportionation reaction that produces sulfuric acid and hydrogen sulfide is carried out by sulfur disproportionating microorganisms:

$$4S^o + 4H_2O \rightarrow 3H_2S + H_2SO_4 \tag{7.69}$$

In summary, according to this mechanism, the SRB corrosion of mild steel in the presence of oxygen is an acid corrosion:

$$\text{Anodic reaction: } Fe \rightarrow Fe^{2+} + 2e^-. \tag{7.70}$$

$$\text{Cathodic reaction: } 2H^+ + 2e^- \rightarrow H_2 \tag{7.71}$$

It is worth noting that hydrogen, the product of the cathodic reaction, can be oxidized by some species of SRB to reduce sulfate and generate hydrogen sulfide, H_2S:

$$H_2SO_4 + 4H_2 \rightarrow H_2S + 4H_2O \tag{7.72}$$

Hydrogen sulfide dissociates to bisulfides:

$$H_2S \rightleftarrows H^+ + HS^- \tag{7.73}$$

which are used in the reaction described by Equation 7.65. Thus, this mechanism involves several loops in which reactants are consumed and regenerated, and the process continues at the expense of the energy released by the oxidation of the metal.

The reactions described above are linked with each other in a network of relations. Figure 7.37 shows the main reactions and the effect of oxygen on the SRB corrosion of mild steel.

7.7.1.1.4 Mechanism 4: Metabolic reactions in biofilms generate chemicals that serve as cathodic reactants. One of the most puzzling aspects of MIC is the change in the electrochemical properties of the stainless steel that occurs as a metal surface is colonized

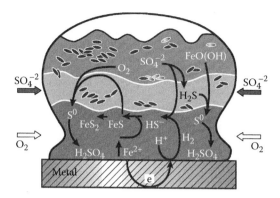

Figure 7.37 The SRB corrosion of mild steel in the presence of oxygen is an acid corrosion. (Reprinted from Z. Lewandowski et al., *Water Science and Technology*, 36, 295–302, 1997.)

by microorganisms in natural water. The dominant effects of colonization are a several-hundred-millivolt increase in the corrosion potential (E_{corr}) to values near +350 mV versus the saturated calomel electrode (SCE) and a 2-to-3-decade increase in the cathodic current density at potentials between approximately –300 and +300 mV_{SCE}. These effects, known as ennoblement, were first observed in the mid-1960s. Since then, numerous researchers have shown that stainless steels and other passive metals in natural waters exhibit a several-hundred-millivolt increase in corrosion potential accompanied by an increase in cathodic current drawn upon mild polarization. This phenomenon has been observed in a wide variety of natural and engineered environments—in seawater, in a freshwater stream, and in a hydroelectric power plant (Linhardt 1996).

The ennoblement of stainless steels in natural waters may influence material integrity: as the corrosion potential approaches the pitting potential, the material integrity may be compromised by localized (pitting and crevice) corrosion. This sequence of events, from an increase in corrosion potential to pit initiation, is well known to material scientists, although the microbial component is new. Because the pitting potential of 316L stainless steel in seawater is around 200 mV_{SCE}, the danger of pitting initiation in such an environment is serious. There is, however, evidence of microbial involvement in the pitting corrosion of stainless steels immersed in fresh waters with much lower chloride concentrations than that found in seawater.

Temporal changes in the corrosion potential of 316L stainless steel coupons immersed in different natural water sources are illustrated by our results in Figure 7.38. In all cases the potentials of 316L stainless steel coupons increased, demonstrating ennoblement of the stainless steel. Several hypotheses have been postulated to explain the mechanism of ennoblement, all suggesting that it is caused by microbial colonization of the metal surface. Ennoblement has been attributed to such diverse factors as the presence of extracellular polymeric substances, increased potentials due to acidification of the metal–biofilm interface caused by protons derived from the metabolic reactions in the biofilm, a combination of acidification and hydrogen peroxide production, and microbially produced passivating siderophores. Although many authors have demonstrated the relationship between ennoblement and biofilm formation, the proposed hypotheses have not been supported by convincing experimental evidence unequivocally demonstrating the mechanism of ennoblement.

We have demonstrated, in the laboratory and in the field, that stainless steels and other passive metals are ennobled when colonized by manganese-oxidizing bacteria

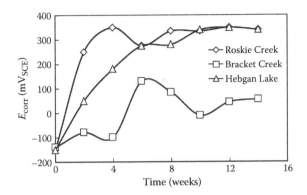

Figure 7.38 Potential of 316L stainless steel coupons exposed to fresh water at three locations in Montana for 4 months. The rate and extent of ennoblement roughly correlated with the amount of biomineralized manganese recovered from the surface after four months (Table 7.1). (Reprinted from K. R. Braughton et al., *Biofouling*, 17, 241–251, 2001. With permission.)

(MOB). While the origin of the manganese-rich material deposited on stainless steel coupons exposed to Bozeman stream water was not rigorously established, mineral-encrusted bacterial sheaths characteristic of *Leptothrix* sp. and mineralized capsules characteristic of *Siderocapsa treubii* were abundant on the surface of the ennobled stainless steel coupons, and manganese-oxidizing bacteria were isolated from the manganese-rich deposits. In parallel with these findings, Linhardt (1996) also demonstrated that manganese-oxidizing biofilms were responsible for pitting corrosion of stainless steel. Although the biomineralization of manganese can be carried out by certain genera of the so-called iron and manganese group—*Siderocapsa, Leptothrix,* and *Crenothrix*—in fact, the property is widely distributed in a variety of organisms including bacteria, yeast, and fungi. These organisms can oxidize dissolved manganese to form highly enriched mineral-biopolymer encrustations. Deposits of manganese oxides form on submerged materials including metal, stone, glass, and plastic and can occur in natural waters and sediments with manganese levels as low as 10–20 ppb.

Because biomineralized manganese oxides are in direct electrical contact with the metal, the metal exhibits the equilibrium dissolution potential of the oxides. The standard potentials ($E°$) for Equations 7.74 through 7.76 were calculated using the following energies of formation from thermodynamic data reported by Stumm and Morgan (1970): $\Delta G_f^\circ Mn^{2+} = -54.5$ kcal/mol, $\Delta G_f^\circ \gamma\text{-}MnOOH = -133.3$ kcal/mol, $\Delta G_f^\circ \gamma\text{-}MnO_2 = -109.1$ kcal/mol, and water $\Delta G_f^\circ H_2O = -56.69$ kcal/mole.

$$MnO_{2(s)} + H^+ + e^- \rightarrow MnOOH_{(s)} \quad E° = +0.81\ V_{SCE} E'_{pH=7.2} = +0.385\ V_{SCE} \tag{7.74}$$

$$MnOOH_{(s)} + 3H^+ + e^- \rightarrow Mn^{2+} + 2H_2O \quad E° = +1.26\ V_{SCE} E'_{pH=7.2} = +0.336\ V_{SCE} \tag{7.75}$$

This leads to the overall reaction:

$$MnO_{2(s)} + 4H^+ + 2e^- \rightarrow Mn^{2+} + 2H_2O \quad E° = +1.039\ V_{SCE} E'_{pH=7.2} = +0.366\ V_{SCE} \tag{7.76}$$

Because this is a newly proposed mechanism, we report the relevant thermodynamic calculations below. The potentials (E') were calculated at a pH of 7.2 and $[Mn^{2+}] = 10^{-6}$ using the constants with the units corrected to make them agree with the unit reported in the source, kcal/mol.

$$E^\circ = -\Delta G_r^\circ / nF$$

where

$F = 96.42$ kJ V^{-1} mol^{-1}; $F = 23.04$ kcal V^{-1} mol^{-1}

1 cal = 4.184 J; 1 kcal = 4.184 kJ; 1 kJ = 0.239 kcal

For the reaction $MnO_{2(s)} + H^+ + e^- \rightarrow MnOOH_{(s)}$,

$$\Delta G_f^\circ \gamma\text{-}MnO_2 = -109.1 \text{ kcal/mol}$$

$$\Delta G_f^\circ \gamma\text{-}MnOOH = -133.3 \text{ kcal/mol}$$

$$G_r^\circ = 133.3 - (-109.1) = -24.2 \text{ kcal/mol}$$

$$E^\circ = -(-24.2)/23.04 = 1.05 \text{ V}_{SHE}$$

$$E^\circ = 0.241 \text{ V}_{SHE}$$

$$E^\circ = 1.05 - 0.241 = 0.81 \text{ V}_{SCE}$$

Potential corrected for pH = 7.2 using the Nernst equation

$$E' = E^\circ - 1/(H^+)^{-7.2} = 0.81 - 0.059 \log [1/(10)^{7.2}] = 0.385 \text{ V}_{SCE}$$

For the reaction $MnOOH_{(s)} + 3H^+ + e^- \rightarrow Mn^{2+} + 2H_2O$,

$$\Delta G_f^\circ Mn^{2+} = -54.5 \text{ kcal/mol}$$

$$\Delta G_f^\circ \gamma\text{-}MnOOH = -133.3 \text{ kcal/mol}$$

$$\Delta G_f^\circ H_2O = -56.69 \text{ kcal/mol}$$

$$\Delta G_r^\circ = -54.5 - (2 \times 56.69) - (-133.3) = -34.58 \text{ kcal/mol}$$

$$E^\circ = 34.58/23.04 = 1.5 \text{ V}_{SHE}$$

$$E^\circ = 0.241 \text{ V}_{SHE}$$

$$E^\circ = 1.5 - 0.241 = 1.26 \text{ V}_{SCE}$$

Potential corrected for pH = 7.2 using the Nernst equation:

$$E' = E^\circ - 0.059 \log ([Mn^{2+}]/[H^+]^3) = 1.26 - 0.059 \log (10^{-6}/(10^{-7.2})^3) = 0.34 \text{ V}_{SCE}$$

For the reaction $MnO_{2(s)} + 4H^+ + 2e^- \rightarrow Mn^{2+} + 2H_2O$,

$$\Delta G_f^\circ H_2O = -56.69 \text{ kcal/mol}$$

$$\Delta G_f^\circ Mn^{2+} = -54.5 \text{ kcal/mol}$$

$$\Delta G_f^\circ \gamma\text{-}MnO_2 = -109.1 \text{ kcal/mol}$$

$$\Delta G_r^\circ = -54.5 - (2 \times 56.69) - (-109.1) = -58.78 \text{ kcal/mol}$$

$$E^\circ = 58.78/(2 \times 23.04) = 1.28 \text{ V}_{SHE}$$

$$E^\circ = 0.241 \text{ V}_{SHE}$$

$$E^\circ = 1.28 - 0.241 = 1.039 \text{ V}_{SCE}$$

Potential corrected for pH = 7.2 using the Nernst equation:

$$E' = E^\circ - 0.059/n \log([Mn^{2+}]/[H^+]^4) = 1.039 - 0.059/2 \log (10^{-6}/(10^{-7.2})^4) = 0.366 \text{ V}_{SCE}$$

These thermodynamic calculations are in good agreement with the observations, as the potential of the stainless steel coupons exposed to river water rose to about 360 mV, as predicted. Our results directly correlate the extent and rate of ennoblement with the amount and rate of manganese oxide deposition on metal surfaces. To determine which environmental factors influence the rate of ennoblement, we exposed 316L stainless steel coupons at three locations, two creeks and a lake, for 100 days. The OCV was monitored periodically, about once a week (Figure 7.38). The coupons in both creeks reached a potential of +350 mV_{SCE} in three weeks. The coupons in the lake reached a final potential of less than +100 mV_{SCE}, and their ennoblement rate was very slow. Manganese oxides were deposited on all metal coupons, and the amounts roughly correlated with the rate of ennoblement, as can be seen in Table 7.1.

The results in Figure 7.38 show that the corrosion coupons were ennobled at a rate correlated with the amount of manganese oxides covering the surface. This observation coincides with our previous observations. In the authors' laboratory, Dickinson et al. (1996,

Table 7.1 Amounts of Biomineralized Manganese Recovered from the Surfaces after Four Months

Source	Bracket creek	Roskie creek	Hebgen lake
Mn recovered (µg/cm²)	9.3	33.6	1.7

1996b) demonstrated that a surface coverage of 3%–5% by biofouling deposits was enough to ennoble 316L stainless steel and that a surface coverage of just 6% by manganese oxides could increase the resting open circuit voltage (OCV) of stainless steels (-200 mV$_{SCE}$) by some 500 mV, which coincides closely with the reported equilibrium potential of the oxides, $+362$ mV$_{SCE}$ at a pH of 7.2. As the potential of the stainless steel increases, it may eventually approach the pitting potential, which would endanger material integrity. Depositing manganese oxides on stainless steels increases their potential to alarming levels, as can be demonstrated by comparing the potentials of the coupons in Figure 7.39 with the pitting potentials of various stainless steels in 3% NaCl shown in Figure 7.40.

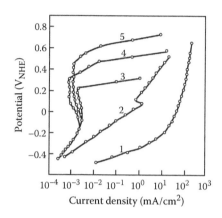

Figure 7.39 Pitting potentials of various metals in 3% NaCl: (1) mild steel, (2) nickel, (3) 430 SS, (4) 304 SS, and (5) 316 SS. The pitting potential of 304 SS, for example, which is a very popular alloy, is about 0.350 mV, dangerously close to the potentials of the corrosion coupons in Figure 7.39. For the meaning of pitting potential, inspect Figure 7.17. The data were taken at 50 mV/3 min at 30°C. (Modified from Z. Szklarska-Smialowska, *Corrosion*, 27(6), 223, 1971.)

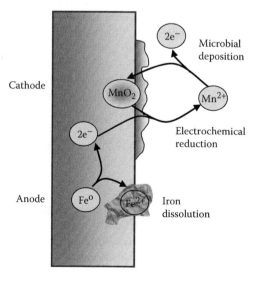

Figure 7.40 **(See color insert.)** Redox cycling on metal surfaces: hypothetical mechanism of microbial involvement in the corrosion of stainless steels and other passive metals.

Thermodynamic calculations demonstrated that the ennoblement of stainless steel was consistent with the deposition of biomineralized manganese oxides. Separate work focused on the microbial and chemical composition of the deposits was conducted to reveal the mechanism of pitting corrosion due to the deposition of biomineralized manganese oxides. Chemical examination of the deposits showed the presence of Fe(III) and Mn(IV), and epifluorescence microscopy revealed the presence of manganese- and iron-oxidizing bacteria. On the basis of these observations and other studies conducted in our laboratory, we suggest that MOB are involved in the corrosion of stainless steels through the following mechanism: the divalent manganese (Mn^{2+}) ions are microbially oxidized to manganese oxyhydroxide, MnOOH, which is deposited on the metal surface; then the solid MnOOH is further oxidized to manganese dioxide, MnO_2. Both reactions contribute to the increase in the OCV because the deposited oxides, MnOOH and MnO_2, are in electrical contact with the surface, and their dissolution potential is determined by the equilibrium of the deposited minerals with the dissolved divalent manganese. The oxides deposited on the surface are reduced to divalent manganese by electrons generated at anodic sites. However, the reduction of the manganese oxides does not stop the ennoblement process, because the reduced products of this reaction, soluble divalent manganese ions, are reoxidized by the MOB attached to the metal surface. The described sequence of events, oxidation–reduction–oxidation of manganese, is a hypothetical mechanism that produces renewable cathodic reactants, manganese oxyhydroxide and manganese dioxide, and their presence on the metal surface endangers material integrity. This mechanism is illustrated in Figure 7.40.

The suggested mechanism relies on the activity of manganese-oxidizing bacteria in biofilms deposited on metal surfaces. The biomineralization of manganese can be carried out by a variety of organisms including bacteria, yeast, and fungi, but it is particularly associated with genera of the so-called iron and manganese group—*Siderocapsa*, *Gallionella*, *Leptothrix-Sphaerotilus*, *Crenothrix*, and *Clonothrix*. These bacteria accelerate the oxidation of dissolved iron and manganese to form highly enriched mineral-biopolymer encrustations. Biomineralized manganese oxides are efficient cathodes and increase cathodic current density on stainless steel by a few decades at potentials between roughly –200 and +400 mV_{SCE}. The extent to which the elevated current density can be maintained is controlled by the electrical capacity of the mineral, which reflects both total accumulation and the conductivity of the mineral-biopolymer assemblage (only material in electrical contact with the metal will be cathodically active). Oxide accumulation is controlled by the biomineralization rate and by the corrosion current, as high corrosion currents will discharge oxide as rapidly as it is formed. It appears that this mechanism may result in the redox cycling of manganese on metal surfaces producing a renewable cathodic reactant, which agrees well with the notion that whenever biofilms accumulate on cathodic members of galvanic couples, a significant increase in the reduction current can be expected. In conclusion, the accumulation of manganese oxides can cause pitting corrosion, as demonstrated in Figure 7.41.

7.7.1.2   *Further implications*

The mechanism by which manganese-oxidizing microorganisms increase the potential of stainless steels can be called an indirect involvement of MOBs in pit formation. The result of their action still depends on the actual pitting potential of the stainless steel in water of a given chemical composition. Our observations also suggest that MOB may be directly involved in pit initiation, in addition to the indirect effects caused by biomineralized manganese oxides. Scanning electron microscopy and atomic force microscopy images given in Chapter 2 (Figure 2.18) show micropits formed on 316L stainless steel

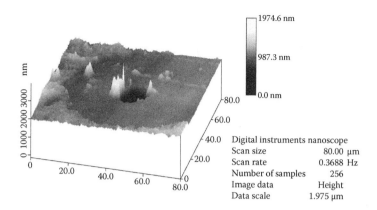

Digital instruments nanoscope
Scan size 80.00 µm
Scan rate 0.3688 Hz
Number of samples 256
Image data Height
Data scale 1.975 µm

Figure 7.41 Corrosion pit on a SS surface covered with biomineralized manganese oxides and immersed in a 3.5% solution of NaCl.

ennobled by *L. discophora* SP-6. This indicates that the pits were initiated at the sites of bacterial attachment and then propagated because of the presence of manganese oxides driving the potential in the noble direction.

Our data show that the manganese oxides deposited on the surface elevate the potential, creating an environment where the pits initiated by microbes cannot repassivate. In light of the pits being initiated at the sites of attachment, it appears that the bacteria initiate the pits and the microbially deposited manganese oxides stabilize the growth of the pits by maintaining a high potential.

In conclusion, biofilms can influence the corrosion of metals (1) by consuming oxygen, the cathodic reactant; (2) by increasing the mass transport of the corrosion reactants and products, and thus changing the kinetics of the corrosion process; (3) by generating corrosive chemicals; and (4) by generating chemicals that serve as auxiliary cathodic reactants. These interactions do not exhaust the possible mechanisms by which biofilm microorganisms may affect the corrosion of metals; rather, they represent those few instances in which we understand the microbial reactions and their effect on the electrochemical reactions characteristic of corrosion. In addition, we can use electrochemical and chemical measurements to detect one or more products of these reactions. An important aspect of quantifying mechanisms of microbially influenced corrosion is demonstrating how microbial reactions exacerbate corrosion processes and, based on this, identifying products of these reactions on surfaces of corroding metals using appropriate analytical techniques. The existence of these products, associated with an increasing corrosion rate, is evidence that the specific mechanism of microbially influenced corrosion is active.

Some mechanisms of MIC other than those described in this chapter involve bacteria that produce corrosive metabolites. For example, *Thiobacillus thiooxidans* produces sulfuric acid and *Clostridium aceticum* produces acetic acid. These two metabolic products dissolve the passive layers of oxides deposited on a metal surface, which accelerates the cathodic reaction rate. Yet other mechanisms may be initiated by hydrogen-generating microorganisms causing hydrogen embrittlement of metals or by iron-oxidizing bacteria, such as *Gallionella*. As indicated above, an important aspect of quantifying these mechanisms is demonstrating how they exacerbate the corrosion processes. There is no universal mechanism of MIC. Instead, many mechanisms exist, and some of them have been described and quantified better than others.

It does not seem reasonable to search for universal mechanisms, but it does seem reasonable to search for evidence of specific, well-defined microbial involvement in corrosion processes. For example, demonstrating the presence of elemental sulfur in the corrosion of mild steel can be considered evidence of SRB corrosion, and demonstrating the presence of manganese oxides in the corrosion of stainless steel can be considered evidence of MOB corrosion. However, even in these examples, there is a possibility that some aspects of microbial participation escape our attention. The deposition of manganese oxides is easy to demonstrate on stainless steels or other passive metals because they are stable on such surfaces. However, if manganese-oxidizing bacteria deposit manganese oxides on mild steel on which oxides are reduced at the same rate as they are deposited, the corrosion rate may increase without evidence of microbial participation in the process, deposits of manganese oxides, being detectable.

7.7.2   Microbial fuel cells

Microbial metabolism, by which a microbial cell gains energy from oxidizing a substrate, takes place in several different modes. For the sake of simplicity, we will consider two modes that are important in microbial fuel cells: fermentation and respiration. Fermentation takes place in the absence of oxygen or other terminal electron acceptors, and it involves mainly redox reactions in which the total (additive) energy of the reactants and products remains nearly unchanged from the energy of the substrate; an example is the fermentation of glucose to acetate and ethanol. Fermentation is an inefficient mechanism for gaining energy, and thus it generally takes place only when respirable electron acceptors are unavailable. Fermentation does not require an electron acceptor, just an electron donor (e.g., glucose). Respiration further processes fermentation products by partially or completely oxidizing them by harvesting electrons contained in chemical bonds and depositing them on an electron acceptor. Respiration usually takes place in a series of reactions called the electron transport chain. During respiration, protons and electrons are liberated from the electron donor, and the transfer of the electrons through the electron transport chain, from regions of lower to higher redox potential, causes the protons to be pumped out of the cell. This creates a potential difference across the cell membrane, which the cell can convert to chemical energy via the production of ATP as the potential difference dissipates. Several different chemicals can act as electron acceptors for different forms of respiration; some recapture the protons in chemical bonds (fumarate or oxygen), and some do not consume the protons at all (Fe(III)). It is important to consider both fermentation and respiration when discussing microbial fuel cells.

Substrates such as glucose can be fermented by planktonic microorganisms in solution whenever it is present, but respiration can only take place in the presence of an electron acceptor. In a chamber with microorganisms, a substrate like glucose, and no oxygen or other chemical electron acceptors, one might assume that only fermentation would take place. However, it just so happens that there are several species of microorganism that can use a solid-phase electrode as a terminal electron acceptor or, rather, use the electrode as part of their electron transport chain.

In a MFC, electron donors and electron acceptors are in different compartments, separated by an ion exchange membrane. Microorganisms capable of using a solid-phase electrode for respiration can transfer the electrons from the fermentation products generated by the fermenters to the electron acceptor in the other chamber through an electrical circuit. When the electrons are transferred through the electronic circuit, the difference in energy between the electrons that leave the cells to go through the circuit, and the energy of the electrons trapped in the chemical bonds of the terminal electron acceptor, can be harvested and subsequently used for other purposes unrelated to microbial respiration. In principle, such a device may serve as a power supply. The path of the electrons from the electron donor through the electron transport chain and through the electrical circuit to the electron acceptor is shown in Figure 7.42. It is important to note that fermentation can take place anywhere in the chamber, but respiration using an electrode must take place at or very near the electrode surface, so the microorganisms capable of this type of respiration form biofilms at the electrode surface. The fermenters and respirers form a symbiotic relationship in which the respirers remove the fermentation products so the fermenters are not feedback inhibited, and the fermenters provide electron donors that can be easily oxidized by the respirers. Because of this symbiotic relationship, biofilms in MFCs are composed of several different species in amounts that maximize the use of the available energy source.

Figure 7.43 shows an example of a MFC in which acetate is oxidized and oxygen is reduced in separate compartments. The redox reactions occurring in the two compartments are as follows.

The oxidation of acetate:

$$CH_3COO^- + 3H_2O \rightarrow CO_2 + HCO_3^- + 8H^+ + 8e^- \tag{7.77}$$

The reduction of oxygen:

$$6O_2 + 24H^+ + 24e^- \rightarrow 12H_2O \tag{7.78}$$

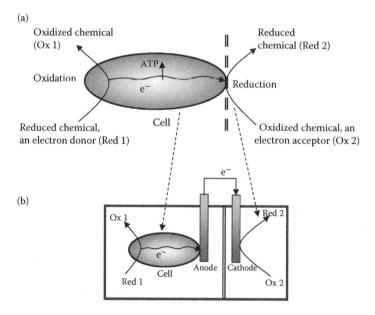

Figure 7.42 (a) Microbial respiration involves two external redox reactions, one in which an electron donor is oxidized and one in which an electron acceptor is reduced. The two chemical reactants are dissolved in the same solution. (b) In a MFC, these two reactions occur in separate compartments connected by an electronic circuit.

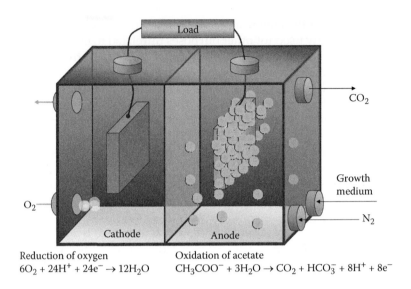

Reduction of oxygen   Oxidation of acetate
$6O_2 + 24H^+ + 24e^- \rightarrow 12H_2O$ $CH_3COO^- + 3H_2O \rightarrow CO_2 + HCO_3^- + 8H^+ + 8e^-$

Figure 7.43 **(See color insert.)** MFC based on oxidizing acetate and reducing oxygen.

The compartments are separated by a membrane, typically a proton exchange membrane, which allows protons to be transferred between the compartments to equilibrate the electrical potential of the solution (Figure 7.43).

By convention, the electrode that accepts electrons from the biofilm is termed the "anode" and the electrode in the opposite compartment, which donates the same electrons to an electron acceptor, is termed the "cathode." The solutions in the two compartments are termed the "anolyte" and the "catholyte." While the mechanism of electron transfer between dissolved chemical reactants and microorganisms is well known and described in textbooks, it is not yet entirely clear how electrons are transferred between microorganisms and solid electrodes. There is good evidence to suggest that some microorganisms transfer electrons directly to an electrode through immobile redox centers or through "nanowires," that some use an excreted mediator compound to transfer electrons, and that some use a combination of both of these approaches. To investigate electron transfer mechanisms, electrochemical techniques can be applied. However, in order to interpret the results of these techniques properly, it is important to understand the kinetics of mass transfer and the reaction taking place at every juncture in the system. Depending on the configuration of an MFC, a number of different processes might limit the amount of current that can pass through the circuit. These include the substrate concentration (mass transfer of substrate into the biofilm cells), the amount of cells on the electrode, the available surface area on the electrode, the cellular metabolic rate, the transfer of protons out of the anode biofilm, the pH of the anolyte, the distance of travel for the protons, the load, the membrane surface area, the cathode surface area, the cathode material, the mass transfer of the cathode reactants to the cathode (protons, oxygen), the pH of the catholyte, and, last, the internal resistance of the solution, which is related to the conductivity and thus the ionic strength of the anolyte and the catholyte. Electrode reactions in an electrochemical system are controlled either by reaction kinetics or by the diffusion of reactants or products. Studying the electron transfer reactions of a biofilm electrode under both conditions helps to uncover information about the reactions taking place. For this reason, studies of electron transfer in biofilms are generally carried out in systems without a membrane and with the anode and cathode placed very close together, so that electrochemical limitations are minimized.

Example 7.5: Calculating the number of electrons available for transfer from the organic compound to the electron acceptor

The number of electrons that are available from oxidizing an organic compound is calculated using the concept of degrees of reduction (Shuler and Kargi 2002). The degree of reduction of an organic compound (say glucose) is defined as the number of available electrons per gram-atom of C. The total number of electrons available from the molecule is calculated by multiplying the degree of reduction by the number of gram-atoms of carbon in the compound. For example, the reduction number of glucose ($C_6H_{12}O_6$) can be calculated as

$$\gamma = \frac{6 \times 4 + 12 \times 1 + 6 \times (-2)}{6} = 4$$

where the oxidation number of C is 4, that of H is 1, and that of O is –2. The number of gram-atoms of carbon in one mole of glucose is 6. Thus, the total number of electrons available is $6 \times 4 = 24$ moles of electrons per mole of glucose.

For lactic acid ($C_3H_{12}O_6$), the reduction number is again 4:

$$\gamma = \frac{3 \times 4 + 6 \times 1 + 3 \times (-2)}{3} = 4$$

and the number of gram-atoms in the lactate is 3. Therefore, the total number of electrons available from lactic acid is $4 \times 3 = 12$ moles of electrons per mole of lactic acid.

Example 7.6: Bench-scale microbial fuel cells

There are multiple variations of MFCs described in the literature. We will focus here on the design that we studied intensively in our laboratory, MFCs that use manganese oxides as cathodic reactants according to the mechanism of stainless steel ennoblement described in this chapter, as mechanism 4 in the section dedicated to MIC. Using biomineralized manganese oxides instead of oxygen as the terminal electron acceptor offers advantages. One advantage is that solid-state manganese oxides do not change their activity as the reaction progresses: as long as they are present at the surface, their chemical activity is close to one. Another is that, because the manganese oxides are deposited on the surface of the metal, their use is not subject to mass transport limitations as that of any other dissolved cathodic reactant would be. Also, manganese oxides are recyclable cathodic reactants. If oxygen is used as the cathodic reactant, then in the cathodic process it is reduced to water and removed from the environment. When manganese oxides are reduced to the divalent manganese ions, $MnO_{2(s)} + 4H^+ + 2e^- \rightarrow Mn^{2+} + 2H_2O$, the manganese ions are released near the metal surface, within the biofilm composed of MOB, which can reoxidize the manganese ions back to manganese oxides. Ultimately, the presence of oxygen is needed to complete this cycle. However, manganese oxides are deposited on surfaces as a result of the metabolic activity of the manganese oxidizers whether the cathodic reaction in the MFC is active or not, which cannot be done with oxygen. Figure 7.44 shows this mechanism of recycling the manganese oxides on the surface of the metal.

We tested the possibility of using biomineralized manganese oxides as cathodic reactants in MFCs using the simple laboratory setup summarized in Figure 7.45. In the

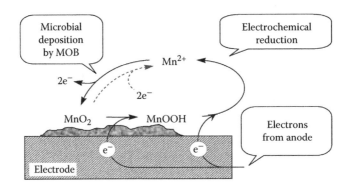

Figure 7.44 Diagram of manganese deposition and reoxidation used as the cathodic reaction.

anodic compartment we used the anaerobic respiration of glucose by *Klebsiella pneumoniae*. To facilitate electron transfer between the microorganisms and the graphite electrode, we used 2-hydroxy-1,4-naphthoquinone (HNQ), following literature findings which suggest that it (1) has a high columbic output and (2) is chemically more stable than other redox mediators. In the cathodic compartment, we used *Lepthothrix discophora* SP-6 and an aerated solution of Mn^{2+}. As a result, *L. discophora* SP-6 grew and deposited MnO_2 on the electrode surface.

To elucidate the differences between manganese oxides and oxygen when used as cathodic reactants, we ran another test using the same arrangement of the anodic compartment as that shown in Figure 7.45 but using oxygen instead of manganese oxides in the cathodic compartment. Figure 7.46 shows the results of those tests. When oxygen was the cathodic reactant the equilibrium potential of the graphite electrodes was

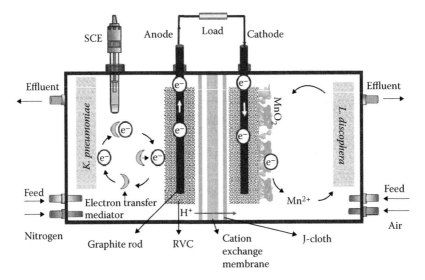

Figure 7.45 **(See color insert.)** Schematic of designed MFC. Glucose was oxidized in the anodic compartment, and the electrons were transferred via an electronic conductor to the cathodic compartment, where they reduced microbially deposited manganese oxides. In the anodic compartment we used a redox mediator, HNQ, to facilitate the electron transfer from the glucose to the graphite electrode. In the cathodic compartment, manganese oxides were deposited on the graphite electrode and reduced directly, without any redox mediator, by the electrons derived from the anodic reaction. (Reprinted from A. Rhoads et al., *Environmental Science and Technology*, 39, 4666–4671, 2005.)

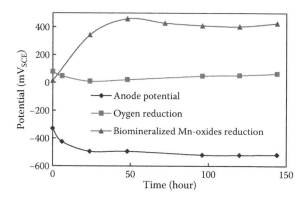

Figure 7.46 Cathode and anode potential variation over time when oxygen or biomineralized manganese was the cathodic reactant. (Reprinted from A. Rhoads et al., *Environmental Science and Technology*, 39, 4666–4671, 2005.)

50.6 ± 30 mV, and when biomineralized manganese oxides were used as the cathodic reactants, the equilibrium potential increased to 382 ± 58 mV$_{SCE}$. Thus, biomineralized manganese oxides increase the cell potential by approximately 300 mV, as compared to the equilibrium potential reached in the presence of oxygen. The power generated was 0.459 ± 0.10 mW when oxygen was used as the cathodic reactant and 17.10 ± 4.25 mW when manganese oxides were used. Thus, the biomineralized manganese increased the power generated by the fuel cell by two orders of magnitude.

To test the reproducibility of our results, we constructed and operated several microbial fuel cells using *Klebsiella pneumoniae* oxidizing glucose in the anodic compartment and *Leptothrix discophora* depositing biomineralized manganese oxides in the cathodic compartment. An example of the results of these tests is shown in Figure 7.46. The fuel cells were operated for up to 500 hours, and they reached an average anodic potential of −441.5 ± 31 mV$_{SCE}$ and an average cathodic potential of +384.5 ± 64 mV$_{SCE}$. The peak power produced by the fuel cells was 17.10 ± 4.25 mW when a 510-Ω resistor was used. We conclude that microbially deposited manganese oxides are more effective as cathodic reactants in microbial fuel cells than oxygen is. The results of these tests were encouraging enough to prompt the design and operation of field-scale MFCs. In conclusion, microbial fuel cells are a promising technology and have been implemented at a scale larger than laboratory scale, as described in the section dedicated to biofilm technologies in Section 1.5.2.

Nomenclature

Subscripts

a   Anodic
c   Cathodic

Roman Symbols

Symbol	Meaning	Usual units
ΔE	Electric potential difference or potential difference between the electrode and the solution or nonequilibrium potential	V
ΔE_{eq}	Equilibrium potential	V
ΔG	Gibbs free energy change in a chemical process	kJ, kJ/mol
ΔG_a	Anodic activation energy barrier	kJ, kJ/mol
ΔG_c	Catodic activation energy barrier	kJ, kJ/mol

$\Delta G_{\text{activation}}$	Activation energy	
ΔG_e	Overall energy barrier	kJ, kJ/mol
ΔG°	Standard Gibbs free energy change in a chemical process	kJ, kJ/mol
ΔG_{Ta}	Sum of energies contributing to the energy barrier for the anodic reaction	kJ, kJ/mol
ΔG_{Tc}	Sum of energies contributing to the energy barrier for the cathodic reaction	kJ, kJ/mol
ΔG_r^o	Standard Gibbs free energy change for a reaction	kJ, kJ/mol
ΔG_c	Cathodic activation energy barrier	kJ, kJ/mol
$E_X^{0\prime}$	Standard reduction potential of the redox couple	V
[ox]	Concentration of oxidant	Mol/m³
[red]	Concentration of reductant	Mol/m³
A	Surface area	m², cm²
A'	Arrhenius frequency factor	s⁻¹, min⁻¹
C	Concentration of electroactive chemical reactant	mM or Mol/m³
E	Potential of an electrode against a reference	V
E_{KA}	Potential at which the current is half the limiting current	V
E°	Standard potential of an electrode or standard emf of a half reaction	V
$E_{S/P}$	Thermodynamic electrode potential	V
f	Grouped term of the Faraday constant, divided by the temperature, and the universal gas constant	F (s A/mol), T (K), R (J/K mol), nF/RT (1/V)
F	Faraday constant: charge of one mole of electrons	C
G	Gibbs free energy	kJ, kJ/mol
i	Current density	A/m², A/cm²
I	Current or current passing between two electrodes	A
i_a	Anodic current density	A/m², A/cm²
i_c	Cathodic current density	A/m², A/cm²
i_{corr}	Corrosion current	A
I_{lim}	Limiting current	A
i_o	Exchange current density	A/m², A/cm²
k	Mass transport coefficient or reaction rate constant	m/s or s⁻¹
k^0	Standard heterogeneous rate constant	m/s
K_1	Ratio of the rate of biochemical substrate utilization to the rate of electrochemical exchange current density	unitless
K_2	Ratio of the rate of product formation to the rate of substrate formation inside the microorganism	unitless
k_a	Reaction rate constant for the anodic reaction	s⁻¹
k_c	Reaction rate constant for the cathodic reaction	s⁻¹
K_M	Substrate affinity constant	mM
K_S	Monod half saturation constant for the electron-donating substrate	mM
L	Thickness of the double layer	m
l^*	Distance between the beginning of the double layer and the location of maximum free energy	m
n	Stoichiometric number of electrons involved in oxidation/ reduction reactions	

P	Power	W
R	Ideal gas constant or resistance	8.31446 J K^{-1} mol^{-1} or ohm
r_a	Anodic reaction rate	mol/s
r_c	Cathodic reaction rate	mol/s
R_p	Polarization resistance	Ohm
T	Absolute temperature	K
t	Time	s
V	Cell potential	V
x	Distance from the electrode surface	m
X_{ox}	Concentration of the oxidized form of the redox couple at the biofilm electrode surface	mM
X_{red}	Concentration of the reduced form of the redox couple at the biofilm electrode surface	mM

Greek Symbols

Symbol	Meaning
η	Overpotential of the electrode
η_{total}	Total overpotential
α	Symmetry coefficient
η_a	Activation overpotential
η_c	Concentration overpotential
γ	Degree of reduction

References

Bard, A. J. F., and Faulkner, L. R. 2001. *Electrochemical Methods: Fundamentals and Applications.* New York: John Wiley.

Bockris, J. O., and Reddy, A. K. N. 2000. *Modern Electrochemistry.* New York: Kluwer Academic.

Borenstein, S. B. 1994. Microbiologically Influenced Corrosion Handbook. Industrial Press Inc., New York.

Braughton, K. R., Lafond, R. L., and Lewandowski, Z. 2001. The influence of environmental factors on the rate and extent of stainless steel ennoblement mediated by manganese-oxidizing biofilms. *Biofouling* 17: 241–251.

Dickinson, W. H., Caccavo, F., and Lewandowski, Z. 1996a. The ennoblement of stainless steel by manganic oxide biofouling. *Corrosion Science* 38: 1407–1422.

Dickinson, W. H., Lewandowski, Z., and Geer, R. D. 1996b. Evidence for surface changes during ennoblement of type 316L stainless steel: Dissolved oxidant and capacitance measurements. *Corrosion* 52: 910–920.

Dickinson, W. H., Caccavo, F., Olesen, B., and Lewandowski, Z. 1997. Ennoblement of stainless steel by the manganese-depositing bacterium Leptothrix discophora. *Applied and Environmental Microbiology* 63: 2502–2506.

Geiser, M., Avci, R., and Lewandowski, Z. 2002. Microbially initiated pitting on 316L stainless steel. *International Biodeterioration and Biodegradation* 49: 235–243.

Hamelers, H. V. M., ter Heijne, A., Stein, N., Rozendal, R. A., and Buisman, C. J. N. 2011. Butler–Volmer–Monod model for describing bio-anode polarization curves. *Bioresource Technology* 102: 381–387.

Lee, W., Lewandowski, Z., Nielsen, P. H., and Hamilton, W. A. 1995. Role of sulfate-reducing bacteria in corrosion of mild-steel—A review. *Biofouling* 8: 165.

Lewandowski, Z., Dickinson, W., and Lee, W. 1997. Electrochemical interactions of biofilms with metal surfaces. *Water Science and Technology* 36: 295–302.

Linhardt, P. 1996. Failure of chromium-nickel steel in a hydroelectric power plant by manganese-oxidizing bacteria. In *Microbially Influenced Corrosion of Materials*. E. Heitz, H. C. Flemming, and W. Sand (Eds.). Springer, Berlin, pp. 221–230.

Nealson, K. H., and Finkel, S. E. 2011. Electron flow and biofilms. *MRS Bulletin* 36: 380–384.

Newman, D. K. 2001. Microbiology—How bacteria respire minerals. *Science* 292: 1312–1313.

Nielsen, P., Lee, W. C., Morrison, M., and Characklis, W. G. 1993. Corrosion of mild steel in an alternating oxic and anoxic biofilm system. *Biofouling* 7: 267–284.

Roe, F. L., Lewandowski, Z., and Funk, T. 1996. Simulating microbiologically influenced corrosion by depositing extracellular biopolymers on mild steel surfaces. *Corrosion* 52: 744–752.

Schmitt, G. 1991. Effect of elemental sulfur on corrosion in sour gas systems. *Corrosion* 47: 285–308.

Sedriks, J. 1996. *Corrosion of Stainless Steels*. 2nd ed. Copyright Wiley-VCH, Verlag GmbH & Co. KGaA.

Shuler, M. L., and Kargi, F. 2002. *Bioprocess Engineering: Basic Concepts*. Upper Saddle River, NJ: Prentice Hall.

Stumm, W., and Morgan, J. J. 1970. *Aquatic Chemistry: An Introduction Emphasizing Chemical Equilibria in Natural Waters*. Wiley-Interscience.

Wang, J. 1994. *Analytical Electrochemistry*. New York: VCH Publishers.

Suggested readings

Acuna, N., Ortega-Morales, B. O., and Valadez-Gonzalez, A. 2006. Biofilm colonization dynamics and its influence on the corrosion resistance of austenitic UNSS31603 stainless steel exposed to Gulf of Mexico seawater. *Marine Biotechnology* 8: 62–70.

Al Darbi, M. M., Agha, K., and Islam, M. R. 2005. Comprehensive modelling of the pitting biocorrosion of steel. *Canadian Journal of Chemical Engineering* 83: 872–881.

Amaya, H., and Miyuki, H. 1994. Mechanism of microbially influenced corrosion on stainless-steels in natural seawater. *Journal of the Japan Institute of Metals* 58: 775–781.

Antony, P. J., Chongdar, S., Kumar, P., and Raman, R. 2007. Corrosion of 2205 duplex stainless steel in chloride medium containing sulfate-reducing bacteria. *Electrochimica Acta* 52: 3985–3994.

Beech, I. B., and Gaylarde, C. C. 1999. Recent advances in the study of biocorrosion—An overview. *Revista de Microbiologia* 30: 177–190.

Beech, I. B., Sunner, J. A., and Hiraoka, K. 2005. Microbe–surface interactions in biofouling and biocorrosion processes. *International Microbiology* 8: 157–168.

Beech, W. B., and Sunner, J. 2004. Biocorrosion: Towards understanding interactions between biofilms and metals. *Current Opinion in Biotechnology* 15: 181–186.

Bolwell, R. 2006. Understanding royal navy gas turbine sea water lubricating oil cooler failures when caused by microbial induced corrosion ("SRB"). *Journal of Engineering for Gas Turbines and Power* 128: 153–162.

Caspi, R., Tebo, B. M., and Haygood, M. G. 1998. c-Type cytochromes and manganese oxidation in *Pseudomonas putida* MnB1. *Applied and Environmental Microbiology* 64: 3549–3555.

Chandrasekaran, P., and Dexter, S. C. 1993. Mechanism of potential ennoblement on passive metals by seawater biofilms. CORROSION/93, Paper 493, NACE, Int., Houston, TX.

Coetser, S. E., and Cloete, T. E. 2005. Biofouling and biocorrosion in industrial water systems. *Critical Reviews in Microbiology* 31: 213–232.

Costello, J. A. 1974. Cathodic depolarization by sulfate-reducing bacteria. *South African Journal of Science* 70: 202–204.

Cramer, S. D., and B. S. Covino Jr. (Eds.) 1987. *Corrosion: Materials*, vol. 13b, ASM Handbook Series. Materials Park, OH: ASM International.

Crolet, J. L. 1991. From biology and corrosion to biocorrosion. In *Proceedings of the 2nd EFC Workshop*, Sequeira, C. A. C., and Tiller, A. K. (Eds.). London, pp. 50–60.

Crolet, J. L. 1992. From biology and corrosion to biocorrosion. *Oceanologica Acta* 15: 87–94.

Dexter, S. C., and Gao, G. Y. 1988. Effect of seawater biofilms on corrosion potential and oxygen reduction on stainless steels. *Corrosion* 44: 717.

Dickinson, W. H., and Lewandowski, Z. 1996. Manganese biofouling and the corrosion behavior of stainless steel. *Biofouling* 10: 79.

Dickinson, W. H., and Lewandowski, Z. 1998. Electrochemical concepts and techniques in the study of stainless steel ennoblement. *Biodegradation* 9: 11–21.

Eashwar, M., and Maruthamuthu, S. 1995. Mechanism of biologically produced ennoblement—Ecological perspectives and a hypothetical model. *Biofouling* 8: 203–213.

Finster, K., Liesack, W., and Thamdrup, B. 1998. Elemental sulfur and thiosulfate disproportionation by *Desulfocapsa sulfoexigens* sp nov, a new anaerobic bacterium isolated from marine surface sediment. *Applied and Environmental Microbiology* 64: 119–125.

Flemming, H. C. 1995. Biofouling and biocorrosion—Effects of undesired biofilms. *Chemie Ingenieur Technik* 67: 1425–1430.

Flemming, H. C., and Wingender, J. 2001. Relevance of microbial extracellular polymeric substances (EPSs)—Part II: Technical aspects. *Water Science and Technology* 43: 9–16.

Ford, T., and Mitchell, R. 1990. The ecology of microbial corrosion. *Advances in Microbial Ecology* 11: 231–262.

Francis, C. A., and Tebo, B. M. 2002. Enzymatic manganese(II) oxidation by metabolically dormant spores of diverse *Bacillus* species. *Applied and Environmental Microbiology* 68: 874–880.

Hakkarainen, T. J. 2003. Microbiologically influenced corrosion of stainless steels—What is required for pitting? *Materials and Corrosion* 54: 503–509.

Hamilton, W. A. 2003. Microbially influenced corrosion as a model system for the study of metal microbe interactions: A unifying electron transfer hypothesis. *Biofouling* 19: 65–76.

Hernandez, G., Kucera, V., Thierry, D., Pedersen, A., and Hermansson, M. 1994. Corrosion inhibition of steel by bacteria. *Corrosion* 50: 603–608.

Hernandez, G., Pedersen, A., Thierry, D., and Hermansson, M. 1990. Bacterial effects of corrosion of steel in seawater. In *Proceedings Microbially Influenced Corrosion and Biodeterioration*. Knoxville: University of Tennessee.

Herro, H. M. 1991. Tubercle formation and growth on ferrous alloys. Paper 84. NACE Int., Cincinnati, OH.

Hossain, M. A., and Das, C. R. 2005. Kinetic and thermodynamic studies of microbial corrosion of mild steel specimen in marine environment. *Journal of the Indian Chemical Society* 82: 376–378.

Ilhan-Sungur, E., Cansever, N., and Cotuk, A. 2007. Microbial corrosion of galvanized steel by a freshwater strain of sulphate reducing bacteria (*Desulfovibrio* sp.). *Corrosion Science* 49: 1097–1109.

Javaherdashti, R. 1999. A review of some characteristics of MIC caused by sulfate-reducing bacteria: Past, present and future. *Anti-Corrosion Methods and Materials* 46: 173–180.

Jayaraman, A., Ornek, D., Duarte, D. A., Lee, C. C., Mansfeld, F. B., and Wood, T. K. 1999. Axenic aerobic biofilms inhibit corrosion of copper and aluminum. *Applied Microbiology and Biotechnology* 52: 787–790.

Lee, A. K., and Newman, D. K. 2003. Microbial iron respiration: Impacts on corrosion processes. *Applied Microbiology and Biotechnology* 62: 134–139.

Lewandowski, Z., and Beyenal, H. 2007. *Fundamentals of Biofilm Research*. Boca Raton, FL: CRC Press.

Lewandowski, Z., Beyenal, H., and Stookey, D. 2004. Reproducibility of biofilm processes and the meaning of steady state in biofilm reactors. *Water Science and Technology* 49: 359–364.

Linhardt, P. 1998. Electrochemical identification of higher oxides of manganese in corrosion relevant deposits formed by microorganisms. *Materials Science Forum* 289–282: 1267–1274.

Linhardt, P. 2004. Microbially influenced corrosion of stainless steel by manganese oxidizing microorganisms. *Materials and Corrosion* 55: 158–163.

Linhardt, P. 2006. MIC of stainless steel in freshwater and the cathodic behaviour of biomineralized Mn-oxides. *Electrochimica Acta* 51: 6081–6084.

Little, B., Lee, J., and Ray, R. 2007. A review of "green" strategies to prevent or mitigate microbiologically influenced corrosion. *Biofouling* 23: 87–97.

Little, B., and Ray, R. 2002. A perspective on corrosion inhibition by biofilms. *Corrosion* 58: 424–428.

Little, B. J., Ray, R. I., and Pope, R. K. 2000. Relationship between corrosion and the biological sulfur cycle: A review. *Corrosion* 56: 433–443.

Mansfeld, F., and Little, B. 1991. A technical review of electrochemical techniques applied to microbiologically influenced corrosion. *Corrosion Science* 32: 247.

Mattila, K., Carpen, L., Hakkarainen, T., and Salkinoja-Salonen, M. S. 1997. Biofilm development during ennoblement of stainless steel in Baltic Sea water: A microscopic study. *International Biodeterioration and Biodegradation* 40: 1–10.

Miyanaga, K., Terashi, R., Kawai, H., Unno, H., and Tanji, Y. 2007. Biocidal effect of cathodic protection on bacterial viability in Biofilm attached to carbon steel. *Biotechnology and Bioengineering* 97: 850–857.

Mollica, A., and Trevis, A. 1976. Correlation entre la formation de la pellicule primaire et la modification de le cathodique sur des aciers inoxydables experimentes en eau de mer aux vitesses de 0.3 A, 5.2 m/s. In *Proceedings of Fourth International Congreso Marine Corrosion and Fouling.* Juan Les-Pins, France.

Olesen, B. H., Avci, R., and Lewandowski, Z. 2000a. Manganese dioxide as a potential cathodic reactant in corrosion of stainless steels. *Corrosion Science* 42: 211–227.

Olesen, B. H., Nielsen, P. H., and Lewandowski, Z. 2006b. Effect of biomineralized manganese on the corrosion behavior of C1008 mild steel. *Corrosion* 56: 80–89.

Olesen, B. H., Yurt, N., and Lewandowski, Z. 2001. Effect of biomineralized manganese on pitting corrosion of type 304L stainless steel. *Materials and Corrosion* 52: 827–832.

Rao, T. S., Sairam, T. N., Viswanathan, B., and Nair, K. V. K. 2000. Carbon steel corrosion by iron oxidising and sulphate reducing bacteria in a freshwater cooling system. *Corrosion Science* 42: 1417–1431.

Romero, J. M., Angeles-Chavez, C., and Amaya, M. 2004. Role of anaerobic and aerobic bacteria in localised corrosion: Field and laboratory morphological study. *Corrosion Engineering Science and Technology* 39: 261–264.

Shi, X., Avci, R., and Lewandowski, Z. 2002a. Microbially deposited manganese and iron oxides on passive metals—Their chemistry and consequences for material performance. *Corrosion* 58: 728–738.

Shi, X. M., Avci, R., and Lewandowski, Z. 2002b. Electrochemistry of passive metals modified by manganese oxides deposited by *Leptothrix discophora*: Two-step model verified by ToF-SIMS. *Corrosion Science* 44: 1027–1045.

Starosvetsky, J., Starosvetsky, D., and Armon, R. 2007. Identification of microbiologically influenced corrosion (MIC) in industrial equipment failures. *Engineering Failure Analysis* 14: 1500–1511.

Tebo, B. M., Bargar, J. R., Clement, B. G., Dick, G. J., Murray, K. J., Parker, D., Verity, R., and Webb, S. M. 2004. Biogenic manganese oxides: Properties and mechanisms of formation. *Annual Review of Earth and Planetary Sciences* 32: 287–328.

Tebo, B. M., Ghiorse, W. C., van Waasbergen, L. G., Siering, P. L., and Caspi, R. 1997. Bacterially mediated mineral formation: Insights into manganese(II) oxidation from molecular genetic and biochemical studies. *Reviews in Mineralogy and Geochemistry* 35: 225–266.

Tebo, B. M., Johnson, H. A., McCarthy, J. K., and Templeton, A. S. 2005. Geomicrobiology of manganese(II) oxidation. *Trends in Microbiology* 13: 421–428.

Videla, H. A. 1994. Biofilms and corrosion interactions on stainless-steel in seawater. *International Biodeterioration and Biodegradation* 34: 245–257.

Videla, H. A. 2001. Microbially induced corrosion: An updated overview. *International Biodeterioration and Biodegradation* 48: 176–201.

Videla, H. A., and Herrera, L. K. 2005. Microbiologically influenced corrosion: Looking to the future. *International Microbiology* 8: 169–180.

Wang, W., Wang, J., Xu, H., and Li, X. 2006. Some multidisciplinary techniques used in MIC studies. *Materials and Corrosion* 57: 531–537.

Washizu, N., Katada, Y., and Kodama, T. 2004. Role of H_2O_2 in microbially influenced ennoblement of open circuit potentials for type 316L stainless steel in seawater. *Corrosion Science* 46: 1291–1300.

White, D. C., de Nivens, P. D., Nichols, J., Mikell, A. T., Kerger, B. D., Henson, J. M., Geesey, G., and Clarke, C. K. 1985. Role of aerobic bacteria and their extracellular polymers in facilitation of corrosion: Use of Fourier transforming infrared spectroscopy and "signature" phospholipid fatty acid analysis. In *Biologically Induced Corrosion,* S. C. Dexter (Ed.). NACE Publications, Houston, TX, p. 233.

Xu, C. M., Zhang, Y. H., Cheng, G. X., and Zhu, W. S. 2007. Localized corrosion behavior of 316L stainless steel in the presence of sulfate-reducing and iron-oxidizing bacteria. *Materials Science and Engineering A-Structural Materials Properties Microstructure and Processing* 443: 235–241.

Zhuang, J., Zhang, L., Lu, W., Shen, D., Zhu, R. and Pan, D. 2011. Determination of trace copper in water samples by anodic stripping voltammetry at gold microelectrode. *International Journal of Electrochemical Science* 6: 4690–4699.

Zuo, R. J., Kus, E., Mansfeld, F., and Wood, T. K. 2005. The importance of live biofilms in corrosion protection. *Corrosion Science* 47: 279–287.

chapter eight

Interpreting results of biofilm studies using the model of stratified biofilms

8.1   Introduction

In the previous chapters, it was tacitly assumed that our knowledge of biofilm processes is refined in the following sequence: advances in understanding biofilm processes lead to more accurate conceptual models of these processes, and more accurate conceptual models serve as a base for building more accurate mathematical models of these processes. However, this sequence is only part of the picture of how knowledge of biofilm processes is refined. Mathematical models are not necessarily the end of the sequence. The remaining part of the picture can be characterized as feedback in which the mathematical models of biofilm processes determine the advances in understanding biofilm processes. The existence of this feedback is immediately obvious if we note that mathematical models are used to interpret the results of biofilm studies. Figure 8.1 shows a flowchart representing the activities refining our knowledge of biofilm processes: (1) conducting empirical studies of biofilm processes, (2) developing conceptual models of biofilm processes, and (3) developing mathematical models of biofilm processes. This flowchart illustrates how our knowledge of biofilms is refined through a sequence of activities. In biofilm studies, the weak part of this process is the interpretation of results of empirical studies, and much of this chapter is dedicated to this activity.

To interpret the results of empirical studies, researchers need mathematical models of the processes they study. The successful development of technologies that use microbial reactions in suspension should be largely attributed to the fact that the designers of these technologies could use accurate, user-friendly mathematical models to interpret the results of experimental studies, such as the models used to quantify microbial growth kinetics. In a similar fashion, biofilm researchers need accurate, user-friendly mathematical models not only to predict the outcomes of biofilm processes but, more immediately, to interpret the results of biofilm studies. Despite the obvious progress in constructing mathematical models of biofilm processes (IWA Task Group on Biofilm Modeling 2006), these models still have difficulty in predicting the long-term effects of important variables, and, more importantly, in accommodating the results of empirical studies. The lack of accurate, user-friendly mathematical models that can be used to quantify effects deduced from the conceptual model of biofilm structure and activity inhibits progress in understanding biofilm processes because of the difficulties in interpreting the results of biofilm studies.

This chapter demonstrates how to use the model of stratified biofilms to (1) interpret the results of biofilm studies and (2) refine the conceptual models of biofilm structure and activity. The conceptual model of stratified biofilms has been conceived to interpret the results of biofilm studies and to deliver data that can be used to model biofilm processes in heterogeneous biofilms. It presents data quantifying biofilm structure, biofilm activity,

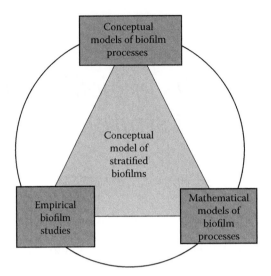

Figure 8.1 The conceptual model of stratified biofilms can be introduced into the flowchart representing the sequence of activities refining our knowledge of biofilm processes at various locations. It can be used to interpret empirical results, it can be used to interpret the conceptual model of biofilm processes, and it can be used to interpret the predictions of mathematical models of biofilm activity and accumulation.

and mass transport in biofilms in a consistent framework of three-dimensional analysis, and the data can be used to construct mathematical models of biofilm activity as well as to interpret the predictions of the existing mathematical models.

Much progress has been made in the mathematical modeling of biofilm processes, and the mathematical models used today include factors reflecting the specificity of the attached growth of microorganisms, factors that have been quantified by countless empirical studies of biofilms in a variety of environments. Early mathematical models of biofilm activity were based on the conceptual model of so-called *uniform biofilms*, depicting biomass uniformly distributed in the space occupied by the biofilm. Formally, these early mathematical models of microbial activity in biofilms imitated the models of microbial activity in suspension, with the addition of mass transport resistance. They balanced the rate of growth-limiting nutrient utilization and the rate of mass transport in one dimension—toward the surface:

$$\left(\frac{\partial C}{\partial t}\right) = D_{fav}\left(\frac{\partial^2 C}{\partial z}\right)_f - \frac{\mu_{max}X_{fav}}{Y_{X/S}}\left(\frac{C}{K_s+C}\right) \quad 0 \leq z \leq L_f \tag{8.1}$$

with the boundary equations

$$\left(\frac{\partial C}{\partial z}\right)_{(z=0)} = 0 \quad t \geq 0$$

$$C_{(x=L_f)} = C_s \quad t \geq 0$$

As time passed and our knowledge of biofilm processes was refined, the mathematical model shown in Equation 8.1 was gradually amended by the addition of various expressions quantifying factors characteristic of biofilm processes, such as the rate of detachment. However, the conceptual model of a biofilm that served as the base for formulating mathematical models of biofilm processes remained intact: a biofilm was viewed as a continuous layer of extracellular polymers attached to a surface, packed with uniformly distributed microorganisms. This conceptual model was used to make predictions, formulate hypotheses and interpret results of experimental studies, and the results of the experimental studies were expected to be consistent with the existing conceptual model of the biofilm structure. However, as these results gradually accumulated, some of them were in obvious disagreement with the conceptual model of biofilms in which microorganisms were uniformly distributed in a continuous matrix of extracellular polymers. A more thorough discussion of this subject can be found in Chapter 2. Because of the disparity between the accumulated experimental evidence and the existing conceptual model of biofilm structure, a new conceptual model of biofilm structure was presented that viewed biofilms as aggregates of microcolonies packed with microorganisms, separated by interstitial voids filled with the solution of nutrients and no microorganisms at all. This conceptual model of biofilm structure is still in use: it is the model of heterogeneous biofilms shown in Figure 8.2.

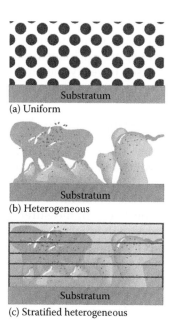

(a) Uniform

(b) Heterogeneous

(c) Stratified heterogeneous

Figure 8.2 Conceptual models of biofilms. (a) The conceptual model of homogeneous biofilms views a biofilm as a matrix of extracellular polymers with uniformly distributed microorganisms. (b) The conceptual model of heterogeneous biofilms views a biofilm as an assemblage of aggregates, called microcolonies, separated by interstitial voids filled with water. The activity of a heterogeneous biofilm is equal to the sum of the activities of the individual microcolonies. (c) The conceptual model of stratified biofilms represents a heterogeneous biofilm as a collection of layers of different densities and activities. According to this model, the overall activity of a heterogeneous biofilm is equal to the sum of the activities of the individual layers.

Accepting the new conceptual model of biofilm structure required modifying the mathematical models of biofilm processes. For example, using the conceptual model of heterogeneous biofilms, the researcher can no longer assume that the mass transport in a biofilm is predominantly in one direction (toward the surface): mass transport in interstitial voids can be in any direction. As a result, mass transport in the space occupied by the biofilm became a subject of study, and the term *intrabiofilm mass transport dynamics* was created to facilitate discussion of the results of such studies.

The conceptual model of heterogeneous biofilms defined new challenges for constructing mathematical models of biofilm activity and accumulation. To quantify biofilm processes using the conceptual model of heterogeneous biofilms, mathematical objects had to be generated that could imitate the structure of microcolonies and interstitial voids. A computer model called *cellular automata* was used to generate such objects. Cellular automata, developed from the Game of Life introduced by British mathematician John Horton Conway in 1970, allow the building of complex structures from simple and repetitive building blocks, called *cells*, following simple rules imposed on the cells. These rules determine the behavior of the computer-generated cells according to the occupancy of spaces adjacent to them. A set of such rules has been developed for generating objects resembling heterogeneous biofilms—microcolonies separated by interstitial voids. These computer-generated mathematical objects serve as matrices on which various biofilm processes are superimposed, such as mass transport of nutrients and microbial growth. This approach, using cellular automata to construct objects resembling biofilms, has been refined by several generations of mathematical models and is now the predominant approach to constructing models of biofilm activity and accumulation. The conceptual model of stratified biofilms is fully compatible with this approach. Indeed, data interpreted using the concept of stratified biofilms can easily be used to verify the predictions of mathematical models of biofilm activity and accumulation based on cellular automata.

8.2   Conceptual model of stratified biofilms

The model of heterogeneous biofilms shows biomass in biofilms concentrated in microcolonies separated by interstitial voids and claims that the building blocks of heterogeneous biofilms are microcolonies. The microbial activities of individual microcolonies can be quantified from microscale measurements. Consequently, to predict the activity of the entire biofilm system from the results of measurements of biofilm activity in individual microcolonies, the activities of individual microcolonies have to be integrated over the entire biofilm. This approach is difficult to implement because each microcolony in a biofilm is different from other microcolonies and the measurements of microbial activity are limited to a finite, and relatively small, number of microcolonies. How to average these individual measurements so that their average can be related to the activity of the entire biofilm system is not clear. The conceptual model of stratified biofilms takes a different approach to the problem of how to average the results of individual measurements over the entire biofilm system: it claims that the building blocks of biofilms are not microcolonies but layers. The conceptual model of stratified biofilms should not be confused with a model of biofilm structure. The conceptual model of stratified biofilms does not modify the model of heterogeneous biofilms: it modifies its interpretation. The results of the microscale measurements are used to quantify the activities of the layers, not the microcolonies, and the activity of each layer is determined from measurements conducted at several locations equally distant from the bottom. Obviously, this approach does not change the fact that the biofilm is composed of microcolonies and interstitial voids: it just assumes that the heterogeneous biofilm can be subdivided into a finite number of uniform layers and that the combined activity of all these layers represents the activity of the biofilm. Integrating the activities of layers is more productive than integrating the activities of microcolonies. Because the activity of each layer can be measured and there is a finite number of layers, integrating their activities is not difficult.

Figure 8.2 shows the progression in the development of the conceptual model of biofilms and its interpretation. The conceptual model of heterogeneous biofilms uses microcolonies as the building blocks of biofilms, which is often referred to with the phrase: Biofilms are composed of microcolonies separated by interstitial voids. The model of stratified biofilms uses discrete layers as building blocks of biofilms, which can be referred to using the sentence: Biofilms can be represented as discrete layers with different microbial activities and different mass transport properties. It is practically impossible to quantify the properties of each microcolony in a biofilm, but it is possible to quantify the properties of a finite number of discrete layers in the biofilm. In this respect, the conceptual model of stratified biofilms makes the structure of a heterogeneous biofilm more manageable for mathematical description.

The conceptual model of stratified biofilms has been developed with a very practical purpose: it provides a framework for interpreting the results of biofilm studies at the microscale. Many tools described in this book can be used to characterize biofilm structure and biofilm. Variables characterizing heterogeneous biofilms, such as microbial activity and biomass density, can be quantified for a small surface area covered by a finite number of microcolonies, but these variables vary from location to location, and it is not clear how to generate a set of representative variables so that they can be used to compute the activity of the entire biofilm at the macroscale. Using the tools described in this book, one can quantify many variables characterizing microbial activity at the microscale. Ultimately, however, it is the macroscale effect of the biofilm—the overall activity of the entire biofilm system—that is predicted. The conceptual model of stratified biofilms gives a rational approach to interpreting the results of microscale measurements in biofilms and provides a framework for scaling up biofilm processes. Thus far, the scales of observation have been determined by the size of the object under study: the microscale measurements characterize the biofilm processes at a scale comparable to the thickness of the biofilm, and the macroscale measurements characterize the biofilm processes at the scale of the reactor. Using the concept of stratified biofilms, the operator determines the scale of observation, which is between the microscale and the macroscale. In the application shown here, a surface area of a size equal to the field of view of a light or confocal microscope is characterized. This is done for practical reasons: in principle, larger areas of the surface can be characterized if the measurements provide adequate sets of data.

As seen in Figure 8.2c the conceptual model of stratified biofilms divides the space occupied by a biofilm into a finite number of layers (strata). Dividing the space occupied by the biofilm into discrete layers is not new in biofilm research: biofilm researchers do this when acquiring confocal images of biofilms. Using the terminology of the model of stratified biofilms, the distance between the images in a stack of confocal images determines the thickness of the layer in the model of stratified biofilms, and the field of view of the microscope determines the size of the surface area. From these dimensions, the volume of each layer can easily be estimated. Microelectrode measurements are made to cover the area of the field of view of the microscope, making the scales of observation used in the confocal microcopy and in the microelectrode measurements equal and under the control of the operator. Not only the surface area but also the distance between layers is under the

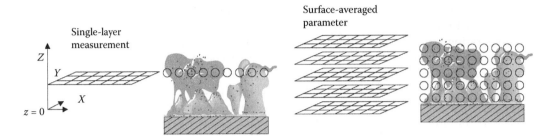

Figure 8.3 Microscale measurements in stratified biofilms. The selected variable (i.e., local dissolved oxygen concentration) is measured at locations where the gridlines intersect. Several such grids are positioned at various distances from the bottom. CSLM images are acquired, and the physical measurements are made at the same distances from the bottom.

control of the operator, just as the field of view and the distance between optical slices are under the control of the microscopist in confocal microscopy. Using the empirical and computational procedures described in other chapters, other variables in the individual layers can be characterized, such as hydrodynamics, mass transport rate, microbial activity, biomass concentration and distribution, and biofilm structure. The results are interpreted using stacks of confocal images taken at various distances from the bottom of the biofilm and stacks of maps showing the distributions of chemistries, rates of mass transport, and microbial activity, all generated at distances from the bottom equal to those distances at which the confocal images were taken. Figure 8.3 illustrates this process.

8.3   Interpreting results of biofilm studies using the conceptual model of stratified biofilms

8.3.1   Measurements at the microscale

To use the conceptual model of stratified biofilms to interpret the results of microscale measurements, the data must be acquired in a format that can be accepted by the model, and this requirement may affect the way the sets of data are prepared. For example, oxygen concentration profiles are measured at several selected locations, one location at a time. If the results of such measurements are to be interpreted using the concept of stratified biofilms, the profiles of oxygen concentration need to be measured on a regular grid of locations precisely defined on the surface of the biofilm and consistent with the field of view of the confocal microscope characterizing the distribution of the biomass in the biofilm (Figure 8.3). The size of the grid determines the lateral dimensions of the strata, and selecting the size of the grid has consequences. The larger the surface area characterized by measurements at the microscale, the closer the estimates based on these results will be to the estimates based on results acquired at the macroscale—those based on the influent and effluent of the reactor. However, the larger the surface area characterized by measurements at the microscale, the larger the deviations of individual measurements from the average are expected to be. The standard deviation of the measurements needs to be accounted for because it reflects the extent of biofilm heterogeneity, which expands the scope of the analysis. The experimental setup we use is shown in Figure 8.4, and the following sections explain how to take measurements and generate sets of data that can be interpreted using the concept of stratified biofilms.

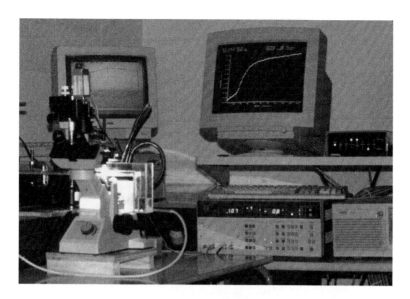

Figure 8.4 Setup for measuring concentration profiles using microelectrodes. The profiles are measured at several locations in the biofilm and at several distances from the bottom. The measurements are taken at the intersections of gridlines precisely located on the surface of the biofilm. From a set of such measurements, we construct maps of the distribution of the measured variable, as illustrated in Figure 8.7 using oxygen concentration profiles. The measurement procedures are described in Chapter 9.

To illustrate the procedure for arranging and interpreting the sets of data, the distribution of oxygen in a biofilm of *Pseudomonas aeruginosa* PAO1 grown in a flat plate biofilm reactor is selected. We start by selecting the locations for the measurements on the surface of the biofilm, and we select a grid size that is appropriate for the measurements. In this example, the selected grid is 5 × 5 gridlines, which makes 25 locations, and the distance between adjacent locations is equal to 100 μm: the grid covers a square 500 μm × 500 μm (Figure 8.5). Oxygen concentration profiles were measured at the locations where the gridlines intersect, and the results are shown in Figure 8.6. The set of oxygen profiles shown in Figure 8.6 was used to generate maps of oxygen concentration at various distances from the bottom (Figure 8.7).

When designing the measurements, it is important to determine the position of the bottom and select the step of the microelectrode movement so that the measurements in each profile are taken at the same distances from the bottom. The procedure for locating the bottom is described in Chapter 9. If we expect to correlate the measurements with the distribution of the biomass determined from a stack of confocal images, the size of the step for which the microelectrode data were acquired must be equal to the distance between confocal images in the stack. In this example, we measured the profiles of oxygen concentration at the locations where the gridlines intersect, and the results of all 25 measurements are shown in Figure 8.6.

The data need to be presented in a format that is compatible with the concept of stratified biofilms. From the oxygen profiles in Figure 8.6, we extracted the concentrations of oxygen that were measured at the same distance from the bottom and assembled these data in new data sets. The number of these data sets equals the number of data points in

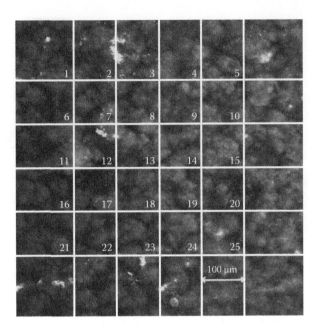

Figure 8.5 Locations in the biofilm where dissolved oxygen concentration profiles and effective diffusivity profiles were measured and biomass distribution was characterized from CLSM images. (From Veluchamy, R. R. A., Structure and activity of *Pseudomonas aeruginosa* PAO1 biofilms, MS dissertation, Montana State University, Bozeman, 2006.)

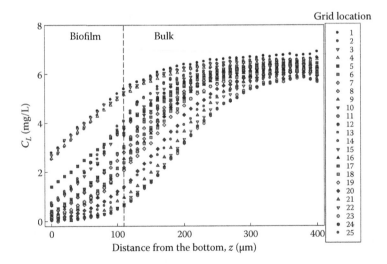

Figure 8.6 Oxygen profiles measured at the locations shown in Figure 8.5. (From Veluchamy, R. R. A., Structure and activity of *Pseudomonas aeruginosa* PAO1 biofilms, MS dissertation, Montana State University, Bozeman, 2006.)

each of the oxygen profiles in Figure 8.6. Each data set is composed of the measurements of dissolved oxygen that were taken at a given distance from the bottom of the reactor, and each data set is used to plot the oxygen distribution in a layer of the biofilm. For practical reasons, all the results are not shown here; selected results illustrating the procedure are shown in Figure 8.7.

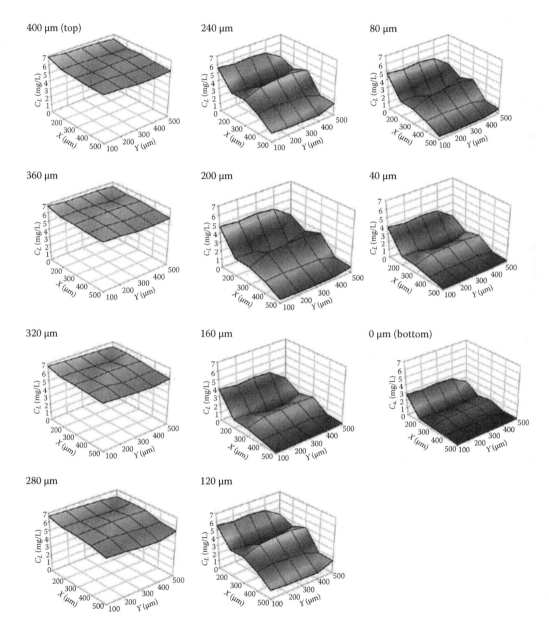

Figure 8.7 Distribution of oxygen concentrations at the selected distances from the bottom of the biofilm. (From Veluchamy, R. R. A., Structure and activity of *Pseudomonas aeruginosa* PAO1 biofilms, MS dissertation, Montana State University, Bozeman, 2006.)

8.3.2   Interpreting the data using the concept of stratified biofilms

The interpretation of the data in Figure 8.7 calls for computing the average oxygen concentration and the standard deviation from the average for each layer of the biofilm. Consequently, for each layer, the 25 measurements of oxygen concentration are averaged and the standard deviation, C_{SD}, is computed as follows:

$$C_{SD} = \sqrt{\frac{\sum\limits_{i=1}^{\text{number of measurements}} (C_{\text{local}} - C_{\text{surface-averaged}})^2}{\text{number of measurements}}} \tag{8.2}$$

The average concentration of oxygen and the standard deviation from the average value are plotted versus distance in Figure 8.8.

The composite profile of oxygen concentrations generated by the average oxygen concentrations of the various layers (Figure 8.8) is considered to be the representative oxygen concentration profile for the area of the biofilm covered with the gridlines, and it is used to compute the flux of oxygen into the biofilm and evaluate the overall biofilm activity. As is seen in Figure 8.8, the standard deviations of the measurements form a regular envelope encasing the representative profile of oxygen concentration. These standard deviations should not be confused with error of measurement: they reflect the heterogeneous distribution of the variable evaluated in the measurement, here the oxygen concentration. The extent of heterogeneity determined from one type of measurement, such as oxygen

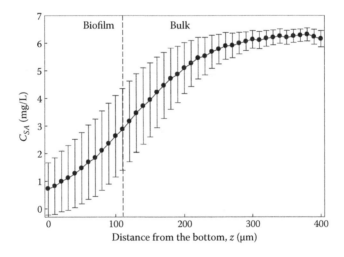

Figure 8.8 Average oxygen concentration and standard deviation computed for each data set in Figure 8.7. The average oxygen concentrations form a representative profile of oxygen concentration, characterizing the area covered with the biofilm, and the envelope of the standard deviation is a measure of the heterogeneity of the measured variable, oxygen concentration in this case. (From Veluchamy, R. R. A., Structure and activity of *Pseudomonas aeruginosa* PAO1 biofilms, MS dissertation, Montana State University, Bozeman, 2006.)

concentration, can be correlated with the extent of heterogeneity determined from other types of measurements, such as local mass transport coefficients, as long as the data sets were acquired on the same grid. Correlating the heterogeneities of various variables is useful in studying the relations among variables measured in a system. For example, to determine whether the heterogeneity in oxygen concentration in a layer is caused by the heterogeneity of the biomass distribution in that layer, the standard deviation for the measurements characterizing the distribution of the biomass in each layer is correlated with the standard deviation for oxygen concentration in that layer.

Because the standard deviation in Figure 8.8 reflects the extent of biofilm heterogeneity, this result will be examined more closely by computing, for each standard deviation in Figure 8.9, the coefficient of variation from the following formula:

$$C_{CV} = \frac{C_{SD} \times 100}{C_{\text{surface-averaged}}} \tag{8.3}$$

where $C_{\text{surface-averaged}}$ is the surface-averaged dissolved oxygen concentration, C_{SD} is the standard deviation, and C_{CV} is the coefficient of variation. The plot of the coefficient of variation versus distance shows that the coefficient of variation of the dissolved oxygen concentration decreases with distance from the bottom in a surprisingly linear fashion.

The distribution of oxygen concentration has been used as an example of interpreting results using the concept of stratified biofilms. The data set subjected to interpretation does not have to be the distribution of concentration of a component: it can be any variable measured at the microscale in a biofilm. In the example in Figure 8.10, mass transport coefficients were measured at selected locations and distances from the bottom, and the data were interpreted in the same way as we described for the oxygen concentration profiles.

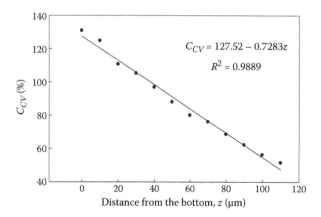

Figure 8.9 The coefficient of variation in dissolved oxygen concentration (C_{CV}) plotted against the distance from the bottom of the biofilm (z). (From Veluchamy, R. R. A., Structure and activity of *Pseudomonas aeruginosa* PAO1 biofilms, MS dissertation, Montana State University, Bozeman, MT, 2006.)

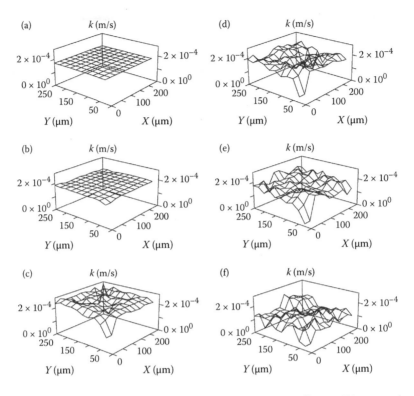

Figure 8.10 Horizontal distributions of the local mass transport coefficient. Distances from the bottom: (a) $z = 1000$ μm, (b) $z = 500$ μm, (c) $z = 300$ μm, (d) $z = 200$ μm, (e) $z = 100$ μm, and (f) $z = 50$ μm. The biofilm was 200 μm thick. The bulk liquid flow velocity was 1.58 cm/s. It is seen that the maps of the local mass transport coefficient become convoluted near the biofilm and progressively more so near the bottom. If an average mass transport coefficient is computed for each layer, the standard deviations of individual measurements in the layers should be related to the distribution of the biomass and interstitial voids in these layers. (Reproduced from Yang, S. N., and Lewandowski, Z., *Biotechnology and Bioengineering*, 48, 737–744, 1995.)

The conceptual model of stratified biofilms can lead to interesting mathematical descriptions of biofilm processes based on the distribution of the variables that are quantified using the model. In this sense, the model of stratified biofilms should be seen as a tool of discovery in interpreting the results of biofilm studies, just as good mathematical models are used as tools of discovery in predicting the outcomes of unknown processes. Section 8.3 interprets the results of effective diffusivity measurements and exemplifies the use of the conceptual model of stratified biofilms in formulating mathematical descriptions of biofilm activity. The distribution maps of relative effective diffusivities shown in Figure 8.11 were plotted using sets of data measured in a biofilm composed of *P. aeruginosa* (ATCC 700829), *Pseudomonas fluorescens* (ATCC 700830), and *Klebsiella pneumoniae* (ATCC 700831). Many more such maps were plotted using these data sets, and the plots in Figure 8.11 exemplify these results (Beyenal and Lewandowski 2000).

The results given in Figure 8.11 were used to compute the surface-averaged effective diffusivities, which were plotted against the distance from the bottom (Figure 8.12).

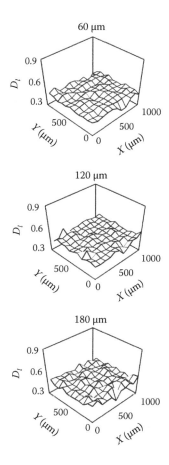

Figure 8.11 Horizontal distributions of local relative effective diffusivity (D_l) in biofilms grown at a flow velocity of 3.2 cm/s and a glucose concentration of 50 mg/L at distances of 60, 120, and 180 μm from the bottom. The surface-averaged relative effective diffusivities were 0.409, 0.426, 0.449, and the standard deviations were 0.0179, 0.0195, and 0.0284, respectively. (Reproduced from Beyenal, H., and Lewandowski, Z., *Water Research*, 200(34), 528–538, 2000.)

The relative effective diffusivity profile in Figure 8.12 is approximated by a straight line, which vastly simplifies the mathematical modeling of diffusional mass transport in this biofilm. A continuous function $(D_{fz}^* = 0.001 \times z + 0.2968)$ is used to correlate relative effective diffusivity (D_{fz}^*) with the distance from the bottom (z). Using the effective diffusivity gradient (the slope of the effective diffusivity profile) within a biofilm, the equation quantifying mass transport in homogeneous biofilms is amended by adding variable diffusivity, a factor related to biofilm heterogeneity. The relative effective diffusivity gradient, dD_{fz}^*/dz in Figure 8.12, can be multiplied by the diffusivity in water of the substance used in the measurement to calculate the effective diffusivity gradient, ζ:

$$\zeta = \frac{dD_{fz}^*}{dz} \times D_w \qquad (8.4)$$

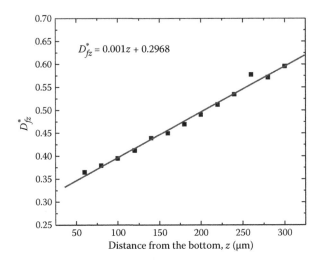

Figure 8.12 Surface-averaged relative effective diffusivity profile. (Reproduced from Beyenal, H., and Lewandowski, Z., *Biotechnology Progress*, 18, 55–61, 2002.) The surface-averaged relative effective diffusivity (D_{fz}^*) is multiplied by the diffusivity of the growth-limiting nutrient in the water to calculate the surface-averaged effective diffusivity (D_{fz}). Because, in the example, the growth-limiting nutrient is oxygen, to calculate the effective diffusivity of oxygen at various distances from the bottom, we must multiply the relative effective diffusivity by the diffusivity of oxygen in water (2.1×10^{-5} cm^2/s).

8.4   Using the model of stratified biofilms to refine conceptual models of biofilm structure and activity

8.4.1   Modeling biofilm processes in stratified biofilms

8.4.1.1   Nutrient continuity equations in stratified biofilms

One of the known properties of biofilms is that the density of biomass increases rapidly toward the bottom; it is not unusual to see biofilms with the density of the biomass near the bottom reaching 100 g/L. This section studies the effect of biomass density increasing toward the bottom of the biofilm on the form of the continuity equation. Because the biomass concentration increases toward the bottom, only the mass transport toward the bottom, i.e., in the direction in which the mass transfer resistance changes, will be considered. With this assumption, the mass balances for nutrients around a differential element, shown in Figure 8.13, are as illustrated.

As described in the previous sections, we are attempting to calculate the average effective diffusivity in a layer Δz thick, covering a known area of the biofilm. By accepting the average properties of the biofilm over the differential volume ($\Delta y \times \Delta x \times \Delta z$), we ignore the variations in the X and Y directions (averaged for each discrete layer), but not in the Z direction. The activity of a biofilm composed of discrete layers will be modeled, and a test will determine whether it is meaningfully different from the activity of a uniform biofilm.

If N is the flux of the nutrient, the rate at which the growth-limiting nutrient enters the differential element along z is

$$\text{nutrient (in)} = N\Delta y\Delta x \tag{8.5}$$

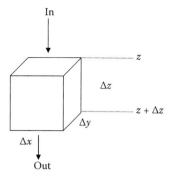

Figure 8.13 A differential element of a biofilm.

Similarly, the rate at which the growth-limiting nutrient flows out of the differential element at $z + \Delta z$ is

$$\text{nutrient (out)} = N\Delta y\Delta x + \frac{dN}{dz}\Delta y\Delta z\Delta x \tag{8.6}$$

The growth-limiting nutrient utilization rate in the differential element is

$$\frac{dN}{dx}\Delta y\Delta z\Delta x = \frac{\mu_{max}CX_{fl}}{Y_{X/S}(K_S+C)}\Delta y\Delta z\Delta x \tag{8.7}$$

where X_{fl} is the average cell density in the differential element.

In summary, the difference between the rates of growth-limiting nutrient flow into and out from the differential element equals the growth-limiting nutrient utilization rate within the volume of the differential element, and the mass balance around the differential element is

$$N\Delta y\Delta x - \left(N\Delta y\Delta x + \frac{dN}{dz}\Delta y\Delta z\Delta x\right) = \frac{\mu_{max}CX_{fl}}{Y_{X/S}(K_S+C)}\Delta y\Delta z\Delta x \tag{8.8}$$

Because one-dimensional mass transport has been assumed, the diffusive flux is given by Fick's first law:

$$N = -D_f\frac{dC}{dz} \tag{8.9}$$

where D_f is effective diffusivity. In stratified biofilms, effective diffusivity changes in the vertical (Z) direction (Figure 8.12) are more noticeable than those in the horizontal (X and Y) directions. Therefore, the effective diffusivity (D_{fz}) in each layer can be averaged over a defined volume of the layer ($\Delta y \Delta x \Delta z$) and described by the surface-averaged effective diffusivity as (Figure 8.12):

$$D_f = D_f(z) = D_{fz} \tag{8.10}$$

D_{fz} represents the average effective diffusivity in the volume of the differential element ($\Delta y \Delta x \Delta z$). Because effective diffusivity is a function of biofilm density, biofilm density also changes in the Z direction: biofilms are denser near the bottom than near the surface. The relation between effective diffusivity and biofilm density can be approximated from the following equation (Fan et al. 1990):

$$D_{fz}^* = 1 - \frac{0.43 X_{fl}^{0.92}}{11.19 + 0.27 X_{fl}^{0.99}} \tag{8.11}$$

When Equations 8.9 and 8.10 are substituted into Equation 8.8,

$$\frac{dN}{dz} = \frac{d}{dz}\left(D_{fz}\frac{dC}{dz}\right) = D_{fz}\frac{d^2C}{dz^2} + \frac{dD_{fz}}{dz}\frac{dC}{dz} = \frac{\mu_{max}CX_{fl}}{Y_{X/S}(K_S+C)} \tag{8.12}$$

As a result of our studies, we conclude that the continuity equation in Equation 8.1 should be expanded using variable relative diffusivity, as shown in Figure 8.12. Also, the conclusions of our study coincide with the model in Equation 8.1, in which the effective diffusivity is a function of distance:

$$D_{fz}\frac{d^2C}{dz^2} + \frac{dD_{fz}}{dz}\frac{dC}{dz} = \frac{\mu_{max}CX_{fl}}{Y_{X/S}(K_S+C)} \tag{8.13}$$

The results in Figure 8.12 show that dD_{fz}^*/dz is the slope of the plot describing the relation between the effective diffusivity and the distance. Note that, similarly, $\dfrac{dD_{fz}}{dz} = \text{constant}$ and dD_{fz}/dz can be calculated from the slope. The effective diffusivity profile in Figure 8.12 can be approximated by a straight line:

$$D_{fz} = a + \zeta z \tag{8.14}$$

When discussing the significance of introducing variable effective diffusivity into the continuity equation, an often asked question is, how much difference to the overall activity of the biofilm can it make that the molecular diffusivity varies across the biofilm by several percent? The answer to this question is that the variation in effective diffusivity is not the only variation that is introduced into the model. The effective diffusivity in a biofilm varies because the biofilm density varies, and biofilm activity is affected both by the variation in effective diffusivity and by the variation in biomass density.

Equation 8.11 gives relative effective diffusivity as a function of biofilm density and may be used, with limited accuracy because this is an empirical equation, to quantify the distribution of biofilm density. The variation in effective diffusivity associated with the variation in biofilm density (Figure 8.14) shows its effect on the overall biofilm activity.

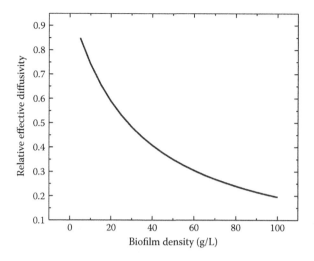

Figure 8.14 Relative effective diffusivity versus biofilm density computed from Equation 8.9.

In this plot, biofilm density varies from 5 to 100 g/L. We consider this range in biomass density in biofilms realistic because independent measurements show that biofilm density near the bottom can reach 100 g/L. From the graph, an increase from 0.2 to 0.4 in the relative effective diffusivity is associated with a change in biofilm density from 100 to about 40 g/L. Although the significance of the effective diffusivity variation across a biofilm may be debatable, the associated variation in biomass density across the biofilm is significant. This variation in density cannot be ignored, because the activity of a biofilm depends on its density.

Figure 8.15 shows the distribution of biofilm density in biofilms composed of *P. aeruginosa* (ATCC 700829), *P. fluorescens* (ATCC 700830), and *K. pneumoniae* (ATCC 700831) grown at a flow velocity of 25 cm/s.

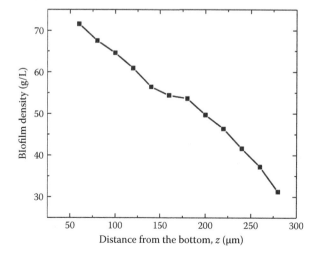

Figure 8.15 Variation in biofilm density with distance from the bottom.

8.4.1.2 Comparing biofilms using the model of stratified biofilms

The surface-averaged relative effective diffusivity (D_{fz}^*) in Figure 8.12 and the D_{fz} in Equation 8.14 can be related by multiplying the relative effective diffusivity by the diffusivity in water ($D_{fz}^* = D_{fz} D_w$). To introduce the variable biofilm density and effective diffusivity, the effective diffusivity gradient (ζ) across the biofilm is defined:

$$\frac{dD_{fz}}{dz} = \zeta \tag{8.15}$$

Inserting Equations 8.14 and 8.15 into Equation 8.12 yields nutrient continuity, which can be used to compute growth-limiting nutrient concentration profiles in stratified biofilms:

$$D_{fz}\frac{d^2C}{dz^2} + \zeta\frac{dC}{dz} = \frac{\mu_{max}CX_{fl}}{Y_{X/S}(K_S + C)} \tag{8.16}$$

Equation 8.16 describes mass transport and activity in real biofilms—biofilms in which density increases toward the bottom and effective diffusivity decreases toward the bottom. Conceptually, it is possible to imagine a biofilm in which the density is uniformly distributed and the gradient of effective diffusivity equals zero. Such a hypothetical homogeneous biofilm is seen differently in the conceptual model of heterogeneous biofilms, where microcolonies are considered to be the building blocks of the biofilm, and in the model of stratified biofilms, which assumes that layers are the building blocks of the biofilm. In the model of heterogeneous biofilms, a biofilm with uniformly distributed density must be uniform because the biomass in the entire space occupied by the biofilm has the same density. In the model of stratified biofilms, however, the density is computed by averaging the distribution of the density in each layer, and two layers can have the same average density even though their densities are differently distributed. Consequently, in the model of stratified biofilms, a biofilm with uniformly distributed density is not necessarily a uniform biofilm. Despite the fact that uniform biofilms are purely hypothetical constructs, such biofilms are important enough to warrant further discussion.

Hypothetical biofilms with uniformly distributed diffusivity and density can be used as standards from which real biofilms deviate to various extents. To simplify the terminology, biofilms with uniformly distributed density and diffusivity, $\zeta = 0$, will be referred to as *uniform biofilms*, with the restrictions on the meaning of this term specified above. Biofilms that exhibit a gradient in density and effective diffusivity will be referred to as *stratified biofilms*.

For uniform biofilms, the continuity equation is simplified to the form:

$$D_{fav}\frac{d^2C}{dz^2} = \frac{\mu_{max}CX_{fav}}{Y_{X/S}(K_S + C)} \tag{8.17}$$

Equations 8.16 and 8.17 are used to quantify growth-limiting nutrient transfer in stratified and, for comparison, in uniform biofilms. The following list specifies the assumptions accepted in these equations:

- The biofilm layers are a continuum.
- Nutrients are transferred by diffusion only and are consumed by microorganisms.
- The diffusion of nutrients obeys Fick's first law.

- The model considers one growth-limiting nutrient at a time, and this nutrient is consumed at a rate described by the Monod equation.
- Effective diffusivity and biofilm density can be computed by averaging their values at the boundaries of adjacent layers.
- The biofilm processes are in a pseudo-steady state, which means that the growth-limiting nutrient utilization rate does not change for a period of time that is longer than the time needed to measure the growth-limiting nutrient utilization rate.
- The growth-limiting nutrient is transported in one dimension only: perpendicularly to the substratum.
- Biofilms grow on impermeable, inactive surfaces.

The following notes address important details in considering the model:

1. Even though mass transport is considered in the Z direction only, when appropriate data (variation of effective diffusivity in X and Y directions) are available, they can be integrated into the model.
2. Monod kinetics are used here to describe microbial growth, but any type of growth kinetics can be used in the model.
3. If microbial growth is limited by multiple nutrients, a continuity equation must be written for each growth-limiting nutrient and the equations must be solved simultaneously.

8.4.1.3 Dimensionless equations for stratified biofilms

Let the dimensionless variables—distance, z^*; concentration, C^*; and Monod half-rate constant, β—be defined as

$$z^* = \frac{z}{L_f} \quad C^* = \frac{C}{C_s} \quad \beta = \frac{K_s}{C_s} \tag{8.18}$$

Plugging these dimensionless variables into Equation 8.16 yields

$$\frac{d^2 C^*}{dz^{*2}} + \frac{L_f \zeta}{D_{fz}} \frac{dC^*}{dz^*} = \frac{\mu_{max} L_f^2}{Y_{X/S} C_s} \frac{X_{fl}}{D_{fz}} \frac{C^*}{(\beta + C^*)} \tag{8.19}$$

X_{fl} and D_{fz} are functions of the distance (Equations 8.11 and 8.14), z, and they may be expressed as dimensionless variables by defining a new variable, Ψ:

$$\Psi = \frac{a}{L_f \zeta} \tag{8.20}$$

Using the new variable Ψ, the expression $\dfrac{L_f \zeta}{D_{fz}}$ can be calculated from the left side of Equation 8.14:

$$\frac{L_f \zeta}{D_{fz}} = \frac{L_f \zeta}{a + \zeta z} = \frac{1}{\Psi + z^*} \tag{8.21}$$

Equation 8.21 can be inserted into Equation 8.19 to yield

$$\frac{d^2 C^*}{dz^{*2}} + \frac{1}{\Psi + z^*} \frac{dC^*}{dz^*} = \frac{\mu_{max} L_f^2}{Y_{X/S} C_s} \frac{X_{fl}}{D_{fz}} \frac{C^*}{(\beta + C^*)} \qquad (8.22)$$

The dimensionless biofilm density, X_f^*, and the effective diffusivity in the biofilm, D_f^*, are defined as

$$X_f^* = \frac{X_{fl}}{X_{fav}} \quad D_f^* = \frac{D_{fz}}{D_{fav}} \qquad (8.23)$$

Combining Equations 8.22 and 8.23 yields

$$\frac{d^2 C^*}{dz^{*2}} + \frac{1}{\Psi + z^*} \frac{dC^*}{dz^*} = \frac{\mu_{max} L_f^2 X_{fav}}{Y_{X/S} C_s D_{fav}} \frac{X_f^*}{D_f^*} \frac{C^*}{(\beta + C^*)} \qquad (8.24)$$

Defining the Thiele modulus as

$$\Phi = \sqrt{\frac{\mu_{max} L_f^2 X_{fav}}{Y_{X/S} C_s D_{fav}}}$$

and combining Equations 8.23 and 8.24 yields

$$\frac{d^2 C^*}{dz^{*2}} + \frac{1}{\Psi + z^*} \frac{dC^*}{dz^*} = \Phi^2 \frac{X_f^*}{D_f^*} \frac{C^*}{(\beta + C^*)} \qquad (8.25)$$

To compute X_f^* and D_f^* as functions of distance z, the average effective diffusivity D_{fav} is first calculated using the following equation, derived by integrating Equation 8.14:

$$D_{fav} = a + \frac{\zeta L_f}{2} \qquad (8.26)$$

Solving for $D_f^* (= D_{fz}/D_{fav})$

$$D_f^* = \frac{2(\Psi + z^*)}{2\Psi + 1} \qquad (8.27)$$

and combining Equations 8.25 and 8.27 yields

$$\frac{d^2 C^*}{dz^{*2}} + \frac{1}{\Psi + z^*} \frac{dC^*}{dz^*} = \Phi^2 X_f^* \frac{2\Psi + 1}{2(\Psi + z^*)} \frac{C^*}{(\beta + C^*)} \qquad (8.28)$$

X_{fl} can be calculated by numerically solving the effective diffusivity (Equation 8.11). The relation between biofilm density and effective diffusivity is a single-valued function, and it can be inverted. Because Fan's equation could not be inverted analytically and the relation between biofilm density and effective diffusivity could not be given explicitly, we used numerical methods and found that

$$X_{fl} = -38.856 + 38.976 \left(\frac{D_{fz}}{D_w} \right)^{-0.7782} \tag{8.29}$$

can be used.

Let κ be defined as

$$\kappa = \frac{D_w}{a} \tag{8.30}$$

D_{fz}/D_w can be calculated as follows:

$$\frac{D_{fz}}{D_w} = \frac{a + \zeta z}{D_w} = \frac{1 + \dfrac{z^*}{\Psi}}{\dfrac{D_w}{a}} = \frac{1 + \dfrac{z^*}{\Psi}}{\kappa} \tag{8.31}$$

Because the relation between biomass density and diffusivity is a one-to-one function, Fan's equation (Fan et al. 1990) can then be rewritten in dimensionless and inverted form:

$$X_f^* = \frac{-38.856 + 38.976 \left(\dfrac{1 + \dfrac{z^*}{\Psi}}{\kappa} \right)^{-0.7782}}{X_{fav}} \tag{8.32}$$

The dimensionless form of Equation 8.18 is calculated below:

$$\frac{d^2 C^*}{dz^{*2}} + \frac{1}{\Psi + z^*} \frac{dC^*}{dz^*} = \Phi^2 \left(\frac{-38.856 + 38.976 \left(\dfrac{1 + \dfrac{z^*}{\Psi}}{\kappa} \right)^{-0.7782}}{X_{fav}} \right) \frac{2\Psi + 1}{2(\Psi + z^*)} \frac{C^*}{(\beta + C^*)} \tag{8.33}$$

8.4.1.4   *Dimensionless equation for biofilms with uniformly distributed density*

Using the Thiele modulus, Φ; the Monod half-rate constant, β; the dimensionless distance, z^*; and the dimensionless concentration, C^*, Equation 8.17 can be written as a dimensionless equation:

$$\frac{d^2 C^*}{dz^{*2}} = \Phi^2 \frac{C^*}{(\beta + C^*)} \tag{8.34}$$

8.4.1.5   Boundary conditions

The concentration of the growth-limiting nutrient at the biofilm surface is defined as C_s. It can be measured experimentally or determined from the external mass transport resistance. Therefore, it is assumed that its value is known. In this case, the dimensionless concentration at the biofilm surface ($z^* = 1$) is equal to "1" as stated in Equation 8.35. Equation 8.36 is a physical condition. Because biofilms are grown on impermeable surfaces, the flux at the bottom is equal to zero. Although the growth-limiting nutrient concentration may or may not reach zero above the bottom, the flux is always zero at the bottom, and Equation 8.36 is always satisfied.

At

$$z^* = 1 \qquad C^* = 1 \tag{8.35}$$

At

$$z^* = 0 \qquad \frac{dC^*}{dz^*} = 0 \tag{8.36}$$

8.4.1.6   Effectiveness factors

Effectiveness factor η is the ratio of the growth-limiting nutrient utilization rate that is diffusion-limited to the growth-limiting nutrient utilization rate that is not limited by diffusion (diffusion-free), as given by

$$\eta = \frac{\text{diffusion-limited nutrient utilization rate}}{\text{diffusion-free nutrient utilization rate}} = \frac{\text{NUR}}{\text{NUR}_0} \tag{8.37}$$

The diffusion-free growth-limiting nutrient utilization rate, NUR_0, needs to be calculated for both uniform and stratified biofilms from

$$\text{NUR}_0 = \frac{\mu_{max} L_f A X_{fav}}{Y_{X/S}} \frac{C_s}{(K_s + C_s)} = \frac{\mu_{max} L_f A X_{fav}}{Y_{X/S}} \frac{1}{(\beta + 1)} \tag{8.38}$$

For stratified biofilms, NUR_0 could be calculated using variable biofilm density. In this case, it would be difficult to compare effectiveness factors for uniform and stratified biofilms (they would be calculated using different NUR_0 values). However, this computation may be approached by noting that the ratio of the activities of the stratified and uniform biofilms is the same as the ratio of the effectiveness factors calculated for these biofilms.

8.4.1.6.1   Effectiveness factor for uniform biofilms.   The growth-limiting nutrient utilization rate in a uniform biofilm is equal to the product of the flux and the surface area of the biofilm. The flux is calculated from Equation 8.33 by first calculating, from the numerical solution, the derivative of the concentration with respect to distance, and then multiplying it by the diffusivity:

$$\text{NUR}_{\text{average}} = A D_{fav} \frac{C_s}{L_f} \frac{dC^*}{dz^*} \bigg|_{\substack{\text{uniform} \\ z^* = 1}} \tag{8.39}$$

Combining Equations 8.37 and 8.39, the effectiveness factor is

$$
\eta_h = \frac{AD_{fav} \dfrac{C_s}{L_f} \dfrac{dC^*}{dz^*}\Big|_{\substack{uniform \\ z^*=1}}}{\dfrac{\mu_{max} L_f AX_{fav}}{Y_{X/S}} \dfrac{1}{(\beta+1)}} = \frac{(\beta+1)}{\Phi^2} \dfrac{dC^*}{dz^*}\Big|_{\substack{uniform \\ z^*=1}}
\tag{8.40}
$$

8.4.1.6.2 Effectiveness factor for stratified biofilms. The growth-limiting nutrient utilization rate in a stratified biofilm is equal to the product of the flux and the surface area of the biofilm, and it is calculated from

$$
NUR_{stratified} = AD_{f\_at\_surface} \frac{C_s}{L_f} \frac{dC^*}{dz^*}\Big|_{\substack{stratified \\ z^*=1}}
\tag{8.41}
$$

The flux is calculated from Equation 8.34 by calculating the derivative of the concentration with respect to distance and multiplying it by the effective diffusivity.

The effective diffusivity at the surface is defined as

$$
D_{f\_at\_surface} = D_{fav} \frac{2(\Psi+1)}{2\Psi+1}
\tag{8.42}
$$

Combining Equations 8.37, 8.41, 8.42, and the effectiveness factor is

$$
\eta_s = \frac{AD_{fav} \dfrac{2(\Psi+1)}{2\Psi+1} \dfrac{C_s}{L_f} \dfrac{dC^*}{dz^*}\Big|_{\substack{stratified \\ z^*=1}}}{\dfrac{\mu_{max} L_f AX_{fav}}{Y_{X/S}} \dfrac{C_s}{(K_s+C_s)}} = \frac{(\beta+1)\dfrac{2(\Psi+1)}{2\Psi+1}}{\Phi^2} \dfrac{dC^*}{dz^*}\Big|_{\substack{stratified \\ z^*=1}}
\tag{8.43}
$$

8.4.1.7 Activity of stratified biofilms

To solve Equations 8.33 and 8.34, we use MATLAB's boundary value solver function (bvp4c). Function bvp4c is a finite difference code that implements the three-stage Lobatto IIIa formula. Mesh selection and error control are based on the residual of the continuous solution. We use MATLAB's defaults to control the precision of the solution. The MATLAB® program "StratifiedBiofilms.m" can be used to calculate the activity of stratified biofilms. The program can also be used to calculate the effectiveness factors given by Equations 8.40 and 8.43. From the solution, it calculates the average effective diffusivity and biofilm density using Equations 8.26 and 8.11 (by using the average values instead of the local values). These average values are used to calculate the growth-limiting nutrient concentration profile and the effectiveness factor for a uniform biofilm.

Example 8.1: Calculation of biofilm activity using the MATLAB program

Assume the following operating conditions, biokinetic parameters and biofilm properties:

$C_s = 0.008$ mg/cm^3
$K_s = 0.002$ mg/cm^3
$D_w = 2 \times 10^{-5}$ cm^2/s
$\mu_{max}/Y_{X/S} = 6.37 \times 10^{-5}$ (1/s)
$a = 0.25 \times D_w$ (cm^2/s)
$\zeta = 0.001 \times 10^4 \times D_w$ (cm/s)
$L_f = 500 \times 10^{-4}$ (cm)

1. Calculate average effective diffusivity.
2. Calculate average biofilm density.
3. Calculate dimensionless groups $\kappa = \left(\dfrac{D_w}{a}\right)$, $\Psi = \left(\dfrac{a}{L_f\zeta}\right)$, and $\Phi = \left(\sqrt{\dfrac{\mu_{max}L_f^2 X_{fav}}{Y_{X/S}C_sD_{fav}}}\right)$.
4. Prepare a table showing the distance from the bottom versus the growth-limiting nutrient concentration.
5. Calculate the activity of the biofilm using (1) the stratified biofilm model and (2) the uniform biofilm model.
6. Calculate the ratio between the activity of the uniform biofilm and that of the stratified biofilm.
7. Calculate the effective diffusivity at the surface of the stratified biofilm.
8. Calculate the biofilm density at the surface of the stratified biofilm.
9. Recalculate the activity of the uniform biofilm assuming its density and diffusivity are equal to those at the surface of the stratified biofilm.
10. Recalculate the activity of the uniform biofilm assuming its density is equal to 5 g/L and its diffusivity is equal to 1.8×10^{-5} cm^2/s.
11. Discuss the results.

Solutions

1. Average effective diffusivity is calculated from Equation 8.26:

$$D_{fav} = a + \frac{\zeta L_f}{2} = 0.25 \times 2 \times 10^{-5} + \frac{0.01 \times 10^4 \times 2 \times 10^{-5} \times 500 \times 10^{-4}}{2} = 1 \times 10^{-5} \frac{\text{cm}^2}{\text{s}}$$

2. Average biofilm density is calculated from Equation 8.29; note that average effective diffusivity is used instead of surface-averaged effective diffusivity:

$$X_{fl} = -38.856 + 38.976 \times \left(\frac{D_{fz}}{D_w}\right)^{-0.7782} = -38.856 + 38.976 \times \left(\frac{1 \times 10^{-5}}{2 \times 10^{-5}}\right)^{-0.7782} = 27.99 \text{ mg/cm}^3(\text{g/L})$$

3. The dimensionless groups are calculated as follows:

$$\kappa = \frac{D_w}{a} = \frac{2 \times 10^{-5}}{0.25 \times 2 \times 10^{-5}} = 4$$

$$\Psi = \frac{a}{L_f \zeta} = \frac{0.25 \times 2 \times 10^{-5}}{0.001 \times 10^4 \times 2 \times 10^{-5} \times 500 \times 10^{-4}} = 0.25$$

$$= \sqrt{\frac{\mu_{max} \times L_f^2 \times X_{fav}}{Y_{X/S} \times C_s \times D_{fav}}} = \sqrt{\frac{6.37 \times 10^{-5} \times (500 \times 10^{-4})^2 \times 27.99}{0.008 \ 1 \times 10^{-5}}} = \sqrt{55.7} = 7.46$$

4. If "StratifiedBiofilms.m" and "UniformBiofilms.m" are used, they will write the dimensionless position, dimensionless derivative, and dimensionless concentration to the "Stratifiedprofile.txt" and "Uniformprofile.txt" files. If the files are opened using Microsoft Excel®, the following table will be obtained:

Stratified biofilm			Uniform biofilm		
x^*	dC^*/dx^*	C^*	x	dC^*/dx^*	C^*
0.00E+00	0.00E+00	2.28E-07	0.00E+00	0.00E+00	1.80E-06
1.72E-02	4.76E-06	2.69E-07	1.72E-02	6.97E-06	1.86E-06
3.45E-02	1.06E-05	3.98E-07	3.45E-02	1.44E-05	2.04E-06
5.17E-02	1.89E-05	6.48E-07	5.17E-02	2.28E-05	2.36E-06
6.90E-02	3.18E-05	1.08E-06	6.90E-02	3.27E-05	2.83E-06
8.62E-02	5.17E-05	1.78E-06	8.62E-02	4.48E-05	3.50E-06
1.03E-01	8.24E-05	2.92E-06	1.03E-01	5.99E-05	4.40E-06
1.21E-01	1.29E-04	4.72E-06	1.21E-01	7.90E-05	5.59E-06
1.38E-01	1.99E-04	7.50E-06	1.38E-01	1.03E-04	7.15E-06
1.55E-01	3.03E-04	1.18E-05	1.55E-01	1.35E-04	9.19E-06
1.72E-01	4.55E-04	1.82E-05	1.72E-01	1.75E-04	1.18E-05
2.07E-01	9.91E-04	4.21E-05	1.90E-01	2.27E-04	1.53E-05
2.41E-01	2.06E-03	9.26E-05	2.07E-01	2.94E-04	1.97E-05
2.76E-01	4.11E-03	1.95E-04	2.24E-01	3.80E-04	2.55E-05
2.93E-01	5.72E-03	2.79E-04	2.41E-01	4.92E-04	3.30E-05
3.10E-01	7.89E-03	3.96E-04	2.59E-01	6.37E-04	4.27E-05
3.28E-01	1.08E-02	5.56E-04	2.76E-01	8.24E-04	5.52E-05
3.45E-01	1.46E-02	7.73E-04	2.87E-01	9.78E-04	6.55E-05
3.79E-01	2.62E-02	1.46E-03	2.99E-01	1.16E-03	7.78E-05
4.14E-01	4.54E-02	2.67E-03	3.10E-01	1.38E-03	9.23E-05
4.48E-01	7.64E-02	4.73E-03	3.22E-01	1.64E-03	1.10E-04
5.00E-01	1.58E-01	1.06E-02	3.33E-01	1.94E-03	1.30E-04
5.52E-01	3.03E-01	2.21E-02	3.45E-01	2.31E-03	1.55E-04
6.03E-01	5.42E-01	4.35E-02	3.56E-01	2.74E-03	1.83E-04
6.55E-01	8.94E-01	8.01E-02	3.68E-01	3.25E-03	2.18E-04
7.07E-01	1.36E+00	1.38E-01	3.79E-01	3.86E-03	2.59E-04
7.59E-01	1.91E+00	2.22E-01	3.91E-01	4.59E-03	3.07E-04
8.10E-01	2.50E+00	3.36E-01	4.02E-01	5.45E-03	3.65E-04
8.62E-01	3.08E+00	4.81E-01	4.14E-01	6.47E-03	4.33E-04
9.14E-01	3.62E+00	6.54E-01	4.25E-01	7.68E-03	5.14E-04
9.66E-01	4.10E+00	8.54E-01	4.37E-01	9.12E-03	6.10E-04
1.00E+00	4.37E+00	1.00E+00	4.48E-01	1.08E-02	7.25E-04

Stratified biofilm			Uniform biofilm		
x^*	dC^*/dx^*	C^*	x	dC^*/dx^*	C^*
			4.60E-01	1.28E-02	8.60E-04
			4.71E-01	1.52E-02	1.02E-03
			4.83E-01	1.81E-02	1.21E-03
			4.94E-01	2.15E-02	1.44E-03
			5.06E-01	2.55E-02	1.71E-03
			5.17E-01	3.02E-02	2.03E-03
			5.29E-01	3.58E-02	2.41E-03
			5.40E-01	4.25E-02	2.86E-03
			5.52E-01	5.04E-02	3.39E-03
			5.69E-01	6.50E-02	4.38E-03
			5.86E-01	8.38E-02	5.65E-03
			6.03E-01	1.08E-01	7.30E-03
			6.21E-01	1.39E-01	9.41E-03
			6.38E-01	1.78E-01	1.21E-02
			6.55E-01	2.29E-01	1.56E-02
			6.72E-01	2.92E-01	2.01E-02
			6.90E-01	3.73E-01	2.58E-02
			7.24E-01	5.98E-01	4.23E-02
			7.76E-01	1.17E+00	8.65E-02
			8.28E-01	2.11E+00	1.70E-01
			8.79E-01	3.50E+00	3.13E-01
			9.31E-01	5.29E+00	5.39E-01
			9.66E-01	6.67E+00	7.45E-01
			1.00E+00	8.16E+00	1.00E+00

5. If "StratifiedBiofilms.m" is used, the following results will be obtained: the flux at the surface of the stratified biofilm is equal to its activity. Stratified_flux = 1.0496 × 10^{-5} (mg/cm^2/s).
6. If "UniformBiofilms.m" is used, the following results will be obtained: the flux at the surface of the uniform biofilm is equal to its activity. Uniform_flux = 1.3057 × 10^{-5} (mg/cm^2/s).
7. The ratio between the activity of the uniform biofilm and that of the stratified biofilm is 1.3057/1.0496 = 1.2439.
8. The effective diffusivity at the surface of the stratified biofilm is calculated from Equation 8.14 by replacing the biofilm thickness (500 × 10^{-4} cm) with z (because the diffusivity at the biofilm surface needs to be calculated).
   D_{fz} at the surface = $a + \zeta \times z = 0.25 \times 2 \times 10^{-5} + 0.001 \times 10^4 \times 2 \times 10^{-5} \times 500 \times 10^{-4} = 1.5 \times 10^{-5}$ cm^2/s
9. The biofilm density at the surface is calculated using the effective diffusivity calculated above.

$$X_{fl} = -38.856 + 38.976 \times \left(\frac{D_{fz}}{D_w} \right)^{-0.7782} = -38.856 + 38.976 \times \left(\frac{1.15 \times 10^{-5}}{2 \times 10^{-5}} \right)^{-0.7782} = 9.67 \text{ mg/cm}^3 \text{(g/L)}$$

10. If $X_{fa} = 9.67$ mg/cm^3 and $D_{fav} = 1.5 \times 10^{-5}$ cm^2/s are used in "UniformBiofilms.m", the activity of the biofilm is calculated to be 9.3993×10^{-6} mg/cm^2/s. (Use lines 89–90 to enter density values; otherwise, the software automatically calculates the averages and uses them.)

11. When $X_{fa} = 5$ mg/cm^3 and $D_{fav} = 1.8 \times 10^{-5}$ cm^2/s are used in "UniformBiofilms.m", the activity of the biofilm is calculated to be 7.373×10^{-6} mg/cm^2/s.

12. The results are summarized below. Assuming that the density of the biofilm equals the density measured near the surface of the stratified biofilm, the stratified biofilm is more active than the hypothetical uniform biofilm. However, if the same average (average density of the stratified biofilm) is used for both, the biofilm with uniformly distributed density is more active. This demonstrates that when the uniform and stratified biofilms are compared, the definition of uniform biofilms defines the results rather than a true evaluation because such biofilms are hypothetical and do not exist. See the section below for a more detailed discussion.

   For $X_{fav} = 27.99$ g/L, `Stratified _ flux` $= 1.0496 \times 10^{-5}$ mg/cm^2/s and `Uniform _ flux` $= 1.3057 \times 10^{-5}$ mg/cm^2/s.

   For $X_{fa} = 9.67$ g/L (the density at the surface of the stratified biofilm), `Uniform _ flux` $= 7.373 \times 10^{-6}$ mg/cm^2/s.

8.5   Computing biokinetics parameters in stratified biofilms

One of the important steps leading to the experimental verification of a mathematical model of biofilm activity is evaluating the biokinetic parameters of microbial growth in the biofilm. All mathematical models of biofilm activity compare the rate of transport of the growth-limiting nutrient to the rate of consumption of the growth-limiting nutrient. Experimental verification of this relation requires empirical assessment of the variables of biofilm processes, which are represented as parameters in the mathematical models of biofilm activity. The conceptual model of stratified biofilms can be used to compute the biokinetic parameters of microbial growth from the concentration profiles of the growth-limiting nutrient measured with microelectrodes, and the following section illustrates the computations.

8.5.1   Solution algorithm

The algorithm we use to compute the biokinetic parameters is shown in Figure 8.16; we followed this algorithm to solve Equation 8.33. To facilitate computation of the biokinetic parameters, we have integrated the algorithm (Figure 8.16) into a MATLAB program, "biokineticparameterestimator.m", which is given on the disk.

The procedures in the algorithm (Figure 8.16) are best explained using a pseudocode; the numbers refer to steps in the flowchart shown in Figure 8.16:

1. Read the sequence of pairs: dimensionless distances and dimensionless oxygen concentrations calculated from experimental data.
2. Enter biofilm variables C_s, a, ζ, and L_f.
3. Assume K_s and $\mu_{max}/Y_{X/S}$.
4. Calculate the Φ, β, and ψ values, and run the minimization search procedure (fminsearch()).
5. The minimization search procedure calls the Stratified_model() function.
6. The Stratified_model() function solves Equation 8.33 for the given boundary conditions. It uses a boundary value solver function (bvp4c). Function bvp4c is a finite

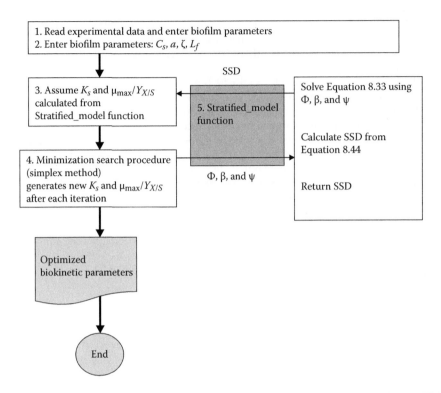

Figure 8.16 The flowchart we use to compute biokinetic parameters in biofilms. The MATLAB program written from the algorithm is given on the disk (biokineticparameterestimator.m).

difference code that implements the three-stage Lobatto IIIa formula. Mesh selection and error control are based on the residual of the continuous solution. We use MATLAB's defaults to control the precision of the solution.

7. The Stratified_model() function determines the predicted concentrations of oxygen, at the same locations where they were measured, and calculates the sums of squared differences (SSD) for the pairs of predicted and measured values as

$$SSD = \sum_{n=1}^{n=n\_of\_data} (C^*_{predicted} - C^*_{experimentally\_measured})^2 \tag{8.44}$$

The minimization search procedure (step 4) continues until it finds the Φ, β, and ψ values that minimize Equation 8.44, which is considered the objective function in the search for optimum Φ, β, and ψ values.

To minimize SSD and calculate the optimum Φ and β values, we use the direct search method (Lagarias et al. 1998) integrated into MATLAB's fminsearh function. The fminsearh routine is referred to as an unconstrained nonlinear optimization routine in MATLAB's help menu and in the work of Lagarias et al. (1998). It starts searching from the assumed Φ and β values, which were calculated from assumed K_s and $\mu_{max}/Y_{X/S}$, and calculates corresponding dimensionless variables and the respective SSD from the solution of

Equation 8.33. The SSD calculation is shown as step 4 in Figure 8.16. We constrain the values of K_s and $\mu_{max}/Y_{X/S}$ to be greater than or equal to zero in the Stratified_model() function because their values cannot be smaller than zero. Then the fminsearh function, using the Nelder and Mead (1965) simplex algorithm, finds the optimum K_s and $\mu_{max}/Y_{X/S}$ values for the next iteration (Nelder and Mead 1965). The iteration stops when the optimum K_s and $\mu_{max}/Y_{X/S}$ values have been found, i.e., when the variables from two consecutive iterations differ by less than 0.00001. We relied on MATLAB's default criterion of convergence. The MATLAB program which uses the algorithm shown in Figure 8.16 is given on the disk (biokineticparameterestimator.m).

Example 8.2

For the following dissolved oxygen concentration profile in dimensionless form at the specified operating conditions, estimate $\mu_{max}/Y_{X/S}$ and K_s using the given MATLAB program (biokineticparameterestimator.m) (1) for uniform biofilms and (2) for stratified biofilms.

$C_b = 0.008$ mg/cm^3, or 8 mg/L
$D_w = 2 \times 10^{-5}$ cm^2/s
$a_0 = 0.5 \times D_w$: Effective diffusivity at the bottom of the biofilm (cm^2/s)
$\zeta = 0.001 \times 10^4 \times D_w$: Effective diffusivity gradient (cm/s)
$L_f = 500 \times 10^{-4}$: Average biofilm thickness (cm)

x^*	C^*
0.00E+00	1.10E-04
1.72E-02	1.17E-04
3.45E-02	1.39E-04
6.90E-02	2.35E-04
1.03E-01	4.31E-04
1.38E-01	7.92E-04
1.72E-01	1.43E-03
2.24E-01	3.28E-03
2.76E-01	7.11E-03
3.28E-01	1.45E-02
3.79E-01	2.77E-02
4.31E-01	4.95E-02
4.83E-01	8.25E-02
5.34E-01	1.29E-01
5.86E-01	1.89E-01
6.38E-01	2.63E-01
6.90E-01	3.49E-01
7.41E-01	4.46E-01
7.93E-01	5.50E-01
8.45E-01	6.59E-01
8.97E-01	7.72E-01
9.48E-01	8.87E-01
1.00E+00	1.00E+00

Solution

After the above profile is entered, `biokineticparameterestimator.m` gives the following outputs:

1. Assuming that the biomass has the same density from the top to the bottom:
   $a = 0.5D_w$
   $b = 1 \times 10^{-10}$, which is very close to zero.
      The program outputs the following values:
   Umy $= \mu_{max}/Y_{X/S} = 6 \times 10^{-6}\,s^{-1}$
   $K_s = 0.00058$ mg/cm^3, or 0.58 mg/L
   SSD $= 0.0128$
2. Assuming that biomass density increases toward the bottom:
   $a = 0.5D_w$
   $b = 10^4 D_w$
      The program outputs the following values:
   Umy $= \mu_{max}/Y_{X/S} = 6.38 \times 10^{-5}\,s^{-1}$
   $K_s = 0.0010$ mg/cm^3, or 1 mg/L
   SSD $= 7 \times 10^{-6}$

As seen from the SSD values and the figures (Figure 8.17) showing the experimental and the predicted data (see below), prediction is more successful when the stratified biofilms model is used.

8.5.2　Using the concept of stratified biofilms to explain the properties of uniform biofilms

We have been asked, on occasion, whether the model of stratified biofilms can be used to predict the properties of uniform biofilms. In principle, the answer to the question is yes, but with some restrictions. Because uniform biofilms do not exist in nature, the model's predictions cannot be verified experimentally. Nevertheless, it is interesting to inspect what the activity of a hypothetical biofilm would be if $\zeta = 0$. There is a practical purpose to this attempt: it would be useful to consider hypothetical uniform biofilms that were equivalent to given heterogeneous biofilms. Such a hypothetical biofilm would serve as a conceptual standard and could be used to measure the deviations of the properties of real heterogeneous biofilms from those determined for hypothetical uniform biofilms. Uniform biofilms have been defined here as those that have uniformly distributed density and diffusivity, and the properties of such biofilms can be considered. However, as pointed out, experimental data cannot be generated: such biofilms cannot be grown to verify their properties, because uniform biofilms do not exist in nature. Uniform biofilms are conceptual constructs that are generated to better understand the properties of real biofilms, which are heterogeneous.

We define equivalent biofilms as biofilms that have the same activities. Consequently, to construct a uniform biofilm that is equivalent to a given heterogeneous biofilm is to construct a biofilm with uniformly distributed density (and diffusivity) such that the uniform biofilm has the same activity as the given heterogeneous biofilm. As discussed in Chapter 1, biofilm activity is defined based on the rate of utilization of the growth-limiting nutrient, and this rate is related to biomass density and diffusivity, the variables we have chosen for testing whether biofilms are uniform or not. However, it is not clear how to select the constant diffusivity and related biomass density for the uniform biofilms so that they have the same effect on biofilm activity as variable effective diffusivity

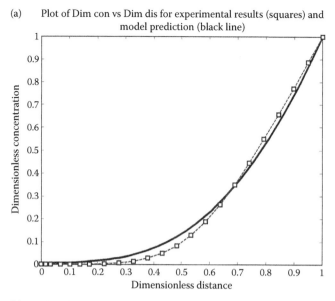

(a) Plot of Dim con vs Dim dis for experimental results (squares) and model prediction (black line)

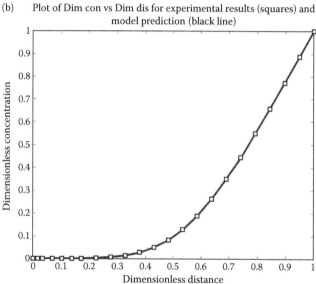

(b) Plot of Dim con vs Dim dis for experimental results (squares) and model prediction (black line)

Figure 8.17 Profiles of the experimental data (squares) and the predicted values (continuous line) for two cases: (a) assuming that the biomass has the same density from the top to the bottom and (b) assuming that the biomass density increases toward the bottom.

and biomass density have on activity in stratified biofilms, and three possibilities are considered:

- Rule 1: A uniform biofilm has an effective diffusivity equal to the average effective diffusivity of the equivalent stratified biofilm.
- Rule 2: A uniform biofilm has an effective diffusivity equal to the effective diffusivity near the bottom of the equivalent stratified biofilm.

- Rule 3: A uniform biofilm has an effective diffusivity equal to the effective diffusivity near the surface of the equivalent stratified biofilm.

As expected, uniform biofilms constructed following these rules behave differently from each other.

To compare the activity of stratified biofilms with the activity of uniform biofilms we have computed the ratio of their effectiveness factors (Equations 8.40 and 8.43).

$$\frac{\eta_h}{\eta_s} = \frac{\dfrac{(\beta+1)}{\Phi^2} \dfrac{dC^*}{dz^*}\Big|_{\substack{\text{uniform} \\ z^*=1}}}{\dfrac{(\beta+1)\dfrac{2(\Psi+1)}{2\Psi+1}}{\Phi^2} \dfrac{dC^*}{dz^*}\Big|_{\substack{\text{uniform} \\ z^*=1}}} \tag{8.45}$$

where β (the dimensionless Monod half-rate constant) does not depend on biofilm structure and has the same value for uniform and stratified biofilms. The term $\dfrac{2(\Psi+1)}{2\Psi+1}$ is always greater than 1, and the dimensionless derivative of the concentration with respect to distance is higher in uniform biofilms than it is in stratified biofilms. The Thiele modulus computed for the uniform biofilms,

$$\Phi = \sqrt{\frac{\mu_{max} L_f^2 X_{fav}}{Y_{X/S} C_s D_{fav}}}$$

can be different from that computed for the stratified biofilms because in uniform biofilms the Thiele modulus depends on the average biofilm density and average effective diffusivity, and the latter can be computed using different rules, as described above.

For each of the three rules for constructing uniform biofilms, the effectiveness factor and activity ratio of the stratified biofilm and of the uniform hypothetical biofilm having $\beta = 0.044$, $\psi = 0.5$, and $\kappa = 4$ were calculated. The results in Table 8.1 show that, depending

Table 8.1 Effectiveness Factors for Different Hypothetical Uniform Biofilms ($\beta = 0.044$, $\psi = 0.5$, and $\kappa = 4$)

Rule	Density of the hypothetical uniform biofilm	η_h	η_s	η_h/η_s Activity ratio of the uniform and stratified biofilms
1	Averaged from the diffusivity profile (Equation 8.26) = 32.45 g/L	0.2050	0.147	1.339
2	Equal to the diffusivity measured near the bottom of the stratified biofilm = 77.8 g/L	0.4356	0.147	2.07
3	Equal to the diffusivity measured near the surface of the stratified biofilm = 9.9 g/L	0.089	0.147	0.6068

Note: The diffusion-free utilization rate is calculated for the average biofilm density calculated for the stratified biofilm ($X_{fav} = 32.45$ g/L). (Reproduced from Beyenal, H., and Lewandowski, Z., *Chemical Engineering Science*, 60, 4337–4348, 2005.)

on how the average properties of the uniform biofilm were computed, its activity could be higher or lower than the activity of the stratified biofilm. It is interesting to note that for rule 1, in which the effective diffusivity of the uniform biofilm was equal to the average effective diffusivity of the stratified biofilm, the activity of the stratified biofilm was lower than the activity of the uniform biofilm. This may seem counterintuitive, but it also demonstrates that selecting properties for a uniform biofilm that represent the behavior of a stratified biofilm is not trivial and involves more than just computing the average effective diffusivity from an experimentally measured diffusivity profile. A comparison of the data in Table 8.1 shows that a uniform biofilm of a slightly lower density than that computed for rule 1 would have the same activity as the stratified biofilm. However, because the activity of most biofilms is defined by the activity of the layer near the surface, perhaps the effective diffusivity near the surface should be used to generate a representative uniform biofilm, which would indicate that the stratified biofilm (Table 8.1) is $1/0.6 = 1.7\times$ more active than the uniform biofilm.

8.6 Mathematical modeling of biofilm processes and experimental verification of model predictions

Whenever mathematical models need to be verified experimentally, there is always a desire to make a loop in which the predictions of the model are verified and the differences between the predictions and the experimental verification are used to improve the model. This idealized situation is rarely possible, although in many instances it can be partially implemented. In biofilm research, the gap between mathematical modeling and experimental verification is deep and very few model predictions can be verified. One reason for this state of affairs is that biofilm models do not accommodate many variables measured experimentally. For example, the tools shown in this book allow measuring biofilm porosity, and we expect that biofilm porosity affects biofilm activity. The effect of porosity on biofilm activity cannot be modeled because the models of biofilm activity do not include biofilm porosity as a control parameter. In such instances, the model of stratified biofilms can still be used to study the effects of biofilm porosity on variables represented in the models of biofilm activity, such as effective diffusivity. We have determined experimentally that biofilm porosity is correlated with surface-averaged relative effective diffusivity for a given distance from the bottom (Figure 8.18). The areal porosity of each individual layer was calculated from a confocal image of the biofilm and was related to the volume of that layer computed by multiplying the surface area (the field of view) by the thickness of the layer (the distance between the images).

Implementing a loop in which predictions of mathematical models are verified experimentally and the differences between the predictions and the data are used to improve the model is possible if the predicted parameter in the model is also a variable measured in biofilm reactors. This has been demonstrated here using effective diffusivity as an example. This is a special case, though, because the measured variable (effective diffusivity) is also a parameter in the mathematical model of biofilm activity. Therefore, it is possible to ascribe effective diffusivities to various layers in the model of stratified biofilms, solve the mathematical model of biofilm activity for several different effective diffusivities, and predict how the effective diffusivity gradient affects biofilm activity. Such predictions can be verified because effective diffusivity gradients in biofilms can be measured using the tools described in this book. There are interesting variables hypothetically affecting biofilm activity that are not represented by parameters in the models of biofilm activity. For example, the fractal dimension of microcolonies is related to the ruggedness of

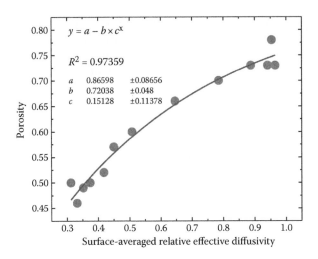

Figure 8.18 Correlation between experimentally measured surface-averaged relative effective diffusivity and porosity for our three-species model biofilm. There is a good correlation between model and experimental data, promising that porosity can be integrated into the description of effective diffusivity and used in the mathematical models of biofilm activity.

their surface. Hypothetically, the more developed the surface area of the microcolonies is, the higher the activity of the biofilm is expected to be. To test this hypothesis, the fractal dimension would need to be manipulated in the same manner as the effective diffusivity gradient. Fractal dimension, however, is not represented by a parameter in the mathematical models of biofilm activity, and this procedure is not possible. The predictions can only be verified with respect to variables that can be measured and that also are represented as parameters in the models of biofilm activity. An interesting possibility for verifying the effects of parameters that are not represented in biofilm models is amending biofilm models with expressions that include the parameters of interest. It would then be possible to follow the delineated procedure—to manipulate the parameter of interest, solve the model for several characteristic values of the parameter, and use these solutions as predictions that can be verified experimentally. In the case of the fractal dimension, the amended model might look like the following expression:

$$\text{local biofilm activity} = F(D_{fz}, z, \mu_{max}, C, X_{fl}, K_s, Y_{X/S}, \text{fractal dimension}) \qquad (8.46)$$

The function of fractal dimension in the above expression is defined by the user. The type of function used would affect the predicted biofilm activity, and the search for the function that represents the effect of the selected parameter may become a research question itself.

In the examples discussed here, the stratified biofilm model is used to characterize a small surface area covered with a biofilm, limited to the size of view of the microscope. However, in principle, the surface area that can be characterized in this manner is not limited by any linear dimensions. The researcher may design the measurements so that the results quantify biofilm processes on 10% of the surface covered with the biofilm, for example. By controlling the surface area to be characterized by the results of microscale measurements, the researcher can use the conceptual model of stratified biofilms to bridge the microscale and macroscale measurements and contribute to solving one of the fundamental problems in biofilm engineering: quantitatively relating biofilm activity at the microscale to the performance of biofilm reactors at the macroscale.

The model presented here has been extended to provide analytical solutions describing biofilm processes considering a continuum of variation of both biofilm density and substrate effective diffusivity, demonstrating the usefulness of our approach (Gonzo et al. 2012).

Nomenclature

Roman symbols

a	Effective diffusivity at the bottom of the biofilm (m²/s)
A	Surface area of the biofilm (m²)
C	Growth-limiting nutrient concentration (kg/m³)
C^*	Dimensionless concentration $\left(= \dfrac{C}{C_s} \right)$
CA	Cellular automata
C_s	Nutrient concentration at the surface of the biofilm (kg/m³)
D_{fav}	Average effective diffusivity $\left(= a + \dfrac{\zeta L_f}{2} \right)$
D_f^*	Dimensionless effective diffusivity $\left(= \dfrac{D_{fz}}{D_{fav}} = \dfrac{2(\Psi + z^*)}{2\Psi + 1} \right)$
D_f	Effective diffusivity of growth-limiting nutrient (m²/s)
$D_{f\,\text{at surface}}$	Effective diffusivity of growth-limiting nutrient at the biofilm surface (m²/s)
D_{fl}	Local effective diffusivity of growth-limiting nutrient (m²/s)
D_{fz}	Surface-averaged effective diffusivity of growth-limiting nutrient (m²/s)
D_{fz}^*	Relative surface-averaged effective diffusivity (dimensionless)
D_w	Effective diffusivity of growth-limiting nutrient in the liquid medium (m²/s)
k	Number of microelectrode measurements
K_s	Monod half-rate constant (kg/m³)
L_f	Average biofilm thickness
L_x	Width of the layer in the X direction
L_y	Width of the layer in the Y direction
n	Integer number
p	Number of layers in the direction perpendicular to the biofilm surface
X_{fav}	Averaged biofilm density (kg/m³)
X_f^*	Dimensionless biofilm density $\left(= \dfrac{X_{fl}}{X_{fav}} \right)$
X_{fl}	Averaged biofilm density in the differential element (kg/m³)
NUR	Diffusion-limited nutrient utilization rate (kg/s)
NUR$_0$	Diffusion-free nutrient utilization rate (kg/s)
NUR$_\text{stratified}$	Nutrient utilization rate for a stratified biofilm (kg/s)
NUR$_\text{uniform}$	Nutrient utilization rate for a uniform biofilm (kg/s)
$Y_{X/S}$	Yield coefficient (kg microorganisms/kg nutrient)
z^*	Dimensionless distance $\left(= \dfrac{z}{L_f} \right)$

Greek symbols

κ	Inverse of the relative effective diffusivity at the bottom of the biofilm $\left(=\dfrac{D_w}{a}\right)$
ψ	Ratio between the effective diffusivity at the bottom of the biofilm and the difference in diffusivity between the surface and the bottom of the biofilm $\left(=\dfrac{a}{L_f\zeta}\right)$
Φ	Thiele modulus $\left(=\sqrt{\dfrac{\mu_{max}L_f^2 X_{fav}}{Y_{X/S}C_s D_{fav}}}\right)$
ζ	Effective diffusivity gradient
η	Effectiveness factor
η_s	Effectiveness factor for a stratified biofilm
η_h	Effectiveness factor for a uniform biofilm
μ_{max}	Maximum specific growth rate (s^{-1})
β	Dimensionless Monod half-rate constant $\left(=\dfrac{K_s}{C_s}\right)$

References

Beyenal, H., and Lewandowski, Z. 2000. Combined effect of substrate concentration and flow velocity on effective diffusivity in biofilms. *Water Research* 34: 528–538.

Fan, L. S., Leyvaramos, R., Wisecarver, K. D., and Zehner, B. J. 1990. Diffusion of phenol through a biofilm grown on activated carbon particles in a draft-tube 3-phase fluidized-bed bioreactor. *Biotechnology and Bioengineering* 35: 279–286.

Gonzo, E. E., Wuertz, S., and Rajal, V. B. 2012. Continuum heterogeneous biofilm model—A simple and accurate method for effectiveness factor determination. *Biotechnology and Bioengineering* 109: 1779–1790.

IWA Task Group on Biofilm Modeling. 2006. *Mathematical Modeling of Biofilms*. London: IWA.

Lagarias, J. C., Reeds, J. A., Wright, M. H., and Wright, P. E. 1998. Convergence properties of the Nelder-Mead simplex method in low dimensions. *SIAM Journal of Optimization* 9: 112–147.

Nelder, J. A., and Mead, R. 1965. A simplex method for function minimization. *Computer Journal* 7: 308–313.

Suggested readings

Biofilm modeling

Arcangeli, J. P., and Arvin, E. 1997. Modeling of the cometabolic biodegradation of trichloroethylene by toluene oxidizing bacteria in a biofilm system. *Environmental Science and Technology* 31: 3044–3052.

Atkinson, B., and Davies, I. J. 1974. Overall rate of substrate uptake (reaction) by microbial films. 1. Biological rate equation. *Transactions of the Institution of Chemical Engineers* 52: 248–259.

Beyenal, H., and Lewandowski, Z. 2005. Modeling mass transport and microbial activity in stratified biofilms. *Chemical Engineering Science* 60: 4337–4348.

Bishop, P. L. and Rittmann, B. E. 1995. Modelling heterogeneity in biofilms: Report of the discussion session. *Water Science and Technology* 32: 263–265.

Boltz, J. P., Johnson, B. R., Daigger, G. T., and Sandino, J. 2009. Modeling integrated fixed-film activated sludge and moving-bed biofilm reactor systems I: Mathematical treatment and model development. *Water Environment Research* 81: 555–575.

Boltz, J. P., Morgenroth, E., and Sen, D. 2010. Mathematical modelling of biofilms and biofilm reactors for engineering design. *Water Science and Technology* 62: 1821–1836.

Campos-Diaz, K. E., Bandala-Gonzalez, E. R., and Limas-Ballesteros, R. 2012. Fluid bed porosity mathematical model for an inverse fluidized bed bioreactor with particles growing biofilm. *Journal of Environmental Management* 104: 62–66.

Chakraborty, C., Chowdhury, R., and Bhattacharya, P. 2011. Experimental studies and mathematical modeling of an up-flow biofilm reactor treating mustard oil rich wastewater. *Bioresource Technology* 102: 5596–5601.

Choi, Y., Hayes, D., and Johnson, K. 2007. Mathematical model for a batch aerated submerged biofilm reactor for organic carbon and nitrogen removal. *Korean Journal of Chemical Engineering* 24: 633–640.

Coelhoso, I., and Rodrigues, A. 1995. Modeling of biofilm reactors with consecutive reactions. *Bioprocess Engineering* 12: 187–192.

Cooke, A. J., Rowe, R. K., Rittmann, B. E., and Fleming, I. R. 1999. Modeling biochemically driven mineral precipitation in anaerobic biofilms. *Water Science and Technology* 39: 57–64.

Dillon, R., Fauci, L., Fogelson, A., and Gaver, D. 1996. Modeling biofilm processes using the immersed boundary method. *Journal of Computational Physics* 129: 57–73.

Dodds, M. G., Grobe, K. J., and Stewart, P. S. 2000. Modeling biofilm antimicrobial resistance. *Biotechnology and Bioengineering* 68: 456–465.

Eberl, H. J., van Loosdrecht, M. C. M., Morgenroth, E., Noguera, D. R., Perez, J., Picioreanu, C., Rittmann, B. E., Schwarz, A. O., and Wanner, O. 2004. Modelling a spatially heterogeneous biofilm and the bulk fluid: Selected results from Benchmark Problem 2 (BM2). *Water Science and Technology* 49: 155–162.

Essila, N. J., Semmens, M. J., and Voller, V. R. 2000. Modeling biofilms on gas-permeable supports: Concentration and activity profiles. *Journal of Environmental Engineering* 126: 250–257.

Frederick, M. R., Kuttler, C., Hense, B. A., and Eberl, H. J. 2011. A mathematical model of quorum sensing regulated EPS production in biofilm communities. *Theoretical Biology and Medical Modelling* 8: 8.

Fuzzato, M. C., Tallarico Adorno, M. A., de Pinho, S. C., Ribeiro, R., and Tommaso, G. 2009. Simplified mathematical model for an anaerobic sequencing batch biofilm reactor treating lipid-rich wastewater subject to rising organic loading rates. *Environmental Engineering Science* 26: 1197–1206.

Gikas, P., and Livingston, A. G. 1997. Specific ATP and specific oxygen uptake rate in immobilized cell aggregates: Experimental results and theoretical analysis using a structured model of immobilized cell growth. *Biotechnology and Bioengineering* 55: 660–673.

Goudar, C. T., and Strevett, K. A. 2002. Computer programs for estimating substrate flux into steady-state biofilms from pseudoanalytical solutions. *Computer Applications in Engineering Education* 10: 26–32.

Han, Y., Zhang, W., and Xu, J. 2011. A simplified mathematical model of multi-species biofilm for simultaneous removal of sulfur dioxide (SO_2) and nitric oxide (NO) using a biotrickling-filter. *African Journal of Microbiology Research* 5: 541–550.

Herald, M. C., Adler, F. R., and Lion, T. G. 2010. A mathematical model of biofilm formation. *Pediatric Pulmonology* 335–335.

Hermanowicz, S. W. 1998. A model of two-dimensional biofilm morphology. *Water Science and Technology* 37: 219–222.

Hermanowicz, S. W. 1999. Two-dimensional simulations of biofilm development: Effects of external environmental conditions. *Water Science and Technology* 39: 107–114.

Hermanowicz, S. W. 2001. A simple 2D biofilm model yields a variety of morphological features. *Mathematical Biosciences* 169: 1–14.

Horn, H., and Hempel, D. C. 1998. Modeling mass transfer and substrate utilization in the boundary layer of biofilm systems. *Water Science and Technology* 37: 139–147.

Kreft, J. U., Picioreanu, C., Wimpenny, J. W. T., and van Loosdrecht, M. C. M. 2001. Individual-based modelling of biofilms. *Microbiology* 147: 2897–2912.

Laspidou, C. S., and Rittmann, B. E. 2002. Non-steady state modeling of extracellular polymeric substances, soluble microbial products, and active and inert biomass. *Water Research* 36: 1983–1992.

Laspidou, C. S., and Rittmann, B. E. 2004. Modeling the development of biofilm density includ-ing active bacteria, inert biomass, and extracellular polymeric substances. *Water Research* 38: 3349–3361.

Laspidou, C. S., Rittmann, B. E., and Karamanos, S. A. 2005. Finite element modelling to expand the UMCCA model to describe biofilm mechanical behavior. *Water Science and Technology* 52: 161–166.

Liao, Q., Wang, Y.-J., Wang, Y.-Z., Chen, R., Zhu, X., Pu, Y.-K., and Lee, D.-J. 2012. Two-dimension mathematical modeling of photosynthetic bacterial biofilm growth and formation. *International Journal of Hydrogen Energy* 37: 15607–15615.

Loney, N. W., Tabatabaie, M., and Jaiswal, R. 2008. ACSAICHE 99056-Mathematical modeling of leaching of heavy metals from biofilm coated cement based waste forms. *Abstracts of Papers of the American Chemical Society* 235.

Malmstead, M. J., Brockman, F. J., Valocchi, A. J., and Rittmann, B. E. 1995. Modeling biofilm bio-degradation requiring cosubstrates—The Quinoline example. *Water Science and Technology* 31: 71–84.

Martins, A. M. P., Picioreanu, C., Heijnen, J. J., and van Loosdrecht, M. C. M. 2004. Three-dimensional dual-morphotype species modeling of activated sludge flocs. *Environmental Science and Technology* 38: 5632–5641.

Montras, A., Pycke, B., Boon, N., Godia, F., Mergeay, M., Hendrickx, L., and Perez, J. 2008. Distribution of *Nitrosomonas europaea* and *Nitrobacter winogradskyi* in an autotrophic nitrifying biofilm reactor as depicted by molecular analyses and mathematical modelling. *Water Research* 42: 1700–1714.

Morgenroth, E., Eberl, H., and van Loosdrecht, M. C. M. 2000. Evaluating 3-D and 1-D mathematical models for mass transport in heterogeneous biofilms. *Water Science and Technology* 41: 347–356.

Morgenroth, E., van Loosdrecht, M. C. M., and Wanner, O. 2000. Biofilm models for the practitioner. *Water Science and Technology* 41: 509–512.

Morgenroth, E., and Wilderer, P. A. 1998. Modeling of enhanced biological phosphorus removal in a sequencing batch biofilm reactor. *Water Science and Technology* 37: 583–587.

Mousseau, F., Liu, S. X., Hermanowicz, S. W., Lazarova, V., and Manem, J. 1998. Modeling of TURBOFLO—A novel biofilm reactor for wastewater treatment. *Water Science and Technology* 37: 177–181.

Nogueira, R., Elenter, D., Brito, A., Melo, L. F., Wagner, M., and Morgenroth, E. 2005. Evaluating het-erotrophic growth in a nitrifying biofilm reactor using fluorescence in situ hybridization and mathematical modeling. *Water Science and Technology* 52: 135–141.

Noguera, D. R., and Morgenroth, E. 2004. Introduction to the IWA Task Group on Biofilm Modeling. *Water Science and Technology* 49: 131–136.

Noguera, D. R., Okabe, S., and Picioreanu, C. 1999. Biofilm modeling: Present status and future direc-tions. *Water Science and Technology* 39: 273–278.

Noguera, D. R., and Picioreanu, C. 2004. Results from the multi-species Benchmark Problem 3 (BM3) using two-dimensional models. *Water Science and Technology* 49: 169–176.

Noguera, D. R., Pizarro, G., and Clapp, L. W. 2000. Mathematical modeling of trichloroethylene (TCE) degradation in membrane-attached biofilms. *Water Science and Technology* 41: 239–244.

Noguera, D. R., Pizarro, G., Stahl, D. A., and Rittmann, B. E. 1999. Simulation of multispecies biofilm development in three dimensions. *Water Science and Technology* 39: 123–130.

Pavasant, P., dosSantos, L. M. F., Pistikopoulos, E. N., and Livingston, A. G. 1996. Prediction of opti-mal biofilm thickness for membrane-attached biofilms growing in an extractive membrane bio-reactor. *Biotechnology and Bioengineering* 52: 373–386.

Perez, J., Picioreanu, C., and van Loosdrecht, M. 2005. Modeling biofilm and floc diffusion processes based on analytical solution of reaction–diffusion equations. *Water Research* 39: 1311–1323.

Picioreanu, C., Kreft, J. U., and van Loosdrecht, M. C. M. 2004. Particle-based multidimensional multi-species biofilm model. *Applied and Environmental Microbiology* 70: 3024–3040.

Picioreanu, C., van Loosdrecht, M. C. M., and Heijnen, J. J. 1998. A new combined differential-discrete cellular automaton approach for biofilm modeling: Application for growth in gel beads. *Biotechnology and Bioengineering* 57: 718–731.

Picioreanu, C., van Loosdrecht, M. C. M., and Heijnen, J. J. 2000. A theoretical study on the effect of surface roughness on mass transport and transformation in biofilms. *Biotechnology and Bioengineering* 68: 355–369.

Picioreanu, C., van Loosdrecht, M. C. M., and Heijnen, J. J. 2000. Effect of diffusive and convective substrate transport on biofilm structure formation: A two-dimensional modeling study. *Biotechnology and Bioengineering* 69: 504–515.

Picioreanu, C., van Loosdrecht, M. C. M., and Heijnen, J. J. 1998. Mathematical modeling of biofilm structure with a hybrid differential-discrete cellular automaton approach. *Biotechnology and Bioengineering* 58: 101–116.

Picioreanu, C., van Loosdrecht, M. C. M., and Heijnen, J. J. 2001. Two-dimensional model of biofilm detachment caused by internal stress from liquid flow. *Biotechnology and Bioengineering* 72: 205–218.

Pizarro, G. E., Garcia, C., Moreno, R., and Sepulveda, M. E. 2004. Two-dimensional cellular automaton model for mixed-culture biofilm. *Water Science and Technology* 49: 193–198.

Pizarro, G., Griffeath, D., and Noguera, D. R. 2001. Quantitative cellular automaton model for biofilms. *Journal of Environmental Engineering* 127: 782–789.

Rao, K. R., Srinivasan, T., and Venkateswarlu, C. 2010. Mathematical and kinetic modeling of biofilm reactor based on ant colony optimization. *Process Biochemistry* 45: 961–972.

Rittmann, B. E., and Brunner, C. W. 1984. The nonsteady-state-biofilm process for advanced organics removal. *Journal Water Pollution Control Federation* 56: 874–880.

Rittmann, B. E., and Dovantzis, K. 1983. Dual limitation of biofilm kinetics. *Water Research* 17: 1727–1734.

Rittmann, B. E., and McCarty, P. L. 1980. Evaluation of steady-state-biofilm kinetics. *Biotechnology and Bioengineering* 22: 2359–2373.

Rittmann, B. E., and McCarty, P. L. 1980. Model of steady-state-biofilm kinetics. *Biotechnology and Bioengineering* 22: 2343–2357.

Rittmann, B. E., Pettis, M., Reeves, H. W., and Stahl, D. A. 1999. How biofilm clusters affect substrate flux and ecological selection. *Water Science and Technology* 39: 99–105.

Rittmann, B. E., Schwarz, A. O., Eberl, H. J., Morgenroth, E., Perez, J., van Loosdrecht, M., and Wanner, O. 2004. Results from the multi-species Benchmark Problem (BM3) using one-dimensional models. *Water Science and Technology* 49: 163–168.

Rittmann, B. E., Stilwell, D., and Ohashi, A. 2002. The transient-state, multiple-species biofilm model for biofiltration processes. *Water Research* 36: 2342–2356.

Rittmann, B. E., and VanBriesen, J. M. 1996. Microbiological processes in reactive modeling. *Reactive Transport in Porous Media* 34: 311–334.

Roberts, M. E., and Stewart, P. S. 2004. Modeling antibiotic tolerance in biofilms by accounting for nutrient limitation. *Antimicrobial Agents and Chemotherapy* 48: 48–52.

Shen, L., Lu, Y., and Liu, Y. 2012. Mathematical modeling of biofilm-covered granular activated carbon: A review. *Journal of Chemical Technology and Biotechnology* 87: 1513–1520.

Smith, D. P. 1995. Oxygen flux limitation in aerobic fixed-film biotreatment of a hazardous landfill leachate. *Journal of Hazardous Materials* 44: 77–91.

Sonner, S., Efendiev, M. A., and Eberl, H. J. 2011. On the well-posedness of a mathematical model of quorum-sensing in patchy biofilm communities. *Mathematical Methods in the Applied Sciences* 34: 1667–1684.

Stewart, P. S., Hamilton, M. A., Goldstein, B. R., and Schneider, B. T. 1996. Modeling biocide action against biofilms. *Biotechnology and Bioengineering* 49: 445–455.

Suidan, M. T., Flora, J. R. V., Biswas, P., and Sayles, G. D. 1994. Optimization modeling of anaerobic biofilm reactors. *Water Science and Technology* 30: 347–355.

Sun, A. K., Hong, J., and Wood, T. K. 1998. Modeling trichloroethylene degradation by a recombinant pseudomonad expressing toluene ortho-monooxygenase in a fixed-film bioreactor. *Biotechnology and Bioengineering* 59: 40–51.

Thalla, A. K., Bhargava, R., and Kumar, P. 2010. Nitrification kinetics of activated sludge-biofilm system: A mathematical model. *Bioresource Technology* 101: 5827–5835.

Wanner, O., Cunningham, A. B., and Lundman, R. 1995. Modeling biofilm accumulation and mass-transport in a porous-medium under high substrate loading. *Biotechnology and Bioengineering* 47: 703–712.

Wanner, O., and Gujer, W. 1986. A multispecies biofilm model. *Biotechnology and Bioengineering* 28: 314–328.

Wanner, O., and Morgenroth, E. 2004. Biofilm modeling with AQUASIM. *Water Science and Technology* 49: 137–144.

Wanner, O., and Reichert, P. 1996. Mathematical modeling of mixed-culture biofilms. *Biotechnology and Bioengineering* 49: 172–184.

Wichern, M., Lindenblatt, C., Luebken, M., and Horn, H. 2008. Experimental results and mathematical modelling of an autotrophic and heterotrophic biofilm in a sand filter treating landfill leachate and municipal wastewater. *Water Research* 42: 3899–3909.

Williamson, K., and McCarty, P. L. 1976. Verification studies of biofilm model for bacterial substrate utilization. *Journal Water Pollution Control Federation* 48: 281–296.

Wimpenny, J. W. T., and Colasanti, R. 1997. A more unifying hypothesis for biofilm structures—A reply. *FEMS Microbiology Ecology* 24: 185–186.

Wimpenny, J. W. T., and Colasanti, R. 1997. A unifying hypothesis for the structure of microbial biofilms based on cellular automaton models. *FEMS Microbiology Ecology* 22: 1–16.

Wimpenny, J., Manz, W., and Szewzyk, U. 2000. Heterogeneity in biofilms. *FEMS Microbiology Reviews* 24: 661–671.

Xavier, J. B., Picioreanu, C., and van Loosdrecht, M. C. M. 2004. Assessment of three-dimensional biofilm models through direct comparison with confocal microscopy imaging. *Water Science and Technology* 49: 177–185.

Zhang, T., and Klapper, I. 2010. Mathematical model of biofilm induced calcite precipitation. *Water Science and Technology* 61: 2957–2964.

Useful experimental data for biofilm modeling

Beyenal, H., and Lewandowski, Z. 2000. Combined effect of substrate concentration and flow velocity on effective diffusivity in biofilms. *Water Research* 34: 528–538.

Beyenal, H., and Lewandowski, Z. 2001. Mass-transport dynamics, activity, and structure of sulfate-reducing biofilms. *AIChE Journal* 47: 1689–1697.

Beyenal, H., and Lewandowski, Z. 2002. Internal and external mass transfer in biofilms grown at various flow velocities. *Biotechnology Progress* 18: 55–61.

Beyenal, H., Tanyolac, A., and Lewandowski, Z. 1998. Measurement of local effective diffusivity in heterogeneous biofilms. *Water Science and Technology* 38: 171–178.

Bishop, P. L. 1997. Biofilm structure and kinetics. *Water Science and Technology* 36: 287–294.

Boessmann, M., Staudt, C., Neu, T. R., Horn, H., and Hempel, D. C. 2003. Investigation and modeling of growth, structure and oxygen penetration in particle supported biofilms. *Chemical Engineering and Technology* 26: 219–222.

Buffiere, P., Steyer, J. P., Fonade, C., and Moletta, R. 1998. Modeling and experiments on the influence of biofilm size and mass transfer in a fluidized bed reactor for anaerobic digestion. *Water Research* 32: 657–668.

Cao, B., Majors, P. D., Ahmed, B., Renslow, R. S., Silvia, C. P., Shi, L., Kjelleberg, S., Fredrickson, J. K., and Beyenal, H. 2012. Biofilm shows spatially stratified metabolic responses to contaminant exposure. *Environmental Microbiology* 14: 2901–2910.

Casey, E., Glennon, B., and Hamer, G. 2000. Biofilm development in a membrane-aerated biofilm reactor: Effect of flow velocity on performance. *Biotechnology and Bioengineering* 67: 476–486.

Hung Duc, N., Cao, B., Mishra, B., Boyanou, M. I., Kemner, K. M., Fredrickson, J. K., and Beyenal, H. 2012. Microscale geochemical gradients in Hanford 300 Area sediment biofilms and influence of uranium. *Water Research* 46: 227–234.

Renslow, R. S., Majors, P. D., McLean, J. S., Fredrickson, J. K., Ahmed, B., and Beyenal, H. 2010. In situ effective diffusion coefficient profiles in live biofilms using pulsed-field gradient nuclear magnetic resonance. *Biotechnology and Bioengineering* 106: 928–937.

Shanahan, J. W., Cole, A. C., Semmens, M. I., and Lapara, T. M. 2005. Acetate and ammonium diffusivity in membrane-aerated biofilms: Improving model predictions using experimental results. *Water Science and Technology* 52: 121–126.

Yang, S. N., and Lewandowski, Z. 1995. Measurement of local mass-transfer coefficient in biofilms. *Biotechnology and Bioengineering* 48: 737–744.

Zhang, T. C., Fu, Y. C., and Bishop, P. L. 1994. Competition in biofilms. *Water Science and Technology* 29: 263–270.

chapter nine

Protocols and procedures

9.1   *Introduction*

Previous chapters have described the conceptual, computational, physical, and virtual tools used to quantify biofilm processes. It has been made clear that to generate reproducible results in biofilm studies, these tools need to be used, to the extent that is possible and practical, in a reproducible manner. This chapter provides the protocols used during research described in this book. Other researchers use similar protocols when using similar tools. It is not realistic to expect that everyone will ever use exactly the same protocols, but it is possible to standardize some procedures within a laboratory, directly affecting the quality of the results. It is important to have these procedures written and to let other researchers know what procedures were used so that if there are differences between the results of similar experiments, researchers can judge to what extent these differences were caused by using different procedures.

Even though each biofilm study is unique and different studies use biofilms with different microbial community structures grown in different reactors and the researchers evaluate biofilm processes using different conceptual, computational, physical, and virtual tools, and perhaps different methods of interpreting the results, many steps in the research procedures are common and repeated from one study to another. For example, in each biofilm study, the researcher will have to acquire the microorganisms, prepare their stock culture, evaluate their growth parameters, preserve them for future use, select the growth medium, select the reactor, etc. This chapter will describe how to make these decisions, and many of the steps described here can be reproduced in other laboratories. The first step in every biofilm study is establishing the goal, and this and related topics are described in Chapter 1. Here, we assume that the goal, objectives, etc., have been determined and setting up the experiments can begin.

9.2   *Preparing the experimental system*

9.2.1   *Selecting the microorganisms*

The selected microorganisms should be biologically safe, grow in biofilms, and carry out the biofilm process the researcher is studying.

Biological safety is obviously a concern in biofilm research, and the researchers should be adequately protected against pathogenic microorganisms if they work with them. Specialized laboratories working with pathogenic microorganisms employ well-trained personnel, and biological safety procedures are strictly enforced there. In the university environment, biological safety is an even more serious concern because students with various levels of knowledge and training in microbiological procedures may be using potentially pathogenic microorganisms in their research. Fortunately, there are clear guidelines regarding biological safety, and they can be obtained from the Centers for Disease Control (CDC) and Prevention Web pages (http://www.cdc.gov/biosafety/). From the biological safety point of view, each type of microorganism belongs to one of four biological safety levels (BSLs). Biological safety level 1 includes microorganisms that do not cause diseases in healthy humans. Biological safety level 2 includes microorganisms that may cause diseases in humans, particularly in individuals who are immunocompromised. Working with microorganisms belonging to these two safety levels, BSL-1 and BSL-2, is common in academic institutions. When using these microorganisms, it is important to observe all precautions specified by the CDC and described on its Web pages at http://www.cdc.gov/ and http://www.cdc.gov//biosfty.htm. Working with higher safety level microorganisms, BSL-3 and BSL-4, requires specially designed containment facilities, which are available at highly specialized research institutions. It is important to check the required safety precautions for dealing with specific microorganisms before attempting to acquire them, and it is important to check the rules regulating biological safety at the location where the specific research is scheduled. Academic institutions involved in biological research have safety officers who should be consulted before any microorganisms are purchased.

9.2.2 Obtaining the microorganisms

Many countries, universities, research centers, and individual researchers have their own collections of microorganisms. We use the American Type Culture Collection (ATCC) (http://www.atcc.org/) and reach out to other sources only when a particular strain of microorganisms is not available from this source. Large, well-established collections, such as the ATCC, offer services beyond holding known microorganisms and delivering them to research institutions. Large collections offer information about the microorganisms they hold and publish procedures for their growth and maintenance. Individual researchers can register their own isolates with such collections, thus securing a reliable source of microorganisms that can be easily shared with others. For example, three biofilm microorganisms that we frequently use are registered strains of *Pseudomonas aeruginosa* (ATCC 700829), *Pseudomonas fluorescens* (ATCC 700830), and *Klebsiella pneumoniae* (ATCC 700831). We isolated these microorganisms from the environment and registered them at ATCC, and we use this consortium whenever we need a reproducible source of microorganisms to form a biofilm. Many procedures described in this chapter were tested using one or more of these three strains, and readers are encouraged to use these microorganisms to test the procedures described here. ATCC provides exhaustive information about the microorganisms in their collection, suggests compositions of growth media, and lists references of research projects in which these microorganisms were used. Even though ATCC satisfies most of our needs, occasionally we use the German Collection of Microorganisms and Cell Cultures (http://www.dsmz.de), Deutsche Sammlung von Mikroorganismen und Zellkulturen, Braunschweig, Germany. Occasionally, we use microorganisms that have been genetically altered, and we obtain these from the researchers who made them, although some of the altered microorganisms can also be acquired from the culture collections.

9.2.3 Preparing and maintaining stock cultures

Microorganisms from the culture collections are not free, and some strains can be quite expensive. Therefore, it is advisable that after the initial purchase, a stock culture of the purchased microorganisms be maintained so they do not have to be bought every time they are needed. The microorganisms from ATCC arrive as freeze-dried or frozen samples, and these samples are used to prepare stock cultures. Preparing a stock culture of microorganisms includes growing them in a solution of an appropriate growth medium, distributing the volume of the growth medium with the microorganisms into smaller vials, freezing the vials, and keeping the vials in a freezer at –70°C. As the vials are gradually used, occasionally one of the vials is used as a source of the microorganisms and the process of preparing the stock culture is repeated. In principle, this process can be repeated for years, although sometimes the microorganisms lose desirable features and a new sample needs to be purchased from the culture collection. If a laboratory uses more than one type of microorganism, it helps to designate a custodian to oversee the collection, to monitor the distribution of the microorganism to individual researchers, and to make sure that the last vial of a type of microorganism is not used before a new stock culture is made.

9.2.3.1 Preparing a stock culture from a freeze-dried sample from ATCC

When a vial with microorganisms arrives from ATCC, the package contains information about the microorganisms and instructions on how to open the vial. Follow these instructions carefully. As an example, the procedure we use to prepare a stock culture of *P. aeruginosa* (ATCC 700829) will be described. The procedure has two steps.

Step one: growing the microorganisms received from ATCC

1. Break the tip of the vial as described by ATCC.
2. Add 0.3–0.4 mL of the growth medium [ATCC medium 18: 30 g/L trypticase soy broth (BD 211768)] using a sterile syringe.
3. Transfer the mixture into a test tube (10–20 mL volume) filled with 5 mL of growth medium.
4. Place the test tube in a shaker operated at a moderate shaking rate.
5. Grow the microorganisms overnight.

On the next day, there is usually visible microbial growth in the test tube; if not, wait longer. After there is visible growth, prepare the stock culture.

Step two: preparing the stock culture

1. Fill a 250-mL flask with 100 mL of ATCC medium [18: 30 g/L trypticase soy broth (BD 211768)]; i.e., weigh out 3 g of trypticase soy broth in a flask and fill it up to 100 mL.
2. Autoclave it for 15 min at 121°C.
3. Let the solution cool down to room temperature.
4. Inoculate the solution with 10 mL of the culture prepared in step one above or, if frozen vials from an individual collection are being used to prepare more vials, use the contents of one vial, which is 1 mL of the frozen stock.
5. Place the flask on a shaker operated at 150 shakes per minute (spm).
6. Grow the bacteria overnight.
7. Prepare cryogenic vials (Fisher®, Denver, CO) by labeling them (the type of microorganism, date, and researcher's name).
8. Prepare a sterile 20% glycerol solution by vacuum filtering (put a 0.2-μm syringe filter in front of a syringe and draw up the glycerol solution for sterilization).
9. Divide the solution, and place the grown culture in two 50-mL centrifuge tubes (the total volume was 100 mL).
10. Centrifuge at 10,000 rpm for 10 min.
11. Pour off the supernatant and add 25 mL of the 20% glycerol solution to the growth medium in the centrifuge vials.
12. Mix them using a vortex mixer.
13. Pipette 1 mL of culture solution into each cryogenic vial.
14. Store the vials in the –70°C freezer.

As a result, approximately fifty 1-mL vials with bacteria should be stored in the freezer. When needed, individual vials are removed from the freezer, thawed in a 37°C water bath, and used to inoculate freshly prepared growth medium. The frozen samples can be thawed at room temperature or in a 37°C water bath.

9.2.3.2 Preparing the growth medium for the selected microorganisms

The compositions of suitable growth media can often be found in the literature, but they may need to be modified to fit the needs of a specific biofilm study. The obvious rules need to be observed when preparing growth media: the microorganisms need electron donors, electron acceptors, and nutrients containing all the biogenic and trace elements the microorganisms need to grow and be able to produce proteins and other vital molecules. Typically, the pH of the growth medium is controlled by using a suitable pH buffer. Tables 9.1 through 9.3 give examples of the components of growth media and their sources.

9.2.3.3 Inoculating biofilm reactors

Biofilm reactors are never inoculated directly using frozen microorganisms. When this has been attempted, problems growing the biofilms reproducibly, or even growing them at all, have resulted. Always start growing the microorganisms in a separate vessel, and use the solution from the vessel to inoculate the biofilm reactors when the microorganisms enter the exponential growth phase. To prepare the inoculum, follow this procedure:

1. Fill a 250-mL flask with 100 mL of the growth medium described in Table 9.3, *not with the ATCC medium*. To prepare the inoculum, use the same composition of growth medium as the one used in the biofilm reactor to grow the biofilms.
2. Autoclave the solution for 15 min at 121°C.
3. Let the solution cool down to room temperature and place it in a flask.
4. Inoculate the solution with the frozen stock culture.
5. Place the flask on a shaker operated at 150 spm.
6. Grow the bacteria overnight.

Table 9.1 Typical Components of a Growth Medium and Sources

Element	Source (examples)
Carbon (organic electron donors)	Glucose, pyruvate, proteins
Nitrogen	NH_4^+, proteins, NO_3^-
Sulfur	SO_4^{2-}
Phosphorus	PO_4^{3-}

Table 9.2 Growth Medium for *Pseudomonas aeruginosa* (ATCC 700829)

Chemical	Concentration (mg/L)
Na_2HPO_4	1830
KH_2PO_4	350
$MgSO_4\ 7H_2O$	10
Yeast extract	10
Glucose	1000

Table 9.3 Stock Solution of Trace Elements

Chemical	Concentration (mg/L)
$MnCl_2\ 4H_2O$	527
$CuCl_2\ 2H_2O$	228
$CoCl_2\ 2H_2O$	317
$(NH_4)Mo_7O_4\ H_2O$	231
$Na_2B_4O_7\ 10H_2O$	127
$ZnCl_2$	363
$FeCl_3$	2160
$CaCl_2$	3700

Note: Prepare a larger volume of this solution, such as 1 L, and add 1 mL of the solution for every liter of growth medium. The growth medium must be prepared using distilled water in a 20-L carboy and sterilized in an autoclave at 121°C and 1 atm absolute pressure for 3 h. Glucose, yeast extract, and $(NH_4)_2SO_4$ must be autoclaved separately, because during autoclaving glucose decomposes. Trace elements can be added to the sterile growth medium using a disposable sterile syringe filter (0.2-μm, Corning).

To inoculate a biofilm reactor, use a volume of the inoculum equal to 5% to 10% of the working volume of the reactor.

The procedure for growing *P. aeruginosa* (ATCC 700829) is given as an example; some deviations from this procedure may be required when other microorganisms are grown. For example, some bacteria grow slower than *P. aeruginosa*, and researchers may wait longer than overnight for the microorganisms to reach the exponential growth phase.

9.3   Quantifying microbial growth

9.3.1   Kinetics of microbial growth in suspension

Although it may not be the most critical part of biofilm studies, try to determine the parameters characterizing the growth of the microorganisms in suspension. It is debatable whether the biokinetic parameters determined for suspended microorganisms can be used to quantify microbial growth in biofilms, but measuring the biokinetic parameters of the microorganisms is considered part of the maintenance of our collection, and it is done routinely. The kinetics of microbial growth in suspension should always be known before the microorganisms are used to grow biofilms. The procedures for measuring microbial growth kinetics in a chemostat are well established, and the one we use to compute the biokinetic parameters of *P. aeruginosa* (ATCC 700829) exemplifies them. Because the procedure for computing biokinetic parameters from experimental data is routine, software has been developed to handle the computations. The procedure and the attached computer program simplifying the computation of the biokinetic parameters can be used similarly for different types of bacteria. Figure 9.1 shows the typical arrangement of a chemostat.

9.3.1.1   Kinetics of P. aeruginosa *(ATCC 700829) growth in suspension*

As an example of the procedures involved in characterizing the growth and activity of microorganisms in suspension, the entire process of measuring and computing the biokinetic parameters of *P. aeruginosa* (ATCC 700829) will be described.

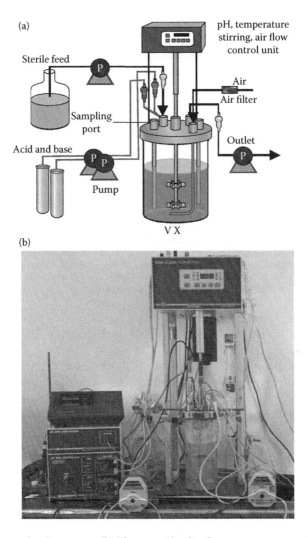

Figure 9.1 (a) Diagram of a chemostat. (b) Photograph of a chemostat.

9.3.1.1.1 Microorganisms. The microorganism, *P. aeruginosa* (ATCC 700829), was originally obtained from the ATCC. Stock cultures are prepared by following the procedures described earlier in this chapter.

9.3.1.1.2 Inoculum. To prepare the inoculum, a 1-mL frozen stock sample in a vial is taken from the stock culture collection (stored at −70°C). It is thawed in a 37°C water bath, and the contents of the vial are introduced into a flask containing a growth medium composed of glucose (5 g/L), yeast extract (0.2 g/L), $(NH_4)_2SO_4$ (1 g/L), and a solution of micronutrients (described in Table 9.3). The total volume of the solution is 100 mL, and the microorganisms are grown for 20 to 30 h in a shaker flask. The flask is placed on a shaker set to 150 rpm, at room temperature, approximately 25°C. To inoculate the chemostat, 200 mL of this solution, which is 10% of the working volume of the chemostat, is used.

9.3.1.1.3 Chemostat. In principle, a chemostat can be any suitable vessel in which microorganisms can be grown in a well-mixed solution at a controlled flow of nutrient solution. However, good chemostats are equipped with many control and measurement devices that make the entire operation easier and the results more reproducible. We use a New Brunswick chemostat (BioFlo 2000) with a working volume of 2 L, equipped with pH, agitation, and temperature controllers. The sensitivities of the control units for pH, temperature, and agitation rate are 0.1 unit, 0.1°C, and ±1 rpm, respectively. Prior to use, the chemostat and the growth medium are autoclaved for 30 min at 121°C. Then, the solution of micronutrients is filtered through 0.2-µm filters (Corning, 431219). The pH is controlled by pumping solutions of 0.2 N NaOH and 0.2 N H_2SO_4. If the pH in the chemostat oscillates, decrease the concentrations of the acid and the base; if excessive amounts of the acid and the base are pumped, increase the concentrations of the acid and the base. The solution in the chemostat is stirred by a blade-type double impeller, and the stirring rate is optimized using the specific oxygen utilization rate (SOUR) as the criterion (see Section 9.3.1.1.4). The dissolved oxygen (DO) concentration is controlled by agitation and purging with either nitrogen (for a lower dissolved oxygen concentration) or oxygen (for a higher dissolved oxygen concentration). All gases added to the chemostat must be filtered. The chemostat is operated at a constant temperature of 25 ± 0.1°C.

After inoculation, the chemostat is initially operated in batch mode for 20 to 30 h and then it is operated as a continuous flow reactor. To establish a steady state, the reactor is run for six or seven retention times; the existence of a steady state is confirmed if the absolute difference between consecutive measurements of effluent nutrient concentration is less than 3%. Several dilution rates are used, up to the washout, and the corresponding steady state data, such as the biomass concentration and the concentration of the growth-limiting nutrient, are recorded. To find a new steady state, the dilution rate is increased from one level to the next level by gradually increasing the flow rate of the growth medium. The microbial culture in the chemostat is periodically tested for contamination by plating on agar plates. Biofilm formation on the reactor walls is constantly monitored, and, when it is necessary, the reactor is shut off to remove the wall growth and restarted.

9.3.1.1.4 Analytical methods. To determine the biomass concentration, the standard total suspended solids method is used [Standard Methods for the Examination of Water and Wastewater, 2540E (Eaton et al. 1995)]. Take 100 mL of solution from the chemostat and centrifuge it. Then pour out the supernatant, resuspend the pellet in 50 mL of distilled water and vacuum-filter the sample through a Whatman® Glass Microfibre Filter, 2.5 cm in diameter, with a 0.2-µm pore size. Prior to filtering, dry the clean filter to a constant weight in a drying oven at 105°C for 24 h and weigh it. Dry the filter at 105°C until a constant weight is observed. The difference between a dry filter with microorganisms and the same filter without microorganisms gives the dry weight of the microorganisms. The total suspended solids is determined analytically, and the microorganism concentration (X) is calculated from

$$X = \frac{\text{Dry weight of the microorganisms (g)}}{\text{Volume of the sample (L)}} \tag{9.1}$$

The concentration of the growth-limiting nutrient, glucose, is measured using Sigma® procedure 510 (Sigma® Diagnostics, St. Louis, MO). The ammonium concentration is measured using a Hatch® ion-selective electrode. The ammonium electrode is calibrated using a standard ammonium solution from Hatch® (catalog no. 24065-49). Dissolved oxygen and pH are monitored using Ingold® dissolved oxygen and pH electrodes integrated with the chemostat. The dissolved oxygen electrode is calibrated in the autoclaved growth medium purged alternatively with pure nitrogen or air. The pH electrode is calibrated at pH 4, pH 7, and pH 10 using pH buffers from Fisher (catalog nos. SB98-1, SB108-1, and SB116-1, respectively).

To estimate the oxygen utilization rate (OUR) in the chemostat, the aeration is stopped and the gas space in the chemostat is flushed with nitrogen to remove oxygen and prevent reaeration. Immediately afterward, the dissolved oxygen concentration in the reactor is recorded versus time. The oxygen utilization rate, $OUR = dS_o/dt$, is determined by multiplying the slope of the plot of oxygen versus time by the volume of liquid. SOUR is determined as OUR divided by the biomass concentration, $SOUR = OUR/X$.

Example 9.1: Computing the oxygen utilization rate

The following example shows how to compute OUR of *P. aeruginosa* (ATCC 700829) grown in the chemostat. The aeration was stopped, and the temporal change in oxygen concentration in the solution was measured; the results are shown in Table 9.4. The biomass concentration (X) was 1 g/L, and the volume of the chemostat was 2 L. Calculate OUR using the data in Table 9.4.

To evaluate OUR, plot the dissolved oxygen concentration versus time and then apply a linear curve fit to the data in the linear range only, as shown in Figure 9.2. The slope of the line is –1.3138 mg dissolved oxygen per minute. Because the microorganism concentration ($X = 1$ g/L) is known, OUR and SOUR can be computed.

$$OUR = -\frac{dS_o}{dt} = 1.3138 \frac{\text{mg oxygen consumed}}{L \times \min}$$

To calculate SOUR, divide OUR by the cell concentration in the chemostat.

Table 9.4 Temporal Variation of Oxygen Concentration in the Chemostat after the Aeration was Interrupted

Time (min)	Dissolved oxygen concentration (mg/L)
0	5.78
0.25	5.644
0.5	5.44
0.75	4.896
1	4.42
1.25	4.08
1.5	3.74
1.75	3.332
2	2.992
2.25	2.72
2.5	2.448
2.75	2.176
3	1.904

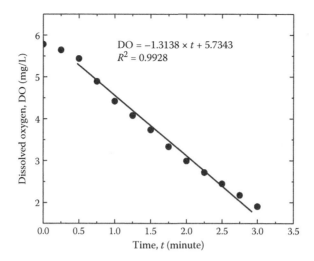

Figure 9.2 Dissolved oxygen concentration versus time.

$$SOUR = \frac{OUR}{X} = 1.3138 \frac{\text{mg of oxygen consumed}}{L \times min} \times \frac{1}{1000} \frac{L}{\text{mg of microorganisms}}$$

$$= 1.3138 \times 10^{-3} \frac{\text{mg of oxygen consumed}}{\text{mg of microorganisms} \times min}$$

SOUR is equivalent to the activity of the microorganism.

Example 9.2: Establishing the time needed to reach a steady state

According to our definition, biological processes in the chemostat are at a steady state when the limiting nutrient is utilized at a constant rate. However, the process of microbial growth should be described by a so-called double kinetic expression, in which the electron donor and the electron acceptor are both growth-limiting nutrients. In this study, glucose is the electron donor and oxygen is the electron acceptor, and at a steady state they are both used at a constant rate. The constancy of the utilization rate is confirmed if the growth-limiting nutrients and the biomass concentration (cell density) in the chemostat remain constant. The existence of a steady state is verified by measuring the concentration of one of the growth-limiting nutrients and the cell density. Because measuring the glucose concentration is tedious, the concentration of oxygen in the chemostat is measured, and the existence of a steady state is assumed when the oxygen concentration in the liquid does not change over time. Using the conditions specified in Example 9.1, the dilution rate is set to 0.24 h^{-1}, and the oxygen concentration in the liquid is measured at the selected time interval. This is different from the measurement of OUR, in that the chemostat is in operation and the aeration is not discontinued, as it was when OUR was measured. The data are listed in Table 9.5, and the question is, "When did the chemostat reach a steady state?"

Solution

The criterion used to verify the existence of a steady state in the reactor is that the results of two consecutive measurements of oxygen concentration, taken a single retention time

Table 9.5 Dissolved Oxygen Concentrations Measured at Different Times

Time (h)	8:00	10:00	12:00	14:00
DO (mg/L)	1.84	1.87	2.05	2.10
Time (h)	16:00	18:00	20:00	22:00
DO (mg/L)	2.18	2.15	2.25	2.20

Table 9.6 Differences in Oxygen Concentration Between Consecutive Measurements

Time (h)	12:00	14:00	16:00	18:00
DO difference (mg/L)	= 2.05 − 1.84 = 0.21	= 2.1 − 1.87 = 0.23	= 2.18 − 2.05 = 0.13	= 2.15 − 2.0 = 0.05
Percentage difference	= (0.21/2.05) × 100 = 10	= (0.23/2.1) × 100 = 11	= 0.13/2.18 = 6	= (0.05/2.15) × 100 = 2
Time (h)	20:00	22:00		
DO difference (mg/L)	= 2.25 − 2.1 = 0.04	= 2.2 − 2.25 = 0.05		
Percentage difference	= (0.04/2.25) ×100 = 2	= (0.05/2.2) ×100 = 2		

apart, do not differ by more than 3%. From the above data, the retention time in the chemostat is $V/Q = 1/D = 1/0.24 = 4.2$ h. This means that the concentration of oxygen should be measured every 4 h. The reactor is at a steady state when the oxygen concentrations in two consecutive measurements differ by less than 3% of the earlier measurement. See calculations in Table 9.6.

Because the measurements of oxygen concentration after 18 h differ by less than 3%, the reactor has reached a steady state after 18 h.

After the reactor has reached a steady state, other measurements, such as the concentrations of glucose and the microorganisms, can be conducted. Actually, the steady state in the chemostat should be determined based on the cell density. Dissolved oxygen concentrations are used instead because this measurement is less time-consuming than measuring cell density. It is assumed that when the microorganisms reach a constant concentration in the reactor, the concentration of glucose in the effluent is constant. However, once we have determined that the reactor has reached a steady state based on the oxygen concentration in the effluent, the existence of the steady state is verified by measuring the variations in glucose and biomass concentrations.

9.3.1.2   Selecting the agitation rate at which to operate the chemostat

Agitation in chemostats has many functions, and one of them is introducing oxygen into the solution. Therefore, it is important to set the agitation to a level that ensures the necessary rate of oxygen delivery to the liquid. SOUR is used to determine the optimum operating conditions in the chemostat. To determine the optimum agitation rate, the chemostat is operated at a fixed dilution rate and the agitation rate is changed stepwise. Figure 9.3 shows SOUR for various agitation rates in the chemostat. It is expected that at low agitation rates, the growth of microorganisms is limited by the mass transport of nutrients to the microorganisms. As the agitation rate increases, SOUR increases, reaches a maximum value, and then decreases. Increasing the agitation rate beyond the maximum SOUR probably injures the microorganisms. The agitation rate that coincides with the maximum SOUR is selected for the operation.

SOURs measured at a fixed dilution rate (0.1 h⁻¹) and a sequence of agitation rates were compared: 150, 250, 350, 450, and 550 rpm (Figure 9.3). For *P. aeruginosa* (ATCC 700829), the

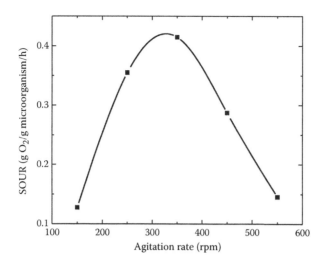

Figure 9.3 SOUR for different agitation rates in the chemostat ($D = 0.124$ h^{-1}, pH = 7.2, $T = 25°C$, $S_{fg} = 5$ g/L, $S_{fn} = 0.1$ g/L, and air flow rate = 3 L/h).

optimum agitation rate was 350 rpm, at which SOUR reached a maximum (Figure 9.3), and 350 rpm was selected as the suitable agitation rate and used to operate the chemostat. Microscopic examination of the dispersed microorganisms showed that at that rate of agitation the microorganisms were distributed uniformly in the chemostat and there was no flocculation.

9.3.1.3 Steady state data for modeling microbial kinetics

Before calculating the growth parameters of *P. aeruginosa* (ATCC 700829), we tested whether the substances used in previous computations, glucose and oxygen, were indeed growth-limiting nutrients. To test whether oxygen was a growth-limiting nutrient, we stopped aerating the chemostat (zero oxygen in the chemostat); cells were washed out from the chemostat. To test whether glucose was the growth-limiting nutrient, we stopped delivering glucose to the reactor; cells were washed out from the chemostat in this case, too. These results demonstrate that both oxygen and glucose were limiting microbial growth. Stopping the delivery of ammonia NH_4^+ did not affect the effluent concentrations of glucose, oxygen, or microorganisms, showing that NH_4^+ was not a growth-limiting nutrient. These observations also demonstrate that both glucose and oxygen influenced the growth kinetics: the growth of *P. aeruginosa* should be represented by a kinetic expression that quantifies the effect of two limiting substrates combined. An appropriate kinetic expression needs to be developed to combine the concentrations of these two substances and to quantify their effect on microbial growth rate. To develop such a kinetic expression, the steady state concentrations of glucose, oxygen, and biomass and OUR are assembled in Table 9.7. Note that in Table 9.7, OUR has been multiplied with the reactor volume to calculate the total oxygen utilization rate.

Before computing the biokinetic parameters describing microbial growth in this reactor, we need to agree on the form of the kinetic expression that reflects these data, which is one reason we need mathematical models to interpret results of experimental studies, as we discussed at length in the opening sections of this chapter. The procedure for finding such an expression is illustrated by the following example.

Table 9.7 Concentrations of the Specified Substances Measured at a Steady State

D (h^{-1})	S_o (mg/L)	S_g (mg/L)	X (mg/L)	OUR (mg oxygen/h)
0.03	1	5	1725	323
0.04	7.2	3.8	3000	424
0.0556	0.5	19.4	2381	581
0.069	7.2	7.1	2820	719
0.118	0.8	45.7	3150	1212
0.124	7.2	15.1	3070	1273
0.162	7.2	22.7	3225	1658
0.187	1.5	69.4	3285	1912
0.24	6.6	255	2760	2565
0.24	2.5	87.4	3105	2440
0.275	3.3	112.65	3090	2799
0.299	5.4	217	2850	2599
0.325	5.6	154.9	3045	3306

Note: $T = 25°C$, pH = 7.2, agitation rate = 350 rpm, $S_{fg} = 5$ g/L, $S_{fn} = 0.1$ g/L, and OUR refers total oxygen consumption in the reactor.

9.3.1.3.1 Using nonlinear regression to calculate the biokinetic parameters: Defining the objective function.　　There are many kinetic equations that can represent our experimental data. The goal is to find the mathematical expression that predicts the experimental data with minimum error. The procedure for finding this expression has four steps:

1. Selecting the kinetic equations that will be tested.
2. Determining the objective function (the one that will be minimized).
3. Fitting the experimental data to each kinetic expression selected in step 1.
4. Selecting the best kinetic expression, the best model.

9.3.1.3.2 Selecting the kinetic equations.　　Several kinetic equations can be used to describe the growth of microorganisms (see Chapter 1). In Chapter 1 we described Monod, Tessier, Moser, and Contois kinetic expressions for predicting the growth rate as a function of a single growth-limiting nutrient. However, our preliminary data demonstrated that the growth of *P. aeruginosa* (ATCC 700829) was limited by two nutrients: glucose and oxygen. The kinetic equations can be modified to fit more than one growth-limiting nutrient, but, as shown in Section 1.4.2.1, there is more than one form in which these growth-limiting nutrients can be combined into a single kinetic equation: they can be combined in (1) an interactive or multiplicative form, (2) an additive form, or (3) a noninteractive form. One of these combinations must be selected. On the basis of the preliminary observations, the additive interactions (Equation 1.17) can be eliminated because it has been demonstrated that both nutrients must be present to support microbial growth. Equation 1.17 does not satisfy this condition: it can give a positive growth rate even if the concentration of one of the growth-limiting nutrients equals zero. For the same reason, Equation 1.18 can be eliminated from the search. Therefore, consideration is limited to the combined kinetic equations described by Equation 1.16, and all possible biokinetic expressions (24 combinations: see the first three columns of Table 9.8) are tested. To simplify computations of biokinetic parameters, a MATLAB® program (on the attached CD) has been developed. This program

Table 9.8 Growth Models, Biokinetic Parameters, SSD, and R^2

Model number	Equation no. for oxygen	Equation no. for glucose	λ_o	λ_g	B_o	B_g	K_o	K_g	μ_{max}	SSD	R^2
1	–	1.9	–	–	–	–	–	31.97	0.30	0.0272074	0.78
2	–	1.11	–	–	–	–	–	39.76	0.26	0.0256887	0.80
3	–	1.12	–	1.06	–	–	–	37.42	0.29	0.027141	0.79
4	–	1.13	–	–	–	1.13E-02	–	–	0.30	0.0308807	0.76
5	1.9	–	–	–	–	–	0.65	–	0.21	0.1055993	0.17
6	1.9	1.9	–	–	–	–	0.50	20.32	0.32	0.0192399	0.85
7	1.9	1.11	–	–	–	–	0.51	20.00	0.21	0.1012759	–
8	1.9	1.12	–	1.49	–	–	0.62	66.67	0.30	0.0174575	0.86
9	1.9	1.13	–	–	–	6.81E-03	0.55	–	0.32	0.021275	0.83
10	1.11	–	–	–	–	–	0.98	–	0.19	0.0980918	0.22
11	1.11	1.9	–	–	–	–	0.85	19.13	0.29	0.016236	0.87
12	1.11	1.11	–	–	–	–	1.18	26.89	0.29	0.0041595	0.97
13	1.11	1.12	–	1.49	–	–	0.96	60.30	0.27	0.0146219	0.88
14	1.11	1.13	–	–	–	1.13E-02	9.9E-06	–	0.30	0.0308807	0.76
15	1.12	–	3.32	–	–	–	0.76	–	0.20	0.0956579	0.24
16	1.12	1.9	2.5	–	–	–	0.40	18.78	0.29	0.0163252	0.87
17	1.12	1.11	–	1.51	–	–	0.78	27.30	0.30	0.0045242	0.96
18	1.12	1.12	2.29	1.47	–	–	0.59	105.56	0.27	0.0154927	0.88
19	1.12	1.13	2.56	–	–	6.36E-03	0.44	–	0.29	0.0176969	0.86
20	1.13	–	–	–	1.97E-04	–	–	–	0.20	0.1126745	0.11
21	1.13	1.9	–	–	1.53E-04	–	–	21.14	0.32	0.0202808	0.84
22	1.13	1.11	–	–	2.05E-04	–	–	25.96	0.29	0.0164883	0.87
23	1.13	1.12	–	1.53	2.00E-04	–	–	76.13	0.30	0.0181868	0.86
24	1.13	1.13	–	–	1.64E-04	7.27E-03	–	–	0.32	0.0232337	0.82

Note: The second and third columns show the numbers of the equations we combined to assemble the double-nutrient kinetics; –, not available.

automatically considers all models (Equations 1.11 through 1.14) and fits the experimental data; our results are given in Table 9.8.

Note that although in this specific example it had been determined that the single-nutrient models could not be used to represent the growth kinetics of the microorganism, the software considers all models. This option is kept available to cover all possible cases, not only the one discussed in this example.

9.3.1.3.3 Determining the objective function. The objective function represents the sum of squared differences (SSD) between the experimentally measured specific growth rates and the specific growth rates predicted from the selected kinetic model for the specific concentrations of the growth-limiting nutrients.

$$\text{SSD} = \sum_{i=1}^{N} (\mu_{\text{experimental}} - \mu_{\text{predicted}})^2 \tag{9.2}$$

The goal is to find the kinetic expression and the associated biokinetic parameters that minimize SSD. There are many procedures for making these computations. The MATLAB program is used to calculate the biokinetic parameters that minimize SSD for each model.

9.3.1.3.4 Fitting the experimental data to the model.   The MATLAB program calculates the objective functions and biokinetic parameters for each model. On the attached CD are four MATLAB programs: (1) `Interactive_and_single_models.m` is the script file that reads the experimental data, calls various interactive models, and calculates the objective functions (Equation 9.2) by calling the (2) `InteractiveObjectiveFunction` function for each model. (3) `NonInteractiveObjectiveFunction.m` is the script file that reads the experimental data, calls various noninteractive models, and calculates the objective functions (Equation 9.2) by calling the (4) `NonInteractiveObjectiveFunction` function for each model.

To minimize the value of the objective function, the MATLAB programs use the direct search method. The following restrictions are applied to verify the results of the search:

1. Models that produce nonrealistic biokinetic coefficients (values that are negative, extremely high, or significantly out of range of biokinetic constants reported in the literature) are discarded.
2. Unstable models producing significantly different biokinetic parameters for insignificantly different initial estimates are ignored as ill conditioned. To test whether the model solution depends on the initial estimates, the programs must be run several times (at least five). Before discarding a model as unstable, consider that changing the initial estimates may change the results of computation: there may not be enough experimental data to make the computation precisely, in which case more data should be acquired.

Table 9.8 shows the results of searching for the best kinetic equation using the kinetic models and the modes of their possible interactions specified in Equations 1.9 and 1.11 through 1.13.

9.3.1.3.5 Selecting the best model.   Table 9.8 shows that the minimum SSD were found for models 12 and 17, with R^2 between 0.96 and 0.97. Model 17 combines Moser and Tessier kinetics. However, according to Moser kinetics (model 17), *P. aeruginosa* should grow in the absence of oxygen, contradicting experimental results. Consequently, the best growth model is double Tessier kinetics:

$$\mu = \mu_{max}\left(1 - e^{-S_o/K_o}\right)\left(1 - e^{-S_g/K_g}\right) \qquad (9.3)$$

Although it was found that the growth of *P. aeruginosa* is described best by double Tessier kinetics, most biofilm researchers use Monod kinetics, and most, if not all, mathematical models of biofilm growth and accumulation use Monod kinetics as well. Considering this fact, Table 9.8 is inspected, and it is found that the experimental data fit double Monod kinetics (Model 6) with $R^2 = 0.85$, which is less than the best fit, with $R^2 = 0.96$. For practical reasons, this difference would probably be ignored and double Monod kinetics selected, even though this is not the best model, because this choice would put the results in direct comparison with the data available in the literature. For the purpose of this example, however, the best model will continue to be used: double Tessier kinetics.

The high correlation coefficient (0.97) demonstrates that the model accurately represents the growth of *P. aeruginosa*. This example also demonstrates that the traditionally used Monod model is not necessarily the best model for describing microbial growth: it is just the most popular model.

For the selected model, the biokinetic parameters are $\mu_{max} = 0.29$ h^{-1}, $K_g = 26.9$ mg/L, $K_o = 1.18$ mg/L, $Y_{x/g} = 0.628$ g biomass/g glucose, and $Y_{x/o} = 0.635$ g biomass/g oxygen. The maintenance factors are $m_g = 0.0078$ g glucose consumed/g microorganisms hour, and $m_o = 0.014$ g oxygen consumed/g/microorganisms hour.

Example 9.3

When the growth kinetics of *Leptothrix discophora* SP-6 were quantified, it was found that microbial growth was limited by pyruvate and oxygen. To determine the biokinetic coefficients, a chemostat was set up using the following operational parameters: temperature = 25°C, pH = 7.2, agitation rate = 350 rpm, $S_{fp} = 1000$ mg L^{-1}, and $S_{fn} = 65$ mg NH$_4^+$ L^{-1}. The results of the steady state measurements are listed in Table 9.9. In the table, S_p and S_o are the pyruvate and oxygen concentrations in the chemostat, respectively. Calculate the biokinetic parameters, and determine the best model. Compare your results with those reported by Yurt et al. (2002).

Table 9.9 Results of Steady State Measurements Performed to Determine the Biokinetic Parameters of *Leptothrix discophora* SP-6

D (h^{-1})	X (mg L^{-1})	S_p (mg L^{-1})	S_o (mg L^{-1})	SOUR mg oxygen (mg microorganism)$^{-1}$ h^{-1}
0.029	87	2	5.7	0.0935
0.052	113	3.6	5.6	0.11
0.071	131	5.2	3.8	0.137
0.081	110	26.9	0.2	0.16
0.129	111	12.8	1.3	0.174
0.163	97	40.7	0.4	0.22
0.24	143	28.9	2.2	0.378
0.48	106	225	6.8	0.425
0.118	134	10.4	2.1	0.156
0.1	104	7.7	3.3	0.151
0.08	175	10.2	0.9	0.152
0.1	109	470	0.1	0.162
0.1	125	8.1	5.1	0.163
0.1	175	10.4	6	0.151
0.047	114	3.4	7.6	0.124
0.055	121	4.5	7.7	0.112
0.03	98	1.9	7.8	0.105
0.11	119	8.1	7.7	0.139
0.188	132	17.5	5.5	0.21
0.5	99	325	6.8	Na
0.3	103	34.1	1.6	0.27
0.35	121	74	0.9	0.31
0.43	113	234	0.65	0.435

9.4 Preparing and operating biofilm reactors

9.4.1 Operating flat plate biofilm reactors

Flat plate reactors are the most often used. Among the advantages of using these reactors are the possibilities of controlling the hydrodynamics, making microelectrode measurements, and quantifying the structure of biofilm. The procedures for assembling and operating flat plate reactors can be easily adapted to other types of biofilm reactors.

9.4.2 Components of the reactor system

The reactor is just one part of the reactor system; pumps, tubing, flow breakers, and other components are needed to support the operation. Table 9.10 lists the items that are used.

Table 9.10 Tools, Supplies, and Instruments Used to Operate Biofilm Reactors

Component	Function	Common suppliers
Tubing	Used to pump growth medium to the reactor, used in the recycle line, used in the waste line, used to connect the air filter, etc.	Fisher, Cole-Parmer
Flow breakers	Used to separate the liquid flow line to prevent the back-contamination of growth medium by bacteria growing in the reactor. They are also used in the waste line to prevent bacterial movement back into the biofilm reactor.	Custom-made
Connectors	Used to connect tubing of different sizes or the same size.	Fisher, Cole-Parmer
Peristaltic pumps	Used to pump medium, recycle, etc. We use variable-speed 6–100 rpm pumps for slow flow rates, and variable-speed 6–600 rpm pumps for higher flow rates. Make sure that the tubing size and the pump head size match. The smaller the tubing size, the less pulsation in the nutrient solution line.	Fisher, Cole-Parmer
Pulse dampeners	When the tube size is large, the peristaltic pump causes pulsation in the nutrient solution line. Pulsating flow affects hydrodynamics and biofilm growth and is undesirable. Pulse dampeners minimize pulsation. They are larger versions of the flow breakers, but the air inside the dampener acts like a pillow and minimizes pulsating flow. A syringe is used to control the amount of air in the dampener.	Custom-made
Flow meters	Used to measure gas or liquid flow rates.	Fisher, Cole-Parmer
Pressure transducers	Used to measure pressure drop.	Fisher, Cole-Parmer
Biofilm reactors	Used to grow biofilms.	All of our reactors are custom-designed and constructed by local companies.

9.4.3 Common procedures used in operating biofilm reactors

9.4.3.1 Measuring flow rates

The flow rates of liquids and gases are controlled variables in biofilm reactors. Two methods are used to measure the flow rates of liquids, depending on the flow rates: (1) calibrating recycling pumps that are operated at high flow rates by measuring the volume pumped in a certain time and (2) calibrating pumps delivering nutrients that are operated at low flow rates by counting the drops per unit time and measuring the volume of the drops. To measure the flow of gases, rotameters are used. However, avoid using these as in-line devices because biofilm growth in rotameters affects their ability to measure and control the flow rates of liquids.

9.4.4 Calibrating pumps

9.4.4.1 Calibrating pumps operated at high flow rates

The setup in Figure 9.4 is used to calibrate pumps used in recycle lines.

1. Prepare a graduated cylinder with adequate volume, 50 mL to 1 L, depending on the flow rates expected.
2. Connect the tubing to the peristaltic pump head using the same length of tubing as is used in the reactor setup.
3. Immerse the influent side of the tubing in a water container and the other side in the graduated cylinder.
4. Set the pump controller to the desired level (1, 2, 3, etc.)
5. Before starting the measurements, pump enough water through the tubing to make sure that there are no air bubbles remaining in the tubing.
6. Mark the initial volume of water in the graduated cylinder, and start the chronometer.
7. Wait at least 1 min or until the graduated cylinder is full.
8. Record time and volume.
9. Subtract the volume of water that was in the cylinder before pumping from the volume of water in the cylinder after pumping and calculate the volume pumped.
10. Divide the volume pumped by the time elapsed and calculate the volumetric flow rate.

Example 9.4

Using a variable-speed 6–600 rpm pump and size 16 silicone rubber tubing resulted in pumping the volumes of water given in Table 9.11. Calculate the volumetric flow rate for each setting of the pump and prepare a calibration curve.

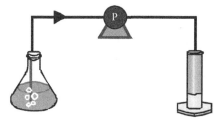

Figure 9.4 Calibrating a peristaltic pump: for each setting of the pump controller, measure the volume of the water collected in the cylinder after a specific length of time.

Table 9.11 Experimentally Measured Data

Pump setting	Volume of water in the graduated cylinder (mL)	Time elapsed (min)
2	50	1
3	135	1
4	206	1
5	289	1
6	382	1

Table 9.12 Calculations

Pump setting	Volume of liquid in graduated cylinder (mL)	Time elapsed (min)	Flow rate (mL/min)
2	50	1	= 50/1 = 50
3	135	1	= 135/1 = 135
4	206	1	= 206/1 = 206
5	289	1	= 289/1 = 289
6	382	1	= 382/1 = 382

Solution

The flow rate is calculated by dividing the volume of water in the graduated cylinder by the time elapsed. The flow rates are calculated in Table 9.12 and shown in Figure 9.5.

9.4.5   Using flow breakers to measure low flow rates

Using flow breakers between the container with the growth medium and the reactor prevents microbial contamination of the growth medium. When the flow rate is low (less than several mL/min), water flows through a flow breaker drop by drop, and the volumes of the drops are equal. The volume of a drop is calculated and used to determine the flow rate. The procedure, given below, is similar to that used when pumps are calibrated, and the setup is shown in Figure 9.6.

1. Get a graduated cylinder (50 mL to 1 L, depending on the flow rates necessary to work).
2. Connect tubing to the peristaltic pump head; be sure to use exactly the same length of tubing that you would like to use in the experiments.
3. On one side, there should be a water container, and on the other side, there should be an empty waste container and a graduated cylinder.
4. Set the pump level to a low value so that the drops can be counted easily.
5. Start pumping water to the waste container.
6. Pump enough water to be sure that there is no air in the tubing.
7. Click the chronometer, and move the tubing from the waste container to the graduated cylinder (these must happen at the same time) and start counting the drops.
8. Count 10–20 drops; then, stop the measurement.

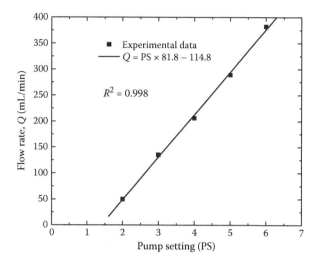

Figure 9.5 Pump setting versus flow rate. This pump can only be used for settings from 2 to 6. Using settings outside this range requires new calibration.

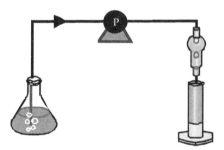

Figure 9.6 Calibrating the flow rate of the growth medium. Water flows through a flow breaker drop by drop. The flow rate is determined by measuring the volume of the water, the number of drops and the time elapsed.

9. Record the time and the volume of water in the graduated cylinder.
10. Divide the volume of water in the graduated cylinder by the number of drops to calculate the volume of each drop.
11. If the volume of water is divided by the time elapsed, the volumetric flow rate can be calculated as described above.

Example 9.5

The measurement shown in Figure 9.6 was performed, and it was found that 100 drops is 10 mL. Calculate the volume of each drop and determine the number of drops per minute that is equivalent to a flow rate of 2 mL/min.

$$\text{Volume of a drop} = \frac{\text{total volume of the collected liquid}}{\text{number of drops}} = \frac{10\ \text{mL}}{100} = 0.1\ \text{mL}$$

Two milliliters is equivalent to 20 drops (2 mL/0.1 mL). Therefore, with the pump set to deliver 20 drops/min, the flow rate will be 20 mL/min. Using a flow breaker between the container with the growth medium and the reactor prevents microbial contamination of the growth medium. When the flow rate is low (less than several milliliters per minute), water flows through a flow breaker drop by drop and the volumes of the drops are equal. We calculate the volume of the drops and use it to determine the flow rate. The procedure is similar to that we use when we calibrate pumps, and the setup is shown in Figure 9.6.

9.4.6   Measuring the working volume of a reactor

For this example a flat plate open-channel reactor is selected. Fill the reactor with water, and operate under operating conditions using water. Then, stop the reactor, and collect all the water in a graduated cylinder. The volume of the water is equal to the working volume of the reactor. This volume may be slightly different from one that was calculated from the geometry of the reactor. Water is typically used to measure the operating volume because it is hard to calculate the correct volume in the tubing, connector, etc.

9.4.7   Sterilizing reactors and other components

If possible, autoclaving reactors at 121°C and 1 atm pressure is preferable. If the reactors are constructed of materials that are not heat resistant, sterilize them using either 20% bleach or 70% ethanol. The decision of whether to use ethanol or bleach depends on the type of glue used to assemble the reactor. Some types of glue dissolve in bleach, and some dissolve in alcohol. For example, reactors made of polycarbonate and glass are glued with silicon rubber, and when such reactors are repeatedly sterilized using ethanol, they start leaking. Therefore, bleach is used to sterilize reactors glued with silicone rubber. The sterilizing agent, bleach or alcohol, must reside in the reactor for at least 2 h, and it must be removed from the reactor before the reactor is inoculated. The easiest way to remove the sterilizing agent from the reactor is to wash it out using sterile water in a volume exceeding 3–6 times the volume of the reactor. Just to be sure that the sterilizing agent has been removed, we pump sterile water through the reactor overnight.

Tubing, filters, flow breakers, and connectors can be autoclaved. The critical moment is when these components are connected to reactors, because sterile components must be handled manually. To minimize the chance of microbial contamination, assemble the reactor setup in a laminar flow hood. Also, clean all components of the setup using 70% alcohol before and after connecting the components.

9.4.8   Preparing the surfaces for biofilm growth

Biofilms are grown on glass microscope slides placed on the bottom of the reactor (Figure 9.7). These slides are removed one by one and treated separately, according to the specific protocol of the experiment. To facilitate this, the width of the reactor is made equal to the width of the microscope slides (2.5 cm). In a typical setup, microscope slides (2.5 × 7.5 × 0.1 cm³) etched with 20% hydrogen fluoride (HF) for 5 s and rinsed with excess deionized water are positioned on the bottom of the reactor at a distance from the entry to the reactor exceeding the entry length. This procedure must be performed in a hood capable of handling HF. Roughening the surface by etching in HF removes films contaminating the glass surface and helps microbial attachment. The slides are placed on the bottom of the reactor and held in place using sterile stainless steel brackets. These prevent the

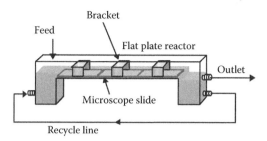

Figure 9.7 Metal brackets holding microscope slides. It is very convenient to move the brackets and take the slides out of the reactor.

slides from rising off the bottom if gas bubbles form underneath them. The slides in the reactor in Figure 9.7 cover the entire length of the bottom. However, when the effect of hydrodynamics on biofilm structure is studied, the slides that are used for the measurements must be placed at a distance from the entry exceeding the entry length computed as shown in Chapter 3.

9.4.9   Inoculating the reactors

To prepare the microorganisms for inoculation, follow the procedure given at the beginning of this chapter. Observations show that microorganisms attach to the surface after they deplete most of the growth-limiting nutrient; the time required may vary from one microorganism to another, and it will depend on the initial concentration of the growth-limiting nutrient.

Example 9.6

Growing biofilms of *P. aeruginosa* (ATCC 700829), *P. fluorescens* (ATCC 700830), and *K. pneumoniae* (ATCC 700831) in a flat plate reactor. To set up the reactor system shown in Figure 9.8, use the following components:

1. Flat plate flow reactor (described in Chapter 3)
2. Size 16 tubing (for recycle, ~1 m)
3. Two connectors, size 16, to the reactor (3.2–5.5 mm, Fisher catalog no. 15-315-28A)
4. Three flow breakers
5. 1.5 m of size 14 tubing (for nutrient solution line; the length of the tubing can be adjusted as needed)
6. 1.5 m of size 16 tubing (for water line; the length of the tubing can be adjusted as needed)
7. Small pieces (3–5 cm) of size 16 silicon tubing
8. Two connectors reducing the size from size 16 to size 14
9. One T connector
10. Four air filters (0.2 µm)
11. Three autoclavable carboys (20 L)
    a.   One filled with growth medium and then autoclaved
    b.   One to collect waste
    c.   One filled with water and then autoclaved
12. Two connectors to connect carboys to tubing (not shown in figure)
13. 2 L 70% alcohol or 20% bleach (not shown in figure)

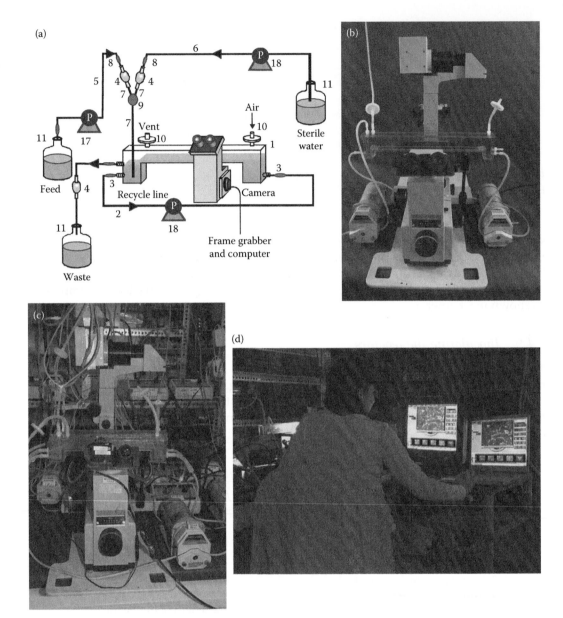

Figure 9.8 (a) Flat plate open-channel reactor operating with recycle. The numbers in the figure correspond to the numbers in the list of components in Example 9.6. (b) Photograph of the setup. (c) The reactor in operation. (d) Collecting images.

14. 500 mL 70% alcohol in a spray bottle (not shown in figure)
15. Six clamps (not shown in figure)
16. Inoculum, at least 10% of the volume of the liquid medium in the reactor (not shown in figure)
17. One variable-speed 6–100 rpm pump
18. Two variable-speed 6–600 rpm pumps
19. One 30-mL syringe and one size 16 (or smaller) needle (not shown in figure)

9.4.10   Sterilizing connectors and tubing

Use the following procedure to sterilize the connectors and tubing.

1. Connect the pieces of tubing and connectors as shown below in Figure 9.9.
2. Cover the ends with aluminum foil (as shown in Figure 9.9).
3. Place everything on a tray.
4. Autoclave at 121°C for 20 min.
5. Remove the tubing and connectors from the autoclave, and let them cool down.

If planning to use the components more than once, make sure that they are cleaned immediately after each use and rinsed with lots of water. If the components are not cleaned for a prolonged time, dry patches of biofilm accumulate on the walls. Such deposits are difficult to remove when dry and may detach unexpectedly, ruining the next experiment. The components must be cleaned with bleach right after the experiment is terminated, rinsed with lots of hot water, and then autoclaved.

9.4.11   Attaching the lid to the reactor

Before sterilizing the reactor, attach the reactor lid using silicone rubber. Here, a general purpose silicone rubber from a hardware store is used, and any ordinary silicone rubber sealant can be used for this purpose. Before applying the silicone rubber to the edges of the reactor, make sure that the surface of the reactor is clean and dry. Use a spoon or a knife (not sharp) to remove the old silicone rubber from the previous experiment, and then clean the reactor with a dishwashing detergent. Apply a layer of the silicone rubber evenly around all edges. Do not mix silicone rubber on the surface; apply one layer evenly and without mixing. Clean the lid of the reactor using the same procedure as the one used to clean the edges. Gently position the lid on top of the reactor, and place some weight (0.5 kg or so) on top of the lid, making sure that the weight is uniformly distributed. Allow the silicone rubber to dry overnight (Figure 9.10).

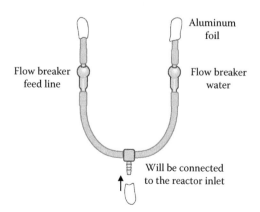

Figure 9.9 Before autoclaving, the ends of tubing and connectors are covered with aluminum foil.

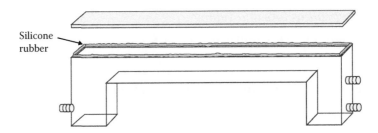

Figure 9.10 Applying the silicone rubber along the edges of the reactor.

9.4.12 Sterilizing a flat plate flow reactor

Flat plate flow reactors are sterilized using the following procedure.

1. Connect three pieces, 5 cm long, of size 16 tubing to the ports at the ends of the reactor.
2. Rinse the connectors with 70% alcohol.
3. Connect the autoclaved connectors and tubing to the reactors.
4. Connect a piece of size 16 tubing, 5 cm long, to the port where the air filter will be located.
5. Connect a piece of size 16 tubing, 5 cm long, to the port where nutrient solution and water will enter the reactor.
6. Place the clamps on the recycle tubing as shown below in Figure 9.11.
7. Fill the reactor completely with 70% alcohol or 20% bleach.
8. Leave the air port open, and introduce the sterilizing agent from the other side until it fills the reactor completely; make sure that all connectors are covered with liquid.
9. Close the tubing in the nutrient solution and air lines using clamps.
10. Allow the alcohol or bleach to sit in the reactor at least 2 h.
11. Remove the alcohol or bleach following the procedure described in Section 9.4.13.

9.4.13 Removing bleach or alcohol from a flat plate reactor

The bleach or alcohol solution is removed from the reactor using the following procedure.

1. Remove the clamp from the air line and insert an autoclaved air filter.
2. Connect the nutrient solution line to the port (do not remove the clamp yet).
3. Remove the clamps on the recycle line.

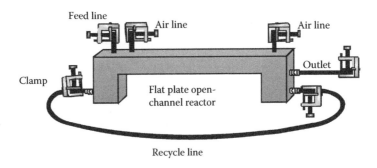

Figure 9.11 Sterilizing the reactor.

   4. Open the drain line.
   5. Start the recycle at a low rate. Make sure that it is running in the correct direc-
      tion. The higher liquid level must be on the side where the solution enters the
      reactor.
   6. Connect the air filter to the air line and start pumping air. Make sure that the drain
      line is open and the air has a place to go: sometimes researchers forget to open the
      drain line and the air does not have any place to go. This builds up pressure in the
      reactor, and it will damage the reactor.
   7. Reverse the recycle line; this will empty the reactor.
   8. Start the water flow at a moderate flow rate.
   9. Return the recycle to normal operating conditions.
  10. Make sure that the entire reactor has filled with water.
  11. When the reactor has filled with water, again reverse the recycle and empty the
      reactor.
  12. Repeat this fill and draw procedure at least five times.
  13. Set the water flow rate to approximately 0.5 L/h, and allow the water to flow overnight.

   After all traces of the sterilizing agent have been removed, the reactor is filled with
sterile water, which needs to be replaced with the growth medium.

9.4.14   Replacing water with growth medium in a flat plate reactor

The following procedure is used to replace the sterile water with growth medium.

   1. Remove the clamp from the nutrient solution line.
   2. Start pumping the growth medium at a moderate flow rate.
   3. Stop the water line.
   4. Reverse the recycle and empty the reactor.
   5. Fill the reactor with growth medium.
   6. Repeat this fill and draw procedure at least three times.

   The reactor is ready to be inoculated and operated according to the following
procedures.

9.4.15   Inoculating a flat plate reactor

The following procedure is used to inoculate the reactor.

   1. Spray 70% alcohol at the pieces of silicone tubing delivering air to the reactor.
   2. Check whether the recycle line is working at the desired flow rate.
   3. Draw 30 mL of inoculum into a 30-mL syringe in a laminar hood, connect a size 16
      needle to the syringe, and slowly inject the inoculum through the silicone tube of the
      air line.
   4. Repeat this procedure for the other bacteria, using a new syringe and a new needle
      each time.
   5. Stop the recycle and wait for 30 min. This will allow the initial attachment of the
      bacteria.
   6. Start the recycle at a very slow rate and increase gradually up to the operating recycle
      flow rate (within a few minutes).

9.4.16   Operating a flat plate reactor

The following procedure is used to operate the reactor.

1. Operate for at least 8 h in batch mode to let the bacteria grow; let it run in batch mode overnight.
2. Start the nutrient pumps and deliver the nutrient solution at the operating conditions.
3. Grow the biofilm.

9.4.17   Removing suspended microorganisms

It is recommended that suspended microorganisms be removed before images of the biofilm in the reactor are taken; this improves the quality of the images. For this purpose, sterile water or a sterile pH buffer solution without any nutrients should be used. Make sure that the biofilm does not change its structure when washed if just water is used. Some biofilms require a pH buffer for rinsing because the microorganisms are susceptible to the changes in osmotic pressure. If the nutrient solution contained a pH buffer, rinsing the biofilm with water once a day is an acceptable procedure. A volume of the rinsing solution equal to five working volumes of the reactor can be used.

9.4.18   Operating a simplified open-channel flat plate reactor

The following components need to be assembled to set up a simplified open-channel flat plate reactor system. The setup is shown in Figure 9.12.

1. A simplified open-channel flat plate reactor (described in Chapter 3)
2. One variable-speed 6–100 rpm pump
3. Various connectors
4. Two flow breakers
5. 1.5 m of size 13 tubing (nutrient solution line; the length must be adjusted as needed)
6. 1.5 m of size 16 tubing (waste line; the length must be adjusted as needed)
7. One T connector

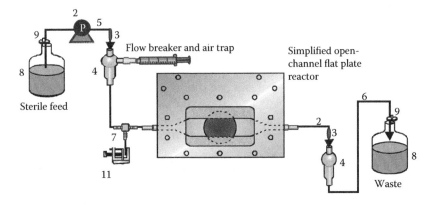

Figure 9.12 Simplified open-channel flat plate reactor. As seen, the reactor is operated without a recycle. The numbers in the figure correspond to the numbers in the list of components in Section 9.4.1.8.

   8. Two 10-L autoclavable carboys
      a.   One filled with growth medium
      b.   One to collect waste
   9. Two air filters (0.2 µm)
  10. 500 mL of 70% alcohol in a spray bottle (not shown in figure)
  11. One clamp
  12. 20 mL of inoculum (not shown in figure)

9.4.19   *Preparing the inoculum for a simplified open-channel flat plate reactor*

Prepare the inoculum following the procedure described for the flat plate reactor. Because the inoculum must be ready when the reactor is sterile, it is advisable to prepare the inoculum while the reactor is being sterilized. Both procedures, sterilizing the reactor and preparing the inoculum, take approximately one day.

9.4.20   *Sterilizing a simplified open-channel flat plate reactor with its connectors and tubing*

Use the following procedure to sterilize a simplified open-channel flat plate reactor and its connectors and tubing.

   1. Connect the tubing to the reactor and connectors.
   2. Make sure that the screws holding the glass slide are loose; otherwise, thermal expansion of the elements of the reactor—glass, rubber, and metal—will break the glass.
   3. Cover the ports with aluminum foil.
   4. Place all components on an autoclavable tray.
   5. Autoclave at 121°C for 20 min.
   6. Let the components cool down.

   As described above, it is advisable to always use new or well-cleaned tubing. If the plan is to use the components more than once, make sure that they are cleaned immediately after each use and rinsed with lots of water. If the components are not cleaned for a prolonged time, dry patches of biofilm accumulate on the walls. Such deposits are difficult to remove when dry and may detach unexpectedly, ruining the next experiment. For best results, the components must be cleaned with bleach right after the experiment is terminated, rinsed with lots of hot water and then autoclaved.

9.4.21   *Inoculating a simplified open-channel flat plate reactor*

Use the following procedure to inoculate a simplified open-channel flat plate reactor.

   1. Start pumping air into the growth medium: the solution must be saturated with oxygen.
   2. Start pumping the growth medium at the operational flow rate. Be sure that air bubbles are not going to the reactor. Stop aerating the growth medium after it is equilibrated with the oxygen in the air. Further aerating will not increase the dissolved oxygen concentration in the medium.

3. After all the tubing and the reactor are filled with the growth medium, pump the growth medium for some time to remove air bubbles from the reactor and from the tubing; then stop the pump.
4. Draw 20 mL of inoculum into a 30-mL syringe in a laminar hood.
5. Slowly inject the inoculum through the T connector (inoculation port) near the entrance to the reactor until it replaces the growth medium in the reactor (the volume of the inoculum should be equal to at least one volume of the reactor).
6. After inoculation, wait for 30 min to allow the initial attachment of the bacteria.
7. Start pumping the growth medium, first at a very slow rate, then increasing it gradually up to the operating flow rate (within a few minutes).
8. If a recycle is used, start the recycle at the same time as the pump pumping the growth medium. As with the growth medium, the recycle flow rate must be initially very low. It should be gradually increased to the operational recycle flow rate within one hour.

9.4.22　*Operating a simplified open-channel flat plate reactor*

Use the following procedure to operate a simplified open-channel flat plate reactor.

1. Operate the reactor in continuous flow mode until the biofilm reaches the desired thickness.
2. From time to time, check the flow breaker and the air trap to make sure that air is not being pumped into the reactor.

If needed, the above procedure can be modified for different microorganisms or growth media. Adding recycle can increase the flow rate in the reactor. If more air is needed, a mixing chamber can be added. However, if such needs emerge, consider using the regular flat plate reactor instead of the simplified one.

Often air bubbles develop near the walls of the reactor, and these may affect the biofilm process. The following may help to prevent the formation of air bubbles:

1. Make sure that the growth medium, tubing, reactor, etc., are all at the same temperature. Temperature differences affect the solubility of oxygen, and air bubbles can develop in the warmer parts of the reactor.
2. Make sure that all connections are airtight. Leaks at connections are the usual cause of air bubbles in the reactor. When a small tubing size is used, peristaltic pumps create a lower pressure in the tubing and the pump may suck in air through the connections between pieces of tubing.

9.4.23　*Operating a modified open-channel flat plate reactor for growing* Geobacter sulfurreducens *biofilms and quantifying electron transfer rates*

This protocol describes the procedure for assembling and operating a modified open-channel flat plate reactor to quantify the rate of electron transfer, or simply current, between a biofilm of Geobacter sulfurreducens and a glassy carbon electrode. A photograph of this reactor is shown in Figure 3.19, and the results of a study completed using this reactor are described in Section 3.5.1.1.2. The components of the reactor are shown in Figure 9.13 and are listed below. An open-channel flat plate reactor is modified to be a three-electrode bioreactor by inserting a working electrode (WE), counter electrode (CE), and reference electrode (RE); these function

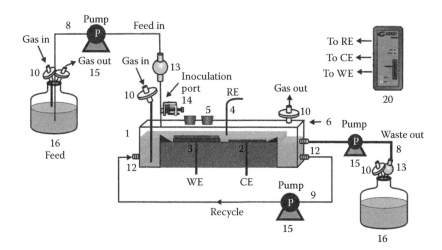

Figure 9.13 A modified open-channel flat plate flow reactor for *G. sulfurreducens* biofilm growth. As seen, the reactor is operated with a recycle. The numbers in the figure correspond to the numbers in the list of components in Section 9.4.23.

as an electrochemical cell and are used to quantify electron transfer rates as current. The *G. sulfurreducens* biofilm is expected to grow on the glassy carbon WE, colloquially referred to as the biofilm electrode. The electrochemical cell is completed by inserting a CE, usually made of graphite, and a saturated Ag/AgCl reference electrode.

The following components are needed to assemble and operate the reactor:

1. A modified open-channel flat plate flow reactor
2. A graphite electrode as the counter electrode (Sigma-Aldrich® 496553-180.7G)
3. A glassy carbon electrode as the working electrode (Structure Probe, Inc. 4370GCP-AB)
4. A saturated Ag/AgCl electrode as the reference electrode
5. Rubber stoppers
6. Silicone rubber (to seal compartments of the reactor and its parts)
7. Conductive epoxy (ITWChemtronics® CW2400, not shown in figure)
8. Tygon® tubing (Cole-Parmer® EW-06475-16, EW-06475-14)
9. Norprene® tubing (Cole-Parmer® EW-06404-16, EW-06404-14)
10. Five autoclavable large-diameter gas filters (Cole-Parmer® EW-02915-28)
11. Autoclavable barbed tube connectors to connect tubing (not shown in figure)
12. Autoclavable fittings that connect the reactor body to tubing at the inlet, outlet, recycle, and gas filters
13. Two flow breakers, one at the inlet and one at the outlet, to prevent back-contamination (reactor to feed, waste to reactor)
14. Autoclavable tubing clamps
15. Three peristaltic pumps and pump controllers
16. Two 10-L autoclavable containers
    a. One filled with *G. sulfurreducens* growth medium
    b. One to collect waste
17. Gas cylinder (with 20% CO_2, 80% N_2) and a regulator (not shown in figure)
18. Syringes and needles for inoculation and sample collection, if required (not shown in figure)

Table 9.13 Gas Permeability of Different Types of Masterflex® Tubing

Tubing formulation	Gas permeability cc × mm × 10⁻¹⁰ (cm² × s × cm Hg)			
	CO_2	H_2	O_2	N_2
Norprene®	1200	–	200	80
Tygon®	270	97	60	30
Viton®	76–79	–	13–15	4.3
Silicone (platinum-cured)	20,132	6579	7961	2763

Source: Cole-Parmer® Web site. (Check company Web site for more up-to-date information.)

19. A multimeter (not shown in figure)
20. A potentiostat
21. Electrical wiring and alligator clips (not shown in figure)
22. 20 mL inoculum (not shown in figure)
23. 500 mL 70% ethanol in a spray bottle (not shown in figure)

Note that the selection of tubing is dependent on tubing life and gas permeation rates. Norprene® tubing has a lifetime of well over 4000 h in a peristaltic pump head, whereas the lifetimes of Tygon® formulations are a fraction of that (source: Cole-Parmer® Web site, http://www.coleparmer.com/TechLibraryArticle/773). Tygon® tubing is typically prone to cracks and leaking within the typical operation time of the three-electrode bioreactor. However, Tygon® is less gas permeable than Norprene® in regards to both carbon dioxide and oxygen. In the three-electrode bioreactor, the reactor volume equilibrates with a 20% carbon dioxide/80% nitrogen atmosphere and thus gas permeation by carbon dioxide and oxygen needs to be minimized. It is advantageous to use Tygon® tubing for long lengths of tubing and short lengths of Norprene® inside pump heads to reduce cracking and subsequent leaking. Another alternative from Cole Parmer® is Viton® tubing; however, this has a limited lifetime and is generally susceptible to autoclave sterilization. Silicone-based tubing should never be used with the three-electrode bioreactor unless absolutely necessary for very short lengths of tubing. Table 9.13 summarizes the gas permeability of relevant types of tubing.

9.4.23.1 Preparing the inoculum
The inoculum is prepared according to the following procedure.

1. Growth medium
   G. sulfurreducens growth medium should be prepared using the following recipe:

Chemical	Concentration (g/L)
Potassium chloride (KCl)	0.38
Ammonium chloride (NH_4Cl)	0.2
Sodium phosphate monobasic ($NaH_2PO_4·H_2O$)	0.069
Calcium chloride ($CaCl_2·H_2O$)	0.04
Magnesium sulfate heptahydrate ($MgSO_4·7H_2O$)	0.2
Sodium acetate ($NaC_2H_3O_2$)	1.64

Sodium fumarate (Na$_2$C$_4$H$_2$O$_4$)*	6.4
Sodium carbonate (Na$_2$CO$_3$)†	2
Additional solutions	**Per 1 L of the medium solution**
Mineral solution	10 mL
Vitamin solution	10 mL

* Sodium fumarate is used as the electron acceptor in the preparation of the inoculum. However, we do not feed fumarate during reactor operation because this would interfere with the electrode being the only available electron acceptor for the biofilm.

† Sodium carbonate (Na$_2$CO$_3$) should be added, adjusting the pH to 6.8, after all the other chemicals have been added but before autoclaving.

2. Sterilizing the growth medium
   a. Autoclave at 121°C for 15 min/L of growth medium.
   b. After taking the medium out of the autoclave, let it cool down and then bubble the sterilized growth medium with 80% N$_2$/20% CO$_2$ for 24 h to ensure equilibrium between the liquid and gas phases.
3. Culturing *G. sulfurreducens*
   a. Transfer 1 mL of *G. sulfurreducens* stock culture from the freezer (kept at −85°C) to the anaerobic chamber and let it thaw. Do not let the stock culture sit after it has thawed; the cells will die.
   b. Inject the 1 mL of stock culture into a 20-mL vial (or larger) of sterile anaerobized *G. sulfurreducens* growth medium.
   c. Leave the culture in the anaerobic chamber; it will be ready for inoculating the reactor in 5–7 days.
   d. Note the following:
      i. *G. sulfurreducens* should be grown at 30°C.
      ii. When properly grown, a *G. sulfurreducens* culture has a doubling time of approximately 6 h.
4. Because the inoculum must be ready when the reactor is sterile, it is advisable to prepare it in advance. Both procedures, sterilizing the reactor and preparing the inoculums, take approximately one day.

9.4.23.2 Assembling the open-channel flat plate reactor

Since reactors are usually used for multiple runs, the first step after a run is completed is to clean the reactors and make them ready for the next run.

1. Clean the reactor parts.
   a. Wash all parts of the reactor using glass cleaning detergent and tap water.
   b. Rinse all the parts using tap water.
2. Prepare the working electrode.
   a. Chemically clean the working electrode. Working electrodes can be used as is from a vendor but it is recommended to clean them chemically. After a successful reactor run in which the working electrode is exposed to medium/biofilm, it *must* be cleaned chemically. Failure to do so will result in irreproducible results, electrochemical artifacts, and in general erroneous results during electrochemical characterization. The surface of the working electrode must be chemically clean, not simply visually clean. *Surface preparation of the working electrode is the single most important step in the entire assembly of the reactor.* After a

working electrode has been received from the vendor, or after the reactor has had an initial cleaning, wash the working electrode with distilled water in copious amounts. Place it in acetone for approximately 15 min. Afterward, rinse the working electrode again with copious amounts of distilled water. It should then be dried and submerged completely in freshly made 1 M H_2SO_4 for at least 24 h. Note that the acetone is used to remove trace organics and the acid wash is used to remove trace metals. It will not efficiently remove large amounts of dirt or visible contamination.

b. For glassy carbon electrodes with a smooth, mirror-like polish (usually created with a final polish using a 0.2-μm alumina slurry on a felt pad), an extra step is necessary. The polished surface must be refinished by polishing with 0.2-μm alumina slurry on a felt pad for at least 5 min using a figure-eight pattern. Refinishing the glassy carbon surface is the best method of obtaining a reproducible surface. Afterward, sonication in distilled water is required to remove both alumina particles and fine carbon dust. Dry with a lint-free cloth.

c. Store the working electrode dry, away from dust.

d. The same procedure can be used for the counter electrode if it is also glassy carbon and being recycled after each run. For graphite counter electrodes, do not polish using alumina slurry; instead use fine-grain sandpaper (1200 grit).

e. Connect an insulated copper wire to the working electrode (Figure 9.14). Connecting electrical wires to the working electrode allows us to make a connection to a potentiostat, which will monitor electron transfer rates. The wires are mounted onto the working electrode using conductive epoxy. The conductive epoxy creates a low-resistance electrical connection between the wire and the working electrode.

f. Decide first where the wire will be mounted onto the working electrode and strip the ends of the (usually) insulated copper wire. Note that the connection must be sealed in waterproofed adhesive/sealant that will not allow water to contact the conductive epoxy.

g. Prepare the conductive epoxy (this step varies with the type and brand used).

h. Immediately apply a modest amount of conductive epoxy between the exposed wire and the working electrode. Allow it to cure for 24 h. Secure the wire so that it does not shift during the curing period.

i. Repeat the procedure for the counter electrode (steps e–h).

j. After 24 h, use a multimeter to measure the electrical resistances of the connection(s). A connection is acceptable if the resistance is smaller than a few ohms.

3. Assemble the reactor. Assembly includes installing the prepared electrodes and sealing the top of the reactor. Note that electrode connections must be sealed in waterproofed adhesive/sealant that will not allow water to contact the conductive epoxy.

Figure 9.14 Wires can be connected either at the bottom of the electrode or through the side.

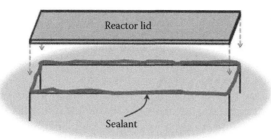

Figure 9.15 After applying sealant around the top of the reactor body, press the reactor lid down on the sealant.

As shown in Figure 9.13, the working/counter electrode with wire connection is affixed to the raised portion of the reactor. Usually, the wire connection is sealed in the adhesive used to affix the working electrode to the reactor bottom, and the wire is routed through a small hole in the bottom of the reactor body.

   a. Following Figure 9.13, affix both the working electrode and the counter electrode to the bottom of the reactor using an adhesive, typically silicone rubber sealant. Route the wires through the bottom.

   b. Using a silicone rubber sealant, apply a continuous line of sealant around the top of the reactor body (Figure 9.15).

   c. Press the reactor lid down on the sealant, making it square with the reactor body. Apply even pressure.

   d. Allow the reactor assembly 24 h to cure and set in place.

9.4.23.3 *Sterilizing the reactor, connectors, and tubing*

1. Place clamps on all air filters.
2. Clamp the inlet stream and any unused lines that were not sealed with silicone rubber.
3. Wrap the clamped inlet stream end and all filters with aluminum foil.
4. Loosen the lid of the waste container to avoid pressure buildup.
5. Place reactor in autoclavable tray.
6. Autoclave at 121°C for 15 min.
7. When autoclaving is complete, take the reactor out, then tighten the waste container lid and remove the clamps from the lid before removing the reactor from the autoclave.
8. Allow reactor to cool to room temperature.

9.3.23.4 *Inoculating the reactor*

We run the reactor in a temperature-controlled incubator.

1. Place the assembled and autoclaved reactor into the incubator.
2. Put the inlet, outlet, and recycle lines through the pump heads on the pumps.
3. Start pumping the growth medium (without fumarate).
4. Start pumping 80% N_2/20% CO_2 gas to the growth medium.
5. Place the Ag/AgCl reference electrode into the reactor as shown in Figure 9.13. Sterilize the reference electrode with 70% ethanol and then rinse it with autoclaved deionized water before placing it into the reactor.

6. Hook the connection wires of the working, counter, and reference electrodes to the potentiostat.
7. Run cyclic voltammetry (CV) to make sure that the working electrode is clean. This step will tell you whether the electrode cleaning procedure is successful. The details of running a CV are provided below.
8. Polarize the electrode to +300 mV$_{Ag/AgCl}$. This polarization potential is chosen so that the limiting current is what is measured (see the following section).
9. Leave the reactor running for 24 h to get a stable background current. This step is critical to ensure that the measured current is coming from the biofilm.
10. Turn off the inlet and outlet pumps (not the recycle) before inoculating.
11. Add 20 mL of inoculum through the T connector into the feed line.
12. Stop the recycle pump and let cells settle on the electrode for about an hour before turning all pumps back on.

9.4.23.5   Operating the reactor
For optimal cell growth and current generation, operate the reactor in continuous mode. On a daily basis, we check the flow breaker and recycle lines to make sure that flow is going in the correct direction and that there is no pressure buildup in the reactor.

9.4.23.6   An example cyclic voltammogram of a G. sulfurreducens biofilm
We use potentiostats from Gamry Instruments©, and the examples below describe the use of these potentiostats with their respective software packages. However, potentiostats from other companies can also be used, and Section 9.4.23.7 will provide rough guidelines for other software. Table 9.14 details example input parameters used to operate a Gamry Instruments Reference 600 potentiostat and obtain a representative CV for *G. sulfurreducens* biofilms. Figure 9.16 shows a screen shot of the input window where these input parameters are entered. The typical value of each input parameter is entered here; these values should be modified slightly to obtain the optimum CV. For example, Figure 9.17 shows the CV obtained before the reactor is inoculated and that obtained after a biofilm has grown on the working electrode.

9.4.23.7   Using the chronoamperometry script to polarize the working electrode continuously
To polarize the working electrode continuously during reactor operations, we use the chronoamperometry script. Although we could write our own script, it is advantageous to use the default scripts so that the output file is compatible with the analysis software included with the potentiostat. The input window for the chronoamperometry script is shown in Figure 9.14. The values shown in the input boxes are the typical values and settings used to grow *G. sulfurreducens* biofilms. Although chronoamperometry is traditionally used as a technique for monitoring the current response to a potential step change (hence the input boxes for step 1 voltage and step 2 voltage), we are using it to apply a constant polarization potential of +0.3V$_{Ag/AgCl}$. For the input parameters in Figure 9.16, the script will take one data point every 10 s, for a total time period of one million seconds (~11.5 days). Usually, it is best to restart the script every 2 to 3 days to prevent the data file from becoming too large. The same rules apply for the chronoamperometry script, as shown for IE range and maximum current in the CV script (Figure 9.18). There is also an extra input parameter to limit the current density, which is shown as Limit I. Limit I acts as a turn-off switch that stops the script once the specified current density is reached. This is different from the maximum current, since Limit I does not affect the choice of IE range in fixed mode (see Table 9.14). Example results obtained using chronoamperometry are presented in Chapter 7 (Figure 7.23).

Table 9.14 Descriptions of the Input Parameters and the Typical Values of Them Used to Run CVs for *G. sulfurreducens* Biofilms

Parameter	Description
Electrode area	Surface area of the working electrode covered with biofilm in square centimeters.
Initial E	Initial polarization potential for the CV. A typical value for *G. sulfurreducens* biofilms is -0.7 $V_{Ag/AgCl}$.
Scan limit 1	The first polarization potential set point that can be either more positive (anodic scan) or more negative (cathodic scan) than *Initial E*. A typical value for *G. sulfurreducens* biofilms is $+0.4$ $V_{Ag/AgCl}$. Therefore, CVs for *G. sulfurreducens* biofilms are typically run in the anodic direction.
Scan limit 2	Set to the same value as *Initial E*. This is the second polarization potential set point; it returns to the value of *Initial E*, completing the CV scan.
Final E	Set to the same value as *Initial E*. Only in atypical CV experiments will *Final E* be different from *Initial E*.
Scan rate	The rate (mV/s) at which the polarization potential is increased (positively or negatively) from *Initial E* to *Final E*. The scan rate determines the total time required for each CV scan; $2 \times (Final\ E - Initial\ E)/(Scan\ rate/1000) = $ time elapsed during one CV scan. Typical values are 1–10 mV/s.
Step size	Determines the number of data points collected for each CV scan. A smaller *step size* provides more data points and sometimes smoother figures. $2 \times (Final\ E - Initial\ E)/(Step\ size/1000) = $ no. of data points. Typical values are 1–5 mV.
Cycles	Number of CV scans performed for each experiment. Typically set to two or more to ensure that the CV characteristics are stable over time.
IE range mode[a]	Set to fixed mode. Auto is not typically needed.
Maximum current	The current value that sets the IE range in fixed mode. The software will choose an IE range that is 11% greater than the maximum current to ensure no overloads occur. The maximum current for a *G. sulfurreducens* biofilm depends on the electrode area.
IR Comp	Set to none. Not typically needed. This option compensates for the internal resistance of the cell, which can be estimated using the script *GetRu*.
PF Corr	When IR Comp is set to none, this value is not used (it is only used when IR Comp is set to *PF*).
Equilibrium time	The amount of time that the potentiostat holds the polarization potential at *Initial E*. A typical value is 10 s.
Initial delay	Set to off
Conditioning	Set to off
Sampling mode	Set to noise reject

[a] IE range is the integer number, n, that determines the internal resistor used to measure current. It follows that for the Reference 600 series, 6×10^n pA determines the maximum current measured for each internal resistor. For example, for an IE range of 5, the maximum current measurable by the Reference 600 series is 6×10^5 pA, or 600 nA. There are a total of 11 IE ranges from 1–11, or 60 pA to 600 mA.

9.4.24 Operating tubular reactors

Tubular reactors are often used to grow biofilms at flow velocities and shear stresses higher than those that can be reached in flat plate reactors. To satisfy the requirements for bacterial growth, these reactors are operated with recycle and with mixing chambers. The example protocol reports a procedure for growing mixed-population biofilms composed of *P. aeruginosa* (ATCC 700829), *P. fluorescens* (ATCC 700830), and *K. pneumoniae* (ATCC 700831)

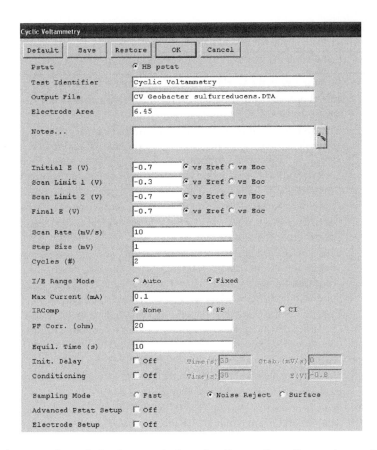

Figure 9.16 A screenshot of the input window for the cyclic voltammetry script on Gamry Instruments© software.

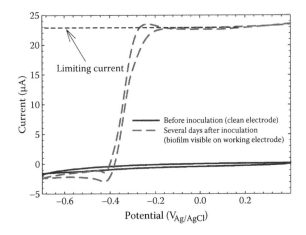

Figure 9.17 Example CV of a clean electrode prior to inoculation with *G. sulfurreducens* cells and after several days of biofilm growth. *Initial E* = −0.7 V; scan limit 1 = +0.3 V; scan limit 2/*Final E* = −0.7 V; scan rate = 10 mV/s; step size = 1 mV; cycles = 2 (cycle 1 not shown); equilibrium time = 10 s. The horizontal dashed line represents the limiting current.

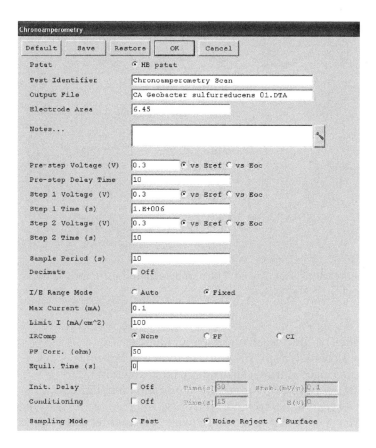

Figure 9.18 A screenshot of the input window for the chronoamperometry script, showing the typical input parameters used to grow *G. sulfurreducens* biofilms.

to determine the effect of biofilm accumulation on pressure drop. The setup is shown in Figure 9.19. Circular tubing is used, and pressure drop is measured across the reactor.

To assemble the reactor system shown in Figure 9.19, the following components are needed:

1. A clear polycarbonate or glass tube with an inside diameter of 0.5 in and a length of 1 m (or any other size and length needed)
2. Size 16 tubing for pumping liquids
3. Various connectors
4. Three flow breakers
5. 1.5 m of size 14 tubing (nutrient solution line; adjust the length as needed)
6. 1.5 m of size 16 tubing (water line; adjust the length as needed)
7. 1 m of size 16 tubing (waste line; adjust the length as needed)
8. Two 50-cm pieces of size 16 silicon tubing (to connect the pressure transducer)
9. 2 T connectors
10. Three air filters (0.2 μm)
11. Three 20-L autoclavable carboys
    a. One filled with growth medium
    b. One to collect waste
    c. One filled with water

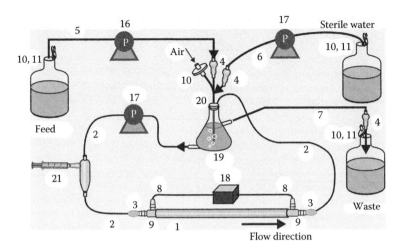

Figure 9.19 Tubular reactor system layout. The numbers in the figure correspond to the numbers in the list of components in Section 9.4.24.

12. 2 L 70% alcohol or 20% bleach (not shown in figure)
13. 500 mL 70% alcohol in a spray bottle (not shown in figure)
14. Several clamps (used during sterilization) (not shown in figure)
15. Inoculum: 30 mL of each microorganism (not shown in figure)
16. One variable-speed 6–100 rpm pump
17. Two variable-speed 6–600 rpm pumps (water line and recycle line)
18. Pressure transducer
19. Mixing chamber (a flask with two exit ports can be used: one close to the bottom and one around the middle of the flask)
20. Rubber stopper that fits the flask with holes for the glass tubes
21. Pulse dampener

9.4.25 Preparing the inoculum for a tubular reactor

Prepare the inoculum following the procedure described in Section 9.1.3.1. Because the inoculum must be ready when the reactor is sterile, it is advisable to prepare the inoculum while the reactor is being sterilized. Completing both procedures, sterilizing the reactor and preparing the inoculum, takes approximately one day.

9.4.26 Sterilizing a tubular reactor with its connectors and tubing and connecting the pressure transducer

Use the following procedure to sterilize the reactor with its connectors and tubing and connect the pressure transducer.

1. Connect all tubing to the reactor and connectors.
2. Clamp tubing for pressure transducer close to the connectors.
3. Fill the system with 70% alcohol or 20% bleach and start operating all the pumps.
4. Make sure that the air has been removed from the tubing.

5. Rinse tubing connections for pressure transducer with alcohol.
6. Connect ports of pressure transducer; make sure that water does not enter the pressure transducer.
7. Make sure that the connection ports are up and water does not get into the transducer.
8. Start pumping filtered air into the mixing chamber. This creates a positive pressure in the mixing chamber, and the liquid is removed from the reactor without a pump.
9. Fill the reactor with autoclaved water.
10. Tilt the reactor to drain the water from the reactor: allow all the liquid to run to the overflow and then fill the reactor with autoclaved water.
11. Repeat this fill and draw procedure at least five times.
12. Allow overnight rinsing of the reactor with autoclaved water.

9.4.27   *Replacing water with growth medium in a tubular reactor*

Use the following procedure to replace water with growth medium in a tubular reactor.

1. Drain the water from the reactor by tilting the reactor. Allow all the liquid to run to the overflow and then fill the reactor with the growth medium.
2. Repeat this fill and draw procedure at least three times.

9.4.28   *Inoculating a tubular reactor*

Use the following procedure to inoculate a tubular reactor.

1. Draw 30 mL of inoculum into a 30-mL syringe in a laminar hood.
2. Slowly inject the solution into the reactor through the air port connected to the mixing chamber.
3. After inoculation, stop the recycle and wait for 30 min; this will allow the initial attachment of the bacteria.
4. Start the recycle pump (first slowly, and then increase the pumping rate to the operating rate within a few minutes) and allow 8 h or overnight growth in batch mode with recycle.

9.4.29   *Operating a tubular reactor*

Use the following procedure to operate a tubular reactor.

1. Continuously pump the growth medium until the desired biofilm thickness or duration of the experiment has been reached.
2. From time to time, check the pulse dampener to make sure that there is enough air to damp the pulses.

When using different bacteria or different growth media, modify the procedure as needed.

9.4.30   *Measuring pressure and pressure drop in a tubular reactor*

The pressure drop is determined as the pressure difference between two locations in a reactor, often between the inlet and the outlet. Two types of devices are used to measure pressure drop: (1) U-shaped manometers and (2) electronic pressure transducers, which convert pressure to an electronic signal. Pressure transducers can be purchased from specialized vendors such as Cole-Parmer. Use the following criteria to select a pressure transducer:

1. Select a transducer that is made of parts that are compatible with the growth medium.
2. Select the range of the expected pressure variation and the required accuracy of the measurements. Selecting a pressure transducer with a range of measurement largely exceeding that expected in the reactor decreases the accuracy of the measurements.
3. Select the type of output signal. There are two analog signals used: 4-20 mA and DC voltage. Transducers are available in both versions. The 4-20 mA signal can be converted to a voltage signal using a resistor.

The selected pressure transducer needs to be calibrated using a U-type manometer.

Example 9.7: Calibrating the pressure transducer

Connect the pressure transducer to the ports of the U-type manometer as shown in Figure 9.20. Note that one of the ports has a T connector and a syringe. This syringe is used to create positive pressure. Connect the pressure transducer to an electrometer and read the potentials for various pressure differences within the range of expected pressure drops in the biofilm reactor. An example of such computations is shown in Figure 9.21 and Table 9.15.

To convert height differences (Δh) to pressure, use

$$\text{Pressure drop} = \rho g \Delta h$$

$$[\rho g \Delta h] = \frac{kg}{m^3} \times \frac{m}{s^2} \times m = \frac{kg}{m \times s^2} = \frac{kg \times m}{m^2 \times s^2} = \frac{N}{m^2}$$

where $1 \text{ kg} \times 1 \text{ m/s}^2 = 1 \text{ N}$.

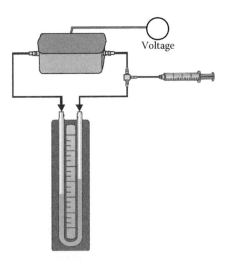

Figure 9.20 Experimental setup used to calibrate a pressure transducer.

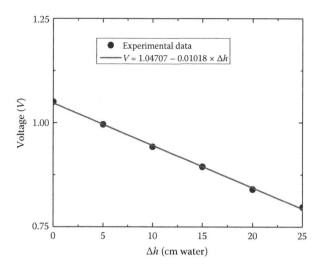

Figure 9.21 Pressure transducer calibration curve.

Table 9.15 Differences in Water Level and Voltages from the Pressure Transducer

Difference in water level, Δh (cm)	Voltage from pressure transducer (mV)
25	0.797
20	0.84
15	0.894
10	0.942
5	0.996
0	1.05

9.4.31 Packed-bed reactors

9.4.31.1 Preparing the inoculum for a packed bed reactor

Prepare the inoculum for a packed bed reactor (PBR) following the procedure described in Section 9.3.9. Because the inoculum must be ready when the reactor is sterile, it is advisable to prepare the inoculum while the reactor is being sterilized. Completing both procedures, sterilizing the reactor and preparing the inoculum, takes approximately one day. The following sections describe how to prepare and operate packed-bed reactors.

9.4.31.2 Preparing a PBR

The following is a list of the components needed to set up a PBR (Figure 9.22).

1. A column reactor
2. One variable–speed 6–100 rpm pump
3. One variable–speed 6–600 rpm pump
4. Various connectors
5. Two flow breakers (not shown in figure)
6. 1.5 m of size 13 tubing (nutrient solution line; the length must be adjusted as needed)
7. 1.0 m of size 16 tubing (recycle line; the length must be adjusted as needed)

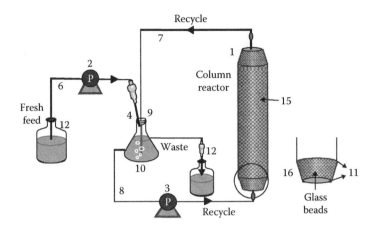

Figure 9.22 Packed-bed reactor with recycle. The numbers in the figure correspond to the numbers in the list of components in Section 9.4.30.3.

8. 1.0 m of size 16 tubing (recycle line; the length must be adjusted as needed)
9. Rubber stopper that fits the flask with holes
10. Mixing chamber (a flask with two exit ports can be used, one close to the bottom and one around the middle of the flask)
11. Sieves at the inlet and at the outlet of the column
12. Two 10-L autoclavable carboys
    a. One filled with growth medium
    b. One to collect waste
13. 500 mL 70% alcohol in a spray bottle (not shown in figure)
14. 30 mL inoculum (not shown in figure)
15. Packing material
16. Glass beads 0.1–0.2 cm in diameter

9.4.31.3 Preparing the packing material for a PBR

A reactor made of clear polycarbonate tubing is used. Before it is filled with packing material, the pore volume must be measured. This can be done as follows:

1. Fill the empty reactor with water and then drain the water into a graduated cylinder to measure the volume of water (V_e).
2. Put the packing material into the water, and let it get wet.
3. Remove the packing material from the water (a sieve can be used).
4. Fill the reactor with this wet packing material.
5. Fill the reactor with water and then drain the water into a graduated cylinder to measure the water volume (V_p).
6. The volume difference between V_e and V_p is the pore volume of the reactor.

Now the reactor can be filled with packing material such as minerals. Then, seal the reactor. To ensure the uniform delivery of the nutrient solution, use flow distributors. Some 0.5-cm glass beads entrapped between two plastic sieves can be used; these are placed in the inlet and in the outlet of the PBR (Figure 9.22). PBRs can be operated with or without recycle. A mixing chamber can be used if needed.

9.4.31.4 Calculating the operational parameters of a PBR

The operational parameters of the reactor usually mean the settings on the respective pumps at which the reactor is operated to obtain the required retention time and the required flow velocity through the porous bed. The computations are illustrated in the following example. A reactor has the following characteristics:

Diameter of the column = 2.0 cm
Length of the column = 40 cm
Pore volume = 100 mL
Nutrient flow rate = 10 mL/h

The reactor will be operated with a recycle ratio of 320. Calculate the retention time and the flow velocity in this reactor.

$$\text{Retention time} = \frac{\text{Volume of liquid in the reactor (pore volume)}}{\text{Volumetric flow rate}} = \frac{100 \text{ mL}}{10 \text{ mL/h}} = 10 \text{ h}$$

If the recycle ratio is higher than 40, the reactor can be considered to be well mixed. If the recycle ratio is set to 320 (very high), the flow rate in the recycle line must be established.

$$\text{Recycle ratio} = \frac{\text{Recycle volumetric flow rate (RFR)}}{\text{Feed flow rate}} = \frac{\text{RFR}}{10 \text{ mL/h}} = 320$$

$$\text{Recycle volumetric flow rate (RFR)} = 10 \text{ mL/h} \times 320 = 3200 \text{ mL/h}$$

$$\text{Total flow rate at the entrance to the column} = \text{Recycle volumetric flow rate} + \text{Nutrient solution flow rate} = 10 \text{ mL/h} + 3200 \text{ mL/h} = 3210 \text{ mL/h}$$

$$\text{Empty reactor volume} = \text{cross-section area} \times \text{length} = \pi \times r^2 \times 40 = 3.14 \times (2/2) \times 40 = 125.6 \text{ cm}^3$$

$$\text{Porosity} = \frac{\text{Void volume}}{\text{Reactor volume}} = \frac{100 \text{ cm}^3}{125.6 \text{ cm}^3} = 0.8$$

This means 80% of the reactor is void and is available for liquid volume. This also means that 80% of the cross section of the reactor is available for the liquid flow (this is the same as the volumetric porosity of the reactor if a homogeneous distribution of the filling material in the column is assumed). Thus, the cross-sectional area available for liquid flow must be calculated.

$$\text{Cross section available for liquid flow} = \text{cross-sectional area} \times \text{porosity}$$
$$= \pi \times r^2 \times 0.8 = 3.14 \times (2/2) \times 0.8 = 2.5 \text{ cm}^2$$

$$\text{Linear flow velocity} = \frac{\text{Volumetric flow rate}}{\text{Cross-sectional area available for flow}} = \frac{3210 \text{ cm}^3/\text{h}}{2.5 \text{ cm}^2} = 1286 \text{ cm/h}$$

9.4.31.5 Growing biofilm in a PBR

The following procedure is used to grow biofilm in a PBR.

1. Autoclave the tubing, reactors, and all containers.
2. Connect the entire system as shown in Figure 9.22. Fill the system with 70% alcohol, and then recycle for 3 h. Be sure that the filling material used does not react with the sterilizing agent. If necessary, change the sterilizing agent.
3. Drain the reactor.
4. Pump 10 L of sterile deionized water through the reactor to wash out traces of alcohol.
5. Drain the reactor again, and then fill with appropriate growth medium.
6. Inoculate the reactor with 30 mL of inoculum.
7. Operate the reactor in batch mode for at least 8 h or overnight.
8. Start the flow of nutrient solution.
9. The biofilm should be visible on the filling material after a few days of operation.

9.4.32 Hollow fiber biofilm reactors

We use hollow fiber biofilm reactors (HFBRs) to grow biofilms and then extract EPS from these biofilms. This section describes how to extract EPS from a biofilm grown in a HFBR. For our purpose, we choose an HFBR because we can obtain large amounts of biomass. An HFBR gives us a large ratio of surface area to volume, which allows biofilm growth. One of the key factors in studying the properties of EPS is that we need to have enough EPS for chemical analysis. Growing biofilms in flat plate reactors or other types of reactors with a small ratio of surface area to volume would not generate enough EPS. The following section describes how to prepare and operate an HFBR and extract EPS. We describe this procedure for batch operation. For continuous operation, the user simply needs to add inlet and outlet ports to the reactor.

9.4.32.1 Preparing a hollow fiber biofilm reactor

To assemble the HFBR system shown in Figure 9.23a, the following components are needed:

1. A hollow fiber membrane module (Zena Membranes, Czech Republic)
2. One variable-speed 6–600 rpm peristaltic pump
3. One flow breaker
4. Various connectors
5. 1 m of size 16 tubing (recycle line; the length must be adjusted as needed)
6. Rubber stopper that fits the flask with holes
7. 1-L flask (or other large flask that can hold the hollow fiber membrane module)
8. Air filter (0.2-μm)
9. 30 mL of inoculum (not shown in figure)

To operate the HFBR, you may use different hollow fiber membranes, including custom-made ones. In this case, make sure that you have enough room in the flask to make connections and that the entire hollow fiber module is immersed in the liquid solution. The hollow fiber is operated in outside-in mode. We always apply negative pressure, and the biofilm grows on the outside of the membranes. For this to happen, one end of the hollow fiber needs to be sealed. Figure 9.23b shows a photograph of a hollow fiber membrane module with one end sealed with silicon. We cut a 10-mL syringe in half and used it to connect the fiber module to size 16 silicone tubing.

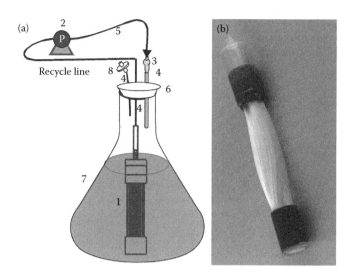

Figure 9.23 (a) Hollow fiber biofilm reactor. (b) Hollow fiber module.

To construct a lid, we used a rubber stopper which fits the 1-L flask. Three holes should be drilled into the stopper. We cut short (~2-inch) glass tubes to make connections through the stopper. When glass tubes are being inserted, gloves and safety goggles should be used to prevent accidents.

Three flasks of the same size should be autoclaved and cooled before the experiment is started. One flask should contain enough medium to cover the fiber bundle, another should contain the same volume of water, and the other should be an empty flask. Because the fiber module we use cannot be autoclaved, we follow the following steps for sterilization:

1. Autoclave all the components shown in Figure 9.23a at 121°C (except the hollow fiber module).
2. Hook the fiber bundle up to the reactor lid and to a flow line to a pump. There should be a flow outlet connected to the fibers, a flow inlet/recycle line, and an air line connected to an external 0.22-μm filter.
3. Fill the flask with 70% ethanol for sterilization. Make sure to prepare the fibers for use in an aqueous environment if they are hydrophobic. (Soak in isopropyl alcohol for 20 min to an hour.)
4. Run 70% ethanol through the system for one hour to sterilize. The flow should be pulled from the flask, into the fiber, through the line, and out the recycle line back into the flask, as shown in Figure 9.23a.
5. Stop the flow. Move the fiber bundle and connected lid to the flask containing sterilized water in a biosafety cabinet or sterile environment. Resume flow for another hour. This step may be repeated to remove trace amounts of ethanol. We generally repeat these procedures at least three times to remove ethanol.
6. After removing the ethanol, stop the flow. Move the fiber bundle and lid to the flask containing the growth medium in a biosafety cabinet or sterile environment. Allow this to circulate for 5–10 min.
7. Add a small overnight culture (~30 mL) to the growth medium to begin biofilm formation and growth.

The longer we grow the biofilm, the more biomass and the more EPS we can obtain. We generally grow the biofilm at least three days and then harvest it for EPS separation. We collect biofilm according to the following procedure:

1. While continuing inward radial flow on the fiber bundle, remove the recycle line and allow the flow to drain to a waste container. Properly cover the waste container to avoid aerosols.
2. Once the medium has drained from the flask, add a small amount of isotonic solution (0.9% NaCl) to clear the fibers and line of trace amounts of medium. Allow this to flow until depletion. Remove any residual liquid from the flask into the waste container.
3. Place the recycle line in a sterilized container of 0.9% NaCl. Reverse the flow into the fibers so that it flows out into the flask and disperses the biofilm from the fibers.
4. Collect a minimum of 25 mL or until cells and biofilm matter become less concentrated. Alternatively, the fiber bundle may be placed in a conical tube with isotonic solution and vortexed to remove residual biofilm material.
5. Once the biofilm material has been collected, continue the outward flow of water, PBS, or isotonic solution through the fibers for about 500 mL.
6. Place the fiber bundle into 70% ethanol (for cleaning and the next experiment), and place on a shaker to remove residual biofilm. Autoclave the lid and line to sterilize.

9.4.32.2   *EPS extraction*

Loosely associated EPS is extracted from biofilm according to the following procedure:

1. Once the biofilm material has been collected from the reactor, place it in a conical tube for centrifugation.
2. Spin at ~4,000 g at 4°C for 15 min or until the cells have pelleted. This supernatant is the first fraction of loosely associated EPS (laEPS).
3. Resuspend the cells in one volume of 0.9% NaCl and centrifuge similarly. Repeat this two more times, to complete three washes of the cells, and save all supernatants in the laEPS fraction.
4. Filter all bound EPS (bEPS) twice through a 0.45-μm filter.

We have two different methods of extracting bound EPS.
EDTA extraction of bEPS is performed as follows:

1. Resuspend the remaining washed cell pellet in a solution of 0.9% NaCl + 2% EDTA to a concentration of 3.2 g of wet cell weight/mL solution.
2. Add an equal volume of 0.9% NaCl.
3. Incubate at 4°C for 3 h.
4. Centrifuge the cells at 10,000 rpms and 4°C for 15 min to pellet the cells. Save the supernatant as the first fraction of bound bEPS.
5. Resuspend the cell pellet in one volume of 0.9% NaCl solution and perform similar centrifugation. Repeat this two more times to complete three washes of the cells, saving all fractions as bEPS.
6. Filter all bEPS twice through a 0.45-μm filter. Discard the cell pellet.
7. Place all bEPS into a dialysis membrane with a MW cutoff of <10 kDa. We use a MW cutoff of about 3.5 kDa.
8. Perform overnight dialysis in 0.9% NaCl to remove EDTA. Afterward, the dialysis solution should be changed for another 6-h dialysis.

Heat extraction of bEPS is performed as follows:

1. Resuspend the remaining washed cell pellet in one volume of sterile water or 0.9% NaCl.
2. Incubate cell suspension for 10 min at 80°C.
3. Centrifuge cells at 15,000 rpms and 4°C for 15 min to pellet cells. Save supernatant as first fraction of bound bEPS.
4. Resuspend cell pellet in one volume of 0.9% NaCl solution and perform similar centrifugation. Repeat this two more times to complete three washes of cells, saving all fractions as bEPS.
5. Filter all bEPS twice through a 0.45-μm filter. Discard cell pellet.

9.5 Common procedures

9.5.1 Determining viable cell concentration, biomass concentration, and biofilm activity

9.5.1.1 Viable cell count

The procedures for counting bacterial cells were originally developed for counting cells growing in suspension, not in biofilms. These procedures need to be modified to accommodate the fact that the microbial cells in biofilms are initially densely packed: appropriate procedures need to be employed to disperse these cells prior to their counting. Once they are dispersed, the procedures developed for counting bacterial cells in suspension can be used. The solution with the dispersed cells is spread over an agar gel plate containing an appropriate growth medium, and the cells grow on the agar surface, forming colonies. If the number of cells in the solution is not exceedingly high, each viable cell can grow and divide to form one colony. The plates are incubated, and after a prescribed time the number of microcolonies is counted. This number is equal to the number of viable bacterial cells present in the volume of the solution spread over the agar gel.

9.5.1.2 Counting bacterial cells in suspension

The following procedure can be used to count bacterial cells in suspension.

1. Take a sample of at least 10 mL from the liquid medium.
2. Centrifuge for 20 min at 6000 rpm to pellet the microorganisms.
3. Pour off the supernatant, resuspend the microorganisms (pellet) in 10 mL of phosphate buffer (the same buffer as was used in the growth medium).
4. Homogenize the sample for 30 s at 20,500 rpm using a probe homogenizer (such as Ika Labortechnik, Wilmington, NC) with a probe diameter of 1.5 cm.

The sample is ready for a viable cell count.

9.5.1.3 Counting bacterial cells in biofilms

Use the following procedure to count bacterial cells in biofilms.

1. Open the biofilm reactor.
2. Stop the nutrient flow.
3. Remove the slides with biofilm from the reactor.

4. Using a Teflon scrubber, scrape the biofilm from the microscope slide aseptically in the phosphate buffer in a 50-mL centrifuge tube.
5. Rinse the slides with phosphate buffer identical to the one used in the growth medium.
6. Note the volume of the phosphate buffer used (10–20 mL).
7. Disperse the scraped biofilm in the test tubes using a probe homogenizer (Ika Labortechnik, Wilmington, NC) with a probe diameter of 1.5 cm.
8. Homogenize the sample for 30 s at 20,500 rpm.
9. Centrifuge for 20 min at 6000 rpm to pellet the microorganisms.
10. Homogenize the sample using a vortex mixer.

The sample is ready for a viable cell count.

The number of colonies growing on each agar plate equals the number of viable bacteria in the sample that was spread over the agar. To prevent overgrowing the plates, the sample needs to be diluted (Figure 9.24) before the cells are spread on the agar plates (Figure 9.25). Dilutions are done in tenfold increments so that they will be easy to compute and so that the results can be presented on a logarithmic scale. To do a tenfold (10^{-1}) dilution, take a 1-mL sample and add it to 9 mL of the same phosphate buffer solution as was used in the growth medium.

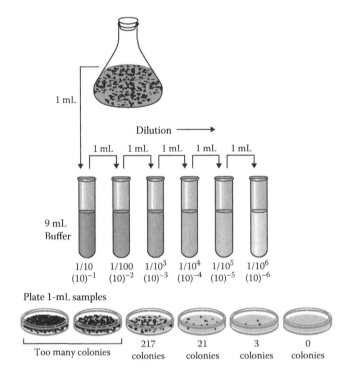

Figure 9.24 Diluting a sample in preparation for a viable cell count. One milliliter of properly diluted culture is spread over the surface of an agar plate using a sterile glass spreader as shown in Figure 9.25. The plates are incubated, and the colonies are counted after 24 h. To count the cells, use three replicates of the measurements. Use R2A agar plates (Fisher Scientific), incubate the plates at 30°C, and count the colonies after 24 h.

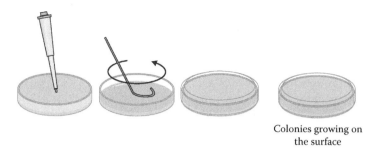

Colonies growing on
the surface

Figure 9.25 Spread plate method. The diluted culture is spread over the surface of an agar plate using a sterile glass spreader. The plate is incubated at 30°C for 24 h, and the colonies formed on the agar surface are counted.

The following example shows how to compute the number of colony-forming units (CFU) using the results shown in Figure 9.24. As shown, when the sample was diluted three times, corresponding to a 10^{-3} dilution, the number of colonies counted on the agar surface was 217. Therefore, the number of colonies in our original sample was

217×10^3 (dilution factor) $= 2.17 \times 10^5$ cells (or CFU) per milliliter of sample

This computation is usually shown in a compact form, as

$$\frac{CFU}{mL} = \text{Number of cells} \times \frac{1}{\text{Dilution}} \times \text{Sample volume} \qquad (9.4)$$

The sample volume is well defined if the sample is taken from a culture of bacteria growing in suspension. However, this biofilm sample was scraped from a coupon and diluted in an arbitrarily selected volume of phosphate buffer. For biofilms, the number of CFU/mL needs to be related to a more relevant factor than the volume of the solution, such as the surface area from which the biofilm was removed. In effect, in biofilms, the relevant number is CFU/cm^2.

Using the data from this example,

$$\frac{CFU}{cm^2} = \text{Number of cells} \frac{1}{\text{Dilution}} \frac{1}{\text{Coupon surface area (cm}^2)} \text{Scraped volume} \qquad (9.5)$$

In the equation, *scraped volume* refers to the volume of the scraped and diluted biofilm. The microscope slide on which the biofilm grows is removed from the reactor, and the biofilm is mechanically removed by scraping and placed in a 5-mL centrifuge tube. Some sterile buffer is added to the tube and the total volume of the biofilm and buffer in the tube is called the scraped volume.

Measuring CFU/cm^2 is an excellent way of expressing the number of microorganisms if it is certain that all microorganisms in the biofilm will grow in the conditions of the test.

9.5.1.4 Determining biomass concentration

The concentration of biomass in a biofilm reactor is measured using the following procedure:

1. Open the biofilm reactor.
2. Stop the nutrient flow.
3. Remove the slides with biofilm from the reactor.
4. Using a Teflon scrubber, scrape the biofilm from each microscope slide aseptically in the phosphate buffer in a sterile 50-mL centrifuge tube.
5. Use a phosphate buffer identical to the one in the growth medium to rinse the slide.
6. Centrifuge for 20 min at 6000 rpm to pellet the microorganisms.
7. Pour off the supernatant and resuspend the microorganisms (pellet) in 10 mL of phosphate buffer.
8. Vacuum filter the sample through Whatman® Glass Microfibre Filters, 2.5 cm in diameter, with a 0.2-μm pore size.
9. Prior to filtering, dry the clean filters to a constant weight in a drying oven at 105°C for 24 h and weigh.
10. Re-dry the trapped cells on filter paper at the same temperature for 24 h and record the weight difference; the weight difference is equivalent to the dry biomass that accumulated on the given microscope slide.
11. Divide the accumulated weight by the surface area of the slide to get the average biomass accumulated on a unit surface area using the following formula:

$$\text{Biomass per surface area} = \frac{\text{Dry weight of biomass and filter} - \text{Dry weight of filter}}{\text{Surface area of biofilm}}$$

$$\left[\frac{\text{mg biomass}}{\text{cm}^2} \right]$$

(9.6)

9.5.1.5 Specific number of viable cells

The ratio of the CFU per surface area to the biomass of the film is called the specific number of viable cells (SNVC), and it is expressed as CFU/mg biomass/surface area.

$$\text{SNVC} = \frac{\text{CFU}}{\text{Surface area of biofilm}} \times \frac{1}{\text{Dry weight of biomass and filter} - \text{Dry weight of filter}}$$

$$\left[\frac{\text{CFU}}{\text{cm}^2 \times \text{mg biomass}} \right]$$

(9.7)

Measuring CFU/surface area provides information about the viability of the bacteria in the biofilm, and it is also a convenient test for checking the effects of any actions undertaken to change the viability of the bacteria, such as using biocides to eradicate the biofilms.

9.5.2 Testing the efficacy of antimicrobials/biocides against biofilms

To test the antimicrobial activity of selected agents, the CFU/cm² is measured before and after treatment. The biofilm sample can be treated in the reactor or it can be removed from the reactor and treated at another location. The samples are handled identically to how they are handled for a viable cell count.

9.5.2.1 Treating biofilm samples with antimicrobial agents

The following procedure is used if the sample is to be treated with an antimicrobial agent in the biofilm reactor:

1. Determine the number of CFU.
2. Add the desired amount of the antimicrobial agent to the reactor. If the antimicrobial agent is to be added to the reactor continuously, add it to the nutrient solution.
3. Wait the desired length of time to complete the treatment.
4. Determine the number of CFU.

It may be impossible to treat the samples in the same reactor where they grew. In this case, the biofilms need to be moved to another location for treatment. In this procedure, biofilm samples growing on microscope slides are removed and placed in 50-mL sterile centrifuge tubes. The desired amount of the antimicrobial agent is added to the centrifuge tube, which is placed in a shaker and shaken gently until the desired duration of treatment has elapsed. When the treatment is completed, measure the number of CFU as described above.

9.5.2.2 Evaluating the efficacy of antimicrobial agents

Log CFU is used as a criterion of antimicrobial efficacy. The numbers of CFU before and after the treatment are expressed as decimal logarithms, and the log reduction is computed as

$$\text{Log reduction} = \text{Log(CFU/ml)}_{\text{untreated sample}} - \text{Log(CFU/ml)}_{\text{treated sample}} \qquad (9.8)$$

9.5.3 Using microelectrodes to characterize local mass transport in biofilms

Although many different microelectrodes are used in biofilm research, the procedures for using them are similar. Of course, there are differences at the stage of interpreting the results, depending on whether dissolved oxygen or pH was measured, but the measurements themselves are done in a similar way. The use of the microelectrodes that measure limiting current density exemplifies these procedures. The results of such measurements can be used to characterize the rates of local mass transport in biofilms. These microelectrodes are versatile, and they are used to measure local mass transport coefficient, local effective diffusivity, and local flow velocity. The major difference between these microelectrodes and many other microelectrodes is that to use limiting current microelectrodes, the solution in the reactor must be modified by replacing the growth medium with a solution of electrolyte. The procedures for using limiting current microelectrodes can easily be modified and applied to other microelectrodes.

9.5.3.1 Inspecting and testing microelectrodes

Before use, each microelectrode is inspected visually and tested electrochemically to make sure that it is in an acceptable operating condition. Inspecting the microelectrode visually under the microscope is useful for detecting obvious problems, such as a broken tip, but it needs to be supplemented with electrochemical testing to detect less obvious problems, such as an unstable current, that may not be detected visually. The electrochemical testing determines whether the microelectrode responds to an electric stimulus in a predictable manner. If the reading drifts or if repeated calibrations fail to give the same results, the electrode should not be used. The sensitivity of microelectrodes to stirring is also tested: the reading of a dissolved oxygen microelectrode must be immune to stirring. Electrochemical testing of a microelectrode includes the following steps:

1. Fill a 100-mL beaker with 25 mM $K_3Fe(CN)_6$ in 0.2 M KCl.
2. Insert a suitable reference electrode, such as SCE, and the limiting current microelectrode to be tested into the solution, and connect them to a suitable electrochemical instrument that can apply the desired polarization potential and measure the resulting current.
3. Connect the measuring instrument to a data acquisition system, and arrange the data acquisition system so that a plot of applied potential versus measured current is displayed.
4. Polarize the microelectrode with a scanning potential between −0.3 and −1.2 V_{SCE} at a scan rate of about 5 mV/s and read the current. The data acquisition system should display a plot similar to that shown in Figure 9.26.
5. From the plot, determine the range of potentials delivering the limiting current, the range of potentials for which the current remains constant.

In Figure 9.26, for applied potentials between approximately −0.6 and −0.9 V, the current remains constant; this confirms the existence of limiting current conditions. The existence of limiting current conditions qualifies this microelectrode as usable, and the microelectrodes show limiting current conditions for the range of applied potential between −0.6 and −0.9 V. At potentials lower than (−)1.0 V, the electrode reduces water, and the additional electrochemical reaction increases the current. On the basis of the results in Figure 9.26, it is decided to polarize the microelectrode at −0.8 V during measurements in biofilm reactors. Selecting such a high negative potential causes some concern: at −0.8 V oxygen can be reduced. However, tests demonstrated that the limiting current generated

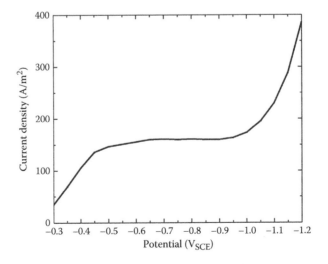

Figure 9.26 Polarization curve for a microelectrode with a tip diameter of 10 μm in stirred solution of 25 mM $K_3Fe(CN)_6$ in 0.2 M KCl.

by reducing ferricyanide to ferrocyanide was not affected by the presence of oxygen. Two reasons may, hypothetically, explain this result: (1) The concentration of ferricyanide in the system, 25 mM, exceeds the solubility of oxygen in water, 0.5 mM, by 50 times, and (2) the reduction of ferricyanide on the electrode is kinetically preferred.

9.5.3.2 Replacing the growth medium in a biofilm reactor with an electrolyte solution

To determine the local mass transport coefficient, local diffusivity or local flow velocity in a biofilm reactor, the growth solution needs to be replaced with a solution of ferricyanide.

1. Stop the nutrient delivery to the reactor.
2. Slowly drain the nutrient solution from the reactor.
3. Slowly fill the reactor with 0.2 M KCl.
4. Let the 0.2 M KCl solution run through the reactor. Use a volume of KCl equal to at least 2–3 volumes of the reactor. For example, if the volume of the reactor is 250 mL, pump 500–750 mL KCl through the reactor. This procedure removes residues of the growth medium.
5. Slowly drain the KCl solution from the reactor.
6. Slowly fill the reactor with a solution of 25 mM $K_3Fe(CN)_6$ in 0.2 M KCl.
7. Allow the electrolyte solution to flow through the biofilm reactor until it equilibrates with the biomass.

The condition that the electrode reaction is the only sink (or source) of electrons for the electroactive substance introduced into the reactor needs to be verified. It is known that the biomass can serve as a source of electrons to reduce ferricyanide and therefore compete with the electrode reaction. Tests show that it takes at least 30 min for the ferricyanide to equilibrate with the biomass. To test whether the system has equilibrated, measure profiles of ferricyanide across the biofilm using ferricyanide microelectrodes. Ferricyanide microelectrodes are constructed the same way as the microelectrodes used to measure mass transport dynamics with one exception: their tips are covered with a 5% cellulose acetate membrane (as is done when the hydrogen peroxide microelectrodes described in Chapter 5 are constructed). An appropriate amount of cellulose acetate is used to make a 5% solution in acetone. The tip of the microelectrode is dipped into the solution and dried overnight. The presence of the membrane makes the electrodes useless for measuring mass transport coefficients, but it makes them useful for measuring the concentration of ferricyanide within the biofilm. The ferricyanide microelectrodes are operated in the same way as the microelectrodes used to measure mass transport dynamics, and they are polarized to -0.8 V_{SCE}.

9.5.3.3 Positioning the microelectrode in the reactor

The procedure for preparing the microelectrode measurements is illustrated in Figure 9.27. It includes the following steps:

1. Attach the microelectrode to the microelectrode holder.
2. Insert a suitable reference electrode into the reactor.
3. Position the inverted microscope with its lens below the location of the measurement (Figure 9.27).
4. Position the microelectrode above the lens of the inverted microscope.
5. Use fiber optic illuminators to illuminate the bottom of the biofilm reactor.

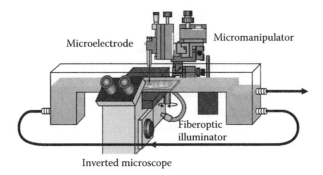

Figure 9.27 Positioning the microelectrode in the reactor. Some biofilm was removed from the bottom to locate the tip of the microelectrode.

Before starting the measurements, it is important to locate the position of the bottom of the reactor. If the position of the bottom is not precisely located, it is likely that the tip of the microelectrode will be driven into the bottom and damaged. To locate the bottom, follow these steps:

1. Use a small wood stick to remove biofilm near the location of the measurement, and make sure that the surface is clean to visual inspection.
2. Move the entire reactor so that the location of the removed biofilm is visible in the field of view of the microscope.
3. Align the tip of the microelectrode and the objective lens.
4. Using the micromanipulator, position the tip of the microelectrode about 2–5 mm from the bottom while monitoring the location of the tip through the side of the reactor.
5. Find the tip of the microelectrode using the microscope and focus on the tip. To find the tip, focus first on the bottom and then above the bottom; the tip is located somewhere in the solution above the bottom.
6. Move the microelectrode left/right/forward/backward to bring it into the field of view of the microscope (Figures 9.27 and 9.28).

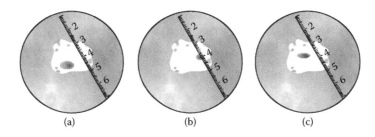

(a) (b) (c)

Figure 9.28 Images seen in the field of view of the inverted microscope as the tip of the microelectrode approaches the bottom. (a) The tip of the microelectrode is in the electrolyte solution. (b) The tip touches the bottom. (c) The microelectrode tip is moved 2000 μm above the bottom. The differences in refractive index among air, water, and glass, combined with the small size of the tip of the electrode, force us to move the reactor during the measurements to better see the tip of the microelectrode. The reactor was moved between images (a) and (b), but it was not moved between images (b) and (c). In image (b), the tip of the microelectrode is almost touching the glass bottom of the reactor. In image (c), we see the tip of the microelectrode through layers of glass, water, and air.

7. Memorize the location of the tip (Figure 9.28). From now on, the microelectrode will be moved using the stepper motor and controller. Manipulating the microelectrode by hand with its tip near the bottom is a recipe for damaging the tip of the electrode.

8. Initially, move the microelectrode in large steps, about 100 μm, but when the tip gets closer to the bottom, lower the step size to 50, 20, and 10 μm. While moving the microelectrode toward the bottom, change the focus level of the microscope to see the tip of the microelectrode clearly. If necessary, slowly move the reactor left/right/forward/backward and watch the bottom.

9. When the microelectrode tip and the bottom of the reactor are clearly visible, the tip is near the bottom. Lower the step size to 5 μm and then to 2 μm.

10. Before the tip of the microelectrode touches the bottom, its image looks diffused. When the tip touches the bottom, the image of the tip is sharp. This occurs because the image in the microscope includes the shadow produced by the tip of the microelectrode. Once the tip touches the bottom, the shadow disappears (Figure 9.28).

11. Be careful when the microelectrode touches the bottom! Moving the electrode further may break the tip.

12. Note the position of the micrometer on the stepper motor: this is the position of the bottom for all further measurements (Figure 9.28).

13. Move the microelectrode up to a distance from the bottom least 2–3 times higher than the thickness of the biofilm. The thickness of the biofilm can be estimated using light microscopy. If it is unclear how much to move the microelectrode, select a large distance, such as 3000 μm.

Finding the bottom of the biofilm requires some practice. Figure 9.28 shows the image seen in the field of view of an inverted microscope as the tip of a microelectrode approaches the bottom. The scale shown in this figure is the micrometer etched in the ocular of the microscope. It helps, at least initially, to polarize the microelectrode during this procedure and monitor the current as the tip approaches the bottom. Near the bottom the readout changes because the presence of the bottom obstructs the mass transfer to the tip of the microelectrode (Figure 9.28b).

9.5.3.4 Selecting the location for the measurement and moving the microelectrode to this location

The microelectrode is not actually moved. The micromanipulators are not rigid enough for that, and if the micromanipulator were touched, it would change location by several micrometers, changing the position of the bottom. Instead, the reactor is moved, and the microelectrode tip stays at the same location. Because the microelectrode is above the biofilm and its exact location (corner of the number 4 on the micrometer) is known, the reactor is moved to align the selected location for the measurement with the position of the microelectrode tip. For the reactor to be moved, it must be rigidly mounted on the microscope stage; the reactor can actually be taped to the microscope stage at several locations, and the microscope stage can be manipulated with the reactor in the horizontal plane.

9.5.3.5 Measuring the profile of local limiting current at the selected location

Before the profile is measured, the step size of the microelectrode movement must be selected. If the distance between the bottom and the microelectrode tip is 2000 μm, as we assumed in the example above, and the biofilm thickness is approximately 500 μm, making measurements every 20 μm is acceptable. Wait a few seconds between measurements to take into account the response time of the microelectrode. The response time of an individual microelectrode should be evaluated in a separate measurement. This is done by inserting the microelectrode into a solution of ferricyanide and monitoring the current; it approaches the final current in a length of time equal to the response time of the microelectrode. The tips of limiting current microelectrodes are not covered with membranes, and their response is very fast. The microelectrode is moved in a 20-μm step 100 times, and the current is measured after every 3 s. If another profile needs to be measured at another location, move the microelectrode up, again by 2000 μm, and move the reactor to the new location.

9.5.3.6 Plotting profiles of local mass transport coefficient and local effective diffusivity from limiting current profiles

Profiles of limiting current density measured under two conditions, with and without flow in the reactor, serve as a source of information about the distribution of local flow velocity, local mass transport coefficient, and local effective diffusivity. Each of these parameters has been separately calibrated with respect to the density of the local limiting current. Because of the nature of the measurements, the response of the limiting current electrode is affected by the presence of the bottom of the reactor. Therefore, the following relations are only valid for measurements taken at a distance of more than about two diameters of the microelectrode from the bottom.

The limiting current density i is calculated by dividing the measured limiting current I by the surface area of the microelectrode, A $(i = I/A)$.

The local effective diffusivity is related to the limiting current density by the following equation (Beyenal and Lewandowski 2000):

$$D_{fl} = 1.12 \times 10^{-10} + 3.69 \times 10^{-12} \ (i) \tag{9.9}$$

where D_{fl} is effective diffusivity (m²/s) and i is current density (A/m²).

Local flow velocity can be estimated from the following relation (Xia et al. 2000):

$$i = 160 + 163 v_l^{0.408} \tag{9.10}$$

where v_l is the local flow velocity (cm/s) and i is the current density in (A/m²). Note that Equation 9.10 uses different units of length on the two sides of the equal sign (square meters to express the current density and centimeters for the flow velocity). This reflects the conventional use of units in the two measurements, current density and flow velocity, in biofilm reactors.

The local mass transfer coefficient can be estimated from the following relation (Yang and Lewandowski 1995):

$$k_1 = \frac{i}{nFC_b} \tag{9.11}$$

In Equation 9.11, C_b is the ferricyanide concentration (0.025 M), F is Faraday's constant (96,500 coulombs per mole), and n is the number of electrons transferred (2).

Example 9.8

Using the results of the limiting current measurements shown in Table 9.16, calculate the local flow velocity, local effective diffusivity, and local mass transfer coefficient at each location.

Equation 9.9 is used to calculate local effective diffusivity (Table 9.17). Equations 9.10 and 9.11, and the results of the measurements with flow, are used to calculate local flow velocity and local mass transport coefficients (Table 9.18).

Table 9.16 Limiting Current Measurements for Example 9.8

No flow		With flow	
Distance from the bottom (μm)	Current density (A/m²)	Distance from the bottom (μm)	Current density (A/m²)
300	160	0	160
250	154.3	50	285.2203
200	141.9	100	331.0243
150	131.4	150	350.1081
100	120.5	200	369.5047
50	111.4	250	372.3414
0	103.2	300	378.0302

Table 9.17 Local Effective Diffusivities Calculated from Measurements Taken at Stagnant Conditions

Distance from the bottom (μm)	Current density (A/m²)	Local relative effective diffusivity, $D_{fl} \times 10^{-10}$ (m²/s)
300	160	$D_{fl} = 1.12 \times 10^{-10} + 3.69 \times 10^{-12} \times 160 = 7.0256 \times 10^{-10}$
250	154.3	6.8152E-10
200	141.9	6.3575E-10
150	131.4	5.97E-10
100	120.5	5.5677E-10
50	111.4	5.2318E-10
0	103.2	4.9291E-10

Table 9.18 Local Effective Diffusivities Calculated from Measurements Taken with Flow

Distance from the bottom (μm)	Current density (A/m²)	Local mass transport coefficient (m/s)	Local flow velocity[a] (cm/s)
0	160	$k_1 = \dfrac{160}{2 \times 96500 \times 0.025} = 0.0331$	0
50	285.2203	0.059113	0.524
100	331.0243	0.068606	1.125
150	350.1081	0.072561	1.458
200	369.5047	0.076581	1.85
250	372.3414	0.077169	1.912
300	378.0302	0.078348	2.04

[a] The local flow velocity is calculated using Equation 9.10 and Microsoft® Excel's solver.

9.5.3.7 Presenting the results in a form accepted by the model of stratified biofilms

The use of the conceptual model of stratified biofilms to interpret the results of measurements has been discussed. Using this model requires that the results of measurements be reported as averages and that the standard deviations of the measurements be taken at selected distances from the bottom of the reactor. The computations below use three profiles of oxygen, measured at various locations, to show how to compute the results. Typically, about 25 profiles are used for such computations; in extreme cases, 100 profiles have been used.

Example 9.9

Oxygen concentrations were measured at the specified distances from the bottom, and the results are given in Table 9.19. Calculate the surface-averaged dissolved oxygen concentration for each distance.

The surface-averaged oxygen concentration at a distance of 100 μm from the bottom is

$$C_{sa} = \frac{6.81 + 6.84 + 6.82}{3} = \frac{20.47}{3} = 6.82$$

The other average oxygen concentrations are computed in the same way, and the results are shown in Table 9.20.

Three profiles of oxygen were used to demonstrate the computations. More realistic examples of such results are shown in Chapters 1 and 8.

Table 9.19 Oxygen Concentration Measured at Various Distances from the Bottom

Distance from the bottom, X (μm)	Dissolved oxygen concentration (mg/L) at location A	Dissolved oxygen concentration (mg/L) at location B	Dissolved oxygen concentration (mg/L) at location C
100	6.81	6.84	6.82
80	5.42	4.25	3.11
60	4.54	3.58	1.15
40	2.19	1.48	0.57
20	1.12	0.47	0.14
0	0.51	0.45	0.0

Table 9.20 Surface-Averaged Dissolved Oxygen Concentrations Computed from the Results Shown in Table 9.19

Distance from the bottom, X (μm)	Surface-averaged dissolved oxygen concentration (mg/L)
100	6.82
80	4.26
60	3.09
40	1.41
20	0.58
0	0.32

9.5.4   Live/dead cell imaging in a biofilm

This section describes imaging biofilms grown in a capillary flow reactor, such as that shown in Figure 3.37. A similar protocol can be used for biofilms grown in other types of reactors. The first step toward obtaining good-quality images of biofilms is to make sure that the biofilms are grown on a surface that is suitable for imaging. Among many conditions for satisfying this requirement, the surface on which the biofilms are grown should not interact with the stain. The best surface for imaging biofilms is glass, but experimental conditions in individual cases may require using other surfaces. This may sound trivial, but it is wise to make sure that the flow cell fits under the objective of the microscope objective before growing the biofilms. The biofilms in the capillary flow reactor should be within the working distance of the microscope objective. The staining procedure needs to be optimized for the actual conditions of the test. Sometimes biofilms are stained before the sample is placed under the microscope, and sometimes they are stained under the microscope. Figure 9.29 shows the steps in the procedure we use to stain biofilms using a Live/Dead BacLight bacterial viability kit (Molecular Probes Inc., Eugene, OR). This consists of SYTO 9 and propidium iodide (PI). SYTO 9 stains all cells (live cells and dead cells, which are those with damaged or compromised membranes), and PI stains only dead cells. Both SYTO 9- and PI-stained cells are excited by the blue laser (488-nm wavelength). The biofilm is grown in a capillary flow reactor operated in a continuous flow mode. After a mature biofilm is established (approximately three days after inoculation) the biofilm is ready to be stained and imaged. We use the following procedure.

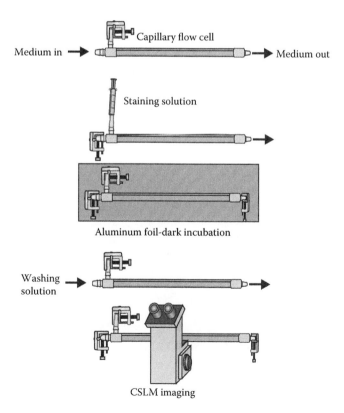

Figure 9.29 Staining procedure for biofilms grown in simplified open-channel flat plate reactors.

1. Stop the flow of nutrients into the reactor. However, the flow cell should remain full of nutrient and there should be no air bubble while the flow is suspended.
2. Prepare a SYTO 9 and propidium iodide mixture by adding 3 μL of each component (from original stocks provided by Molecular Probes) to 1 mL of DI water.
3. Inject the mixture of SYTO 9 and propidium iodide. Note that the 1-mL solution volume is larger than the volume of the flow cell. Ensure that the entire flow cell is filled with the staining solution.
4. Close the tubing on both ends of the flow cell with clamps.
5. Cover the reactor with aluminum foil to prevent light penetration, because most of the fluorescent probes are light-sensitive.
6. Wait 20 min for the stains to penetrate the biofilm.
7. Wash out the excess stain by pumping fresh nutrient solution through the reactor for 20 min.

The time allowed for staining and washing depends on the volume of the reactor and the amount of biofilm in the reactor; it should be optimized for each case. Using either an excessive amount of stain (too low a ratio of biofilm volume to the amount of stain added) or an insufficient amount of stain (too high a ratio of biofilm volume to the amount of stain added) can result in poor-quality images. Figure 9.30 shows two images: a good-quality image, which was obtained when the amount of stain was optimized (Figure 9.30a), and a bad-quality image, which was obtained when the amount of stain used was not optimized (Figure 9.30b).

Fluorophores are stimulated using monochromatic blue laser light at 488 nm. The emitted light has two different colors, green and red, and these can be separated by monitoring the green and red channels in the RGB image. The green channel shows the live cells, while the red channel shows the dead cells. The image in Figure 9.30 shows only the green channel. The images of live and dead cells in the different channels are then combined to show the locations of the live and dead cells. Figure 9.31 shows an example of an image of a biofilm obtained using a Nikon DS-Qi1Mc camera mounted on an inverted microscope (Nikon Eclipse Ti-S, 40x ELWD objective). The biofilm was stained using the procedure described above.

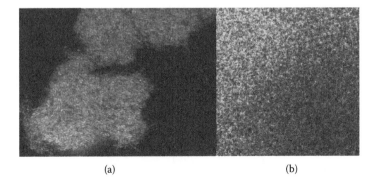

(a)   (b)

Figure 9.30 (a) Properly stained cells look crisp in a CSLM image. (b) Improperly stained biofilm gives a noisy signal in a CSLM image. (Both images were taken by Deepak Sharma at the Center for Biofilm Engineering.)

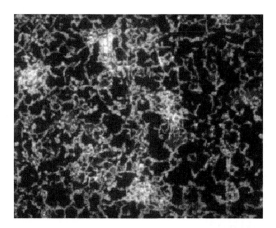

***Figure 9.31* (See color insert.)** Live/dead image of *P. aeruginosa* PAO1. The red cells are dead, and the green cells are alive.

9.5.5   Preparing biofilms for scanning electron microscopy

This section describes procedures for preparing samples of *Geobacter sulfurreducens* biofilms grown on electrodes for imaging using scanning electron microscopy (Figure 9.32). The biofilms in the example were grown in the reactor shown in Figure 3.19.

9.5.5.1   Fixation protocol

Follow the steps listed below to fix the biofilm.

1. Remove the biofilm electrode from the modified open-channel flat plate reactor (Section 3.5.1.12). Use tweezers to remove the electrode with biofilm from the reactor. Make sure that the tweezers were sterilized to avoid contamination of the sample. We should note that we use a small amount of silicone rubber to glue the electrode to the bottom of the reactor. Therefore we can remove the electrodes from the reactor easily.

2. Gently place the biofilm electrode in an appropriate container, where liquid can be added to cover all sides of the sample completely and the container can be sealed and closed. Use tweezers to move the biofilms from the surface on which they were

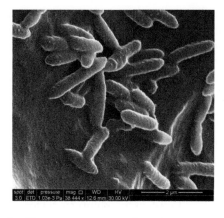

Figure 9.32 *G. sulfurreducens* biofilm grown on a graphite electrode in a modified open-channel flat plate reactor.

growing. Make sure that the tweezers were sterilized to avoid contamination of the sample.

3. Add the fixating solution of 2.5% gluteraldehyde and 2% paraformaldehyde in 0.1 M sodium phosphate buffer. One liter of buffer contains 27.6 g of NAH_2PO_4 and 28.4 g of Na_2HPO_4. (When working with the fixation solution, always work under a hood and wear gloves.)
4. Seal the top of the container with parafilm and then close the container to prevent contamination and evaporation of the fixation solution.
5. Allow to sit overnight, undisturbed, at 4°C.

9.5.5.2 Dehydration protocol

The biofilm sample is dehydrated during a series of 10-min incubations in a set of increasingly concentrated ethanol solutions. All steps should be performed under a hood, and gloves and a lab coat should be worn.

1. Slowly remove the fixation solution from the container to minimize disruption to the sample. Dispose of the solution in an appropriate waste container.
2. Carefully add 0.1 M sodium phosphate buffer (1 L of buffer contains 27.6 g of NAH_2PO_4 and 28.4 g Na_2 of HPO_4) to cover the sample, let it sit at room temperature for 10 min, then remove the buffer solution as in step 1. This is the first sample rinse. Repeat twice for a total of three rinses.
3. To begin the dehydration, remove the last of the buffer rinse. Following the same procedure as for rinsing, incubate the sample in a series of increasingly concentrated ethanol aqueous solutions. The first solution should be 30% (v/v) ethanol, followed by 50%, 70%, and 95%. Last, there will be three incubations with 100% ethanol. Each incubation should last 10 min before the solution is removed.
4. After the last 100% ethanol rinse, add hexamethyldisilizane (HMDS) (SPI, no. 02852-AB) to dry the sample overnight in a hood.
5. After the sample is thoroughly dry, it should be mounted on a stand for SEM analysis and coated with gold by sputter coating. Each sputter coater will have a different protocol, but we aim for a gold layer thickness of 150–200 A.

9.6 Disclaimer

The authors make no warranty whatsoever regarding any outcome obtained from the use of these protocols. Any decision regarding safety, applicability, marketability, effectiveness for any purpose, or other use or disposition of said research outcome shall be the sole responsibility of the user.

Nomenclature

Roman symbols

A	Surface area (m²)
B	Constant in Contois model
B_g	Constant in Contois model for glucose
B_o	Constant in Contois model for oxygen
CFU	Colony-forming unit

C_b	Bulk ferricyanide concentration (M)
C_{sa}	Surface-averaged oxygen concentration (mg/L)
D	Dilution rate (h^{-1})
D_{fl}	Local effective diffusivity (m^2/s)
DO	Dissolved oxygen (mg/L)
F	Faraday's constant (C/mole)
g	Gravitational constant (Nm^2 kg^{-2})
i	Limiting current density (A/m^2) or total number of growth-limiting nutrients
K_g	Monod half-saturation constant for glucose (g/L)
k_l	Local mass transfer coefficient (m/s)
K_o	Monod half-saturation constant for oxygen (g/L)
K_{SM}	Monod half-saturation constant (g/L)
K_{sMZ}	Moser half-saturation constant (g/L)
K_{sT}	Tessier half-saturation constant (g/L)
m_g	Maintenance factor for glucose (h^{-1})
m_o	Maintenance factor for oxygen (h^{-1})
n	Number of electrons transferred
N	Number of experimental data
OUR	Oxygen uptake rate (mg oxygen/h)
Q	Flow rate (L/h)
R	Regression coefficient
S	Nutrient concentration (g/L)
S_{fg}	Concentration of glucose in fresh feed (g/L)
S_{fn}	Concentration of ammonium sulfate in fresh feed (g/L)
S_{fp}	Concentration of pyruvate in fresh feed (mg/L)
S_g	Concentration of glucose in chemostat (g/L)
S_i	Concentration of nutrient i (g/L)
SNVC	Specific number of viable cells (CFU/mg biomass/cm^2)
S_o	Concentration of dissolved oxygen (g/L)
SOUR	Specific oxygen uptake rate (g oxygen/g microorganism/h)
S_p	Concentration of pyruvate in chemostat (mg/L)
T	Temperature (°C)
t	Time (h)
V	Reactor volume (L) or Potential (V)
v_l	Local flow velocity (cm/s)
X	Microorganism concentration in chemostat (g/L)
$Y_{x/g}$	Yield coefficient for glucose (g microorganisms/g glucose)
$Y_{x/o}$	Yield coefficient for oxygen (g microorganisms/g oxygen)

Greek symbols

μ	Specific growth rate (h^{-1})
ρ	Density (mg/m^3)
λ	Moser's constant
$\mu_{experimental}$	Experimental specific growth rate (h^{-1})

λ_g	Moser's constant for glucose
μ_{max}	Maximum specific growth rate (h^{-1})
λ_o	Moser's constant for oxygen
$\mu_{predicted}$	Theoretical specific growth rate (h^{-1})
Δh	Height difference (m)

References

Beyenal, H., and Lewandowski, Z. 2000. Combined effect of substrate concentration and flow velocity on effective diffusivity in biofilms. *Water Research* 34: 528–538.

Eaton, A. D., Clesceri, L. S., and Greenberg, A. E. 1995. *Standard Methods for the Examination of Water and Wastewater*. Washington, DC: American Public Health Association.

Yang, S., and Lewandowski, Z. 1995. Measurement of local mass transfer coefficient in biofilms. *Biotechnology and Bioengineering* 48: 737–744.

Yurt, N., Sears, J., and Lewandowski, Z. 2002. Multiple substrate growth kinetics of *Leptothrix discophora* SP-6. *Biotechnology Progress* 18: 994–1002.

Suggested readings

Babauta, T. J., Nguyen, H. D., Harrington, T. D., Renslow, R., and Beyenal, H. 2012. pH, redox potential and local biofilm potential microenvironments within *Geobacter sulfurreducens* biofilms and their roles in electron transfer. *Biotechnology and Bioengineering* 109: 2651–2662.

Babauta, T. J., Renslow, R., Lewandowski, Z., and Beyenal, H. 2012. Electrochemically active biofilms: Facts and fiction. *Biofouling* 28: 789–812.

Beyenal, H., Davis, C. C., and Lewandowski, Z. 2004. An improved Severinghaus-type carbon dioxide microelectrode for use in biofilms. *Sensors and Actuators B-Chemical* 97: 202–210.

Beyenal, H., and Lewandowski, Z. 2001. Mass-transport dynamics, activity, and structure of sulfate-reducing biofilms. *AIChE Journal* 47: 1689–1697.

Beyenal, H., and Lewandowski, Z. 2002. Internal and external mass transfer in biofilms grown at various flow velocities. *Biotechnology Progress* 18: 55–61.

Beyenal, H., and Lewandowski, Z. 2004. Dynamics of lead immobilization in sulfate reducing biofilms. *Water Research* 38: 2726–2736.

Beyenal, H., Sani, R. K., Peyton, B. M., Dohnalkova, A. C., Amonette, J. E., and Lewandowski, Z. 2004. Uranium immobilization by sulfate-reducing biofilms. *Environmental Science and Technology* 38: 2067–2074.

Christensen, B. E., Ertesvag, H., Beyenal, H., and Lewandowski, Z. 2001. Resistance of biofilms containing alginate-producing bacteria to disintegration by an alginate degrading enzyme (AlgL). *Biofouling* 17: 203–210.

Jackson, G., Beyenal, H., Rees, W. M., and Lewandowski, Z. 2001. Growing reproducible biofilms with respect to structure and viable cell counts. *Journal of Microbiological Methods* 47: 1–10.

Jesaitis, A. J., Franklin, M. J., Berglund, D., Sasaki, M., Lord, C. I., Bleazard, J. B., Duffy, J. E., Beyenal, H., and Lewandowski, Z. 2003. Compromised host defense on *Pseudomonas aeruginosa* biofilms: Characterization of neutrophil and biofilm interactions. *Journal of Immunology* 171: 4329–4339.

Lewandowski, Z. and Beyenal, H., 2001. Limiting-current-type microelectrodes for quantifying mass transport dynamics in biofilms. *Microbial Growth in Biofilms, Part B* 337: 339–359.

Lewandowski, Z. Beyenal, H., and Stookey, D. 2004. Reproducibility of biofilm processes and the meaning of steady state in biofilm reactors. *Water Science and Technology* 49: 359–364.

Marsili, E., Beyenal, H., Di Palma, L., Merli, C., Dohnalkova, A., Amonette, J. E., and Lewandowski, Z. 2005. Uranium removal by sulfate reducing biofilms in the presence of carbonates. *Water Science and Technology* 52: 49–55.

Xia, F. H., Beyenal, H., and Lewandowski, Z. 1998. An electrochemical technique to measure local flow velocity in biofilms. *Water Research* 32(12): 3631–3636.

Index

Page numbers followed by f and t indicate figures and tables, respectively.

For Product Safety Concerns and Information please contact our EU
representative GPSR@taylorandfrancis.com Taylor & Francis Verlag GmbH,
Kaufingerstraße 24, 80331 München, Germany

Printed and bound by CPI Group (UK) Ltd, Croydon, CR0 4YY